TED KENNEDY

ALSO BY JOHN A. FARRELL

Richard Nixon: The Life

Clarence Darrow: Attorney for the Damned

Tip O'Neill and the Democratic Century

TED KENNEDY

A Life

John A. Farrell

PENGUIN PRESS

NEW YORK

2022

PENGUIN PRESS
An imprint of Penguin Random House LLC
penguinrandomhouse.com

Copyright © 2022 by John A. Farrell
Penguin Random House supports copyright. Copyright fuels creativity,
encourages diverse voices, promotes free speech, and creates
a vibrant culture. Thank you for buying an authorized edition
of this book and for complying with copyright laws by not reproducing,
scanning, or distributing any part of it in any form without permission.
You are supporting writers and allowing Penguin Random House to
continue to publish books for every reader.

Image credits appear on pages 709 and 710.

LIBRARY OF CONGRESS CATALOGING-IN-PUBLICATION DATA

Names: Farrell, John A. (John Aloysius), author.
Title: Ted Kennedy : a life / John A. Farrell.
Description: New York : Penguin Press, 2022. |
Includes bibliographical references and index.
Identifiers: LCCN 2021060432 (print) | LCCN 2021060433 (ebook) |
ISBN 9780525558071 (hardcover) | ISBN 9780525558088 (ebook)
Subjects: LCSH: Kennedy, Edward M. (Edward Moore), 1932–2009. |
United States. Congress. Senate—Biography. | Legislators—
United States—Biography. | United States—Politics
and government—1945–1989. | United States—
Politics and government—1989–
Classification: LCC E840.8.K35 F37 2022 (print) |
LCC E840.8.K35 (ebook) | DDC 973.92092 [B] —dc23/eng/20220525
LC record available at https://lccn.loc.gov/2021060432
LC ebook record available at https://lccn.loc.gov/2021060433

Printed in the United States of America
1st Printing

Designed by Amanda Dewey

For Javier, and for Adriana

In time, when yet very young, he became chief mate
of a fine ship, without ever having been tested by those
events . . . that show in the light of day the inner worth of
a man . . . not only to others but also to himself.

"I shall be faithful," he said . . . letting his eyes wander
upon the waters, whose blueness had changed to a
gloomy purple under the fires of sunset.

JOSEPH CONRAD
Lord Jim

CONTENTS

TED KENNEDY

One

THE LAST OF THE
KENNEDY BOYS

Notice was sent, not to the applicant, but to his father. "Your son has been admitted to Harvard College," wrote the dean of freshmen, Delmar Leighton, to Joseph P. Kennedy in July 1950. He scribbled in a postscript, "Happy to be sending you another of these letters!"

Kennedy, a Harvard alumnus and benefactor, took the university's admittance of his eighteen-year-old son, Edward, as his due. At sixty-one, the patriarch was extraordinarily wealthy, after a rollicking career as a Wall Street tycoon, diplomat, Hollywood studio chief, real estate mogul, purveyor of forbidden liquor, and adviser to President Franklin Roosevelt.

"I suppose it would almost be a sacrilege," Kennedy wrote back, "not to have the last of the Kennedy boys attend the school where his father and brothers went."

The corsair closed his letter with cajolery. Someday he might need Leighton's help again. "It's a rather difficult job today to be Dean of Freshmen at a college like Harvard, with all the problems that the youths of today have to face," Kennedy wrote. "We are delighted that Teddy is in your hands."

UNSPOKEN, BUT KNOWN TO BOTH, was Harvard's expansive criteria for accepting Edward Moore Kennedy to the Class of 1954. It wasn't because his academic record showed flair. Like so much in his life, it had to do

with family. The university was a place where clans like the Adamses, Roo-
sevelts, and Lodges sent their sons—prodigies, rakes, and dolts alike—to
be certified for rank and lives of privilege. Even in the 1950s, when the
leveling effects of World War II were strong and programs for young
veterans like the GI Bill democratized the yards of the Ivy League, Harvard preserved its traditional allotment of each year's class for boys of
wealth and stature. Ninety percent of the applicants from the better prep
schools, and an equal proportion of the sons of Harvard alumni, were
admitted in 1950.

College administrators called them "the gentlemen" or (with smiles they
shared among themselves) "the paying guests." Along the redbrick walks
of Cambridge, on the gold coast of Mount Auburn Street, in clubs with
names like Spee or Fly, the "gentleman's C" was respectable. In some of
the clubhouses or athletes' suites, where eggheads and day students grinding for grades might find themselves the subject of mockery, academic
indifference was a mark of honor. Yet there were always a few of the legacy
sort who, for lack of effort or talent, or temperament, would come to ill-
starred ends, face suspension, and place the school in an awkward position. Leighton sought, in his letter to Joseph Kennedy, to head this off.
"While we believe that no students have been admitted to Harvard who
do not have the capacity to do good college work, the transition to university conditions is not always easily made," wrote the tactful dean. "We ask
for your cooperation in notifying us if . . . you have reason to believe your
son is having difficulty."

"Write us about him, as fully as you are willing, with references to his
individual qualities and needs," the dean urged Kennedy, "in case he has
deficiencies in his earlier education or weaknesses in character or health
we ought to know about."

IN FACT, there was reason for Joseph to believe that Edward Kennedy—
Ted or Teddy, sometimes Eddie, to family and pals—might find the tran-
sition difficult. It's not that Ted was not gifted. Far from it. The last of the
Kennedy boys was tall and handsome, with a robust physique, arboreal

quads, a million-dollar grin and an exuberant sense of humor. His thick, wavy dark brown hair would last a lifetime and the mighty Irish jaw was assertive—if prone to be enveloped in times of plenty by the chipmunk cheeks of the Fitzgeralds, his maternal line. His eyes were expressive: not probing like his older brother John's, but vulnerable, and eloquent in times of sorrow. He was a warm, playful human being who loved dogs, good times, song, and devilry. "To find Ted Kennedy, listen for the laughter," a friend of his would say. He said his prayers and went to church; a Sermon on the Mount—not a Ten Commandments—Catholic.

He was more than intelligent, but no intellectual. His brother John called Ted a "gay illiterate." When motivated—most notably by his father's prodding—he'd invest the needed hours in the study halls and carrels. As the last of nine children, he had sometimes been coddled, but often neglected. He knew loneliness, having spent much of his childhood shuttled off to boarding schools. By the time he got to Harvard, he had attended ten different schools. (Or was it nine? Or eleven? His mother could sometimes not remember.) The experience left him unsure. He stumbled over words, a cognitive tell. He did better when rehearsed, and he knew it. Throughout his life, he would compensate via intense preparation and relentless effort. It made for an intricate, and complex character—that marvelous affability joined with drive and perseverance; insecurities addressed by toil, and anxiety salved by self-indulgence. He would spend that life seeking "to catch up" to his siblings. "The disadvantage of my position is being constantly compared with . . . brothers of such superior ability," he would say.

As a Kennedy, he had formidable advantages—and just as formidable expectations. His grandfathers were men of note in Boston. Each was the son of an Irish immigrant father who died young in the new land, leaving the boys to sustain their families; each found his way into politics. Tight-lipped Patrick J. Kennedy, an East Boston barkeep, tavern owner, and liquor distributor, served in the state senate and on the Democratic Party's "board of strategy," which sought to arbitrate disputes among the town's fractionate Democrats. There, he recurrently found an ally in garrulous John Fitzgerald, who would ascend from the North End to the U.S.

Congress and to City Hall, where he served two terms as Boston's mayor. Their families gathered for picnics on Old Orchard Beach in Maine. And Patrick Kennedy's son Joseph married John Fitzgerald's daughter Rose.

Rose was a fine catch: Irish American royalty, "rocked to sleep to political lullabies," she would say. Joseph was a lone wolf, with a lean and hungry look, who set out to build a fortune in finance. "Tenaciously independent," a reporter wrote in his notes. "A cold-blooded predilection to bet against the crowd," wrote another. "When you get out on The Street, you have got to be a cold appraiser, or you die," Joseph told the scribes.

Fine advice, not always followed. Joseph Kennedy was a temperamental sort—self-made, gifted, sensitive and prickly, reliant on instinct, which sporadically failed him. He could rage, engage in torrid love affairs, crush rivals—and be overpowered by emotion when seeing the polio-stricken children who shared the rehabilitative swimming pool with the disabled Roosevelt at Warm Springs, Georgia. While serving as the U.S. ambassador to Great Britain at the outset of World War II, Kennedy had scuttled his yen to be the first Roman Catholic president when he split with Roosevelt over the threat posed by Nazi Germany and got vilified as a herald of appeasement. His designs for a Kennedy presidency fell upon his sons.

Ted's three older brothers—Joseph Patrick Kennedy Jr. (Joe Jr. to the tribe), John Fitzgerald Kennedy (Jack), and Robert Francis Kennedy (Bobby)—had excelled at Harvard. The two oldest then left Cambridge for war, and memorable acts of heroism. Joe Jr. had been groomed to lead clan and country but died in a perilous mission in the skies over Europe. John—renowned for his gutsy efforts to save the crew of his sunken torpedo boat in the South Pacific—took up the family's drive for power.

Joseph and Rose Kennedy expected that the boys—that all their children—would excel. They were dispatched to elite schools—Harvard, Princeton, Stanford—taught to ride, sail, waltz, and ski, and shine at golf and tennis. Amid the Great Depression, they savored prime rib suppers on Sundays at Longchamps, had their teeth straightened by the best Manhattan orthodontists, and canoodled with film stars on the zebra-patterned booths at El Morocco. Seated around the family dinner table, the boys faced intense interrogation from their father on current events, politics, and history. Visitors to the Kennedy estates in Palm Beach, Florida, and Hyannis Port, Massachusetts, found a gorgeous crowd of young folk, furiously engaged in sailing, touch football, waterskiing, and other athletic pursuits, teasing, laughing, and goading one another in play. "They were like carbonated water, and other families . . . flat," John's wife, Jacqueline, recalled. "They bring out the best then they all bounce off each other." After surviving her introduction, and a broken ankle suffered in one of their football games (from which she thereafter abstained), she nonetheless found them "wonderful . . . gay . . . stimulating . . . [and] gallant."

WHEN JOSEPH WAS NAMED as ambassador to the Court of St. James's in the months before the war, his wife and children had joined him in Great Britain. The handsome family beguiled the British and American press, which recorded their sojourns to London's teas and dances, to kiss the Blarney Stone in Ireland, to Saint Moritz to ski and skate in winter, and to the cabanas of Cannes in summer. The Kennedys arrived in England in March 1938, when Ted was six, and Rose and her children stayed through the first weeks of the war, in September 1939. They settled at 14 Princes Gate, a thirty-six-room mansion near the Albert Memorial, bequeathed to the U.S. government by another famous American financier, J. P. Morgan, as a residence for its ambassador. It had an elevator, which Ted commandeered; a large garden where he and Robert, twelve, rode their bicycles; and a view of Hyde Park, where their father went horseback riding. Robert was old enough to wear trousers; Ted was consigned to knee socks and shorts. They attended a party at Windsor Castle and danced with the princesses, Elizabeth and Margaret. Ted wrenched a knee learning to ski in Switzerland, was goaded by his older brothers to leap into the Mediterranean from the high embankment at Eden Roc, and received his First Communion from the newly inaugurated Pope Pius XII, a family friend, in Rome. "I hope you will always be good and pious as you are today," the pontiff told Ted.

"I wasn't frightened at all," the boy told the press. "The pope patted my head and told me I was a smart little fellow. He gave me the first rosary beads from the table before he gave my sister any."

Atop the ladder, in those years before the war, were Joe Jr. and John and high-spirited Kathleen, who was called Kick and would marry into the British aristocracy. "To us they were marvelous creatures, practically god-like, and we yearned to please them and be acceptable," said Eunice, a middle child. The youngest Kennedy, nurse Luella Hennessey would remember, was "bubbly and happy." The ambassador reserved times to visit with each of his sons. He and Robert would have a sober discussion, and then after Robert left, "Teddy would come in and the atmosphere of the room would completely change," said Hennessey. "Teddy was like the sunshine, lighting up everything in sight and keeping his father young. Through the corridors, you could hear them laughing." He was the "complete antithesis" of the brooding, more reticent Robert, said their mother.

The outbreak of war sent Rose and the children home to the Kennedy mansion in Bronxville, New York. London was not safe during the Nazi air attacks. The family had been chastised by the air raid wardens after Ted ripped a blackout curtain.

"We are up in Bronxville now . . . we had a dead skunk in the pool," Ted wrote his father, who remained in England.

"We had a Halloween party lost week Afterwards Igot dressed up like a ghost and went all the way down the road I didn't scare because you said not to scare anyone because they may have a weak heart," Ted reported.

"It snowd on Friday," Ted wrote. "I hope not many bombs have drop near you . . . my reading is beter in school, love, Teddy."

And, "Dear Daddy. We are down in cap-card [Cape Cod] mother has gone to jacks graduain [graduation]. joe is here. The wether is very dad [bad]. Would you get me the kings autograh [autograph] for me."

In September 1940, amid the Battle of Britain, Joseph took the time to write a long letter to his youngest son:

> I don't know whether you would have very much excitement during these raids. I am sure, of course, you wouldn't be scared, but if you heard all these guns firing every night and the bombs bursting you might get a little fidgety.

I am sure you would have liked to be with me and seen the fires the German bombers started in London. It is really terrible to think about, and all those poor women and children and homeless people down in the East end of London all seeing their places destroyed. I hope when you grow old you will dedicate your life to trying to work out plans to make people happy instead of making them miserable, as war does today. . . .

Well, old boy, write me some letters and I want you to know that I miss seeing you a lot, for after all, you are my pal, aren't you?

Love Dad

The summers of his youth took on an idyllic status for Ted: the family together on the Cape or the Riviera; those handsome, laughing brothers teaching him to swim, to sail, to ride a bicycle. The children looked to one another for closeness and camaraderie; the notion that age or marriage—much less death—would end it seemed absurd. "My family did not so much live in the world as comprise the world," he remembered. "It was all here; all here." This idealized family moment would be his lifelong touchstone—something he would desperately miss and, incessantly and incapably, seek to renew. "We were enormously happy together. Our best friends were our brothers and sisters," he recalled. It was "our space and time."

But with those breezy summers came that unabating expectation. "Our family was the perfect family," Rose told her journal. "Boys brilliant, girls attractive and intelligent, money, prestige, a young father and mother of intelligence, devoted, exemplary habits and successful in the education of the children." Joe Jr. and John were warriors. Robert was too young to serve in wartime combat, yet he—the shortest and scrawniest of the brothers—surpassed them on the football field, winning his Harvard letter by playing in the Yale game, on a fractured leg. There was "no crying" in his house, Joseph Kennedy famously decreed. "I would not have allowed the children to express grumpiness," Rose said.

After Joe Jr. was killed in an aerial attack on a Nazi U-boat base, their father's calculations prevailed, and John moved to the head of the line.

Ted remembered how the family received news of the eldest son's death—from priests who arrived on a summer day at the Cape—and how it shattered their father, and how John had stepped in as leader, to suggest that they go sailing, for "Joe wouldn't want us sitting here crying." John Kennedy entered "politics not because it was natural to him or that it was his desire," Joseph wrote to Representative John McCormack a few years after the war. "As the next oldest, Jack took up a great many . . . obligations and desires of Joe's."

Singularity was discouraged. "If a member of the family has nothing to offer in a conversation, or has accomplished nothing, then the rest of the family rather ignores him," Rose wrote. "If everyone campaigns for Jack and he has done nothing, then the other members do not want to talk with him. If he does not want to play tennis, golf, ski or ride then he sits by himself." There was, Eunice would remember, "a lot of pressure, all the time." Her father had a saying: "Not for chalk, money or marbles will we take second place."

In this silken, Darwinian environment, Ted Kennedy craved a secure footing. He was awed by the achievements of his father and brothers and vexed by self-doubt. His solicitations of affection had an urgency. He was avid, yet sometimes failed to show good judgment. He was wont to take risks that, in retrospect, were reckless. All his life, he would see himself as the "fuck-up" in the clan. "Ted—he was the ninth child, after all—did not get the attention the others got. Always felt inadequate because of his brothers," said his cousin Joseph Gargan.

"What is of interest to people who might study him," said Patrick, his youngest son, "is this conflict in his life between this idea of who he was supposed to be . . . and who he was. And I think who he was, was just an amazing, authentic person who loved a good time, loved people, was very gregarious and social and yet, in a way, felt encumbered . . . [by] the sense of *I have to be something else and be serious-minded if I'm to be successful, taken seriously.*"

If nagged and pressed, he was also spoiled. As those who knew them well remarked, there were rules for Kennedys and rules for everyone else. When a child of his blundered, Joseph Kennedy might stomp and storm, but his clout ensured a bailout was at hand. To avoid Joseph's hard glare and displeasure, the boys grew adept at dodging responsibility. After being reported for a road rage incident in which he repeatedly bumped the car in front of him, John asked his friend Kirk Lemoyne "Lem" Billings to lie to the police and take the blame. When Robert was caught in a cheating scandal at Portsmouth Priory, a Catholic prep school in Rhode Island, he was permitted to leave quietly and resume his schooling elsewhere. When Ted conducted a nighttime raid on a chemistry lab at Milton Academy—to rig the equipment so that an instructor's planned experiment failed the next morning—there was agita but no expulsion.

Within Ted's life of privilege, there was tension. When he was nine, his mentally handicapped sister Rosemary was given a lobotomy and vanished from their home. Ted wondered if he, too, might be disappeared.

"You can have a serious life or a non-serious life, Teddy. I'll still love you which ever choice you make. But if you decide to have a non-serious life, I won't have much time for you," his father told him when he was a teenager. "You make up your mind."

Over time, Ted chose sailing as his avocation—leaving the stringent standards of the crowded shore for the liberty of wind and water. Here he found solace in troubled times. His metaphor for life became a search for a "true compass"—a steady course, fixed by the unshakable stars, to guide him through tumult.

The sea was salve and getaway. As a man, he would display on his dresser a framed bit of dialogue from the playwright Eugene O'Neill, in which the dissolute Edmund Tyrone speaks of his escape to deep water:

> I dissolved in the sea, became white sails and flying spray, became beauty and rhythm, became moonlight and the ship and the high dim-starred sky!

Ted had applied to Harvard from Milton, one of the country's finer preparatory schools, which traced its history, in the countryside outside Boston, back to 1798. His work there was satisfactory, but his education overall was haphazard: Milton was the last of those ten primary or secondary schools he attended by the time he turned sixteen. His parents were rich, busy people whose relationship was characterized by the long stretches they spent apart—apart from each other, and from their nine children. Rose dealt with Joseph's marital infidelities by spending his money on jewelry and clothes and traveling about the world.

"Gee, you're a great mother to go away and leave your children all alone," John scolded when he was five years old and Rose was leaving for a six-week vacation. "His mother really didn't love him," Jacqueline told a writer from *Life* magazine in the days after John's death. "She likes to go around talking about being the daughter of the Mayor of Boston or how she was an ambassador's wife. She didn't love him." When a measles epidemic struck Boston and imperiled her brood, Rose left Joseph and the family nurse to deal with it. "My mother didn't touch me—but you can't give what you didn't get," Maria Shriver would say of her mother, Eunice, and Eunice's relationship with Rose. "Ghastly family," author Gore Vidal, a relative of Jacqueline, recalled. "What an awful woman [Rose] was. Never went to see [John] in the hospital—he was sick most of the time he was at school. She never showed up."

The boys were delivered as boarders to chilly institutions like Choate or St. Paul's, and the girls (like Rose before them) dispatched to convent schools. The older sons—Joe Jr. and John—left home as teenagers and had relatively stable educations. But by the time Ted, the youngest, came along, his mother, Rose, was weary of reading books, playing games, or devoting too much time to a child. "We tried to keep everything more or less equal, but you wonder if the mother and father aren't quite tired when the ninth one comes along," she would say. "It takes an effort to tell a bedtime story which has been told dozens [of] times," she confided to her journal. "It is sort of a chore to go out on a frigid hill to watch a child's ski lesson."

Rose tried, unsuccessfully, to enroll Ted in kindergarten when he was four, and in first grade at five, and ultimately dispatched him to his first boarding school at the age of seven. More than once, when she wanted to get to Palm Beach for the season, Rose yanked her son out of his cold-weather school and placed him in a strange Florida classroom. It's not certain that he ever finished third or fourth grade. "You spent your time just sort of finding how you get to your classroom, where your bed was," he remembered.

So he bounced from school to school. He was deposited at seven in Portsmouth Priory where the rest of the students were five or more years older, and bullied him. They dug up the dead pet turtle he had buried and threw it in his bed with him one night, then played catch with it around the hall.

"I was in the wrong grade . . . you couldn't have friends," he remembered. "Suddenly this wonderful, nurturing family is . . . divided. Suddenly . . . there was real separation and sense of confusion. And wondering. You wondered were you going to ever see these people again." It was "a rather lonely existence . . . very difficult . . . bleak."

"At nine years old I went off to boarding school at Riverdale Country, and I got whooping cough and almost died," he remembered. "The underpinnings . . . of the family and support and faith weren't there." He reached for a sailing analogy. "You're losing your mooring."

Much of the time, his native buoyancy prevailed. "Teddy is just the same," Rose wrote her children in a letter from Palm Beach in 1941. "He went roller skating all by himself the other day and enjoyed it thoroughly." A year later, she reported how Ted "goes confidently off without bothering anyone" when he wished to see a movie. "I remember him when he was seven or eight as being overweight, terribly good natured, laughing constantly and an incessant tease," Eunice remembered.

Yet, as a schoolboy, Ted was given an assignment to write a short story. Many years later, he showed it—to illustrate his childhood—to James Young, a University of Virginia professor. "It was a story about a boy at school who was very sad and who didn't like it at school," Young recalled. "He was just so sad and . . . he got his little bag together and tried to run away. They caught him and all the things in his bag spilled off and rolled down the hill."

By Kennedy's account, it was not until he arrived at Milton, at the age of fourteen, that his anxiety eased. He learned to make a friend, met his first girlfriend—learned to learn—and the loneliness started to dissipate. He played football, and was a member of the school debating squad that gloriously defeated a team of Harvard freshmen.

But parental abandonment remained a running theme. "I'm sending these flowers to you even though you sent me to boarding-school when I was 7," Ted would write on Mother's Day in 1973.

"Have sent flowers to New York and called Palm Beach and Boston," wrote his sister Jean. "No wonder I am so insecure. Where are you Mommy?"

The boarding school regimes were strict, at times Dickensian. At the Riverdale Country School in the wealthy suburbs of New York, Ted and the other boys suffered degrees of sexual molestation at the hands of a dormitory master and his stooges. At the Fessenden School in Newton, Massachusetts, he was paddled thirteen times in four years. Some classmates found the spankings "absolutely horrendous," he later recalled, but when the school asked for parents' permission to employ corporal punishment, "My father was the first one to send it back, approved."

His parents shrugged off danger signs. "Changing schools is always something of a handicap no matter how successfully the person is handled," warned Julia Markham, the principal of his Bronxville, New York, elementary school. "Interruptions at this point in his progress are apt to prove difficult and will no doubt result in slowing up his advance," wrote the heads of the nearby Lawrence Park West Country School, upon hearing that Ted would be leaving only months after arriving.

Ted's namesake, Edward Moore—an adjutant for Joseph Kennedy—and Moore's wife, Mary, were often called on as surrogate parents. His father's office staff helped the youngster gather the correct gear, from the proper clothing stores, for the latest academy. He had problems focusing. When he was ten, his parents had him evaluated, and hired a tutor. "Ted is much more quiet and considerably deflated," Rose reported to the family, then quipped, "which most of his brothers and sisters consider an improvement." Friends of the family did what they could—taking Ted and his brother Robert in for Thanksgiving dinner or to the theater in Boston. Robert, who was similarly shipwrecked, kept in touch with Ted on the telephone and reported to his parents. "Sorry you didn't get to Boston as expected but I expect you were busy with the welfare of all the other little children," Robert wrote his father.

"I was struck by what a complicated role [Ted] played in that family," said Harvard Law professor Laurence Tribe, a friend and adviser, years later. "Rose was merciless with him, joking in various ways, making fun of him. . . . After a few drinks he would say, 'Mom, you always left me behind.' . . . It was really remarkable to watch the family tensions."

Among "the biggest thrills" of his childhood, Ted would recall, was the time that Robert and he stole away to Hyannis Port on Easter weekend, camped out in the empty garage—the house was boarded up for winter—hiked the beach, cooked their own meals, and slept on cots.

Rose concluded that, for the most part, Ted just needed to apply himself. Her easygoing son could, she feared, cross the line to fat and lazy. His siblings called him "Biscuits and Muffins" and the family correspondence was chock-full of gossip about his weight. "Teddy has to go on a diet. Miss Dunn has to get extra-large suits for him," his sister Jean tattled to their father. "Get that fat little brother of yours to write more frequently," Joseph told her.

Rose knew what strings to tug. "Your diagnosis is undoubtedly correct, as you are on the scene," she wrote the concerned staff of the Fessenden School. She urged them to ratchet up the pressure. "The constant reminder to him that his three brothers all did excellent work in their schools (and that you know his father is placing great dependence on him) might help do the trick."

Within the family, it was expected that "he was never going to amount to much," his friend and aide David Burke would later recall. But then, what did it matter? Ted was the comic, the jester, the afterthought. It was crazy to think that the weight of the crown might ever rest on those blithe shoulders.

AMONG THOSE WHO FILLED in as parental figures was Ted's grandfather John Fitzgerald. "John F" or "Honey Fitz," as the former mayor was known, would take Robert and Ted to lunch on Sundays and then walk with them through the city, discoursing at length on the sites and monuments. Fitz-gerald whetted Ted's interest in history and impressed him with the glad-handing way he greeted the common folk—the help they encountered in restaurant kitchens, the passersby and workmen on the Common and street corners.

The old man's disquisitions stoked a sentiment that Ted and his broth-ers and sisters had inherited from their parents: a kinship with the little guy, despite the family's elite status. Fitzgerald told his grandsons about the days when "No Irish Need Apply" signs welcomed job seekers, and the Protestant Yankee "Brahmins" and Irish Catholic immigrants squared off in ruthless enmity. In 1910, Henry Adams, a scion of the city's other, es-teemed presidential sept, had met the news of Fitzgerald's election as mayor by writing to a friend, "Poor Boston has fairly run up against it in the form of its particular Irish maggot, rather lower than the Jew, but more or less the same in appetite for cheese."

Rose told the children how she founded an "Ace of Clubs" society so that Irish American girls, snubbed by the proper Bostonians, could have their own social circle. And Joseph, though he publicly professed to have moved beyond such grievances, let his sons know that he moved to New York in the 1920s to escape Boston's parochial gridlock. He had felt the sting of prejudice at Harvard, and his grand seaside home was in Hyannis Port, and not in Cohasset nearer to Boston, because the Protestants there had blackballed him when he tried to join their country club. Boston "was no place to bring up Irish Catholic children," Joseph would recall. "I didn't want them to go through what I had to go through. . . . I know so many Irish guys in Boston with real talent and ability that never got to first base only because of their race and religion."

Thomas Fitzgerald, the children's great-grandfather, had fled the Great Famine and the oppression of British rule. He arrived in Boston in the 1850s, worked as a peddler, and raised his children in a three-story tenement house on Ferry Street crammed with nine families. They slept on pallets of straw and shared a toilet with three dozen neighbors. Family traits made their appearance, among them fecundity (Thomas and his wife, Rosanna, had twelve children), enterprise (he found wealth in the liquor trade, after investing with his brother in a grocery and saloon), tragedy (a baby girl died of cholera), dependency (three of his children became slaves to drink), and ambition (John F. was accepted at Harvard Medical School and, with the backing of his clan, soon excelled in politics). Joseph Kennedy also had immigrant grandparents. His widowed grandmother, Bridget Murphy Kennedy, and her hardworking son—Patrick Joseph—had used a notions store and a saloon to secure their family foothold in East Boston.

Adams defined politics as "the systematic organization of hatreds," and nowhere was this truer than in Boston at the turn to the twentieth century, as the native elite reacted from contempt and fear, and with resolve, to stop the Irish from taking power. It was a doomed endeavor, as the immigrants poured ashore in unrelenting number and Catholics gave birth at a rate surpassing the Brahmin gentry. But the competition dominated society, commerce, and politics for much of a century, and left a lasting scar on the newcomers. "It was symbolic. The business establishment, the clubs, the golf course . . . that was what I was told at a very young age," Robert Kennedy would recall. "Both my parents felt very strongly about the discrimination."

Joseph said he wanted to raise his children free from all that. "What the hell do I have to do to be an American?" he muttered. In 1927, he put his family on a private railroad car and set off for Wall Street. The youngest children, Jean and Ted, were born New Yorkers. Their childhood home was the mansion in Bronxville, in Westchester County, New York. The gabled white house in Hyannis Port—fourteen rooms on a seaside bluff that would grow into a six-acre compound with sauna, swimming pool, tennis court, and private movie theater—was purchased in 1928, and an oceanfront villa in Palm Beach acquired in 1933.

Kennedy "moved in the intense, secretive circles of operators in the wildest stock market in history, with routine plots and pools, inside information and wild guesses," said *Fortune* magazine in a 1937 profile. But he kept his Democratic affiliation, shifted his gaze from finance to politics, and in 1934 Roosevelt named him to lead the newly created Securities and Exchange Commission, to regulate Wall Street. Who better than a fox to guard the chickens?

"I wanted power," Kennedy would recall. "I thought money would give me power and so I made money, only to discover that it was politics—not money—that really gave a man power." Where Rose had chosen to duplicate the Brahmin institutions, historian Arthur Schlesinger Jr. wrote, Joseph resolved to infiltrate their core. His sons came away with the edge of outsiders. With a sympathy for rebels. With an empathy for the dispossessed. Joseph Kennedy's boys were "well fed underdogs, with pretty good bite," said Charles Daly, who worked with them all.

TED ARRIVED AT HARVARD after spending the summer of 1950 on a splendid jaunt through Europe. He and his cousin Joseph Gargan, who was two years older and studying at Notre Dame, left for Italy from New York after the week of festivities surrounding Robert's wedding to Ethel Skakel in Greenwich, Connecticut. While in Europe, Ted and Gargan missed a storied moment when the high-spirited Kennedys dunked Senator Joseph McCarthy of Wisconsin, a friend of their father, in Nantucket Sound. "They gave him the boat treatment, i.e., throwing him out of the boat, and then Eunice, in her usual girlish glee pushed him under. To everybody's concern and astonishment, the Senator came up with a ghastly look on his face, puffing and paddling. The wonder of it all was that he did not drown on the spot . . . coming from Wisconsin he had never learned how to swim," Rose wrote Robert.

Kennedy and Gargan alighted in Rome, rented a Fiat convertible, and toured Naples and Sorrento before turning north and traveling through Austria and Germany to France. They visited Pompeii, went boating in the Blue Grotto of Capri, took a sliding, twisting trip over Mount Vesuvius, and had to be rescued after capsizing their canoe on Lake Como. They toured the World War II battlefield at Monte Cassino, and Hitler's "Eagle's Nest" at Berchtesgaden, and were moved by the bombed-out ruins of Aachen and Cologne. A survivor guided them through the bleak grounds, the huts and crematorium at the concentration camp in Dachau.

They were innocents: Catholic boys who on most mornings rose early to attend Mass, and alleged to be baffled by the bidets in the bathrooms. But they were eighteen and twenty, and so there was room on the itinerary for young ladies—a lovely Rose Marie who stole Gargan's heart in Venice; eighteen-year-old Elizabeth Taylor, whose path they crossed as she honeymooned poolside at the Hotel du Cap-Eden-Roc on the French Riviera (the young actress "really is the business," Ted told his diary, somewhat embarrassed by the "maneuvering" he had performed to get her photograph and the cold eye he and Gargan had gotten from her husband, Conrad "Nicky" Hilton), and the American girls they met in Paris, who showed them its cultural attractions by day and joined them at the Moulin Rouge and other cabarets at night. No scene of them carousing, watching the bare-breasted showgirls, was included in their letters home to Rose.

They may have done better, girl-wise, had Ted not forgotten his swimsuit and been forced to purchase an ancient woolen bathing garment at the Lido as a substitute. "It takes Ted ten minutes to squeeze into it, because he isn't getting any lighter eating this food," Gargan wrote Joseph and Rose. The suit led to a run-in with the law. After breaking into a private cabana to change, they were rousted by police and escaped by sprinting, arms full of clothes, through the thickets of beach chairs, blankets, and umbrellas on the strand. They sailed home on the luxurious ocean liner SS *America*. For Gargan it was "one laugh after another." Ted wrote in his diary, "Sensational time. Best trip ever."

In Cambridge, Ted was assigned to room in the Wigglesworth dormitories, on the south side of Harvard Yard. He came to Harvard in his mother's blue coupe, but quickly switched to a sporty Pontiac convertible, with a horn that bleated like a cow. "I considered that fairly stylish and amusing," he would remember. "I was still a kid in many ways." His father, who kept close tabs on his children, heard of Ted's noisy cruises through Harvard Square, and lectured his son about deportment. You might do this sort of thing as a prole, Joseph told Ted, but not as an epitome of Irish America. To be a Kennedy was to be different. "When you exercise any privilege that the ordinary fellow does not avail himself of, you immediately become a target," Joseph wrote. "It's alright to get ahead of the masses by good works, by good reputation and by hard work, but it certainly isn't by doing things that [prompt others to say] 'Who the hell does he think he is?'"

HARVARD WAS ALL TED hoped for. He was six feet two inches tall and weighed 210 pounds and made the freshman football team, where he won kudos for rambunctious play. His father was delighted, and paced the sidelines in coat and beret, shouting encouragement. Ted made lifelong friends among the Harvard athletes and—had he not already done so in Europe that summer—lost his chance at the $1,000 his parents promised the Kennedy boys if they made it to twenty-one without drinking. "Making cleat marks and crashing into other solid bodies on the same field where my brothers had played—it didn't seem that life could hold anything better than that," he would recall.

There were shadows that fall. John Fitzgerald died—a sad landmark commemorated by impressive ceremonies, laments, and retrospectives in the Boston newspapers. There were tales of death from Korea as well, where, as Kennedy and Gargan frolicked in Europe, the communist regime of North Korea had launched a surprise attack on South Korea, seizing Seoul and corralling the beaten American and South Korean defenders in a corner of the peninsula. The U.S. troops were told to stand or die; there would be no miraculous evacuation, like Dunkirk.

The allied commander, General Douglas MacArthur, reversed the course of the war with a brash amphibious landing at the port of Inchon in mid-September, flanking the North Koreans and driving them back deep into their homeland. But MacArthur's success led to the third act of the conflict, as hundreds of thousands of Red Chinese troops crossed the border. With flares, screaming trumpets, and gongs, the Chinese troops attacked at night, sending the allies in a reeling retreat south. Casualties soared at the frozen Chosin Reservoir and amid the blood-soaked rocks of Hoengsong. President Harry Truman, prompted by MacArthur, considered the use of nuclear weapons.

On December 15, Truman declared a national emergency, and called for full mobilization and an army of 3.5 million men. Joseph Kennedy had lost one son to war. Not irrationally, he feared that this Cold War wildfire would spread to the plains of Europe and across the Pacific islands. He sent a letter to Ted, warning him to mind his grades and secure his deferment from service: "Keep after the books if only to keep the draft away from your door," he told his son.

With the help of brother John's congressional staff, Ted explored his options. He could enlist in the Navy ROTC program and ensure that upon graduation he would serve in an officer's uniform, but the naval training cruises might interfere with the plans he was crafting for a bigger, better version of the previous summer's escapades with Gargan. His father's employees had hammered out a nine-week itinerary, and applied for the necessary visas, after asking Ted what he wished to see. Kennedy and Gargan would start in Paris and range across the continent—to Normandy and Bordeaux, then Spain and Morocco, and back up through Provence and Burgundy to Amsterdam, Berlin, and Scandinavia before sailing home on the luxury liner *Île de France*. His father would buy a car for them and have it waiting in Paris. Did he prefer another convertible? European-made, or an American brand?

The plans for his vacation were enticing, as were his hopes of playing football for Harvard as a sophomore. His father and all three of his brothers had sought glory on the gridiron. Ted was too slow to be a star, but his physical gifts exceeded theirs. And "I loved being part of a team—I didn't want to lose that," he remembered. As his freshman year drew toward a close, he grew anxious over an upcoming Spanish exam, lost his nerve, and resolved to cheat. "I worried that if I flunked or made a D on the final exam, I wouldn't be eligible to play football in the fall," Kennedy recalled. "I didn't think it through."

It was a heedless decision and an imbecilic scheme. "They were freshmen. They were stupid," said George Abrams, a classmate. A friend, William Frate, agreed to pose as Ted and take the exam. Earlier that year, the ruse had succeeded. This time, a proctor recognized the impostor and turned the culprits in. Dean Leighton booted them from school, though with a condition that after two years of appropriate reflection and good deeds, they might apply for readmittance.

Ted feared what Joseph would say. He called John, who agreed to break the news to their father. ("Jesus Christ," the exasperated congressman told an aide. "Teddy's caught cheating at Harvard.") Ted made the long drive down to Cape Cod and met his dad in the sunroom.

Joseph had been spending the spring and early summer consulting Eisenhower and MacArthur about politics and world affairs and mulling whether John should challenge the incumbent senator Henry Cabot Lodge in 1952. Now he switched between forlorn disappointment and eruptive fury at the actions of his youngest. "See what happens when you do these things?" he barked. From time to time, John or Robert would call on the phone to mollify their father, but Joseph would be just as furious when he hung up.

Joe Jr. had been the golden firstborn. Robert was steel and steady—a classic runt. John was more of a miscreant—but one of those charmed and charming individuals who glides away from difficulty. "A child of fate," who could slip on a banana, his father liked to say, and win the crowd's applause for the grace with which he fell. But this youngest boy seemed clueless. "There are people who can mess up in life and not get caught," he told Ted. "You're not one of them." A decade later, in an interview with a journalist, Joseph Kennedy called Ted the most attractive of his sons—but regretted that he was also the least intelligent.

There was "a lot of disappointment. Disappointing him. Disappointing my brothers. Disappointing my family," Ted remembered.

The European adventure was scrapped. A secretary wrote the steamship company, canceling the reservations. There was gossip in the faculty club, but the world was not told why Ted Kennedy left Harvard.

TED DECIDED, as his redemptive deed, to enlist. He had lost his deferment, and enlistees had a wider range of choices in how they would serve. Joseph Kennedy had pulled strings to win John a combat assignment during World War II, and Robert a post on a U.S. Navy destroyer christened to honor Joe Jr. Now his father kept Ted safe from the battlefields in Korea. He stayed in touch with his contacts in the military, connecting on even trifling decisions like Ted's Christmas and Thanksgiving leaves.

The unfairness troubled Ted—enough that, as "a necessary phase of my atonement," he considered volunteering for service in Korea. The war was a gory standoff, with the two sides clashing along the 38th parallel in battles memorialized as Bloody Ridge, the Punchbowl, Heartbreak Ridge, and Pork Chop Hill. The fighting would not end for months. He met with Robert and John in New York to explain his plan. They told him to forget it. "Mother and Dad have suffered enough," his brothers said.

Joe Jr. was lost in 1944. Rosemary had been dispatched to seclusion in Wisconsin. And the family had been devastated when, after much heartache over her marriage to a Protestant (a nobleman killed in battle during the war), Kathleen died in a plane crash in 1948. Ted had heard the news at Milton. "Even though it was spring," he would write, "I remember that morning as exceptionally cold and dark. I waited alone for a long time before Jack arrived to pick me up and take me to Hyannis Port."

John and Robert persuaded him. "I realized I was being selfish and was risking unspeakable grief for my parents," Ted recalled. He made the best of it. He had moved on from Nancy Burley, his Milton girlfriend. Soon he was driving his sister Patricia's Pontiac convertible and dating Marjorie McDonnell, a young lady from New York's Irish American royalty.

Kennedy was assigned to three months of basic training at Fort Dix, New Jersey. "It is really hot down here. This getting up at four thirty in the morning is quite a change but am making the best of it," he told one of his father's assistants. Hotter still when he accused a fellow soldier of shirking duty and ended up brawling in the barracks. After additional training as a military policeman in Fort Gordon, Georgia—in which he drew more extra duty for accidentally setting his sleeping bag on fire during a cold nighttime deployment—Ted made it to Europe after all.

Others were sent to war. But after a long ride on a ship whose chow was so awful that he lost "considerable poundage," Kennedy joined the honor guard for the newly formed North Atlantic Treaty Organization command in Rocquencourt, outside Paris. "He was a perfect physical specimen,"

Matty Troy, a friend from Fort Gordon, recalled. "And so fiercely competitive that if the sergeant would tell him to do ten pushups, he would do 20."

In a letter to his parents, he gave a description of the leveling effect of army service. "When I happened to read my name as one of the hundred and eighty-seven out of a possible three thousand men who were to have KP every other day the whole way over, I then decided to make a supreme effort to get off that ship in Norfolk and return to New York. However, upon considering my welcome back in New York by my family and especially Mrs. McDonnell I concluded that to make the crossing now was the only thing left to do," he wrote. "On the way over . . . it became quite rough with the result that most of the troops were rather sick. Your ninth, however, was so busy washing the total of twenty-five thousand trays during the voyage that he didn't have much time for anything else."

IN PARIS, Kennedy patrolled the perimeter, took French language lessons, and enjoyed the local wine and cuisine. Before he left home, Rose—not knowing that Ted had been drinking beer at Harvard—suggested that his parents suspend the $1,000 wager over smoking and drinking while their son was stationed in France. His father, by now, knew him well: "Rose: Are you out of your mind?" he asked.

The nature of Kennedy's service was captured in a New York newspaper. The headline declared, "'Miss Shape' Is Crowned," and the body of the piece related how "Pfc. Edward Kennedy, 20 years old, of the 520th Military Police Service Company, assigned to special security duty at Supreme Headquarters, Allied Powers in Europe, presided tonight at the second anniversary ceremony of his unit. . . . The highlight of the occasion was the crowning of Miss Nanette Blanchette . . . as Miss SHAPE 1953." She was, a *Time* magazine correspondent cabled his editors, a "shapely . . . brunette English model."

On a weekend trip to Switzerland, Kennedy won a bobsled race for novices. He was arrested in Pamplona after throwing his seat cushion into the ring to protest a listless Spanish bullfight. His sisters Patricia and Jean joined him in Austria for a week of skiing to celebrate his birthday. Intent on exposing her youngest to high society, Rose stopped in Paris while vacationing in Europe. She had a limousine pick Ted up at his base and bring him to her suite at the Ritz. From there they went to the Hotel du Golf, a seaside resort in Normandy.

"Dearest Joe," she told her husband. "Everything is going very well & Ted looks wonderful & seems to be enjoying it. His girl, the nurse, is to come over this week & his girl from Texas has left, so he is lucky as usual."

"Dear Everyone," she wrote the other children, "I introduced your frere to the social set & you know how that went over—If you do not, he will be describing it for the next ten years. Among those present was a de Cuevas ballerina & last seen last night Ted was on the way with the troupe not the troops."

It was a nice visit, marred only when Ted had the limousine drop him several hundred yards from the base to avoid the ribbing he would get for being a rich man's son. "I almost made it. I'd walked through the gate and was headed for the barracks when I heard rapid tiny footsteps and a familiar voice behind me," he would recall. "Teddy, dear! Oh, Teddy, dear! You forgot your dancing shoes!" Rose called.

KENNEDY RETURNED HOME in March 1953. One of his first stops was Washington, where brother John—a congressman when Ted shipped off to France—was now Senator Kennedy, having defeated Lodge in the 1952 election. Ted took the night train, climbed the hill from Union Station, and arrived at the Senate Office Building at 7:30 a.m. The door to John's office was locked, so he sat on his suitcase in the corridor until the intense, early-rising occupant of a neighboring suite—Vice President Richard Nixon—came by and invited him in. Nixon at the time was a friend of John Kennedy. The future rivals would dine together, talk foreign policy, and later that year Nixon and his wife, Pat, would be invited to John's wedding to Jacqueline Bouvier. The conversation was light and cordial. "I thought he was the nicest person. He was interested in what I was doing in school, and liked my brother, and it was just an amazing half hour," Kennedy recalled. Then John arrived and gave his brother a backstage tour of the Capitol and the Supreme Court Building across the street. Ted walked out on the Senate floor for the first time. It left an indelible impression. So did his brother's parting words: "Now that you've seen the buildings, you ought to take an interest in what happens in the buildings."

Kennedy also visited with Dean Leighton, who reported to Joseph, "I was favorably impressed by Ted's appearance and attitude in my recent talk with him. It looks to me as if he had made good use of these last two years." Harvard would absolve the prodigal son.

"I am very happy that Teddy is going back to Harvard and I am sure he will do a great job," Joseph replied. "I do appreciate your understanding and consideration in this matter from the beginning."

Ted was twenty-one. A veteran. An ex-cop. His military service had opened windows for him on class and race and human behavior. The boy who had bobbed to get a film star's autograph was now the man who ran girlfriends through Paris and charmed prima ballerinas. He had three more years to complete his education at Harvard, but it was time to consider a vocation.

His father, thinking business, sent Ted on an inspection tour of the family's properties in oil and real estate, out to Tulsa and Chicago. Jean Kennedy had not yet married Stephen E. Smith, and Joseph had no clear successor at administering the family fortune. Or Ted might have chosen to head the Kennedy philanthropic foundation. Giving away money was a fulfilling task. Eunice was a few years away from founding the Special Olympics, which would revolutionize society's care and treatment of the mentally handicapped. Ted might have followed his sister Patricia, who married the actor Peter Lawford that spring and moved to a beach house in Malibu. He could have bought a sailing boat and coasted cerulean waters.

John urged their father to let Ted be a playboy. He and Robert could carry the family standard; they had done so in 1946 and 1952, winning tough elections. He suffered from debilitating illnesses, and part of him lived vicariously through his robust younger brother. Still another part of him bristled at how "Pappy's eyes on the back of my neck" had compelled him to take up the family quest after Joe Jr. died. Let the cup pass, John told his dad.

No one knows how Joseph Kennedy would have reacted if Ted had opted for indolence and splendor. But he had told Ted long before that he would have no time for him if he chose a life that was not interesting. And those political chevaliers, John and Robert, were Ted's idols. To be in their company, to campaign in their cause, was an irresistible proposition. It wasn't business, he told his father when he returned from his inspection tour. It would be politics.

AND SO, one night that summer, as the news photographers jostled for position and reporters scribbled in their notebooks, Ted Kennedy sat on the dais at the state's great fund-raising dinner for the war on childhood cancer. In the starbursts of flashbulbs, Ted handed a $50,000 check from the Joseph P. Kennedy Jr. fund—the evening's single biggest contribution—to the honorary star of the event: the slugger Ted Williams, home from aerial combat in Korea.

A thirty-eight-car caravan had toured Boston that evening, bearing the Red Sox hero through all points of the city. Crowds five deep lined the sidewalks, and the cheering when Williams took the stage in the ballroom at the Statler Hotel was "the greatest public ovation ever tendered a major-league ballplayer," one Boston newspaper insisted. His Sox teammates were in attendance, Ed Sullivan was the toastmaster, and the crowd was dotted with sports figures, politicians, and movie stars. Williams—famously, stubbornly casual—even wore a tie. That new phenomenon, television, carried the scene across the country.

Ted Kennedy—not Joseph or John or Robert, or Rose or any daughter—watched, grinning, as Williams passed the $50,000 sliver of the Kennedy fortune to cancer's resolute foe, Dr. Sidney Farber, there in the spotlights, the dazzle and the flash. To everyone in the hall, and all those who read the story on the front page of the next day's newspapers, the night was about a good cause, a hometown team, and one terrific ballplayer. The ugly war was over, and summer's sweet shadows crept Fenway Park.

The night marked something else as well, though no one knew it then: the beginning of Ted Kennedy's political career—a journey of glories and grief that would span more than half a century and multiply, by a factor of millions, the aid and sustenance that his father's $50,000 check could bring to the sick, the disabled, the downtrodden, and the dispossessed. Kennedy would become one of the greatest U.S. senators, ever—as sublime at his work as Williams was at his—preserving and advancing progressive ideals through decades of political peril, and brokering bipartisan bargains in a hyperpartisan age. And though he would not cross the river himself, Kennedy would be the prophet who witnessed, in his final days, the fulfillment of the century-old liberal vision of health care as a right— not a privilege—of every American.

WHO COULD HAVE KNOWN? In June, Ted sent his parents a telegram from the French Riviera, where he was hot in pursuit of an actress who caught his fancy.

"Having barrels of fun," it said. "Send money for more barrels."

Two

HIGH HOPES

T ed Kennedy got his second chance at a Harvard education, and made more of it. He prepared by taking courses in government, his proposed major, in summer school. He followed his brother John's advice to always be toting and reading a book. He strayed no more into disciplinary danger.

His grades had been erratic on his elementary school report cards and sufficient—Cs and Bs—at Milton Academy and in his middle years at Harvard. With a B average in his senior year, he climbed into the top half of his college class. "I've heard people say, 'Oh, he's a quick study,' but that simply isn't true," Kennedy said. "I've got to go at a thing four times as hard and four times as long as some other fellow."

Kennedy was a grinder. He "would really think through things, even though he didn't have the raw intellectual horsepower to make them easy," said Laurence Tribe, the Harvard law professor who worked with him years later. Like the rest of the Kennedys, and much of increasingly prosperous Catholic America, he had middlebrow tastes in music, food, and literature. Standing around a piano, laughing and singing Irish songs or show tunes, was his idea of a grand time, as were the family's sparky parlor games, sailing contests, and cutthroat bouts of touch football. As a member of the Silent Generation, that cohort that followed the World War II generation but preceded the Baby Boom, he was not weaned on television.

All in all, he was a happy-go-lucky Fifties jock from Winthrop House, whose hours at practice were rewarded in the 1955 football game against Yale, in which he pulled in a touchdown pass. Harvard lost, 21–7, and the locker room was gloomy until Joseph, John, and Robert arrived and marched into the showers to boisterously celebrate Ted's achievement—an explicit demonstration of how family, for Kennedys, superseded other loyalties.

He won a wager with a classmate by taking a perilous walk across the frozen Charles River in a late winter thaw without plunging through the ice. During the summers, he augmented his time on Cape Cod with trips to California, where he dabbled as a park ranger, waterskiing instructor, and, in 1955, a crewman on a trans-Pacific sailing race to Hawaii. "A red-bearded sunkeneyed 185 pound shadow has arrived in Waikiki," he wired his parents. He had no need to worry about paychecks: at the age of twenty-one he had received a million-dollar trust fund from his father. Ted graduated, at the age of twenty-four, in 1956.

HIS RELATIONSHIP with John and Robert was changing. He had been teased, unrelentingly, by his brothers as a child: "They never ceased this for many years." Joe Jr. had tossed him overboard while sailing, and Joe Jr. and John would throw footballs at his legs until they knocked him down and made him cry. When John ran for Congress in 1946, fourteen-year-old Ted was too young to do much but run errands, and was thrilled when his brother invited him to tag along to lunchtime speeches. To show what a generous guy he was, the candidate—rail thin from chronic illness—would tell his audiences that when the Kennedys sat down at the table he always passed the food to the younger children, to make sure they had enough to eat. To prove it, John would then have husky Ted stand up. "I always got great joy out of it," Ted recalled, "until I began to realize I was the brunt of the joke." Robert had come in for his own share of torment from Joe Jr. and John and shrugged off Ted's plea to save him from an assault by the bullies at Portsmouth Priory. "You've got to learn to fight your own battles," he advised.

But there was warmth and affection as well. When Ted, as a boy, resolved to leave home, it was John who suggested that they go to the movies, and then Ted could "run away in the morning." By the following day, whatever family storm had passed. John ignored the Navy's regulations and took Ted on a verboten, thrilling ride on a PT boat in Florida. With the passage of time, they grew closer. John was fifteen years his senior, but willing to throw Ted passes, advise him on his football moves ("Always run back to the huddle"), and compete with him in a family painting contest. As John recuperated from a near-fatal back surgery, Ted would visit him in the hospital, cook him scrambled eggs, read drafts of the book—*Profiles in Courage*—that John was writing, or, with a Harvard pal, Claude Hooton, serenade the hero with an off-key version of "Southie Is My Home Town." As a singer, Ted was loud. While John recovered at the Cape, he and Ted took turns reading Stephen Vincent Benet's epic poem "John Brown's Body" aloud. When Ted had a tooth knocked out in the Bucknell game, it was John who ordered him to a dentist immediately. And just as when Robert and Ethel were married, Ted was an usher when John wed Jacqueline. In 1954, when Ted and his college buddy John Culver traveled to Washington to watch Robert's performance as an aide at the Army-McCarthy hearings, they bunked with the newlyweds. Jacqueline asked Ted to help her craft a question about politics that she could pose to her husband, to impress John with her savvy.

The three brothers had variant personalities. John's usual detachment favored irony and distance. Robert and Ted were more fervid. In the annual Labor Day softball clash between the Kennedy clan (the "Barefoot Boys") and the WASPs from Pennsylvania (the "Pansies") whose big white homes surrounded the compound in Hyannis Port, it was Ted and Robert who argued with the umpires and scrapped with their foes and John who infuriated his brothers by tossing slow fat pitches for the Pansies to clobber. "Jack was always friendly," one of the Pansies recalled, "Bob and Ted seemed rotten spoiled." Robert stepped between his intemperate younger brother and a weekend athlete on another playing field, fighting the belligerent outsider until both were bloodied. After being taunted by some supercilious yachtsmen in Northeast Harbor, Maine, Ted climbed aboard their boat and, with the help of a friend, tossed them in the water.

In the intrafamily competition, the enlistment of ringers was fair game. Upon hearing that Robert had recruited Hall of Fame quarterback Johnny Unitas to play against Ted's team in touch football, Ted went out and found another Baltimore Colt—fullback Billy Pricer—who scored six touchdowns on that snowy afternoon. When Cardinal Spellman offered to join in or umpire a Labor Day softball game, however, both the Barefoot Boys and the Pansies agreed that his holy presence would put a damper on the zeal and profanity—and perhaps land someone in hell for disputing a call. He stayed a spectator.

Like John, Robert had advice for Ted—about his younger brother's carousing. "I talked to Dad last night and he agreed with me that you really made a fool of yourself New Year's Eve," the young puritan wrote Ted in January 1955. When Robert's book about corrupt labor bosses, *The Enemy Within*, was published, he inscribed Ted's copy with the biting "To Teddy, who has his own enemy within."

HARVARD'S AMENITY TO Joseph Kennedy ended at the undergraduate admissions office, and Ted did not qualify for Harvard Law School. He considered Stanford University, where John and Eunice had found California so pleasurable, but that was far from Massachusetts, where the Kennedys had built a political constituency that Ted might one day tap. Instead, he followed Robert to the law school at the University of Virginia, a fine "public ivy," founded by Thomas Jefferson, where Ted could stay in touch with his brothers in Washington and join them if John launched a national campaign.

Virginia boasted of its hundred-year-old honor system, however, a self-policing code administered by students against lying, cheating, and other ungentlemanly acts. Should its law school admit a man who had been expelled for cheating elsewhere? There was precedent for taking applicants with such blots on their records, but it was unsettled law, and there were those who looked upon the Kennedys as arrivistes. Ted's application plunged the faculty and alumni into Talmudic debate, which was ultimately decided by a "divided—and secret—ballot" to admit Ted, and a resolution by university officials that this was the last time they would make this exception.

The family's politics may have been what made Ted less than welcome. The South was controlled by segregationists. As a law student at Virginia in 1951, Robert Kennedy had ignited a controversy by inviting the Black American diplomat Ralph Bunche to speak in Charlottesville. Bunche refused to address a segregated audience, and Robert led a successful campaign to compel the university to integrate the hall. No doubt that memory lingered with the white supremacists.

BEFORE HEADING TO CHARLOTTESVILLE, Ted fulfilled another family rite of passage by visiting Tunisia, Morocco, and war-torn Algeria as a wire service correspondent. Joe Jr. had covered the fall of Madrid in the Spanish Civil War. John had toured Nazi Germany and worked as a journalist after the war. Robert had written stories from the Middle East. Now Ted and Frederick Holborn, a Harvard teaching fellow who was conducting research on the Algerian independence movement for John Kennedy, toured North Africa for a month in the summer of 1956. They interviewed the premier of Tunisia, traveled with the sultan of Morocco, admired the weapons and rode the horses of Berber tribesmen, dodged terrorists on the roads of Algeria, and accompanied the French combat troops who were battling Algerian rebels.

"They say the trip is quite safe as long as the Liberation Army knows you are American and so the first stop in the morning is the [U.S.] Army base [to] collect the biggest flag they have," Ted wrote his father before entering Algeria.

"Glad to hear everything is exciting but be careful," Joseph replied. "You were accepted for Virginia Law School session to start September 14th. If you like, send your article to me here. I will whip it up. . . . Keep that American flag all over the car but learn to duck."

When Ted arrived home, a researcher at Joseph's office in New York helped him prepare articles on the "adamant, fierce, burning nationalism" he had witnessed in North Africa. They were published by a Hearst newspaper agency, the International News Service. The danger for America, Ted concluded, was its identification as an ally of the imperialist regimes in Africa, Indochina, and elsewhere. The French soldiers he joined in the Algerian bush used American-made helicopters and equipment. "They are being used to snuff Nationalist movements, and all the Arab world knows it," he wrote. "The United States is suffering irreparable damage here."

Holborn returned to the United States, but Ted joined his father in the south of France, and so missed John Kennedy's stirring, if unsuccessful, campaign to claim the vice presidential nomination at that summer's Democratic National Convention. Ted listened as his dad, who had originally opposed the venture, now joined in, counseling John and Robert on the telephone and making calls to Democratic bosses on his son's behalf. He, and most everyone in American politics, concluded that the loss was not consequential—it was the dash and vigor of the candidate that folks would remember. "Jack," his father liked to say, "has lucky stars."

The charmed son arrived in France, where he and Ted joined lobbyist William Thompson and some young women on a rented yacht for a pleasure cruise along the Riviera. In their quieter moments, the brothers discussed Algeria and what Ted had learned there, and John made it clear that after his promising debut as a national political figure at the convention, he was looking at the presidency. Ted believed, with no small amount of pride, that their conversations helped inform a celebrated speech John gave some months later endorsing Algerian independence and skewering French and American foreign policy. The voyage ended badly. The press discovered that John was cruising the Mediterranean when Jacqueline, back in New England, had started to hemorrhage, underwent an emergency operation, and lost their stillborn baby girl.

WHEN TED KENNEDY ARRIVED at law school in September, he met another first-year student with a wealthy and famous father. John Varick Tunney was the son of Gene Tunney, the former heavyweight boxing champion, and Mary "Polly" Lauder, an heiress of the Carnegie steel fortune. Tunney and Kennedy became intimate friends, roommates, and teammates in the moot court competition, a "bare-knuckled intellectual prizefight," in which pairs of students wrote briefs and argued fictional cases before tribunals of judges. They played golf and tennis, traveled together, in time became godparents to each other's sons. They shared a rich kid's sensibility about life, and the burden of fulfilling their parents' aspirations at a tough school like Virginia. "There was . . . anxiety," Tunney would recall. "That first year . . . both of us thought that we might get left behind."

The two shared "a fear," said Tunney, "that we wouldn't match up to the standard that we felt had been established for us. We talked about that a great deal." It was "very much a question of fathers," said Tunney. "We had developed . . . the kind of dynastic sense of where we should be as a result of our . . . family history. . . . We had a blowtorch at our hind quarters and we'd better make good, otherwise we would rue the day." Ted was all of twenty-five, and still a nervous first-year law student, when his father made a prediction, in a national magazine, that one day Ted would serve in the U.S. Senate. At Virginia, Ted developed an ulcer.

Kennedy completed his first year of classes in the spring of 1957. He set off to Europe with Tunney, to take a course on international law in The Hague and spend their downtime chasing romance and adventure. Tunney, who had done some mountain climbing in college, hired guides and booked them on the Rimpfischhorn, a twelve-thousand-foot mountain in the Swiss Alps. It was an elementary ascent for skilled climbers but perilous for novices. Near the peak, as the rock face became vertical, Kennedy lost his footing, fell, and was left swinging in the air. In Tunney's account, Kennedy kept his wits and coolly munched on orange slices to recoup his strength. As Kennedy told the story, it was Tunney who pulled him to safety, and showed the saving presence to lead them to the top.

Joseph wrote his son in the Netherlands, congratulating him on compiling a "very satisfactory" record in Charlottesville, and telling him how John Kennedy's speech on Algerian independence had "raised hell all through France." Almost immediately, Ted got in a car crash on a French highway. "Oh, my God. No. Not in France, and this week of all times," John groused.

Ted was earning a reputation as a careless driver. His nickname at Virginia was "Cadillac Eddie." He returned to school that year, worked on his studies, and hosted, with Tunney, memorable parties for their classmates. He toured the Blue Ridge foothills in a beat-up Oldsmobile convertible, too often at excessive speeds, and was charged with a series of offenses, including speeding and reckless driving and attempting to evade arrest, in 1958. A sheriff's deputy alleged that Kennedy cut his lights, turned off his engine, and was hiding in his car when the officer found him.

"Dear Teddy. If you're going to make the political columns let's stay out of the gossip columns," his father wrote him.

John had married, so had Robert, and so had sisters Eunice, Pat, and Jean. Ted visited John and Jacqueline, and Robert and Ethel, on weekends in Washington. They all seemed happy. He turned twenty-six in February 1958. He was content, dating young sophisticates from New York and New England. But getting married, it seemed, was a thing to do.

KENNEDY'S APPROACH TO WOMEN was in keeping with a well-chronicled family heritage. He was strikingly rich and filthy handsome, consummately mannered and an excellent companion. He raced sailboats in Nantucket Sound, wintered in Palm Beach, swam at Acapulco, spent holidays skiing at Stowe and Sun Valley. While in Charlottesville, he took flying lessons and acquired a pilot's license. He had his own cook, and other retainers, to free him from life's tedium. In an era when Hugh Hefner's centerfolds and Ian Fleming's secret agent were casting the hunt for sexual pleasure as recreational sport for the men and women of the Silent Generation, Ted Kennedy was superbly equipped to play Don Juan and very well may have, John Kennedy told his friend Arthur Schlesinger Jr., had not Joseph interceded.

"My father wasn't around as much as some fathers when I was young,"

John told Schlesinger, "but, whether he was there or not, he made his children feel that they were the most important things in the world to him. He was so terribly interested in everything we were doing. He held up standards for us, and he was very tough when we failed to meet those standards. That toughness was important. If it hadn't been for that, Teddy might just be a playboy today. But my father cracked down on him at a crucial time."

But Joseph also taught his sons that accomplishment need not deprive one of pleasure. The father's extramarital sex life was "formidable," said family friend William vanden Heuvel, and the old man made no effort to disguise it. Why should a Kennedy be bound by standards harsher than those that governed a Roosevelt or a Rockefeller? "Irish Catholics in America have been, if anything, puritanical about sex," wrote historian Garry Wills, "and [Joseph] wanted people to know he had escaped that particular form of ethnic narrowness; that he was a man of the world, making his own rules, getting what he wanted, ready to indulge without guilt the one sensual pleasure that interested him."

Ted's Mediterranean sailing trip with John would have taught him, on the slight chance he did not already understand, that Kennedy men viewed wedding vows with more than a little elasticity. "Jack liked girls. He liked girls very much. He came by it naturally. His daddy liked girls. He was a great chaser," said Senator George Smathers, a Kennedy pal.

Sex outside of marriage was a mortal sin for Roman Catholics. John and Ted would commit this offense while honoring other obligations of their religion, like saying their prayers, declining meat on Fridays, and attending Sunday Mass. They ignored the contradiction. By keeping to the rituals, a Catholic retained a connection to the faith that could be valuable in hard times, John told a friend. At moments "when you really needed our religion, you would feel that you really belonged, and that this was a very worthwhile thing," he said. Once you abandoned your faith, "then you don't know where you would finish up."

Rose had left Joseph, but just once, and only briefly. Her father, who had his own relaxed standards of marital fidelity, had lectured her about wifely duty. She returned to Joseph's bed, bore the rest of their nine children, and found escape in travel, shopping, and prayer. This required, or elicited, some measure of coldness. When in Paris together, Rose and her husband stayed in different hotels, not just different rooms and beds. Their relationship, played out before the children, was transactional. For every night of splendor as guests of the king and queen at Windsor Castle ("Rose, this is a helluva long way from East Boston," Joseph said), there was an incident of awful humiliation, like the day he brought a mistress, actress Gloria Swanson, to the Cape.

Rose "willed the repugnant knowledge out of her mind," wrote historian Doris Kearns Goodwin. She "seemed to have what she wanted in her marriage: children, wealth, and privilege. At the same time, the marriage satisfied what may have been her own desire for sexual distance." It was not strange, then, that Rose Kennedy's boys sought warmth in women's arms. Or that, striving to emulate their father, and to win his attention and regard, they mimicked his attitude toward women. He more than encouraged them.

"Dear Teddy," Joseph had written when Ted was twenty-three, "I don't know whether you know it or not but the reports of your goings on with all these beautiful women . . . is slowly but surely driving your oldest brother insane. There was a time when I think he thought I was a little strict with you by insisting that you have something else on your mind besides girls, but having heard [of] you at the airport with a more beautiful girl than Grace Kelly, Jack, I am sure, has changed his whole outlook."

"He hasn't expressed it to me as yet, but from hints being dropped, I gather he feels that I should take a much stricter hand and [that] if there are so many beautiful girls looking around for a Kennedy, it should be the oldest brother and not the youngest," the father wrote. At the time, John had been married for two years. Yet Joseph told Ted, "He will be . . . knocking at your door before long now to get your list."

The family correspondence, even Rose's chatty, round-robin letters, is chock-full with such scorekeeping—like her reports of Ted's romantic conquests in Paris. The sisters did not hold it against their brothers. The second wave of the feminist revolution was years away. It was fine to be a cad. "I can't really understand why I like Englishmen so much as they treat one in quite an off-hand manner and aren't really as nice to their women as Americans," Kathleen wrote brother John, "but I suppose it's just the sort of treatment that women really like. That's your technique, isn't it?"

Ted's technique mirrored that of brother John. He began dating at Milton, where he met girls at school occasions, "which couldn't please me more," he reported to his father. With Richard Clasby, the captain of the Harvard football team, Ted had taken dazzled socialites and career girls from *Seventeen* magazine to night spots like the Stork Club in Manhattan. He "won a small reputation as a date who would take out a girl, make clear his expectations of the evening, and either happily realize them or accept defeat with as much surprise and curiosity as disappointment," biographer James MacGregor Burns wrote. It was in keeping with the general sexual mores of the day, at least for the Kennedys and their class. "Part of the father's aggressive charm, passed on to the sons," said Wills, "was a merry effrontery, a freshness and candor of rapacity." The boys "were expected by their father to undertake a competitive discipline of lust."

In Washington, in the Eisenhower years and the advent of the New Frontier, "flirtation was rampant. Sex was a diversion . . . smoking and heavy drinking were the norm, and a certain kind of sophisticated sin was synonymous with life in the capital," wrote Nina Burleigh, the biographer of one of John Kennedy's mistresses. "A quick act of love shared between a willing man and a willing woman, whether married or not, was one of the small pleasures of a life well lived. It was accepted that one code of behavior applied to the peasants and middle class, another to the sophisticates, who were better equipped to handle certain emotional ambiguities."

NO ONE HAD BRIEFED Joan Bennett.

She and Ted met on a day in October 1957. Ted had received a call from John's office: the senator could not make it to Manhattanville College of the Sacred Heart, in the town of Purchase outside New York City, to dedicate a gymnasium in honor of their sister Kathleen. Ted agreed to take his place.

Virginia Joan Bennett was a "willowy blonde," as the press would come to call her, a twenty-one-year-old classical music and English lit major who had done a touch of modeling. She was the daughter of a New York advertising executive and his wife, who, like many families rising to prosperity in the 1950s, sought to add a bit of polish by sending their girls to college, in this case, with the Sacred Heart nuns in Westchester County. Rose, Jean, and Ethel were Manhattanville alumni; Eunice had attended before heading to Stanford.

Jean introduced Joan to Ted at a reception held after his speech. There was an instant attraction. "She was young and beautiful and went to college where my sisters went," Ted Kennedy would remember.

Ted phoned often, but theirs was a long-distance romance. The couple saw each other sporadically, and their dates were tame affairs. She was a Catholic and a debutante. "I had to be chaperoned everywhere," she remembered. "Nobody slept together. Nobody spent time alone . . . at least if you were a Manhattanville girl." At a New Hampshire getaway with the Bennett family, Ted charmed all by taking over and calling the steps at a square dance in the barn. Joan was impressed by how patient he was when teaching her to ski. During the summer of 1958 they spent a week with Rose on the Cape. They strolled the beach; Ted played golf, and Joan walked the course with him. The matriarch signaled her approval—this was a Catholic lass from Manhattanville who knew classical piano, after all— but called Mother Eleanor O'Byrne, the college president, to verify Joan's character.

Ted proposed, somewhat gawkily, on the beach in Hyannis Port over Labor Day weekend. After an audience with Joseph, who had just returned from his yearly escape to the south of France, the accords were decided and the wedding scheduled for November. Rose had, customarily, switched continents with Joseph, and was at the Ritz in Paris. She dashed off a congratulatory note to Joan, erroneously addressing her as "Connie."

JOAN AND TED did not spend much time together between Labor Day and their wedding rites, except for their engagement party, where Ted gave her a diamond ring selected by his father. Ted was busy with his law school coursework, in the moot court competition, and as "campaign manager" for John's 1958 reelection. The Republicans nominated a nobody. Ted held the fort, making speeches around the commonwealth, watched over by professionals like Lawrence O'Brien and Kenneth O'Donnell, as John toured the nation, seeding the ground for the 1960 presidential race. "I was the nominal manager," Kennedy recalled. "Steve [Smith] was the new brother-in-law assigned by dad to help me out. But it was not long before everyone knew that I was the figurehead and Steve was really running things."

"One day, when [Smith] had just undone the latest series of dubious decisions I had made, he said that when he signed on to the campaign, he didn't realize babysitting the baby brother was part of the job description," said Kennedy. "You looked in the wrong place," Ted told him. "Dad put it in your wedding vows."

Apathy was their actual foe. John's performance in the Democratic primary was less than optimal, and Ted and the others had to redouble their efforts in the general election to impress the party chiefs and the national press corps. Ted's unique contribution was to target the towns of Washington in the Berkshires and Mashpee on Cape Cod, two little burgs whose inhabitants voted early to receive an instant of fame in the afternoon newspapers. They were Republican strongholds that "would vote for Mao Tse-tung if Mao was running on the Republican ticket," John's aides warned him. But Ted "staged a personal crusade . . . visiting the homes of the people, becoming personally friendly with all of them," and delivered both on election day.

A highlight was election eve. The Democrats, as was the custom, assembled at the G&G restaurant, a Dorchester delicatessen. The Honey Fitz in Ted was always ready to surface, but John and Robert were generally more reserved campaigners. Not this night. "Jack got up in front of the crowd that was gathered there and said that it had been a long campaign and the issues had been discussed. Now he was going to do something that hadn't been done in this whole campaign," Ted recalled. "He invited Bobby and me . . . and we sang a song." They joined in a tune they knew as "Heart of my Heart."

JOHN WON WITH THE requisite landslide. But all the politics took Ted away from Joan. Their romance could not qualify either as a sensible or, conversely, a madly intense courtship. "Joan and I were young and naïve," he would recall. "We didn't want to wait. We thought we were in love. . . . I was keen to join my brothers as a married man, a family man. I certainly wished to be a family man." And so "we did what young people do at that time, and we got married."

On the eve of the wedding, Ted shared grievous doubts—"babbling in his martini" to two friends—about his impending marriage. Yes, Joan punched all the right tickets—he would never find another girl like her, he said. But he was only twenty-six, a player like his brother John, and wanted to wait before settling down. Joan had similar trepidation and persuaded her father to ask Joseph Kennedy for a postponement. But the patriarch would not hear of it. Events were in motion: the Kennedys would not be humiliated by the qualms of a young woman.

And so on a cold November day in 1958, at a church in the New York suburbs, at the hand of Francis Cardinal Spellman himself, Ted and Joan were married. Afterward, watching the photographer's movies of the ceremony, Joan heard John—the best man, who forgot he was wearing a microphone—assuring Ted that fidelity was elective. The four-day honeymoon was a bit of a dud. They spent it at the Nassau home, and on a tiny Caribbean islet owned by the seventy-nine-year-old Lord Beaverbrook, a British peer and friend of Ted's dad. The island was deserted, hot, and buggy. There was little but the obvious to do, and they really did not know each other.

JOAN HAD JUST TURNED twenty-two. For the final six months of Ted's law school career, the couple played house in Charlottesville. Like Jacqueline, and unlike Ethel, Joan did not fit well in the rowdy, ultra-competitive Kennedy clan. David Hackett, a prep school friend of Robert Kennedy, offered a glimpse of the demanding life that she confronted—and what had driven Jacqueline to the sidelines—in a compendium called "Rules for Visiting the Kennedys":

Prepare yourself by reading the *Congressional Record, U.S. News and World Report, Time, Newsweek, Fortune, The Nation,* "How to Play Sneaky Tennis," and the *Democratic Digest.* Memorize at least three good jokes. Anticipate that each Kennedy will ask you what you think of another Kennedy's (a) dress, (b) hairdo, (c) backhand, (d) latest public achievement. Be sure to answer "Terrific." That should get you through dinner.

Now for the football field. It's "touch" but it's murder. If you don't want to play, don't come. If you come, play, or you'll be fed in the kitchen and nobody will speak to you.

Don't let the girls fool you. Even pregnant, they can make you look silly. If Harvard played touch, they'd be on the varsity.

Above all, don't suggest any plays, even if you played quarterback in school. The Kennedys have the signal calling department sewed up, and all of them have A+ in leadership. If one of them makes a mistake, keep still. Run madly on every play, and make a lot of noise. Don't appear to be having too much fun, though. They'll accuse you of not taking the game seriously enough. . . .

Don't criticize the other team. . . . It's bound to be full of Kennedys, too, and the Kennedys don't like that sort of thing. . . .

To become really popular you must show raw guts, fall on your face now and then. Smash into the house once in a while going after a pass. Laugh off a twisted ankle or a big hole torn in your best suit. They like this. It shows you take the game as seriously as they do. But remember. Don't be too good. Let Jack run around you now and then. He's their boy.

Joan tried. "Now I can do everything that is required," she proudly told a journalist after completing Kennedy basic training and learning tennis, golf, skiing, and waterskiing. A decade later she confessed, "This family can be overwhelming. . . . I went along with everything they said because I didn't dare do otherwise."

"Oh, what a beautiful girl! Beautiful girl. But she was so scared to death," said Betty Taymor, a Kennedy ally in Massachusetts politics. "The whole thing was just too much for her. She was always trembling. . . . She really gave it the best she had. She really did. It was just too much."

Joan felt the expectation, from Ted and his clan, to match up—in childbearing, appearance, athletic zeal, and political savvy—with her overachieving sisters-in-law. "I had very good legs and lots of blonde hair," she remembered. But she was by nature sensitive and shy and a bit wispy—"vulnerable" was the word she would use to describe herself. And she was quickly overwhelmed by her new life. "I was very smitten by her graciousness, her gentleness, her beauty," Tunney would recall. "She was such a sweet girl, but totally incapable of being a Kennedy."

"When she got into that . . . environment, it just crushed her," he said. "Was it the Kennedys' fault? No. They are what they are. Was it Joanie's fault? No. She didn't know what she was getting into."

The Bennett family, her high school crowd, and the "nun bunnies" who taught her music at Manhattanville had paid little attention to politics. Before she met Ted, "I took no interest in current affairs. I had never even heard of the Kennedys," she remembered. Now her husband was consumed by political duties, and she was left to conjure the elements—good-looking children, lovely home, the guise of perfect mom, hostess, and style-setter—for the campaign brochures, shiny magazines, and "women's sections" of the daily newspapers.

Ted felt the pressure as well. He had "all the physical apparatus of being rather easygoing . . . taking life easy," John Kennedy confided to Burns, but the surface calm was deceiving. "He got an ulcer," said John, "because he didn't know if he was going to be able to stay in law school, because he's not terribly quick." "Could you imagine Teddy a lawyer?" Jacqueline asked one of his professors.

With his father, brothers, and sister-in-law making it a practice of telling friends, scholars, and journalists that Ted was not too sharp, it is unsurprising that his self-image suffered. "He loved and trusted those who had doubtful views of his capacities," one aide recalled.

But then Kennedy and Tunney made it to the moot court finals in the spring of 1959, where, before a star-studded Law Day audience, they were victorious. Friends and family gathered around, offering praise and congratulations. Recruiters dangled jobs at fancy New York law firms. In the final act of his formal education Ted Kennedy was a spectacular success. "He won the toughest contest at one of America's best law schools," an aide and friend, Thomas Rollins, would remark. "All winners of such an event must work hard at it—you [also] have to enter the ring with some serious smarts." The outcome of the moot court trials, the time he spent working on brother John's campaign—and, perhaps, the likelihood that he might be the president's brother—impressed the law school faculty. They overlooked his failing grade in a final semester class on securities law and regulation. Kennedy graduated, though he chose not to attend the ceremonies or collect his diploma.

Ted was nothing if not tenacious, John acknowledged, especially when "induced by outside pressures" like their father's demands. "It's gotten to him now," said John. "He's doomed to this treadmill too."

JOHN, meanwhile, had set off to win the White House. After Ted and Joan toured Mexico and South America on a second honeymoon, Ted joined in the all-day strategy sessions, the nonstop phone calls, and the grueling travel of a national campaign. In an October 1959 meeting at the Kennedy compound on Cape Cod (John and Robert had by now bought homes adjacent to the "big house"), Ted was assigned the western states and given Robert Wallace and Hyman Raskin, two veteran political operatives, as tutors and companions.

Soon, Ted was sending memos to the candidate (John) and the campaign manager (Robert) with the insights gained through nonstop travel. "Senator LBJ did not make much ground in his appearance" in Arizona, Ted reported to Robert in a typical message that December. "To date no one is really taking him seriously except [former] Sen. McFarland, [who] is generally discredited throughout the state." Don't be put off by Ted Kennedy's youth, campaign aide Pierre Salinger told a friend in California: the candidate's little brother was "an agreeable young man who understands the facts of political life."

Ted's territory sprawled across the Great Plains and the Rocky Mountains to the Pacific Northwest, the desert Southwest, California, Hawaii, and Alaska. As the one American region that did not field a presidential candidate in that year's Democratic primaries, it proved more competitive, and significant, than expected. The western Democrats were fragmented, and Ted's challenge was often distilled to gripping a hand, applying charm, and picking up delegates, one by one. "It was conventions, delegates . . . who was going to go, what they cared about, what the contacts were, who influenced them," he would remember. "I was challenged to get them stirred up about my brother."

John Kennedy and his aides Theodore Sorensen and Robert Wallace had focused on the West, laying the groundwork in earlier travels. By the beginning of 1959, John had visited Utah three times. So Ted found a loose network of allies in place. Mostly he was doing what the Kennedys were known for in Massachusetts: building their own political organization from World War II veterans, up-and-comers, and ambitious young Turks. They found Joseph Dolan and Byron White in Colorado, Stewart and Morris Udall in Arizona, Teno Roncalio in Wyoming. Ted would jet from state to state, switch to a car or a private aircraft, and—smile and a shoeshine—hit towns like Show Low, Arizona; Thermopolis, Wyoming; and Rock Springs, Montana, to assure local Democrats that John did indeed have farm and water policies. He made seven trips to Wyoming alone.

"He was so cute," Mary Kelly, an Oregon organizer, recalled. "We had pictures taken, and he came back three or four times." The intense pace bred risk. Sometimes, like the day the weather forced his plane to make an emergency landing on a dirt road outside Price, Utah, the aircraft and pilots were loaned them by supporters. Other times, like the day Ted landed in Show Low in a heavy storm, he flew the little planes through the volatile skies himself.

He was tapped, as well, as a surrogate speaker. When his brother faced win-or-go-home primaries in New Hampshire, Wisconsin, and West Virginia, Ted joined his mother and sisters, making appearances at Eagle halls and Elks lodges, ice fishing contests, bowling alleys, factory gates, and coal mines. On one Saturday night, he hit seven Milwaukee dance halls. "He has the Kennedy trademark—the calculated unruly hair and energy spilling over the gunwales," a *Boston Globe* journalist, following him through Wisconsin, reported. The campaign left Ted with a splendid collection of memories. In Wisconsin, he accepted a sponsor's dare and—as ten thousand roared and honked their car horns—soared down a ski jump for the first time in his life. At a Montana rodeo in August, he risked broken bones (and ruptured his groin in the violent dismount) on a five-second ride upon a bucking bronc named Skyrocket. In West Virginia, after John Kennedy lost his voice from nonstop campaigning, he wrote "Get Ted" on a pad, and the youngest brother gave the candidate's speeches.

The road is a lonely place. It is not known when Ted Kennedy first broke his wedding vows, or when Joan first suspected him, or if she confronted him. But when Joan was at home, coping with the last weeks of her first pregnancy in early 1960, Ted was in Las Vegas, earnestly seeking to seduce a young woman. "When [Joan] first got to meet Teddy, she fantasized and projected it onto a screen, things that Teddy wasn't, things that he couldn't be," said Tunney, "and a lifestyle that was out of a romantic Hollywood movie and not the way that life really is."

The woman in Nevada was an actress, Judith Campbell. Her account placed Ted at John Kennedy's side on February 7, 1960, when she met the two brothers at a party hosted by Frank Sinatra in the Sands hotel lounge. The younger brother was "such a rosy-cheeked little boy. Very good-looking, a great teaser with a ready laugh, and eyes that never stopped flirting. But he had nowhere near the charm and sophistication or just plain likeability of Jack," she recalled. "Teddy was the baby brother walking in his older brother's shadow."

Ted took her for a stroll around the city and escorted her to her room, where, in a courtly manner, he suggested he might stay the night. She was twenty-five and Ted was twenty-seven. Campbell declined. Ted flew on to Denver. The next morning, John Kennedy called and invited Campbell to lunch. A few weeks later, they began their affair. The president reveled, Campbell said, at having beaten Teddy to the prize.

On February 27, 1960, after returning to her parents' home in Bronx-ville for support not afforded by her roving, busy husband and his family, Joan gave birth to Kara Ann Kennedy. Ted flew to New York from New Hampshire and arrived at the hospital in time for the delivery. "I had never seen a more beautiful baby, nor been happier in my life," he remembered. "Kara's name means 'little dear one' and she was then and always has been my precious little dear one. Soon afterward I reluctantly left Joan and Kara and hurried to Wisconsin."

WHEN THE WISCONSIN AND West Virginia primaries were over, and the Kennedys had shown that the country's lingering anti-Catholic sentiment was no match for their cash and dash, the contest came down to a ground war for delegates. Senator Hubert Humphrey of Minnesota was Kennedy's leading challenger before losing those two contests. Senator Lyndon Johnson of Texas then emerged as a rival. If Johnson could find enough votes out west, and couple them with his strength down south, he might yet keep Kennedy from a first-ballot victory at the Democratic convention. "To whittle down the Johnson total in the mountain states, to isolate and portray Johnson as the Southern candidate, was essential to Kennedy," wrote campaign chronicler Theodore White. "Let Kennedy be stopped . . . on the first ballot or two and this crescent [of South and West] would close on the Northern delegates and roll east to victory."

John Kennedy threw himself at the West, down rows he had sown and given Ted to cultivate. "He felt that it was extremely important that he be successful on the first ballot. . . . If it was possible to block him on the first ballot, he'd have a very difficult time," Ted would remember. And "to be successful on the first ballot, he had to have some strength in the western states." Teeth were flashed and deals were made. The Alaska delegates sought a Yukon River dam. Senator Frank Church of Idaho wanted to be keynote speaker. The Cheyenne National Bank craved Joseph Kennedy's business. Ted urged Robert to lobby Anaconda, the giant mining company, for votes in Montana, and to muscle the railway unions in Colorado.

Sweet-talking and horse-trading, and warning wavering delegates that the train was leaving, Kennedy's troops stole four delegates from Johnson at the New Mexico state convention. Stewart Udall stunned the political world by ambushing the "old gang" in Arizona and corralling all of the state's seventeen votes for Kennedy. Dolan and Byron White beat formidable odds in Colorado, undermining the state's established leaders and emerging with a dozen and more delegates. They were, they liked to say, a band of brothers like those who fought alongside Henry V at Agincourt.

"Let's be honest," John told Ted and White as they dragged their tired selves into the Durango, Colorado, airport. "Just how many delegates did I get for this 2,000-mile flight? A half of one?"

"But you cheered us all up," said White, who would serve on the U.S. Supreme Court as a reward for his efforts in the 1960 campaign.

TED KENNEDY'S PEAK EXPERIENCE as his brother's lieutenant arose at the Democratic convention in Los Angeles. John and Robert were adamant: they had to cinch the nomination on the first ballot, lest sentiment trigger a run to Adlai Stevenson, or doubts about a Catholic candidate spur a surge for Johnson. "If we don't win tonight, we're dead," Robert told his troops.

A candidate needed 761 votes to secure the nomination. If John had 700 votes after the state of Washington voted, Robert figured, a first-ballot victory was in reach. The Kennedys watched the count as, fueled by a better-than-expected showing in the western states, it hit 710 once Washington declared its favorite. West Virginia and Wisconsin would nudge that total to 748. They were running out of alphabet, but Wyoming, with its 15 votes, could give Kennedy victory.

Early in the day, Ted was assigned to ask the splintered Wyoming delegation if they would unite behind Kennedy if, by doing so, they would put him over the top. "Sure. Sure," said national committeeman Tracy McCraken, presuming that it was an unlikely scenario. Now the unlikely was real. On the floor of the convention, Ted stood with the cowboys, reminding them of their promise. "Finish this tonight," he urged them. "Let's vote."

Ted was on his own. Raskin was off pleading with the Kansans, and Robert Kennedy, on the telephone, was sending word to the governor of New Jersey—who had forgone his own opportunity to cast the deciding votes—to go fuck himself. The television cameras focused on Ted, in the Wyoming delegation. From the press row, newsman David Broder could read Ted's lips. He was saying, "Do it. Do it. Do it." A delegate shouted, "Let's go!" Others waved their arms in assent. Watching the balloting in his hotel suite, seeing Ted enjoining the delegates, John Kennedy murmured, "This may be it."

At 10:50 p.m. the clerk called "Wyoming." The white-haired McCraken, a Cheyenne newspaper publisher, did not bury the lede: "Wyoming's vote will make a majority for Senator Kennedy," he declared. The Democrats erupted, drowning out McCraken as he announced that "Wyoming casts all fifteen votes for the next president of the United States." Ted hugged McCraken, and then Governor John J. Hickey. The state's delegates shouted, "Hooo! Hooo!" and pounded one another, and Ted, on the back. "I waved the Wyoming standard alongside people who'd been strangers just weeks earlier, but were now dear friends," Ted remembered. The band

played "High Hopes," the Kennedy campaign song. In the Texas delegation, Johnson's friend and mentor Sam Rayburn, the Speaker of the
House, grimaced and blinked back tears.

The next night, at the Kennedy victory party, Ted and his pal Hooton
challenged Sammy Davis Jr. and Frank Sinatra to a singing contest. Present as well were Judy Garland—who joined the competition with a rendition of "Somewhere Over the Rainbow"—and Nat King Cole. When the
velvet-voiced Cole began to sing, Hooton told Kennedy, "Maybe we should
have quit when we were ahead."

TED'S ROLE CHANGED IN the general election. He spent less time on organizing and more time making speeches. In the last six weeks of the
campaign his schedule took him from the Pacific Northwest to New Mexico and Colorado, to Los Angeles and Hawaii and back to California; he
then embarked with press and aides in a shiny leased DC-3 on a nine-day
"Air Hop Tour" of college campuses in twelve western states, and closed
the campaign at the head of a weeklong car caravan through Southern
California, winding 950 miles from Ventura to Barstow and down to San
Diego, stopping in every small town and city on the way. His final event
was in Richard Nixon's hometown of Whittier. His grueling schedule may
have brought out voters in one of the closest and most exciting of American presidential races, but it was not enough to win the West. The western
states had given overwhelming support to Dwight Eisenhower in the last
two presidential elections, and ten of the thirteen (all but New Mexico,
Nevada, and Hawaii) now went with Ike's vice president, Nixon.

The Democrats might have done better. In California, the state's
Stevenson-loving liberals detested the Kennedys' choice to head the campaign: Democratic boss Jesse Unruh. It is unlikely that a man of Ted Kennedy's age and experience, even with his pedigree, could have overcome such
infighting. Ted "was quite young and quite inexperienced and, I think,
not too effective," said Democrat Don Bradley. "He finally decided . . .
that the organization of California was way beyond his comprehension."

"The intensity of the feelings between individuals was extremely evident," was how Kennedy put it. But the campaign made tactical errors as well. Ted's choice for a finance director was a flop. He conceded later that they should have paid more attention to the issue of John's religion, and to courting the transplanted Okies of the Central Valley. Most egregiously, the Democrats neglected the absentee balloting, which the Nixon campaign used to overcome the election day results and clinch a thin victory in the Golden State.

Nixon's stoppage-time triumph stirred suspicion in the Kennedy camp that the Republicans may have stolen California. The state had split roughly 50–50 at the polls on election day, with Kennedy ahead by 37,000 votes. But the 243,000 absentee votes went heavily to Nixon, reversing the outcome and giving him a 35,000-vote margin of victory. "We were very careless about doing the job that had to be done on the absentee ballots," said Raskin. "More than the normal number came from [Nixon's home turf in] San Diego, Orange County, and Los Angeles." The margins in California, which Nixon won, and Texas and Illinois, which went to Kennedy, were so narrow that the Kennedys dispatched Ted to Los Angeles to prepare to contest the California results should Republican recounts prove fraud elsewhere. In the end, only Hawaii switched camps due to a recount—and it went from Nixon to Kennedy.

"If we had carried California," Ted would recall, thinking of how that would have impressed his father and his brothers, "I could have done no wrong."

TED WENT EAST IN time to vote in Boston and join the family on election day in Hyannis Port. They gathered in Robert's home, where the sunroom had been transformed into a master phone bank, a bedroom was filled with wire service tickers, and a pink-and-white upstairs children's bedroom was incongruously devoted to statistical analysis. It was a seesaw night, and not until late the next morning, as John and Ted returned from a walk along the beach, did they learn that Nixon would concede, and that John F. Kennedy would become the thirty-fifth president of the United States.

On one swing through Las Vegas, Ted had placed a wager that his brother would win. He hoped to buy an Aston Martin DB4—the forerunner of the car used by James Bond in the movies—with the proceeds. "I made the mistake of telling Dad about it, and he hit the roof," he recalled. Ted never collected.

Three

IF HIS NAME WAS
EDWARD MOORE

John Kennedy's election brought the burden of choice to Ted and Joan Kennedy. In other times and circumstances, they may have had the freedom to take the road that beckoned in 1960: to go west and build their lives in New Mexico or Wyoming or California, two drifters off to see the world, away from the family and its expectations. It was a romantic notion: He would be a young lawyer, making his own way. She would be at his side. "In a new state he would have to succeed or fail on his own," Joan said. The couple had "just about decided," Joan remembered. Ted took her on a western tour. "We fell in love with Arizona."

But that did not account for Joseph Kennedy's aspirations. John, at his father's urging, chose Robert to serve as attorney general. And Joseph bridled at giving up the Massachusetts Senate seat. "I urged Ted not to move out West, as he thought of doing, but to dig our roots even deeper in Massachusetts," Joseph wrote a friend a month after the inauguration. "I am glad to see that he is doing just that."

"Get your fat asses up to Boston. You guys are going to run for the Senate," Joan remembered, or reimagined, her father-in-law saying. "Joansie, you go up and rent a house." She had never performed that kind of chore—and leased a cramped garret in Beacon Hill. "We felt," she said, "like we were a part of *La bohème*." When a newsman asked Joseph what problems Ted might encounter, the patriarch steepled his fingers and said, "None."

IN FACT, the obstacles were formidable. In 1958, John Kennedy had won reelection to a six-year Senate term. In case of a vacancy, the laws of the commonwealth gave the power to make an interim appointment to Governor Foster Furcolo. The interim senator would need to face the voters, or give way to other aspirants, in a special election in 1962, and again in the regular election of 1964. Since Ted would not meet the constitutional qualification of thirty years of age until February 1962, he could not be the temporary appointee. Thus the family needed to find, and compel Furcolo to appoint, a compliant politician who would hold the seat for two years, then surrender it. Ted had to be tutored on the complexities of arms control, taxes, defense appropriations, agriculture, foreign affairs, and— closer to home—the politics of fish, shoes, and textiles. He would need to deal with the inevitable disclosure of the Harvard cheating scandal. And the Kennedys must engineer this as critics and foes savaged them for treating their state as their kingdom and the Senate seat as a bauble, to be given to an idle prince.

This last factor alone left John and Robert queasy. O'Donnell, O'Brien, and the other White House aides with political portfolios—charged with ensuring that John Kennedy got reelected in 1964—were adamantly opposed to making Ted a senator. "Kenny didn't think Ted's running for the U.S. Senate . . . was a good idea," their mutual friend Paul Kirk recalled. "It was too much Kennedy, too much dynasty, and not helpful to the president." Ted resented O'Donnell, who added to the animus by curbing Ted's requests for the president's time. Politically, the mess "is just awful," Richard Donahue, another member of the "Irish Mafia," told a reporter, holding his head and grimacing.

But Ted believed in what he had learned about politics, and about himself, while working with his father and his brothers over the previous three years. And he relished the opportunity to become Joseph Kennedy's project. "I'd worshipped my father as a young boy," he recalled, and watched enviously as his "energy had been focused on the older brothers." Now Ted would be Joseph's focus. On a boat ride off the Cape, the patriarch told his son that the older brothers were "well set in terms of their political lives." It was Ted's turn. "I'll make sure they understand," Joseph promised. "For the first time in my life," Ted would remember, "the two of us [were] together as men, sharing a common purpose."

Kennedy was certain that no one would outwork him. "Listen, this thing is up for grabs," he told one journalist. "The guy who gets it is the one who scrambles for it and I think I can scramble a little harder than the next guy." To another correspondent, Ted cited John Kennedy's example: "Keep hustling, and if the opportunity presents itself, take it."

Ted and Robert had vacationed together after the election—diving off Acapulco and skiing Smuggler's Notch. But then Robert, averse to Ted's candidacy, was found saying nice things about one of his brother's potential rivals. Ted was swift to gripe. "You can see what I am up against here Dad," he wrote his father. At first, John offered contingent support. Ted traveled to Washington and talked about working with CIA director Allen Dulles. Or was there another job in the new administration, Ted asked his brother, where he could build a record in international affairs? No, said John. Go back to Massachusetts and start shaking hands. We will know quickly enough if this is real.

A Senate delegation was making an arduous fact-finding tour of Africa—John sent Ted to join them. "The golf and swimming are not too good here," Ted reported from Nigeria to their parents. He lost thirteen pounds, and asked them to send the family cook to meet him in Liberia. But it gave him something to talk about as he made the rounds back home. Begin with the small-town chambers of commerce, John advised, and work your way up to the State Club and the Catholic Alumnae Association. Soon, the brothers were conferring every week. When Ted reported how audiences seemed to lose interest in his hourlong speech about African affairs, the president told him, "If I could do the State of the Union in 23 minutes, you can shorten up Africa. Just talk for 20 minutes and answer a couple of questions."

Garrett Byrne, the Suffolk County prosecutor, found room on his staff for an assistant district attorney who, for the salary of one dollar a year, could handle drunk driving cases and petty larcenies while spending lunch hours giving speeches to Rotarians about Ghana. (His colleagues took to calling Ted's office "the Africa desk.") Kennedy broke even on his first court case, failing to persuade a jury to find a man guilty of driving under the influence, but getting a conviction for driving to endanger. "I'll never vote for that son of a bitch," said one convicted defendant as he was led away to jail.

Francis X. Morrissey, a municipal court judge who had participated in all the previous Kennedy campaigns in Massachusetts, took Ted around to meet the boyos, doing for Ted what he had done for John. Kennedy's older brothers were trying to ease Morrissey, a "bouncy and embarrassingly mediocre little guy," out of the picture, a reporter told his editors. But "whenever I was home, the phone would ring, and my father would talk to Morrissey," Ted recalled.

"Dear Dad. Frankie is keeping me on the go day and night," Ted wrote to Joseph. "The reaction has been quite good except for a few cynical old pros. I have found some old Irish stories that Grampa used to tell which have really helped out during the activities of St. Patrick's Day."

Ted reenlisted in the Cancer Crusade, the United Fund, the Massachusetts Centennial Committee of Italian Independence, and the like, extending his reach around the state. Giddy civic leaders were delighted at the crowds that came out to see the president's handsome little brother. John had run for the Senate with "the Kennedy secretariat"—a personal organization of stalwarts. Ted had come to know many of them in 1958, and he now toured the commonwealth, distributing commemorative medals, thanking them for their contributions to the New Frontier, and cementing their allegiance.

Ted and Joan moved out of their garret. After buying a town house on Charles River Square, and a home on Squaw Island, just down the beach from the Kennedy compound on the Cape, they had established their Massachusetts residency. He took over the family's customary campaign office space in a four-room suite at 122 Bowdoin Street and filled his nights and weekends at a fundraiser in Winchester for the Medical Missionaries of Mary, a dinner for the Greater Boston Association for Retarded Children, a father-son night at St. Joseph's Church in Somerville, a Knights of Columbus communion breakfast at the Immaculate Conception Church in North Easton, and the General Casimir Pulaski Skyway Committee banquet in Dorchester, where, as a *Time* magazine reporter looked on, he "quoted part of Poland's national anthem in Polish, [and] enthusiastically danced the polka with a score of girls."

They would campaign, Joan remembered, in "any Rotary Club that would have us. . . . We felt it was us against the world." As soon as Ted discovered she could draw a crowd, Joan was sent off on her own. "Those were the good years of our marriage," she said. "I was needed and wanted." Ted remembered something else. He found Joan unsteady from drink before an important political event. He pushed his concern aside: there would be time to deal with it after the election.

BENJAMIN SMITH, the president's Harvard roommate and a former mayor of Gloucester, agreed to keep the Senate seat warm. Furcolo, arm sore from the twisting, made the appointment. For a year, as Mr. Smith served in Washington, the press carried stories about Ted Kennedy contemplating . . . inching toward . . . or sure to launch a Senate campaign. The impression of the writers who tailed him through the state was that it was all a bit of a game for the attractive but lightweight candidate. "As opposed to the President's intellectuality and aloofness, young Kennedy appeared to have no overwhelming enthusiasm for ideas, for which he compensated with enormous life-of-the-party exuberance, gregariousness and willingness," wrote Thomas Morgan in *Esquire* magazine.

Kennedy crossed the ocean to visit the homelands of the commonwealth's immigrant tribes—Ireland, Israel, Poland, Germany, Italy—but he did not help himself when the newspapers carried reports that during a party celebrating Robert and Ethel Kennedy's eleventh wedding anniversary, Ted had joined revelers, fully clothed, in the pool. "Wonderful," said his father. "Everybody in Massachusetts wants to vote for somebody who jumps into a swimming pool wearing a tuxedo."

In the summer of 1961, Kennedy made a visit to South America to burnish his foreign policy credentials. Joan was at home, expecting their second child, Edward M. Kennedy Jr., who would be born in September. Ted wrote a series of earnest stories about the region, which were published in the *Boston Globe*. But American diplomats in Chile passed word to the FBI of how Ted, a "pompous and a spoiled brat," had invited his embassy driver to join him in an all-night escapade at a rented brothel. Ted's luck held; the FBI report was not leaked. Nor did journalists publish reports they were collecting of Ted hanging out with Sinatra and the Rat Pack or bellowing bawdy songs in an all-night tour of Parisian bars and dinner clubs with Porfirio "Rubi" Rubirosa, a Latin playboy of worldwide notoriety.

KENNEDY'S TEST, or perhaps a saving grace, was that he was not the only Senate candidate from a celebrated family. Running as an independent "peace candidate" was H. Stuart Hughes, grandson of Charles Evan Hughes, a former chief justice of the United States. On the Republican side, George Cabot Lodge loomed as the likely nominee—setting up the possible rubber match between the Lodge and Fitzgerald-Kennedy dynasties, who had split the 1916 and 1952 Senate contests. And to earn the Democratic nomination, Kennedy would need to defeat the Massachusetts attorney general, Edward J. McCormack, the nephew of John McCormack, the new Speaker of the House of Representatives.

Teddy versus Eddie, the headlines yawped. McCormack was a fine attorney general—a graduate of the U.S. Naval Academy, a liberal with a splendid record on civil rights and liberties, with solid support in working-class neighborhoods like Dorchester and South Boston, as well as in scholarly Brookline and Cambridge. The young rivals were, *Life* magazine exalted, "manifestly designed by nature to fill the role of hero. . . . Each is handsome and clean-limbed, vigorous and virile, bold and spirited, ambitious and persevering, intelligent and forthright. Each is happily married to an attractive wife and has attractive children." It was a twentieth-century war of the roses, the writers said, between the state's own houses of Lancaster and York.

Boston's pols could not believe that President Kennedy would split the party and imperil his legislative agenda by antagonizing the Speaker. "Gouts of political gore" would stain "the porticoes of the White House," wrote Ted Kennedy's Harvard schoolmate and biographer Burton Hersh. The families had already clashed in 1956, when the Kennedys wrested control of the Democratic state committee. Surely the Kennedys would move Ted to a less prestigious race—perhaps the contest for attorney general—and let him acquire seasoning.

McCormack's support among Democratic regulars cut both ways, however. After a series of well-publicized scandals, the commonwealth of Massachusetts had earned a reputation as an entity rank with corruption. In a now famous speech, given to the legislature before embarking to Washington for his inauguration, John Kennedy had warned the statehouse denizens not to mortgage their honor. "We must always consider that we shall be as a city upon a hill," Kennedy said. "For of those to whom much is given, much is required," he added, supplementing John Winthrop with the Gospel of Luke.

McCormack was untouched by the waves of scandal, but with the candidate's pompadour, the family's roots in parochial Southie, and colorful kinsmen like Eddie's father, "Knocko"—a former stevedore and prizefighter, bartender, and bookie—and brawling brother "Jocko," there was just enough of an association with the old as to make the Kennedys seem shiny, bright, and clean. And that was a considerable, and lasting, advantage for Ted Kennedy.

"The Boston Irish politician has been stereotyped as a crook by many Irish and non-Irish," wrote Boston University political scientist Murray Levin. "Americans of Irish extraction have been excluded from the 'right' clubs and, until recent years, forced to play a secondary role in the state economic and cultural life.

"The Kennedys, however, 'proved' that Irish Americans can be statesmen," Levin wrote. The family had "power, money, glamour and—what is most important to the Irish—class and respectability. . . . By identifying with them, the Irish of Massachusetts can fulfill in fantasy the American dream."

Levin's theory was confirmed by the Kennedy campaign polling. Maggie, a sixty-five-year-old respondent who had arrived in Boston from Ireland as a girl, would never forget how the Lodge family had found her a job as a housekeeper and helped her become a citizen. But when asked by a pollster who she favored, she answered, "I'm for Kennedy. He's more of my own kind. He is the best next to his brother . . . and his father is a fine man." The Kennedy family's success was a "liberating" influence for the Irish in Massachusetts, pollster John Kraft noted, and a significant factor in Ted's popularity. "Ted should be the whole show, no question about it. But let's not obscure or bury that part of the story which clearly seems to give so much."

ONCE HIS POLLSTERS PERSUADED the president that Ted could win, the Kennedys went all in. To keep from seeming imperious, John had publicly vowed not to meddle. The Irish Mafia—O'Brien, O'Donnell, and the others—ostensibly stayed at their posts in Washington. But the hands-off pose was a sham. In his first months as president, John Kennedy had been given lessons in humility from Nikita Khrushchev, Fidel Castro, and the South's miscreants in Congress. He could not risk the defeat of his brother in their own state. "It was sort of like the Bay of Pigs," aide Dan Fenn remembered, likening the administration's clandestine aid to Ted Kennedy to the CIA's ill-fated invasion of Cuba. "Our enterprise, but we don't want our fingerprints on it." The Kennedys dangled a bunch of carrots to lure McCormack from the race. They offered to back him if he ran for governor and promised him a presidential appointment—like assistant secretary of the Navy—should he lose. He declined.

It was "another Kennedy political adventure, with some problems but with the same determination to win," *Time* magazine's Hugh Sidey advised his editors. The Kennedys could be counted on to use "every device, skill and energy that can be mustered and effectively employed." As for the candidate, "assuming that a reasonable amount of brains, energy, high connections, noble purpose and guts are the ingredients necessary to be a decent senator, then we guess that Teddy Kennedy would be okay," Sidey said.

Stephen Smith set up house in Boston's Ritz-Carlton hotel and proceeded to direct the campaign with the same meticulous care by which John Kennedy had won the Democratic presidential nomination. Joseph Kennedy's fortune was tapped. Pollsters were hired and surveys conducted. Experts at Harvard were enlisted to draft a platform. The Kennedy campaign card catalogues were updated and augmented. Television and radio ads and billboards carried Ted Kennedy's name to the people. Ted peppered the White House with requests for favors—federal jobs, executive pronouncements, presidential visits—that would aid his campaign. Sorensen drafted remarks and wrote out answers for Ted to give inquiring reporters. McCormack's military service records were pulled from the archives and scoured for signs of malingering.

Kennedy faced three hurdles, and if he faltered at any step in the process, his candidacy was finished. The state's Democratic party leaders and professional politicians would render the initial verdict, at the state convention on June 8. Rank-and-file Democrats would then certify or overrule that decision in a statewide primary on September 18. Then the general electorate would weigh in on election day, in November. In the spring of 1962, when it appeared that Ted was having problems with the first hurdle, and that McCormack had taken the lead among delegates to the convention, the president got involved. On April 27, John Kennedy convened a council of war at the White House, where he made it clear to a gathering of his aides and their Massachusetts henchmen that his brother absolutely needed to, and was absolutely going to, win this election. "Jack told them that this . . . was really important to him and that he wanted everyone to be pitching in and doing what had to be done, and that it made a great deal of difference to him," Ted recalled. "From that point on, it seemed that we really started moving in high gear." The president called for "a discreet mobilization of the resources of the federal government to put over Teddy's nomination," White House aide and historian Arthur Schlesinger Jr. told his diary.

Ted's candidate for campaign manager—Gerard Doherty, a rumpled lawyer-legislator from Charlestown—had been flown down from Boston and smuggled into the White House under an assumed name. John Kennedy seized on a green briefing file that Doherty had compiled and compared his own encyclopedic knowledge of the Massachusetts political terrain with Doherty's assessments. The president was satisfied, and went off to greet the British prime minister, but Doherty needed to repeat the performance the following morning, when he was grilled by Robert Kennedy at the Department of Justice. Only then did he get the authority to proceed.

The president closed the doors to the Oval Office and personally rehearsed Ted before his younger brother appeared on *Meet the Press*. He spent hours of their time at the Cape with Ted, coaching and discussing strategy, and took the Washington press corps for a boat ride with the candidate on the presidential yacht *Honey Fitz*. Robert Kennedy and Sorensen traveled to Hyannis Port to brief Ted on the issues. "Have no fe-ah, we are he-ah!" said Robert upon arrival. John dictated the campaign slogan ("He can do more for Massachusetts") and sketched the design of the *Kennedy '62* tie clips. It is a matter of debate, but Ted Kennedy believed that his brother acceded to his many requests and named Anthony Celebrezze to the cabinet, as secretary of health, education, and welfare, in part to court the Italian vote in Massachusetts.

"Where are you going today?" John Kennedy asked Ted.

"To western Massachusetts, to the big Polish festival," Ted replied.

"I'll give you a great quote," the president said.

John Kennedy had made a postwar visit to the battlefield at Monte Cassino in Italy, where a free Polish corps suffered horrific casualties storming the Nazi stronghold. At the cemetery, with its thousand graves, was an inscription that John employed with Polish American audiences, and now passed on to Ted, in both languages: "We soldiers of Poland gave our soul to God, our life to the soil of Italy, our hearts to Poland."

"That is a pretty good one," Ted said. The thousands gathered near Lenox were thrilled when he delivered it in Polish. The family's old friend Cardinal Cushing said Mass, and as the novitiates from Saint Stanislaus came up to kiss his ring the prelate told them, "Don't kiss me, kiss Kennedy."

At a meeting of the Polish American club in Worcester, the two rivals, Ted and Ed, answered questions while behind them—dead center—hung an epic picture of John F. Kennedy.

As the Democratic convention in Springfield approached, White House aides proffered patronage jobs and other gifts to the delegates for votes. It was "a knock-down, drag-out battle for political supremacy," the *Boston Record* said—a good time to be a ward committeeman who wanted a job as a postmaster, or whose brother was up for parole—and not so good a time to be a McCormack delegate with tax or immigration problems. "At the ward and city committee level of Massachusetts politics, a U.S. postmaster is an exalted public station—and the pay is good," *Time* correspondent Neil MacNeil informed his editors. Snap surveys, by the *Globe* and other news organizations, now cast doubt on McCormack's boasts that he would carry the convention. "If the McCormack people have counted this badly all over the state, he's in for a big surprise," said MacNeil. Ted, meanwhile, was reminding the pols, "Remember. Win or lose, I'm handling the patronage here in Massachusetts." It was "non-nonsense stuff, and indicates a pretty tough fiber in the candidate," the newsman concluded.

"They're cold," said Knocko of his son's unrelenting opponents. "It's pressure, pressure, pressure, post office, post office, post office."

JOHN KENNEDY'S ASSISTANCE WAS essential that spring because in December 1961, Joseph Kennedy had suffered a stroke while playing golf in Florida. The patriarch was unable to stand or speak.

A few weeks earlier, in a Thanksgiving entry in her diary, Rose had written of how Jackie ("in a Schiaparelli pink slack suit") taught the others how to dance the Twist, as Joan played ("jungling-rumbling music") on the piano and Jack laughed at Ted's dancing. ("Ted has great sense of rhythm but he is so big & has such a big derriere it is funny to see him throw himself around.") The only shadow was Joseph's fragility. "For first time," Rose wrote, "I have noticed he has grown old." His sons still had the use of his money, but his influence and acumen were gone.

For Ted, who heard the news of his father's stroke at work and rushed to join his brothers and sisters in Florida, it was a special loss and a "very powerful blow." He spent a week sleeping at the hospital. In the Senate race he had become "much, much closer" to Joseph, he said. "I remember my brothers calling him when they were facing challenges, and he always had some good advice for them. And here I was, talking to him on the same kind of plane.

"It was a very exhilarating time . . . then suddenly this person who had been my kind of right hand and principal figure was struck down," Kennedy said. "They thought he was going to get better, you know; this thing was going to be temporary—it was all going to get better but it just never, it just never did."

In the months before his stroke, Joseph had initiated a process for handling the Harvard cheating story by engaging the noted Washington lawyer Clark Clifford to assess the matter. The eminent fixer met with all three Kennedy sons and with William Frate, who had taken the exams for Ted at Harvard. The cheating did not bother Clifford so much as Ted's youth and inexperience. He advised the Kennedys to get the story out on the best terms they could dictate. The Irish American voters would be understanding, Clifford's law partner, John Sharon, reasoned, because, "hell, most of those Back Bay Boston Irish voters' sons could never get through Harvard unless they cheated their way through." The president approached the issue from the other side of the ethnic divide, telling his friend Ben Bradlee, "It won't go over with the WASPs. They take a very dim view of looking over your shoulder at someone else's exam paper. They go in more for stealing from stockholders."

With Joseph sidelined, it fell to John Kennedy to summon Robert Healy, a friend and columnist at the *Boston Globe*, to the White House to negotiate the placement—on the bottom of the front page, with a modest headline—of the news that Ted had been tossed from Harvard. The story had been kicking around Boston, but Healy had not been able to persuade the college to confirm it.

John broke the news to Ted. "Teddy, I think it's good if we get that Harvard story out," he said.

"What do you mean?"

"Get that whole story out, from beginning to end," John said. "Get it out in the early part of this campaign."

Easy for you to say, Ted thought.

Healy's story was published, and Ted felt humiliated. "I just spoke to him on the phone," the president told Bradlee. "He's really singing the blues."

"I thought that was the end of the whole campaign," Ted recalled. At an evening event in Milford, he froze outside the hall, dreading to face several hundred people. But they welcomed him with a cheer. "Maybe I can get through this," he decided.

At Harvard, some remembered Ted Kennedy and felt outraged that he would start his political career with a campaign for the U.S. Senate by trading on his brother's name. Mark DeWolfe Howe, a leading light at Harvard Law School, called Ted "bumptious" and "reckless" and "childish" and "irresponsible"—even "corrupt"—"to seek an office that would now be manifestly beyond his reach were he not the president's brother."

"His academic career is mediocre," Howe wrote, seeking to rouse the opposition across the state. "His professional career is virtually non-existent. His candidacy is both preposterous and insulting."

McCormack called it "the chutzpah issue." But then there was that Irish pride, and a feeling among Democratic voters that Ted had done his penance in the army, been accepted back by Harvard, and graduated with no further incident and credible grades. The cheating saga was viewed as a boyish mistake and seemed not to hinder Kennedy's momentum as he neared the state convention. A handful of politically oriented professors—Samuel Beer of Harvard, Robert Wood of MIT, and others—elicited his promise to help them reform the Democratic Party in the state, and their subsequent endorsement served to counter Howe's attacks.

At one point, Howe cornered Wood and launched into a tirade about Ted's imperfections. "Mark! Mark! Hold off!" Wood said. "We're only trying to make him a U.S. senator, not a Harvard professor."

Ed McCormack made his pitch to the delegates via intermediaries, or over the telephone. Ted Kennedy personally visited 1,300 of the 1,719 slated to vote at the convention. One day that summer, he made twenty-three stops. "We know where every single vote is," said Doherty. "You can give me anybody's name and I can tell you when they've been talked to, who talked to them and what Teddy has to do—some personal contact, telephone calls—so that we have left nothing to chance." If a delegate said he was 100 percent committed, Doherty put him down as "undecided." Only the "150 percent committed" were classified as certain.

"No candidate ever worked harder," wrote Stewart Alsop in the *Saturday Evening Post*. "Here is the grandson of Honey Fitz, enjoying the smell and feel of the crowd" and showing "a kind of bubbling, superbly confident ebullience, an almost overpowering vitality."

Preparation was key. Kennedy had done enough speechmaking and advance work in 1958 and 1960 to recognize the elements of an effective campaign. "He knew every alley in Boston," one aide, Charles Tretter, recalled. If Kennedy was going to give a talk at 4 p.m. on a Friday afternoon, his advance team would visit that location at 4 p.m. on the previous Friday, observing the scene, the traffic, and the crowds so there would be no surprises. "He knew when you didn't know. . . . He would ask an open-ended question, sense your hesitancy, and push. You could feel his eyes on you as you tried to explain."

Kennedy worked them to debility. He was amply motivated by the fears of shaming his family and damaging his brother's presidency. He was "big and strong," Tretter recalled. "Had tremendous energy. Very health conscious—he would eat half a sandwich—and not a heavy drinker. He was scrupulous about bedtime." The Kennedy family remedy for exhaustion was a hot evening bath before the night's campaign events. If that meant knocking on a stranger's door in the wilds of western Massachusetts to ask if Ted Kennedy could use the bathtub, that's what his advance team did. McCormack's supporters were left shaking their heads. Kennedy has "been in places like . . . Gill. Who ever goes to Gill? This guy went to Gill to see one delegate," a McCormack man told Levin. "Most people wouldn't know where Gill was, including Eddie McCormack. . . . Anybody in this room know where Gill is? Well, Ted Kennedy has been to Gill."

The Kennedy campaign preparations for the June 8 convention were extensive and efficient. Knowing that the Springfield phone circuits were subject to crashing under the intense demand (as soon they did), the campaign had its own twelve-line switchboard installed at the hotel headquarters, and another at its command center in the convention hall—and then, just to be sure, equipped its troops with walkie-talkies.

Before the balloting, Stephen Smith had Doherty write down a prediction of the final vote and seal it in an envelope. Doherty took the game a step further and handed out his hard count to the brace of national political reporters who arrived from Washington to watch democracy work. Bradlee was out on the convention floor when a page summoned him to the telephone. It was the president of the United States, asking how things were going in his brother's campaign, and offering to dictate the newsman's story: "It almost has to be something about Teddy's First Hurrah, doesn't it?" Kennedy's suggestion "really bugged me," Bradlee would remember, as he had already written: "For fledgling politician Edward Moore Kennedy, 30, the First Hurrah rose from a steaming, smoking auditorium in Springfield Mass. at 12:25 a.m." He knew that he would never persuade John Kennedy that it was not the president's idea.

"Their day is gone, and they don't know it," said the president of John and Ed McCormack's ward heelers. The opposition surrendered midway through the roll call, when Kennedy led by the landslide count of 691 to 360. By folding his tent, McCormack freed the rest of his supporters from the painful duty of crossing the Kennedys in a losing cause. Smith opened the envelope. Doherty was right on target.

Ted watched intently as McCormack conceded. Beside him was Joan. "She was aglow now," an observer saw, and "smiling up lovingly at her hero husband, who didn't notice she was there."

MCCORMACK HAD ONE FINAL opportunity. The convention's endorsement was an invaluable asset, as it sent a strong, well-publicized signal to loyal Democrats across the state. But it did not prevent a losing candidate from taking his case to the people in the September 18 Democratic primary. Few succeeded, but such was McCormack's hope.

To have any chance of prevailing, McCormack needed to score a knockout at one or both of the two scheduled debates. "We should be prepared for a purely personal attack," wrote an adviser to Kennedy in an internal memo. "McCormack knows that public interest can't be excited by . . . a few nitpicking differences. . . . Nothing less than a clean shot at our jugular can bring about the dramatic swing in voter attitudes he desperately needs."

In an act of bravado, Smith and Doherty agreed to schedule the Boston showdown at McCormack's alma mater—South Boston High School—on August 27. The second debate would be in Holyoke, as a nod to the voters of western Massachusetts, on September 5. "Tell them why you're interested in public life," Robert advised Ted. The brothers had all made the choice not to manage Joseph's money, not to follow him to Wall Street or Hollywood, but to seek the common good in the pursuit of public service. "Tell them why you don't want to be sitting on your ass in some office in New York."

Those who attended the Southie debate remember the electric atmosphere, akin to a title fight or a championship game. McCormack was the aggressor, calling his opponent "Teddy" throughout and sneering in his opening statement, "You never worked for a living."

"I say we need a senator with a conscience, not with connections. We need a senator with experience, not arrogance," McCormack said. "The office of United States senator should be merited, and not inherited."

McCormack worked to trigger Kennedy's emotions, hoping his opponent would show his immaturity. Kennedy had attended a segregated law school, McCormack charged. He had failed to vote in state and municipal elections, except for those occasions when his brother was on the ballot.

His slogan—"He can do more for Massachusetts"—was a paean to nepotism. Kennedy's international travel, so ostentatiously political, said McCormack, had been marred by clumsy incidents in Europe and South America.

Kennedy held his own, at best. He had been warned by brother John and other handlers not to stray from his stance of lofty purpose. In his closing remarks, looking shaken, he docilely responded to McCormack's onslaught. "We should not have any talk about personalities or families," Ted said. His voice cracked. "We should be talking about the people's destiny in Massachusetts."

By lot, McCormack had the final word. He used it to throw what those in the hall viewed as a mortal blow. Kennedy's aides shuddered.

"If his name was Edward Moore, with his qualifications, with your qualifications, Teddy, if it was Edward Moore, your candidacy would be a joke," McCormack said, pointing at his rival, an arm's length away on a small, crowded stage.

The crowd erupted, though there were boos amid the roar. Kennedy studied the floor. He was thoroughly dejected. It was "a very Catholic image—like Saint Sebastian with the arrows going into him," the *Globe*'s Martin Nolan remembered.

"What do I do now?" Kennedy asked Doherty as they conferred afterward.

"You were terrific," said Doherty, ever-faithful corner man.

"I'm going to punch that sonofabitch in the nose," said Kennedy.

"That's the one thing you can't do," said Doherty.

Outside the high school, Ted and Joan hailed a cab. On the way home, the mood was somber. Almost everyone in the Kennedy camp thought that the debate had been a debacle. "Ted was convinced he had blown it," said his young press aide Terri Robinson. McCormack, meanwhile, was thrilled. "Shock therapy" had worked. This could be the turning point.

The president called to find out how it went. "I still, at that point, was numb," Ted recalled. "I wasn't sure whether we'd been knocked out of the race." He handed the phone to an aide, Milton Gwirtzman. Their guy had maintained his demeanor, Gwirtzman told the president, yet McCormack had done well.

"Don't give him an objective analysis," the president said. "He has to go out tomorrow morning and shake hands at the docks. Tell him he was great."

SOME SENSED THE SEA change from the callers who phoned in to the radio talk shows that night; others heard from the women manning the campaign switchboards. It was gospel by the time the next day's afternoon newspapers hit the street. The verdict was not what it seemed. McCormack had lost his cool. McCormack had snarled. McCormack was a bully. His liberal and female supporters were especially disappointed. He had reminded people what they didn't like about the state's coarse politicians.

A poll the next day brought confirmation. An "extremely high percentage" of Massachusetts households had seen the debate on television. When asked which candidate made the most favorable impression, 44 percent said Kennedy, 34 percent said both, and only 22 percent chose McCormack. McCormack had "used poor taste," and "slandered Kennedy," and "was insulting to the Kennedy family," the viewers told the pollster. McCormack was sarcastic and "knife-stabbing" and "not a gentleman." He stood "not for anything, just anti-Kennedy."

"There is no doubt that Ted Kennedy made a more favorable impression than Ed McCormack in this debate," pollster Joseph Napolitan concluded. "McCormack apparently made a serious tactical mistake attacking the Kennedy name and Kennedy family as sharply as he did."

Ted, on the other hand, had responded with decorum—like a senator. He had declined the bait. He had looked "very young" but reminded people, Irish people—the state's Irish mothers in particular—what they liked about his family.

It had been McCormack's final gambit—to provoke Ted into some sort of unseemly reaction. He reminded Schlesinger of "a fighter who knows he is behind on points and is gambling everything on a knockout."

"Eddie has some good points about Teddy's lack of experience," John Kennedy told Schlesinger. "But he should have made them calmly and dispassionately. His mistake was in making it all so personal—in pointing his finger at Teddy and acting like a prosecutor. All that suggested malice. . . . It will boomerang."

In the Holyoke debate that followed, McCormack was markedly polite, but this approach—the "high-road pillow fight," as the *Globe* called it—was no more effective. He lost the primary by a two-to-one margin. Kennedy won 559,303 votes and McCormack 247,403.

A LOVELY STORY, which has taken on the status of scripture in Massachusetts, emerged from Ted Kennedy's 1962 campaign.

He always insisted it was true: that on the morning after the South Boston debate with McCormack—who had scorned "Teddy" for not working a day in his life—Kennedy campaigned in a bakery on the North Shore.

"Hey Kennedy," one of the bakers called out. "They say you haven't worked a day in your life." Kennedy braced himself, ready for the jab that was sure to follow.

"Lemme tell you," said the baker. "You haven't missed a thing."

NOW ONLY A LODGE stood between John F.'s grandson and the U.S. Senate. Given the state's huge Democratic advantage in registered voters, any Republican candidate entered the general election facing formidable odds. The Democrats who chose Kennedy in the primary were "about as solid in their support for him as can be," pollster Kraft reported. Kennedy started the fall with a 17-point lead. Across the commonwealth, the voters gave Lodge high marks for knowledge, but prized Kennedy's "influence, party loyalty, vigor and family." The president was wildly popular, with a favorability rating of 89 percent inside Boston and 81 percent in the rest of Massachusetts.

Though it narrowed a bit in October, Ted Kennedy retained that double-digit advantage. And on the night of October 22, as Kennedy and Lodge squared off at a forum in Worcester, John Kennedy appeared on national television to inform one hundred million viewers that the USSR had been caught installing nuclear-armed missiles in Cuba. The Cuban Missile Crisis froze every political race across the country—and gave a huge boost to Democrats once John Kennedy persuaded the Soviets, peacefully, to remove the weapons.

The November results gave Ted Kennedy 1.1 million votes and Lodge 887,000.

"That was the question: Was there anybody there?" as Stephen Smith told Hersh. "Turned out there was."

BACK IN SEPTEMBER, on primary day, John Kennedy had ducked into Boston by helicopter, a veritable fugitive, to cast his vote. He was in and out of the city in twenty-three minutes, not wanting to link his White House to Ted's campaign. He joked about wearing a clown disguise.

For the general election, and Ted's certain victory over Lodge, John arrived in Air Force One, with Speaker McCormack at his side, and camped out in the presidential suite of the Sheraton Plaza hotel, downtown at Copley Square.

That evening, he motored out to Dorchester and called upon his ninety-seven-year-old grandmother Josie, the seamstress girl whose husband, John Fitzgerald, had lost the race for a Senate seat to Henry Cabot Lodge in 1916.

Four

THE NEW FRONTIER

Benjamin Smith was a trouper, and resigned his Senate seat in November so that thirty-year-old Ted Kennedy and Massachusetts would earn extra seniority. Getting there early and staying late was all and everything in the U.S. Senate. It was then a sump of aged men with liver spots, claws, and bourbon breath, who strode the chamber with reptilian gait and hailed one another with mellifluent courtesies. Of all the checks and balances that America's founders installed in their marvelous political machinery, none was so designed to slow things down, gum things up, and apply the brakes like the Senate. The name itself derives from *senex*, which is Latin for "old man."

The Senate was conceived, said James Madison, as "an anchor against popular fluctuations," and designed to curb "fickleness and passion." It was not until ratification of the Seventeenth Amendment, in 1913, that senators were elected by the direct vote of the people. The amendment was a product of the Progressive Era, but did little to make the Senate progressive. It did not address the terms of the "Great Compromise" of 1787—the deal in the Constitutional Convention that gave small states the same representation in the Senate as their more populous counterparts. It did not alter the sheltering effects of the six-year terms that senators served—longer than presidents and three times longer than members of the House of Representatives. It did not change the Senate's hidebound ceremony—its veneration of seniority, reliance on committees, and rules of debate. Nor did it address the volatile, profound, and seemingly perpetual vexation of race. The Senate at mid-twentieth century was "a defiant fortress barring the road to social justice," wrote Robert Caro in his biography of Lyndon Johnson. "For almost a century it had not merely embodied but had empowered, with an immense power, the forces of conservatism and reaction in America."

The Senate as Kennedy found it was run by its committees, and the chairmen who controlled the famous panels—such as Richard Russell of Georgia at Armed Services, James Eastland of Mississippi at Judiciary, J. William Fulbright of Arkansas at Foreign Relations, Harry Byrd of Virginia at Finance—were mostly southern, and courtly, and old and racist. They had earned their gavels via seniority. Though they thought of themselves as gentlemen, as opposed to demagogues like George Wallace or Theodore Bilbo, all of them had signed the "Southern Manifesto" in 1956, vowing to defend segregation "with all lawful means." The system rewarded what the one-party South was adept at: picking a young man with promise, dispatching him to Congress, and reelecting him, again and again and again. Seniority ruled on committee assignments, subcommittee chairmanships, the order of questioning witnesses at hearings, assignment of the Senate's mahogany desks—even office space and parking places. Chairmen had the sway of little despots, able to kill legislation by pocketing bills and denying hearings.

Seniority, the committee system, and the filibuster rules, which gave any senator, or small group of senators, the ability to talk a bill to death, gave the segregationists power beyond numbers. It took a two-thirds vote of the Senate to invoke "cloture" in those days—to end debate, shut down a filibuster, and move to a roll call. The eleven states of the old Confederacy and the five pro-slavery border states gave the South a starting bloc of thirty-odd votes, which conservative senators from the sparsely populated Great Plains and West, mindful of their own prerogatives, historically joined. The Senate, as William S. White wrote in 1956, was "the South's unending revenge upon the North for Gettysburg."

"Once it had been a place of leaders, men who conceived daring solutions to daunting problems," wrote Caro. But "decades of the seniority rule had conferred influence . . . not on men who broke new ground but on men who were careful not to." Progressive legislation languished and decayed. Federal aid to education, health care for the elderly, and civil rights measures ranked high among the casualties. From Reconstruction to World War II, some four thousand Black Americans were lynched in the United States, and blessed were those who met a quick end through hanging instead of a cruel and agonizing death by burning, disfigurement, disembowelment, and other torments. Yet when antilynching bills passed the House of Representatives in the 1920s and 1930s, they died in the Senate, prey to southern filibusters.

Northern, more liberal Democrats made gains in 1958, and fresh blood like Phil Hart of Michigan, Edmund Muskie of Maine, and Eugene McCarthy of Minnesota joined the Senate. Ted Kennedy's class of 1962 included Birch Bayh of Indiana, Gaylord Nelson of Wisconsin, and George McGovern of South Dakota. In two more years, Walter Mondale of Minnesota and Joseph Tydings of Maryland would arrive. The Senate still reeked of pine tar, mint, hate, and molasses when Kennedy took his seat. But at least a trace of change was in the wind.

EDWARD MOORE KENNEDY fit right in. His brother John, cool and smart, had not been cut out for the Senate's stultifying culture. "Black Robert," as the president called the attorney general, was a Holy Joe. But Ted had a different makeup. He was gregarious, glad-handing—as affable as an Irish cop, his father liked to say. John Kennedy objected to a magazine's description of Ted's "sardonic" smile. He and Robert could smile sardonically, Kennedy told a friend, but Ted would need more experience. And as the youngest of nine, Ted knew how to cope with seniority. "Briefed and overbriefed, he marched the marble corridors . . . humbly paying his respects to the aging titans," journalist Meg Greenfield wrote.

He was wonderfully fun-loving. Boston congressman Tip O'Neill liked to illustrate the difference in brotherly temperaments by comparing the parties the Kennedys hosted. You would get one drink off a waiter's silver tray at John Kennedy's house, and then they would show you the door. But when Ted was your host the food and drink flowed, the mood was convivial, there was singing and talk and laughter, and he was likely to stop you from leaving. The police came to one of Ted's louder parties—his brother, the attorney general of the United States, deftly slipped out a door. Ted's staff discovered that the unforgivable sin was not in scheduling a two-hour lunch with a constituent, but in not inviting the boss along.

He knew his place in the constellation of power, and was sure enough to make sport of it. "Some pipeline I have," Ted said, with a rueful smile, to journalist Ben Bradlee. "One thousand men are out of work in Fall River, four hundred men out of work in Fitchburg. And when the army gets that new rifle, there's another six hundred men out of work in Spring-field. And you know what [the President] says to me? 'Tough shit.'"

"Amiability, adaptability, risk-taking, self-deprecation . . . what did all this signify?" asked James MacGregor Burns. "Did he know himself?" Like his brothers, the Senate's newest member was a centrist and a realist, with a bundle of liberal ideals, drawn from his Irish affinity for the underdog and the edicts of Saint Matthew and Saint Luke. As with his brothers, Ted's ability to learn through experience—to extend his concern and grow in office—would be a defining trait. "He had a collection of religious and political beliefs, but he had no rounded political creed or coherent doctrine," Burns said. "He was late-born—and thus the most vital influences on him lay ahead."

The Senate club was leery. Would the president's brother spy and tattle, toss his weight around, display an attitude? John Kennedy had seen enough of the Senate to warn Ted against such predilections. Get to know "the Old Bulls," he told his brother. Join them in the Senate gym and steam room, in the cloakroom and prayer breakfasts. Ted called upon Russell, the South's commander in chief, ingratiatingly noting that Russell was also in his thirties when he came to the Senate. Yes, Russell replied, but by then he had already served as Georgia's governor. Kennedy watched, with growing horror, as portly Jennings Randolph of West Virginia, a candidate for cardiac arrest, grew red like a beet as they schmoozed in the steam room. And Kennedy staggered back to his Senate office, thoroughly drunk at noon, after he and Eastland downed scotch after scotch while conferring about subcommittee assignments.

"The new senator is expected to keep his mouth shut," Donald Matthews, a scholar of Senate folkways, observed. All the more if you were thirty-one years old and had never held elective office. "The long custom of the place impels him, if he is at all wise, to walk with a soft foot and to speak with a soft voice, and infrequently," White noted.

Kennedy, in these early years, was spellbound, well aware how a false move or mistake would cost him—and his brother's presidency. He moved carefully, focusing on Massachusetts. "Teddy stayed submerged a long time," *Time*'s MacNeil remembered. The records of the Judiciary Committee's executive sessions, where much of the work was done, show how, unlike other freshmen, Kennedy refrained from impassioned speeches or barbed retorts, but might be found at the end of a debate, summing up a compromise, so that all understood the terms of the deal. "Kennedy's critics on the Hill, especially those youthful Senators and their staffs who adhere to a sort of liberalism a Go Go, contend he is a plodder," wrote Greenfield, "and . . . too readily avoids a scrap." But the Old Bulls approved. Know your place, work hard—"Don't avoid the ditch-digging," Eastland told him.

The Mississippi senator would play a determining role in Kennedy's initial years in the Senate. The White House had petitioned Senate leaders and consulted with Bobby Baker, the crafty Senate secretary, to get Ted his committee assignments. He was seated on the Labor and Public Welfare Committee, which had jurisdiction over health care, labor, and education, but was then in a sort of quiescence, and Eastland's Judiciary, which had jurisdiction over seething matters like civil rights and immigration, as well as antitrust law, gun control, constitutional amendments, Supreme Court nominations, and the federal judiciary.

"You've got a lot of Eye-talians. Now, the Kennedys are always talking about immigration and always talking about Eye-talians," Eastland had told Kennedy at their midmorning scotch-drinking conclave. Thus he was awarded a seat on the immigration subcommittee. "You Kennedys always

care about the Negras. Always hear about you caring about those," said
Eastland. So Kennedy was seated on the subcommittee for constitutional
rights.

A stout, cigar-smoking buddha of a man, Eastland lived on a five-
thousand-acre plantation in the Mississippi Delta where the Black inhabitants of the Jim Crow South were not treated too significantly better than
their enslaved ancestors. His grandfather had been wounded at Gettysburg, his mother chaired the local chapter of the United Daughters of
the Confederacy, and his father once led the lynch mob that had tortured
a fugitive Black man and woman, then burned them alive. Eastland spent
much of his time on parochial political matters, or on his investments in oil
and gas drilling operations. But the Kennedy brothers enjoyed the Mississippi rogue and knew how he could bury legislation or stall the nomination
of federal judges. It was "how the trains run around here," Ted concluded.

It was a complex relationship. Eastland was clearly a bigot, who would
one day startle a fellow senator by referring to Representative Barbara
Jordan, the regal Democrat from Texas, as "that nigger." But he was also
a Democrat, friendly to John, Robert, and Ted, and generally wanted his
party to succeed. He had clashed with the Ku Klux Klan when supporting
the first Roman Catholic presidential candidate, New York governor Al
Smith, in 1928. He lionized Franklin Roosevelt and, though he worked
well with the GOP grandees on the Judiciary Committee—conservative
lawmakers Everett Dirksen of Illinois and Roman Hruska of Nebraska—
had no wish to surrender his gavel to anyone from the Party of Lincoln.
When Senator Birch Bayh of Indiana sought to memorialize the birthplace of the socialist Eugene Debs in his home state of Indiana, Eastland
stuck by his young Democratic colleague. Debs may have been a radical
and a socialist, but he was "from [Bayh's] hometown, boy," Eastland told
Republican senator William Scott of Virginia. "Sit yo' ass down."

When John and Robert faced civil rights crises in Mississippi, Eastland
gave them unvarnished advice, worked with Robert to limit violence, and
always kept his word. "I found it much more pleasant to deal with him
than many of the so-called liberals," Robert would remember.

ROBERT AND TED WERE not everyday fixtures at the president's dinner table. They all had duties, and wives of different tastes and stature, and children. But the younger duo got invitations to state dinners and other White House events, and joined in family celebrations, like a spirited cruise down the Potomac in the presidential yacht *Sequoia* to mark John's forty-sixth birthday. They saw each other often at the Cape. Joan was bedazzled. "When there is no tragedy in your life and you're 26 years old, and you are the sister-in-law of the President of the United States, and your husband has just become the senator from Massachusetts, and your other brother-in-law is the Attorney General, and you move to Washington . . . I mean, how glamorous can life be?" she recalled. "And you're just a part of all this, the enthusiasm, the excitement, the . . . years Jack was President. I didn't have to do an awful lot of thinking—I was just being, you know, engulfed by this exciting, stimulating life." The exceptional event, in those first few months of Ted's Senate career, was a miscarriage she suffered in May 1963.

Common purpose brought the brothers together, but primogeniture prevailed. If there was conflict in their political lives, the younger gave way to the elder. At one point, Jacqueline took to worrying about what she and her husband would do after he left the presidency. She asked Robert to inform Ted that he might then need to return the Senate seat to John. Robert dutifully conveyed the message. And Ted acceded. When the president found out, he chastised his wife: "How could you think I would do such a thing?" Jacqueline should not make Ted think of himself as a seat-warmer, John told his wife—his younger brother's confidence would suffer. But Jacqueline found Robert's loyalty to John admirable, and Ted's willingness to sacrifice "touching," because the Senate seat "was the highest thing that I think Teddy could ever have hoped for."

Kennedy's legislative files show his preoccupation with fulfilling his campaign slogan—and doing more for Massachusetts. His eager aides did not wait for the new year before announcing, in December 1962, that to stock the fallout shelters, and prepare for nuclear war, the Pentagon had ordered 5,428,000 pounds of survival crackers from the Educator Biscuit Company of Lowell. But the list of needs was long. Northeast Airlines needed a profitable new route to Florida. The Boston Navy Yard in Charlestown needed to be shielded from military budget cuts. The state's shoe factories and textile mills needed protective tariffs. The residents of Lawrence needed a new hospital.

The rookie had mixed success. After much haggling, Northeast got the blessings of the federal Civil Aviation Board. With Speaker McCormack's help, ships were ordered from the Charlestown and Quincy shipyards. But the White House could do little for the state's mills and factories, which were being pummeled by low-wage offshore rivals. The most noteworthy plum that Kennedy harvested was a NASA research center for Cambridge. It looked toward the future, to a time when the computer and electronics firms along Route 128 would transform the state's economy.

IT WAS A BUSY, historic spring and summer for John Kennedy. He wrestled the communists in Berlin, Vietnam, and Cuba—but signed an atmospheric test ban treaty with the Soviet Union and gave a memorable address on the dangers of the nuclear arms race at American University. "In the final analysis, our most basic common link is that we all inhabit this small planet," he said. "We all breathe the same air. We all cherish our children's future. And we are all mortal."

The very next night, Kennedy spoke to the nation on civil rights—and bound his presidency to the cause of racial equality.

The movement had been on his agenda. He had raised the plight of Black America in the most important hour of his presidential campaign, the first televised debate with Nixon. But it was never at the top of his priorities. As Robert said, "That was not a particular issue in our house. . . . We weren't thinking of the Negroes in Mississippi or Alabama, what should be done for them." Said civil rights activist Andrew Young, "They didn't even have black maids."

In his first years in office, John Kennedy "very carefully calculated civil rights," said Burns. "The question was whether, if there should be some great moral issue that was beyond the possibilities of calculus," Kennedy would side with "overriding moral purpose." Over lunch at the Century Club, Schlesinger and Theodore White listened as newsman Edward R. Murrow wondered if Kennedy had any deep beliefs at all. The president "has unlimited power to express the moral sense of the people," Schlesinger told his diary. "In not doing so, he is acting much like Eisenhower used to act when we denounced him so." Like Ike, Kennedy feared the social turmoil, and the political price, of implementing integration. As a tactical matter, the president needed the southern chairmen in Congress, Burns said, and "as long as he held back from civil rights he had a trading relationship."

The violent confrontations at Ole Miss in 1962, and at the University of Alabama, and in the streets of Birmingham in 1963—with televised footage of police dogs biting Black children, and teenagers braving a barrage from fire hoses—persuaded John and Robert that a civil rights bill must pass the Congress. Aides advised against it, but the brothers pushed ahead. "I'd like to say how brave it was of us to do it, but it was just clear," Robert recalled. "We needed to do something. . . . These demonstrations were going to continue. They were going to spread. There was going to be more violence." A grassroots movement, launched by the despised and powerless, had stung the conscience of Americans, and nudged the brothers leftward. On June 11, John Kennedy put his domestic agenda, his legislative hopes, his legacy, and his reelection at risk.

"We are confronted primarily with a moral issue. It is as old as the scriptures and is as clear as the American Constitution," John Kennedy told a national television audience in an address that was in part extemporaneous. "The heart of the question is whether all Americans are to be afforded equal rights and equal opportunities, whether we are going to treat our fellow Americans as we want to be treated.

"If an American, because his skin is dark, cannot eat lunch in a restaurant open to the public, if he cannot send his children to the best public school available, if he cannot vote for the public officials who will represent him, if, in short, he cannot enjoy the full and free life which all of us want, then who among us would be content to have the color of his skin changed and stand in his place? Who among us would then be content with the counsels of patience and delay?"

With bipartisan support, Robert's dilligence, and the president's lobbying, the Kennedy civil rights bill started to move. It was approved by the House Judiciary Committee that fall. "The one thing President Kennedy didn't want to do, really, was to become involved in civil rights legislation; he hoped that this matter would work itself out," Majority Leader Mike Mansfield of Montana remembered. "But once he acted he went all the way and his heart was really in getting . . . legislation."

John Kennedy told an aide that until he met southern hatred first-hand in 1962 and 1963, he believed that the Radical Republicans of the Reconstruction era, whom he had portrayed as fanatics in *Profiles in Courage*, were men of "vicious bias." Now, having witnessed the racists at work, said the president, "I'm coming to believe that Thaddeus Stevens was right."

"Mr. Eisenhower's administration had been like an enormous national tranquilizer. Nobody was begging for leadership. Everybody was saying just leave us alone, don't bother us," said columnist Joseph Alsop. "To start, as Kennedy did start, the country down a new path in those circumstances was a most extraordinary feat. And he did. He made us think about a whole series of things."

TED, the rookie, played no role in the drafting or advancement of the Civil Rights Act in 1963. But he and John enjoyed each other's company that summer. "Obviously when he was 20 and I was six, we were naturally not as close," Ted said, "but during his political career we were enormously close as brothers. By the time I arrived in the Senate and he was President, the sense of great age difference had almost disappeared."

They played cutthroat games of checkers. When the president returned from a triumphant tour of Ireland, it was Ted who sat with him in the family theater, watching film of the visit, over and over. When John and Jacqueline lost an infant son, Patrick, in his first week of life, Ted flew to Massachusetts to console the devastated president and First Lady. "He tried to keep inside of him, as well as he could, his feelings" of grief over

Patrick's death, Ted remembered. "But it was very evident to those of us who were very close to him."

On one occasion, they took off on a Sunday and toured a Civil War battlefield. Sometimes, when their wives were away, John summoned Ted to the White House. They would swim in the pool, share a drink or cigars on the Truman Balcony, and have comfort food for dinner. "Some of the happiest days of my life," Ted would recall. "There seemed no limit to the splendid quests . . . that lay ahead."

ON OCTOBER 19, Ted introduced the president to the audience at a Democratic fundraising dinner at the National Guard armory in Boston. "My last campaign, I suppose, may be coming up very shortly," the president told his longtime colleagues and friends. "But Teddy's around and therefore these dinners can go on indefinitely." Ted was then due to join John in Palm Beach for a sunny weekend off in mid-November, but a foul-up in the senator's schedule, and a speech he had agreed to give in Michigan, kept him away. When they spoke on the telephone, "he said that I was missing some good weather and we'd get together soon," Ted recalled.

Ted was serving as the Senate's presiding officer in the early afternoon of Friday, November 22. He was tidying up his correspondence and looking ahead to the evening, as he and Joan had planned a grand party to celebrate their upcoming fifth wedding anniversary. Guests were already arriving in town. And Saturday was the Harvard-Yale game. Shortly after 1:40 p.m., an ashen-faced clerk ran into the chamber, went from one Senate leader to the next, then climbed the dais and told Kennedy, "Your brother. Your brother the president. He's been shot."

Kennedy hastened to the wire service teletype machines in the lobby, where crowds were gathering to read the bulletins from Dallas. He went to his office, where, to his immense frustration, the phones were not working. Fragments of news arrived. Things were "really uncertain," he remembered. His aides were listening to transistor radios and—stunned—staring at him with horror.

For a moment, Ted deceived himself with a "disbelief that this thing was going to be real, you know, terribly serious." With an aide and a friend, he drove to his Georgetown home but found the house empty; Joan was getting her hair done and Kara and Ted Jr. were at the White House for a play date with little John F. Kennedy Jr. The telephone circuits were still jammed. He went from house to house, knocking on doors in the neighborhood, trying to find a dial tone.

Finally, he got through to Robert.

"He's dead," Robert said, before Ted could ask. "You'd better call your mother and our sisters."

At that, Ted remembered, "The world lurched apart."

Robert and the new president, Lyndon Johnson, met Jacqueline and her husband's body at Andrews Air Force Base that evening. She wore the same pink suit, stained with his blood, that she had been wearing when John Kennedy fell over, shot, dying and senseless, into her lap in the limousine in Dallas. Joan was terrified and huddled at home most of the weekend. Ted and Eunice were dispatched to Hyannis Port.

Rose had heard the reports on the television, but no one had told Joseph Kennedy of his son's death. All feared the news would kill him. They stalled until Saturday morning—Ted at one point ripping the wires from his father's television set—and even then the young man stumbled, as Eunice wailed beside him.

"There's been a bad accident," he told his father. "The president has been hurt very badly. As a matter of fact, he died."

TED RETURNED TO WASHINGTON, to march beside Robert and Jacqueline in the funeral on that bright cold Monday, with the world leaders, the skirl of bagpipes and the thrum of drums, the Irish Army rifle team and Black Jack, the riderless horse. At Arlington, he and Robert and Jacqueline lit an eternal flame.

It was John Jr.'s third birthday. Back at the White House, the adults tried to appear cheerful. There was cake and a party, and at Jacqueline's request,

Ted and David Powers joined in "Heart of My Heart," the tune that Ted and John and Robert sang at the G&G Restaurant on election eve in Dorchester in 1958.

Robert, stricken, rushed from the room.

Sometime that winter, Ted accompanied the disinterred bodies of John Kennedy's two dead infants—Patrick and the stillborn daughter—to Arlington and saw them buried with their father. In February, Ted Kennedy turned 32.

Five

MORE OF US THAN
TROUBLE

To Robert, the dauphin, now flowed privilege and dominion. He was seven years Ted's senior, had run a presidential campaign, scrapped with Joe McCarthy, faced down corrupt labor leaders and racist southern governors, and counseled a president at the brink of war. There would be no challenge from the younger brother: the attorney general led the Kennedys. It was Robert who donned President Kennedy's old leather bomber jacket, took President Kennedy's seat on the family airplane, and accepted on his family's behalf a twenty-two-minute ovation given by the Democrats at the 1964 national convention.

It was an extraordinary moment. Robert stood moved and vulnerable before millions, his voice catching as he sought to introduce a film about his brother.

"When there were periods of crisis, you stood beside him," Robert told the delegates, as they finally let him speak. "When there were periods of happiness, you laughed with him. And when there were periods of sorrow, you comforted him." John Kennedy was more than a Cold Warrior, his brother said. "He wanted to do something for the mentally ill . . . for those who were not covered by Social Security; for those who were not receiving an adequate minimum wage . . . for our elderly people who had difficulty paying their medical bills; for our fellow citizens who are not white," he said. "To all this he dedicated himself."

Robert closed with a passage, suggested to him by Jacqueline, from *Romeo and Juliet*:

When he shall die,
Take him and cut him out in little stars,
And he will make the face of heaven so fine
That all the world will be in love with night,
And pay no worship to the garish sun.

Robert's enhancement of John's liberal resolve was accepted by the Democrats. It was natural to attribute, when mourning a slain hero, fine grails and finer purpose. Robert recognized, in his brother's unmet aspirations, a legacy to nurture and employ. The garish sun, to those steeped in the politics of 1964, was reckoned a reference to Lyndon Johnson—the usurper invested at that convention, there on the boardwalk in Atlantic City, New Jersey. John Kennedy's body had not left Dallas before the Kennedy clan had clashed with Johnson and his people over real and concocted slights. In the months that followed, the New Frontiersmen split between those whose distaste for the less elegant Texas president compelled them to plot a Kennedy restoration, and those who saw, in Johnson's skilled conniving and the power of the moment, a path to succeed where John had failed.

Ted set a foot in both camps. He saw it as his duty to support Robert's ambition *and* John's platform, and not one at the expense of the other. If Robert was a sinker, pulling them toward darker depths in the next five years, Ted was a bobber, resisting. "They didn't always agree . . . their natures were so totally different," said John's friend Charles Spalding. "Teddy has never had Bobby's . . . appetite for meeting things just head on in such a way that could only provoke argument, dissent, and eruption. And I think Teddy sometimes was impatient with that."

THE KENNEDYS HAD GRIEVED when Joe Jr. and Kick died, but not like Robert grieved now. His vague affinity with life's underdogs grew into a fierce empathy for the dispossessed. With a spirit born in his own suffering, Robert visited and allied himself with striking Latino farmworkers in California, the victims of apartheid in South Africa, immigrants, impoverished Indians on forgotten reservations, and malnourished Black infants in Mississippi. On a visit to a Catholic home for the aged in Kansas City, he stole away for an hour, sitting by a bedside of a dying woman in a ward for the terminally ill. "I watched with tears in my eyes as the 'ruthless' Bobby Kennedy stroked this unknown woman's hand, and spoke to her in a near whisper," Ben Bradlee recalled.

They had been so close—Jack the candidate and Bobby the campaign manager; John the president and Robert the attorney general. In the crises of the New Frontier—the integration of the Universities of Mississippi and Alabama, the Cuban missile showdown with the Soviet Union—the bond between them was a defining feature. Ted was in Massachusetts, campaigning for his Senate seat, for all but ten months of his brother's presidency; shared in no crises or momentous decisions, and only some social occasions. He had grown from the jester's role, but slowly. While waiting for Ted to emerge from one visit to the White House, two of his aides had relieved themselves in the shrubbery, an act not missed by the Secret Service. "I have a message from the President," a mortified Ted told them: "Piss on your own lawn." When honored with a dinner by Mayor Willy Brandt in Berlin in 1962, Robert had merry Ted and his friend Claude Hooton play the fools—singing "Won't You Come Home Bill Bailey" to the puzzled Germans—while reserving the serious speechmaking for himself. An American in the audience called it "one of the most embarrassing occasions I ever witnessed."

Then an instant, gunshots, and so much lost. Robert turned to poetry, and the ancient Greek playwrights, for solace. Watching him mourn, fearing for his brother's well-being, Ted set aside his own deep grief: "It veered close to being a tragedy within the tragedy," he would remember, as Robert "seemed to age physically. He would spend hours without speaking a word. . . . Hope seemed to have died within him, and there followed months of unrelenting melancholia."

Robert and Ted would spend most of the next five years shoulder to shoulder in national politics. From the experience, and that of shared loss, they grew close in a manner that, while different from the iconic relationship between John and Robert Kennedy, was evocative in a less Olympian way. When Robert visited a Washington orphanage in the holiday season that followed John's assassination, the children froze when he came into the room. "Your brother's dead!" one of the orphans blurted. Realizing he had erred, the boy burst into tears. Robert hugged him. "That's all right," he said. "I have another brother."

AS MUCH AS ATTENTION was focused on Robert, Ted's grief was neglected. He was, after all, the happy-go-lucky one. After John's funeral, Ted was master of ceremonies at the family Thanksgiving in Hyannis Port: Robert could not bear the memories of the Cape and spent the holiday in Florida. This left the youngest to organize the traditional football game, and a raucous Celtic wake. The governess quit the next day, aghast at the indecorous all-night ceilidh of laughter, drink, stories, and song. In Washington, a few weeks later, Robert and his wife abruptly left a dinner party at newsman David Brinkley's home after Ted began to play a tape of an Irish raconteur from Boston telling stories about John Kennedy. "Perhaps more than the others, [Ted] seemed to believe that grief could be conquered by talk and comradeship," wrote Burns. Pain was suppressed. "I just pushed it down further and further inside," Kennedy recalled. "Hour by hour, I learned to contain my grief, to not give way to it." Grown men—Kennedys—did not seek counseling; Ted Kennedy's therapists were windswept strands and waves.

It seemed reasonable, then, for Robert to ask his seemingly less affected brother to serve as the family representative and be briefed on the findings of the Warren Commission's investigation of John's assassination. Robert had warred with some of the suspected conspirators—the chieftains of organized crime and Fidel Castro—and was haunted by the thought that by doing so he may have brought on his brother's death. Ted had no connection to his elder brothers' crusades against Mafia racketeering, or to Operation Mongoose, the Kennedy administration's program to topple Castro. Chief Justice Earl Warren gave Ted a four-hour briefing and persuaded him that Lee Oswald acted alone. Unacknowledged was the impact on the youngest brother—a searing immersion in the forensic details of a loved one's murder that would ceaselessly repeat in the years to come, as Hollywood and the news media milked each conspiracy theory and rebroadcast the gruesome imagery. His son Patrick would liken it to post-traumatic stress.

As sorrowful, if more consoling, were the duties that Ted Kennedy took on to plan and raise money for a presidential library and museum to honor his brother. He suggested to Jacqueline that the library focus on John Kennedy's capacity to inspire young Americans—a suggestion that, in time, would take shape as the John F. Kennedy School of Government at Harvard. In May, Ted left the country to thank the Europeans for the sympathy they had conveyed to his family, and to raise funds for the library. He met with Harold Macmillan in London, Georges Pompidou in France, the pope in Italy, and Konrad Adenauer in Germany. On the way home, "with . . . sad glamor," diplomat Sean O'Huiginn recalled, Kennedy stopped in Ireland. A hundred thousand lined O'Connell Street in Limerick to greet him on a warm sunny day. At a mournful dinner, Sinéad de Valera, the wife of the Irish president, recited a bit of the Irish lament "Johnny We Hardly Knew Ye." When John Kennedy left Ireland in 1963, he had promised to return in springtime. That promise would not be met, Ted told the Irish. "My brother will not be able to come back and enjoy any more spring days."

JOHN KENNEDY'S LIBERALISM HAD been informed by the discrimination that confronted Boston's Irish, by the family's association with Roosevelt and the Democrats, by the poverty John witnessed when campaigning in Appalachia in 1960, and by the hatred he beheld in his efforts, as president, to peacefully integrate bus lines, lunch counters, and campuses. He had arrived in office preoccupied with foreign policy, but the energy of the civil rights movement had compelled him to tend to the liberal planks in his domestic agenda as well. "John . . . grew as his horizons expanded," said his lyricist, Sorensen. "When he was a member of the House . . . he knew almost nothing about civil rights, he knew almost nothing about poverty and economic and social justice, inner cities and failing cities. But as he campaigned . . . he learned a lot more about the plight of the poor, about the discrimination against blacks. He began to see the similarities between the discrimination that Irish Catholics had once suffered and the discrimination faced by blacks."

Now it fell to Robert and Ted to take up their brother's causes. Transfixed by pain and loss, they, too, needed to grow. Together, they would push the New Frontier farther than their brother ever conceived—far, far down the course he set toward racial justice, aid for the poor, health care for all, a hike in the minimum wage, and arms control. In one of John Kennedy's last cabinet meetings, he had scrawled the word "poverty" a half dozen times amid his doodling. Robert had the paper framed, and hung it on his office wall.

"There was a parallel" with the younger brothers, Sorensen said. "Bobby started out very close to his father in every sense of the word, ideologically and in terms of personality. . . . He learned as Attorney General, first from the civil rights problem, which was in his lap . . . and then from his world travels. And Jack's death very much changed Bobby, in a way humbled him, took some of the so-called ruthless arrogance that he was accused of out of him. He became a gentler, warmer personality. . . . Ted had some of all that. He started out very young, very inexperienced. But he gained years, he gained experience, he began to specialize in certain issues like health care and mastered them."

John's murder was one of a dozen appalling tragedies to define Ted Kennedy's life. Like Robert, he grew more sensitive and receptive after Dallas. He was always good-hearted and convivial, but now was born the "empathy," said one aide, "that many people in positions of power and influence and wealth tend not to have. They rarely have experiences that create that foundational capacity to understand pain and suffering." Ted had those experiences and "on an almost spiritual level, he understands."

ROBERT AND TED WERE AIDED, in their journey, by the man their brother had called "Riverboat." Assessing the great outpouring of sorrow that followed the gunshots in Dallas, Lyndon Johnson knew he would be judged by history—and by the voters in the 1964 election—by how effectively he made use of "the Kennedy aura" and propelled the late president's program through Congress. The challenges—civil rights, poverty, federal aid to education, and health care for the aged—were formidable, but so was the opportunity.

"All I have I would have given gladly not to be standing here today," Johnson told Congress in a televised address the day after the funeral, but "let us continue. This is our challenge, not to hesitate, not to pause, not to turn about and linger over this evil moment, but to continue." Atop his list of prescriptions was the tartest of the medicaments he aimed to have Congress swallow: passage of Kennedy's civil rights bill, to outlaw segregation and ban discrimination in public venues. "No memorial oration or eulogy could more eloquently honor President Kennedy's memory" than action on civil rights, Johnson told Congress. "We have talked for one hundred years or more. It is time now to write the next chapter, and to write it in the book of law."

In bus stations, classrooms, and luncheonettes, from Greensboro to Oxford to Birmingham, the courage of the demonstrators, the righteousness of their cause, and the eloquence of their leaders had roused America's religious denominations, labor unions, and liberal activists. In the parlance of Capitol Hill, this was "the outside game"—the education and incitement of the electorate and the subsequent application of public pressure on elected officials.

John and Robert Kennedy's ardent lobbying for a civil rights bill in the summer and fall of 1963 had epitomized "the inside game" on Capitol Hill. They dealt, reasoned, and bargained with both Democrats and Republicans, persuading them to join and move a bill through the House Judiciary Committee. On the other side of the Capitol, Robert appeared before the Senate nine times, in long sessions marked by southern salvoes.

"Isn't it true, if we pass this bill, we confer the power of a dictatorship?" Jim Eastland asked, intent on interring the legislation.

"There is no doubt that this bill . . . would confer the power of a dictator upon the president," Senator Sam Ervin of North Carolina replied.

In keeping with his unpretentious entry to the Senate, Ted had ducked the limelight on civil rights. When he expressed his wish to attend the August 1963 March on Washington, at which Martin Luther King Jr. talked so powerfully of a dream, John had told Ted to stay away, lest he be identified with Black radicals or caught up in an outbreak of violence. The president met with the leaders of the march at the White House; Ted watched it on television. But now he had an opportunity to drop his self-effacing pose—and make a mark on history.

THE CIVIL RIGHTS BILL passed the House, 290 to 130, in February 1964, thanks to an effective collaboration of President Johnson, Robert Kennedy's Justice Department, and Speaker McCormack—and 138 Republican votes. A week later, the Senate majority leader, Mike Mansfield of Montana, employed a parliamentary rule to rip the bill from Eastland's jurisdiction and move it to the Senate floor.

The battle was far from won. In an election year, the congressional calendar had huge blocks of time reserved for the national conventions and the fall campaign. The South's best weapon was delay. The southerners kept the bill from consideration until March 30, and then began to filibuster.

"Would it not be fair to ask what kind of fix the colored folks would be in if they had not been brought to this country, but had been allowed to roam the jungles, with tigers chasing them . . . compared with the fine conditions they enjoy in America?" asked Louisiana's Russell Long, heir of the Kingfish, in one Senate colloquy.

"The Negroes are much better off," Senator Strom Thurmond of South Carolina averred, and "the people who are primarily responsible for the progress of the Negroes are the Southern people."

The white South was not going to surrender its privilege and supremacy without a struggle. There were twenty-one southern Democrats. To beat the filibuster, Johnson had to have Republican votes.

As THE GREAT DEBATE RAGED, Ted's name won him an appearance on *Meet the Press*, where he ably parried journalists' questions about Johnson, the Senate, the state of play and civil rights. Robert's thorny relationship with the president had been aggravated when a rogue Kennedy operative launched a write-in campaign on behalf of the attorney general in the New Hampshire primary. When pressed by his inquisitors, Ted dismissed the reports of enmity. Johnson appeared to be tending his flanks—or seeing if he might drive a wedge between the brothers—when he called to praise Ted for his performance.

"[President Kennedy] would have been so proud of you," Johnson told him. "I just thought you just hit a home run every time they asked you a question."

"It's just a matter of survival," Ted said. "You want to come out of the program and not have sort of left yourself wide open."

"You can take my job any time that you're ready," said Johnson. "Nobody is going to come in between us. . . . I'm just a trustee. . . . We're going to put over [John Kennedy's] program and he's going to be proud of it, if we all survive. Then we're going to go on to better things, and you'll always have me in your corner."

On APRIL 9, 1964, Kennedy chose civil rights as the topic of his first notable Senate address—his "maiden speech," he called it, though he had spoken other times, on minor matters. His wife, his sisters, and members of the Washington press corps watched from the gallery, but he made his address—as befit his place in the Senate's pecking order—to a nearly empty chamber. His remarks were printed in the *Congressional Record* alongside a Texas senator's treatise on the peerless pecans of the Lone Star State.

"Mr. President. It is with some hesitation that I rise to speak on the pending legislation before the Senate. A freshman senator should be seen, not heard; should learn, and not teach," he began, with the kind of obsequiousness that tradition then demanded. "This is especially true when the Senate is engaged in a truly momentous debate."

Kennedy followed with a parochial nod, assuring the voters that he had not forgotten his campaign promise to do more for Massachusetts. "I had planned . . . to make my maiden speech . . . on issues affecting industry and employment in my home state," he said. But "to limit myself to local issues in the face of this great national question would be to demean the seat in which I sit." And so he got to civil rights—which he addressed with much the same caution that had characterized John's and Robert's initial approach. He supported his brothers' legislation, and no more.

"The basic problem the American people face in the 1960s in the field of civil rights is adjustment," said Kennedy. "It is the task of adjusting to the fact that Negroes are going to be members of the community of American citizens, with the same rights and the same responsibilities as every one of us." Lauding his home state's prowess at assimilating immigrants, he avowed with misplaced optimism, or stunning naivete, that "if America has been able to make this adjustment for the Irish, the Italians, the Jews, the Poles, the Greeks, the Portuguese—we can make it for the Negroes."

"In 1780, a Catholic in Massachusetts was not allowed to vote or hold public office. In 1840, an Irishman could not get a job above that of a common laborer," Kennedy told the Senate. But the "noble characteristic" of "fairness and good will" had prevailed in "the minds and hearts of men" in Massachusetts and would again for Black Americans. The Civil Rights Act was not a sledgehammer, but an enticement. It would bring brotherhood "out in every person, so in the end the prejudice will be dissolved."

Kennedy waded through the titles of the legislation and read into the record the letters he'd received from hometown religious leaders on its behalf. But then, finger to the wind, he catered to the instincts of a different constituency by declaring his opposition to the mandatory desegregation of schools—which the NAACP in Boston was demanding and the Boston School Committee, chaired by the redoubtable South Boston segregationist, Louise Day Hicks, was resisting.

Kennedy did not recognize the fierce urgency of now. The southern senators had alleged that liberals from the North were hypocrites—ready to run the buses through Richmond and Atlanta, but not in their own segregated communities. There was a difference, Kennedy argued. While it was true that Boston's schools were segregated, it was by custom, not by law, he said. It was eminently reasonable for white parents in South Boston and Charlestown to cling to "the sound and historic principle that children of the same neighborhood should attend the same school." Improvements in economic opportunity for Black Americans would, in time, desegregate the towns and cities and neighborhoods of the North. There was no need to bus children across district lines. Goodwill, in time, would prevail.

Kennedy did not choose to tell the Senate how, three weeks earlier, during Boston's St. Patrick's Day parade, a float sponsored by the NAACP—with an icon of John F. Kennedy and slogans equating the Irish and Black struggle in America—had been the target of bricks, cherry bombs, beer cans, and racist insults, until Ted had been compelled to dispatch his own police escort to protect it. One group of youths shadowed the float through South Boston with their own shamrocked banner: "Go Home Nigger. Long Live the Spirit of Independence in Segregated Boston."

It was only in Kennedy's peroration that he strayed from the mundane and the artful—and tendered his brother's legacy as a reason to enact the law. "My brother was the first President of the United States to state publicly that segregation was morally wrong. His heart and soul are in this bill," Ted said. "If his life and death had a meaning, it was that we should not hate but love one another; we should use our powers not to create conditions of oppression that lead to violence, but conditions of freedom that lead to peace." His voice broke and, up in the gallery, Joan wiped tears from her eyes.

The press focused on this moment. Kennedy's go-slow approach to integrating schools was not noted in the next day's newspapers. The gushy encomiums of his colleagues were, as befit Senate tradition, transparently effusive. It was a "magnificent address," said Paul Douglas of Illinois. "I have never heard the principles of the bill or the tenets of civil rights stated more succinctly." Young Ted was "a worthy continuer of the great tradition of the seat which he occupies in the Senate, beginning, I believe, with John Quincy Adams, Daniel Webster, and Charles Sumner . . . to his beloved and lamented brother."

MANSFIELD HAD CHOSEN Senator Hubert Humphrey to be the floor manager for the bill. A small group of senators, including Kennedy, were enlisted as "floor captains." Ted had little to do but listen and learn and help his staff corral colleagues for the quorum calls—he spent eight days of the civil rights debate soliciting funds for the Kennedy library in Europe—but his membership on the Judiciary Committee sometimes put him in a room where it happened: where Robert and his advisers, Burke Marshall and Nicholas Katzenbach, were dealing with Humphrey, the staff of the Senate leadership, and the man who would determine the bill's success or failure, the Republican leader, Senator Everett Dirksen of Illinois.

Dirksen was a midwestern conservative, the son of German immigrants, from the little town of Pekin in southern Illinois. His heavy, horn-rimmed eyeglasses, rumbling baritone, and languid wit left a memorable impression. He was a reporter's favorite. And as Johnson often reminded him, Dirksen was from the Land, and the Party, of Lincoln. Like the other members of the Republican congressional leadership, he knew what was fair and what was not, had voted for antilynching measures and voting rights for Blacks, and would play an indispensable role in carrying the Civil Rights Act over its final hurdle.

The civil rights forces needed sixty-seven votes to shut down the southern filibuster. Unless Dirksen would help them enlist the support of some two dozen of the thirty-three Senate Republicans, they had no chance. Before Kennedy's death, Dirksen had warned civil rights leaders that the section of the bill banning discrimination in public accommodations, like hotels, restaurants, rooming houses, and barbershops, would not likely survive. But Dallas changed things. Dirksen "wants to do what is right," said Humphrey. "We've just got to help him along a little bit."

Humphrey began by ceding Dirksen center stage. "What we want to do is get some blue lights and pink lights and dress up this little spot on the stage," Humphrey told an aide. "And when everything is set, we want to have Everett Dirksen walk out there, stand in that spotlight, and be the man who rescues the whole operation."

The Republican leader—a former actor and playwright—was adept at masking his concessions and finding victory in compromise. The liberals, and their allies in the administration, recognized that Dirksen would need changes—fig leaves, mostly, but lots of them—to provide cover for his fellow Republicans. Katzenbach would say later that Dirksen's greatest legislative accomplishment was to persuade the Republican caucus that "refinements in punctuation" were substantive adjustments.

Suffering from a bleeding ulcer, in and out of the hospital, reliant on bourbon and cigarettes, Dirksen went from one Republican colleague to another citing Victor Hugo: Stronger than any army is an idea whose time has come. Modest alterations were negotiated, the bill was amended, and the conservative coalition shattered. By an overwhelming margin, the Senate Republicans voted with the liberal Democrats for cloture. It was a moment fraught with feeling, no more so than when Democratic senator Clair Engle of California, suffering from brain cancer and carved by surgery, was wheeled into the chamber. When his name was called, he lifted a shaky finger and pointed to his eye. Senator Engle votes "aye." The final score was 71–29. Not before, in all the years since Appomattox, had civil rights supporters been able to shut down a filibuster.

The experience left vivid impressions on Ted, lessons about the Senate that would guide him in the years ahead: the importance of the outside and inside games; how, with bipartisan support, even the unimaginable can become real; and, finally (evident in how Humphrey handled Dirksen), that there were few limits to what one could achieve if you were willing to let others take credit.

Kennedy's last duty in the passage of the Civil Rights Act was ripe with symbolism and emotion. He was taking his turn in the chair, a freshman presiding over the chamber, when Richard Russell made his closing argument against the bill.

"The moving finger is writing the final act of the longest debate and the greatest tragedy ever played out in the Senate of the United States," the Georgian said. He seemed intent on exceeding the time limit set by the leaders. It had indeed been the longest Senate debate ever. The South had used every hateful argument, over and over. It needed to stop.

"The time of the senator from Georgia has expired," Kennedy said.

Russell looked stunned. Kennedy's words could be read two ways. The Georgian's eyes glistened. "I have been gagged," he said.

Kennedy checked with the clerks. The liberals had toed the time limit. Russell needed to stand down. His time, the South's time, the time of segregation had expired.

On Friday, June 19, the senators voted. The Civil Rights Act of 1964 passed the Senate, 73 to 24.

THAT SUMMER'S PASSAGE OF the Civil Rights Act was a delineating moment in American politics. The Party of Lincoln stood at a crossroads, wrote Theodore White, with its leaders confronted by a prospect "tantalizing in the extreme." The Republicans could make a Faustian bargain and shift their organizing principle to "racial fear," White said. If so, "the South can be theirs for the asking and with the South, if it comes permanently to Republican loyalty, could come such solid addition of electoral strength as would make Republicans again, as they were for half a century, the majority party of the nation."

Among the six Republican senators who voted "No" on the civil rights bill was Barry Goldwater, the hard-right Arizonan who would claim the party's presidential nomination and steal five states of the old Confederacy from the Democratic Solid South in November. Among the twenty-one southern senators who voted "No" was John Tower of Texas, the first Republican to win a Senate seat from the South since Reconstruction. Richard Nixon supported the civil rights bill, but Tower and Goldwater and George H. W. Bush and Ronald Reagan did not. The Republican Party's steady, deliberate abandonment of its first principles, and return to majority status, would be a dominant current in Ted Kennedy's political future, and in the American story for the next fifty-six years. As this is written it is race—not economic equality, opportunity, or class—that remains the prevalent theme.

KENNEDY DID NOT LINGER in the chamber. He was due to address the Democratic state convention in Springfield that evening and to bring Senator Birch Bayh, the guest speaker, to the gathering with him. But it was one of those nights when, as politicians say, everything had been said, but not everyone had said it. The speeches, and the final roll call, continued until 7:40 p.m. "We were having the final vote on the civil rights bill. It went on and on and on," Bayh recalled. The two U.S. senators hurried to the airport and boarded a chartered airplane with Bayh's wife, Marvella, and Kennedy's aide Edward Moss. It was a storm-struck night. At around 10:50 p.m., as pilot Edwin Zimny was following a directional beacon some three miles from the Springfield area airport, he allowed the aircraft to drift down and to the left in a dense fog. The plane clipped a stand of trees on a hilltop and plunged into an apple orchard, coasting like a toboggan atop the branches before breaking into pieces on the rocky ground.

The boughs likely saved three lives. But Zimny, the pilot, was killed instantly. Moss had begun the flight in the passenger section with Kennedy and Bayh but had climbed into the seat beside the pilot to give them room to work on their speeches. He, too, bore the brunt of impact, and would die that night from his injuries. He had served as Ted's advance man in 1962, and the two had drawn close in all their hours on the road.

When they had started to descend, Ted—a licensed pilot—had turned in his rearward-facing seat to watch the landing. "For some reason or other he had taken off his seatbelt and was up talking to the pilot," Bayh remembered. Kennedy watched the altimeter register their descent—1100 . . . 1000 . . . 900 . . . 800 . . . 700—yet all that appeared through the window was fog. At 600 feet, the sky cleared, and Kennedy saw the dark line of trees.

The impact broke Kennedy's back, punctured his lung, and left him in shock with internal bleeding. In their forward-facing seats in the rear of the airplane, the Bayhs suffered lesser injuries: Marvella cracked vertebrae, Bayh a torn-up hip. Prompted by the reek of aviation fuel and the threat of fire, Bayh was able, through what can accurately be described as a heroic effort, to find the 230-pound Kennedy in the wreckage, pick him up, and pull him to safety.

Bayh brought Kennedy down a hill. Marvella covered him with a raincoat, pulled the weeds away from his face, and then the Bayhs stumbled off through the drizzle to find help.

Kennedy had fleeting awareness. When lying in the wreckage, he had heard Bayh shout his name, but could not at first focus and reply. Then came Bayh and Marvella, talking about a fire—and that gave Ted the strength to call out. Bayh had seen a white cuff and reached in to grab him. Kennedy draped his arms around Bayh's neck as they lurched from the wreckage. He had no feeling in his legs.

The scene was eerily lit by the flashing red taillight of the airplane. Lying in the grass, as rescuers arrived and tried to save Moss, the thought came to Kennedy that he, too, was going to die. "You could just sort of feel everything go out of you," he would remember, "that the tide was just going out." He asked for water. He struggled to breathe. The adrenaline wore off. Came the pain. Mercifully, he lost consciousness.

JOAN, rebounding from a second miscarriage, was at a friendly Democrat's home nearby, and the first of the family to get to the hospital. "Hi Joansie," said Kennedy as, dazed by fear, she arrived at his bedside. Bayh called Robert Kennedy in Hyannis Port, where Jean had roused the household after hearing the news on the television.

"Is he dead—we haven't lost him too?" Robert asked.

Robert and Jean reached the hospital before dawn. Patricia Kennedy Lawford and Stephen Smith and Lem Billings followed. "Is it true that you are ruthless?" Ted asked his brother. He told Pat, who hated to fly, "Maybe you've got the right idea." Away from the requisite joshing, Robert, pale and drawn, paced the hospital corridors and grounds. The journalist Jimmy Breslin caught up to him in the hospital coffee shop at midday.

"Is it ever going to end for you people?" Breslin asked.

"I guess the only reason we've survived is that there are too many of us," Robert replied. "There are more of us than there is trouble."

He stared down at the counter. "I was just thinking . . . if my mother did not have any more children after her first four, she would have nothing now. My brothers Joe and Jack are dead and Kathleen is dead and Rosemary is in the nursing home," said Robert. "She would be left with nothing if she only had four."

It was a warm, sunny summer day, but with echoes of Dallas. "Everywhere there was this chill, and all the people in the hospital and most of the ones standing outside were quiet because this plane crash and this hospital brought them all back to a day last November, and nobody mentioned it, but it was with everybody," Breslin wrote. In his hospital bed Ted, too, felt "these flashbacks . . . of the loss again. Of 1963."

Just past death was the prospect of paralysis. When Kennedy was wheeled into Cooley Dickinson Hospital in Northampton that Friday night, the emergency room staff had found him in shock, his pulse irregular and his blood pressure negligible. He was stabilized, X-rayed, given transfusions, and put into an oxygen tent. The doctors made a list of his injuries: a collapsed and punctured lung, a bruised kidney, two broken ribs, one shattered and two fractured vertebrae, several lesser fractures of the spine, lacerations to his legs and arm, and the troublesome internal bleeding from ruptured blood vessels around his spleen.

Lyndon Johnson phoned from California, where the news of the plane wreck had stilled a roistering crowd at a Democratic Party dinner. The president ordered specialists from the Walter Reed Army Medical Center to Massachusetts. Throughout that weekend, Johnson tracked Kennedy's progress.

"There's not any question about him dying, is there?" the president asked an aide, Walter Jenkins.

"Doctor said he didn't think so . . . although his pulse was not strong and he was in and out of shock, and that he had a broken back," Jenkins said.

"What does that mean?" Johnson asked. "Do you recover from that?"

"Yes, sir. Perhaps not completely."

That was the fear—that Ted would not walk again. But by Saturday evening, when the president reached his attorney general, the doctors had shown some optimism.

"How's Teddy, Bob?" Johnson asked.

"He's got a lot of broken bones and his back is in bad shape, but he's not paralyzed," Kennedy said. "It's going to take anywhere from six months to a year, but he's going to be fine."

"Looks like you have more than we can bear," Johnson told Robert, and said it again to Jacqueline Kennedy when she got on the phone. Jacqueline, still in mourning and wearing black, seven months after losing her husband, visited his brother in the hospital on Sunday.

KENNEDY WAS EXTRAORDINARILY FORTUNATE. "The vertebrae kind of exploded," he would remember. "They all broke into a lot of pieces" that came short of severing his spinal column. There was no debate over his initial treatment. His spine needed to be immobilized so that the shattered bones might knit together. "I had a goal in life," he would remember. "I would walk again by Christmas."

He was bound in a Stryker frame, which had replaced the old-time plaster body casts. It was a rotisserie-like contraption of canvas, leather straps, and steel that kept Kennedy secured, like a fowl on a spit, and allowed his nurses to flip him, to avoid bedsores and other complications. In time, a gyroscopic element was added so that he could be tilted up and back and regain his sense of balance. There were cutouts for bedpans fore and aft. He would not leave its confines for five months.

The nights were worst. He found it difficult to sleep and fell into a pattern of dozing and waking. When Johnson phoned him on June 30 and assured him that adversity builds character, Kennedy told the president that may be so, but that so far he didn't much like the terms of the transaction.

On July 9, Kennedy was taken by ambulance to the Lahey Clinic at New England Baptist Hospital in Boston. The doctors told him not to expect much; there was still a chance that he might not walk again. A summit was arranged with the clinicians in Massachusetts, the specialists at Walter Reed, and orthopedic experts from around the country. They determined that it might be helpful if Kennedy had surgery to fuse the damaged vertebrae. But Joseph Kennedy, who had watched John Kennedy skirt death after a similar operation, and seen Rosemary suffer irredeemable injury, made his controlling opinion known with an emphatic "N-o-o-o!" On August 6 the clinic issued a statement: "All of these eminent and highly experienced physicians were fully in accord that fusion is not indicated and that very satisfactory normal healing is taking place."

Because he was a Kennedy, he had visits from Cardinals Cushing and Spellman and the president of the United States—who arrived at 1 a.m. and, when departing, kissed Ted on the cheek. "I understand that even one of our Republican doctors down the hall came out in his night shirt to pledge his vote for you," Kennedy wrote Johnson afterward.

Ted had the best suite at the clinic, with its own sunlit porch. In an emptied room across the hall, members of his staff set up phone lines, desks, and typewriters. Joan handled the personal appearances in this, an election year, but Ted campaigned by note and letter as best he could, and conducted an October press conference lying prone and smiling for the reporters, who applauded when he finished.

Two sergeants, on loan from Walter Reed, flipped him in the Stryker bed and supervised physical therapy sessions. With his torso immobilized, he could only exercise arms and legs. He withered a bit and lost thirty pounds. He used prismed eyeglasses to read books balanced on his chest. There was a ridge in the floor on the way to the porch, and he marked his progress by how much it hurt when they wheeled him over that bump each day.

He picked up a long-handled paintbrush—as John Kennedy had when recovering from his own back surgery—and worked on still lifes and seascapes. Aides brought dinners from swank Locke-Ober and rum cake from the North End. His dad came by in his wheelchair. Ted called Kara, now four, and the toddler Ted Jr. at bedtime each night to give them the latest installment, complete with chirpy voices, of an ongoing saga he was crafting about Freddy the Crocodile, Gobble the Turkey, Leo the Lion, and their friends. The children's artwork covered the walls of his room. So he would not be lonely, they brought him a frog.

Kennedy studied the *Congressional Record*. On a call to Johnson in August, he expressed his support for the Gulf of Tonkin Resolution, in which Congress gave the president the authority to wage war in Vietnam. He read biographies of Irish statesman Daniel O'Connell and other famed men, and James Madison's record of the Constitutional Convention—from which Kennedy would quote throughout his life. It is not known, but unlikely, that he followed his mother's advice to read passages from the books aloud, to recognize "the difference between the succinct dramatic expressions of the author," as she put it, and "your own discursive dull recital."

Doherty came by some evenings with a treat not generally available to hospital patients—reels of first-run motion pictures that they ran on a projector while eating bowls of ice cream. Kennedy was aware that his standard of treatment was exceptional. He quizzed Doherty, who had spent two years in a sanatorium with tuberculosis as a young man, about the financial effects of catastrophic illness. The Kennedys could afford the best. As Arthur sang in *Camelot*, Ted asked, What did the simple folk do?

KENNEDY PROPOSED THAT he follow John's example and devote the days of his recuperation to scholarship. "I have been contemplating how to spend these next few months," he wrote Harvard professor John Kenneth Galbraith in July. "Perhaps, sometimes when you are down in Boston, you will drop in."

Galbraith replied immediately: "Count on me for any help I can give you on reading—or writing. (Perhaps I can get Harvard to knock off a course if I take you on as a tutee.)"

When drawing up a reading list, Galbraith pulled no punches. "This will get you started on foreign trade and the balance of payments," he wrote Kennedy in a note accompanying an intimidating stack of materials. Kennedy assembled a private grad school, with the biggest names in Boston as his personal faculty. He asked Galbraith, Schlesinger, Robert Wood, and Sam Beer for syllabi, plowed his way through their lists of books, and took one-man tutorials, two nights a week, from experts at Harvard and MIT. "Teddy's recovery from an airplane crash is remarkable, and I am sure that in retrospect his interlude will turn out to have been one of the luckiest things that ever happened to him," Schlesinger told his diary.

Kennedy found it rough sledding. "I've been trying to read that list of books which Jack said were his favorites," he told Schlesinger. "Could [Jack] really have enjoyed those books? I tried to read [Samuel Flagg] Bemis on John Quincy Adams and Allan Nevins on the coming of the Civil War and I just couldn't get through them."

Cued by George Wallace's success in the Democratic primaries, and by Goldwater's rise as the Republican nominee, Kennedy proposed to write a book on right-wing extremism. It might even be structured like *Profiles in Courage*, Schlesinger suggested, with chapters on the Know-Nothing movement, the Klan, and the John Birch Society.

"An excellent idea," Schlesinger wrote him. "Underneath the good-natured surface of American politics there has always been a dangerous susceptibility to extreme acts. Our social equilibrium . . . has always been precarious; and extremism remains a chronic threat—something whose existence we like to deny to ourselves."

"What most of these movements did have in common was a determination . . . to exclude proscribed groups from the American community," Schlesinger told him, "and to transform this country from a republic of diversity."

"Your initial bibliography was excellent and very helpful," Kennedy replied. He read and thought and wrote, and in early October he sent Schlesinger and Galbraith an article he proposed to submit to the *Saturday Evening Post*. "I hope this can be published prior" to the November election, he told the historian.

Galbraith found Kennedy's writing "sensible and interesting," but—"with all the offensive tendencies of the candid friend"—he told his student that the article was too slow and wordy. It was not published.

Galbraith and Wood suggested less taxing theses: in Wood's case, a "corny" book on politics for young adults, while Galbraith proposed a volume of essays, which Kennedy would edit, called *The Political Art*, with an introduction and chapters by Kennedy and contributions from Sorensen on speechwriting, Schlesinger on style, Robert Kennedy on campaign management, and so on. *The Fruitful Bough*—the book that ultimately emerged from Kennedy's convalescence—was more intimate. It contained vignettes on his father's life, similar to a volume that John had assembled on their lost oldest brother, *As We Remember Joe.*

Robert, meanwhile, had entered the race for a U.S. Senate seat in New York. When Ted received worrisome reports from Galbraith and Schlesinger on how the campaign was faring with Manhattan's liberals, he interceded with the White House. Testing Johnson's professed affection, Kennedy asked the president to help Robert in New York. The White House dispatched a liberal darling, Adlai Stevenson, to campaign on Robert's behalf.

"Ted Kennedy called to ask if you could be made available to assist Bob's campaign," Johnson's aide Bill Moyers wrote Stevenson. "The President has asked me to tell you that we would be pleased to have you do everything possible."

ON NOVEMBER 3, Ted Kennedy won election to his first full term—by more than 1.1 million votes. Not Christ nor Saint Patrick could have beaten a Kennedy in Massachusetts that year, or so the saying went, but Joan deserved credit for her excellent work as Ted's surrogate.

A month later, Ted walked—stepping gingerly from an upright bed and doing a slow shuffle across the floor. "I took my first steps today and my back held together," he wrote Johnson. The newspapers chronicled each happy stage of his recovery: the December day he limped out of the hospital, his arrival in Palm Beach, the hug Ted Jr. gave him, his first swim in the pool under Joseph Kennedy's loving gaze.

There were retrospective accounts, as well, about a private trip Kennedy had taken at 5 a.m. on the day he left New England Baptist. It was to the cemetery in Andover where Moss was buried. Leaning on a cane, in ten-degree weather, Kennedy made his way up an icy hill and said prayers for his friend at the grave.

Six

EDDIE AND ROBBIE

On January 4, 1965, Ted Kennedy's car stopped on the way to the U.S. Capitol to pick up his brother. Robert met him with a prizefighter's bob and weave, a handshake, and a grin. Robert took the wheel, turned to Ted and asked, "Which way?" That morning, with the help of a black teak cane and a steel brace he wore beneath his clothing, Ted returned to the Senate. And now Robert was with him. Overcoming the charge of carpetbagger, riding Lyndon Johnson's coattails, he had beaten a Republican incumbent and clinched the Senate seat from New York. For the first time since the 1800s, two brothers would serve as senators together.

The press found one quirk irresistible—the younger of the brothers was the senior senator. But there was no need to teach Robert the ropes. He had been a Senate staffer, and testified before Congress regularly while serving as attorney general. A suspiciously apt anecdote spoke of Robert's post-election visit to Ted's hospital room. A photographer asked him to step back, for he was "casting a shadow on Ted." Said the younger brother, "It'll be the same in Washington."

There was never, ever, a doubt about primacy. Ted would clear his actions with Robert, but Robert—though he often asked for advice—did not clear his moves with Ted. "He's going to drive us crazy," Ted Kennedy told his new aide, David Burke. "He'll have us doing this and doing that—

we really have got to get cracking because he really is going to be all over me if we don't have everything on the ball and we aren't really accomplishing things." Burke was dubious, but when Robert took his seat "it was like a hurricane arriving . . . like an electric charge."

Johnson's landslide drove the Democrats to a two-to-one margin in the House of Representatives, and a filibuster-proof majority of 68–32 in the Senate. "These are the most hopeful times in all the years since Christ was born in Bethlehem," said the president as he lit the White House Christmas tree in December. During that landmark 89th Congress the Democrats would employ those big majorities to transfigure American education, old age, and health care; to declare a war on poverty; and—with the Voting Rights Act and the Immigration Act of 1965—to inalterably recast the ethnic, racial, and political complexion of the United States of America.

They would also dispatch thousands of U.S. combat troops to Vietnam—an act that would inexorably serve to wreck the progress, smash the consensus, and poison the good will of that Congress and that Christmas season. President Kennedy's two younger brothers would play a role in all these historic measures. They linked their offices with a telephone line and spoke every day.

THE ILL-MADE RELATIONSHIP BETWEEN Robert Kennedy and Lyndon Johnson had continued to deteriorate through 1964, and Johnson—conspicuously—kept sweet-talking Ted. "It is lucky that Teddy has such strong loyalty to Bobby," Schlesinger told his diary after lunch with Robert. "LBJ and Teddy get along well, and I am sure that the White House will do its best to give Teddy preferential treatment in order (a) to show that LBJ loves the Kennedys and (b) to dish Bobby.

"The same thing will happen in the Senate," Schlesinger wrote. "Bobby's first appearance there was greeted by visible coldness on the part of his colleagues. Bobby will never be a Senate insider, any more than JFK was; but Teddy is liked by the old-timers and will inevitably become a member of the Club."

Ted laughed it off. "There were times that Johnson tried to play Bobby off against me, which was totally bizarre," he remembered. "There was no way that a Kennedy would side with an outsider against another Kennedy." Their father had taught them: a family's success was measured by "its loyalty to one another."

Robert's and Ted's approaches to politics were most definitely different, however. Robert Kennedy's talents were as an adversary—he was not well fit for the Senate's lubricious blather. "No one understood practical politics better," Richard Goodwin said, "yet the imagining heart was always in the hills, leading some guerrilla army, without speeches or contaminating compromise."

If the question in the Senate cloakroom was whether Ted Kennedy would get the necessary fifty-one votes on a legislative measure or be stopped at forty-nine, said Senator Gale McGee of Wyoming, the question about Robert Kennedy was whether he could summon a dozen votes at all. "He never developed any rapport in the Senate, and they would vote against his stuff," said McGee, "not because it was necessarily unwise, but because he introduced it."

Robert had "passionate feeling . . . a sense of injustice and a great dislike of bullies," said vanden Heuvel. The "passion and the fire" had been stoked by John Kennedy's death, and Robert's own experience as attorney general. He "was not a senator by temperament . . . never interested in being in the club." Ted, by contrast, truly "loved the Senate," said vanden Heuvel. He "had an instinct for bringing people together and resolving confrontations, whereas Bobby sort of welcomed confrontation." Ted's was "a very natural calling . . . the classic Irish politician."

The two younger Kennedys declared as much in another anecdote, fed to the public by their aides, about "Eddie" and "Robbie."

"Is this the way I become a good senator—sitting here and waiting my turn?" asked Robbie.

"Yes," said Eddie.

"How many hours do I have to sit here to be a good senator?" Robbie asked.

"As long as necessary, Robbie," Eddie replied.

—————

ROBERT'S ARRIVAL IN THE Senate served to expedite an upgrade in Ted Kennedy's staff. With Texans taking over the White House and the agencies, Kennedy could fill his corral with prize stock from the New Frontier. Bright young men arrived on Capitol Hill to help him lift his game. Burke came from the White House as top strategist. James Flug arrived from the Justice Department to be a legislative tactician. Milton Gwirtzman, who had worked as a wordsmith for both John and Robert, offered his talents to Ted. And George Abrams, a Harvard classmate, became lead counsel of the Judiciary subcommittee that Ted now chaired, assessing the impact of the Vietnam War on Vietnamese civilians.

Burke joined Ted Kennedy in early 1965 and quickly won his confidence. As the grandson of a fireman and the son of a Boston cop, "I had every credential out of old Boston mythology," he said. While a graduate student at the University of Chicago he had impressed a professor—George Shultz, a future secretary of state—who had helped him find work in the Kennedy White House. Flug was from Brooklyn. He had graduated magna cum laude from Harvard, and from Harvard Law School, where he was editor of the *Harvard Law Review*. Kennedy and Burke gave him the freedom to roam, he recalled: "It was fairly open. You could do just about anything you wanted." Gwirtzman was a summa cum laude graduate of Harvard, with a law degree from Yale. He had worked as an issue adviser for John in 1960, for Ted in 1962, and Robert in 1964, and now, as a Washington lawyer, donated his time as crisis manager, adviser, and speechwriter. Abrams was Harvard and Harvard Law, and had already started on his lifelong avocation as an international collector of art.

The four were prototypes for dozens of similarly shrewd, brainy aides who would work for Kennedy over the years. "Very smart, very ideological, very hard-driving, very sure of themselves—and difficult," is how Senator John Danforth, a Republican from Missouri, would come to describe them.

What Kennedy didn't have, in the first half of his career, were women with executive authority. Barbara Souliotis, Angelique Voutselas, Nance Lyons, Melody Miller, and Terri Robinson were formidable professionals, but were relegated to administrative duties, constituent service, or press relations. "The AA's [administrative assistants, in the days before the top Senate staffers became known as chiefs of staff] tended to be very male chauvinistic," said Souliotis, "that is just the way it was." Their senator was no different. "You can't give women [voters] too much. They get confused," Kennedy had told a reporter during his first campaign.

Kennedy was not unique—Capitol Hill was still "the planet of the guys" when she arrived a decade later, said Representative Patricia Schroeder of Colorado. But Ted was most comfortable with men with whom he could relax—like Charles Tretter, John Culver, or Jack Crimmins, a crusty Irish bachelor who served as his driver. The senator didn't need the complication of having professional women around. Across the Capitol, Representative Tip O'Neill was shaking things up, obtaining floor privileges for Judith Kurland, a female aide. But when Kennedy's staff suggested that he blaze a path and appoint a young woman as a Senate page, he killed the idea with a curt dismissal. And in keeping with his Roman Catholic faith, in these days before *Roe v. Wade*, he was fervently against abortion. The Kennedys felt no need to blaze this trail. John Kennedy's White House and Robert Kennedy's Justice Department were white male domains. Eunice and Jean would accomplish great things in the years to come, but their early role in the family business was hosting teas for the menfolk's campaigns.

Joan's role was to be "the Dish," as John Kennedy called her; "Too Beautiful To Use" was the inscription on a silver cigarette case he gave her after the 1960 campaign. She was ogled, sometimes pawed, by lowlifes at political events. Joan was lonely, suffering from depression, her heart riven by John's murder and by the miscarriages of 1963 and 1964. Her old pals, seeing her march across the society pages, assumed she was happy. "I had to make an extra effort to let [them] know that I really needed their friendship more than ever," she recalled. "It wasn't all sweetness and light." After causing a family stir with some mildly indiscreet comments about Jacqueline's wigs and John's bad back during the presidency, she tensed up around reporters, and lived in fear that Ted would disapprove of her replies to their questions.

It was during this time that her predisposition to drink, which Ted had noticed in the 1962 campaign, became more pronounced. "She had a problem with alcohol and it was getting much more serious," Terri Robinson would recall. "It was a hidden problem. . . . We were innocent staffers, we thought maybe Joan was tired or maybe she didn't feel well . . . but she had a lot of difficulty getting out of bed."

Ted and Joan would be cheered by the birth of their third child, Patrick, in 1967. They resolved to make a fresh start and purchased a stunning six-acre lot on a bluff above the Potomac River in McLean, Virginia. An architect drew plans for a sprawling home with swimming pool and tennis court, a central living and dining section for public entertainments, a slate patio with a view of the water, and wings of bedrooms for the family and the help, which now included a governess, a gardener, a cook, a social secretary, and a cleaning woman. The builders scoured four states for vintage barn timbers to support the living room's vaulted ceiling and then, to Ted's chagrin, painted the rugged hand-hewn beams a designer white.

The master bedroom was tailored for Joan, all pinks and greens, with white silk walls, to befit "the American Blonde," the designer told *Architectural Digest*. "I have a strong feeling that bedrooms should be very feminine," he said. "After all, it's the woman's brain center of the house."

KENNEDY'S MANAGEMENT STYLE DID not change over the years. He hired the best and brightest, set them loose, and it did not matter that they were smarter or more credentialed than he was. "The smarter you are, the more he'll drive you," Burke said. "He had a level of expectation. You'll do the right thing . . . without [him] telling you." His aides had direct access to the senator, and the power to wield Kennedy's name to craft progressive policy and negotiate with the capital's other loci of power. Preparation was key. If Kennedy was working weekends, or nights, or rising at 6 a.m. to study briefing books, so was his staff.

Loyalty was paramount and discretion a virtue. The Senate was renowned for its drunks and womanizers, and Kennedy's revelery was shrugged off by the men of the *Playboy* decades.

A "culture of alcoholism . . . pervaded the Senate through much of the 20th century" and "took its toll in the form of diminished judgment, erratic behavior and recurrent health problems," wrote historian Lewis Gould. "The prevailing ethos was that real men, as were most senators in their own minds, played hard and drank even harder."

"At the time, it wasn't unusual that you were fucking other women," said Richard Goodwin. "Everyone was doing it." The grueling demands and artificiality of modern American politics "tested marital bonds," said Gould. "Men in the Senate were ambivalent about infidelity." To the voters, Kennedy's colleagues waxed about the sacred bonds of marriage and family. Privately, "in an era before sexual harassment was even a concept in most men's minds, a certain amount of senatorial privilege was expected," Gould said. The press would describe senators as "fun-loving," or say that they "enjoyed a good time." These were euphemisms "for aggressive philandering and pursuit of the young women who flocked to Capitol Hill for jobs."

What angered Kennedy was failure. As he would sometimes tell aides, "As you may have noticed, I'm quite good at it." He had very little patience for lousy staff work and would bark or make a biting wisecrack—like, "Gee, I don't remember my brother ever having a problem getting a speech"—and then Burke would have to walk the corridors of the Senate office buildings, comforting some summa cum laude graduate of Harvard who had "just been destroyed" by the putdown. The cloud would pass, Kennedy would share a joke or extend an attaboy to the ego-wounded aide, or call the aide's mother on her birthday. The ties were recast, "and all would be good," said Burke. There was no master strategy. Like most Kennedy ventures, there was improvisation. "You take the recommendations coming from these very intelligent people who all have hearts of gold," said Burke.

The Kennedy brothers did not spare each other. They would laugh, needle, and laugh some more. Ted would make fun of Robert, the ruthless and unbeloved carpetbagger. "Stay off the floor," Ted would tell his brother. "I need some votes."

"When I shake my head from side to side and you nod your head up and down, does this mean I will vote no and you agree? Obviously not," Robert wrote in a joking note to Ted after a breakdown in the semaphore. "I should have nodded my head up and down—you would have shaken your head from side to side—then I would have known."

Beyond the humor, Ted Kennedy felt the weight of elevated expectations with Robert in the Senate. "No one's radar is more sensitive than his in what you think of him," Burke said of his boss. "He was under pressure" to show he had the tools. And "he was under pressure from Bobby because Bobby was 'smarter' than him."

Kennedy now assessed his career. He had been a member of the U.S. Senate for two years—albeit while spending six months in the hospital—with relatively little to show for it. There was his maiden speech on civil rights, and he would soon cast his vote for the Kennedy-Johnson proposal to extend federal aid to public schools. An idea that Ted and Robert helped to foster—the formation of a national "teachers corps," made up of idealistic volunteers, like those serving in the Peace Corps—was incorporated in the Great Society. From the White House, Ted received souvenir pens used by the president to sign historic legislation, which recognized the young senator's contributions to the community health and mental health services acts, funding of the National Endowments for the Arts and for the Humanities, and the creation of Medicare and Medicaid. But Kennedy still felt the need to distinguish himself. He did so successfully, using two momentous civil rights bills as his vehicles.

FIRST UP WAS THE Voting Rights Act. As Kennedy lay in his Stryker bed, Martin Luther King and the civil rights movement had banked the gains of the Montgomery and Birmingham protests and shifted the field of battle to Selma, Alabama. There, though eligible Black residents made up half the population of Dallas County, only 2 percent had been able to pierce a wall of hostility and register to vote.

It was the same across the South. In Jim Eastland's Sunflower County in Mississippi, there were 13,500 eligible Black residents, but only 160 of them had been able to register. The Negroes were too old, the local officials said, or illiterate, or too poor, or too uppity. When Blacks climbed the courthouse steps to register, they were met with profanity, duplicity, violence, or arrest. The door of the registrar would be locked on the two days a month that registrations were scheduled. They would be forced to pay an onerous poll tax. Or they would be confronted by impenetrable questions ("If a person charged with treason denies his guilt, how many persons must testify against him before he is convicted?") on literacy tests. Some were disqualified for not writing their full middle name in their signatures, or for using "St." for "Street" when listing their address.

King was jailed leading the protests in Selma. Civil rights activists and journalists covering the drama were assaulted, and Jimmie Lee Jackson, a twenty-six-year-old Black man protecting his mother, was shot and killed by white police. On "Bloody Sunday," March 7, Hosea Williams and John Lewis, leading a group of marchers from Selma to Montgomery, were met by Governor Wallace's state troopers with tear gas and nightsticks on the Edmund Pettus Bridge. Lewis emerged with a fractured skull. Several days later, James Reeb, a minister from Boston who had traveled to Selma to join the movement, was clubbed to death. America's attention was focused on the South as Johnson addressed Congress and a national television audience.

"Outside this chamber is the outraged conscience of a nation," Johnson told the lawmakers. "What happened in Selma is part of a far larger movement which reaches into every section and state of America. It is the effort of American Negroes to secure for themselves the full blessings of American life.

"Their cause must be our cause too," Johnson said. "Because it is not just Negroes, but really it is all of us, who must overcome the crippling legacy of bigotry and injustice." And here he leaned toward the cameras. "And we *shall* overcome."

Johnson urged Congress to pass the legislation without delay. It would ban discrimination in voting. The worst-offending jurisdictions would be put under federal supervision and need the Justice Department's preapproval before making changes in election laws and procedures.

Whereupon, to the wonder of many, Ted Kennedy threw sand in the gears.

KENNEDY SOUGHT A ROLE, and Joseph Rauh, a leading civil rights and labor lawyer, had furnished the notion. When crafting the Voting Rights Act, the Johnson administration omitted any mention of the poll tax. The device was a bane for civil rights activists and liberals in the Senate, but had been preserved for decades by the threat of southern filibusters. Now Rauh told Burke, and Kennedy agreed, that the Massachusetts senator should lead a movement to ban such taxes.

It wasn't that Johnson approved of the poll tax. His bill was silent on the issue because there was a question among lawyers as to whether a mere statute could outlaw the contrivance, or whether a constitutional amendment was necessary. A pending case, which might settle the issue, was moving toward the Supreme Court. Nicholas Katzenbach, a New Frontiersman who had replaced Robert Kennedy as attorney general, decided not to complicate things and left the poll tax out of the bill.

The Voting Rights Act was otherwise a strong measure. "The question was," Ted Kennedy recalled, "how much can this train take?" But scholars led by Harvard Law School dean Erwin Griswold, the U.S. Commission on Civil Rights, the NAACP, and other civil rights organizations saw no reason why the tax should be omitted from the debate. Kennedy took up their cause. "There is a battle to be fought here," he told a delegation of Massachusetts civil rights leaders, who called on him after Reeb was slain.

Lyndon Johnson was mightily irritated.

"I told the attorney general . . . I was against the poll tax," the vexed president complained to Birch Bayh. But "he feels this is going to mess up the bill."

"This man's been Bobby's lawyer, he's been Teddy's lawyer, and he's been my lawyer. They asked me to keep him and I have kept him and I'm following what he says," said Johnson.

There was "no reason why the Kennedys can't get along with Nick Katzenbach," Johnson grumbled. "He lo-v-ves them, and he's loyal to them."

BUT KENNEDY HAD CALLED upon his stable of tutors in Cambridge and Washington and explored the constitutional issues. "There were a number of us believed it wasn't as strong as it should be," he remembered. Defying the murderer's row of Johnson, Katzenbach, Majority Leader Mike Mansfield, Minority Leader Dirksen, and Eastland, Kennedy joined with the liberal Jacob Javits, a Republican from New York, and urged the Judiciary Committee to ban the poll tax.

"I never thought Teddy would have the guts to buck Lyndon," a fellow senator marveled in the *Boston Globe*. "We felt he was too soft."

Not soft, but "a very nervous person" who now held "endless preparations at his home," Burke recalled. At the very least, Kennedy told his colleagues, getting Congress on record against the poll tax could sway the justices of the Supreme Court. Kennedy and Javits rallied the committee liberals, and prevailed, on a vote of 9–5.

"WHEN IT'S GOING GOOD and it's high and mighty, it's a bill that's drafted by the Kennedy boys' attorney general," Johnson now griped to labor leader Walter Reuther. "But when the son of a bitch gets in trouble, it becomes the Johnson bill!

"I'm not going to be president long, but while I am president, brother, I'm going to take care of voting in this country. Everybody's going to be able to vote. . . .

"I don't give a damn how ignorant they are," Johnson vowed. "They got enough instinct to know how to vote because they've been voting for me all these years: a lot of ignorant people."

Katzenbach shared the president's wrath, and went to work with the Senate leaders to foil the upstart. Mansfield and Dirksen introduced a substitute bill—without a poll tax ban—which Kennedy and Javits tried to block on the Senate floor. In mid-May, Kennedy and Javits lost that show-down, 49–45.

Not since Bunker Hill had defeat earned the kind of acclaim that now was showered on Kennedy. Outmanned, he had gone into battle on the side of the angels, shamed his elders, and very nearly prevailed. "His mastery of the issue has been complete," Mansfield acknowledged. "His presentation and argumentation have been lucid and compelling. . . . He almost—but not quite—persuaded me."

Kennedy had proven himself, if not yet a Senate whale, then at least a Senate shark. With "a dash of charm, an ounce of tact, and gallons of 100-proof learning," wrote one correspondent, "the 'new boy'—the once sheltered darling of the Senate, had come into his own."

A year later, the Supreme Court confirmed his good sense by outlawing the poll tax—and crediting the argument, which Kennedy had made, that Congress had possessed the authority to do so.

Only five states levied a poll tax. And Kennedy lost, after all. But his little revolt unveiled tactics he would employ, again and again, in the years ahead. He had charged his bright and ambitious staff to find a noteworthy issue, consulted with lawyers and scholars, prepared himself with arduous study, rallied liberal interest groups, assembled a coalition of like-minded senators, and enlisted a leading Republican to give his cause bipartisan heft.

The names of the Republicans—Javits, Baker, Hatch, Quayle, Kassebaum, Dole, Brownback, Simpson, Thurmond, Laxalt, McCain, Enzi, Weicker, Graham, Jeffords, Gramm, Kyl—would change over the years, but almost always one would be there at his side, giving political cover to their Republican colleagues, and to Democrats from conservative states. Republican presidents and governors—Ford, Nixon, Romney, Reagan, Bush—joined with Kennedy as well. What did they get by allying with the right wing's bête noire? There was the expertise of his staff, the Kennedy name, which brought attention to their cause, and a bloc of liberal votes he could deliver—all raising their prospects for success. And should they prevail, there would be recognition as a statesman or stateswoman in the history of their times. In a chamber of one hundred titanic egos, this last factor was no small matter, and Kennedy used it deftly.

"The tendency has been to write off Ted as intellectually the least able of the Kennedy brothers, but such a judgment may be hazardous," William Shannon wrote in the *New York Times* that summer. "When the poll tax fight had ended, so had Kennedy's Senate apprenticeship. . . . His near-victory against heavy odds climaxed a year and a half of rapid personal growth under the forced draft of adversity."

The Voting Rights Act had profound effects on American politics. Johnson tracked its impact on the South, personally studying each monthly count of new voters and prodding civil rights and civic groups to run registration drives. In the first week after passage, 381 new Black voters joined the rolls in Selma; many more followed, and Sheriff James Clark, who had led the local white resistance, was driven from office to take up a career selling mobile homes. Momentum grew as word spread among the Black population: they would no longer be met by violence or intimidation at the registrar's office, but by dutiful civic servants, working at convenient hours. Johnson's reports told the story. In the first month, 42,000 new Black voters were registered in Alabama, Louisiana, and Mississippi. The week of January 22, 1966, was marked by particularly severe weather in the South, but 7,000 Black people braved storms to register in a single Alabama county. On the act's first anniversary, the White House released its totals: the number of Black voters had doubled in Alabama, quadrupled in Mississippi, and a million Black citizens were now registered to vote in the five states of the Deep South.

As impressive were these gains for Black Americans, as historic and worthy was the Voting Rights Act, no legislation from the 1960s would change the complexion of American society in such transformative ways as Kennedy's next initiative. The issue was immigration, and this time he served not as Johnson's irritant, but as his lieutenant.

The 1960 census had shown how little America had changed in the decades since World War I. The white population stood at 85 percent, where it had hovered for most of the twentieth century, and the cohort of the foreign-born was in single digits. Fifty years later, in a large part due to the 1965 Immigration Act, and Kennedy's later efforts on behalf of refugees and immigrants, the share of white America had fallen to 64 percent, and the percentage of foreign-born citizens had tripled. Not for a century, since the great surge of immigration before the world wars, had the proportion of foreign-born Americans been so high.

Like so many of Ted Kennedy's legislative causes, immigration reform was a family legacy, which he made a specialty and pursued for a half century. As a child, Ted had heard of the day in 1897 when Representative John F. Fitzgerald confronted Senator Henry Cabot Lodge on the floor of the Senate, denouncing the Brahmin's bill to mandate a literacy test for immigrants.

"You are an impudent young man," Lodge was said to have told Fitzgerald. "Do you think the Jews or Italians have any right in this country?"

"As much right as your father or mine," Fitzgerald was said to have replied. "It was only a difference of a few ships."

John F. claimed to have helped persuade President Grover Cleveland, a fellow Democrat, to veto the legislation. It was a good story, family lore. More important, for Ted, was the fact that immigration reform—along with civil rights, health care for the aged, and disarmament—were unrealized goals of John's New Frontier. As senator and president, John Kennedy had coupled a sentimental embrace of the immigrant cause with his Cold War conviction that American democracy—lily-white and hostile to the foreign-born and swarthy—must change to win the contest with communism among the peoples of Latin America, Asia, and Africa. One of the four books John Kennedy authored in his life—*A Nation of Immigrants*—made the case for reform, and in July 1963 he had sent legislation to the Hill that called for "urgent and fundamental" revisions in immigration policy. "He had tried," his brother Ted remembered. "This was something that was alive and evident . . . I was always very much aware."

There were chips on those insouciant shoulders. It was an innate sensibility, not something drilled day by day into Joseph Kennedy's wealthy sons by the social settings they navigated with such ease, but nonetheless real.

Ted kept an antique sign from Boston—"No Irish Need Apply"—on his wall as a reminder. "We had a sense about discrimination against ethnic groups, and that there were laws that perpetuated it."

Immigration was one of the topics that Kennedy studied in the hospital as his broken back mended. "It was obviously a civil rights issue, and although the civil rights issues as we think of them are rooted in a different tradition, when you look at this, the basic fundamental elements of hostility and bigotry and prejudice and discrimination were the same," he said.

The system the Kennedy brothers hoped to liberalize dated back to the 1920s, when American isolationists enacted laws to end the unbridled flow of immigrants. "National origins" quotas were put in place to cap the overall number of newcomers at fewer than 200,000 a year, and to freeze America's ethnic makeup by basing future immigration on the proportion of the U.S. population that had already arrived from each foreign land. The 1890 census was chosen as the official baseline—to favor Anglo-Saxon types and limit the number of Jews, Italians, and other eastern and southern Europeans who made up later waves. These quotas were recodified during the Red Scare of the 1950s.

The oldest immigrant flocks, like those from the British Isles, made out well. But more recent aspirants felt shortchanged. The quota for Italy was 5,666—which left a waiting list of 260,000. The waiting list for aspiring Poles grew to 80,000 and for Greeks to 105,000. Jews and southern Europeans could console themselves that they were treated better than aspirational travelers from Africa or the Pacific Rim—where Asian immigration had been virtually eliminated. Japan had a quota of 185 immigrants a year, China and Korea, 100 each. All these, and India, Pakistan, Southeast Asia, Taiwan, the Philippines, and Indonesia were lumped together in a so-called Asia Pacific Triangle, with capped total immigration from the region at 2,000 per year. The entire continent of Africa was allotted 1,000 visas. "What was the real central challenge we were facing? It was the issue that our Founding Fathers failed on," Ted recalled. "Racial discrimination."

And Latin America? For most of the twentieth century, America's southern border was an outback of little concern. Without the huge water projects, defense installations, and air-conditioned suburbs that would fuel its transformation, the Southwest was scarcely populated and held little lure to the peoples of Latin America. When the authors of the 1920s laws completed their work, the border was still open, with no cap on the number of immigrants admitted from Mexico, Canada, Cuba, and the rest of the Western Hemisphere. At midcentury, a temporary worker system—the Bracero program—was instituted to address America's need for migrant field workers. Mexican pickers came across the border, sent their wages back to their families, and returned to their own homes and farms when the harvest was over.

THIS, then, was the creaky and discriminatory system that the Kennedys proposed to reform. Johnson, who had felt the bite of poverty as a young man, and taught school to Mexican children in Texas, shared their commitment.

When compared to civil rights and Medicare and the Great Society's other landmark achievements, the liberalization of immigration policy was then viewed as something from the second tier. The Johnson administration's bill, sponsored by Phil Hart in the Senate and Representative Emanuel "Manny" Celler of New York in the House, proposed to end the "national origins" quotas, and so remove race as a criterion. It capped legal immigration from outside the Western Hemisphere at 170,000 a year but kept the open borders with Latin America and Canada. Preferences were given to immigrants with valuable skills and to those with family ties. No single nationality could receive more than 20,000 entry visas. "Our cities will not be flooded with a million immigrants," Kennedy assured the public as the hearings opened. "The ethnic mix of this country will not be upset."

Quick passage was predicted. The conservative coalition had been shattered, the liberal tide was running high, and the Bourbon barons were exhausted. Eastland was picking his battles, and concluded that he wanted no public role blocking the proposed reforms. He gave the bill to Ted Kennedy to manage.

Kennedy, who had just turned thirty-three, proved up to the task. He took up the gavel of the Judiciary subcommittee on immigration and called fifty-six witnesses in two dozen hearings, most of which, broken back and all, he chaired. The panel heard from brother Robert, whose Justice Department had written the original legislation in 1963, Secretary of State Dean Rusk, Attorney General Katzenbach, and Secretary of Labor Willard Wirtz. Kennedy allowed the wily Sam Ervin, the leading skeptic on the subcommittee, to call witnesses from nativist organizations like the American Coalition of Patriotic Societies and the Baltimore Anti-Communist League.

"This country happens to have been settled chiefly by Nordic types," said Mrs. Charles Ralph Nichols of the Federation of Republican Women, in the August 3, 1965, subcommittee hearing. "They brought a language, which happens to be the English language, along with its literature, based on Shakespeare and Chaucer and Milton. . . . Is it so terrible . . . ? Must we deliver these legacies to the hordes of Red Chinese, Indians, Congolese cannibals?"

"It has come to a point in America if a man has any racial pride, especially if he happens to be an Anglo-Saxon, he is accused of racial prejudice," Ervin complained. He contended that the northern European countries "gave us our language, they gave us our common law, they gave us most of our political philosophy." The proposed bill was "discriminatory against those people . . . because it puts them on exactly the same plane as the people of Ethiopia are put . . . and I don't think, with all respect to Ethiopia, I don't know of any contributions that Ethiopia has made to the making of America."

"Frankly," Ervin said, "if it came down to the choice of people from Congo and those from Ireland, I am going to discriminate in favor of the people from Ireland because they have been a real contribution."

This last point worried Burke. How was his boss, "this [descendent] of Irish immigrants, going to handle the cutback on Irish numbers?" he wondered. Hecklers from Irish American interest groups began to confront Kennedy at public events. He ignored their protests and marched ahead. "That was my first surprise with him, that there were certain things that he is deaf on, and one is political advice like, 'I'd stay away from that issue, that's a killer.' That's not a good way to open a conversation with him," said Burke. "He just looks at you sort of with a wonderment." It fell to Burke to use the hockey skills learned in a Boston childhood to check the demonstrators out of Kennedy's way.

THERE WERE MOMENTS WHEN Kennedy's mouth got ahead of his brain—an early public sign, perhaps, of a lifelong strained relationship with syntax. "Do you not think that—as I understand it—under the Fair Share, by removing this from the mandate of the United Nations, still you could outline for, and perhaps you do, the procedures by which these refugees are even admitted?" he asked one witness.

Yet he was viewed as a just and capable chairman, who showed "scrupulous tact." The only notable clash occurred when Kennedy chided Javits, a fellow supporter of the bill, for going beyond the bounds of Senate decorum when maligning their opponents as bigots.

Kennedy warned Johnson that the more serious challenge to the legislation lay in the House, where Celler, the chairman of the House Judiciary Committee, was engaged in a war of wills with Representative Michael Feighan of Ohio, the chairman of two panels on immigration.

"That Feighan is a tough cookie," Kennedy said.

"We'll have to work on him," the president promised.

Feighan and his allies had found considerable support for closing the Mexican border and limiting immigration from the West Indies. They proposed to impose a ceiling on newcomers from the Western Hemisphere. After losing by a hair in the House, the idea was revived by Dirksen and Ervin in the Senate, where, with Eastland's help, they pushed it through over Kennedy's objections. "These bastards," Celler said.

Feighan also suggested that the first preference for granting an entry visa should be family reunification—a sly way, he thought, to perpetuate the national origin quotas. "Since the people of Africa and Asia have very few relatives here, comparatively few could immigrate from those countries," Celler fumed. *The American Legion* magazine assured its nativist readers that, thanks to Feighan's legislative sleight of hand, "the great bulk of immigration henceforth will not merely hail from the same parent countries as our present citizens, but will be their close relatives."

KENNEDY DIDN'T YELP AT all of Feighan's proposed revisions: uniting families was a humane act, reflected in all liberalization measures, including his brother John's original proposals. What distressed the Kennedy brothers, Hart, and other liberals was the ceiling on immigrants from the Western Hemisphere. It was a "historic step backward," they said. When they turned for relief to their ally in the White House, however, they found that Feighan and Ervin and Dirksen had gotten there before them, and persuaded Johnson and Attorney General Katzenbach that the only way to muster the votes to pass the bill was to close the border with Mexico. It was a bitter dose. Hart, a sponsor of the legislation, all but disowned it. But Ted and Robert had no choice but to accede. Like Celler, they accepted the deal as a part of the legislative process. "If you want the rainbow, you must take the rain," Celler would write in his postmortem notes. "If you want the rose, you must put up with the thorns."

Kennedy was learning more than just how to bang a gavel. He was seeing Congress as the huge institution that it is, with factions and interests representing a range of human fears and hungers. And Johnson was teaching him the law of compromise—not to let the perfect be the enemy of the good. When John Kennedy began the crusade in the 1950s, his objectives were to end the national origin quotas and do away with the curb on immigrants from Asia. These goals were now achieved. Brother John would have bridled at the gratuitous slap to Latin America, the region he had tried to assist with the policy he called an Alliance for Progress. But that, as Ted wrote in his own postmortem assessment, was the price of a deal.

The Johnson administration "acquiesced . . . seeking at all times to avoid an open struggle" with Feighan, Kennedy wrote. "It was felt in many quarters . . . that the administration perhaps paid a needlessly heavy price." The White House "continued to oppose a ceiling on Western Hemisphere immigration," he said, but "it was unwilling to wage a battle for this cause.

"It was believed that, given the general parliamentary situation and the strong support voiced by Senator Dirksen for a curb in Western Hemisphere," the cap "was necessary to get the bill out of committee."

AND SO WHEN THE final legislation reached the Senate floor, Kennedy was there to defend it, most notably from an attack by Senator Spessard Holland of Florida, who objected to the expansion of African immigration.

"Why for the first time are the emerging nations in Africa to be placed on the same basis as our mother countries?" Holland asked Kennedy. "We have not learned anything at all about the difficulties which have risen from the racial admixture in our country."

Kennedy stirred. The sleepy Senate debate "came alive," one onlooker recalled, as Kennedy challenged Holland with "a sudden soaring of emotion." His "words same rushing out in a rough eloquence," commanding the attention of those in the chamber.

"One of the most laudable aspects of the entire bill is the elimination of the racist factor," Kennedy said. "If there is one guiding principle to this bill, it is that we are going to treat all men and women who want to come to this country as individuals, equal in the eyes of the law . . . and we are not going to ask where they come from or who their fathers werc."

Robert Kennedy rose at his desk in the back row, eager to join in the altercation. African Americans, imported for generations as slaves, had helped build America, Robert said. Weren't their homelands our mother countries too?

Maybe, but after talking to "a great many" Black Americans, Holland said, he had not been able to find a significant number who "have the slightest idea as to what tribe or area or nation or region their people came from." It was white people, he maintained, who proudly knew their ancestry.

"The fact that I might know that I come from Ireland," Robert said, "does not make me any better than a Negro."

"The senator may not be," Holland sneered, "but I shall let him be the judge of that."

Ted had helped ignite the fireworks, but as manager of the bill, he now had the duty to suppress a debate that could wreck the consensus. Liberals were on the floor, seeking recognition. Kennedy moved among them, whispering, soothing, and urging restraint. He was successful. The final roll call, in support of the act, was 76–18. Kennedy "was big—real big—on the immigration bill," Neil MacNeil told his editors.

OVER TIME, Celler's rain and thorns, rainbows and roses would produce confounding, and far-reaching, unintentional results. The changes pushed by Feighan, Ervin, Dirksen, and their allies would ultimately act not to reduce the number of newcomers but to accelerate immigration at quantum rates. The bill was now a blueprint for a demographic revolution, as the foreign-born population in the United States leapt from 9.7 million in 1960 to 40 million in 2010. A relative few of the newcomers were from the "mother nations" of western Europe.

Feighan failed to recognize that, far from capping non-white immigration, a family preference clause might result in a phenomenon that nativists labeled "chain migration." An engineer from Taiwan, admitted to the United States for his skills and expertise, would be allowed to bring his wife and children and parents and siblings to America. They, in turn, could bring other members of the extended family to join them. And so, mathematically, the admission of a single individual could lead to the migration of an entire clan. Refugees were another favored class in the new legislation. The Cold War persisted, and newcomers fleeing communism, natural disasters, or political persecution in Cuba, Southeast Asia, and Central America arrived, forging more chains of migration.

Some of the unintended results revealed themselves quickly. In 1966, Kennedy's office obtained data from the Johnson administration on comparable periods before and after the law's passage. The number of visas issued to the Irish dropped in the sampling from 1,036 to 82, and those to the West Germans dropped from 3,813 to 515. Meanwhile, visas issued to the Chinese rose in number from 81 to 2,220, and the number issued to residents of the Philippines leapt from 7 to 1,203.

As for Mexico, Feighan and his allies were correct to anticipate that the growing population in Latin America would create an immense demand for migration within the Western Hemisphere. But to think that a legal ceiling would triumph over human needs and yearnings—with a two-thousand-mile border to guard—was folly.

The Bracero program had ended in 1964, in large part because liberals believed the farmworkers were being abused. "If you ever knew of a group that was as exploited, intimidated, treated effectively almost like slaves [it] was the Bracero program," Kennedy would recall. On the other hand, having the program as a relief valve had "effectively halted the illegal immigration." Closing this portal cut off a legal source of entry for hundreds of thousands of guest workers just as air conditioning, mammoth public water projects, and modern farming methods were fueling a surge in housing and agriculture in the American Southwest. Though legally dismantled, the old system left a network of farmers, affiliated employers, and middlemen in place—who made sure that workers, legally or illegally, kept crossing the border. Over time, as the number of subsistence farms in Mexico dwindled, and the population shifted toward the cities, fewer migrants arrived in the United States with a plan to return to the family homestead. They were mesmerized by the opportunities and wonders of American life. A vibrant subculture of Mexican America awaited them in Texas and California. Crisscrossing the border was bothersome and hazardous. Why not just stay?

UNINTENDED CONSEQUENCES ARE A risk of writing laws. When a rascally southern chairman, hoping to kill the bill, slipped the word "sex" into the categories of discrimination prohibited by the civil rights act in 1964, it blew open doors, like a morning sea breeze, for millions of American women. So it was with immigrants and the 1965 act.

Johnson signed the bill on October 3, on Liberty Island in New York harbor, in the lee of the Statue of Liberty, with Ted and Robert Kennedy and a dozen others standing by his side.

"This . . . is not a revolutionary bill. It does not affect the lives of millions. It will not reshape the structure of our daily lives," Johnson said. He, the Kennedys, Feighan, Ervin, Hart, Celler—all of them—could not have been more wrong.

Seven

LOYALTIES

The cold-weather states of New England bred a class of political flunkey who carried the velvet-collared chesterfields of men of higher stature. They became known as "coat-holders," a term that grew to encompass all political minions of slight gifts and consequence. Such a man was Francis Joseph Xavier Morrissey. In 1965, as a reward for his years of service as a Kennedy family coat-holder, Morrissey was nominated for a prestigious federal judgeship on the U.S. district court in Boston. The exercise did not fare well. Ted's skirts got muddied. Coming hard on the heels of his success on voting rights and immigration, it was just the sort of self-inflicted wound he had worked hard to avoid.

While not particularly lofty, neither were Kennedy's motives—affection, and loyalty to a faithful retainer—condemnable. Early in the proceedings, he had gone to his friend and tutor, Senator Phil Hart, the "conscience of the Senate," and asked him if the concept of Frank Morrissey on the federal bench was so abominable. The privilege of filling judicial vacancies was then the preserve of U.S. senators, some of whom had salted the federal bench with cronies, Mob lawyers, and racists from the South. Morrissey's nomination would not be the worst, Hart assured his younger colleague.

In Morrissey's rise from meager stirrings, there was much to admire. He was one of eleven children, raised in a Charlestown tenement by a longshoreman and his weary wife. He took to the streets on a corner selling newspapers, played the games of Irish American politics, and—through ceaseless work and night school classes, as a teller in a bank, a clerk in an insurance firm, and positions "on the state"—crowned his career as a judge on Boston's municipal court, ordaining judgment on shoplifters, drunk drivers, and yeggs.

"He was not . . . Clarence Darrow," said one bar official. But "he learned the basic rudiments of adversary trial. No one has to show him where the courthouse is." Morrissey was a father of seven; short, plump, and personable, and willing to apply himself. "A lively, gregarious foxy little guy," a correspondent would describe him. "Incompetence is too strong a word. . . . He simply is not a man of any great intellectual attainment." Charles Dickens would recognize the type: the soul of a clerk with an eye for a chance.

When John Kennedy returned to Boston to claim Curley's old congressional seat in 1946, Morrissey was his Sherpa, and then served as the congressman's chief aide—"secretary," it was called—in the district. He was avidly mindful of Joseph Kennedy's wealth and authority, and others in John's entourage tagged him as the old man's spy. But the Kennedys trusted him: when John's suitcase was stolen from his car in Washington, Morrissey was assigned to replace the drugs it carried, which Kennedy took to treat Addison's disease, his secret illness.

Throughout John Kennedy's time in Congress, Morrissey moved around the state, serving as Joseph's eyes and ears, acting as his liaison with the Democratic hierarchy and doling out money to churches, causes, ethnic groups, and candidacies. "Last Friday, Judge Tomasello and Judge Fox had me up in their chambers and expressed a wish that Jack and you would prevail upon Ed Hanify to run for governor," he wrote Joseph in May 1954. And "I thought that you might like to know that your suggestion about taking the representatives of the Colored Press to the Dedication of the Kennedy Center in Harlem has had excellent results as far as the negroes in Boston are concerned."

"I think on this gift to the Don Orione Home, Mr. Kennedy, with your permission, I can build this up to a tremendous thing among the Italians," Morrissey told Joseph a week later, after quietly conferring with the local monsignor about a $65,000 donation to an East Boston old folks' home. Morrissey also reported from the Boys' Club in Roxbury, "They have a gymnasium and swimming pool that apparently should be enlarged and remodeled. They feel they could do this for $25,000. This club has a membership of about 2,400 boys from the surrounding Roxbury neighborhood. . . . They comprise twenty-seven different nationalities."

As John rode to the New Frontier, and Ted toward the Senate, Morrissey changed mounts. He was Ted Kennedy's sponsor when he applied to the Massachusetts bar in 1959 and helped Ted land the job as assistant district attorney. When Kennedy embarked on his luncheon and after-hours speaking engagements, it was Morrissey who arranged them. He was "the person who got me started," Ted remembered.

SOMETIME IN THIS COURSE of events, Joseph Kennedy's sons were informed that their father wished to reward Morrissey with the seat on the federal bench. The new president and his brother, the attorney general, recognized that their stature would be diminished by the appointment of a legal gallant who twice failed, and took twelve years to pass, the Massachusetts bar exam, and had no experience as a trial lawyer. Word of Morrissey's candidacy was leaked; there were cries of hackery from the bar associations, the midlands, and the press, and Joseph was informed that, regrettably, it could not be done.

When Joseph Kennedy suffered his stroke in 1961, it was Morrissey who visited, sat by his side, and brought him tidings and gossip. "Frank . . . was very faithful in that respect. He came to see him almost every week," Milton Gwirtzman recalled. The Morrissey nomination was revived and pending in 1963, when John Kennedy flew to Dallas. In the summer of 1964, Attorney General Robert Kennedy—on the way out of office and feeling the tug of familial obligation—sent a note to President Johnson urging him to name Morrissey to the federal bench. Ted nagged the White House too, and, since the job was for a U.S. district court in Boston, became Morrissey's primary advocate. Johnson called each brother to the White House, and in separate meetings asked them if they were sure they wanted to proceed.

"Do you really want this?" Johnson asked Ted, when Kennedy went to see him.

"I do," Kennedy told him.

Johnson then called Joseph Kennedy, who was overcome with emotion when the president gave him the news.

The president handed the phone to Ted. "Dad," he told his father, "it looks like you're the man with all the influence still."

Before Johnson could make the official announcement, the word leaked out. The *Boston Globe*, the American Bar Association, the Boston Bar Association, and Judge Charles Wyzanski, the chief justice of the federal district court, all urged the Senate to reject the nomination.

"I cannot overlook the obvious fact that the ONLY discernible ground for the nomination of Judge Morrissey is his service to the Kennedy family," Wyzanski wrote to Chairman Eastland. America was past this form of "feudalism," he said. "To confirm Judge Morrissey would be to corroborate the cynical view that judicial place goes not to those who will honor it but to those who by service have bought it." The ABA called Morrissey the most unqualified candidate it had ever evaluated. He lacked the "intellectual capacity," scholarship, knowledge, and legal experience, the bar association said.

"Teddy, this is not going to be easy," aide George Abrams told him, after a preliminary fact-finding mission through Boston.

"You're telling me," said Kennedy.

Lights flashed and alarums sounded. All hands were called to duty. Respected figures from the Massachusetts judiciary issued fulsome praise, commending Morrissey's Runyonesque affinity with the little guy. Ted defended him on the Senate floor. Speaker John McCormack and the pols on Beacon Hill fell dutifully into line. "Frank Morrissey has been loyal to the Kennedys," the Speaker said. "What's wrong with rewarding your friends?" Morrissey was no Harvard scholar, all said, but he understood the human heart. Eastland was poised to move the nomination when the serendipitous intervention of unlikely allies—the liberal-leaning *Boston Globe* and Republican leader Everett Dirksen—brought the parade to a halt.

Dirksen had spent the last two years helping Johnson push three celebrated civil rights bills through the Senate. What better way to mend
fences with the Goldwater wing of his party than to give Johnson and the
Kennedys a good whacking? He sauteed Morrissey in committee.

"So . . . virtually all of your trial experience has been on minor felo-
nies and misdemeanors," Dirksen said to Morrissey. "And if there were
civil cases, they were rather inconsequential?"

"I would say that is a fair statement," the hapless judge replied.

"Senator Kennedy . . . do you regard the federal court as an in-training
course, where you train after you are appointed?" Dirksen asked his colleague.

Under questioning, Morrissey admitted that after failing to pass the
bar in Boston in 1933, he had moved to Georgia. There, he took a three-
month course from "Southern Law School," an evanescent two-room citadel of learning, declared himself a Georgia resident, and obtained his
license to practice law. He could not make a go of it, he said, and eventually moved back to Boston. "Dirksen made mincemeat out of him," Gwirtzman said. "We were not at all prepared" and "knew nothing about the fact
that he had gotten a funny law degree."

"I came up the hard way myself," Dirksen muttered to a friendly correspondent, but "it never occurred to me to go to some goddamn diploma
mill."

ALL THIS WAS BAD ENOUGH. Then the *Globe* (which would win a Pulitzer
Prize for its coverage of the nomination) discovered that Morrissey could
not have been living and practicing law in Georgia if, as he attested when
campaigning for the state legislature in Massachusetts at the same time,
he was a registered voter and yearlong resident of the commonwealth.
Nor, the *Globe* reported, had Boston College had an evening law school in
the year that Morrissey said he took classes there. It was not the most
grievous sin—fudging facts on a job application—but the round-faced
Morrissey was an awkward witness when Dirksen demanded he explain

himself. He admitted to forgetting many crucial details, like whether his alma mater had a library.

There was a limit to loyalty, even for Kennedys. This nomination was making national news—the bad kind—for the family. To Robert's irritation, a high-minded speech he gave about American policy toward China got swallowed by the din. Robert, "very angry and very unhappy," Burke recalled, called on Dirksen to see what could be done. Their meeting turned into a Wild West "shootout," Gwirtzman said. There was more to come, Dirksen told Kennedy, and handed him a folder with a photograph of Ted Kennedy and Morrissey vacationing on the isle of Capri in 1961—in the company of mobster Michael Spinella. "A bombshell: the President's brother, a Mafia figure, and Morrissey," said Gwirtzman. It was an innocent grip and grin—but who wanted to spend the time and political capital explaining why Morrissey had introduced them?

"You just hate all the Kennedys," Robert told Dirksen.

"Why," said Dirksen, "I don't believe I know all the Kennedys."

TED HAD BEEN LEADING the charge, pressing colleagues for votes, defending Morrissey on the floor and in committee—and digging a deeper hole. There were unwritten rules about such matters—the first was that senators get to pick federal judges in their states, and that colleagues should respect and ratify those selections. But the second rule held that a senator, if he wanted to retain the affections of those colleagues, should not make them walk a plank on his behalf. "He has wrapped an albatross around his neck which will weigh down his career for years to come," said a *New York Times* editorial. If they persevered, his fellow senators would "wrap this albatross around their necks too."

The brothers and their staffs conferred at midnight, before the vote. The wise thing to do, Robert told his brother, was to pull the nomination. They did not have the votes. Even if they could twist enough arms, cut enough deals, and call in enough chits, it would not be worth it.

One of Ted's advisers asked: What of their commitment to Morrissey?

"I think we've more than fulfilled our commitment to Frank Morrissey," Robert Kennedy snapped.

And so on October 21, Ted Kennedy rose to address the hushed Senate chamber. He spun the tale of Morrissey's humble origins and beneficent character.

"He was young, and he was poor—one of 12 children," Kennedy said, his voice breaking, as Joan and Ethel and Eunice watched from the gallery. "The family living in a home without gas, electricity or heat in the bedrooms, their shoes held together with wooden pegs their father made."

Then Kennedy freed his colleagues from the hook by requesting that the nomination be buried, indefinitely.

"All because he didn't go to Harvard," Kennedy told Gerard Doherty, as they killed Frank Morrissey's dream.

POLITICOS AND JOURNALISTS AT the time, and historians since, have proposed that the Morrissey nomination was a snare employed by Johnson to embarrass the Kennedys, who had only been going through the motions for their loving Da. It is more likely that Johnson acceded to their sincere requests, reckoning he would profit from their gratitude should it pass— or laugh at Ted's and Robert's bruises if it failed. "Work hard on this one," Johnson told his aides. "This boy [Ted] is going to get his ass whipped and . . . I want to make goddamn sure that he doesn't accuse anybody here of not supporting him, not fighting for him when it happens."

Ted Kennedy suffered a "grievous loss of prestige and dignity," Tom Wicker concluded in the *New York Times*. The young Galahad's armor, "gleaming during this session as a result of his careful handling of such matters as his anti-poll tax amendment," had been "permanently tarnished," said a *Time* magazine correspondent. "It's inescapably a shabby business."

Kennedy's "wooden pegs" speech did not stop Dirksen from leaking the Mafia story to the press. But the old fox also stood and praised Ted for the grace and collegiality he displayed in quitting the ring. Robert, knowing how his brother was suffering, had quietly asked Dirksen to do so. Robert had a different response for Joe Tydings, and it said much about how the family viewed a declared opponent, like Dirksen, versus a sunshine patriot.

The Maryland senator owed the Kennedys: he had gotten his start when John and Robert named him as the U.S. attorney in the state, and the brothers supported him against the wishes of the state's congressional delegation. Tydings and Robert Kennedy had campaigned together, gone fox hunting, and sailing off the Cape. In the Senate, he had joined Ted Kennedy in what senators and aides called the "Fearless Foursome"—Kennedy, Tydings, Bayh, and Hart—who challenged Eastland in the Judiciary Committee.

"I was considered a third Kennedy brother," Tydings recalled. "Whichever way they went, I went. And that was the way it should be."

But the Morrissey appointment was excruciatingly difficult. Tydings had fought his way through Maryland's corrupt politics as a reformer and an outspoken advocate for judicial independence. "Morrissey was a gofer for the old man," Tydings recalled. "I'm a leader in court reform. This was my arena."

He tried to dissuade his friend. "Teddy, you shouldn't do this. He's not fit," said Tydings.

"No, we need it. We've got to have it. The family wants it," Kennedy told him.

"I can't do it," Tydings said. When he spoke in the Senate about the need for federal judicial reform, he didn't mention Morrissey by name, but everyone in the Capitol knew how he would vote.

Amid defeat, seething at the fix that he and Ted had put themselves in, Robert lashed out at Tydings when they crossed paths on the Senate floor.

"Judicial reform? That wasn't on top of your list when you wanted to be U.S. Attorney in Maryland," Robert Kennedy told him. "We made you." When Tydings tried to reason with him, Robert gave his friend a hard shoulder in the chest.

"BOBBY GOT OVER IT," Tydings would recall, "but Teddy didn't."

The tension between them didn't ease as they embarked on a long-planned CODEL trip through Southeast Asia. "The person seated next to me was Joe Tydings—all the way to L.A., all the way to Vietnam," Kennedy said. In Saigon, "they put us in the same room for four days and nights. It was about as hard a jaw biting as I've had."

Kennedy sometimes used foreign trips as recreational interludes. So it was in Saigon where, partying in a nightclub with a group of American war correspondents, Kennedy met an alluring Vietnamese courtesan and proposed to take her back to their hotel in the embassy car. Tydings objected. It was a crazy risk. What if they had an accident, or were ambushed?

"It would be devastating," Tydings said. "Have her go with your friends in the press and meet you there and you can do whatever you want. But, my God, you can't take a chance like this."

"You can't tell me what to do," Kennedy said, his anger spilling out. "This is CODEL Kennedy. You wouldn't be here if it weren't for me."

Kennedy would need to knock him down, said Tydings, before he would let the girl in the automobile. The two had it out, two U.S. senators jawing on the sidewalk in Saigon, until Kennedy relented and dispatched the woman to his hotel by a different car. Ultimately, he and Tydings parted.

Vladimir Lehovich, Kennedy's embassy escort on that trip to Vietnam, broadened the story. If the senator had difficulties finding a consort, his superiors had told Lehovich, he was to "dip into your private stock. It is that important" to keep Kennedy on board as a supporter of the war.

"The 'private stock' was a rather flattering presumption that I had a stable of my own lovelies who would come whenever I told them," Lehovich recalled. The Kennedys' old rival, Henry Cabot Lodge, was then the American ambassador, and laughed when he heard of Lehovich's discomfort.

"You really got stuck with the dirty job," said the ambassador. "Let me tell you something about those Kennedy boys. Those brothers are all the same. They want one thing. They want one thing only. They want it every night. Your job? Make him crawl for it."

And so Lehovich paled when Kennedy called him to his room one night, saying, "I need something and I need it real bad."

The diplomat exhaled after learning that the senator had aggravated his injured back. "Aspirin," said Kennedy.

SOME MONTHS LATER, when Dun Gifford interviewed for a job on Ted Kennedy's staff, he was asked to sit down with Ted and Robert Kennedy.

"You know our rules?" Robert asked, referring to the family's political bylaws. There were two, said Robert: "Don't get mad, get even," and "Forgive, but don't forget." Topping the list of unforgettable offenders, said Kennedy, was Joe Tydings.

"Loyalty is a cardinal axiom of the way they did business," said Gifford. Tydings "was not loyal, and he made political capital at their expense. And they did not like that."

The coat-holder fared better. After returning from his trip to Vietnam, Ted Kennedy turned heads when he walked into the Parker House, the Boston hotel that served as a haunt for the city's politicians, and sat down at a conspicuous table—with Francis X. Morrissey.

Eight

A SENATOR TO BE
RECKONED WITH

Through no design of his own, Kennedy's 1965 jaunt through Asia, with its five-day tour of South Vietnam, would launch his long reappraisal of brother John's war. The four young members of Congress who assembled in Saigon—Kennedy, Tydings, Tunney, and Culver—had all served in the victorious U.S. military in the years after World War II. They felt at ease in the army gear and slouch hats they were given by their uniformed hosts in Vietnam, in the green bunting of jeeps and helicopters that bore them and their military guides to preselected sites in the countryside, and in swaddled visits with the gung-ho U.S. officers and Vietnamese government officials they met in the field. Away from the temptations of Saigon, Kennedy was earnest and dutiful. He and his friends had planned their visit with an overriding belief in the righteousness of the cause, and nothing their hosts showed them demolished that faith, not even the disclosure that hamlets they visited had been constructed, like Potemkin villages, for their benefit.

Which is not to say he didn't have questions. Kennedy had taken over as chairman of the Judiciary panel's unheralded subcommittee on refugees, where he retained two aides, Dale de Haan and Jerry Tinker, and added Abrams as counsel. They were bighearted experts who understood the damage done to civilian populations by war, revolutions, and other crises, and who maintained close ties to the nongovernmental organizations that ministered to the South Vietnamese people. Kennedy made them into a hub of expertise and influence on the war.

Kennedy, his staff, and many in the NGOs believed in John Kennedy's final word on the conflict in Southeast Asia: that the cause of freedom was noble, but that it could not be won if the South Vietnamese would not join the battle. The Pentagon's counterinsurgency experts agreed: in guerrilla warfare, victory lay in capturing not territory, but the "hearts and minds" of the people. John Kennedy's escalation of the war, to sixteen thousand U.S. servicemen, left his brothers in an awkward position. "The problem they had was they owned it," said Charles Tretter. "It went bad and it was theirs."

In the summer and fall of 1965, as Johnson dispatched tens of thousands more U.S. combat troops to South Vietnam and filled the skies with bombers, Ted Kennedy chaired thirteen hearings to determine how the Vietnamese people were faring. The first eleven hearings focused on the plucky ("fantastic . . . marvelous," said Kennedy at one point) U.S. and international aid organizations that were conducting relief efforts, despite the depredations of the Viet Cong. Some questions in the early hearings fit nicely with the Pentagon propaganda: Were the communists terrorizing the inhabitants of the countryside to inundate the South Vietnamese government with refugees? Were the columns of refugees a "Trojan Horse" that allowed guerrillas to infiltrate the cities?

The Marines had just splashed ashore at Danang. Anti-war protests were small and mostly confined to college campuses. Kennedy had been warned by Carl Marcy, the chief of staff of the Senate Foreign Relations Committee, to limit his inquiry to the plight of the displaced civilians and not stray onto geopolitical turf. Kennedy was not to call any top administration officials, like Secretary of State Dean Rusk, or ask questions about broader topics like the U.S. bombing of North Vietnam. Chairman Fulbright was under pressure from Senate liberals to investigate the U.S. conduct of the war but, though he was himself a critic, did "not believe such an investigation would serve any useful purpose" at the time, Marcy said.

As loyal Democrats, they didn't want to "kick the only president we got in the teeth."

Kennedy kept to his brief, focused on refugees, and achieved immediate success in rousing the administration to remedial action. Before he broached the subject, "very little was known about the refugee problem and even less was being done," *Time* magazine's Washington bureau reported to its editors in New York. "The quietly and adroitly voiced concern of the subcommittee raises no visible irritation on the part of affected AID [Agency for International Development] and State Department officials," and "both agencies agreed that the subcommittee had proved itself very valuable."

It was not until late September, just before he left for Vietnam, that witnesses in Kennedy's final two hearings challenged the U.S. conduct of the war. On September 21, Stephen Cary, testifying on behalf of the American Friends Service Committee, suggested that the military's "no sanctuary" and "open target" policies, which subjected villagers to random artillery and air attack, was counterproductive, and the feature of the war that most alienated Vietnamese civilians. On September 30 the panel heard from Roger Hilsman, a West Point graduate, World War II hero, and former State official with expertise in Southeast Asia and wars of liberation.

Hilsman urged Congress not to escalate the conflict, but to negotiate with the communists, even if it meant settling for a neutral Laos, Cambodia, and Vietnam. The United States had to resist the impulse to meet Viet Cong success with more, and increasingly more lethal, firepower. "An effective counterguerrilla program must avoid the large-scale military operations that bring destruction and hardship to the people," he told Kennedy. "Artillery and airpower must be used with extreme discrimination—for to bomb a village, even though the guerrillas are using it as a base for sniping, will recruit more Viet Cong than are killed." Yet Johnson's commanders seemed increasingly intent on wiping out the communist cadres in sweeps and battles that terrorized the peasantry. Counterinsurgency was an alien strategy for an army that, since Gettysburg, had triumphed via firepower and attrition.

Kennedy then left for Vietnam with Tydings and the others. He returned home in November, where an assignment from *Look* magazine awaited. Its editors wanted him to assess the war, and he approved the first draft of a bullish essay, supporting the American commitment, that would have pleased Lyndon Johnson. Aides Burke and Abrams balked. Given what they had heard in their final round of hearings, shouldn't Kennedy maintain his independence, instead of being a cheerleader?

Tunney, meanwhile, had returned with doubts and a hunger for more information. Back in Washington, his conversations with Bernard Fall fueled his reappraisal. Fall, a Vienna-born historian and journalist whose mother had died in Auschwitz and his father at the hands of the Gestapo, had displayed his hatred of authoritarianism by joining the French Resistance as a teenager during World War II. As a young scholar, he had written the classic *Street Without Joy* about the French disaster in Indochina. He was teaching at Howard University and putting the final touches on an account of the French defeat at Dien Bien Phu when Tunney called and quizzed him.

Burke and Abrams had heard about Tunney's misgivings and sent him a draft of the *Look* essay. He joined them at Kennedy's home, lobbying for a rewrite. If he took the safe route, Tunney told Kennedy, it could come back to haunt him. Fine, Kennedy told his staff, draft a new version. Abrams and Burke stayed up all night to meet the magazine's deadline. The article, published in February 1966, caused no great stir at the White House or the Pentagon, as the tone was more of worry than opposition. Kennedy made no mention of the "open target" and "no sanctuary" tactics and included just a fleeting suggestion that refugees were fleeing "bombs from our planes." His article focused mostly on the plight of the people.

"The second conflict in Vietnam—the struggle for the hearts and minds of the Vietnamese people themselves—has not been waged with the same ferocity" as the war in the field, he warned. "Whatever social institutions once existed for the benefit of the Vietnamese are now crippled or totally ruined." Kennedy had found a million refugees in Vietnam, and no U.S. commitment to deal with the problem. Instead, there was sleight of hand. Blankets distributed to refugees were repossessed by the authorities after Kennedy and the others had departed. "Construction was started on seven refugee camps in anticipation of my visit," he wrote. "Work stopped when my plans were temporarily altered. It began again when it was finally possible for me to go."

The most noteworthy impact of Kennedy's trip to the war zone was not what he was shown in Vietnam, but in how it exposed him to a growing school of expert doubt after he returned home. Now Ted, too, sought out Bernard Fall. At a dinner in the scholar's home, Fall challenged Kennedy's assertion—bred by the briefings the senator had gotten in Vietnam—that the territory around the city of Hue had been scoured of Viet Cong. Fall went to his bookshelf and returned with a U.S. government report showing that the price of rice in that area had soared by 600 percent. "So, do you think they're pacifying that road?" Fall asked Kennedy.

"Whoom!" Kennedy recalled. The briefers had lied. "That really took me. I read everything after that with a great deal more care and concern."

COMING ON THE HEELS of his success on the poll tax and immigration, and his graceful surrender on Morrissey, Kennedy's measured approach to the Vietnam War—supporting the endeavor while critiquing its execution—won him the regard of his Senate colleagues. It also allowed him to take the first awkward steps toward breaking with his brother John's Cold War outlook and rhetoric. His subcommittee marched ahead, investigating the plight of the civilian population, holding hearings, and confronting the Johnson administration on the rising toll of displacement, injuries, and deaths. In John Kennedy's era, the United States had made "a cool appraisal" of Vietnamese nationalism, Kennedy said later. Under Johnson's more frantic leadership, "we fell into all-out war."

"Our frustration and impatience with progress in South Vietnam, especially in the most difficult year of 1965, caused us to retreat to the common solutions and the techniques of warfare that were familiar to us," Kennedy now told audiences. "We lost sight of the special nature of this war and began to undertake operations and procedures directed to the annihilation of the Viet Cong and the troops of the North rather than the winning of the hearts and minds of the people in the South. What became important was the number of Viet Cong killed, and the 'other war' was reduced in meaning to press releases and plans on paper."

In time, Kennedy and his little panel earned a reputation as a haven for skeptics. His staff introduced him to then-unsung rebels like John Paul Vann and Daniel Ellsberg. Still, it was a halting evolution.

"I have been to Vietnam. I have seen what our boys are doing there and I know the pride you feel as the mother of two fighting men," he wrote to a hawkish constituent on March 17, 1966. "I have stated, without any reservations, that I support the President. . . . I have never called for a withdrawal from Viet Nam; I have never stated that the Viet Cong should be in any future government."

That same day, however, Kennedy replied to a critic of the war, the historian Henry Steele Commager, in more qualified terms. "I do basically support our current position in Viet Nam but . . . I think certain barriers to negotiations could be removed," Kennedy wrote. "It was in this light that I called for direct contact with the Viet Cong and the recognition of them as a party to negotiations."

Kennedy was threading a needle, but his approach seemed successful. It also kept him out of Robert's way. As befit the elder brother, Robert was assessing American foreign policy on a grander scale and, by inch and step, publicly taking a critical view of the Johnson administration's strategy in Southeast Asia. The plight of the Vietnamese civilians was something that could be left to Ted. As was another thriving wartime controversy: the draft.

MASSACHUSETTS WAS HOME TO more than a dozen major colleges and universities, and Johnson's determination to fill combat units with draftees, instead of reservists, brought the war to the campuses quickly. In May 1965, just a few weeks into the buildup of U.S. forces, Kennedy had brushed off the complaints made by the early peaceniks. In 1966 and 1967, as the number of U.S. troops in Southeast Asia swelled to hundreds of thousands, this was no longer possible. Conscriptions tripled. The random inequities of the Selective Service System were galling to young men, adding to the growing antiwar movement.

Kennedy entered the Selective Service debate, backed by Robert, in early 1966. To their credit, the brothers' efforts were not aimed at securing deferments for the boys of Harvard or Princeton, but at reforming a system administered by local draft boards, and prey to manipulation when it came to clout, class, and race. "The draft and who was fighting the war: It was all the poor and the blacks," Kennedy recalled. More fortunate young men received "the education deferment, the marriage deferment, the skill deferment." The inequities were stark in Massachusetts. Of twenty thousand undergraduates who attended Harvard and MIT between 1962 and 1972, fourteen were lost in battle in Vietnam, one survey concluded. In the same span, South Boston High School, with a tenth of that student population, had twenty-five graduates killed in action.

Kennedy proposed that young men be subject to a lottery, as in World War II. It would add fairness to the system and certainty for potential draftees. Soon, he was debating General Lewis Hershey, the head of the Selective Service System, on national television. Congress declined to act, but Kennedy kept at it.

"We have a system which allows professional athletes to join National Guard units which neither train nor guard. We have a system of local boards which apply widely different rules—which result in calling up married men in some states, while tens of thousands of single men in other states remain untouched," he told an audience at the National Press Club in early 1967. "We have a system which sends tens of thousands of young men into the army because they cannot afford to go to college; one which lets seventy-five percent of those wealthy enough or bright enough to go on to graduate school escape military service completely."

Prodded, Johnson established a commission, chaired by Kennedy family adviser Burke Marshall. It endorsed a lottery. With a newly aggressive demeanor ("Move in for the kill. I'm behind you—way behind," Robert wrote him during one floor debate), Ted used the rubric of "manpower" to stage hearings on the draft in a Labor subcommittee, and to offer reform measures on the Senate floor. He lost a showdown in June 1967 but corralled two dozen votes and Armed Services chairman Russell's regard. Kennedy would return to the issue in the months ahead, until the country switched to a lottery, and ultimately to a volunteer army. But for now, Russell and Kennedy shared a drink. The Georgian told Kennedy he had impressed his elders and earned some legislative courtesy—unspecified concessions that would be granted the next time the Senate took up the draft. He recognized the pressure the senator must be feeling from liberal Massachusetts, Russell said, and "I don't like you to go away empty-handed." He also suggested that Kennedy might help him on an appropriation for the port of Savannah. Of course, said Kennedy, happy to collect a chit: "We're a Navy state and a Navy family."

IN THAT SAME YEAR, 1967, Ted and Robert Kennedy struck another blow for equality, and exacted a measure of revenge against Dirksen, who had humiliated them on the Morrissey nomination.

Five years earlier, in a ruling that Chief Justice Earl Warren would rank as the most significant of his tenure, the Supreme Court had concluded that the equal protection clause of the Fourteenth Amendment applied to the formation of legislative districts. The court's endorsement of a "one man, one vote" principle was a mighty blow to lawmakers who represented lightly populated rural counties or townships and thus, under the old rules, wielded similar or greater power as those representing metropolitan districts with far larger populations.

Since rural voters tended to be more conservative and Republican than their counterparts in the cities, the court's ruling—*Baker v. Carr*—also seemed to favor Democrats, minorities, and labor unions. Dirksen made it his mission to steer a constitutional amendment through Congress to nullify the Supreme Court's actions. He came close from 1964 to 1966, amassing a huge campaign war chest from American business interests and using it to employ one of the country's premier political consulting firms, Whitaker & Baxter.

"At stake is who—labor-dominated big city political machines or all of the people through fair representation—will make the decisions," said one of the firm's appeals to American corporations. On the table were corporate tax rates, welfare benefits, oil and gas drilling, unemployment compensation, food safety standards, and labor relations. Donations were solicited from Ford and General Electric, DuPont and U.S. Steel, Standard Oil, United Airlines, IT&T, the Chase Manhattan Bank, and other blue-chip firms. A quiet little dinner in Washington, organized by Clem Whitaker and hosted by Dirksen, sought to raise $700,000—the equivalent of almost $6 million in 2021, after factoring for inflation. That kind of money underwrote a major public relations campaign. Two million pamphlets titled "Let the People Decide" were distributed, 46,000 news releases were issued, and film clips were sent out to 194 television stations around the country. "My dear Senator Dirksen. Enclosed is a Ford Motor Company Check in the amount of $20,000, made payable to The Committee for Government by the People," wrote Rodney Markley, who ran the auto firm's Washington office. "I want you to know how much we appreciate the dedicated effort on your part."

In 1965 and 1966, a majority in the Senate voted in favor of Dirksen's proposed constitutional amendments to allow bicameral bodies to use factors other than population to fill legislative chambers. But a simple majority was not enough; by seven votes one year and nine votes the other, Dirksen failed to collect the two-thirds needed to pass a constitutional amendment and send it to the states for ratification. Ignoring the moral of Pandora's box—and failing to recognize that the tactic would stir widespread alarm—Dirksen and his allies then turned to the never-used provision that allows the states to petition for a new constitutional convention, which would take up any changes its members fancied. The battle moved to state legislatures; at one point Dirksen's side came within two states of the two-thirds needed.

As this tack also failed, Dirksen tried a third strategy: to slide a law through the Senate allowing the population of House districts to deviate by as much as 35 percent. Dirksen had the help of Sam Ervin and the rural South. Kennedy opposed them in the Judiciary Committee and, in 1967, stepped in to stop Dirksen on the Senate floor, in a shootout as wounding for the Illinois senator as the Morrissey business had been for Ted and Robert.

———

REPRESENTATIVE JOHN CONYERS OF Michigan had alerted Ted and urged him to stop Dirksen's latest meddling. Kennedy was becoming a go-to guy for liberals. "If something needed doing, and it wasn't clear that someone else was going to do it, we had to do it," James Flug recalled.

Ted enlisted Robert. It was not a hard sell, as this was the ground of legacy. John Kennedy, when a senator, was a fierce advocate for fair reapportionment. "The urban majority is, politically, a minority and the rural minority dominates the polls," he had written in a magazine article, "The Shame of the States," in 1958. "Apportionment . . . has been either deliberately rigged or shamefully ignored so as to deny the cities and their voters that full and proportionate voice in government to which they are entitled." In California, Kennedy had noted, thirteen thousand rural citizens had as many state senators as four million urban residents.

The redistricting cases were a major preoccupation—and accomplishment—of John Kennedy's administration. His solicitor general, Archibald Cox, had argued for the winning side in *Baker v. Carr.* Attorney General Robert donned the traditional morning coat and striped pants and made his only personal appearance before the Supreme Court—with First Lady Jacqueline, brother Ted, wife Ethel, and other family members in attendance—in a related case from Georgia.

"We used to have a saying in my home city of Boston: 'Vote early and vote often,'" Robert told the justices. "In Georgia, if you lived in a rural area . . . you accomplished the same result."

In the course of his argument, Robert became the first attorney general to use the phrase "one man, one vote" before the Court. His side carried the day.

Now together in the Senate, Ted and Robert teamed up to foil Dirksen. Don't get mad, get even.

"Do you want to ask a question or make a speech?" Ted, smiling, asked Robert, who had arrived in the chamber with a request that his younger brother yield the floor.

"I want to make a speech," Robert said. "I thought the senator from Massachusetts understood that."

Robert started talking. Ted gave him a moment and interrupted.

"How much time does the senator from New York want?" he asked.

"How much time does the senator from Massachusetts want to yield to me?" said Robert, grinning at the needle.

"Twelve minutes," Ted said.

"I thank the senator for his courtesy," Robert said.

KIDDING ASIDE, the Kennedys needed Republican votes. At Robert's suggestion, Ted enlisted the help of Senator Howard Baker, a freshman Republican from Tennessee, as an ally. As younger men, Robert and Baker had served together as Senate staff in the Army-McCarthy hearings.

"I'm going to fight this. Would you help me?" Ted asked.

"Absolutely," said Baker.

The Tennessee senator was Dirksen's son-in-law, but he had generational differences with the old man. He came armed with statistics showing how the Republican Party could make up in the suburbs what it lost in the farmlands. Tennessee Republicans had used the "one man, one vote" argument against the rural Democratic courthouse machines. It was "a hard thing for me" to take on Dirksen, Baker recalled. "I went from adoration to opposition." Nor was he ever very close to Ted Kennedy. But Baker was up to the task. He rounded up Republicans, demonstrating the political skills he would employ over the next three decades as a senator, majority leader, and White House chief of staff.

Kennedy's staff stuffed a briefcase—"the Bag"—with statistics, scholarly analyses, and constitutional arguments. He spent the Memorial Day weekend studying, then rehearsed with Flug at night at home. Their goal was to block Dirksen's bill allowing wide disparities in congressional districts. When the Senate reconvened in June, the Kennedys and Baker won on a 44–39 vote, and by 55 to 22 when the notion was resurrected, in a bastardized form, in November.

The June debate took place as Israel, under the leadership of the one-eyed defense minister Moshe Dayan, was heading to a stunning victory over Arab armies in the Six-Day War. At a party in his Senate office, celebrating their triumph over Dirksen, Kennedy presented Flug with an eyepatch like that worn by Dayan.

It was the kind of victory, against long odds, on an important but popularly obscure issue, that spurred the capital's press corps to strut. In the *Washington Post*, columnist David Broder called the victorious Ted Kennedy–Howard Baker alliance "one of the bright spots" in the "long and rather dreary record" of the 1967 session. "All this was done by young men, who gambled against heavy odds in challenging the elders of their parties," he wrote.

"While it is impossible for any Kennedy to be overlooked, this one has surely been underestimated," Broder said of Ted. "To the general public he appears to be a tail on Bobby's kite, the young fellow who used the family name and family fortune to win election to his late brother's seat, and then put forward for a federal judgeship a family crony. . . .

"But within the Senate, Kennedy has long since overcome the skepticism that greeted his election and the embarrassment of the Morrissey nomination fight. His cheerful acceptance of the routine chores handed a junior senator and his skillful leadership on immigration and civil rights legislation have earned him high marks from his colleagues. Without this standing he could never have done what he did on the redistricting bill."

When he arrived in the Senate, "Ted's sole assets seemed to be a princely phiz and a kingly cognomen," said *Time* magazine. But "the reputed intellectual lightweight who was once expelled by Harvard because of hanky-panky on an examination, turned out to be a glutton for legislative homework" and "a senator to be reckoned with."

Nine

ROBERT'S TIME

The Kennedy brand had been tarnished by the Morrissey affair, and in 1966 it was marred again when Jacqueline and Robert stumbled into a public fray with the author William Manchester, whom they had commissioned to write an account of John's assassination. The book contained personal details that she wanted cut, and it strayed, in ways that were politically awkward, into unflattering comparisons of Johnson and Kennedy. "The Texans in their polka-dot dresses and bow ties are seen as newly arrived scum—plucked from the dung heap by magical Jack," the book's editor, Evan Thomas, admitted. The Kennedy family's lawsuit against the writer made them look like bullies, infringing on artistic freedom.

Camelot was starting to cut both ways. The Kennedys had been "extraordinarily skilled, led by their dad, in manipulating their imagery," a young broadcaster from South Dakota, Tom Brokaw, would later recall. "I didn't know anybody who skied, I didn't know anybody who had a private airplane . . . and suddenly there were these handsome men and women who were sailing on weekends, and throwing each other in the swimming pool, and dressing very stylishly, and hanging out with movie stars."

In time, the breathless accounts of John and Jacqueline and the glamorous court of the New Frontier made Kennedy coverage—good or ugly—a commodity. Thanks to the boundless appetite of television, and its part in the "cocktail of celebrity, technology and collective memory," the lives of "Bobby" and "Teddy" and "Jackie" and the others passed into the surreal realm inhabited by Marilyn, Elvis, the Beatles, and a few other superstars, a Kennedy of the next generation would recall. Anything was game: their sins, their sex lives, their autopsy photographs. For the rest of his career, Ted would be judged by a very different public standard than that applied, in life, to his brothers. The reporters and editors of John Kennedy's generation had protected and promoted their young hero. As time passed, the media was infiltrated by younger journalists who showed less deference to tradition, courtesy, or authority. Infused with the certainties of youth—and influenced by the rights and liberation movements, the stylistic upheaval of the 1960s, and resistance to the Vietnam War—they viewed the American establishment with a less forgiving eye. By 1967, there were veiled references in the gossip sheets to Ted's associations with pretty young women.

As chieftain of the clan, Robert Kennedy was a focus of journalistic attention. Aspiring stylists filled the slick, shiny pages of American magazines with soulful accounts of Robert climbing Mount Kennedy in the Canadian Yukon, breaking a fast with Cesar Chavez and his striking farmworkers in the fields of California, or choked with emotion as he held starving babies in the Mississippi Delta. The enmity between "RFK" and "LBJ," meanwhile, was catnip for the lazier sort in the political press corps. As things went sour in Vietnam, and Robert's criticism of the Johnson administration grew harsh, the narrative was distilled to an insistent question: Would Kennedy challenge Johnson in the 1968 election?

Ted fervently wished not. Only one elected American president, Franklin Pierce, had ever been defeated by a challenger from his own party—and that was amid turmoil on the eve of the Civil War. The Democrats seemed imperturbably ascendent once Johnson whipped Goldwater in 1964, but a troublesome trend—a backlash among blue-collar voters over civil rights—had surfaced in George Wallace's success in the Democratic primaries that year, where he won a third or so of the vote in Wisconsin and Indiana and 43 percent in Maryland. Ted was wounded by the payback in Boston when he changed his stance on busing, and endorsed the mandatory transfer of black and white students to achieve integration of neighborhood schools. Why let the Republicans back in the game, Ted asked Robert, by further fracturing the Democratic Party over issues as combustible as race and Vietnam? With the right preparation, Ted believed, Robert could claim the Democratic nomination in 1972, when Johnson would be gone and the war would most surely be over. Robert was influenced by Ted's counsel. If he played the role of spoiler, the press would attribute it to personal pique. If he split the party, the collateral damage could include its liberal Senate candidates. If he challenged Johnson, it would be seen as a repudiation of John Kennedy's foreign policy. When asked how he would reply when journalists pressed him about his brother's responsibility for the war, Robert answered, "I don't know what would be best: to say that he didn't spend much time thinking about Vietnam, or to say that he did and messed it up." Then he threw a hand toward heaven and said, "Which, brother, which?"

At the end of 1965, Robert McNamara, the secretary of defense, had confided to Robert Kennedy that a victory of arms was not possible—a political solution must be found. "If we regard bombing as the answer in Vietnam," Robert said in his January 1966 speech, "we are headed straight for disaster. In the past, bombing has not proved a decisive weapon against a rural economy—or against a guerrilla army. And the temptation will now be to argue that if limited bombing does not produce a solution, that further bombing, more extended military action, is the answer . . . the first in a series of steps on a road from which there is no turning back—a road which leads to catastrophe." A few weeks later he suggested that, as part of a negotiated settlement, the communists might have a voice, and share power, in the government of South Vietnam. He was attacked for this apostasy.

TED SAILED IN HIS brother's lee. He admired Robert's passion, even as he questioned his timing. "Make sure that they announce that it's the Kennedy from New York," Ted teased as Robert readied a blast at Johnson's conduct of the war. At the conclusion of Robert's March 1967 speech, in which he called for an end to the U.S. bombing of North Vietnam, Ted had a page carry a note to his brother in the Senate chamber. "I'm not

leaving," Ted wrote. "I'm afraid to go outside." But Ted was quietly building his own record of concern. He followed up on the *Look* magazine article by releasing a 337-page report on the refugee crisis in Vietnam. He led
more hearings in 1966, and this time grilled leading administration officials. He backed Robert's call for negotiations with the Viet Cong. And, in
1967, he adjusted his focus on civilian refugees to emphasize the toll of
Vietnamese dead. The argument was no longer about counterproductive
tactics, it was over the morality of the carnage. Kennedy and his staff "focused their concerns on an area that had not attracted public attention:
South Vietnamese civilians killed, wounded and displaced by U.S. military actions," Frank Mankiewicz, Robert's press secretary, would recall.
"Until Ted Kennedy began to ask questions, no one in the U.S. government even pretended to try to count such casualties."

"When you watched the strikes from 25,000 feet, you can bomb anything and it doesn't bother you," said David Burke. "Teddy knew what was
going on down below . . . and what he should know about and should care
about. . . . He was doing it on behalf of innocents."

Kennedy no longer trusted the Pentagon's estimates. He had his staff
contact the scores of doctors who had served in Vietnam, and cashed in
chits with Eastland to obtain the funds to send teams of physicians to
tour South Vietnam. The Johnson administration estimated that fifty
thousand civilians would be treated for war-related injuries in 1967. In a
front-page story, the first of a series by correspondent Neil Sheehan and
colleagues at the *New York Times*, Kennedy doubled that number. He attributed most of the bloodshed to American and South Vietnamese artillery and air attacks.

On he marched, down the path from ingenue to oracle. In early 1967,
he had Representatives Culver and Tunney join him for an hours-long
lunch with Richard Holbrooke, a young American diplomat with experience in Vietnam. The number of U.S. military personnel had risen by
then to 375,000.

"I assured them the U.S. troops . . . were as gentle and fair with the
people as any army has ever been in such a difficult situation," Holbrooke reported to his superiors. "Kennedy asked our opinion of prog-

ress in Vietnam. I gave him the standard line. . . . He obviously didn't buy this."

"When he was out there in November of 1965, he said, he had heard exactly the same line. He said that he expected to hear the same line five years from now," Holbrooke wrote, and conceded, "It might well be true."

When Richard Goodwin made a speech castigating U.S. policy, Kennedy passed it to Tip O'Neill and encouraged him to declare against the war. To Johnson's dismay, O'Neill—a Democratic wheelhorse and rising House leader—announced his opposition in September 1967. Launching a new round of hearings that fall, Kennedy spoke again of "the other war" in Vietnam—the political conflict that the United States was in danger of losing as the people of both countries grew exhausted and repelled by the seemingly endless shambles. He had appealed to Johnson and his advisers via "quiet discussion," but in vain, he said. And so "it is both appropriate and necessary that the entire question of civilian casualties in South Vietnam be fully aired." He hiked his estimate of civilian casualties to as many as 150,000 a year.

A highlight of the hearings was a confrontation between Kennedy and Assistant Secretary of State William Bundy, who had testified that communist infiltration into South Vietnam had been brought to a halt by U.S. forces. Bundy did not know that Kennedy possessed leaked Pentagon documents that proved otherwise.

"My figures," said Kennedy, show infiltration "in the first half of 1967 . . . going up quite noticeably."

"Well now," Bundy said condescendingly, "I am not sure of the source of your figures . . ."

"My figures are from the Department of Defense," said Kennedy.

MORE RELEVANT TO THE question of the death toll and casualties was Roger Hilsman's testimony. "Artillery and air power must be used with extreme care and discrimination," he told the committee, and yet 85 percent of allied artillery salvos were in the form of blind "interdiction" shelling. "These free fire zones and interdiction bombing; unobserved shelling of suspicious movement or of suspicious installations, goes against the principle that the effective way to deal with a guerrilla war is to win the allegiance of the people."

Civilian aid worker Donald Luce also returned to testify. When he appeared in 1965, he said, refugees were fleeing violence initiated by the Viet Cong. Now the source of deaths, injury, and alienation was American "bombing in an area where someone thinks there may be Vietcong [and] in the harassment and interdiction firing—the 105 and 155 howitzers firing at night into the rural areas . . . to just keep things stirred up out there and perhaps make the Viet Cong nervous," said Luce. "There has been a very definite swing . . . from support and respect for America to one of resentment." A Vietnamese friend had formerly used his native word for "wrong" to describe American tactics, Luce said. Now his friend employed the Vietnamese word for "evil."

Kennedy was quiet, circumspect as chairman. He let the grim statistics, and pessimistic testimony, speak for him. Robert, influenced by the testaments of Ted's witnesses and others, was more given to outrage.

"Do we have the right, here in the United States, to say that we're going to kill tens of thousands? Make millions of people, as we have . . . refugees? Killing women and children?" Robert asked on national television. "Those of us who stay here in the United States, we must feel it when we use napalm, when a village is destroyed and civilians are killed. . . . When we say we love our country, we say it for what it can be and for the justice it stands for . . . and that is what I think is being seriously undermined in Vietnam."

For Robert, the war had become "something central" in "his life and his politics," Ted would remember.

TWO YEARS HAD PASSED since Ted had visited Vietnam. It was time, he reckoned, to go again. The pictures in his mind were of Vietnamese civilians—mostly women, the elderly, and children—killed and maimed by napalm; swept from their homes and into camps as their farmland was transformed into free-fire zones; or terrorized by the army's "harassment and interdiction" fire. He could not rely on American officials to show him such things; on this trip he would need a different approach. A four-man advance team, drawn from his and Robert's stable of advisers, would precede him—some of them by weeks—and draw up an independent itinerary. Kennedy would dodge the buoyant briefings and spend his time in the field, traveling from the Mekong Delta in the south to First Corps in the north. He and his staff would spotlight not only the condition of the refugees, but the forces that displaced them: the rules of engagement, the accuracy of airstrikes and artillery barrages, and the selection of targets. He would test the will of the Vietnamese people to continue the war. And this time he would not be wearing shiny new fatigues and a rakish army slouch hat.

KENNEDY FLEW FIRST CLASS to Asia, accompanied by Dr. John Levinson, an expert on refugee medicine. They broke briefly for dinner on New Year's Eve, but otherwise spent the long flight studying their briefing materials. As they began to take off from a refueling stop in Guam, their airplane blew an engine and hurtled down the runway, stopping just short of the fence at the edge of the airport. Kennedy gripped the armrest and muttered, "I've been through this before."

Burke joined them in Vietnam. The trip is best remembered for the overpowering conviction it left with Kennedy: of the malaise of the elites, corruption in the cities, and the bankrupt American strategy. "Once you see and experience it," he would say, "it has real meaning." He was there for twelve days. "It was an awful trip because we saw things that you shouldn't see," said Burke. "Napalm burns on a child. Bones—arms frozen to the side of the body by the melted skin." At one point Kennedy begged Levinson to stop showing him such filth and gore and sorrow. "It's too much," he said. "It's too much."

The casualties were "not people who are around when a terrible battle erupted" and got caught in a crossfire between the good guys and the bad guys, said John Nolan, one of Ted's advance men. "Civilian casualties in this context means . . . civilians who are wounded or killed because of us—the United States. . . . We have all of the artillery. We have all of the naval gunfire support. We have all of the air."

It was not surprising, then, that "in the most meticulously reported and recorded war in the history of warfare, any statistic dealing with civilian casualties was avoided," Nolan said. "Not recorded. Even talking about it was regarded as kind of subversive."

A TORRENT OF SCENES seared the senator. In Saigon, it was the "thousands of young men 18 and 19 years old" cruising the streets on motorbikes, "wearing cowboy hats and leather gloves, exempt from the war and oblivious to the sacrifices of others," Kennedy would recall. He wondered how he could tell the parents of the dead American draftees that their son had died as "the Saigon cowboy" and "the profiteer" and "a small, privileged segment of Vietnamese society is thriving in this . . . war economy . . . content with the status quo."

In the Mekong Delta, Kennedy's advance team received word from American relief workers of how U.S. and South Vietnamese aircraft had bombed a farming village, killing ten innocents, including four children. "A community of 33 families was wiped off the map. Their homes were mostly destroyed along with their boats and livestock. The survivors arrived in the market with nothing but the clothes they were wearing," wrote aid worker David Gitelson in a detailed report. "Perhaps the essence of the matter is that the Vietnamese and American military don't feel any mistake has been made." When Gitelson asked a senior American officer if the rules of the war did not leave civilians as "just so much foliage to shoot through," the officer readily agreed. "The people [in the village] were lucky," the officer said. "If the helicopters had been in proper strafing position, no one would have got out alive."

Kennedy came south to investigate, but as the aid workers prepared to welcome him, two bombs were detonated, destroying their vehicles and compelling them to cancel the meeting. Kennedy huddled with Gitelson at a nearby U.S. headquarters instead, where they discussed American tactics and Vietnamese corruption. Gitelson was a U.S. Army veteran—an idealistic former medic who had volunteered to go to Vietnam as a civilian relief worker. He rambled around the delta alone, with a shaved head, in jeans and flip-flops, playing a concertina and winning the trust of the peasants, who called him My Ngheo—the poor American. Two weeks after his meeting with Kennedy, he was shot and killed.

"WHOLE AREAS WHICH HAVE been bulldozed to the ground are commonplace, and so are wide corridors of defoliated forests, and fields that once produced food," Kennedy wrote in his diary. "Here and there are compounds of long sheds with shiny tin roofs—the refugee camps where thousands upon thousands of people have been herded together, uprooted from all they ever knew or wanted."

His encounters spoke of the phantasma, Vietnam. "Mad, it was crazy, it was nuts," said Nolan. Inside Saigon, Kennedy found a city of the dead—a Catholic cemetery where five thousand refugees sought shelter by stringing hammocks between tombstones, stripping caskets from the mausoleums, employing the stone shelves as beds, and building tarpaper hovels atop the graves. In these hovels, he was stunned to see, many had hung photographs of his brother John. The refugees chanted "ken-uh-dee" as he walked by. Outside the city, the Quakers ran a camp where two hundred Vietnamese children were waiting for artificial legs; it distributed seven thousand a year but could not keep up with the demand.

In Quang Ngai, a young American air controller choked back tears as he told Kennedy how he called in air and artillery bombardments, as ordered, on groups of Vietnamese wearing black pajamas, the uniform of the Viet Cong. But "that's what the peasant wears," he told the senator. "They all wear black pajamas."

Kennedy snapped at a callous artillery officer firing random interdiction rounds into civilian territory. Thinking that the senator would appreciate the honor, the gunners had scratched his name on a shell.

"Where did that shell go?" Kennedy asked. "Coming in here on the helicopter, we were surrounded by farmers in the fields and rice paddies."

"This is a free fire zone," the officer said.

"Where are you from? Illinois, or Iowa? You wouldn't shoot it off in your hometown, would you? Who is that hitting?"

They spent a night at John Paul Vann's house. After dinner and drinks, he took Kennedy on a hazardous midnight ride through the jungle to an asylum for the mentally ill whose patients were fed with slop dumped on the floor. "If you lost your spoon you were dead," said Levinson.

On one of Kennedy's final stops, he met with General William Westmoreland, the commander of allied forces, who assured him that the death and wounding of civilians was an isolated, inadvertent problem—because his army had been told to be careful.

"Contradictions. Glaring contrasts. Inconsistencies," Kennedy told his diary. "Friend and foe are truly indistinguishable."

Robert Kennedy had become friends with New York journalist Pete Hamill. At their suggestion, Ted looked up Hamill's brother John, serving in the 173rd Airborne in the Central Highlands, for an unvarnished account of the war's progress.

Kennedy arrived with Burke and no entourage. He was dressed in a Ban-Lon shirt, jeans, and work boots. "He looked you in the eye," Hamill remembered. "He was like Bobby's scout."

"So, what do you think?" Kennedy asked.

"I told him it was a mess," Hamill recalled. "What a clusterfuck it was. I told him, 'You guys got to end this thing.'"

"I AM FORCED TO report to you, and to the people of the commonwealth, that continued optimism cannot be justified," Kennedy told a Boston audience upon his return home.

With himself, he was candid. "I left Vietnam with one further thought in my mind: I could no longer support this atrocity of a war," he would remember.

They drank "a great deal of liquor" on the long flight home.

ROBERT WAS IMPRESSED BY his brother's trip, and the reports he received from Ted and his companions. They spoke of "the futility of the military situation, the extent to which we were destroying the countryside, the extent to which the commitments made to the refugees had all fallen through, the corruption at every level," said E. Barrett Prettyman, one of Robert's former aides, who had been on Ted's advance team.

Johnson also kept track of Ted Kennedy's travels. Soon after their return, Kennedy and Burke met with the president for ninety minutes in the Oval Office. Johnson cowed Burke, but Kennedy retained his wits and offered the president a litany of dissent, ranging far beyond the treatment of refugees.

"The senator seemed less concerned with the management or adequacy of [refugee] programs than with broader issues of . . . corruption and U.S. military strategy," a White House record of the conversation noted. "He had begun to wonder whether 'round eyes and white skin' could solve Asia's problems."

Kennedy did not call for a unilateral withdrawal, but he urged Johnson to turn the American military mission back to clearing and holding the countryside—instead of, as Kennedy had witnessed, the search-and-destroy campaigns, and harassment and interdiction fire, of a war of attrition.

They parted with civility, but Kennedy's public critique in a speech the next day spurred the president to mobilize his frontline advisers and respond. Westmoreland and Ambassador Ellsworth Bunker took Kennedy to task. The senator's public comments were "based in a large part on incomplete, biased or false information," Bunker assured the White House. "It appeals heavily to the emotions and is in no sense a sober evaluation of our policy, our tactics, and our progress in Vietnam. . . . It would appear, mainly to fit an already conceived theme."

Others were not so sure. Kennedy "has used figures we cannot legitimately attack," Secretary of State Dean Rusk told the president. "Corruption is a tough one to deal with."

Vice President Humphrey told National Security Adviser Walt Rostow that "there obviously is some merit to some of Ted Kennedy's complaints. . . . During my visit with President Thieu, he expressed concern over our search-and-destroy operations."

McNamara sympathized with Kennedy's comments about the Saigon cowboys and the South Vietnamese will to win. "There is no excuse for the Vietnamese not lowering their draft age," he told Johnson.

"There is truth in what he says about corruption and three-hour siestas," even Lodge acknowledged.

Johnson's aides suggested that they rob Kennedy of his thunder by declaring new anticorruption measures and announcing reductions in the random bombardments and artillery fire. The State Department prepared two documents: a "sanitized discussion" of the South Vietnamese government's corruption-fighting efforts for public consumption and a "sensitive and detailed" internal discussion, which confirmed many of Kennedy's concerns, but shrugged them off. "Corruption is brought on by the poverty and poverty is brought on by the war," Lodge wrote. "Once the war stops the poverty will go down and so will the corruption."

Ultimately, Johnson dismissed Kennedy, and the warnings of other Cassandras. All governments, including that of the United States, experienced political thievery, he told the Joint Chiefs of Staff. "We have corruption here" in Washington, the president said. "We cannot have perfection."

Johnson's staff was making plans to attack Ted Kennedy for unpatriotic "demagoging" when the president, and the country, learned just how far from perfection the United States had strayed.

ON JANUARY 30, as Johnson and his advisers were debating how to handle Kennedy, the first of a series of disturbing reports arrived from South Vietnam, elbowing its way onto the agenda and eclipsing the senator's trip. Catching the Americans unaware, the communists had launched a general offensive, timed to take advantage of the Tet holidays, with attacks on more than a hundred South Vietnamese cities and towns. The American embassy in Saigon came under assault. The ancient imperial capital of Hue was seized. The allied forces would ultimately win the battle—and crush the Viet Cong, as a fighting force—over the next six months. But the psychological shock to the American public, conveyed by the televised evidence of the enemy's capabilities—after their leaders had assured them how splendidly the war was going—transformed the debate.

Word then reached the press and public that the military wanted another 206,000 troops, above the 530,000 already deployed to fight the war. The news was almost as shocking as the Tet Offensive itself.

Johnson was terribly downcast. On March 26 he met with two of his top generals, Earle Wheeler and Creighton Abrams, and described the dark maze in which he dwelled. "Our fiscal situation is abominable," he began. "There has been a panic in the last three weeks. It was caused by Ted Kennedy's report on corruption and the [Vietnamese government and army] being no good. And now a release that Westmoreland wants 206,000 men. . . . That would cost $15 billion. . . . The country is demoralized. . . . We have no support for the war. This is caused by the 206,000-troop request, leaks, Ted Kennedy and Bobby Kennedy."

"We need more money in an election year, more taxes in an election year, more troops in an election year and more cuts in an election year," he said. "I will have overwhelming disapproval in the polls and elections."

"I will go down the drain," he said.

ROBERT KENNEDY HAD BEEN FEELING unrelenting pressure to challenge Johnson in the presidential primaries. Friends like Allard Lowenstein, Schlesinger, Goodwin, and Pete Hamill believed it was a moral duty, and younger staffers like Adam Walinsky and Peter Edelman agreed. More pragmatic advisers, like Theodore Sorensen, Fred Dutton—and Ted Kennedy—wondered what kind of moral obligation required them to destroy the Democratic Party and, by doing so, elect Richard Nixon. "Teddy Kennedy was the most reluctant, and the most practical," Kenneth O'Donnell remembered. "I think he saw the peril in it very clearly."

"I had reservations about it because I thought it was very important that Bobby be president, and I thought it was inevitable that [someday] he would," Ted remembered. Challenging Johnson was "high risk" and could lead to the loss of the White House and the defeat of "good liberal members of Congress." He knew, as well, how the Kennedy haters would cast it. "It was going to be blind personal ambition for power . . . because the Kennedys thought they were entitled," Ted said. "It was going to reaffirm a view about Bobby being particularly aggressive and ruthless . . . trying to seize power in a war which his brother had gotten started.

"These are big-time differences," he said, "and some of us thought they could very well be the destruction of Bobby."

Ted's opposition was meaningful to Robert, who told Schlesinger that Ted was "the strongest opponent" to his running. At a lunch with Edelman and California's Jesse Unruh, Robert lamented that he did not have a brother who would do for him what he had done for Jack. "My brother thinks I'm crazy," Robert told a friendly journalist. "But my brother . . . you know, Teddy and I are such different people. We don't hear the same music."

After months of private talks, in or without his presence, in which the question had been chewed and chewed, Robert decided not to make the race. "Around the country antiwar activists said to hell with it and set to work for Eugene McCarthy," Schlesinger recalled. The Minnesota senator launched a peace campaign at the end of 1967.

THE TET OFFENSIVE, however, reopened the debate at Hickory Hill. Ted was intransigent, set in opposition to his brother's candidacy. Robert sent Goodwin to speak to him, and they spent a long evening together, arguing in Boston. Robert had but a one-in-five chance of winning the Democratic nomination, they concluded. But they agreed as well that all of Robert's instincts told him to run and that he would be miserable if he did not.

"He usually follows his own instincts and he's done damn well," Ted acknowledged.

What, Goodwin asked him, would Jack advise?

"I'm not sure about that," Ted replied, "but I know what Dad would have said. . . . Don't do it."

Ted thought further. "Jack would probably have cautioned against it," he told Goodwin, "but he might have done it himself."

The Kennedy brothers huddled with Dutton and O'Donnell. "All four of us felt that Bob could not win," said Dutton, "but that he now had to try."

At this point, a curious thing occurred. Robert had asked Ted to notify McCarthy—before New Hampshire voted on March 12—that Kennedy was intent on joining the race. Ted, dreading this outcome and perhaps sensing Robert's final residue of uncertainty, chose not to do so. This left McCarthy and his supporters with an unshakable belief that Robert's candidacy—which was not announced until after they had done the hard work of fighting Johnson to a draw in New Hampshire—was an opportunistic course of action. "Other politicians were afraid," McCarthy charged. "They were willing to stay up on the mountains and light signal fires and bonfires and dance in the light of the moon. But none of them came down."

The final council convened in Stephen and Jean Smith's apartment in New York on March 14. Ted chaired the meeting and somberly outlined the alternatives until, at 7 p.m., they stopped to watch Robert give an interview on the evening news. He all but declared his candidacy.

"I don't know what we are meeting about," Ted said. "He has made all the decisions already, and we're learning about them on television."

The substance of the gathering, Ted recalled, changed from "Should he?" to "What are we going to do?" It was a turning point. "He knew what was in his soul," Ted remembered. "We spent the rest of the evening dividing up assignments."

Still, Robert hesitated. Responding to a feeler from McCarthy's aides, he sent Ted to Wisconsin to ascertain if the antiwar senators might yet find a way to work together. Robert was "90 percent in" but might yet stay on the sidelines if McCarthy adopted a forceful platform to meet the needs of the inner cities, Ted was to tell McCarthy. If not, then maybe they could join together to defeat Johnson, by dividing the upcoming primaries, and then going head-to-head in California. McCarthy was asleep, and his wife, Abigail, wavered at waking him, letting Ted cool his heels in a nearby motel until 2 a.m. When they finally met, McCarthy ended the discussion before Kennedy could retrieve his proposals from a briefcase.

Kennedy got back to Hickory Hill at dawn. Bill vanden Heuvel asked how things had gone. "Abigail said no," said Kennedy.

"Why not come out for McCarthy?" Schlesinger asked Robert, who was now awake and wandering the house in pajamas. "He can't possibly win, so you will be the certain inheritor of his support."

"I can't do that," Robert said. "It would be too humiliating. Kennedys don't act that way."

Short on sleep, with misgivings, aghast at the lack of preparation and dreading the prospect that somewhere out there was another assassin, who would leave Robert's children without a father, Ted threw his arms up in the air. "I just can't believe it. It is too incredible," he said. "I just can't believe that we are sitting around the table discussing anything as incredible as this."

"I'm going ahead," Robert said, "and there is no point in talking about anything else."

He left to get dressed. "He's made up his mind," said Ted. He echoed his brother John's advice in the hours after the 1962 debate against Ed McCormack. "If we discuss it any longer, it will shake his confidence and put him on the defensive. He has to be at his best at the goddamned press conference. So we can't talk about it anymore."

A barber showed up to tame Robert's notoriously bushy hair, a symbol of Sixties rebellion. "Don't pay any attention to anything he says," Ted told the stylist. "Cut off as much as you can."

Ethel was holding up neckties for Robert to choose. Ted grabbed Burke and set off for a walk around the property. Dallas was not far from his thoughts. "I'm really afraid," Kennedy told Burke. "I have a terrible feeling about this whole thing."

Yet the deed was done, Ted said. As the best-known of the devil's advocates, he and his staff would be scrutinized for any lapse in enthusiasm. There could be no sign of ambivalence, he told his aide.

A few nights later, at a New York dinner party, Jacqueline Kennedy took Schlesinger aside.

"Do you know what I think will happen to Bobby?" she asked.

"No," said Schlesinger.

"The same thing that happened to Jack," she said.

ROBERT KENNEDY SPED OFF to campaign in college field houses, city streets, chaotic motorcades, and rope lines where thousands reached out to touch, to grasp, to rip his shirt and steal his cuff links and leave his wrists bloodied, scratched, and raw. If Ted disapproved of the campaign, he must have recognized his own responsibility for it, hearing how what he had discovered in Vietnam—accounts of corruption, and the deaths of innocents—regularly appeared in Robert's speeches. Where Ted spoke of doctrinal errors, Robert now raged like an Old Testament prophet.

"Can we ordain to ourselves the awful majesty of God—to decide what cities and villages are to be destroyed, who will live and who will die, and who will join the refugees wandering in a desert of our own creation?" he asked students at Kansas State University in his first campaign address.

Ted's initial assignment was in Washington. His aides were dispatched to find a campaign headquarters and set up phone banks. He worked the telephone, talking to lawmakers and governors, mayors and state chairmen, union leaders and activists, and reporting his findings to the "boiler room girls," a group of sharp young women who ran the delegate-tracking operation from a locked and windowless chamber of bulletin boards, maps, desks, and telephones. They, in turn, kept him busy with "action items" to allot. The calendar did not look promising. Robert's indecision had cost them the chance to compete in the Democratic primaries in New Hampshire, Wisconsin, and Massachusetts—which Ted had long since ceded to McCarthy's brigades, after declining to run as a stand-in for Johnson. California and New York, in June, were naturals—but to get there Robert would have to run, and win, in conservative Indiana and Nebraska.

In late March, Ted Kennedy dispatched Gerard Doherty to Indianapolis to gauge Robert's chances in the Indiana primary. Doherty and the three Hoosier volunteers who met his plane had less than a week to collect more than five thousand valid signatures from districts scattered around the state and get Robert on the ballot. Michael Riley, thirty, the leader of the state's Young Democrats, was the highest-ranking state party official to offer his help. "I started talking about congressional districts and our contact people. And we didn't have any contact people," Doherty would remember. "I talked about getting petitions. They didn't have any petitions. I talked about getting voting lists. . . . There were no voting lists."

Riley had been recruited by Ted Kennedy. He did not believe that the caller with a heavy Boston accent, phoning him out of the blue and asking him to lead Robert's cause in the state, was actually a Kennedy. It had to be a practical joke. It was only after a follow-up call from Mankiewicz that Riley was persuaded he had been on the phone with the candidate's brother.

Doherty's mind was always churning. In Indianapolis that first trip, he saw Black students wearing Crispus Attucks sweatshirts. As a Massachusetts pol, he knew that Attucks was a man of color whom the British shot and killed in the Boston Massacre in 1770. So Doherty phoned the Crispus Attucks High School principal to see if its marching band would escort Robert Kennedy to the statehouse when he filed the papers for his candidacy. The principal was thrilled. Doherty waited for most of a day, called the principal back, and told him that he was sorry but that, due to a lack of volunteers, the signature drive seemed hopeless and there would be no Kennedy parade for the band to lead. Then, as if the idea had just struck him, Doherty wondered if teams of band members, in uniform, might be willing to stand outside the city's Black churches on Sunday and collect the needed signatures. Of course, said the principal, and the Kennedy campaign's entry into the Indianapolis Black community—and subsequent collection of two thousand signatures—was sealed.

Several of Robert Kennedy's advisers urged him to bypass the state. It was too conservative, they said—an ancestral home to the Ku Klux Klan and the John Birch Society; host to the national headquarters of the American Legion, with hostile right-wing newspapers—and the site of one of brother John's worst showings in 1960. Governor Roger Branigin, running as a favorite son, would be a popular stand-in for Johnson. The governor commanded the state party machinery and treasury, and the resources of most labor unions. "For a Democratic politician to stand up and be counted for Kennedy . . . would be very hazardous," an internal

CBS News political memo, predicting Kennedy's defeat, noted. "The party establishment doesn't want him and in this state the machinery for punishing the mutinous is very efficient."

But Doherty was convinced they could win. Yes, the local registrars were hostile. The Notre Dame "Students for Kennedy" had been roughed up by party regulars as they collected signatures on the streets of South Bend. The local machine had locked Lake County up, forcing the Kennedys to bring in volunteers from Chicago. But these incidents only impressed Doherty of his team's commitment. Seminarians, Black preachers, high school kids were chipping in. "If RFK gets on the ballot," he told Ted, "we can beat Branigin."

Ted backed his man Doherty. They needed to defeat Johnson and McCarthy somewhere. Robert agreed. "If I'm not as good as I think I am, I should find out sooner rather than later," he told his staff. A victory on supposedly hostile terrain could convince the skeptics—doing for Robert what the West Virginia primary accomplished for John in 1960. "The campaign began in Indiana. . . . It was the search for a domino," David Halberstam would write. "Charging in, hoping that somehow Indiana would come around and then topple Nebraska; and then they would topple Oregon which would topple California, which would topple Chicago mayor Richard Daley, the fifty-first state."

Robert campaigned furiously, in city streets and rural courthouse rallies; he paid reverence to local historical sites and took the press corps for a train ride on the Wabash Cannonball. In a year when law and order was a premier issue, he reminded white voters that he was once the country's "chief law enforcement officer." The press accused him of pandering, but African American allies, like Richard Hatcher, the mayor of Gary, just grinned and stuck by him. Most of the gut chores—circulating petitions, organizing, scheduling, registering voters—were handed to Ted Kennedy's people. He had given Doherty the keys, and Indiana rang with Boston accents. "Don't send me any brains" from the New York staff, Doherty told Burke. "I want legs" from Massachusetts. Said Burke of Doherty, "He just keeps walking around like an unmade bed and he gets things done."

"Everybody we had, friends we had, just stayed—lived in that state,"

Ted recalled. As was the case at national headquarters, there was generational and stylistic friction among Ted Kennedy's folks, Robert Kennedy's Senate staff, and the lingering veterans of the New Frontier. "Bobby's people were slash and burn and run riots through a city or a state, whereas the Teddy Kennedy people got Christmas cards for years after from people they had met on the campaign," said Burke. Ted dispatched John Douglas, the son of Illinois senator Paul Douglas, to Indiana as a general peacemaker. "Does Gerry know what he's doing?" Robert asked. Oh yes, Ted would say, and then get on the phone to Doherty and growl, "Gerry, I hope you know what you're doing."

TED WAS IN INDIANAPOLIS on March 31, meeting with Doherty and other local supporters. They paused to watch Johnson's national address on Vietnam, which the president brought to a stunning conclusion. He would focus on peace, said Johnson, and not be a candidate for reelection. Kennedy and the others hustled to Riley's law offices, where they could make phone calls to Democratic leaders around the country. They discovered profound ambivalence. The raison d'être for Robert's campaign had been to topple Johnson. And while it was too late for Humphrey to win the nomination in the primaries, the vice president had many IOUs, from two decades of serving the Democrats, to aid him in the party caucuses and conventions. As John Kennedy's enforcer, Robert had alienated more than his share of these functionaries. He was, moreover, a lightning rod in this electric year. The men on the other end of the telephone were keeping their powder dry.

"Key is in Indiana," Sorensen told a strategy meeting at Hickory Hill. Victory there was now indispensable.

Four days later, as he was leaving Muncie for Indianapolis, word reached Robert Kennedy that Martin Luther King Jr. had been shot in Memphis. Rioters were burning America's cities. The local officials told Kennedy that they could not guarantee his safety if he insisted on making a scheduled appearance in the Black section of Indianapolis. John Lewis, the civil rights activist who, with Walter Sheridan, had advanced the event, argued the opposite: someone had to console the crowd.

Standing on the back of a flatbed truck, in an overcoat that once belonged to his brother John, Robert Kennedy gave perhaps the finest spontaneous address since Agincourt. He spoke about John's assassination, and how a line from Aeschylus, the Greek poet, had comforted him after that awful loss: "Even in our sleep, pain which cannot forget falls drop by drop upon the heart until, in our own despair, against our will, comes wisdom through the awful grace of God."

Then he told the grieving crowd, "What we need in the United States is not division; what we need in the United States is not hatred; what we need in the United States is not violence and lawlessness but love and wisdom and compassion toward one another and a feeling of justice towards those who still suffer. . . .

"Let us dedicate ourselves to what the Greeks wrote so many years ago: to tame the savageness of man and make gentle the life of this world."

There were no riots in Indianapolis that night. Ted thought it one of Robert's finest moments. He included its sentiments in his own talks and speeches many times in the years that followed. When friends and aides would ask him what, amid all his sorrows, was the grail he pursued, he would reply, "To make gentler the human condition."

IN THE EIGHTY-FIVE DAYS that Robert ran for president, Ted took on many chores. He joined Robert, Ethel, and Jacqueline at King's funeral in Atlanta, where the ushers sat him beside Nixon. He spent many nights in Indiana. He had a choice corner suite in the executive offices at the campaign headquarters in Washington, which reflected his position as one of its directors. He shared the duty, with O'Donnell, of acting as a liaison with union leaders, big-city bosses, and other party musclemen in the nonprimary states. He reached out to fellow senators like George McGovern and Fritz Hollings and members of Congress like Dan Rostenkowski of Illinois, Tom Foley in Washington, and Wilbur Mills in Arkansas. Ted and his mother and sisters were prized as surrogates. Often he mixed all these roles, as in the campaign's unavailing effort to stop Humphrey at the Pennsylvania state convention.

Ted's faith in Doherty was repaid on May 7, when Robert Kennedy won the Indiana primary. As Robert watched on election night, McCarthy told his television interrogators that it didn't matter who finished where.

"That's not what my father told me," Robert said. "I always thought it was better to win. I learned that when I was about two."

Charisma, and cash, had prevailed. Riley recalled the day that Leo Racine, a longtime aide to Joseph Kennedy and Stephen Smith, asked him to tag along on an errand. A pilot flew them in a private plane to Chicago, where Racine picked up two suitcases, packed with currency, to take back to Indiana. Jerry Kretchmer, a New Yorker ordered to help organize Gary for the Kennedys, was handed signed blank checks and told to spend what was needed. Robert Fitzgerald, the Kennedy brothers' cousin, traveled to the city with an attaché case of cash. "We would sit in Mayor Hatcher's office. We would see the captains. We would have the cash and we would give them the money," Kretchmer recalled.

As the primary approached, Smith called the Kennedy district leaders to a meeting in a room at the Indianapolis Athletic Club. On a table, in bundles of all denominations, was $100,000 or more. Each local captain stated what was needed to get out the vote—$14,000 for the Eighth District, $10,000 for three wards in Marion County, and so on—and left with that amount in a paper grocery sack. By the end of April, the campaign had shipped 955,000 tabloid pamphlets and flyers, 412,250 bumper stickers, 109,000 posters, and 489,600 photographs of RFK to Indiana. Some 15,000 Kennedy block captains, and thousands of student volunteers, were invited to "thank you" parties on the Sunday before the voting, given a pep talk, and told how to provide babysitters, and rides to the polls, on election day. The wash of cash did not stop Ted and Robert Kennedy, who never carried money, from turning to Riley and having him make the offering when the collection plate was passed at St. John the Evangelist.

But more than money fueled the victory. The candidate had given everything, spoken from the heart, preached movingly of love and justice, and demonstrated his ability to pull votes both from Black communities and from white folks who still believed in Kennedys. "Our greatest strength lies among blue collar workers [and] Negroes," one internal memo noted.

ON MAY 14, Kennedy won over the farmers of Nebraska, where he gave McCarthy—the midwesterner—a 52-to-31-percent drubbing. But McCarthy's cool mien was the better fit for misty Oregon, and two weeks later he handed the Kennedys their first defeat, 44 to 38.

"In Oregon our people did the best they could. They were a little out of place . . . pine trees and eagles . . . and it's nice and there's no hurly-burly," Burke remembered. "It's not like Indianapolis where you've got tough ethnic groups and if you don't buy a $5000 ad in their paper they'll editorialize against you. The real tough stuff . . . our guys knew how to handle very well. Oregon was sort of different. There was too much sun and air and not enough [smoke-filled] rooms."

The primary season was nearing an end. Kennedy needed to put McCarthy away in California. Then, he reasoned, he would have a body of evidence to take to party regulars like Daley, who, while fond of their ebullient vice president, doubted that Humphrey could beat Nixon.

"Bobby was by this time a hot campaigner. . . . He felt the surge that was moving for him. He identified with the people who were going out and supporting him. He enjoyed the enthusiasm," Ted recalled. "It was just a fit between Bobby and California. That whole momentum, all of it, just took off, and we could feel it, see it, and it caught him up."

Ten

TO SAIL BEYOND . . .
THE WESTERN STARS

T he election night rally was rowdy, with that tension which marked the last days of the Sixties, when heroes were dying and the search for transcendence veered toward the desperate. "The drinks were free," wrote San Francisco's bard, Herb Caen, "the bartenders hard-working and heavy-handed." When Ted Kennedy entered California Hall to claim victory in the state's presidential primary on behalf of his brother Robert, he walked into delirium. It was a near-run thing, and the new electronic vote-counting system had proved balky, delaying results almost until midnight, but Robert Kennedy had defeated Eugene McCarthy.

The hall was a monstrous *rathaus* on the fringe of the Tenderloin, built by German immigrants for dances and vaudeville in the decade after the 1906 earthquake and fire. In a city famous for its gay population, it had served as San Francisco's own Stonewall Inn—the site of a costume ball on New Year's Eve 1964 whose gay attendees, harassed by police, battled back. More recently, despite its lame acoustics, it hosted rock concerts—benefits for legal marijuana and sexual freedom with headliners like the Grateful Dead or Janis Joplin. The Hells Angels partied there. By the summer of 1968 rock and roll music had an edge, as did the politics, and the drugs. The groovy days were passing, the decade's hopes for social justice and peaceful change dissolving in a tide of killing—the 1963 slaying of John Kennedy, the 1965 assassination of Malcolm X in New York, and the murder of King in Memphis.

Militance aimed to take King's place. David Burke would remember that as the senator took the stage in California Hall, there were signs hanging from the balcony on behalf of the Oakland Seven, a group of activists opposed to the draft and the war in Vietnam who had battled the police in the streets. Others in the hall chanted "Free Huey!" in support of Huey Newton, the Minister of Defense of the Black Panther Party—due to face trial for murder after a confrontation with police that left an officer dead. Two young men, identified as Panthers, would be arrested that evening for tossing firebombs into McCarthy headquarters.

It was a smashmouth year. The Left had split when Robert Kennedy joined the race; McCarthy's legions saw him as an opportunist. "Sorry I can't join you," the New York columnist, Murray Kempton, had said in a telegram to Ted. "Your brother's announcement makes clear that St. Patrick did not drive out all the snakes from Ireland." There were ominous portents in the Golden State. Robert was spat on at San Francisco State University and cursed by the Panthers in a confrontation in Oakland. An underground paper had advised its readers not to waste their vote on Kennedy: "They're going to kill him." Before leaving for Los Angeles on election eve, his caravan had inched through San Francisco's Chinatown, where the sudden rip of firecrackers caused friends and loved ones to recoil.

As Robert celebrated victory in Los Angeles, Ted was in San Francisco because John Seigenthaler, the Northern California coordinator, had needed a dose of charisma onstage to reward the faithful.

"Send me a Kennedy," he had told Robert.

"Great. Who do you want?" the candidate had asked.

"If he'll come, Teddy is best," Seigenthaler said.

Though known for his love of a good time—with Joan away in Paris, he had been spotted by the local newspaper partying with the city's smart set and a lovely young woman named Helga Wagner that week—Ted

Kennedy chose not to linger in the frenzy at California Hall. "The whole night started off terribly," Burke recalled. They were shoved and jostled as the senator made his way through "a noisy crazy crowd." In those days "there was no security . . . there was a balcony with overhanging signs— free the such-and-such five or something . . . [people] yelling at us. . . . We realized we had to get out of there."

The campaign had a bank of three television sets offering the election results onstage, and after watching his brother claiming victory ("Now it's on to Chicago, and let's win there!") at an equally raucous rally in the Ambassador Hotel in Los Angeles, Ted Kennedy gave his thank-yous and pushed his way to the exit. He left with Burke for the Fairmont Hotel, some fifteen blocks away.

Seigenthaler, following them, heard the news on the radio in his car. Robert Kennedy, while making his way through a hotel kitchen pantry at fifteen minutes after midnight, had been shot three times. "I was shattered and torn to hell and back," Seigenthaler remembered. "Had a hard time driving."

Kennedy and Burke made it to the Fairmont, unaware of what had happened in Los Angeles. In the senator's hotel room, they switched on the television for updates. The screen showed shrieking women and weeping, grim-faced men; it took Kennedy a moment to ascertain that he wasn't watching the San Francisco rally he had just left, but the ballroom at the Ambassador in Los Angeles. Someone had been shot. His brother. Ted Kennedy's mind went black.

"WE HAVE TO GET down there," Kennedy told Burke. A local congressman, Phillip Burton, had the Air Force ready a passenger jet. After talking to Humphrey on the telephone—who agreed to have the military fly a first-rate brain surgeon from Boston to California—Kennedy made ready to leave. There was jostling and pushing, and lights and cameras, as he made his way through the marbled pillars in the Fairmont lobby at 1:15 a.m. On the drive to Hamilton Air Force Base, Kennedy sat up front in a Highway Patrol car, controlling his emotions, silent and staring ahead as they crossed the Golden Gate Bridge into Marin County.

By the time he climbed aboard the airplane with his cousin Robert Fitzgerald, Burke, and Seigenthaler, Ted had spoken by telephone with the Kennedy entourage in Los Angeles. It wasn't hopeless, Ted told Seigenthaler— there was that expert neurosurgeon en route from Boston—but it didn't look good either. Kennedy remained silent on the short flight south; it was hard to speak above the engine noise in any case, and the passengers stayed lost in thought, or quietly weeping. "I couldn't console him. I didn't know how," said Seigenthaler. "But boy he sure knew how to help me through it and I was crying some of the time and I guess he was too. . . . And I mean, you know, here's somebody who is in his own mind going through questions about who and why, twice lightning has struck. . . . I stopped thinking about him as a younger brother."

Just before 3 a.m., about the time that Ted was arriving in Los Angeles, Robert Kennedy was taken into an operating room. For almost four hours the surgeons tried to remove the fragments of bullet and bone that extended to the core of his brain. They concluded that, "given the damage, even if Kennedy could survive the initial insult, his neurological outcome would be tragic," the patient's charts said. He would no longer be Robert. Ted arrived at the hospital in a state of frozen grief and fury. He first saw his brother in recovery. The side of Robert's head was shaved, sutured, and bandaged, his face bruised and blackened. He lay on an iced cooling blanket, connected by tubes and wires to life-maintaining machinery. The surgeon from Boston offered little hope. By evening, Robert Kennedy's brain waves were flat. He died after midnight.

Ted Kennedy had spent that day making phone calls to his parents and other members of their family, talking to the medical staff, and kneeling in prayer at the foot of Robert's bed. "You didn't want to believe the worst. I didn't want to believe the worst and wouldn't believe the worst," he remembered. "Then you're confronted with the reality of his presence, and my presence, in the room. Then it's the reality and . . . you have a difficult time letting him go." He spoke like that in painful times—slipping into the second person—guarded against revelation, distancing himself from feelings.

Mankiewicz, the press secretary, had the duty to convey word from the family, gathered around the deathbed, to the world. After paying his own last respects to his dying friend, he had passed the adjoining bathroom, where Ted Kennedy stood bent in semi-darkness, his hands gripping the sides of the sink. "I had never seen—nor do I expect ever again to see—a human face so contorted in agony. Ted's face twisted, his eyes unseeing and beyond tears, beyond pain, truly beyond any feeling I could bring myself to describe."

As Kennedy and John Tunney rode the hospital elevator to the morgue with Robert's body, the doors opened and Allard Lowenstein joined them. "Bobby's gone," Lowenstein told Kennedy. "You're all that we've got."

So soon, and "shaken to my core," Kennedy would remember, "I was implored to rejoin the political whirlwind." He made to follow his brother's body to the autopsy table, but Tunney stopped him. "Remember him the way he was," said the congressman. "Don't look."

TED JOINED HIS SISTERS Jean and Pat; Jean's husband, Stephen; and Robert's widow, Ethel, to plan the funeral. They would hold a Requiem Mass at St. Patrick's Cathedral in New York and bury Robert next to John in Arlington National Cemetery. A train would carry Robert's body from New York to Washington, DC. Ted went to a funeral home with Burke, and chose the coffin, of African mahogany. He was addled by grief, could not deal with a funeral director trying to sell him a fancier model. For part of the day, he paced the blacktop hospital parking lot with Charles Evers, whose own brother Medgar, a civil rights leader, had been murdered in Mississippi in 1963.

Joan had been visiting Eunice and her husband, Sargent Shriver, the American ambassador to France, in Paris; the three of them were soon on a jet airliner, crossing the Atlantic. Jacqueline Kennedy joined them all in Los Angeles. At the hospital, she met up with Mankiewicz. "Well, now we know death, don't we—you and I," she said. Johnson had dispatched a presidential aircraft to bear Robert Kennedy's body to New York. She refused to board until she was assured it was not the same silver-and-blue Air Force One that had carried her and her husband's body home from Dallas.

In New York, an assortment of Kennedy aides and friends met to handle the scores of details. Michael Schwartz, an aide to Robert, was taken aback as the older hands drew on their experience from President Kennedy's funeral. "It was such a moment of horror," he would remember, and "they had a precedent."

ON THE FLIGHT TO New York from Los Angeles, Ted and Ethel— pregnant with her eleventh child—snatched bits of sleep in the compartment of the airplane that bore the mahogany casket. A few friends were invited to spend time there; they found Ted cold with anger at a society that gave birth to faceless crazed assassins. In New York, he helped carry his brother's coffin from the airplane and rode in the hearse from LaGuardia Airport to the cathedral, past the thousands dotting the sidewalks of middle-class Astoria, the projects of Spanish Harlem, and the posher precincts of the Upper East Side. Inside the cathedral, he comforted the sobbing Jacqueline and then, sitting, kneeling, or pacing with a rosary in hand, joined an honor guard of Robert's friends as they started an all-night vigil. Before morning, red-eyed and his face swollen from grief and lack of sleep, he stopped in at the Kennedy family business office, in the Pan American Building, to supervise the funeral arrangements.

So Thursday passed to Friday, the day that a hundred thousand people walked by the bier to pay their respects, shuffling in a line that stretched more than a mile among the skyscrapers of midtown Manhattan. "World statesmen in formal dark suits stood next to Harlem school boys in torn Levi's and sneakers; Wall Street stockbrokers with morocco briefcases under their arms walked behind flower children with daisy chains in their hair," wrote J. Anthony Lukas, the lead writer for the *New York Times.* "Suburban housewives in trim fashionable suits waited side by side with young Puerto Rican girls who fingered worn rosary beads."

It was hot, humid. Some waited for eight hours before their time came to genuflect or kneel and say a prayer or touch the flag-draped coffin in the cool cathedral. "Most striking of all," Lukas wrote, "was the response from the poor and the underprivileged, the racial and religious minorities . . . as well as the young." On the same front page, in a story about the political aftershocks of Robert's assassination, was a nod to the growing "emotional appeal" among Democrats for "his brother to take his place."

Early on Friday, Ted met in a hotel room with Tunney and Milton Gwirtzman, the family speechwriter. He had decided to speak at his brother's funeral, and they met to share thoughts on what he should say. The eulogy would feature Robert Kennedy's words, they agreed, but Ted wanted to add something personal. He wanted to say something about the love he felt for his brother, and the love that Robert had shown for the dispossessed.

After a night of preparation and some sleepless wandering about the city, Kennedy opened Saturday's funeral Mass with a selection from one of his brother's finest speeches—the "ripple of hope" address Robert gave in South Africa in 1966. But it was Ted Kennedy's closing words—those that Gwirtzman shaped for him, words about love—that echo through the years.

"My brother need not be idealized or enlarged in death beyond what he was in life," Kennedy said. "He should be remembered simply as a good and decent man, who saw wrong and tried to right it, saw suffering and tried to heal it, saw war and tried to stop it."

His voice quavered; he seemed on the verge of losing his composure. Millions—the congregation of the notable, the prelates in the chancel, the worldwide television audience—willed him the strength to go on.

"Those of us who loved him and take him to his rest today," he said, "pray that what he was to us and what he wished for others will someday come to pass for all the world."

Then he closed with the quote, from George Bernard Shaw, that his brother had used to wrap up his speeches in the campaign.

"As he said many times, in many parts of this nation, to those he touched and who sought to touch him:

"'Some men see things as they are and say why. I dream things that never were and say why not.'"

ROBERT KENNEDY'S BODY WAS borne in the last car of a funeral train that, passing through clusters of mourners—color guards, Little Leaguers, nuns, Scouts, women in curlers, workmen of all races—took eight hours to make it to Washington, DC. At times Ted would step out onto the rear platform and make grief-stifled nods of acknowledgment to the crowds.

At Arlington, in the misty night, Robert was buried. John Glenn, the astronaut, handed the flag from the casket to Ted, who turned and gave it to his brother's son and widow. Vanden Heuvel, a friend to both brothers, saw it as the transfer of more than a banner.

"Much against his will," vanden Heuvel remembered, Ted Kennedy "was suddenly the head of this extraordinary family, a position he never aspired to and never expected."

Eleven

WILDNESS

A week after Robert Kennedy's funeral, Ted and his parents filmed a message to the nation from the lawn at Hyannis Port. Joseph sat mutely in his wheelchair as his grieving Hecuba and the last of their sons spoke.

"We cannot always understand the ways of Almighty God, the crosses which He sends us, the sacrifices which He demands of us. But we know His great goodness and His love, and we go on our way with no regrets," Rose said.

Ted was weighted with, and weighing, obligations. He told the country nothing of his plans. "Each of us will have to decide in a private way, in our own hearts, in our consciences, what we will do in the course of this summer and in future summers," he said.

At Kennedy's direction, Dun Gifford—an aide and able yachtsman—chartered a sixty-one-foot yawl, the *Mira*, for Ted. On a shakedown cruise from its berth on Long Island, Kennedy startled Gifford and the boat's Bahamian captain by insisting that he steer the twin-masted craft through unfamiliar waters to a mooring in New London, Connecticut, closing with the dock at a breakneck rate, then spinning the wheel so that the boat gently nestled into place. Kennedy shrugged. "It is your name on the charter contract," he told Gifford.

The *Mira* carried Ted, Joan, and their two children and his nephew John Kennedy Jr. to Rhode Island to see a sailing spectacle: the start of the annual Newport Bermuda Race. It bore Ethel and her children to Martha's Vineyard on a Sunday morning, where they all scrambled off the boat and toddled down the dock to Mass. Kennedy took day sails, for bonfires and cookouts, to tiny Muskeget Island, an uninhabited skerry of dunes halfway between Nantucket and Chappaquiddick. He sailed, as John and Robert had liked to sail, along the fringed coast of Maine.

With cousin Joseph Gargan, he moored for a night of revelry in Hadley Harbor, in the Elizabeth Islands. He traveled to Greece with Jacqueline Kennedy to meet with her prospective husband, the shipping magnate Aristotle Onassis, and, in the presence of a *Life* magazine correspondent, to chat up two women. One was a blonde with "cerulean eyes," the journalist reported. "There are some things, I am sure, in hindsight, he wished hadn't happened that summer and did," said Gifford. "But so be it."

There were other occasions when Kennedy fled the *Mira*, took the tender to shore, and walked the dunes alone. In late July, he traveled to Capitol Hill, but, once outside the Senate Office Building, he could not find the will to enter.

The violence, death, and loss he had experienced in the space of five years had reshaped him. Indelibly. The impish, lighthearted Teddy could still declare himself. At his core was that joie de vivre that drink and song and fellowship could revive. But, incredibly, at thirty-six, he was the unready heir of all things Kennedy: a legacy, a faction, a clan—and memories. Sadness was now a constant companion—sadness and its consort, despair.

"Whatever justice there was, whatever the meaning of life in terms of spirituality and reliance and source of strength that would come from my faith—I found it was pretty empty," he would recall. "I mean . . . the losses, his loss. All these children growing up without the kind of extraordinary human beings that both of my brothers were. . . . I just sort of checked out."

He took Robert's eldest son to Spain. He grew a beard with strands of red. He called contingents of family advisers to Hyannis Port to discuss, over chowder, plans for a memorial to Robert, and his own political future. He went drinking with a detachment of Green Berets who had come to demonstrate their skills, rappelling on the gables of the family home. After draining their glasses at a local tavern, they smashed them on the floor—a Kennedy tradition. He spoke of quitting politics. "He had a hard time," Gifford recalled. At times, at home, he might instantly, quietly start to weep.

"Devastation," Kennedy called it. "My only defense against giving in to it was to keep active, keep moving, keep churning forward. I feared that despair and darkness might overtake and smother me." If his bond with the sea was not fixed already, it was sealed in grief that summer.

I surrendered myself to the sea and the wind. . . . I let my mind drift, when it would, from my sorrows to a semblance of the momentous joy I have always felt at the way a sailboat moves through the water. . . . On these nights in particular, my grieving was subsumed. . . . The darkness helped me to feel the movement of the boat, and the movement of the sea, and it helped displace the emptiness inside me with the awareness of *direction*. . . .

A sail from Cape Cod to Maine, with a southwest breeze, is a glorious adventure, and it's a trip that Bobby and I had enjoyed together in years past. . . .

The North Star guides you through the evening. Its light is the most definite thing you can see on the surface of the dark water. And so you have the North Star, and the sound and swell of the shifting water. And sometimes the fog will come in and you must go by the compass for a period. But you are always waiting to see the North Star again, because it is the guide to home port; it is the guide to home. . . .

You are a part of the beginning, you are a part of the end. You are a part of the ship and a part of the sea. I gazed at the night sky often on those voyages, and thought of Bobby.

FINALLY, more than two months after Robert's death, Ted Kennedy returned to public service, with a speech at Holy Cross College in Worcester.

He began by thanking his constituents for their concern, including

the many who, fearing a third assassination, had urged him to leave political life "for safety's sake, and for my family's sake." He spoke of how he
had "spent much of my time with the sea; clearing my mind and spirit."

"But there is no safety in hiding," he said. "The only path is to work, in
whatever way we can, to end the violence and the hatred, and the division
that threatens us all."

He would not retire from politics and take his shattered family toward
whatever recovery, and happiness, was attainable in private life.

"Today I resume my public responsibilities," he said. "Like my brothers before me I pick up a fallen standard. Sustained by the memory of
our priceless years together, I shall try to carry forward that special commitment to justice, to excellence, to courage that distinguished their
lives."

The "fallen standard" speech was, otherwise, about the war in Vietnam. The Democratic Party was still riven, with Humphrey, its prospective
presidential nominee, defending Johnson's policies against the clamorous
antiwar forces. The Democratic convention was scheduled to convene the
following week, and the war's critics sought to use the party platform as a
vehicle for dissent. Kennedy's speech put him squarely in their camp.
Crafted by his brothers' writers, it was a template for a Democratic "peace
plank"—with a call for a cessation of U.S. bombing and a withdrawal by
American and North Vietnamese forces.

That week, in a private meeting at his McLean home, Kennedy
spurned Humphrey's pleas to join him on the ticket.

"Unequivocal?" Humphrey asked.

"It is," said Kennedy.

"Is the door ajar, is the key in it, or is it locked?" Humphrey asked him.

"The door is locked," said Kennedy.

Given what followed, locking that door seems a squandered opportunity. A Humphrey-Kennedy ticket may well have united the party, defeated
Nixon, maintained the Democratic hold on the working class, wound
down the war, and advanced the liberal cause. Senior Democrats would
have welcomed it. Kennedy could have signed on with Humphrey without
risking his Senate seat and, had they won, grown as a national candidate

and vice president. But Robert Kennedy's supporters were wounded and wretched, dead set on ending the war, and in no mind to make peace with Johnson and Humphrey.

Or with McCarthy. The Minnesota senator was unnerved by Kennedy's assassination. Instead of working to unite the Left, he squandered the summer, and the faith of his young rebels, in ever-higher zeniths of ambivalence. "McCarthy just tuned out entirely," supporter John Shattuck recalled. Instead of rallying and uniting the antiwar forces, and leading them to Chicago, the senator gave up. "He just became utterly monastic. . . . What little personal fire there was in him about the campaign . . . just died completely."

Some of the war's opponents rallied around the hasty, surrogate candidacy of Senator George McGovern of South Dakota. Others, who had lost faith in organized politics, filled the lakeside parks and streets of Chicago, preparing to march on the convention hall and into battle with Mayor Daley's police. There things stood on the eve of the convention when a notion of astonishing simplicity—Ted Kennedy for President!—roared through the toddlin' town.

EARLIER THAT SUMMER, IN the last week of July, Kennedy had taken friends on a cruise to Maine. It was a family tradition—to sail by day, then crowd ashore for food and drink, hot showers, and softer bedding at the summer estates of wealthy folk like the Tunney family, IBM chairman Tom Watson, or former Treasury secretary Douglas Dillon. Among such stops, word reached Kennedy that Chicago mayor Richard J. Daley wished to speak to him. He went ashore and called the mayor from a dockside pay phone in the little port of Stonington.

Daley was the last all-powerful big-city boss. His alliance with the Kennedys went back to the 1960 presidential campaign, when "with a little bit of luck and the help of a few close friends," he had delivered just enough votes from Chicago to give Illinois to the Democrats. Now the mayor was worried about the 1968 election. He had scanned the landscape, made

phone calls, heard from pollsters, and concluded that the Kennedy name
on the national ticket would go a long way toward bringing his party together in victory. Daley wasn't talking about Kennedy for president—not
yet. He wanted to know if the senator was open to running for vice president. It would add five million votes, a Harris poll had concluded. "Adding Teddy Kennedy to the ticket would result in a Democratic landslide,"
Lyndon Johnson's pollster told the president.

Kennedy was evasive. And so Daley told the press that Kennedy was
"considering" the prospect, igniting the intended sensation. Kennedy, unhappy, made another visit to the village pay phone, and his office issued a
statement saying that the senator was flattered—but would not accept the
second spot. Daley went to ground for several weeks. But the mayor was
back on the eve of the convention, promoting another idea to excite Democrats. Since Kennedy was a uniquely unifying figure, Daley decided, the
senator should be its nominee for president. Kennedy was wary that the
mayor was scheming to lure him back to national politics, only to saddle
him with the vice presidential nomination. But he sent an emissary, Stephen Smith, to Chicago.

Kennedy had no plans to attend the convention. He had turned down
the opportunity to introduce a filmed tribute to Robert, which, thought
those who remembered John Kennedy rousing a convention in 1956 and
Robert Kennedy in 1964, might have triggered insurrection in the hall.
On Friday, August 23, with the convention set to convene on Monday,
Smith met with the mayor, and returned to the Cape with the word that
Daley's offer was sincere. On Saturday, Daley called Kennedy, urging him
to come to Chicago, or signal his willingness to accept a draft. Kennedy
put him off and went sailing. Daley kept pushing. On Sunday, the Illinois
delegation unexpectedly declined to endorse Humphrey, and the mayor
met with the California delegation's leader, Jesse Unruh, to promote a
Kennedy candidacy.

Kennedy sent Smith back to the Loop. The senator was tantalized,
swayed by the telephone calls he was receiving from Democratic figures,
urging him to run. He asked John Tunney to sleuth around as well. His

instructions to Tunney were clear. "If it was possible," Tunney recalled, "we would put something together. . . . I didn't go there for my health."

Kennedy "had not yet slammed the door," Richard Goodwin remembered. The news spread through the city, and its effect was electric—an "emotional spasm," Goodwin called it. Ten thousand "Draft Ted" lapel stickers were distributed in a day. Columnists weighed in on "Kennedymania." Even McCarthy seemed amenable. He sent promising words via emissaries like Ken Galbraith and Goodwin. "Of course, he's young, but then, those fellows in the Revolution were young too—Jefferson and Hamilton," McCarthy told Goodwin. "Let's see how things develop."

For most of three days, working the phones, taking a count, meeting with McCarthy and other Democratic leaders, spied on by the press and inspiring speculation, Smith served as Kennedy's pathfinder. He was aided by Unruh, Tunney, Doherty, Seigenthaler, David Hackett, Fred Dutton, and others. He came to believe, and reported to Ted, that it was real; it could be done. "The momentum was there . . . the madness was in the air," said Burke. Kennedy would have felt it, would not have been so conflicted, if only he had gone to Chicago, said Lowenstein. Daley brought them Illinois. Unruh was the key to California. To that formidable beginning they could add Robert's delegates from New York, Indiana, Nebraska, and South Dakota. And McGovern's troupe. And—though the haughty McCarthy told Smith that while he was willing to stand aside for Ted, "I could never have done it for Bobby"—they might count, in the end, on McCarthy's delegates from Massachusetts, Oregon, New Hampshire, and Wisconsin. "There were legitimate inquiries made and potentialities explored," Kennedy acknowledged.

After Russell Long told William vanden Heuvel that Louisiana would swing from Humphrey to Kennedy, vanden Heuvel placed a call to the Cape. They could do it. They could stop Humphrey on the first ballot. The presidency was a mighty peak, he told Kennedy, and they might never climb so high again.

"No," Kennedy told vanden Heuvel, and Smith, and others who urged him to run. "I'm not going to do it."

WITH THE PASSAGE OF years, and wisdom earned, Kennedy looked back at Chicago and 1968 and cited the sentiments of Brutus, from Shakespeare's *Julius Caesar*, a play with worn pages and underlined stanzas that he kept upon his desk.

> There is a tide in the affairs of men.
> Which, taken at the flood, leads on to fortune.
> Omitted, all the voyage of their life is bound in shallows and in miseries.

Kennedy sensed the passing tide—the "tyranny of time" he called it—at Hyannis Port that summer, but made from it a jest.

"You know, someday I'm going to be in Coos Bay, Oregon, or someplace like that, and I'll just have blown my last chance at the nomination, and I'm going to call you and remind you of what we decided here," he told Burke as they shut down Kennedymania. "You'll regret it ten years from now, when you're nobody and you could have been and this could have been, and I could have been."

So many could-have-beens. But it is difficult to see how Kennedy could have made a different choice. "I was too vulnerable," he would tell a reporter six months later. He was just one year past the constitutional requirement for the presidency, and years younger than his brother John was when he took office at forty-three. Ted had shown fortitude, grace, and resilience to the world in the days after John's assassination, during his recuperation from the 1964 plane crash, and at Robert's funeral in June. He had displayed promise in his six years in the Senate. He could bring talented cadres of New Frontiersmen to the White House to help him. But the challenges he would face—ending the war, racial strife—would ultimately destroy the presidencies of Lyndon Johnson and Richard Nixon, two far more experienced, wily politicians. And Ted was a broken man. And knew it.

"Here would appear . . . the opportunity to carry out in the most effective way possible the things Bobby had lived and died for," he told his old Harvard friend Burton Hersh. "On the other side was the complete real loss of spirit in terms of willingness to run. I just didn't have the stomach for that. I didn't feel I was personally equipped for the race; I thought it was much too great a burden to place on my family. . . . People would be considering the candidacy for entirely the wrong reasons."

"They'd say that I was just an overly ambitious thirty-six-year-old kid, trying to make it on a wave of sympathy over Robert's death," Kennedy told Stephen Smith.

"He was afraid because all of a sudden, there it was, right in front of him. It could possibly happen," said Burke, "and he wasn't ready and he knew it. . . . His brother had just been murdered, and he was a hurt person."

THEN THERE WAS THIS. Hundreds of miles from the arena floor, Kennedy could ask distanced, informed questions about the motivations—and arithmetic—of his giddy well-wishers, spies, and operatives. And the solidarity of the Humphrey delegates was impressive. There were few deserters from the vice president's strong hold on regular Democrats and union delegates in Pennsylvania and the industrial Midwest. The South, whipped by Johnson's lieutenants, stayed in line. And with each passing hour, as the Chicago police bludgeoned antiwar demonstrators in the streets, a Daley-McCarthy-Kennedy alliance seemed more unlikely. The party was being ripped apart. Even if they managed to deny Humphrey on the first ballot, what was to stop Johnson from arriving in Chicago to reassert order, or to claim the nomination himself? For that was the other mad rumor sweeping Chicago.

The media, especially the television networks, were delighted to have a story; there was ratings gold in a Kennedy surge. It was "inescapably romantic," Theodore White wrote. "The prince returning to claim his inheritance, his people on the floor rising to reclaim honor from chaos and squalor." But the surge was also "leaderless, incohesive . . . [and] insubstantial." And Kennedy, "with impeccable correctness, braced by the clarity which distance gave him, behaved well and wisely."

"You were probably the only winner," Galbraith wrote Kennedy, when the chaos of a convention was over. "I . . . for two or three hours allowed myself to think there might be something there. But by my mathematics Hubert still had the votes and nothing could hurt you as much as a false try or . . . a draft that failed.

"Delegates have their minds made up . . . by themselves or someone else, by the time they get to the convention, and only the amateurs and the television men suppose otherwise," Galbraith wrote. "At Chicago I don't think Jesus himself . . . could have picked up more than twelve and a half votes, always assuming he could have gotten in with the beard.

"You were right to stop it," Galbraith wrote. "I for one was greatly relieved when you did."

As ALWAYS, there was family—family to exemplify, family to safeguard, family to lead. Joseph Kennedy was a wraith; Joe, Jack, and Bobby gone. Joan was terrified by the violence in Chicago. Once Ethel gave birth to her last child, Rory, in December, Ted would have thirteen fatherless nieces and nephews and his own three children to mentor. Had they all been the brood of an Irish workingman, the load would be heavy enough. But anonymity was not theirs. They were, all of them, *Kennedys*—blessed and consigned to privilege and celebrity. Every move would be scrutinized, every misstep or weakness or sin exposed. There was no pause for counseling, no time for grieving. "Either you survive or you succumb," Rose said coolly. "If you survive, you profit from the experience. . . . I made up my mind that I wouldn't allow it to conquer me." Jacqueline and Ethel did their widow's duty, she said approvingly. "They have never really distressed us by an undue demonstration of grief or sorrow."

Ted was now the flagbearer. It was not supposed to be this way. He was never raised to lead. Who could have imagined—three brothers and a sister dead. "He was having to say . . . 'I'm the oldest. Now what? What am I going to do?' That's the thing," said Gifford. "Grieving is one thing . . . but then you think, *Oh my God, now what? Now they're all going to be looking at me.* And they were, everybody."

"EVERYBODY" included the hate-filled and the crazy.

Assassination was not an exclusively American malady, but the country's virulent mix of accessible firearms, fomenting media, and startling cultural change incited deadly violence throughout the 1960s. Of the candidates running in 1968, Reagan and Nixon and Wallace would all be targets of bloody assassination attempts during their careers. In the coming years, two armed assassins would enter Kennedy's Senate office but be thwarted by Capitol security. It was realistic to expect that in a crowd, or from a window, shots would be fired by a mad individual intent on killing the last Kennedy brother. "When they got Jack," Ted told vanden Heuvel, "that was perhaps an accident of history, but when they killed Bobby, that was not."

It was not that he believed in the conspiracy theories, said vanden Heuvel, "he just felt that there were forces in motion that were so dark and so determined to destroy what the Kennedys represented that he would be the immediate target." It was a prevalent fear for Joan and Rose, and among the senator's aides, and friends and family members, and for his children as they grew.

Amid the boom at the Chicago convention, Lowenstein had come upon Charles Evers—the civil rights activist whose brother Medgar had been murdered by white supremacists in Mississippi—and sought to sell him on a Kennedy candidacy.

"Uh-uh," said Evers. "You're not going to do it to that family a third time."

There was a sense "that we would send him off to get assassinated, and that was not right," Lowenstein recalled.

Hardball politics . . . duty and family . . . assassination. There were sound, tangible reasons for Kennedy not to run in 1968. But there was, as well, an ineffable factor that stayed his hand and helps to explain the chaotic months and years that followed. Depression, despair, anxiety, and darkness are the words that he, and his intimate friends and family, used to describe his mental state. He was by all accounts a psychological wreck. By the following spring his friends would add "reckless" to their characterizations. "T.M.B.S.," he would murmur to his aides—Too Many Blue Suits—as he felt himself encircled, crushed by obligation.

Robert's death had wrecked Kennedy's internal gyroscope, torn him from his moorings, cost him his faith, left him adrift, abandoned, with a hunger for ameliorating sensation. He harried Senate aides and women reporters for dates, lost himself in "the frencticism of booze and sex," a friend recalled. In the wake of the assassinations, Joan's reliance on alcohol increased. "In the months and years after Bobby's death, I tried to stay ahead of the darkness. I drove my car at high speeds; I drove myself in the Senate; I drove my staff; I sometimes drove my capacity for liquor to the limit," Kennedy remembered. "I might well have driven Joan deeper into her anguish but the sad truth is that she needed no help from me."

Friends tried, but there was no reaching him. "Ted weathered Jack's assassination really quite well, as I look back on it, because Bobby was there," Tunney would say. Robert "was a colossal human being, and I think that Teddy felt great comfort, quite frankly, in knowing that Bobby was there, the head of the family, and he didn't have to assume that role. He could be just good old Teddy, fun, laughter." Then Robert Kennedy was murdered. And Ted Kennedy's life turned. "Robbie and Eddie" had sustained each other in the years after John's assassination. Their camaraderie in the Senate and their work in Robert's presidential crusade brought them closer still. And so the toll of losing Robert was "exponentially greater" than that of losing John, Ted Kennedy's son Patrick came to believe.

"It's the re-traumatization that exacerbates the original trauma," Patrick said. Over and over, the media promulgated grisly scenes of gunshots, bleeding wounds, and bloodied flowers. And the near-death experience of the 1964 airplane crash—with its own terrors, violent fatalities, and trauma—left Ted in chronic pain, fueling his need for self-medication.

"Ted was deeply hurt by Jack's death, deeply hurt," said Tunney. "It was really very psychologically damaging. But Bobby's death was much worse. . . . He adored his brother, he admired his brother, talked to him all the time. . . . Where you have so much of your soul and spirit embedded in your brother's existence and friendship and companionship, and then to have that taken away in the way that it was. . . .

"He was not able to function effectively for a while," said Tunney. "Part of his brain was not working, and it was because of this extraordinary grief."

Kennedy came to call it "the time of greatest questions."

A PART OF HIM found release in women, fast cars, and alcohol. He and Tunney purchased Pontiac convertibles, and Ted carried on a relationship with Helga Wagner—a carefree, Austrian-born blonde artist and athlete who skied, liked scuba diving, and flew helicopters, and whose appetite for fun matched his. She had entered Ted Kennedy's orbit in the early 1960s when, via one of John Kennedy's golfing partners, she was invited to lunch in Palm Beach to meet the president and got introduced to Ted as well. After marrying a wealthy corporate executive, she moved to San Francisco, where she fell in with Ted's California social set, and the two became romantically involved. She delighted in playing pranks on him—mischievously showing up at his public appearances in a fetching disguise or buzzing him at a football game in her helicopter. "He was a pretty strong presence in my life," she would recall. "When you looked at him . . . he was handsome, wasn't he?" And caring, she decided.

But the premier anodyne for Ted was work. It filled his mind, crowded out the bad thoughts, and fulfilled his sense of obligation. "I have to do work. Work, work, work. Then I can have fun. And when I have fun, it's none of your business. And then I have to work, work, work, work, work," said David Burke. "Work is the answer to a lot of things. You can't be all bad if you're working hard."

The Senate suited him. The chamber was, as Lyndon Johnson once observed, "the right size" for men of certain abilities. Kennedy knew how to employ the advantages bequeathed him by fortune and family. He understood how to leaven his performance with generosity, humor, and bonhomie. He studied his fellow senators, identifying their political needs and ambitions, until he knew just who to ask for help, or who to invite into an alliance, or who was a lost cause, to be battled at all costs. No one out-worked Kennedy and his zealous, top-notch staff. "If he had not been so good at politics, he would not have survived," said Patrick. "He felt that terrible about himself."

THE YEAR 1968 MARKED the start of two decades, and six presidential election cycles, when Ted Kennedy was a recognized candidate, an-nounced or unannounced, for the American presidency. In all the coun-try's history, very few American leaders experienced the demands, the pressure, the expectations of such scrutiny for so long. From the time he was thirty-six until his final withdrawal from presidential contention at the age of fifty-three, he was more than a luckless combatant like Henry Clay, Adlai Stevenson, or William Jennings Bryan. He was a Kennedy, flag-bearer for a restoration. At times, he was said to epitomize his party's soul.

In November 1968, amid the shambles of Humphrey's defeat, Ken-nedy had Gwirtzman draft a five-page memo, to be circulated among other top advisers, on how to prepare for a presidential campaign in 1972. It included tactical details, like the need for a "political person" in every state to represent Kennedy's interests (and the current lack of such a per-son in Texas and the South), the naming of a new press secretary, selection of an ad agency, and what changes he might seek in the party's delegate selection process. There was a broader discussion as well, about the strength and weaknesses of his image.

"Being known, being liked and respected, appealing to various age groups—all these are in very good shape. The only one on which you could be vulnerable is the requirement of age and experience . . . that regardless of views or personality, the candidate can do the biggest job," Gwirtzman wrote. "You are the youngest man ever to be seriously consid-ered for the Presidency, and if you ran at 40 the youngest ever to be elected."

Kennedy was advised to acquire foreign policy and national security credentials, to cultivate the titans of American culture (Billy Graham), labor (George Meany), and business (David Rockefeller) and stage weekly practice sessions for dealing with the press. "It was in him and in the situation," David Burke recalled. "In him because his name was Kennedy, in the situation because he was growing in strength in the Senate. He was gaining a reputation of his own, and the tragic deaths of his brothers placed him in an historic setting.

"From 1968 on, it was a governing factor in his mind. He wanted to someday be the President, and as long as he took care of himself, he could do it rather easily."

So 1968 passed. To the dismay of the Kennedy family, Jacqueline married Onassis in Greece. Ted did not attend. He grew woozy in the operating room as Ethel, in a Cesarean delivery, gave birth to Rory. He returned to the Senate floor to sound an alarm about civil war and famine in Biafra. He was infuriated—the veins stood out in his neck—when he welcomed Humphrey to Boston during the campaign and was met with cascades of catcalls and profane chants from antiwar demonstrators jamming the streets at Downtown Crossing. He got a better reception when, with passion and conviction, he condemned the racist Wallace—the Alabaman who had stood in the schoolhouse door against his brothers—who was running as a third-party candidate that fall. The outcome of the race was so close—Nixon 43.4, Humphrey 42.7, Wallace 13.5—that Kennedy diehards studied the electoral rules that might toss the election to the House of Representatives.

THEN CAME 1969, which Kennedy welcomed with victory.

Over Christmas vacation, Burke had spoken with Charles Ferris, a son of Massachusetts who was now the top aide to Majority Leader Mansfield. Senator Edmund Muskie of Maine had given some thought to challenging Russell Long, the Democratic whip, but decided against it. Might Mansfield look kindly on a Kennedy candidacy? Burke asked. He would indeed, said Ferris.

Ferris was acting, covertly, in Mansfield's interest, and on behalf of Senate liberals in general. Like Kennedy, Long was the heir to a dynasty. He had arrived in the Senate at the age of thirty, and was savvy, ambitious, and a silver-tongued speechmaker. Yet while he had a populist streak—he was, after all, the flush-faced son of the "Kingfish," Huey Long—it did not extend to Black Americans, whom he maligned as ignorant, lazy welfare cheats. Soon after his election as whip (he replaced Humphrey in 1965), Long's seniority gave him the chair of the Finance Committee, where he zealously took to guarding the interests of the oil and gas industry and its right-wing multimillionaires.

The "Princefish," as they called him, was erratic and unpredictable. "Perhaps the son has never equaled his father's famous oration on the virtues of 'potlikker and cornpone,' but few leave the floor or the galleries when Russell Long rises," one scholar noted. He drank too much ("drunk from early in the morning till late at night," the usually circumspect *New York Times* would report) and would wander onto the floor, inebriated and without shoes, offending the sensibilities of traditionalists like Georgia's Richard Russell or John Stennis of Mississippi.

Long was a source of irritation for Mansfield because once he had secured the Finance barony he neglected his duties as whip, which basically ran to watching the floor, adjourning the Senate, and helping the leader count votes—"washing the sweatshirts," as the old ballplayer Eugene McCarthy put it. The whip's job was "not giving orders, but . . . carrying out orders somebody else has left," Long griped, "just a grueling, day-to-day, thankless, time-consuming job of being around when nobody else cares to be." He had decided not to seek another term, until word of Muskie's prospecting stirred Long's competitive juices and moved him to stand for the office again. His resolve was not shaken when his foe turned out to be Kennedy.

Kennedy was on a family vacation, skiing in Sun Valley, Idaho. After speaking to Burke and Ferris, and making calls to Muskie, Humphrey, and Mansfield, he rousted his staff from their holiday snogs and firesides. Furiously, he worked the phone, tracking down Senate colleagues from his room at the Sun Valley Lodge. The Senate was scattered for the holidays. It would not be a race of backroom deals, sealed with a handshake in a wood-paneled office over a drink at dusk. For the most part, Kennedy campaigned on the telephone.

Aside from not being Russell Long, Kennedy offered youth and vigor and a sprinkle of glamour to a Democratic congressional leadership dominated by the well-loved but taciturn sixty-five-year-old Mansfield, and seventy-seven-year-old Speaker John McCormack, which would soon have to take on Richard Nixon. Sugarplum dreams of a Kennedy campaigning at their side danced for the twenty-five Democratic senators facing reelection in 1970. The Fearless Foursome and their liberal colleagues sprang at the chance to shove a southern conservative off the leadership ladder. Just the same, it was a late, and impromptu, action. Kennedy had "little or no chance" of winning, the *New York Times* declared.

On the phone from Mississippi, Eastland sounded puzzled.

"Kinndy! Wha'chew want, Kinndy?"

"I'm calling to say that I'm running for whip of the Senate . . ."

"That job ain't vacant."

"I know. But I want to run anyway."

"Wha'chew wanna run against Russell Long fo?"

"I think I should. I'm calling to solicit your vote, Senator."

"Shee-it."

But Richard Russell, with a nod and a wink, let Kennedy know that while the southerners might not vote for him, neither would they bleed for Long.

"I will put no stone in your path," said Russell.

Kennedy publicly declared his candidacy on December 30, four days before the vote. He set up a command post in his home, and the Kennedy network of donors, state officials, ward heelers, activists, and advisers were soon lobbying the Democrats in the Senate.

A Republican presidency would require fresh tactics, Kennedy told his colleagues, and with his famous name and visage he could give the whip's job, and liberal causes, a profile. He believed this, and so, ultimately, did thirty of his fellow Democrats, forgetting why they were dissatisfied with the incumbent. Nobody asked, if Kennedy was off grandstanding, who was going to wash the sweatshirts. But it was enough to beat the preening Long, who at one point thought he had forty votes, but ended with only twenty-six.

_____

NIXON WAS SWORN INTO office on January 20. Kennedy met him with a challenge. China had become a nuclear power in 1964, prompting Johnson to proceed with plans for an anti–ballistic missile shield (known as the ABM) to protect American cities. On February 1, Kennedy sent a letter to the new defense secretary, Melvin Laird, stating his opposition to the program. It would ignite a new arms race, Kennedy said, and it was "political folly and a serious technical mistake" to believe that such a system would work—or stay anywhere in the region of its proposed $5.5 billion price tag.

Kennedy's opposition was incited by scientists at MIT, Harvard, and elsewhere, who told him that the Pentagon technology was inalterably flawed—and by fifteen hundred people who turned out on a winter night in the Boston suburbs to protest the installation of radar and missiles near Andover. Colleagues across the country, whose own suburban constituents did not care to live next to Soviet missile targets, joined Kennedy. All politics is local.

Nixon deftly parried. To quell the suburban opposition, he abandoned the goal of protecting the cities and proposed to build two ABM sites on the northern Plains, to guard U.S. ICBM silos. The ABM and a companion program to put multiple warheads on a single offensive missile (the multiple independently targetable reentry vehicle, known as MIRV) were essential chips in arms control bargaining with the USSR, the president said. The name of the ABM program was changed from Sentinel to Safeguard, but its critics were not assuaged. Kennedy joined a group of his brother John's former arms advisers in composing an independent analysis—a "Summa Theologica" on the ABM—that was published as a bestselling book. But Kennedy now discovered how his presence—via a kind of political quantum effect—warped the arguments, the outcome, and the stakes.

Kennedy's aide Wayne Owens wrote him on April 10, warning him of the emerging "apprehension" among ABM foes about Kennedy's high profile. There was a growing public feeling "that ABM will be the first skirmish in the Nixon-Kennedy '72 campaign," said Owens. In the Senate, "some are envious of your publicity but they are concerned, too, about the fight becoming a partisan issue and the consequent loss of Republican support."

Furthermore, "there is some sensitivity," Owens said, among senators who worked on arms control or other issues over the years, only to discover that "you had then come along and made a speech on the subject, had gotten a great deal of publicity and immediately, the issue became important and you were a leader." He urged his boss to stay "in the wings" and focus on doing "effective work with the senators themselves . . . while purposely avoiding the frontman role."

Nixon recognized Kennedy's dilemma and exploited it. He saw Kennedy as the Democratic front-runner for 1972, and with the help of some prodding by White House aides, so did the press. The *New York Times* had three articles in the first eight days of April on ABM and the Nixon-Kennedy rivalry. As Nixon's chief of staff, H. R. Haldeman, wrote in his diary, the ABM fight "is the first battle of '72, vs Teddy Kennedy and we *must* win." The spotlight was on the Senate's new whip, the Republicans and conservative Democrats were unsettled by his motives, and the debate would persist all summer.

KENNEDY WAS NOT ONE to stay in the wings. He had no more inclination than Long to be the "legislative concierge," as Burke described it, and tend to mundane chores. The new whip was the last Sixties figure who could lend a marquee name to a cause. Mansfield was being reduced to "a Kennedy legionnaire," a White House lobbyist reported to Nixon. In April, against the wishes of aides and advisers, Kennedy braved threats of violence and flew to seething Memphis to mark the one-year anniversary of King's assassination. As the senator spoke to a crowd of some ten thousand people from the steps of City Hall, the mayor of the city, responding to intermittent rioting and looting, was compelled to impose a curfew and cut off sales of alcohol and firearms. Kennedy was selected to speak first so that he might leave quickly and safely. "We want to save and preserve him," said civil rights leader Ralph Abernathy, "because one day he will be the President of the United States." Kennedy demurred, and stayed for the whole ceremony.

On a Saturday in May, on impulse, Kennedy grabbed Burke and flew off to Los Angeles to join Cesar Chavez and the farmworkers on a long, hot, dusty march for better working conditions. He brought joy and pride to the marchers. The Kennedys "bring you in the front door. They don't make you use the back door," organizer Dolores Huerta remembered. "He came and asked, 'What can I do to help?' It was such an important question." It was the first time he had returned to the city since Robert died, and he arrived as a judge was prepared to sentence the assassin, Sirhan Sirhan. That night, in his hotel room, Kennedy composed a hand-written letter asking the state to spare the killer's life.

"My brother was a man of love and sentiment and compassion," Kennedy wrote. "He was a young man totally committed to life and living. He stood against injustice, poverty and discrimination, for those evils lessened life. He grew to despise war for war denies the sacredness of life.

"We all realize that many other considerations fall within your responsibility and that of the court," he told the judge, "but if the kind of man my brother was is pertinent, we believe it should be weighed in the balance on the side of compassion, mercy and God's gift of life itself."

Kennedy's staff was scrambling to keep up. "You make the best case you can—he does what he wants," Burke said. "Cesar Chavez wants him to come to California. We all say no, couldn't possibly, no security. I spent the whole day reiterating the argument. He called me up at five-fifteen: the plane left at six. Or Memphis. The Martin Luther King funeral anniversary. You go to Memphis, you may not go home. Bricks. Tear gas. He goes."

There were other entailing duties in his role as family patriarch. He set aside time for graduations and other milestones. His staffers rolled their eyes but complied when the next generation of Kennedys asked for help on their term papers. A gang of teens led by some of his nephews was joyfully tormenting their Hyannis Port neighbors: painting graffiti and shooting pellet guns, hijacking bicycles, racing speedboats through the harbor, setting off fireworks, throwing eggs at passing cars. After a country club manager rebuked them for setting fire to their food in the club dining room, someone slashed his tires three nights in a row, and he quit and left town. Kennedy overreacted, defending the cubs like a bear, bullying the complaining neighbors, and calling on IBM counsel Burke Marshall, a former assistant attorney general, for assistance.

"I need not remind you that one is not completely at liberty to make a public distribution of unproven charges against a group of children," Kennedy wrote the concerned neighbors. "Even as juveniles they are protected by law against libel. . . . I cannot see how a meeting with your group would be appropriate or honorable." Over time, the neighbors would be vindicated. Lax supervision, the temptations of youth, and perhaps a genetic predisposition led several of the nephews to addiction.

KENNEDY AND BURKE WOULD differ over who took the initiative—perhaps it occurred to both of them that morning—but on May 20, outraged by accounts of a battle in the Ashau Valley in South Vietnam, Kennedy took the Senate floor—and accosted Nixon on Vietnam. Keeping with tradition, Kennedy had maintained a quiet and supportive posture for four months. No more.

U.S. troops had suffered grievous losses in the ten days and twelve assaults it took to conquer a three-thousand-foot massif near the Lao border, only to turn and march away and relinquish the heights to the enemy. The name of the hill was Dong Ap Bia—the "mountain of the crouching beast." The military planners knew its whorls as Hill 937. The airborne troops who bled and died came to call it Hamburger Hill. Of the 450 men of the 3rd Battalion, 187th Infantry of the 101st Airborne Division who led the fighting, some 320 were killed or wounded.

Kennedy "had worn the army green, and I think the needless slaughter of all those young men really moved him," Gifford recalled. "He was *angry*. . . . We loved that day. It was one of the best days we ever had in that office. Ted took the gloves off, said the right things. We were thrilled. It helped change the debate."

"President Nixon has told us, without question, that we seek no military victory, that we seek only peace," Kennedy told his colleagues. "How then can we justify sending our boys against a hill a dozen times or more, until soldiers themselves question the madness?"

Republican senators responded. The White House joined the fray. Antiwar senators rose to back Kennedy.

"It has been possible for the past six months to nearly forget about the war, push it to the back of the mind," Ward Just wrote in the *Washington Post* on the day after Kennedy roused the Senate. Hamburger Hill "brought us back to reality."

Life magazine published a special issue, with photographs of the 242 Americans who had died in Vietnam the previous week. Kennedy and others followed up. By the fall the conflict would be "Nixon's War."

As with the ABM, Kennedy's status as the Democratic Party's presidential front-runner led some to wonder, in the Senate and the newsrooms, if he was being too aggressive.

"Edward Kennedy has changed," wrote James Reston in the *Times*. "The paralysis of last year is over. He is moving. He has taken up a position, and in the process, he is dominating the Democratic opposition. No doubt events will decide whether he was wise to move so fast and so boldly."

TED KENNEDY'S FEELINGS OF inadequacy, of being an unworthy and unintended heir, could not be assuaged by easy success. His brothers were icons, frozen in youth and time. To him now fell a more arduous duty: to carry that fallen standard, over decades, and deliver.

"The causes with which they were so closely identified have, to a great extent, become my causes," he told the press, "and I am attempting to carry on as best I can."

"We carry on, because we have to, because our loved one would want us to, and because there is still light to guide us in the world from the love they gave us," he would write, years later, to a grieving widow.

To carry on, but not to catch. When he broke with courses charted by his ghosts, it was generally in response to the Democratic Party's ongoing shift leftward. He distanced himself from John's famous challenge to land men on the moon by questioning the cost of the manned exploration of space. He criticized his brothers' use of wiretaps, as the details of their surveillance of King became public. But mostly he honored John and Robert, throughout his public life, by espousing their causes: immigrants, health care, a decent wage for workers, civil rights, hunger, poverty, and disarmament.

For America's Indians, he assumed Robert's mantle as an advocate for the tribes. With all his other duties, and with little political payoff, he took it on himself to wedge Indian health and education, land and water rights, and other tribal issues onto his agenda and daily schedule. "I generally managed to keep my public duties and my private anguish separated," he would write in his memoirs. "Whatever excesses I invented to anesthetize myself, I could almost always put them aside in my role as senator. Almost, but not always."

That spring, Kennedy's involvement in Indian affairs took him to Alaska, at the head of a bipartisan delegation and a posse of two dozen reporters, for a three-day, thirty-six-hundred-mile tour of villages in the bush country, capped by a hearing on Native American education in Fairbanks. He exulted, out north of the Arctic Circle, landing on frozen rivers and riding snowmobiles and dogsleds under the northern lights, but got ambushed by three Republican senators who had accompanied him when they walked out on the trip. They complained that the exercise was a Kennedy "publicity stunt paid for at the taxpayers' expense," with camera crews and reporters traipsing through villages and exploiting the native Alaskans' poverty. Their mutiny "was not an isolated incident," *Time* magazine reported. "Since his emergence . . . Republicans have been treating him like an opposition candidate."

Kennedy was tasting the pressures that Robert endured in 1967 and 1968. He was spotted by the press taking nips from a silver hip flask. "First time I've used it," he told a reporter, unconvincingly.

"He had tried most of the other strategies already by that time, the raffishness, the playfulness, the fond exaggerations," wrote Hersh. "But the world, the self, was getting harder and harder to outsmart." When the hearing in Fairbanks was over, and the business part of the trip had ended, he let go—drinking heavily in the hotel bar, at the airport, and on the airplanes home. He roamed the passenger compartment, leading chants of "Eskimo power! Eskimo power!" The reporters, as was custom-ary at the time, kept word of Kennedy's antics from their copy. Several, however, wrote confidential memos to their bosses urging them to pre-pare for an imminent disaster.

"He's living by his gut," Sylvia Wright told her editors at *Life* magazine. "Something bad is going to happen."

"Part of Ted hasn't kept pace in growth with the rest of him," wrote *Newsweek*'s John Lindsay in a memo to his editors. "He doesn't drink well. He gets giddy, sort of out of control, his voice rising rather sharply. . . . This could be a serious problem."

Friends were thinking the same thing. "After the passing of those two heroes in his life, Jack and Bobby, especially after Bobby's assassination, he almost looked like he had a death wish," said Edmund Reggie, a long-time Louisiana associate of the family. "He was just going lickety-split . . . like he didn't care."

"He was throwing himself into these issues with abandon, but almost with reckless abandon. He had almost superhuman energy to be able to do what he was doing, but he hadn't healed. He hadn't healed at all," said Tunney. "I was very worried about Teddy. . . . I could tell that there was a wildness in his brain."

IN EARLY JUNE, an Associated Press reporter shared an airplane ride with Kennedy to the Cape, while preparing a feature story on the senator and the 1972 presidential race. "He is eye deep in politics, moving at a dead run, spreading himself thin," wrote Joseph Mohbat. Swirling a drink as he gazed out the window, Kennedy confessed to a deadening of his soul.

"You know, those kinds of things pretty much turn me off now," said the family's most natural politician, on the daily chores of politics. "The kicks aren't . . . I mean, meeting Molly Somebody and hearing all about her being Miss Something. What's it all for? I used to love it. But the fun began to go out of it after 1963 and then after the thing with Bobby, well."

"I'm really very unresolved right now," he said. Would the country be receptive? Was it the right thing for him and his family? Could he make a contribution as a candidate, as a president?

He needed to catch his breath. To get out on the water. To break his breakneck pace and reflect.

"Maybe over the summer . . . some sailing . . . the family," said Kennedy, half-sentences dangling, with a shrug. "I think perhaps by fall I'll be settled, have some idea . . ."

Twelve

CHAPPAQUIDDICK

The initial contingent of boiler room girls arrived on Martha's Vineyard at midday on Thursday, July 17. They were Esther Newberg, twenty-six, who had found work after the campaign at a Washington think tank; Rosemary "Cricket" Keough, twenty-three, an assistant at the Children's League, a Kennedy family project in the capital; Susan Tannenbaum, twenty-four, a congressional aide; and Mary Jo Kopechne. The four were joined on Friday morning by Maryellen Lyons, twenty-seven, an assistant to a Massachusetts state senator, and her sister Nance, twenty-six, who worked on Ted Kennedy's Senate staff.

Kopechne, the oldest, was a week short of her twenty-ninth birthday. After helping Robert Kennedy's family with the sorrowful chores that followed the assassination, she had found work as a political consultant with Matt Reese, the hulking organizer whose troops had helped John F. Kennedy win the 1960 West Virginia primary. Her ancestors were immigrants and coal miners, from the anthracite belt of northeastern Pennsylvania, but Kopechne grew up in white working-class neighborhoods in Newark and East Orange, New Jersey. Later, her parents—Joseph, an insurance salesman, and Gwen, a stay-at-home-mom—made a classic postwar trek to Berkeley Heights, New Jersey, the suburban community famed as the home of Bell Laboratories.

Mary Jo was a chubby-cheeked, wide-eyed child with a high forehead, blonde hair, blue eyes, and a sly grin. She had no brothers or sisters and so was treated to a new baseball glove, or full cowgirl regalia, at Christmas. "If we were to have only one child, God surely chose the very best one for us," Joseph said. The Kopechnes were Roman Catholics, and so she was schooled at Our Lady of the Most Blessed Sacrament elementary school and Our Lady of the Valley High School and graduated from the Caldwell College for Women, a Catholic institution run by the Dominican order, in 1962. She studied business administration and was remembered in her yearbook for her "perfectionist's touch" and "dauntless charm." Kopechne could be quiet, her cousin Georgetta Potoski recalled, but she took to the stage in college plays and loved to dance. The music, "the swinging and swaying and turning and dipping," had the power of "setting her soul free," Mary Jo said. She liked to swim as well. "She was a rare type; never phony and always honest," a college boyfriend remembered.

A grandfather had been crippled working in the Pennsylvania coal mines. Her father found a paycheck in the Civilian Conservation Corps, a New Deal work project, during the Great Depression. So Mary Jo had a feeling for underdogs (her childhood favorites were the Brooklyn Dodgers) and a spirited idealism that drew her to Democratic politics. She spent a year on a faith-based mission, teaching typing and other skills at the Montgomery Catholic High School in Alabama, amid the turmoil of the civil rights era. The faculty was comprised mainly of nuns, and finding neither the teaching nor the convent amenable, she moved to Washington to serve the New Frontier. During the summer of 1963 she joined the staff of Senator George Smathers, a Democrat from Florida with a reputation as a playboy. She seemed an odd fit, and quickly the Hill had its jest: on an office staff known for its "chic, sleek" women, it was said, only Kopechne could take dictation.

She was seen by other Senate staffers as attractive but not gorgeous—it depended on her hair, or how the light caught her face—but not less than pretty. She was five feet two inches tall and barely topped a hundred pounds. She was smart, serious, and worshipful, with framed pictures of the Kennedy brothers on her desk. On a trip to Ireland, she made a pilgrimage to the Kennedy ancestral home in New Ross. "Stopped in to see the Kennedy relatives today," she wrote her parents. "Have kissed the Blar-

Young Ted, about to turn three, on the lawn of the family's
Palm Beach estate in January 1935.

The P. J. Kennedy and John Fitzgerald families at Old Orchard Beach, Maine, when Rose was sixteen. Rose, third from the left, is sitting with her father, John, on her left and her future father-in-law, P. J., on her right. The young man sitting second from the right is Joseph P. Kennedy, her future husband.

Mayor John "Honey Fitz" Fitzgerald waving his hat to the crowd while crossing the field at the newly opened Fenway Park with builder Charles Logue in 1912.

Joe and Rose, leaving the church on their wedding day, in October 1914.

The Kennedy family posing in Palm Beach at Christmas, 1937. Front row, left to right: Patricia, Jean, Rose, Robert, Ted in sailor suit, Kathleen. Back row, left to right: Joe Jr., Joseph, John, Eunice, Rosemary.

Ambassador Joseph Kennedy at his desk, with young Ted standing at his side, in a photograph taken in England in 1939.

Joe Jr., Kathleen, and John on their way to Westminster in September 1939 to hear Britain declare war on Germany. Said biographer Doris Kearns Goodwin: "Little could this golden trio have imagined . . . how much each would lose by the war that was about to begin."

The Kennedy children had busy parents, and the family was tended by a sizable staff of servants and caretakers. Here Ted, Robert, Jean, and Patricia take a trip to a Florida orange grove in the spring of 1934 with nanny Katherine Conboy on their right and governess Alice Cahill behind them; Joseph and Rose (in a fur and a diamond tiara) prepare for a banquet in London in 1938; and Ted rides his bicycle near the residence in London under a watchful eye, just before the outbreak of war in the summer of 1939.

As children, Kennedys were taught to compete. Here is Ted, center left, in a boxing match in an outdoor ring at the Sea Spray Club in Palm Beach around the time of his third birthday, and (below) as a teenager with his brother John on Cape Cod, learning the ropes on the sailboat *Victura*.

His two older brothers were heroes in World War II, but only one came home alive. Here Ted poses with cousin Joseph Gargan in Hyannis Port with John and his PT boat crewmates, and (below) watches, glumly, as Rose accepts a posthumous decoration for Joe Jr. with her husband and children Patricia, Robert, and Jean.

Ted and Rose, in Palm Beach, on the day of his confirmation in 1942. A devout Roman Catholic, she made sure her children had religious instruction.

Ted, circa 1942, in the Hyannis Port home, standing above Rose and four siblings, as Joseph Kennedy, characteristically, watches over them from afar. Seated on the couch, left to right, are Patricia, Robert, and Kathleen. Behind them are Rose, Ted, and Jean.

In the postwar era, the Kennedys defined charisma. Photographs like this one, from *Look* magazine, dotted the glossy pages of major publications. From left to right, Robert, John, and Ted emerge from the surf in 1957.

When John married Jacqueline Bouvier in 1953, five of the surviving Kennedy children—left to right: Robert, Patricia, Eunice, Ted, and Jean—were captured with the bride and groom.

Ted Kennedy (top center) and, to his left, John Tunney, hands in pockets, the acclaimed victors in the moot court competition at the University of Virginia law school.

Ted in uniform, number 88, with two Harvard teammates. Worried about losing his eligibility for football, Kennedy cheated on a Spanish exam. He was caught and asked to leave the university.

These two photographs capture a scene from the West Virginia primary in 1960. Amid this critical campaign against Hubert Humphrey, John Kennedy's voice gave out. Ted was summoned and, after some one-on-one counseling from his older brother, took over at the podium.

The three Kennedy
brothers, after the
primaries but before
the convention, on
July 1, 1960, in
Hyannis Port.

Ted rides a bucking bronc
in Miles City, Montana,
while leading the western
states campaign for his
brother John against the
Republican nominee,
Richard Nixon.

Happy days in the New Frontier. Ted and Joan Kennedy with babies Kara and Ted Jr. in their laps in 1962.

President Kennedy lounges in an armchair as a group of the family stands behind him singing a silly song during Joseph Kennedy's seventy-fifth birthday party. In print pants is Patricia Lawford and to her left are Lem Billings, Ethel Kennedy, Robert Kennedy, Eunice Shriver, Ted Kennedy, and Joan Kennedy.

The 1962 Senate campaign. A young woman runs out to shake hands with Ted Kennedy as he walks in the "God and Country" parade in Lawrence, Massachusetts.

The young candidate addresses a group of factory workers.

Attorney General Edward McCormack points his finger at a grim-faced Kennedy in the closing moments of the August 1962 debate in South Boston. "If your name was Edward Moore," said McCormack, "your candidacy would be a joke."

In their last political appearance together, a fundraiser at the armory in Boston a month before his death, President Kennedy applauds Senator Kennedy.

John Kennedy Jr. salutes his father's coffin as Caroline stands with Ted, Jacqueline, and Robert, struggling with their grief.

The smashed airplane in the western Massachusetts orchard. Ted Kennedy's back was broken, and the pilot and another passenger were killed.

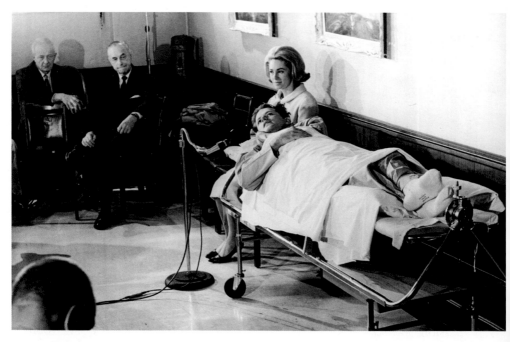

Ted's recuperation took six months. Here, in a hospital bed with Joan beside him, he answers questions from the press in the fall of 1964.

ney Stone, so watch out." After Dallas she endeavored, and was thrilled, to find work with Robert Kennedy.

Kopechne was a usual Hill rat, one of hundreds of young people staffing congressional offices, mostly ill-paid, lured by the politics of the era. She shared a house in Georgetown with three roommates. She drove a Volkswagen Bug. She played catcher on the office softball team. "She was a normal red-blooded American girl . . . she was funny . . . she wore short skirts like all the rest of us did," Keough recalled. "She wasn't a saint. She was a nice, lovely girl who was very dedicated to what we all were dedicated to. It was a time of great commitment."

In Robert's time, the Kennedys were less clan and more tribe. Children, pets, staff, advisers, celebrities, and reporters drifted through Hickory Hill. An aide was as likely to be asked to watch the kids as to help craft a speech on the Vietnam War. At one point, not knowing that Robert had promised the property to the city of New Rochelle, Kopechne told a group for the mentally disabled that they could have access to surplus army land on an isle in Long Island Sound. "Given away any islands today?" he henceforth teased her. But she could give as good as she got. When the staff presented Kennedy with an illuminated globe, he said, "Gee, just what I wanted." And Kopechne right quickly razzed him: "Yes—the world."

The great moral causes of the Sixties grew complex as the decade neared its end and the consensus of the Great Society was frayed by urban riots, the Black Power movement, and the Vietnam War, yet the struggle for peace and civil rights still had the power to move Kopechne and the others. At her office on Wednesday, before leaving for New England, she had joined in the talk about the upcoming Apollo 11 landing on the moon. She spoke of the iconic photograph of Earth rising over the lunar surface, taken by the crew of Apollo 8 at Christmastime in 1968. "Just imagine. Someone took a picture of the whole world," she said. "Everything is there, the war, prejudice, everything. And we're just hanging there in the blackness of space, and one wrong move and that would be the end."

Politics is a voracious calling: then and now an aberrant life of highways, telephones, and tarmacs; eighty-hour weeks of frantic intensity fueled by passion, loyalties, and late-night scotches in hotel bars. The boiler room "girls" were career women, reaping new freedoms delivered by the women's movement and the availability of oral contraception in the early 1960s. They were smart, ambitious, and committed—not there to find a husband. "We were all single," because the 1968 Kennedy campaign only assigned single women to the boiler room, Keough would remember. "You can't be married because you're going to have to be here at all hours," they were told. "And you can't have kids or anything." Indeed, they were all beyond the median age of first marriages, which for American women at that time was a few months past twenty years. It became a running joke—how the game of politics was so not conducive to romance—that the men from the 1968 campaign had staged a party, a "bachelor's ball," promising dual suitors for every lass, in January. "We were considered to have kind of the hippest staff. The Robert Kennedy staff was very hip and cool," Keough would recall.

Kopechne had handled Rust Belt states—Indiana, Pennsylvania—in the 1968 campaign. She could talk the language of blue-collar politics and had just returned, in that summer of 1969, from an unenviable stint in gritty Jersey City, advising Thomas Whelan, a Democratic mayor. She was looking forward, like the others, to a sunny weekend in a tony locale with a gang of old friends with whom she shared a unique bond. She told her office not to expect her back until Tuesday.

THE SIX WOMEN DID not know the details of the weekend, aside from that there would be sailboat races, and Ted Kennedy would attend. They hoped to recreate a restorative occasion from the previous summer. Ted had been too distraught to join them in the weeks after Bobby's death, but he had loaned them a chartered sailboat for a trip to Nantucket; his wife, Joan, had held a cocktail party for them on Squaw Island, and his cousin Joseph Gargan and his wife, Betty, served up steak at a cookout. There had been other reunions: at one of them, the bachelor's ball in January, Kennedy had lost his composure. "There was a special relationship between the boiler room girls and Teddy. It was a place that he was comfortable," Nance Lyons recalled. "I think it's the first time he cried in public. . . . He broke down and I thought afterward that maybe that was good."

They traveled as a group, hoping to find comfort in fellowship, and maybe to meet intriguing guests, drawn by the glamour of the Kennedys. They'd seen the array of astronauts, writers, athletes, and movie stars who visited Hickory Hill. "Joan knew every one of these girls. Betty Gargan knew every one of these girls and loved every one of them," said Paul Redmond, a Massachusetts lawyer who would marry Keough. "These weren't five international, jet set high priced hookers who had been flown in from all over the world for Ted's carnal amusement."

The early arrivals went shopping in Edgartown on Friday, then headed for the beach. Joan Kennedy would not be joining them; after two miscarriages, she was pregnant again, and acting with an abundance of caution. Gargan, the organizer of the weekend, had failed to find a house for the Friday night festivities near South Beach, where the women were bunking at the Katama Shores Motor Inn. All he could get was a cottage on Chappaquiddick, the rougher, rural island (year-round population: 12) that sat across from Edgartown, separated by the harbor channel from the Vineyard proper. There, on the secluded East Beach, the group went swimming. To get there, they crossed the harbor on the little *On Time* ferry and took Chappaquiddick Road, and then unpaved Dike Road, eastward toward the sea. Just before the beach, they crossed a long one-lane humpbacked bridge, which angled sharply to the left as it crossed Poucha Pond, the saltwater lagoon that ran behind the dunes. The pond had once been diked, but now was open to the strong tidal currents. The Dike Bridge, as it was known, was crude, made from thick planks and timbers, and used mainly by fishermen. There were no guardrails, warning signs, or reflectors.

Just after lunch, the women were joined by Ted Kennedy, who had been driven to the cottage and then to the beach by his driver, Jack Crimmins, in a heavy black Oldsmobile sedan. The senator had flown up from Washington that morning looking, said his seatmate Tip O'Neill, like the most tired man in the nation's capital. He took a short swim. Before 3 p.m., Kennedy was back in Edgartown and at the helm of *Victura*, the twenty-five-foot blue-hulled sailboat that had come to him from his brother Jack, who had received it as a gift from his parents on his fifteenth birthday. It was a Wianno Senior—a gaff-rigged sloop with triangular sails—designed and built for the special conditions of shallow, windswept Nantucket Sound. Sailors on the Cape and islands had been racing the low, sleek daysailers for years. Kennedy was easy to spot: his tricolored spinnaker was a replica of the Irish flag. Alone among the skippers, he wore a back brace.

The sultry conditions were no good for racing: that, at least, was Kennedy's excuse for finishing ninth in a field of thirty-one, behind the victorious *Bettawin*, skippered by a longtime friend and rival, Ross Richards. Kennedy was not a "ghoster"—he raced best in heavy weather. The six women watched the race from a charter boat (Kopechne urged its skipper to cruise by the *Victura*, so they all could cheer and wave), then returned to their motel to change clothes.

The regatta weekend was a traditional, high-spirited event, with partying that began after the afternoon races and carried on into the early morning hours—Joe Jr. and John Kennedy had spent a night in the Edgartown lockup in the 1930s, according to local lore. Ted drank a beer while racing. He dropped by the *Bettawin* to congratulate the winner and downed what one onlooker remembered as three rum-and-Cokes. The senator may have had a beer at Edgartown's Shiretown Inn as he checked in to the room he was to share with Gargan that night. There was no tub, only a shower, so they crossed to Chappaquiddick, where Kennedy soaked his broken back in the bathtub at the cottage, and Crimmins fixed him a rum-and-Coke. In the course of the evening, Kennedy later testified, he would replenish that cocktail once. Others said twice.

It was not a great party. The turnout was smaller than expected, the cottage a drab two-bedroom shingled house in the brambles, the night thick and sticky. Campaign pals like Dave Hackett and Dun Gifford failed to show. Gargan had trouble with the frozen cheese and sausage hors d'oeuvres, the charcoal proved difficult to light, and the grill was too small to hold all the steaks. They ate in shifts, drank as would befit a party, sang songs, and told stories about Robert Kennedy. There was a crescent moon, circled by a spacecraft that would fulfill John Kennedy's vow and land Americans on the lunar surface on Sunday.

If the women longed for glamour they were disappointed by the five decidedly unglamorous men who attended the cookout with Kennedy. They were drab campaign regulars. Ted's driver Crimmins was sixty-three, a cranky retired state police investigator. Paul Markham was a former U.S. attorney for Massachusetts; like Gargan he was thirty-nine and sometimes crewed on the senator's boat. Ray LaRosa was forty-one, a fireman and civil defense official who did odd political chores. Charles Tretter, a thirty-year-old former Kennedy staffer, was closest to the women's age but, like all the men but Crimmins, had a wife at home.

"It was as if they were in an army platoon that had all gone to war together. They weren't people who had been dating each other. Some were married, some were not, some were aged. It was just a whole mishmash of folks getting together to have a reunion, even a mourning of Robert Kennedy, and to tell war stories," said Melody Miller, another Kennedy aide. "It was also something that Joey Gargan wanted to host for these gals, to keep them as a cohesive unit . . . to remind them they were appreciated, just in case Edward Kennedy was going to run in the coming Presidential campaign. . . . That's who these folks were, and I knew almost every one of them."

Tretter and Keough took the senator's Oldsmobile back to Edgartown to get a radio, so that the guests could dance. She left her purse—a lunchbox type with mod decorations—in the car when they returned. The partygoers wandered in and out, alternately trading the coolness of the night for the protection from mosquitoes offered by the window screens. Many took walks. The well-stocked bar proved popular. It was the Sixties—the Woodstock summer—and young men and women were known to have sex in those days. But this was no bacchanal. "It was a steak cookout, not a Roman orgy," an exasperated Newberg later told the press.

Yet grief, shared, can nurture intimacy. Kopechne, after several drinks, grew emotional as she spoke with Ted about Bobby. His grief welled up as well. "I needed to get out of that party," Kennedy would recall. "I needed to get outside, to breathe some fresh air." Kopechne said she, too, wished to leave.

Kennedy asked Crimmins for the car keys. The old grouch was staying in the cottage that night and happy to comply; he wanted to get to bed. By the reckoning of the witnesses, it was sometime between 11:30 p.m. and 12:30 a.m. when Kennedy and Kopechne slipped away. She left her room key and her purse behind. With Kennedy at the wheel—weary, emotional, after hours of intermittent drinking—the Oldsmobile came to a juncture and turned off the paved road, away from Edgartown and the ferry. Christopher Look, a deputy sheriff on his way home from work, would recall that he saw and approached a dark sedan at that intersection, which sped off down the washboard dirt surface of Dike Road toward the beach. The moon had set; the night was black. Kennedy passed a house, where the inhabitants—Sylvia Malm and her daughter—would recall a car moving fast, toward the sea, around midnight.

Then Dike Bridge was in the headlights, with its iniquitous angle to the left. Kennedy slammed the brake pedal. The car left the bridge, flipped, and crashed roof-first against the surface of the water. The driver's side window was open. The passenger side windows were shattered on impact. Instantly, the Olds filled with water and sank to the bottom of Poucha Pond.

Automobiles did not have seat belts in 1969, much less airbags. Mary Jo would have been tossed by the crash: forward and down—which was now toward the roof. Kennedy felt her thrashing beside him. She ended with her head in the footwell of the backseat, beside the shattered window through which she might have escaped. Perhaps she found a pocket of air; perhaps she never realized that the car was upside down. Deep in black water, seeing nothing, Kennedy at least had the steering wheel to grasp and get oriented. He was terrified, felt himself drowning, dying. Experts later theorized that the crash sprung open a door, or that the torrents sweeping through the car helped push him through a window.

He called out "Mary Jo!" and made futile dives to the submerged car. "I knew there was a girl in that car and I had to get her out. I knew that," he'd recall. The current pushed him away. Defeated, he crawled onto the shore.

KENNEDY'S SUBSEQUENT BEHAVIOR QUALIFIED as craven. In his defense, he had taken a blow to the head, suffered a concussion, nearly died, and no doubt was in shock. Crazy thoughts beset him—that his family was cursed, that Jack and Bob had come, as spirits, to guide him from the wreck. "Ted found the idea that the girl had died psychologically unacceptable," his brother-in-law, Stephen Smith, would say. "He had got out in some unexplained way; she must have got out too."

As Tunney and others feared, Kennedy's precarious emotional state had been drawing him toward this sort of crack-up. In six years, two brothers had been gunned down by assassins, his back had been broken in an airplane crash that killed the pilot and one of his aides. Now he'd had a pounding car wreck, the terrifying sensations of drowning, and was compelled to recognize that a vibrant young woman was dead by his hand. He was thirty-seven, crushed by the expectations of his father, his family, his allies, of Camelot; aghast at the thought of telling her parents, his parents, his wife. "I just couldn't gain the strength within me—the moral strength," he would confess.

There are acts of reasoned—and spontaneous—courage in Kennedy family history. There was also a carelessness, bred by wealth, about laws that applied to others, but not to them. There was recklessness. There was evasion, to escape a father's anger or, worse, his threatened withdrawal of affection. John had asked a pal to take the blame for his highway violations; Ted had hidden from the Charlottesville police. And while the sin is not unique to Kennedys, there was a family history of perjurious behavior in the service of ambition; John had lied to cover up his Addison's disease, even to his friends.

Kennedy got to his feet and jogged and stumbled back to the party, passing houses and an unmanned but well-lit volunteer fire station, with a fire alarm, on the way. Once at the cottage, he did not alert the boiler room girls—*I drove off the bridge! Mary Jo is missing! Call for help!*—but crawled into the backseat of a rented Plymouth Valiant parked in the driveway. Without a word about the accident, he told LaRosa—a qualified rescue worker—to bring him two lawyers, Gargan and Markham. The duo heard Kennedy's jumbled explanation and sped off with him, back down Dike Road to the bridge.

Afterward, proposing a rationale for their behavior, Gargan spoke of a code on the water. If you saw another sailboat capsize, you didn't head for shore and a pay phone, you rescued the crew yourself. Perhaps. But by the time that Kennedy trudged back to the cottage, summoned Gargan and Markham, and returned to the bridge, Kopechne had been in the water for more than half an hour. Gargan was expecting to see a car half-immersed in the shallows, with a stunned or bleeding Mary Jo caught in the wreckage. When he saw the position of the Oldsmobile, he lost hope quickly. "Holy God!" Markham said. To himself, Gargan thought, "This is over. This is done."

Yet they tried. They played the Valiant's headlights out upon the water, and Gargan and Markham stripped and dove. The open windows in the flipped car were now at the bottom of the channel. Gargan managed to poke his head and shoulders into the wreck. He did not see Kopechne, above and beyond him, behind the front seats. He had no mask, no weight belt, no air tank. The strong currents—bitter black tidewater laden with sand and silt—blinded him.

Markham gave limited assistance; he had hurt his leg that day and been drinking at the party. Kennedy was no help at all. After shouting, "Can you see her?" he lay back on the bridge, knees raised, his arms splayed above his head, moaning and rocking. "Oh my God," he said. "What am I going to do?" It had happened, like everyone thought it would. There were folks who could get away with things, his father had told him. Ted was not one of them.

A FORGIVING INTERPRETATION OF Kennedy's behavior over the next nine hours—the time that passed before he reported the accident—is that he was fixed in dazed disbelief. He and the others climbed back into the Valiant and drove up Dike Road to the ferry landing. "This couldn't have happened," he said. "Can you believe it? I don't believe this could happen to me."

"Well it did happen and it has happened," Markham told him.

"What am I going to do? What can I do?"

"There is nothing you can do," said Markham.

Kennedy could not face it. "Even though I knew that Mary Jo Kopechne was dead and believed firmly that she was in the back of that car, I willed that she remained alive. . . . I was almost looking out the windows trying to see her walking down that road," he would testify. He had "sort of a thought and the wish and desire and the hope that suddenly the whole accident would disappear."

"At bottom I knew, I guess, it wasn't so," he'd confide to Stephen Smith. "But I kept figuring out how it might be so."

A LESS CHARITABLE EXPLANATION is that Kennedy sought—at first frantically, and then coolly—to shirk the blame for Kopechne's death, to save himself from prison and maintain his career. The Massachusetts motor vehicle code was a mess, old and riddled with loopholes. But a drunk driver, speeding down an unsafe road, who drove off a bridge and killed a passenger might well be convicted of manslaughter or vehicular homicide. Despite its dangers, the Dike Bridge had existed for thirty years without anyone running off it. Reporting the accident would bring police, with tests that could measure the alcohol in his blood.

His "feverish" inclination, Kennedy later confessed, was to concoct "scenarios" that would absolve him. Why, he asked Gargan and Markham, did the world have to know that he was driving the car? Couldn't Mary Jo have driven off the bridge herself? It was magical thinking. Kennedy and Kopechne had been seen leaving the party together. He had taken the keys to the Oldsmobile from Crimmins. He had been seen, soaking wet, a half hour later by LaRosa. Then Kennedy and Gargan and Markham had driven to the bridge, turned their headlights upon the water, and splashed around, just a hundred feet from the nearest occupied house.

Gargan was a defense attorney and knew the motor vehicle law. Markham was a former U.S. attorney. Kennedy had told them that he was driving. Even if they could put loyalty above honor (which neither was willing to do), they recognized that once the cover-up crumbled, as it surely would, they could lose their licenses and livelihoods, and maybe join the senator behind bars. They advised him, urged him, told him to report the accident to the police.

Gargan hammered away at his reluctant cousin as they sat at the ferry landing. The harbor was dotted with sailboats; the lights of Edgartown, and the happy sounds of the last late-night parties, lay five hundred feet away. There was one final angry exchange: "You take care of the girls," Kennedy said. "I will take care of the accident." Then, clothed, he plunged into the water and swam across the harbor.

The confounded duo assumed that Kennedy was heading to the police station. Maybe he would call his parents, or his chief of staff, or contact Burke Marshall, a former member of Robert Kennedy's team at Justice, before turning himself in, but he was going to report the accident. When they got back to the cottage, Gargan slept by the front door, assuming he would be greeting rescue personnel before morning. The young women were miffed at being stranded—there was speculation that Kennedy and Kopechne had slipped off to the beach, where their car got stuck in the sand.

It was now well past 2 a.m., and Kopechne's body was still in Poucha Pond. If the thought haunted Kennedy, he didn't show it when, dry and dressed, he appeared to ask the clerk at the Shiretown Inn for the correct time, or when he joined Ross Richards and his wife for a chat about sailing before breakfast the next morning.

He was there, neat and showered, when the bedraggled Gargan and Markham arrived, took him aside, and, newly enraged, resumed the previous night's argument. "I'm going to say Mary Jo was driving," Kennedy told them. They tried to pound it home: no one else could take the blame. Finally, after using pay phones to call Helga Wagner and David Burke, Kennedy saw the *On Time* carry a tow truck from Edgartown to Chappaquiddick. An island resident told him that his car had been discovered. There was no time left for consultations. Gargan was dispatched to clean up the party site, inform the young women their friend was dead, and get them off the island. Then, finally, Kennedy headed to the town hall and the police.

"He called me around 8 o'clock in the morning. He told me what happened, and that he desperately tried to save her," Wagner would remember. "He was supposed to go to the police and all that but it didn't occur. . . . He was confused about it all. He said, 'I don't know what to do.

What shall I do?' It was like a feeling of lostness because neither Steve nor his sister Jean were anywhere near and usually when anything happened, Stephen Smith, he would take care of everything."

In retrospect, Kennedy's behavior looks like the actions of a man who wants to establish an alibi as his friends concoct a story that absolves him. Or, alternately, a drunk driver waiting for the alcohol in his bloodstream to diminish.

Not just enemies wondered. "It . . . encouraged suspicions—especially that he might have been drunk and postponed reporting the accident until the alcohol could be absorbed in his system," Arthur Schlesinger told his diary. "It was as unfortunate as hell, that nine-hour period," Lawrence O'Brien told Neil MacNeil, the *Time* magazine correspondent. "Very bad. It seemed obvious that the fellows were trying to figure out what to do. Appalling."

Kennedy "could not accept the idea that this was running against him—that he was caught, tagged, faulted. And so tagged, he didn't know how to react. He didn't know how to accept the blame," MacNeil wrote his editors. "The golden boy had mud on his shoes, and he didn't know what to do about it. It wasn't supposed to happen that way."

KENNEDY'S ARRIVAL AT THE Edgartown police station, on the first floor of the white clapboard town hall, at around 10 a.m. on Saturday had been met by awed local authorities. He was not merely the state's U.S. senator, he was a Kennedy, the scion of a family beloved in Massachusetts, and a leader of the Democratic Party.

They resolved to treat the accident as they would handle any summer mishap: as a regrettable but accidental drowning, with charges pressed against the driver for leaving the scene. It was a misdemeanor, punishable by two months to two years in jail. For a first-time offense by a young man with a clean record, the proposed outcome—a negotiated guilty plea followed by a suspended sentence and probation—was not atypical. A plea bargain would save the state from the moth-eaten motor vehicle code by which, a skilled defense attorney could argue, Kennedy was absolved by reporting the accident to Gargan and Markham. He had not left the scene to evade prosecution—he had gone and summoned help. Remarkably, the code did not insist that a driver in such circumstances must alert the police.

Serious charges, like manslaughter or vehicular homicide, carried a heavier burden of proof: the prosecutors would need to show that Kennedy was drunk or speeding recklessly down Dike Road. The skid marks at the bridge were not determinative but indicated to the authorities that his car had been traveling at least twenty miles per hour. And while the medical examiner could test Kopechne's blood and conclude she had been drinking, the isolated location of the accident, the late hour, and Kennedy's wanderings allowed traces of the drinks he'd downed to leave his system.

And so the state's response to Mary Jo Kopechne's death came in stages, tugged this way and that by press and public opinion, in a process that served neither Kennedy nor the public well.

At first, the police, medical examiner, and prosecutors bent over backward to give their U.S. senator a break. They were encouraged by his apparent compliance. He had appeared at the station, however belatedly, waived his right against self-incrimination, given an inculpatory account, and accepted blame. There were no other witnesses, so Kennedy's statement was the essential piece in any prosecutor's case against him. And he had handed it to them.

But as the hours and days passed, and Kennedy hunkered down at Hyannis Port with his lawyers and political advisers, the constabulary's initial failure to ask basic questions—Was Kennedy drinking? Had he been at a party? What was he doing from midnight until midmorning?—incensed the army of reporters and cameramen who had descended on Martha's Vineyard. Their editors were demanding a full account of the accident; Kennedy wasn't talking, and the police seemed cowed or clueless.

The authorities started to feel like chumps. Chagrined, they swung in the other direction. Pressed and harassed, they staged three extraordinary judicial forums in the coming months—a two-day exhumation hearing, a four-day inquest whose record ran to eight hundred pages, and a brief grand jury probe. There were plenty of rumors, some damnatory contradiction, and much speculation, but no case to sustain a conviction for something more serious than leaving the scene. If Kennedy's behavior had been, as he said, "indefensible," it was also effective. By not summoning rescue workers to Poucha Pond, Kennedy had preempted any prosecutorial opportunity to put him in the Barnstable County House of Correction.

THE SUNKEN OLDSMOBILE WAS spotted by fishermen shortly after 8 a.m. The Edgartown police chief, a sunny giant named Dominick "Jim" Arena, was at work in his two-room station, got the call, and took the case. He drove to the bridge, borrowed a swimsuit and a diving mask, and dove into a current that stunned him with its power. In daylight, with a mask, he could not see into the car, much less explore its interior. He used his car radio to summon a fire department diver and had a subaltern call in the numbers from the license plate. It took the diver twenty minutes to arrive. In the meantime, Arena learned that the owner of the car was Kennedy.

The diver, John Farrar, brought Mary Jo Kopechne's body to the surface. From how he found her, with her hands gripping the backseat and her head in the footwell, he was convinced that she had been alive, breathing from a pocket of air, for a time. Had Kennedy gone straight to a nearby house and called for him, Farrar came to believe, they may have had Kopechne out of the car in forty or fifty minutes. Yet tacking on the time taken by Kennedy's initial efforts to rescue her, Kopechne would have had to survive for more than an hour in that pocket as the tidal current surged through the car. It was not impossible, nor was it likely.

From the purse found in the car, Arena presumed that the dead young woman in his arms was Keough. He had a hearse, the medical examiner, and a tow truck summoned and ordered his force to look for Kennedy. Just before 10 a.m., after hearing the senator had been spotted at the ferry, Arena called the station to have someone fetch him. "He's right here, chief," the dispatcher said. Kennedy asked if they could talk at the police station. Arena headed to Edgartown, where he found Kennedy in his office, using the phone as the first news reporters gathered.

"I'm sorry about what happened," Arena said.

"Yes, I know," said Kennedy. "I was the driver."

Startled, Arena asked Kennedy how they might contact Rosemary Keough's next of kin.

It wasn't Keough, Kennedy told him. "It's Mary Jo Kopechne. I've already notified her parents."

Arena asked him how to spell "Kopechne." Kennedy admitted that he did not know.

"What would you like for me to do?" Kennedy asked. "We must do what is right or we'll both be criticized for it."

Years later, Arena recalled the scene. "Nothing in my prior career as a police officer had prepared me for standing in a wet bathing suit and shaking hands with a United States senator—and a Kennedy—who tells me he is the driver of a car from which I have just removed the body of a beautiful young girl," he said. "I was stunned. . . . I'm standing in a puddle of water in a state of confusion thinking I had only minutes before broken the news of a personal tragedy he's now telling me quite calmly he knows all about." Arena had lost his equilibrium. He "fell back on years of police training and began to process the matter as though it was a routine traffic case," he remembered. It was anything but. He led Kennedy and Markham to an empty town office, where the senator could compose a statement:

On July 18, 1969, at approximately 11:15 p.m. in Chappaquiddick, Martha's Vineyard, Massachusetts, I was driving my car on Main Street on my way to get the ferry back to Edgartown. I was unfamiliar with the road and turned right onto Dike Road, instead of bearing hard left on Main Street. After proceeding for approximately one-half mile on Dike Road I descended a hill and came upon a narrow bridge. The car went off the side of the bridge. There was one passenger with me, one Miss Mary ___, a former secretary of my brother Sen. Robert Kennedy. The car turned over and sank into the water and landed with the roof resting on the bottom.

I attempted to open the door and window of the car but have no recollection of how I got out of the car. I came to the surface and then repeatedly dove down to the car in an attempt to see if the passenger was still in the car. I was unsuccessful in the attempt. I was exhausted and in a state of shock.

I recall walking back to where my friends were eating. There was a car parked in front of the cottage and I climbed into the back seat. I then asked for someone to bring me back to Edgartown. I remember walking around for a period and then going back to my hotel room. When I fully realized what had happened this morning, I immediately contacted the police.

As Kennedy and Markham worked on the statement, Arena returned to the bridge and helped take measurements at the scene.

THE ASSISTANT MEDICAL EXAMINER, Dr. Donald Mills, was marginally more cognizant than the police chief. Summoned to Dike Bridge, he took ten to fifteen minutes to examine Kopechne's body and conclude she drowned. "Death by drowning. Not a question about it," he told the rescue workers. It was not an unreasonable conclusion—her body had been found in a submerged car, and water leaked from her nose and mouth—and an autopsy in such circumstances seemed unnecessary. But because it was the car of a famous entity, Mills sent word, via the state police, to the office of District Attorney Edmund Dinis: Did they want him to hold the body for an autopsy? Via the state police, the word came back: Not if you're confident in your ruling.

Accordingly, Mills released Kopechne's body to the funeral directors. Much heartache was to follow this decision. An autopsy would not have added to the legal case against Kennedy, but it would have been more precise, reinforcing the cause of death, and ruling out some of the lurid claims that soon were stirring: that Kopechne was murdered, and the accident faked to protect the killer. For the press, an autopsy might have answered questions that cast light on Kennedy's character: Had he and Kopechne gone to a local lover's lane and had sex that night? Had she died of asphyxiation during the night, when a pocket of air she was breathing dissipated?

Dun Gifford, a friendly supervisor of the campaign boiler room, was the Kennedy staffer assigned to help the family with her body. He watched the undertakers as they did their work on Saturday and accompanied the casket on Sunday, when it was flown to Pennsylvania for the funeral and interment.

ARENA, after finishing at the bridge, returned to the police station, where he took Kennedy's handwritten statement and typed it out. The chief had questions, and so did inspectors from the state Motor Vehicle Registry, who had been called to the scene. The senator needed to consult with his lawyer, Burke Marshall, said Markham. Could they please hold the statement and questioning until then? It was Kennedy's right to decline interrogation—he had already made his most significant admission, identifying himself as the driver of the car. It seemed they could trust him. They wanted to be helpful. They agreed.

Arena took the next routine step and, like Mills, used the state police to report the accident to the district attorney. George Killen, the chief investigator for Cape Cod and the islands, was preoccupied by a sensational serial killer case. If Arena needed help, the chief was told, the higher-ups would happily assist. If not, he could handle it himself. Arena then helped Kennedy and Markham slip out a back door, where the registry inspectors drove them to the airport for a chartered flight to Hyannis.

On the way, one inspector remembered, Kennedy kept mumbling, "Oh my God, what has happened?"

Thirteen

INQUEST

A rthur Schlesinger returned to his New York home from a European vacation in the week after the crash on Chappaquiddick. The historian found the world turned upside down. Ted and Joan and Ethel Kennedy had led a glum troupe of family and friends to Plymouth, a small town outside Wilkes-Barre, for Mary Jo Kopechne's funeral on Tuesday. It was the only glimpse the nation had of the senator in the days immediately after the accident. Joan had looked composed. Ted was a wreck—and scorned in the media, and even by friends, for sporting a cervical collar around his neck: it was seen as a contrived bid for sympathy.

Only Kennedy's statement, handed to Chief Arena in Edgartown on Saturday morning, gave the public an account of Kopechne's death. Details of the boiler room girls and the party—which Kennedy had not mentioned to the police—were unearthed by reporters. Absent information, loud rumor spoke. Schlesinger phoned liberal confidants and lunched at the Century Club with James Reston and Tom Wicker, two journalists from the *New York Times*. According to one raging rumor, they said, Kopechne had been done in by Kennedy just as Clyde Griffiths killed Roberta Alden in *An American Tragedy*. An autopsy was forgone, the gossips were saying, because it would reveal that Kopechne was pregnant.

The reports from the Kennedy clan were almost as disconcerting. Those who had seen the senator at the funeral described him as moving "in a catatonic trance." Friends bemoaned his feckless behavior, said it showed a lack of character. Some wondered if Kennedy had brought it down upon himself, as an act of self-destruction, to make himself ineligible for the presidency and flee the burden of his family's expectations.

Slowly, Schlesinger assembled the shards. As a former aide to John Kennedy and an intimate friend of Stephen and Jean Kennedy Smith, the historian was a trusted family confidant.

After talking to her shaken brother, "Jean thinks that he panicked—that he hoped . . . he could find some way to cover it all up," Schlesinger told his diary.

"It was not, she says, that he was worried about the Presidency: 'He didn't want to be President. He was sure that he would be killed if he became President.'"

"It was rather that he could not bear the thought of letting down the family, of destroying all that Jack and Bobby had done," Schlesinger wrote.

Ted "told the others to say nothing and do nothing until they heard from him. Then, in some confused way, he made his appearance before the hotel clerk, perhaps to establish an alibi."

Word came from Hyannis Port that until his sister Eunice enjoined him, Kennedy had proposed to announce that he would never seek the presidency. When Schlesinger spoke to Ethel Kennedy and told her he hoped Ted would not resign from the Senate, she replied, "You will never know how close it was."

After stepping from the plane in Hyannis on Saturday, Kennedy had been examined by a doctor who found a patient with symptoms befitting a car crash. The blows to the head had left a scrape and a lumpy bruise. Kennedy's back had been wrenched and his neck sprained. After talking with him and testing his gaps in memory, Dr. Robert Watt concluded that the senator suffered a concussion as well. "Impairment of judgment and confused behavior are symptoms consistent with an injury of the character sustained," the physician reported. Car wrecks are random things, and human behavior unpredictable. Just as people survive in submerged cars, there are instances of crash victims, dazed and traumatized, wandering away from accidents, intent on getting home.

Kennedy's shaken condition made life difficult for the company of advisers who were now en route to Cape Cod. Burke Marshall was first to arrive, and he quickly assembled a team of specialists in motor vehicle law. They were aghast at the news that Kennedy had already admitted to driving off the bridge, as it would undercut their leverage in plea negotiations with the Dukes County prosecutors. They insisted that Kennedy say no more, lest his own words put him in further jeopardy. Stephen Smith, who arrived to take charge of the compound on Tuesday, recalled their priority: "Our prime concern was whether or not the guy survived the thing; whether he rode out the still-possible charge of manslaughter." Kennedy faced "real legal peril," his friend William vanden Heuvel recalled.

Kennedy's political advisers had their differences with the lawyers, which grew as the days went by. They wanted their guy to talk: to fill the news vacuum with a rational explanation. They wanted him, in fact, to go on television and tell all—just as vice presidential candidate Richard Nixon had done in 1952, parrying accusations of financial misfeasance and saving his spot on the Republican ticket. In the course of that address, Nixon cited a gift he had taken from a political supporter—a cocker spaniel puppy named Checkers—and so the speech was named. It was maudlin but effective.

"I fear I looked at it as primarily a political problem, even though it was an intensely personal one; a young woman dead at the prime of life," one of Kennedy's confidants, Milton Gwirtzman, recalled. "My entire career and a lot of my life had been invested with him over the past ten years. I couldn't believe someone who was that fine a person . . . would let this girl drown. There must be some reason for it, and he should tell what his reasons were."

By midweek the compound was brimming with family members, big names from past crusades—Robert McNamara, Richard Goodwin, Theodore Sorensen, Marshall—and Ted Kennedy's core advisers, like Gwirtzman, John Tunney, and David Burke. McNamara and Sorensen were there to safeguard Camelot. ("I obviously felt very sorry for Ted and wanted to help, but that was not a great place to be for anybody who had a future," Sorensen would recall.) Their presence, and the secrecy imposed by the lawyers, served to escalate the crisis. They made it seem "as if he felt himself in a terrific jam and could not afford to tell the truth," Schlesinger told his diary. And "as if he thought, as a Kennedy, he should get special and favored treatment."

Kennedy was making everyone's life difficult. As his advisers argued at the compound, he kept to his Squaw Island home with Joan, who was coping with the crisis, its lurid implications, and her own raw feelings—while trying to avoid another miscarriage. She was advised to stay in her upstairs bedroom. "It was the worst experience of my life. I couldn't talk to anyone about it," she recalled. "No one told me anything."

At one point that week, Joan picked up the telephone and overheard Ted talking to Helga Wagner. "Nothing ever seemed the same after that," Joan would recall. Wagner was noteworthy among her husband's girlfriends, Joan said later, in that the relationship with Kennedy lasted for years. She was of a type—European, blonde, artistic—that Kennedy was drawn to. He was "a very good person at heart," Wagner remembered. By the time of Chappaquiddick, his marriage was in deep trouble, Wagner said.

Kennedy was maddeningly inconsistent—telling his doctor he had escaped through a window and others that he could not remember how he got out of the sunken car. He told Markham that he had recognized he made a wrong turn onto unpaved Dike Road, and others that he did not realize it until he drove off the bridge. "Steve says that he has heard Teddy give three different versions of the events that terrible night, two within an hour—different not because of manipulation on his part but because of the extreme difficulty he finds in reconstructing the sequence of events," Schlesinger confided to his journal. "It is sad again in perhaps an even more painful way; for what happened to John and Robert Kennedy was beyond their control, while Edward Kennedy's wounds are self-inflicted. . . . He is accusing and punishing himself."

"The diving was very difficult: the water was black, the current swift and filled with blinding sand. None of them could see the body," Schlesinger wrote. "Everyone agrees that Ted was not drunk in any serious sense. But he did have three drinks, and it might be argued that this amount of liquor, small as it was, constituted the margin that propelled the car off the bridge. As Ted himself wryly says, 'No other car had ever gone off the bridge.'"

Kennedy was strung out, slowly recovering from shock and "post-shock trauma," Sorensen remembered. For weeks the senator would find it hard to look friends in the eye. He would watch them "tentatively, seeking signs of loyalty or defection." At signs of kindness, he'd sob and embrace the well-wisher. At one point, in that first week in the compound, he proposed that he leave politics altogether. "What are you going to be?" Burke challenged him. "The Duke of Windsor?"

ON WEDNESDAY NIGHT, evading reporters with a surreptitious gathering at Walter Steele's fishing camp, Arena and Steele danced the necessary legal tango with Kennedy attorney Robert Clark. There were weaknesses in the case on each side, nobody wished to see Kennedy in jail, and everyone wanted a neat resolution that would serve the many interests. Steele, who had been a colleague of Kennedy in the Middlesex district attorney's office in the early 1960s, might have recused himself—but it would be hard to find a Massachusetts official who didn't have some ties to the state's first family.

Early on the morning of Friday, July 25, the Kennedy cabin cruiser, *Marlin*, emerged from the mist of Nantucket Sound and docked on Martha's Vineyard. Ted and Joan Kennedy proceeded to the Edgartown courthouse, where he stood before Judge James Boyle and pleaded "Guilty" to the crime of leaving the scene of a motor vehicle accident that had caused a personal injury. Kennedy had to say it twice: his first plea was so soft that few in the courtroom heard it. Arena told the judge that there was "no evidence of negligence on the part of the defendant"—a necessary element for a more serious charge.

Boyle asked a pointed question: Had Kennedy tried to hide the fact that he was driving the car?

"Not to my knowledge," Arena replied.

The judge gave his consent and delivered the minimum sentence: two months, suspended, and a year probation. "He has already been and will continue to be punished far beyond anything this court can impose," Boyle said.

The proceeding took all of nine minutes. It served its legal purpose. There was an admission of guilt, and a sentence imposed. But the hearing had added little to the public understanding of Kopechne's death. The pressure was immense—on Kennedy, and the legal authorities—for answers. He would supply them, he promised the reporters gathered outside the courthouse, in a televised address that evening.

AS A PAROCHIAL EMOLLIENT the speech that Kennedy gave that night was effective: he was returned to the Senate by the people of Massachusetts every six years until his death. In a broader sense it failed. It did not lay to rest the questions about the accident, or doubts about his character. It was clumsily manipulative, which undermined its impact. Far from laying things to rest, it spurred recurrent reexaminations of the tragedy, by the courts and in the media, for decades.

The initial section outlined the events of the previous weekend. For the first time Kennedy spoke about the party ("a cookout I had encouraged and helped sponsor for a devoted group of Kennedy campaign secretaries") and gave his account of the accident. ("The car overturned into a deep pond and immediately filled with water. I remember thinking as the cold water rushed in around my head, that I was for certain drowning; then water entered my lungs and I actually felt a sensation of drowning; but somehow I struggled to the surface alive.")

He introduced Kopechne ("a gentle, kind, and idealistic person. . . . All of us tried to help her feel that she still had a home with the Kennedy family") and denied that they had left the party with amorous intent. A tone of righteous umbrage crept into his speech. ("There is no truth whatever to the widely circulated suspicions of immoral conduct that have been leveled at my behavior and hers that evening. . . . I know of nothing in Mary Jo's conduct . . . that would lend any substance to such ugly speculation.") He assured his listeners that he had not been driving under the influence of alcohol. He spoke about his second attempt, with Gargan and Markham, to rescue Kopechne, his swim across the harbor, and his 2:30 a.m. meeting with the hotel clerk.

Kennedy was frank in discussing the charge of leaving the scene of the accident. His mea culpa was as tough and unforgiving as any politician ever employed to describe their own actions. At the height of the nuclear arms race, with Americans at war in Southeast Asia, the words he selected to describe his behavior ("indefensible . . . irrational . . . fear . . . panic . . . confusion") as good as declared that he could not be trusted with the presidency.

"I regard as indefensible the fact that I did not report the accident to the police immediately," he said. "All kinds of scrambled thoughts . . . went through my mind during this period. They were reflected in the various inexplicable, inconsistent, and inconclusive things I said and did—including such questions as whether the girl might still be alive somewhere out of that immediate area, whether some awful curse actually did hang over all the Kennedys . . . whether somehow the awful weight of this incredible incident might in some way pass from my shoulders. I was overcome, I am frank to say, by a jumble of emotions—grief, fear, doubt, exhaustion, panic, confusion, and shock."

With the introduction of the family "curse," Kennedy pivoted toward the second segment of the speech: a more mawkish plea for forgiveness, directed to the voters of Massachusetts. He put aside his text and folded his hands. Sitting in the library of his father's home, he read from cue cards while seeming to be talking straight from the heart. He spoke of family, of the New Frontier, of the "very sad" days after the assassinations. His peroration came from John Kennedy's book *Profiles in Courage*.

"It has been written: 'A man does what he must—in spite of personal consequences, in spite of obstacles and dangers and pressures—and that is the basis of all human morality. And whatever may be the sacrifices he faces if he follows his conscience—the loss of his friends, his fortune, his contentment, even the esteem of his fellow men—each man must decide for himself the course he will follow. The stories of past courage cannot supply courage itself. For this each man must look into his own soul.'

"I pray that I can have the courage to make the right decision. Whatever is decided, whatever the future holds for me, I hope I shall be able to put this most recent tragedy behind me and make some future contribution to our state and mankind."

Gwirtzman had written this segment. "I did the end, which was referred to as . . . the Nixon Checkers speech thing. It was generally decried as tasteless and out of place, but it worked," he recalled. "He got 100,000 letters . . . from people in Massachusetts, urging him to stay in office."

KENNEDY'S SPEECH MAY HAVE persuaded the voters of Massachusetts that this was, indeed, only an awful accident. "Your statement was too long and was a bit contrived toward the end. But it wholly served its purpose . . . it answered the basic questions," economist J. Kenneth Galbraith wrote him. "A year from now, six months from now, it will have reduced itself to that miserable accident that Kennedy had—one that could have happened to me."

But that was more magical thinking. The nation's press was still skeptical—and scanned the text for inconsistencies. The New York Times, in an editorial, called the address "a partially irrelevant and totally unsatisfactory ex parte account." There were "many gaping holes . . . he has so assiduously avoided filling."

One of those craters commanded special attention. By introducing the nation to Gargan's and Markham's rescue attempt, Kennedy had fortified his contention that he did all he could to save Kopechne. It raised a question of timing, however. If Kennedy and Kopechne left the cookout to catch the last ferry, and it was his car that the renters of the Dyke House said they heard at midnight, there was plenty of room in his timeline for him to dive and try to save Kopechne, trudge back to the cottage, recruit his two friends, spend another forty-five minutes at the bridge, go to the ferry landing, swim the harbor, and appear in the hotel lobby.

But in light of Kennedy's expanded account, the incidental testimony of another witness became relevant. Sheriff's deputy Christopher Look, driving home from a night shift, had seen a car at the intersection of the roads to the cottage, bridge, and ferry at 12:45 a.m. He described it in some detail and told Arena how it had lurched down Dike Road when he approached. The police chief had disregarded Look's testimony because, as a legal matter, it brought nothing to the case: Look could not identify the driver, or say if he was speeding, or drunk—or even how many passengers were in the automobile.

But to the scores of irritated, skeptical reporters roaming Martha's Vineyard, Look's story was a gift from the heavens. It gave them—and their journalistic descendants—cause to raise prurient questions. Had Kennedy seen Look approach and, fearing he would be nabbed for drunk driving with a tipsy young woman in the car, sped off toward the bridge? If Kennedy and Kopechne were still on Chappaquiddick an hour after the last ferry departed, what had they been up to? Was there room in this new timeline for the second rescue attempt? Or had Kennedy embellished that story to excuse his failure to call the police?

"What's keeping this case alive, besides politics, is the public wants to know what the hell is a United States Senator doing on the island of Chappaquiddick having a few pops and ending up on a lonely road with a blonde," Steele would grumble. "Now that's very interesting but it's not a criminal matter."

ON THE WEEKEND OF THE ACCIDENT, District Attorney Dinis, the lead prosecutor for southeastern Massachusetts, had chosen to let the police chief and the county attorney conduct the investigation and negotiate the plea. Dinis could have asserted his prerogative at any time in those first hours but chose not to do so. As the days passed, however, the prosecutor—an elected official—became a target of scathing criticism and felt forced to take control of the case. He would ask the courts to conduct an inquest, he announced. As a first step he moved to exhume Kopechne's body from her Pennsylvania grave and have it examined for signs of foul play—for proof, as the court documents said, "as would cause one in authority to conclude that the death of Mary Jo Kopechne resulted from a cause other than drowning." State police chemists had found traces of blood on the dead woman's clothing, Dinis declared, and her body needed to be reexamined. Perhaps, his now-zealous staff suggested, she had been struck or strangled.

Kennedy's lawyers, who had been careful to seem cooperative when the charge in question was leaving the scene of an accident, were transformed into bulldogs at the suggestion Kopechne's death might be categorized as homicide. They were mindful as well that the senator might still be charged with manslaughter—for "willful, wanton or reckless" conduct. And if there was no clear-cut proof that Kennedy was drunk or speeding when his car flew off the bridge, there was case law in Massachusetts—including a notable precedent laid down in the wake of Boston's Cocoanut Grove fire, in which 492 people perished when flames swept through an overcrowded nightclub—that could open Kennedy to a charge that he showed "wanton or reckless disregard" for his passenger.

IT WASN'T JUST SOMETHING that happened, and then it was all over with," Joan would remember. It seemed to "drag on. I mean it went on for months." In the course of this long nightmare, she lashed out at unctuous sympathizers. "I don't need . . . I don't want your sympathy," she would say. Some were well-meaning, even good friends. Others, insisting it was for "her own good," passed on the gossip about her husband's extramarital activities. "They would insinuate that your life was pretty miserable," she remembered, "and they would name all the rumors that were going around."

The exhumation hearing was held in Wilkes-Barre, Pennsylvania, in October. The Kennedy attorneys and the Kopechne family lawyers, joining in opposition to Dinis, prevailed. Officer Look, Chief Arena, and diver Farrar told their stories under oath. A pathologist testified that Kopechne "lived for a certain time under the water . . . she breathed, that girl, she breathed . . . she wasn't dead instantaneously." But the traces of blood were attributed to a phenomenon in drowning cases—the presence of a bloody foam bubbling up from the lungs—and the judge (a Democrat facing reelection in a Democratic district) ruled that the questions raised at the two-day hearing were not relevant enough to override the Kopechne family's opposition to a "violation of the sepulchre."

Arena's testimony absolved Kennedy of negligence. Mills stuck by his July conclusion. Look's testimony was compelling, but "the fact that the vehicle operated by the driver may have entered the water at 12:40 A.M. . . . rather than at 11:15 P.M. . . . does not suggest a cause of death other than death by drowning," Judge Bernard Brominski ruled. They were not going to exhume a young woman's body and dissect her remains to see if she had had sex. Kennedy's account of the accident contained inconsistencies, but "these discrepancies do not alter the determination of the cause of death." Even if the body was exhumed, and a broken neck, ruptured organ, or fractured skull discovered, "none of these would be incompatible" with an automobile accident. It would only "give loose rein to speculation."

THERE WOULD BE NO exhumation. Kennedy's legal team triumphed as well in the jockeying over the inquest, an archaic appendage of Massachusetts law with no established ground rules. The family's iconic status in the commonwealth gave them the advantage. As his lawyers requested, the state supreme court ruled that the inquest would be closed to the press and public. A state police detective quietly contacted Smith and outlined the district attorney's evidence.

Judge Boyle retained the case and called the proceedings to order in the Edgartown courthouse on January 5. For four days of bracing cold, besieged by hundreds of reporters, the boiler room girls and their lawyers shared meals and work and waiting time on Martha's Vineyard. The young women had arrived on a plane together, and were famously photographed, healthy-looking American girls in short skirts and smiles, crossing the snow-swept tarmac. With their lawyers' coaching, they prepared to offer testimony.

The purpose of the inquest was to hear from witnesses, examine the evidence, and see if there was reason to charge Kennedy with manslaughter, vehicular homicide, or other offenses. The judge would reach a conclusion and write a report; it would then be left to Dinis to decide how—or whether—to take further legal action. Kennedy and the others would swear to tell the truth: unlike his unsworn report to Chief Arena, or his televised speech, he would be subject to prosecution for perjury if he lied.

Boyle had not flinched when insisting that Kennedy take the stand. But the senator was given the courtesy of testifying first. He stuck to the story he had told on television: he had two rum-and-Cokes before he and Kopechne left the cottage around 11:15 p.m. He had never stopped, never seen Deputy Look. He made a wrong turn and drove off the bridge. He had felt Mary Jo "struggling, perhaps hitting or kicking me" after getting "a half gulp" of air as the "pitch black" water poured in on him. His final thoughts, he said, before "pushing pressing and coming to the surface," was that they were drowning, and that no one would look for them until the next morning. "I have no idea in the world how I got out of that car," he said. He told of walking back to the party, and summoning Markham and Gargan, and of their fruitless rescue efforts. Dinis asked him why they had not then summoned police to the scene. Kennedy requested, and was granted, the opportunity to tell the story his way.

"Different thoughts came into my mind . . . about how I was going to really to be able to call Mrs. Kopechne at some time in the middle of the night to tell her that her daughter was drowned, to be able to call my own mother and my own father, relate to them, [and] my wife," he testified. "Even though I knew that Mary Jo Kopechne was dead and believed firmly that she was in the back of that car I willed that she remained alive," he said. "I was almost looking out the front window and windows trying to see her walking down that road. . . . I also had sort of a thought and the wish and desire and the hope that suddenly this whole accident would disappear."

Markham and Gargan had insisted that he must report the accident, and at the ferry slip, before swimming the channel, he had left them with the promise that he would go to the police. But as he swam to Edgartown "all the nightmares and all the tragedy and all the loss of Mary Jo's death was right

before me again," he said. By the time he reached the shore, he had "no further strength" and succumbed to the urge "that I just had to go to my room."

"I somehow believed that when the sun came up and it was a new
morning that what had happened the night before would not have happened," Kennedy said. "I just couldn't gain the strength within me, the
moral strength, to call Mrs. Kopechne at 2 o'clock in the morning and tell
her that her daughter was dead."

It was a genteel procedure: there was no testimony about Kopechne's
relationships with men or Kennedy's marital infidelities, and no thorough
examination of how much he had had to drink. The judge cut Farrar off
when the diver prepared to speculate about air bubbles and young women
submerged in cars. Look's story was persuasive, though analysis would
show how it grew ever more certain, and took on elaborations, over time.

A telling concession that emerged from the hearing, though not noted
at the time, came from the judge's questioning of the boiler room girls on
the final day. What, he asked Maryellen Lyons, did the partygoers think
when Gargan and Markham took off in the middle of the night? They
guessed that the senator's car had got stuck in the sand, said Lyons. But
there was no sand on the paved road to the ferry. The sand was at the beach.

Boyle found the witnesses credible. He did not resolve the questions of
how long Kopechne survived in the car, or whether Kennedy tried hard
enough to save her. Based on the testimony before him, he decided that
Kennedy had not been drunk. That said, Boyle's final report was damn-
ing. The judge concluded that Kennedy had lied under oath when he
testified about why he and Kopechne left the party. They had been heading to the beach, Boyle surmised, and when Kennedy failed to exercise
the proper caution on Dike Road, his negligence led to her death.

> I infer a reasonable and probable explanation . . . is that Kennedy
> and Kopechne did <u>not</u> intend to return to Edgartown at that time;
> that Kennedy did <u>not</u> intend to drive to the ferry slip and his turn
> onto Dyke Road was intentional. . . .

Dyke Bridge constitutes a traffic hazard, particularly so at night, and must be approached with extreme caution. A speed of even twenty miles per hour, as Kennedy testified to, operating a car as large as this Oldsmobile, would at least be negligent and, possibly, reckless.

If Kennedy knew of this hazard, his operation of the vehicle constituted criminal conduct. Earlier on July 18, he had been driven over Chappaquiddick Road three times and over Dyke Road and Dyke Bridge twice. I believe it probable that Kennedy knew of the hazard that lay ahead of him on Dyke Road but that, for some reason, not apparent from the testimony, he failed to exercise due care as he approached the bridge.

I, therefore, find there is probable cause to believe that Edward M. Kennedy operated his motor vehicle negligently . . . and that such operation appears to have contributed to the death of Mary Jo Kopechne.

A finding of negligence—a crucial ingredient to a manslaughter case—had been made. But Judge Boyle left it there and did not release his findings or the transcript of the inquest to the public until spring. He was a few months short of retirement. "As a legal scholar, he was a good golfer," one writer would conclude.

WHILE HIS LAWYERS WERE traversing the legal shoals, the man in the mirror had to reckon with himself. Ted Kennedy had failed to summon "moral strength"—the quality of courage that his brothers so admired. This tragedy was unlike the others that had beset his family. This time he was fortune's agent.

Years later, he was accosted by a woman as he took the underground passage between the Capitol and the Senate Office Building.

"Don't you ever think about that poor girl you killed?" she snarled.

"Every day of my life," he told her.

And yet it was an accident.

"I shouldn't have been there. I shouldn't have been in a car when I've had a few drinks," he told Tunney at the compound. Yet, "I don't feel guilty," he said. "I tried to save her but I couldn't. I tried to dive down and couldn't."

He had not had sex with Kopechne, he insisted. "I can be faulted terribly . . . but . . . it was an accident."

Leaving a party with a young woman "was one of those awful judgments that he displayed," Tunney said later. And "then he went back up to the house and was badly advised by others who had probably had too many drinks as well. So everything fell apart."

ON AUGUST 25, while Ted was away on a camping trip with his children, Ted and Kara, and his nephew John Kennedy Jr., Joan suffered the miscarriage she so feared.

She "was terrified to lose another baby by leaving her bed," her son Patrick would recall, but "she joined my father at the [Kopechne] funeral, because it was felt it would look bad if she wasn't at his side. She miscarried."

It was, Joan wrote a friend, "a very sad summer."

ROSE REACTED WITH CUSTOMARY stoicism. ("I always try to look at any situation in a quiet, composed, and calm way," she liked to say.) She had heard about the accident from Ann Gargan and canceled plans to attend a charity bazaar at the nearby St. Francis Xavier church.

"I did not understand why Joe Gargan or Markham did not report the matter to the police even if Ted did not have sense enough . . . especially when the body of the girl was in the car," Rose told her diary. "That is what seems so unforgivable and brutal to me." It was a feeling shared by the Kopechnes.

The press was being rough on Ted, Rose noted. "The criticism put in a question is, 'What would he do under stress as President, when he was so unstable in this predicament?'"

July was "unusually sunless," she wrote. "The worst season in years."

———————

TED'S FATHER, whose deterioration had seemed to accelerate after Robert Kennedy's murder, was freshly devastated at the news of Chappaquiddick.

Ted had gone to his father's room that Saturday afternoon looking "drawn, downcast, intimidated," Joseph Kennedy's nurse, Rita Dallas, recalled.

"Dad. I'm in some trouble," Ted said. "There's been an accident, and you're going to hear all sorts of things about me from now on. Terrible things. But, Dad, I want you to know that they're not true. It was an accident. I'm telling you the truth, Dad; it was an accident. . . . Dad, a girl was drowned."

Joe clutched Ted's hand and held it to his chest. In the hours after the accident, he must have "gone a little crazy," Ted confessed. The old man nodded, patted his son's hand, and shut his eyes. In the days that followed "I would see Ted stumbling around the compound," Dallas recalled. He was heartbroken, confused, despairing, "in a stupor, more alone than I had ever seen him."

JOSEPH KENNEDY DECLINED RAPIDLY. He "looks so helpless, bereft of even that minimal spark that used to light up when Ted approached," Rose told her diary.

Joseph's eyesight failed. He stopped eating. As summer turned to fall, and then toward winter, the patriarch succumbed. On November 16, Jacqueline and Ted, propped in chairs with blankets, spent Joseph's last night at his bedside. The next morning, as his family gathered around his bed and recited the rosary—they got as far as the Joyful Mysteries—he died.

Ted blamed himself for Joseph's unhappy deterioration. "I killed my father," he told Burton Hersh.

"As I SETTLED BACK into the Senate, into something like a state of equilibrium, I recognized that I had grown almost completely devoid of a state of mind I'd taken for granted since my early childhood," Kennedy would write in his memoirs. "That state of mind was joy."

"What amazing fun it had all once been. What adventures, what friendships and laughter and travels I had shared with my brothers and sisters," he wrote. "What a lift it had been, watching Jack and then Bobby soar into the stratosphere of world events, and to watch each of them accomplish mighty and good things; and then, incredibly, to join them on that plane, standing with them to engage history, with laughter and good cigars and the pranks we still played on one another. No more."

"THERE'S SOMETHING ABOUT ME I had hoped you would understand," he told a reporter in 1971. "I can't be hurt anymore."

Fourteen

UNLIKELY SAVIOR

On August 3, 1969, President Richard Nixon returned to the United States from an exhilarating circumnavigation of the planet. On the deck of the aircraft carrier *Hornet*, he had watched Neil Armstrong and the crew of the Apollo 11 moon mission splash down safely in the South Pacific. He had met with foreign leaders in Southeast Asia, India, Pakistan, and Europe, and mingled with the grunts in Vietnam. He had employed the Romanian government to send a secret signal to Beijing: The United States would welcome warmer relations. Nixon would go to China.

It was a dazzling trek, made sweeter still by the news from Chappaquiddick. Nixon's foremost Democratic rival, the greatest threat to his reelection, was ensnarled in seamy scandal. The president's men knew of Kennedy's proclivities. "See if the passenger was a girl," was the first thing speechwriter Pat Buchanan told an underling when the initial bulletins of an unnamed fatality reached them. Nixon was aghast at Kennedy's recklessness. "In the backseat!" he marveled.

The presidential party was in Guam when Kennedy made his mea culpa speech: in those pre-internet days, an aide in Washington held a phone up to a radio so the White House chief of staff, H. R. Haldeman, could listen and take notes. As they roamed the globe, Nixon and Haldeman weighed the repercussions like touts at a racetrack. "Obviously [Nixon feels] he was drunk, escaped from car, let her drown, said nothing until police got to him," Haldeman told his diary. "Shows fatal flaw in his character, cheated at school, ran from accident. . . . Feels it marks the end of Teddy."

But Nixon had regard, born of scaring experience, for the Kennedy name and muscle. He commanded his aides to make sure the senator did not slip the noose. "Nixon was mesmerized by Ted Kennedy. Even after Chappaquiddick," Tom Korologos, who lobbied for the administration on Capitol Hill, recalled. "The Kennedys had screwed him in 1960. He had a syndrome. He didn't want it to happen again. He was paranoid. Really. Paranoid." Kennedy sometimes played on Nixon's fears. "Nixon was apoplectic about the possibility that Ted was going to run," one of Kennedy's aides, Paul Kirk, remembered. "The senator didn't mind leaving him in that state. . . . If Nixon was awake at night worrying about it, that would be fine with him."

The rivalry with Kennedy fed a dark side of the president's personality, nudging him toward historic disgrace. Within hours after news broke of the accident on Chappaquiddick, a private detective—an ex–New York City cop named Tony Ulasewicz—was dispatched to Edgartown to pose as a reporter, collect gossip, and toil as provocateur. In the next three years, as a bagman and snoop, Ulasewicz would travel to twenty-three states investigating Kennedy, other prominent liberals, and newsmen. He went on to handle the payoffs in the Watergate cover-up, making so many calls from secluded pay phones that, like an ice cream man, he took to wearing a coin dispenser on his belt. In one fantastical scheme hatched by the Watergate tricksters, an actor was to lure Mary Jo Kopechne's friends to a midtown New York apartment where, in the act of seduction (or blackmail, as the flat would be fitted with a hidden camera), they would confess their secrets.

On issues like health care, hunger, draft reform, arms control, and U.S. relations with China, the slightest sign of a Kennedy initiative would spur a countermove from the Nixon administration. "Keep the offensive on this. Don't let Teddy grab it," Nixon scribbled to his aides. His taped conversations and correspondence with advisers reveal, time and again, his concerns that Kennedy would seize an issue and wield it against him in the 1972 presidential campaign. The dynamic was often good for the Republic: it spurred Nixon toward his historic opening with China, to cite but one example.

On August 4, Nixon welcomed the leaders of Congress to the White House to brief them on his voyage. In the Oval Office, he pulled Kennedy aside. The president, who knew something about comebacks from near annihilation, tried in his awkward manner to show empathy. It was just the two of them, and no notes were kept, but speechwriter William Safire found handwritten sentiments about Kennedy in a sheaf of papers used by the president. "Defeat—doesn't finish a man—quit—does," Nixon jotted. Then he had polished and woven the thoughts together: "A man is not finished when he's defeated. He's finished when he quits."

TWO DAYS AFTER NIXON'S avuncular chat, the president gave Kennedy a taste of defeat. With Vice President Spiro Agnew presiding and casting the fifty-first vote, an epic legislative battle wound to an end when the Senate approved funding for Nixon's ABM system. Rivals were exploiting Kennedy's debility. In early October, his protests were brushed aside as he watched the Senate carve exemptions in the Gun Control Act of 1968. In a debate on reforming the federal tax code, Kennedy's proposal for a minimum tax survived, but he lost on two well-crafted amendments which would have enhanced a bill from Russell Long crammed with special interest goodies. No one in Massachusetts or Washington missed the meaning when NASA announced it was closing its heralded electronics research facility in Cambridge, or when the Senate began hearings on changing the name of Cape Kennedy back to Cape Canaveral. Kennedy was hemorrhaging clout. "His enormous power and prestige in the Senate, supported by the reluctance of his colleagues to oppose a young man so likely to occupy the White House . . . and by their eagerness to curry favor with one who could so readily lend glamour and attract money to their personal causes, collapsed overnight," the *New York Times* reported. In the months that followed Chappaquiddick, "Kennedy's record of non-accomplishment in the Senate" was "truly astonishing."

"The wound was grave, politically and also personally, in terms of self-esteem, his view of how others saw him," said Robert Peabody, a scholar who was embedded on the Hill, studying Congress, at the time. Once again, Kennedy considered quitting; once again, his nature would not let him. "If all of us who share this belief walk away in disgust," he wrote a disillusioned young constituent who, furious with events in Vietnam, was planning to leave the country, "then there is little room for hope."

THE STRUGGLE BETWEEN DISTRICT Attorney Dinis and Kennedy's lawyers over the exhumation of Kopechne's body and the ground rules for the inquest had kept Chappaquiddick in the headlines. It also kept Kennedy from playing a public role in the battle over two of Nixon's nominees to the U.S. Supreme Court: a federal appellate judge from South Carolina by the name of Clement Haynsworth, and one from Florida named G. Harrold Carswell. Their appointments were bows to the South, a part of the Republican southern strategy that was reshaping American politics.

The South had been reliably Democratic from the days of Reconstruction through the years of World War II, but Republican Dwight Eisenhower, the general who had led the allied forces that liberated Europe, swept up prizes like Florida, Texas, Tennessee, and Virginia in his victorious presidential campaigns in the 1950s. Once Kennedy and Johnson pushed the Civil Rights Act through Congress, the segregationists surged toward the Republicans. Mississippi communities that gave Nixon only 9 percent of their votes in 1960 handed conservative Barry Goldwater 90 percent of their ballots when he ran for president in 1964. Over time, the growth of the southern suburbs, fueled by the spread of air-conditioning and the migration of retirees from the North, would give younger, moderate Republicans like George H. W. Bush of Texas, Howard Baker of Tennessee, and Linwood Holton of Virginia an opportunity to topple the courthouse Democrats in congressional and statehouse contests as well. Racism, if it emerged in a campaign, was cloaked in euphemisms like "welfare" or in opposition to unpopular race-mixing remedies like compulsory school busing. Otherwise, this new brand of Republicans ran on platforms that stressed a strong national defense, low taxes, school prayer, law and order, and other sturdy conservative issues. The Supreme Court's tenure under Chief Justice Earl Warren—with its landmark liberal rulings on civil rights (*Brown v. Board of Education*) and criminal justice (*Miranda v. Arizona, Gideon v. Wainwright*), and assertion of the one-man, one-vote principle (*Baker v. Carr*)—became a preferred target.

"By 1968 you can't say 'Nigger.' That hurts you, backfires," said Republican strategist Lee Atwater. The southern strategy shifted to "coded racism . . . busing . . . a Supreme Court judge."

In 1968, when Chief Justice Warren sought to orchestrate his retirement so that Lyndon Johnson could replace him with the liberal justice Abe Fortas, the Senate Republicans had rebelled. Fortas had history on his side: only one nominee had been rejected by the Senate in the previous seventy-four years, and none since 1930. Supreme Court nominations were genteel affairs—Warren had not even bothered to attend his own confirmation hearing. But control of the court was starting to become an ideological, and partisan, struggle. If the Republicans could stall the Fortas nomination, then a new president—Nixon—could name a conservative chief and steer the court to starboard. The Republicans slammed Fortas as a Johnson crony, a coddler of hoodlums and smut, and a jurist whose ethics left much to be desired—some of which was arguably true. And so, for the first time, a Supreme Court nomination was defeated by a filibuster.

Nixon named federal judge Warren Burger, a Republican from Minnesota, to take Warren's place. Under the direction of Attorney General John Mitchell and his assistant, William Rehnquist, the Justice Department unearthed evidence of how Fortas had accepted the munificence of a Wall Street swindler. They compelled him to resign. Now Nixon had a second vacancy to fill. As he had promised the South, he named one of their own—Haynsworth—to the court.

If not for the hard feelings left by the Fortas scrap, Haynsworth, fifty-six, may have been quickly confirmed. He was a courteous old-line gentleman of the South Carolina upstate, who addressed his wife as "Miss Dorothy," and could trace his American ancestors back to the Revolution.

The judge was markedly hostile to unions, and two of his civil rights opinions—allowing a private hospital to refuse to treat Black patients, and permitting a Virginia county to close rather than integrate its public schools—showed his Old South sensibility. Yet his overall record was the handiwork of the temperate, southern, Harvard-educated Eisenhower Democrat he was. Kennedy knew him slightly from his days at the University of Virginia law school: Haynsworth had been one of the judges who chose Kennedy and Tunney as the victors in the moot court competition.

The tactics used to ruin Fortas had liberals seething. "We had entered the politics of vendetta," Eastland's top aide, John Holloman, recalled. And with Warren and Fortas gone, the court's liberal core had shrunk to four. "People began to focus on how narrowly the court was divided." The struggle for control of the Supreme Court had begun: for fifty years it would ebb and flow, but never cease.

Organized labor and civil rights groups, opposing Haynsworth, looked to the Fearless Foursome. Phil Hart had drained his political capital in an unsuccessful defense of Fortas, and Joe Tydings was a Haynsworth family friend, so Birch Bayh took the lead. His staff fretted: constitutional reform was the senator's métier, and they needed the help of southerners like Eastland and Ervin to pass a pending measure to abolish the Electoral College. But organized labor had been there for Bayh when he faced a challenge to his reelection from a formidable Republican candidate in 1968. Bayh took the assignment.

As is often the case in contested nominations, the battle was not waged—publicly—on ideological grounds. As with Fortas, the assaults upon the nominee were powered by makeweight ethical issues. The MacGuffin in the Haynsworth nomination was a lawsuit involving a vending machine company, where the judge failed to disqualify himself, though he had a $450,000 investment. "It wasn't the conflict of interest that motivated the opposition, it was his ideology," Bayh acknowledged years later. "But what defeated Haynsworth was the conflict of interest."

Why Bayh and not Kennedy? Haynsworth had been nominated one month after Chappaquiddick. Kennedy was stumbling, barely able to function, and preoccupied with guilt and legal jeopardy. The war on Nixon's nominee would be fought on the terrain of personal behavior, and this was no longer Kennedy turf. His "moral armor was in bad repair," wrote newsman William Eaton, who would win a Pulitzer Prize for his coverage of the nomination. "This was right after Chappaquiddick," Jason Berman, an aide to Bayh, recalled. "You can understand, if you were going to make the fight on grounds of ethics and morality, why Teddy would not have been the best candidate."

Not for the last time in his Senate career, Kennedy's off-night behavior gagged him in an historic debate. He did, however, make a notable contribution to the cause. He unleashed his aide, the indefatigable James Flug, to work as a gumshoe with the liberal staffers and labor lawyers who were pawing through Haynsworth's million-dollar portfolio. Soon Flug and his cohorts had unearthed additional conflicts of interest. The trick was to drip and dribble the damaging evidence, to keep the press and the public enthralled. They were "cutting off a dog's tail, inch by inch," Senator Charles "Mac" Mathias, a Maryland Republican, recalled.

Haynsworth might have survived if Everett Dirksen had not died in September, leaving the Republican leadership in the hands of Senator Hugh Scott of Pennsylvania, a more liberal minority leader, and whip Robert Griffin of Michigan, who had spearheaded the opposition to Fortas and feared being seen as a hypocrite if he did not apply the same exacting standards to a Republican nominee. Ultimately, they both would vote to reject the nomination, and Haynsworth was defeated, 55 to 45 on November 21.

THE LOSS ENRAGED THE PRESIDENT. At one point, Bayh had sought the help of Senator William Fulbright, who warned, "Listen Birch . . . I know this president. If you beat this nominee, you will get someone worse." So it was. When Nixon nominated Carswell, who had most of Haynsworth's flaws and not many of his virtues, people assumed that the president was spitting in the Senate's eye. "The appointment was an act of vengeance," wrote the legal historian Henry J. Abraham.

Carswell was Georgia-born, had served in the Navy during World War II, and then worked as a U.S. attorney. He had been recommended to Mitchell by Burger, but had been on the appellate court for less than a year. Unlike Haynsworth, he had no august alma mater or record of legal scholarship to add sparkle to his résumé. He was a graduate of the Mercer University law school who liked to hunt and garden and play bridge with "the plantation crowd"—the white Tallahassee upper crust.

Carswell was nominated on January 19, 1970. Within a week the press had unearthed a speech he gave in 1948 while campaigning for the Georgia legislature. "I am a Southerner by ancestry, birth, training, inclination, belief and practice. I believe that segregation of the races is proper and the only practical and correct way of life in our state," Carswell had said. "I yield to no one . . . in the firm vigorous belief in the principles of white supremacy."

Mitchell had botched the vetting process. But Nixon did not withdraw the nomination. He had concluded that his path to reelection lay through confrontation and division. They would force-feed Carswell to the Senate. If they succeeded, they'd have kept their promise to the South. If they lost, they could use the defeat to their advantage, turning South against North, liberal against conservative, and Black against white.

In the Senate, the liberals were making their own assessment. Few looked forward to a second clash. The mood, said Bayh, was "God, don't put us through that again!" Bayh wished to move to other issues; Tydings was in a tough reelection campaign; organized labor was not very interested; and Kennedy was AWOL. Kennedy took David Burke aside and voiced his fear that should they persist, they might permanently alienate Eastland. "The chairman's been good to me, Dave, you know," he said. "Maybe we call Flug off a little."

Civil rights leaders saw it differently: They had bled to stop Haynsworth, how could they let Nixon succeed with someone worse?

When Burke tried to rein him in, Flug erupted. "I had an awful row with Flug. . . . We both wound up in tears. Me trying to call Flug off. It was impossible," Burke remembered. "Teddy says, 'Jesus, Dave, can you calm Jimmy down?' Well, we couldn't and we didn't. And he succeeded again.

Thank God." Flug was a genius at creating a jungle and forcing Kennedy to hack his way out, another of the senator's aides, Carey Parker, concluded.

His views on race aside, Carswell was a pedestrian jurist. Nearly 60 percent of his decisions had been reversed by higher courts, more than twice the average rate for district court judges in the South. Marian Wright Edelman, an adviser to the Leadership Conference on Civil Rights, dispatched an investigator to Florida, who found another blot on the judge's record. As a U.S. attorney in 1956, Carswell had drawn up the papers of incorporation for a public golf course in Tallahassee so it could transform itself into a private, whites-only club and evade a Supreme Court ruling prohibiting segregation in municipal facilities.

Nixon had "again nominated a mediocre candidate with no indications of particular intelligence, leadership, insight, or respect among his brethren," Flug reported in a memo to Kennedy. "His official record is quite consistent with the notion that he is a segregationist and white-supremacist."

Eastland was determined to approve the nomination before the liberal opposition could get organized. He scheduled the first hearing for January 27. The judge received a warm welcome—the lovefest marred only by news of the Tallahassee country club, which was published in that morning's newspapers. In a private interview with the American Bar Association the previous evening, Carswell had acknowledged that he helped craft the club's letter of incorporation. But when the question was raised in the public hearing, the judge said, "No, sir." Kennedy brought the discrepancy to light. It would be taken as a sign of the judge's bad faith and give wavering senators cause to oppose him.

"Carswell took an active role, not a passive role, in transfer of the Tallahassee municipal golf course to a private club," wrote conservative columnist James Kilpatrick. "Forgive my incredulity, but if Carswell didn't understand the racial purpose of this legal legerdemain, he was the only one in north Florida."

Kennedy was influenced by Flug's argument—in a memo titled "How to Beat Carswell"—that the votes were there to defeat the nomination. Flug began, "I smell blood." The liberals were impressed as well by the forceful speech given by Kennedy's seatmate, Republican senator Ed Brooke, the chamber's lone African American, in opposition.

CARSWELL'S OPPONENTS WERE GATHERING, but needed time to conduct research on the judge's record, to rile up the public and to halt Eastland's efforts to ram the nomination through. The southerners and conservatives were proven masters of delay; now the Senate liberals showed that they could exploit the calendar as well.

The Judiciary hearings ended on February 3. The first two weeks in March, by common consent, had been reserved to debate and vote on an extension of the Voting Rights Act. If Carswell's foes could postpone a vote on his nomination until after the debate on voting rights began, they would get the time they needed to rally the country.

But could they stall for all of February?

The liberals got help from an unlikely source when Strom Thurmond launched a mini filibuster in committee on February 3, to block consideration of Bayh's measure to abolish the Electoral College.

Eastland then tried to schedule a committee meeting on February 4, during hours when the Senate was in session—a move that, under the rules, required unanimous consent. Kennedy and Hart objected.

Eastland vowed to convene his committee after the Senate adjourned, no matter how late they stayed. Tydings threatened to take the floor and keep the Senate in all night.

Eastland retreated. The next day, February 5, Tydings took advantage of a committee tradition that gave individual senators the power to delay any vote for a week.

That pushed matters to February 12, which, because of the Lincoln's Birthday recess, became February 16.

Finally, Eastland got his vote. As expected, the Judiciary Committee approved the nomination, 13–4, with the Fearless Foursome alone in opposition. But the liberals then took every day of the ten they were allotted by the Senate rules to write a minority report, kicking the can to the morning of February 27, a Friday.

Technically, there were still two days—Friday and Saturday—to squeeze in a debate and a vote on Carswell. But any senator could employ a Senate courtesy and ask that a measure be held for a day, and it would take unanimous consent to call the Senate together on Saturday. The race to March 1 was over, and the liberals had won.

Majority Leader Mansfield announced that he would schedule debate on Carswell after the Senate finished with the Voting Rights Act. If the South wanted a quick vote on its judge, it would have to forgo an extended debate on voting rights. When an Alabama senator launched a filibuster against the voting rights bill (and the Senate took its Easter recess), the vote on Carswell was pushed back to April.

The liberals had secured the time they needed to persuade their colleagues that Carswell should, and could, be beaten.

AND NOW, help arrived from an unexpected quarter. The nation's legal establishment stunned itself, and the capital, by rising in opposition. It wasn't so much that Carswell was a bigot, the lawyers said, it was that he was so second-rate. In making the appointment, Nixon had insulted and riled the profession. The uprising began in Manhattan, and spread like a contagion to the Ivy League, to the UCLA and University of Virginia law school faculties, to students at Columbia, the deans of Harvard, Yale, and Penn, the heads of bar associations, judges, and the counsels for federal agencies. Two of Carswell's southern colleagues, the venerated judges Elbert Tuttle and John Minor Wisdom, who had braved white vilification for their support of civil rights, came out against him. Flug efficiently leaked the news.

Nixon's aides began to fret. "They think Carswell's a boob, a dummy," White House lobbyist Bryce Harlow told the president. "And what counter is there to that? He is."

After hearing that Tuttle opposed the nominee, Republican senator

Roman Hruska went "reeling off the Senate floor and into the presence of a radio interviewer," wrote Richard Harris, a correspondent for the *New Yorker*. Hruska stepped right up to the microphone and declared, "Even if he were mediocre, there are a lot of mediocre judges and people and lawyers. They are entitled to a little representation aren't they?"

"The remark was to go down as one of the greatest political blunders in the history of the Senate, and, in the opinion of those most intimately involved in the battle over the nomination it contributed as much as any other factor to Carswell's defeat," Harris wrote. Nixon reacted badly. He refused to plead with wavering senators for their votes. He insisted, publicly, that they be rubber stamps. He banned independent-minded Republicans from White House social functions.

The public galleries, the press gallery, and the Senate floor were jammed with onlookers on April 8. The atmosphere was "tense, electric, nervous," one witness recalled, as the Senate rejected Carswell by a vote of 51 to 45. A key vote was that of Margaret Chase Smith, who was incensed to learn that the White House was deceptively citing her as a Carswell supporter to pressure other Republican moderates. Not much liking being so used, she voted "No."

The president took a day to let his molten anger harden, then went before the nation to declare that his two southern nominees were victims of a hostile, liberal elite. As long as the Senate was so constituted, he said, "I will not nominate another Southerner and let him be subjected to the kind of malicious character assassination accorded both Judges Haynsworth and Carswell. . . . I understand the bitter feelings of millions of Americans who live in the South about the act of regional discrimination that took place in the Senate."

With his appeal to white southern victimhood, Nixon made converts below the Mason-Dixon line. He would sweep the region when running for reelection in 1972. But liberals came away from the Haynsworth-Carswell wars with a long-lasting victory as well. Nixon's next nominee was Harry Blackmun, a Minnesota Republican—he had been the best man at his friend Burger's wedding—who was quickly, unanimously confirmed. In January 1973, Blackmun would write the majority opinion in the case of *Roe v. Wade,* upholding a legal right for abortion. More than any other, the *Roe* case guaranteed that the struggle for the court would continue for decades.

Carswell went back to Florida to mount an unsuccessful campaign for the Senate, in which he salted his stump speech with references to Chappaquiddick. "Most of the opposition to me was engineered by ultra-liberals like Teddy Kennedy," he told his audiences. "He was driving the whole thing. . . . Er . . . I shouldn't say that. He doesn't drive too well." Carswell might well have stayed away from the subject of moral behavior. In 1976, he was arrested by a vice squad after soliciting sex from an undercover agent in a Florida men's room.

Nixon's appeal to white southern grievance was his public response to the Carswell fiasco. There was a covert reply as well. The president "wants us to step up political attack. Investigators on Kennedy and Muskie plus Bayh," Haldeman told his diary on April 9. "Have to declare war." Nixon would be frustrated on this count too. Before the month was out, his mismanagement of the conflict in Vietnam would help save Kennedy's career.

THE PRESIDENT'S INITIAL ATTEMPTS to end the war—offering the warmongers in Hanoi an olive branch in an armored fist—had failed. Huge antiwar demonstrations in 1969—the Moratorium to End the War in October and the Mobilization in November—resulted. In response to those who marched that fall, the president retreated to seclusion, pulled out a yellow pad, and wrote a speech calling on "the great silent majority" to defeat his critics.

Nixon dispatched Agnew to attack the "radical liberals" in American society—those "effete" and "decadent" intellectuals, student protesters, professors, broadcasters, and members of Congress who dared to challenge a president. Americans should "separate them from our society with no more regret than we should feel over discarding rotten apples," the vice president said. He called for polarization. "Dividing the American people has been my main contribution to the national political scene," he would boast a few months later. "I not only plead guilty to this charge, but I am somewhat flattered by it."

Winter turned toward spring. Communist forces had long used neighboring Cambodia, and Laos to its north, to funnel arms and ordnance to their armies in South Vietnam. In response, Nixon had ordered U.S. warplanes to launch a clandestine air campaign in Cambodia. The Pentagon hid the bombing from all but a handful of the members of Congress, via falsified records and top-secret classification. It was not enough. In a televised speech on April 30, Nixon announced that fifty thousand allied troops—including thirty-one thousand Americans—would invade Cambodia.

As a military tactic, the incursion was a mixed success, but Nixon and his aides were surprised and unnerved by the force of the reaction it ignited at home. There were strikes and protests at hundreds of campuses, and a hundred thousand demonstrators marched on the capital. Nixon dismissed the striking students as "bums" three days before thirteen students were shot by National Guard troops at Kent State University in Ohio. Two of the four who died were only walking to class. The president and his national security team had now reached the point of "psychological exhaustion," Kissinger recalled. Nixon took off on a solitary predawn ramble to the Lincoln Memorial, trying in vain to reason with the student protesters. In the Senate, the war's critics proposed legislation to cut off funds for the Cambodian operation and terminate funding for combat operations across Indochina. The debate would rage for weeks.

As bedlam gripped Washington and turmoil shook the country, the transcript of the closed-door Chappaquiddick inquest, and Judge Boyle's ruling on Mary Jo Kopechne's death, became public. For a day, they shared a place on the nation's front pages with the war, then vanished in the storm over Cambodia, the campuses, and the Kent State shooting. The reaction in the Senate was "almost nil," the *Boston Herald* noted, as news from Southeast Asia "dulled the political impact of the inquest finding."

KENNEDY HAD BEEN LUDICROUSLY LUCKY, as Boyle's report was potentially ruinous. The judge had ruled that the senator was reckless and negligent—necessary elements for a charge of manslaughter. But, transfixed by the dramas in Kent State and Cambodia, no major news organizations hammered District Attorney Dinis to follow up.

"Kennedy Calls It Madness" was the headline in the *Herald* when the senator made his first visit home after the release of the inquest report. The "madness" was not his behavior on Chappaquiddick—it was that of Nixon in Southeast Asia. He "concentrated . . . on attacking President Nixon's action in Cambodia" and "brushed aside newsmen's questions about the Kopechne case" as he spoke about the war before audiences of broadcasting executives, firefighters, teachers, dentists, and college students in the first week of May. "Today we have all been jolted back into more important things," Kennedy told the broadcasters. "We are back to war and more war and there does not seem to be an end to it."

Without public pressure, the Massachusetts authorities were content to let things slide. Boyle "failed to exercise his statutory power and order Kennedy's arrest," the *Boston Globe* Spotlight team concluded, after an exhaustive review of the case. And then "Dinis, in an apparent abuse of his authority, steered the grand jury away from pursuing Kennedy."

To be fair, it was unlikely that Dinis, with no hard evidence of drunk driving or recklessness, could have persuaded a Massachusetts jury to convict Ted Kennedy of manslaughter. But the prosecutor's unwillingness to try reflected Kennedy's stature in the state. "We were dealing with deities," Dinis told the Spotlight team.

Fifteen

BUBBLE AND TOIL
AND TROUBLE

Robert Byrd was not one to forget. He never forgot the Christmas mornings without gifts, or missing Sunday school for lack of socks, or wearing his sneakers through mountain winters because his parents could not afford to buy him shoes. He was raised in a West Virginia hollow—"Away out there in a world of loneliness," he recalled—by a miner and his wife. She never once kissed the boy, and maybe that was the way of the mountain folk, but he'd heard the taunts at school that she wasn't his real mother at all.

The closest town was Wolf Creek, near Sinks Grove and Pickaway in the southeastern part of the state. The Byrds had no car, no indoor plumbing. He studied beneath an oil lamp. His only diversion was the fiddle that his father had bought him, for $27, on a trip to Beckley. "It took him a long time to save that much money working in a coal mine," Byrd remembered. "I can remember coming back home. . . . The moon was shining, and I was hugging that fiddle under my arm."

The family raised hogs. It was Robert's job to beg neighbors for their garbage, which they would leave outside for the boy to collect in a bucket. In winter the slop would freeze, and he would have to chop at it and mix it with feed and warm water before giving it to the hogs. When the time came to butcher the swine, it was Robert's job to slaughter them. His father gave him a .22 rifle, and Robert looked down its sights and shot each hog in the head.

As a teen, he learned that he was not who he thought he was. He was born Cornelius Calvin Sale Jr., not Robert Carlyle Byrd. While he was an infant, his mother had died of the Spanish flu, and been hastily buried in an unmarked grave. Vlurma Byrd, the woman who raised him, was his real father's sister. His father lived in North Carolina. He went once to meet them—his dad, his sister, and his three brothers. Cornelius Sr. wept. It must have been an emotional experience, an interviewer suggested many years later. "Not for me," Byrd said, "but for him it was." Byrd lingered a week and returned to West Virginia.

He took work as a butcher in the town of Crab Orchard, and then, like many from Appalachia, left the mountains to work in the factories during World War II. It was during the war that he joined the Ku Klux Klan as a regional organizer—a Kleagle. The local Grand Dragon concluded that this young man, all canniness and resolve, had the stuff of a leader, and urged him into politics. Byrd was an outsider, with no help from the unions or the local Democratic Party machines. He campaigned with a band of musicians. He would start fiddling "Old Joe Clark" and set feet tapping, and after an appreciative crowd had gathered, Byrd would make his pitch. "I grew up in a coal miner's home, married a coal miner's daughter, ate from a coal miner's table, slept in a coal miner's bed," he would tell them. "Are you going to vote against a man like that?"

They sent him to the state legislature, to the House of Representatives, and to the U.S. Senate. He never lost an election.

AT ONE POINT IN THE 1960s, Byrd got it in his head that the post of Senate majority leader was a fine job indeed. So he maneuvered to claim the bottom rung of the leadership ladder—the thankless chore of secretary of the Senate Democratic Conference—and assigned himself the pedestrian tasks that Mansfield had given to four assistant whips: corralling

votes, arranging the calendar, and generally ensuring that the Democratic majority was present and accounted for. The four were happy to
turn over their duties to the solicitous Byrd; so was Long, then struggling
with his marital and drinking problems. Mansfield was aging. Byrd could
see the path before him.

If anyone crossed Byrd in his laborious climb to power, well, he would
not forget that either. And the Kennedys ranked atop his list. When Ted
Kennedy ran off the bridge at Chappaquiddick, Byrd saw his opportunity
to wound the privileged son, and took it. The events in Cambodia and
Ohio may have sheltered Kennedy from the harshest fallout of the inquest, but it would not prevent his colleagues from rendering their own
verdict.

THE ANIMOSITY BETWEEN BYRD and the Kennedys went back a long
way. When Byrd arrived in the Senate in 1959, Majority Leader Lyndon
Johnson had been a mentor, and found him a seat on the Appropriations
Committee, the perch from which, for almost half a century, Byrd would
assiduously steer federal spending to West Virginia. Byrd had represented
Johnson's interests in 1960, when John Kennedy squared off against Humphrey in the West Virginia primary. With unfailing energy, Byrd campaigned across the state. "This primary may be your last chance to stop
Kennedy," he told the crowds. He was fourteen years removed from the
Klan and swore that his previous association with the Catholic-hating
group was not influencing his actions, but that didn't stop him from raising John Kennedy's religion as an issue.

After joining the bloc of southern senators who opposed the landmark civil rights bills, Byrd then tangled with Robert Kennedy. Byrd had
held the floor for fourteen hours in the filibuster against the Civil Rights
Act, and voted against the Voting Rights Act and the nomination of Thurgood Marshall to the Supreme Court. Kennedy parried, moving to block
Byrd's nominees for the federal bench and accusing the West Virginia senator—who was overseeing the District of Columbia's budget—of

contributing to the decline of the capital's public schools, with their largely African American student bodies. Then came a clash, on the Senate floor, that neither side—nor those who witnessed it—would forget.

IN THE CLOSING DAYS of the 1967 session, Robert and Ted Kennedy and a group of fellow liberals were using the approaching holiday recess for leverage—by threatening to filibuster a Social Security bill that the White House endorsed and many of their colleagues wished to pass and boast about back home. The Kennedys were fully supportive of the Johnson administration's desire to increase the retirement benefits, but opposed the House version of the bill, which imposed work requirements on welfare recipients. In the House-Senate conference, Russell Long had caved, in favor of the House. Now the conference report was back in the Senate, awaiting final passage. Johnson and Mansfield pleaded with the liberals to let the bill pass, promised to eliminate the offensive requirements in the coming session, and even threatened to cut them off from Democratic donors—all to no avail. "This is the time for some moxie," Robert told a friend.

As the session neared its December 15 adjournment, the liberal senators appointed watchmen to stake out the Senate floor. If Mansfield, Long, and Byrd tried to pass the conference report, the liberal assignee was to object and start a little filibuster. With all the senators itching to leave town, "we would have eventually won," Senator Fred Harris, a liberal from Oklahoma, recalled.

On Tuesday, December 14, the Senate convened at 9 a.m. with the customary tedium. Mansfield asked that they dispense with the reading of the journal. A bill to compensate Greene County, Mississippi, the sum of $46,455 for maintaining U.S. Forest Service roads was passed, as was a measure to name a new Bronx post office after Charles Buckley, a former congressman. Senator Frank Lausche of Ohio spoke, relaying a complaint from a constituent that the national anthem was no longer played in movie theaters on U.S. Army posts.

Mansfield momentarily left the floor. At his seat in the back of the chamber, Joseph Tydings—the liberals' watchdog—was sifting through the office mail. Robert Kennedy, assured by the leadership that the Social Security bill would not come up that morning, was chairing a hearing on Indian education. He paused to phone Harris to see how things were going.

As Harris spoke to Kennedy he saw Mansfield's aide Charles Ferris burst from the chamber, waving his arms and shouting, "They passed it!"

"Passed what?" asked Harris.

"The Social Security bill," said Ferris.

"Where was Joe Tydings?" Harris asked.

"Sitting on his ass," said Ferris.

THE LIBERALS WERE UNDONE.

Once Mansfield departed, Long and Byrd, from their front-row roosts, had quietly asked unanimous consent to begin legislative business and make the Social Security bill the matter at hand.

"The question is on agreeing to the motion of the senator from Louisiana," said the clerk. No one objected.

"The question now is on adoption of the conference report," said the clerk. No one objected.

The Senate rules allow for votes to be retaken if the winning side accedes, and so Long moved that the vote be reconsidered. Just as swiftly, Byrd moved to table Long's motion. No one objected.

The Social Security bill had been passed, the opportunity for reconsideration ended, and liberal victory lost. It all took ninety seconds.

Long's supporters gathered to pat him on the back. But Mansfield was aghast. And the liberals were aflame.

"I was unavoidably absent from the Senate chamber when, like a flash of lightning, the conference report on the Social Security bill was agreed to," said Mansfield after reclaiming the floor. "The way it was done raises a most serious question. . . . There is such a thing as decorum and dignity."

Long declined to bend. "I have done a lot of filibustering in my day," he replied, putting the blame on Tydings. "If you do not want the Senate to vote, you better start talking."

Robert Kennedy believed that he had a commitment from Mansfield and Long that, at the very least, he would get a chance to debate the bill. He was seething when his turn to speak arrived.

Long had departed, but Byrd was there to take the beating, and Kennedy framed it in ways that the West Virginia senator would not forget. The yokels, Kennedy said, had shown a lack of class. The liberals had been denied "that elementary consideration and decency that exists among men," said Kennedy. It was "a reflection not only on the Senate but also on the integrity and honesty of those who participated."

"There was no attempt to do anything here this morning that was indecent," Byrd replied. He called on Kennedy to withdraw his insult.

Kennedy refused to do so. Instead, he piled on. "I thought I was dealing with men," he said.

Don't get mad; get even. Byrd resumed his duties, content in his alliance with Long and his place in the line of succession. And then Ted Kennedy struck in 1969, stripping Long of the whip's job and stomping on Byrd's fingers where they gripped the leadership ladder.

"I did not like Ted Kennedy," Byrd would recall, the memory of moment etched as if by acid more than thirty-five years later. "He did not like me."

"I didn't like him from the start," Byrd said. "He didn't come up the ladder like I did. I was a poor boy . . . I had to scratch my way up. I was made fun of, called a hillbilly."

Kennedy "leapfrogged over me," Byrd remembered. "All of a sudden came this scion of wealth." Now "Kennedy was the whip," said Byrd. "And I despised him because he leapfrogged over me and I thought he looked down on me."

"And so," said Robert Byrd, "I began to plan."

BYRD'S PLAN WAS AS old as Aesop. He would be an ant, prepping for winter, as Kennedy played the grasshopper, a wastrel singing through the days of summer.

The West Virginian "lurked and he festered over this," David Burke recalled. "Bubble and toil and trouble."

Kennedy's concept of the whip job was elastic. Like Mansfield, he loathed the drudgery of tending to the caucus and managing the floor. Colleagues griped. Committee chairmen, who had spent years learning details and contours of their turf, bridled when Kennedy brought in experts from Harvard to instruct them. His fellow senators viewed his field hearings and fact-finding missions as typically Kennedy, hunting for glory.

He had publicly disavowed any race for the White House in 1972, but those with their own ambitions never quite believed it. The events on Chappaquiddick would have snuffed any other senator's prospects, but the power of the Kennedy name and myth would preserve his status as a potential president until America's voters had an opportunity to express their judgment about his character. And so as he dashed to Paris or Geneva, the donkey work was left to the irked, impatient Mansfield.

"Teddy's heart wasn't in it," Ferris said. He "knew what the job entailed and was almost subconsciously—Who will rid me of this nuisance?"

Byrd saw that Kennedy was vulnerable. "I worked the plan. I took my time. I followed the plan to the limit, and nobody knew it but me," he would recall. He looked at Kennedy's back and thought, "I'm coming after you. You may think I'm nothing but a piece of dirt, but you're going to find out."

CONGRESS WAS EVOLVING, and this gave Byrd an opportunity. Dirksen was dead, Russell dying, Ervin in his final term. The big-city political machines were disintegrating as voters convoyed to the suburbs. The South had become a two-party battleground. Vietnam, desegregation, and the Great Society, and the taxes to pay for it all, had fed political awareness. Senators were now independent entrepreneurs, prima donnas who wooed constituents via television and direct mail appeals—not winter coats, turkeys at Christmas, or jobs on the state.

The issues were complex, the number of special interest groups and news reporters swelling. The days of elaborate courtesies and sacred tradition, when a few shuffling bulls could gather in an office off the floor, sip bourbon, and set the agenda, were nearing an end. Senators wanted to chair their own committees and subcommittees, as forums for newsworthy hearings and platforms from which to promote legislation. They needed to be busy raising money, to buy advertising time on television. They had to travel—back home, and around the country—to hike their profiles. They no longer could get by with two legislative assistants and a couple of "girls" who answered the mail. Staffs inexorably expanded, and by the end of the 1960s, Congress was a billion-dollar business, employing thirty-one thousand people; the days in session had grown by a third, and the number of recorded votes had soared.

In such demanding times a senator might well appreciate a party leader who came to his assistance. Someone who washed the sweatshirts. That is what Byrd set out to do. That was his plan.

When a senator needed to attend a fundraiser, it was Byrd who adjusted the Senate schedule. When a senator needed to give a speech downtown, or have lunch with a constituent, it was Byrd who ensured that he didn't miss an important roll call, or arranged to "pair" him with another absentee from the opposing side, so that their positions were recorded. When a senator wanted material inserted in the *Congressional Record*, or a parking ticket fixed, Byrd made it happen. When a senator coveted a committee assignment, it was Byrd who helped secure it. When a senator needed to rush for the airport at the end of the week, or before a recess, it was Byrd who called the taxi. The joke went around the Senate club: If you left your shoes outside your door, Bobby Byrd would have them shined.

He worked nights and weekends, memorized the rules, haunted the floor, guarded prerogatives. During the time they served together, George Smathers employed an array of enticements to try to get Byrd to visit Florida. Byrd always declined until, finally, he felt the need to explain. "I have never in my life played a game of cards. I have never in my life had a golf club in my hand. I have never in life hit a tennis ball. . . . I don't know how to swim," he told Smathers. "I don't do any of those things. I have only had to work all my life."

By "personal temperament" Byrd was "better suited for the house-keeping aspects," one observer wrote. Byrd "understood, far better than Long or Kennedy, how small personal favors performed for other Senators might build a credit balance that could be put to other uses." Often, after doing a favor, Byrd might remind a colleague with a letter, and record it in the notebook he carried, with a page devoted to each fellow Democrat. His avidity was cloaked in unctuous humility, and in time he was likened to Uriah Heep. "No one has mastered the art of tickling senatorial vanities better," said the *New Republic*.

Byrd would ambush Kennedy, just as Kennedy had once bushwhacked Long. "I didn't make an open campaign, but every time the subject came up, I made some headway," Byrd recalled. "As the time went on encouragement became commitment and commitments became . . . firm."

KENNEDY, meanwhile, eyed Byrd with fateful complacency. He had returned to the Senate after Kopechne's death, then took leave again to bury and mourn his father, to deal with the inquest, to recover from a bout of pneumonia, and to make several trips to Europe. He was running hard for reelection in 1970—the first time he would face the voters after Chappaquiddick—and packing his schedule with days and nights in Massachusetts. He appeared on the *Today* show, his first such interview in two years, and on *Meet the Press*. He accepted an invitation to serve as a guest narrator for the Boston Pops Orchestra as it performed Aaron Copland's *Lincoln Portrait*. He was a speaker at the Kent State memorial services and testified before a presidential commission on campus unrest. He badgered his staff to find issues that would impress the liberal press and demonstrate to voters that he was still an effective voice in Washington.

In March, Kennedy went to Dublin, where he had been invited to give the bicentenary address to the College Historical Society at Trinity College, a speech and debating club whose roots went back to the time of the

Whig philosopher and statesman Edmund Burke. In the tumult of their own times, Kennedy told the audience, there was a lesson to be taken from Burke's antipathy toward the radicals of the French Revolution. "History is a harsh judge of those so caught up with revolution that they forget reformation," said Kennedy. "Change . . . will not come through random acts of violence and disruption."

For Burke and, by extension, for lawmakers like Ted Kennedy, "a lifetime of thought and action consumed by the slow labor of improving the human condition was more valuable than all the rhetoric of destruction and impossible visions," Kennedy said, in a speech he had personally worked and reworked. This was "no time for moderate men to be in retreat," but to act, with dedication, and to persevere.

Though the great civil rights laws struck down legal barriers, they did not address lasting in equities in wealth, housing, education, and employment, said Kennedy. This "illusion of progress" had led to disenchantment, and violence, among disadvantaged minorities. Their intemperate response, in turn, fed an anger that Wallace and Nixon and Agnew exploited.

"Frustrations and impatience gave rise to a new militancy and a harsh rhetoric fearful to many [average white Americans]—and those fears were played upon by forces of reaction," Kennedy said. "The tide has shifted in America." He expressed foreboding about the Nixon playbook, "the present reactions—the words of law and order, the trials and jailings, the . . . name-calling by men in high places."

"The future will either be one of increasing justice for our fellow man and the liberation of the individual to enrich his own destiny," said Kennedy, "or it will be a future of increasing repression and control, if a future at all. Discontent must either be met or suppressed. To meet it is liberation. To suppress it is the end of liberty."

IT WAS A FINE SPEECH, but on his return to Washington Kennedy found that his standing in the Senate continued to erode. A project he had been working on, to win younger Americans the right to vote, had been pilfered by Mansfield and his staff.

The rationale for changing the law was basic: If young men could be drafted to fight and die in Vietnam at the age of eighteen, then they must surely be mature enough to vote. But—and here there were echoes of the poll tax fight—the Democratic congressional leaders believed they needed a constitutional amendment to lower the voting age, with the arduous requirement that it be ratified by three-fourths of the states.

Archibald Cox, a Harvard law professor whose ties to the Kennedys dated back to the 1960 campaign, had suggested that the voting age could be lowered by a simple act of Congress. His proposal was refined by Carey Parker, another of the bright young men who came to Washington to work on Kennedy's staff. Parker was a graduate of Harvard Law School and had clerked for a Supreme Court justice. He was a Rhodes Scholar, with a PhD in biological science. He served Kennedy as a wordsmith, speechwriter, and policy wonk.

Parker would compile a stellar record as the senator's chief legislative strategist over the next four decades and emerge as something of a Senate legend. Hauteur was not his style. But he was new to the staff, and well aware that Kennedy ached to secure the lion's share of the credit for lowering the voting age in this post-Chappaquiddick election year. When Kennedy found that Mansfield's office had assumed control of the issue, Parker and his boss bridled. It was "the only time I ever saw Mansfield do anything unseemly," Wayne Owens, another Kennedy aide, fumed. "He stole the issue away. Because it was coming. And it was Teddy's issue."

Mansfield had the measure attached to the pending extension of the Voting Rights Act. When his assistant Charles Ferris recruited Barry Goldwater and other senators to broaden the base of support, Parker and Kennedy, furious at the prospect of diluted glory, took turns berating him. Did the senator want to pass the law, Ferris countered, or was he only interested in the publicity? Kennedy slammed down the phone in fury. The capital was learning that affable Teddy could throw an elbow.

The legislation passed. Kennedy, to stake his ownership, took on the role of the Senate's lawyer, and personally argued in the federal courts on behalf of the measure. Ultimately, the issue landed with the Supreme Court, which agreed with Kennedy's legal reasoning—but only as it applied to federal elections. To standardize the process, Congress and the states responded in record time, passing and ratifying the Twenty-Sixth Amendment, which extended the franchise to thirteen million young Americans in state and local elections as well. All in all, it was one of Kennedy's more notable, lasting accomplishments.

MASSACHUSETTS, meanwhile, seemed poised to forgive. On St. Patrick's Day in Southie, Kennedy was welcomed like a rock star. Shouting and crying, "We love you, Ted," some 250,000 "turned the streets of South Boston into a merry mob scene, clamoring for autographs, handshakes, hugs, kisses" as Kennedy passed by, the *Boston Globe* reported. "He was mobbed and touched and kissed and congratulated and wished good luck over every step of the way. People, by the score, broke through police lines just to be near him."

It was the same when he marched in Lawrence, where "middle-aged Irish women broke from the curb to grab his hand and kiss him and mother him," and at the St. Clare Catholic Women's League in Lawrence, the Democratic District Club in Wakefield, the Emerald Club's corned beef and cabbage dinner in Worcester, and the Friendly Sons of St. Patrick in Everett.

"He's in disrepute . . . and the little old ladies are coming up and throwing flowers at him, hugging him, kissing him," marveled Martin Nolan of the *Boston Globe*, who was watching from a Boston sidewalk with newsman David Broder when Kennedy saw them and came over to say hello. "In Southie," said Kennedy, "they love you when you're down." It was an Irish thing, Nolan concluded: the more grievous flaw was perfection. Kennedy had transformed the election into "a referendum on whether the Kennedy family had suffered enough."

Others agreed. "Here we have a man with no obviously unusual strengths of character, beaten upon by unimaginable disasters, left as surrogate father to a dozen children, loaded by strangers with surrogate responsibility for a whole nation, then brought to a crisis in the water in the dark of the night; and we dare to blame him because he could not react with the automatic elan of a man with no experience with the fatality of life," wrote columnist Murray Kempton. "There is no defense for what he did. But every excuse cries out to us."

The Republicans in Massachusetts cooperated, with a contested primary that left Kennedy facing a weak opponent—Josiah Spaulding, a blueblood and a gentleman who deigned not to raise Kopechne's death as an issue. Taking nothing for granted, campaigning like a dervish, with Joan at his side, Kennedy won another term by 486,000 votes. "It was very important . . . that I go everywhere with him," Joan recalled. But it was different from her happier experiences in the campaigns of 1962 and 1964. This time, "I felt used rather than needed."

For a Massachusetts electorate that harbored such sympathy for his star-crossed family, and still viewed John and Robert as martyred saints, Kennedy's mea culpas had bought him the requisite political cover. It wasn't so much that the voters believed him, it was how much they wanted to. "People were uncomfortable" and conflicted, said a veteran Massachusetts pollster, looking back; they wanted to "put it behind them as fast as they could."

THE SENATE'S DEMOCRATS WERE conflicted as well. "Come here, right back where you belong," Mansfield had said, taking Kennedy's arm and pulling him to his side when his whip returned to the floor twelve days after Chappaquiddick. But there was no denying that the accident, and Kennedy's behavior, had wounded him—and liberalism. "He took us with him over that bridge," said Walter Mondale, "because he was sort of our star."

Many friends stood by him. Galbraith wrote often and Mankiewicz thanked him for not abandoning Robert Kennedy's causes. Birch Bayh lectured more than one nasty constituent, "Judge not lest ye be judged." But Kennedy had been wounded, and there were jackals, hungry to take him down.

Byrd led the pack, openly using his knowledge of the Senate rules to embarrass his rival. "One day they had a particularly bloody exchange, where Teddy just came off holding his head in his hands," his aide Wayne Owens remembered.

"You know, I really feel sorry for you," Kennedy told Owens, a Mormon, who was driving him home that night. Why was that? Owens asked.

"Because you can't go drink a huge glass of Scotch in a hot bath and forget what happened today," said Kennedy.

In the end, Chappaquiddick did him in.

"Ted didn't realize the effect of Chappaquiddick on his colleagues," Tydings remembered. "After Chappaquiddick I could not support him."

"I remember how shattered Ted was. . . . I don't know how he got the courage to walk on the Senate floor," said Mondale. But much as he admired Kennedy for soldiering on, "I couldn't justify Chappaquiddick. . . . It was a humiliation, a horrible embarrassment. . . . We were, I would say, ashamed for him."

Some of Kennedy's staff shared the feeling. Burke would not desert his boss before the 1970 campaign, but when it was finished he departed. "Chappaquiddick was a bad event for me," Burke would recall. "It tore a lot of foundations away that had been holding me up. His behavior had been on and off, errant on many occasions." But whenever Burke had confronted the senator, Kennedy would say, "That's alright. We'll always see our way through."

Nolan got the scoop while sharing an airplane ride with Senator Thomas McIntyre, a New Hampshire Democrat and erstwhile Kennedy ally.

"Bobby Byrd's going to run against Kennedy," the senator told the journalist.

"Do you think that's a problem?" Nolan asked.

"Yes."

"Who are you voting for?"

"Bobby Byrd."

After the November election, the Senate returned to Washington for a lame-duck session. There was not much else to write about, and the press corps focused on the whip race.

Belatedly, Kennedy attended to his duties—as tranquil as a caged tiger, schmoozing with his colleagues with "resolute casualness," Nolan reported. When Byrd stood to offer a motion to adjourn, Kennedy would arrive, interrupt him, and make the motion himself.

"It was more than rivalry, it was enmity," Byrd recalled. "It was a little thing, but still it was enough to incite my slowly rising anger. The little foxes spoil the vine."

Byrd "has become Kennedy's own personal bird of prey," Mary McGrory wrote. "He circles the chamber endlessly." Right up to the end, Kennedy remained confident, so much so that he journeyed to a NATO meeting in Brussels and then joined his family on a Caribbean vacation. "Ted was off playing . . . down in the islands," Smathers recalled. "Bob was up here calling on the phone. . . . When Teddy got back to town, Teddy didn't know what hit him. It was already over."

IN THE DEMOCRATIC CAUCUS, each man had his base: Kennedy the northern liberals, and Byrd the southern conservatives. There were more of the former than the latter, and that was the cause for Kennedy's confidence. He worked the phones and the Senate floor, lining up commitments. To help keep wavering Democrats in line, Kennedy sent labor lobbyists, or major party donors like shipbuilder George Steinbrenner or lawyer-banker Louis Susman, to plead for him.

Kennedy found trouble out west. He was feuding with Alaska senator Mike Gravel, a freshman who had voted for Long in 1969 and then, at Kennedy's hands, lost a seat he craved on the Commerce Committee. Montana's Mansfield was irritated by Kennedy's absences. Gale McGee of Wyoming was "unfriendly, if not hostile" to Kennedy after getting a chunk of the $18,000 Byrd had passed out to senators running for reelection that fall. By the time Kennedy's aides got to Joseph Montoya, the New Mexico senator was already pledged to Byrd, who had helped him land a coveted seat on the Appropriations Committee.

The two senators from the state of Washington—Henry "Scoop" Jackson and Warren "Maggie" Magnuson—had not forgiven Kennedy for siding with environmentalists in a December vote against the SST, a federal supersonic aircraft project that would have brought thousands of jobs to Boeing in Seattle. Kennedy dispatched an official from the machinists' union to lobby Jackson, who had long ties to the Kennedys and had given the seconding speech for Ted when he won the whip race in 1969. Aide Paul Kirk reported back to Kennedy that the meeting had not gone well. Their envoy "got about 30 minutes of wrath."

"Why doesn't Kennedy worry a little bit more about the thousands of machinists who will be out of work if SST fails instead of his lousy job as whip?" Jackson had barked. "You can tell him I said that."

Kennedy and Owens went to see Jackson. He kept them waiting, staring at the floor in the outer office. "It was embarrassing," Owens remembered. "We stood there drawing in the dust with our toes." Finally, Jackson and Kennedy conferred. Kennedy emerged, shaking his head, saying, "Scoop's against us."

Nordy Hoffman, a Kennedy intimate who served as the director of the Democratic Senate campaign committee, was dispatched to see Lawton Chiles, the incoming freshman senator from Florida. "Steinbrenner gave him $10,000 at end of his campaign and visited him yesterday with Nordy," Kirk reported to Kennedy. "After his visit, George sent Nordy back to Chiles' office to remind him [of] that $10,000. . . . George feels that Chiles got the message." Yet Chiles would not commit.

Vance Hartke of Indiana spurned a United Auto Workers lobbyist sent to persuade him. Lou Susman had vassals send Hartke a reminder that Susman and his friends "are liberal contributors to his campaign, and . . . would be greatly disappointed if he did not support you," Kirk reported to Kennedy. But Hartke gave them no commitment: Byrd had offered to help pay off his campaign debt.

Fulbright was said to have voted for Kennedy in 1969, but this time around he was leaning toward Byrd—a bit of Kennedy grandstanding over Vietnam had nettled the turf-conscious chairman.

As the Democrats convened at 10 a.m. on January 21, Byrd feared he would fall one vote short of victory. The seventy-four-year-old Richard

Russell lay dying at Walter Reed Army Hospital. In the last official act of his career, he had signed a proxy ballot for Byrd. But if Russell passed away before the vote, his ballot would not count.

Early that morning, Byrd inquired and found that Russell was breathing. The West Virginian fretted as the caucus went through the time-consuming formality of electing Mansfield for another term as majority leader. At 10:53 a.m., as the whip contest was about to begin, Byrd checked again. Russell was still alive. Entering the chamber, Byrd nodded at his seatmate, Jennings Randolph, who rose to put Byrd's name in nomination.

Russell died at 2:25 p.m. But it was over by then. Robert Byrd had defeated Edward Kennedy. Byrd took Richard Russell's proxy, framed it, and hung it on his office wall.

THE VOTES WERE CAST as handwritten ballots. The counting was done, in accordance with Senate custom, by the four new freshman senators. Going in, Kennedy thought he had thirty-one firm commitments, three more than necessary. In the end he received just twenty-four votes; it was Byrd who had the thirty-one. Kennedy had lost Chiles, and Hartke, and Jackson and Magnuson and Fulbright. And maybe Mansfield, who never publicly declared his preference.

Russell Long reveled. By challenging him in 1969, Kennedy had set a precedent for Democratic fratricide, Long said. "Two years later, after Chappaquiddick, he was hoisted by his own petard."

"It was a huge humiliation within the Senate—a very personal thing that happened to him that senators rarely do to each other," Mondale recalled. "Chappaquiddick got him." Kennedy could find reasons for his loss—Fulbright's tantrum, the SST, the two freshman senators who wrote "Bird" on their ballots—but no excuses. It was an extraordinary personal rejection. He knew its cause.

"Here you are living to try and make a difference in other people's lives, carry forward the unfulfilled mission of your brothers . . . your pathway of life," he said. But instead "you're going back . . . bearing the shame of that incident."

"You're conscious of what it means to the Kopechne family, and what it means to your family. . . . These are body blows . . . underneath the rib cage . . . particularly cruel and difficult and painful," he said. "It never goes away."

Sixteen

A FORTUITOUS PREOCCUPATION

After losing John and Robert, "Ted's grief was palpable; his responsibilities to a frightened family multiplied," his aide Paul Kirk remembered. "The Chappaquiddick tragedy compounded his heartache and sense of loss." And then his father died. The 1972 election was looming, but as in 1968, "Ted knew he lacked the intensity and the fire needed to mount a presidential campaign."

A growing file at the FBI gave testament to the threats posed by the crazed and hateful who lurked in his backyard, or at his office door, or otherwise communicated their intent to kill him. Friends and aides were struck by moments when the backfire of a passing car or some other loud bang caused him to blanch, duck, or drop to the ground. His family had become "numb" and "brutalized," he told journalist James Wechsler. Even Rose despaired. It was agony on a biblical scale, like the suffering in the Book of Job. Grimly, said Kennedy, "I suppose all our kids can see themselves standing in Arlington cemetery again three years from now."

Wechsler was editor of the *New York Post* and had been a confidant of Robert Kennedy. In April 1971, Ted called him to the family's New York pied-à-terre on Central Park South, with its stunning view of Olmsted's fields and lake, for a drink and some blandishment about health care.

Their talk drifted far afield—to the topics of faith and death and duty. At one point Kennedy questioned his decision to remain in public life, but "again and again he talked about how, after Bobby's death, he felt his major obligation was to carry on Bobby's fight," Wechsler remembered. Kennedy seemed torn, but fatalistic.

"He was saying, 'For Kennedys the die is cast.' I could not bring myself to ask him whether that meant he was committed to seeking the presidency, one way or another, or whether it was a more macabre observation," Wechsler recalled.

After their meeting, Wechsler wrote down his impressions. "He looked very alive and animated, with a faint tint of red on both cheeks; as he talked I was struck by how many of his facial mannerisms, gestures and even tones were reminiscent of Bobby. . . .

"I found him more interesting, spirited, articulate and warmer than I had expected," Wechsler said. "He is obviously a very troubled, even tormented guy and there were moments when I wondered whether he isn't masking almost unbearable tensions."

Publicly, Kennedy kept an open door to a campaign for president in 1972. If nothing else, the speculation about his potential candidacy brought attention to his causes—a prominence he would lose if he convincingly renounced all executive ambition. Privately, he wondered. There were liberating times, suited for the challenge of New Frontiers, and there were eras of retrogression or consolidation, ill-cast for Kennedys. Did the country now prefer "to go along quietly?" he asked people.

In 1971, he took two dozen trips around the country. He gave speeches, met with party leaders, while wearing his brother's golden cuff links, engraved with the initials "J.F.K." A North Dakota Democrat asked a reporter, "If he isn't a candidate, why did he bring his wife way the hell up here?"

Joan went along, dreading the prospect that Ted would be murdered. Ten-year-old Ted Jr. was obsessed with the fear, and Ted called to reassure him every day. Kennedy tried, in his fashion, to be a good father. When he was home he carved out time for his children in the morning, and after he returned from the Senate at night. "He made the most of the time he had with us," said Kara. "Every morning at breakfast, he was up early, he was with us, and also at dinner." They joined him in the bathroom as he shaved, or soaked his back. He joined with them in costume parties, card games and football, chocolate cake, sledding, and ice skating on the frozen C&O Canal. If an important visitor came for dinner or a briefing, the children were invited to listen. "He wanted us to get an education and . . . he wanted us to learn about what his life was like," said Ted Jr. "He was away a lot" but "made a huge effort, given all of his time commitments." He encouraged them to take a stand on issues, and played the devil's advocate to bring out their talents for debate and persuasion.

Yet the cloud was always there. "All you hear about the Kennedy family pressuring Ted to run—what family?" Joan demanded of one writer. "What's left of the Kennedys besides Ted? Only women and children. You don't seriously think we want Ted to be President, do you? To have the only Kennedy man . . . risk having happen to him what happened to his brothers?"

SOME OF THE TENSIONS Wechsler saw in Kennedy could be traced to the senator's marriage. Joan was a prototypical "good wife" who had stood by her man at Kopechne's funeral, and again on his day in the Edgartown court. But it was a hellish experience. She was heart-torn by the miscarriages, which fed her conviction that she was not measuring up to the expectations of her husband and his family. She was haunted by the loss of Jack and Bob, and by the thought that she would one day be compelled to act like Jacqueline and Ethel, called to play widow on a national stage. Her mother was an alcoholic and her father a drinker. It is reasonable to assume there was a genetic component to Joan's alcoholism. Acquaintances told stories of finding her drunk at parties. Her children giggled nervously when their mom, driving under the influence, swerved on the road. "I knew Joan before Teddy did," said Tunney. "You have to have stronger mettle than she had. . . . She was very fragile and she also had

this terrible disease called alcoholism. And the . . . feedback loops of insecurity, fragility and booze just brought her right down."

As the wife of Ted Kennedy, well-known rake, public humiliation sustained Joan's demons. She tried to act oblivious but was not so fierce a
person as Jacqueline Onassis or Lady Bird Johnson or Eleanor Roosevelt,
whose husbands' infidelities had at least been concealed by an acquies-
cent press. Years later, Joan would own up to acting out and pleading for
attention when she showed up in short skirts and see-through blouses and
other provocative outfits at Nixon White House social events.

Ted's gamboling, Joan's attire, and the first arrests of misbehaving
nephews on drug charges were affecting the family's image. They had always been rich, but seemingly wholesome, and with that Irish underdog
chip on their shoulders. Now "there is a vision developing of the Kennedys
as a glittering elite—apart from and above the people at large," a worried
Galbraith wrote to Kennedy.

"Jackie's reference to Camelot gave it a name. Washington, which has
the world's most sycophantic and most worshipful society, added to it by
investing a lot of crap," Galbraith said. "Various gatherings and parties
add to the legend."

"The American people will, sooner or later, react against any elite," he
advised. "Government in a Republic should be identified with the people—
many poor, many awkward, many black, many ill-at-ease—and not with a
lot of coiffured rhinestoned women with big artificial smiles. . . . There
must be no privileged class of beautiful people."

"WEIRD," Nixon said, after hearing about one of Joan's outfits. "What the
hell's the matter with them? What's she trying to prove?"

"Whatever it is, she ain't gaining them many votes," said Haldeman.
"The super swinger jet set types are going to be with them and not for you
no matter what happens. [For] Middle American folk . . . [Joan's attire
was] desecration of the White House."

"She has to have some sort of hang-up herself personally," the press secretary, Ron Ziegler, offered. "She knew what Teddy was doing out there with that girl, running her into the water, you know, and what he's been doing."

"That family is used to that," Haldeman said. "That's the price you pay when you join that club."

"They do it all the time," said Nixon.

"They all know that. Ethel, Jackie, and all the rest of them."

"They gotta expect that," the president said.

"If you want to get in their ballgame," said Haldeman, "you play by their rules."

BUT KENNEDY WAS NOTHING if not resilient. After losing the whip job to Byrd, he surveyed the political wreckage and proposed to reporters that it might be a good thing: it would liberate him from the housework of the Senate and free him for more lofty tasks. Prime among those challenges, he decided, was the troubled state of American health care.

Until 1971, Kennedy's preferred base was the Senate Judiciary Committee, where he had scored victories for immigrants and refugees, weighed in on Supreme Court nominations, and maintained an effective opposition to the Vietnam War. His refugee subcommittee would continue to serve, and Judiciary would be a rewarding forum for years to come. But a series of serendipitous changes at the Committee on Labor and Public Welfare— his other major committee assignment—now offered opportunity.

The first tile to fall was Senator Lister Hill's retirement in 1969. The Alabama populist, a surgeon's son, had served as the unchallenged champion of public health and research on the Senate side of the Capitol for most of his forty-five-year career in Congress. He had been chairing the Labor Committee, and its health subcommittee, since Ted Kennedy was catching passes for Harvard. Hill also led the Senate appropriations subcommittee that had jurisdiction over health care. He could authorize, and fund. Now he was gone.

Another southern Democrat, Senator Ralph Yarborough of Texas, sought to fill the role. Yarborough was a liberal maverick whose feud with Democratic governor John Connally had brought John Kennedy to Dallas on the fatal political peacekeeping mission in 1963. Yarborough was another populist—his campaign vow was to "put the jam on the lower shelf so the little people can reach it"—and so a prime target of the surging Texas Republicans. His preoccupation with a Republican challenge may have blinded him to the danger of the Democratic primary, where he was upset in May 1970 by former congressman Lloyd Bentsen, a lawyer-businessman from the party's conservative wing.

Yarborough's loss left the health subcommittee chairmanship vacant again. Next in line were Senators Harrison Williams of New Jersey and Claiborne Pell of Rhode Island. Organized labor, and other liberals, persuaded Williams to chair the labor subcommittee and helped to convince Pell that the education subcommittee was more attractive. It was a good fit for the patrician Pell and his country; for generations, the sons and daughters of American families have been able to attend college with the help of the grants that bear his name.

And so, after all these dominoes toppled, the gavel of the Senate's health subcommittee came to Ted Kennedy. He was all of thirty-nine years old.

KENNEDY HAD CHOSEN HEALTH care as a cause in his earliest years in Congress. In 1966, he became an advocate for community health centers after visiting a trailblazing clinic in the Columbia Point public housing project in Boston. The concept, the doctors told him, was to free the poor from medical neglect by bringing health care to their neighborhoods. Through prevention and early intervention, the human and financial toll of serious illness could be constrained. Kennedy was impressed. He spent hours talking to the staff and patients.

Stars were in line. His brother-in-law Sargent Shriver was then head of the Office of Economic Opportunity, and he and Ted joined with Lyndon Johnson, Robert Kennedy, and others to move the first authorizations and appropriations for community health through Congress. Ted received one of Johnson's souvenir pens for his role. Eunice Shriver made her own contribution, inviting the head of the American Medical Association, Dr. Charles Hudson, to breakfast at the Shriver estate and welcoming him like this: "Dr. Hudson, I want to meet you. Very nice to see you. And I am delighted that you are here, because I think the American Medical Association ought to be helping on developing good health care for the poor. And I have to warn you that if you don't, my brothers will, and they don't know anything about it."

Though largely overlooked amid the tumultuous events of 1968, Kennedy had assembled a series of proposals on health care planning, hospital construction, aid for education of doctors and nurses, and targeted assistance for rural America. He expected "great ferment" in health care, and proposed to take a leading role, he told Galbraith. Toward the end of that year, Walter Reuther, the visionary leader of the 1.6 million members of the United Auto Workers, traveled to Boston to enlist Kennedy for the new "Committee of 100 for National Health Insurance," a group of medical and civic leaders whose goal was to move the United States from its reliance on patchwork private insurance to a universal plan, guaranteed and administered by the federal government.

"I was always sort of fascinated by him," Kennedy said years later about Reuther. "No one could not have been, who was interested in politics . . . and he was enormously persuasive. It was an area I was interested in . . . the policy issues were interesting, and I thought he had the vision." The National Governors' Conference and the AFL-CIO signed on to the concept, the Nixon administration agreed to study it, and by the end of 1969 Kennedy promised an audience of medical professionals in Boston that he would devote himself to the cause.

Reuther died in an airplane crash in May 1970, but Kennedy followed through and introduced a Health Security Act three months later. It was a single-payer plan—a Medicare for all—calling for full replacement of all public and private health insurance with a federal system run by the Social Security Administration. "Publicly financed and damn the taxes," said a Senate aide, James Mongan. "Better because people ultimately pay less than what they're paying in their premiums, and those insurance companies won't be ripping off their share. . . . He believed all of that."

The rationale for federally subsidized health insurance would remain much the same for the next fifty years. When compared with other
industrialized nations, all of which have embraced some sort of government-
assisted health care, the American system was both expensive and under-
performing. The United States ranked third in health expenditures yet
lagged behind a dozen other nations in life expectancy and infant mortality.
It did not cover twenty-seven million people at all, and millions of others
were underinsured and exposed to fearsome catastrophic illness. It was
"the fastest growing failing business in the nation," Kennedy said. He predicted action within the decade. By January 1971, his bill had twenty-three
Senate sponsors.

AMONG THOSE CHEERING KENNEDY was Mary Lasker, a remarkable crusader who did for medical research what Margaret Sanger had done for
birth control and Jane Jacobs was doing for neighborhood preservation.
They were of a class of twentieth-century women who, with the more traditional routes to power blocked by men, identified a need, assigned themselves to meet it, overcame seemingly unscalable obstacles, and achieved
great things. Lasker was a cum laude graduate of Radcliffe who built a
career as an art dealer (she organized the first showing of Marc Chagall's
art in the United States), fashion designer, and philanthropist in New York
before the war. Ultimately, she became an activist, a networker, a fundraiser—
an indefatigable mink-clad lobbyist for health care causes, particularly cancer research; in 1950, her husband had died from the disease. Lasker's ties
to the Kennedys dated back to the New Frontier, and her medical consigliere
was Dr. Sidney Farber, the biggest name in medicine in Massachusetts, who
had revolutionized the field of chemotherapy. "Farber needed a political
lobbyist as urgently as the Laskerites needed a scientific strategist," wrote
Siddhartha Mukherjee in his history of cancer. "It was like the meeting of
two stranded travelers, each carrying one-half of a map."

Farber had led Children's Hospital, taught at Harvard Medical School,
and founded what would become known as the Dana-Farber Cancer Institute. Kennedy knew him well, after twenty years of helping the children's

cancer fund-raising drive, the Jimmy Fund—yet another Farber innovation. "When hope is matched with genius, the result is progress," Kennedy
had said at a testimonial dinner for Farber in the summer of 1969. It was
his first major address after the accident on Chappaquiddick.

The National Institutes of Health was one grateful beneficiary of Lasker's lobbying and philanthropy, as was its bureaucratic affiliate, the National Cancer Institute. Research budgets grew as mortality rates and fear
of cancer soared in the postwar years. But the cost of the Vietnam War
was cramping federal spending by the end of the 1960s and Lasker's team,
getting on in years and impatient at the lack of progress, bridled at the
NIH preference for conducting basic research rather than targeted assaults on specific maladies. Lasker had gotten Yarborough to set up a
blue-ribbon panel of consultants to evaluate federal efforts against cancer.
The chair of that panel was yet another Kennedy intimate—Republican
businessman Benno Schmidt, who had worked with Robert Kennedy on a
public-private development project in Bedford-Stuyvesant, a depressed
Brooklyn neighborhood. The Schmidt report, which was released in
Washington on December 4, 1970—with Lasker, Farber, and Kennedy in
attendance—called for far higher funding for cancer research. It also
made the contentious claim that a national cancer institute should act
independently of NIH bureaucratic, philosophical, and budgetary restrictions. When the new Congress convened in January, launching a war on
cancer had joined universal health care atop Ted Kennedy's agenda.

THIS SERIES OF EVENTS did not go unnoticed at the White House, where
Nixon looked upon Kennedy with the kind of dread that Neverland's tick-
ing crocodile evoked in Captain Hook. The president was preparing to
run for reelection and maneuvering to strip Democrats of appealing
issues. With a bold environmental agenda, Nixon had parried the appeal
of Edmund Muskie, the father of the Clean Air Act of 1970. Now Nixon
worried that the other Senate Democrat atop the polls—the cursed Ted
Kennedy—might ride health care to the nomination. His aides had carefully tracked the progress of Yarborough's blue-ribbon panel. A war on

cancer "is something we might be able to steal," domestic adviser John Ehrlichman concluded. Despite Chappaquiddick, despite the whip race, Nixon—author of the greatest comeback in American politics—was not counting Kennedy out. "The likelihood now is that Teddy Kennedy will be nominated by the Democrats," the president warned his aides in the spring of 1971. "Jesus Christ!"

Pharmaceuticals mogul Elmer Bobst—yet another of Lasker's allies on the cancer panel—happened to be Nixon's friend and benefactor. It was Bobst who had lured Nixon to New York and a lucrative job as a corporate lawyer, which served as staging area for his political resurrection. Bobst and Benno Schmidt now persuaded the president to launch a preemptive strike on cancer. In the State of the Union address on January 22—three days before Kennedy could file his own legislation—Nixon called for $100 million to mount a "war on cancer" that would match such feats of engineering as NASA's lunar landing or the Manhattan Project, which gave birth to the atomic bomb. The nation saluted, the press gushed, for the threat was real. "In the next year alone, 650,000 new cases of cancer will be diagnosed in this country and 340,000 of our people will die of this disease," Nixon told Congress in a "National Health Strategy" report in February. "Incredible as it may seem, one out of every four Americans who are now alive will someday develop cancer unless we can reduce the present rates of incidence."

Yet cancer, at the time, was a mystery. Research on atomic energy and space travel had progressed so that the Manhattan and Apollo programs were for the most part giant engineering projects. Scientists knew the innards of the atom, and the Newtonian principles of how propulsion moved a spacecraft through space. There was no similar consensus on what turned cancers on—or might switch them off. Was it even one disease, or many?

Nixon recognized this, and warned that in Apollo, "the challenge was technological; it did not require new theoretical breakthroughs. Unfortunately, this is not the case in most biomedical research." But Farber and Lasker, excited by the progress they were seeing in hospitals and clinics, wanted the federal government to wage a war to keep breast and colon and other cancer patients alive, to issue public health advisories that steered consumers away from cancer-causing behavior and substances, to develop new chemotherapy drugs and other therapies. Only a new, independent cancer institute—dedicated to a single mission, freed from the current half dozen levels of bureaucracy and built along the lines of NASA— could do this, they declared.

At NIH, the scientists resisted. They believed that basic research in molecular biology, cell biology, genetics, biochemistry, virology, and other biomedical sciences was the key—that you didn't launch spaceships toward the moon until you had a thorough knowledge of lift and drag, cosmic rays, atmospheric resistance, lunar geology, and gravity. It was vital, the men in white coats at NIH argued, to keep any war on cancer under their big tent. If cancer was spun off, then why not heart disease? Victims of other diseases, each one with passionate patients, poster boys and girls, and ad campaigns, would demand targeted funding. The whole concept of NIH could come under fire. Creation of a new cancer agency would "unleash forces of a divisive character which would quickly destroy the integrity of the NIH," warned a former director, James Shannon. "Orderly governance would be replaced by anarchy. . . . Program emphasis would be entirely determined by uncritical zealots."

NIH had its way. Instead of creating an agency like NASA, Nixon proposed to leave the new "Cancer Conquest Program" under the authority of the NIH director, who in turn reported to the secretary of health, education, and welfare. They would "enlarge the effort a little bit with a small amount of money, but not making any big effort to get away from bureaucratic control in HEW," Lasker griped. This put the president on a collision course with Kennedy, whose own bill—the "Conquest of Cancer Act," cosponsored by New York senator Jacob Javits—reflected the Lasker-Schmidt-Bobst preference for an independent agency. Freeing the new cancer institute from top-heavy bureaucracy would "maximize the chances to make real progress," Kennedy asserted as he opened hearings in March. As his subcommittee staff director, Leroy Goldman, recalled, this notion "was profoundly unsettling, not only to NIH but to most of the biomedical research community."

THERE IS A VENERABLE maxim in the capital city: If one is willing to distribute the credit, there is no limit to what can be accomplished.

There is another informal axiom, crafted as a question: Do you want a law, or do you want the issue?

Kennedy wanted a law and was willing to relinquish the credit.

The turning point arrived when Bobst persuaded Nixon that the NIH research centers were "a bureaucracy, incestuous, with a bunch of third-rate scientists . . . goddamn doctors [who] sit over there draining down money with mice and goats and never do a goddamn thing," as the president put it to his aides. Bobst urged his old friend to insist on a separate authority, lest Kennedy claim the laurels. Nixon's reaction was predictable. "Piss away the $100 million? Bullshit!" the president told his aides. "Teddy Kennedy is going to get credit for this! He is going to get credit because he is presenting it as a separate agency." His staff didn't understand the need for "pizzazz," Nixon griped. They were "absolutely without balls. They're eunuchs. We've got a bunch of goddamn eunuchs—that's what we've got." They were not showing "guts, balls, strength," the president said. Worst of all, "it reflects on the man at the top!"

In an April 2, 1971, letter to Kennedy, HEW secretary Elliot Richardson proposed a compromise—an administrative structure that kept the cancer program within NIH but raised its profile and authority. Nixon added autonomy—the new agency would have an independent budget, and its director would report to the president himself. The elements of a deal were there. But who would get the glory? "Unless we take immediate action Senator Kennedy will claim and receive credit for your initiative," his staff warned Nixon. "The Lasker forces are working very heavily to not only secure enactment of the bill but to see that it is Senator Kennedy and not our Administration who receives the credit."

As he left a meeting in the Oval Office, Schmidt was pulled aside by Kenneth Cole, a White House aide with a domestic affairs portfolio. "You can't ask this President to support a Kennedy-Javits bill," Cole told him. "You've got to get the names changed."

The press was portraying the debate over the cancer institute's independence as a showdown between Kennedy and Nixon. Bloodied by Byrd and Chappaquiddick, Kennedy desperately needed a celebrated victory. Yet to change the narrative and clinch the deal, Schmidt and Lasker asked Kennedy to give Nixon the glory. This, he agreed to do. Kennedy took the title of the administration's bill, which had been introduced by Senator Peter Dominick, a Republican from Colorado, and pasted it onto the Kennedy-Javits bill. Though entitled to have his name on the historic legislation, Kennedy suggested that he be omitted and Dominick be listed as the sponsor: "Peter, why don't you report the bill?"

It passed the Senate on a vote of 79 to 1. "It was extremely amiable of him to be willing to give up the bill in name and . . . let Dominick's name be on the bill," Lasker would remember.

Kennedy was slogging back. The Nixon administration, working with the Democrats in Congress, would pour hundreds of millions of dollars into the new war on cancer—a down payment toward a hundred billion dollars spent across the decades that followed. Cancer guards its secrets well, and the crash program never yielded a capstone like a lunar landing or an atomic bomb. Lasker did not live to see her dream. But a focus on prevention, screening, and early detection, and a few revolutions in treatment led to a notable decline in cancer death rates. Cancer became, bit by bit, a disease to be survived.

Nixon signed the National Cancer Act into law in an East Room celebration in December 1971. Standing far in the background in the ceremonial photographs was Ted Kennedy.

THE WAR ON CANCER was not the only serendipitous offshoot of the Nixon-Kennedy rivalry. The president's preoccupation with his presumed foe extended to international affairs, where it nudged Nixon toward his greatest achievement—the opening of China.

Nixon had entered office with the conviction that, just as Ike had settled the Korean War, he could brandish America's nuclear lance and the communists in Moscow and Beijing would pressure their North Vietnamese clients to make peace. But he found the two Red giants at odds, competing for eminence in their world and reluctant to bend. Nixon's solution was "Vietnamization." Under cover of a savage bombing campaign—the heaviest aerial bombardment the world has ever seen—he would bring home U.S. ground troops. Nixon pared U.S. draft calls and reduced the number of Americans in combat as Kissinger sent a signal to Moscow and Beijing that America would settle for a "decent interval" in which it could withdraw with flags flying and some fragment of prestige before South Vietnam fell to the communists. The abandonment of South Vietnam was a jaundiced exercise—a bit of realpolitik that Nixon justified as the price for a stable world order based on a multicentered balance of power among the United States, the USSR, Europe, Japan—and China.

The opening to China was not uniquely Nixon's idea. Mansfield, Fulbright, McGovern, and others were among the prominent American leaders who had urged the country to break the grip of the right-wing "China lobby" on U.S. foreign policy and coax China from its hostile isolation. So was Ted Kennedy. In foreign policy, as in many areas, he had a brain trust of former New Frontiersmen and academic specialists to consult. They swapped ideas in correspondence, and in relaxed "issue dinners" at private homes and faculty clubs. "I think we have found a good long-run policy issue in this area and I am going to pursue it," he wrote his old Harvard friend Sam Beer about China. He raised the matter with his Japanese hosts on his trip through Vietnam and Asia in the fall of 1965, and with a select group of academics from Cambridge at the MIT faculty club the following March. Four months later, he was consulting with Galbraith on what Kennedy called a matter "of great importance to me." Acknowledging the political minefield, he nonetheless suggested that a "blue-ribbon foreign policy commission" be appointed to stimulate "greater public discussion of our China policy" because "Vietnam aside, it is important that the public fully understand the overall foreign policy challenges we face in Asia in the long run." In a July 1966 Senate speech, Kennedy proposed that China be admitted to the United Nations.

"In the crucial period of 1966–79 . . . Ted Kennedy played a significant role," a foreign policy adviser, Jerome Cohen, recalled. "He saw a need and an opportunity to stake out a foreign policy issue where he could leave a mark." Galbraith and others urged Kennedy on. "Your China speech was first rate," Galbraith told the senator. "The problem of our China policy has not been knowledge but courage." Another Harvard professor, Stanley Hoffmann, echoed the sentiment: "It is the staleness of our foreign policy thinking that frightens me most . . . hence the fruitfulness of your suggestion." By the time of Nixon's own landmark contribution—a seminal article titled "Asia After Viet Nam" in the October 1967 issue of *Foreign Affairs*—Kennedy was in the field.

IMMEDIATELY AFTER TAKING OFFICE in late January 1969, Nixon ordered Kissinger to revive the moribund low-level U.S. diplomatic talks with China. The new president had not missed the fact that Kennedy was scoring headlines by promoting a more open policy. "The United States must take creative action in an effort to break down the great wall of estrangement which exists," Kennedy said at a two-day conference on China in Santa Barbara, just a few days after Nixon's inauguration. On March 20, at a gathering of leading China experts in New York, Kennedy gave the marquee address, and used the spotlight (and a front-page story in the next day's *New York Times*) to prod Nixon to act. "If the new administration allows this time to pass without new initiatives," he said, "if it allows inherited policies to rush unimpeded along their course, it will have wasted this opportunity. . . . If nothing changes, we Americans will have to live with the consequences of arms and fear and war. We owe ourselves, we owe the future, a heavy obligation to try."

Nixon's own vision for a "structure of peace" became real when the Soviets and Chinese, already feuding about communist doctrine, stumbled into an undeclared war over tracts of near-worthless Siberian tundra on the Soviet-Sino border. The USSR shifted its armored divisions from Europe to the East and drew up plans for a preemptive strike on China's nuclear weapons program. Nixon recognized a splendid opportunity to play one against the other. The breakthrough came in the spring of 1971, when Zhou Enlai sent Nixon an invitation to visit China via a secret channel maintained by Yahya Khan, the president of Pakistan.

In Pakistan, once again, Nixon ran into Kennedy. The country was then divided into eastern and western limbs, as if the giant awl of India, a thousand miles wide, had been hammered through its core. Western Pakistan was the home of power, the capital city of Islamabad, and the ruling Punjabi minority. The more numerous people of East Pakistan were largely Bengali and, though most shared the Muslim religion with their countrymen in West Pakistan, chafed under its rule.

Kennedy's involvement in Southwest Asia began in November 1970, when a cataclysmic typhoon brought massive death—from 240,000 to half a million were lost—and misery to East Pakistan. It was a land of seven hundred rivers, few hills, and no mountains—a vast alluvial lowland subject to flooding, composed of silt borne down from the Himalayas. The storm made landfall in a region of peninsulas and islands, crowded with migrant harvest workers. A million people were left without food. A disproportionate number of the dead were children. A week later, Kennedy—the Senate's man on refugees—took to the floor, criticizing the Pakistani government and the international community for fumbling the response and accusing Nixon of "grandstanding and tokenism."

"Reports from East Pakistan continue to tell a horrifying story of massive human suffering made all the more horrifying by the mounting evidence of confusion and inexcusable delay," Kennedy said.

In December, the people of East Pakistan rose at the polls, inflamed by their government's callousness, and won a majority—and thus the right to govern all of Pakistan—in the national assembly. Yahya refused to cede office. In March 1971 he launched an armed campaign of murder, rape, and repression in East Pakistan. U.S. officials in India and Pakistan warned Washington that the slaughter bordered on genocide. The estimates of the dead were stunning, ranging from 250,000 upward. Joined by Archer Blood, the American consul general in East Pakistan, the diplomats took the extraordinary step of signing a protest cable of "strong dissent" to the Nixon administration's "moral bankruptcy."

Millions of refugees fled across the border into neighboring India, which joined the conflict as a covert supplier of arms and aid to the Bengali insurrectionists. The Bengalis proclaimed their independence, in a new nation to be called Bangladesh. "Your 'charges' of indiscriminate killing with U.S. supplied weapons, execution of dissident political elements and students and a threat of mass famine and epidemic were fully confirmed," Kennedy's aide Dale de Haan told him after a State Department briefing. "The situation is deteriorating."

The violence in East Pakistan brought Kennedy to the Senate floor time and again. "It is a story of indiscriminate killing, the execution of dissident political leaders and students, and thousands of civilians suffering and dying," he said on April 1. "It is our military hardware—our guns and tanks and aircraft—which is contributing much to the suffering. . . . Shouldn't our government condemn the killing?" On June 18, he accused the Nixon administration of "whitewashing" human tragedy. He sent letters of protest to the State Department and called on the government to cut off economic aid and arms sales to Pakistan. He was fast becoming the leading congressional critic of Nixon's policy. On June 28, he had Blood testify before the refugee subcommittee. The hearing took place amid a raging summer thunderstorm, with thunder and lightning bolts that jolted the senators.

NIXON, who bore a grudge against the Brahmins of India for petty slights in his past—he spoke of how "repulsive" he found Indian women—feared for Yahya Khan, his conduit to Mao Zedong and Zhou Enlai. "To all hands. Don't squeeze Yahya at this time," the president ordered his staff. He underlined the word "don't" three times. "The White House policy [on Pakistan] had a China aspect to it that made our position on refugees not particularly palatable," Kissinger deputy Harold Saunders would later concede.

In early July, on a trip to India and Pakistan, Kissinger feigned illness to shake off the press and, with Yahya's help, secretly flew from Islamabad to Beijing. The preliminary negotiations were successful. On July 15, Nixon stunned the world by announcing he would visit China.

Nixon basked in just acclaim, but Kennedy, other Democrats, and the world's press kept calling attention to Bangladesh. The cause got a boost on August 1 when two of the Beatles—George Harrison and Ringo Starr—joined Bob Dylan, Eric Clapton, and others at Madison Square Garden for a benefit. It was the first all-star rock concert for humanitarian relief, a model for others to come. Then, on August 10, after a flight that took most of two days, Kennedy landed in India.

KENNEDY'S TAPE-RECORDED DIARY of his visit does not list what political motivations weighed on his decision to make the trip. It does, however, reveal his empathy for the Bengali people, and the searing effect of what he saw. "He *cared*," said Nevin Scrimshaw, an MIT professor and expert on nutrition who accompanied him. Kennedy had hoped to visit East Pakistan, but on the eve of his journey the Pakistani government revoked its proffered visa. Instead, he toured the refugee camps along the long Indian border, where ten million had fled.

"Genocide is being committed in East Pakistan . . . there cannot be any doubt about it," Kennedy told his tape recorder. "I have seen it in the faces, the eyes, the bodies of scores of children. I have seen it in the lost limbs of women and old men." The disaster would "be written as one of the great errors in chapters of human suffering in the history of mankind," he said. "The suffering and the misery defies any description.

"It is the malnutrition and undernourishment of some 250,000 children under the age of five who in the matter of hours or days can easily be lost to death for lack of nutrition. It is a small boy quivering in a refugee camp . . . quivering as he has quivered for three months, in the state of continued shock after seeing his mother and father butchered by the savagery of the Pakistani troops.

"It is a boy in Chalagary hospital, 14 years of age, whose face is contorted but not by any birth defect or by any external measure, but only from the continued pain and anguish and suffering that he's experienced when he saw his parents shot before his eyes and received a bullet in his spine which has paralyzed him for life, never to be able to utilize his limbs again. His limbs today are wrapped in gauze bandages, covered with white powder," Kennedy said, "but the bedsores continue to grow as the overtasked staff in the hospital tries to provide some release but, what is more important—some hope for the cause of a hopeless boy."

"We drove hour after hour" as "the lines of people that crowded the streets lined up, became more intense. And then the rains came. The scores of children without any covering, exhausted old men and old women, literally in the last hours of their lives."

"The rains and monsoons descend on these areas, these fields, in many cases former rice paddies, which are close to the ground and close to the water level. And you see the sweep of water moving across, through the refugee camps. And you hear the screams of mothers and children as the water creeps up and floods their sleeping areas. Then you walk ankle deep, and even knee deep, through the refuse of the latrine trenches . . . then you hear the cough of the children and you hear about the continued problems of nutrition and diarrhea that these children have and you know that death for them is just around the corner."

At the Salt Lake camp, Kennedy said, "I asked the refugee camp leader what his first need was [and] he said a crematorium."

KENNEDY AND A SMALL GROUP of aides and advisers traveled over four days to some twenty refugee camps along the thirteen-hundred-mile East Pakistan border. Off came the coat and tie, on went a pair of desert boots. "*Zindabad Kin-a-dee!*" (Long live Kennedy!) roared the crowds in the camps, their clenched fists raised. Long days in the field, often in monsoon rains, were followed by nighttime visits to hospitals and river crossings and meetings with Bengali officials and guerrillas. It was as if, by sheer effort on behalf of those suffering, like some latter-day Lord Jim, he would find redemption. To make sure he was getting an unvarnished look, he abandoned the official schedule and showed up where he was not expected. "At lunchtime he was appalled by the suggestion that we stop at a government . . . bungalow to eat our box lunches," John Lewis, a Princeton University dean who accompanied him, remembered. "Not, by God, when there were still refugees to see out there in the rain. We would eat as we drove. Within minutes he was afoot again."

"He persistently questioned individuals—able-bodied men, old men, broken men who had lost their wives or children, wives who had lost their husbands . . . younger children, one by one, dozen after dozen, eventually hundred after hundred," Lewis recalled. "When had they come? Why? What happened to them? Why did they think they were molested, or their relatives or friends killed? Had their troubles come from soldiers or collaborators or both? Was food available in their villages?"

Scrimshaw remembered the human feces everywhere, the stench of the open latrines, the diarrhea and dysentery and the blindness brought on in children by vitamin deficiency; the dead and dying boys and girls lying under rags in tents or cornstalk huts, and how Kennedy was visibly affected. Television crews and news photographers, lured by his presence, conveyed the scene around the world.

Home seemed far away, except on the day that their caravan stopped along the side of the road. "What is the matter?" Kennedy asked an Indian escort. They had taken a "wrong turn," he was told.

"Story of my life," he said.

Kennedy capped his trip in Delhi. He had a series of meetings with Prime Minister Indira Gandhi and other officials and responded ably when called upon to give an impromptu press conference, and a speech to the Indian parliament. The U.S. embassy would sum up his Asian odyssey as a "tour-de-force." At a reception of Indian officials and international diplomats at the embassy, "I . . . gave Bobby's quote from Camus," he told his diary. "Maybe we cannot have a world in which children are not tortured, but we can have a world in which we reduce the number of tortured children."

KENNEDY AND HIS ENTOURAGE left Asia with the knowledge that without some dramatic intervention by outside forces, India and Pakistan would soon be at war. Back in Washington, he lit into the Nixon administration's indifference in a speech at the National Press Club. He had spoken, in the months after Robert's assassination, of how he was now father to sixteen children—his own and those of his brothers. It was to the children of the refugee camps that he kept returning.

"It is difficult to erase from your mind the look on the face of a child paralyzed from the waist down, never to walk again . . . or the anxiety of a 10-year-old girl out foraging for something to cover the body of her baby brother who had died of cholera a few moments before our arrival," he said. "It is time—it is past time—for Americans to understand what has produced this massive human tragedy, and to recognize the bankrupt response by our own nation."

"You may say that we have no business getting involved—that we cannot police the world. That may be true," he said. Kennedy knew as well as anyone that Americans would not tolerate another intervention, another war, in Asia. "But the cold fact is that we already are involved in East Bengal. Our guns are involved. . . . Let President Nixon make personal representations to President Yahya Khan about every aspect of the crisis."

The most immediate benefit of Kennedy's involvement in the affairs of East Pakistan was a change in Indian policy to allow distribution of a nutritional formula, recommended by Scrimshaw, that was easier for the severely malnourished infants and young children to digest. But the publicity about his trip, and the political pressure he and others sought to apply, brought results back home. He had raised awareness, and "considerable public revulsion," for U.S. policy, Christopher Van Hollen, who led South Asian policy at the State Department, recalled. Nixon and Kissinger, reading the currents of public opinion, moved to increase aid. "We've got to have a big program . . . of relief" to counter Kennedy's charges, Kissinger told his boss on August 11, as the senator toured the camps. "I want a big, big, big package," Nixon agreed. In late September, Kennedy asked the Senate to authorize $400 million for refugee relief. On October 1, Nixon countered with a $250 million request.

Kennedy's involvement in Southwest Asian affairs thoroughly irked Nixon. So did news that Kennedy was trying to get into China before the Nixon visit; the president told Kissinger to convey their extreme displeasure at such an idea to the Chinese.

"He's after us every day," Nixon griped to White House aide Charles Colson.

"All of a sudden Kennedy has emerged. He's on every issue," Colson agreed. "He's speaking out on everything, all the way from medical care to the Supreme Court to aid to Pakistan. . . . He's the one figure Democrats rally around."

"Smear the hell out of him," Nixon told his aide.

THE ARMED CONFLICT THAT Kennedy and others had predicted arrived that fall. India backed the Bengali guerrillas and prepared for war—prompting a retaliatory attack from West Pakistan on December 3. Nixon and Kissinger viewed this long-standing regional, ethnic, and religious conflict as a Cold War showdown, with China and Pakistan as good guys, and the USSR and India as aggressors. The president famously "tilted" toward Pakistan. He urged the Chinese to move troops to threaten India in the Himalayas. He sent the USS *Enterprise*, a nuclear aircraft carrier, and its battle group into the Bay of Bengal and conspired with Kissinger to break the law and ship fighter jets to Pakistan. "Hell," the president told Kissinger. "We've done worse."

Kennedy condemned Nixon for promoting the violence by siding with Yahya throughout the yearlong crisis. "This war began on the bloody night of March 25 with the brutal suppression by the Pakistani army of the results of a free election," he told the Senate. "At no time has any official of our government, including the president, condemned the brutal and systematic repression."

The Pakistan armed forces were no match for the Bengali insurgents and India's military, which quickly secured East Pakistan and was attacking in the west when the United States and the Soviet Union brokered a cease-fire. Yahya had paid dearly for his cruelty: East Pakistan became the independent People's Republic of Bangladesh. He had lost half his country, and resigned in late December.

Nixon shrugged; his historic trip to China was still on—it took place in February. He followed it with another foreign policy triumph that spring: the first visit of a U.S. president to the Soviet Union.

Kennedy was left with the less momentous but gratifying task of welcoming Bangladesh to the community of nations. "The people of Bangladesh will remember with gratitude your deep personal concern for them during our struggle for liberation against the fascist Pakistan occupation army," the new country's leader, Sheikh Mujibur Rahman, wrote him. "Your visit was a source of inspiration and succor." On February 14, after a few days skiing in Gstaad with the Tunneys, Kennedy and Joan and nephew Joe landed to a hero's welcome—instantly bedecked in garlands of flowers by crowds that at times seemed ready to crush them—in Dacca, the capital of Bangladesh.

As with the war on cancer, it is not possible to say how Nixon would have acted on China, or the crisis in India and Pakistan, if a Kennedy had not been stalking, prodding, and heckling him. Statesmen don't like to admit that domestic political concerns are driving forces in international diplomacy. Yet it is equally impossible to ignore the continual preoccupation, by a famously insecure and competitive president, over Kennedy's role in Asia.

Seventeen

A DRAMATIC PUBLIC PROCEEDING OF HISTORIC PROPORTIONS

The war in Vietnam raved on, and Kennedy remained a prominent critic, using his refugee subcommittee to throw light on the conflict's toll on the people of Southeast Asia. His little panel did not close up shop as American ground troops were withdrawn; it became, perhaps, even more significant—as a clearinghouse for data from NGOs and peace groups, and an authoritative source for journalists. "Although Vietnamization has reduced American participation in the war, to the average Vietnamese civilian the war still exacts the same high toll in human life," aide Jerry Tinker wrote Kennedy.

Nixon was changing the color of the corpses. In a twelve-month span from 1969 to 1970, some 50,000 civilians died, and an additional 225,000 were wounded by artillery and small-arms fire or the round-the-clock sorties of U.S. aircraft dropping napalm, high explosives, and cluster bombs, which scattered toy-like bomblets over wide areas. In Quang Tri province, only 11 of 3,500 villages remained unbombed by the end of the war. More than a third of South Vietnam's population—some six million people—had been driven from their homes to crowd the cities and refugee centers. B-52 strategic bombers, modified for use in tactical warfare, could devastate concentrations of North Vietnamese troops. But, flying so high, they were murderous to civilians. "From a Vietnamese civilian viewpoint,

all of [the] Vietnam [War] is an atrocity," Kennedy's staff informed him.
"While people are regarded as the key to victory in Vietnam, they too
often become a secondary consideration when the choice is between saving them or securing a military objective."

The Cold War premises of deterrence, credibility, and prestige—the
foundations of John Kennedy's foreign policy—were now hollow, if not
sinister, abstractions for his younger brother. "I cannot be deterred from
my abhorrence of the Vietnam war by the . . . strange logic that says that
every Asian child who dies becomes a ghostly messenger to Moscow, warning the Marshals of the Soviet Union that they must go easy," Kennedy
wrote in a letter of reply to columnist Joseph Alsop, a supporter of the war.

"We have had enough of war, and death. What goal do we have in
mind, what prize so enviable, that this great nation must pursue Asians
through endless jungles, across borders, in and out of their burning villages, to give and take human life?"

"What once was rationalized, in the atmosphere of a decade ago . . .
has deteriorated into a monumental and historic catastrophe," Kennedy
said, not sparing his brother's role in the debacle. "Now we know it was an
error—and now we must not only end it, but never commit that error
again."

Kennedy was tenacious, furnishing the media with statistics, GAO reports, and eyewitness testimony. At the White House, Nixon and his aides
called killed civilians "slop over" and quipped among themselves that one
dead Asian was indistinguishable from another. Kennedy put faces on the
slain. "Are we as a nation so morally bankrupt?" he asked.

In the spring of 1971, John Kerry, a Navy lieutenant from Massachusetts, led the Vietnam Veterans Against the War to Washington and an
encampment on the National Mall. Kerry had been inspired by John Kennedy, and as a boy played a minor role in Ted Kennedy's 1962 campaign.
Now Kennedy showed up on the Mall to offer his support to the Vietnam
vets, share a tent and sing protest songs, and thoroughly irritate the White
House. As May Day marchers sought to shut down the capital with acts of
civil disobedience, Kennedy spoke out against the Nixon administration's
illicit mass arrests, and his aide James Flug made sure the hundreds of

detainees had water and fruit while they were confined in the makeshift jail of an arena.

A few weeks later, the *New York Times* published the first installment of the Pentagon Papers—a secret government history of U.S. involvement in Vietnam. It had been leaked to the newspaper, with the peripheral help of Kennedy's friend and former aide Dun Gifford, by Daniel Ellsberg, a defense analyst and former adviser to Kissinger, Ted and Robert Kennedy, and others. The Justice Department rushed to federal court, and obtained an injunction to silence the newspaper, but Nixon's outrage was selective. Even as he sought to enjoin the *Times*, he was ordering his aides to leak the damaging segments in the Pentagon Papers that concerned John Kennedy. "The Kennedy stuff should get out. Leak it to some other paper," Nixon told his aides, with no apparent irony. "The public is entitled to know." After the *Times* and then the *Washington Post* were stopped by the courts, the *Boston Globe* stepped up and, to Nixon's delight, published the chapters on John Kennedy and Vietnam. Once again, Ted Kennedy issued a statement acknowledging his brother's mistakes. "There was writhing in pain in the streets of Boston," the gleeful White House aide, Charles Colson of Massachusetts, told his boss.

The U.S. Supreme Court ended the affray with a six-to-three decision on behalf of the press. The Pentagon Papers became public, and the American people learned of the duplicitous behavior of their government. Nixon sulked. Under his direction, his aides set up a Special Investigations Unit to plug leaks that might be damaging to the president (they would become known as the Plumbers) and collect dirt with which to smear Ellsberg, the Kennedys, and others. Howard Hunt, a former CIA agent, forged phony diplomatic cables that blamed South Vietnamese president Ngo Dinh Diem's assassination on John Kennedy, and the counterfeit evidence was peddled to the press. Diem was a Catholic, and the goal was to tarnish Ted Kennedy with Roman Catholic voters. The senator now believed that his telephone was tapped.

Nixon pressed his staff for dirt on Kennedy's sex life. Enterprising aides learned, like housecats, to bring mice to the master's door. Hunt was sent to New England, trolling for smut about Chappaquiddick. Haldeman put a spy on Kennedy's Secret Service detail. "Plant one . . . plant two guys on him," Nixon had ordered. "One that can cover him round the clock, every place he goes. . . . Just might get lucky and catch this sonofabitch."

"Amanda Burden," Haldeman said, nodding, referring to a New York City activist romantically linked to Kennedy by the press.

"Is the Teddy story being properly kicked around about the woman?" Nixon prodded Haldeman. "Nail the goddamn thing."

Colson brought Nixon photographs of Kennedy at a Parisian nightclub beside an Italian princess. Kissinger regaled the president with gossip of how Kennedy had pursued, like "a total animal," the actress Candice Bergen and the socialite Cristina Ford. The president's men lacked hard evidence, however. As Kennedy journeyed home from his visit to the refugee camps in India, he stopped in Hawaii, where the White House placed him under surveillance.

"We had a guy on him," a chagrined Ehrlichman reported to Nixon, but Kennedy "was just as nice as he could be the whole time."

"Watch him," Nixon replied. "What happens to fellows like that who have that kind of problem is that they go for a while and then . . ."

Joan, meanwhile, was aware of Ted's philandering, and received advice from Rose. "It was quite well known that Ted was having an affair with a married woman," Joan remembered. But Rose told her that she should not believe everything she read in the press, and besides, it was not Ted's fault, because "women chase after politicians."

Joan found her mother-in-law's advice "dear" but "after the fact." Rose "was telling me not to pay attention," she said.

NIXON'S FEBRUARY 1972 TRIP to China was a planet-shaking triumph. So was the Moscow summit. He was not just the first U.S. chief executive to shake hands with Mao, he was also the first to visit the Soviet Union, where he signed two landmark nuclear arms treaties—one on strategic arms, and the other on ABM systems. But all was not well in Nixonland. Nixon had always played Iago to his own Othello; now his insecurities prevailed.

Nixon's great fear—that the public craving for a restoration of Camelot would derail his bid for reelection—had waxed and waned in his first term. He could do wonderfully nice things, like hosting Jacqueline Kennedy Onassis and her children at the White House for a private preview of John Kennedy's presidential portrait. But other times he seemed off his rocker. After spotting photographs of President Kennedy as he toured the White House complex, Nixon ordered a "sanitization" of the Executive Office Building and had aides investigate the loyalty—not just to Nixon, but to her country— of a GS-9 employee who had a picture of Kennedy on display.

Nixon professed fear, to his slithery courtiers, of what Ted Kennedy might be like as president. "He is soft," Nixon said. "Jim Eastland said Jack was bright and Bobby was tough. This fellow is neither bright nor tough." But White House strategists fueled Nixon's obsession with long memos analyzing Kennedy's assets and the likelihood he would run in 1972.

If "Kennedy would ask Americans to help him finish what his brother began, the voting population would once again become a victim of that 'old Jack magic.' A Kennedy campaign would convey nostalgia and emotionalism," noted one memo, passed by deputy campaign director Jeb Magruder to his boss, John Mitchell. The senator, more than any other Democratic candidate, could unite a divided party. Kennedy was strong with young voters and Blacks and Latinos—yet more than acceptable to labor and the old guard, and, with his new focus on health care, had an issue with which to court the elderly. Despite Chappaquiddick, he was third in the polls of most admired Americans, after Nixon and evangelist Billy Graham. "Kennedy has often been called an intellectual lightweight," but that was "in the past," the memo warned. A top-notch staff kept him well briefed and he "has gained a certain degree of intellectual maturity." It would be perilous to underestimate him. "Kennedy must be eliminated now."

Speechwriter William Safire, who had been with Nixon since before the 1960 campaign, sent a similar warning to Haldeman. The Kennedys had a proven method of rebounding from disaster, said Safire: their allies would maintain that the brothers learned from their mistakes. "The Bay of Pigs changed JFK, enabling him to rise to greatness at the Cuban Missile Crisis. Bobby, too, underwent an enormous change from . . . ruthless and coldblooded, to the warm and compassionate friend of the underprivileged," said Safire. "Similarly, the story will go, Teddy went from the high-living, irresponsible boy pre-Chappaquiddick, to the 'man of the family' after being deeply sobered by that tragedy."

"Kennedys traditionally overcome their pasts," Safire wrote. "The 'record' has never been held against them, and . . . will not be this time."

On May 28, 1971, Nixon ordered Haldeman to proceed with a campaign of bugging and surveillance. "I want, Bob, more use of wiretapping," Nixon said. "Kennedy . . . Maybe we can get a real scandal on any one of the leading Democrats."

"Scandal or improprieties," Haldeman echoed.

"Now you're talking," Nixon said.

KENNEDY FED NIXON'S OBSESSION WHEN, on the president's return from China, the Senate Democrats charged the president with scandalous behavior in the "IT&T affair." It was a flap that flamed and fizzled but served as a precursor for Watergate. "The same players, the same atmosphere, the same activities," Kennedy would recall.

Jack Anderson, the muckraking columnist, triggered events by publishing a memo, purportedly written by a lobbyist named Dita Beard, revealing that in return for a $400,000 donation from the International Telephone & Telegraph (IT&T) corporation to the Republican Party, the Nixon administration would drop its opposition to a merger that the company had planned. Much of this was true. Nixon personally ordered his new attorney general, Richard Kleindienst, to have the Justice Department's antitrust division relinquish its objections. "The IT&T thing—stay the hell out of it. Is that clear? That's an order," Nixon told Kleindienst. "Drop the goddamn thing."

Quid pro quos are hard to prove, however, and Nixon's commands,

captured on the White House taping system, would not be made public for
another two years. Yet Kleindienst, in a mindless move, insisted that his
confirmation hearings be reopened so that he could defend his reputation. This led to the longest such sessions in the nation's history, and
enough razzle-dazzle to keep the press hooked for weeks. Beard fled to a
Denver hospital, claiming to be suffering from a heart condition, where
she was quickly followed by, first, Howard Hunt in a wig and disguise, to
urge her to recant, and then by Kennedy and other liberal senators, who
interrogated her at bedside until her doctors intervened.

"Her blood pressure went up, the arrows of all the machines went to
high gear, and she gasped and grasped and every other thing she could
do," Kennedy recalled. "Phil Hart said he was not going to interview her
again. He was scared to death that she would collapse or die."

The IT&T scandal smudged Nixon's Beijing halo, and forced Kleindienst and Mitchell to lie under oath. "I was not interfered with by anybody
at the White House. I was not importuned. I was not pressured. I was not
directed," Kleindienst told Kennedy at a March 8 hearing. For that false
testimony, Kleindienst would become the first attorney general in U.S. history to be convicted of a crime committed in office. It was "a blatant, flagrant lie," Kennedy remembered. Ultimately, Kleindienst cooperated with
a special prosecutor, pleaded guilty, and wept in court when sentenced.

In that same eventful spring, the North Vietnamese launched what
became known as the Easter Offensive. The North's early success gave
rise to fear in the Oval Office that South Vietnam would collapse and
take Nixon's hopes for a second term with it. "There is a very good chance
that sitting in this chair could be somebody else," the president told
Kissinger. Humphrey was "a gibbering idiot," he grumbled; Reagan was "a
lightweight," and the prospect of Kennedy "unbelievable."

"What the hell is the matter with Teddy?" Nixon asked Kissinger. "I
don't think it's a sex business. . . . Don't you think it's the booze? He can't
resist. . . . Bobby and Jack, everybody knows it, had their own ladies. They
were a hell of a lot more discreet."

Nixon's dirty tricksters picked up the pace, with schemes to wreak
havoc at the Democratic National Convention in Miami, to break into

Democratic candidate George McGovern's headquarters in Washington, and to bug Democratic headquarters at the Watergate office building. On June 17, at the Watergate, they got caught.

THE COVER-UP WAS SUCCESSFUL, at first. With perjury and payoffs, Nixon and his aides cloaked the president's involvement.

The *Washington Post* kept the story alive in the summer and fall of 1972. So, warily, did Kennedy. His staff probed, gathered incriminating information, and spurred headlines. But Kennedy, worried that an aggressive investigation would be viewed through a partisan lens, and revive discussion of his own behavior at Chappaquiddick, declined to confront Nixon. To the considerable exasperation of McGovern's presidential campaign aides, and some on his own staff, Kennedy chose not to give the voters a full account of the Watergate break-in and other dirty tricks before the November election.

"A gigantic fraud is being perpetrated upon the American people, and anyone who has it within his power to help expose that fraud has a responsibility to the public and to himself to do so as soon and as dramatically as possible," a member of Kennedy's staff argued in an internal memo. "If we are going to stand quietly in the face of both a scandal of historic proportions and a politically motivated effort to . . . cover-up that scandal until after Election Day, then we deserve the kind of government we are getting."

Watergate was the ultimate jungle to which James Flug took his boss, daring him to find a pathway out. The vehicle was Kennedy's third, oft-forgotten subcommittee. In addition to the refugee panel and the subcommittee on health, he chaired an all-purpose toolbox with jurisdiction over the federal government's administrative procedures and practices. Known as Ad Prac, its charter was basically anything that Ted Kennedy could convince James Eastland to approve. "It was bottom-up work," staffer Thomas Susman recalled. The staff brought their groundwork to the boss. He then made the choice to join, or to skip, a scrap.

Flug was the Ad Prac counsel. By mid-August, he was thoroughly versed in Watergate, "finding connections and weaving patterns that were just sort of mind-boggling," Kennedy would recall. The aide was one of the first investigators to interview Alfred Baldwin, the man who monitored the Watergate wiretaps and served as a lookout on the night of the break-in. Flug told Kennedy, in a long August memo, how Nixon's men were succeeding, via perjury and other means, at covering up the ties between the burglars and the White House. "The information in the indictments will probably not provide much real detail on the who, what or how of the plot," Flug wrote. "The indictments will be better than nothing, [but] they will be of very limited utility in bringing out the whole story."

Meanwhile, the Democrats had chosen McGovern to face Nixon. Kennedy gave a rousing speech at the national convention but turned McGovern down when asked to be his running mate. Kennedy's family was worried about his safety, and he instinctively recoiled from the inconsequential duties of the office. "I am not cut out that way," he told the *Boston Globe*. "The vice presidency is good for some people. However, I don't need that kind of exposure."

Performing a mitzvah for the party might have been a smart move. By declining to serve, Kennedy squandered an opportunity to be immunized, on a national stage, for his behavior at Chappaquiddick. "You do the penance, as they say, as a vice presidential candidate," *Boston Globe* editor Robert Healy told Colson. "You do the bit for the party and then in '76 you have done it and because you've done it Chappaquiddick fades away. . . . I think that really makes some sense."

"That's the one rationale," Colson agreed.

McGovern accepted Kennedy's decision but bristled at the selfishness Kennedy displayed *after* declining the offer. Like a wolf marking his territory, Kennedy helped blackball McGovern's second choice, Mayor Kevin White of Boston. If Kennedy wished to run for president himself someday, he did not see the sense in raising another Irish Catholic from Massachusetts to national prominence. Pressed for time, and with cursory vetting, McGovern picked Senator Thomas Eagleton of Missouri as his running mate. Two weeks after the convention, Eagleton admitted that he had received electroshock therapy for nervous exhaustion and depression. Once again, McGovern begged Kennedy to join the ticket, save the Democrats, defeat Nixon, and end the war. Again, Kennedy declined. Despite Kennedy's opposition—there was room for only one Kahuna in the Kennedy clan—McGovern enlisted Sargent Shriver to replace Eagleton.

It was a disastrous start for McGovern's fall campaign. Nixon had the economy on fire, a string of foreign policy successes, and was able to portray the Democratic nominee (a bomber pilot who flew thirty-five missions against the Nazis in World War II) as an irresolute radical. McGovern's final hope, it seemed, was Watergate. Kennedy faced circumstances much like those that silenced him in the Haynsworth and Carswell battles. Did he have the credibility, after Chappaquiddick, to launch a highly public investigation of corrupt acts by others? "My natural inclination, like yours, is to go—it's too meaty a thing to stay away from," Flug urged his boss. "But for the same reason, it could backfire big."

Nixon and his aides would credit "the fine hand of the Kennedys" with the creation of the Senate Watergate Committee, the appointment of Special Prosecutor Archibald Cox, and the president's eventual downfall. McGovern's advisers, however, were just as agitated by what they perceived as Kennedy's failure to act. Upon examination, McGovern may have had the better cause to complain.

THERE WERE, to be sure, complications. To start, there was Kennedy's proposed use of Ad Prac. Some in the Senate objected to his view of the panel as an unfettered hunting license and argued that a Watergate investigation would be better launched from a committee with clear jurisdiction like Government Operations. On the other hand, Kennedy had held hearings on the threat posed to civil liberties by wiretapping long before Watergate, and so had precedent on his side. A month before the election, the leading alternative—Senator Sam Ervin, who chaired Government Operations and a Judiciary subcommittee—took himself out of the running. He encouraged Kennedy to unmask the cover-up with a televised public hearing—Kennedy vs. Nixon—that would guarantee blanket coverage and commentary. They had a prize catch in Baldwin, who could spin a gripping blow-by-blow account of the burglary, the bugging, and the involvement of Nixon campaign officials. "I want to urge you to consider hearings," said Ervin. It would be "a perfectly proper congressional inquiry into how the Justice Department is performing its obligation to the American people."

As a dean of the Senate and a voice from the South, Ervin carried weight. He was "bad on civil rights," but "incredibly good on civil liberties," Kennedy recalled. Ervin's imprimatur would keep peace in the Senate, but it led Kennedy to other questions: Would his investigation be deemed credible by the press and the voters? Could he lose more than he might win? Kennedy had Flug poll the family advisers. Calls went out to Burke Marshall and others from Robert Kennedy's staff, and to McGovern, David Burke, Richard Goodwin, and Lawrence O'Brien. Attorney Edward Bennett Williams and his partner Joseph Califano, whose firm represented the *Washington Post* and the Democratic Party, were consulted. Kennedy's allies on the subcommittee—Hart, Tunney, Bayh, and North Dakota senator Quentin Burdick—were canvassed as well.

On September 28, Flug sent Kennedy three memos. Written by different advisers, and signed "X," "Y," and "Z" to encourage candor, each outlined a course of action.

The first memo, by "X," gave the case for restraint. Putting Baldwin on the stand would be "a dramatic public proceeding of historic proportions," X admitted. But it could make it impossible for the other Watergate burglars to get a fair trial. "The most outrageous dimension of the Nixon Administration has been its constant readiness to sacrifice principles . . . [in favor of] short-run pragmatic expediency. To fight such cynicism and opportunism by partaking of it ourselves would be hypocrisy of the first order." Principle aside, there was politics to consider. "We would be playing in a rough league, and we would have to be prepared to play rough," wrote X. Baldwin's testimony would be one man's story, and it relied in part on hearsay. They needed hard proof that the White House was involved or that "the fix is in" at the Justice Department. "Right now we don't have it."

The second memo, from "Y," gave the bullish point of view, and was titled "Why Ad Prac should announce Watergate Hearings Now." Here was the case for a full-fledged assault before the election. "Even if Baldwin is our only witness, his story is one of ruthless lawlessness by employees of the [Nixon] Re-Election Committee," said Y. They had a moral obligation to expose Nixon's transgressions.

The final memo, by "Z," offered a middle approach, outlining a path that Kennedy ultimately selected: to keep investigating, but to forgo hearings. It was temperate, responsible—and timorous. Comparisons to Chappaquiddick were inevitable, Z warned. "I think the public should get as many facts as possible before the election, but I see no reason why we have to be the ones who do it . . . if our doing it is going to raise a serious collateral issue."

And so the moment passed. Baldwin would not tell his story that fall. Americans would not hear before the election what he could say: that Attorney General John Mitchell and other high-ranking officials were involved in the break-in, that McGovern headquarters had also been targeted for bugging, and how the cover-up began.

"I don't want a circus or to look like a headline hunter," Kennedy told a reporter from *National Journal*. Things seemed settled. But then, on October 10, the *Washington Post* disclosed that the Watergate break-in was just part of a widespread campaign of political sabotage and espionage, coordinated by White House officials.

This gave Kennedy a second opportunity—and this inquiry would not threaten the defendants' rights in the upcoming Watergate trial. His staff would launch a "preliminary inquiry," Kennedy announced. Flug went back to work. The *Post*'s Carl Bernstein was invited to interview the senator. "I know the people around Nixon," Kennedy told him. "They are thugs." But he had no illusions about what he could accomplish, this late in the election. At best, his investigation would be a "holding action," he said, to keep Nixon's crew from destroying the evidence, and to keep heat on those running the cover-up. Politically, there was "no percentage" in it, Kennedy told Bernstein. The White House would go "with everything it had to smear him," he said. He was vulnerable on Mary Jo Kopechne's death and other "nickel-and-dime stuff."

Indeed, Nixon's allies—Republicans Strom Thurmond, Barry Goldwater, and Clare Boothe Luce—would soon raise Chappaquiddick and the Harvard cheating episode. "There is still that little truism which says people who live in glass houses should not throw stones," Goldwater said. In an op-ed in the *New York Times,* Luce quoted the bumper sticker slogan: "Nobody was drowned at Watergate."

Flug was allowed to proceed. Subpoenas were issued. Bank records were collected. Kennedy's staff ran down the head trickster, Donald Segretti, and the paymaster—Nixon's personal lawyer, Herbert Kalmbach. But, once again, no hearings were held. At a meeting with his staff in December, Kennedy decided to put off the confrontation. "Since the expected outcome was so uncertain, and the prospect of EMK falling on his face was so possible, no decision was made," an internal memo noted.

At the White House, the president and his men chortled. Kennedy was backing off, Haldeman told Nixon, because he had been compromised at Chappaquiddick. On Nixon's birthday, in early January, his staff sent him a joke telegram. Allegedly from Kennedy, the "Director of Water Safety," it invited Nixon to "a quiet weekend at Chappaquiddick" for a "homey family barbeque," and added, "P.S. Bring your bathing suit."

KENNEDY, MEANWHILE, was adding to the "nickel-and-dime stuff" that left him politically vulnerable, and timid. On the weekend after Thanksgiving, he joined Arthur Schlesinger and other friends and family at his sister Jean's country home in Pawling, New York. They played tennis and talked politics and analyzed Nixon's landslide victory over McGovern. Kennedy "agreed with the view that race was the hidden issue of the campaign and felt rather pessimistic about the possibility of stopping the drift of low-income whites, who feel threatened by racial change, into the Republican Party," Schlesinger told his diary. "Ted was especially scornful of Nixon as the first President since Hoover who did not move the racial justice issue forward, if even a little," and instead "threatened to undo a good deal of the progress that has been so painfully made."

With McGovern's loss, Kennedy was a favorite for the Democratic presidential nomination in 1976. As a former counselor to John and Robert, Schlesinger was often asked to advise their younger brother. That Sunday morning, Kennedy pulled him aside. He had been giving much thought to issues like trade, and the effects of globalization on American workers, Kennedy said. How should he best occupy himself over the coming months? What travel, what speeches, what moves within the party did Schlesinger recommend?

"It was evident that he had already thought about it very carefully and intelligently," the scholar wrote. The senator seemed "a much-changed person from the Ted Kennedy of a decade ago. He . . . still likes physical movement and is entirely capable of noise and boisterousness; but he is fundamentally much more serious, and . . . consistently comes back to issues . . . trade, Ireland, his health program."

Schlesinger had a publisher's deadline to meet and left early that morning for his Manhattan home. His wife, Alexandra, stayed behind. Just before lunch, she and the Smiths were joined by "a gorgeous Hungarian girl," Alexandra reported to her husband. "This turned out to be a girl Teddy had picked up on the train from New York to Pawling." The romance, Alexandra said, "was moving fast."

Ted Kennedy was married and the father of three children. His presidential hopes had been quashed in 1972 by the scandal over Mary Jo Kopechne's death. His foes then, and ever after, would wield his repute as a womanizer to wound him. But here he was, three years after Chappaquiddick, romancing a young stranger on a public conveyance, bringing her to lunch at his sister's home, and enlisting friends and family in his antics.

"How is one to put together the senator, so serious about issues, so absorbed by political strategy, with the playboy, picking unknown Hungarian girls up in trains?" Schlesinger asked his diary. "If fornication were the purpose, he could undoubted find plenty of girls he knows already. Why run the extra risk? Do tensions build up inside him that require this particular outlet? Or is it an inherent lack of self-discipline? Or perhaps he is unconsciously seeking another disaster that might rule him forever out of the Presidency?"

It was the perplexing riddle, the source of "a flaw in someone who has become otherwise a most able and impressive man," Schlesinger wrote.

MANSFIELD FINALLY ACTED. Convinced that a probe led by Kennedy would be seen as politically motivated, the majority leader wrote to two committee chairmen—Ervin and Eastland—proposing a return to regular order and asking how the Senate might best meet the "imperative" of fielding a "single instrument of investigation" into "the Watergate Affair." On February 7, after seeing the burglars convicted, and hearing Judge John Sirica accuse the administration of a cover-up, the Senate voted, unanimously, to establish a select committee to investigate "illegal, improper or unethical activities" in the 1972 presidential election. It quickly became known as the Senate Watergate Committee, or the Ervin Committee, after the man chosen to chair it.

At the time, and in the years to follow, Kennedy expressed relief and gratitude to Ervin for assuming the duty. Had Kennedy kept hold of the investigation, "it wouldn't be so much about Nixon, as about me and Nixon. It would all be political without getting to the substance," he would say. At the White House, "they were always trying to say this was a political witch hunt." He passed his subcommittee's findings and files to Ervin. It is hard to believe that Kennedy was not disappointed, however, when Mansfield and Ervin named the members of the select committee and he was not among them. Flug had come up with several proposed lineups of senators that included Kennedy. All were rejected.

KENNEDY WAS ON THE SIDELINES, so it seemed. But then Nixon gave him a platform by sending the nomination of L. Patrick Gray, acting FBI director, to the Senate for confirmation. The nomination went to the Judiciary Committee, where Gray was grilled by Kennedy, Byrd, Ervin, Tunney, and Hart. They trapped Gray in a series of damaging admissions about Watergate, which brought the name and activities of the White House counsel, John Dean, to public attention. Dean, a piranha in a tank of sharks, having seen how fall guys fell in the Nixon administration, joined the prosecution as a cooperating witness. Magruder was right behind.

The cover-up was finished. Dean told the prosecutors all about Watergate; how Nixon had approved a comprehensive plan to conduct illegal break-ins and bug dissenting Americans, and how the White House, wanting to smear Daniel Ellsberg, had dispatched Hunt and an imbecilic sidekick, Gordon Liddy, to Los Angeles in 1971 to burglarize the office of Ellsberg's psychiatrist. A desperate Nixon fired Ehrlichman, Haldeman, and Kleindienst and named Elliot Richardson as the new attorney general.

Once again, the Judiciary Committee Democrats were in the spotlight, conducting Richardson's confirmation hearings. Kennedy and his allies made the most of it, holding the nominee hostage until Nixon agreed to appoint a special prosecutor. It was "a quid pro quo," the senator would recall. Kennedy helped dictate the prosecutor's broad charter, with its guarantees of independence, and approved Richardson's selection of Archibald Cox.

Cox, a professor at Harvard Law School, had been a research director for John Kennedy's race against Nixon in 1960. He had served as the solicitor general in the New Frontier. Ethel and Ted Kennedy attended his swearing-in ceremony as special prosecutor. It is too facile to make the claim, as have some Nixon aides, that Kennedy orchestrated a plot to unseat the president. But, like Ervin at the Senate Watergate Committee, Cox stippled his staff with veterans of the Kennedy Justice Department. Eight of the dozen senior attorneys on Cox's "Watergate Special Prosecution Force" had worked for Robert Kennedy. Nixon, who at first dismissed Cox as a bow-tied cluck, now found him unabating. When a White House aide told the Watergate Committee about the president's secret taping system, Nixon's doom came down to a single question: Could Cox pry the tapes from the president?

While the courts wrestled with that issue, Nixon suffered another setback. Vice President Agnew admitted that he had taken bribes in office, and resigned. The vice presidency was still vacant—and House Speaker Carl Albert next in the line of succession—when Nixon lit a political inferno by firing Cox on Saturday, October 20. Nixon knew what was on the tapes—and decided that he could not let Cox hear them. In a long meeting at Kennedy's home that weekend, Cox gave the senator and his aides a full rundown of Nixon's crimes.

Americans were outraged by the "Saturday Night Massacre." Talk of impeachment stirred the capital. If there had truly been a plot to steal the White House, the elements were now in line: the Democratic Congress could stall the confirmation of a new vice president, impeach and find Nixon guilty, and swear in Speaker Albert—the next in the line of succession—as president. Or, since there is no constitutional requirement that the Speaker of the House be a member of the House, other prominent Democrats—like Ted Kennedy—could replace Albert and become president. "Get off your goddamn ass, and we can take this presidency," the diminutive but importunate representative Bella Abzug of New York told Albert, poking him in the chest. Theodore Sorensen sent Albert a twenty-page "contingency plan" for a Democratic takeover. The rumors were wild—enough so that Kennedy felt compelled to issue a statement.

"One of the most troubling aspects of the current national crisis is the increasingly whispered White House accusation that Democrats may be seeking to delay action on the nomination of Gerald Ford as Vice President, as part of a partisan plan to reverse the 1972 election results," he said. "I want to go on public record now, as emphatically and unequivocally as I possibly can, to say that the last thing this country needs in the present turmoil is a partisan debate over the motives of Congress. . . . I hope continuing expedited action on the [Ford] nomination will be made the Senate's highest business."

Congress did the right thing and confirmed Ford, the House Republican leader, as vice president. The Republic stumbled on.

The events of autumn 1973 seemed to be propelling Kennedy toward victory in the presidential election of 1976. He need only to remain visible, harrying Nixon as impeachment took its course, to reap the prize. But the year was not finished with its shocks. On November 17 surgeons in Washington removed Ted Kennedy Jr.'s leg at the knee. Stricken by cancer, the boy was fighting for his life. Instead of Iowa and New Hampshire, the Kennedy family would spend the coming months in antiseptic hallways and gloomy hospital waiting rooms. And, in the spring of 1974, Ted Kennedy and Richard Nixon would join in a quixotic effort to provide all Americans with comprehensive health insurance. That they failed does not diminish their astonishing quest.

Eighteen

HEALTH CARES

W hen Ted Kennedy took control of the Senate health subcommittee, he did what he usually did, and hired from the best young men in the field. If they were physicians, they learned that their duties included Kennedy family doctoring. And so Philip Caper, MD, summoned while on his way to a formal occasion after work, had arrived at his boss's home in a tuxedo on a night in early November 1973. Kennedy met him at the door. The family housekeeper, Teresa Fitzpatrick, had alerted them to a hard and painful lump a few inches below the knee on Ted Jr.'s right leg.

The soreness persisted, and the doctor had the twelve-year-old visit Georgetown Hospital for X-rays. Joan was in Europe, said to be attending a music festival in Austria. Kennedy cut short a scheduled trip to Boston and found Caper waiting at the airport in Washington with a gruesome report. It looked like cancer. Specialists were summoned from the Mayo Clinic, the Armed Forces Institute of Pathology, and elsewhere; a biopsy confirmed the diagnosis. Kennedy was overwhelmed. He faced the unimaginable. Three brothers, a sister; now his son might die young too.

The recommended course of treatment was amputation above the knee. Because they were Kennedys, word leaked. But with the help of a sympathetic press, they kept the news from Ted Jr. until the day before the operation. His leg was "very sick," Kennedy told his son. It had "a kind of cancer inside it."

"Does that mean I am going to die?" the boy asked.

No, but to stop the cancer from spreading through his body, "Son, they're going to have to take your leg off," Kennedy said.

THE SURGERY BEGAN AT 8:30 on a Saturday morning and was over in ninety minutes. Three blocks away, at Holy Trinity Church, Robert Kennedy's eldest daughter, Kathleen, was to be married at 11:00. Ted Kennedy arrived at the church, haggard but in time to walk his niece down the aisle and join the congregation in a bittersweet chorus of a family favorite, "When Irish Eyes Are Smiling." Then he returned to his son's bedside.

Ted Jr. made a steady recovery. By mid-December, outfitted with a prosthesis, he joined his dad and made the rounds at Washington's Children's Hospital, where they distributed many of the get-well gifts that had arrived from around the world. After spending Christmas with the family in Palm Beach, the senator mounted an aggressive campaign of consultation with specialists from the nation's finest cancer-care centers. He convened a meeting of experts at his McLean home, where they reached a consensus that the potential benefits of an additional course of chemotherapy outweighed the risks. At three-week intervals over the next two years, Ted Jr. spent three days at Boston Children's Hospital taking massive infusions of methotrexate, a toxic anticancer drug, followed by doses of citrovorum factor, an antidote administered to protect his healthy cells. The senator and his son would fly to Massachusetts on a Friday afternoon and spend the weekend in the hospital together. Ted learned to give his boy injections.

"A few months after I lost my leg, there was a heavy snowfall," Ted Jr. would remember. "And my father went to the garage to get the old Flexible Flyer and asked me if I wanted to go sledding down the steep driveway. And I was trying to get used to my new artificial leg, and the hill was covered with ice and snow."

The boy slipped and fell. "I . . . can't do this. . . . I'll never be able to climb up that hill," he told his father. "And he lifted me up in his strong, gentle arms and said . . . 'I know you can do it. There is nothing that you can't do. We're going to climb that hill together, even if it takes us all day.'

"He held me around my waist and we slowly made it to the top," Ted Jr. remembered. "At age 12 losing your leg pretty much seems like the end of the world, but as I climbed onto his back and we flew down the hill that day, I knew he was right. I knew I was going to be okay."

The Kennedy regimen of vigorous exercise for body and soul carried father and son—and magazine photographers—to the ski slopes of Vail in February, and to Moscow in March. "Teddy never cries, and he never talks about either his illness or his missing leg," *Good Housekeeping* reported. "I have to be brave for Dad," the boy told his mother.

BEYOND THE UPBEAT, the song was bleak. Joan had not been attending a festival in Austria when Ted called to give her the news of their son's illness. She was at a clinic in Switzerland, where she was being treated for alcoholism. The disease had taken control of her life. Jean Kennedy Smith compared her brother's home to that of the wretched Tyrone family of *Long Day's Journey into Night*, with its haunted, addicted mother, Mary. "You can't imagine that household. It's like something out of Eugene O'Neill. Teddy comes home to this hopelessness, night after night," she told a friend. A story was fed to the press that fall: Ted and Joan had reached an agreement to have an "open marriage" with room for personal growth and relationships outside the home. Joan was photographed at a ball in Venice, dancing with an Italian publicist.

Then Ted Jr. got sick. Joan believed, mistakenly, that he had but a 25 percent chance at survival. "I often tried to imagine four beautiful, cheerful young twelve-year-olds like Teddy—and I fought back the tears when I realized that three of them would die," she recalled. His parents bought Ted Jr. a telescope as a birthday present and spent time with him as he scanned the night sky. "I wondered what kind of universe it is that strikes down a little boy with cancer—and then reaches out to him with the stars while giving him so little hope," she would remember.

In May, Joan fled the family for a three-week stay in rehab at the Silver

Hill psychiatric hospital, a fashionable Connecticut clinic where her mother had once sought treatment. Several weeks after being discharged, Joan was back in Silver Hill. In September, she checked into a California clinic. The nation's women's magazines and pages began to publish sympathetic stories that nonetheless linked her to tranquilizers, alcohol, and flirtations. On October 9, Joan was arrested for drunk driving after ramming the car in front of her on a street near their Virginia home.

The assassinations. A plane crash. Chappaquiddick. Infidelity, money, drink, and drugs. It took Patrick Kennedy "a long time to even begin to understand how we were affected by all of this," he would recall. "I knew there was huge suffering going on in my family. But it was never spoken of when I was growing up." Joan spent much of his childhood in her room, "doing little but drinking and surviving," Patrick remembered. She might emerge at midday in a nightgown or robe, in front of guests, and be scolded by her husband. She asked Lester Hyman, a state Democratic Party chair, to fill her water glass with vodka when her husband was not looking. She cast a pall at dinner parties. She collapsed at a family gathering in Manhattan. On one occasion, Ted took a journalist to where Joan had passed out in a car, to have the reporter see what he was facing. John Tunney described the breakup of the Kennedy marriage as "more like a Chinese water torture than it was a dramatic event." It went on for years.

Ted had an old-school attitude, Patrick said, and could not understand why Joan could not just suck it up. He would groan, "Here she goes again . . . oh my god . . . I can't believe it!" But Kennedy's philandering was an element in Joan's decline. "They went to the core of my self-esteem," she would tell a writer for *McCall's* magazine when asked about reports of his infidelity. "It was difficult to hear all the rumors. And I began thinking, well, maybe I'm just not attractive enough or attractive any more . . . and it was awful easy to then say, Well, after all, you know if that's the way it is, I might as well have a drink.

"Rather than get mad, or ask questions concerning the rumors of Ted and his girlfriends, or really stand up for myself at all, it was easier for me to just go and have a few drinks and calm myself down as if I weren't hurt or angry," she said. "Alcohol could sedate me. So I didn't care as much. And things didn't hurt so much."

Kennedy managed his own increasing use of alcohol. When confronted by political necessities, he could swear off rich food and drink and lose a dozen pounds. John and Robert drank sparingly. Ted "is the only one who seems to be affected," Schlesinger wrote. He "becomes a little high in an entirely merry way, lurches a little, his face grows a little flushed, and he wants to sing." But no one explained to the children why Joan "was walking through the house like a shadow in the middle of the day," Patrick said. "My father went on in silent desperation for much of his life, self-medicating and unwittingly passing his unprocessed trauma on to my sister, brother and me." Kara had emotional difficulties, and would run away from home. All three of Kennedy's children would be treated for substance abuse at some point during their lives. His family life was, indeed, unfolding like an O'Neill tragedy.

BEFORE TED JR. BECAME ill, Kennedy had been preparing for the 1976 election with characteristic diligence, pocketing chits from forty-two Democrats in twenty-four states by appearing with them in the 1972 campaign. Kennedy had stumped for McGovern, too, winning glowing notices in the press as "the Selfless Star, defender of a losing cause" and "the Voice for the Voiceless," whose aides "moved . . . like an elite cadre" as he simultaneously courted "old pols, labor, big city bosses," and the young folks and minorities in the McGovern coalition. Until the voters disabused them of the notion, the nation's pollsters and political reporters remained enthralled with the prospect of another Camelot. Even those, like Georgia governor Jimmy Carter, who believed that Kennedy's faults would leave him vulnerable in the post-Watergate era, had small doubt he would run.

On St. Patrick's Day 1973, Stephen Smith gathered a half dozen of his brother-in-law's advisers at his New York apartment, where they considered a lengthy campaign blueprint drawn up by Theodore Sorensen. It was based on a list of premises, reminiscent of those that John Kennedy faced in 1960, including:

1. That you want the Presidential nomination and election in 1976 badly enough to undertake the personal sacrifices, risks and commitments necessary;

2. that the obstacles and opposition to your nomination and election are fierce, 3-1/2 years may already be too little time to overcome them, and only part-time attention to this task even this year will assure failure;

3. that you will nonetheless, no matter what you do, be regarded as the front-runner, with all the political risks, publicity and attacks that accompany that position;

4. that you will have to run hard for the job, and cannot await or arrange a draft, or leave it in "the lap of the gods";

5. that, if nominated, your November 1976 opponent will have the most lavishly financed, skillfully merchandised, powerfully organized and ruthlessly expedient campaign in history.

Sorensen went on to list the tasks that Kennedy would have to address. He needed to burnish his foreign policy credentials, to appear as an "international statesman and leader." His image needed buffing as well, so that he came across like John Kennedy—as "mature, sound, wise, thoughtful, serious, self-confident, cool . . . moral, religious, trustworthy, honest." They must buttress Ted Kennedy's image as a patriot: "no appeaser, no crawling or begging or retreating, no equivocation on flag or anthem." And, in an increasingly conservative climate, they needed to disassemble his reputation as a high-taxing, big-spending liberal and rebuild it as a "responsible" moderate, a candidate "not for swift or drastic change, or soft on crime, drugs, welfare, pushy youth or pushy women or pushy minorities."

Kennedy would need to reduce the "personal" stories in the press, watch his weight, and tone down the emotion in his public appearances. He should vacation with his family in "non-elegant" sites like Yellowstone

Park or Mount Rushmore. He should write a scholarly book—but carefully, so as not to appear dependent on his staff, or too hastily, as "a mediocre or political-appearing book can only hurt." He should publicly criticize his fellow liberals, and be seen taking advice from "judges, generals, businessmen, scholars, Southern Senators, Republicans, bankers [and] hawks." When choosing his issues, he should embrace mainstream proposals, and disregard the "popular fads, the temporarily chic [and those] issues more dear to the *Globe, Times* [and] *Post* than [to a] Kansas City welder."

The senator needed to "assail abuses of Medicare and particularly Medicaid," said Sorensen. "Pursue the . . . thesis that pouring more money into certain cherished social programs of the New Deal, Fair Deal, New Frontier and Great Society brings nothing but more inflation." He suggested that the campaign hire Richard Scammon, whose book on the wooing of aggrieved white voters had been a Nixon political bible. And it would be wise, Sorensen said, to have the state legislature change the law so that Kennedy could run for president and senator at the same time and thus not risk his seat.

Sorensen urged Kennedy to ready himself for the inevitable attacks on Chappaquiddick, potentially "the largest and most difficult hurdle." He needed to secure all embarrassing records. In concluding, Sorensen warned, "You cannot afford to provide any grounds for rumors about your personal conduct, or to risk any accidents, or to assume that others will not talk. . . . Your best friends in the press will betray you first and damage you most."

KENNEDY HAD ACCEPTED Sorensen's recommendations and ordered Milton Gwirtzman and other aides to trim his liberal sails. In the summer before Ted Jr. fell ill, Kennedy made a well-publicized pilgrimage to a "Spirit of America" festival in Alabama, where he embraced George Wallace as a fellow populist before some ten thousand southerners and a traveling press corps of a hundred journalists.

"I did not come here to lecture you about that racial injustice which has proven to be as deeply embedded and resistant in the cities of the North as in the counties of the South," he said, as Wallace—paralyzed in 1972 in an attempted assassination—looked on from his wheelchair. "If there is one thing George Wallace stands for," Kennedy said, comparing the demagogue to his brothers John and Robert, "it is the right of every American to speak his mind and be heard."

Civil rights groups were stunned. The Southern Christian Leadership Conference denounced Kennedy's appearance as "the height of political opportunism" and a concession to "racism, police statism and mob rule." The SCLC reminded Americans that "more churches and houses have been burned and bombed during the administration of George C. Wallace than in the history of the state." But the South would be an important battlefield in 1976, and Kennedy wanted to temper the region's hostility.

When jousting with Strom Thurmond at a Senate hearing over amnesty for Vietnam War resisters, Kennedy noted, correctly, that President Abraham Lincoln had supported amnesty for Confederate soldiers guilty of treason. But comparing Johnny Reb to long-haired draft dodgers would not play well in the South. Some political trimming was needed. "At no time did Senator Kennedy say he believed those who fought for the Confederacy during the Civil War were traitors," his administrative assistant, Edward Martin, took pains to note. "Any such inference is inaccurate, unfair and contrary to the Senator's long-held beliefs that courage and bravery and dedication to a cause were equally evident among those who fought and sacrificed their lives on both sides of that unfortunate war."

KENNEDY ALSO ACTED TO fortify his résumé on foreign policy. He had some experience as a member of an organization of legislators from NATO states, and as Senate floor leader on the ABM. Now he hired Robert Hunter, the editor of *Foreign Policy* magazine, as an adviser and scheduled trips to Great Britain, France, West Germany, Israel, Jordan, the USSR, and Portugal. Because of his state's large Portuguese community, Kennedy had an interest in the ongoing transformation in Lisbon from dictatorship to democracy. He helped persuade Congress to nurture the new civilian government. He took the opposite tack when investigating the atrocities committed by the right-wing government of Chile—which the Nixon administration had abetted to install General Augusto Pinochet and depose the socialist president Salvador Allende. Political prisoners were subjected to beatings, electric shock, and water torture, and thousands of Allende supporters were executed or "disappeared" in the 1973 coup. At a hearing of his refugee subcommittee in 1974, Kennedy distilled the findings: "Violence and executions in the early days and the apparent continuation of torture and repression." Yet Nixon had voiced "no sense of outrage, no sense of distress," Kennedy said. The senator worked, successfully, to have Congress cut off U.S. military aid to Chile. Before Presidents Gerald Ford and Jimmy Carter raised the banner of "human rights" as an American priority in international affairs, Kennedy's refugee subcommittee was a focal point on Capitol Hill.

Kennedy's weeklong voyage with his family to the Soviet Union in April 1974 proved valuable, as it included a four-hour meeting with Soviet leader Leonid Brezhnev, in which they discussed a comprehensive ban on nuclear weapons tests. Ted was carrying on a brother's legacy—John Kennedy had signed a partial test ban treaty with the Soviets. The American ambassador, Walter Stoessel, reported to his diary that Kennedy was "effective" and "charismatic" in a luncheon with other Soviet leaders at Spaso House, the ambassador's residence in Moscow. "Not too clear in his exposition," Stoessel wrote, "but his ideas are good."

Kennedy spoke on arms control in Moscow, toured Georgia, and met with students at Moscow State University. Less successful was a stop in Leningrad, where the Soviets foiled his attempts to meet with dissident Polina Epelman. Boldly, Kennedy and Joan made a late-night visit to a group of prominent refuseniks gathered in a Moscow apartment. At the behest of conductor Leonard Bernstein, Joan asked Brezhnev to give the renowned cellist Mstislav Rostropovich an exit visa. As the Kennedys prepared to depart for home, word came that Rostropovich had been given the freedom to leave.

In time, other dissidents like Rostropovich were granted exit visas—

including Epelman, who emerged from a crowd to surprise the senator during Kennedy's trip to Israel six months later. In February 1975, Rostropovich gave a memorable performance at the Kennedy Center, with a post-performance visit to McLean. He hugged and handed Joan a box of roses and offered to teach Teddy Jr. how to play the cello. It was the start of something good for Kennedy: on subsequent trips to the Soviet capital, he would bring a list of dissidents to set free. But he was upset with Joan for raising the Rostropovich visa on her own. "I didn't share with Ted that I wanted to bring this up," she recalled. When Brezhnev asked what he might do for her, she acted on her own. "Ted was in a state of shock, he was so angry."

AND THEN THERE WAS health care. Kennedy was being tutored by other parents of stricken youths about the costs of medical care and treatment. "Those parents would be in the waiting room—they had sold their house . . . or mortgaged it completely, eating up all their savings, and they could only fund their treatment for six months, or eight months, or a year—and they were asking the doctor what chance their child had if they could only [pay for] half the treatment. Did they have 50 percent chance of survival? A 60 percent chance of survival?" Kennedy recalled. "This is about as stark as you can get."

Nixon, meanwhile, needed to demonstrate that his administration was not paralyzed by Watergate. His advisers had shaped a plan to guarantee health insurance for all. It was not a single-payer system like Medicare, which Kennedy favored, with government assuming the costs. Instead, Nixon offered to extend the coverage of private insurance via a system of mandates and government subsidies. The ideological gulf seemed wide, yet both men saw an opportunity.

Each of them was moved by personal experience. As a boy, Nixon lost two brothers to early deaths. His baby brother Arthur was consumed in days by a strain of tubercular encephalitis and their elder brother, Harold, took years to die of a more classic case of tuberculosis. The illness drained the family's finances and dictated its actions for years. On the eve of Ted

Jr.'s surgery, the young man had a surprising phone call: the president of the United States wanted to wish him well. The Kennedy family was touched by Nixon's kindness.

Kennedy's single-payer proposal was a "screwball scheme" that could end up costing $60 billion, Nixon told the president of the American Medical Association, but "we shouldn't blind ourselves to the problem." He described Harold's demise. "My parents . . . they borrowed, they sold property. They did everything. They put him in hospitals. They took him to Arizona for two years. He stayed in a very expensive hospital and then he finally died," Nixon said. "I know what it did to that family."

There were formidable obstacles to a Nixon-Kennedy collaboration— most notably a jurisdictional hurdle that would frustrate the senator throughout his career. The Senate Finance Committee held sway over Social Security, Medicare and Medicaid, and taxes. As such, it had extensive, and primary, jurisdiction over the American health care system. "There was this very large obstacle to his objective of enacting national health insurance, because the committee platform that he chaired was one that did not have direct legislative jurisdiction," aide LeRoy Goldman remembered. And the Finance Committee chairman who had the jurisdiction— Russell Long—was no friend of Ted Kennedy. Long's committee was packed with senators attentive to the oil, securities, pharmaceutical, insurance, and other industries, and its snug little hearing room was routinely jammed with lobbyists. Medicare and Medicaid were popular successes, but soaring costs were raising demand for higher taxes.

Over the years, Kennedy finagled, threw his weight around, and used his own committee's jurisdiction over public health issues—like scientific research, medical education, medical manpower, pharmaceutical regulation, and disease control—to outflank the Finance panel. In May 1974 he held hearings on how the major drug companies bribed customers— doctors, pharmacists, and hospitals—with color televisions and other gifts to increase business. "It smacks of payola," Kennedy said.

"But what we couldn't do was report the bill and have the Senate act on it," said Goldman, "because that required concurrent action by the Senate Finance Committee . . . the killing field for national health insurance."

There were, however, other dukes on Capitol Hill. If he could not get the Finance chairman, Kennedy might corral the next best thing. In the spring of 1972, he formed an alliance with Wilbur Mills, chairman of the House Ways and Means Committee, the godfather of Medicare and Medicaid.

"Russell Long was sitting there like a troll on the top of the Senate Finance Committee bridge," but then Mills "got the bug" and declared himself a candidate for president, Goldman recalled. A candidate for national office might appreciate the attention that would flow from an alliance with Kennedy. The senator found Mills was "approachable . . . austere . . . and very bright. . . . I went over [to the Ways and Means offices] frequently, and would talk to him." The two had made a joint appearance before the Democratic Platform Committee in June 1972. The lawmakers and their aides negotiated for two years—and in April 1974 they had a bill.

NIXON HAD A MIX of motivations. Early in his presidency, he had watched the environmental movement snowball from a few tweedy conservation groups to a national phenomenon. His strategy was to co-opt. With an array of bill signings and executive orders, he fended off the efforts of Democrats like Muskie to monopolize the field. His instincts told him that health care was the next big domestic issue.

"Nothing that politics abhors more than a vacuum," he told his cabinet. "Here we come to health. If the media can make the environment an issue, then they sure as hell will make health an issue—with the help of Teddy Kennedy." He needed something that he could support, the president told his aides, if only to parry Kennedy.

"What we're playing in the health game is really a defensive maneuver," Nixon said. "In addition, of course, to trying to deal with the real problem effectively." A "game plan" was drawn up by his aides. Its top priority was to persuade Americans "that the President can do more to solve the health care problem than anyone else." Its next priority was "to ensure that the Kennedy plan is blocked." Presidential advisers wrote long papers analyzing Kennedy's arguments. "You simply can't fight something with nothing," Nixon told his domestic council.

Defensive, yes. But once the idea was introduced, those assigned to developing a plan became, as human beings are wont to do, invested in the process. Nixon's team dreamed up two big ideas to expand the role of the federal government in health care. The first was the health maintenance organization (HMO). As a native Californian, Nixon was familiar with the Kaiser Permanente Health Plan, which brought a range of medical practices together beneath one roof to limit costs. The second big idea was a mandate. Kennedy wanted a single-payer program along the lines of Medicare. Nixon's plan would instead require that employers provide health insurance to their employees.

Kennedy had no objection to an HMO experiment. He helped the White House secure the necessary legislation and funding—a significant and historic bipartisan collaboration. But he did not consider a mandate worthy—until the president, desperate to shift the spotlight from scandal ("One year of Watergate is enough," Nixon told Congress and the country in the State of the Union address), sweetened the deal in early 1974.

Nixon's new proposal—the Comprehensive Health Insurance Plan— still had its employer mandate, but it now limited the amount of "out of pocket" costs that employees would pay, offered generous standard benefits, and provided a public option for those who could not obtain private coverage at the workplace.

"The time is at hand—this year," Nixon told the nation in that State of the Union speech. And for a moment, it seemed he was correct. Nixon's proposal, and Kennedy's alliance with Mills, made national health insurance "a realistic possibility," a young economist, Alice Rivlin, wrote at the time. "The congressional barons were in motion, and their ponderous minuet created an opening," judged the medical historian David Blumenthal.

KENNEDY NOW HAD MILLS, and a willing Nixon. But to the senator's chagrin, he no longer had Labor. It was organized labor, in the person of Walter Reuther, who had first recruited Kennedy to the cause of national health care. But Reuther was dead, killed in that plane crash. His replacements contended that the compromises Kennedy made to get the cost-conscious Mills on board had violated the spirit of the dream. "Creeping incrementalism is not the answer," Reuther's successor, Leonard Woodcock, declared.

In a face-off in Kennedy's office, Andrew Biemiller, the head lobbyist for the AFL-CIO, scoffed when Kennedy told him, "This is the best deal we're ever going to get." Biemiller and the other labor leaders urged Kennedy to abandon Nixon and return to the issue after the 1974 midterm elections when, presumably, they would have veto-proof majorities.

Kennedy parried, listing the conservative senators who would still be serving in 1975—especially those on the Finance Committee. "Tell me which ones you're going to defeat in the upcoming elections," he challenged Labor's representatives. "The same people that you have now [will still be] pulling the strings."

The time was ripe, Kennedy argued. "Here we've got the Ways and Means Committee, with Mills," he said, "and the president is in such a weakened condition, we may just make him sign this."

The unions did not budge. If Kennedy forged ahead, they promised to brand him a sellout.

"Well, you're just going to have to call me a traitor," Kennedy replied. The meeting ended on that acrimonious note.

Kennedy ignored Labor's threats—kept talking with Mills and Nixon—and was jeered by union officials in Boston and Washington for "abandoning" them. "The strength of their feeling should not be underestimated," a Massachusetts ally who witnessed the display of anger wrote to Kennedy. The Kennedy-Mills proposal was "not a compromise," it was "a surrender," said a Cambridge-based newsletter for liberal health care professionals. "Senator Kennedy has bargained away the support of millions of Americans at a politically inopportune time. The Watergate scandals promise to change the complexion of the next Congress, making it more liberal and more Democratic. The time to compromise would have been after the elections, when the senator could have faced Mills with a substantially stronger bargaining position."

They were "holding out for the perfect," Kennedy would remember, citing another legislative adage, "rather than dealing with the good."

Reuther had foreseen that the resurgent economies of western Europe and Japan, equipped with national health care systems, would be able to undercut U.S. manufacturers burdened by soaring health care and pension costs. By the turn of the century, General Motors would have $62 billion in health care liabilities. But not all labor leaders shared his foresight. The labor hierarchy, and many of its member unions, had grown complacent in the postwar era, and were now aligned culturally with Nixon's "silent majority." In 1968, Reuther had pulled the UAW out of the AFL-CIO.

"Reuther led an almost ascetic life. He took few vacations, had little interest in food or drink, and believed that union leaders should share the lifestyle of the workers they represented," noted sociologist Jill Quadagno. But AFL-CIO president George Meany "drew a large salary, had gourmet tastes in wine and food, smoked expensive cigars, and played golf, a rich man's hobby. He held AFL-CIO annual meetings at a luxurious Miami beachfront hotel and spent his free time nightclubbing, lounging around the pool and playing gin rummy."

Health care benefits were something the union leaders won for their members in contract negotiations: Why undermine their own stature and authority? Kennedy questioned Labor's sincerity. "You had lip service," Kennedy said. "You had some who were very strongly for it . . . others who said they were for it and really were not; and others who basically sat on their hands."

Undeterred, Kennedy plowed ahead. Stuart Altman, representing the Nixon administration, and Stan Jones, an aide to the senator, devised a possible compromise during a cable car ride up Sandia Peak while in Albuquerque to discuss health care at a conference of state officials. After returning to Washington, amid the turmoil of impeachment, Altman and other Nixon aides joined their counterparts from the Kennedy and Mills staffs in secret meetings in the basement of St. Mark's Episcopal Church. Kennedy "wanted to get something and I wanted to get something," Caspar Weinberger, the HEW secretary, remembered. "We were quite close."

Kennedy agreed to adjust the package of benefits and copays to conform with the Nixon proposal, and to give the insurance industry a role in administering the system; he also accepted a phased-in program, which would start with coverage for children. He and Mills sat down with Weinberger in July. But Nixon's team would not budge from the employer mandate, nor agree to fund a program with federal payroll taxes. And that, Kennedy could not accept.

"You have to compromise," Mills told him.

"I can't bring Labor any further. You can't file this bill," Kennedy replied.

"Oh yes I can," said Mills.

"I'll kill it in the Senate," Kennedy told him.

It was the last hour—stoppage time—of the Sixties. The costs of the Vietnam War and Nixon's politically self-serving economic policies were coming home in the high price of beef, soaring interest rates, and lengthy gas lines. America's liberal leaders, spoiled by affluence, did not recognize that this would be their last chance, for decades, to provide the capstone to the New Deal and the Great Society, and complete the social democracy imagined and conceived by Franklin Roosevelt, Harry Truman, John Kennedy, and Lyndon Johnson.

In retrospect, Kennedy said, he should have taken Nixon's 1974 proposal, with its employer mandate, and worked to perfect it in the future. It was his worst tactical mistake, he would say, of all his years in Congress.

NIXON RESIGNED IN AUGUST. In his first address to Congress, Gerald Ford endorsed his predecessor's health care initiative—then quietly let it slide from his list of priorities.

Mills kept on, but he worked by consensus. He corralled support for a bill in the Ways and Means Committee, yet only by a single vote. Kennedy watched from the back of the hall, struck by the power that the health insurance industry wielded on the congressmen. The chairman shelved the bill for 1974—but promised to revive it the following year, when they would have that big post-Watergate Democratic majority.

In the predawn hours of October 7, an inebriated Mills, sixty-five, was riding in a car with its headlights off with Annabella Battistella, thirty-eight, a striptease artist whose professional name was "Fanne Foxe, the Argentine firecracker." Police pulled them over and she leapt, or fell, into the Tidal Basin. A few weeks later, Mills wandered out from the wings as she stripped at the Pilgrim Theatre, a burlesque house in Boston's Combat Zone. His career was finished. So were the chances of a grand bipartisan bargain on health care. "We got very close," Weinberger recalled. "When Mills got into all those terrible problems, the issue kind of curled up and died."

IN THE MEANTIME, as Sorensen had warned and Carter predicted, Kennedy found a target on his back for journalists out to prove they were not, in the wake of Watergate, in the tank for Democrats. At the fifth anniversary of Mary Jo Kopechne's death in the summer of 1974, the *New York Times* published a blistering magazine piece, "Chappaquiddick + 5" by Robert Sherrill, the Washington correspondent for *The Nation*.

The story had no fresh findings. It was a specimen of the "raises questions" genre, in which a politician's actions are said to "raise questions" among unnamed skeptics by writers lacking on-the-record sources or fresh evidence. It purported to address the "mystery" of why a skilled politician like Kennedy "refused to clear the air" of innuendo and gossip, which Sherrill outlined in great detail.

Kennedy's "reputation as a wild driver and . . . a ladies' man provided a marvelous culture for growing virulent rumors," Sherrill wrote, and proceeded to spread them through the pages of the *Times*: "There were whispers that Miss Kopechne was pregnant and that her death was no accident. When her parents later moved into a much more expensive home, it was hinted that Kennedy had paid them for silence." Instead of being seen as deplorable, the way the wily Nixon had dispatched his goons to Chappaquiddick was evidence, said Sherrill, that "Kennedy may now be vulnerable." The fact that Kennedy garnered "only" 64 percent of the vote in the 1970 Senate race was a signal that "something dramatic has happened" to his popularity. Sherrill's article set a pattern for scores of pieces that followed—counting the ounces of liquor consumed at the party, checking the timeline with stopwatches, bemoaning the lack of an autopsy.

The Watergate investigations that Kennedy had facilitated were having, in the end, a perverse effect on his own presidential hopes. "The scandal raises profound questions about the morality and credibility of public men," wrote Harry McPherson, former aide to Lyndon Johnson. Longtime friends and allies, like John Glenn of Ohio and Wayne Owens of Utah, declined Kennedy's offer to campaign with them. It was not an auspicious season for a candidate who had left the scene of a fatal accident, wrote Kennedy's friend William Shannon. "In going over the side, Richard Nixon may have taken Edward Kennedy down with him," Shannon said. "After the public has rebelled against a cover-up at Watergate, will it buy a cover-up at Chappaquiddick?"

TED JR. HAD CANCER. Joan was in and out of rehab. The press would give Kennedy no quarter. Sorensen had advised him that the only way to clinch the presidency was by selling out the "pushy" women and minorities, and underplaying John's and Robert's legacy. And inevitably, one day, in a downtown plaza or a hotel kitchen, a gunman would fire and Ted Jr. and Patrick and Kara would join their fatherless cousins, and Joan the famous widows. "If you talk about the personal . . . you had someone who had been flawed, A, by Chappaquiddick, B, I guess by a lot of stories about drinking himself," said Gwirtzman. "He's got an alcoholic wife, and a son with an iffy, a very serious medical problem . . . and a lot of people would like to shoot him."

By the close of the summer of 1974, Kennedy had begun to spread the word among his advisers. He would not run in 1976. He made it official at a Parker House press conference in September.

The bicentennial year was likely, looking back, Kennedy's best opportunity to be elected president. The Republicans were in rank confusion and the Democratic nomination would eventually be captured by Carter, a one-term, unknown governor from Georgia. It was a moment of slack water, before the conservative tide.

Nineteen

ROAR

Senator Edward Kennedy had reason to believe, as he climbed upon the small green wooden stage outside City Hall, that the people of Boston would listen to him. He had heard boos in Massachusetts—directed by antiwar protesters at him and Hubert Humphrey as they campaigned together in 1968. But the white working-class folks of South Boston and Dorchester, East Boston and Charlestown, were not left-wing agitators. They who stood before him were Kennedy folk. They had elected John Kennedy, forgiven Ted for Chappaquiddick, and bathed him in affection on St. Patrick's Day four years earlier.

This was Boston, family turf—cradle of American democracy. Within hailing distance were Faneuil Hall, the graves of Sam Adams, Paul Revere, and John Hancock, and the old City Hall, where Mayor John Fitzgerald had reigned. The several thousand protest marchers gathering on that September day in 1974 had assembled on the Common near the statues of the abolitionists Charles Sumner and Wendell Phillips and the bas-relief tribute to the 54th Massachusetts: the all-Black regiment, those "warm blooded champions of a better day for man," who charged the Confederate guns at Fort Wagner, South Carolina, in 1863.

Like their forebears, the crowd this day talked long and loudly about rights. But theirs was a different cause. They were the troops of ROAR—Restore Our Alienated Rights—a militant organization dedicated to keeping the Black working-class schoolkids of Roxbury apart from the white working-class schoolkids of neighborhoods like Southie. Kennedy, and several on his staff, were not entirely unsympathetic. There was rot in closed neighborhoods like Charlestown and South Boston, and complacency and hatreds brewed by insularity. There was fear, spurred by bigotry and the deteriorating industrial economy. But there was also warmth, and shared memories and Irish and Italian traditions in the clapboard three-deckers, and a feeling that, in a fearsome and often hostile world, here was home.

To these white Americans, unrequested, had come a charge to stay racial injustice. John and Robert Kennedy in the years before their awakening in 1963 had viewed the civil rights movement as an irritant, not a cause. They knew few Black people and thought civil rights leaders like Martin Luther King were impudent and politically naive. But John Kennedy's assassination had left Robert vulnerable and open to the suffering of others—and so a friend to Blacks, Latinos, and Indians, who became his most passionate supporters in 1968. Robert's death left Ted with two martyrs to honor, and both law and liberal dogma called for the immediate integration of schools, by crosstown busing if necessary. Ted's maiden speech in the Senate, during the debate on the 1964 Civil Rights Act, had opposed busing—but as doctrine had evolved, so had he.

Led by the formidable Louise Day Hicks, who insisted that the problems of Black children could be traced to their families and culture, the Boston school committee had opposed even voluntary pupil transfer programs. The Black population of Boston grew, and grew aspirational, but its schools were deliberately underfunded, separate, and inferior. Arthur Garrity, a federal district judge, had responded in June 1974 with an order to desegregate the schools. His decision surprised no one. The judge's reading of the Supreme Court's rulings was proper, and his liberal credentials—as a Harvard Law graduate who had worked in Jack Kennedy's presidential campaign—were unassailable. His name had been submitted to Lyndon Johnson by Ted Kennedy for the judgeship denied to Frank Morrissey.

The question, in retrospect, was whether the commonwealth's political leadership should have—or could have—reached a consensual solution, forestalling Garrity's arithmetical order. Garrity's decision did not extend to the leafy suburbs that ringed Boston. It left resolution of an incendiary social issue to the harried working class, Black and white. Southie was described by the Department of Justice as "an isolated area . . . marked by narrow streets . . . multiple family dwellings, high unemployment . . . an abundance of bars and taverns," and high school students who specialized as dropouts. Roxbury was "black, lower class, the ghetto section," with streets that looked like "London after the blitz."

"The busing is a scandal," Harvard psychiatrist and sociologist Robert Coles told the *Boston Globe*. "It's working-class people who happen to be white and working-class people who happen to be black . . . poor people . . . both of whom are very hard pressed; neither of whom have got much leverage on anything. They are both competing for a very limited piece of pie, the limits of which are being set by the larger limits of class which allow them damn little." The "middle-class, privileged, well-to-do, well-educated" suburbanites were not affected, those "who have . . . plenty of money in the bank, who have summer homes down on the Cape," Coles noted. It all left working-class whites feeling victimized and powerless. "To talk about it in terms of only racism is to miss the point."

"I don't want to be critical of the court," said Representative Tip O'Neill, a sociologist of another sort, "but instead of busing children from one ghetto area to another he would have done better to bus them from a ghetto area to a much more affluent area."

"I think this is correct," Kennedy wrote, in the margin of a letter he received from Edward Logue, administrator for the Boston Redevelopment Authority, who was also pressing for a solution that involved suburbs and city.

IN 1966, when Kennedy traveled to Mississippi to address the Southern Christian Leadership Conference, King had warned him that the hate he had experienced in Cicero, a working-class suburb of Chicago, exceeded any that he witnessed in the South. They would soon discover, King said, that racial bias was profoundly universal. In the South, it was just more obvious. Now the weight, the penance for old sins, had fallen on a few

poor and clannish neighborhoods in the city. This was the challenge presented to Kennedy by Mike Barnicle, the *Boston Globe* columnist, in an
"open letter" in the newspaper. He reminded Kennedy of how brother
Robert had touched the heartbroken crowd in Indianapolis on the evening King was killed. Ted Kennedy had ties to the families of South Boston and Charlestown. He could reach them.

> Most of these people are left only with their fears. To them, busing
> is a plot, concocted by "the liberals" and the suburban hypocrites
> who preach equality from the front porch of gilded white neighbor-
> hoods. . . . And now they feel that their children are being taken
> from them by a judge who doesn't know them. . . .
>
> Senator, you are the one man who can help heal the divisions that
> have arisen over the issue of busing. You have the one voice that can
> help keep this city calm, leaving the clear ring of justice and common
> sense in homes and streets where people sit, uncertain. . . . You, more
> than anyone else, could stand and speak about the consequences of
> violence.
>
> And to you, Senator Kennedy, they would listen.

But Barnicle's faith in the people of Boston was misplaced. It was too
late. To Senator Kennedy, they would not listen.

KENNEDY HAD SPENT THE summer sailing wide of the busing issue. Garrity's order had brought him "unshirted hell" from his constituents, he
recalled. The senator and his seatmate, Ed Brooke, were conscientious,
battling antibusing measures in Congress, but "have been conspicuous
for their absence in Boston," the *Globe* reported. Many noted how Kennedy's own children attended elite private schools. When pressed by reporters, Kennedy dodged the issue, ultimately arriving at the formulation
"I'm for quality education" but "not for busing just for the sake of busing."
His decision to attend the ROAR rally, after stopping at high schools
in Dorchester and South Boston that morning, was spontaneous, and

perhaps inspired by Barnicle's reference to Robert and Indianapolis in 1968. He would try. "I felt . . . a responsibility," Kennedy would say. "It was my city." He had arrived in Boston from the Cape that morning looking tired and uneasy. At Government Center, he skipped a meeting with march organizers and went right to the stage. There, two men with chicken masks (one mask was black and the other white) were mocking the nation's only biracial Senate delegation. Kennedy arrived with a single policeman as an escort. He was jostled at the platform. When he tried to speak, the crowd booed, then turned their backs. "No, no, we won't go," they chanted—then sang "God Bless America."

Stymied, Kennedy climbed down the wooden stairs and headed toward his office in the twenty-six-story John F. Kennedy Federal Office Building, a hundred yards away, on the north side of the plaza. Things turned ugly, fast. "Pig!" they shouted. "You're a disgrace to the Irish." The crowd shoved and elbowed to get right up in his face. He tried to keep a frozen half-smile. A wadded-up newspaper sailed toward him. Then a tomato. His suit was splattered. Eggs. Stones. Sneers.

"Why don't you put your one-legged son on a bus to Roxbury . . ."

"Yeah, let your daughter get bused there so she can get raped . . ."

"Why don't you let them shoot you like they shot your two brothers . . ."

Years later, Kennedy remembered his tormentors as "nasty . . . cowardly." Once he was safe inside the building, the guards locked the doors. The crowd surged, yelling and banging and kicking at the glass walls. A panel shattered, and shards and splinters scattered across the lobby floor. He rode the elevator to his office on the twenty-fourth floor with his nephew Joseph.

"Well, what did you think of that, Joe?"

"I think you had about half of them," his nephew replied.

MANY OF ITS INSTITUTIONS failed Boston that fall: the school committee, the dissipating Brahmins, the Catholic hierarchy, the downtown business community, and, arguably, the federal judge. Garrity's ruling was announced in late June, with little time before school began in the fall; he implemented an off-the-shelf state desegregation plan that bused eighteen thousand students and paired the overwhelmingly Black Roxbury High School with lily-white South Boston High School—two of the poorest, worst-performing schools in the city. The protests and rioting and assaults, stabbings and random gunfire carried on for months.

"Nothing had prepared the black children for the ugliness of the crowd that ambushed the buses. As they sat inside, terror-stricken and in some cases hysterical, all they could see was the sudden rush of angry people. . . . The faces of the crowd were distorted with taunts and jeers, their arms were upraised in obscene gestures or acts of rock or bottle throwing," the *Globe* reported. "All the black children could hear were their own screams, the tattoo of missiles against the buses and the crack of shattering glass." On the last day of school at South Boston High, the public address system played Handel's "Hallelujah" chorus.

The next school year was no better. On September 8, 1975, the Brookline birthplace of John Kennedy was firebombed, and "Bus Teddy" painted on the sidewalk. Years later, the culprit was identified as Whitey Bulger, a leader of organized crime in Boston and the brother of state senator William Bulger, an antibusing champion.

Kennedy must be added to the list of those who failed Boston. In the crisis, he seemed "distracted and not well-informed" and at times "rambling," said the *Globe*. Kennedy tried, he said years later. "My own sense was I could have no influence with the racists but some influence on people who were concerned and bewildered and troubled." In the end, he conceded, his efforts had but "marginal" effect. Mayor Kevin White and his aides, who bore the brunt of the peacekeeping in the weeks that followed, fumed at Kennedy's appearance at the ROAR rally. Kennedy had given the protesters worldwide exposure, fueled their bravado, and overshadowed the efforts of the mayor and police to keep order. "He raised the level of tension. He brought the rally back to life," said Kirk O'Donnell. "Maybe it was good for him, but it was not good for this city," said O'Donnell's colleague Robert Kiley.

After talking with reporters (his hand trembling as he poured milk into his coffee), Kennedy left for the airport and a flight back to Washington. He would not remain in Boston, nor return to the city that week.

"It must be nice being in Washington and eating breakfast in the Senate dining room," Mayor White told a journalist early on the morning the buses rolled.

Kennedy had no solutions.

"What can I do?" he asked the press.

THE CONFRONTATION AT City Hall Plaza took place on Monday, September 9, 1974: one month after Nixon resigned, and two weeks before Kennedy announced that he would not be a candidate for president in 1976. To the extent it played any role in his decision, it was as further evidence that the times were, once more, changing. Kennedy recognized that Watergate was a momentary eddy within deeper currents of public opinion, represented by the combined Nixon-Wallace vote—57 percent—in 1968 and Nixon's landslide victory, with 61 percent, over McGovern in 1972. Nixon and his aides employed issues like busing to drive a wedge between liberals like Kennedy and the Democratic Party's blue-collar constituency. The White House proposed a moratorium, and then a constitutional amendment, to stop the practice. According to a 1971 Gallup poll, mandatory busing was opposed by three out of four Americans, and two out of four Black Americans. Kennedy, to his credit, consistently voted against Nixon's dodges. He proposed to give segregated school systems extra federal funding to ameliorate the difficulties of integration. It was not enough.

The skirmishing between Kennedy and ROAR persisted for months. He was heckled outside the Copley Plaza Hotel, interrupted at a field hearing on airline deregulation, and trapped, on another occasion, at a fundraiser inside Anthony's Pier 4 restaurant. Hicks was a big woman who drove around in a golden Cadillac ("You could spot her a half a mile away," Kennedy recalled), but Elvira "Pixie" Palladino, of East Boston, was a darting barracuda. "Short, pitch-black hair and flaming eyes," Kennedy remembered. She "always came out of nowhere . . . you walked into some hotel lobby and—boom!—she was there . . . standing in front of you, not letting you move." The most menacing confrontation took place on a Sunday morning in the spring of 1975, after the senator attended a Knights of Columbus breakfast in Quincy. He emerged to find the tires of his car slashed and the windshield and door handles smeared with excrement. Someone took a swing at him; another protester tried to kick him. A woman jabbed at him with the point of a small American flag, and mothers blocked his car with their children.

"There were several hundred of them. So I start to walk, and I don't know where the hell I'm walking," he recalled. The crowd was "taunting and yelling" and following him, growing bigger and nastier, waving pickets torn from nearby fences, as his aides, police, and Knights of Columbus linked arms around him. "Keep calm," he told them. "Try to act nonchalant." Ultimately, the state's senior U.S. senator turned and dashed for the nearby subway station, where aide James King held the gate shut, keeping the protesters at bay. They settled for pelting Kennedy's train with rocks.

"I told him how proud we were of his brother Jack when he walked the streets of Charlestown in the Bunker Hill Day parades," the town's Pat Russell, a ROAR leader, told the *Globe* that day. "I told him how my grandmother invited Jack into our house during the parade. . . . I asked him, how could he let the court take away Charlestown's identity."

"I cried for his brothers," said Flossie O'Keefe, a South Boston antibusing organizer. "But today I'd dance on his grave."

Garrity maintained control of the schools for more than a decade. By the mid-1980s, South Boston High School, and schools like it, were no longer sacred turf for white, working-class communities. Busing changed the complexion of the classrooms—but in part because many white parents fled to the suburbs or chose to send their children to private or parochial school. "In 1973, roughly 60 percent of the students in the [Boston] public schools had been white. By 1980 the percentage had dropped to 35, by 1987 it was 26," wrote historian Ronald Formisano. Was the quality of education better? "By 1988 nearly 40 percent of the system's ninth graders were dropping out before [high school] graduation." Support for busing among Black parents plummeted.

AMERICANS WERE LOSING FAITH. The electorate was "more alienated and more cynical than at any point in modern time," Gerald Ford's pollster, Robert Teeter, told him. "These feelings . . . are directed at all major institutions—the government, businesses, unions, school systems, media, churches."

The Watergate scandals played a central role in casting the national mood, but they were not the only cause of disillusionment. The assassinations of the Sixties had broken hearts; so had race riots in Watts, Detroit, Newark, and Washington, DC. Peaceful protesters—white and Black—gave way to more militant counterparts like the Black Panthers, or to violent nihilists like the bomb-throwing Weathermen or the Symbionese Liberation Army, a ragtag bunch of losers who kidnapped the heiress Patty Hearst and capped their "revolution" in a fiery suicidal shootout with police. Economic challengers from western Europe and Asia bit into American manufacturing. Aging factories, union wages, and generous benefits put U.S. firms at a disadvantage in their competition with government-subsidized, low-wage foreign rivals. Overnight, it seemed, the everyday things of life—automobiles, shoes, televisions, pianos—were manufactured overseas. Nixon's flawed economic policies, the bill for the war in Vietnam, and the truculence of an international oil cartel brought on an unbridled inflation, with soaring prices at the gas pumps and grocery aisles. The movies grew dark and conspiratorial, and pop music hedonistically frothy. And poison, still, was Vietnam.

In 1972, Kennedy had assembled a study team of experts to visit North Vietnam and assess the impact of U.S. bombardments on the civilian population. Their visit was delayed when Nixon launched the "Christmas bombing," a brutal air campaign against the North. Kennedy wrote an op-ed for the *New York Times* decrying the air assault and, once more, reminding Americans of the costs of war. In 1972 alone, he wrote, the number of civilians who died in South Vietnam exceeded the number of American soldiers killed in action during the entire war. A million tons of bombs had been dropped, and one-fourth of the two hundred thousand civilian casualties were children. "As we gather with our families during these special days of peace on earth and good will toward men, how can we help but think about this war?" he wrote. "How can any American be proud?"

The air assault appeared to work—as the North and South then joined with the United States in the Paris Accords, liberating American prisoners of war and bringing a cease-fire to Southeast Asia. Kennedy said all the right, supportive things about the treaty, but his investigators stayed in the field.

The peace settlement was tissue thin. It left two hundred thousand North Vietnamese troops on South Vietnamese soil and gave them a respite in which to rearm. North and South quickly violated the accords. Kennedy dubbed it "The Ceasefire War." In Cambodia, nearly half the population—some three million people—had become refugees since the destabilizing U.S. incursion in 1970, and the communist Khmer Rouge encircled Phnom Penh.

Congressional critics had spent years attempting to cut off funding for the wars in Southeast Asia. In May 1974, Kennedy led the Senate in its first successful bid to reduce military aid to South Vietnam, defeating Nixon's attempt to send another $266 million to the Saigon government. Kennedy's efforts were an irritant to the administration diplomats, who believed that the senator and his aides, de Haan and Tinker, were overtly sympathetic to the North Vietnamese. "It would be the height of folly" to give the senator "the tactical advantage of an honest and detailed answer to the questions of substance" that Kennedy was raising, the U.S. ambassador to South Vietnam, Graham Martin, advised Kissinger. The White House would blame Congress for the tragedy that followed. But Nixon signed the legislation that cut off the funding for all U.S. military operations in Southeast Asia. By the spring of 1975, there was consensus: even conservative stalwarts like Barry Goldwater said "Enough."

"The people of America want peace . . . a durable peace, so that our nation can finally turn all its resources to all the other things that command our attention," said Kennedy, in support of the cutoff. "The time has come for Americans to stop sending its bombers to produce a war that is called peace, and to end our role in the violence and bloodshed."

The North Vietnamese, hoping to make military progress in 1975 and finish off South Vietnamese president Nguyen Van Thieu in 1976, discovered that the South Vietnamese military was as likely to flee as fight, and adjusted their timetable. President Ford appeared before a joint session of Congress and begged for half a billion dollars in emergency aid. Kennedy helped lead the opposition: "Let us not pretend that the crisis in Vietnam can be solved by a few dollars more, after pouring in some $140 billion over the last decade," he said. Instead, he called for $100 million in humanitarian assistance to ease civilian suffering in the coming denouement.

The sorry scenes of those last days—desperate Vietnamese at the embassy gates, helicopters landing on rooftops or being shoved into the sea from the decks of U.S. ships—brought shame to Americans and contributed to the national discontent. The genocidal Khmer Rouge captured Phnom Penh on April 17, and Saigon fell on April 30. Most of the American political class chose to close the book on Vietnam. It would have been easy for Kennedy to join them. He did not. His subcommittee, working with the Ford administration, became an advocate in Congress for Southeast Asian refugees. In the next eighteen months, more than 150,000 were resettled in the United States. In 1980, at Kennedy's urging, U.S. immigration law was adjusted to replace the old quota for refugees and allow up to 50,000 each year.

As the Republic of South Vietnam succumbed there was more dispiriting news—for the country and Kennedy. In December 1974, the *New York Times* had run a shocker of a story about widespread illegal CIA spying on American citizens. Ford, trying to get ahead of the unfolding scandal, promised a full investigation. In the process, he told newsmen that U.S. intelligence agencies—working under Dwight Eisenhower and John and Robert Kennedy—had plotted to kill Fidel Castro and other foreign chiefs of state. For the next two years, as a presidential commission and two congressional committees—most prominently a Senate panel led by

Frank Church—conducted investigations, Americans were treated to a diet of startling, often sordid reports about what U.S. intelligence agencies had been up to in their name.

The raft of wrongdoing was astonishing. The federal agencies had a seemingly inexhaustible appetite for spying on Americans—opening their mail, reading their telegrams, following them around, listening in on phone calls, and bugging offices and hotel rooms. Lists of dissidents were compiled, including twenty-six thousand of allegedly questionable allegiance who were tagged for preventive detention in the event of a "national emergency." The FBI had half a million "domestic intelligence" files; the CIA kept a computerized index of nearly one and a half million suspect Americans. Among those under surveillance were the NAACP, the conservative Young Americans for Freedom, *Playboy* magazine, and the ACLU—and celebrities like Joan Baez, Sammy Davis Jr., Norman Mailer, John Steinbeck, Ted Kennedy, and the pre-presidential Richard Nixon. The merely spied upon were lucky, as the government agents grew skilled at burglary, infiltration, and disruption of dissenting organizations. The programs went by bureaucratic jargon—COINTELPRO and ZR/RIFLE—or whimsical code names like Shamrock, Minaret, Mockingbird, and Mongoose.

That was the framework of fact. The flourishes left Americans shaking their heads: the brothels that the CIA operated in San Francisco, where unwitting patrons could be studied after being fed doses of LSD; the wiretapped recordings of King's sex life; and the various secret agent gadgets—an exploding seashell, a contaminated wet suit, a poisoned ballpoint pen—designed for use against Castro. And then there was the biggest thunderbolt of all: news that President John Kennedy had shared a mistress with a Mafia boss, at the same time that the CIA was employing Mob leaders to help them kill the Cuban dictator. Democrats controlling Congress had relished the opportunity to expose more Nixon-era wrongdoing. They were dismayed to find that John and Robert Kennedy were exposed as well.

Ted Kennedy gave his testimony to the Church Committee, under oath, on September 22, 1975. It was a session best described as circumspect. Kennedy had only served in Washington for ten months of his brother's administration, he reminded his colleagues, and was not in the loop when John and Robert discussed affairs of state. Two witnesses testified that President Kennedy had asked them about the advisability of killing Castro, and there was no doubt that Robert Kennedy had overseen the anti-Castro Operation Mongoose. But when Robert was briefed about the CIA-Mafia plot, the Church Committee concluded, he was informed it had been terminated. Ted told the committee that he had never heard his brothers speak of assassination. "They would have deplored it and ceased it," Kennedy said. As a matter of courtesy, Ted was not questioned about his brother John's relationship with Judith Campbell Exner, the girlfriend the president had shared with Chicago Mob boss Sam Giancana. Her public account of a two-year relationship appeared in the summer of 1975, and as a published memoir in 1977. It would spur a cascade of exposés, of varying reliability, about the infidelities of all three Kennedy brothers.

What did it all mean? The biggest casualty of the post-Watergate scandal season was faith in government. But as more and more evidence of the family's recklessness reached the public, it gave Ted Kennedy a louche reputation that some found immaterial—but others thought deplorable. Tintagel was tawdry. "The notion of Camelot, always overblown and romanticized, has barely survived, if it has at all, allegations and disclosures about assassination plots and Mafia women [and] wiretaps," wrote Tom Wicker in *Esquire* magazine.

KENNEDY WAS NOW WELL into the middle stage of his career—when his powers were augmented by his role as a candidate, torchbearer, and potential president. He was not John and Robert's kid brother anymore, listening respectably to his elders, going along to get along. If he saw a juicy issue, he lunged to seize it. He led stirring campaigns, in and out of Congress, to block elements of Republican presidential agendas. He took jaunts around the world to burnish his foreign policy credentials, pushed progressive ideals like national health insurance, and served as the frontman for liberalism. Ted Jr.'s cancer and Joan's setbacks had taken him out of the 1976 presidential race, but he was only forty-four, with years of opportunity ahead.

In the meantime, reinforcements arrived. Liberals like the Fearless Foursome were no longer lonely rebels. They were fortified, in House and Senate, by regiments of new men and women, the "Watergate babies." These were independent-minded Democrats like Gary Hart of Colorado, Al Gore of Tennessee, and Bill Bradley of New Jersey, or the man who became Kennedy's seatmate in 1978, Paul Tsongas. "We were a conquering army," Congressman George Miller of California would recall. "We came here to take the Bastille." In the years after Watergate, they clamored for reform, and Kennedy played prime roles in the enactment of historic legislation to control the secret flow of money into campaigns, limit presidential war powers, open government files to the public, manage the intelligence agencies, reform the budget process, and otherwise limit what was now being called "the imperial presidency."

Nixon, for example, had imposed his own priorities when vetoing spending bills and impounding funds. The budget was not Kennedy's usual bailiwick, but Sam Ervin—looking for star power—invited him to testify on the constitutional issues. "Recent events have made it imperative that the Congress address itself to this issue, without delay, and reassert its 'power of the purse' in the appropriations and budget process," Ervin wrote Kennedy. The "crisis" was far-reaching, Ervin warned. A "somnolent unconsciousness" on Capitol Hill had left a vacuum for presidents to fill. "The Executive has moved with a boldness unmatched in our history to grasp and to consolidate power."

"Obviously you should do something unique and spectacular," aide Thomas Susman advised Kennedy. "I don't know yet what that will be, but we'll come up with it."

Congress passed the Congressional Budget and Impoundment Control Act of 1974, clarifying the budget process and asserting its authority. And Kennedy came up with his "spectacular" gesture. He challenged the Nixon administration in federal court and personally argued the case. Though judges are inclined to give U.S. senators a courteous reception, it was no small risk for a politician battling the impression that he did not measure up to his brothers. Lawyers, clerks, and reporters packed the courtroom. At issue was the pocket veto, a device by which presidents allow legislation to wither to death during a congressional adjournment, thus depriving Congress of the opportunity to override a formal veto. Nixon had used a pocket veto during a five-day Christmas break to kill a Kennedy favorite—a $225 million bill to meet a national shortage by training doctors in family medicine. The Constitution allowed presidents to use the device, Kennedy contended, but only during long periods of adjournment—not in short-term recesses. He won; the administration appealed—and Kennedy made another appearance as a courtroom lawyer in the august U.S. Court of Appeals for the District of Columbia. Once again, he prevailed. The government chose not to take the case to the U.S. Supreme Court, and *Kennedy v. Sampson* became the prevailing precedent.

Kennedy had no central part in the passage of the War Powers Act of 1973, which bridled future presidents' ability to take the country into undeclared wars. But he did make a significant contribution to a new law limiting the government's ability to cite national security as a justification to eavesdrop on American citizens. He was a midwife to the Foreign Intelligence Surveillance Act (FISA) of 1978, which required that the National Security Agency and other intelligence services obtain court orders for electronic surveillance. The FISA process would be a framework for decades, most notably when employed against terrorists after the 9/11 attacks in 2001.

Though not the original sponsor of the Freedom of Information Act, which authorizes citizens' access to public records, Kennedy played a consequential role in strengthening the statute when it was amended and expanded in 1974. FOIA, as Americans came to know it, had been around for almost a decade, but its reach had eroded due to hefty fees, delays, and resistance. Ford vetoed the corrective legislation, but Kennedy led a successful effort to override the president's veto, and the bill became law.

THE POST-WATERGATE REFORMS FADED over time. Presidents would declare them inconvenient, ignore their strictures, and dare Congress to do something about it. Congress, run over roughshod by special interests, would cower. Fear of terrorism outweighed civil liberties. Lobbying disclosure laws rotted amid years of neglect. The independent counsel statute was discredited, after it led to hideously expensive, politically inspired, corrosive investigations. The budget act became a casualty of Washington's willingness to run up mammoth deficits. FOIA delays became a punch line. But the greatest failure, and a root of other failures, was the deterioration of campaign finance reform.

Kennedy was a central figure in the passage of a landmark 1974 law, which brought on an Elysian moment in American politics. For a brief time, the country had spending limits for presidential and congressional contests, optional public financing of presidential campaigns—and a working enforcement agency, the Federal Election Commission. The *New York Times*, in a front-page story, called it "the first effective curbs in American political history on the influence of the rich in government."

Kennedy was resolute: "A tiger," reformer Fred Wertheimer remembered. "The people who won battles in the institution were people who just never went away and were aggressive about it and forceful about it. And had great intensity about it. And that was . . . Ted Kennedy."

Kennedy had sensed an opportunity when Republican leader Hugh Scott of Pennsylvania, after Watergate, showed a willingness to support meaningful reforms. Kennedy "was prepared when he went to the floor. He was constantly pushing. He did not give. He pushed the Democrats hard in conference. He pushed his own allies," said Wertheimer. At one key moment, before passage, Kennedy met privately with a leader of the House opponents to break a stalemate. "In a single stroke," Scott and Kennedy promised, "we can shut off the underground rivers of private money that pollute politics at every level of the federal government." Just as the War Powers Act would lead to "no more Vietnams," they declared, the campaign finance bill "means no more Watergates."

This was regrettably optimistic. Their foes went to court, and in 1976, in *Buckley v. Valeo*, the Supreme Court declared that the expenditure of money is considered speech and protected by the First Amendment. If you have more cash, you get a louder voice. Kennedy would support later efforts, like that of Republican senator John McCain of Arizona and Democratic senator Russ Feingold of Wisconsin, to work around the ruling and curb the impact of political action committees, corporations, and other deep-pocketed donors. But the Supreme Court remained willfully blind to the dangers of corruption. In 2010, the conservative majority adopted Gilded Age thinking and, in *Citizens United v. FEC*, found that corporate "speech" was equal to human speech, and so corporate expenditures cannot be curbed. With a series of other rulings, the Court helped foster a system in which "dark money" donators can make limitless contributions without needing to disclose their identities. As of this writing, America has returned to the status of the early Nixon years, with secret donors funneling hundreds of millions of dollars of "dark money" into politics, while the public financing provisions of the law grow increasingly irrelevant. "The pieces that created the Watergate scandal," said Wertheimer, "secret money, unlimited donations—have been brought back to life."

Twenty

DEACON

On the first weekend in May 1974, Ted Kennedy journeyed south to give a Law Day address at the University of Georgia. This otherwise negligible visit was made notable by the counterculture journalist Hunter S. Thompson, who tagged along to gather string for a story on the 1976 presidential race. Thompson would describe to the readers of *Rolling Stone* how Governor Jimmy Carter, quoting from Bob Dylan and Reinhold Niebuhr and Leo Tolstoy, had skewered the Georgia bar for its injustice and complacency, and thoroughly eclipsed Kennedy with a "king hell bastard of a speech." Carter, said Thompson, was an anti-politician, and a very cool and laid-back fellow. The governor's ruminations about a lapse of national spirit—a "malaise," Carter called it in that speech—fit neatly with the thoughts of the gloomy, bourbon-swilling Thompson, pining for the liberations of the Sixties.

Kennedy had strolled into an ambush. The governor "had nothing but scorn—moral, intellectual, political, whatever—for Ted Kennedy," Carter speechwriter Patrick Anderson recalled. The speech was explicitly directed at Thompson, *Rolling Stone*'s top correspondent, for precisely the resultant effect. "If Carter's speech was fascinating," said Anderson, "it was also pious and self-serving, inspired less by populist idealism than by his determination to outshine a politician he despised."

James Earl Carter had many fine qualities: a good Christian faith, determination, smarts—and audacity. It would soon dawn on Kennedy and the rest of the political class that this one-term governor and South Georgia peanut farmer actually believed he could be president of the United States. By the time of their face-off in Athens, Carter had been nurturing his ambition for years. With stealth and calculation, he had identified Kennedy as his primary impediment. Eventually, political competition and human nature being what they are, Carter developed a fine contempt for his rival.

For Carter had less admirable traits as well. In politics, your strengths are often weaknesses. The flip side of piety was priggishness. His engineer's mind, trained in nuclear physics at the Naval Academy, could become ensnared by details. The loyalty shown by his young, southern staff could show itself as insolence. He and his boys flaunted their outsiderness, which could present as cluelessness. And the other side of audacity was blinding self-regard. This was a man who helped lead an anybody-but-McGovern movement in the summer of 1972, then proposed to be McGovern's running mate.

THE GOVERNOR AND HIS advisers framed his presidential campaign around themes, not issues. It fit the post-Watergate era, and bridged the Democratic Party's differences. "I will never lie to you," Carter promised. He would give the country "a government that is as honest and truthful and fair and idealistic and compassionate and filled with love as are the American people." Late in the primary season, when opponents and a scrap-hungry press criticized the governor for trying to be all things to all men, Kennedy agreed that, yes, the candidate could be imprecise on issues like health care. Carter's response was over the top. "I'm glad I don't have to depend on Kennedy . . . or people like that to put me in office," he told a reporter. "I don't have to kiss his ass."

Kennedy shrugged it off and distanced himself from the last-ditch anybody-but-Carter movement, publicly warning the leaders of his party that it would be undemocratic to deny the nomination to a candidate who compiled the most delegates. The Carter aides showed no gratitude, and ostentatiously shut Kennedy out of a meaningful role at the 1976 convention. "I never had a relationship with him, nor did he reach out," Kennedy would recall. "We weren't . . . included. . . . He was going to do it his way."

Once Kennedy withdrew from the 1976 race, there was no reason for Carter to view him as an adversary. And yet he did. These footling slights, reverberating in the press—as the participants knew they would—strained an already taut relationship. "I don't know the man," Kennedy told a Boston reporter when asked about Carter. "He's looking over his shoulder at me, although God knows why."

THE RANCOR PERSISTED. In December, before Carter had taken the oath of office, his pollster, Pat Caddell, sent him a long memo identifying potential centers of resistance to the incoming administration. First off, said Caddell, was Kennedy and the rest of "the liberal establishment," for whom "there is little risk in challenging an incumbent president coupled with overwhelming desire to do so. There are already rumblings from Senator Kennedy—privately—that he senses problems with Governor Carter and that Carter is unnecessarily antagonistic to him. He and others may develop a mindset that enables them to build up seemingly rational arguments for . . . instigating political opposition." With prescience, Caddell identified the party's midterm convention in Memphis, two years away, as a possible "scene of a major attack on the administration."

The debacle that followed was a turning point in American politics and government, the course of American liberalism, the pursuit of social justice, and the outcome of the Cold War. There were other avenues that these two proud men might have taken, roads that might have brought them somewhere but to the wretched confrontation that split their party, crippled the progressive cause for a generation, cost the Democrats their hold on Congress, and put Ronald Reagan in the Oval Office. Yet the personal prevailed. Neither man summoned greatness—of spirit, or of vision—where the other was concerned.

For his part, Kennedy had little reason to take Carter's success personally. Kennedy chose not to enter the 1976 contest for his own valid reasons. His wife and son were very sick, she with alcoholism and Ted Jr. with cancer. The Watergate-era press had resurrected Chappaquiddick, and the threat of assassination lingered. He was the elder now: "If something happened to me, what was going to happen to the family?"

He had no cause to resent Carter for seeking to fill the vacuum left by his departure—any more than he resented his friends Morris Udall, Frank Church, and Henry Jackson or his brother-in-law Sargent Shriver when they joined the 1976 race. Kennedy knew that leaving the White House to a fellow Democrat would postpone a restoration for years, and possibly turn the party in a different direction. Perhaps he felt cheated by Providence, which had visited his family with such sorrows, but that was not Carter's doing. There were ways to serve the Democratic president— as a counselor or legislative partner—that could keep the senator in a line of succession.

Kennedy chose instead the single most destructive path: to challenge a president of his own party, with all the predictable enmity and debility, and harm. Bob Byrd might have read him the words from the Book of Proverbs 16:18: "Pride goeth before destruction, and a haughty spirit before a fall."

And Carter? Well, he knew his Bible too. What possible aid to his agenda, political prospects, or legacy did he discern in stoking a feud and alienating Kennedy? He could have learned from the last southern president about the folly of that approach. John Kennedy had been cool and wise to select Lyndon Johnson—so unalike in style and upbringing and loathed by party liberals—as a running mate who could court Texas and the South and help him win in 1960. But Johnson let his insecurities, and a paralyzing hatred of Robert Kennedy, ruin his own time in office and bring on a destructive rift in the party. The Georgian might have taken instruction from the Texan's debilitating paranoia; instead, Carter aped it. And then, like Johnson, he doubled down by choosing a northern liberal—Walter Mondale—as his vice president and likely successor, leaving a Kennedy in the wilderness, wounded and angry, rummaging furiously for paths to power.

"This is . . . clearly civil war, Georgia . . . and Boston . . . a cultural void," said pollster Caddell, who worked for both men during his career.

"People from Massachusetts saw a guy from Georgia as the enemy, people in Georgia knew the people from Boston are automatically not our friends." Carter believed that Kennedy "was undermining him all the time. And Kennedy thought that Carter treated him like a pariah." In the years ahead, Carter would decry Kennedy's drinking and damn him as "a woman-killer." What the world came to witness was "the congenital disinclination of a south Georgia farm boy to kowtow to some Massachusetts pol who had inherited everything he had, from his political career to his bank account," said the president's spokesman, Jody Powell.

Carter would not hear, did not care to dicker and deal. Instead, the president perfected "the appearance of listening," Kennedy complained. If concession and compromise and frank talk were the signs of a healthy alliance, "ours was not healthy." It did not help that the abstemious president's social hours at the White House were liquor-free affairs, and built around a lecture by Carter that, however informative, seemed designed to impress guests with the president's broad range of knowledge. To Jimmy Carter, schmooze was a dirty word. To John Fitzgerald's grandson, it was life.

Caddell tried to mediate: "I spent four futile years of being run over by two . . . trains, determined to crash." It was more than civil war, he decided, it was "suicide." He wrote privately to Carter and to Kennedy, urging restraint. Even if he beat Carter, the pollster told the senator, the result would be malice, carnage, and ruin. Carter wasn't so sure. It might get his team in fighting shape for the general election. If you put a barracuda in a tank of fish, Clark Clifford told him, you may lose three or four of your fish, but the rest would be lean and agile.

IN THE BEGINNING, Kennedy was supportive of the new administration. Carter's problems in that first year lay with other congressional leaders—Speaker Tip O'Neill and Senate Majority Leader Byrd—and their colleagues on the Hill. The White House expected Democrats to fall into step. Carter and his aides didn't comprehend that the get-along, go-along Congress was a thing of the past. Absent the umbra of a popular president, the members of this House and Senate felt a keen need to star: to sponsor headline-grabbing bills, to appropriate funds for their districts or states, to pay back their supporters with jobs, and to show up in the media. In his lone term as Georgia's governor, Carter had bickered with the legislature. He had no knack at leading a broad coalition or setting its priorities. He saw things in black and white and expected others to follow suit. If the country needed action, then it was a president's task to analyze the issue and design a fix, and the duty of Congress to enact it. Much had been deferred in the Watergate presidencies, and much that had been deferred was politically unpalatable. But Carter never considered that "we just sent two really hot potatoes up there" and so maybe they should "send something that helps Democrats," Jordan would recall.

Flocks of arrears came due on Carter's watch. Inflation topped the list, fueled by the soaring cost of energy. In the go-go years of the 1960s and early 1970s the country's thirst for oil—to run cars, power factories, and heat or cool American homes—outgrew domestic production. Imports tripled. After Nixon rescued Israel in its 1973 war with Egypt, the Muslim regimes of the Persian Gulf retaliated. The Arab states slapped an embargo on the United States, and the OPEC cartel—the Organization of the Petroleum Exporting Countries—moved to double, then quadruple, the price of oil.

The oil embargo added to the "witches' brew" that Carter inherited from his predecessors, said his domestic affairs adviser, Stuart Eizenstat. In its last flush of post–World War II grandeur, the American economy had been jazzed by arms production and Johnson's desires to launch new social programs while deferring the costs of Vietnam. Nixon then fed the Great Inflation with expedient actions in the months leading up to the 1972 election. He levied wage and price controls, while bullying Fed chairman Arthur Burns to rev the economy. Carter thus inherited a bedeviling 1970s phenomenon called "stagflation." In classic Keynesian economics, inflation and unemployment countered each other, giving government options to slow or boost growth. With stagflation the two ills held sway together, like the wicked sisters of Oz. "The rules of economics are not working the way they used to," a chastened Burns told Congress.

The liberals of the Democratic Party viewed unemployment as the greater evil. But Carter was a puritan, and a businessman. Inflation ran against his grain. He clashed with his party over full employment legislation, pork barrel water projects, and the regulation of oil and gas. He had been told by Caddell that the New Deal coalition was fragmenting and that Democrats needed to hunt for votes in suburbia. There, homeowners were up in arms over rising costs and soaring taxes. In 1978, after California voters endorsed Proposition 13, capping property taxes and rocking the political world, Carter reacted by proposing cutbacks in the federal budget.

KENNEDY WAS NOT HOSTILE to Carter's foreign policy initiatives. They worked together on guaranteeing human rights in Latin America and eastern Europe, extending diplomatic relations to China, defending the rights of the Roman Catholic minority in Northern Ireland, opposing construction of the B-1 bomber, and negotiating a strategic arms agreement with the USSR. During a showdown in the Senate over the Panama Canal treaties that Carter negotiated—which, to the disgust of right-wing America, gave control of the waterway to the Panamanians—Kennedy and John Culver cornered Senator James Abourezk in a phone booth and threatened to burn it down if Abourezk didn't return to the floor and cast his vote.

Kennedy also aided Carter on domestic issues, like immigration. He shepherded the president's hospital cost containment bill through his committee. And to the dismay of his friends in the civil rights community, he backed Carter's appointment of Georgia lawyer and fixer Griffin Bell as attorney general. The nominee was a member of segregated clubs and had angered civil rights leaders as a federal judge when ruling on desegregation cases. "I am of the personal opinion that Bell is a true mediocrity, an old-line states righter, a politico, careful, and unfriendly to most of what we would like to see in the area of civil rights," aide Thomas Susman told Kennedy. "If he were a Republican appointee, I would push to generate outright opposition." But Bell was a Democrat. Kennedy told disappointed civil rights leaders like Aaron Henry, Clarence Mitchell, and Jesse Jackson that he needed to side with his president.

Carter and Kennedy bristled at Russell Long's kneading of the federal income tax, a system so larded with special breaks and loopholes that candidate Carter had drawn no admonishment for describing it as "a disgrace to the human race." Months before Proposition 13, through the spring and summer of 1976, Kennedy battled Long on tax reform. With Carey Parker, and the imported expertise of Boston College Law School professor Paul McDaniel, Kennedy scheduled private tutorials on arcane tax loopholes and subsidies—like the "Mexican vegetable rollover" or the "kumquat tax shelter"—on nights and weekends at his McLean home. Kennedy's team organized two dozen Senate liberals and their staffs, held weekly strategy meetings, and published a book. Kennedy testified before Long's committee, offered amendments, and worked the floor for hours, enduring the pain from his fissured back, to expose the tax code's defects and defacements. Though the Senate liberals lost more than they won (after an 89–1 whupping by the oil and gas industry, Kennedy asked McDaniel, "Why in the world did we offer that?"), he and his insurgents led a successful defense of the minimum income tax and the capital gains tax and left Long with a weaker hand when he went to meet the more liberal House members in conference. The final bill curbed special interest tax breaks and tax shelters for the wealthy by $1.6 billion, while giving all Americans a tax cut.

CARTER ALSO JOINED IN Kennedy's push for cheaper airfares, a crusade the senator had launched during the Ford administration. Conceived and directed by then Harvard Law School professor Stephen Breyer—and gussied up as "deregulation" for the press—it gave Kennedy a talking point when critics portrayed him as an unrepentant liberal. But it was real. Deregulation would transform the way Americans traveled. It marked, as well, the beginning of Kennedy's partnership with Breyer. Throughout his career, Kennedy played a leading role in the confirmation process of Supreme Court justices—in blocking some appointees, and in trying but failing to stop others. Breyer was the standout on the other side of the ledger: the jurist who would rise to the high court via Kennedy's patronage.

The partnership dated back to 1974, when Kennedy needed to replace Flug on the Ad Prac staff. Breyer had met Kennedy the previous fall, when he traveled to Washington to brief the senator at an issues lunch on energy. Breyer was the token free marketeer at the table, the one who believed that "regulation caused the [natural] gas shortage and that deregulation is the answer," Susman advised Kennedy. The thirty-six-year-old professor was Stanford, Oxford, Harvard Law, and a member of the *Harvard Law Review.* He had clerked for Supreme Court justice Arthur Goldberg and served in the Watergate special prosecutor's office, supplying expertise to Archibald Cox on the ITT scandal. He knew Carey Parker's brother from their time together at Oxford. In the somewhat random way that Kennedy recruited staff, Breyer touched more than the usual bases.

The professor's specialty was government regulation, and he studied how federal agencies could become captive of the industries they purportedly regulated. He and Kennedy agreed that the trucking industry, with its still-powerful Teamsters Union, was a target best saved for another day. But the airlines! As targets they offered glamour and sport and populist appeal. Faced by the decade's higher fuel and capital costs, the airlines had raised fares and sought to woo customers—especially businessmen on expense accounts—with advertising that stressed amenities like legroom, cuisine, décor, and lovely stewardesses wearing tight skirts or hot pants. The average Joe, hoping to take the kids to Disneyland, was denied the option of no-frills flights.

"You're having a hearing on *airlines?* I have never been able to fly," one antibusing protester in Boston told Kennedy. "Well, that's why I am having a hearing," Kennedy replied. After twelve years of haggling with the Civil Aeronautics Board (CAB) over gates at Logan Airport and routes for

Eastern or Northeast Airlines, Kennedy knew the bureaucracy. He was looking for a way to handle antitrust issues by promoting competition, Kennedy recalled. Breyer "caught my imagination." Parker offered the professor a job as special counsel. Breyer was interested. He believed that the airlines—and other transportation, communications, financial, and power concerns that relied on public resources—operated under regulatory provisions that sheltered companies from competition and its consumer-pleasing effects, like innovation, price cuts, and efficiency.

By choosing the airlines as a target, Kennedy was once more marching the Ad Prac banner onto another senator's turf. In this case there were two Senate chairmen to anger: Commerce Committee chairman Warren Magnuson (D-Boeing) of Washington, and Senator Howard Cannon from Nevada, who chaired the Commerce subcommittee on aviation and, as Democratic chairman of the Rules Committee, controlled the budget for the Senate's investigations. Kennedy needed to get their clearance for Breyer's crusade, and it did not come easy.

It wasn't just turf (though "proper jurisdiction," as the two senators put it, was certainly an issue): Pan American World Airways, the nation's largest international carrier, was facing bankruptcy. If Kennedy held hearings on federal regulation of the airlines, it could "cast doubt in the minds of the financial community" and be "read as a signal" that Washington was in "disarray and confusion," the senators warned Kennedy. It was not the most subtle threat: If he held his hearings and Pan Am collapsed, they would blame it on him.

Kennedy wrote back, agreeing to a short delay, but using his reply to list the failures of the CAB—insinuating that Magnuson and Cannon had not been the keenest watchdogs. Breyer, meanwhile, had been huddling with Ford administration officials. The accidental president was looking to build his own record for reelection. Regulatory reform—paring back government to unleash the market—seemed like a winner. A Republican president working hand in hand with a Democrat named Kennedy? Magnuson and Cannon had to calculate: Was the price of resistance worth it, or should they get on board? Cannon grumbled, but gave Ad Prac the money to proceed.

WHY DID KENNEDY CHASE deregulation? He still felt a need to be seen as a man of substance. Flug had done a fine job running Ad Prac as a "fire brigade for liberal causes." From Carswell to Watergate, he had kept Kennedy in the headlines. And on the legacy issues—health care, Indians, farmworkers, civil rights, and arms control—Kennedy had kept faith with his brothers. But Ad Prac's agenda lacked thematic consistency. Kennedy had been "rushing feverishly from one conflagration to another, leaving the rebuilding and analysis of source and solution to others," a reform group led by Ralph Nader noted. Repeatedly, in long conversations, Kennedy told Breyer that he would rather be "quietly effectual than publicly applauded." With deregulation, Kennedy could do meaningful work, instead of indulging in what Susman called "staff frolics."

"Breyer is right that no one else is really doing this; that few on the Hill even understand the process and the choices . . . that this is not a natural for publicity or visibility," Susman advised Kennedy. But "the lessons learned could be applied time and again to other areas . . . [and] we need a more unifying theme and long-range approach to maximize effectiveness."

Breyer analyzed the congressional hearing process. An effective hearing, he concluded, had gobs of fresh data to insert in the record, a captivating narrative, dramatic face-offs, and a tangible result to cap the day's events. Media coverage would then generate interest, persuading overextended lawmakers that the matter was worth the time it would take to master the issue. A hearing should unfold like a story, Breyer advised, and put a spotlight on a quick-witted chairman, who would nail opposing witnesses in privately rehearsed exchanges known in Ad Prac as "zingers." Kennedy would need to master the material, so that he could seize advantage of the moment and not, like many senators, come across as a ventriloquist's dummy, mouthing what aides whispered in his ear. Over time the preparations would become canon law for the senator's staff, right down to the number of water glasses and the placement of the cushion for Kennedy's back.

Kennedy, freed from the obligations of the 1976 presidential campaign, took on the challenge and put in the hours. One of the more accessible lines of reasoning he developed drew on the experience of two states—Texas, with the new Southwest Airlines, and California, with Pacific Southwest Airlines—that were big enough to have routes within their borders, and were thus unaffected by CAB regulation. These upstarts pared costs without sacrificing safety and lured more passengers with cut-rate fares. It cost $41.67 to fly from Washington to Boston, but only $18.75 to fly Pacific Southwest from Los Angeles to Sacramento. When a CAB member argued that the California airline operated with the same percentage of empty seats as the federally regulated airways, Kennedy zinged him.

"You left out a very important point, have you not?" Kennedy said. "How many seats are on the PSA planes?"

Pacific Southwest had installed more seats in its planes, making each flight more efficient and allowing the firm to cut fares. The percentage of filled seats might be the same, the senator knew, but not the number of passengers.

"Considering what you left out," said Kennedy, the witness was comparing "apples with oranges," wasn't he?

Zing.

THE AD PRAC HEARINGS drew blood fast, and often. The flamboyant Freddie Laker, president of Laker Airways, chronicled the struggle his no-frills airline faced when competing with the CAB-approved cartel. Fred Smith, the future CEO of FedEx, told how the board frustrated cargo carriers. The committee exposed a secret CAB moratorium on competition, and a Justice Department official told the panel that the board's actions were illegal price fixing, a cross for consumers, and inflationary. Southwest president Lamar Muse told how folks in Texas, who used to carry chicken coops on the roofs of their cars, didn't do that anymore: air travel was so cheap that they put them on airplanes. "No one says it's fun, flying in an airplane filled with chicken coops," Breyer would recall. "But nonetheless, if people want to pay the low prices for that kind of service, they should have the opportunity." At one point, Ad Prac staged what became known as "frozen dog day," revealing how abuses (like how pets, stuck in cargo holds, often arrived icy stiff) were ignored by CAB inspectors. The director of CAB enforcement committed suicide two days before he was scheduled to testify, after discovering how his board's investigation of Watergate-era campaign donations by the airlines had been whitewashed.

Ford's aides described the "catalytic role" the senator was playing on the Hill, and Kennedy was welcomed by the president at the White House. Ford promised to dilute the CAB's regulatory authority, stimulate competition, and open prime routes to new carriers. The CAB, the airlines, and manufacturers like Boeing and its unions gave way. Breyer returned to Cambridge to write a 328-page report. His place on Kennedy's staff was filled for a time by another future super-lawyer, David Boies. Ford, and then Carter, appointed CAB chairmen receptive to competition and discount fares. Cannon saw where things were going and joined with Carter and Kennedy to craft legislation. They followed it all up with a law deregulating trucking.

Eizenstat reported to his diary that he found Kennedy "dynamic, charismatic, very knowledgeable and hardworking," if sometimes given to fragmented thought and jargon, which could make him difficult to understand. The administration would need to subsidize rural air service, Kennedy warned, given how the Senate was preposterously tilted toward small states, with the five hundred thousand inhabitants of Wyoming and the six hundred thousand people in Vermont getting the same representation as California's millions. But the government was getting out of the airline business. The era of stews in hot pants, linen napkins, and spacious legroom was over.

Pan Am, Eastern, and other airlines staggered into bankruptcy, and passengers bitched as they were herded from overcrowded terminals into cramped, worn seats without treats and comforts. But more than 700 million Americans took advantage of cheaper airfares to travel by air in 2010, up from 107 million in the early 1970s. Before Carter signed the bill, only a fourth of the American public had taken a commercial airline flight, Eizenstat noted, but by 2014 that number had tripled. The average cost of air travel was halved. It was a revolution, the first dismantling of a major government regulatory scheme since the New Deal, ignited in Ad Prac by Kennedy and his zingers.

When Kennedy traveled to the White House on October 24, 1978, to attend Carter's signing of the Airline Deregulation Act—and the next day watched Carter affix a presidential signature to the FISA surveillance law that the senator had sponsored—this was evidence that the two men could cooperate.

THE TRIGGERING EVENT FOR the catastrophe that followed was Carter's retreat on health care. The labor leaders who scuttled Kennedy's deal with Nixon in 1974 had assured him that a post-Watergate Congress and a Democratic president would put this last, missing piece of a modern democracy—guaranteed federal health insurance for all—into place. In the course of the 1976 election, they had wrung that vow from Carter. As president, however, Carter ranked energy deregulation, work requirements for welfare recipients, and hospital cost containment over expanded health care. The country needed to eat its peas before it could have dessert. "There was a Jeremiah quality to Carter," Eizenstat admitted. Carter backpedaled, delayed, and diluted his proposal. "He had four years" to get something passed, said Kennedy, "and effectively had either misrepresented or misstated what his commitment on that would be." Carter "said he had to do energy," the senator recalled. "That took a long time, and it was not very well done."

Kennedy wanted a broad approach, aimed toward the working-class and middle-class constituencies of the Democratic Party—the thirty million low-income working men and women who were not adequately insured at work, or via government old-age or poverty programs, and the millions more unionized workers whose benefits were imperiled by low-wage foreign competition. A systemic solution was expensive to launch,

Kennedy acknowledged, but would save billions of dollars in the long run by giving the federal government the regulatory clout to limit soaring health care costs. Carter came to favor a cheaper, more targeted approach like that offered by Russell Long—expanding Medicaid for the poor and offering government insurance for catastrophic illness as a first phase of coverage for all.

Kennedy and Carter staked out their positions in the spring of 1977 and met several times to discuss the issue. Early in 1978 they were said to have agreed on "general principles." Kennedy went to work on the labor chieftains, urging them to accept a compromise. But at a meeting that summer Carter informed the senator it would be "many, many years" before the budget would allow him to act. Kennedy stalked away and called a press conference to blast the administration's "failure of leadership." Carter accused him of bad faith but did not mourn the demise of their alliance, or the knock it gave to health care reform. He confided to his diary, "In the long run . . . it helped because we've been dreading the liberal image of putting forward an expensive health care system, and Kennedy made us look responsible and conservative."

Their dance had kept Kennedy in the disagreeable role of supplicant, trying to keep pace, making concessions, tugging the unions to the table. He had tried to accommodate the president's concerns about the cost of the program by dropping the liberal preference for a single-payer system, such as Medicare, in favor of an employer mandate. "We had to work hard . . . to get labor . . . a great deal of time," he recalled. He agreed on the need to control costs. He ground his teeth and nodded when Carter proposed a phased rollout, over as long as a decade.

The final dose, which Kennedy could not digest, was Carter's refusal to commit to a timetable. The White House plan was contingent on improved economic conditions, and left passage of the full legislation to future Congresses. These were "self-destruct buttons," Kennedy complained. "Health care is a right," he said. "If this is conditioned on a set of circumstances, that really isn't a right at all." Nor, in Carter's plan, was there money in the budget. Without statutory deadlines or allocated funding, the president and his successors could kick the can down the road.

As a candidate, Carter had promised to defeat inflation, curb unemployment, and launch a new federal health care program—all while balancing the budget. Unless he was willing to raise taxes, something had to give. He chose to honor his promise to balance the budget. He sidled to the right, and let employment, health care, and social programs languish. Word leaked of his proposed cuts in social services.

BY THE TIME THE Democrats gathered in Memphis for their midterm convention in December 1978, the party's liberal base was seething. Carter's Friday night address, preaching austerity, landed with a thud. More than a few attendees, thumbing through the program, earmarked a Saturday afternoon "workshop" on health care, starring Kennedy, Eizenstat, and Health and Human Services secretary Joseph Califano. The moderator was a bright up-and-comer, Governor Bill Clinton of Arkansas. The convention organizers moved it to their biggest hall.

Califano led things off, minimizing the effects of the proposed budget cuts. Kennedy was up next. What followed, Califano would recall, was "grand political theater." It was "the most electric speech I had ever heard him give," he remembered. "Half-rim glasses perched on the end of his nose, fist pounding the podium, fingers alternately jabbing at the . . . charts he held and the audience he faced."

Kennedy was tired of being jerked around, tired of trying to find common ground with a White House that didn't want a deal, tired of watching Carter renege. He fired a warning shot: a ringing, full-throated defense of liberalism, to an adoring liberal crowd of more than a thousand people—many sporting newly minted blue-and-white Kennedy buttons. He was "a man transformed by passion, power and fluency," Eizenstat recalled, and the audience was "transfixed."

"We are not a party of reaction or retreat," Kennedy began, suggesting that this is where Carter was taking the Democrats. It might well be a time of caution and uncertainty, he said. But "sometimes a party must sail against the wind. We cannot afford to drift or lie at anchor. We cannot heed the call of those who say it is time to furl the sail."

Surely it was "wrong that prices are rising as rapidly as they are," he said, "but it is also wrong that millions of our fellow citizens are out of work . . . and it is wrong that millions who are sick cannot afford the care they need.

"I support the fight against inflation. But no fight against inflation can be effective or successful unless the fight is fair."

And with that, *boom*, came the shot across the bow: "The party that tore itself apart over Vietnam in the 1960s cannot afford to tear itself apart today over budget cuts in basic social programs."

No one in the hall missed the threat, and many welcomed it. If Carter continued on his abstemious path, then he, like Lyndon Johnson in 1968, could face a Kennedy in the primaries.

Kennedy was rolling. On he went, defending labor unions, the dispossessed, minorities, and the cities that were vying against corporate America, tax cheats, and the military-industrial complex. He itemized the costs, gaps, and basic unfairness of America's private health care system.

At the end, he made it personal. With the audience behind him and rising to its feet—even junior White House aides, hopping and bopping at the rear of the hall—he talked of his father's stroke, his son's cancer, his own near death in the 1964 airplane crash.

The Kennedys were rich, he said, and so their care was excellent. They did not have to mortgage their home, their hopes, their children's future to meet a medical emergency. The lofty top percent of Americans, "the tip," enjoyed a superlative level of care, he bellowed. The duty of Democrats, he said, was to represent the broad unseen base—those for whom he'd fight for decent health care, "as a matter of right, not of privilege."

KENNEDY'S PERFORMANCE, wrote Myra MacPherson in the *Washington Post*, was "a shouting, stomping, pounding battle cry" that electrified the otherwise "nigh catatonic" convention. "It was not to have been Kennedy's party, his year, his anything. But beefy, red-faced Kennedy, the only claim to charisma currently floating in the Democratic party, made it his."

Kennedy was surprised at the impact of that speech. "It caught a moment," he would say. Looking back, he called it a watershed in his career, the "defining moment" that established him as the leader of the liberal wing of the party. The following night, at the Kennedy Center in Washington, DC, the president and his wife shared a box with the senator at a fund-raising event for sister Eunice's Special Olympics: the premiere of the movie *Superman*. There were no reported unpleasantries: Carter had preached on "forgiveness" that morning at a local Baptist church. But the president saw the Memphis speech as more than a warning shot. It was a declaration of war—a "throwing down a gauntlet," he recalled.

Jody Powell had watched the performance from the back of the room, where he sat on a table nursing a beer and a cigar. The South has no monopoly on demagogues, he told the press.

In the White House councils, Eizenstat urged the president to yield. The struggle over health care reform was a symbolic exercise, he contended: everyone knew that Kennedy didn't have the votes. Neither Congress nor the electorate shared the senator's sense of urgency in this era of limits. And besides, Long's Finance Committee had jurisdiction. Why give a Kennedy a rationale to challenge the president in the Democratic primaries? Throw him a bone.

But Kennedy's rip-snorting speech had persuaded the president's most important strategist that the breach was irreparable. "There is no question in my mind that Senator Kennedy will challenge us for the nomination in 1980 if he believes that there is a very good chance that he can win," Hamilton Jordan told Carter a month after Memphis. It would not help to offer concessions—it would only make the president look weak. "The absolute worst thing that we can do is to behave in a way that suggests we fear a Kennedy candidacy," he told his boss.

Seeking to look strong, Carter looked petty. Despite Kennedy's years of interest, his 1977 goodwill tour of China, and the help he had given Carter on diplomatic recognition for Beijing, the White House ostentatiously left Kennedy off the list of invitees (which included even Richard Nixon) to a state dinner with Chinese leader Deng Xiaoping. When Archibald Cox was proposed by Carter's own advisers for an open seat on the federal appeals court in Boston—Cox was "a national treasure" and an American "folk hero," his staff advised the president—Carter scuttled the appointment. And in a sophomoric act that left many in Washington shaking their heads, the White House leaked word of the president's boast that if Kennedy challenged him in 1980, he would "whip his ass."

Richard Moe, the vice president's chief of staff, urged Carter and Mondale to reconsider before the hard feelings brought on a brawl that would only benefit Ronald Reagan. Kennedy had been amused by the "whip his ass" comment but disturbed by the glee with which the Georgians promoted it with the press, Moe told them in an August 1 memo. The senator's "instincts are for the party" but he was getting "enormous pressure" from his Senate colleagues to run. "He doesn't want to run but feels the White House is sniping at him and thinks, why go through four more years of this?"

The opportunity for reconciliation was slipping away, Moe said: Kennedy would likely make his decision on the Cape in August. "I think we are unnecessarily contentious with him, and appear outwardly to be uptight, petty and sometimes paranoid," Moe told Carter and Mondale. "Too often we let our emotions govern our reason when it comes to Kennedy; *It's in our own political interest to be friendly to him and keep him out of the race*; in our present position we can't afford [the] luxury" of spite. "It could well be the deciding factor which compels him to run," Moe warned, and "that would be tragic."

The repudiation of the sixty-seven-year-old Cox was especially irksome. It spurred Kennedy, red-faced and waving his arms, to personally berate Attorney General Bell. Carter was loyal to his Georgians—he was steadfast when his brother, Billy, or advisers like Hamilton Jordan and Bert Lance, were tainted by reports of scandalous behavior. Yet when allies like Ted Kennedy, Tip O'Neill, or Representative Dan Rostenkowski of Chicago asked for favors for their retinues, the Deacon (as the Secret Service called the president) responded with disdain. Carter didn't appreciate, he would later admit, that others also felt the pull of "ancient loyalties."

By humbling Cox, Carter appeared vindictive. When he informed Kennedy that he would not make the appointment, the president rubbed it in. "He said he knew [Cox] was close to our family" and showed a "sense of pleasure" in rejecting him, Kennedy recalled. The ostensible cause was Cox's age. The reason Carter gave to Kennedy in their one-on-one meeting was Cox's support for Udall in the 1976 presidential primaries. Kennedy left the White House furious at the humiliation, persuaded that Carter "was just doing it to jam me."

Carter declined to help Kennedy on a land preservation plan for the islands of Nantucket Sound. "Jimmy Carter just wouldn't do anything about it. He spent $62 million to preserve the Chattahoochee River [in Georgia] . . . but he just wouldn't do it," Kennedy recalled. Carter told him, "I'm . . . not going to do it, not going to appoint Archie Cox . . . and I'm not going to support national health insurance. I know that's the thing you care most about."

"Okay," Kennedy would recall. He chuckled at the memory of his internal response: "See you in Iowa."

CARTER AND JORDAN MAY have been spiteful, but they were not fantasists. By the time he got to Memphis, Kennedy had added Carl Wagner, a talented campaign organizer, to his Senate staff, and spoken to gatherings of the UAW, the NAACP, the National Organization for Women, the AFL-CIO, the Congressional Black Caucus, and the ACLU. In mid-February 1979, the senator welcomed advisers to a strategy session in McLean to discuss the ifs and whys of challenging the president in the 1980 primaries. They met again on Memorial Day in New York, and by then the idea had moved enough along so that Joan's alcoholism was a topic of discussion: Could she take the stress and pressures of a campaign?

Carter's woes were spiking. Inflation and interest rates were in double digits, and the price of gasoline—when you could find it, without waiting in lines—was at an all-time high. The Iranian people, stirred by Islamist revolutionaries, had overthrown their cancer-ridden shah, Mohammad Reza Pahlavi, who fled to Mexican exile and soon would request passage to New York for treatment. The strikes and protests cut Iranian oil production, contributing to a worldwide shortage. On one June weekend, more than half of the gas stations in America were closed. The president was "full of melancholy at America's psychic landscape and misgivings about his own hitherto small powers to alter it," *Newsweek* reported. Carter's standing in the polls collapsed, and Democratic leaders in New York, California, Minnesota, Ohio, New Jersey, and Oregon called on Kennedy to run or be drafted.

Caddell stepped in and made history. With a series of long memos, he persuaded Jimmy and Rosalynn Carter that the fault was not in OPEC or the stars, but in ourselves. America was suffering a midlife crisis, the pollster said, a collapse of confidence, an illness of the spirit—a national malaise. The president should talk in cosmic themes, after building suspense by retreating to the mountain at Camp David, there to sprawl in blue jeans on the floor and confer for eleven days with wise men and rabbis, pop culturists, financiers, and other Big Thinkers. The resultant speech was pretty good. Then Carter asked for wholesale resignations and replaced half his cabinet. Americans viewed the bedlam as a sign of idiocy. "It went from sugar to shit right there," said Mondale.

The Fates and Furies and the Seven Holy Angels had Ted Kennedy right where they wanted him.

Twenty-One

THE CAUSE OF
THE COMMON MAN

E dward M. Kennedy ran for president in the worst way. He entered thirty-four primaries and lost twenty-four. He contested twenty-five state caucuses and prevailed in five. Carter got 51 percent of all Democratic votes cast; Kennedy 38 percent.

It was not for lack of effort. Kennedy made more than two thousand appearances, traveled three hundred thousand miles, and touched down in thirty-nine states. It is true that he was met by calamity not of his making; it is also true that presidents—or presidential candidates running under the banner of supplying better "leadership"—are judged by how they respond to the unexpected.

Having made the decision to challenge Carter in the summer of 1979, Kennedy misspent the precious days of fall and was thrashed in the contests of winter. It took him six months—six months of mouthing centrist slush—to voice a defendable rationale for his candidacy.

Bewitched by promising public opinion polls and the pleadings of Democrats who feared, rightly, that Carter would lead them to ruin, Kennedy misjudged the impact that "Chappaquiddick"—an all-purpose word that had come to stand for recklessness, panic, infidelity, and duplicity—made on voters concerned about presidential temperament in an era of prospective Armageddon. Carter and Brezhnev had hugged and kissed, the Soviets and Chinese had feted Kennedy, but grave peril lingered. Tens of thousands of nuclear-armed missiles, stashed in silos or borne by submarines or aloft in planes, were aimed at foes around the globe. There were whiffs of smoke in Iran, Afghanistan, and Nicaragua.

"It's the enduring problem of character," said author Barbara Tuchman, one of John Kennedy's favorite historians, when asked about brother Ted. "Might a person who reacted so inadequately to a desperate personal situation react inadequately in other situations? To put into the Presidency a man whose moral fiber, whose decision-making apparatus, whose capacity for panic all bring up grave questions—is it something we really want to do?"

The White House knew that Carter would lose a referendum on his performance. The winning game was to cast the campaign as a choice between two men of different character—one of whom would occupy the Oval Office, and carry the nuclear war codes, for the next four years.

As they walked to the mansion from the White House tennis court on a sultry June afternoon in 1979, Jordan told a colleague, "Kennedy is going to run and we'll beat him bad."

"You know what the one issue will be?" said Jordan as he stepped into a White House elevator.

The colleague shrugged. "Kennedy!" said Jordan as the doors closed. "And we're going to be geniuses again."

It was only in the spring of 1980, as the country came to recognize the grit with which Edward Kennedy took defeat, that voters voiced appreciation for his advocation of social justice, liberal ideals, the dispossessed, and the working class. His was "the cause of the common man," he would tell an adoring audience at the Democratic National Convention in New York in August.

But by then he had lost the nomination. And helped elect Ronald Reagan as president of the United States.

THE CONVENTION SPEECH WAS a fine address—one of several that Kennedy gave in that election cycle. If little else succeeded in his campaign, the speechwriting clicked. Yet just as memorable was Kennedy's faltering reply, at the beginning of his odyssey, to the fattest of journalistic pitches: "Why do you want to be president?" It was tossed by newsman Roger Mudd in September, 1979. And Kennedy could not answer it. He rambled about the country's great resources, in a poor imitation of his brother John's 1960 exhortations to get America moving again. Because it came to typify Kennedy's woeful start, that CBS News special report, *Teddy*, played a larger than warranted role in the 1980 election.

It was "more than the disintegration of a personality, it was the destruction of a political myth . . . of Kennedy invincibility, of strength and competence, of eloquence and articulateness, of the keeper of the family flame restoring the lost days of glory," said one postmortem in the *Washington Post*.

The Mudd interviews—the first time Kennedy had cooperated for a feature-length broadcast on his life and career—called for a forceful performance that would demonstrate to a national audience that the candidate had the stuff to be president. For Kennedy, preparation was always a crux. He should have been well rehearsed, surrounded by staff, keen at the gate. Instead, he winged it. When Mudd showed up at Squaw Island in late September, asking basic questions like, "What is the present state of your marriage, Senator?" the senator should not have been surprised. Yet he was.

"Well I think that, uh, it's a, uh, we've had, uh, ah some, uh, difficult, uh, ah times, but I think we've, uh, have, uh, ah we've, I think ah been able to make some uh very good progress, and uh, uh it's, uh, I would say that it's, uh, it's, it's, uh—I'm delighted that we're able to, to uh, share the time and the relationship that we, uh, that we do share," Kennedy replied.

The *Teddy* documentary, after months of preparation, was broadcast at the start of the week in which Kennedy officially declared his candidacy. CBS chose *Appalachian Spring* as the musical score. Offsetting the interviews were clips of Ted Kennedy at work, of him teasing his mother, and shots from a summer camping trip—in a lumbering RV packed with next-generation Kennedys—through Massachusetts. One of the advertisements hailed the success of a new little fuel-efficient car called a Honda, imported from Japan. There was a probing quarter-hour segment on Chappaquiddick, with eerie nighttime video and the feel of a Hollywood horror film.

Kennedy would claim that Mudd sandbagged him—that the CBS team had described the proposed documentary as a gauzy trip to Camelot. "I have no staff, no nothing, because we're just going to talk about the sea," he would insist. But he had no excuse for a second abysmal performance two weeks later, when Mudd showed up in the Senate office and lobbed him the softball about the presidency.

Or for this reply, when Kennedy was asked just how his leadership on specific areas would be different from Carter's: "Well, it's ah, on, on what, on, you know you have to come to grips with ah the—the different issues that, we're—we're facing. I mean we can, we have to deal with each of the various ah questions that we're—we're talking about whether it's in the questions of the economy, whether it's in—in the areas of energy."

"I'll never understand that," said a colleague, Senator Warren Rudman of New Hampshire. "It's almost as if somebody injected him with a numb drug. . . . There was something holding him back . . . there was something psychologically going on. . . . It's as if he had one foot in and one foot out and it was holding him back."

THE CONCLUSION, reached by more than a few professional Kennedy watchers, was that the senator did not want to be president, but was going through the motions out of a sense of obligation to his parents and brothers and sisters.

"I mean, starting from law school, always getting himself prepared, prepared, prepared, prepared," said John Tunney. "And then he starts off on the biggest campaign of his life and he doesn't prepare himself. . . . It's almost as though he felt that he had to run but really didn't want to."

"There's always been a question with Ted Kennedy whether he really wanted to do what he was doing: Was he driven into it by the sense of his family and his two brothers' deaths and he was sort of going through the motions and figuring he had to do it?" said newsman Anthony Lewis, a family friend. "And maybe not even figuring, just . . . it's happening. It was something that was happening to him and it had to be."

The threat of assassination, terrifying to his children, surely added to Kennedy's ambivalence. On November 28, a woman waving a five-inch hunting knife charged into his office, shouting wildly, and was tackled by the Secret Service. One agent was wounded; Kennedy was not harmed. Several months earlier, another disturbed woman had tripped the burglar alarm at Kennedy's home. On yet another occasion, a crazed man assaulted the senator's receptionist. At the start of the campaign, Kennedy sat down and wrote letters to his children, to be opened if he was murdered.

The closer he got to succeeding in his presidential campaign, the more Ted Kennedy fumbled. The longer the odds—the more the White House retreated from his reach—the better he performed. And once he'd lost he was at his best. It was a pattern to stir speculation that Kennedy's intrinsic insecurities—or an impulse to escape the burdens he bore—were presenting as self-sabotage.

AND YET THAT WAS only part of Kennedy's story. He didn't need to fail to be free. He always had the option of walking away and spending his life sailing. His children, and the nieces and nephews he tried to mentor, may have been better for it. Nor, given the ups and downs of the thirty years that followed, did losing seem to liberate him.

Kennedy was more than John Fitzgerald's buoyant grandson, he was Joseph Kennedy's son—a political thoroughbred, with high regard for power. That was Joseph's portrait hanging in the foyer of Kennedy's home. Being "effective" or "having an impact" were the gracious ways he phrased it, but by 1979 he had been operating at the highest levels of American politics for sixteen years. His father had taught him: if there was cake on the table, take it. And the polls in that summer and fall of 1979 said there was cake. So, too, did the parade of Democratic officeholders who arrived at his office, waiting in line to beg him to run and save their careers from the ruins of Carter's presidency. And then there was Governor Jerry

Brown. If the weakened president was going to be challenged by California's young executive in the primaries anyway, then the onus of splitting the party would not fall on Kennedy. It was a salient argument for Kennedy, who had watched his brother Robert make the crippling mistake of letting Eugene McCarthy step ahead of him in 1968.

So, yes, Ted Kennedy wanted it. "You have to want it, so bad, and know you are the best because otherwise you could be deterred," said Joan. "You just have to have that vision straight ahead. Ted has that. Otherwise, how could you take it? Because it's a bitch, frankly."

Was the legacy a shackle for the youngest brother? Certainly. There were millions of Americans whose memory and measurement of John and Robert Kennedy were transformed by the circumstance of their lives and deaths. (They "freed a lot of people, but it seems the good, they die young," sang a pop balladeer.) With high hopes came duty. But Joe Dolan, an aide to Robert Kennedy, liked to say that the Republican Party would always find a place for a bright and handsome guy willing to defend the interests of the wealthy class. It took a different sort of character, whether rich man's heir or poor man's child, to devote their gifts to the cause of freedom riders and farmworkers, union laborers, and the starved and desperate children of a Sioux reservation or the Mississippi Delta.

Rich as they were, spoiled as brats, the sons of Joseph Kennedy picked up on the rancor he harbored as an Irish Catholic who had faced discrimination. It was reinforced by Rose and her father and the stories she told as she tucked them into bed about the bigotry their kind had faced in Boston. In the 1960 campaign, they witnessed it themselves, saw themselves as that band of brothers, warriors for the working day. It left them with empathy for the common man. "Call it mystique," said newsman Robert Healy, who knew them all well, "but don't underestimate commitment."

So this was a Kennedy legacy, too. For Ted, who revered his brothers and the time they had shared, political achievement was more than dutiful: it was not letting brothers down, it was honoring them, it was keeping them alive. Kennedy had not been invited to join Carter's mystical retreat at Camp David. He watched the president's speech alone. When he heard Carter speak of a crisis of spirit, a time of limits and a muted trumpet, it was "contrary and in conflict" to all he knew. "I'm tired of listening to a president and an administration that wrings its hands and says no one can do any better," he would tell his audiences in the months ahead. "That runs alien to everything that I believe, everything I grew up with."

"This . . . this *outsider* can't solve our problems," Kennedy raged privately. "He doesn't know how."

No two-mast schooner could bear Ted Kennedy away from the mix of loss and love that shaped this obligation to his brothers and their causes. His reaction to Carter's "malaise" speech was visceral. The great deeds of the New Deal, the New Frontier, and the Great Society needed a champion. "If the thing doesn't work out," Kennedy told Paul Kirk, "I think I'll just be able to live with myself better for having taken up the cause that's drifting away."

A TWENTY-YEAR-OLD FANTASY PREVAILED that fall, of a fine-tuned Kennedy machine ready to take down a president. In fact, there never was such a contraption, and the world of American politics had significantly changed since John Kennedy's primary victories persuaded the Democratic bosses to give him the nomination in 1960. Carter's team, having navigated that landscape in 1976, knew that the democratized party rules rewarded time, preparation, and depth. But Kennedy spent August charging his batteries, talking to advisers, and securing the support of his mother and his children. By the time Stephen Smith started building a campaign, Carter's men had been at work in Iowa, New Hampshire, Florida, and elsewhere for a year.

Smith was subsumed by the challenge of opening a headquarters, kick-starting the fund-raising, arranging travel, and recruiting a staff. Key positions went unfilled for months. There were no clear lines of authority, and little appreciation of how the Democratic Party's recent reforms—the abolishment of winner-take-all primaries, for example—gave Carter's hardened organization the advantage. By the time Kennedy declared his candidacy, the primary calendar had been jiggered by Carter's men to ensure that even if the president lost a state, he would split the delegates from that contest—and offset what was lost with lopsided victories in the South or other friendly turf that day.

Kennedy had never used the sort of detailed polling that Caddell performed for Carter, Robert Teeter did for Nixon and Ford, or Richard Wirthlin was conducting for Reagan. Nor, after watching Carter's reliance on Caddell, did Kennedy want to cede such influence. He began his campaign without in-depth data on his political liabilities and strengths. Aside from the horse-race polls in the media, Kennedy had no idea, as he opened his quest for the presidency, what the voters thought of him. This reluctance to relinquish control—Kennedy "ran his campaign out of his hip pocket," the ABC correspondent Catherine Mackin recalled—afflicted the campaign in general, which never had a strong hand to rival his on the tiller. "We didn't have a media guy," said Kirk. "We didn't have a media plan. We were raising money—it was coming in one door, going out the other."

"As soon as we opened our door it was nothing but ragtime," said Smith, who tried to play the role of campaign manager but was instantly overwhelmed. It took them three weeks to get the phones wired. "We were going off in 50 directions . . . all happening to us at once . . . all moving too quickly . . . just a lot of ragtime." It was, Gerard Doherty recalled, "like being in a washing machine with no water."

Kennedy's first draft of a rallying cry was a failure, too. His advisers reckoned that since the public polls showed him routing Carter, there was no need to rouse the party's liberal base. It was better to prepare for a general election campaign—a year away—by offering centrist bromides. "We are making a clean break with the New Deal and even the 1960s," Kennedy told a Wall Street audience. "There is now a clear consensus, which I share, that government intervention into the economy should only come as a last resort."

Robert Shrum was an early objector to the strategy. "We are running a general election campaign in primary season. We are failing to raise several issues that can stir intensity among Democratic primary voters and that in fact reflect your own longtime convictions," he wrote in one memo. "We seem afraid to offend the business community . . . we barely mention poor people."

As a matter of good manners and professional courtesy, Kennedy felt he could not declare his candidacy until after Carter gave the keynote address at the dedication ceremonies for the new John F. Kennedy Presidential Library on October 20. "That meant a lot to me," Kennedy remembered. "I wanted that done—and done right." The day arrived. The president more than held his own. "We have a keener appreciation of limits now," Carter said, entombing the New Frontier. "The world of 1980 is as different from the world of 1960 as the world of 1960 was from that of 1940."

Carter's false note came when he tried to plant a friendly kiss on Jacqueline Onassis, who recoiled. Kennedy's own speech was warm with nostalgia, with an ending he would rework in memorable moments to come. "We recall those years of grace, that time of hope," he said. "The spark still glows. The journey never ends. The dream shall never die." At the glittery dedication dinner, the band played "Camelot."

Kennedy chose November 7 to make his announcement. The Mudd show was broadcast on November 4. That same day, word came from Tehran: Islamic radicals had seized the American embassy. No one recognized it yet, but Ted Kennedy's campaign for the presidency was finished before it began.

Kennedy declared his candidacy in Boston, at Faneuil Hall. The speech he gave contained lines that would have been nice, had he been able to summon them, for the Mudd interviews. "Before the last election, we were told that Americans were honest, loving, good, decent, and compassionate," Kennedy said, reminding his audience of Carter's 1976 campaign. "Now the people are blamed for every national ill and scolded as greedy, wasteful, and mired in malaise."

"Did we change so much in these three years?" he asked. "Or is it because the present leadership does not understand that we are willing, even anxious, to be on the march again." He cribbed from Franklin Roosevelt, adding, "The only thing that paralyzes us today is the myth that we cannot move."

But Kennedy discovered, instantly, how the drama in Tehran had reset all calculations. The American public, done with post-Vietnam timidity, surprised everyone by taking inordinate interest in the fate of the sixty hostages. The broadcast networks rushed to gratify their audiences with film of crazed Iranian mobs, a solemn tolling of each passing day since the embassy was seized, and other jingoistic flourishes. Jordan saw the political potential of the crisis, and Carter, watching his approval ratings soar as Americans rallied around the flag, put a bellows to the flame. And the Iranians, noting how this impulsive act commanded Jimmy Carter's attention, went all in for the rest of his presidency.

"Just every single evening there was twelve, fifteen, eighteen minutes of national television focused on the hostages," Kennedy recalled. "It was the dominance of that issue in the news . . . not just any issue but an issue . . . that touched the hearts and souls of the American people, and also reached the matter of national honor."

FOR CAMELOT'S HEIR, there were no off-Broadway rehearsals, no previews in New Haven. It took two airplanes to carry all the journalists who accompanied him on his first campaign swing. In the small towns of Iowa or New Hampshire, the size of his entourage—aides, media, security— was itself off-putting. A hundred Iowans might gather in a church, to be pushed and shoved by twenty-five Secret Service agents trying to keep the last Kennedy brother from getting shot, and by thirty cameramen intent on filming it when he was. "The more I went to Ottumwa, the more I fell behind," the candidate lamented.

Kennedy was rusty—and catching flak for his inelegant syntax. "Teddy is very hard to deal with," a colleague, William Cohen of Maine, would say. He "is a very effective legislator. He has great staff work, does his homework, but he's not articulate and he can't complete thoughts. . . . You just get a sense in talking to him that there's no continuous thought process . . . he just seems to be incoherent." A raft of news stories cited the candidate's garbled concern for the "fam farmilies" of Iowa. Then, on December 2, he was asked to respond to Reagan's assertion that the shah of Iran was a noble ally whom Americans should proudly harbor. Nonsense, said Kennedy, the shah was a tyrant who tortured and robbed his own people.

Reagan's remarks were rash; they might well have provoked the Iranians and endangered the hostages—but Kennedy was the one who felt the heat. His appraisal of the tyrant's flaws did not fit the national mood, not when Americans were tying yellow ribbons around their trees. Within hours, Kennedy canvassers in New Hampshire were assaulted and spat upon. His remarks fit the definition of a political gaffe—the truth told at an inopportune time.

Americans were seeing Kennedy as an individual, with his own flaws, beliefs, and passions, and not a member of some holy trinity. "The expectations left by his brothers, that memory and history had enlarged . . . were real factors to contend with, and we fell far short," said Kirk.

"He seemed to be in a shell, a shield in front of his eyes," said Walter Isaacson, who covered the race for *Time* magazine. "He was just a shadow figure," gesturing and shouting, going through the motions with varying degrees of enthusiasm, said T. R. Reid, who followed Kennedy for the *Washington Post*. "You never got the sense that he was a person."

Kennedy was working on his flaws, trying to claw his way back, and rebounding a bit in Iowa when, over the Christmas holidays, the next brace of bad news arrived: the Soviet Union had sent tanks, fighter-bombers, and helicopter gunships to subdue the rebel Muslims in Afghanistan.

The "implications of the Soviet invasion of Afghanistan could pose the most serious threat to the peace since the Second World War," Carter declared—overlooking wars in Southeast Asia and Korea, the Cuban Missile Crisis, the construction of the Iron Curtain, and the divisions of Palestine, India, China, and Berlin. The president withdrew from a scheduled Iowa debate after unctuously declaring that despite "the adverse political consequences" to his campaign, the crises in the Middle East required his constant attention. He would stay in the White House and be a president.

Even his insiders called the ploy Nixonian. But thus did roses become Jimmy Carter's lotus blossoms. The flag, the flag. It was wonderful, comforting, warm. It imbued its wearer with the valor of warriors and the stature of heroes. Question the man who bears the flag, as Kennedy had questioned U.S. policy toward the shah, and you trod on patriot graves. Tap the feelings of fury and pride, as Carter chose to do in the winter of 1980, and even he could be Teddy Roosevelt, or Andy Jackson—at least for a time. There was no need to join Kennedy in the barnyards of Iowa, or to stand onstage and debate all those dreary insoluble problems— inflation, gas lines—that had driven the president's approval ratings down. Carter was winning by being no more than an American president in a time of crisis. For half a year, Carter clung to his Rose Garden strategy. "Fuck the fat rich kid," an adviser to the president told the *Washington Post*.

In one campaign ad in Iowa, Carter sat before a map of a blood-red USSR. "On Monday night, Iowa will send a clear signal to the world," the narrator said. "Do we or do we not support the president?" Carter's State of the Union address was short and bold, with a warning that he would consider any attempt to seize control of the Persian Gulf "as an assault on the vital interests of the United States of America . . . [to be] repelled by use of any means . . . including military force." He called for a boost in the defense budget, and resumption of the military draft.

The president was shameless, and lucky. After declaring that the United States would boycott the Summer Olympics in Moscow (thus crushing the dreams of America's warm-weather athletes), he soaked in the revelry and the cheers of *U-S-A!* when, just days before the New Hampshire primary, the American ice hockey team beat the favored Soviets in the Winter Olympics and went on to win the gold medal, a "miracle" that *Sports Illustrated* would anoint as the most memorable sports moment ever. On the eve of the voting in hockey-mad New Hampshire, Carter welcomed the Olympians to the White House, and all the nation cheered.

The American public did not discover until years later how Carter's vacillations helped bring on the Iranian crisis, and that he had known for months of the Soviet Union's designs in Afghanistan. Indeed, Carter signed a presidential finding providing covert aid to the Afghan mujahideen six months before the Soviet invasion, as his advisers nurtured hopes that the USSR would invade and get mired in a Vietnam-like quagmire.

And Kennedy? He had cut his payroll, dropped his fancy airplane, and was answering questions about the midnight tides and washboard roads of Chappaquiddick. When asked by Caddell's interrogators to envision Kennedy as a potential president, voters had replied approvingly. They saw him as an effective leader. (Carter told Caddell to take those results and burn them.) But those same voters, asked to compare the two men's character, found Carter the better person. Character was the killer. And Kennedy, without a campaign pollster, or a thematic plan for the campaign, or a strategy to fall back on if he lost in Iowa, was staggered by the focus of the press and public.

KENNEDY HAD MARKED THE tenth anniversary of Mary Jo Kopechne's death, in the summer of 1979, by granting a round of interviews to reporters. Though they were overshadowed by the news of Carter's Camp David séances, Kennedy's advisers hoped this show of openness would serve as an immunization.

The president and his wife, Rosalynn, had quickly tested the theory, suggesting to audiences that Kennedy would panic in a crisis. Carter then apologized ostentatiously, ensuring that the charge got further play. Powell slyly added to the flap: "We cannot be fairly precluded from talking about the positive aspects of this president just because someone may incorrectly interpret them as being a negative reference to someone else," he said.

"Husband, father, president—he's done these three jobs with distinction," one Carter television ad declared. A Carter canvasser in Iowa was more direct: "I tell them Ted Kennedy's led a cheater's life—cheats on his wife, cheats in college." Mondale had called his old friend Kennedy to warn him. "As civil as you and I think this is going to be, it won't. We don't intend to leave voluntarily," said the vice president.

Carter's opposition research team had been accumulating information on Chappaquiddick and Kennedy's womanizing for years after Jordan had identified this, in the post-Vietnam and Watergate eras, as the senator's Achilles' heel. "Perhaps the strongest feeling in this country today is the general distrust of government and politicians at all levels," Jordan had informed Carter in a November 1972 memo. "The unanswered questions of Chappaquiddick" run "contrary to this national desire for trust and morality in government."

Now the media joined in, obsessed. The *Washington Star* published a special section, and the *Washington Post* a three-day series. Even *Reader's Digest* weighed in on Chappaquiddick. The National Conservative Political Action Group bought full-page ads in the *Washington Post* and the *Boston Globe*, and the editors at the *Wall Street Journal* ran long attacks on Kennedy's account of the accident.

The media would not be satisfied unless Kennedy confirmed what so many reporters and editors believed, and almost all continued to insinuate: that he was drunk and out for sex that night. This, Kennedy would not do. Frustrated by his denials, with no witness but the senator to what really happened, the press seized on peripherals to suggest he was lying. There was no clock in the Valiant. The tides were not running as Kennedy described. Kopechne was not carrying her purse or room key. The phone company withheld records from the inquest.

"There is not going to be any new information that is going to challenge my testimony . . . absolutely none," Kennedy declared on *Meet the Press*. "If there was ever going to be any new information that was going to be different or challenge the sworn testimony that I gave, there would be absolutely no reason that I should consider . . . remaining in public life, let alone run for the presidency."

Feminists added their concerns. Joan Kennedy and Mary Jo Kopechne were not independent women and agents of their lives, some contended—they were the victims of a predatory playboy. Iris Mitgang, the chairwoman of the National Women's Political Caucus, acknowledged that Kennedy was good on women's issues but said that his history as a "known womanizer" certainly "raises questions" about character. And in a widely read essay in *Washington Monthly*, Suzannah Lessard contended that the issue of Kennedy's relationships with individual women was grist for feminists to weigh before they entered the voting booth.

"The type of womanizing that Kennedy is associated with is a series of short involvements . . . lunch and a dalliance, over and out, on with the pressing schedule," Lessard wrote, citing unnamed sources from "the world of politics and journalism." She continued, "What it suggests is a severe case of arrested development, a kind of narcissistic intemperance, a huge babyish ego that must constantly be fed. Certainly, it suggests an old-fashioned, male chauvinist, exploitative view of women as primarily objects of pleasure. It gives me the creeps."

There was some truth in Lessard's description: like the other men of the Silent Generation, Kennedy was an old-fashioned chauvinist. But the women who slept with him were portrayed by Lessard only as victims—dazzled by the Kennedy magic and left crushed and wounded when the prince rode back to the castle.

"There are two pathologies here," she wrote, sounding much like the Bible-Belt scold she professed not to be. "Success in this kind of activity must depend a lot of the time upon a sense of inadequacy in the women involved—a desire to upgrade themselves by association with a powerful male." It was as if the sexual liberations of the late 1950s and the 1960s and women's claim to agency and sexual freedom never happened.

KENNEDY'S PLAN FOR PARRYING such questions relied to a great extent on Joan. Before he announced his candidacy, he and his staff convened a conclave of psychiatrists, physicians, and relatives, who reviewed her medical history to decide if her mental frailties could withstand the pressures of a presidential campaign, or a term as First Lady. "I wasn't going to get into it unless it was something that people who reviewed all of the medical conditions were satisfied could work," he said. "Not just that it was dicey, but that they thought there was a much better chance than not that she would make it through and be satisfactory."

Joan looked forward to the challenge—this was something she was doing for herself, she would say—but she had few illusions at the start that the breach in their relationship would heal. As befitted a woman separated from her husband, she had entertained suitors. She and Ted shared the same bedroom on the campaign trail—but only to mislead the press. "Ted Kennedy is being nice but he doesn't even talk to me," Joan told a confidante. "He calls and says you've got to come or I'll lose the election, but when I get there he doesn't notice me or say I look nice or thank me or ask my opinion on anything." His advisers had to urge him to demonstrate affection in public. "The tension and the apathy were chilling," wrote Marcia Chellis, Joan's aide, in her journal of the campaign. "Mom and Dad weren't doing well," Kara would remember.

The notion of an alcoholic First Lady was not totally new: Betty Ford had confessed to an addiction to painkillers and alcohol in 1978. The campaign press corps found Joan likable, and frail. Her presence was a mixed bag. Said *Newsweek*'s John Walcott, "Every time you see Joan you see . . . Mary Jo Kopechne." The first response that Joan elicited from Kennedy's audiences was, "Isn't she nice?" said Walcott. The next was, "What a shit he is to treat . . . this nice vulnerable woman like that." Her Secret Service code name was "Spectator."

MILTON GWIRTZMAN AND OTHERS prepared briefing sheets for the couple, framing possible questions about her drinking, his womanizing, Chappaquiddick, and reports of family drug use.

Kennedy was advised to answer any question about recreational use of cannabis or cocaine with a curt "No." If pressed about adultery, he was to reply, "Those of us in public life necessarily come in contact with a variety of different women in many contexts, which often become the subject of gossip. It is hard to accept or justify this, but we have to learn to live with it, and my family has learned to live with this gossip because we are a close-knit family."

Kennedy's team had learned from the Mudd disaster; some of the rehearsal questions were tougher than the ones actual newsmen asked.

Query: "You panicked at Harvard, panicked when the police chased your speeding car [at the University of Virginia], panicked at Chappaquiddick. What assurance do the American people have that you would not panic in a crisis if you were President?"

Reply: "I lost two brothers under the most terrible and traumatic circumstances possible. I didn't panic. I managed to help their families go on. . . . Six years ago, the doctors told me my son had cancer, with little chance to survive. I had the inner strength to see him through. . . . Any one of these crises could have paralyzed many people, but I kept on. I concede that in the one instance of Chappaquiddick I responded irrationally; but I would place the whole record of my life against any candidate."

Query: Hadn't his womanizing fueled Joan's drinking?

Reply: "Alcoholism is an illness. . . . It's impossible to assign particular causes to that illness. . . . I don't know whether the course of our lives together—the illness of my son, the deaths of my brothers or the pressures of public life, my being away—may have contributed."

Aides Martin and Gwirtzman had met with Joan and her staff before Kennedy's formal announcement in November. A question written by the senator's staff was planted with a friendly journalist for the press conference that followed his speech at Faneuil Hall. All worked as planned. Kennedy called Joan to the microphone where, gallantly, she conveyed her determination to stand by his side. Her first individual press conference, a few weeks later, also went well.

KENNEDY'S CHILDREN, a bit reluctantly, joined the campaign. "He wanted us to love it," Ted Jr. remembered. "He always viewed politics as a . . . family enterprise."

The kids learned early. Once, when Patrick hurt his leg while skiing in western Massachusetts, his father told him to "Stay down. Stay down" until the ski patrol arrived to carry him off the mountain. "I couldn't figure out why he was so insistent," Patrick remembered, until they reached the lodge and found mobs of photographers. "It was on the front page of every paper in Massachusetts . . . the ski patrolman . . . carrying him with Dad," Ted Jr. recalled. "I had done my job," said Patrick.

Kara was now twenty, Ted Jr. nineteen, and Patrick twelve. They scattered about the primary states. Patrick would be in Iowa with their father, and "I'd go to New Hampshire," Ted Jr. recalled, and "Kara would go to California." She and Ted Jr. found it tiring, and lonely, to be handed from one campaign coordinator to the next, and to sleep in the spare bedrooms of supporters, instead of a more private hotel room. At times, they met ugliness and hostility as they worked the crowds. Patrick had a better experience—traveling with his dad, keeping a diary, playing crazy eights on the campaign trail—except for the day that their plane was diverted and forced to make an emergency landing in St. Louis when the youngster suffered an asthma attack.

"I was not crazy about him running for the presidency. . . . I didn't think he needed to be president," Ted Jr. recalled. But "I really didn't want to be the one who denied him . . . because there were very few people who ever get the chance to even run for president. . . . I didn't want him to go the rest of his life thinking he could have been president but he never gave it a shot."

"He thought he had to do it," said Kara. Patrick agreed. In 1980, their father went out and "exorcised that angst," said the younger son, that "very strong sense of his own obligation to carry out this historic legacy and mandate of his generation . . . that sense that he had to carry it, to keep it all together."

"He really was very insistent about using his political capital for good purposes, not just to go along and get along," said Patrick. "He imparted to us that you don't waste this thing called a legacy."

THE PRESS DID NOT exhaust itself until it had confronted Joan face-to-face about Chappaquiddick. The Iowa caucuses were a few days away when the initial question at an airport press conference in Sioux City was directed to her. What about the reports in the *Star* and *Reader's Digest*— did she really believe her husband's story? It was not a planted question. She had not rehearsed.

Joan paused, biting her lip. "Yes," she said finally. "I believe my husband's story, which he told me right after the incident . . . and so I don't believe that these stories in the last few days will come up with anything new." She continued, voice trembling, "We really should be discussing the important issues. It just seems a shame that, you know, it all has to come out again."

Joan walked back to Ted. "Good, that was good," he said, though he did not reach out or hug her.

"Mrs. Kennedy had defended her husband many times before," the *Washington Post* reporter T. R. Reid would recall. "But her faltering and obviously heartfelt response that day was so moving that nobody present could say a word . . . nobody asked another question. . . . Finally everybody just walked away. The press conference was over."

A network producer broke the spell.

"Great television," they said.

THE PRESIDENT'S AIDES KNEW that at some point the American people would recover their proper skepticism—see through Carter's imperial trappings—and remember their displeasure with his performance. But the weeks ticked by, with Carter victories on January 20 in Iowa (59 percent to 31 percent), February 26 in New Hampshire (47–37), and March 18 in Illinois (65–30). Inflation and interest rates hovered near 20 percent; economists warned of an approaching recession. Newsmen Walter Cronkite and Ted Koppel marked the calendar, tolling each day of American disgrace at the hands of the mullahs. But Carter kept winning.

After losing in Iowa, Kennedy gave thought to quitting. His campaign had "spent itself virtually out of existence in the first month of 1980 because of a series of poor management decisions," the *Washington Post* reported. Donations had dwindled—the campaign sold prints donated by Andy Warhol, Jamie Wyeth, and others to make ends meet. Kennedy had to forfeit his personalized jetliner, with a customized commander's chair, which he had once felt flush enough to leave sitting on the tarmac, at $5,000 a day, over the Christmas break. Now he spent two days in a rolling debate about his future. "This was a raw meat campaign . . . the senator was being almost, you know, destroyed personally in terms of how the nation looked at him," Kirk remembered. Smith warned him that the fall-out from the dismal start was affecting his standing in Massachusetts, where polls showed that he had fallen behind Carter. "If he beats you in Massachusetts," Smith said, "your career is gone. Finished. . . . You have no money and I don't know what's going to turn this thing around." At one point, eight advisers in the room voted, and found they were tied, four to four, on whether to continue.

"When I got in, didn't I say it was because the country was in a mess?" he asked the naysayers. "So why would I now say I was getting out?" He decided to recast his quest, in a speech at Georgetown University. "If I am going to stay in this race—and I am—I'm going to do it on my terms," he told his aides.

ON JANUARY 28, amid the carved wood and frescoes of Gaston Hall, Kennedy turned his furies on the president. He began by confronting Carter for the administration's failures in foreign policy. Eighty-six days, and Americans were still hostages in Iran. It was, he said, a "time to speak the truth." It was not rash or disloyal to differ with a president, it was a patriotic duty. Silence and acquiescence had led to Vietnam. The real danger was in Washington, he said, where an administration was exploiting a crisis to try to persuade the voters to "rally around its failures."

Kennedy pilloried Carter for failing to recognize the warnings—the tide of intelligence reports, the slaying of the U.S. ambassador to Afghanistan, and a previous takeover of the embassy in Iran—of danger in the region. When Carter did act, it was little and late. The president "drew a line in the dust that was already rising from the tread of Soviet tanks," said Kennedy. "It is less than a year since the Vienna summit, when President Carter kissed President Brezhnev on the cheek. We cannot afford a foreign policy based on the pangs of unrequited love." Kennedy moved on, to the fathomless state of American economic discontent, and his own raison d'être for running. In an attack that would be mirrored by the Reagan campaign that fall, Kennedy noted how Carter had concocted a "misery index" by adding the rates of unemployment and inflation to taunt President Ford in 1976. The misery index was 13 percent under Ford, said Kennedy, but soared under Carter's stewardship to 19 percent in 1980.

Carter offered oil companies and defense contractors "a bright future of expansion and profit," said Kennedy, at the expense of "the middle class, the blue-collar workers, minorities and every victim of discrimination by race or sex or age." These forgotten Americans were "out of work or about to lose their jobs, families who cannot buy a home, parents who cannot send sons and daughters to college, the sick who cannot pay their bills . . . and the elderly who must now choose between heat in their apartments and food on their tables.

"When the unity of our present fear fades, when the crowds stop cheering and the bands stop playing, someone has to speak for all the Americans who were ignored in the State of the Union Address," said Kennedy. "It is their union too, and the state of their lives deserves to be addressed.

"If my candidacy means anything it means a commitment to stand and speak for them. Today I reaffirm my candidacy for President of the United States. I intend to stay the course."

He had found a voice, he had found his cause, and from this point on in his long, august career, he had a star to steer by.

KENNEDY'S SPEECH TRIGGERED NO stampede of Democrats away from the president in New England or Illinois. But it marked, to borrow a Churchillian construct, the end of an awful beginning.

"What a pleasure it is to see an overconfident, top-heavy favorite get knocked on his ear," wrote columnist William Safire, the former Nixon aide. "What an even greater pleasure it is to see the chastened man shake his head clear, get up off the floor, and—by dint of the intellectual and emotional effort of a powerful speech—give his political campaign life and give his political life meaning."

By embracing "a cause other than himself," Kennedy gave his campaign coherence and motive, said Safire. "The trend in wolf-pack journalism is to savage Mr. Kennedy while treating Mr. Carter's Rose Garden campaign with awe and reverence," he wrote. "As one who has kicked Mr. Kennedy when he was up, I want to salute his first performance as an underdog. He showed class; perhaps even character."

Donors returned and morale improved. The candidate seemed happier. "When my grandchildren ask me 20 years from now why I ran for President in 1980, I'll be able to tell them," Kennedy told aides. Now he joined with ABC and CBS, publicly flagging each day that passed with the hostages imprisoned. He compared Carter's campaign to Nixon's refusal to engage in debate in 1972 and reminded the voters what happened then. "No president should be reelected because he happened to be standing there when his foreign policy collapsed around him," he said in a talk at Harvard.

Pietistic as ever, Carter returned fire in a nationally televised press conference at the White House: "The thrust of what Senator Kennedy has said throughout the last few weeks is very damaging to our country."

To which Kennedy responded, "We will all rally around the flag, but we need not, must not, rally around the failures."

ON MARCH 17, Kennedy and his wife marched through snow and rain and vituperation in the St. Patrick's Day parade in Chicago. The hatred ("Where's Mary Jo?"), obscenities, and firecrackers directed toward Ted and Joan buckled the knees of those who witnessed it. "A very tough, mean, nasty reception," Kennedy would recall. It had become a campaign "out of Kafka, by way of James Joyce," one writer noted. "It's as if he is doing some awful penance for his sins."

Yet the accounts of the day, widely circulated, added to a swelling sense of sympathy. Many in the press shared Safire's sentiments. Reporters watched, and empathized, as Secret Service agents held chairs against Kennedy's shattered back to keep him from buckling in pain. He was coming across as plucky, winning for losing.

"Week after week, loss after loss, he has bounced back with a smile, a bit of graceful depreciation and a vow to try harder," said the beat reporter from the *New York Times*. The candidate's suits shone at the elbows; he was flying tourist and sleeping in hotels that "have seen better days," but there was an "inner peace and self-confidence that he appears to have acquired in adversity."

Perhaps. If Kennedy had found inner peace, he remained distant, wary, and guarded. When discussing himself, he used the first-person plural "we" or the second-person "you" or the third-person "this campaign."

"It's always been a paradox," said Cohen. "He's kind of the guy who'll come into a room and slap you on the back and with a big booming voice and you have the impression of this Irish pol . . . [but] there's a wall there thicker than marble and you never get close to him."

"You were never allowed to feel that Kennedy was hurt," said his pollster Peter Hart. "Instead, it was a marvelous veneer." Such self-imposed isolation must have come at a high cost, said Hart, for "every loss is not a victory."

AFTER VICTORY IN ILLINOIS, Carter had an overwhelming lead in delegates. The jaded reporters in Jody Powell's briefing room staged "The White House Press Corps Gin Rummy Tournament." But outside Washington, Americans had begun to view Carter as manipulative and unsporting. He was too busy to debate Kennedy, but he could find half an hour, several times a day, to phone Iowa truck drivers or host newspaper reporters from Baltimore? The press had begun to call the Rose Garden strategy hypocritical and duplicitous. Caddell warned his colleagues: there would be hell to pay once Carter lost the flag. Voters would say, "I was tricked. I was fooled. I was had," said Caddell. "A level of personal hostility to the President began to enter our surveys that had never existed before."

One week out, and New York looked bad for Ted Kennedy. His speechwriter, Robert Shrum, drafted a concession speech, and aides booked a hall in the Parker House in Boston, where Kennedy could announce he was abandoning the race. "You don't let your mind go in those directions in the course of the campaign," said Kennedy, but after Illinois he was "peering down into the grave." It was good news for the Democrats. Carter, it appeared, would have all spring and summer to unite the party and prepare for the contest with Reagan.

It was not to be. New York was a home of modern liberalism, and the sleaze and swagger of the Big Apple was always a poor fit for Carter, the cloying Baptist farmer, who had finished fourth in the 1976 presidential primary there. ("It's a unique state, with a habit of sucking at the federal budget tit," the sore-losing president wrote in his diary.) New York's Democrats had a growing feeling that the primaries should not end in a quick coronation of a leader whose performance seemed at best quotidian. And the Carter administration had infuriated Jewish voters by supporting a United Nations resolution chastising Israel.

New York, California, and other cosmopolitan states, with sizable minority populations, knew the Kennedys and had come to terms with Ted Kennedy's character—at least more so than their counterparts in Cedar Rapids or Laconia. By taking his lumps in a manly way, for fighting on in a foredoomed cause, Kennedy was demonstrating strength and purpose, and the New York City scribes, itching for a scrap, hailed him for it. Kennedy was doing what the Carter team most feared, since Memphis and forever: assembling a coalition in the heart of the party of blue-collar families, Black and white; unions; Latinos; and liberals from the coasts.

Victories in New York (Shrum rewrote the speech, and the Parker House reservation was canceled) and Connecticut persuaded Kennedy to stay in the race. They were followed by triumphs in Pennsylvania, Arizona, Michigan, Vermont, New Jersey, the Dakotas, New Mexico, and California. Indeed, the latter stages of the Kennedy campaign suggest that liberalism was in better shape than historians, writing backward through the gauze of the Reagan years, generally attest.

Now it was Carter showing signs of panic. As the polls were about to open for the Wisconsin primary, he called reporters to the Oval Office at 7 a.m. to promote claims of a breakthrough that would free the hostages. There was no breakthrough, but "at least there was good news from

Wisconsin . . . we defeated Kennedy," Jordan would recall. Those sorts of victories are Pyrrhic. "We paid a price for that—a real price," said one of Carter's advisers. "Carter no longer seemed decent and honorable." At the end of April, despite a calamitous failed rescue mission—which the ayatollahs exploited, on television, by desecrating the remains of American soldiers—Carter pronounced that the Iranian crisis was "manageable" and that he would leave the White House to campaign.

The president's campaign went to work on a new round of ads, attacking Kennedy's character. It was a fateful decision, Caddell recalled—like calling in artillery fire on your own besieged position. It all but guaranteed that the Democrats would be riven for the rest of the election, he said, and deliver the White House to Reagan.

Carter never had to run an ad with gloomy music and a silhouette of the Dike Bridge. Instead, his media team filmed and culled "man in the street" comments from voters expressing doubts about Kennedy's character. Caddell wrote Kennedy a private note, explaining the tactic as best he could. But he also told the senator's angry aides to suck it up: they were playing for the presidency. The ads clicked on Main Street. The president's triumph in Ohio was what he needed to counterbalance Kennedy's late victories in California and New Jersey.

Kennedy remained in the race, praying that inflation and a midsummer lobbying scandal involving the president's brother, Billy, would accomplish what he had failed to do. The president, equally petulant, spurned Kennedy's request for a face-saving debate that might have set the stage for unity before the New York convention. "I never really resented Kennedy's challenge to us, for, at the time he decided to run, it seemed that he had good prospects for winning," Jordan wrote. "Later, as it became mathematically impossible for him to be nominated, I developed an enormous resentment of what his continuing in the race would do to our chances of beating Reagan." In his diary, Carter called Kennedy "a spoiled brat." The long competition and human nature had led to a predictable result: the political had become personal.

"You went out and ran against me," Carter told Kennedy when they met in early June. "You had a lot of hard words to say about me."

"Those ads of yours didn't handle me with kid gloves," Kennedy replied.

Senator Daniel Inouye of Hawaii, who won the Medal of Honor and lost an arm fighting the Nazis in World War II, walked in on a preconvention negotiating session between the Carter and Kennedy staffs. "There is a certain smell when men go into battle," he told them. "I smell it in this room today."

ON AUGUST 11, the first night of the Democratic convention, the Kennedy forces challenged a rule that bound pledged delegates to candidates. After a thrashing, Kennedy ended his campaign. He secured a prime-time speaking opportunity on Tuesday, the second night, with a promise that his troops would let Carter's coronation proceed smoothly. The president's captains saw Kennedy's speech as a necessary interruption in their scheduling, but they were not prepared for the power of the moment.

As augury it was limited by a failure of Kennedy's imagination: Who could grasp the coming years of greed, called liberty? Of hate, masked as family values? Of bigotry, cloaked in nostalgia? But the topic of his speech was economic justice—"the cause of the common man," as he said—and in that, at least, it was prophetic. As John Kennedy had spoken on freedom at the height of the Cold War, and Robert Kennedy had spoken about peace and civil rights in the 1960s, Ted Kennedy now spoke about shuttered factories, besieged unions, lost health care, and stagnant wages.

His odyssey had informed him. He had spent a night in the home of a laid-off autoworker in Anderson, Indiana—once home to ten General Motors plants and twenty-two thousand well-paid employees. Globalization and industrial ruin would cost the city all of those factories and jobs. He had listened to anguished workers in South Gate, California, where the GM plant that produced Buicks before World War II had been retooled to make the B-24 Liberators and other warplanes to win the conflict—but now was doomed by Japanese imports. If Kennedy foresaw how the Republicans would so deftly use race to divide the hard-pressed working class, he did not say so. But he had no doubts about where the

Democrats needed to stand when it came to choosing sides between Wall Street and the Heartland. Work was more than a paycheck, though paychecks were important: work gave Americans pride and confidence, lives of meaning, leisure time with family, and faith in the future.

"I have seen the closed factories and the stalled assembly lines," he said. "I have seen too many—far too many—idle men and women desperate to work.

"To all those who are idle in the cities and industries of America, let us provide new hope for the dignity of useful work," he said, echoing Franklin Roosevelt. "Democrats have always believed that a basic civil right of all Americans is their right to earn their own way. The party of the people must always be the party of full employment. To all those who doubt the future of our economy, let us provide new hope for the reindustrialization of America.

"Together a President and the people can make a difference," he said. Americans should "reject the counsel of retreat and the call of reaction." The Republican Party's proposed tax cuts for the rich would "redistribute income in the wrong direction," he warned. And only the Democratic Party's commitment to guaranteed health care could ensure that "the state of a family's health shall never depend on the size of a family's wealth."

IN THE THOUSANDS OF miles between Gaston Hall and Madison Square Garden, Ted Kennedy had found his mission. He had summoned his party; recalled it to first principles. Now it was time to say farewell.

"What golden friends I had," he said. "Someday, long after this convention, long after the signs come down and the crowds stop cheering, and the bands stop playing, may it be said of our campaign that we kept the faith.

"May it be said of our party in 1980 that we found our faith again.

"And may it be said of us, both in dark passages and in bright days, in the words of Tennyson that my brothers quoted and loved . . . :

"I am a part of all that I have met . . .
Tho' much is taken, much abides . . .
That which we are, we are—
One equal temper of heroic hearts . . . strong in will
To strive, to seek, to find, and not to yield."

These were lines from Tennyson's poem "Ulysses," the Kennedy family favorite, in which the hero of the *Odyssey*, restless in old age, sets sail from Ithaca on a last adventure.

"For me, a few hours ago, this campaign came to an end," Ted Kennedy said. "For all those whose cares have been our concern, the work goes on, the cause endures, the hope still lives, and the dream shall never die."

It was a splendid, resonant address, with a spectacular peroration: Ted Kennedy's stellar moment in that election year, taking a place with the Miracle on Ice and the yellow ribbons, the chanting mullahs, with *Nightline* and gas lines and malaise—supplanting the stammers of his first days on the trail. It legitimized his candidacy and gave it meaning. He had ripped his party apart; now history knew why.

It would be nice to leave him there, Joan at his side, basking in a forty-minute ovation and the adoration of the political press. It was not to be. He closed out the campaign with petulance.

CARTER WAS THE FOIL. When the president finished his acceptance speech on Thursday night, the plans called for Mondale, O'Neill, Kennedy, and other party leaders to join him on the podium. But Carter's choreographers did not account for New York traffic; the balloons did not drop from the rafters, and the demonstration began to sag long before Kennedy arrived at Madison Square Garden.

"We want Ted!" the delegates chanted. All eyes were on Kennedy when he finally took the stage, shook Carter's hand several times, but departed without joining the president in the traditional hands-gripped, arms-raised salute of vanquished and victor. Kennedy gave "a seigneurial wave of goodbye, as if he had appeared at the wedding of his chauffeur," wrote Theodore White, "and was gone."

Kennedy's performance was accurately interpreted by the press as a slight. And he would display that same tepid enthusiasm when campaigning for Carter in the fall, after Jordan, cocky to the last, told the press that "we could do it without him. . . . He doesn't matter so much." The Georgians gnawed on the episode for years; the First Lady was particularly incensed, and a fable grew in Carter's mind that Kennedy, drunk, had refused to shake his hand.

Twenty-Two

REAGAN

On a warm June morning in 1981, Ronald Reagan stood on the steps to the Rose Garden with his wife, Nancy, and Ethel Kennedy. Before and around them were Ted Kennedy and a hundred Kennedy courtiers and relatives. It was the thirteenth anniversary, almost to the hour, of Robert Kennedy's death, and they had gathered to see his widow accept a special gold medal, authorized by Congress in 1978 in his honor. The medal had been struck by the U.S. Mint and delivered to the White House, but the Carter administration never got around to scheduling a ceremony during the 1980 election. "Mrs. Kennedy," Reagan told Ethel, "this medal has been waiting patiently." Ted offered words of thanks, and as white-coated waiters served iced tea and cookies, the president mingled with the clan. Almost twenty years had passed since Caroline Kennedy had left the mansion, but she recognized and greeted several members of the staff.

"He roused the comfortable," Reagan said of Robert Kennedy. "He exposed the corrupt, remembered the forgotten, inspired his countrymen, and renewed and enriched the American conscience." It was an especially affecting moment for his audience, who knew Reagan was still healing from the gunshot, fired by a crazed young man, that had almost claimed his life that spring.

"Those of us who were with Robert Kennedy when he died in 1968 felt a special sense of relief . . . at your own recovery," Ted told the president.

He had been among the first to place a call to Reagan in the emergency room, moments after the attempted assassination. In time, Kennedy would learn that the gunman, John Hinckley Jr., had visited the senator's office, stalked him on the Capitol grounds, and prowled the corridors of the Senate Office Building before, impatiently, deciding to shoot Reagan instead.

The Rose Garden ceremony was a typically gracious performance by Reagan, a gift to the family of a man who, in life, was not his friend. More than a few of those mingling in the crowd were struck by the contrast between this president and his predecessor. Reagan and his staff were outsiders, like Jimmy Carter's Georgians, but they came to town to charm and rule.

Reagan had shared a table with Ted Kennedy at the Irish embassy on St. Patrick's Day, and he had invited him to the White House, to talk about gun control and the troubles in Northern Ireland. Later that year, he would host Rose Kennedy on her first visit to the mansion since her son John's death. At Ted Kennedy's request, Reagan authorized the burial of longtime family aide and friend Timothy "Ted" Reardon in Arlington National Cemetery.

Before his time in Washington was over, Reagan would welcome John and Caroline Kennedy to the Oval Office—and grant their wish that he join with their mother in a fund-raising dinner at Ted Kennedy's house to raise several million dollars for the John F. Kennedy Presidential Library. Because it had no living president to woo donors with such galas, the children needed a surrogate to build the library's endowment.

"I only wish Jack could have been there, too, last night," Ted wrote the president after the dinner. "Your presence itself was such a magnificent tribute to my brother. And your generous and beautiful remarks made his memory come alive again for all of us. The country is well served by your eloquent and graceful leadership. . . . My prayers and thanks for you as you lead us through these difficult times."

REAGAN WAS A STRANGER to Ted Kennedy, and to Speaker O'Neill, whom he likewise courted, after hours, in Washington. They bared teeth and fought like curs over issues—taxes, the Pentagon budget, the communist threat in Central America—yet both sides respected the other's beliefs, duties, and commitment. The three men, and the best of their talented staffs, were politicians as John Kennedy described the finest of the breed, committed to a full use of their powers, along lines of excellence, in a life of scope. "Whatever difference that you might have had with him," Ted Kennedy would say of Reagan, "you had the sense of a restoration of the institution and the role of the Presidency."

Reagan had carried forty-four states, including Massachusetts, and the Senate had fallen to the Republican assault. Some of Kennedy's best friends—John Culver, George McGovern, Birch Bayh, Frank Church—were among the nine Democratic incumbents swept from office. Yet the president and his aides, and those advising Kennedy and O'Neill, had no illusions that Americans had decided, after twenty years of voting to expand the modern welfare state, to suddenly tear it down. Turnout had been dismal, and while those who bothered to vote were scornful of Carter, leery of high taxes, and angered by events in Iran, that did not mean they wished to forfeit Social Security or abandon Medicare or forsake the minimum wage. Over half of the electorate had voted to keep the House in Democratic hands, and a shift of just fifty thousand votes, distributed among seven key Senate contests, would have left the Democrats with a 54–46 advantage.

Reagan and his men knew what they had won: an opportunity. They had watched Carter flounder and resolved not to make his mistakes. They drew up a concise agenda—to cut taxes and the budget, while shifting spending to defense—and relentlessly pursued it. Then they stood back and let Federal Reserve chairman Paul Volcker wring inflation from the economy, accurately anticipating a robust recovery ("It's morning in America," their ads would call it) by the reelection year of 1984. They laughed at Carter's sententious urge for balanced budgets and propelled the economy with deficit spending. They relentlessly wooed Democrats, especially southern and western Democrats, and those representing blue-collar districts in Congress. "We courted the Congress assiduously," then White House chief of staff James Baker recalled. "We stroked and we stroked, and we stroked and we stroked, and we stroked and we traded, and the president was very good at that, and willing to do it all day and night."

Kennedy recognized Reagan's skills and admired his daring, his inspirational references to American history, and the cadences in the president's rhetoric. There was no meekness or hand-wringing or talk about limits when Reagan spoke—his words had the carry of Franklin Roosevelt and John Kennedy. And all that work paid off. The charming, assertive president, his approval ratings ratcheted to heroic heights by his return from the attempted assassination, rallied Republicans, and just enough Democrats, to embrace the conviction, expressed in his inaugural address, that it was time for Americans to "dream heroic dreams" again. It was Reagan's program, not his performance, that stoked Ted Kennedy's resolve to fight him. "Government is not the solution to our problem; government is the problem," Reagan said. Income taxes were slashed, especially for wealthier Americans, and the budgets for working-class social programs like Pell college grants and food stamps axed.

KENNEDY SHOWED THE REAGANITES he was no ideological scold. He had been in the Senate for almost twenty years, now. He knew his way around the capital, recognized political realities, and was willing to work and deal.

Stuart Eizenstat was surprised when, during the presidential transition period after the November 1980 election, Kennedy had proposed that the White House appoint Stephen Breyer to an open seat on the federal court of appeals in Boston. Eizenstat saw two major barriers to the plan—his boss, Jimmy Carter, who was not in a mood to perform favors for Kennedy, and the Republican Party, which would want a conservative nominee on the bench. Why would the incoming Judiciary Committee chairman, Strom Thurmond, give Kennedy this plum?

"You take care of the president," Kennedy told Eizenstat. "I will take care of Strom."

So Eizenstat went to see Carter. "Forget who requested this," he told the president. Given the alternative of handing Reagan a judgeship, Carter went along.

And Thurmond? While Kennedy had been out campaigning in 1980, Breyer had led the staff of the Judiciary Committee, where he worked well and fairly with the Senate Republicans, laying out the day's schedule at breakfasts with Thurmond's staff, springing no surprises. They knew Breyer as a liberal voice on social issues, but his embrace of deregulation sent a signal to the business community, forever and always the preeminent Republican constituency, that he would rule like a moderate on matters of commerce. Thurmond was old school: willing to honor senatorial prerogative and give Kennedy say on the Boston-based appellate court. And besides, Thurmond's kids and Breyer's kids went ice skating together.

Thurmond cleared the nomination with Reagan, the word was passed, and Kennedy joined Republican senators Thurmond, Orrin Hatch of Utah, and Reagan's good friend Senator Paul Laxalt of Nevada to cut off a filibuster launched by Senator Robert Morgan, a Democrat from North Carolina. "He was upset," Kennedy would recall. "I was getting my judge and he wasn't getting his." Thus Kennedy—with the help of Ronald Reagan and Strom Thurmond—put Breyer in the seat that Carter had denied to Archibald Cox, and on a path to the Supreme Court. "This was a political world far from today's polarized and polluted arena," Eizenstat remembered.

KENNEDY WORKED WITH THE Republicans on another Judiciary Committee matter in Reagan's first year in office—an extension of the landmark Voting Rights Act. His deal-making partner this time was Senator Robert Dole of Kansas. The act had been extended twice since its passage in 1965. Under its protections, more than one and a half million southern Blacks had qualified to vote. In Mississippi, to cite a pronounced example, the percentage of the eligible Black community registered soared from 7 to 70 percent. The law put an onus on segments of the country—mainly but not exclusively in the South—with a history of voter suppression. It demanded that such jurisdictions obtain preapproval from the Department of Justice or the federal courts before changing the rules of the electoral process. White southerners bristled at the federal intrusion and argued that their region was unfairly singled out. This was getting to be like original sin, they griped. How long would it go on?

Extension of the act was universally perceived as the most important civil rights issue in the 97th Congress. Kennedy was a sponsor, with Republican senator Charles Mathias of Maryland. Chairman Thurmond led the opposition. The South had atoned enough, the old Dixiecrat argued. If the southerners could not delete the preclearance requirement, they wanted to extend it to the entire country—and so dilute enforcement. Kennedy predicted (and he was proven right after a Supreme Court dominated by Republican appointees struck down the preclearance requirement in 2013) that the Republican Party would exploit any dilution of the law to suppress minority voting. "Without . . . preclearance," he warned, "the advances of the past decade could be wiped out overnight with new schemes and devices."

Privately, Kennedy was stunned that the act's opponents would seek to abridge such a basic right. It was "absolutely sobering . . . an extraordinary wakeup . . . that on issues of civil rights you have to win them again and again and again and again, even on something that is as fundamental as voting rights," he would remember. His brothers were gone. The Fearless Foursome was no more. Phil Hart had died of cancer in 1976. Birch Bayh and Joe Tydings had lost bids for reelection. The duty was now Ted Kennedy's, to lead the defense, to nobly save, the cause of civil rights. His senior staff fretted, urged him to be cautious, but Kennedy chose the most aggressive tack.

The voting bill's supporters got a boost when witnesses before a House subcommittee described the "schemes and devices" still in use to discourage voting in the South. Registrars closed their offices; polling places were eliminated in minority neighborhoods; voter rolls got purged; district boundaries were warped by gerrymandering; and secret ballots were denied Black voters, who too often faced intimidation from the police when trying to vote in polling places situated in white business establishments. The House passed its version of the bill, 389–24.

Reagan, conflicted, endorsed the legislation. The South hollered.

Reagan backed off. He called for a federal study. "It came to me, with ex-cruciating clarity, that this was going to be a monumental kind of task," Kennedy recalled. To keep Thurmond from burying the legislation in the Judiciary Committee, Kennedy and Mathias employed the little-used rule to move the House bill directly to the Senate floor. With the help of the Leadership Conference on Civil Rights and Ralph Neas, its new director, Kennedy and Mathias enlisted sixty-one cosponsors—enough to break a filibuster—as a show of strength. To bring along the White House, the civil rights forces turned to Dole.

Dole was a skillful lawmaker whose thirty-six-year career in Congress roughly coincided with that of Kennedy. Few matched their gifts as legislators—their ability to read colleagues, skewer foes, see the lay of common ground, and cut the deal that made a law. They were dark comics, employing jest to mask the hurt that drove them to succeed. Both were lone wolves, with a gift of steering the herd. Outside the Senate, the two men did not have much else in common, except that each aspired, and would fail, to get elected president.

Dole's wit was the more caustic, and it got him into trouble more than once in his career. He had grown up handsome and athletic in Russell, Kansas, a classic American small town where, after he was horribly man-gled by Nazi shellfire during World War II, his neighbors kept filling a cigar box, there on the counter at Dawson's drugstore, with enough small change and bills to help pay for his three years of recovery. His wounds left his right arm virtually useless; he carried a pen in his clenched fist to keep folks from trying to execute that most elemental political rite, the handshake.

Never close, always wary, Dole and Kennedy would nonetheless join on several occasions to champion the cause of the hungry, dispossessed, or wounded, with results that defy superlatives. The Voting Rights Act was one such instance. In the spring of 1982, Dole endorsed a compromise that let Reagan save face. "Dole offered an amendment, came on and sort of sealed it," Kennedy recalled. The Senate approved the legislation, 85–8. Reagan, making the best of it, claimed the act as his accomplishment and signed the bill in a White House spectacle with civil rights icons like

Jesse Jackson, Coretta Scott King, Ralph Abernathy, Clarence Mitchell—and Ted Kennedy—in attendance. The bill maintained the preclearance section and extended the law for twenty-five years.

THE FUROR OVER THE Voting Rights Act gave Kennedy the opportunity to take the measure of another western Republican with Dickensian attributes: Orrin Hatch of Utah. Hatch had arrived in the Senate in 1977 and landed on the Labor and Judiciary panels beside Kennedy. "One of the three or four [colleagues] I find basically nothing good to say about," Hatch told his diary. "A total demagogue."

They had clashed on measures to give the District of Columbia full voting rights in Congress (Kennedy was for it; Hatch against), on labor law reform, and on Bayh's proposed constitutional amendment to abolish the Electoral College. "The Electoral College is a product of its time—America in 1787," Kennedy argued, but Hatch, a leader of the opposition, had prevailed.

Prim, square, upright, and impeccably dressed, Hatch sang in a barbershop quartet, wrote religious pop songs, and looked the part of a Mormon bishop; few guessed that he, like Dole, had a tender side. In his hardscrabble childhood, Hatch had suffered the bite of poverty and the loss of a brother to war. He had won notice as a conservative gadfly, but now, with his party's capture of the Senate, he was wielding gavels.

Their years of fruitful cooperation lay over the horizon when Kennedy and Hatch jousted over the Voting Rights Act. As chairman of the Senate Judiciary subcommittee that held hearings on the legislation, Hatch had emerged as a keen critic of one specific clause, added by House liberals. In a 1980 case, *Mobile v. Bolden*, the Supreme Court had ruled that the claimants in civil rights cases must prove they were victims of discriminatory *intent*, not merely a prejudicial *result*. Hatch and his allies argued that a standard based on results would give birth to quota systems. Kennedy, and his allies in the civil rights community, saw this as a dodge. A part of Dole's compromise, disavowing racial quotas, gave the combatants a face-saving solution to the standoff, but not before Chairman Hatch gave Sponsor Kennedy a grilling in a subcommittee hearing.

Framing his question as "hypothetical," Hatch described how things then stood in Boston's municipal government. Suppose a 22 percent minority population had 11 percent representation on a city council, he said: What did Kennedy think of that?

"Suppose . . . a purely hypothetical thing, of course," Hatch smirked, "but I would like to have your response."

"Supposing you write it out for me," Kennedy spat back, "and I will give you a written answer."

KENNEDY WON THE VOTING rights battle. Even Thurmond and Hatch voted for the Dole-Reagan compromise. But Kennedy and his Democrats did not fare as well in the other great fight they joined—against Reagan's proposed tax and budget cuts.

The House remained in Democratic hands, so the lion's share of the public's attention was devoted to Speaker O'Neill's leadership of the liberal resistance. But Kennedy was the other most recognizable Democrat in Washington, and the media focused on what he said and did. When aides gave him contradictory advice on whether he should vote for the Reagan tax plan, a politically appealing measure that would pass the Senate with overwhelming support, Kennedy told them, "You guys have your discussion, but I'm voting against it."

Through most of 1981, Kennedy and Hatch tussled for the support of two liberal Republicans from New England—Lowell Weicker of Connecticut and Robert Stafford of Vermont—who held the swing votes on the Labor Committee. In the long, seesaw battle, Reagan won much of what he requested. Scores of federal programs faced cutbacks, and others were repackaged as block grants, with lower funding levels, to state and local governments. Congress pared the federal budget by almost $40 billion, cut taxes over five years by $749 billion, and added $18 billion for defense, resulting in a $100 billion budget deficit.

Yet, in the end, Reagan's revolution was attitudinal. The sinews of the New Deal and the Great Society emerged intact. Those who suffered were the working poor—the folks who "catch the early bus" to low-wage jobs, as Jackson then described them. Tightened eligibility standards for food stamps, college grants, and other social programs left them with less help. It wasn't fair, the Democrats argued, and the "fairness" issue helped Kennedy's party recoup some of its 1980 losses in the 1982 midterm elections. Washington returned to form.

KENNEDY'S WILLINGNESS TO COMPROMISE with his conservative colleagues was not always without cost. In no case was this more evident than in the decade-long campaign he conducted to reshape the criminal justice system, which culminated in passage of the Sentencing Reform Act of 1984. In doing so, he contributed to a calamitous leap in incarceration, particularly for young men of color. It was another case, like the 1965 Immigration Act, where the finest motives led to unexpected consequences and unforeseen upheaval. "What began as a modest, technocratic reform proposal . . . resulted in the most radical, controversial and disliked sentencing system in American history," wrote scholar Michael Tonry, who watched the disaster unfold.

When Senator James Eastland retired in 1978, and Kennedy became chairman of the Judiciary Committee, reform of the clunky, outworn federal criminal code was a leading priority. It was an era when soaring crime rates, in part due to the movement of the Baby Boom generation through the crime-prone years of their teens and twenties, had put law-and-order on the national agenda. He hired a former prosecutor, Kenneth Feinberg, to be committee counsel. "Violent crime is spreading like a national plague," Kennedy wrote in a get-tough op-ed for the *New York Times*. Breaking with longstanding liberal sentiment, he declared it was a "fallacy . . . that crime cannot be controlled unless we . . . eliminate poverty and discrimination." He called for "certainty of punishment and imprisonment," and mandatory sentences "without the possibility of probation or parole" for a variety of violent offenses, including those involving firearms and narcotics, and crimes committed by repeat offenders.

This agenda met the recommendations of Kennedy's political advisers—that he distance himself from "pushy" minorities in a conservative era. When liberal critics from the American Civil Liberties Union and other such organizations objected, Kennedy stifled yawns. "The ACLU thinks that it defines liberalism in this country," he said. "*I* define liberalism in this country."

Kennedy found wide support for reform, in part because sentencing had emerged as a concern of both Left and Right. Each side was concerned that magistrates of the rival persuasion—bleeding-heart liberals or hanging-judge conservatives—were abusing their discretion. He was moved by the arguments of liberal judge Marvin Frankel, and other scholars, who contended that disparate sentencing, bail, and parole procedures led to unsurety, which discouraged both rehabilitation and deterrence. A group of them made the case effectively to Kennedy at an issues dinner at his home.

Kennedy came close, but could not steer a comprehensive bill to rewrite the criminal code through Congress. It would pass in the Senate but die in the House. But an important chunk of the legislation—sentencing reform—did become law as a stand-alone measure. The Sentencing Reform Act of 1984 abolished federal parole and created a federal commission charged with promulgating binding sentencing guidelines. Kennedy was the chief sponsor. By the time the law was enacted, the Right had returned to power. Reagan was in the White House; the Senate was controlled by the Republicans, and Thurmond chaired the Judiciary Committee. Kennedy needed to make concessions, and the legislation became more punitive. He and Thurmond pledged, once they reached a deal, to defend it from both Left and Right. With Joseph Biden and Laxalt, they became known as "the junta" that controlled the law's fate. The alliance was crucial to the bill's success. "Kennedy was overly eager to be regarded as an effective legislator," wrote federal district judge Lynn Adelman in an analysis of the act for the American Bar Association journal, *Litigation*. The senator "accepted numerous harmful amendments."

"The Sentencing Reform Act abolished parole, curtailed 'good time,' and discouraged alternatives to incarceration, with enormous consequences," wrote Naomi Murakawa in a study of the act's history and effects. The act achieved the goal of uniformity—but it was uniformity of a harsh and arbitrary kind. The new commissioners, appointed by the president, followed the conservative signposts in the act—and ignored those left in place by liberals like Kennedy. The commission built a forty-three-level grid of crimes and factors that became known, scornfully, as "the sentencing machine." Prosecutors acquired more leverage and "probation officers, who formerly were the social workers of the criminal justice system," were reduced to being "guardians of the guidelines," Adelman wrote. As the commission conducted its initial deliberations, Congress raced ahead and, with Kennedy's support, passed laws that created mandatory minimum sentences for drug-related offenses.

Kennedy quickly had misgivings. Within months he was issuing unheeded warnings about excessive sentencing, reliance on incarceration, and the costs of new prisons. But in a series of crime-fighting bills over the next decade, small-time drug dealers would be targeted like kingpins, and third-time offenders marked for life terms. The number of crimes with mandatory sentences soared, and offenses that qualified for capital punishment grew by the score. The U.S. government, by offering incentives to state and local authorities, spurred a wave of construction of jails and prisons. In the process America, "land of the free," began to jail its citizens at rates like those reached by authoritarian regimes in Russia or Iran. "America, with less than five percent of the world's population, accounts for around 25 percent of the world's prisoners," *The Economist* reported in 2015.

Kennedy and his colleagues had helped trigger "a serious overpunishment problem," Adelman concluded. "The country embarked on a shift of penal policies, tripling the percentage of convicted felons sentenced to prison and doubling the length of their sentences." A disproportionate number of those convicted were from minority neighborhoods, Adelman noted, where mass incarceration produced "deep social transformations" among poor, urban, and African American young men. By the year 2000, the rate of young Black males behind bars was ten times the rate of their white counterparts. By the time they reached middle age, one in four Black American men had spent time in prison. In some poor communities, incarceration was so prevalent that it became a common rite of passage, wrecking the paths to higher education, remunerative employment, home ownership, and a family life. More than a million Black children had a father in a jail or prison cell. To return to the levels of incarceration that existed in the early 1970s, noted author Ta-Nehisi Coates in 2015, the United States "would have to cut its prison and jail population by some 80 percent."

In time, Democrats like Bill Clinton and Biden, who played their own leading roles in the anticrime crusades, regretted their part in the debacle. They joined with Kennedy to try to eliminate some of the more egregious flaws—like the disparity between sentences for the possession of crack cocaine, sold in poorer neighborhoods, and powdered cocaine, used by wealthy drug users. "The harsh sentences for crack cocaine were intended to punish those at the highest level of the drug trade—the kingpins and the traffickers," Kennedy said, when testifying before a Senate subcommittee chaired by Biden in 2008. But "the overwhelming majority of those convicted were low-level offenders, and their harsh sentences had only a limited impact on the drug trade. The mass incarceration resulting from such sentences has done nothing to reduce drug use."

A National Research Council report in 2014 found blame enough to go around. Washington had been swept up in a national political hysteria, which Kennedy and his contemporaries had joined. "The unprecedented rise in incarceration rates can be attributed to an increasingly punitive political climate . . . in a period of rising crime and rapid social change," the report concluded. "This provided the context for a series of policy choices—across all branches and levels of government—that significantly increased sentence lengths, required prison time for minor offenses, and intensified punishment for drug crimes."

As he headed toward his second term, Reagan turned to international affairs. Kennedy followed, as both critic and facilitator. By virtue of his famous name, Kennedy played a unique role—one of a very few senators not serving on the Armed Services or Foreign Relations committees who had the know-how and experience to credibly participate in world affairs. By the time Reagan took office, Kennedy had helped craft America's response to refugee crises in India, the Middle East, and Southeast Asia. He had helped spur the opening to China and provoked U.S. interest in the persecution of Catholics in Northern Ireland. He had helped save a revolution in Portugal, spoken against repression in Chile, and won freedom for dissidents in the Soviet Union. In 1974, Kennedy had played a quietly important role in reassuring the Soviet leadership that American governance, and foreign policy, would be stable through the denouement of Watergate.

The roots of Kennedy's interest ran deep. His father was an ambassador, his brother a president, his mother a consummate globetrotter. Ted had lived in an ambassador's residence, attended school in England, sailed the Riviera, and spent a term studying international law in the Netherlands. He spoke passable French and knew the finest restaurants and nightclubs in Paris, Brussels, and Geneva.

In foreign affairs, as in domestic policy, Kennedy soldiered for "legacy" causes, as his staff called them. He maintained John's and Robert's interest in immigration, in the struggle for social justice in Latin America, and in opposing apartheid in South Africa, and pushed to expand John Kennedy's atmospheric test ban to include all testing—both above and below the ground. Kennedy told Soviet ambassador Anatoly Dobrynin that John Kennedy's talk of a "missile gap" during the 1960 campaign had been a "tragic mistake." The arms industry, said Ted, had exploited the claim and fueled an insane nuclear arms race.

In the sweeping and historic events that ended the Cold War, Kennedy would play noteworthy roles: prodding the president on arms control, opposing the administration's intervention in Nicaragua and other "Third World" disputes, defending human rights—and serving Reagan as a backchannel messenger to the Soviet leadership.

KENNEDY STARTED HIS DANCE with Reagan by promoting the nuclear freeze. He was facing reelection in 1982, and though the Republicans would ultimately field a weak foe, the senator was on the lookout for issues to galvanize the liberal base. Race, taxes, and abortion were still resonant themes for middle-class voters in the state; Reagan had carried Massachusetts in 1980 and the governor, Edward King, was a ham-fisted conservative who had deposed a liberal Democratic incumbent, Michael Dukakis. Kennedy's seatmate, Senator Paul Tsongas, was one of the party's "neoliberals," who prospered by tapping the concerns of more moderate, especially suburban, voters. During Kennedy's 1980 campaign against Carter, Tsongas had given the last rites to the New Deal in a speech before the liberal Americans for Democratic Action, in what was perceived as a slap at his seatmate.

So Kennedy needed to rally his faithful. When a group of professors and activists from Massachusetts began pushing a proposal that the United States and the Soviet Union take a first step toward reducing the risk of nuclear war by freezing the testing and development of new weapons, Kennedy enlisted as its champion. He gave the cause instant recognition.

The notion of halting the arms race in midstride, with some sort of unilateral or bilateral stroke of the pen, had been kicked around for years, and its proponents dismissed as naive. In December 1979, Randall Forsberg, a veteran peace activist, PhD candidate at MIT, and member of an informal collective known as the Boston Study Group, presented the argument in a fresh context in a speech to a conference of several hundred fellow peaceniks. The arms race had morphed into such a perilous phenomenon, fueled by its own lunatic theology, she said, that a freeze was a rational first step—and a concept the peace movement might sell to the middle class. The idea had appeal, and in 1980 Forsberg and her Brookline-based Institute for Defense and Disarmament Studies published a "Call to Halt the Nuclear Arms Race" that, in the lingo of a later age, went viral.

Kennedy remembered a young mother who came up to him on a snowy day in Leominster and demanded that he justify the arms race. He could not. On March 10, 1982, Kennedy joined Republican colleague Mark Hatfield of Oregon—who had been among the first U.S. military officers to tour the ruins of Hiroshima in 1945—to introduce the freeze resolution in the Senate. The two senators put their names on a mass-market paperback, *Freeze! How You Can Help Prevent Nuclear War*, drafted by Carey Parker and Robert Shrum.

The campaign had made progress in New England town meetings and local referenda, yet in the media there was "dead, dead silence," Forsberg recalled. Then Kennedy climbed aboard. "Suddenly there burst on the scene the fact that there was a movement out there," she said, and "it began to be reported in a big way." Kennedy staged an extravagant press event at American University—where his brother John had spoken on nuclear disarmament—and recruited experts like Frank Church, Averell Harriman, Henry Cabot Lodge, William Colby, Gerard Smith, and Paul Warnke to join him. The campaign spread like a California wildfire, fanned by cultural events like the publication of Jonathan Schell's stark little book on nuclear winter, *The Fate of the Earth*, and the televised nuclear doomsday film *The Day After*, which even Reagan watched. In June 1982, some 750,000 to a million people jammed Central Park and midtown Manhattan on behalf of the freeze: a bigger crowd than any other civil rights, peace, or Vietnam War protest.

"The tenet of the Reagan buildup was that you could have winners. . . . This whole debate and [freeze] discussion contributed in a very important way in saying that [in a nuclear war] there weren't going to be any winners," Kennedy recalled. "It really turns out to be how high the rubble is going to bounce. . . . Six hundred [warheads] on each side is enough to end humanity."

The "people power" on display in Central Park was matched in the cities of western Europe, where hundreds of thousands took to the streets to protest a NATO buildup of intermediate-range nuclear missiles, and the prospect of war on European soil. When the president took office there were fifty thousand nuclear warheads in the superpower arsenals, poised to incinerate hundreds of millions of people. In the best case, humanity would retreat to Stone Age hunter-gatherer status; in the worst case, the race faced extinction. But Reagan had looked out upon this arsenal and said "More." He was an anticommunist of long standing, convinced that the USSR was an "evil empire" dedicated to world domination.

Since the first days of the Cold War, American strategy had been built upon the thesis that the Soviet Union's economy was intrinsically flawed and, when competing with the capitalist West in the provision of weapons, food, and consumer goods, would eventually crumble in rot and contradiction. Reagan sought to accelerate the process. From his intelligence briefings, the president had discerned that the Soviet economy "was a basket case, partly because of massive spending on armaments." He pondered "how we as a nation could use these cracks in the Soviet system to accelerate the process of collapse." An expensive arms race might do the trick. The Pentagon budget became a gift list for the arms industry, with a bundle of fantastically expensive strategic weapons systems, including the B-1 bomber, the MX strategic missile, the neutron bomb, cruise missiles, midrange Pershing nuclear-tipped missiles, stealth technology, and the Trident submarine.

Reagan's shopping list bore a political price when zealots in his administration started talking in earnest about a limited world war, and the distribution of shovels, so that the average American family could cover a backyard foxhole with a roof of dirt and survive a nuclear exchange. As Reagan prepared to run for reelection in 1983, his pollsters warned him that the single greatest concern among the voters, dwarfing other issues, was the fear that he would bring on a nuclear holocaust. Always nimble, Reagan dealt with this liability—and his own revulsion for "mutual assured destruction," the guiding tenet of American deterrence—by promoting the Strategic Defense Initiative (SDI), a space-based antimissile system. "What if free people could live secure in the knowledge that their security did not rest upon the threat of instant U.S. retaliation to deter a Soviet attack—that we could intercept and destroy strategic ballistic missiles before they reached our soil?" he asked.

Kennedy and other critics ridiculed the proposal by nicknaming it "Star Wars." But Congress added Star Wars to the shopping cart.

"REAGAN REACTED IN TWO big ways to the freeze movement. The first was to pull out the SDI proposal out of nowhere [but] the second was to start negotiating with the Soviets," said Forsberg. "All of a sudden the rhetoric started changing."

The president was a man of parts. He shared his hatred of communism with a mystic belief that he had a heroic—perhaps even biblical—role to play in saving the world from nuclear Armageddon. "He had a sense of the world as it would be and as it might be, not merely of the way it was," his biographer Lou Cannon wrote. "Reagan wanted a world without nuclear weapons, and a world without walls and iron curtains." His administration was divided. There were anti-Soviet zealots, especially at the Pentagon, and more pragmatic types at the State Department and the White House (including Nancy Reagan) who tended to Reagan's political standing, his place in history, and his prospects for reelection. The popularity of the freeze movement, and the presence in the front ranks of Ted Kennedy, a prospective challenger in 1984, caught the eye of both groups. He would do the freeze one better, Reagan declared. They would not just lock the deadly arsenals in place but eliminate them entirely—or render them worthless with his Star Wars shield.

And when Mikhail Gorbachev, a reformer, became leader of the Soviet Union, Ronald Reagan had someone to talk to.

IN THE EVENTS THAT FOLLOWED—the Soviet Army's withdrawal from Afghanistan, the fall of the Berlin Wall, the liberation of eastern Europe, the dissolution of the USSR, and the unification of Germany—no piece was as important as Gorbachev. The new Soviet leader recognized that his nation's sclerotic economy could not sustain a competition with the West, or match Reagan's initiatives to expand and modernize the American military. Gorbachev gambled and pressed for reforms. But Reagan stood beside him. And so did the American public, who had manned the watchtowers against the authoritarian regimes in Beijing and Moscow for forty years, paying the price in blood and money until the bankrupt communist systems, as predicted, collapsed.

Kennedy, too, stood with the peacemakers. The senator was no longer just a sponsor of the freeze and a vocal foe on the Senate floor. As Reagan's priorities changed and the president reached out to Moscow during his second term, Kennedy served as an envoy.

As a potential president, Kennedy had been well received by the Soviets in his 1974 and 1978 trips to the USSR. He had met with Brezhnev on both occasions, traveled around the country, and focused attention on the plight of Soviet dissidents. Since the freeze called for both superpowers to halt the production and deployment of nuclear weapons, it was reasonable to appeal to Moscow, and in 1983 he had proposed to the Soviets that he and Mark Hatfield come for a visit.

Times and roles changed, however. Brezhnev had died in 1982, leaving power to the aged, ailing Yuri Andropov. And Kennedy was no longer a likely president, or candidate. He would become Reagan's ally and not, as many had anticipated, his opponent in the 1984 election.

KENNEDY'S DECISION NOT TO run for the presidency in 1984 was consequential. He was not yet forfeiting all his hopes of one day serving in the Oval Office, but he was bowing out at an auspicious moment, when Carter and Mondale were besmeared by their landslide loss to Reagan and Kennedy, having captured the hearts of so many liberal Democrats in 1980, seemed a favorite for the nomination.

"He was the only party leader of national prominence who evoked any obviously emotional support from traditional Democratic constituencies," wrote Jules Witcover and Jack Germond. "He had moved beyond his position as the heir to his brothers' politics to a recognition in his own right as the leading exponent of liberal causes in American politics. And he was clearly the dominant personality in the party." The country was battered by recession, and unemployment had reached a forty-year high. The Democrats had picked up twenty-six House seats in the midterm elections. "The prospects of a Democratic comeback in the presidential election of 1984 appeared to be infinitely brighter."

Tempering these auspicious vibes was a reality that faced any presidential contender in the late twentieth century: a campaign for the White House was an unceasing, soul-sucking ordeal for a candidate and their

family. "Public people almost eagerly dehumanize themselves. They allow
the markings of region, family, class, individual character and, generally,
personhood that they once possessed to be leached away," the journalist
Meg Greenfield would write in her 2001 book *Washington*. "They construct a new public self that often does terrible damage to what remains
of the genuine person."

Kennedy had been campaigning almost nonstop for nearly four years
when, in December 1982, he called the press together to announce he
would not challenge Reagan. It was too much. Kennedy's three children
were against it: he had sounded them out privately while sailing that fall.
"I could tell by their faces . . . that each was deeply troubled by the prospect, more troubled than I had realized," he would remember. He invited
them to join him and other family members at a summit of sorts with
political advisers on the Friday after Thanksgiving. Brother-in-law Stephen Smith was there, and sisters Jean and Pat, niece Kathleen Kennedy
Townsend, and nephews Joseph P. Kennedy II and Stephen Smith Jr.

The younger generation was properly skeptical—they remembered
how the pollsters had rated Kennedy so highly in the summer of 1979,
when beating Carter was purportedly a slam dunk. His children also recalled the ordeal—how all-consuming that race had been; how hateful the
jeers, how prying the press and public. They had not wanted to deny their
father, not wished to be the ones to leave him saying, "What if?" But they
had given him that shot in 1980, and so this was different. Their lives, and
their mother's life, did not need more angst and strain.

"They made it very clear that they'd much prefer that I not run," Kennedy recalled. The family had gathered in the living room of John Kennedy's house in the compound at Hyannis Port. "I'm not concerned about
the poll data," one of Robert Kennedy's children had said. "I'm concerned
about what it is going to do to *us*." After hearing them out one last time,
Kennedy walked out on the porch with his aide Lawrence Horowitz and
said, "That's it."

Kennedy made the call to dismantle his campaign after hiring staff,
authorizing months of planning, and conducting an expensive reelection
advertising blitz that had the benefit of changing how presidential

primary voters in southern New Hampshire—who lived within the Boston media market—viewed his character. But his heart was not in it, and his family was against it. "We had a good organization, message. And I was a stronger and better candidate, and there was a lot going for us at that time. But the power of the children was overwhelming," Kennedy would recall. He left the chase to Mondale and played a role as party elder, bringing the nominee together with his vanquished opponent, Gary Hart, at the end of the primary season.

It was more than just the children. "He decided that he could, if he continued to work at it, be a great senator, and I think that emotionally he just didn't want to go through with another presidential race," said Tunney. Kennedy's work in the Senate, "psychologically, was very comforting to him because he had achieved excellence" in that setting.

IF HIS NEW STATUS made Kennedy's motives for a trip to Moscow purer, it was equally true that his declining stature made the prospect of a meeting on the freeze less attractive to the Kremlin. "The question of receiving Kennedy raises doubts in my mind," Andropov wrote to his foreign and defense ministers. "If the time comes to talk to Democrats, then it would be better to meet some of the presidential candidates, the more so since Kennedy has recently reduced his political profile." But Kennedy took the cold shoulder in stride and persisted, employing an emissary—Horowitz, his administrative assistant—to visit and speak with the Soviets.

Reagan, meanwhile, was having his own problems communicating with Andropov. Some early harsh exchanges led Jack Matlock, the Soviet affairs expert for the National Security Council, to search for other avenues. "It was obvious that the United States needed more channels of communication if it was to inject any positive element into the U.S.-Soviet relationship," he recalled. Matlock and his boss, Admiral John Poindexter, were intrigued when Horowitz returned from a trip to Moscow in January 1984 with a message for Reagan. Kennedy's aide had met with Vadim Zagladin, a deputy minister. The differences between the two countries were real, Zagladin had told him, but there were opportunities to be had—like a ban on the use of chemical weapons, to start—if the great powers would give each other "elbow room."

Mondale, Jackson, and Hart were then battling for the Democratic presidential nomination, and so Kennedy was viewed by the Reagan White House as a political noncombatant. "Kennedy considered these matters above politics," Matlock recalled. In the months ahead, Horowitz "continued to keep us informed of contacts with Soviet officials." These "were always handled responsibly by Senator Kennedy," Matlock said. "At a time when other Democrats were telling Ambassador Dobrynin that Reagan was dangerous, Senator Kennedy's quiet coordination with the White House helped convince the Soviets . . . that Reagan was serious about negotiation."

Then Andropov died. Matlock attended the funeral and, with the blessings of Reagan and Secretary of State George Shultz, followed up with Zagladin. He informed the Soviets that the United States was not seeking to exploit a cornered USSR and hoped to proceed with the chemical weapons ban and discussions about nuclear weapons. "We considered this a signal breakthrough in establishing direct communication with the Soviet leaders," Matlock recalled. Before Reagan could meet with him, Andropov's successor, Konstantin Chernenko, died as well. It was then, in the spring of 1985, that Gorbachev took power.

Reagan and Gorbachev met in Geneva in November, where it was clear that the Soviets, in economic straits, were willing to make massive reductions in the number of strategic weapons. Reagan refused to trade away Star Wars, but otherwise impressed the Soviet leader. Though no final deal was struck, the two left Switzerland with a goal of cutting their nuclear arsenals in half. Two months later, Gorbachev proposed that they eliminate all nuclear weapons. Reagan's reluctance to abandon his space-based shield doomed that proposal, but the deteriorating Soviet economy compelled Gorbachev to make unilateral concessions. The arms race, if not over, was on a course to ending.

In Gorbachev's first years in office, both Soviet and White House officials used the Kennedy back channel, and it played a noteworthy role in keeping them apprised of the other's positions and attitudes. Gorbachev

employed Kennedy and Horowitz to send word of his plans to withdraw
Soviet troops from Afghanistan, to signal changes in his negotiating
stance on regional and strategic nuclear arms, and, on at least one occasion, to offer Reagan an important concession on the Strategic Defense
Initiative. Kennedy played signal roles in the release of dissident Natan
Sharansky and, when the Soviets were considering a military crackdown
on the unruly Baltic states, in warning Gorbachev that it would be a catastrophic mistake. "We were of some value," Kennedy would say.

KENNEDY WAS LESS COOPERATIVE, and outright confrontational, when
it came to human rights—clashing with Reagan and other conservatives
over revolutionary movements in Latin America, and the future of apartheid in South Africa.

The struggle for social justice in Latin America was a popular cause
for Democrats from New England. Speaker O'Neill and Massachusetts
representatives Edward Boland and J. Joseph Moakley were leaders of the
resistance to Reagan's policies in El Salvador and Nicaragua in the House,
and Kennedy's friend Senator Christopher Dodd of Connecticut led efforts in the Senate. Senator John Kerry, who replaced Tsongas as Kennedy's seatmate in 1984, made a quick name for himself investigating CIA
ties to the right-wing Contra resistance to Nicaragua's leftist Sandinista
regime. Kennedy was another stalwart in Congress, where the struggle
with the Reagan administration over U.S. policy seesawed back and forth.
Kennedy took several noted individual initiatives: saving the Miskito Indians from the violence in Nicaragua, working to prohibit the CIA mining
of Nicaraguan harbors, and standing against the right-wing dictator Augusto Pinochet in Chile.

In January 1986, Kennedy arrived in Chile as part of a tour of South
America, despite warnings from CIA officials that the Pinochet government was organizing a hostile reception. He was met at the airport at
Santiago by demonstrators who blocked the highway to the city. They
threw stones, chanted, and carried signs that said "Death to Kennedy" or
featured photographs of Mary Jo Kopechne. He was not an enemy of

Chile, Kennedy said in his remarks, he was an enemy of "torture, kidnapping, murder [and] arbitrary arrest." The U.S. ambassador raised a ruckus, and the government provided helicopters to fly the senator and his entourage to the city, where he dodged more protests and gave rallying speeches to the Chilean resistance.

Two years later, in a national plebiscite, the Chilean people ended Pinochet's harsh rule. Kennedy returned, to attend the restoration of democracy. He long recalled a scene from this trip, which was staged in the soccer stadium where Pinochet's henchmen had once slaughtered their foes. The field now was filled by the families of those who had been tortured and executed. "All of the families that have lost people, they came in. Husbands who had lost wives came in, the wives who lost husbands came in—and they danced by themselves," Kennedy recalled. "And you look out there and you see all of these people doing this folk dance, all by themselves, representing the people that they have lost. It was just absolutely, absolutely moving."

As in Chile, Kennedy placed himself in personal and political danger when intervening in the affairs of South Africa. He is remembered for a tense and violence-filled trip that contributed, in time, toward an epochal victory for human rights, and the fall of the apartheid state.

Kennedy's involvement in South Africa went back to the 1960s but was notably revived in the fall of 1984 when he hosted the Black clerics Desmond Tutu and Allan Boesak at a lunch in Washington. Tutu asked Kennedy to lend his famous name to the war against apartheid and to visit South Africa.

Robert Kennedy had given one of his finest speeches on a 1966 visit to the country, but he had gone there to inspire student rebels—there had been no hope his visit could bring about an end to apartheid. Two decades later, the anti-apartheid movement had amassed considerable power, and Ted Kennedy knew he would be measured on how, with this trip and subsequent actions, he helped topple the evil practice. Despite the daunting expectations, he signed on to the cause. "I urge you to change course," he wrote Reagan in 1984. "To remain silent about recent events in South Africa would confirm the suspicion that the United States of America only cares about the human rights of white people, that when black people arc killed, beaten and arbitrarily imprisoned, the United States can be expected to remain silent."

Before landing in South Africa, Kennedy took Kara and Ted Jr. on a Christmas journey to Ethiopia and Sudan, where famine was killing thousands. The scenes of dying parents and starving infants unnerved Eileen McNamara, a superb, tough columnist for the *Boston Globe*. Kennedy pulled her aside in the desert night. It was not about him, not about her, he said. They were instruments—celebrated and privileged—whose presence might compel the world to address the misery they witnessed. To do that, he told her, they would be strong.

Kennedy and an entourage—he brought friends, aides, press, and family—landed in Johannesburg in January, and plunged into controversy. They were met at the airport by hostile representatives of warring sides: U.S. ambassador Herman Nickel, representing the Reagan administration, and protesters from the Azanian People's Organization (AZAPO), a militant anti-apartheid group, who believed the outsiders detracted from the purity of Black Africa's struggle. Discord would mar the trip throughout, denying Ted a triumphant moment like his brother Robert's 1966 address. Claiming that they could not assure his safety, the police at first kept Kennedy from visiting Tutu's home in Black Soweto. The government then refused to let Kennedy see Nelson Mandela, the imprisoned leader of the African National Congress. Ambassador Nickel insulted Kennedy as an attention-seeking dilettante. The South African press coverage was vicious. The Black factions squabbled. And a speech in Soweto had to be canceled for fear of a clash between AZAPO and the police.

Kennedy soldiered on as best he could, joining a protest outside the walls of Mandela's prison and visiting Mandela's wife, Winnie, in the remote village where she had been exiled. His unsparing rhetoric infuriated the government. At a mass meeting in a Cape Town stadium, he warned white South Africans that change was coming and that those "who comfort themselves that Ambassador Nickel speaks for the American people have some surprising and painful days ahead." The scenes of his trip, carried on worldwide television, reminded viewers how the apartheid government was only sustained by its brutal security forces. "We were faced with a vicious system, which basically was controlling the media," said Tutu, "and we had to find all sorts of stratagems to be able to tell our story."

Kennedy's journey told the story and boosted Black morale. But the reviews were harsh. In much of South Africa and the United States, the trip was perceived as a stunt by a politician running for president. "From the time that I arrived there," he would remember, "the South African government, enormously skillfully, portrayed that trip as having little to do with apartheid and everything to do with the election—just rife, with that whole sense all during the time that I was there . . . every report, every speech."

And so the family scene from Thanksgiving 1982 was reprised in 1985. Kennedy spent the holiday consulting with his children and summoned Shrum to the Cape in mid-December to craft a speech—a short, taped television address—declaring that he would not run for president in 1988. The news stunned his aides, who had hoped to run a victorious campaign against Vice President George H. W. Bush, and then staff a Kennedy White House. Once again, Kennedy had prepared—hiring staff, plotting strategy, helping Paul Kirk get elected as the Democratic Party chair—only to decide against it. You cannot keep doing this, said Shrum, and they agreed to insert the words "I know that this decision means that I may never be President. But the pursuit of the Presidency is not my life." Whatever contribution Kennedy would make he would make in the Senate.

And on his list of priorities was South Africa.

Tutu and others had advised Kennedy that the worldwide campaign to level economic sanctions against South Africa seemed the most promising way to transform the regime. Kennedy embraced the strategy. In March he joined Lowell Weicker and a group of other senators on a bill prohibiting further American investment in South Africa, banning loans and sales of computers and the importation of golden Krugerrands. As a parade of nonviolent demonstrators and celebrities took turns getting arrested at the South African embassy in Washington, the Reagan administra-

tion and its loyalists in Congress promised to work for gradual change—
a policy called "constructive engagement"—but repression in South Africa
continued.

A Republican filibuster led by Senator Jesse Helms of North Carolina
blocked the move for sanctions throughout 1985. Kennedy's response was
to propose even tougher measures—legislation imposing a trade embargo
passed by the Democratic House, which would require that all U.S. companies cease doing business in South Africa. On July 21, 1986, in an op-ed
piece in the *New York Times*, he lambasted Reagan as the free world's chief
defender of apartheid. The following morning, he renewed his call for
sanctions in testimony before the Foreign Relations Committee. The Senate's patience was running out. Biden lashed out at Secretary of State
Shultz for supporting a policy that lacked "a moral backbone." The Republican chairman of the committee, Senator Richard Lugar of Indiana,
endorsed the sanctions and legislation passed the Senate, 84 to 14, in
August.

When Congress returned for a short preelection session in September,
it fell to Kennedy to visit the House and urge the members of the Congressional Black Caucus to give up their hard-won embargo bill and support the Senate sanctions instead. It was the only way, he told them, to get
action in the few weeks remaining. They accepted his reasoning, and the
House passed the Senate bill, knowing that even this gentler measure
would attract a Reagan veto. So it did, and the confrontation over American policy on apartheid now reached its apogee.

"Apartheid is not just a 'codified system of segregation' as President
Reagan described it in the cool detachment of his veto message," Kennedy told the Senate. "It is much, much more—and much, much worse. It
is the torture of children and the use of terror against their parents. It is
the total disenfranchisement of an entire population. It is midnight arrests and disappearances. It is the forced relocation of entire villages. It is
attacks on innocent neighbors with bombs and bullets and planes. It is
starvation, disease, and early death. It is genocide, a crime against humanity."

The import of the moment was clear. Instead of milling around the chamber, as in most roll call votes, each senator rose at their desk to say "Aye" or "No" when their name was called. Reagan's veto was overridden, 78 to 21.

The sanctions were effective, and "constructive engagement" was discredited and discarded. Mandela was released from prison in 1990. In 1994 he was elected president of South Africa. "Sanctions passed and we overrode Reagan's veto," Weicker would recall. "I have no doubt that it was because of Kennedy's efforts that it took months rather than decades for that system to disintegrate."

A FEW RIGHT-WINGERS ON Reagan's National Security Council staff, meanwhile, had been selling U.S. arms to Iran and sending the profits to the Nicaraguan Contra rebels, in defiance of congressional bans. The Iran/Contra scandal, as it became known, erupted a few weeks after Reagan's veto of the South African sanctions, on the eve of the 1986 election. The voters dumped several of the Republican mediocrities who had ridden to office on Reagan's coattails in 1980. The Democrats now had control of both houses of Congress. Kennedy, newly dedicated to the Senate, had to decide which gavel he would wield.

The choices were the Labor and Human Resources Committee, or his familiar stomping ground, the Judiciary Committee, which he had chaired for two years in the late 1970s. His choice was telling. The Judiciary chair was the more high-profile post, with Supreme Court nominations and constitutional debates on provocative issues like abortion or prayer in school, which could lure television coverage for a presidential prospect. The Labor Committee was where things could be done, where Kennedy could help the average American family cope with stagnant wages, soaring health care costs, disease, jobs, and education. Campaigns taught candidates, Kennedy would say, and he had seen, campaigning across America in 1980, "human conditions that cried for attention." It left an impression "in my own psyche."

To make the selection, Kennedy and his top aides gathered on the Cape for an exchange of views. His new chief of staff, Ranny Cooper, warned them: this was not to devolve into an adversarial exercise. But Thomas Rollins, the staff director at the Labor Committee, pretty much ignored her. He came equipped with a thick binder of what Kennedy could accomplish for the American people in the fields of health, education, and employment, and argued that the impact of defeating a Supreme Court nominee was overrated.

"Do you remember the Haynsworth and Carswell fights?" he asked Kennedy.

Of course, the senator replied.

"What was the name of the man who eventually filled that empty seat?" Rollins asked.

Kennedy drew a blank. (It was Harry Blackmun.)

"A defeated nominee is a replaced nominee," said Rollins. "A public law is a thing of joy forever."

Anthony Podesta, a liberal lobbyist, disagreed. He paid a call on Kennedy, urging him to stay on Judiciary and keep judges like Carswell off the Supreme Court.

"I didn't get into politics to stop people from getting on the bench," Kennedy told him. "I got into politics to help people."

Kennedy chose to chair the Labor Committee. Years later, he would call it the turning point in his career.

Twenty-Three

VEHEMENCE
AND VITRIOL

B efore the events of the 1980s, the affliction known as Kaposi's sar-
coma, a cancer that announced itself with ugly purple skin lesions,
plagued only a few old men around the globe. *Pneumocystis* pneumonia was another ailment of the elderly. Thrush was something that new
mothers worried about—a white coating in a baby's mouth, which went
away as the infant's natural immunity evolved.

In the first days of the decade, these and other opportunistic illnesses
appeared with sudden frequency on the medical charts of young gay men
in Los Angeles, San Francisco, New York, and other cities. They complained of night sweats, swollen glands, diarrhea, skin disorders, and malaise. Blood work showed that their disease-fighting T-cells were being
decimated by an unknown agent. On June 5, 1981, the federal Centers for
Disease Control published an article, *"Pneumocystis* pneumonia—Los Angeles," by two California physicians, describing the cases of five gay men,
in the agency's *Morbidity and Mortality Weekly Report*. It didn't yet have a
name—they called it GRID (gay-related immune deficiency) or "the gay
plague" in those first months—but this was the U.S. government's first
report of acquired immunodeficiency syndrome (AIDS) and the human
immunodeficiency virus (HIV), which caused it. In the coming years,
more than thirty-six million human beings—including seven hundred
thousand Americans—would die from the virus.

———

To the extent that a society's response to an epidemic is influenced by political currents, the 1980s was an opportune era for AIDS to flourish. Its initial incursions were in reviled populations—gay male lovers, intravenous drug users, and Black immigrants from Haiti—whose gratifications could result in transfers of blood or semen. It required politicians to be well versed in perturbing topics like anal gonorrhea, dirty heroin needles, and bathhouse sex. In the era of "family values," it would be hard to design a disease more certain to scare off an elected official.

It was not a happy time to be gay. In mid-decade, in a Texas case, the Supreme Court upheld state laws that criminalized gay sex. Reagan was in the Oval Office, and an influential segment of the Republican coalition that put him there were "social conservatives," a vocal breed whose resistance to modernity dated back to the tide of Fundamentalism at the turn to the twentieth century. They had responded to the disorienting change of the 1960s and 1970s with a renewed investment in politics. Televangelists Jerry Falwell and Pat Robertson, the antifeminist Phyllis Schlafly, the gay-baiting Anita Bryant, the Reagan administration's Gary Bauer, North Carolina senator Jesse Helms, and others identified pornography, recreational drug use, extramarital sex, birth control, feminism, abortion, and the gay rights movement as sin-soaked features of permissiveness.

"The sexual revolution has begun to devour its children. And among the revolutionary vanguard, the Gay Rights activists, the mortality rate is highest and climbing," wrote conservative columnist and future Reagan communications director Pat Buchanan in a 1983 column. "The poor homosexuals—they have declared war upon nature, and now nature is exacting an awful retribution."

The AIDS virus was insidious in that its victims, once infected, could go years before showing its death-dealing effects, and thus pass it to many others. The initial fatality tolls were low, even as the number of those contracting the disease soared. Federal health workers were advised by complacent Reagan administration officials to voice sympathy and hope, but not to ask for too much money to combat the disease. Some protested. "Our government's response to this disaster has been far too little," an eminent AIDS expert, Dr. Donald Francis, warned his superiors at NIH in a 1983 letter. "The inadequate funding to date has seriously restricted our work and . . . deepened the invasion of this disease into the American population."

These were rough seas for the nascent gay political movement to navigate in Reagan-era Washington, yet with each death and day it was clear that the crisis required a federal response. The House remained in Democratic hands, and Representative Henry Waxman of Los Angeles held the first congressional hearing in 1982. But the Senate was controlled by Republicans, who backed Reagan's plans for cutting federal spending and taxes—and harbored baying bigots like Helms. "There was so much misinformation in those days. We didn't know what caused it until 1983 and didn't have a test for it until 1985," said Dr. Lynn Drake, the AIDS expert on Robert Dole's staff. "Could you get it from saliva? Tears? Kissing? People were terrified. By 1985 we were getting more confidence in the science, but that is when the real hostility arose." In an op-ed published by the *New York Times*, conservative publisher William F. Buckley Jr. called for the tattooing of those who tested positive for the disease: gay men on the buttocks, and addicts on the arm. The gay community needed paladins. Kennedy became their knight.

KENNEDY'S INVOLVEMENT WITH GAY politics dated back to at least 1975, when his staff was approached by activists endeavoring to add sexual orientation to the categories—race, gender, and so on—of individuals protected by the Civil Rights Act. A staff memo warned Kennedy he would encounter "knee jerk hostility" from those in his working-class constituency who hated the "fags," but urged Kennedy to "join, if not lead, this one if you think it can be done without too much political backlash."

Kennedy was amenable. Though the Roman Catholic Church had always characterized homosexual behavior as sinful, in the Manhattan, Hollywood, and European circles in which he and his siblings socialized,

The two Kennedy senators. It was the first time in more than a century that two brothers served together.

President Lyndon B. Johnson signs the landmark 1965 immigration act with the New York skyline behind him, and Ted and Robert Kennedy to his left, at his side.

Kennedy's deference won him the regard of his colleagues. Above, he stands with senators (left to right) Thomas Kuchel, Philip Hart, Mike Mansfield, Everett Dirksen, and Jacob Javits after a victory in the battle over the Voting Rights Act of 1965. After being elected as the Democratic whip in 1969, however, he ran afoul of Robert Byrd, seen (below) at right with Kennedy and Mansfield. Byrd ambushed Kennedy two years later and took the whip's job for himself.

Kennedy's position on the Vietnam war changed over the years. In a 1965 visit to the war zone, he seemed gung ho, outfitted in army fatigues and a slouch hat. By 1966, he was showing concern and fatigue during a White House briefing on the war. By the spring of 1971, Kennedy was joining Vietnam veterans against the war at a protest on the National Mall with a future Senate seatmate, John Kerry, seen in upper left.

As 1968 began, Robert Kennedy made plans to challenge Lyndon Johnson in the Democratic primaries. Ted Kennedy, just back from a visit to Vietnam, added to the president's woes in an Oval Office meeting by declaring his opposition to the war.

Robert Kennedy's campaign peaked with victory in the California primary in June. Moments after this photograph was taken, he was shot while leaving the ballroom.

On a misty June evening, astronaut John Glenn hands Ted Kennedy the flag from Robert's coffin during burial ceremonies at Arlington National Cemetery.

Joan Kennedy, in a newsworthy miniskirt, greets the Nixons and Vice President and Mrs. Agnew on a White House receiving line in March 1969. Years later, she said that her flamboyant outfits were a cry for attention.

The bridge at Chappaquiddick, with Ted Kennedy's wrecked Oldsmobile after it was pulled from the water, the morning after the fatal accident that claimed the life of Mary Jo Kopechne.

Mary Jo Kopechne, on the far left, with other members of Robert Kennedy's staff and the senator in 1967.

Ted Kennedy, wearing a cervical collar, on the trip to Mary Jo Kopechne's funeral with his wife, Joan.

Kennedy campaigned furiously for reelection in the year after the Chappaquiddick accident, often with Joan at his side, and was usually met by forgiving crowds. Here (right) they joined Charlestown's Bunker Hill Day parade in June 1970, and (below) stopped to greet a group of nuns, whose banner said, "God Bless Our Ted!"

Kennedy found that he could work with Richard Nixon, so long as he was willing to yield the spotlight to the president. Here, Nixon signs the war on cancer legislation, with Kennedy tucked away, behind him, in the back.

It was during the Nixon years that Kennedy became recognized as the champion of national health insurance. Here he addresses a union audience in 1971.

The liberalism of the Sixties provoked a conservative reaction, especially when it came to race. Here Kennedy, with *Boston Globe* columnist Mike Barnicle on his right and screaming anti-busing protesters gathering around them, is surrounded in Boston on September 9, 1974.

Kennedy's 1980 campaign peaked at the Democratic National Convention in New York when he stirred the crowd with a speech that promised, despite his own defeat, "The dream shall never die."

Kennedy marred Jimmy Carter's hour of triumph by waving at the president and shaking his hand, but not raising Carter's arm in the traditional salute to the victor.

Kennedy learned how to work with the opposition in the Republican era—and they with him. Here Kennedy, Ronald Reagan and his wife, Nancy, Jacqueline Kennedy Onassis, Ethel Kennedy, Caroline Kennedy, and John F. Kennedy Jr. pose at a 1985 fundraiser that Reagan agreed to headline for the John F. Kennedy Presidential Library.

Kennedy's taste for cigars and the fine life, and their stark ideological differences, did not prevent Senator Orrin Hatch, the straitlaced Mormon Republican from Utah, from joining his colleague in landmark collaborations.

Discredited by his association with the 1991 Palm Beach rape trial of a nephew, William Kennedy Smith, Kennedy showed discomfort while sitting in judgment of Anita Hill's charges that she was sexually harassed by Supreme Court nominee Clarence Thomas.

Kennedy's marriage to Victoria Reggie brought him love, support, and a peacefulness he needed. She was a shrewd adviser as well, and happy to help him change his image as he faced a tough reelection battle in 1994.

Kennedy needed the boost that his marriage provided as he faced
Mitt Romney, a hard-charging young Republican, in the 1994
election. The two are seen here, squaring off in their second debate.

Kennedy won reelection but tragedy continued to stalk the family. He is seen here
with Patrick, Ted Jr., and others at the recovery of the remains of John F. Kennedy
Jr., his wife, Carolyn, and her sister Lauren, all killed in a plane crash in 1999.

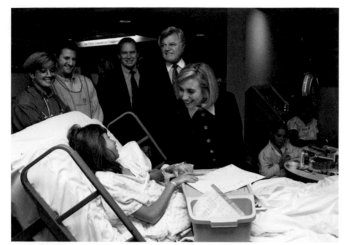

Bill and Hillary Clinton failed to push "Hillarycare," a major health care reform bill, through Congress. It was a major disappointment for Kennedy, and a political disaster for Democrats.

Kennedy was a stalwart defender of Bill Clinton when a majority-Republican House impeached the president in 1998 for lying about an affair with a White House intern. But for Kennedy, it was not a comfortable chore.

No Child Left Behind

George W. Bush collaborated with Kennedy on passage of the landmark No Child Left Behind education act in 2001, but their relationship suffered when the president led the country into war with Iraq, and Kennedy became a fierce critic. Here, from seats on the Armed Services Committee, he and an old rival, Robert Byrd, prepare to interrogate administration officials. Byrd came to admire Kennedy, and greatly mourned his passing.

As he settled into his role as the "Lion of the Senate," Kennedy turned speeches into performance art. Here are snapshots of a Kennedy tub-thumper.

His constituents returned Kennedy to the Senate over and over again. In Massachusetts, he was "Teddy," an institution, seen here as a guest conductor for the Boston Pops during the Democratic National Convention in Boston in 2004.

Kennedy and his three children, wife Vicki, and her son in Ted's hospital room on the morning after a May 2008 seizure signaled the presence of brain cancer. From left to right: Patrick, Curran Raclin, Ted Jr., Ted, Kara, and Vicki.

Kennedy went from his hospital room to the helm of his sailboat, the *Mya*, joined by wife, Vicki, and their Portuguese water dogs.

Kennedy had to marshal his fading strength but could not be kept from the White House deliberations on enactment of the Affordable Care Act—Obamacare—in the last months of his life.

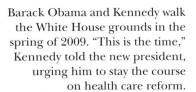

Barack Obama and Kennedy walk the White House grounds in the spring of 2009. "This is the time," Kennedy told the new president, urging him to stay the course on health care reform.

Presidents paid their respects at Ted Kennedy's funeral. From left to right are Patrick Kennedy, Kara Kennedy, Ted Kennedy Jr., Vicki Kennedy, Bill and Hillary Clinton, George Bush, Barack and Michelle Obama, Joe and Jill Biden, and Rosalynn and Jimmy Carter.

gay men like Lem Billings and Gore Vidal were accepted. Kennedy signed on as a cosponsor. Then, after some debate among his staff, Kennedy made the decision to campaign for the gay community's support in the 1980 presidential race and attended a California fundraiser with wealthy activists. When one of the donors, Sheldon Andelson, rebuked him for excluding the press, Kennedy was happy he had made a last-minute change and brought the political press corps with him. He pointed at a balcony, where the scribes and camera folk had gathered, and introduced them: "Sheldon, that's Cassie Mackin from ABC . . ."

Which is not to say he was totally hip, or that the process of acceptance—on both sides—was immediate. The gay community could spot a phony and would know it "if you twinge," one organizer instructed him. At a California press conference, he faced an unexpected question about immigration restrictions on homosexual lovers. *I can't wait to see what I have to say on this one,* he told himself. But the ghost of John Fitzgerald prevailed. He felt rapport—"a lump in my throat"—at the injustice. "Of course" he opposed the restriction, he told the press. "We can't have discrimination in immigration."

At the Democratic convention that year, Kennedy delegates pushed for a gay rights plank. "What do I call you?" he asked them. "Is it just gay? Or lesbians and gays? Or gay men and gay women?" The campaign was the turning point in his "personal evolution," he would say. "At the end of the campaign I was very much in their corner."

Some of his aides saw trouble in the prospect of the louche Kennedy aligning himself with men and women who were finding liberation in felonious, and at times orgiastic, indulgence. Kennedy saw things differently. His reputation gave him freedom that more straitlaced politicians lacked. "It's the upside of my downside; nobody thinks I have a self-interest," he told his advisers.

His response to the AIDS epidemic can be broken into two stages: the years 1981 through 1986, when he and a handful of Senate colleagues, in a somewhat clandestine manner, began to do the right thing; and the years 1987 and after, when he moved major legislation, with mighty price tags, through the Senate. In both eras, Kennedy's willingness and ability to cooperate with politically bold Republicans like Robert Dole, Orrin Hatch, and Lowell Weicker was critical.

IN THE FIRST YEARS of the decade, as the virus secured its foothold in the United States, the Senate Democrats were in the minority and Kennedy was hors de combat. "Once he got religion, he was great, but it took him a while to get there," gay rights activist Vic Basile recalled. Kennedy had been alerted to the disease in its early days by the gay veterans of his 1980 campaign, and by family friends like Mathilde Krim, a cancer researcher who led one of the first national AIDS organizations. But when a young physician named Mona Sarfaty joined his staff in 1985, "HIV was unaddressed . . . almost a taboo subject" in the Senate, she recalled. Kennedy was interested and concerned; his heart went out to the victims, who "were being treated like lepers." He signed Dear Colleague letters, urging more AIDS funding, to Senate appropriators. But he had lost his title, his gavel, and the lion's share of his committee staff in the Reagan landslide.

"A warm pitcher of spit is great compared to being in the minority in the Senate," his committee staff director, Thomas Rollins, would recall. "It's a perfunctory responsibility." At one point, when he objected to something the Republicans were planning, Rollins was told by the majority staff director, "Oh, Tom, that's a great point. Tell you what, let's have a meeting of the committee and we'll count how many people are on our side of the committee and how many are on your side."

"The work of . . . Kennedy's side of the committee was almost entirely reactive. . . . There was no clear agenda about what we wanted to get done," Rollins said. And Kennedy? "He seemed to be going through the motions. . . . He was unbelievably stung by the loss in 1980 . . . [and] by the loss of the majority. . . . He just seemed kind of disconnected and dissolute."

But "did I ever hear Kennedy worry about the political consequences" of the AIDS battle? "Not once," said Rollins. "And I heard him worry about such matters in many other contexts. The circumstances, the context of this issue, made it radioactive . . . [but] the senator charged into the fray."

In the spring of 1987, in a speech to AIDS activists in Washington, Kennedy apologized for the tardy response. "The federal government has wasted precious time. . . . We would not be facing a crisis of this magnitude today if Congress and the administration had listened earlier," he told them. "You have endured the insensitivity—and, worse, the insults— of a society that too often in the past has failed the test of character, of a nation that sought at first to turn its back and ignore your pleas for help and action."

But until 1987, this was a Republican Senate. Dole rose to be majority leader; Hatch chaired the Labor Committee; and Weicker was chairman of the appropriations subcommittee that allocated money to the National Institutes of Health, the Centers for Disease Control, and other public health agencies. The hero in those first years of the plague was Weicker, a liberal Republican from Connecticut who would slip out to NIH and confer with officials to discover how much money the research community could use and absorb. He would then convene a public hearing, listen to the parsimonious Reagan budgeteers, ignore their stingy requests, and appropriate what the NIH scientists had privately advised. On Weicker's watch, AIDS funding grew from $61 million in 1984 to $925 million in 1988—twice what the Reagan administration requested. In his last days as a chairman, in September 1986, Weicker was visited by a delegation of gay activists who begged him to fund experimental use of a cancer drug, AZT, that had the potential to save lives. The end of the fiscal year was approaching. As the gay lobbyists wondered whether their pitch had succeeded, they received word that Weicker was on the Senate floor, with a $47 million appropriation. "At least 10,000 people can live six extra months, and I'm not coming off the floor of the United States Senate until I get the money," Weicker said.

But Kennedy needed more than liberals as allies. He needed Hatch, and at some point he would need Dole, to give other Republicans the political cover to vote for the sort of preventive measures—distribution of condoms, public health curricula with detailed descriptions of gay sex, provisions to supply drug addicts with clean needles—that the experts recommended, but that left politicians and their constituents uneasy.

Republican senators could persuade the Republican White House to sign, not veto, legislation.

"Kennedy had a vision in mind, and he was going to do what he had to do to get there," said Dole's top legislative aide, Sheila Burke: "Find the coalition." Kennedy liked to compare American politics to a river, said his aide Nancy Soderberg. There were 99 other senators and 435 representatives, a president, and nine judges. The river would surge and overpower, and make its own way, said Kennedy, but one man with a cause could sometimes "change the course."

Republicans like Dole knew that if they got Kennedy's name on a bill, he would protect the legislation from attacks in the Democratic caucus. "If he made a deal, it would stick," said Kennedy aide Jeff Blattner. There were also the matters of ego, and accomplishment. "What this meant to his Republican colleagues was that if they wanted to enter the law books, or the history books, they could do it."

Republicans like Hatch, Dan Quayle, and others were swayed by Kennedy's aura, said Christopher Dodd. "Teddy knew how to marshal his celebrity. . . . He was a Kennedy, an iconic figure. With two assassinated beloved brothers. There was a realization: you were talking with history, not just a colleague." A visit to Kennedy's Senate office, or hideaway, or home, invariably featured a personal tour, given by the senator, of the snapshots, funny notes, and other family mementos that hung on the walls and bestrewed the sills and tables. "When Ted Kennedy showers you with attention, it has an effect. You start to believe you are more of a person than you thought you were," said Chris Jennings, a Washington health care expert. "And remember, politicians are in it for love."

Kennedy worked endlessly to understand the legislative goals and political needs of his GOP colleagues, and to know all there was about their states or districts and ambitions, and to come up with ways to accommodate them. His celebrity might lure them to the table, but the deal-making "would not have lasted ten minutes if he didn't have something more to offer," said Dodd. His staff, especially Parker, were matchless assets. Kennedy's rule was to hire brilliance, not specialty, and to give it rein. "A smart person can learn the issue," Kennedy would say. "But someone who knows the issue, but isn't smart, doesn't help me. And I don't need to hire people who agree with me. I can agree with myself."

HATCH HAD BUILT HIS REPUTATION leading conservatives into battle against civil rights measures like fair housing. But there was an area of the Labor Committee's jurisdiction—health—where he was susceptible to liberal appeals. Before the Republicans lost control of the Senate in the 1986 midyear elections, Chairman Hatch recognized that government had a role in combatting AIDS, especially as it moved beyond "the high-risk groups" to threaten children and adults needing blood transfusions. Hatch had a health staff director—Dr. David Sundwall—who had been tipped off by California Republicans as the disease spread on the West Coast. The senator was an early promoter of the AIDS-fighting CDC director James Mason and of Surgeon General C. Everett Koop, whose nomination was resisted by Kennedy and other liberals because he opposed abortion, but who stunned Washington in 1986 with a fierce, no-nonsense report on the perils of AIDS.

Hatch and Dole had national ambitions, and moved discreetly, wary of hysteria. But they were resolute: when a program to help AIDS victims passed the House, Hatch quietly moved it to the Senate calendar, so that conservative rabble-rousers could not seize the forum of a Labor Committee hearing and spew hatred. When Helms proposed mandatory testing for large swaths of Americans, Dole rebuked him on the Senate floor. To assuage fears that the disease could be spread by casual contact, Hatch posed for news photographers with his arm around Nathan Smith, a hemophiliac who had testified before the committee.

Kennedy and Hatch agreed that AIDS was a crisis for which they would face the judgment of history. "They were seen almost as a team," Dr. Anthony Fauci, the government scientist, recalled. They found common ground in a fixed approach: to define AIDS as a threat to public health—not anything that demanded that politicians issue a moral judgment. And when a deal was made, they promised each other, they would defend it together from Left and Right. "People just did not want to deal with this issue at all," Michael Iskowitz, another Kennedy aide, recalled. But "if Kennedy and Hatch were standing up there together, and the two of them agreed to it, that was fine, and they could just vote."

"People couldn't say this is some cockamamie left-wing thing that Kennedy wants to do," Rollins said. With Hatch, "you had enormous credibility."

IN JANUARY 1987, within days of taking over as the committee chairman, Kennedy convened his first hearing on AIDS. "In five years we will have approximately 270,000 people with active cases in the United States," he said. "Unless a cure is found, every one of those Americans will die."

Koop testified, and stressed the need for public education and safe sex practices to stop the virus from spreading. "We have neither a drug for cure nor a vaccine for prevention," he told the sobered panel. Kennedy vowed to seek "all out action" by the government. The "vehemence and the vitriol" against gays was "just extraordinary," he would later recall. "It was a very volatile, hate-filled moment . . . just a mean, nasty time."

Kennedy was fully engaged: questioning and studying and learning until Fauci was warning his administration colleagues not to fall back on their usual pap in Senate hearings, because it would only infuriate the new chairman. Fauci was not immune to Kennedy's truculence—but when the hearing was over, the senator would throw an arm around the doctor's shoulders and say, "Nothing personal, Tony, but we've just got to get things moving."

Said Fauci, "He was very good at that . . . at making his point. You know, not being mean, but being tough." Other senators routinely asked witnesses a staff-written question and moved on without listening to the answer. "They [don't] have a clue of what it is they're asking," Fauci said. Not Kennedy. "When he asks a question, he wants an answer to it."

Washington was developing a fresh appreciation for Kennedy. "He's not doing it because he wants to be president. He's not doing it because he wants to be majority leader," said Fauci. "He's doing it because this is what he believes in."

THE POLITICAL CLIMATE WAS CHANGING, with a million infected and 16,500 AIDS deaths, and an increasing number of transfusion patients and heterosexuals who were contracting the disease. Kennedy had his own moment of terror when he remembered all the liters of blood he had been given when hospitalized for a serious case of hepatitis in 1985. To his considerable relief, tests showed the blood was not contaminated, but "I was scared to death," he would recall. "My God, what the outcry would be."

Rock Hudson, a Hollywood star who died of AIDS in the fall of 1985, was a friend of Ronald and Nancy Reagan. The disease opened doors to many such closets. Like thousands of other American families, the president and his wife were discovering that sons and nephews and cousins and friends were gay. Celebrities like Elizabeth Taylor were raising funds and lobbying the government for action. Kennedy spoke regularly to Mathilde Krim and added two gay men—Iskowitz and Terry Beirn—to his staff. "They were superstars," he recalled. Beirn, an AIDS activist and former television news reporter, was loaned to Kennedy by Krim when Kennedy took over the Labor Committee. Kennedy requested "a retired, university president type," she recalled. Instead, Krim sent him a pit bull. "There were then no federal AIDS policies, no legislative initiatives underway and ridiculously insufficient federal funding of AIDS research," Krim remembered.

Beirn and his colleagues lured senators to picture-taking sessions with Taylor, then signed them up as cosponsors. Using their newfangled fax machines, they built a national network of supporters who could be triggered to call Congress at a moment's notice on an impending vote. Beirn introduced Kennedy to Ryan White, who was banned from attending grade school in Indiana after contracting AIDS via a blood transfusion. The two gay aides outlined legislation on the back of a restaurant place mat. When the bill was approved by the Labor Committee, Kennedy murmured, "This is for you, Ryan." The remark was overheard and picked up by the press. White died a few days later.

Kennedy hosted small dinners with five or so colleagues at his home to encourage candid conversations about what should be done. He had experts talk to senators and staff at issue lunches in the Senate office. He chaired public hearings in New York, Los Angeles—and rural Georgia. He insisted that the Reagan administration professionals, like Koop and Fauci, give "the right answers, not the Far Right answers."

Dole, meanwhile, was emerging as a profile in courage among the Republican candidates for president in 1987, refusing to let politics stampede the science. He pushed, successfully, for a presidential commission on AIDS. Together, he and Kennedy convened a senators-only briefing that summer (even staff were barred by a guard at the door) where Koop, Fauci, and others moved the Senate through stages of fear and hysterics toward truth and health and science. When Drake asked him how the closed-door briefing went, Dole responded with his customary growl. "Good," he said. "Lots of questions." He worked with Kennedy to find consensus. "Respectful of one another's experience and one another's skill . . . they were so different in style," Burke recalled. "Kennedy . . . the classic stereotypical Irish Catholic. Lots of arm waving, lots of loud talk. Dole is midwestern, very steady on, never raised his voice, could get very stern. . . . It was like watching two really skilled combatants, and when they come together, it works."

"Reagan used to say, 'If you can't get me 100 percent, give me 90 percent or 80 percent, or even 70 percent, and I'll get the rest later.' Kennedy was in that mold," Dole remembered. "He came from a different view, but you could talk to him and work out differences."

When a conservative columnist asked him why he had gotten out in front on AIDS, Dole's answer was revealing: "If I make a public policy decision on banking, it costs people money. When I make a policy decision on this, what's at stake is lives," he said. When the interview had ended and the scribe was leaving, Dole murmured to Drake, "Sometimes you just have to do what is right."

That left Helms. Given the Senate's rules—that an individual senator could speak, hold the floor, and offer bundles of amendments—it didn't take more than one loud, pompous jerk to expose his unnerved colleagues to politically toxic roll call votes. Fear of his "killer amendments" stalled progress for years: Hatch and Kennedy could craft all the aseptic public health legislation they wanted, but Helms would insist that the Senate offer judgment on sinful behavior. How could public health officials promote the safe sexual practices that would hold AIDS at bay if, as Helms and his amendments insisted, they were banned from describing the sexual practices that were dangerous?

"We must not treat people infected with the virus as villains," Kennedy said. "AIDS is spreading like wildfire, and ideology cannot stop it." The nation was failing a test of character. "We will never win the battle against AIDS if we permit ourselves to lose our humanity in the struggle."

KENNEDY HAD MEMORABLE RUN-INS with Helms before the AIDS era. They bickered on the floor in 1983, when the North Carolinian cited the Kennedy administration's eavesdropping on Martin Luther King Jr. as a reason not to make King's birthday a national holiday.

"Senator Kennedy's argument is not with the senator from North Carolina," Helms said, referring to himself in the third person, as was Senate custom. "His argument is with his dead brother who was President and his dead brother who was Attorney General."

It was a surefire way of provoking Kennedy. He rose, seething, and accused Helms of making "inaccurate and false" statements. The North Carolinian appealed to the chair, who studied the precedents and officially "silenced" Kennedy—banned him from talking—for imputing that his fellow senator was a liar.

"The senator needs to learn the rules," Helms taunted.

Mathias came to Kennedy's defense, and then–majority leader Howard Baker rushed into the chamber to ask that the antagonists back down before the confrontation reached a point that could "blow up in our face." Kennedy agreed to strike the word "false" from his remarks. He regained the floor, and with care of the Senate's rules, and allowable synonyms, accused Helms of cowardice.

"I am appalled at the attempt of some to misappropriate the memory of my brother, Robert Kennedy, and misuse it as part of this smear campaign," said Kennedy. "Those who never cared for him in life now invoke his name when he can no longer speak for himself."

Helms's attack on King was but "the vestiges of old hatreds," said Kennedy. King's dream of justice and equality "must live on, if America is to live."

THUS, Kennedy and Helms had a history when the North Carolinian ambushed Kennedy on an October day in 1987. Helms seized upon a safe sex comic book, published by the Gay Men's Health Crisis, a disease-fighting organization in New York, as cause for a devious attack. The group received federal funds, Helms noted, fallaciously implying that the comic book's illustrations of naked gay men fondling each other's erections was paid for by the hard-earned tax dollars of the God-fearing folk of Mayberry.

"The comic book promotes sodomy!" Helms declared. He had sent it around to fifteen or twenty senators in a brown envelope marked "Personal and Confidential: For Senators' Eyes Only," lest young staffers be corrupted. "I have seen a lot of things. I served four years in the Navy," Helms said. But at the gay group's suggestion that there were erogenous areas of the body outside the genitals, "I get embarrassed. . . . I may throw up." Why, he had carried the comic book to the Oval Office, said Helms, where Reagan was so enraged as to smite the Resolute Desk in anger.

The virus was not the cause of the epidemic, said Helms, it was the sodomites: "Every AIDS case can be traced back to a homosexual act." The only cure that government should promote was "abstinence outside of a sexually monogamous marriage." It was time for a sexual lockdown— time to "slam the door on the wayward, warped sexual revolution."

It is a testament to the tenor of those years that Helms won this round by a vote of 94 to 2, with an amendment to an appropriations bill prohibiting the government from distributing explicit instructions on safe sex. To recognize the homosexuals' plight was to condone their behavior, Helms insisted. The best that Kennedy could do was negotiate a compromise so that the CDC could continue with its educational work, so long as it did not "promote" homosexuality. Kennedy vouched for the deal, absolving the Senate's cowardly lions. The compromise language "is toothless, and it can in good conscience be supported by the Senate," he said lamely.

But there was no disguising it. Kennedy had gotten a whipping. The U.S. Senate had gone on record, amid an epidemic that was slaughtering gay men, as deploring the afflicted. The CDC and other agencies began the process of purging their sex-ed material. Gay activists in Boston and around the country cried out in hurt and anger. The movement's leaders, demoralized by the ninety-two-vote scope of the shellacking, wondered if the cause was doomed—if America had turned its back on them, content to let them die. "Trust and fear are major issues," Kennedy's small band of AIDS aides wrote him. "We . . . share a sense of alarm and disappointment" after the Helms amendment, which was "essentially seen as an up or down vote" on whether gay lives were worth saving.

Six months would pass before Kennedy would dare bring the first major AIDS-fighting measure to the floor—six more months the virus employed to extend its reach. But because he was Kennedy, and because they were his staff, he and his aides analyzed how they had failed, and what they needed to do to win.

KENNEDY HAD A BILL in hand—the HOPE Act. It was a game-changing measure—the first big swing that Congress would take at the virus—that would allocate $1.8 billion for research, prevention and education, and medical, hospice, and home care for sufferers. But the Senate needed educating, Kennedy and his team concluded. A whip count showed them that there were sixty-five to seventy sympathetic but pigeon-hearted senators out there, whose fears of a thirty-second ad in the next election cycle would need to be addressed. Kennedy's aides organized seminars for the legislative assistants who would be framing the issue for their bosses. They went through each title of the legislation, easing doubt and fear. And to make sure the senators and their advisers knew that both sides in the argument wielded political clout, Kennedy's team rallied the gay groups and civil rights organizations and put them to work inundating Senate offices with calls and letters and telegrams. When the senators left Washington over the Christmas holidays there was no respite; they were met by local mayors, doctors, and public health officials demanding that the Senate act on AIDS. By April, having tilled the ground, Kennedy was ready to take the HOPE Act to the floor.

Dealing with Helms, and his parliamentary devilry, was a different matter. When Helms had thrashed him in October, Kennedy had planned to replace any poisonous amendments with a "second-degree" substitute that would render the toxic changes inoffensive. But Helms, getting word this might happen, had struck quickly, caught Kennedy off guard, and countered with a parliamentary ploy. As winter turned toward spring, Kennedy and his team studied and prepared to combat Helms. They would be "far more vigilant to mischief," his staff promised Kennedy.

Robert Byrd was in his last term as majority leader and prided himself as a parliamentary wizard and defender of Senate traditions. He was no great friend of gay Americans, but Kennedy met with him, obtaining his approval for a detailed strategy that met the Senate rules. Byrd and Kennedy had grown close in the years since the 1971 whip contest. "Kennedy was one of the best," Byrd said. "He loved the committee work. He went about his work with great zeal. He knew the subject matter on any bill that came out of his committee, and he was loyal to me [when Byrd led the Senate Democrats in the Carter and Reagan years] . . . loyal to the core.

"I gave him his due and he was due a lot," said Byrd. "He was a senator in every sense of the word." When fortune turned on Kennedy, "he proved himself to be a man."

Kennedy's staff did whip counts on potential Helms amendments, to know which ones would have to be defeated outright, and which ones would require a second-degree replacement so that timorous senators could go on the record voting for something that sounded pro-family, without hurting the war on AIDS. By mid-April Kennedy was ready, and so was the AIDS network. Majority Leader "Byrd will receive 500 telegrams requesting that he call the bill up immediately. We are up to 49 cosponsors and hope to have 51 by the end of the day," Kennedy's aides informed him.

KENNEDY'S MACHINATIONS PREPARED the field for gay America's unlikely champion: Orrin Hatch.

On April 28, Helms offered an amendment to the HOPE Act, insisting that any federal education programs must emphasize "abstinence from sexual activity outside a sexually monogamous marriage, including abstinence from homosexual sexual activities." It passed the Senate easily.

But this time Kennedy was ready with a second-degree amendment, to replace the Helms measure with language that sounded vaguely similar but was harmless in its effect, and abstruse enough for almost any colleague to support. Federally funded health programs should stress "the public health benefits of a single monogamous relationship," the amendment said. The wording was loose enough to include homosexual or heterosexual relationships, in and out of marriage. Furthermore, "nothing shall restrict the ability of the education program to provide accurate information on reducing the risk of becoming infected with the etiologic agent for AIDS." If safe sex could save Americans, and unsafe sex could kill them, the government was going to have the freedom to talk about safe sex.

This time it was Helms who was caught unprepared. Kennedy's amendment was drawn so that a senator could vote for it and be on the record as being in favor of monogamy and against AIDS.

"What the senator from Massachusetts is saying is that we should stress monogamous relationships, meaning shacking up, just do it one at a time, do not get married," Helms sputtered. The Senate would not be on record, as Helms so desired, as saying that sexual gratification was the rightful, moral province of married heterosexual couples. "I do not know how to inform the Senate . . . that they are being snookered."

Kennedy did not respond. Hatch did. He and Helms "both wish that there were not homosexuals. He and I both wish that we could get everybody to live decent moral lives in a marital relationship," Hatch said. But "this is a pandemic. We are not talking about some little narrow problem here. We are talking about the Number One public health problem in America."

"I do not agree with their sexual preferences," said Hatch of gay Americans. "That does not mean I do not have compassion for them; that I am just going to write them off and tell them to forget it, go ahead and die, because they are different from me."

"If we put in 'heterosexual married monogamous relationships' we exclude the largest group of people that are being devastated by this illness," said Hatch. It "does not make sense . . . to subject this whole country to a widespread pandemic."

Helms was irate—and mean as an adder. "There is not one single case of AIDS reported in this country that cannot be traced in origin to sodomy," he declared. "The point is, we should not allow the homosexual crowd to promote and legitimize their lifestyle in American society," he said. "That is exactly what is going on."

And then, here was Hatch at his best—standing up for the despised and powerless, in an election year, as the C-SPAN cameras carried the debate to Utah.

"I am not sure that homosexuals chose to be the way they are, or that anybody else fully chooses to be who or what they are," he replied, but gently. "I have known homosexuals that I liked, and I have known homosexuals that I disliked. . . . Some of them are just as fine human beings as anybody . . . in the United States Senate."

"That is true of Senators, too. Some of them are very fine and some of them . . . are not as fine as they could be. . . . Who are we to judge anyway? Let him who is without sin cast the first stone. . . . We have to tell homosexuals more than simply to become heterosexuals. . . . Let us quit judging and let us start doing what is right."

Though they lost the votes of too many good men who knew better—Dole, Alan Simpson, John McCain among them—the Kennedy-Hatch alliance prevailed, on a 61–29 vote, to replace the Helms amendment. When the HOPE Act came up for a final roll call vote, the 87–4 vote for passage was testament to the hard work by the forces of light. Over six months they had turned a ninety-two-vote deficit to an eighty-three-vote triumph.

And Hatch's empathy and eloquence? "Every now and then they get under enough pressure, that they stop being politicians and they turn into themselves," said Rollins. "He had turned into himself."

KENNEDY AND HATCH WERE called upon again, two years later, in another fight with Helms. The measure at hand was the capstone of their collaboration: it set aside a billion dollars to fight AIDS, and has served as the keystone of federal policy since. It was named after Ryan White, the thirteen-year-old victim of pediatric AIDS.

"At the time that the Ryan White legislation was passed . . . it was still predominantly a disease of gay men," Fauci recalled. Naming the legislation after White broadened the political appeal of the bill. "People who are fundamentally reticent to do something for the gay population could point to hemophiliacs as the so-called—I hate to use the word—innocent victims, as opposed to the people who 'did some bad thing' to get infected. So if that's what it took to get certain lawmakers . . . fine. It was almost as if Kennedy really didn't care what you hung your hat on . . . as long as it gets approved, because he realized that we desperately needed a Ryan White CARE Act. . . . He pushed for it, and he got enough votes to get it."

Helms, however, was up to his old tricks. "Ryan White was an innocent victim of *these people*," he sneered. "It is about time that this Senate addressed the moral issue. . . . What we have is another legislative flagship for the homosexual segment of the AIDS lobby and its apologists in and out of Congress.

"The AIDS lobby and its allies . . . are unwilling to say that Ryan White would never have contracted AIDS had it not been for the perverted conduct of people who are demanding respectability."

"The taxpayers' money is being proposed to be used to proselytize a dangerous lifestyle," Helms claimed. "Millions of other Americans, gravely ill with Alzheimer's or cancer or diabetes . . . are being cast aside."

Again, Hatch replied. Helms was wrong, he said. The disease did not originate in the homosexual community—research showed that the virus had likely made the leap from African monkeys to native hunters, and then via heterosexual sex to the rest of the world.

"The American people have developed a better understanding about how we can and should be dealing with this particular disease," Kennedy added. After complimenting Hatch for how he "again demonstrated how much he cares about Americans who are suffering," Kennedy noted that "this legislation will not end the pain and sorrow unleashed by this killer. What it can and will do is diminish the devastating toll that AIDS has taken."

The tide had turned. Helms could no longer cow his colleagues. The bill had sixty-five sponsors and passed the Senate, 96–4.

More than little, but late. In the nine years since the illness was first reported, a million Americans had become infected by the HIV virus, 128,000 had come down with full-blown cases of AIDS, and 78,000 people had died. Terry Beirn was among them. "There would have been no legislation named after Ryan White, no help for cities and states overburdened by AIDS, no federal funds to help people with HIV/AIDS buy life-extending drugs were it not for Terry," said Krim. Working with Sarfaty and Iskowitz, Beirn "gave six years of grueling, unrelenting work to the framing of federal AIDS legislation—the last six years of his short life." He died of the disease in 1991.

Kennedy asked Hatch to speak at the memorial service. It was interrupted when Helms offered another of his amendments, spurring a call from Majority Leader George Mitchell to the mourners, who scrambled to the chamber to resist.

WHEN ASSEMBLING THE ELEMENTS of the HOPE Act, Kennedy and Hatch had put off action on matters regarding privacy and discrimination. These were serious issues, and high on the agenda for activist groups, but could be misrepresented by Helms as protecting AIDS patients at the expense of healthy Americans. Kennedy and Hatch wanted a big tent, and moving through the Senate on a separate track was a vehicle that could meet such concerns—an antidiscrimination bill promoted by advocates for the disabled. If AIDS victims could be included as "disabled," then passage of the historic Americans with Disabilities Act could protect them, among millions of other handicapped Americans.

Kennedy supported the bill, which was the work of two of his committee members—Republican Weicker and freshman Democrat Tom Harkin of Iowa. Kennedy had watched his sister Rosemary's decline, seen his father suffering from the crippling effects of a stroke, watched Ted Jr. learn to ski on one leg—and spent enough time in the Stryker frame in 1964, learning to walk again—to enhance even his consistent enthusiasm for far-reaching civil rights acts. Then a series of twists called him out to center stage. The understudy took on the starring role.

The first turn came in 1987, when the Democrats took over the Senate. There were extra seats to fill, and to lure Harkin to the Labor panel, Kennedy promised him the chair of a subcommittee on the disabled. Harkin agreed, even though the two men did not especially get along. As a freshman with a seat on the Appropriations Committee, Harkin had found Kennedy "overbearing" and "demanding." He was stunned when Kennedy, in a disagreement over one appropriation, with "one of his famous temper tantrums . . . storm[ed] out of the room."

Kennedy regretted the outburst and a few days later asked if he could call on Harkin in the Iowan's office. "I need your help," Kennedy said when the door was closed.

"The way he did it was classy," Harkin recalled. He was beginning to appreciate his famous colleague, a titan willing to show humility. "If he wants something, my God, he'll do anything to get it. Do anything."

It was fortunate for both men that they reached an accommodation. In the 1988 election, Weicker was defeated by an inferior Democratic challenger. And Harkin, meanwhile, was facing his own reelection campaign in 1990; the Republican White House had no wish to give him a legislative trophy to carry around Iowa. Suddenly, the disabled needed a paladin—the more powerful and savvy the better. With Harkin fretting about his status back home, Kennedy stepped in as an ADA cosponsor and strategist.

"I'm only there in my first term and this is Ted Kennedy . . . and he's running interference for me," Harkin remembered. "He's doing the blocking, he's working out the deals without me there, but he's always checking with me, making sure this is okay. . . . He couldn't have been better. He just did it all. . . . He always kept pushing them, because they would do anything they could to slow it down."

"They" were hostile members of the White House staff, which was divided over the issue. Momentum for an ADA had been building for years, as activists for the disabled, Republicans and Democrats alike, clamored for federal protection and picked up allies in the greater civil rights community. The new president, George H. W. Bush, had put the ADA atop his list of domestic priorities. The bill was opposed, however, by Main Street: the small businesses and local government agencies that groaned about the cost and the regulatory burden of making properties and services accessible. Conservatives in the House of Representatives, aiming to take power on an antigovernment platform, were hesitant; so was White House chief of staff John Sununu, an egotist with something of a political tin ear, and new to Washington. The task for Harkin and Kennedy was to craft as strong a bill as they could, accommodate sympathetic Republicans like Hatch and Dole, Attorney General Richard Thornburgh, and White House counsel C. Boyden Gray—and douse resistance from skeptics like Sununu.

Kennedy drove things at a furious pace. The legislation was introduced in May, hearings were conducted in May and June, and by the start of summer Kennedy had enlisted Dole and Hatch and was engaged in talks with the White House. His chief negotiator was Carolyn Osolinik, who handled civil rights issues. She was a typical Kennedy staffer, unintimidated by the opposition, ready to bluff, stomp, or deal. "One of the toughest negotiators I have ever seen," said Pat Wright, advocate for the disabled. When the White House representatives balked at her opening bid—that whatever agreement they reached would be binding on congressional Republicans—Osolinik walked out. Sununu called on Kennedy to replace her. "There could be no higher compliment in Kennedy's mind than to have John Sununu, particularly on this issue, asking him to change his staff person," she remembered. Kennedy refused, and the talks carried on through July. Her boss was "always more than happy to commit his staff to work day and night," she recalled.

On July 28, in Dole's conference room, "the principals," including the leading senators and Sununu, Thornburgh, and Gray, gathered to approve or amend the blueprint their aides had designed. Sununu was his smug self, berating Harkin aide Bobby Silverstein for daring to correct him on the impact the bill might have on small businesses.

"Jesus, he's going after my staff person. And I'm thinking to myself I can't let this go, I've got to do something," Harkin remembered.

Before Harkin could speak up, Kennedy rose out of his chair, leaned toward Sununu, pounded the table, and said, "Goddamn. Don't you ever yell at my staff. You want to yell about something, you yell at me! You want to yell at me? Huh? C'mon, yell at me."

"Jesus Christ. I thought Kennedy was going to punch his lights out," Harkin recalled. "Veins are popping out on Kennedy's head. Sununu didn't know what the hell to say. I think it really scared him." Dole rolled his eyes in amusement and suggested that the two sides settle down. Sununu sat silent as Thornburgh and the others took over the negotiating for the White House.

In the ensuing talks, Kennedy posed as the conciliator, making pre-planned concessions that Harkin appeared to resist. "We are close now," Kennedy urged the group. "We can get this solved."

"Kennedy . . . starts yielding," said Harkin. "Gives this up, gives that up . . . [but] then he gets basically what he thought he might get in the beginning. . . . He was using me as a foil."

Three days later, in a smaller meeting of Thornburgh, Harkin, and Kennedy, the two sides reached what Kennedy called "a fragile compromise." On August 2, the Labor Committee, with a unanimous vote, sent the ADA to the floor where, somewhat stunned at its rapid progress, the Senate approved the legislation by a 76–8 vote. When Harkin and Kennedy left the chamber, they found that the Senate reception room was jammed with their fellow human beings—all afflicted by disabilities, all cheering, some clapping as best they could, some with tears coursing down their cheeks. It was a remarkable demonstration of legislative skill. In eight months, Kennedy and his allies had moved a landmark civil rights bill through the Senate.

The only shadow was cast, predictably, by Helms. He and Colorado Republican William Armstrong strove to exclude disabilities with "mental disorders" or a "moral content"—like kleptomania, bisexuality, or homosexuality—from the new law's coverage. Kennedy countered with the public health argument: AIDS victims would hide their illness, and so endanger others, if they knew they would face discrimination. In the end, the two sides (with Hatch at a typewriter) drew up a list of various ailments—like kleptomania—not covered by the bill. They did not exempt AIDS or homosexuality.

That issue was revived, in a different guise, in the House of Representatives, when lobbyists for the restaurant industry asked Congress for the right to exclude AIDS patients and others with communicable diseases from handling food. There was no science to suggest that cooks or waiters could transfer AIDS at the workplace. But the amendment sounded good and so had strong support. The bill was sent to a House and Senate conference with the restaurant industry's measure a prime issue of contention, and Helms on the attack. He won a test vote in the Senate.

The advocates for the disabled were presented with a harsh choice: sell out the nation's AIDS patients or lose the bill. Kennedy chaired the conference committee, where he and Harkin stood fast. So did the disabled. They would abandon their long-sought legislation, they said, if AIDS sufferers—targets of an amendment with no scientific validity, that only codified hate and fear—were excluded from its protections. At a White House meeting, Bush's staff urged the ADA forces to compromise—to not let the perfect be the enemy of the good. One by one, the representatives of the various groups in the coalition refused to abandon the victims of AIDS. Robert Williams, a wheelchair user, sitting next to Gray, suffered from cerebral palsy. He had been turned away from restaurants for scaring away customers. Now he pointed to the letters on the board he carried to spell out his thoughts. "I.T. A.I.N.T. C.I.V.I.L. A.N.D. I.T. A.I.N.T.

R.I.G.H.T," he spelled. And as he did so, the advocates for the disabled, anticipating what he would say, called out the letters with him.

The conference report reached the Senate on July 11, 1990. Hatch once again played a pivotal role. He had initially cast his lot with the restaurant owners but came to recognize the injustice. In a meeting with Iskowitz and the advocates for the disabled, he proposed a science-based compromise, in which the government would publish a yearly list of truly communicable diseases, which restaurant owners could use to restrict food handling in their establishments. AIDS would not be on that list. The Hatch amendment prevailed, 99 to 1, with Helms the only dissenting vote.

Bush signed the ADA into law on July 26. Three weeks later, the president put his signature on the Ryan White Act.

Kennedy had reclaimed his chairmanship in 1987. In the span of three years, working with Hatch, Dole, and other allies, he and his committee had made historic strides for equality and inclusion on behalf of society's most vulnerable and preyed-upon outcasts. Kennedy had loaned them his strong voice, his lawmaking skills, and the muscle of his bright and driven staff. His brothers would have teased him—with pride.

Twenty-Four

ROBERT BORK'S AMERICA

Toward the end of the twentieth century, death and retirement claimed members of the U.S. Supreme Court at the worst possible times for liberalism and the Democratic Party. In the four years that Jimmy Carter led the land, no justice passed away or stepped down. Richard Nixon, in contrast, replaced four justices on the court, Gerald Ford named another, Ronald Reagan made three appointments, and George H. W. Bush two more. The Supreme Court was shuffling right.

Reagan's nominees were illustrative. Soon after his election, he named an Arizona conservative, Sandra Day O'Connor—the first woman justice—to the court. The Senate consented, 99 to 0. In Antonin Scalia, the president then tapped the pride of Italian America, and (after New York governor Mario Cuomo gave his personal assurance to Senate Democrats that Scalia was no ideologue) the feisty Scalia sailed onto the court by a 98–0 vote. Even Kennedy voted for the conservative Scalia as Senate liberals, in a deliberate calculation, chose to fight William Rehnquist's elevation to chief justice instead. They failed. Kennedy could not attract enough votes to sustain a filibuster, and Rehnquist was confirmed by the Republican-controlled Senate, 65–33, in 1986. By then, only three quite elderly justices from the Warren court remained.

There things stood when Kennedy came to the Senate floor on July 1, 1987—less than an hour after hearing that Reagan had named federal appeals judge Robert Bork to the Supreme Court.

Bork "stands for an extremist view of the Constitution," Kennedy told the Senate. "In the current delicate balance of the Supreme Court, his rigid ideology will tip the scales of justice against the kind of country America is and ought to be." Then came the thunderbolt.

"Robert Bork's America," said Kennedy, "is a land in which women would be forced into back-alley abortions, blacks would sit at segregated lunch counters, rogue police could break down citizens' doors in midnight raids, schoolchildren could not be taught about evolution, writers and artists could be censored at the whim of government, and the doors of the federal courts would be shut on the fingers of millions of citizens for whom the judiciary is—and is often the only—protector of the individual rights that are the heart of our democracy."

His friend Alan Simpson, the Republican from Wyoming, waylaid Kennedy as he left the floor.

"What the hell are you doing?" said Simpson. "I never heard you rant like that."

"We cannot have him," Kennedy said.

KENNEDY'S ATTACK WAS TENABLE. A cadre of conservatives in the Reagan Justice Department, with allies on the campuses and in Republican think tanks, were pushing a right-wing view of the Constitution called originalism. Bork was its premier champion. The Constitution was not a living document, with basic principles that courts could interpret and apply to a society swept by change over the centuries, they said: it was more like the Ten Commandments, etched in stone. The job of a judge was to discern the original intent of the authors, no matter that assault weapons had replaced the musket over the fireplace, or that women—with freedoms garnered by the suffragettes and the science of contraception—were surging into the workplace, or that the government's power to eavesdrop and harass had grown with technological advances the Founders could never imagine, or that minorities faced persisting discrimination that cried out for judicial intervention. All these things were addressable, said Bork, Scalia, and their ideological kindred, but by legislative majorities—not by judges finding "rights."

Originalism was itself a theoretical invention. The Bill of Rights states plainly that the rights of the people are not limited to those enumerated in the Constitution. But Bork's theory acquired political clout, and devotees, because many of the rights "discovered" by the postwar-era courts dealt with tinderbox topics like race, sex, gender, faith, crime, and abortion. Liberal-leaning decisions on the rights of criminal defendants, on police misconduct, on prayer in public schools, on pornography and sexual practices, and on interracial marriage, affirmative action, and busing had made control of the court a vibrant political issue. And American corporations and business executives, chafing at decisions that upheld federal regulation, were pleased to underwrite the Republican campaign. The war that had begun with the filibuster against Abe Fortas and continued through the Haynsworth and Carswell nominations was set to erupt again.

"We would be hard pressed to explain why our ideal vision is not in fact of Judge Bork in action," the White House counsel's office advised Reagan. "He is decidedly unawed by misguided precedent . . . [and] an extraordinarily articulate advocate" of a philosophy "that he himself has greatly helped to define and popularize.

"For Bork there is a clear dividing line . . . between rights contained in the Constitution and rights the courts have made up," the counsel's memo said. "He is solicitous of the former . . . and contemptuous of the latter."

BORK'S NOMINATION WAS A sign of how American politics was becoming acrid in the later Reagan years. The justice he would replace, Lewis Powell, was a reliable voice for prosecutors, corporations, and puritans. But by 1987 he was perceived as moderate because he had been a swing vote, siding with the liberal minority, on issues like abortion, integration, and affirmative action.

Bork, on the other hand, was a provocateur, a witty contrarian, an intellectual. At sixty, the former Yale Law School professor and Nixon-era solicitor general had helped craft the creed for the Right's own "Movement." He had questioned, for instance, the requirement in the 1964 Civil Rights Act that a restaurant owner serve both Black and white patrons. For the state to impose such an onerous requirement on an innkeeper, a barber, or other businessman, Bork wrote in the *New Republic*, was "a principle of unsurpassed ugliness."

Back-alley abortions? In an academic journal in 1971, Bork had attacked the Supreme Court ruling in *Griswold v. Connecticut*, a 1965 case that overruled a state statute banning the use of contraceptives, even by married couples. In the *Griswold* case, the court had found a right of privacy in the Constitution, which was to serve as a foundation for abortion rights in *Roe v. Wade*. Bork called *Roe* "an unconstitutional decision, a serious and wholly unjustifiable judicial usurpation."

Evolution? Bork insisted that the First Amendment applied only to political speech, not literary, scientific, or educational expression, and that it did not bar the practice of religion in public schools.

Rogue police? Bork deplored the rules by which courts excluded evidence tainted by police misconduct.

"Bork . . . was the political operative: brilliant, articulate, opinionated, a scholar, writer, lecturer. He was always in the wings," Kennedy would recall. "They were seeking out judicial activists. . . . [It was a] politicization of the judicial process." Some of the judicial decisions Bork frowned upon were dear to Kennedy. As a senator he had played roles in eliminating the poll tax, passing the Civil Rights Act, regulating government surveillance and defending the Supreme Court's one-man, one-vote decisions. Kennedy saw America as an unfolding promise to folks of all sorts—a progression of inclusion from the white male property owners of the Revolution to emancipated women, Blacks, and other minorities—which Bork and Reagan would curb in favor of a clamoring white, Christian majority. Aide Jeff Blattner had taken the first swing at writing Kennedy's July 1 remarks, and then passed his draft to Carey Parker. "When I got it back it had a zing like biting a jalapeño," Blattner remembered. Kennedy had ordered up "the toughest language he could sustain" after hearing Bork might be named.

———

JUST AS THERE WAS a basis for Kennedy's biting rhetoric, so there was a tactical necessity. At the White House, where Bork and others watched Kennedy's speech over celebratory glasses of champagne, Reagan's advisers had dismissed it. Kennedy had said similarly nasty things about Rehnquist, and where did that get him? He was a political dinosaur—had admitted as much by withdrawing from presidential politics. In the first of many missteps, they missed what was occurring. Kennedy was not barking at the Right—he was pulling a fire alarm for the Left. He was rousing the liberal base, announcing that this was a fight worth making, to which Ted Kennedy would devote his name and talents and organizing skills. He was acting quickly, before wary moderate Republicans and Democrats could announce their approval of the nomination. And he was doing it to inject some political adamantium in the spine of senators who might otherwise want to duck the fight—in particular, the new Judiciary Committee chairman, Joseph Biden of Delaware.

A son of working America with no fancy Ivy League degrees or fortune, Biden was given to insecurity and bouts of braggadocio. In that vein, after taking up the gavel, he had told a reporter from the *Philadelphia Inquirer* that he was not beholden to liberal interest groups and might find his way to vote for a conservative scholar like Bork, just as he had voted for Scalia. "I'm not Teddy Kennedy," Biden said. His days, furthermore, were crowded by a campaign for the presidency, which took him to Iowa, New Hampshire, and elsewhere around the country. Once Kennedy had declared jihad, Biden and his advisers saw that there was hay to be made in the Democratic primaries if he kept Bork off the court—and hell to pay if he did not.

"I spoke right away on Bork . . . to hold people in their place . . . so they had to understand that they were going to have a battle . . . they were going to have accountability on it," Kennedy recalled. "Otherwise, the rhythm of these battles flows in favor of the nominees."

"I wanted to make clear what was at stake," Kennedy said. "The statement had to be stark and direct so as to sound the alarm."

THOUGH A YOUNG TED KENNEDY, in the Fortas wars, had ascribed great sway to President Johnson's authority to choose Supreme Court judges, he and Biden now contended that an acute change in the ideological makeup of the court was reason for the Senate to reject the nominee. Though he failed to stop Rehnquist, Kennedy had succeeded at laying the political groundwork for that argument the previous fall, in the Rehnquist hearings. "We are making headway on the issue of the Senate's right to consider Bork's ideology, since the President so obviously nominated him because of his ideology," Kennedy wrote his old friend Archibald Cox. "But on a vote as close as this is likely to be, there will inevitably be Senators who hesitate." An early head count showed the arduous task ahead: there were thirty-seven senators opposed to Bork, but fifty-eight of their colleagues were already for or leaning toward confirmation.

Biden and Kennedy threw themselves into the fight, Kennedy making call after call after call to liberals, union leaders, and civil rights activists, and Biden huddling with scholars and advisers on how to frame the arguments for the televised hearings ahead. Kennedy's staff prepared briefing books on Bork's swivel-eyed positions, tailored to the interests of individual senators. They kept daily track of unaligned senators and "everything going on in those states and offices" and appointed "constituency captains" to organize the civil rights and women's groups, and other grassroots allies.

During Watergate, in the Saturday Night Massacre of 1973, it had fallen to Bork—the third-ranking official at the Justice Department—to follow Nixon's orders and fire the special prosecutor, Archibald Cox. Kennedy now asked Cox to testify, but Cox demurred, fearing it would look like a personal vendetta. "It was good to talk with you," Kennedy wrote to him in August. "I'm reluctant to press the point further in light of your obviously strong feeling. . . . but the outcome is by no means certain."

"If you don't in some way indicate your opposition, then Bork may well prevail," Kennedy said. "America still remembers you from that day, Archie, and I will not ask you to do something that you feel will tarnish the incredible lesson in integrity you have given the country. But even Yankees come down from Olympus sometimes."

Cox declined. But disarray on the Republican side helped Kennedy's cause. The Reagan administration could not decide if it should sell the judge as a centrist or as a right-wing crusader. Moderates in the White House feared that after losing the Senate and getting tarred by the Iran/Contra scandal, Reagan was in no shape to launch a divisive, ideological war upon individual rights. Instead, they pitched Bork as a "mainstream jurist" in the mold of Lewis Powell, and spent weeks compiling research for that unpersuasive argument. It puzzled their base, baffled the nominee, and inspired a Democratic riposte: Who was the real Bork? "They tried to mask it," Kennedy remembered. Bork was accused of undergoing a "confirmation conversion."

As the Republicans diddled away the August recess, their liberal foes targeted Democratic senators from the South, who now owed their elections to biracial coalitions. Kennedy's office sent personalized letters to sixty-two hundred Black elected officials. His phone calls from the Cape that summer, to civil rights leaders like the Reverend Joseph Lowery, chairman of the Southern Christian Leadership Conference, helped trigger a clamor that reverberated, via telephone calls, letters, and telegrams, in the offices of Democrats Howell Heflin of Alabama, Lloyd Bentsen of Texas, John Breaux of Louisiana, and others.

"Bork is a radical activist dedicated to undoing constitutional law in pursuit of his own reactionary vision," Kennedy wrote the civil rights community. "Everything we have worked for in the past quarter century may be jeopardized if Bork is confirmed and . . . the narrowly divided Supreme Court of today shifts in the direction of Bork's extremist ideology."

In Black churches across the country, preachers took time in Sunday services to help members of their congregation compose letters to their senators. By the time Congress returned in September, even some of Bork's most dedicated backers believed the nomination was in jeopardy. "Kennedy was doing for the anti-Bork effort what the White House political operatives, out of fear of using scarce political capital . . . refused to do" for their nominee, said Biden's counsel, Mark Gitenstein. A dramatic intervention by Reagan might have turned the tide, but he seemed consumed by his own political troubles and his dealings with the Soviets. If Bork was to be saved, the judge would have to save himself.

So STARTED TWELVE DAYS of televised hearings, conducted in the grand arena of the Senate Caucus Room, that high-ceilinged, columned home to historic investigations of the Watergate and Teapot Dome scandals, the sinking of the *Titanic*, the attack on Pearl Harbor, the Vietnam War, organized crime, and the sins of Joc McCarthy. Kennedy had prepared for his role in briefings and dinners with constitutional experts like Kathleen Sullivan of Harvard and Philip Kurland and Cass Sunstein of the University of Chicago. Laurence Tribe, the Harvard law scholar, played Bork in a staged rehearsal. "You can laugh—you're not going up against him tomorrow," Kennedy said to Blattner, when the aide chuckled at one exchange.

A few days before the hearings began, Kennedy sought to soften up the target and flesh out his opposition with a speech at the Georgetown University law school. "Rarely have we had such a combination of circumstances: a Supreme Court so closely divided—and a president so consciously seeking to bend it to his will; a justice resigned who held the decisive balance on many critical issues, yet who defied any ideological category—and a justice nominated who tilts consistently toward one narrow ideological point of view," Kennedy said.

Bork testified for five days, coming across as a fidgety, bearded professor with ideas that, if not merely extreme, at times seemed to border on the kooky. In the first round of questioning, Biden focused on the right of privacy and the *Griswold* ruling. Kennedy followed up on *Griswold*, voting rights, and the one-man, one-vote cases. Bork seemed cold and stilted. Kennedy was relentless. Away from the cameras, Biden doodled scorecards after each exchange: "Kennedy 30, Bork 0."

"Kennedy felt very strongly," Simpson recalled. "He was full bore. He was going to get this guy out of there, by God, and he did. He was never more passionate and never more stubborn. In the hearings he was as close as you could get to punching the guy's lights out."

Kennedy's second-round queries were directed to Bork but aimed at Majority Leader Robert Byrd, who needed coaxing. Byrd, ever watchful of senatorial prerogatives, came out against Bork after Kennedy grilled the judge on past writings extolling the power of presidents at the expense of Congress. In his final turn as an interrogator, Kennedy played a tape of a speech Bork had given in 1985, in which the judge stated, "I don't feel that . . . precedent is all that important" when compared with a justice's ability to contrive "what the framers were driving at." It confirmed some of the worst fears about Bork's own activism.

CONSERVATIVE SCHOLARS AND COMMENTATORS, citing Kennedy's rhetoric and the smooth-running liberal campaign that defeated the judge's nomination, maintain that the nominee was "borked"—a phrase that has entered the political lexicon, implying that someone is a victim of an unfair portrayal. "Kennedy painted a nightmare of fascist repression and attributed it to me," Bork said after his defeat. "Even for a political campaign, it set record lows in mendacity, brutality and intellectual vulgarity."

The truth is, Bork's wounds were self-inflicted. The judge had declined to participate in the full course of staged rehearsals—"murder boards"—recommended by his White House handlers. "It was my fault," said administration lobbyist Tom Korologos. "I should have grabbed him by the lapels and thrown him up against the wall. But everyone thought Bork was going to be brilliant in the hearings. He was the Einstein of the law."

As tens of millions of Americans watched, Bork botched question after question—even softballs lobbed by friendly GOP senators like Hatch and Simpson. At one point, hoping to save Bork from appearing like a heartless egghead, Simpson asked him to tell America why he wanted the job. Oh, it was the clash of ideas, the absorbing debate, the "intellectual feast" of the court, Bork replied. It reinforced the judge's image as a cold fish.

"Instead of saying, 'I want to do justice and show mercy and protect the rights of individuals,' he says, 'It will be an intellectual feast.' And most people said, 'Who's the dinner?'" said Gitenstein.

"Bork came across on television as coldhearted and condescending," wrote the television critic Tom Shales, in coverage that helped him win a Pulitzer Prize. "A dazzling intellect, if that's really what he has, doesn't necessarily guarantee television stardom. . . . [The] shortage of compassion on Bork's part seemed palpable."

If anyone borked Bork it was Bork. "He was not enormously appealing," Kennedy said. "By nature, and disposition, he is arrogant, intellectually arrogant. The stamp on him was that he's an academic elitist who isn't sensitive to the legal problems of ordinary people. That's what nailed him, I think finally, as much as anything." The Senate rejected his nomination 58 to 42, the largest margin of defeat in the history of Supreme Court nominations.

The White House and the Senate ultimately settled on federal appellate judge Anthony Kennedy as the man to fill the empty Supreme Court seat—where he took on Powell's role as a swing vote. Advocates like Ralph Neas still shiver when they think how the aims and brains of a Rehnquist-Bork-Scalia troika might have transformed American jurisprudence. Ted Kennedy "saved us," Neas said. "He bought us twenty-five years."

Kennedy remained sensitive to the charge that his broadside in July had unfairly transformed the terms of Supreme Court confirmation fights, or even that he had strayed from the bounds of fairness.

"I understand the posturing going back and forth in the post-mortem, but I continue to believe that Bork got a fair shake by the Judiciary Committee," he wrote to Simpson when it was over. "He was his own worst witness before the committee.

"Liberals did not beat Bork, and they certainly did not beat him unfairly," wrote Kennedy. "Bork beat Bork."

Twenty-Five

RELAPSE

When he relinquished his presidential ambitions, Kennedy had worried he'd lose influence in the Senate. But in the combat over AIDS, South Africa, the Bork nomination, and other issues in Reagan's second term, Kennedy had shown he was once more, and more so, "a senator to be reckoned with." He had time to focus on his work in the Senate and was freed from the need to scuttle for headlines.

The list of Kennedy's accomplishments after abjuring presidential ambition in December 1985 was considerable. In 1986, he helped orchestrate the vote to override Reagan's veto of economic sanctions on South Africa, to facilitate the Reagan-Gorbachev dialogue, and to extend health insurance coverage via the COBRA program to the nation's unemployed. He also deserves credit for the Emergency Medical Treatment and Active Labor Act (EMTALA), passed that year, which prohibits hospitals from turning away emergency patients and women in labor because they lack health insurance.

In 1987 Kennedy contributed to Bork's defeat. In 1987 and 1988 he helped pass a Civil Rights Restoration Act (overriding a Reagan veto); 1988 also saw passage of the first major AIDS legislation, a bill banning most use of lie detectors by employers on their workers, legislation requiring employers to give workers advance notice of plant closings (circumventing a Reagan veto), and fair housing legislation.

In 1989 Kennedy steered a hike in the minimum wage into law, and in 1990 he followed up with the Americans with Disabilities Act and Ryan White AIDS legislation, and a landmark bill on breast and cervical cancer screening. His decision to chair the Labor panel was paying off: he was leading there, while still playing an influential role on Supreme Court nominations, civil rights, immigration reform, and other issues that came before the Judiciary Committee.

"I have always thought of legislators as people I should persuade," Galbraith wrote him. But now, "repeatedly I pick up the paper and find you articulating the position that I feel I should already have taken."

"In a way it is your misfortune that you are part of such a prodigious family," said Galbraith. "Alone, no one would imagine you had an equal."

THE NEW CHIEF OF STAFF, Ranny Cooper, had brought a new element— whip-smart women—into Kennedy's office. Cooper "put women in high positions," Kennedy's longtime aide Barbara Souliotis would recall. It was "a huge change." Kennedy endeared himself to women's rights activists by sustaining abortion, defeating Bork, and defying Reagan with the Civil Rights Restoration Act. This last was the congressional reply to a Supreme Court ruling involving Grove City College, a small Christian campus in western Pennsylvania. The school accepted no federal money, but the U.S. government contended that because its students took advantage of federal tuition grants and loans, the college was still subject to antidiscrimination law and other regulatory measures. The Supreme Court ruled that the federal laws only applied to the school's admission and student aid office. Liberals petitioned Congress for redress.

Women's groups were particularly concerned. Women had scored great gains in the years since 1972, when Title IX of a federal education law— banning sex discrimination in academic and athletic programs—was adopted. In the decade after Title IX's passage, the number of athletic scholarships for women had leaped from zero to fifteen thousand, and women were entering law and medical schools in record-setting numbers. Kennedy had helped defend Title IX when it came under fire during the

Ford administration, and after Birch Bayh was defeated for reelection in 1980 it was Kennedy who "picked up the mantle" as Title IX's protector, activist Marcia Greenberger recalled.

At first, the Reagan administration held Congress at bay. But then the Democrats took control of the Senate in 1987, and the Restoration Act, with the help of the Leadership Conference on Civil Rights and other liberal organizations, moved through both chambers. "Senator Kennedy's Grove City legislation . . . will change our way of life more drastically than Lyndon Johnson's Great Society programs ever did," the White House warned Republican lawmakers, but Reagan's veto was overridden in 1988, 73–24.

As KENNEDY WAS MAKING the productive transition from presidential candidate to Senate workhorse, away from the Capitol his life was a jumble.

"I don't think he had any psychological thing going that kept him off balance," said Senator John Warner, whose marriage to Elizabeth Taylor had ended in divorce. "He liked to blow off steam. He liked people. Had that Irish blood. And women were attracted to him as an imposing man and a powerful personality. . . . There were women and drink and I joined in both." Others were less sure. "The sense I had," said his old friend and aide Charles Tretter, "was that he was just willing himself to hold it together."

Their friend was "terribly lonely," John Culver recalled. "He'd go back to that big house alone."

Kennedy's divorce had been approved by the courts. Joan had periods of stability, but periodically showed up in police reports, or in traffic court. Ted Jr. and Kara finished college and were out on their own. Teenaged Patrick, after a brief turn living with Ted in McLean (where he would mischievously click the household intercom on and off to disrupt his father's "aggressively single lifestyle"), ultimately left for boarding school. The senator noticed, but chose not to act on, the 3 a.m. withdrawals that Patrick made from ATM machines to buy drugs.

"My dad had a drinking problem and was deeply in denial about it, but, well, he did still function as a U.S. Senator, and a powerful one. So it is unsurprising that he didn't believe in abstinence," Patrick wrote in his memoir, *A Common Struggle*. "Even after I had been in rehab at eighteen, he didn't seem concerned about my drinking. . . . He seemed mostly concerned that I not get into trouble or attract any negative attention to the family." In the decade ahead, all three of Kennedy's children faced substance abuse problems, as did several of their cousins. The brew of celebrity and expectation, death and grief, riches and entitlement and parental instability took a toll. Kennedy strove to maintain family solidarity, attending graduations and weddings, taking his nephews and nieces on trips to the Berkshires or Civil War battlefields or on river rafting excursions. When Caroline Kennedy married, Ted walked her down the aisle. But, if beloved by the next generation, he was a damaged role model. "The killings of my uncles were these giant catastrophic events. The mythic proportions somehow dehumanized the actual events and prevented any real human association," nephew Christopher Lawford recalled. "We had no tools for dealing with any of it, and those who might have provided some were far too devastated themselves to be much help. The only way to survive was to escape."

The Kennedys were celebrated as upbeat, tireless achievers. Acknowledgments of weakness would breach the family code. For many reasons—Irish reticence, the Roman Catholic custom of private confession, Joseph Kennedy's all-consuming focus on victory and imagery—there was no tradition of soul-searching conversation, or contemplative introspection. "In our family, we haven't been the best communicators or the best sharers of feelings," said Kara. In memoirs and interviews, the members of her generation habitually return to this culture of silence, and how it affected them. "Perhaps it was his Irish Catholic upbringing that made it difficult for him to easily talk about intimate feelings," Ted Jr. added. And after Joe Jr., John, and Robert died, "everyone in our family was relying on him to be the strong guy. I think he felt he had to be stoic, even though he was an emotional man."

Kennedy found it challenging to rest. To sail was to relax, but in part because there was a score of things—wind, lines, lunch, currents, political gossip, Neil Diamond on the tape deck—to command his attention and leave him happily spent. "He never relaxed," said Kara. He tried to fill each moment with "activity, fun, laughter."

"We just couldn't go for a normal snorkel or a normal swim . . . or even maybe rent a cottage by the ocean and go down and sit on the beach," said Ted Jr. "He had this beautiful beach on Cape Cod . . . [but] we never once, not once, went down and actually sat on the beach." When a *Boston Globe* reporter compared him to a great white shark, ceaselessly moving to stay ahead of feelings, Kennedy sent back a note with a doodle of a great white, and signed it "Ted the Shark." So the years passed, with unresolved discord.

THE 1980S WERE SOMEWHAT empty years emotionally for the bachelor Kennedy. "You need to deal seriously with your image," wrote Nancy Korman, a friend and Democratic fundraiser, midway through the decade. "Men over 50 who date women under 30 are seen as immature and silly. . . . It is very important to couple Kennedy glamour with some social maturity and cultural substance. You are old enough to have a grown-up social life. Give up the boys, the beer and the playmates."

Kennedy had female friends from his generation, and relationships with accomplished women. He "couldn't have been a sweeter, kinder suitor," said author and diplomat Elizabeth Shannon, the widow of a longtime family friend, whose relationship with Kennedy lasted several years. But she found that he had difficulty articulating feelings and emotions, and preferred raucous times, surrounded by guests, singing and drinking, instead of private moments.

It was "hard for him to relate to women in the way that you would hope that a man in your life would. That relationship is just elusive for him," Shannon said. "He had a lot of, I thought, hangers-on friends who would come and just be there, and he'd have to be on stage for them in a way, to be the way they expected him to be. There were very few times that we got to go off and be by ourselves, and that's when I really enjoyed him the most."

"He likes being surrounded by people. I think that gives him comfort.

If you're alone, you can get a little introspective, and maybe that's not his best role," said Shannon. "So there really was no time to create the kind of intimacy that most people like and seek in a relationship." Korman agreed, and saw Kennedy's reticence as a political liability as well. "You still stumble and stutter whenever you confront a question that has to do with your feelings," she scolded him. "If you do not begin to just talk to women you will not be able to ever deal easily with emotional subject matters."

YOUNGER WOMEN WERE less demanding, and easily moved by his charm and celebrity. "He was an attractive man. He was a Kennedy. There were groupies just like for a rock star," said Melody Miller, a longtime assistant. "Women just followed him." His dalliances with twentysomething blondes, actresses, socialites, and middling Euro-royalty dotted the gossip columns. So did a growing number of occasions when he embarrassed himself in public.

Many stories were harmless, like the accounts of Kennedy and Chris Dodd fencing with gladiolas, or dancing and stomping on each other's framed photographs in the foyer of La Colline, a French restaurant on Capitol Hill. *Laissez les bons temps rouler* was how Kennedy chose to inscribe the portrait he sent to the restaurant as a replacement. Hatch caught Kennedy and Dodd staggering in for a late-night vote in the Senate and elicited Kennedy's promise to host a gathering of the Mormon missionaries at Faneuil Hall in Boston. "Orrin. What else did I promise?" Kennedy asked him the next morning.

Some of his antics might have cost him his career had they happened in a different, less forgiving era. In 1985, while their dates were in the ladies' room, Kennedy and Dodd manhandled a waitress at La Brasserie, a restaurant near the Capitol. After tossing her across a table and into Dodd's lap, Kennedy lewdly rubbed himself against her. In the same establishment, two years later, he was seen having sex on the floor of a private dining room with a woman lobbyist. "There was a lot of stuff slowly eating away at his reputation," said Tunney. "Look at the facts, that's the case."

"This is about relieving the pain," said Patrick Kennedy. "People have this mistaken notion that you get high. What you're really getting is relief from the low."

In the summer of 1987, Kennedy ran his yacht aground late on a Sunday night, prompting panicky guests to call the Coast Guard. At the 1988 Democratic convention in Atlanta, Kennedy showed up smelling of alcohol at a breakfast with *Boston Globe* reporters and editors. In January 1989 at the American Trash bar in New York City, Kennedy got into a sidewalk brawl with another patron in the predawn hours. Paparazzi photographed him atop a young woman in a speedboat on the Riviera. Drunk and unsteady, he challenged his nephew Lawford to a fistfight outside a bistro in Saint Moritz. Editors at the *Washington Post* received evidence of Kennedy using cocaine but chose not to pursue it unless he ran for president.

THE *BOSTON HERALD* WAS particularly adept at chronicling Kennedy's imperfections. The paper's gossip maven, Norma Nathan, tracked his blonde companions, while columnist Howie Carr seared "Fat Boy" for his appetites and staged a remote broadcast of a talk-radio show at the Chappaquiddick cottage. The *Herald* was the tabloid descendant of a long line of Boston's Republican-leaning newspapers. It had been purchased in 1982 by the conservative Australian-born press lord Rupert Murdoch, who brought a cynical business model—dividing Americans and monetizing fear—to the United States and the Fox News Channel at the end of the twentieth century.

To enter the American television market, Murdoch became a U.S. citizen in 1985, and purchased stations in several cities—New York and Boston, most notably—where he also published newspapers. These actions breached a Federal Communications Commission rule that prohibited cross-ownership of newspapers and television stations. The Reagan-era FCC gave Murdoch waivers, and announced its plans to do away with the regulation. Encouraged by Kennedy, Democratic senator Fritz Hollings of South Carolina slipped an amendment into a year-end spending bill. It ordered the FCC to keep the rule in place, and to terminate Murdoch's waiver and compel him to divest. It was passed without debate as part of the larger measure.

Don't get mad, get even. The press lord and his minions bleated that they were the victims of a Kennedy vendetta, orchestrated in the dead of night. But "the people of Massachusetts know what Kennedy did," wrote *Boston Globe* columnist David Nyhan. "The *Herald* has repeatedly and consistently insulted and mocked Kennedy. The *Herald* puts Kennedy through the sheep dip every chance it can, and Kennedy got even. It's called settling a score."

Murdoch went to court and won a preliminary legal skirmish, but ended up selling the television station (which he repurchased later) and keeping the *Herald* (which he ended up selling).

IT IS FAIR TO ask why Kennedy, so skilled at the craft of politics, thought he was immune to the public consequences of his actions. His son Patrick came to believe that resilience in the face of tragedy had a flip side: it persuaded Kennedy that almost any catastrophe was governable and gave him a false sense of impunity. "He managed his life in a way that was full of turmoil, but he always managed to survive, which reinforced his sense that this [the flawed private life] was manageable," Patrick wrote in his memoir. But with each escape, the odds for ruination were catching up.

"Up close, the face is a shock. The skin has gone from red roses to gin blossoms. The tracery of burst capillaries shines faintly through the scaly scarlet patches that cover the bloated, mottled cheeks. The nose that was once straight and narrow is now swollen and bulbous. . . . The Chiclet teeth are the color of old piano keys. The eyes have yellowed too, and they are so bloodshot, it looks as if he's been weeping," wrote journalist Michael Kelly in February 1990. "For his hard public drinking, his obsessive public womanizing and his frequent boorishness he has become a late-century legend . . . a Senator Bedfellow figure, an aging Irish boyo clutching a bottle and diddling a blonde."

—————

KENNEDY'S CONDUCT in Palm Beach over Easter weekend in 1991 was in keeping with Kelly's description. On Wednesday, he picked up a woman at a shopping center nightclub called Au Bar and brought her back to the Kennedys' seaside estate. On Good Friday, he woke up his son Patrick and nephew William Kennedy Smith and asked that they return with him to Au Bar for more post-midnight revelry. There, he picked a fight with Anne Mercer, a striking but dull blonde who was mocking Patrick.

Meanwhile, her friend Patricia Bowman, a single mom of twenty-nine years, was dancing with the thirty-year-old Smith, and accepted his invitation to go back to the Kennedy villa. Smith and Bowman walked on the beach and had sex on the mansion grounds. Later, he claimed their lovemaking was consensual. But she was distressed. She telephoned Mercer from the mansion and said she had been raped. The police, doctors, and rape counselors who examined Bowman believed her.

"Let's face it," William vanden Heuvel told his friend Arthur Schlesinger, when accounts of the incident dominated the news. "Teddy is an alcoholic."

"He is . . . a formidable figure, a model for the young Kennedys and no doubt they feel they must match him, drink for drink," Schlesinger wrote in his diary. "One cannot escape the feeling that Ted has some impulse of self-destruction buried within. Yet such a fine senator. It is all too sad."

On Easter Sunday, after church, Ted Kennedy was seen at a Palm Beach bar downing several drinks in rapid order. That afternoon, when the police called at the mansion to interview him, a family friend who answered the door told them—falsely—that he was not home. For that, Kennedy came under investigation for obstructing justice. Ultimately, no charges were pressed against the senator, but Smith was charged with rape and battery. Three more young women came forward with accusations, each describing how Smith had sexually assaulted her. One said she was raped, the other two said they fought him off.

The scandal attracted the biggest collection of reporters and cameramen since that winter's Persian Gulf War. Patrick had also brought a young woman home on Friday night, and she told reporters a weird tale of a pantless Ted Kennedy tipsy and leering and wobbling around the grounds of the estate clad only in a shirt or nightshirt. The nation's comedians had sport with that image for weeks. "Ted's many virtues as a public man are being subverted and destroyed by his many frailties as a private man," Schlesinger told his diary. "I feel more keenly than ever that the best thing he can do for himself, for the Kennedys, for all American alcoholics and for the country would be to declare himself an ill man, go to Hazelden, dry out and sober up, and stay off the sauce forever. But how to persuade him to do something like this?"

Kennedy's life was the story of "the youngest son of a famous family who is surrounded by death and disappointment and, somewhere within, must feel so diminished, so unworthy of his brothers' accomplishments, that he runs for liquor or for women," wrote another friend, Mike Barnicle, in the *Boston Globe*. The Palm Beach affair was "quite simply, the end of Edward Kennedy's life in politics. If he indeed runs again, he will positively be beaten by any credible candidate." Kennedy's reelection campaign polls showed him losing to Massachusetts governor William Weld in a prospective matchup.

AMID ALL THIS, Justice Thurgood Marshall announced he was retiring from the U.S. Supreme Court. On July 1, President George H. W. Bush named Clarence Thomas, a federal appellate judge, to replace him. With his own behavior under scrutiny, Kennedy would now be asked to pass judgment on a conservative nominee who, as it turned out, had character issues of his own.

His biography was the most compelling reason Clarence Thomas was named to the Supreme Court. "The mythology of Clarence Thomas [was] a mythology that every American could identify with," said his friend Phyllis Berry Myers. He was born in a shanty in Pin Point, Georgia, to a teenage mother, then raised in his grandfather's home in Savannah and educated in all-Black Catholic schools. He briefly considered the priesthood before graduating with honors from Holy Cross College and enrolling in law school at Yale. As a young lawyer, he found a mentor—Missouri's attorney general and soon-to-be senator, John Danforth—and joined the Republican Party. He embraced conservative principles, and when Reagan captured the White House, Thomas joined the administration. He hired a fellow Yale law graduate, Anita Hill, for his staff, and she followed him to the Equal Opportunity Employment Commission when he was named its chairman in 1982. In 1990, George H. W. Bush had made Thomas a judge.

When facing the Senate, Bush's first Supreme Court nominee, New Hampshire judge David Souter, had used a technique very different from that employed by Bork. When asked in his confirmation hearings about contentious issues, Souter had not taken the bait. Instead of debating the senators, he contended that the call of judicial objectivity required he not answer. To assure the senators that he was no radical, he promised to honor precedent. Kennedy decided to vote against him, but not to lead a full-scale campaign. Upon hearing that news in a phone call, Republican senator Warren Rudman of New Hampshire hung up and told his friend Souter his confirmation was assured.

Thomas followed much the same strategy when he came before the Judiciary Committee in the summer of 1991. He met with Kennedy in the senator's hideaway office in the Capitol, accompanied by Danforth. In a forty-five-minute session, the senator sought to form a bond by describing his family's own encounters with anti-Irish discrimination. He found Thomas open and accessible, but somewhat overwhelmed. He tried, without success, to get Thomas to reflect on issues he would face as a Supreme Court justice.

The judge was no Bork—no legal scholar with a paper trail for Kennedy and others to scrutinize. Nor was Kennedy—the butt of late-night monologues and attack ads funded by right-wing groups—in a position to summon liberals to arms. The Democrats had built a commanding advantage—57 to 43—over the Republicans in the Senate. But the NAACP and other civil rights organizations initially balked at opposing a Black nominee and thus risking the African American presence on the Supreme Court. And Danforth, who was serving as a Sherpa for Thomas in the Senate, was an ally with Kennedy and Senate liberals in their struggle with the Bush administration over the pending Civil Rights Act of 1991 which, among other provisions, provided a legal remedy to the victims of sexual harassment. Thomas was not a movement conservative, only an opportunist, the SCLC's Joseph Lowery assured Kennedy: "Clarence drove up the right lane because the left lane was crowded." As the Left temporized, the White House capitalized on its hesitance. Thomas waffled on the issue of abortion, which alarmed women's groups, but it seemed too late to stop the nomination. The Senate seemed poised to give its consent.

What happened next became the subject of an FBI probe, a new round of Judiciary Committee hearings, and a special counsel's investigation. While working for Thomas before he was a judge, Hill had felt sexually harassed. Thomas had pressed her to date him, she said, told her graphic accounts of the pornographic films he enjoyed, and boasted of his sexual prowess. She was twenty-five years old. Ultimately, she left his staff and moved to an Oklahoma law school.

Hill had told her story to just enough friends that her name surfaced on the Washington grapevine. Ricki Seidman, who was working for Kennedy as a committee investigator, chanced upon the tale while checking out Thomas's background. Seidman spoke to Hill but was told by her bosses to stand down: with Willie Smith's trial scheduled to begin that fall, Kennedy and his advisers concluded that the senator was in no position to be grilling anyone about sex. Seidman referred Hill to Biden's staff; the chairman then notified the White House and called in the FBI. The story broke in the press on October 5 and the protagonists were called to testify.

THE BORK-SLAYER—the senator with impeccable civil rights credentials and a demonstrated ability to rally the liberal community—would sit it out. Slouched next to Biden, looking grimly uncomfortable, Kennedy "wasn't there for us," Judith Lichtman recalled. "Viscerally and visually he was getting smaller and smaller . . . just sinking into his chair . . . becoming

TED KENNEDY

a little shriveled man." Had it not been for Ted Kennedy's Palm Beach transgressions, Thomas might well have been kept off the Supreme Court.

Both Thomas and Hill were Black. But Thomas successfully cast his ordeal in racial terms. On prime-time television on a Friday night he denied all of Hill's accusations, denounced the Senate, and claimed to be the victim of "a high-tech lynching for uppity blacks." The tactic worked. "As the overnight polls showed, by playing the race card . . . Thomas could win the victim sweepstakes. A professional woman's complaints about sexual mistreatment on the job had no chance against a black man's claim to being lynched simply because he dared to think independently," wrote journalists Jane Mayer and Jill Abramson.

The hearings, however, had become a climactic moment in the changing relationship between American men and women. Over the course of the previous quarter century, women had been rising in number and prominence in politics, the press, and other professions, and few had not encountered some sort of discrimination, rude treatment, or harassment from boorish colleagues or predatory bosses. Hill's story rang true to these women. The aging male senators "just don't get it," they said. A squad of congresswomen marched across the Capitol grounds, intent on disrupting the Senate's comfy club. Major media outlets dropped their weekend lineups to cover the hearings.

If evidence was needed to support the feminist complaint, the Republicans now supplied it. They cast Hill as "a little bit nutty and a little bit slutty," as one conservative polemicist wrote. She was a woman whose affections had been spurned by Thomas, his defenders contended. Or she was a liberal tool, or suffered from fantasies, or frustrated ambition, or a psychological disorder called "erotomania," said otherwise decent men like Simpson and Danforth.

Meanwhile, Kennedy's strategy of maintaining a low profile backfired. Seated beside Biden, he was constantly on camera, absently doodling (sailboats), frowning and conspicuously silent. When he objected to the tone of one of Republican senator Arlen Specter's questions, the Pennsylvanian mocked him: "If Senator Kennedy has anything to say, let him participate in this hearing." Kennedy's discomfort was so striking, and the chorus of criticism grew so loud—not least among the women on his staff—that he felt compelled to change his tactics on Sunday, the last day of the hearings. A friend of Hill, watching television with her, was startled and blurted out, "He speaks!"

"I hope we are not going to hear a lot more comments about fantasy stories," Kennedy said, referring to the Republican line of questioning. "I hope we can clear this room of the dirt and innuendo . . . about over-the-transom information . . . about proclivities. We heard a good deal about character assassination yesterday, and I hope we are going to be sensitive to the attempts of character assassination on Professor Hill. They are unworthy. They are unworthy."

Two days too late, he dismissed Clarence Thomas's claim of being victimized by a high-tech lynching. "I hope we are not going to hear a lot more about racism," said Kennedy. "The fact is that these points of sexual harassment are made by an Afro-American against an Afro-American. The issue isn't discrimination and racism. It is about sexual harassment, and I hope we can keep our eye on that."

But Simpson, Hatch, and Specter knew they had won. They grinned at Kennedy as he made his remarks. They were ready for him, too, when he deplored their "shameful" tactics in a speech on the Senate floor.

"Are we an old boy's club—insensitive at best, and perhaps something worse?" Kennedy asked.

Specter roasted Kennedy as a hypocrite—the last one in the chamber to be talking about moral standards. "We do not need characterizations like 'shame' in this chamber from the senator from Massachusetts," he said.

And Hatch piled on. If anyone believed Kennedy, "I know a bridge up in Massachusetts that I'll be happy to sell to them," he said.

It was a disaster all around. The embittered Thomas was confirmed by an historically slender margin of 52 to 48. The writers at *Saturday Night Live* portrayed Kennedy as an addled skirt-chaser, offering Thomas tips on technique: "Another good thing is to get them out on your boat for some reason," said the Kennedy character to the actor playing Thomas, "because then it's really hard for them to get away."

"There were a lot of people who were disappointed," said Hill. "Here is somebody who has been so outspoken, and so well spoken, in the past and he put himself in the position of allowing people like Arlen Specter to silence him."

"It really did come to a head in those hearings: this disconnect between many of the principles he had espoused publicly and the things that he had allegedly done personally," Hill recalled. "If you really care, you better live it. And if you don't, if you're not willing to live it, then someone's going to come around and point out that you're a hypocrite."

ATTENTION WAS NOW FOCUSED, as at no time since Chappaquiddick, on Kennedy's lifestyle. In June, the *Boston Globe* sent a reporter to confront the senator: Did he have a drinking problem? Was his bloated, red-faced countenance the result of alcoholism, or other illness? Was he well enough, and did he possess the dedication, to serve another term?

"I have never felt I had a problem," Kennedy said. He vowed to run again in 1994. His drinking was under control, he insisted. He promised to "be a little more attentive to behavior," but "I don't know what they're driving at," he said of friends who had shared their concerns with the newspaper.

"He's a sick man. . . . His life is a true tragedy, and true tragedies end tragically," a friend had told the *Globe*. Another said, "Ninety-five percent of the time he's working hard. The other five percent of the time, he has a need to anesthetize the pain."

Kennedy bristled and answered, "No," when asked if he had sought professional help or joined Alcoholics Anonymous. He agreed to release his medical records, but by evening he had reneged on that promise. Instead, adviser Larry Horowitz was made available to answer questions about his former boss's use of liquor. "My definition of an alcoholic is someone who seems dependent and unable to function unless alcohol is available," the doctor said. "I don't see how, by any definition, that fits him. How ever could he function in that fishbowl over that long a time? You cannot hide his public performance."

Years later, another aide, Ronald Weich, turned the question around.

"He had alcohol issues," said Weich. "He struggled with alcohol." But the tragedy and hardship in his life left him a workaholic as well. "Work was a balm to him. . . . He was constantly, constantly working."

It was a fallback position for pols like Kennedy: however much they drank, it did not interfere with their public duties. He was a big man, with a mighty thirst, and a capacity that in most instances matched his appetite. "Does he drink? Sure. Teddy obviously drinks," Richard Goodwin told the newspaper. "Does he drink too much? To keep himself from being effective? Well, he seems to be as effective as can be in the Senate."

"He likes women. I've seen him with a lot of women. I've never seen him treat women disrespectfully," said Goodwin. "I mean, if they want to go to bed with a guy, should they be deprived of that right? It's sort of antifeminist, actually, to not have that attitude because it implies that somehow women are helpless victims of Teddy. And as far as I know they are all mature and what they are doing is voluntary and even desired."

Aides like Thomas Rollins, colleagues like Thomas Harkin and Wyche Fowler, and nephews like Anthony Shriver all shared memories with a common theme: of being flabbergasted by the alcohol they would see Kennedy consume, and still find him functioning the next morning— hard at work or whipping them in a 7 a.m. tennis match.

The Thomas hearings, however, told a different story. However much he denied it, his private behavior was affecting his public performance. Kennedy was at the halfway mark in his six-year term, and his actions caused the liberal editorial page of his hometown paper to wonder if he deserved another.

"Those who have generally supported Kennedy over the years—and we include ourselves in that number—have maintained that his private behavior, however reprehensible one judges it to be, has not adversely affected his performance as a public official," the *Globe* wrote. "Sadly, that contention can no longer be made." Chappaquiddick, Palm Beach, "and other, periodic reports of reckless behavior by Kennedy have diminished his moral authority."

"Sen. Kennedy is up for reelection in 1994 and has said he will run again. He will have to do so realizing that neither he nor his supporters can again assert that his private life has had no impact on the discharge of his public duties."

Kennedy was scheduled to speak at Harvard that week, at the twenty-fifth anniversary celebration of the Institute of Politics at the John F. Kennedy School of Government. People depended on him to "fight the good fight," and his drinking was affecting his ability to do so, he conceded. "I recognize my own shortcomings," he said, and promised that "I am the one who must confront them."

The reviews were not uniformly good. "What he was on the day of the speech was an almost 60-year-old divorced man who drank too much, an aging father and uncle who was the caretaker of a spectacular array of functional and dysfunctional children, and that was all he was, and the barstools are full of them," Charles Pierce, an admirer, would write in the *Boston Globe*. "By then the woman in the car had been dead for 22 years . . . and if this was an epiphany it was a damn slow one."

There was pathos in his testimony, and his countenance, when Kennedy took the stand at the Smith trial in December. During pretrial motions, Judge Mary Lupo excluded the testimony of the three women who alleged that Smith had on other occasions assaulted them. The ruling scuppered the prosecution's case. The victim's friend, Anne Mercer, was an awful witness, admitting on the stand that she had sold her story to the tabloid news shows and otherwise undermining Patricia Bowman's testimony. Bowman was persuasive, but after Smith took the stand and insisted the sex was consensual, the jury was left with reasonable doubt, and voted swiftly to acquit.

Kennedy was a witness, called by the prosecution. Ranny Cooper, Carey Parker, and the staff—and former aide Greg Craig, a Washington lawyer—had exhaustively prepped him. He had not seen Smith and Bowman at the mansion, Kennedy testified, and could contribute nothing but an account of how the night's events began. Haltingly, he told the jury that he had spent the evening hours reminiscing with his sister Jean and others about Robert Kennedy and her husband, Stephen, who had died of cancer in 1990. Overcome with emotion and unable to sleep, he rousted Patrick and Willie to return to the pickup bar. "I wish I had gone for a long walk on the beach instead," he said.

Willie Smith went free, but immense damage had been done. Florida had a strong open-records law, and the investigative reports and depositions were all released to the media. It seemed a sordid tale about the appetites of trashy rich folks and the pilot fish who swam among them.

KENNEDY WAS, FUNDAMENTALLY, UNREPENTANT.

"There came a point in my own life when I had to admit that I'd stopped looking forward to things . . . especially experiences that involved new personal commitments," he wrote in his memoirs. The pain of so much loss had seared him. Yet "I am an enjoyer," he said. "I've enjoyed books and music and well-prepared food, especially with a generous helping of cream sauce on the top. I have enjoyed the company of women. I have enjoyed a stiff drink or two or three.

"At times I've enjoyed these pleasures too much," he wrote. "It was all part of my desire to escape, to keep moving, to avoid painful memories. And so I lived this string of years in the present tense, not despondently, because that is not my nature, but certainly with a sense of the void."

He was also disingenuous. "My friends didn't tell me that my drinking or my private life was getting out of control, but maybe that's because we were all having too much fun," he wrote. In fact, John Culver had warned him, and been cut out of Kennedy's life for a time for daring to say so. And after the Palm Beach verdict his children confronted him at his McLean home.

"Looking back, what we were saying was a pretty modest, watered-down intervention," Patrick recalled. "We had our heads between our knees, almost, saying, 'Dad, we're concerned, we're worried about you and we think you're drinking too much.'" They told him that his drinking threatened to drive the family apart. "And then we all cried."

It didn't register. "He took it the exact opposite way we had hoped," Patrick recalled. They were abandoning him, Kennedy said. They were taking sides with the critics, who could never comprehend how much he had endured. He stalked from the room. On New Year's Day, Kennedy sent Patrick a six-page letter. He told his son that he had been undergoing counseling from a doctor, and a priest. But he raged against the notion that his behavior endangered the family.

"What in heaven's sake does anyone think has been on my mind day and night, in restless dreams and sleepless nights—My God, Our family— my sisters and the cousins and the brutality of treatment to John and Bobby and I wonder how much I am to blame for all of this," he wrote. He suggested that he and Patrick not see each other for a while. "This letter sounds like it's written in bitterness. It isn't. It's written with great disappointment and enormous sadness and I thought 1991 was over. Love, Dad."

Though Kennedy softened his stance, Patrick told his dad that he would not attend the upcoming birthday celebrations unless the senator agreed to stop drinking. "When he wouldn't agree to get treatment, I didn't go to any of his sixtieth-birthday parties," Patrick would recall.

Twenty-Six

A DIFFERENT KIND
OF DEMOCRAT

When Ted Kennedy gave his "shortcomings" speech at Harvard, few had noticed, and none commented upon, the dark-haired woman in attendance. It was not until March 1992, after her six-year-old daughter spilled the secret on a Washington, DC, playground, that word of an impending wedding made its way to the *Washington Post*. When columnist Lois Romano called Paul Donovan, the senator's spokesman, he chuckled. If his boss was getting married, he assured her, he would know. But after checking up the line, the startled Donovan and his colleagues started working the telephone, calling the national and Boston media with an announcement. The boss was indeed engaged.

The dark-haired woman was Victoria Reggie. She was a talented lawyer, thirty-seven, of Lebanese ancestry, divorced, and the mother of two young children, Caroline, six, and Curran, nine. Her parents, Edmund and Doris Reggie of Crowley, Louisiana, were longtime political allies of the Kennedy family, a bond that dated back to the 1956 Democratic convention when Edmund had joined in the unsuccessful drive to get John Kennedy the vice presidential nomination. Twenty years later, after Vicki graduated magna cum laude from Sophie Newcomb, the women's college at Tulane University (she would hike that to summa at the Tulane law school), the straight-A student—"She made a B once in school and we [still] hate that teacher," her father said—spent a summer, unnoticed, as an intern in Kennedy's Senate office.

In the early 1980s, the Reggie family bought a home on Nantucket. When sailing to the island, Kennedy regularly dropped by—on one occasion with three young women as his shipmates, to have Doris rechristen his new boat with a bottle of champagne. Vicki was there on a 1987 visit—a picnic on the beach—and heard him talk about the Bork nomination. She was interested. This was a side of Ted Kennedy, she told herself, that she had not seen. "He was a person who prepared and thought and was intellectual," she recalled. "I found that very intriguing." As for Vicki, then a married mom, Kennedy still "didn't even know who she was," her father remembered.

It was not until June 1991, when she hosted a fortieth anniversary dinner for her parents at her Washington home, that their relationship began. They had run into each other around town, where he was his usual buoyant and flirtatious self. But she had expected Kennedy to bring a female companion that evening, and when he showed up alone at her doorway, she teased him, "What's wrong? Couldn't you get a date?" Now he was intrigued. He helped her prepare the meal and, as they said good night, invited her out to dinner. The next day he sent flowers. They dated all summer. By September he was stopping by her home most every night, and they were attending Mass together on Sunday. One evening, when she was repeatedly called from the dinner table to a child's bedside, he told her not to worry. "A child calling 'Mother' is the most beautiful sound in the world," he said.

It was a unique courtship. She needed to be with the kids most nights, and so they spent hours just keeping each other company, talking mostly about family and life. Her home was a welcome, quiet getaway from the tumult of the Willie Smith saga. Her mother urged her to be careful—a man like that could give you sorrow. But her father believed that Kennedy was "coming out of his black period," had resolved to stop "being a bad boy," and that Vicki could lug him the last few yards. Ted promised her exclusivity but cautioned that it might take a little time for him to politely close down his other relationships.

Before their public debut as a couple, Kennedy was snappish and quarrelsome with his staff. "Then Vicki arrives," aide Trina Vargo recalled. "He immediately was the calmest, nicest person and I realized that he might have been nervous about her . . . [because] the minute he saw her, everything was okay. . . . She calmed him, relaxed him, gave him something else."

Kennedy asked her to marry him at a performance of *La bohème* at the Metropolitan Opera in New York in January, two weeks after his children had pleaded with him to change. He was about to turn sixty, in counseling, and, evidently, serious about what he had told the audience at Harvard that fall: he would be more attentive to his personal life. Rather than spend Easter at Palm Beach, Kennedy took Vicki to the Virgin Islands, where, while snorkeling, he pointed at an engagement ring he had set among the coral. She was with him when he hosted Gorbachev at the John F. Kennedy Library in May. On July 3, at his home in McLean, they were married.

There was tension, as in many second marriages, with Kennedy's older offspring. Patrick did not attend the wedding. And though Kennedy's three children were quick to give Vicki credit for helping him turn his life around, they found it hard to acknowledge their father's affection for a new wife and family. "I was surprised when he made the decision to get remarried," Ted Jr. recalled. "I mean, he dated a lot of wonderful women, he had wonderful friends, he had a wonderful family, loved spending time with them, so my thinking was, *why do you need a wife*—Right?—*when you have all of that?*" At the same time, "Vicki was really helpful. . . . I think she really helped him work harder and focus and direct himself." Kara came to see Vicki "as a partner in everyday life or in political life. She's smart. She's a great sounding board."

"His personal life was becoming a big issue, and Vicki really was somebody who gave him some stability," Patrick concluded. "She was a great source of strength and political stability, definitely, no question about it. And I think personally, there's no question that she was very helpful to him in bringing some focus . . . back on what he loved to do so much in his work."

———

Vicki loved deeply and saw in Ted a generous, and wounded, human being. "Lonely. He was always lonely," she said. They shared a love of laughter, and she learned to share his love for sailing. He gave her a small sailboat, named *La Bohème*, and followed her in a tender, calling out instructions as she circled inside the breakwater at the Cape. She was his greatest fan and defender and champion, and—he would discover, and marvel at how much the discovery meant to him—she insisted that he learn to forgive, and accept, and love himself.

Vicki leaped to her feet and silenced him with an epithet when he started to tell a roomful of friends and advisers how they, and the family legacy, deserved the credit for a hard-fought victory.

"This victory isn't about me," he was saying.

"Bullshit!" she said, then called him out. "If you had lost, it would've been you that lost. It wouldn't have been your family. . . . *You* would've lost," she said. He needed to give himself credit. "*You* won. *You* won! Not your family. You."

He never forgot. "Her message to me was one I needed to hear," he would say. "One I'd yearned to hear."

"Kennedy was at his best when he was uninhibited and confident in being able to speak the way he felt and say what he believed," said former aide Gregory Craig. But "when people surrounded him, making him feel as though he was on thin ice . . . he could embarrass himself or he would humiliate himself or wasn't up to the job. . . . One of the greatest things Vicki Kennedy ever did for Edward M. Kennedy was to release him from his own sense of inadequacy."

Each year at his office Christmas Party, Kennedy dressed in a silly costume. Now he and Vicki came as couples: as Scarlett and Rhett, or, in 1993, as Beauty and the Beast. There were lame jokes about how he had been tamed, and the horns he wore, which kept slipping from his head.

At one point she reached up to reposition his wig, paused to stroke his cheek, and murmured, "Poor beast." He left the party with a mighty grin, waddling down the corridor, Beauty at his side, shouting instructions over his shoulder to aides about a memo on health care reform.

By his new children's account, he was a fine stepfather. He made it home for dinner at 7:15 p.m. He played cards with Curran and Caroline and taught them the time-efficient game of Kennedy speed chess. He showed up at their sports events and brought them to Cape Cod to meet their new pack of cousins. To help Caroline through the sometimes Darwinian family rites and rituals, he would challenge her: "Don't you want to be a ruff-tuff-'em? I'm a ruff-tuff-'em. He's a ruff-tuff-'em. Let's go all be ruff-tuff-'ems."

Curran and Caroline entered a world where it was not remarkable to find Shelby Foote engaged as their tour guide at Civil War battlefields, Broadway stars singing at Ted's birthday parties, or Robert Caro sleeping in the guest room after offering Kennedy and his Senate colleagues a seminar on the history of the filibuster. When they grew older and angered their mother with (the usual) high school transgressions, they trusted Ted to intercede. "All right," he would say, "this is what you are going to do," and then he would sketch out a plan of action, based on his own considerable experience.

Once, when Vicki took Caroline for a stern talking-to in her car, Ted followed behind in a van with Curran. "Ted gets behind the driver's wheel," Curran remembered, "and he goes, 'Curran, my boy, there are few places and few times in your life that you will be happier than you are right now. . . . Remember this, when you think it's always bad. It's not always bad. You're in the van today.'"

Ted and Vicki were dog-lovers. They adopted two-year-old Splash, and then Sunny, a puppy, both Portuguese water dogs. Kennedy brought Splash to work, where he sat by his master's side and followed him around all day. In fine weather, the senator could be seen on the Capitol grounds, carrying a poop bag and hitting balls with a tennis racket for the dog to chase. Returning from a funeral with Senator John Kerry, and claiming that his back was ailing, Kennedy had a limo driver stop the car so that Kerry could hit a few fungoes and move Splash to relieve himself. Kerry rolled his eyes—but complied.

VICKI WAS SAVVY ABOUT men and marriage. She took no guff, was protective and vigilant: the era of boozy nights at American Trash or Au Bar was over. No matter the strength of their attraction, she said, she would not have a man whose behavior would hurt her children. They sold the McLean house and moved into the city, to a fine home amid the embassies in northwest Washington. Friends from Kennedy's playboy past, like Tunney, were bruised by her decision that their visits were an unwelcome influence. But they could not deny her contribution to his well-being.

In the years before Vicki, his friend Ted suffered "an ever-increasing sense of despair," said Tunney—a feeling by Kennedy that he was "heading down a road that's going to end in catastrophe, either . . . eliminated by some wild man who wants to take out the third Kennedy boy, or just self-destruction."

"Vicki represented . . . a way out. . . . That relationship, that love that developed . . . was a much more mature feeling than the love that he might have had for others . . . when it was more fun and games," said Tunney. "Vicki . . . had a bad marriage and she was divorced. She's attractive looking and she's smart as hell and she's got a very lovely way of emoting and facilitating conversation, and she's warm," said Tunney. "I think that Teddy . . . was definitely looking for a sea anchor to windward—and all of a sudden the radar . . . begins to focus.

"If it had come about ten years earlier it might not have been there, you see—his radar may not have been turned on." But "he had a terrific political sense and he had to know that he was heading into the seas between Scylla and Charybdis and that those clashing rocks were going to sink him if he didn't get some change of focus and direction. It's the kind of thing that no man could ever really get him to do. I don't think even his father could have gotten him to do it. I don't think Bobby or Jack could have gotten him to do it. . . . It took a woman like Vicki to do it. She was there and she loved him.

"I think that she deserves a huge amount of credit for having given him the stability and the constancy and the love that he needed to bring him through this extraordinary period. It wasn't major despair—because if it had been major despair it could have killed him. But it was a minor despair that he had to come to grips with . . . and he did, when he had her at his side."

KENNEDY DIDN'T STOP DRINKING, but he got his thirst under control. With Vicki, he had found a warmer, richer anodyne for pain. "She has brought me . . . emotional stability," Kennedy said in the fall of 1993. He added, lapsing into Tedspeak, that their relationship had "an enormously constructive impact on my life and my happiness." If Kennedy now indulged, it was at the dinner table. "Sauces? I know what I like and, unfortunately, the more the better," he admitted: béarnaise on the tenderloin and hollandaise on the broccoli. As he settled into his more sedate sixties, his natural inclination to put on weight caught up with him and he was captured by photographers in unattractive poses: big-bellied on the dock on Cape Cod or catching his breath on a bench in Boston. For years he had performed a Lenten fast, dieting and cutting back on alcohol, subsisting on salads or protein shakes. Now he found it too oppressive, and the pounds accumulated.

VICKI WAS ALSO A CATHOLIC, and Kennedy's faith began to play a more important, and comforting, role in his life. He asked the church to annul his marriage to Joan so he could participate in the sacraments. After one argument left Ted and Vicki irate and fuming, he called home at midmorning to see if she would join him at a midweek Mass on Capitol Hill. At the point in the liturgy where the faithful "offer each other the gift of peace," they embraced and forgave.

His lack of introspection and self-reflection troubled her. "As gregarious

as he might have seemed, in many ways Teddy was basically a shy person,"
Vicki said. "Small talk and self-revelation were not his strong suits."
Kennedys were Irish, stoics, fatalists. She regretted he would not discuss
feelings. Lamenting loss, he said, was "bellyaching." On the other hand,
"he was never, *never* bitter," she recalled. "He could have checked out.
Why didn't he? He fundamentally really did believe Luke 12. ["To whom
much is given, much is required."] Deeply."

His stepchildren were impressed. "He never talked about himself . . .
[he] sacrificed himself," said Caroline Raclin. "I'm not saying Jesus here,
but I'm saying he spent a lot of time helping other people, when it might
have been more beneficial—more selfish, more beneficial to himself—to
spend that time on him. He wore himself thin."

LIKE TED, Vicki had grown up at a lively dinner table where, in the jawing with her parents and five siblings, politics was a staple. She accepted
that her husband had a need to repair his image. Over Labor Day weekend in 1992, the couple led a steady march of camera crews, television
correspondents, and feature writers through the compound in Hyannis
Port. With inexhaustible vitality, they told the story of their courtship over
and again, as if for the first time every time: the meeting at her parents'
doorway; the Halloween night that he took her children trick-or-treating;
the daffodils he painted and gave her as a wedding present; the big grou-
per that swam by in the Virgin Islands, and how Ted feared it would eat
the engagement ring.

Their performance was so effective that it dimmed, for all but a few
cynics, the notion that the marriage was staged for political effect. It was
surely not. Yet she was a political partner, not just a mate. "Alone, on the
campaign trail, without Vicki, Kennedy might seem nothing but spectacle, all bloat and tremor," the *New Yorker* reported.

In the summer of 1993, they joined President Bill Clinton and his wife,
Hillary, and Jacqueline Onassis and her companion, Maurice Tempelsman, on Tempelsman's seventy-foot yacht, the *Relemar*, for a luncheon
cruise from Menemsha on the Vineyard.

"Teddy, you go down and greet the president," Onassis told him.

He wavered. "Maurice is already there," he said.

"You do it," Onassis ordered. "Maurice isn't running for reelection."

No, he was not. Ted Kennedy was the one running for reelection, and despite the Ted and Vicki show, he was not faring well.

SOME OF KENNEDY'S TROUBLES could be traced to his yachting guests. He was a latecomer to the Clinton telenovela. Massachusetts had a wealth of political talent and ambition and to keep peace in the house, Kennedy made it his practice to endorse presidential candidates from the commonwealth. In 1992, he had signed on with his former seatmate, Paul Tsongas, who battled Clinton in the primaries. The touts believed that George H. W. Bush, riding high in the polls after drubbing Iraq in the Persian Gulf War, had his reelection clinched. But after Clinton disposed of Tsongas, Kennedy urged his national security adviser, Nancy Soderberg, to accept an invitation to go to Little Rock and work for the Arkansas governor's campaign.

"You've got to do it. He's going to win," Kennedy said.

"You're a hopeless romantic," she replied.

"I may be a hopeless romantic," he said, "but on this one I'm right."

"Are you serious?"

"Yes," he said. "Go do it."

She did. Clinton claimed the nomination. And in the fall campaign, Kennedy and the band all did what they could do. The Democrats regained the White House after winning a three-way race against independent businessman Ross Perot and Bush, whose domestic tribulations overshadowed his foreign policy achievements.

Clinton impressed the Kennedys when, on the eve of the inauguration, he joined them in prayer at the graves in Arlington. When Kennedy asked the new president to name Jean Kennedy Smith as the U.S. ambassador to Ireland, Clinton went along. In doing so, Kennedy squelched the hopes of his friend, Elizabeth Shannon, and of Representative Brian Donnelly of Dorchester, an ally in Congress. Kennedy told Shannon he felt compelled to do it, to patch things up with his sister after he had enlisted her son Willie in the night of ribaldry in Florida. "Jean is furious with me," he said. Smith had no foreign policy or diplomatic experience, but her performance as America's ambassador was outstanding, and so something good came from the Palm Beach fiasco.

IT TOOK TWO ATTEMPTS, but Kennedy won a coveted promotion for his former aide, Judge Stephen Breyer, as well. In the spring of 1994, Clinton named Breyer to fill a vacancy on the U.S. Supreme Court—in part because of Kennedy's mastery and tenacity.

Kennedy had lobbied Clinton on Breyer's behalf in 1993, when Justice Byron White retired—but the seat went to Ruth Bader Ginsburg, whose passion for justice stirred Clinton's admiration. The White House vetting team had found Breyer intelligent and scholarly, but somewhat bloodless, especially on civil rights and liberties issues. "There is such a lack of vigor in his jurisprudence that one suspects he does not have (or refuses to utilize) any innate sense of justice. . . . He clearly prefers the plodding application of law," they wrote. "Quite clearly, he is a rather cold fish. . . . Conservatives will be thrilled." Kennedy knew and accepted Breyer's temperament, but Clinton was not awed by the judge when they met: Breyer's wits were dulled by the pain meds he was taking after falling off a bicycle in Harvard Square.

Kennedy was disappointed, but not disconsolate. He stood outside the West Wing after Ginsburg was named, took questions, and praised her as a superb selection—an act of political professionalism that was marked and remembered in the Oval Office. Privately, he told Breyer to be ready for the next opening.

When Justice Harry Blackmun announced his retirement in the spring of 1994, Kennedy made sure that he got next to Clinton—in a hotel hallway at a labor convention—to fill the president's ear. A year had passed since Ginsburg was appointed, partisan fevers were running high, and Breyer's moderation was now an advantage. He was highly regarded by

Thurmond and Hatch, from their years together at the Judiciary Committee. They would vouch for him.

Kennedy was happy for Breyer, but he came to wonder, over time, if the Democrats should have waged war for justices who were not so bloodless and analytical. In contrast to the Republicans, who constructed an assembly-line-like process to stock the federal courts with ideologues, the Democrats missed their opportunity to salt the judiciary with smart, red-blooded liberals like those who had served on the Warren court. "That's where Democrats have been," he said. "Playing it safe rather than taking the chance on someone who has unlimited capability and awareness."

CLINTON SUFFERED FROM ROOKIE MISTAKES, but the Democrats controlled the White House and both chambers of Congress, and that set Kennedy's pulse racing: the stars and planets were aligned for national health insurance. When campaigning for the presidency, Clinton had promised to seek universal coverage—and to send a bill to Congress in his first one hundred days. As a sign of his commitment, he named Hillary to lead a health care task force. It seemed the finest opportunity since the summer of 1974, when Kennedy came up short with Nixon.

For Americans confronted by illness and soaring medical bills, things had grown worse in the intervening years; they now had the unique distinction of paying roughly twice as much for health care as the residents of Western democracies like Canada and Great Britain, while still lagging in standard measurements like life expectancy and infant mortality. The number of uninsured Americans was nearing forty million, and the middle class was anxious about the risk of losing coverage. Health care costs were a $225 billion anchor on American businesses, and General Motors and Ford each spent more on health care each year than on steel. "There is no doubt that while our health care system is among the finest in the world, it is nonetheless in real trouble," Dole's top adviser, Sheila Burke, informed him in a memo. "Costs are continuing to escalate at an alarming rate yet there are a great many people . . . who cannot obtain even minimal care."

In the opening days of 1993, a grand bipartisan bargain—like the Civil Rights Act of 1964 or the ADA in 1990—seemed within reach. Dole and the new Senate Finance chairman, Daniel Patrick Moynihan of New York, sat with Kennedy at a White House dinner on February 22, talked about health care, and joined in a rousing chorus of "Happy Birthday" when the president surprised Kennedy with a cake. American companies seemed ready to accept a government-supported system like those that were giving rivals in Germany, Korea, or Japan a competitive advantage. Joseph Biden told Kennedy how the management of DuPont, his state's most important employer, had lectured him in 1972 on the evils of nationalized health care. Now they had come begging, Biden said, with charts and a briefing that concluded with the plea, "We have to have national health insurance."

Kennedy felt that "in life . . . a lot of it is . . . being at the right place at the right time. Whether it is in love or politics." There were progressive cycles in the 1930s and the 1960s, he believed, and now, perhaps, a new one had arrived. He had high regard for the Clintons as policy wonks: "This is the first time we've had a real president that understands this issue," he said. Kennedy had no irrefutable demands, nor excessive pride in authorship, nor overriding preference. A mandate on employers to provide coverage for their workers, like the "play or pay" measure he had moved through the Labor Committee in early 1992, was as good to him as a federal single-payer system like Medicare. He could teach it round or flat.

"At heart he is a pragmatist," Hillary Clinton's aides advised her in a memo, "and the bottom line for him is enacting health care reform."

"For many years, Senator Kennedy favored a single payer plan. . . . We believe now, however, that the best way to reach that goal is to enact a universal 'play or pay' system," his aide Nick Littlefield wrote Senator Harris Wofford of Pennsylvania. "If we thought we could get to single payer tomorrow, we'd be for that."

What was indispensable, Kennedy believed, was speed. It was crucial to get a bill "up and moving quickly," he told Clinton. "The longer we delay, the more difficult passage will be." The president's political and health care advisers agreed. "The more time we allow for the defenders of the status quo to organize, the more they will be able to marshal opposition to your plan, and the better their chances of killing it," consultant James Carville warned.

Kennedy and George Mitchell had made progress in 1992 with a bill that called for an employer mandate, with government subsidies. Now Kennedy and other Democratic leaders urged the Clintons to take the available components off the shelf, assemble them in a manner of their choosing, and use a parliamentary trick called reconciliation—freeing the bill from the threat of a Republican filibuster—to ram the measure through Congress before the opposition could organize. Which was what the Clintons did not do.

Hillary, a Methodist from Park Ridge, Illinois (who had joined in a Republican canvass of Chicago in 1960, trying to prove that the Kennedys stole the election from Nixon), had converted to earnest liberal at Wellesley College. She went on to Yale Law School, where she met and fell in love with the similarly brilliant (Georgetown, Rhodes Scholar, Oxford) lad from Arkansas. Clinton had campaigned as a "New Democrat" or a "different kind of Democrat"—different, that is, from Democrats like Kennedy. The Arkansas governor, and his vice president, Al Gore, were charter members of the Democratic Leadership Council, an organization founded in the Reagan years to nudge their party from left to center. The Clintons would do things their way.

"The proper approach would have been to gather a Kennedy and a Mitchell—people like that—and say, 'Okay, here's our goal, what's the best we can do?'" said Mitchell's aide John Hilley. Instead, the Clintons gave Congress an ultimatum: "Here's this immaculate conception."

Hillary's task force—over six hundred people at one point—huffed and puffed; the hundred-day deadline came and went, giving her enemies time to assemble. "My strong suggestion was the earlier the better," Kennedy would reflect. "Time was essential . . . [but] it went on for months." And while nothing in American health care is simple, the relatively straightforward "play or pay" and "single-payer" models were rejected in favor of a complicated, cost-controlling option called "managed competition."

The Democrats had been out of power for more than a decade, and it showed. Instead of focusing, like Ronald Reagan had, on select priorities,

Clinton followed Jimmy Carter's example with a mishmash of liberal offerings on gays, race, and the environment, and conservative nods to free trade, fiscal conservatism, and welfare reform. The president's economic advisers insisted that health care take a back seat to a deficit reduction package that would please Wall Street. Liberal interest groups, convinced that health reform was as good as won, shipped their oars and focused on getting plums for their constituencies. Kennedy would go to the White House and cry, "Now! Now! Now!" but the momentum "dissipated," he recalled. And Byrd, haughty as always and a stickler for Senate rules—especially the "Byrd rule" he had authored, which barred extraneous matters from reconciliation—refused to make an exception for health care reform. Clinton and Kennedy made personal pleas, but "Bob just wouldn't move," Kennedy said.

CLINTON WAS OVERWHELMED, MEANWHILE, by crises in Somalia, Bosnia, and Haiti, and by Republican operatives rummaging through the record of his days in Arkansas for evidence of financial and sexual impropriety. After twelve years of Reagan and his successor, the Republicans found it impossible to accept that an adulterous, draft-dodging, pot-smoking small-state governor, who had carried only 43 percent of the popular vote, had put an abrupt and unexpected end to their dominion. Many refused to recognize his legitimacy. The Cold War had ended, and with it the bonds of fear and purpose that brought Americans together in the face of a foreign enemy. Clinton got no honeymoon. "I'm up to my ass in alligators," he told his diarist, Taylor Branch. With the aid of a compliant press corps—for after twelve years of covering Reagan and Bush, journalists were quite snuggly with the Republicans—the GOP ginned up teapot tempests over spurious allegations, mythical cover-ups, and, in one particularly despicable ploy, the suicide of Vincent Foster, a White House lawyer who suffered from depression.

"They attacked him in every possible way," Kennedy recalled. Clinton "got himself in trouble and made it easy, but nonetheless, it was a fierce assault." It all fell under the heading of "Whitewater," after a money-losing real estate deal the Clintons had made in Arkansas. "Whitewater is about health care," talk show host Rush Limbaugh candidly told his audience. "This is . . . to stop health care."

If the Democrats made good on their vow to bring peace of mind about health care to American families, the Republican Party strategists warned, the country's march toward a European-style social democracy would accelerate. Dole was running for president, and 1996 was getting closer. "While Dole's initial instinct was, 'Let's figure out whether we can make a deal here,' he ultimately sided with the majority of his caucus," Sheila Burke recalled. Hope for a bipartisan solution fizzled. "The early hope of . . . 'Kumbaya together' . . . deteriorated."

"They drew blood on Whitewater," Clinton aide George Stephanopoulos recalled. "And then when they drew that blood they began to believe that they could stop health care. . . . It was a psychological break."

Kennedy soldiered on. The Labor Committee was the first in Congress to mark up and pass a health care bill. As a gesture of good faith, he accepted Republican amendments, though they did not fetch him votes for the final measure. And by going first, to restore the bill's momentum when the White House needed help, Kennedy fell on his sword for the Clintons: once he had done his thing, he became an afterthought, and his clout was diminished.

As always, the committee with primary jurisdiction was Finance— dominated by conservatives, friendlier to the special interests, and led by the brilliant, erratic Moynihan. ("He knows all the facts, and he's against all the solutions," Robert Kennedy had once said.) Moynihan was fresh to the issue, a scholar, and, said Hilley, "as a legislator, not competent." Moynihan questioned the need for major change, and thus was less inclined to seek it. He believed the bill's prospects were poor, and that it was essential to strike a deal with the Republicans. "My object, self-evident to a legislator, was to build a consensus," he would recall. But that opportunity had passed, Kennedy believed. With the small business and insurance lobbies leading an effective opposition, the prospects for a grand bipartisan bargain had dimmed, and Moynihan's strategy would cede control of events to Dole. Even Democrats were starting to waver. In the

House, two formidable Democratic nobles, Energy and Commerce chairman John Dingell and Ways and Means chairman Dan Rostenkowski, failed to move the bill through their committees.

By the early summer of 1994, the cause of national health care reform was withering in both chambers. "The tide had started moving. And with such rapidity," Kennedy groused. Like a latter-day Canute, he staged rallies for reform in the Labor Committee hearing room, met and pleaded with moderate Republicans, and urged Mitchell to bring the bill to the floor and compel their colleagues to go on the record in an election year. But the Republicans were good at muddying things. "We've killed health reform," Senator Robert Packwood of Oregon, the ranking Republican on the Finance panel, told his GOP colleagues. "Now we have to make sure our fingerprints aren't on it."

Kennedy's distress spilled over. He was "difficult . . . anxious," aide Ronald Weich recalled. "He recognized this was a unique opportunity . . . he was frustrated . . . he would bark at us." The senator showed his choler in aberrant confrontations—in the Democratic caucus with Senator Robert Kerrey of Nebraska, and in a bellowing tantrum on a Sunday morning directed at the director of the Congressional Budget Office. When aide Jeff Blattner advised him that the prospects of success were dim, Kennedy didn't want to hear it. "We're going to have this debate on the Senate floor before the American people!" he barked.

In August, a jury-rigged bill assembled by Mitchell made it to the floor. It was the first time in its history that the U.S. Senate debated national health insurance. Kennedy had always believed that if confronted with an up-or-down vote, his foes would bow to popular support. But the measure had become so politically toxic that Republicans were delighted to vote against it, and swing state Democrats facing reelection pushed to see it quietly interred.

Packwood led the opposition. At the time, he was facing a wide-ranging investigation of sexual harassment charges involving almost a dozen women. He could ill afford to break with his party's conservatives. Kennedy and Packwood had clashed early in the process over health care jurisdiction.

Now, after one of Packwood's maneuvers, Kennedy confronted him on the Senate floor.

"What are you trying to do?" Kennedy growled. Packwood didn't know how to respond. Moynihan and his aide Lawrence O'Donnell were stunned. Kennedy was "as red and trembling with rage as I've ever seen anyone who has not thrown a punch," O'Donnell recalled.

"We are going to throw you out of here, so fuck you," Kennedy told Packwood, then stalked away.

Moynihan put a hand on Packwood's shoulder to calm the shaken senator. "I was horrified," said O'Donnell. "Senator Moynihan was horrified. It was an out-of-control moment that was pure ugliness."

Kennedy was "very smart, wise, insightful, thoughtful—and very Irish," O'Donnell would recall. "My full picture of him includes a really Irish kind of anger."

"Kennedy believed longer," said Steve Richetti, the White House congressional liaison. His grief was commensurately deeper. "It is his nature, I think, to believe that you still try to do what you can do."

But Mitchell had to concede defeat—and announced that the Senate would cease work on the legislation.

Twenty-Seven

SWEET JACK FALSTAFF

Kennedy was now in unfamiliar territory: fretting about reelection. With no health care bill, he and the Democrats would slink home that fall with little to show America's working families. Some of the measures the Democrats had passed—tax hikes, handgun controls, and a ban on assault weapons—aroused the Republican base. Others, like the North American Free Trade Agreement, and yet another crime bill that promoted incarceration, failed to wow Democratic constituencies. It was hard to tell just what the Democrats stood for. And that included Kennedy.

It was not that Kennedy neglected Massachusetts. The federal share of a $6 billion cleanup of Boston's harbor, defense contracts for jet engines and the Patriot missile, and $12 billion in federal aid to tear down and replace the traffic-choked Fitzgerald Expressway with a modern road and tunnel project were outturns of the clout borne by Kennedy, Tip O'Neill, and the other members of the Massachusetts delegation. After his Vineyard boat ride with the president and First Lady, Kennedy was asked by reporters what they had chatted about. The presidency? International affairs? No, the senator said. He had pressed Clinton about a defense installation that would bring jobs to the town of Southbridge.

At the opening of a conference committee meeting, convened to resolve differences between the Senate and the House, Kennedy would sometimes introduce an issue—an earmarked appropriation for Massachusetts, or some other parochial matter—that was demonstrably not germane. "I just raise it. I just want to make sure that I have the right to bring it up," he would tell his fellow conferees. To move things along, they would promise to hear him out at some point down the road.

Then, generally at a late hour, with adjournment looming, having reached a final deal on the major matters of contention, they would groan as Kennedy brought up his pet project. And then they would wave it through. "Sure as hell, just as you were getting ready to close the conference," Representative George Miller remembered. "Everybody's heading for the airplane . . . home, and so they'd say, 'Okay Ted, just put it in.'"

Kennedy could run the clock the other way as well. Once he sensed a deal at hand, he would press to clinch the agreement before others changed their minds. "He's got his . . . amendments tucked away," Miller recalled. "He's now believing this bill is going to the Rose Garden, and now he's not going to let it not go to the Rose Garden." At this point Miller would turn to his staff. "Let's clean up," he would whisper. "We're going to be going to bed in half an hour."

Kennedy's ardent preparation enabled him to buffalo his colleagues. "Sometimes he would be reading from a memo," said Miller—a memorandum or report that the other conferees had missed or ignored, but Kennedy had war-gamed beforehand with his staff. "He would start to take control, because once it became clear to him that you weren't prepared, you were just bait." Or he would invite a fellow lawmaker to his hideaway office, with all the Kennedy memorabilia on the walls. "He had a lot of resources. He was a Kennedy," Miller recalled. "He'd go into the hideaway and . . . Honey Fitz this and that and . . . his brother Jack," and he would "own [a colleague] in another five minutes."

THE NATION'S EDITORIAL WRITERS knew about Kennedy's skills and tactics, and of his essential work on the Civil Rights Restoration Act, the Bork nomination, the Americans with Disabilities Act, medical reforms at NIH and the FDA, and the war on AIDS. But most people see life from their kitchen table, as his colleague Representative J. Joseph Moakley of South Boston liked to say, and the senator's causes didn't seem to help working folks pay the bills in the unsettling economy. Since 1988, Massachusetts had lost four hundred thousand jobs—14 percent of all employment in the state. They needed "to visibly re-connect EMK with Massachusetts, its people and its concerns," Robert Shrum told the senator's campaign brain trust, and then "to demonstrate that EMK's first priority is to fight for the middle class/working families . . . for their jobs and their standards of life."

The Democratic Party's role as a warden of the national economy was recast by century's end. It had long been the party of work—of keeping paychecks flowing, especially to blue-collar families—if necessary, in hard times, via federal jobs programs. It wasn't just the money—it was also the purpose that work supplied.

"Work must be found for able-bodied but destitute workers," Franklin Roosevelt had told a nation hammered by the Depression. "The lessons of history, confirmed by the evidence immediately before me, show conclusively that continued dependence upon relief induces a spiritual disintegration fundamentally destructive to the national fiber. To dole out relief in this way is to administer a narcotic, a subtle destroyer of the human spirit. It is inimical to the dictates of a sound policy. It is in violation of the traditions of America. . . . We must preserve not only the bodies of the unemployed from destitution but also their self-respect, their self-reliance and courage and determination."

Under Roosevelt's leadership, and that of Harry Truman, the Democrats emerged from the Depression and the Second World War with those values intact. It was the easy times that followed that induced spiritual disintegration. America dominated the postwar scene—it pumped 62 percent of the world's oil, produced 57 percent of its steel, and built 80 percent of its automobiles. The country might face challenges to its economic primacy one day, Dwight Eisenhower told a friend, but that day lay over the horizon. Unions demanded better benefits and wages, and the corporate chieftains complied. "A rising tide lifts all boats," John Kennedy said. "And for the golden decades after World War II, this was true," Ted Kennedy added, decades later. Workers had homes, two cars, a boat, a summer cottage; they grew complacent, and socially conservative. Liberals focused on those left behind—the poor, minorities, women—and vilified the military, big business, the police, and other symbols of conformity and order.

The Kennedys—especially the empath, Robert—played a significant role in the reshaping of liberal priorities. "Having swung over to the cause of social change, he was constantly on the verge of calling for social upheaval," Moynihan lamented, in a letter to Ted Kennedy in the summer of 1968. The Kennedys "descended from a tradition of stable, working class urban politics. . . . That tradition is very much isolated now, and very much in trouble. . . . In a word, the people of South Boston and Dorchester ought to be as much in our minds as those of Roxbury or Bedford-Stuyvesant or whatever. Those are your people, they were Bob's people before he got religion, they have been abandoned and our politics are much the worst for it. No one is much interested in them, no one admires much less likes them, no one tries to help them break out of the sour and self defeating attitudes which they have acquired."

Ted Kennedy had watched with alarm as Nixon and Reagan made effective pitches to blue-collar America: to what came to be called Nixon's "silent majority" and then the "Reagan Democrats." For such voters, "liberalism came to connote . . . the favoring of blacks over whites and permissiveness towards drug abuse, illegitimacy, welfare fraud, street crime, homosexuality, anti-Americanism, as well as moral anarchy among the young," wrote political analysts Thomas and Mary Edsall. To meet the well-financed Republican assaults, the Democrats, too, went hat in hand to the boardrooms for donations. The traditional paradigm—of a two-party system in which one party represents Capital and the other stands for Labor—was broken.

Meanwhile, the world rebuilt. The factories of Asia and Europe boasted modern equipment and management techniques; they were subsidized and protected from foreign imports by government, and their workers—sheltered by an inclusive social safety net—accepted lower wages than their American counterparts. In 1971 a young Nixon aide, Peter Peterson, had drafted a 133-page memo, later published, titled *The United States in the Changing World Economy*, which warned that the golden postwar time had ended. "Most of our thinking and most of our rhetoric about international economic policy have been carried over from another era," Peterson wrote. Americans felt snug with the view "that the international superiority of the U.S. was an unalterable fact of life." But "our perceptions lagged reality."

The times would be defined by "great competition between countries," Peterson wrote. He called for federal intervention, and "a conscious effort to shape our country's future rather than to resign ourselves to whatever it may bring." But while he filled his *cri de coeur* with grave warnings ("We must dispel any 'Marshall Plan psychology' or relatively unconstrained generosity. . . . This is not just a matter of choice but of necessity."), Peterson failed to stir a commensurately effective response from his countrymen. Imports continued to fill stores and showrooms. American factories closed. Iconic companies—RCA, U.S. Steel, Chrysler—were decimated, and with them many communities.

Ted Kennedy had a family history here. John Kennedy and his aides had been free traders: in the "long twilight struggle" against communism, the reborn nations of western Europe and the Pacific Rim could be strong allies. But the captains of the New Frontier recognized that U.S. companies and workers would ultimately pay a price. It was not fair, John Kennedy said, for one class of Americans to bear this burden alone. He proposed, and Congress created, a trade adjustment assistance program that would provide money and retraining for displaced workers. It was a smart and effective approach, other nations discovered, if fervently embraced by government and private enterprise. Peterson endorsed the concept as a key part of "a coherent strategy for the new era." Ted Kennedy would take it as a model. Yet market ideologues, and many in industry, refused to accept aggressive federal intervention. In the think tanks and ivory towers, the concept of adjustment was dismissed as costly, clunky, "picking winners," or protectionist. In the Reagan era, Republicans targeted the program for extinction.

By the 1990s, the Democratic Party's new breed of leaders were comfortable and cozy with its corporate donors. The Clintons and their like were highly educated members of a new American meritocracy, who called themselves "New Democrats" or "neo-liberals," in search of a "Third Way" unshackled by liberal shibboleths. In the 1992 election, Clinton sold himself as "a different kind of Democrat" who would execute criminals, "end welfare as we know it," and carry the flag for free trade. "The era of big government is over," he proclaimed in 1996. The nation's politics became thoroughly muddied. The Reagan-era dismantling of federal regulatory limits helped fuel the stunning growth of the American financial industry. "Finance became the epicenter of the American economy," Clinton's first-term labor secretary, Robert Reich, noted. The financiers focused intently on immediate returns for shareholders, not on the long-term health of a company, its employees, or the community that had nurtured its growth. The number of "disabled" U.S. workers claiming federal benefits tripled as factories closed. Union membership dropped. Economic inequality reached levels unseen since the Roaring Twenties.

Kennedy saw it happening. "Today's rising tide is lifting only some of the boats—primarily the yachts," he warned. "The vast majority of economic gains are being channeled to the wealthy few, while the working men and women who are the strength and soul of this country and its economy are being shortchanged." From the end of the Second World War until 1973, Americans grew wealthy together, Kennedy noted. In the next twenty years, the lowest 60 percent of wage earners had watched their real family income lose ground, as income for the top 1 percent doubled. Corporate executives, in that same twenty years, saw their salaries leap from 40 times that of the average worker to 190 times more. "Can this be called fair?" he asked. It was "economically unjustified, socially dangerous, historically unprecedented and morally unacceptable."

"A storm is coming," Kennedy warned. "Only the short-sighted, who look only to the next quarterly report, can be content."

Yet the best the Democrats could offer was palliative care: insisting that workers be given advance notice when employers closed a factory; or time off (without pay) in the event of a family or medical emergency; or that job training programs for dislocated workers be streamlined; or that disabled Americans be free to work more hours without losing their government benefits. "All these policies were helpful but frustratingly small in light of the systemic changes that were occurring," Reich concluded.

The political and economic trends joined in 1993 when Clinton led a Republican-Democratic crusade to promote a Reagan favorite: the North American Free Trade Agreement. Kennedy voted for NAFTA, though he knew it would cost American breadwinners jobs. There is much to be said for free trade and globalization. It weaves the economic interests of nations together, reducing the chance of war. It raises the standard of living and education levels of the peasantry in developing nations, encouraging peaceful change. It reduces the cost of goods in wealthy countries, delighting consumers with low-cost smartphones, flat-screen televisions, video games, and other gimcracks. But the price for postwar American families was fierce. A way of life ended for workers who cast steel, or built automobiles, heavy appliances, and other products—who *built stuff*.

"Uselessness will kill strong and weak souls alike, and kill every time," said Kennedy aide Thomas Rollins, quoting novelist Kurt Vonnegut. "We've been willing to give away people's purpose in exchange for cheaper stuff imported from elsewhere." When Bethlehem Steel folded and Mack Truck moved to non-union factories in South Carolina, it was easy to say to the ransacked families of Bethlehem, Pennsylvania, that they must find opportunity elsewhere, for that is what the laws of economics required. But the change was wrenching, and their homes and community would never be the same. Palliative steps were humane. Workers could buy food and pay rent with unemployment checks and food stamps. But the dole was, as Roosevelt said, a destroyer of the human spirit. In depressed inner city neighborhoods, throughout Appalachia, and on the Indian reservations, "we have created an entire subculture of dependency, alienation and despair," Moynihan warned. "It is in truth the way we cope with this kind of problem. As against giving the men proper jobs and a respectable place in their community and family." It left huge swaths of America ripe for crack and opioid salesmen and political demagogues.

Workers without college degrees "have seen their economic prospects shrivel over the past 15 years," said then–labor secretary Reich in 1994. "This isn't the way it is supposed to be in America. Unlike more fatalistic cultures, Americans have always had a deep faith that efforts will be rewarded, that you reap what you sow. In other words, you can earn your fate. That was the American credo."

"Middle-class families tried every means they had of holding on," said Reich. "Spouses went to work. Both parents worked long hours or they took multiple jobs. They decided to have fewer kids. They pushed these coping mechanisms about as far as they can go and they still feel that they are losing the American dream."

"We are on our way to becoming a two-tier society composed of a few winners and a larger group of Americans left behind, whose anger and whose disillusionment is easily manipulated," Reich warned, with prescience. "Once unbottled, mass resentments can poison the very fabric, the moral integrity, of society—replacing ambition with envy, replacing tolerance with hate."

Through all this, Kennedy was chairman or ranking member of the Senate Labor Committee, and must bear some responsibility for failing to lead an aggressive campaign to rescue America's workforce. His ability to offer more than alleviation was limited by jurisdictional hurdles, however. The Finance and the Banking committees handled trade and taxation and supervised Wall Street, banking, and overseas investment, and were dominated by the industries they were presumed to regulate. Kennedy was left with a handful of prescriptions to help the out-of-work voters of Massachusetts and elsewhere. He aimed to fortify the safety net by preserving and improving federal health and education programs, adding health insurance coverage for working families, ameliorating some of the immediate shocks of job dislocation, and raising the minimum wage.

But first he had to be reelected.

KENNEDY'S MARRIAGE, and turn toward sobriety, had neutralized some of the toxins from the Willie Smith trial and the Thomas-Hill hearings. So did the swell of sympathy after Jacqueline Onassis died of cancer in May 1994 at the age of 64. Once again, Kennedy excelled at a eulogy.

"During those four endless days in 1963 she held us together as a family and as a country," Kennedy said. "In large part because of her, we could grieve and then go on. She lifted us up . . . in the doubt and darkness."

But bestselling books were chronicling, with salacious excess, Ted Kennedy's years of dissipation—his "disgrace-defying high-wire act, reeling between honorable public service and egregious self-abasement," as the *Washington Post* book critic Jonathan Yardley cast it. "The magic of the family name is still there, but it has been compromised and diminished and soiled."

Martin Nolan, in the *Globe*, marked Kennedy's stature as the commonwealth's longest-serving U.S. senator with a long essay that compared him to Sir John Falstaff, Shakespeare's dissolute knight, asking Massachusetts for forgiveness just as Falstaff had begged Henry V: "If to be old and merry be a sin, then many an old host that I know is damned. . . . For sweet Jack Falstaff, kind Jack Falstaff, true Jack Falstaff, valiant Jack Falstaff, and therefore more valiant, being, as he is old Jack Falstaff, banish him not . . . banish plump Jack, and banish all the world."

There was a feeling among Massachusetts voters that the senior senator was in need of a thwack. "There was a nastiness out on the street that was palpable," his nephew Michael, the 1994 campaign's early manager, recalled. "A rough surliness." The voters had not necessarily decided to dump Kennedy—when he seemed in true peril, the polls showed their support returning—but neither were they pleased with his performance. Tax-loving "Big Government" Democrats were not in vogue. Health reform had been caricatured by the deft Republicans as a program for ne'er-do-wells, rather than a safety net for the working and middle classes. And in any event, it had failed. "They were ready to put the spurs into him, and pitchforks," Tunney recalled. Kennedy would need to win them back. And this time, in contrast to his five previous reelection campaigns, he had a formidable opponent.

Mitt Romney, at forty-seven, was much like a young Ted Kennedy. He was handsome and wealthy, the Harvard-educated scion of a famous political family, with ingrained principles, skill, and nigh-faultless comportment. The race, said the *Boston Globe*'s Ben Bradlee Jr., would be "Pat Boone against Dean Martin."

Romney would rise to serve as a governor, a U.S. senator, and, in 2012, the Republican presidential nominee. He had made his fortune as a venture capitalist for a Boston-based investment firm called Bain Capital, and promised to employ his skills and business acumen to bring jobs and prosperity to the state. He was a fine-looking alternative for those swing voters—women, independents, and suburban voters in the new high-tech industry—who could determine the outcome. In the spring and summer of 1994, as Romney coasted to victory in the Republican primary, his advertising pummeled Kennedy as soft on crime. There was no effective response from the senator's campaign, despite polls that showed crime was a surging concern. Kennedy was mired in Washington, and then he and Michael made a mess of things when, in an ill-advised effort to save money, the campaign stopped advertising that summer. "Nobody watches TV in August," said Kennedy. "They are all at the beach."

The consequence was clear in September, when a *Boston Herald* poll showed Romney had taken the lead. Democratic pollsters verified the findings. An independent poll had Kennedy down by a dozen points. "You don't know what it's like out there," he told Senator Claiborne Pell. The press described him as standing at "the abyss" or "a Democratic dinosaur" facing extinction. To bolster the candidate's morale, Shrum had Kennedy's own poll results tailored so that they showed them one point ahead, instead of the actual point behind. Now, when Michael brought up cost-saving measures, his uncle brushed them aside. They would spend whatever was necessary, Kennedy said, and he took out a mortgage on his home. For a time, "it looked like Teddy was going to lose," David Burke remembered.

Money (he would ultimately spend north of $10 million on the race) helped. So did the hours that Kennedy devoted to day-and-night campaigning. Few were as good at giving set speeches, and he reminded the voters who he was and what he stood for in a stirring declaration of liberal principle in Faneuil Hall. "I reject the laissez-faire notion that all government has to do is get out of the way, and kind, caring, generous, unselfish, wealthy private interests and power will see to it that prosperity trickles down to ordinary people," he said.

When Shrum suggested that Kennedy reef his sails and endorse stern limits on welfare moms, the senator told him to cram it. He would rather lose, he said, than win on the backs of children. "I don't want to hear the results of the poll," he told his chief of staff, Paul Donovan. "No. . . . It is aimed at the mother and hits the child. I won't do it." Another staff proposal, that he trim his opposition to capital punishment, was similarly rejected. "He was very staunch. . . . He understood that once you put a chink in the armor, the armor is gone," aide Ronald Weich said. "On a moral question like the death penalty I never saw him yield." On an earlier occasion, renowned on Capitol Hill, their colleagues had to step between Kennedy and Florida Senator Bob Graham when their argument about capital punishment grew alarmingly loud and heated. "I opposed the death penalty for the man who killed my brother!" Kennedy had shouted.

THE CAMPAIGN BROADCAST ALL-POINTS bulletins for help, and the state's Democratic political talents and ex–Kennedy staffers arrived like minutemen. Two former chiefs of staff headed the reinforcements: Cooper took a leave of absence from her consulting firm to impose order at headquarters, and Burke, who had led Kennedy's staff in the 1960s and spent the interim years as the president of ABC News, assumed the inglorious but vital chores of senior body man, traveling with Kennedy in a van to events, providing counsel, calm, and reassurance.

The fates convened and concluded that Kennedy was due for a break. Romney's job in venture capitalism required more than judgment—it called for a certain ruthlessness. To whip companies into shape, Bain's managers were known to cut payrolls, wages, and benefits. That was the creed of free-market capitalism, exalted by Romney and other raiders. Vicki Kennedy, knowing the score from her years as a corporate lawyer, suggested that Romney might be vulnerable in an era when closed factories and jobs shipped overseas were symbols of American economic distress. The campaign was thus primed when a representative of a paper workers' union phoned and was connected to the research desk. He told of how a Bain subsidiary, the Ampad Corporation, had taken over a paper and stationery firm with a plant in Marion, Indiana. Ampad had cut pay and benefits, increased weekend hours, and laid off workers, prompting the employees to go on strike. With a script for a campaign ad in hand, Shrum's partner, Tad Devine, was dispatched to Indiana. He reported back with welcome news: the strikers were eloquent and authentic—and furious at Bain Capital. Devine tossed his script, turned on his cameras, and let them speak from the heart.

Kennedy had never used negative ads in Massachusetts. Now he plastered the airways with angry Ampad workers, and an advertisement smacking Romney for not providing health care coverage to the employees of another Bain acquisition, Staples, the office products company. "Come out here to Marion, Indiana, and see what your company has done to these people," said an Ampad worker in one advertisement. "I would like to say to the people of Massachusetts—You think it can't happen to you? Think again, because we thought it wouldn't happen here either." A half dozen striking Ampad employees arrived in the state to tail and taunt Romney on the campaign trail. The Kennedy camp "characterized me as a cold-hearted unfeeling robber baron," he recalled.

Campaigns sometimes turn on a moment or an episode that captures the heart of the contest, or reveals a candidate's limitations. Michael Dukakis and John Kerry were each scarred by not countering fierce Republican attacks in the 1988 and 2004 presidential elections. As Kennedy's ads slashed at Romney, and the senator marched through every harvest fair and union hall in the commonwealth, the voters looked to the young businessman to gauge his mettle. But the Republican campaign responded with a languor akin to that shown by Kennedy in summer. Romney's standing slipped among independent voters, and Kennedy moved ahead in the polls.

"There are some people who, when the circumstances are mediocre, they can be mediocre," Kennedy's old friend Gerard Doherty said. "But if it's do-or-die, they can catch the ball behind their back. My experience is that [Kennedy has] been able to do that, time and time again."

The debates in October cinched the outcome. Kennedy, his girth masked by a plus-sized podium that his aides had contrived to install in

Faneuil Hall, was well prepared and animated and exceeded expectations. For weeks the voters had been hearing from an imprudent Romney
campaign and a hostile media that Kennedy was afraid to debate. Some
of Kennedy's staff believed it—that the senator was too old and out of
touch, and that he dared not face Romney onstage. "Are you here to see
your guy destroyed?" a *Boston Globe* reporter taunted Shrum. The nation's
political press corps, alert for the scent of blood, came to Boston for the
estocada.

"The event was tied to the notion that Romney would destroy Kennedy
and the old progressive who has fought consistently for liberal programs
would come crashing down. More than the political end of the last Kennedy brother, it would have been a strong score for the end of liberalism
in America," wrote the *Globe*'s Bob Healy. "It didn't happen." That night,
Romney was Romney: bright and handsome and a shade superficial. But
Kennedy, who had spent the afternoon before the debate communing
with his ghosts at the John F. Kennedy Presidential Library, was not the
stumblebum that so many in the crowd expected.

"The Kennedys are not in public service to make money. We have paid
too high a price," he growled at Romney after the challenger repeated a
far-fetched charge about a shady family real estate deal. Kennedy had rehearsed the line, and Romney had marched into the trap.

A few nights earlier, Kennedy had stood at a mirror and, apropos of
nothing, turned and told Vicki, "I'm ready, you know."

"Yeah, I know," she told him.

Kennedy was nervous nonetheless as he rode the campaign van to the
hall at Holyoke Community College for the second debate, two nights
later. This was Romney's last stand; Kennedy's last hurdle.

Burke knew to get his man laughing.

"So, Senator," Burke said. "Steve Breyer worked for you, and he's sitting on the Supreme Court. I worked for you, and I'm sitting in this fucking van."

On election day, Massachusetts returned Kennedy to the Senate. He
beat Romney 58 to 40 percent.

In the end, said Tom Kiley, Kennedy's pollster, "The voters kind of turned and said, 'My God, we're proud of him. We didn't realize we were, but we are.'"

But Kennedy was an outlier. The Republicans picked up eight seats in the Senate in 1994, and when two Democrats switched parties, the GOP majority stood at 54 to 46. Republican cadres led by Representative Newt Gingrich of Georgia seized the House of Representatives, ending forty years of Democratic rule.

Ted Kennedy would return to Washington, but he had lost another opportunity to give Americans health care coverage as a right, not a privilege. He would need to find another way.

Twenty-Eight

CATSKINNING

To an extent he did not publicly acknowledge, Ted Kennedy was dismayed by Bill and Hillary Clinton for having booted the grand opportunity handed them in 1992. Their performance had led to the Republican takeover of Congress, and abruptly put the Democratic Party in a dire, defensive crouch. The Republicans had picked up fifty-four seats in the House. Speaker Tom Foley, and Governors Mario Cuomo of New York and Ann Richards of Texas, were among the casualties. The enemy was on the banks of the Tiber, preparing to loot the Palatine—and Kennedy thought Clinton an improbable Horatius.

The leader of the "revolution" was Gingrich, an audacious former professor of history from West Georgia College. Broad-faced and portly, with a shaggy helmet of grey hair, he was a mirror image of Bill Clinton, his fellow Baby Boomer, with a similarly traumatic childhood and proclivity for self-absorption and marital faithlessness. In politics, Gingrich was shameless. He "spoke in sweeping sentences bursting with adjectives and adverbs that rendered his world oversized and absolute," wrote two contemporary observers: His foes' mistakes were "classic." Their philosophy was "grotesque." His truths were "unequivocal."

Though creatively adorned and tactically impressive, the core of Gingrich's movement was the sturdy Nixonian politics of grievance. His pseudo-scholarly patter was designed to persuade a querulous white majority that its troubles were brought on by contemptuous elites in league with minorities. He had come to lead the House Republicans by offering them power through means his predecessors had rejected: he renounced civility and slandered the Democrats as traitorous and corrupt. Liberalism was an enslaving evil, he declared, and that justified his tactics. "One of the great problems we have in the Republican Party is that we don't encourage you to be nasty," Gingrich told potential disciples.

"The politics of division," Kennedy called it. "What's happening is a real threat to the core meaning of what it is to be an American." Gingrichism was "a very practical philosophy to enhance power for power's sake, and exploitation, and the accumulation of resources and money to the wealthiest special interests."

"They turned family values on their head," Kennedy said of the Republicans. "There's very little sense of the religious teaching of Matthew about feeding the hungry and giving a cup to the thirsty or clothing the naked and welcoming the stranger and visiting the poor or the imprisoned. It has all been tied into a message of greed, and all about Me and Myself."

SEVERAL OF GINGRICH'S LIEUTENANTS moved from House to Senate, bearing the pathogen with them. More would follow, changing the tenor of the chamber. Their sanctimonious bearing made traditionalists like Dole fidget, but as a presidential hopeful he could not afford to buck them. The partisan use of the filibuster soared, and the number of Democrats who voted with Republicans, and Republicans who voted with Democrats, began to slide toward zero.

More was at stake than tax cuts and defense contracts, the staples of the Reagan era. The new breed was grandiose by nature—and inebriated by victory. The goal, one of Gingrich's co-plotters would say, was to reduce the size of government until they could "drown it in the bathtub." They targeted food stamps, college aid, the Environmental Protection Agency, the school lunch and Medicaid programs for dismemberment or death.

Giant cutbacks in Medicare would pay for mammoth tax breaks, and Gingrich boasted how Medicare would "wither." They proposed to bring prayer back to the public schools and repeal gun controls. Gingrich wondered aloud if the children of the poor might not be better off in orphanages, and if women were not disqualified for combat by their reproductive cycles. The incoming chairman of the House Ways and Means Committee suggested that the country abolish the progressive income tax. The Berlin Wall had tumbled, the Iron Curtain crumbled. Americans, absent the existential threat of communism, were free to indulge in fits of political fratricide.

KENNEDY HAD AN INSTINCTUAL and immediate reaction to the Republican victory. He began to plot a counterrevolution. After being serenaded by Carol Channing, the star of the musical *Hello, Dolly!*, at a morning-after breakfast for staff and supporters at campaign headquarters (*Hello, Teddy, well Hello, Teddy, It's so nice to have you back where you belong*), he flew to Washington and called in Carey Parker and Nick Littlefield, his top aides.

"There will now be a long and difficult struggle for the soul of the Democratic Party," he told them. Seared by the election day results, centrist Democrats from the South and West would feel the urge to "be more like the Republicans," said Kennedy. "We must convince them that the election was not a mandate for a drastic scaling back of government." His own reelection was proof. "The best strategy," he said, "is to identify the issues that matter to working families—health care, education, jobs and wages—and hold every Republican action and every Democratic initiative to the standard of how it affects middle- and low-income Americans."

Kennedy didn't need to name the most important centrist Democrat. He launched a yearlong campaign to enlist Bill Clinton in the resistance.

Kennedy started, as always, by preparing. "With Teddy it was always practice, practice, practice," said his wife, Vicki. "He was a prepare-aholic." The senator scheduled meetings with a range of experts—speechwriter Richard Goodwin and author Doris Kearns Goodwin; economist John Kenneth Galbraith; historian Alan Brinkley; journalist Robert Kuttner and Democratic pollster Mark Mellman. From Harvard came Robert Coles and Michael Sandel and Robert Blendon. He visited with Democratic leaders in the House and Senate, Massachusetts politicos like John Sasso and Representative Barney Frank, and administration officials like the budget director, Alice Rivlin, and White House chief of staff Leon Panetta.

Kennedy found unanimity. "The Republicans' appeal to the middle class is a fraudulent way to release resources to the rich," said Galbraith, who had been advising Kennedys since the 1950s, in a typical response. The mandate Gingrich claimed was figmental, Galbraith told Kennedy, over tea and cookies in the professor's Cambridge home. Democratic turnout had cratered on election day. Only 38 percent of eligible voters had gone to the polls, and so, even with the dubious assumption that all Republicans understood what they were voting for, the verdict represented the wishes of but 20 percent of the electorate. The most reassuring meetings were those that Kennedy held with the new Democratic leaders of the House (Richard Gephardt of Missouri) and the Senate (Thomas Daschle of South Dakota), who agreed with Galbraith's math, endorsed Kennedy's views and encouraged him to induce Clinton.

"Democrats must keep working on measures the government can take to help working families adapt to the economic insecurity which is now built into our economy," Kennedy wrote Brinkley. "I'm . . . going to be very clear about those issues on which we simply will not give in."

KENNEDY AND CLINTON MET on a December evening in the president's private workspace—the Treaty Room in the White House residence—where John Kennedy had signed the test ban treaty and Clinton had hung the George Tames photograph *The Loneliest Job*, showing John Kennedy bent over a table, as if wracked by the strain of a mighty decision. Ted told Clinton that brother John had actually been reading the *New York Times*—and swearing at the coverage—when the famous picture was made.

Word had reached Clinton of Kennedy's intent, and the president had been consulting with experts and pols of his own. He kicked things off by saying, "I take it you want us to stick with the working family themes."

Yes, said Kennedy. He had a memo for the president on the Massachusetts election and how it applied to their immediate future. The upcoming
budget would be a defining political document. No matter how conciliatory Clinton tried to be, the Republicans would pronounce it dead on
arrival. Its great value, then, was as a statement of principles. So, no cuts
in Medicare, or college aid, Kennedy began. Incremental reform for health
care—

Clinton interrupted. "Why don't we talk about raising the minimum
wage?" he asked. It was high on Kennedy's agenda, and Clinton had gotten there before him.

The two men left the meeting as allies, yet Clinton, like many a fine
politician, had a way of saying things that led one to believe—at times
mistakenly—that you had his inviolable commitment. When Clinton announced his "middle-class bill of rights" two days later, it did not include
an incremental health care bill or a hike in the minimum wage. To keep
Clinton and other wavering Democrats on course, Kennedy made the
case again, this time in public, in a speech at the National Press Club.

"If Democrats run for cover, if we become pale carbon copies of the
opposition and try to act like Republicans, we will lose—and deserve to
lose," Kennedy said.

"If we fall for our opponents' tactics, if we listen to those who tell us to
abandon health reform, or slash student loans and children's programs,
or engage in a bidding war to see who can be the most anti-government
or the most laissez-faire, we will have only ourselves to blame," he warned.
"As Democrats we can win, but only if we stand for something."

KENNEDY'S ALLIANCE WITH CLINTON was tested when the president, in
the spring, announced his plan for a balanced budget, enabled in part by
reductions in Medicare. Kennedy had shown up at a White House ceremony and wangled an uninvited hour to try to persuade Clinton that this
was a bad idea. But the president believed that the progressive cause
would be more credible, the impact on the economy more beneficial, and
his standing in a fight with Dole and Gingrich firmer if he revived his

"different kind of Democrat" persona. Kennedy grumbled—"You guys are fucking up!" he told the White House congressional liaison, Pat Griffin—but otherwise kept his feelings private.

At this point, Gingrich and his band would have shown wisdom to declare victory, but wise was not their nature. Instead, they insisted that Clinton bend to a more draconian approach, with cutbacks in federal health, environmental, education, and hunger programs. The Republicans passed their budget; Clinton vetoed it; the Democrats in Congress stood with him, and in the resulting impasse, all but the most essential functions of the U.S. government ground to a halt. "If you're going to pass your budget, you're going to have to put somebody else in this chair," Clinton told the Republican leaders.

The world, meanwhile, was showing signs that despite the end of the Cold War, humanity retained its savagery. Right-wing extremists, spouting nonsense about an invasion by United Nations troops in "black helicopters," were coddled by zealots in the House Republican caucus. The United States suffered its deadliest act of domestic terrorism when a bomb assembled by antigovernment radicals destroyed the Alfred P. Murrah Federal Building in Oklahoma City in April 1995, killing 168 people, including 19 toddlers in a daycare center. In November, a right-wing assassin murdered Yitzhak Rabin, the Israeli prime minister.

Rabin, a Nobel Peace Prize laureate, was a friend to Kennedy. Ted and his son Patrick joined Clinton and Gingrich on Air Force One for the journey to the funeral in Jerusalem. On the way to the airport, Ted and Patrick stopped at the gravesite in Arlington and scooped soil from the plots of John and Robert Kennedy to mix with the dirt of Rabin's grave. Clinton had handled the Oklahoma City attack superbly, with eloquent speeches about the folly of violence. Gingrich botched the trip to Israel, whining to the press that he had not been treated with the stature and deference he felt due. The Speaker came across like a spoiled child.

The government shutdowns went on for weeks before the Republicans capitulated in early 1996. Most Americans blamed Gingrich, as Dole had shrewdly played the role of grown-up in the room. By the end of March, the Kansas senator had clinched the Republican presidential nomination.

Kennedy now contrived to stop his surge. He chose a two-track strategy. "We have to be very clear about where we are going to fight," he had written Sasso. "But . . . as in the past, I should also work closely with Republicans where there is a chance to make progress on issues that we . . . care about."

First up on the fight track was a hike in the minimum wage—a tough, rough battle that displayed Kennedy's talent for partisan combat. On the progress track was a health care bill, crafted with Dole's Republican seatmate, Nancy Kassebaum of Kansas—an act of bipartisan collaboration. Each left Dole bedeviled.

THE MINIMUM WAGE WAS a trap that Dole might easily have avoided. Kennedy had persuaded Republicans to support a ninety-cent raise back when President George H. W. Bush was president. Dole could easily have gone along with another hike now, but he worried about the rampaging conservative wing of his party, and hesitated. Stagnant wages were a potent issue, but Republican dogma held that small businesses would cut payrolls if saddled with compulsory pay hikes.

The Democratic canon brooked no such worries. Prodded by Kennedy, Clinton had endorsed the pay raise in his 1995 State of the Union address. Kennedy prepared the necessary legislation. There things stood when Rose Fitzgerald Kennedy died at the age of 104.

Her youngest and only surviving son had done his best to break through the fog of senescence in Rose's final years. On Sunday afternoons he would have a musician come to the house in Hyannis Port and bang out the show tunes and Irish ditties she loved on the piano, as he and others sang. Her death came as a shock nonetheless. Joseph Sr. had lit the blowtorch on Ted Kennedy's hindquarters, but it was Rose who gave him his faith, manners, sense of obligation, and Irish identity. It was she, not Joseph, who quoted Luke 12 to her children.

"Having a purpose-driven life was something from his father—he felt it from a young man on," Vicki Kennedy recalled. "The things his father said had enormous impact on him." But both his parents felt a special love for the chubby, endearing baby of the clan. And Ted retained an abiding affection for his mother. He savored and displayed the letters Rose sent him to correct his grammar or chastise him for use of profanity. The funeral was held in the North End, at St. Stephen's Church, a few blocks from where she had been born. Orrin Hatch, other colleagues, and dozens of her descendants attended, on a cold but sunny day.

For a week, Kennedy stayed away from Washington. Aides said he was still affected when he returned to keep an appointment with Daschle and the other Democratic leaders and make his pitch for the minimum wage. It was a classic, proven solution—a justified response to the corrosive effects of globalization and economic inequality. But their strategists had advised them to drop it—there was no way, it was thought, that they could push it through a Republican-controlled Congress.

Kennedy arrived and was infuriated to hear his seatmate, John Kerry, wonder if the measure sent the right signal to the voters, as it was yet another benefit for the poorer people.

Kennedy responded with what Littlefield called "a tirade." He was laying down a marker: it was Memphis redux—a "Robert Bork's America" kind of moment, but unfiltered by any speechwriter. He had spent the last week with his dead. "He was still on edge, his emotions raw," Littlefield recalled. "He clearly felt that everything that he believed about the Democratic Party was on the line."

"I can't believe what I'm hearing!" Kennedy roared. "If we are not going to fight for the wages of working people, who will?" On he went, red-faced, volume rising. "The minimum wage will only help the poor, so we can't be for it?"

"If we won't fight for this cause, what will we ever fight for?" he asked. "If we don't, we don't deserve to call ourselves Democrats."

When he finished, said Littlefield, "there was a long silence, as if he had sucked the air out of the room." Senator Dick Durbin of Illinois broke the spell. "Well," he said, "I guess we understand how Ted feels about this."

———

CLINTON, KERRY, DASCHLE, and Gephardt came on board, but the struggle over the budget and the government shutdowns—and Dole's decision to shut the Senate down while he stumped in Iowa and New Hampshire—foreclosed all opportunities to debate the minimum wage until March 1996, when the majority leader returned to the Senate, low on campaign funds and hoping to use his leadership post and the chamber's friendly confines to display his gifts and talents. Kennedy got the nod from Daschle to proceed. Their tactics required patience, and knowledge of the rules. As liberal groups and labor unions built public support—the outside game—for raising the minimum wage, the Senate Democrats pushed Dole for a vote by exploiting the rules that let any senator propose an amendment, even to extraneous legislation. As majority leader, Dole had the power under other rules to parry such attempts—by adding his own amendments, or amending amendments, or proposing substitutes to entire bills, or by dropping unpalatably amended legislation from the calendar altogether. The goal for Kennedy was to tie up the Senate so that Dole looked ineffective, or was compelled to give them an up-or-down vote on the minimum wage. In either case, Dole would lose.

The first engagement of the general election would thus be staged in the U.S. Senate—on Dole's home turf—with Kennedy serving as Clinton's proxy. The Democrats were cheered on by White House aides, who urged that they get Dole "bogged down in the muddle" of the Senate floor. In a series of test votes, Kennedy had shown he had the support of a majority of their colleagues. Dole should have seen where this all was heading; he should have pivoted and cut a deal. It was what Robert Dole did best. Inexplicably, he did not.

And so, with a bit of legislative chicanery, Kennedy forced Dole to pull a national parks bill off the floor in March. In April, he boxed Dole in on a landmark immigration bill.

"Minimum wage is killing me," Dole told friends.

The Senate was mired in the "Dole-drums," Kennedy declared, defined in the dictionary as "a state of inactivity or stagnation . . . a dull, listless depressed mood . . . a vessel almost becalmed, her sails flapping about in every direction."

Dole had to weigh every move, on every measure, for how his foes might use them to promote a raise in the minimum wage. "The Senate was completely bollixed up. Kennedy had the minimum wage wrapped around the axle," Trent Lott, a Republican from Mississippi, recalled. On May 15, Dole surrendered—and not just on the minimum wage. He shocked the political world by announcing that he would resign his Senate seat and pursue the presidency as "a private citizen, an American, just a man." A national poll showed that, by a 60-to-35 ratio, the voters now disapproved of the Republican Congress. Lott, the new majority leader, was a Gingrich type who had come over from the House, but he had the foresight to recognize that the Republicans running for Congress in November needed to alter their "do nothing" status. In July the Senate voted, 74 to 24, to raise the minimum wage. The House concurred, and in August Clinton signed it into law.

Kennedy took considerable satisfaction. "You know . . . you hope to halt discrimination, or you hope to stop the war—those issues are more than just legislation, you have to change minds," he would say. But a raise in the minimum wage "is a very concrete, measurable, quantifiable twenty dollars a week more for the working people, and it makes a difference." As he once told Rollins, when the Senate's Republican royalists objected to a measure that would raise the family income of a class of union workers from $20,000 to $22,000 a year, "God forbid that a working man would make an extra $2,000 a year."

"The saga of Kennedy and the minimum wage over the course of his Senate career is nothing short of legendary," Littlefield professed. "Four times he led the fight. . . . Each time he faced fervent opposition, even from some Democrats. Each time he prevailed. History will record that he was responsible for increasing wages for the poorest Americans from $2.30 an hour in 1978 to $7.25 in 2009." A typical U.S. senator, compiling that record over thirty years, would be celebrated as an effective and accomplished, big-hearted public servant. For Kennedy, it is almost an asterisk—as he would then go on to demonstrate.

———

KENNEDY HAD NOT FORGOTTEN health care. "We were looking for targets of opportunity," he recalled. Amid the ruins of the Clinton plan, two categories of Americans were readily identified, in Kennedy's office and at the White House, as candidates for incremental help. One group, some twenty-five million, needed a cure that Washington, in its shorthand, called "insurance reform." These were workers trapped in dissatisfying jobs who hesitated to move on to better opportunities (or lived with the terror that their current workplace might lay them off) for fear that the insurance industry would deny them coverage due to preexisting medical conditions. The second group was children. If they could not find a way to pass comprehensive change, a coalition of Democrats and moderate Republicans believed they should at least "do something" for the kids— for ten million children of households that earned too much money to qualify for Medicaid, but not enough to buy private insurance.

Fine causes, readily identified, but someone had to do the work. Someone had to find sponsors in the new Republican majorities, unite the Democrats, and enlist the president. Kennedy was the someone. "He became a master of the ability to move things through the process as it existed," George Mitchell would recall, "not as we might wish it to exist." Kennedy saw and dealt with colleagues as "real, live, breathing human beings, each one different, each one with strengths and weaknesses, understanding how to deal with people, how to get along with them, how to create a sense of trust and confidence," Mitchell said. "Ted was good at it, one of the best."

Having relinquished the freight of his presidential hopes, the jovial, buoyant Ted could surface. "His real strength as a person, his success here on the Hill was the fact that he could bring any one of his colleagues into that sense of joy that he had," Patrick said. "He loved people, he loved the game. . . . His greatest strength—and [key to] his success legislatively— was his ability to befriend . . . to share his joy, his love, for him to connect with people. . . . That's what he was so good at, that connecting."

Kennedy liked Nancy Kassebaum, and she liked Ted Kennedy. Their Senate offices had been for many years across the hall from each other. Often they had strolled together to vote: the Cape Cod gannet and the midlands sparrow. The bond grew stronger when Hatch left the Labor Committee to serve on Finance, leaving Kassebaum as the ranking Republican. She and Kennedy sat beside each other, talking, through the months their committee weighed the Clinton health plan.

Kassebaum was a daughter of the Heartland, with staunch Republican credentials. Her father, Alf Landon, had run against FDR in the 1936 presidential election. She was Dole's seatmate and would soon marry Howard Baker. Working with Ted Kennedy, she would admit, was "like working with the Wicked Witch of the East." Yet this was an era when American politics, though en route, was not quite yet so vicious. In their conversations, she identified the issues of preexisting conditions, and the portability of insurance, as a fight they could make together. He agreed. So was born the Health Insurance Portability and Accountability Act (HIPAA), known as "Kassebaum-Kennedy."

Kassebaum was an efficient chairwoman, and much of the ground had been harrowed in the previous two years. The Labor Committee gave unanimous approval to the legislation in the summer of 1995, and the bill seemed ready for a vote when it was blocked by a small gang of Republicans using a Senate rule that let individual senators put secret "holds" on measures they disliked. Kennedy urged Clinton to champion the legislation in the State of the Union speech, the media was alerted to what was happening, and Dole, campaigning for president, felt compelled to promise that he would end the secret holds and bring up the bill that spring.

As on other occasions—when Kennedy and Hatch joined hands on the landmark AIDS bills, or Thurmond and Kennedy joined forces on sentencing reform—Kennedy and Kassebaum agreed to oppose any changes, from Left or Right, that would alter the nature of their legislation. Their alliance was tested when, amid all the wrangling over the minimum wage bill, Dole proposed to amend the Kassebaum-Kennedy bill to give a tax break to Americans who opened private medical savings accounts (MSAs).

Conservatives applauded, but Kassebaum was true to her word and joined with Kennedy to defeat Dole's proposal. Their legislation then passed the Senate on a 100–0 vote.

There was no time for celebrating. The House version of the bill included the MSA tax break, and after Lott took over from Dole, he broke with the usual Senate practice by excluding Kassebaum and appointing MSA proponents as Senate conferees. Kennedy parried, using the rules to block them from meeting. "Ted Kennedy doesn't run the world," Lott snapped to reporters. But after arduous negotiations, and some necessary soothing of White House aides, who wanted an election-year bill-signing ceremony, and congressional Democrats—many of whom questioned if they would not be better off by employing the Republicans' scorched-earth tactics and killing the bill—a deal was reached, with a short-term MSA pilot program.

"After the health care reform disappointment of 1994, few Members of Congress had any appetite whatsoever for engaging this issue. The two exceptions were Senator Kassebaum and Senator Kennedy," the White House staff informed Clinton. "As a result, workers will no longer be locked into 'second-choice' jobs because their (or their families') preexisting condition makes them live in fear of losing health insurance coverage. . . . Senator Kassebaum played the role of instigator and primary author. . . . Senator Kennedy played the role of tireless advocate, protector of reasonable policy, but end-game deal-maker."

If there was a moment in time that signified Ted Kennedy's revival from the mess of his private life in the 1980s, and the annus horriblis of 1991, it was the third week of August in 1996. On Tuesday, Clinton signed the law raising the minimum wage. On Wednesday, in a second ceremony on the White House lawn, the president signed the Kassebaum-Kennedy Act. Underscoring both events was the growing sense that the Gingrich revolution had died aborning, and that Clinton was now the favorite to win reelection over Dole, the master lawmaker who had been chased from the Senate.

Kennedy "always helped me never to despair," Clinton would recall. "He was one of the first and most aggressive believers . . . that there was still a lot that could be done."

The press had begun to call Ted Kennedy the "lion" of the Senate. "As the minority party's most visible strategist," the *Washington Post* reported, "he's bedeviling the new majority with a host of hot-button economic issues that fuel his impassioned populism and give the Republicans fits."

His colleagues agreed. "I don't know anybody who contributed more," said Daschle. "He's having a royal, riotous good time," said a chagrined Alan Simpson.

Twenty-Nine

IRELAND

The clamor of the 1996 election scotched hope for Kennedy's other favored reform—health care for America's children—for the rest of the year. But it didn't keep Kennedy and Clinton from collaborating on a foreign policy tour de force, bringing peace to Northern Ireland.

The story requires some history. When Ireland won its independence from the British in 1921, six counties in the northern province of Ulster, dominated by Protestant majorities, remained in the United Kingdom. In the years that followed, Catholics there faced poverty and discrimination. Kennedy had come to the issue in the fall of 1971, after civil rights demonstrations by the Catholic minority were suppressed by government security forces, kindling thirty years of violence. The British government response to murderous Catholic and Protestant paramilitary gangs featured military occupation, internment without trial, and torture. While on a trip to study European health care systems, Kennedy was approached by an Irish woman in London. He had voiced his outrage over Kent State and Vietnam, she said: Why wouldn't he speak up for his own people, the Catholics of Northern Ireland?

It was just the sort of question—touching on loyalty to a clan, family history, and a cry for social justice—to trigger a reaction in Kennedy. Until John Kennedy's trip to Ireland in 1963, the Kennedy family seemed ambivalent about their thatched-roof Paddy roots. Kathleen had even married into British aristocracy. But the boys' relationship to Ireland had been influenced by their jaunts with Grandfather Fitzgerald, and the tumultuous welcome given John and Ted Kennedy by the Irish people in the 1960s clinched it. They developed an emotional attachment to the island.

Kennedy ripped into British policy. Ulster was "Britain's Vietnam," he declared. He cosponsored a resolution calling for the withdrawal of British troops and unification of the North with the Irish Republic in the south. "Internment is a cruel and abhorrent policy. The random midnight round-up of suspects . . . the knock on the door, the violent entry, the arrest in the dark of night," he told the Senate. "Three hundred Catholics have been arrested, and not a single Protestant."

"The conscience of America cannot keep silent when men and women of Ireland are dying," he said. "Britain has lost its way, and the innocent people of Northern Ireland are the ones who now must suffer."

The British government and the British press responded with spite and fury. Britain had conquered, ruled, and exploited the island for most of four centuries, the Irish diplomat Sean O'Huiginn noted, and retained an "extraordinary neuralgic nerve" over any indication that the Irish in America, "the monster of their nightmares," would exercise their political clout and turn the United States against the United Kingdom.

"In his grotesque outburst . . . Senator Kennedy showed no more regard for the truth than he did after the drowning of Miss Kopechne on Chappaquiddick," the British *Daily Telegraph* declared. Prime Minister Edward Heath called Kennedy's speech "an ignorant outburst" and the U.S. State Department, an Anglophilic organization that had nurtured a "special relationship" with Britain for decades, ignored Kennedy's protest. Then, on Sunday, January 30, 1972, British paratroopers fired into a Catholic rally in Londonderry, killing thirteen demonstrators. The Bloody Sunday massacre received widespread news coverage in the United States. A mob set fire to the British embassy in Dublin. Kennedy was the lead witness in House committee hearings, where he pushed his Vietnam analogy further. "Just as Ulster is Britain's Vietnam, so Londonderry is Britain's My Lai," he said.

BUT THOUGH HE DISPLAYED such certainty in public, Kennedy was restive about Northern Ireland, and uncomfortable with the rote stance ("Brits Out!") of Irish and Irish American republicans. Kennedy dispatched an aide to Northern Ireland to gauge the political climate, who returned with the verdict that things were too tense for the senator to visit. Kennedy then resolved to bring Ireland to him. When the telephone rang in John Hume's Londonderry home and the fellow on the other end, in a broad Massachusetts accent, identified himself as Ted Kennedy, Hume thought he was the target of a practical joke. "Pull the other leg," he said. But it was Kennedy, asking the Irish lawmaker to meet with him in Bonn, where the senator was headed to a NATO meeting.

The British had shut down the Northern Ireland government, leaving Hume—a social democrat who worked tirelessly to bring peace to the province—as a jobless parliamentarian. He had to swing a loan from his local credit union for the airfare, but he met with Kennedy at the home of the Irish ambassador to West Germany. "That's where John began the great education of Edward Kennedy about Northern Ireland," Kennedy would recall. Within the year, Kennedy published an article in *Foreign Policy* magazine, adopting Hume's nonviolent philosophy and condemning the Irish Republican Army's use of terrorism.

Hume "had a profound influence on me," Kennedy recalled. "He was eloquent and passionate and on the ground and demonstrated extraordinary personal courage. . . . It's important to listen to the ones who are risking their lives."

"The real border in Ireland is not a line on a map. It's in the minds and hearts of people," Hume would say years later. "You can't get rid of that in a week or a fortnight. You need a healing process. So we have to create the structures in which the people will work together rather than shooting each other. . . . As we spill our sweat and not our blood, we will break down the barriers of the past and a new Ireland will evolve. That's a strategy, but it's clearly a long-term strategy. . . . It's a strategy that Ted Kennedy and his colleagues . . . have given their strongest support."

Before Hume schooled him, Kennedy and the forty million other Americans of Irish ancestry viewed Ireland through the mists of Irish nationalism. They broke out the shamrocks, marched in parades, sang about the Minstrel Boy, and cheered the IRA as freedom fighters. The war in the North was seen as a final chapter, the last battle for reunification. Donations from Irish Americans in Boston and New York and other American cities helped the IRA buy the AR-15 rifles and Semtex plastic explosives employed against their Protestant counterparts, the Royal Ulster Constabulary and the British Army. Pubs, parks, and shops were ripped by the gunmen and their bombs, and the death toll climbed into the thousands. "Americans send money over to Ireland and they think that they are sending us help. They are sending us death," Betty Williams, a leader of one northern peace group, told a journalist.

In 1975, the Kennedys got their own spine-chilling lesson in the politics of terror when a car bomb exploded outside the London home of a member of Parliament where Caroline Kennedy, then a student, was staying. By chance, she escaped injury—her host, who was to drive her to class, was delayed by a phone call—but a famed British oncologist, passing by, was ripped apart in the blast.

THE IRISH REPUBLIC, meanwhile, was undergoing a transformation. In May 1972 the voters, by better than a four-to-one margin, chose to join the European Economic Community, the forerunner of the European Union. Multinational firms, attracted by the republic's low corporate tax rates, educated workforce, and access to the European market, were eager to open operations in Ireland. The "Troubles" in the North—bombings, kidnappings, and shootings—were seen as bad for business.

A small contingent of Irish diplomats shared Hume's insight that one path toward a solution might run through Washington, DC, where Irish American politicians had risen to high office. Tip O'Neill was Speaker of the House; Kennedy was perceived as a likely president; Representative Hugh Carey would be governor and Pat Moynihan a U.S. senator of the Empire State of New York. In the short term, such men could persuade

Irish America to stop funding the IRA terror campaigns; in the long term, they might pressure the British government to ease its thickheaded stance. The strategy received a boost when Hume won a fellowship to Harvard and spent a semester in the United States, with ready access to O'Neill and the others. Kennedy hosted a reception in his honor and gave him tours of the Lincoln Memorial and other monuments.

Thus inspired, on March 17, 1977, O'Neill, Kennedy, Carey, and Moynihan issued a declaration that urged the paramilitary groups to "renounce their campaigns of death" and implored Americans to stop sending money "that promotes the current violence." The Four Horsemen, as they were christened, received worldwide coverage in the press—and vicious condemnation from IRA sympathizers in New York and Massachusetts. They followed with a successful appeal, via Speaker O'Neill, to Jimmy Carter. The president's 1977 statement on Northern Ireland—the first by an American chief executive—was an intrusion into a longtime ally's internal affairs, but was sweetened with a promise of U.S. economic aid.

WITH REAGAN'S ELECTION, and Margaret Thatcher's ascent to power in Great Britain, the influence of the four Democrats waned. "Teddy stuck with it," said Bertie Ahern, a future Irish prime minister, though "there were no real signs of getting anywhere." The State Department was its stodgy Anglophilic self. Yet the Horsemen and their Irish confederates kept trying. They feted Reagan as a fellow Irishman, encouraged him to visit his ancestral home in Tipperary, and shared his fondness for Irish jokes and stories. In Reagan's friend and national security adviser, William Clark, they discovered an ally. He was an Irish American, with an educated interest in Irish affairs. "I was looking for openings," Kennedy remembered. "We found . . . a fellow by the name of Clark."

Kennedy rejected one quid pro quo. If he and O'Neill would ease their opposition to American support for the right-wing Contra armies in Nicaragua, they were told, Reagan would intercede with Thatcher and U.S. aid would start flowing to Ulster. Kennedy could not accept that trade-off, but made a counteroffer: If Thatcher helped resolve the Troubles in the North, the Irish Republic might abandon its long-standing neutrality and participate in NATO's defense of western Europe.

In the end, the Irish American leaders had just enough charm and clout to get Reagan to "nudge" his friend Thatcher. At Camp David in 1984, Reagan urged her to leave her unbudgeable position. She had lost close friends to the IRA, dodged its bombers, and generally refused to deal with terrorists. But prodded by Reagan and O'Neill, she acceded that the Troubles were more than an internal police matter. In 1985, she accepted the Anglo-Irish Agreement, giving Dublin a voice in the affairs of Ulster.

The IRA continued its atrocities, but enough of the hard men were growing tired, or nurturing misgivings about their strategy, that Gerry Adams, the political face of the North's republicans, was authorized to confer with Hume. Over time, the British and Irish governments also held secret talks with the IRA and Sinn Fein, its political front. Adams reached out to Irish American business leaders, who invited him to a forum in New York, for which he would need a visa.

Clinton, who identified as Irish (his mother's maiden name was Cassidy), had watched the Catholic civil rights movement while studying as a Rhodes Scholar at Oxford in the 1960s. While campaigning for the Democratic nomination in 1992 he had promised, if elected, to grant Adams a visa. But in his first year in office, apoplectic resistance from the Departments of Justice and State kept him from keeping that promise, especially after Adams was photographed as a pallbearer for an IRA bomber.

SO MATTERS STOOD WHEN Ted and Vicki Kennedy came to Dublin in December 1993, on what they thought was a family vacation, to discover that Ambassador Jean Kennedy Smith had engaged in some productive backstage scheming. She had arrived in the embassy at Phoenix Park in 1993 with a photograph inscribed by Ted: "For Jean, who is going back in the springtime"—a reference to their brother John who, just before his death, had left Ireland with a promise to return. Ignoring the advice of skeptical and stodgy U.S. diplomats, Smith had sought and won the confidence of the republicans. In their clandestine code she was

"Speir-bhean," the Gaelic name for a mythic female personification of Ireland. Ted was, more prosaically, The Brother.

Smith told Kennedy that Adams wished to halt the violence, but needed some sort of gain or accomplishment to prove to his cadres that the path would yield results. They had to persuade Clinton to grant Adams a visa to visit the United States, Smith said. Kennedy bridled. Adams was the front man for IRA terrorists—the thugs who nearly killed their niece. He and Clinton would look like saps if they did favors for Adams and the IRA launched fresh attacks. But Smith had anticipated her brother's hesitancy and weighted his itinerary with visits to her fellow conspirators. The Irish prime minister, Albert Reynolds, gave his strong backing for a visa when Kennedy came to call, as did writer Tim Pat Coogan, an expert on the IRA, when he and the Kennedys dined.

"Tell Teddy what you told me about the visa," Smith prompted Reynolds.

Adams was "our best hope," Reynolds said.

The senator met as well with Father Alec Reid, a Redemptorist priest who had brought warring parties together in Ulster and was a favorite of the ambassador. "Jean had a big influence," Reynolds recalled. "Without her I don't think [Ted] would have swung behind it."

Kennedy was aware that "conversations were taking place," he remembered. "But what impressed me was Jean's observation of the strong commitment that Adams had of ending violence."

"This woman who was patronized" as a lightweight "who would be shortly and drastically out of her depth, was the one who, with absolute acumen, read the situation in Ireland," said Irish diplomat Sean O'Huiginn. "She reminded me of William Yeats' line about Lady Gregory: she could keep a swallow to its first intent . . . a resolute persistence in bringing people to do her will."

In early January, when Hume traveled to Boston for Tip O'Neill's funeral, he and Kennedy went to dinner at Locke-Ober, that ancient Boston landmark known for its scrod, lobster stews, and polished silver hollowware. They spoke for hours. Hume gave the plan his imprimatur, and Kennedy, now committed, went all in. Within days, Smith had formally advised the president—and Kennedy, Moynihan, Kerry, and Dodd had written the White House in her support—to give Adams a visa.

The Departments of Justice and State objected. "The British Embassy was using all its influence to keep Adams out," Kennedy recalled. But on Kennedy's side was his former foreign policy aide, Nancy Soderberg, who had moved on to the White House and, given that she knew the players, managed the Irish portfolio for the National Security Council. She came to have a pivotal role in a covert chain of communication between Sinn Fein and the White House, which ran through Kennedy's office. Adams would talk to Niall O'Dowd, an Irish American newspaper publisher, who would relay word to Kennedy aide Trina Vargo, who would then inform Soderberg, who reported to Anthony Lake and Clinton. When Adams was pressed to renounce violence—something the IRA could not yet accept—the Americans helped him parse a statement that would pass muster with the gunmen while also assuring Clinton that Sinn Fein was sincere. "It was all being filtered through a Kennedy prism," O'Dowd recalled. "The levers were very simple when you were dealing with Ireland on Capitol Hill: get Kennedy, and Kennedy got everyone else."

Two days before Clinton granted the visa, some dud practice grenades were found in British-themed shops and the federal courthouse in San Diego. Kennedy and Soderberg pressed O'Dowd to have Adams denounce what was clearly an amateurish effort to derail his visit. Adams sighed, agreed, and showed a sense of humor. "Does this mean I have to apologize every time an Irishman gets into a fight with an Englishman in a pub?" he asked O'Dowd.

With Kennedy leading the lobbying and providing political cover, Clinton took the risk. "It occurred to me that it was one of those points where there had to be some tangible evidence that there would be a reward for . . . beginning to walk toward peace," the president recalled.

Roderic Lyne, the private secretary to Prime Minister John Major, typified Britain's outrage. "The movement in which Gerry Adams has long been a leading figure has murdered not only thousands of its own countrymen, but also one member of our Royal Family, one Cabinet Minister's wife, two close advisers to Margaret Thatcher and Members of Parliament, two British ambassadors—and small children in our shopping centres," Lyne wrote National Security Adviser Anthony Lake. "It is sad, paradoxical, and misguided of the Kennedys, having lost two brothers to acts of terror, to be pressing you to admit a terrorist leader without an end to terrorism or even a commitment to end terrorism." The British press went bonkers. Much of its ire was directed at Soderberg and Kennedy. When Clinton griped about the flak he was catching, Kennedy told him, "Don't worry about it. It's what the Brits have been saying about the Kennedys for years."

Adams traveled to New York on a forty-eight-hour visit, made a speech, gave a round of television interviews, and met privately with Vargo, who carried word from Kennedy: "There is no free lunch." The IRA was expected to deliver. Adams went home to tell his comrades that if they showed a commitment to peace, they could enlist the world's only superpower as their cornerman. "It gave him a chance to visualize," said Clinton, "what we might be able to help them reap." With the Irish and American governments involved, the Catholics in the North would have patrons and could negotiate with Great Britain with confidence. There was something worth calling "the peace process."

IT WAS NO EASY road. Within weeks of Adams's visit, a series of mortar rounds were fired at London's Heathrow Airport. All failed to explode, but Moynihan wrote Kennedy, "Have we been had?"

Seven months passed before the IRA announced an indefinite ceasefire, and only then after Smith and Kennedy helped win another visa—for Joe Cahill, a hardened old IRA fighter who could swing the army council to the Adams strategy.

"Did you see this guy's CV?" Clinton asked Kennedy.

"Well, I never told you that he was an altar boy," the senator replied.

Kennedy and his Irish American colleagues in Congress then advised Clinton to grant Adams a more expansive visa, which would allow him to tour the country, and let Sinn Fein raise funds in the United States and open an office in Washington.

Kennedy and Vicki led the welcome delegation at Logan Airport when Adams returned to the United States. Vargo fretted that the news photographers would capture the senator and the terrorist in a friendly embrace.

"Whatever you do, don't let Gerry Adams hug you," she told Kennedy.

"Trina, he's Irish," said Vicki. "They barely hug their wives."

The Sinn Fein leader was honored instead with an invitation to spend his first night in Washington at Hickory Hill, the former home of John and Robert Kennedy. Nor were the loyalists forgotten. The doors to the White House and the U.S. government were opened to them as well.

"I never thought I would see the day," said Protestant James Molyneaux, leader of the Ulster Unionist Party, "that Senator Edward Kennedy would sit across the table from me and ask, 'Mr. Molyneaux, what can we do for you?'"

In the days to come were magical moments, like the St. Patrick's Day parties at the White House when Northern Ireland's unionists and republicans, awed and delighted at Clinton's invitation to roam the executive mansion—which had been designed, the president noted, by the Irish architect James Hoban—spoke and drank together and sang into the night; or the trip that Clinton took to Ireland and Northern Ireland at the end of 1995, to meet joyous receptions in Belfast, Derry, and Dublin. He would later call it the greatest journey of his presidency.

But there were grim days as well, like February 9, 1996, when IRA dead-enders, impatient with the lack of progress in negotiations, triggered a massive explosion at Canary Wharf in London, killing two and ending a cease-fire that had lasted seventy-five weeks. It was followed by further attacks, more marching, and riots, requiring all sides to dig deep to repair the shattered process. At the Republican convention that summer, former secretary of state James Baker ridiculed "Gullible's Travels" and accused Clinton of damaging relations with Great Britain. On the campaign trail, Robert Dole scorned Clinton as the man who "invited a terrorist to the White House." Before the Canary Wharf attack, Clinton had appointed George Mitchell as an economic envoy to Northern Ireland; he expected to serve for 130 days. When the IRA reverted to violent tactics, Mitchell's task became more encompassing, and far more difficult.

Kennedy refused to meet with Adams until the cease-fire was restored. It was not until August 1997, after seventeen months of further bloodshed, that the republican gunmen announced their second cessation of violence.

As Mitchell steered the ever-stubborn northerners toward a peaceful settlement, Kennedy did what he could to support his old colleague. "Teddy was a huge show of strength," Ahern recalled. "There were periods where the IRA and Sinn Fein tried to get out of some of the responsibilities, and Teddy went on a limb against the IRA, against Adams, saying implement the agreement."

"He never changed," said Ahern. "He was the one who didn't just chip in with the weather. He was there all along."

In January 1998, Kennedy finally got to visit Ulster. He toured Belfast and Derry, sat in on the peace talks, called for the decommissioning of arms and paramilitary organizations, and took his turn at the annual Tip O'Neill memorial lecture at the Guildhall in Derry. On Good Friday that spring, a peace agreement was signed.

Thirty

TROUBLED WATERS

The telephone rang in the night. It was late, but the message was urgent. John Kennedy Jr., his wife, Carolyn, and her sister Lauren were missing. They had last been seen in his small Piper airplane with John at the controls, leaving an airport outside New York, destined for Martha's Vineyard. Now Ted Kennedy needed to call out the naval and air search teams, and to prepare himself and his family for the staggering possibility that their lives had been struck once more by horror and grief. Many of them were with him in Hyannis Port: they had gathered that Friday evening, July 16, 1999, for his niece Rory Kennedy's rehearsal dinner. The wedding was to take place Saturday. John was on his way to join them.

At midday, a beachgoer on the Vineyard spotted a garment bag in the waves. It was found to contain Lauren's clothes. So ended the hope that there had been some grand misunderstanding and that John would walk through the door with a grin. The National Transportation Safety Board's investigation would conclude that the young pilot, with little night-flying experience, became disoriented after making the turn from the New England shoreline toward where the island, the sea, and the sky faded to black. His frantic response put the plane into a fatal spiral until, nose first and accelerating, it drove into the sea.

Kennedy worked the phones that night and day and weekend. He prayed with the family in funereal vigils held in the white tents erected for

Rory's wedding. Just eighteen months earlier she had held her dying brother Michael in her arms, after he crashed into a tree while skiing with his family in Colorado. On Sunday Kennedy flew to New York to console John's sister, Caroline. He called Robert Shrum, who had written Kennedy's eulogy for Jacqueline Onassis, and told him, "You better get started."

Late Tuesday, the airplane was found in 120 feet of water, seven miles short of the island. Kennedy and his sons were carried by a Coast Guard helicopter and cutter to the Navy salvage ship USS *Grasp* on Wednesday, and were there when the bodies were brought to the surface. "Over the previous few days, we had been consumed—and perhaps even a little distracted—by the technical details of the search, which were provided to us in the depersonalized language the military adopts," Patrick remembered. "But when we were out on that cutter, just my brother and me flanking my dad, it was starting to become more and more real.

"I thought about how many tragedies like this my father had been forced to confront and process. . . . I understood, intellectually, how those traumas had formed him and my family over the decades. But I had no real understanding of that moment of incomprehensible pain and isolation, what it probably felt like when my father flashed back—until we heard on the radio that they were going to start bringing up what they had found and the winch began cranking.

"My father couldn't really react except to put his hand on my shoulder," Patrick recalled. "He was so deep inside himself that he was just shut down. He couldn't comprehend what we were witnessing; it was too much, so raw."

For TED KENNEDY AND the generation that followed his, their journey of splendor and loss had appalling costs. Introspection and self-reflection were not on the Kennedy palette. "It wasn't a family big on . . . allowing you to grieve," Maria Shriver said. Her parents' generation "all walked around with a lot of grief and a lot of sadness which would pop out in different ways, as emotion or rage, because they kept getting hammered."

"I grew up among people who were geniuses at not talking about things," Patrick remembered. "There was huge suffering going on in my family. But it was never spoken of."

Some in the family—notably Jacqueline Onassis and Sargent and Eunice Shriver—recognized how lives could be warped and took steps to shelter their children. Others were left to find their way. Ted Kennedy had reacted to his son's drug problems with much the same impatience as he had to Joan's drinking. What Patrick needed was "a good swift kick in the ass," his father said.

Kennedy was surprised—and then proud and encouraging—when Patrick, as a student at Providence College, and recuperating from surgery to remove a tumor on his spine, ran for a seat in the Rhode Island state legislature and won. After graduating from college, Patrick set his sights on one of Rhode Island's two congressional seats and claimed it in 1994. Patrick was thrilled to have his father's respect and regard, but he admired his brother, Ted Jr., for choosing a different path as well. Kennedy had pushed his older son to run for John F. Kennedy's old congressional seat in Massachusetts, which came open when Tip O'Neill retired. After moving to the district, Ted Jr. had concluded that he wasn't ready, and told his dad he would not be a candidate. Letting their father down took "incredible courage," Patrick said.

IF HE STRUGGLED TO convey his feelings in private, Kennedy was superb at the public expression of loss. With John's death, he was called, once more, to give a eulogy. Kennedy "shines brightest in the darkest suit," *Time* magazine reported. "In the practiced cadences, the defiant wit, the stubborn Catholicism that insists on seeing all the way to the gates of heaven." On July 22, Ted and a small group of family watched from the deck of a U.S. Navy destroyer as John Kennedy's ashes and those of his wife and her sister were scattered on the ocean off Martha's Vineyard. The next day they gathered with a bigger group, led by President Clinton and his family, for a memorial service at the Church of St. Thomas More on the Upper East Side of Manhattan.

Ted began with a story. There came a time, he said, when John was asked what he would do if he went into politics and got elected president. John had replied, "I guess the first thing is call up Uncle Teddy and gloat."

"I loved that," said Kennedy as the mourners laughed. "It was so like his father."

"He had a legacy, and he learned to treasure it. He was part of a legend, and he learned to live with it," Ted said. "Above all, Jackie gave him a place to be himself, to grow up, to laugh and cry, to dream and strive on his own."

"John was one of Jackie's two miracles," the senator said. "He was still becoming the person he would be—and doing it by the beat of his own drummer."

"We dared to think, in that . . . Irish phrase, that this John Kennedy would live to comb gray hair, with his beloved Carolyn by his side," he said. "But like his father, he had every gift but length of years."

So, with a line from Yeats, they said goodbye to John Jr., the "boy who grew into a man with a zest for life and a love of adventure."

John's death was the last, almost surreal, of the century's tolls on the Kennedys. His evoked the fall of Icarus, and stirred exegesis about curses and risk and hubris. Some years later, a memoirist from his generation gave credit to his family for bequeathing the cousins "an appreciation for life, a passion for living each moment fully."

"There is an honesty and vitality to sucking the marrow out of life that is exhilarating," Christopher Lawford wrote. "It is also dangerous."

TWO WEEKS AFTER John Jr.'s death, one of Kennedy's aides, David Sutphen, lost his mother. He went home to Milwaukee for her funeral, where he kept receiving phone calls from the senator. These were not work calls—not a boss asking, "Where is this report?" or "When will you be back?" Kennedy was checking in, to see if Sutphen was okay.

Dozens of friends, advisers, and acquaintances could tell the same story: how the telephone would ring, or the door to the church or funeral home would open, and there was Ted Kennedy, offering compassion.

"I had never lost anybody close to me before," said Sutphen. "It helped a lot, because I thought to myself, *As bad as this feels for me, if he can do this and can have done it as many times as he has and seemed to get his life back together and go on and stay strong . . .* "

We.ll then, maybe, Sutphen thought, he could make it through and soldier on as well.

BILL CLINTON HAD TAKEN heat from his critics for the costs of the extended search and recovery efforts he approved after John Kennedy's plane was reported missing, and for the Navy ship used in the ocean burial. It was part of a complex relationship between the two families, which was showing signs of wear in Clinton's second term. The senator and the president were steady allies on Northern Ireland, and in a legislative effort to provide health care coverage to working people with disabilities, and on a measure known as "the patients' bill of rights," which aimed to end abuses by health maintenance organizations. But they bickered during Clinton's impeachment, and openly clashed over Kennedy's signature issue of the late 1990s—the Children's Health Insurance Program (CHIP).

The idea of extending coverage to the ten million American children not covered by public or private health insurance was not new. The Kennedy and White House staffs had talked of its potential in Clinton's first months in office, and again as an incremental step after the president's health care reform bill was defeated. Once Clinton was reelected, the issue showed up on each man's to-do list for 1997. Their differences came down to cost. Clinton wanted to include a modest benefit for children as part of a balanced budget agreement with the Republicans. Kennedy wanted a bigger program, funded by a tax hike on tobacco.

The Republicans controlled Congress, and so Kennedy needed a conservative cosponsor who would stand up to the party's pushback. After intense negotiations in the winter of 1996–97, Orrin Hatch agreed to join his old ally on a program that would raise $30 billion in taxes on tobacco products, with $10 billion applied to deficit reduction and $20 billion for insuring children. The Utah Republican was an amateur songwriter, and to soften him up Kennedy had Nick Littlefield (who had once sung on Broadway) break the tension with a stirring a cappella version of a Hatch melody. Hatch smiled. "Nice move, Teddy," he said. Ultimately, the two senators struck another of their pacts, swearing to resist all challenges.

They quickly met resistance from Majority Leader Lott, who didn't much like the Hatch-Kennedy freelancing, and from Clinton, who needed Lott to sign off on a balanced budget resolution. Kennedy's approach was "maddening," White House aide John Hilley recalled. "We offered to work with him . . . [but] he was off on his own, he and Hatch and a bunch of Finance and Labor compatriots."

The deal that Clinton could reach with Lott and the Republicans was relatively meager: no tobacco tax, and only $16 billion for children, to be raised through the consolidation of other programs. Kennedy and Hatch defied them, but in May the president and the majority leader twisted enough arms to defeat the CHIP amendment, 53–47. "There we were, being forced to lobby . . . against the damn Kennedy-Hatch amendment," Hilley remembered. "The President, me, everybody making calls and lobbying senators to vote against this damn thing, which on policy grounds we were very much in favor of, all because they decided this was their time and they were going to go for it."

KENNEDY WAS INCENSED. He believed that Clinton had betrayed him, and the nation's children, for the callous goal of a balanced budget. The White House "resisted and resisted and resisted," he would gripe. But Hatch rounded up enough support on the Finance Committee to keep their alternative alive. In June, Hatch got the Finance panel to agree to raise the tobacco tax, and to add $8 billion more for children's health care to the $16 billion that Lott and Clinton had settled on.

Kennedy—upset at sweeteners Hatch was compelled by his Finance colleagues to include in the deal—accused his partner of treachery. "I called up Orrin and laid into him that I thought he was selling out," Kennedy remembered.

Don't be ridiculous, Hatch shot back: they had been shooting for

$20 billion for kids. He had secured $24 billion. Kennedy was "blind . . . unappreciative . . . damn dense."

Kennedy sulked for a night, came to his senses, and recanted. The full Senate then voted to approve the Finance Committee package.

Kennedy and Hatch were making progress, but their work was not finished. The House and the White House were standing by their opening bid of $16 billion and vowing to chop the Senate version in the conference negotiations. With Hillary Clinton's help, and after Kennedy and the president had a heart-to-heart, the White House finally embraced the Senate's $24 billion figure, and the House and Senate conferees hammered out a deal. Clinton signed his balanced budget bill on August 5, 1997. It included the $24 billion over five years for CHIP—the biggest new social program approved by Congress since 1965. "That was Kennedy's role," said Hilley.

This "increment" of health care reform was huge. After factoring in the families covered through CHIP, and new Medicaid enrollees who were attracted by publicity about the CHIP program, by 2010 only 10 percent of American children remained uncovered by public or private health insurance. Kennedy and Hatch had seen to it. Kennedy "had at last integrated his wonderful human qualities . . . his generosity, his empathy, his good fellowship, his sense of humor. . . . He was able to blend those together with . . . the ideals that motivated his public life," said Tunney. "And that made him a powerhouse."

CLINTON NEEDED THE VICTORY. In February 1997 the Whitewater special prosecutors, frustrated at their failure to find the president and First Lady culpable of financial misdeeds, and having wasted several million dollars reinvestigating Vincent Foster's suicide (only to find that the White House lawyer, suffering from depression, had indeed taken his own life), faced the unwelcome prospect that this chapter in their careers was going to be a titanic failure.

Panicky at the prospect, Kenneth Starr and his gang of would-be Javerts set their dogs on Clinton's sex life. They found their own Madame

Thénardier—a disgruntled secretary, Linda Tripp—who posed as a friend to a White House intern by the name of Monica Lewinsky. Tripp learned that Monica and Bill had been having consensual sexual play dates. Starr's right-wing allies questioned the president about Lewinsky during a deposition in an Arkansas harassment case, filed by a woman named Paula Jones. Clinton lied, under oath, and Starr used all the powers of his office to compel Lewinsky to confess. It was a shabby, shameful performance all around. But Gingrich had his wish. The Republicans had embraced the nasty.

The independent counsel statute that Starr abused had been crafted with Kennedy's aid. In the fall of 1973, in the days after Richard Nixon's Saturday Night Massacre, Kennedy had been borne along by the frenzy. He and his colleagues, playing to the press, failed to see that this extra-constitutional barnacle, with its lack of accountability and limitless resources, could be a source of evil mischief in the hands of men like Starr, whose office spent five years and $50 million to prove that Clinton had lied about breaching his marriage vows.

The whole "sordid tale," as *Time* magazine's cover described it, broke in early 1998. Starr followed up with a 450-page report, and thousands of pages of appendices, that chronicled every presidential whisper, caress, and ejaculation. Kennedy was a rock throughout. He stood at Clinton's side in Massachusetts when the president made his first public appearance after confessing, on national television, that he had had an affair with Lewinsky. The witless Republicans in Congress, failing to see the potential for self-destruction—as many were adulterers themselves—impeached the president. They misread a disgusted electorate: the House Republicans lost seats in the fall election and dumped Gingrich as their leader. The Senate nevertheless had a duty to perform, and convened to put a president on trial, for the second time in American history.

KENNEDY WAS A FRIEND to Clinton in what followed, though the president did not always see it that way. The strategy of the Senate Democrats was to maintain a pose of impartiality and let events play out, knowing that the Republicans were nowhere near the constitutional hurdle—a vote by two-thirds of the Senate—needed to drive Clinton from office. Lott knew the math, and worked with his Democratic counterpart, Thomas Daschle, on a process that would reach a conclusion in a brisk and respectable manner. Most dreaded a polarized chamber, with Democrats and Republicans snarling for months over every salacious detail. Kennedy played a key role in an early test of the grand design.

On January 7, 1998, the senators assembled for a rare nonpartisan caucus in the Old Senate Chamber, just off the Rotunda. In this ornate room of gilt and marble columns, beneath its half-dome ceiling, their predecessors had debated the fate of slavery and failed to slow the descent toward civil war in the years from 1819 to 1859. "It was here, on the first day of the historic Clinton impeachment trial, that Republicans and Democrats forged a plan to save the nation (and themselves) from ruination," an historian of the day reported.

"Heavenly Father, we are in trouble and we need your help," said Senator Daniel Akaka of Hawaii in the opening invocation. "We've come to a point where we don't know what to do."

Intellectually, the senators knew what was best for them and for the country, but in their discussion about the trial the tugs of partisan rivalry inevitably emerged. The House managers were pressuring their Republican colleagues in the Senate. The White House wanted its Democratic allies to stonewall. Consensus was elusive, though the questions were relatively simple: What evidence would the Senate consider? Which and how many witnesses would testify? Too few, and they would look feckless; too many, and they would seem crass. "The White House has sullied itself. The House has fallen into the black pit of partisan indulgence," warned Robert Byrd. "The Senate is teetering on the brink of that same black pit."

Phil Gramm, the conservative Republican from Texas, rose and referred, like several senators before him, to the ghosts of great men who once stalked that chamber. Daniel Webster had pleaded for the Union, "not as a Massachusetts man, nor as a Northern man, but as an American," Gramm told his colleagues. There were standard Senate rules on calling witnesses, he told them—the question didn't need to divide them now.

Then Kennedy rose to speak. Gramm was right, he said. Begin the trial. Start the opening arguments. See how things go, and deal with the issue of witnesses later. They didn't need to get to home plate today. "We can get to second base together," he told his colleagues. He proposed that they just agree to agree.

The sight of the liberal lion, lying down with the conservative Gramm, moved their colleagues. Senators cried, "Hear! Hear!" and thumped the desks. "Seal the deal!" someone shouted. Kennedy and Gramm dramatically shook hands, and Lott seized the moment. "If we've got an agreement between Gramm and Kennedy, we ought to be able to wrap this up," he said. "Let's not talk ourselves out of something." He declared the debate over, grabbed Daschle by the arm, and headed for the door.

With "the Gramm-Kennedy Miracle," the Senate had dodged a partisan bloodletting. But several senators and aides were puzzled. Just what was the agreement? Something needed to get put on paper. Kennedy and Gramm joined Lott and Daschle and a handful of other senators to prepare a resolution. In the end they agreed that the Senate would choose which witnesses to approve, and not hear "extraneous" testimony about the president's infidelity. The measure passed, 100 to 0.

It was a good deal for the Democrats. Over time, the Senate would agree to three witnesses, on videotape, whose testimony would be limited to the Lewinsky affair. She would testify, but on tape—not from the well of the Senate. Clinton, who saw any conciliatory moves by Senate Democrats as a conferral of legitimacy on the proceedings, viewed Kennedy's action as a betrayal. The president called up Senate Democrats. "You guys fucked us!" he said. His fears were ungrounded. The Republicans failed to collect a simple majority, much less the two-thirds they needed to convict the president. All but the most hateful partisans agreed that it was a fair and thorough trial. Or at least that it was fair and thorough enough.

Thirty-One

FORTUNATE SONS

Relatively few Democrats had griped when Kennedy's alliance with Republicans like Orrin Hatch supplied a bipartisan umbrella for votes on social issues like AIDS, Title IX, or civil rights. But as the House, and then the Senate, were populated by Gingrich acolytes, the comity in Congress faded. Right-wing talk radio hosts like Rush Limbaugh had arrived on the scene in the late 1980s, and Fox News made its debut in 1996, striving for ratings by flagrantly stoking the fears and resentments of white America. The sort of lawmakers who could bridge differences—moderate southern Democrats, and liberal northeastern Republicans—were endangered species. "To the extent you are in the center of the road, you are roadkill," said Kennedy's friend Christopher Dodd. Kennedy bemoaned "the corruption of the Senate" and "the withering away of collegiality and sense of collective mission."

The new, polarized era was not the best time for deal-makers. "It was the beginning of the intransigence," his wife, Vicki, remembered. Democratic partisans began to question whether Kennedy's hunger for achievement made him too accommodating—too focused on his legacy. As he continued to forge alliances with conservatives like Lauch Faircloth of North Carolina, Sam Brownback of Kansas, or John McCain of Arizona, more than a few Senate Democrats grumbled that the Republicans were taking advantage of him. His drive to build a record as one of the Senate's all-time great lawmakers deprived the Democrats of popular issues, they believed, and led to ill-advised compromises. The child health battle was one example: To enlist Republican allies, Kennedy had agreed to construct CHIP as a block grant, susceptible to the whims of government, instead of as a sturdier federal entitlement like Social Security or Medicare.

Kennedy's collaboration with a centrist like Clinton was tolerable for liberals. But then, after a most bitter struggle that carried to the U.S. Supreme Court, Texas governor George W. Bush claimed the presidency over Clinton's vice president, Albert Gore, in 2001. Lines were drawn. For most of his final years in office, Kennedy would have to choose between hotspur opposition or trading with the enemy.

"It was one of those moments when he had to reteach himself where he was," said Moynihan's aide Lawrence O'Donnell. "He didn't just want to sit there and stare at Republican control. . . . That was just not going to be an interesting workday for him. He saw the reality. He found his spots."

"If it was easy, he wouldn't have had fun doing it," Chris Jennings agreed. Kennedy had many strengths, but perhaps his unique advantage was to recognize possibilities, to see the moment. "He sensed energy and potential quicker than others—and got ahead of it."

BUSH INHERITED A GRAND economy and a world at peace. The Clinton administration had launched cruise missiles at suspected terrorist sites in Afghanistan and Sudan after Al Qaeda, an Islamic terror group, bombed two U.S. embassies in Africa, but the jihadist threat had been eclipsed by Gingrich's antics and Ken Starr's circus. The airstrikes were dismissed by many as Clinton's crude attempt to serve up a distraction from his troubles. Bush and his national security team brushed aside the CIA's distinct warnings that Al Qaeda was primed to strike again, and at the American homeland.

Bush focused on domestic affairs. For the Republican donor class, he pushed a huge package of tax cuts through Congress. To fulfill a campaign promise to reform public education, he asked Kennedy and other congressional Democrats to join him in crafting the No Child Left Behind Act. The president believed that low-income students suffered from a "soft bigotry" of lowered expectations, and that schools in poorer neighborhoods would profit from tough federal standards, increased standardization, and accountability. This mirrored Kennedy's beliefs. Federal aid to education "had evolved into a two-tier system, where the low-income kids were just expected to learn the basics, whereas middle class and affluent kids were expected to master an increasingly complex society and acquire higher order skills," said Kennedy's friend and adviser William Taylor. During the Clinton years, Kennedy became a sponsor of the notion that "there ought to be high standards for all kids." It wasn't enough to send bundles of federal money to the schools: Washington needed to demand results.

Bush followed the Reagan template in wooing Kennedy, inviting the senator and his family to the White House for burgers and barbecue and the screening of a new film on the Cuban Missile Crisis in February, and hosting them again that fall at a ceremony renaming the main Justice Department building after Robert Kennedy. As heirs of political dynasties, Kennedy and Bush had something in common. Alan Simpson had warned each of them that they would like the other. Kennedy was "one of the orneriest sons of bitches around," Simpson told Bush on Inauguration Day, "but if he tells you he'll do something, you can count on it. You can trust him." At the White House movie premiere, Bush said to Kennedy, "I like to surprise people. Let's show them Washington can still get things done."

Kennedy wrote back the next day: "Like you, I have every intention of getting things done, particularly in education and health care. We will have our differences along the way, but I look forward to some important Rose Garden signings."

"I was excited," Bush recalled. "No Child Left Behind stood a much better chance of becoming law with support from the Lion of the Senate. It was the beginning of my most unlikely partnership." Kennedy joined him in exploratory strategy sessions, and in Bush's first public appearance to promote the bill, at an elementary school in northeast Washington. "All of these things . . . were about this trust developing, this mating dance, this relationship, this common cause of getting something big done," Bush adviser Margaret Spellings recalled. "It didn't take long to figure out that here [in Kennedy's support] were the keys to the kingdom."

For his part, Kennedy saw an opportunity to substantially enlarge the federal role in education—a break from Republican intransigence that dated back to Eisenhower. "We were elected to do something," Kennedy would remember. "If we had a shot at education reform . . . well, I was going to try to seize it." He was impressed by the president's preparation and commitment. Kennedy would return from the White House meetings with Bush and tell his staff, "This guy knows what he's talking about." In May, after Senator James Jeffords of Vermont left the Republican Party, caucusing with the Democrats and giving them the Senate majority, Kennedy became the bill's manager, embracing and defending it on the Senate floor, where it passed 91 to 8, and thrashing out differences with the House in the conference committee.

The wings of both parties were wary of the Bush-Kennedy collaboration. Conservatives objected when Bush dropped Republican demands for school choice and voucher programs, while liberals feared that the higher expectations for schools in poorer neighborhoods would not be accompanied by the necessary financial resources. In a closed-door meeting of Senate Democrats, Kennedy and Senator Paul Wellstone, the liberal Democrat from Minnesota, had an angry exchange. Wellstone accused Kennedy of falling for a presidential con job: Bush would *never* provide the funds he had promised, the Minnesotan said. "It became very divisive," Daschle recalled. "The two of them got into a terrible screaming match. They just both lost control of their emotions."

"It was a classic example of the concern everybody had at that time: Why did Ted settle for so little?" said Daschle.

Kennedy prevailed and helped usher the bill to the president's desk. It was signed in January 2002. Kennedy joined Bush at the ceremony, and on a victory lap they took through New England. The president gave Kennedy credit for standing firm against the teachers' unions and other powerful liberal interest groups. The legislation authorized billions to support its requirement that failing public schools start meeting higher standards.

Authorizing and appropriating are two different things on Capitol

Hill, however. Wellstone's fears were valid. Kennedy and his Democratic counterparts in the House seethed at the invariably low funding levels included in Bush's budgets. In the fiscal year of 2006, the funding authorized by Congress was $22.75 billion, but Bush requested an appropriation of just $13.3 billion. They had been snookered. They accused the president of betrayal, of breaking his word. Kennedy "was ripshit. Outraged. Furious," his aide James Manley remembered. But by then Bush had moved on to the Global War on Terror, which, for all its grim demands, offered a sure path toward reelection.

To PROMOTE THE NO CHILD LEGISLATION, Bush was attending a staged event—reading a children's book to second graders at an elementary school in Florida—when two hijacked airplanes flying out of Boston slammed into the World Trade Center in New York on September 11, 2001. First Lady Laura Bush, a former teacher, had an appointment in Kennedy's office that morning, to prepare to testify before the Labor Committee on early childhood education. By the time Kennedy greeted her, they both understood that the United States was under attack. His office television carried the images of the burning twin towers, but he made every effort—with small talk, the presentation of a gift, and his usual guided tour of the memento-laden office—to ignore the scenes from lower Manhattan.

She found it eerie. "I felt trapped in an endless cycle of pleasantries," she would recall. "He may have feared that if we actually began to contemplate what had happened in New York, I might dissolve into tears." But she also wondered "if the small talk that morning was Ted Kennedy's defense mechanism, if after so much tragedy—the combat death of his oldest brother in World War II, the assassinations of his brothers Jack and Robert, and the deaths of nephews, including John Jr., whose body he identified when it was pulled from the cold, dark water off Martha's Vineyard—if after all those things he simply could not look upon another grievous tragedy."

For his part, Kennedy viewed their quiet conversation as a signal to the world that the U.S. government was unshaken and functioning. Then came news that another hijacked jetliner had struck the Pentagon. The Secret Service, guns drawn and rifles ready, hustled the First Lady through hallways and stairs and to their fortified downtown headquarters. A fourth hijacked aircraft was headed toward Washington, mostly likely to destroy the Capitol. It crashed into a Pennsylvania field after its passengers attacked the terrorists in the cockpit. The Capitol and White House were evacuated and Kennedy, battling the traffic that knotted downtown Washington, went home. He returned to the Hill that night, when the Senate held an evening session to demonstrate that it would not be intimidated.

IT WOULD REQUIRE A nobler man than George W. Bush to resist the political temptation that followed the terrorist attacks. In an unprecedented outpouring, the country and the world offered their sympathy and support to the American president as daring CIA and U.S. Special Forces, with a minimum of casualties, toppled the Taliban regime and sent Al Qaeda's leaders scurrying from their outposts in Afghanistan. Bush showed panache while standing amid the rubble of the World Trade Center, dignity at the memorial service in Washington, and unity when hugging Democratic leaders on the floor of Congress. His administration's failures to heed the warnings as the system blinked red before 9/11 were overlooked, perhaps because there were so many who shared the blame. By a 98–0 margin, the Senate voted to authorize the use of force against terrorism; by a 98–1 margin, with Kennedy joining both majorities, the Senate passed the Patriot Act—a far-reaching revision of the FISA legislation that Kennedy had sponsored in 1978—granting burly powers to U.S. intelligence and security agencies.

Bush's approval ratings soared, and he and his advisers grew haughty and bold. A White House aide scorned "the reality-based community" who "believe that solutions emerge from . . . judicious study of discernible reality." Not so, the adviser said. "We're an empire now, and when we act, we create our own reality."

The Patriot Act's provisions were pushed to the limit of the law, and beyond, at the expense of civil liberties. The administration defended the use of indefinite detainment, extraordinary rendition, and the torture of prisoners. When a Democrat-led effort to create a new Department of Homeland Security—a move the president's party opposed—stalled in Congress over concerns voiced by organized labor, the Republicans brazenly flip-flopped, embraced the plan, and accused the Democrats of craven temporizing. The Republicans won a Senate seat in Georgia by questioning the patriotism of incumbent Max Cleland, who had lost an arm and both legs in Vietnam, where his heroism had earned him a Silver Star, Bronze Star, and Purple Heart. Yet these were minor attainments, dwarfed by the administration's triumphant campaign to take the United States into a preemptive war with Iraq.

From the first days after 9/11, Bush had sown the ground. The next time the terrorists struck, the White House warned, the smoking gun would be a mushroom cloud. Time would expose the flaws and fissures in the administration's rationalizations for war. Iraqi dictator Saddam Hussein did not maintain arsenals of nuclear or biological weapons, nor did his regime shelter and abet Al Qaeda. Iraq did not flourish once Saddam was deposed, nor was the Middle East transformed by a surge of democracy. The American war against Iraqi insurgents would last far longer and cost far, far more in lives and treasure than Bush and his aides so blithely projected.

KENNEDY'S ACCESSION TO THE national mood went just so far. He had lived through a similar period of nationalistic excess after the Iranians seized the U.S. embassy in 1980 and knew that, in time, the country would return to its senses. When the Patriot Act came up for reauthorization, Kennedy joined in a filibuster to force changes. He railed at the news that the Bush administration had been eavesdropping, without court orders, on American citizens. And in September 2002, as the Bush administration was starting to chant its Iraq war prayer, Kennedy gave a speech at the Johns Hopkins School of Advanced International Studies in Washington and called on Americans to resist. "We've been down that road before and a lot of people died," he told a friend in Massachusetts, referring to Vietnam. "I'm not going down that road again."

The Bush administration "has produced no persuasive evidence" of a menacing Iraqi nuclear weapons program, Kennedy told his Washington audience, or of Iraqi collaboration with Al Qaeda. An invasion of Iraq, he said, would siphon attention and resources from the war against the real enemy, Osama bin Laden and his gang, and from the ongoing campaign to pacify Afghanistan. It would require an "immense" postwar commitment to impose order and create a stable, democratic Iraq. The talk of war was already poisoning American politics, said Kennedy, as the administration accused critics of doubtful loyalty. Two weeks later, Kennedy was one of only twenty-three senators to vote against the resolution authorizing war against Iraq.

Like his brother Robert, who had argued during the Cuban Missile Crisis that airstrikes against Cuba would put America in the same shameful category as the Japanese attackers of Pearl Harbor, Kennedy opposed the "dishonorable treachery" of a preventive war. A preemptive strike against enemy forces massing on a country's border might be justified, Kennedy said, but America's leadership had wisely, and morally, suppressed the impulse to launch nuclear attacks on the Soviet Union, Communist China, or other hostile states during Cold War crises. "Might does not make right," said Kennedy. "The administration's doctrine is . . . the antithesis of all that America has worked so hard to achieve in international relations since the end of World War II."

KENNEDY WAS DISTRACTED BY the news that his daughter, Kara, at the age of forty-two, was suffering from what at first was diagnosed as incurable lung cancer. She, the firstborn of his children and the one he had the greatest difficulty reaching as a parent, was the third of his offspring to contract a form of cancer before the age of forty-five. Ted Jr. had been twelve when his leg was amputated. Patrick, whose childhood was marred by asthma, was twenty when doctors carved a tumor from his spinal column. "Kara was a bit left out because the two boys were so ill, and having so many crises," her father's aide Melody Miller recalled. And "Joan was ill, so Kara did not always have . . . a mother who was there for her."

Now the Kennedys were back in the world of toxic chemotherapy and long-shot surgery. Doctors at Johns Hopkins told them that Kara had best go home and prepare for death, that she had just a 15 percent chance of survival. Her father told his overwhelmed daughter not to abandon hope.

"That is what they said about Teddy," Kennedy told his daughter. "Do not believe what they say. Stay strong."

Ted and Vicki started calling experts, without success. Friends and advisers thought it hopeless.

"Every time you see a doctor they tell you the same thing," one told him.

"That's fine," Kennedy said. "I want to hear each one of them tell it to me."

They persevered, and found a team of specialists at Brigham and Women's Hospital in Boston who, reviewing the test results, decided that the prognosis was incorrect. It was in fact a treatable cancer, and it had been discovered early. They subjected Kara to a three-part course of treatment that included surgery, chemotherapy, and radiation. Ted and Vicki spent hours in the hospital with her, and he often attended daily Mass, praying for her recovery. Five years later, Kara was cancer-free and running five miles a day. "She lived ten more years," Vicki would remember. "He made that happen. He gave her hope. He wouldn't take no for an answer."

THE U.S. MILITARY'S "shock and awe" assault, and the quick capitulation of Baghdad and the regime, muted Kennedy and other Senate critics—like his friend and ally Robert Byrd—but only for a time. The Bush administration was clueless in victory, and unprepared to administer its conquered territory. An Iraqi insurgency took root. American soldiers were killed and maimed by roadside bombs, mortar and rocket attacks, and soon, open combat in Fallujah and other cities.

Kennedy took it upon himself to fix one Pentagon blunder. At Arlington National Cemetery for the funeral of PFC John Hart, a Massachusetts constituent killed in Iraq, Kennedy heard from the boy's parents, Brian and Alma, how the troops were moving through hostile territory, short on body armor and riding in lightly armored Humvees, prey to ambushes and improvised explosive devices. In Defense Secretary Donald Rumsfeld's war plans, the Humvees were never to be used for occupational duties against a guerrilla army, but for a quick dash to Baghdad and a victory parade home. Kennedy used his seat on the Armed Services Committee to expose the danger and compel the Pentagon to procure armor for the vehicles. On the morning of the first anniversary of John Hart's death, Ted and Vicki joined the soldier's parents at the cemetery. "He told Alma that early morning was the best time to come to Arlington. It was quiet and peaceful and the crowds wouldn't be there yet," said Brian Hart. "He had flowers for my son's grave."

Kennedy was known for such gestures. He held the hands of Frank Church and Phil Hart as they lay dying. He called the families of every passenger from the doomed airplanes that left Boston on 9/11, and the families of every Massachusetts soldier lost in Afghanistan and Iraq. He showed up at John Kerry's doorstep when Kerry's father died, and at George McGovern's door when the South Dakota senator lost his daughter, and at Birch Bayh's home on the day Marvella succumbed to breast cancer. When Joseph Biden was stricken with an aneurysm and hospitalized in critical condition, Kennedy "was the guy who took the time to take the train by himself to Wilmington," Biden recalled, "the guy who . . . just came and made himself available, hung out all day and spent 15, 16 hours at my house and in the pool with my kids, in the kitchen with my wife, talking about how this was all going to work out and then, without me knowing it, got on the train late at night and headed back."

KENNEDY CONTINUED TO SPEAK against the war—in speeches at Washington think tanks, or remarks on the Senate floor, that were regularly overlooked in the jingoistic ruckus. His September 2002 address was roundly ignored by the press, as were a series of speeches he made in 2003, after Bush made a contrived appearance in military gear on a U.S.

aircraft carrier with the banner "Mission Accomplished" displayed behind him.

"All the administration's rationalizations as we prepared to go to war now stand revealed as double talk," Kennedy insisted. "The American people were told Saddam Hussein was building nuclear weapons. He was not. We were told he had stockpiles of other weapons of mass destruction. He did not. We were told he was involved in 9/11. He was not. We were told our soldiers would be viewed as liberators. They are not. We were told Iraq could pay for its own reconstruction. It cannot. We were told the war would make America safer. It has not."

"It was cooked up. They were going to go to war in Iraq regardless, and this was their excuse," Kennedy's foreign policy adviser Sharon Waxman remembered. "The thing . . . that really struck me was how personal it was for him. How passionate and how intensely focused he was on really trying to stop it. . . . He just knew. . . . He knew that it would go wrong, and he really wanted to stop it. . . . Nonstop. The pace was relentless. It was every day . . . every second. . . . The way the president laid this out to the public was just so dishonest that it infuriated him, especially because Americans were sent to war, to their death."

Kennedy's critique broke through in September 2003, after he incautiously told a reporter that the White House had staged the war for political motives. "There was no imminent threat. This was made up in Texas, announced in January to the Republican leadership that war was going to take place and was going to be good politically," he said. "This whole thing was a fraud."

But it was not until 2004, when Kennedy slammed the calamitous occupation as "George Bush's Vietnam" and compared the president to Richard Nixon, that the media and the White House paid consistent attention to the rampaging lion. "Nuclear weapons. Mushroom cloud. Unique and urgent threat. Real and dangerous threat. Grave threat. This was the administration's rallying cry for war," Kennedy said in March. "But these were not the words of the intelligence community. The community . . . never suggested the threat was imminent, or immediate, or urgent."

Kennedy used his perch on Armed Services to grill Rumsfeld. At a

Judiciary Committee hearing in June, Attorney General John Ashcroft was on the searing end of Kennedy's cross-examination about America's use of torture. In September, Kennedy warned that the United States had become "bogged down in a continuing quagmire with no end in sight." His demand for expertise and information was "insatiable," Waxman recalled. She contracted tendinitis from writing so much and had to dictate while a colleague typed. Kennedy and Waxman had begun from scratch, with no expert advisers. By the end of Bush's term their list of critical generals, diplomats, Iraq combat veterans, and Middle East analysts was twenty-seven pages long. There were endless expert meetings, dinners, and lunches. But Kennedy was alone in the Senate, or in a small minority, in his opposition. "There were very lonely times," Waxman said. "The Democratic Party, for the most part, was going along with the war." Kennedy became the first prominent elected official to call for an American withdrawal. John Kerry might have profited by following his seatmate's steadfast course. As the Democratic presidential nominee in 2004, Kerry was disparaged and bruised for shape-shifting on Iraq.

To THE DISMAY OF his Democratic colleagues, Kennedy did not let his differences over the war in Iraq stop him from working with Bush on two politically freighted issues, however—the need to add a prescription drug benefit to Medicare, and a law to address illegal immigration. His detractors revived the charge that Kennedy was acting like Alec Guinness, who had played the co-opted British officer Lieutenant Colonel Nicholson in the motion picture *The Bridge on the River Kwai*. "Kennedy made the decision that this was going to be a pretty bleak eight years unless somebody tried to find common ground," Daschle remembered. And in the Democratic caucus, "common ground for many was too high a price to pay."

The Medicare drug benefit had been a consistent element in Kennedy's plans for national health insurance, going back thirty years. Now that he had come up with solutions for preexisting conditions, insurance portability, and child health care, it was the next logical step in his strategic campaign of incremental reform. When Medicare was adopted in 1965, the role of prescription drugs in medicine had been ancillary, and so coverage was not thought necessary. By the turn of the century, advances in the science had made pharmaceuticals a standard, expensive treatment for many ills. Bush contained his anger over Kennedy's criticism of the war in Iraq (the president didn't much like being compared to Nixon) and asked him if he and the senator might work together again, as they had on education. Kennedy had many reasons not to trust the president, the Republicans, and the stakeholding pharmaceutical and private insurance industries, but the goal, he believed, was worth the risk. After finishing up with CHIP, Kennedy had made the decision that drugs for seniors was "the next big thing," said aide David Nexon, and he lured the chief executive officers of major pharmaceutical firms into private meetings, in a search for mutuality. They ultimately arrived at a formula of "Democratic benefits through a Republican delivery system," in which the beneficiaries, using government subsidies, chose from competing private firms for coverage.

"It had to get done. The question was how," said Chris Jennings, who had advised Bill and Hillary Clinton on health care. "Democrats care so much about the outcome that they will compromise with Republicans, time and again, to let private insurers deliver the benefits, even if it means more inefficiency and more cost. That's how health care reform has gotten done." On the other hand, "do you not do anything? Ted Kennedy said it's immoral not to do something," Jennings said. "He made the deal . . . which the Left of the party hated."

Bush promised to allot $400 billion, and Kennedy signed on. At a Democratic caucus, and in the Senate debate, Kennedy urged liberals to support the Bush plan as a "down payment" on which they could build. "When he spoke out in favor of it," said Senator John Breaux, the Democrat from Louisiana, "a lot of people who you would normally expect to be opposed had to fold their tent." The Senate passed the bill by a healthy margin, and it narrowly escaped defeat in the House, where liberals objected to how the Republican-sponsored subsidies favored managed care companies and private insurance firms. "Teddy was *way* out there trying to cut a deal," Daschle recalled. And even though Kennedy kept the Democratic leadership informed, "I was very worried."

"You're playing with the devil," Daschle told his friend. Sure enough, the House-Senate conference tilted wildly toward the House Republican version. Kennedy and other liberals felt compelled to abandon the bill. He opposed the legislation with the fervor with which he had endorsed it, as if he was doing penance for leading the Democrats into this cul-de-sac. The legislation was enacted—it passed the House after one 3 a.m. vote was extended for three hours for Bush and party leaders to twist the arms of Republican conservatives. Among those who criticized Kennedy— publicly told him to "Get some spine"—was one of the party's young stars, Illinois senator Barack Obama.

The result was paradoxical. People snickered at how Kennedy got fleeced in the endgame, but in the years afterward Nexon, his longtime health policy expert, ranked the drug benefit as one of Kennedy's greatest and most far-reaching achievements. "It was Kennedy who made it possible for the Senate to pass a bill," another adviser, Rashi Fein, remembered. Without Kennedy, there would have been no bill to take to conference. It is true that he "got snookered. . . . He didn't realize that these guys played a different kind of hardball." But in the long term, little damage was done. The inroads by private industry into Medicare proved less of a threat to the popular program than liberals feared. And when the next Democratic president took up the cause of national health care, President Obama would discover that the task had been considerably simplified, and the price tag significantly reduced, by the four incremental reforms—on portability, preexisting conditions, children's health, and prescription drugs for seniors—that Kennedy championed after Clinton's health care crusade collapsed.

ALAN SIMPSON RETIRED FROM the Senate in 1996, depriving Kennedy of his cardinal collaborator on immigration. Republican Sam Brownback of Kansas stepped in and worked well with Kennedy—until the 9/11 attacks stirred fears of foreigners and focused attention on border security, instead of the needs and problems of U.S. employers and the swelling immigrant workforce. Kennedy and Brownback helped guide a border bill through Congress, in part by mollifying Byrd, who was miffed at the Republicans for some past slight. But they failed to prevail against rising anti-immigrant sentiment when they pressed for a grand compromise to meet the quandary of illegal immigration. Even a more limited "DREAM Act," to extend protection to the children of undocumented immigrants, stalled in Congress.

In 2004, John McCain, the GOP senator from Arizona, took Brownback's place. Once more, Kennedy was working with a Republican president and Republican senators on an issue that many Democrats hoped to hang around their adversaries' necks. "He is here to get things done," his top aide on immigration, Esther Olavarria, explained, "and sometimes others . . . are more interested in having an issue for the campaign than a bill." Kennedy and the Democratic leadership had "serious disagreements," she said. It was "a huge problem," as was opposition from the AFL-CIO to a guest worker program proposed by the Republicans, which the unions feared would suppress American wages.

Like the prescription drug issue, immigration reform had become necessary because of lengthy but persistent change. The immigration legislation that the young Ted Kennedy had steered through the Senate in 1965, with its "chain migration" provision, had yielded its unintended results. Extended families from Asia, southern Europe, the Caribbean, Latin America, and elsewhere exploited its provisions to gather legally in the United States. Their numbers were boosted by waves of illegal immigration from Mexico and the rest of Latin America. The Bracero program had long since ended, but American employers still wanted low-wage workers, and Latino breadwinners and aspiring youngsters continued to cross the border to work in the fields, kitchens, gardens, shops, and small factories of Texas, California, and elsewhere.

Lured by America's prosperity and promise, and with no guest worker plan to guarantee their return, many of the "illegals" decided to stay, and were joined by spouses, children, nieces and nephews, and other relatives.

They settled, like immigrants before them, in their own communities, speaking the language of home and transforming the local culture as it went to work transforming them. Their numbers were augmented by compassionate refugee policies, supported by Kennedy, that brought displaced Cubans, Central Americans, Haitians, and Southeast Asians to America. Many white Americans were still struggling to cope with the cultural effects of the civil rights and women's movements when, increasingly, the faces in stores and schools were a different, darker hue, and the lilt of different tongues and melodies and the marvelous scents of exotic cooking once more filled the air. In the United States, the number of Hispanics alone leaped from under ten million in 1970 to more than fifty million in 2010.

Their faith, devotion to family, and enterprising nature made Hispanic and Asian Americans natural recruiting targets for Nixon- and Reagan-era Republicans. Upper-middle-class and wealthy Americans were glad to have gardeners and maids. Business owners hired low-wage immigrants to pick fruits and vegetables, work on meatpacking and other assembly lines, bus tables, or wash dishes. But other elements—social conservatives and blue-collar whites caught up in the culture wars—were persuaded that minorities were receiving unfair preference. By the time that Washington confronted its problem on the border, a wing of the Republican Party—and its caucus on Capitol Hill—was stridently anti-immigrant.

Kennedy had returned to the issue, with Simpson, in the 1980s. Kennedy opposed the final version of his friend's 1986 bill to regulate illegal immigration because he felt its employment provisions were discriminatory, but helped Simpson in the process of drafting the legislation and supported Simpson's provision of amnesty for five million undocumented immigrants then living in the United States. The approach they endorsed was to freeze things as they were by legalizing the illegals, and then end the system that had trapped them in limbo by securing the border, making the employment of undocumented workers a crime, and, over time, setting up a foreign worker visa program. "Ted Kennedy was co-manager of the bill. He kept a steady pace and did not go into any histrionics as in the past," Simpson reported to his diary. He regretted that Kennedy did not attend the bill-signing ceremony at the White House. "Ted was of immeasurable help through the six and a half years, guiding me through issues with the ACLU, Hispanic groups and other concerned parties."

Two years later, in 1988, Kennedy and Simpson joined to update and bring order to the country's legal immigration policies. They encountered resistance but nudged their bill through the Senate and into law. As the years passed, however, it became clear that the Simpson legislation had not sealed the porous border. By 1994, California had more than a million undocumented immigrants living in the state. Proposition 187, a ballot initiative backed by Republican governor Pete Wilson, proposed to cut off funding for education and other social services for the undocumented workers and their families. The debate took ugly turns, and Hispanic voters deserted the Republican Party in significant numbers.

Bill Clinton worked with Simpson to crack down on undocumented workers with an election-year law in 1996 that civil libertarians and immigration activists thought draconian. "We have stuff in there that has everything but the rack and thumbscrews for people who are violating the laws of the United States," Simpson told the press. The measure, which Kennedy helped to temper before voting "Nay" on final passage, targeted immigrants for jail and deportation, took a hands-off approach toward employers, and proved no solution. "A disaster," Kennedy called it. "We put in place these deportations, these horrendous deportation provisions. . . . [It included] some of the most horrific violations of individual rights and liberties." The illegal population continued to soar.

AND SO, when Kennedy met the new century by joining forces with Bush and Brownback, and then McCain, they faced formidable challenges. In the xenophobic wing of the Republican Party, any proposal that hinted of "amnesty" was politically poisonous. Yet Bush and the business wing of his party had no appetite for rounding up the undocumented immigrants—whose number from Mexico had reached five million—and putting them in internment camps, or on buses to Juárez, as part of a massive deportation campaign. And the Democratic Party's leaders, reaping votes from Hispanic America, would just as soon have no reform if the ultimate fix did not include a path for the undocumented to gain U.S. citizenship. The strategy voiced by Senate Democrats was, "Let's not have a bill . . . [then] blame the Republicans . . . and pick up the pieces with Hispanics," said Kennedy.

When the new Congress convened in 2005, McCain and Kennedy went to work. They proposed that the United States issue four hundred thousand guest worker visas to alleviate the pressure on the borders, and that undocumented immigrants living in America be given an opportunity to register, obtain visas, and work toward legal status. Kennedy called it "earned legalization." The anti-immigration forces countered with a House bill authorizing a seven-hundred-mile, $2 billion fence along the border with Mexico, and a crackdown on illegals living in the United States. "You have some of the finest trained people in the world . . . highly disciplined border guards that are chasing gardeners around the desert in southern California," Kennedy complained.

As SENATE COLLEAGUES, Kennedy and McCain had not gotten off to the best of starts. On a memorable occasion in the Clinton years they had mixed it up in an acrimonious debate that peaked when they stripped off their microphones and left their desks to clash like rams in the well of the Senate.

"Fuck you, Ted," said McCain, as deliriously joyful congressional reporters leaned from the gallery to record the scene.

"Fuck you, John," said Kennedy. "Why don't you act like a fucking senator?!"

"Why don't *you* act like a fucking senator?!" McCain replied.

The two men shared the happy sentiment, McCain was to recall, that "a fight not joined is a fight not enjoyed." As they left the chamber, Kennedy threw his arm around his colleague's shoulders and said, "John, I think we got a little carried away this time, don't you?"

Their relationship grew warmer. Kennedy was a supporter of McCain's successful crusade, with Senator Russ Feingold of Wisconsin, to reform the campaign finance system. When McCain and Feingold were honored by the John F. Kennedy Presidential Library with the Profile in Courage award for political valor in 1999, Kennedy arranged to have a Coast Guard cutter take McCain and his son—who was celebrating a birthday—on a ride around Boston Harbor, complete with cake. McCain was grateful for the gesture, honored by the award, and thrilled that Kennedy was recognizing him as a senator of stature, a fellow lion: "One of the guys who last, and get things done."

The Kennedy and McCain bill had bipartisan support, could be sold as homeland security, and would have given the Bush administration the momentum it lacked in his second term. After leaving office, Bush would regret that he did not make it his leading priority after reelection. Instead, Bush declared his intention to privatize Social Security—a polarizing plan that died a quick, deserved death. It was a fateful and unfortunate choice.

Immigration was left to founder. A march for reform brought thousands to Washington, many who listened to Kennedy cheer them on. "We will never give in!" he said, and closed with the celebrated rallying cry of Cesar Chavez, Dolores Huerta, and the United Farm Workers: "Si se puede!" We can make it happen. Bush made an Oval Office address to the nation, and threw his weight behind the bill. And in June 2006, the Senate passed legislation, 62–36, that combined the sensibilities of the McCain-Kennedy approach with increased funding for border security. "Ted Kennedy, as the principal Democratic sponsor, kept his word again and again by voting with the Republicans when Democrats proposed amendments that would have undone some of the compromises," McCain's aide and speechwriter, Mark Salter, recalled. The House, cruelly, balked, and the 109th Congress ended without final action.

Kennedy liked to say that it took six years to move legislation from an idea to a signing ceremony. The Democrats recaptured the Senate and the House in the 2006 election, so Kennedy—theoretically—had more influence. "Let's prove the skeptics wrong again," Bush told him, and vowed to work with him on immigration in 2007. McCain was off running for president, so Kennedy found new allies: Senators Jon Kyl, another Arizona Republican, and Republican Lindsey Graham of South Carolina.

The bipartisan coalition joined with the White House and packed the bill with enforcement and border security measures—but found that congressional Republicans were thoroughly spooked by the nativist campaign wreaked by Representatives Tom Tancredo and James Sensenbrenner in the House, and by right-wing commentators like Rush Limbaugh and Lou Dobbs in the media.

The Left, meanwhile, was no more helpful. Labor and its Senate allies were still opposed to an expansive guest worker program. Kennedy and his Democratic cosponsor, Senator Ken Salazar of Colorado, found themselves in the uncomfortable space—viewed with alarm by their own Democratic leaders—that Kennedy had occupied in the No Child Left Behind and Medicare drug battles. Kennedy had been snookered by Bush then, and would be snookered again, Majority Leader Harry Reid told them. Better to have the issue than the bill. They clashed over Reid's tactics, which Kennedy believed were fated—if not designed—to alienate Republicans and kill chances for passage. The Senate had moved into a harsher, more polarized era, and what Kennedy was proposing was a throwback to a time when senators were independent actors, not parliamentary partisans.

The contest was intense, but in May a group of centrist members from both parties reached a "grand bargain" that seemed to have enough support to guarantee passage. It was "the last best chance," Graham told reporters. If it failed, "it will be years before you can recreate this." Kennedy urged Reid and others to move quickly. On May 21 the bill survived an initial cloture vote, but opponents from both Left and Right returned after the Memorial Day break with fresh resolve. They tore the grand bargain apart with poisonous amendments.

Kennedy would not surrender. As Congress was preparing to leave town for the Independence Day recess, he called the White House and urged Bush to press Reid to keep the Senate in session. He pleaded with the majority leader. They were just a vote or two away, Kennedy said. Reid refused. Had they stayed, said Kennedy, the bill would have passed. "The Senate is a chemical place," he said, employing a term he liked to use. "There's a lot of emotion. There's feeling. There's timeliness in how the Senate works and if you lose the rhythm and lose the balance you lose in a tough and difficult fight, and that's what was lost." There was ample blame to share. The Democrats had been partisans—the Republicans not enough so, when deserting their president. U.S. senators who could not stand up to the likes of Limbaugh showed rank political cowardice, Trent Lott said. "The three issues that bring out the worst in terms of the functions of the Senate are civil rights . . . gay rights, and immigration," Kennedy said. "Immigration starts out as reasonably sanitized and then, as we have seen . . . in 2006 and 2007, basically deteriorates into racist amendments and racism on the floor of the Senate. . . . It's blatant and flagrant."

Throughout his Senate career, Kennedy was known for his often-garbled syntax, and bombast on the stump or the floor. "When you're dealing with him he'll come up and say, 'Bill, gee, about that, yeah, have we got that right, and I hope you're okay on this,' and you don't know what the hell he's talking about," said Senator William Cohen of Maine. "He knows the subject matter and I don't know whether he is overstaffed or whether he's got too much going but you just get a sense in talking to him that there's no continuous thought process that goes from A to B to C to D. And so it's hard to follow."

It was an indication, no doubt, of how much Kennedy had invested in immigration reform—and how disappointed he was in the results—that in the pitch of this debate, he had no problem being eloquent. To show how tough it was, the Bush administration launched raids and rounded up undocumented immigrants in New Bedford, Massachusetts, that spring. "They went in and pulled probably 300 or so people out of the plant and separated these families," Kennedy recalled. "A lot of them had children at home, children in school, small children. Some of them were single moms . . . and the mothers were being taken and shipped out to detention centers."

Reporters cornered him in a Capitol corridor. There was no stammer, no bombast. "It has left children bewildered, confused and alone," Kennedy said, with true feeling. "It has to stop."

Justice Sandra Day O'Connor announced her retirement from the Supreme Court in July 2005. Bush named John Roberts, a federal judge, to replace her. When Chief Justice William Rehnquist died in September, the president chose Roberts for the chief's seat on the high court, and selected federal judge Samuel Alito as his other nominee. Roberts and Alito were both from a phalanx of young conservatives that the Right had groomed to stock the federal judiciary.

Roberts came to Kennedy's office, for a courtesy call, on July 21. The senator had warned his staff that the Harvard-educated Roberts was bright and appealing, and so represented the "worst case scenario" for liberals. They chatted about their alma mater, and of Ireland—where the Roberts family had a cottage just a few miles down the road from the old Fitzgerald homestead in Limerick, and the judge had discovered a passion for Irish dance and music. Kennedy sought not to interrogate the nominee, but to make a connection, and reason with him.

America's history was an unfolding saga, said the seventy-three-year-old senator, who had witnessed so much of it—twelve presidencies—himself. From the days of Lincoln and Black emancipation; to Martin Luther King and the civil rights movement; to passage of the historic civil rights, voting rights, and immigration acts of the 1960s; to the liberation of women, and now gay and disabled Americans, Kennedy told Roberts, progress had been in one direction, toward liberty and equality. "That has to be our continuum," Kennedy told the younger man. Without it, "we'd be a lesser country, a lesser land." Freedom for others had always met opposition, "rooted in a similar kind of hostility and suspicion and, in many instances, bigotry," said Kennedy. As chief justice, Roberts would help determine how far that march progressed. He would have to pick a side. "This is the real question for you," Kennedy told the nominee, "whether you're going to be a part of this whole movement for progress, or if there's going to be a retrenchment."

Roberts remained "collected and contained," Kennedy told his diary. The judge gave "a sort of a stock answer." He believed in judicial "modesty" and restraint.

"I didn't feel I was making much progress," Kennedy reported. He tried another tack, trying to reach Roberts through their common Roman Catholic religion. The judge called his faith "something more powerful and bigger than myself . . . a guiding hand in terms of my life and the people I cared about."

"I said my philosophy is motivated by the Beatitudes and by Matthew 25:40 about the 'least of these,'" the senator told his diary. "But he didn't want to talk much about that. He's very bright and smart and glib, and I would have thought he'd be able to talk about those things . . . about where we are in the country, [but] he didn't want to get into that at all. He's very cautious."

Alito was no more forthcoming in his private meeting with Kennedy. Like Roberts, when he was asked about abortion rights and the *Roe v. Wade* decision, the nominee vowed to "adhere to" precedent. "I believe that there is a right to privacy. I think it's settled," Alito assured him. "I'm a believer in precedents." And briefed, perhaps, by the White House Sherpas, Alito replied to Kennedy's "special interest on civil rights" (as the senator put it in his diary) by assuring Kennedy that though "we may have differences about how we're going to get there," he believed in "a race-free, prejudice-free, discrimination-free society."

In the end, alarmed by their political backgrounds, writings, and rulings, Kennedy voted against both nominees and joined—in those days before the so-called "nuclear option" ended the tactic for judicial nominations—in an unsuccessful filibuster against Alito. The Republicans controlled the Senate, however, and both men took their seats on the Supreme Court where, Kennedy was to allege in 2007, they broke the vows they made under oath in the confirmation hearings. "Instead of substantive answers," he said, "Roberts and Alito worked hard to give the impression of moderation. Over and over, they assured us they would not bring an ideological agenda to the bench." But once they were confirmed, "we saw an entirely different side . . . they have begun to reveal themselves as ideologues." The politicization of the Court continued. As with the members of the once-bold Senate, the justices took to behaving, with dismayingly few exceptions, not like independent statesmen or stateswomen, but as party apparatchiks. In time, one found the need to make a public declaration that she and her colleagues were not "partisan hacks."

KENNEDY WAS NOW WELL into his seventies—and attuned to the passing of time. On a day when the Senate was gripped by spite and intrigue over the "nuclear option," he took time to record some gentler thoughts in his diary.

"I think I've finally got it straight," he wrote. "The crocus' come up first in January and they are the great courageous little flowers, resisting the snow. Then we have the wonderful daffodils that last about 10 days and just when they are going down, we have the tulips that are coming out. And they last about eight or nine days, and just as the tulips are fading, we have the . . . dogwoods that are just emerging and our lilac bush came out . . . and just when the dogwoods and the lilacs are fading, the azaleas are coming into bloom. And wherever the sun is going, they are . . . stronger and stronger.

"All of which makes Washington the loveliest city in the world in springtime," Kennedy wrote. "So there you go."

Thirty-Two

THE FIRES OF SUNSET

Ted Kennedy celebrated his seventy-fifth birthday in February 2007. He was lined and bent and dealing with high blood pressure and unhealthy levels of cholesterol. Toward the end of the year, he underwent surgery to clear a blocked artery in his neck—an unnerving episode for a man whose father had suffered a crippling stroke.

The sand in the glass was running. He was at her side when his sister Rosemary died in 2004, and with Patricia when she succumbed in 2006. Yet Kennedy had watched Ronald Reagan, Supreme Court justices, and colleagues like Strom Thurmond continue in office through their eighth decades, buffered by staff, structure, and routine. Retirement was unthinkable, Kennedy's children told one another. They reckoned he would run again in 2012.

Vicki was playing a greater role in Kennedy's life, sheltering him from the demands of his staff, offering advice on strategy and speeches, trying to guard his health.

Substance abuse still stalked the family. Joan's concern over Kara's cancer no doubt contributed to a series of relapses. At one point she was found on a street in Boston, bloodied and suffering from a concussion and a broken shoulder. Her children were compelled to seek guardianship. In 2006, after running his car into a police barrier on Capitol Hill, Patrick opened up to a writer for the *New York Times*. He confessed his lifelong addictions and spoke of the cross of being a Kennedy. "When you grow up in my family, being somebody meant having power, having status. The compensations you got were all material and superficial," Patrick said. "I've come to realize . . . that that life made me feel all alone."

His father was infuriated—the front-page article was published on the day before his sister Pat's funeral and reporters were calling the grieving senator with probing questions about the family's use of drugs and alcohol. He cornered Patrick at a wake. The article was a *disaster*, he said. How dare he talk about the family this way? "I stood there on the verge of disintegration," Patrick said, until Maria Shriver came to his defense. The family needed more communicating, more openness—not secrecy—she told their uncle. Patrick continued to work, successfully, in the family profession, and his father expressed hope to see him in the Senate. Together, they labored to wrangle legislation through House and Senate to end discrimination in the treatment of alcoholism, drug addiction, and mental illness. The "Mental Health Parity and Addiction Equity Act," the bill was called.

At one family gathering, Ted joined a group of the next generation of Kennedys. He had devoted his life to sustaining the dreams of P. J. Kennedy and John Fitzgerald, Joe and Rose, and Jack and Bob. No drive was more powerful than family. But soon his time would end, he told his nieces and nephews. And, he predicted, "When you guys are my age, the whole thing is going to fall apart."

One of the nephews, Christopher Lawford, was struck by Kennedy's words. "What Teddy understood better than anyone was how much effort it took to keep it all together, because he has been doing it since 1968 when it all fell on him. If he hadn't stepped up and carried us all on his back for the next thirty-plus years, the family would have disintegrated," Lawford said.

But while Ted Kennedy "never had a choice but to give his life to his family," Lawford wrote in a memoir, the next generation was diffused. Many would go out to find their own lives. "And in doing so, what he had spent his life holding together would cease to exist."

That was all right, Lawford believed. The newer generations of Kennedys had a platform to sustain them, and the choice of how to live—because Ted had kept it all together.

The patriarch still loved to sing, and to laugh. If he could live his life over, he told the younger Kennedys, it would be as an opera singer. "Can you imagine going up into those little Italian villages, learning those songs, and having pasta every day for lunch? Singing at La Scala in front of three thousand people throwing flowers at you? Then going out for dinner and having more pasta?" But he had chosen politics, he lamented, where "I can't eat and I don't sing!"

If, to Vicki's dad, members of the Kennedy staff, and certain contemporaries, he was The Commander, to his nieces and nephews he was The Grande Fromage. He enjoyed both nicknames.

THERE WAS A DEEP field of candidates for the Democratic presidential nomination in 2008. It included five of Kennedy's Senate colleagues—Barack Obama, Joseph Biden, Hillary Clinton, John Edwards, and Christopher Dodd. The winnowing was quick, and when his pal Dodd withdrew from contention after a lackluster finish in Iowa, many assumed that Kennedy would fall in line as the party coalesced behind Clinton. Kennedy stunned the world, and rocked the race, by endorsing Obama instead.

It was a pivotal moment, said David Axelrod, the Obama campaign strategist. With an acclaimed keynote speech at the 2004 Democratic convention in Boston, and victories in the Iowa caucuses and the South Carolina primary, Obama had demonstrated his appeal—enough so that voters were preparing to look at him as a serious alternative. But there were also skeptics. Obama had a decade in politics, but only two years of service at the federal level. The "weighty imprimatur" of a warhorse like Kennedy, said Axelrod, would be "a powerful rejoinder to those who questioned whether Barack had the experience."

It was a rejoinder, as well, to the many who wondered if a Black man named Barack Hussein Obama could actually claim the presidency. "He can't win. He can't win. He can't win," Hillary Clinton was telling Democratic fence-sitters. Kennedys were not shy, but neither were they known for suicide missions. With Clinton favored to capture the Super Tuesday states of New York and California, a Kennedy endorsement was a major lift for Obama, as the campaign schedule shifted toward a long and grinding delegate-by-delegate competition.

Most important, though few but Kennedy and Obama saw it then, theirs was the compact that pushed the cause of the senator's life—health care for all—to the top of the future president's agenda, and one day into law as the Affordable Care Act.

KENNEDY HAD SPENT THE years at century's turn looking for vehicles to expand health care coverage. Most of his efforts—Kassebaum-Kennedy, CHIP, and the Medicare prescription drug benefit—had kept him in Washington, in the confines of the Senate. But in 2006 he chose to travel a "Massachusetts avenue" toward universal health care—and helped steer a model for the nation through the statehouse on Beacon Hill. In an unlikely partnership with an old antagonist, Mitt Romney, Kennedy helped in the forging of "Romneycare"—a health care plan that would lead the way to historic change.

After losing to Kennedy in the 1994 Senate race, Romney had leveraged the success he attained when rescuing the 2002 Winter Olympics from financial catastrophe and made a successful run for governor in Massachusetts. Health care was not high on his agenda—he barely mentioned it in the campaign. But after taking office—and confronting the billion dollars the state was paying for the treatment of uninsured patients—he decided to tackle the issue. Kennedy was a factor from the start: someone in Washington was needed to procure some $385 million a year from federal coffers to keep Romneycare solvent, and the senator's blessing would go miles toward persuading the legislature's Democratic suzerains that the governor's plan was a fine idea.

Romney discarded the "play or pay" model, with its employer mandates, that was a core feature of the Nixon and Clinton health care proposals. Instead, Romney placed the burden, and the mandate, on the individual. Most working families received health insurance from their employers as part of their compensation and benefits; the elderly had paid into Medicare all their working lives. So why, Romney asked, should a relatively small percentage of free riders get treatment with no ante? It was a matter of personal responsibility, Romney said, and personal responsibility was a key Republican principle.

"No more free riding," Romney said. "It's the ultimate conservative idea, which is that people . . . don't look to government to take care of them if they can afford to take care of themselves." To help curb costs, the program would provide another conservative innovation—a one-stop shopping venue called an "exchange" where insurers would compete with one another for customers, and so keep costs and prices down.

Romney's plan was supported by the state's business community, brimming with prestigious health-related firms, institutions, and expertise. But the $385 million was a key and necessary element—an annual subsidy paid by Washington to Massachusetts for an experimental program to cover working families and their children. Kennedy had helped former governor William Weld secure and preserve the federal waiver for the experiment, and he was an essential player in retaining it in different form for Romneycare. "This looks pretty good," Kennedy told his staff. "Let's work with him." Together, he and Romney met with George W. Bush's health and human services staff and secured the administration's support.

Kennedy and Romney joined efforts, as well, when the bill stalled in the Democratic legislature. The lawmakers preferred an employer mandate, but with Kennedy's help the logjam was broken. The signing ceremony was held in April 2006 in Faneuil Hall, on the stage where Kennedy and Romney had debated in 1994. "This for me feels like the *Titanic* returning to visit the iceberg," Romney said. Kennedy was invited to stand beside the governor as Romney ensured that every Massachusetts resident would have access to health insurance. They were a few blocks from the hospital corridors where Kennedy had once listened to the distress of the hard-pressed families with loved ones who, like his sons and daughter, had been stricken by cancer.

Massachusetts, of course, was just a single state. But Kennedy's antennae were too fine-tuned to miss the import of its action. "This is a moment to savor . . . for all the people of our commonwealth, and perhaps for the rest of America too," he teased the crowd in Faneuil Hall. "We intend to make the most of it."

When the Clintons launched their health care campaign in the early 1990s, there were about thirty-seven million Americans lacking coverage. Now there were almost sixty million Americans who at one time or another in any given year were without health insurance: a quarter of the non-elderly population. Another twenty-five million were underinsured—subject to copayments, deductibles, and caps that placed them one serious illness away from bankruptcy. The need, the constituency, was there. Kennedy told his staff to prepare, and they began to gather the activists, congressional experts, and representatives of the major stakeholders—AARP, the AFL-CIO, the Business Roundtable, the AMA, and others—for closed-door discussions aimed at forming a consensus. The strategy of incremental reform had had its moment. It was time to go big again.

KENNEDY WOULD REMEMBER WHERE he was in 2007—aboard the *Mya* in Tarpaulin Cove, a favorite summer swimming spot in the Elizabeth Islands—when the conversation turned to Obama. His niece Caroline and her children were on board, and he was stirred by their enthusiasm. In the weeks to come he would hear from others in the younger generations of Kennedys, who told him how inspired they were by the Obama campaign, with its promise of generational change, racial justice, and liberal ideals.

Kennedy was struck as well by an intuitive feeling that the wind had changed: that after thirty years of conservative alignment, the time in the cycle for progressive change had arrived once more. He could accelerate the cycle by endorsing Obama, or impede it by opting for a safer choice. This could be his final opportunity to reshape the future. He asked himself, "How much longer do you have?"

Kennedy had recruited Obama for the Labor Committee in 2004 and worked with him, sometimes uneasily, on immigration reform. The younger man had come to Kennedy in the spring of 2006 and told him he was thinking of running for president. Like Robert Kennedy, Obama was

restless in the Senate, and Reid and other Democratic leaders, recognizing this, had suggested he run sooner rather than later.

Obama recalled the traditional office tour, and then sitting as friends
as Kennedy spun stories. Then, "I hear there's talk of you running for
president," Kennedy said. Unlikely, said Obama, but asked for his counsel
nonetheless.

"Yes, well, who was it who said there are one hundred senators who
look in the mirror and see a president?" Kennedy said with a chuckle.
"They ask, 'Do I have what it takes?' Jack, Bobby, me too, long ago. It
didn't go as planned, but things work out in their own way, I suppose . . ."

He trailed off, lost in thought. Obama watched, and "wondered how
he took the measure of his own life, and his brothers' lives, the terrible
price each one of them had paid in pursuit of a dream. Then, just as suddenly he was back," Obama would recall, "his deep blue eyes fixed on
mine, all business."

"I won't be wading in early," Kennedy told his young colleague. No
endorsement. "Too many friends."

"But I can tell you this, Barack. The power to inspire is rare. Moments
like this are rare. You think you may not be ready, that you'll do it at a
more convenient time," said Kennedy. "But you don't choose the time, the
time chooses you."

Kennedy knew his tides; he remembered 1968, 1972, and 1976. And
he knew his *Julius Caesar.* "Either you seize what may turn out to be the
only chance you have," he told Obama. "Or you decide you're willing to
live with the knowledge that the chance has passed you by."

KENNEDY WATCHED HIS COLLEAGUE for the rest of that year, and the
next, and his regard for Obama grew. He readily forgave the Illinois senator when a tape surfaced in which, during the Medicare drug battle,
Obama had complained that Kennedy was old and tired.

Obama called to grovel. "Start the conversation," Kennedy barked.
Then he laughed. It's okay, he said. Why, he had once called his colleague
Osama.

Obama's victory speech on the night of the Iowa caucuses moved Kennedy. "Hope is that thing inside us that insists, despite all the evidence to the contrary, that something better awaits us if we have the courage to reach for it and to work for it and to fight for it," Obama had told the nation.

"That was a speech," Kennedy would recall. "That was a speech."

There was, however, a factor that gave him pause. On Kennedy's great cause—health care for all—Obama could sometimes seem clueless. It wasn't that, starting out, the candidate's plan was bad—it was that he didn't have one, or even see the need to craft one. And when criticizing his rivals' proposals, he was short on fact and long on bluster. At an early health care policy briefing with his staff, Obama had spent the time fiddling with his BlackBerry. At a forum in Nevada in 2007, Obama's lack of knowledge about health care was glaring; he embarrassed himself and ordered his staff to come up with a proposal. It was a political document, with no mandate for coverage. "Shame on you, Barack Obama!" Hillary Clinton scolded him when he maligned her call for an individual mandate as a Big Government intrusion. "Since when do Democrats attack one another on universal health care?"

But American presidential campaigns work both ways: the candidates speak to the people, and the people educate the candidates. Obama was hearing from the common folk who came to his town halls or cornered him on a rope line to describe the health care catastrophes striking their families and to plead for his help. The cool man's heart was touched.

Kennedy, weighing an endorsement, needed more. The specifics were not as important as a vow of intent: what Kennedy had to have was Obama's word that a universal health care plan would be a top priority. Obama and his team signaled his willingness. The two men clinched the deal in a phone call on Thursday, January 24. "Is there room on that train for old Teddy?" Kennedy asked.

Though few foresaw it, the world was headed toward economic calamity—the financial crisis of 2008. It would compel the new president to reorder priorities. Aides would urge Obama to abandon his health care covenant. There was no space for a new, dreamy progressive initiative. He needed to focus, they told him, on steering the country through the worst recession since the Great Depression. But Obama did not waver. There were moments of quiet despair, when events upset him and all seemed doomed. But first to last he remembered and honored the promise he had made to Ted Kennedy, and the Americans on those rope lines, and ordered the fleet to sail on.

KENNEDY'S ENDORSEMENT WAS ACCOMPANIED by Caroline's op-ed in that Sunday's *New York Times* declaring her support for Obama. For four days, the endorsements commanded the campaign news cycles.

In the rally at American University, before a raucous and ecstatic audience, Kennedy cocked his head and said, "I feel change in the air." Like the legions of the New Frontier, "we, too, want a president who appeals to the hopes of those who still believe in the American dream and those around the world who still believe in the American ideal and who can lift our spirits and make us believe again," Kennedy said. "I have found that candidate."

In the months before, Obama had taken a hands-off approach with Kennedy, calling the senator from time to time or having a mutual friend, Thomas Daschle, make the case. When Obama arrived, alone and unnoticed, at one of Kennedy's birthday parties, he smiled wryly at how Bill and Hillary, who had sauntered in before him, commanded the attention of Ted and his guests.

The Clintons, on the other hand, had badgered Kennedy—a high-pressure sales approach that irritated him. Nor did he much like it when Hillary, making the case for her own experience, praised Lyndon Johnson as the master chief executive who rescued the proposals of John Kennedy. And then there was a series of taunts and jeers aimed at Obama by the Clintons and their allies that, in Kennedy's eyes, sailed too close to intolerance. Clinton associates made references to Obama's youthful drug use, and the couple dismissed him as just another Jesse Jackson: a symbolic Black candidate who could not win. When Bill Clinton told Kennedy in a private conversation that Obama was barely fit to fetch them coffee, the senator simmered, and took issue with the Clinton campaign slurs.

Racism was the country's original sin, he told Clinton. It was a constant threat, a dormant volcano like Mount St. Helens. Hatred was "a-burning" and men of good faith needed to suppress it, yet Bill and the others were fanning the flames. "Let's get the hell off of this thing," said Kennedy. The Clintons had had their chance, Kennedy believed. The Clinton presidency had seen too much squandered opportunity. The new era, with its progressive possibilities, called for a bold approach. Hillary, he felt, was the past.

Belling the cat was another matter. The former president took the news quietly and the phone call ended. Kennedy heaved a sigh of relief. Then Clinton, anger building, called back. The Clintons had campaigned and raised money for Kennedy when he desperately needed allies in 1994. Clinton had named Kennedy's sister as the ambassador to Ireland. The Clinton administration had allocated hundreds of millions of dollars for Massachusetts and done scores of smaller favors. How could Kennedy do this?

HILLARY CLINTON WON NEW York, New Jersey, and California by narrow margins on Super Tuesday. She carried Massachusetts. But, in the kind of strategic oversights that would keep her from the presidency, her campaign neglected the little states. By packing the halls and sweeping up delegates in contests like the Idaho caucuses, the activists of an emerging "Obama coalition" won more states, and a virtual tie in votes and delegates that Tuesday—the day that was meant, but failed, to secure Clinton's status as inevitable.

Kennedy followed his endorsement with commitment—taking campaign swings through the West, Northeast, and Southwest that added to his already intense schedule. He broke down, emotionally, and could not finish one speech after making a reference to his brother Robert. He was two hours late to a dinner party at his home in mid-May: he had stayed in the Senate, brokering a deal to protect the rights of unionized first responders. The following Saturday morning, at the house in Hyannis Port, he felt dizzy, sank into a chair, and suffered a seizure.

Kennedy was taken to a hospital in Boston. He and his family were hopeful: many ailments can bring on convulsions. "Let's have Legal Sea Food and watch the Red Sox," he said. He was alert and feeling better the next morning. But the test results were grim. They revealed a deadly cancer, a malignant glioblastoma, in the upper left part of his brain. It was not an encapsulated growth, but the sort of aggressive tumor that migrates and reaches. He opted for a new course of treatment, a combination of chemotherapy, radiation, and neurosurgery offered at Duke University. It could give him a year or more, the doctors said. Without it, he had weeks. He stretched it to fifteen months.

Kennedy was awake during the surgery, so the doctors could check with him and ensure that they were not robbing him of speech or sight. Despite their care, he lost the facility to form some words, and his range of eyesight narrowed. "I can take this," he told Vicki. "Nothing is worse than having your children have cancer. . . . Maybe I can be an example, of how to face adversity. Maybe [what science and medicine will learn from] my treatment can end up helping somebody else." The radiation treatments were administered at Massachusetts General. He drove up each day from the Cape. "He would see tots and youngsters dying of childhood cancers. Very sick, small children with brain tumors," Vicki recalled. "He never felt sorry for himself. He said prayers for those kids."

WHEN KENNEDY RETURNED FROM his post-surgical recuperation in May, he met with his aides.

"Oh, Jeff, hi. How are you doing?" he would say, as he worked his way through the staff. "Oh, hey, Melanie. How are you doing?"

Then he came to David Bowen, who had been charged with producing the health care legislation.

"Where's my bill?" Kennedy asked him.

Kennedy's way of dying was to set goals; to cross each off his list and move on to the next. As Obama was clinching the Democratic nomination, Kennedy spent much of that summer of 2008 on the Cape, drawing strength from home, sailing, and his family, and reporting to Boston for treatment. But in July he made a most notable, surprising, and emotional return to the Senate to cast a needed vote on a Medicare measure. Leaning on a silver-tipped cane, he was escorted into the chamber amid tears and cheers by son Patrick, Obama, Dodd, Kerry, and Reid. It was a grand moment, but not without a price. His plane back to Boston was delayed on the tarmac, and, stuck in his seat, he suffered a pulmonary embolism, a blood clot in the lungs. In his frail condition, it might well have killed him if an alert nurse had not fretted over changes in his vital signs.

He raced his boat, threw out the first pitch at a Red Sox game, attended the Harvard-Yale game, and collected an honorary degree from his alma mater up in Cambridge. The queen of England, whom he had met when they were little children, bestowed a title: Knight of the British Empire. He led a sing-along from a chair beside the piano at Thanksgiving, grew a beard at Christmas and delighted the youngest Kennedys as Santa Claus.

"It's the goal of every Irishman to be able to be a witness at your own eulogy," Dodd said of the tide of honors. "This is sheer heaven for him."

His grails "gave him purpose," his wife, Vicki, remembered. A preeminent goal was to travel to Denver and speak at the opening session of the Democratic National Convention in August 2008. His illness left him grasping for words at times and using pronouns without antecedents (so what else is new, those close to him said), and so he needed to arduously prepare. "This is what I want to say," he told speechwriter Robert Shrum, who dropped by every morning and carefully constructed a speech with words his friend could enunciate. After finishing the speechwriting, they rehearsed with a teleprompter in the big house at Hyannis Port.

To limit the risk of embolisms, Kennedy was flown on a larger jet—with space for him to recline—to Colorado, only to be stricken by intense pain while airborne and rushed to the hospital in Denver. There he was examined, as he put it, "by every ologist known to man." The diagnosis was reassuring—kidney stones, perhaps a by-product of his chemotherapy. His treatment required an intravenous injection of a narcotic painkiller, but, having gotten that far, Kennedy insisted on proceeding. "Once they knew what was wrong—and that it was something he could tough out," his son Patrick remembered, "he was even more committed to appearing . . . [though] he knew he was going to walk onstage in excruciating pain and still at risk for a seizure."

His remarks were pared in half by Shrum, which negated Kennedy's preparation. He was now to give "a speech he had never seen," Vicki recalled. After an evocative film by documentarian Ken Burns, and Caroline's introduction, Vicki helped him to the podium.

"I have come here tonight to stand with you to change America, to restore its future, to rise to its best ideals and to elect Barack Obama president," he told the delegates.

"This November, the torch will be passed again to a new generation of Americans," Kennedy said. "The work begins anew. The hope rises again. And the dream lives on."

THE DREAM, Kennedy had told the delegates, included "the cause of my life . . . decent quality health care as a fundamental right and not a privilege." Back in Washington, Kennedy went to work, directing his health care staff to meet with their counterparts on the Senate Finance Committee, to negotiate with stakeholders, and to settle on a plan that avoided the debilitating rivalries which had caused such mischief in 1994. He was upset to hear talk that Hillary Clinton, who served on his committee, was maneuvering in the void caused by his illness to appropriate the issue.

"You're not going to take this away from me," Kennedy told Harry Reid. He was prepared to take it to the caucus for a vote, he told the Democratic leader. "Call the roll! Call the roll! I am going to do this."

"Well, I guess you are," said Reid.

Nevertheless, facing death, Kennedy was a realist. He prepared Dodd, and Finance chairman Max Baucus of Montana, to pick up the standard when he fell. With his approval, they fashioned a proposal along the lines of Romneycare, with an individual mandate, insurance exchanges, and subsidies for low-income working families. There would be many adjustments along the way, as the measure wound through House and Senate in the coming months—a single-payer "public option" was included and then deleted; abortion regulations were painstakingly negotiated; and some Democratic senators would request special treatment (the "Louisiana purchase" and the "Cornhusker kickback") for their states before they would join the majority. But the blueprint for the Affordable Care Act was ready when Obama took office.

KENNEDY'S NEXT NOTEWORTHY APPEARANCE exposed the risks he had taken in Denver. On a cold bright day in January 2009, bundled and wearing a natty black fedora, he sat with other senators on the west steps of the Capitol to watch the first American president of African descent take the oath of office. Then, inside Statuary Hall, at the Inaugural luncheon, while laughing and swapping stories with Walter Mondale, he muttered, "I'm cold, I'm cold," and suffered a seizure. He was embarrassed, not injured, and took time the next day to call Biden's grandchildren, who were shocked and frightened by his collapse, to assure them he was all right.

KENNEDY CALLED HIS OLD friend Joseph Califano and urged him to serve in Obama's crusade for health care.

"I'm seventy-one!" Califano said.

"I've got brain cancer," Kennedy shot back. "I'm still fighting."

DEMOCRATIC POLLSTER PETER HART wrote Kennedy a note, praising the courage that it took, and the difference it made, when the senator endorsed Obama. Kennedy wrote back to his old hand from the 1980 campaign, "The fight was ours together."

KENNEDY SPENT THE WINTER in Florida, to sail upon the waters of warmer seas on a sailboat trucked down from Cape Cod. "He sailed every day," Vicki remembered.

In March, he traveled to Washington to make a brief, affecting appearance at Obama's side at a daylong conference on health care in the White House. He looked gaunt, and tottered, but was hoping his presence would move the participants. In that he succeeded. In the days ahead, good and bad, Obama would fall back on what Kennedy told him as they waited to enter the East Room: "This is the time, Mr. President. Don't let it slip away."

THE ECONOMY HAD COLLAPSED. The cores of American finance and industry—Wall Street, the auto industry—were in dire need of bailouts. Things had changed, his staff told Obama: people would understand if he went back on his promise to enact a national health care program.

"This could blow up in our faces," said Rahm Emanuel, his chief of staff.

"If we lose," said Axelrod, "your presidency will be badly weakened."

"We better not lose, then," said Obama.

AMERICA'S IS A GOVERNMENT of men and women, not automatons. Even hardened politicians, made cynical by the years, retain the capacity for sentiment and emotion, for honor and obligation.

The impact of Kennedy's illness in no way rivaled the national state of grief and shock that followed his brother John's assassination—which Lyndon Johnson had employed to pass their legislative agenda. Yet some, seeing the sorrow that Ted's demise evoked among Democratic leaders and the rank and file, believed they heard an echo in history.

It would be wrong to suggest that, in the bruising months of striving that ended with the passage of the Affordable Care Act, tough-minded politicians like Nancy Pelosi, Harry Reid, Max Baucus, and Barack Obama were obsessed by a teary need to do something for Ted. But neither, as they said often throughout and after the process, was he long absent from their thoughts. Nor, while he had the strength, did he let them forget it.

Stepping in for Kennedy on the Labor Committee, while still heading his own Banking panel, Dodd performed superbly, in a legislative season

for the ages. He helped steer the bank rescue bill (the $700 billion Trou-
bled Asset Relief Program, known as TARP), the Kennedy father-son
mental health parity legislation, the Dodd-Frank financial sector reforms,
and the Affordable Care Act into law.

IN MID-APRIL, the Obama family's lives were brightened by the arrival of
Bo, a Portuguese water dog that Ted and Vicki sent them as a gift. When
the president phoned to thank the senator, Kennedy was too frail to take
the call. In May, he started talking about his funeral—though he still
swam his therapy laps in the pool.

He saw himself as blessed. He installed a television camera in the
house at Hyannis Port to teleconference with colleagues in Washington.
He welcomed old friends for goodbyes at the Cape, he cruised on the *Mya*
and sang songs—"spontaneous song syndrome," his stepdaughter, Caroline, called it—with his family at dinner.

After Vicki and Larry Horowitz informed him that the tumor was inexorably migrating through his brain, Kennedy told them, "I have to write
a letter to the president." He had one last card to play—a plea to Obama
to stay the course. It would be touching—and unrelenting. It would be
given by Vicki to Obama as a stirring, binding posthumous call to arms:

> *When I thought of all the years, all the battles, and all the memories of*
> *my long public life, I felt confident in these closing days that while I will not*
> *be there when it happens, you will be the President who at long last signs into*
> *law the health care reform that is the great unfinished business of our society.*
> *For me, this cause stretched across decades; it has been disappointed, but*
> *never finally defeated. It was the cause of my life. And in the past year, the*
> *prospect of victory sustained me—and the work of achieving it summoned my*
> *energy and determination.*
>
> *There will be struggles—there always have been—and they are already*
> *underway again. But as we moved forward in these months, I learned that*
> *you will not yield to calls to retreat—that you will stay with the cause until it*

is won. I saw your conviction that the time is now and witnessed your
unwavering commitment and understanding that health care is a decisive
issue for our future prosperity. But you have also reminded all of us that it
concerns more than material things; that what we face is above all a moral
issue; that at stake are not just the details of policy, but fundamental
principles of social justice and the character of our country.

And so because of your vision and resolve, I came to believe that soon,
very soon, affordable health coverage will be available to all, in an America
where the state of a family's health will never again depend on the amount of
a family's wealth. And while I will not see the victory, I was able to look
forward and know that we will—yes, we will—fulfill the promise of health
care in America as a right and not a privilege.

Kennedy wrote to the pope, asking for his blessing and forgiveness. But not all his concerns were spiritual. Another letter, a very practical letter, went to the governor of Massachusetts, asking that the laws of the commonwealth be adjusted to keep Kennedy's seat in Democratic hands until a special election could be held: the party needed sixty votes to cut off a filibuster and pass the Affordable Care Act.

HIS SISTER JEAN CAME to stay the summer. Ted worked diligently on the autobiography he had started before his illness. Many days, he sat on his porch, looking out over the great lawn on which he and his brothers and sisters had played, at the boats rocking at their moorings, the osprey nest on the piling offshore, and the sea.

"I guess I was . . . always running to keep ahead of the darkness," he told his friend James Young, the historian in charge of Kennedy's extensive oral history program.

Kennedy was thrilled, and proud, to watch from the Cape as the Labor Committee became the first congressional panel to approve the health care act. He "was hooting and hollering" when Dodd called him. And he was touched when his son Patrick wrote him: "There is no one I know who could have endured more emotional heartache than you have in your life and yet you've managed to keep living and loving." In a poignant moment out on the water, Ted absolved Patrick of any obligation he might feel to stay in politics. "Do what makes you happy," he told his son.

He was fading, depleted, and struggling with reading, speech, and memory. He took it upon himself to try to lighten the mood with jokes and wisecracks. "All of us would get pensive or depressed, and he would be the one to think of something funny," his stepdaughter, Caroline, recalled. "It really should have been the other way around, but I guess that's who he was."

He spent parts of his days in early August watching old James Bond films. When Eunice suffered a stroke and passed away, Ted could not attend the funeral. On one bleak day toward the end, a day of no laughter or energy, stepdaughter Caroline whispered in his ear, "You're a ruff-tuff-'em," and was rewarded with a smile.

On August 25, as friends and family gathered in a nearby hotel conference room, planning his funeral, the crisis arrived sooner than expected. On their way home that afternoon, they received messages from Vicki summoning them to return. He succumbed that night, at the age of seventy-seven.

The rites he had decreed before his death were modest when compared to those he had led for John and Robert in 1963 and 1968. The funeral was held at the basilica, in Boston, near the hospital where Kara had been treated for cancer—where Kennedy had often come to pray.

"He was not perfect, far from it," Ted Jr. told the mourners. "But my father believed in redemption."

Obama's eulogy conveyed a similar sentiment and a selection from one of Kennedy's favorite poems.

"As tempted more, more able to endure," William Wordsworth had written. "As more exposed to suffering and distress, hence also more alive to tenderness."

Then the president read a note from Jacqueline Kennedy Onassis to Ted, which she had written after her brother-in-law walked her daughter, Caroline, down the aisle. Ted had had it framed.

"On you, the carefree youngest brother, fell a burden a hero would have begged to have been spared," Onassis had written. "We're all going to make it because you're always there with your love."

He was buried with John and Jacqueline, and Robert, on the hillside in Arlington, between two maple trees.

Sources and Acknowledgments

In 2017, after my biography of Richard Nixon was published, an editor asked if I would like to tell Ted Kennedy's story. I seemed a likely candidate. I am versed in twentieth-century American politics and the course of contemporary liberalism. Having written books on a president and a Speaker, I thought that tackling the life of a celebrated senator would complete a trifecta. The Senate is a compelling setting: a place where six-year terms, the large constituencies of statewide office, sturdy traditions, and a relatively small cast can sometimes evoke nobility. As one who covered Kennedy for his hometown newspaper during interesting times in the 1990s I knew him, watched him under fire, contributed to his oral history project at the University of Virginia, and served as a source for previous biographers. But there were questions I needed to answer before devoting six years of my life to a study of his. Was there room—something fresh to say? Was there a need—something instructive in his career—to make the study worthwhile? Were archival resources available?

At the fiftieth anniversary of John Kennedy's assassination, the then executive editor of the *New York Times*, Jill Abramson, estimated that there were 40,000 books on the thirty-fifth president of the United States and his family. To this imposing total one must add the multivolume reports of three major government investigations (by the Warren Commission, the Church Committee, and the House Select Committee on Assassinations), a half dozen Hollywood movies, television miniseries, documentaries from the Public Broadcasting System, and many, many long-form stories in the press. It seemed, at first glance, that the market was overstocked.

The Kennedys are more than sensational, they are schismatizing as well. Thousands of these accounts are adoring, casting the days of John Kennedy's New Frontier as an Arthurian epic. By the reckoning of this school, "the grace he displayed . . . was more than matched by his coolness under fire," noted Marc J.

Selverstone in an introduction to the 2014 historiographical study *A Companion to John F. Kennedy*. Inevitably, a "dark side of Camelot" emerged from revisionist authors and conservative polemicists of various taste and tact, who portrayed the Kennedys as shallow and dissolute: rash risk-seekers who, as part of their legacy, left us disasters like the Vietnam War. The result is a certain murkiness. "The historical Kennedy remains elusive," said Selverstone. The story has "yet to generate a satisfactory consensus."

As with President Kennedy, there is "interpretive instability" in portrayals of Ted Kennedy's life and times. Here, too, there is dialectical opposition. The youngest Kennedy is unique among the brothers in that he was granted the gift of years. This exposed him, however, to the deconstruction of the New Frontier, a reshaping of media standards, and the colossal proliferation in celebrity scandalmongering in the last half century. Americans view John and his brother Robert in the context of "a president, and a presidency, forever young," said Selverstone. Not so with Ted. The world got to see him comb gray hair. Positive tropes—Lion of the Senate, King of the Hill—vied with depictions of a reckless drunkard and philanderer—Fat Boy, Teddy Bare, Bad Ted. His flaws and mistakes lent themselves to easy moralizing and comedic punch lines. He became a prize target for the conservative movement: Teddy, the caricature of liberal excess, whose appearance in right-wing fund-raising appeals was guaranteed to fill its coffers. The Republican senator Orrin Hatch of Utah, arriving in Washington at the dawn of the Reagan era, knew two things: that he hated what Ted Kennedy stood for, and that he'd go to any length to stop him.

Kennedy reacted to the newly aggressive media, to the focus on his lifestyle and the change in the partisan temper by being more guarded. He sponsored an excellent oral history program, but it's marred by redactions, and most of his diaries and letters are locked away. Only a small segment of his Senate papers has been processed for release by the John F. Kennedy Presidential Library. In early 2020, that process came to a halt in the COVID-19 pandemic.

I admit that I weighed surrender. But something kept me going, even as the virus shut down the Kennedy Library, the National Archives, and the Library of Congress. The venture was meeting my three criteria: There was something fresh, and important, to say and—with a little archival digging—the stuff with which to say it. The liberal ideals that the Kennedys championed have come under fire from the forces of reaction and authoritarianism. It is apt to examine the liberal cause—to learn from its achievements and reversals, power, and defects—and Ted Kennedy's life is an optimum lens.

Kennedy was a consequential legislator from the time of the New Frontier and the Great Society in the agitational 1960s, through the conservative reaction of the Nixon, Reagan, and Bush eras, to the election of Barack Obama and the crafting of the Affordable Care Act—the missing keystone in the liberal edifice—in 2009. In the history of the American republic, only four men have served longer than his forty-six years in the Senate. Given the collaborative nature of American government, and especially Congress, it means little to cite the thousand bills and amendments that bore Kennedy's name. He could not have done it alone. But one can list the causes to which he made a major contribution. And it is no small list.

Can immigrants of all races come and bring their families to America? Are hotels, airports, trains, stores, and restaurants open to darker-skinned, disabled, and gay Americans? Do young people, Blacks, and other minorities have full rights of citizenship? Is the right to vote secured for all? Do women get their fair share of athletic and academic scholarships, and are they otherwise treated as equal to men? Is abortion regulated, safe, and legal?

Do America's seniors have affordable medical care and access to prescription drugs? Have the world's nuclear arsenals been reduced from their menacing Cold War status? Do public schools get federal aid? Have the inequities of the Vietnam-era draft been replaced by a fairer, volunteer army? Do the National Institutes of Health stand guard against diseases like AIDS, or COVID-19? Has the minimum wage remained a tool for economic justice?

Can Americans gain access to their government's deliberations and records? Are lie detectors, and wiretaps, and prosecutors properly governed? Are there rules to safeguard the subjects of scientific, medical, and pharmaceutical testing? Do poorer folks, children, and working families have access to affordable health care?

This last—the crusade for universally accessible health care—was "the cause of his life," said Kennedy. He spent twenty-eight of his forty-six years in Congress during conservative Republican presidencies—playing defense against their sustained assault on liberal principles. He managed, like a courier bearing a vital message through the shot and hellfire of a World War I battlefield, to keep that cause intact and take part in its attainment. When Barack Obama signed the Affordable Care Act in 2010 his thoughts were of his mother, who died young, and of Ted Kennedy, who had succumbed to brain cancer the previous summer.

In our current divide, in this time of great polarity, it is enlightening—indeed, startling—to study Kennedy's legislative success, and particularly his ability to reach across the Senate aisle and recruit Republican partners and cosponsors. In

1970, he made a speech at Dublin's Trinity College about Edmund Burke, the Irish parliamentarian who preached forbearance in an age of revolution. Kennedy embraced Burke's prescription of the long, productive haul. "A lifetime of thought and action consumed by the slow labor of improving the human condition" is more valuable "than . . . impossible visions," said Kennedy. "History is a harsh judge of those so caught up with revolution that they forget reformation."

Orrin Hatch came to Washington loathing Ted Kennedy—and ended up making history with Kennedy as his partner.

For anyone who endures hard times, Kennedy's life is a towering, parabolic lesson of resilience. Through a life of grief and guilt and physical suffering, he spurned despair. He persevered. He endured. His goals, as even his ideological foes came to recognize, were generous and compassionate—"to make gentler the human condition"—he liked to say, echoing the ancient Greeks.

And so, I concluded, his was a story I wanted to tell. His life offers instruction on the political, and the personal. I gave myself the time to surpass the archival obstacles. I discovered that, with the help of an array of good people—Kennedy's contemporaries, staff, and family, and archivists from Boston to Palo Alto—it was not impossible to forge a well-grounded account that might put an end to the "interpretive instability."

My wife, Catharina, may be jaded by the credit I give her in all these books, but it is inescapably hers. She is loving and patient and keeps me focused. And, for this book, she came to work as a full-time researcher and cross-country traveling and working companion. Caitlin and John, our children, are our delight.

David Black, my agent, has been a friend and counselor for thirty years, four books and counting. I had a new team at Penguin Random House for this project—and my thanks go out to my editor, Scott Moyers, to Ann Godoff, and to Helen Rouner, Mia Council, Carlynn Chironna, Roland Ottewell, and Darren Haggar. Their faith and patience in the plague years was especially valuable.

My work on this book was also supported by a grant from the Dirksen Congressional Center in Pekin, Illinois—a generous sponsor of my study of Congress over the years. Frank Mackaman and Tiffany White were gracious hosts who led Catharina and me through the prize collections there, just before the virus shut down research rooms across the nation. I am grateful, as well, for a grant I received from the Association of Centers for the Study of Congress and for the support of the Biography Institute at the University of Groningen in the Netherlands.

I have been fortunate, in telling this story, that the project engaged the interest of Thomas Rollins, a lawyer, entrepreneur, and former aide to Kennedy, and Robert Shrum, who crafted many of the senator's best-known speeches. They read drafts of the manuscript early and often in the last four years, adding insight and perspective and insisting on precision. So did Nigel Hamilton, author of the finest biography of the young John Kennedy, and two sharp-eyed members of the faculty at the University of Groningen: Professor Hans Renders and Professor Doeko Bosscher.

Victoria Reggie Kennedy led a group of folks who knew Ted Kennedy and his work and also were willing to read all, or parts, of the manuscript. For their generosity, I thank her, Ralph Neas, Timothy Leland, Stephen Kurkjian, Thomas Gargan, Jeff Blattner, David Nexon, Trina Vargo, Ronald Weich, Gary Bass, Paul Kirk, Robert Schlesinger, Burt Wides, and Daniel Ellsberg. In many cases, I took their advice; in others I did not. In all cases, the call was mine, as are any errors in fact or reasoning.

Steven Clevenger, Mark Garfinkel, Kathy Kupka, Nicky Lockman, Jan Grenci, and the estate of Robert Lerner helped me furnish the photographs that illustrate this volume. I owe special thanks to Jennifer Quan and Maryrose Grossman at the John F. Kennedy Presidential Library and Foundation for their archival work and assistance, and to Brian McGrory, William Greene, and Chloe Grinberg, who helped me track down the photos taken by the exceptional photojournalists at the *Boston Globe*.

In writing the laws that govern the disposition of congressional records, Congress has been protective of its members and alumni. Personal, political, and office files remain the property of a senator, while the records of the Senate and its committees, stored in the National Archives, can be sequestered for decades. Yet decades have now passed for many of the historic events that took place in Ted Kennedy's life. With some digging in the Senate Judiciary Committee and Labor Committee files at the National Archives—with archivist Adam Berenbak as my Sherpa—I found fresh details from the passage of the historic Medicare and Medicaid, immigration, and civil rights legislation of Lyndon Johnson's Great Society; the origins and waging of the Vietnam War; the Supreme Court nomination battles over Abe Fortas, Clement Haynsworth, and G. Harrold Carswell; the Watergate scandals and the partisan warfare over health care that occurred during the Clinton presidency.

The presidential libraries of Presidents Johnson, Nixon, Ford, Carter, Reagan, and Clinton offered more archival bonanzas. The Senate Judiciary Committee files on the Supreme Court nomination of Robert Bork, for instance, will be closed at the National Archives until 2037. But on our visit to Simi Valley, California, we discovered that the Reagan presidential library has extensive material from White House files on Bork's defeat, as well as on Kennedy's involvement in

civil rights, voting rights, and the troubles in Northern Ireland. The Reagan collection, and others we surveyed, allowed me to write a thorough account of the
Senate's tardy, contentious response to the AIDS epidemic, and Kennedy's heroic
role in that history.

The Carter library in Atlanta, Georgia, has a rich record on the break between
Kennedy and Carter over health care, and their battle in the 1980 presidential
primaries. The Ford library in Ann Arbor, Michigan, holds records on airline deregulation, busing, and health care. The Johnson library in Austin, Texas, offers
rich resources on Kennedy's 1968 trip to Vietnam, and the ill-fated nomination of
Judge Francis X. Morrissey. The Nixon library in Yorba Linda, California, has a
fine collection of presidential tape recordings, an abundance of material on Watergate and Vietnam, and detailed records on Kennedy's collaboration with Nixon on
health care.

Kennedy donated his Senate papers to the John F. Kennedy Presidential Library instead of to Harvard or the University of Virginia, his alma maters. At either of these institutions, so rich a resource would have been processed quickly
and opened with a gala announcement and ceremony. That is how Boston College, for instance, welcomed the papers of Tip O'Neill. Sadly, even famous siblings rank low on the list of priorities at the presidential libraries, where the
shortage of funding provided by Congress qualifies as a national shame. But if
the pace of processing Ted Kennedy's papers at his brother's library can best be
described as glacial, this is not the case at the archives of his colleagues. Many
lawmakers, like O'Neill, donated their papers to home state universities, and so
did Kennedy aides like Nick Littlefield, who led the Labor Committee staff for
more than a decade, and Thomas Susman, who held a similar position on the
Judiciary panel.

If one is willing—as we were—to travel to places like Pekin, Illinois (Everett
Dirksen), Chapel Hill, North Carolina (Sam Ervin), Indianapolis, Indiana (Birch
Bayh), Lawrence, Kansas (Robert Dole), St. Paul and Minneapolis, Minnesota
(Hubert Humphrey, Walter Mondale, and Eugene McCarthy), or Laramie, Wyoming (Alan Simpson), the records of Kennedy's Senate allies—and those of his
rivals—will enrich and supplement the material available from the National Archives and the presidential libraries. My thanks go to the archivists and staff who
welcomed us to the University of Massachusetts, Boston; Harvard University; Boston College; Boston University; Northeastern University; Columbia University;
the New York Public Library; Kent State University; Princeton University; the
University of North Carolina; the Robert J. Dole Institute of Politics at the University of Kansas; Indiana University; the Minnesota Historical Society; Northwest-

ern University; the University of Wyoming; the University of Utah; the University of Virginia; the University of Michigan; the Hoover Institution at Stanford University; Drew University; the University of Wisconsin and the Wisconsin Historical Society; the Library of Congress; and South Dakota State University.

In Boston, Joseph Sciacca kindly opened the morgue at the *Boston Herald* to us. Isobel Ellis and George Condon helped me access the fine work of the *National Journal* in Washington, DC. Betty Koed, Heather Moore, and Katherine Scott welcomed me at the Senate Historical Office. The good folks at the New York Historical Society were, as always, welcoming, warm, and generous in their support. Robert, Stephen, and Andrew Schlesinger gave me permission to quote from the unpublished volumes of an American historical treasure: the diaries of Arthur Schlesinger Jr. A brave young scholar, Brian Robertson, and the indefatigable Ryan Pettigrew helped me find my way at the Nixon presidential library. Gail Hyder Wiley supported my efforts to open some of the closed oral histories at the Miller Center in Charlottesville, Virginia. For these and other courtesies, I thank them all.

Amid these far-flung collections, I found unpublished selections from Kennedy's diary—on Vietnam, the war between Pakistan and India, Supreme Court appointments, and other matters—and samplings of revealing correspondence on Watergate and Kennedy's announced and unannounced 1972, 1976, and 1980 presidential campaigns. In Schlesinger's unpublished diaries I discovered that the historian had recorded Kennedy's private account of the accident on Chappaquiddick, and the senator's panicky efforts to concoct an alibi.

A group of good-hearted souls opened personal collections to me. My thanks go out to Adam Clymer, Thomas Rollins, Thomas Susman, Ralph Neas, Donald Ritchie, Walter Oleszek, Jeff Blattner, Gary Bass, Timothy Phelps, Suzy Chaffee, Michael Putzel, Tad Devine, Patricia Keefer, Patricia Gibbons, Kai Bird, Michael Enright, and the family of Richard Drayne.

Dozens of generous individuals agreed to sit for interviews for this book, including Adam Clymer, Ann Blackman, Ralph Neas, Barbara Souliotis, Thomas Rollins, Robert Shrum, Barry Sussman, Birch Bayh, Burt Wides, Burton Hersh, Charles Daly, Charles Tretter, Christine Sullivan Daly, Trixie Burke, Christopher Dodd, Gary Bass, Chris Jennings, Clark Hoyt, Daniel Ellsberg, Joseph Califano, David Axelrod, David Nasaw, David Nexon, Patrick Kennedy, Victoria Reggie Kennedy, Dolores Huerta, Don Luce, Donald Ritchie, John Warner, Eileen McNamara, George Abrams, Gerard Doherty, Michael Putzel, Gerard O'Neill, Stephen Kurkjian, Timothy Leland, Gregory Craig, Helen O'Donnell, Henry Hubbard, Jack Corrigan, James Manley, Michael Reilly, Janet Heininger, Jason Berman, Jeff

Blattner, James Doyle, James Flug, Robert Nickels, Joseph Tydings, Ricki Seidman, John Hamill, Michael Schwartz, John Siegenthaler, Kandy Stroud, Kathleen Kennedy Townsend, Kenneth Feinberg, Lawrence O'Donnell, Lee Annis, LeRoy Goodman, Louie Mahern, Robert Caro, Lynn Drake, Mark Gearan, Mike Barnicle, Mark Shields, Matthew Storin, Maureen Byrnes, Melody Miller, Nance Lyons, Norm Ornstein, Patricia Keefer, Paul Donovan, Paul Kirk, Peter Canellos, Peter Edelman, Peter Hart, Ranny Cooper, Richard Arenberg, Richard Baker, Stephanie Cutter, Richard Cohen, Roger Mudd, Rosemary Keough Kerrebrock, Stuart Altman, Bob Woodward, Terri Robinson, Vic Basile, Timothy Phelps, Timothy Westmoreland, Thomas Gargan, Thomas Korologos, Thomas Susman, Trent Lott, Wallace Johnson, Walter Oleszek, and William vanden Heuvel.

Others—Antonin Scalia, Trina Vargo, Ronald Weich, Stuart Eizenstat, Charles Green, Walter Robinson, Rick Perlstein, Jonathan Alter, Walker Nolan, John Mulligan, John Walcott, Kai Bird, Madelyn Kelly, Kathleen Sullivan, Dan Moldea, Kitty Higgins, Larry Tye, Peter Gosselin, Tim Naftali, Ray Boomhower, Richard Stearns, Seymour Hersh, Todd Purdum, Mark Feeney, Howie Carr, Peter Lucas, Gregory Moore, Thomas Oliphant, Curtis Wilkie, David Maraniss, John McCain, Mark Salter, George Lardner, Dale DeHaan, Laurence Leamer, Maurice Fitzpatrick, Kitty Kelley—answered my questions when our paths crossed, or replied to specific inquiries via email or a quick phone call, or thoughtfully sent a recollection my way.

In writing this book, I have drawn on interviews I conducted for my Nixon biography with Pat Buchanan, Frank Gannon, George Shultz, Geoff Shephard, Morton Halperin, Leonard Garment, Richard Ben-Veniste, Stanley Kutler, Jack Anderson, and Ben Bradlee.

I also have tapped interviews that I conducted when covering national politics for *National Journal*, the *Denver Post*, and the *Boston Globe* with Lee Atwater, Niall O'Dowd, Nancy Pelosi, John Lawrence, Gary Hart, John Kerry, Karl Rove, Alan Simpson, Orrin Hatch, George Mitchell, Richard Goodwin, Gerry Adams, Nancy Soderberg, Stephen Breyer, Newt Gingrich, Larry Horowitz, John Ehrlichman, William Taylor, Bill and Hillary Clinton, George Stephanopoulos, Harold Ickes, and Tom Tancredo.

Interviews for my biography of Speaker Thomas P. "Tip" O'Neill were especially valuable, as they included figures from Massachusetts and national politics who knew of, or worked with, the Kennedy brothers, including David Nyhan, John Kenneth Galbraith, Robert Healy, Richard Goodwin, Richard Donahue, David Cohen, Barney Frank, Nick Littlefield, Mary McGrory, William Gibbons, Mark Dalton, Dan Rostenkowski, Chris Black, Robert Drinan, Thomas Winship, Frank

Mankiewicz, William Sutton, Theodore Sorensen, Jerome Grossman, James Cannon, Arthur Schlesinger, Lester Hyman, David Powers, Martin Nolan, Elliot Richardson, and Neil MacNeil; and players from the Carter and Reagan eras, including Jimmy Carter, Hamilton Jordan, Jody Powell, James A. Baker III, George Miller, Jim Wright, Howard Baker, Hugh Carey, William Clark, Tony Coelho, John Culver, Michael Deaver, Sean Donlon, Brian Donnelly, Kenneth Duberstein, Garret FitzGerald, Al From, Stanley Greenberg, John Hume, Jacob Lew, Michael Lillis, Edward Markey, Chris Matthews, Frank Moore, Kirk O'Donnell, Patricia Schroeder, and Alan Simpson.

I was fortunate to have had formal interviews with Ted Kennedy several times over the years, and many exchanges in congressional hallways, hearing rooms, and press galleries. Transcripts of these interviews will make their way, with the rest of my papers, to the archives at the University of Virginia.

The digitalization of our history proceeds. I traveled 30,000 miles or more to far-flung courthouses and archives for my 2011 biography of Clarence Darrow; today I could conduct that research without leaving my desk at home. The online collections of Bowdoin College (George Mitchell); Suffolk University (J. Joseph Moakley); Shepherd University (Robert Byrd); the William J. Clinton and George W. Bush presidential libraries; the Office of the Historian at the U.S. Department of State; the FBI; the CIA; the U.S. presidential oral history program at the Miller Center at the University of Virginia; and the National Security Archive are terrific assets, as is the American Presidency Project at the University of California, Santa Barbara.

For various kindnesses, a final word of thanks goes out to Thomas Hayes, Adam Shoop, Ian Frederick-Rothwell, William Arthur, Carla Braswell, John Keller, Steve Branch, Aimee Muller, Sarah Barca, Tim Holtz, John J. O'Connell, Randall Flaherty, Brian Shetler, Susan Halpert, Michael Greco, Bryan Kasik, Jody Brumage, Jay Wyatt, Timothy Johnson, Mackenzie Ryan, Jennifer Kleinjung, Kathleen Cruikshank, Senator Chris Van Hollen, Karen Robb, Molly Brown, Brigid Hogan, Lee Grady, Maria Schleuder, Jessica Holden, Meghan Bailey, Laura Russo, Yvonne Spura, Richard Lehr, Joseph Kahn, Jenny Littlefield, James Concannon, Denis Hamill, Jeff Greenfield, Michael Beschloss, Tom Putnam, and Raymond Smock.

Last, but not least, I thank Michael Desmond, Karen Abramson, Abbey Malangone, Stacey Chandler, Sharon Kelly, James Hill, Stephen Plotkin, Laurie Austin, Michelle DeMartino, and Christina Fitzpatrick at the John F. Kennedy Presidential Library.

Notes

The following abbreviations are used for some of the more frequently cited persons and primary sources.

AC-JFKL	Adam Clymer papers, JFKL
ADST	Association for Diplomatic Studies & Training
AS-NYPL	Arthur Schlesinger Jr. papers, New York Public Library
AW-JFKL	Adam Walinsky papers, JFKL
BA	*Boston American*
Bayh-IU	Birch Bayh papers, Indiana University
BG	*Boston Globe*
BH	*Boston Herald*
BM	*Boston* magazine
BM-JFKL	Burke Marshall papers, JFKL
BR	*Boston Record*
Byrd-SU	Robert Byrd Center, Shepherd University
CQA	*Congressional Quarterly Almanac*
CQW	*Congressional Quarterly Weekly*
CR	*Congressional Record*
CS-MHS	Carl Solberg papers, Minnesota Historical Society
Dole-KU	The Robert J. Dole Institute of Politics at the University of Kansas
EB-MHS	Edgar Berman papers, Minnesota Historical Society
ED-DC	Everett Dirksen papers, Dirksen Congressional Center
EMK	Edward M. Kennedy
EMKI	Edward M. Kennedy Institute
EMK-JFKL	Edward M. Kennedy papers, JFKL
EMKOH-JFKL	EMK oral history, JFKL
EMKOH-UVA	EMK oral history, Miller Center, UVA
EMK TC	*True Compass*
EM-MHS	Eugene McCarthy papers, Minnesota Historical Society
FM-Utah	Frank Moss papers, University of Utah
FRUS	*Foreign Relations of the United States*, Office of the Historian, U.S. Department of State
GFL	Gerald Ford Presidential Library
GM-Princeton	George McGovern papers, Princeton University
Hart-UM	Phil Hart papers, University of Michigan
HJ-UW	Haynes Johnson papers, University of Wisconsin
JAF	John A. Farrell
JBK	Joan Bennett Kennedy
JCL	Jimmy Carter Presidential Library
JFK	John F. Kennedy
JFKL	John F. Kennedy Presidential Library
JKG-JFKL	John Kenneth Galbraith papers, JFKL
JKO	Jacqueline Kennedy Onassis
JMB-WC	James MacGregor Burns papers, Williams College
JPK	Joseph P. Kennedy

JS-JFKL	Jean Stein papers, JFKL
KFP-JFKL	Kennedy family papers, Joseph and Rose Kennedy collections, JFKL
LBJL	Lyndon B. Johnson Presidential Library
LD-KS	Leo Damore papers, Kent State University
LD-WYO	Lester David papers, University of Wyoming
LHJ	*Ladies' Home Journal*
LOC	Library of Congress
LT-CU	Larry Tye papers, Columbia University
NJ	*National Journal*
NL-UMASS	Nick Littlefield papers, University of Massachusetts, Boston
NM-DC	Neil MacNeil papers, Dirksen Congressional Center
NSA	National Security Archive
NYHT	*New York Herald Tribune*
NYT	*New York Times*
OH	Oral histories
RC	Robert Coughlan
RCP-NW	Robert Coughlan papers, Northwestern University
RFK	Robert F. Kennedy
RK	Rose Kennedy
RNL	Richard Nixon Presidential Library
RRL	Ronald Reagan Presidential Library
SEP	*Saturday Evening Post*
SFE	*San Francisco Examiner*
SHO	U.S. Senate Historical Office
SJC-NARA	Senate Judiciary Committee, National Archives
SLC-NARA	Senate Labor Committee, National Archives
TB-UNC	Taylor Branch papers, University of North Carolina
TCF-Harvard	*Time* correspondent files, Harvard University
TCF-HI	*Time* correspondent files, Hoover Institution
TCF-NYHS	*Time* correspondent files, New-York Historical Society
TD-SDS	Thomas Daschle papers, South Dakota State University
TNR	*New Republic*
TNY	*New Yorker*
TON-BC	Thomas P. "Tip" O'Neill papers, Boston College
TP-DC	Todd Purdum papers, Dirksen Congressional Center
TS-JFKL	Theodore Sorensen papers, JFKL
TS-UMASS	Thomas Susman papers, University of Massachusetts, Boston
TTR	Rose Kennedy, *Times to Remember*
TW-Harvard	Theodore White papers, Harvard University
TW-JFKL	Theodore White papers, JFKL
UCSB	Public Papers of the President, American Presidency Project, University of California, Santa Barbara
UVA	Miller Center, University of Virginia
WCL	William J. Clinton Presidential Library
WP	*Washington Post*
WS	*Washington Star*
WSJ	*Wall Street Journal*

One: The Last of the Kennedy Boys

1 **Notice was sent:** Leighton to JPK, July 20, 1950; JPK to Leighton, July 21, 1950, KFP-JFKL.

1 **Harvard's expansive criteria:** Leighton to JPK, July 20, 1950; KFP-JFKL. JAF interviews with EMK classmates George Abrams, Burton Hersh. For admittance procedures at Harvard and the Ivy League see Karabel, *Chosen.*

3 **"for the laughter":** JAF interview with Christopher Dodd. On his chipmunk-like cheeks, see EMKOH-UVA, citing JFK inscription on a photograph of

EMK: "Honey Fitz's grandchild stores nuts for the winter."

3 **a "gay illiterate":** As in fun-loving. JFK to K. LeMoyne "Lem" Billings, Feb. 20, 1945, LeMoyne "Lem" Billings papers, JFKL, cited in Hamilton, *Reckless Youth*, 683. On Rose and schools see TCF-NYHS, Nov. 14, 1961, Sept. 21, 1962.

3 **"being constantly compared":** LHJ, Oct. 1962. JAF interviews with Victoria Reggie Kennedy, Paul Kirk, Adam Clymer. Edward Moore Kennedy was born on Washington's birthday, Feb. 22, 1932.

4 **"a cold appraiser":** "lullabies," "Tenaciously," and "The Street" quotations are from TCF-NYHS, June 1, 3, 4, 1960. The "lone wolf" description is from RK, undated reminiscence, KFP-JFKL. For EMK ancestral roots see Goodwin, *Fitzgeralds.* There was never a single Democratic machine in Massachusetts but rather, as Representative Edward Boland would say, "a loose federation of personal loyalties." See TCF-NYHS, June 1, 1962.

4 **herald of appeasement:** See Nasaw, *Patriarch,* and Whalen, *Founding Father.* The author consulted JPK papers at the JFKL and Whalen's papers at the Hoover Institution at Stanford University. JAF interview with David Nasaw. On polio victims see TCF-NYHS, June 3, 1960.

5 **a gorgeous crowd:** JKO interview, RCP-NW. On parental expectations see RK to Coughlan, July 30, 1973, RCP-NW. See also EMKOH-UVA and Voutselas to Sanderson, July 12, 1973, KFP-JFKL. On El Morocco see Joe Jr. to JPK and RK, 1942, KFP-JFKL; JFK to RFK, Nov. 14, 1943, cited in Donovan, *PT-109,* 152. On broken ankle see TCF-NYHS, Nov. 19, 1955.

5 **months before the war:** The family's adventures in Europe in the months before the war are captured in Swift, *Kennedys Amidst,* and Joseph Kennedy's relationship with Franklin Roosevelt in Beschloss, *Kennedy and Roosevelt.* See also *Herald Statesman* (Bronxville, NY), Oct. 3, 1939. BG, May 9, 1939. BA, March 14, 1939. *Life,* Dec. 20, 1937. Jerome Beatty, "Nine Kennedys and How They Grew," *Woman's Day,* April 1939. On Princess Elizabeth see EMK-TC, 52. For the visit with the pope, see JPK diary, March 12, 13, 15, 1939, JFKL, reprinted in Smith, ed., *Hostage,* 316–20, and Ball to Scott, Nov. 7, 1958, with JPK affidavit, KFP-JFKL.

6 **Atop the ladder:** "marvelous creatures": TTR, 122, and RC interview of Eunice Kennedy Shriver, RCP-NW. Hennessey remembrance is from Goodwin, *Fitzgeralds,* 539. "antithesis": RK to family, March 27, 1942, KFP-JFKL.

6 **The outbreak of war:** EMK to JPK, undated, fall and winter 1939, April 8, 1940, and undated, June 1940, and JPK to EMK, Sept. 11, 1940, KFP-JFKL, reprinted in Smith, *Hostage,* 397, 403, 416, 437, 470–71. Kick Kennedy September 1939 reminiscence of blackout is from Smith, *Hostage,* 371.

7 **"comprise the world":** EMK-TC, 18, 31.

7 **"the perfect family":** RK journal notes, fall 1968, KFP-JFKL. See also RK to Sister Paulus, March 27, 1973, on the need to frame photographs of her mentally disabled daughter Rosemary in clothes that don't make her look so fat, KFP-JFKL. "no crying": EMK-TC, 41, 86. "grumpiness": RK edits to TTR, RCP-NW.

7 **their father's calculations:** Joseph Kennedy's Aug. 8, 1951 letter to John McCormack is published in Smith, *Hostage,* 656–57. See also JPK, TCF-NYHS, May 7, 1957, and JFK tape, dictation belt 39, JFKL: "I never thought—school or college—I would ever run for office myself. One politician was enough in the family and my brother Joe was obviously going to be that politician. I hadn't considered myself a political type and he filled all the requirements for political success." The duty of succession was clear within the

family, and JPK stated it plainly in a letter to a cousin in 1945: "With Joe gone and Jack still a long way from being well, there is plenty of slack for Bobby to take up." See JPK to Kane, March 19, 1945, KFP-JFKL, reprinted in Smith, *Hostage,* 619.

8 **Singularity was discouraged:** RK journal notes, "No Laggard in the Family," KFP-JFKL.

8 **"a lot of pressure":** Eunice Kennedy Shriver interview, RCP-NW. "chalk, money or marbles": TCF-NYHS, June 3, 1960.

8 **the "fuck-up":** JAF interview with Patrick Kennedy. On EMK insecurity see JAF interviews with Burton Hersh, Barbara Souhotis, Trixie Burke, Charles Tretter, Greg Craig, James Manley. Gargan quote is from Joseph Gargan interview transcript, LD-KS. In his memoir, EMK used the word "screwup."

8 **"amazing, authentic person":** Patrick Kennedy OH, UVA.

9 **adept at dodging responsibility:** JFK to LeMoyne "Lem" Billings, Feb. 10, 1938, LeMoyne "Lem" Billings papers, JFKL. RK to RC, undated, KFP-JFKL. Billings recalled yet another occasion, when JFK was caught in a speed trap on Cape Cod and had them switch places so that Billings was behind the wheel when the policeman handed them the ticket. Lem Billings OH, JFKL. See also Ellis Mottur OH, UVA. The Portsmouth Priory cheating story is explored in Thomas, *Robert Kennedy,* 36–37.

9 **handicapped sister Rosemary:** Hersh, *Intimate,* 522: "I thought that I had better do what Dad wanted or the same thing could happen to me."

9 **"a non-serious life":** EMK-TC, 40. See also EMKOH-UVA: "I remember my father talking to me and saying, 'We've got a lot of children. If you want to try and do something with your life I'm going to be here to help you and if you don't want to do something with your life, you've got older brothers and sisters who do, and I'm going to have to spend time with them. So think about that a little bit.' I went back in my bedroom after talking to him and made my mind up."

9 **sea was salve:** JAF interview with Victoria Reggie Kennedy. The framed quotation was from Eugene O'Neill's play *Long Day's Journey into Night.* EMK learned to handle and race a sailboat in the summer of 1940, at Hyannis Port, when he was eight years old. See Jean Kennedy Smith to JPK, June 20, July 21, 29, 1940, KFP-JFKL.

10 **"an awful woman":** Gore Vidal interview by David Pitts, LT-CU. See also Hamilton, *Reckless,* for its account of JFK's childhood, and Martin, *Hero,* quoting JFK: "My mother was either at some Paris fashion house or else on her knees in some church. She was never there when we really needed her. . . . [She] never really held me and hugged me. Never!" The transcript of the JKO interview with *Life* magazine writer Theodore White is in TW-JFKL. The Maria Shriver quote is from Meg Grant, "Maria Shriver Opens Up About Love and Loss," *AARP The Magazine,* Dec. 2013/Jan. 2014.

10 **"the ninth one":** RK journal note, "Older Children Influence Younger Children," KFP-JFKL. See also TCF-Harvard, Sept. 14, 1962: "There was seventeen years between my oldest and my youngest

child, and I had been telling bedtime stories for twenty years," Rose sighed. The older siblings "seem to be more important in a family, and always the ones who have the best rooms, and the first choice of the boats." Mary Moore, the wife of EMK's namesake and a regular family guardian, added, "You sometimes forgot little Ted."

11 **"You're losing your mooring":** EMKOH-UVA. James Young OH, UVA. RK to children, Jan. 12, Feb. 16, March 27, 1942; Frank Hackett to EMK, Jan. 16, 1942; Hackett to JPK, June 1, 1942; King to RK, Nov. 5, 1936; Markham to RK, April 21, 1937, KFP-JFKL. EMK-TC, chapter 4, "Boarding School Boy." JAF interview with Victoria Reggie Kennedy. The most detailed account of EMK's schooling is in Burns, *Camelot Legacy*, 36–39, 42, 352. "The biographer looks in vain for indications of potential greatness," Burns wrote, 33.

11 **"a boy at school who was very sad":** Native Buoyancy: RK to children, Jan. 5, 1941 and March 27, 1942, KFP-JFKL. Tease: William Peters, "Teddy Kennedy," *Redbook*, June 1962. EMKOH-UVA. Short story: James Young OH, UVA. Parental abandonment: EMK to RK, Mother's Day 1973; Jean Kennedy Smith to RK, Mother's Day, undated, KFP-JFKL. Years later, EMK described his childhood to Elizabeth Shannon, a longtime friend with whom he had developed a romantic relationship. "It was just a series of nannies and nursemaids and being shuffled here and shuffled there," she said. "His mother would go off and leave him for long periods of time. She'd go down to Florida when he was up here, or she'd go to Europe with her girlfriends and leave him here. Certainly his father was not ever around much . . . so it was a lonely childhood." See Elizabeth Shannon OH, UVA.

12 **regimes were strict:** JAF interview with Victoria Reggie Kennedy. EMK notes, RC edits, RCP-NW. EMK-TC, chapter four, "Boarding School Boy," 60–65, 72. EMKOH-UVA.

12 **shrugged off danger signs:** Markham to RK, April 21, 1937; Major and Martha Collen to JPK, Jan. 7, 1940; Rose secretary to Ford, Sept. 14, 1942; Tutoring bill, June 13, 1942, "Consultation, Diagnostic Testing and Evaluation," Dr. Hazel Bradbury; RFK letters to parents, November or early December 1942 and undated 1941–1943; EMK notes, RC edits, all KFP-JFKL. On EMK's focus see academic appraisals, Lawrence Park West Country Day School, NY ("At first his powers of concentration were weak"), and Gibbs School, London, 1938, KFP-JFKL. For "deflated" see RK to family, Dec. 5–6, 1941, KFP-JFKL.

See also JPK to EMK, Jan. 31, 1946, KFP-JFKL, reprinted in Smith, *Hostage*, 624, chastising his son for poor penmanship and spelling, and with a typical family jibe about weight: "Skating is not 'scating': it is 'skating,' and tomorrow you spell wrong. You spell it 'tommorow': it is 'tomorrow.' You spell slaughter as slauter. . . . You are getting pretty old now [EMK was about to turn fourteen] and it looks rather babyish," JPK wrote. "I am sorry to see that you are starving to death. I can't imagine that ever happening to you if there was anything at all to eat around, but then you can spare a few pounds."

On weight see also Joe Jr. to JPK, May 5, 1940; JFK to JPK, Aug. 1940; Ethel Kennedy Shriver to JPK, May 1940; Jean Kennedy Smith to JPK, May 29, July 29, 1940 ("Teddy thinks he will go on a diet. He has been thinking that since he came down here"), and JPK to Jean Kennedy Smith ("fat little brother"), Sept. 11, 1940; RK to family, Feb. 16, March 27, 1942, all KFP-JFKL. See also EMKOH-UVA. Laurence Tribe OH, UVA. Hyannis Port camping story from EMK contribution to *That Shining Hour*, a privately printed collection of reminiscences edited by Patricia Kennedy Lawford.

13 **strings to tug:** RK to Fessenden School, Dec. 8, 1944, KFP-JFKL. JPK used the same tactic when ladling expectations. "I . . . got your report from school and, boy, it is the worst one you ever had. In the fifth of your class you didn't pass in English or Geography and you only got 60 in Spelling and History," he wrote EMK when the boy was eleven. "That is terrible—you can do better than that. You wouldn't want to have people say that Joe and Jack Kennedy's brother was such a bad student." See JPK to EMK, Oct. 5, 1943, KFP-JFKL, reprinted in Smith, *Hostage*, 569.

13 **those blithe shoulders:** David Burke OH, UVA.

13 **"John F" or "Honey Fitz":** EMK-TC, 77–82. EMKOH-UVA. In Boston political lore, there is a lovely story of Ted as a youngster, wandering the city with his grandfather Fitzgerald, who is sparing the boy by toting his bookbag. They encounter Fitzgerald's mortal foe, James Michael Curley, who greets them saying, "Hello Fitz. Still carrying your burglar's tools, I see." The tale made it into print in the Kenneth O'Donnell and David Powers book on JFK, in a William Manchester memoir, and in a Lester David biography of EMK. But in his autobiography, *I'd Do It All Again*, Curley said the target of his wit that day was a former Brahmin mayor, Nathan Matthews, not Fitzgerald.

14 **"particular Irish maggot":** Henry Adams to Elizabeth Cameron, Jan. 24, 1910, in *The Letters of Henry Adams, Volume VI: 1906–1918*, ed. J. C. Levenson et al. (Cambridge, MA: Belknap Press of Harvard University Press, 1988). In the early decades of the nineteenth century, Boston was "a comfortable and well-to-do city in which the people managed to lead contented and healthy lives," wrote Oscar Handlin. But that "atmosphere of cultural homogeneity" would prove "rigidly forbidding to aliens," especially once the number of impoverished Irish arrivals soared from 443 in 1836 to 65,556 in 1846, in the first wave fleeing the Irish famine. See Handlin, *Boston's Immigrants*, 52, 89.

14 **"Ace of Clubs":** On discrimination see McCarthy, *Remarkable Kennedys*, 19. See also TTR, 49–52. For EMK's parents' experiences see Goodwin, *Fitzgeralds*, 202–4, 213–16, 325–27.

14 **oppression of British rule:** The RFK quote on discrimination is from RFK to Mooney, Aug. 18, 1966, JFKL, cited in Schlesinger, *Robert Kennedy*, 5–6. The Adams quote on politics is from *The Education of Henry Adams*, chapter 1: "Politics, as a practice, whatever its professions, had always been the systematic organization of hatreds, and Massachusetts politics had been as harsh as the climate."

JFK noted, "All of us of Irish descent are bound together by the ties that come from a common experience; experience which may exist only in memories and in legend, but which is real enough to those who possess it." See Remarks of Sen. John F. Kennedy before the Irish Fellowship Club, March 17, 1956, JFKL. See also Joseph Biden, in *Irish Times*, Feb. 4, 2021: "I was a Catholic schoolboy, Irish Catholic, Jean Finnegan's son," Biden remembered. "The first reaction [to JFK's election] was: My God, this may be the final validation of us Irish Catholics, that we're totally accepted. I know this sounds strange, that Irish Catholics in the '60s would think somehow they were second class, but that's how it was. There was a sense of exclusion from certain areas of social and public life."

The story of the famine, the Irish immigration to Boston, the clash between the newcomers and the Brahmins, and the ascent of the Fitzgeralds and Kennedys has been told many times. Among the best accounts, employed here, are Goodwin, *Fitzgeralds*; Handlin, *Boston's Immigrants*; Woodham-Smith, *Great Hunger*; Beatty, *Rascal King*.

A significant difference marked Boston's integration of Irish Catholic immigrants. Unlike New York and other cities, the influx of Irish into Boston dwarfed that of all other foreign nationalities. New York's immigrants entered a true melting pot, of many creeds and cultures. "In Boston," wrote journalist William Shannon, the struggle was "two dimensional, involving only the Irish and the Yankees. . . . Social antagonisms were not easily diverted, diffused, and blurred. It was all too easy to keep one's hostilities in focus on a single target." See Shannon, *American Irish*.

There is no book, "The Hannons and the Hickeys," that honors EMK's grandmothers and their clans, though they contributed as much to his genetic makeup (and that of JFK and RFK) as the famous P. J. Kennedy and John Fitzgerald. Rose's mother, Mary Josephine "Josie" Hannon, came from Irish immigrants who settled on a farm in Acton, some twenty-five miles from Boston. Her family was related to the Fitzgeralds and haunted, as well, by alcoholism and tragedy. A shy woman, she watched her husband rise to mayor of Boston, and lived to see her grandson John inaugurated as America's thirty-fifth president. See Goodwin, *Fitzgeralds*, 77–91. Joseph's mother, Mary Augusta Hickey, was a formidable woman, the daughter of a well-to-do Irish immigrant who got his start as a saloon keeper and went on to become a prosperous contractor. Her three brothers wound up as a mayor of Brockton, a Boston police captain, and a Harvard-educated doctor. The family provided financial resources that helped Joseph get his start in banking. They were "lace curtain Irish"—"a family that has fruit in the house when nobody is sick," wrote Joe McCarthy in *Remarkable Kennedys*, 30. See Goodwin, *Fitzgeralds*, 227, 254, and Nasaw, *Patriarch*, 10, 12.

16 **"well fed underdogs":** JAF interviews with Charles Daly, Paul Kirk, Kathleen Townsend. Elizabeth Shannon OH, UVA. Loretta Kennedy Connelly to JPK, Sept. 19, 1961; Fayne to EMK, Dec. 15, 1961, with attachments; Ball to RK, May 14, 1965, KFP-JFKL. See also Burns, *Political Profile*, 16, 19. Schlesinger is from *Robert Kennedy*, 5. *Fortune*, Sept. 1937. "born here": NYT, Jan. 28, 1957. "I wanted power": see Hutschnecker, *Power*, 55; also cited in Beschloss, *Kennedy and Roosevelt*. Joseph left his sons feeling "that this money he had made for them gave them the opportunity to really do something important—and that opportunity didn't just include making more money," said John Jay Hooker, a friend and political associate of RFK, in his JFKL oral history. On JPK and underdogs see Raymond Kravis in *Kennedy, The Fruitful Bough*, a privately printed collection of reminiscences edited by EMK, 56.

16 **summer of 1950:** EMK to JFK, undated (spring 1950); Kenneth O'Donnell to JFK, June 21, 1950; JFK to Daniel O'Connell, July 11, 1950, JFK-JFKL. Joseph "Joey" Gargan and his sisters Mary Jo and Ann were the orphaned children of attorney Joseph Gargan and Rose's younger sister Agnes Fitzgerald Gargan, who died in 1937. The elder Gargan was a Notre Dame quarterback who fought in the Marines at Belleau Wood in World War I. When he died in 1946 the Kennedys took his children into their care, but their roles in the family were subordinate to those played by the Kennedys. Joe Gargan was an aide to John and Ted, and Ann a nurse and companion to Joseph after his 1961 stroke.

17 **"Best trip ever":** EMK diary, summer 1950; Joseph Gargan to JPK and RK, July 4, 1950; EMK to JPK and RK, undated, June and July, 1950, KFP-JFKL. JAF interview with Thomas Gargan. The European tour was a family tradition: JFK, for instance, had toured with Lem Billings in 1937 in a new Ford convertible that was shipped from the United States to France. See Billings OH, quoted by Blair and Blair, *Search*, 63. The Joe McCarthy drowning story is from a July 13, 1950, letter, RK to RFK and Ethel Kennedy, published in Smith, *Hostage*, 643.

EMK would befriend Taylor later in life, after the movie star married John Warner, a senator from Virginia. Warner told a story of how Taylor, after refusing to use the foul bathroom of a bus the couple had been forced to take because of inclement weather, was dismayed to find a locked pay toilet in the terminal. At a dinner with Warner and EMK, she prevailed upon them to pass bipartisan legislation banning pay toilets. "We'll be teased like hell for this," EMK told her, "but I'll do it." The legislation was taken up in 1979. JAF interview with John Warner. NYT, Dec. 2, 1979.

17 **lectured his son about deportment:** Cow horn letter from *Fruitful Bough*. See also EMK-TC, 94.

18 **freshman football team:** On football see RFK to JPK ("Teddy was really rough"), Dec. 1950, KFP-JFKL. See also EMK-TC, 95. Ted's European diary from the summer of 1950 reports a "beer incident" and a "wine incident" that might have cost him the $1,000 Joseph Kennedy offered to pay his sons. Ted never collected the money for not drinking. See EMK diary, summer 1950, KFP-JFKL.

18 **tales of death from Korea:** For Korean War generally see Patterson, *Grand Expectations*. The January

9, 1951, letter from JPK to EMK about the draft, KFP-JFKL, is reprinted in BG, Feb. 15, 2009. A fine *Globe* retrospective—"Ted Kennedy"—was presented in the newspaper and its web page, with photographs, video, and graphics, in February 2009. The series was published in book form as English et al., *Last Lion*.

19 **explored his options:** Capt. D. V. Gladding, U.S. Navy, to EMK, July 25, 1950; EMK to M. G. "Woody" Woodward, early 1951; JPK office to EMK, April 21, 1951; Gargan to Paul Murphy, May 8, 1951; Katherine Donovan to EMK, May 15, 1951; Murphy to EMK, May 15, 1951; Henry Haehn to Murphy, May 22, 1951, with "Suggested Itinerary"; Donovan to JPK, June 4, 1951, all KFP-JFKL.

19 **resolved to cheat:** EMK interview, AC-JFKL. EMKOH-UVA. JAF interviews with George Abrams, Robert Healy. EMK-TC, 96. Cleo O'Donnell interview, LD-KS. Melody Miller OH, UVA. Clark Clifford, the noted Washington lawyer, was asked by JFK to investigate the cheating incident in 1961, when Ted was preparing to run for public office. EMK and Frate admitted that this was the second time they had cheated in this manner, but Clifford wrote JFK: "Mistakes in judgment are not uncommon in boys in their teens, and I dare say there is hardly a man who has not committed some similar type of blunder in his youth." See Clifford, *Counsel*, 368–370, with excerpts of Harvard letter to EMK, and Clifford letters to JFK and EMK. Hersh, in *Intimate*, 72, describes yet another cheating episode that spring, involving Kennedy, his pals, and a physics exam, which Hersh attributes to an anonymous source.

20 **"a lot of disappointment":** JPK to JKO, Aug. 25, 1957, KFP-JFKL. JPK memo to file, interview with Eisenhower, April 1951; memo to file, interview with MacArthur, June 27, 1951; JPK to Cornelius Fitzgerald, July 19, 1951, Smith, *Hostage*, 646–54. EMK recollections of telling his dad are from EMKOH-UVA; TTR, 141; EMK-TC, 96; and JAF interview, Robert Shrum. On Ted's intelligence, see Cannon notes, AC-JFKL. See also John Knowles OH, JFKL.

21 **his redemptive deed:** JAF interview, Robert Healy. On JPK and sons' military service see Frank Bedell to Harvard Trust Co., July 24, 1951; Donovan to L. Lepee, Aug. 6, 1951; RFK to JFK, Jan. 1, 1945; telegram, McInery to JPK, Oct. 5, 1951; telegram, Army to EMK and JPK, Dec. 19, 1951, KFP-JFKL. See also JPK to Sir James Calder, Dec. 31, 1952; Smith, *Hostage*, 660. Richard Reeves, "Matty Troy and the Politics of Lying," *New York*, March 5, 1973. EMK interview, AC-JFKL. EMKOH-UVA. Hamilton, *Reckless*, 503–5. Hersh, *Education*, 79–83. Burns, *Camelot Legacy*, 44–46. See also Capt. Alan Kirk papers cited in Blairs, *Search*, 125–28, for example, Kirk to Kennedy, Aug. 8, 1941: "Dear Mr. Kennedy . . . It was no trouble to me to be helpful with such fine young men as yours." If his father needed further evidence of Ted's floundering nature, it came when they examined the enlistment papers and discovered that Ted had put in for a four-year hitch, not the two-year minimum. With some finagling, the error was redressed. "Don't

you look at what you sign?" Joseph barked. See Burns, *Camelot Legacy*, 45.

21 **"risking unspeakable grief":** On "selfish" see EMK-TC, 99. EMKOH-UVA. On the loss of Kick see EMK-TC, 90. He was given the news by the headmaster at Milton Academy. See also JPK to self, May 14, 1948; to the Duchess of Devonshire, Sept. 1, 1948; and to Pamela Churchill, Dec. 21, 1948, all KFP-JFKL, reprinted in Smith, *Hostage*, 636–38.

On EMK military experience see EMK to Paul Murphy, undated, summer 1951; General Accident insurance company to Provost Marshall, Ft. Holabird, Nov. 7, 1951; telegram RK to Murphy, Dec. 7, 1951, KFP-JFKL. Kennedy enlisted on June 25, 1951, was assigned to Fort Holabird, Maryland, on Nov. 10, 1951, sent to Fort Gordon, Georgia, on Jan. 7, 1952, arrived in Paris on June 4, 1952, and returned to the United States and was released from active duty in March 1953: see Ball to Duris, Kennedy for Senator Headquarters, with EMK military service record, July 11, 1962, JFKL.

EMK's original assignment at Fort Holabird, in Baltimore, was to be trained as a counterintelligence officer. But those plans were KO'd when the army discovered that he had been expelled from Harvard and/or, as a dubious report later alleged, was suspected by the FBI of consorting with communists at school. The slur was reported to JPK by columnist Drew Pearson in May 1954 and attributed to Roy Cohn, a foe of RFK and aide to Senator Joe McCarthy. The leak may have flowed from, and/or fueled, the mutual hostility between RFK and Cohn, which spilled over in a famous public shoving match a month later. See EMK-TC, 100.

JPK contributed in his own way to EMK's atonement. He offered scholarships to Notre Dame to the ninety West Point students who were caught in a cheating scandal that spring. See *Newsweek*, Sept. 12, 1960; Nasaw, *Patriarch*, 649–50.

On Burley see EMK-TC, 87. Marjorie McDonnell see telegram RK to Murphy, Dec. 7, 1951, KFP-JFKL. This is presumably the sister of Charlotte McDonnell, a close friend of Kick Kennedy and girlfriend of JFK, and daughter of Irish American financier James F. McDonnell "of Park Avenue and Southampton" and his wife, Anna Murray McDonnell, whose family considered themselves a cut above the nouveau Kennedys. See Stephen Birmingham, "The Upward Social Climb of America's Irish Rich," *New York*, Oct. 15, 1973; John Corry, "Golden Clan," NYT, March 13, 1977.

22 **"KP every other day":** EMK to parents, May 1952, KFP-JFKL. Matty Troy interview, AC-JFKL. Brawling: EMK-TC, 98.

23 **rich man's son:** EMK-TC, 100–103, 106. Rose to "Everyone," Aug. 18, 1952; Rose to Joe, "Monday AM," undated, KFP-JFKL. Miss Shape: NYT, Jan. 18, 1953; TCF-NYHS, Jan. 19, 1953. Ballerina: In his memoir, EMK identified the dancer as the prima ballerina Maria Tallchief, of the Grand Ballet du Marquis de Cuevas. Her marriage to choreographer George Balanchine would be annulled that year; EMK-TC, 103. Pamplona: see EMKOH-UVA.

23 **Vice President Richard Nixon:** In 1970, EMK told writer William Honan that his chance meeting with Nixon took place in the spring of 1953, after he returned from the army and Europe but before he went back to Harvard. Years later, in an oral history with the University of Virginia, he said that the incident took place while he was a law student at UVA. See Honan, *Survivor*, 113. EMKOH-UVA.

JFK's first impulse, on hearing he had defeated Lodge, was to call EMK. In a telegram, EMK sent JFK some congratulatory doggerel, in French: "Il est fatigue et triste / ses yeux sont rouges / ce que vous feisiez [*sic*] a Lodge / ne devrait pas arriver aux morts. (He is tired and sad / his eyes are red / what you did to Lodge / should not happen to the dead)." EMK to JFK, 1952, in Smith, *Hostage*, 660.

On Nixon and the Kennedys see JKO to Nixon, Dec. 5, 1954; Nixon to JKO, Nov. 23, 1963; JKO to Nixon, n.d., late 1963; transcript of telephone conversation, Nixon to Herter, Sept. 22, 1958, RNL. Farrell, *Nixon*, 84, 312. Dictated memorandum by JFK on conversation with Richard Nixon about Vietnam, April 1954, in Widmer, *Listening In*, 235.

24 **the prodigal son:** Leighton to JPK, May 6, 1953; JPK to Leighton, May 11, 1953, KFP-JFKL.

25 **It would be politics:** Rose Kennedy, Notes for Autobiography, dictated Oct. 30, 1972, KFP-JFKL. Fay, *Pleasure*, 152. EMK-TC, 106. *Life*, Aug. 1, 1969, quotes Jean Kennedy Smith: "Jack adored having him around, got a vicarious pleasure out of Teddy's doing things that he couldn't do." Playboy: Martin, *Hero*, 439.

26 **"barrels of fun":** Cancer dinner: BG, BP, Aug. 18, 1953. Barrels: Patricia Kennedy to RK and JPK, June 4, 1953, and RK to Patricia Kennedy, June 19, 1953; telegram, EMK to JPK, June 20, 1953, KFP-JFKL. "By the time I was in . . . law school, I knew I wanted an active career in politics," EMK would tell a reporter. See *Look*, March 4, 1969.

Two: High Hopes

27 **"a quick study":** *Look*, March 4, 1969. For his 1976 biography, James MacGregor Burns requested and got access to EMK's scholastic records. Family publicists had told the press that EMK received honors in history and government (see, for example, *Time*, Sept. 28, 1962), but Burns noted, "The transcript of the grades does not show honors grades." See Burns, *Camelot Legacy*, 49, 352–53.

27 **"raw intellectual horsepower":** See Laurence Tribe OH, UVA. "There are people who have natural gifts in terms of analytical skills," said Tribe. That was not EMK, who was "serious and thoughtful" and had "core insights and deep values . . . without having necessarily the intellectual horsepower."

28 **a happy-go-lucky:** Yale game: see EMK-TC, 108–9. JAF interviews with schoolmates George Abrams, Burton Hersh. EMKOH-JFKL. Richard Clasby, John Culver OH, UVA. Hawaii: see JPK to Dineen, Aug. 6, 1955, in Smith, *Hostage*, 667–68, and Waikiki telegram, undated, Rose Kennedy collec-

tion, KFP-JFKL. Frozen river: TCF-Harvard, Fred Holborn interview, Sept. 14, 1962. California: *Los Angeles Herald Examiner*, July 9, 1954. Trust fund: TCF-NYHS; see also Harold Martin, "The Amazing Kennedys," SEP, Sept. 7, 1957: "I fixed it," JPK said, "so that any of my children, financially speaking, could look me in the eye and tell me to go to hell."

28 **had been teased, unrelentingly:** EMKOH-JFKL. This long, valuable oral history, which had been sealed since 1964, was opened by the library at the author's request. Overboard: EMK notes and transcript, "We Remember Joe" file, JFKL. On Kennedy rituals see Charles Spalding OH, JFKL: "You just got pushed down and pushed down and stuffed under the sofa and into the closet and under the water and off the court until you finally figured out how you would win yourself." Portsmouth Priory: EMK interview, AC-JFKL. "It seemed I could never do anything right with my brothers," EMK recalled; see Nancy Gager Clinch, "Why Ted Kennedy Will Never Be President," *Washingtonian*, Jan. 1973.

28 **warmth and affection:** JFK and EMK: EMKOH-JFKL. On PT boat ride, running away, and JFK recuperation: JAF interviews with Victoria Reggie Kennedy, Robert Shrum; EMK-TC, 69, 76. Claude Hooton OH, JFKL. John Culver OH, UVA.

29 **brothers had variant personalities:** JFK and EMK: EMKOH-JFKL. Softball games, Spellman, and Unitas: see TCF-NYHS, May 30, 1960, and Feb. 2, 1961. It is a gauge of how seriously Robert took the competition that even though Unitas failed to show and quarterback his team, they still won one of the two games that day. Bloodied: Schlesinger, *Robert Kennedy*, 108. Yachtsmen: RFK's friend David Hackett told the story of the summer day when EMK and he were taunted in Northeast Harbor, Maine; see McCarthy, *Remarkable Kennedys*, 110. On RFK as puritan see Walter Sheridan, Pierre Salinger, William Orrick OH, JFKL. On New Year's Eve see RFK to EMK, Jan. 11, 1955, RFK papers, JFKL, cited in Leamer, *Kennedy Men*, 334. On "enemy within" see Kennedy and Fried, *Common Struggle*, 14.

30 **University of Virginia, a fine:** On EMK's process of selecting UVA see EMKOH-JFKL. The account of EMK's admittance at UVA comes from Burns, *Camelot Legacy*, 50. EMK seemed to have enjoyed his time at UVA, and ultimately chose the university's Miller Center to administer his oral history program. The Bunche controversy is covered by RFK in his JFKL oral history and by Schlesinger, *Robert Kennedy*, 85–87. Harvard Law School: In *Kennedy Men*, 386–87, Leamer quotes correspondence between Archbishop Richard Cushing and JPK on their unsuccessful attempt to persuade Harvard president Nathan Pusey to allow EMK into Harvard Law. Pusey "was just as much surprised as I was that Teddy didn't get over the 'hurdle' of the aptitude test," Cushing wrote JPK. "If there is anything else I can do for the boy let me know. Like yourself, I think he has an abundance of latent abilities and a fascinating personality."

31 **family rite of passage:** EMKOH-JFKL. Frederick Holborn OH, JFKL. JFK to JPK, July 13, and

undated, July 1956, and JPK to EMK, July 18, 1956, KFP-JFKL, reprinted in Smith, *Hostage*, 676. The final versions and initial drafts of several articles that ran under the byline of Edward M. Kennedy reveal how the newspaper articles were assembled. "I secured the names of a couple of places you visited from film you sent back. Knowing you would be pressed for time I gathered information from my sources and put together the enclosed copy," a researcher on JPK's payroll, Al DeCrane, wrote EMK on Sept. 5, 1956. "If you are interested in getting something published, you might use this as a basis. By adding some personal comments and feelings . . . it should have an audience." EMK kept a diary during his travels, added his observations to what DeCrane had composed, and the resultant copy was sent to Kingsbury Smith at the International News Service, where it was further edited before distribution. See JPK files on EMK and Burgess to DeCrane, Sept. 17, 1956, KFP-JFKL.

32 **a pleasure cruise:** EMKOH-JFKL. Frederick Holborn OH, JFKL. JFK to JPK, June 29, 1956; JPK to EMK, July 18, 1956; JKO to RK, undated, 1956, KFP-JFKL, reprinted in Smith, *Hostage*, 672–77. Goodwin, *Fitzgeralds*, 785. Kelley, *Jackie Oh!*, 54. WP, Aug. 25, 1956. EMK-TC. George Smathers OH, SHO. JAF interview with Kitty Kelley. Although several authors have listed Smathers and/or Congressman Torbert Macdonald as crewmates on JFK's cruise, Smathers told the Senate historians he did not join the Kennedys, and EMK names Thompson, but not Smathers or Macdonald, as their yachting companion in his 1964 oral history for the JFKL. The "lucky stars" quote is from TCF-NYHS, May 7, 1957.

33 **fulfilling their parents' aspirations:** EMKOH-UVA. John Tunney OH, UVA. Frederick Holborn, a friend and tutor at Harvard, found EMK "extremely nervous" about his family's expectations. See Holborn interview, TCF-Harvard, Sept. 14, 1962. For the JPK prediction—he foretold JFK's presidency, and Robert's service as attorney general as well—see Harold Martin, "The Amazing Kennedys," SEP, Sept. 7, 1957, cited in TTR, 433, and by Clymer, *Edward M. Kennedy*, 26. Ulcer: "Summary of Annual Physical Examination," Nov. 7, 1979, Office of Senator EMK, JFKL. Bareknuckled: JAF interview with Thomas Rollins.

33 **romance and adventure:** On mountain climbing see EMK-TC, 112–14. John Tunney, Richard Clasby OH, UVA. John's speech on Algeria: JPK to EMK, July 8 and 19, 1957, KFP-JFKL. Cadillac Eddie and gossip columns: JPK to EMK, May 2, 1958, KFP-JFKL, reprinted in Smith, *Hostage*, 680; Thomas Morgan, ". . . And Teddy," *Esquire*, April 1, 1962; *Charlottesville Daily Progress*, Aug. 27, 2009. "He had independent wealth. He lived a more dramatic life than most of us," Reid Moore, a classmate at UVA, recalled. "That translated to an Oldsmobile convertible, often with the top down and large dogs in the back seat." See Moore, BM, Nov. 30, 2009.

34 **to play Don Juan:** Schlesinger, *Thousand Days*, 79–80.

35 **extramarital sex life:** JAF interview with William vanden Heuvel; Wills, *Kennedy Imprisonment*, 19, 30. See also Goodwin, *Fitzgeralds*, 391–92, 426. "History would later record a connecting link between the risks Joseph Kennedy took . . . and the sexual daring that would be observed again and again in his sons," Goodwin wrote. "It would seem almost as if, in repeating their father's behavior, they were unconsciously trying to gain some sort of mastery over this early trauma that had nearly destroyed everything they had."

35 **a mortal sin for Roman Catholics:** Lord Harlech (David Ormsby-Gore) OH, JFKL.

36 **"all these beautiful women":** On Rose, her father, and Joseph's infidelity, see Goodwin, *Fitzgeralds*, 303–7, 396, 426. "a helluva": TTR, 221. See also JPK to Houghton, Sept. 19, 1921 ("I hope you have all the good-looking girls in your company looking forward, with anticipation, to meeting the high Irish of Boston, because I have a gang around me that must be fed on raw meat"), KFP-JFKL, reprinted in Smith, *Hostage*, 30–31. On Swanson see Beauchamp, *Joseph P. Kennedy Presents*, 146, 273, and Swanson, *Swanson on Swanson*, 356, and Damore, *Cape Cod Years*, 21. "insane": JPK to EMK, Sept. 3, 1955, KFP-JFKL, reprinted in Smith, *Hostage*, 670–671.

John Fitzgerald's hopes for a third term as mayor were quashed by Curley in 1913 when Curley sent a letter to Fitzgerald's wife, Josie, threatening to expose her husband's relationship with Elizabeth "Toodles" Ryan, a cigarette girl at a dance hall called the Ferncroft Inn. As part of his campaign to force Fitzgerald from the race, Curley announced that he would be giving a series of lectures on graft and immorality, including one with the title "Great Lovers in History: From Cleopatra to Toodles." See Goodwin, *Fitzgeralds*, 246–53, and Beatty, *Rascal King*, 136–39.

37 **"just the sort of treatment":** KK to JFK, July 29, 1943, reprinted in Smith, *Hostage*, 566. Dating: EMK to JPK, April 25, 1948, KFP-JFKL. Richard Clasby OH, UVA. For JPK imprint on his sons, see Wills, *Kennedy Imprisonment*, 16–24 and Elizabeth Shannon OH, UVA. On EMK's approach to women see Burns, *Camelot Legacy*, 48, and Hersh, *Intimate*, 70, 77. On sexual mores in Washington see Burleigh, *Very Private*, 187–88. Mirrored: JFK seemed to enjoy seeing EMK behave in ways that he, because of ill health or political sensibility, could not. After watching JFK urge EMK to dance with a "scantily clad" songstress at a charity ball, Rose concluded that "Jack . . . delighted in having Teddy do what he could and should not do himself." See RK, "Notes for Autobiography," KFP-JFKL. Mimi Alford, a nineteen-year-old White House intern who carried on an affair with JFK, said he "playfully" urged her to service his younger brother Ted as the president watched. She refused. See Alford, *Once Upon a Secret*, 102, 124.

38 **Virginia Joan Bennett:** JAF interview with Patrick Kennedy. EMKOH-JFKL. EMKOH-UVA. Manhattanville was also known for fostering a sense of social justice in its exemplary graduates.

38 **long-distance romance:** JBK interview, AC-JFKL.
JBK interview, LD-WYO. JBK remembrance, RCP-
NW. RK to JBK, 1958, KFP-JFKL.

39 **John's 1958 reelection:** EMKOH-JFKL. Thomas
Winship OH, JFKL. Tribute by EMK to Stephen E.
Smith, St. Thomas More Church, New York, Aug.
21, 1990, AC-JFKL. O'Donnell and Powers, *Memories*, 42, 144–45. The complete title of the song is
"The Gang That Sang 'Heart of My Heart,'" a revival by the Four Aces that was popular in the
1950s.

40 **Joan had similar trepidation:** EMK-TC, 183. Clymer, *Edward M. Kennedy*, 23–24. Doubts: TCF-
Harvard, Daniel Donahoe interview, Sept. 14,
1962. Microphone: JBK, in an interview with Clymer, confirmed the report of JFK and the overlooked microphone, as related in Leamer, *Kennedy
Men*, 399–400. JBK told Clymer that the exchange
was cited as evidence, years later, in EMK's successful plea to have their marriage annulled; see AC-
JFKL.

42 **Joan tried:** EMKOH-JFKL. John Tunney, Betty
Taymor OH, UVA. The Hackett "rules" are from
McCarthy, *Remarkable Kennedys*, 109–10, and Har-
old Martin, "The Amazing Kennedys," SEP, Sept. 7,
1957. For JBK remarks see *Redbook*, June 1962, and
Betty Hannah Hoffman, "Joan Kennedy's Story,"
LHJ, July 1970.

43 **"doomed to this treadmill":** UVA School of Law
news release, May 18, 2014. *Virginia Law Weekly*,
April 23, 1959. An unpublished but credible report from TCF-Harvard, Oct. 10, 1962, states that
EMK, busy with home life and eager to join John's
presidential campaign, failed the "Securities Regulation" course his senior year—but was permitted,
after a faculty discussion, to graduate. "doomed":
JFK interview with Burns, JMB-WC, cited in
Leamer, *Kennedy Men*, 398–99. On moot court see
JAF interview with Thomas Rollins. For JKO and
"lawyer" see Mortimer Caplin, BM, Nov. 30, 2009.

43 **all-day strategy sessions:** EMKOH-JFKL. On the
Cape Cod meeting see White, *Making, 1960*, 53–
62; see also minutes, "Meeting at: Haynnisport . . .
Oct. 28, 1959," 1960 Campaign Files, and Hyman
Raskin OH, both JFKL. On travel see EMK to RFK,
Dec. 23, 1959; EMK to RFK, Smith and Wallace,
Nov. 23, 1959; Salinger to Hines, Aug. 1, 1960;
"Summary of JFK Activities in Idaho," March 1960,
all JFKL; and Lindsay to Kosner, re Alaska, *News-
week* correspondent file, April 9, 1969, AC-JFKL.
Second honeymoon: The couple went skiing,
ocean fishing, boating, and sightseeing in Chile,
Mexico, Argentina, and Peru; see EMK to RK, July
13, 1959; EMK to RK and JPK, summer 1959 and
Aug. 1, 25, 1959, KFP-JFKL.

44 **Ted's territory sprawled:** EMKOH-UVA. Though
geographically in EMK's bailiwick, California was
so big, complex, and important that the big decisions were handled by JFK and the national campaign. See Oliphant and Wilkie, *Road to Camelot*,
176–78.

The 1960 campaign files at the JFKL contain an extensive collection of notes and memoranda that
chronicle EMK's far-ranging travels and duties.
See EMK to RFK, re Alaska, Oct. 30, 1959; EMK to

RFK and Wallace, re Montana, Nov. 16, 1959; EMK
to RFK, re New Mexico, Nov. 23, 1959; EMK to
RFK and JFK, re Idaho, Dec. 22, 1959; EMK to
RFK, re Arizona, Dec. 23, 1959; EMK "Memo for
file," re Alaska, Jan. 4, 1960; EMK to RFK, re Montana, Jan. 25, 1960 and Prouty to JFK, re EMK appearance in Napa, CA, Oct. 31, 1960 to cite a few.

44 **network of allies:** On strategy see Wallace to JFK
and Sorensen, "Preconvention Grass Roots Campaigning; Kennedy Clubs," Jan. 29, 1959; Wallace,
"Outline of Basic Organization," March 31, 1959;
Wallace, "memorandum of State Contacts and Organization," April, 22, 1959; Udall to JFK, re Arizona, Nov. 24, 1959; Sorensen and Wallace to JFK,
"The Colorado Picture," July 14, 1959; Wallace to
JFK, re the West, "Telephone Calls," Oct. 8, 1959;
EMK to RFK and Wallace, Nov. 16, 1959; Roncalio
to "Jack or Ted," April 23, 1960, all 1960 presidential campaign files, all JFKL. See also Mary Kelly,
Hyman Raskin, Dean Anderson, Clinton Anderson OH, JFKL. On the Utah and Arizona airplane
landings see TCF-NYHS, May 27, June 6, 1960.

45 **a surrogate speaker:** JAF interview with Charles
Daly. EMK-TC, 128–31, 140–41, 145, 148. *Life*,
March 28, 1960. *Time*, July 11, 1960. BG, March 27,
Sept. 4, 1960. *Miles City Star*, Bucking Horse Sale
edition, May 1992; a photograph of EMK on Skyrocket ran in the Aug. 28–29, 1960, newspaper
and, like the ski jump story, was reprinted many
times. On the groin rupture see *The Missoulian*,
Aug. 26, 2009, and Claude Hooton, BM, Nov. 30,
2009. In his memoir, Kennedy mistakenly wrote
that the bronc ride took place during the primaries. On Milwaukee and Wisconsin, see TCF-
NYHS, Feb. 19, 1969.

45 **his wedding vows:** On Judith Campbell, see
Hersh, *Dark Side*, chapter 18, "Judy," and Kitty Kelley,
"The Dark Side of Camelot," *People*, Feb. 29, 1988.
Exner and Demaris, *My Story*, 87. By the time her
account was made public, she had married, and
became Judith Campbell Exner. On Kara see
EMK-TC, 138.

46 **ground war for delegates:** Robert Caro offers
EMK's analysis of JFK's western strategy and describes LBJ's fatal dawdling in *Passage*, 58–108. The
West was "very sympathetic to" LBJ, EMK told
Caro. "They sweet-talked me about my brother. But
they said, 'The reality is: This is Johnson Country.
We know how he stands on minerals, on grazing
issues. . . . We know he's been a friend of the
West . . . ' He could have locked that place up without any difficulty at all." But Johnson, fatefully,
temporized; see Caro, *Passage*, 59–60.

On West Virginia and Kennedy money, see Wallace to
RFK, May 27, 1960, JFKL: "Press reports to date
have implied that Kennedy forces bought votes.
The actual vote-buying, as we know, was done for
local offices—especially sheriff. However, the reports indicate that JFK was 'slated' by at least
some of the groups who bought votes. The implications for JFK are not good. The facts are that
both sides bought votes. This is not a point we
should make, however."

On Yukon River dam see "Delegate Situation," Alaska,
spring 1960, and Meekins to EMK, April 15, 1960;

on keynote see Wallace to JFK, "Telephone Calls," Oct. 8, 1959; on Cheyenne bank see EMK to Roncalio, March 7, 1960; on Anaconda see EMK to RFK, Nov. 2, 1959, all 1960 presidential campaign files, JFKL. On state-by-state campaigning, see also EMKOH-JFKL and Hyman Raskin, Mike Mansfield OH, JFKL.

On New Mexico, Colorado, mountain states, and Durango exchange see White, *Making, 1960*, 156–57. On "cheered us up" see TCF-Harvard, June 19, 1960. Another *Time* correspondent wrote on June 23, 1960, that EMK was "galloping around Durango and the convention hall with all the vigor of a fine 2-year-old stud on a blue grass horse farm on a fine Kentucky morning." See TFC-NYHS.

On the Arizona coup see Stewart Udall strategy letter outlining "cohesive action by the small county chairmen," Udall to JFK, Nov. 24, 1959; Sorensen to JPK, July 1, 1959; Wallace to RFK, Jan. 1, 1960; Wallacep to JFK, May 21, 1960; and Scoville to EMK with Scoville to Wallace, May 20, 1960, attached, all 1960 presidential campaign files, JFKL. See also *Arizona Republic*, May 1, 3, 1960; *Tucson Citizen*, May 2, 1960; *Arizona Daily Star*, May 5, 1960.

48 **the Wyoming delegation:** EMKOH-JFKL. White, *Making, 1960*, 185. EMK-TC, 148–50. Schlesinger, *Robert Kennedy*, 206. Of the 172 votes from the Mountain West, Kennedy received 119. David Broder OH, UVA. Gale McGee OH, JFKL. TCF-NYHS, June 14, 1960. O'Donnell and O'Donnell, *Irish Brotherhood*, 357.

49 **a singing contest:** EMK-TC, 152. See Hooton, BM, Nov. 30, 2009.

50 **the Golden State:** In addition to New Mexico, Nevada, and Hawaii, EMK had hoped to add California, Alaska, and Montana to his brother's winning total in the Electoral College. Kennedy "Campaign Report," Oct. 3, 10, 17, 24, 31, 1960, presidential campaign files, JFKL. For California, see Don Bradley OH, JFKL; Hersh, *Education*, 138; and *Esquire*, April 1962. See also TCF-Harvard, Sept. 24, 1960.

On 1960 vote and recounts See EMKOH-UVA; EMKOH-JFKL; EMK interview, AC-JFKL; and Hyman Raskin OH, JFKL. See also Hutcheson to Nixon, Dec. 16, 1960; GG to Finch, "Voting Irregularities," Dec. 22, 1960; Arends to Nixon, Nov. 16, 1960; Adamowski to Nixon, Feb. 24, 1961; Hillings to Nixon, Dec. 21, 1960, RNL. See also NYHT, Nov. 11, 12, Dec. 4, 6, 1960. On California results see Eugene Lee and William Buchanan, "The 1960 Election in California." *Western Political Quarterly*, March, 1961, 309–326. Raskin's comparison of the absentee ballots to the election day voting results is suggestive, but Gellman, in *Campaign*, 261, notes that Kennedy campaign counsel Harold Leventhal wrote RFK on Dec. 7, 1960, downplaying the prospects of proving Republican "hanky-panky" in California.

EMK played a role in one bit of California intrigue that would reverberate for more than a decade. Toward the end of the campaign, he took a phone call from an attorney who offered him "hot" information that could influence the outcome of the election. EMK met the lawyer in Los Angeles, where the man asked for $500,000 in return for evidence that a big defense contractor had bribed Richard Nixon.

A Washington attorney named James McInerney, a friend of RFK, was then representing a California accountant in a dispute involving the Hughes Tool Company, a big defense contractor owned by the billionaire Howard Hughes. When the accountant heard, via EMK, that an opportunist in Los Angeles was seeking half a million dollars for information that he also possessed, he came clean. In a secret transaction, Hughes had loaned Nixon's brother Donald $205,000 to save the family grocery and restaurant business from bankruptcy.

McInerney leaked the story. It is doubtful that the late-breaking "Hughes Loan" scandal swung the 1960 election to Kennedy. But the possibility gnawed at Nixon, and in 1962, when he ran for governor in California, his Democratic opponent raised the issue, and Nixon lost that race, too. Nixon maintained his secret, corrupt dealings with Hughes, which he feared would be revealed after a veteran Kennedy hand, Lawrence O'Brien, went to work for the billionaire. It was one reason that Nixon's men were caught burglarizing O'Brien's offices at the Democratic National Committee headquarters in the Watergate office building in 1972.

The most comprehensive account of the Hughes loan, and how it came to light, was written by James R. Phelan in *The Reporter* magazine of Aug. 16, 1962. See also TCF-NYHS, Jan. 18, 1962. See also NYT, Jan. 24, 1972, Oct.1, 1973, May 16, 1974. WP, Jan. 27, 1974, Jan. 14, 2011. *New York World Telegram*, Oct. 27, 1960. *New York Post*, Nov. 1, 3, 1960. Drew Pearson, Hughes Loan files, Drew Pearson papers, LBJL. Gielgud to Salinger, Oct. 31, 1960, 1960 presidential campaign files, JFKL. See also J. Anthony Lukas, "The Hughes Connection," NYT, Jan. 4, 1976, and Farrell, *Nixon*, 290–91, 307, 469–71.

50 **family on election day:** White, *Making, 1960*, 16–17, 20, 379. O'Donnell and Powers, *Memories*, 225. Chronology of election results, Edward Morgan, ABC News, Nov. 9, 1960, TW-JFKL. "Remarks of the Vice President at 12:18 a.m. PST, Grand Ballroom, Ambassador Hotel, Los Angeles," RNL. Aston Martin: EMK-TC, 158.

Three: If His Name Was Edward Moore

52 **burden of choice:** JAF interview with Robert Shrum. JBK interview, AC-JFKL. *Redbook*, June 1962. EMKOH-UVA. John Culver, Milton Gwirtzman OH, UVA. Ted mentioned this possibility so often out west in 1960 that journalists saw it as a transparent bid for western votes. But Joseph Kennedy confirmed it: see TCF-NYHS, June 3, 5, and 23, 1960. Apologies to Johnny Mercer and Henry Mancini.

52 **the Massachusetts Senate seat:** JBK interview, AC-JFKL. Harold Martin, "The Amazing Kennedys," SEP, Sept. 7, 1957. *Esquire*, April 1, 1962. BG, Dec. 18, 1960, Dec. 6, 1961. BH, Dec. 6, 1961. *Boston Traveler*, March 14, 1962. Stewart Alsop, "What Made Teddy Run?," SEP, Oct. 27, 1962. JPK to

Galeazzi, Jan. 6, 1961, KFP-JFKL, reprinted in Smith, *Hostage*, 695–96; JPK to Steele, Feb. 20, 1961, KFP-JFKL.

53 **obstacles were formidable:** JAF interviews with Charles Tretter, Barbara Souliotis, Helen O'Donnell. Paul Kirk, John Tunney, John Culver OH, UVA. EMKOH-UVA. Donahue, JFK, and RFK qualms: TCF-NYHS, Nov. 13, 1961, and TCF-Harvard, Sept. 14, 1962: "We have it . . . from three different major sources within the White House . . . that both the president and Bobby were appalled at the idea of Teddy's running, realizing the potential damage from the dynasty issue, the possible adverse reaction to Teddy's . . . starting at the top." See also TCF-NYHS, Sept. 11, 1961. NYT, Nov. 24, 1960. BA, Dec. 27, 1960.

54 **It was Ted's turn:** EMKOH-UVA. EMK-TC, 162, 170, 178. Nasaw, *Patriarch*, 766.

54 **offered contingent support:** EMK to JPK, July 1961, KFP-JFKL. EMKOH-JFKL. EMKOH-UVA. BG, Dec. 24, 1960; *Esquire*, April 1, 1962. On JFK and RFK reaction see also TCF-NYHS, Feb. 15, 1961, and undated file by White House correspondent John Fentress, quoting Pierre Salinger. On CIA: EMK to Dulles, Feb. 3, 1961, and Dulles to EMK, Feb. 10, 1961, CIA archives.

54 **tour of Africa:** EMK to RK and JPK, undated, Dec. 1960; EMK to JPK, Dec. 13, 1960, KFP-JFKL. Frank Moss travel diary, African trip, 1960, FM-Utah. Gale McGee OH, JFKL. EMKOH-UVA. EMK-TC, 169.

55 **an assistant district attorney:** For ADA job and first court case, see *Esquire*, April 1, 1962; BG, Dec. 20, 1960, Feb. 8, Feb. 18, 1961, and TCF-NYHS, Feb. 17, 27, 1961. For EMK's illusory description of that case, see EMK-TC, 167–68, and EMKOH-UVA.

55 **"on the go":** EMK to JPK, March 1961, re Frank Morrissey, TTR, 408–9. See also TCF-NYHS, Oct. 20, 1961. JBK interview, AC-JFKL. Levin, *Campaigning*, 4–5. *Time*, Oct. 27, 1961. NYHT, May 16, 1961. John Culver, Milton Gwirtzman OH, UVA. Joseph Feeney OH, JFKL. A "peculiar kind of tittilation" swept over EMK's audiences, due to his youthful good looks and association with the popular president, wrote Levin, 121. "Large crowds cheer him enthusiastically, scream at him as they do at the Beatles, and want to touch him." See also BA, Dec. 24, 1960. BR, Sept. 8, 1962. BG, Feb. 5, Dec. 3, 1961. For Joan and first signs of drinking, see EMKOH-UVA.

56 **attractive but lightweight:** EMK to JPK, July 1961; Eunice Kennedy Shriver to JPK and RK, July 26, 1961, KFP-JFKL. BH, Dec. 6, 1961. BG, July 23, 1961. Joseph Page, "The Precocious Ted Kennedy," *The Nation*, March 10, 1962. EMK wrote a series of stories on his trip for the *Boston Globe*, which were published Sept. 17–21, 1961. Smith: BG, Dec. 20, 21, 1960; Milton Gwirtzman OH, JFKL. Swimming pool: John Seigenthaler OH, UVA; Schlesinger diary, June 18, 1961, AS-NYPL, reprinted in Schlesinger, *Journals*, 122. Exuberance: *Esquire*, April 1962; see also *Redbook*, June 1962. Alsop: See SEP, Oct. 27, 1962. Brothel: BG, March 1, 2011. Rat Pack and Rubirosa: TCF-NYHS, Sept. 26, 1961, Feb. 23, 1962.

57 **a celebrated family:** In 1916, John F. Fitzgerald challenged, and was beaten by, incumbent senator Henry Cabot Lodge, a Senate titan. In 1952, JFK evened the score by upsetting Lodge's grandson, the incumbent senator Henry Cabot Lodge Jr. In 1962, George Cabot Lodge—son of one U.S. senator, and great-grandson of another, defeated U.S. representative Laurence Curtis for the Republican nomination and the opportunity to face EMK.

57 **The young rivals:** *Life*, June 29, 1962. Each had perfected "the Boston shift," *Life* noted: "the technique of shaking hands warmly and at length with one prospective supporter while carrying on a cordial conversation with another, leaving each with the feeling that he has had a full measure of personal attention."

58 **waves of scandal:** John F. Kennedy, "City upon a Hill Speech," Massachusetts State House, Jan. 9, 1961, JFKL. JFK "certainly wasn't the kind of guy you'd go up to and say, 'Hey, Joe needs a thirty days on the state,'" said state Senate leader Maurice Donahue. (When families hit hard times, finding short-term government patronage jobs—"a thirty days on the state"—was a duty of the street-corner pols.) On this and on corruption, see Levin, *Campaigning*, 8–9, 16–17, 24–25, 105–7, 110. EMK's youth, meanwhile, "contributed to his image as a political innocent and non-politician, his wealth was interpreted as an indication that he would not steal from the public till," wrote Levin, 120. BG, July 23, 1961. On political gore see Hersh, *Education*, 157, and TCF-NYHS, Dec. 22, 1960, March 15, 1962. EMKOH-UVA. On the McCormack family, see the rich and definitive Nelson, *McCormack*, 58–62, 614, 618, and O'Neill, *Rogues*, 122–23.

59 **a "liberating" influence:** Kraft to Smith, "Post Primary Report Number 9," and "Post Primary Report Number 13," both undated, John Kraft 1962 campaign papers, JFKL.

59 **the Kennedys went all in:** Dan Fenn OH, UVA. In early 1961 CIA-trained Cuban rebels landed in Cuba at the Bay of Pigs in a doomed attempt to overthrow Cuban premier Fidel Castro. On Kennedy offers to McCormack see Nelson, *McCormack*, 613, and John McCormack OH, LBJL. On Irish Mafia and Sidey see TCF-NYHS, Jan. 8, 1962, and March 15, 1962.

59 **"Kennedy political adventure":** TCF-NYHS, March 30, April 23, May 10, 1962. Red Fay, JFK's wartime shipmate and undersecretary of the Navy, oversaw the search of McCormack's service records. See Reeves, *President Kennedy*, 711.

60 **council of war:** JAF interview with Gerard Doherty. EMKOH-JFKL. Lincoln to O'Donnell, April 23, 1962, and JFK "Memorandum" to staff on "Teddy's campaign," undated, JFKL. Gerard Doherty, Betty Taymor, Milton Gwirtzman OH, JFKL. EMK announcement of candidacy and candidate biography, March 14, 1962, EMKI. Dan Fenn, Nance Lyons OH, UVA. Schlesinger diary, Sept. 4, 1961; "Draft Files," April (27) 1962, AS-NYPL. SEP, Oct. 27, 1962. NYT, March 15, 1962. Drew Pearson radio script, n.d., Drew Pearson papers, LBJL. English et al., *Last Lion*, 81.

61 **Polish American audiences:** EMKOH-UVA. Milton
Gwirtzman OH, UVA. Celebrezze, slogan, tie clip:
EMKOH-UVA and EMKOH-JFKL. Worcester: see
TCF-NYHS, June 1, 1962. There could be downsides to having a brother in the White House. By
the spring of 1962, JFK and RFK were being drawn
into the struggle for Black equality by the civil
rights movement. The racist White Citizens' Council of Little Rock, Arkansas, sought to embarrass
the brothers by offering bus fare to poor Black families with the promise that the Kennedys would
provide jobs and housing when they disembarked
in Hyannis. EMK greeted the first arrivals warmly,
but dozens of poor folk kept coming, and the president had to call upon an old Senate colleague—
EMK said Senator James Eastland of Mississippi,
but it was as likely Senator John McLellan of
Arkansas—to get the practice stopped. See BG,
May 4, June 11, 1962; EMKOH-UVA.

62 **proffered patronage jobs:** Boyle to O'Donnell,
July 23, 1964, JFKL. Thomas Costin OH, UVA.
Time, June 16, 1962. BR, March 15, 1962. Paul
Driscoll, "Jack Was Asking About You," TNR, June
4, 1962. TCF-NYHS, June 8, 1962. Levin, in *Campaigning,* 30–37, 62, 76–77, offers a portrait of how
the Kennedy forces, while capitalizing on the
middle-class reform impulse, also used the president's clout and patronage to win over remnants
of the old machine politics: "Regardless of how
well-organized or disorganized, how active or passive, how rich or poor, were Kennedy and McCormack, the dynamics of the 1962 convention were
ultimately determined by the fact that the President of the United States and his Attorney General were infinitely more powerful than the
Speaker of the United States House of Representatives," he wrote. "The arithmetic of presidential
power, more than any other factor, structured the
situation." For more on White House support see
TCF-NYHS, May 2, 31, June 1, 1962, and TCF-
Harvard, Sept. 14, 1962.
Not all of Doherty's efforts were successful. Early in the
campaign, EMK and Doherty took South Boston
legislator William Bulger and a handful of colleagues to the Locke-Ober restaurant for lunch.
Committed to McCormack—and seeing it would
do no harm to soak the Kennedys—Bulger ordered Lobster Savannah, the signature dish.
When Kennedy picked up the check, he told
Doherty that he was just as happy that Bulger was
not joining them: "We can't afford him." JAF interview with Gerard Doherty.

62 **had suffered a stroke:** EMKOH-UVA. BG, Dec. 20,
1961. NYT, Dec. 20, 1961. BG, Dec. 20, 21, 22,
1961. RK diary entry, "Thanksgiving, 61," KFP-
JFKL, reprinted in Smith, *Hostage,* 698–99. *Time,*
Dec. 29, 1961. TCF-NYHS, Dec. 21, 1961.

63 **Harvard cheating story:** JAF interview with Robert Healy. EMKOH-UVA. John Sharon OH, JFKL.
Clifford, *Counsel,* 368–370. *American Experience,*
"The Kennedys," PBS. Bradlee, *Conversations,* 67–
68. In his oral history for UVA, Milton Gwirtzman
recalls how a classmate confronted EMK in Harvard Yard after the story broke. "Ted, you are a
disgrace to the class of 1954," the man said. "I'm

sure there are others who probably agree with
you," EMK replied.

64 **"the chutzpah issue":** *The Reporter,* July 19, 1962.
Levin, *Campaigning,* 128–29. BG, May 23, 24,
June 3, 1962. EMKOH-UVA. See Sam Beer,
Betty Taymor OH, JFKL. Chutzpah: see *Life,*
June 29, 1962.

65 **Kennedy personally visited:** JAF interviews with
Charles Tretter, Terri Robinson. Levin, *Campaigning,* 52, 54. EMK schedules for 1961 and 1962,
1962 campaign files, JFKL. "every alley": Ed Martin OH, UVA. TCF-NYHS, May 31, July 12, 1962.
In its June 29, 1962, cover story on the race, *Life*
hailed EMK's "healthy animal vigor." EMK on fear
of shaming the family, see *Life,* Jan. 15, 1965. EMK
got the vote of the delegate from Gill, a tiny town
in the Connecticut River valley.
In his oral history for the Miller Center at UVA, EMK
read from and commented on his schedule from
several typical days of campaigning in 1962. Here
it is from one such day, notable for the three old-
fashioned street rallies in Everett, Malden, and
Medford, with searchlights, majorettes, and marching bands:
"October 23rd. We leave Charles River Square at seven
in the morning. We arrive at 7:40 at the Transitron
Electronic Corporation gate in Melrose. There are
300 people. Then we go to the Melrose fire station
at 8:30. At 8:45, the Melrose police station; Melrose Free Press at nine o'clock; Melrose City Hall at
9:15.
"And then we're on our way to Stoneham. We stop at
the Maryland sandal division of BGS Shoe Corporation, and tour that at 9:40. They have 300 people, and Mr. Schubert wants to know about
Japanese imports; they're affecting his business.
What do you have to say about that? At 9:55, meet
Maynard Moore in Stoneham; the store is right
next to the above. They have a hundred people;
you can tour that. Then you tour Stoneham Town
Hall at 10:10 and go the Stoneham Press at 10:30.
Leave the Stoneham Press, an independent, at
10:45.
"You're in the newspaper for 15 minutes, then you arrive at the Wakefield Daily Item. Bill Lee will meet
you there. Bill Lee was President Kennedy's coordinator in Wakefield, a wonderful person. You
walk through City Hall with him. At 11:15 you
leave for the Copley plants on Water Street in
Wakefield. Bill Lee will accompany you. The three
plants are located at the same site, a total of 500
people. You'll arrive at 11:20 a.m. You tour there
for 50 minutes, then leave the Copley plant at noon
and arrive again at the Transitron Electronic Corporation in Wakefield. You'll visit the cafeteria.
They have a thousand people employed in the
plant, and you go down to the cafeteria and meet
and greet. You'll leave there 25 minutes afterward
and arrive at the American Mutual Insurance
Company cafeteria in Wakefield at 12:35. You'll
leave there at one. So you're there for 35 minutes,
another cafeteria with a thousand people.
"At 1:10 you'll arrive at the Ridgestone Shopping Center, Route 28, and stay there for fifty minutes,
meet and greet. At 2:10 you'll arrive in front of

Wakefield High School and greet students and teachers gathered there. At 2:30 you'll leave Wakefield. You'll arrive in Malden at John McCarthy's office and leave thirty minutes later and arrive at Converse Rubber Corporation. People leave in different shifts. This is when the largest group leaves, over a thousand employees. Stay there from 3:40 to 4:15, then go to the Malden News at 4:15. Arrive at station WHIL in Medford at 4:50. "Then you return to Boston. You'll get in sometime around 5:45, and your first rally is in Everett Square at 7:30. The band will assemble in the parking lot in the rear of the city hall. Then at eight o'clock, go to Malden Square in Malden. The band is to assemble in front of the Sacred Heart Church. Finally you go to the rally at 8:30 in Medford Square, Medford."

66 **"Teddy's First Hurrah":** JAF interview with Gerard Doherty. EMKOH-JFKL. Bradlee, *Conversations*, 106–9. Levin, *Campaigning*, 42–44. "Five months before the convention it would have been difficult to find many Democratic politicians in Massachusetts who believed that Kennedy would soundly defeat McCormack for the party's endorsement," said Levin. EMK won because of a "heroic" personal effort and "the candidate's seemingly inexhaustible capacity to contact, cajole and charm delegates." On postmasters, tax, and immigration see Douglas Cater, *The Reporter*, July 5, 1962. On phones, and Joan, see TCF-NYHS, June 8, 9, 1962.

67 **one final opportunity:** McCormack's gambit was not unthinkable. In 1964, Lieutenant Governor Francis Bellotti would challenge Governor Endicott Peabody for the Democratic gubernatorial nomination, lose at the state convention, but prevail in the primary. See NYT, Sept. 11, 1964. JAF interview with Gerard Doherty. Clancy memo, EMKOH-UVA. Milton Gwirtzman OH, UVA. To spur EMK to debate, and otherwise harass him, young Michael Dukakis and Barney Frank were among those who picketed Kennedy's campaign headquarters on McCormack's behalf. See Doherty, Frank, and Dukakis reminiscences, BM, Nov. 30, 2009.

67 **McCormack was the aggressor:** JAF interviews with Gerard Doherty, Robert Nickels, George Abrams. John Culver, Milton Gwirtzman, Martin Nolan OH, UVA. Levin, *Campaigning*, 187, 190. NYT, Aug. 28, 1962. TCF-NYHS, Aug. 29, 1962. Fay, *Pleasure*, 244.

68 **mood was somber:** JAF interviews with Gerard Doherty, Terri Robinson, Charles Tretter. Levin, *Campaigning*, 211–13. SEP, Oct. 27, 1962. NYT, Aug. 29, 1962. EMKOH-JFKL. TCF-NYHS, Aug. 29, 1962.

68 **president called to find out:** Milton Gwirtzman OH, JFKL. Milton Gwirtzman OH, UVA.

69 **the sea change:** JAF interviews with Gerard Doherty, Charles Tretter, Terri Robinson, Robert Nickels, George Abrams, Barbara Souliotis. Ed Martin, John Culver OH, UVA. "Survey on Reaction to Kennedy-McCormack Debate," Aug. 28, 1962, AC-JFKL. Levin, *Campaigning*, 223. EMKOH-UVA. BG, Aug. 28, 29, 1962. NYT, Aug. 28, 1962. "Teddy to me looked like a little boy lost . . . and every mother loves a little boy who's lost and

wanted to cuddle him," one of McCormack's own advisers told Levin. "I felt the same way. I'm pretty soft-hearted and an emotional guy. I almost wanted to pick him out and take him home." The Irish American mothers stuck by EMK, the prodigal son, throughout his career. Hersh described them as "that league of ladies broad in the beam but chipper, the ones with petunias on their housecoats whose ankles hurt a lot by two in the afternoon, whose husbands spent most nights working on the beer." See Hersh, *Education*, 172.

70 **McCormack was markedly polite:** Schlesinger diary, Aug. 28, 31, 1962, AS-NYPL. NYT, Sept. 6, 1962. BG, Sept. 6, 19, 1962.

70 **"a day in your life":** JAF interviews with Barbara Souliotis, Charles Tretter. The provenance of the "worked a day in your life" story is somewhat shaky. Several of EMK's aides and associates, like John Culver and Robert Fitzgerald, claim in their UVA oral histories that they were with him at the time it happened, but recall the location as a factory floor, or a plant gate. Gerard Doherty and Ed Martin said it occurred at the Charlestown Navy Yard. Levin, in *Campaigning*, puts it at a "large industrial plant." Yet Barbara Souliotis, a credible source, insists it is a true story, and so did EMK. The dialogue appeared in print in the *New York Times* on Sept. 3, 1962, as an anonymous contribution from the Washington bureau, which said the anecdote had made its way to the nation's capital from Boston and was circulating around town. In his memoir EMK says the joker was a "laborer." In his oral history, EMK said that it happened in a North Shore bakery. "I was shaking hands, and I had trouble. The people were putting the jam on the bread and things like that, and you . . . don't know whether you're shaking hands or not. And that's where one of the workers just leaned over [and said]. . . . 'I heard what they said about you last night: You never worked a day. You didn't miss a thing.'"

71 **"Was there anybody there?":** Kraft to Smith, "Post Primary Report Number 5," and "Post Primary Report Number 7," and "Post Primary Report Number 8," and "Post Primary Report Number 16," and "Post Primary Report Number 18," and "Post Primary Report 19," all undated, Kraft 1962 campaign papers, JFKL. George Cabot Lodge OH, UVA. EMKOH-UVA. LHJ, Oct. 1962. Hersh, *Education*, 168.

71 **the seamstress girl:** Edward Martin OH, UVA. NYT, Nov. 5, 1962. TCF-Harvard, Nov. 7, 1962.

Four: The New Frontier

72 **everything in the U.S. Senate:** Caro, *Master*, xxiii, 9. Fluctuations: James Madison, *Federalist* No. 63. Fickleness: Madison, Debates, June 26, 1787. See also MacNeil and Baker, *American Senate*, ix, and Gould, *Most Exclusive*, viii, x, and Sinclair, *Transformation*, 9–10, 23. See also Mark J. Oleszek and Walter J. Oleszek, "Legislating in the Senate: From the 1950s into the 2000s," author's collection. When the 88th Congress convened in Jan. 1963, southerners chaired twelve of eighteen committees in

the Senate and twelve of twenty-one committees in the House. See Mackaman, *Idea*, 8.

73 **the filibuster rules:** EMK-TC, 187. Manatos to O'Brien, May 30, 1964, LBJL. White, *Citadel*, 68. *Time* correspondent files, May 4, 1965, NM-DC. See also Clapp, *Congressman*. Sen. Robert Byrd, "The Senate Filibuster—1917–1989," CR, Nov. 19, 1989. John Culver OH, UVA. Caro, *Master*, 52.

74 **antilynching bills:** On lynching see Walter White, "The Burning of Jim McIlherron: An NAACP Investigation," *Crisis*, May 1918, and "The Work of a Mob," *Crisis*, Sept. 1918, and additional *Crisis* reports: "The Waco Horror," July 1916; "The Burning at Cyersburg," Feb. 1918; and "Memphis, May 22, A.D., 1917." See also "An American Lynching: Being the Burning at Stake of Henry Lowry at Nodea, Arkansas, Jan. 26, 1921, as Told in American Newspapers," New York, NAACP, 1921. In "Lynching: America's National Disgrace," *Current History*, Jan. 1924, the NAACP's James Weldon Johnson placed the toll in the four decades around the turn of the twentieth century at four thousand Black Americans. On the congressional response and the fate of antilynching bills see the U.S. House of Representatives: History, Art & Archives, "Anti-Lynching Legislation Renewed," https://history.house.gov/Exhibitions-and-Publications/BAIC/Historical-Essays/Temporary-Farewell/Anti-Lynching-Legislation, and NYT, Dec. 3, 1922, Feb. 22, 1938, and WP, March 18, 2021, and Gould, *Most Exclusive*, 106–7.

74 **fit right in:** JAF interview with Charles Tretter. EMK-TC, 190–95. Meg Greenfield, "The Senior Senator Kennedy," *The Reporter*, Dec. 15, 1966. NYT, June 26, 1965. Parties: Clymer, *Edward M. Kennedy*, 45–46. "sardonic": Bradlee, *Conversations*, 113. Sinclair, *Transformation*, chapter 3, "The Impact of a Change in Membership: The Democratic Classes of 1958–1964."

75 **a defining trait:** Burns, *Camelot Legacy*, 70–71.

75 **Senate club was leery:** EMKOH-UVA. EMK-TC, 190, 193. Matthews, *U.S. Senators*, 93. White, *Citadel*, 82, 108. Burns, *Camelot Legacy*, 98–99.

76 **the Old Bulls approved:** Senate Judiciary Committee, records of executive sessions, SJC-NARA. Neil MacNeil, David Burke OH, UVA. Greenfield, *The Reporter*, Dec. 15, 1966. BG, Dec. 30, 1962. Eastland: Baker with King, *Wheeling and Dealing*, 100.

77 **Eastland was clearly a bigot:** JAF interviews with J. Lee Annis, Kenneth Feinberg. RFK-OH, JFKL. Gale McGee OH, JFKL. EMK-TC, 190–95. John Culver OH, UVA. Greenfield, *The Reporter*, Dec. 15, 1966. Manatos to O'Brien, Jan. 14, 1963; O'Brien to Manatos, Jan. 12, 15, 1963, with list of committee preferences, JFKL. On Eastland's life and times, see Annis, *Big Jim Eastland*, 6, 9, 19. On the relationship of southern Democrats with other senators and the national party, see MacNeil and Baker, *American Senate*, 107. Some of the New Deal's most important Senate champions were from the South. See Zelizer, *On Capitol Hill*, 23–25. On Debs see Annis, and also Blaemire, *Birch Bayh*, 53–54, 63. A stunned Senator Orrin Hatch recorded Eastland's comment about Barbara Jordan in his diary; see Roderick, *Leading the Charge*, 124. See also Donald Ritchie, "Where Is

Ted Kennedy When We Need Him? The Possibilities for Legislating in a Polarized Congress," speech given at U.S. Embassy, Dublin, Ireland, June 22, 2017.

78 **Joan was bedazzled:** JBK interview, LD-WYO.

78 **younger gave way:** Bradlee, *Conversations*, 129. On EMK relinquishing the Senate seat to JFK, see JKO OH, JFKL, and EMKOH-UVA. On stature and wives, see Charles Spalding OH, JFKL.

79 **list of needs:** EMKOH-JFKL. "Senator Kennedy Reports," April 1964, re NASA research center, and other EMK constituent correspondence files, EMK-JFKL. EMK to LBJ, June 19, 1964; EMK to O'Brien (shipyard), June 15, 1964; O'Brien to Johnson, with attachment, EMK to O'Brien, June 19, 1964; Feldman to EMK (shoes), Jan. 7, 1964; Manatos to O'Donnell (shoes), Feb. 18, 1964; Manatos to O'Brien, Feb. 27, 1964 (base closings), April 29, 1964, LBJL. NYT, Dec. 17, 1962, Aug. 3, 1963. Desautels to O'Brien, March 6, 1963, JFKL. "Electronics Research Center," NASA history archive, NASA. William Orrick (Northeast) OH, JFKL.

79 **wrestled the communists:** JFK, Commencement Address at American University, Washington, DC, June 10, 1963, JFKL. Vietnam: EMK made the front page of the *New York Times*, to the Kennedy administration's consternation, when he was photographed in deep conversation with Mrs. Ngo Dinh Nhu, the sister-in-law of South Vietnamese president Ngo Dinh Diem, at a parliamentary conference in Yugoslavia. EMK did not know it, but the United States was at that moment building support for a November coup to oust the imperious Diem, in which Diem and his brother would be assassinated. NYT, Sept. 14, 1963.

79 **nation on civil rights:** RFK, James MacGregor Burns OH, JFKL. Andrew Young, Harris Wofford interviews, LT-CU. Murrow: Schlesinger diary, Oct. 17–Nov. 8, 1960, AS-NYPL.

81 **Kennedy civil rights bill:** JFK, Report to the American People on Civil Rights, June 11, 1963; RFK OH, JFKL.

81 **witnessed the racists:** Mike Mansfield OH, JFKL. JAF interview with Robert Shrum, Charles Daly. JFK on Thaddeus Stevens: Schlesinger diary, June 1963, AS-NYPL; Kennedy, *Profiles in Courage*, chapter 6. For a day-by-day account of the passage of the Civil Rights Act, see Mackaman, *Idea*.

81 **"enormous national tranquilizer":** Joseph Alsop OH, JFKL.

81 **each other's company:** EMKOH-UVA. EMKOH-JFKL. EMK-TC, 173, 202, 204. "Ted Kennedy's Memories of JFK: A Conversation with Theodore Sorensen," *McCall's*, Nov. 1973. On Ireland see Carroll, *Ourselves*, 178.

82 **staring at him with horror:** JAF interviews with Barbara Souliotis, Thomas Korologos. EMK-TC, 208–10. Manchester, *Death*, 197–99, 255, 373, 501, 505. "Joan found the mere contemplation of violence crippling," wrote Manchester. Mary Frackleton, Terri Robinson OH, UVA. EMKOH-JFKL. *McCall's*, Nov. 1973. WP, Nov. 23, 1963.

83 **in the funeral:** Manchester, *Death*, 618, 628. "Remarks of Senator Edward M. Kennedy, Tribute to Dave Powers," St. Catherine of Siena Church, Charlestown, Massachusetts, April 1, 1998. The

name is not on the burial marker, but Jacqueline took to calling her lost daughter Arabella.

Five: More of Us Than Trouble

86 **the garish sun:** Charles Spalding, John Jay Hooker, John Siegenthaler OH, JFKL. Robert Kennedy's five-year odyssey, and the roots of the Johnson-Kennedy conflict, are covered in Schlesinger, *Robert Kennedy*, and vanden Heuvel and Gwirtzman, *On His Own*; in biographies of RFK by Evan Thomas and Larry Tye, and in William Manchester's account of John Kennedy's assassination. Many notable writers, among them Jack Newfield, David Halberstam, William Shannon, Richard Goodwin, Jules Witcover, and Pete Hamill, have written about the years between the assassinations; see bibliography. The RFK-LBJ feud is examined in Shesol, *Mutual Contempt*, and by LBJ biographers Robert Dallek, Doris Kearns Goodwin, and Robert Caro.

87 **Ted was in Massachusetts:** Bradlee, *A Good Life*, 296. Vanden Heuvel and Gwirtzman, *On His Own*, 3. On Berlin see Schlesinger diary, Feb. 22, 1962, AS-NYPL, and Marian Cannon Schlesinger, *I Remember*, 166. Robert "no longer was a militant, hostile character fighting everyone who didn't agree with him," Neil MacNeil remembered in his UVA oral history. "He had made himself a spokesman for the hapless and the hopeless and the helpless."

87 **so much lost:** EMK-TC, 210. JAF interview with Charles Tretter. Peter Maas remembrance: Stein, *American Journey*, 147.

88 **Ted Kennedy's therapists:** JAF interview with Victoria Reggie Kennedy. David Brinkley remembrance: Stein, *American Journey*, 146; a transcribed segment of the original interview is in AS-NYPL. Burns, *Camelot Legacy*, 107. EMK-TC, 210, 213. Her husband suppressed "a Mount Vesuvius of grief," said Victoria.

89 **the gruesome imagery:** JAF interviews with Patrick Kennedy, Victoria Reggie Kennedy, Walter Sheridan. Kennedy and Fried, *Common Struggle*, 32. On the Warren Commission see EMK-TC, 211–12. On RFK's feeling of guilt, see Thomas, *Robert Kennedy*, 283–84. See also Schlesinger diary entry, Dec. 1963, AS-NYPL: "I asked [RFK], perhaps tactlessly, about Oswald. He said that there could be no serious doubt that he was guilty, but there was still argument whether he did it by himself or as part of a larger plot, whether organized by Castro or by gangsters. He said that the FBI thought he had done it by himself but that [CIA director John] McCone thought there were two people involved in the shooting."

89 **return in springtime:** On the JFK school, see JKO to Arthur Schlesinger, Dec. 3, 1963, AS-NYPL. The selection of a site for the presidential library was an arduous process. The original intent, to build a library and museum at Harvard, met resistance from the faculty and residents of Cambridge, who feared an influx of "Bermuda shorts and Winnebagos." The eventual locale, on Columbia Point, was proposed by Robert Wood, president of the University of Massachusetts, Boston, and ratified by JKO and EMK, who were im-

pressed by the seaside location and the vista of Boston when they toured the property. In the car that day JKO told EMK that for Irish Americans and Harvard, "there are three stages of maturity." The first is awe, "when you get off the boat you want to go to Harvard." The second is pride, "when you go to Harvard." The third is when you have the self-assurance to shit on Harvard and its pretensions. See Larry Hackman, Dan Fenn, John Stewart, William Moss OH, JFKL. NYT, May 30, 1973, Nov. 25, 1975; Gerry Nadel, "Johnny, When Will Ye Get Your Library?," *Esquire*, Jan. 1975. On Ireland see William vanden Heuvel, Sean O'Huiginn OH, UVA; SEP, July 11, 1964; Carroll, *Ourselves*, 172.

89 **John Kennedy's liberalism:** Theodore Sorensen OH, UVA. Doodle: Bohrer, *Revolution*, 159.

90 **sensitive and receptive:** David Sutphen OH, UVA.

91 **"let us continue":** Lyndon Johnson, "Address Before a Joint Session of Congress," Nov. 27, 1963, UCSB. LBJ and Smathers, Johnson White House tape, Nov. 23, 1963, LBJL—transcript in Beschloss, *Taking Charge*, 25. "BW" to Bayh, Dec. 19, 1963, "Comparison of President's Civil Rights Message (6-19-63) and HR 7152 (Civil Rights Bill)," Bayh-IU. Strober, *Begin*, Joseph Dolan interview, 25. Robert Caro, in *Passage*, 428–36, gives a detailed account of the speech and its effect, as does Todd Purdum's fine volume on the Civil Rights Act, *An Idea Whose Time Has Come*.

91 **for a civil rights bill:** In his oral history for the JFK Library, EMK said he heeded JFK's warning and so missed seeing King's speech in person. See also Anne Strauss OH, UVA. In his 2009 memoir, EMK said that he slipped away from the Capitol and walked down to the Reflecting Pool to look at the crowd at the Lincoln Memorial, but then returned to his office to watch King speak on television: "If I hadn't been before, from Grampa's lessons of discrimination, from my own awakening to the plight of African Americans in our own nation, I was, that day in Washington, DC, fully baptized into the civil rights movement. . . . His dream had become my own." On JFK and RFK lobbying for the Civil Rights Act in the House see Risen, *Bill of the Century*, chapter 4.

92 **South's best weapon:** CR, April 14, 1964. Republican votes: There were twenty-two senators from the old Confederacy. One, John Tower of Texas, was a Republican who would vote against the bill. Of the twenty-one southern Democrats, only Ralph Yarborough of Texas would vote for it. The final Senate vote was 27–6 for the bill by the Republicans, and 46–21 by the Democrats.

93 **appearance on *Meet the Press*:** LBJ to EMK, March 30, 1964, Johnson White House tapes, LBJL; transcript available in Beschloss, *Taking Charge*, 301–2. LBJ was concerned about the Kennedys that day. After hanging up with EMK, he phoned JPK in Palm Beach, and again vowed to "pass the program and . . . not . . . let them ever divide us." LBJ "liked Teddy," said Nicholas Katzenbach, who worked for RFK at Justice and went on to serve as attorney general, in his oral history for the JFKL. "Johnson was a great admirer of Joe Kennedy and I think he was not averse at all to helping his young boy. . . . So I

think they did have a relationship which I don't think Bobby ever had." For other evidence of warmth in the EMK-LBJ relationship, see EMK to LBJ, April 23, 1963; Carpenter to LBJ, n.d., 1963; LBJ to EMK, Nov. 30, 1963; LBJ to EMK, March 24, 1964, LBJL.

93 **his "maiden speech":** CR, April 9, 1964. BG, April 9, 1964. Two weeks later, in a speech at a Democratic dinner in Philadelphia, EMK again assailed compulsory desegregation. See "Senator Kennedy Opposes Busing of Students," *Philadelphia Inquirer*, April 23, 1964. The scene at the St. Patrick's Day parade in Southie is from Lupo, *Liberty's*, 145–46. EMK's own accounts of his maiden speech do not include his opposition to busing; inexplicably, neither do those of his other biographers.

96 **Senator Everett Dirksen:** Republicans Thomas Kuchel in the Senate and William McCulloch, Charles Halleck, and Clarence Brown in the House also played pivotal, politically courageous roles in the passage of the Civil Rights Act. See Hubert Humphrey, "Memorandum" on Civil Rights Bill; Clarence Mitchell, John Stewart interviews, CS-MHS. Nicholas Katzenbach interview, TP-DC. EMKOH-UVA. Joseph Rauh interview, Robert Loevy papers, Dirksen Congressional Center. The Johnson administration lobbyists dangled every possible plum to pass the civil rights bill, including water projects for Arizona and the striking of silver dollars for Nevada; see Manatos to O'Brien, May 11, 25, 1964, LBJL. EMK's role in the passage of the 1964 act was little more than minor. His name is notably absent from the notes of the key leadership meetings taken by Stephen Horn, the legislative assistant to Kuchel, the Republican whip. See Horn, "Periodic Log Maintained During the Discussions Concerning the Passage of the Civil Rights Act of 1964," Carl Albert Center, University of Oklahoma. See also Katzenbach, *Some of It*, 143, Caro, *Passage*, 561–68, and MacNeil, *Dirksen*, 219, 223–34. On Russell see Purdum, *Idea*, 308. CR, June 18, 1964. The axiom about letting others take the credit is said to have been a favorite of Harry Truman, George Marshall, Ronald Reagan, and others.

98 **a delineating moment:** White, *Making, 1960*, 222, 392. When White House aide Bill Moyers was called to the residence by Johnson on the night the president signed the bill, LBJ was in bed, reading the bulldog edition of the *Washington Post*, with its account of the day. "I think we just delivered the South to the Republican party for a long time to come," he said. Bill Moyers, "What a Real President Was Like," WP, Nov. 13, 1988.

99 **The plane clipped:** JAF interviews with Birch Bayh, Charles Tretter, Barbara Soliotis, William vanden Heuvel. BG, June 20, 21, Oct. 20, 1964. *Indianapolis Times*, June 20, 21, 1964. Hospital statement, The Cooley Dickinson Hospital, June 22, 1964, Bayh-IU. *Time* correspondent files, Oct. 19, 1964, TW-JFKL. Crash report, docket # 2-0058, Civil Aeronautics Board, 1964, Vol. 302, 42–43. The CAB report concluded that Zimny, forty-nine, an experienced pilot, made an "improperly executed instrument approach . . . in which improper altitude control resulted in descent below

obstructing terrain." The accounts of the accident are uniform, except for one detail: EMK said that he retightened his seat belt in the seconds before the crash; Bayh said EMK had his seat belt off when he turned to watch the pilot land the plane. Since the other four remained strapped to their seats during the crash, but not EMK, Bayh may well have been correct.

100 **he lost consciousness:** JAF interviews with Birch Bayh, Robert Shrum. EMKOH-UVA. Bayh said that after smelling fuel, he told Marvella, "I've got to go back for Ted." She urged him not to. "But the plane might catch fire," he said. "All the more reason not to go," she said. In the 1980 presidential campaign, when EMK's aides fumed about Bayh's support for Jimmy Carter, EMK told them to stifle their objections. "Listen, the guy braved flames to pull me out of that plane," he said. See Shrum, *No Excuses*, 89. Said Shrum, "Bayh had a pass, and always would."

101 **echoes of Dallas:** JAF interview with Birch Bayh. Hand to Bayh, June 22, 1964, Bayh-IU. Breslin column, BG, June 21, 1964. BR, Dec. 18, 1964. For miscarriage see BR, June 1, 1964. *Boston Traveler*, June 1, 1964. EMKOH-UVA. TTR, 458.

101 **Just past death:** LBJ and Jenkins, June 20, 1964, and LBJ and Robert and Jacqueline Kennedy, June 21, 1964, White House tape recordings, LBJL, transcribed in Beschloss, *Taking Charge*. *Time*, July 3, 1964. WH Situation Room to Clifton and Reedy, June 20, 1964; "YB" to LBJ, June 20, 1964; WH Situation Room to LBJ, June 21, 1964, LBJL. Associated Press, June 22, 1964.

102 **severing his spinal column:** LBJ and EMK, Johnson White House tape recording, June 30, 1964, LBJL, transcript available in Beschloss, *Taking Charge*, 445. Dr. Herbert Adams, New England Baptist Hospital, statement, BG, Aug. 6, 1964. William Shannon, "How Ted Kennedy Survived His Ordeal," *Good Housekeeping*, April 1965. BR, Dec. 21, 1964. LBJ to EMK, July 9, 1964, LBJL. EMKOH-UVA. "They turn you over like a piece of meat on a grill," said David Burke in his UVA oral history.

103 **the best suite:** JAF interview with Gerard Doherty. Milton Gwirtzman OH, UVA. Rose to EMK, 1964, KFP- JFKL. EMK to LBJ, Sept. 29, 1964, and LBJ to EMK, Oct. 12, 1964, LBJL. LBJ and EMK, Johnson White House tape recording, Aug. 13, 1964, LBJL, transcript available in Beschloss, *Taking Charge*, 514. On Madison, see Jeff Blattner OH; UVA and JAF interview with Jeff Blattner. Recovery details: BH, July 26, Oct. 18, 1964. BR, Dec. 18, 19, 1964. Milton Gwirtzman OH, UVA. *Life*, Jan. 15, 1965.

"dull recital": EMK loved his parents, but JPK was "Daddy" and RK was always "Mother," his second wife recalled. Borrowing a phrase, Victoria Kennedy said that her husband suffered from "the soft bigotry of low expectations" within his family. JAF interview with Victoria Reggie Kennedy.

105 **private grad school:** "I'll try to pick those that aren't the equivalent of sedatives," Robert Wood promised. See Wood to EMK, June 30, 1994, Robert Wood papers, JFKL. EMK to Galbraith, July 14, 1964; Galbraith to EMK, July 21, Aug. 20, Sept. 4, Oct. 30, 1964, JKG-JFKL. EMK to Schlesinger,

Oct. 2, 1964; Schlesinger to EMK, Aug. 17, Oct. 10, 1964, Arthur Schlesinger papers, JFKL. Schlesinger diary, Jan. 20, 1965, AS-NYPL, partially reprinted in Schlesinger, *Journals*, 236. On the SEP article, Schlesinger, too, gave EMK a middling grade. "The introduction is well done; and I think that your definition of extremism . . . is accurate and important," Schlesinger wrote. "My one doubt, which unfortunately is rather fundamental, is that you do far too much honor to present-day extremism by placing it in the tradition of the Hartford Convention and of South Carolina nullification. Harrison Grey Otis and John C. Calhoun were—however mistaken—men of ability and stature. . . . The extremists of 1964 don't deserve to be mentioned in the same breath."
The proper analogue, said Schlesinger, "would not be these intelligent men but the aimless, mindless mobs who harried the Masons, lynched the Abolitionists, burned the convents and persecuted the Mormons." Burns has a list of the tutors and their subjects in *Camelot Legacy*, 122. See also *Life*, Jan. 15, 1965.

106 **worrisome reports:** JAF interview with Victoria Reggie Kennedy. Moyers to Stevenson, "Personal and Confidential," Oct. 16, 1964; LBJ to EMK, Oct. 6, 1965, LBJL. Wood's suggestion: Wood to EMK, Aug. 8, 1964, Robert Wood papers, JFKL. *Fruitful Bough*: The privately printed tributes became a family tradition. Milton Gwirtzman was drafted to help EMK put together the book on JPK. After RFK's death, Patricia Lawford would assemble a privately printed book, *The Shining Hour*, on RFK. EMK would follow with *Words Jack Loved* in 1977.

106 **each happy stage:** EMK maintained his interest and would serve as the guest speaker at graduation ceremonies for all three of Ed Moss's children. EMKOH-UVA. EMK to LBJ, Dec. 3, 1964, LBJL. NYT, Dec. 4, 1964. BG, Dec. 16, 17, 18, 1964. Hersh, *Education*, 208.

Six: Eddie and Robbie

108 **two brothers would serve:** NYT, Jan. 5, 1965. *Life*, Jan. 15, 1965. *Time* correspondent files, June 24, 1965, NM-DC.

108 **was the senior senator:** Adam Walinsky OH, JFKL. NYT, Jan. 4, 1965. O'Donnell, *Common Good*, 493.

109 **employ those big majorities:** Lyndon Johnson, "Remarks at the Lighting of the Nation's Christmas Tree," Dec. 18, 1964, UCSB, quoted in Perlstein, *Nixonland*, 6. On 89th Congress see Patterson, *Grand Expectations*, chapters 18, "Lyndon Johnson and American Liberalism," and 19, "A Great Society and the Rise of Rights-Consciousness."

109 **sweet-talking Ted:** William vanden Heuvel OH, UVA. "They retained the provincial quality that strong family ties cause," vanden Heuvel would recall. "Their first relationships were with each other, and that was the primary relationship and nothing broke that." Loyalty: JPK to John W. McCormack, Aug. 8, 1951, Smith, *Hostage*, 657. LBJ and the Club: Schlesinger diary, Jan. 20, 1965,

AS-NYPL. "Teddy is a fine fellow," Schlesinger told his diary, "but he is much further below Bobby in ability than Bobby is below JFK." EMK-TC, 227–29.

110 **approaches to politics:** William Orrick, Gale McGee OH, JFKL. Vanden Heuvel and Gwirtzman, *On His Own*, 64. Vanden Heuvel OH, UVA. The "as long as necessary" anecdote has been reprinted in Schlesinger, *Robert Kennedy*, other biographies, and journalistic profiles. EMK-TC, 227–29. Goodwin quoted in Schlesinger, *Robert Kennedy*, 802. Lippman, *Senator Ted Kennedy*, 29–30.

111 **expedite an upgrade:** BG, Dec. 24, 1968. David Burke, John Danforth OH, UVA.

112 **"very male chauvinistic":** Owens to EMK, April 28, 1970, with EMK handwritten reply, JFKL. JAF interviews with Patricia Schroeder, Judith Kurland. Family attitude: see McNamara, *Eunice*, 406. On women voters see Thomas Morgan, "And Teddy," *Esquire*, April 1962.

113 **"woman's brain center":** *Architectural Digest*, Sept./Oct. 1973. JBK interview, LD-WYO. Cigarette case: JBK interview, AC-JFKL. Drinking: EMK-TC. EMKOH-UVA. JAF interview with Terri Robinson. Terri Robinson, Betty Taymor, Lester Hyman, Mary Frackleton OH, UVA. McLean House: WP, May 19, 1967, March 3, 1968. NYT, May 10, 1970. Fresh start: Kennedy and Fried, *Common Struggle*, 33.

114 **Loyalty was paramount:** Richard Goodwin interview, LT-CU. David Burke OH, UVA. Gould, *Most Exclusive*, xii, 181, 188–89.

115 **Beyond the humor:** JAF interviews with Jeff Blattner, Thomas Rollins, James Manley. David Burke, Anne Strauss, John Danforth OH, UVA. NYT, July 26, 2011, April 26, 2014. WP, April 29, 1990, Dec. 15, 2020. Semaphore: RFK to EMK, undated, JFKL; see also *Life*, June 1988. Lippman, *Senator Ted Kennedy*, 31.

115 **assessed his career:** O'Brien to EMK (with pens used by LBJ to sign legislation), Dec. 19, 1963, July 14, 15, Aug. 2, 4, 5, Sept. 29, 1965, LBJL. On Teachers Corps, see Lippman, *Senator Ted Kennedy*, 38–40, and William vanden Heuvel OH, UVA.

115 **First up was the Voting Rights Act:** Lyndon Johnson, "Special Message to the Congress on the Right to Vote," and "Special Message to the Congress: The American Promise," March 15, 1965, UCSB. White to LBJ, "Notes for Meeting with Dr. King on March 5," March 4, 1965; Watson to Johnson, with draft letter and statistics by Goodwin, March 19, 1965, LBJL. Congressional Research Service, "The Voting Rights Act of 1965: Background and Overview," July 20, 2015. Clymer, *Edward M. Kennedy*, 65. For details on Selma and the crusade to pass the Voting Rights Act see Watson, *Lion*, 646–59; Waldman, *Fight to Vote*, 142–55; Mann, *Walls of Jericho*, 449–64; Williams, *Eyes on the Prize*, chapter 8.

117 **left the poll tax out:** EMK interview, AC-JFKL. David Burke OH, UVA. Caro, *Master*, 97–98. "Gist of Informal Discussion Between Senator Edward M. Kennedy and Massachusetts Council of Churches Delegates RE Selma, ALA. Crisis," March 12, 1965, AC-JFKL. Katzenbach to LBJ, "Reasons Why the Department of Justice Has

Favored the Mansfield-Dirksen Approach to Elimination of the Poll Tax," May 21, 1965, LBJL.

117 **was mightily irritated:** LBJ and Birch Bayh, White House tape recording, May 7, 1965, LBJL, with transcript in Beschloss, *Reaching*, 313–14.

118 **Committee to ban the poll tax:** EMK interview, AC-JFKL. BG quoted in Burns, *Camelot Legacy*, 127. David Burke OH, UVA.

118 **"the Johnson bill":** LBJ and Reuther, White House tape recording, May 14, 1965, LBJL with transcript in Beschloss, *Reaching*, 323.

119 **had proven himself:** JAF interview with Andrew Glass. David Burke OH, UVA. Katzenbach, *Some of It*, 173. Glenn Reichardt and William Mates, "The Voting Rights Act of 1965: Congress and the Voting Rights Act," JFK School of Government, case study, C94-75-115. WSJ, June 17, 1965. For details on the debate: EMK to Hart, April 14, 1965, with attached statement; Hart to Humphrey Feb. 12, 1965; "Meeting of non-southern members of Senate Judiciary Committee," memorandum, April 2, 1965; Mitchell to Hart, April 5, 1965; Wilkins to Hart, May 5, 1965; Leadership Conference to Hart, May 13, 1965; Katzenbach to Mansfield, May 19, 1965; Leadership Conference on Civil Rights, Aronson to Cooperating Organizations, May 31, June 14, 1965, all Hart-UM. Wilkins to LBJ, telegram, April 26, 1965; Rosenthal to Valenti, April 27, 1965; Watkins to LBJ, May 6, 1965; White to LBJ, May 12, 1965; White to Wilkins, May 12, all LBJL. Clarence Mitchell, Memorandum, "Two Vital Amendments Needed in the 1965 Voting Rights Act," undated; Katzenbach statement, SJC hearing, March 18, 1965; transcript, executive session, SJC, April 6, 1965; Vincent Doyle, "A Brief Comment" on literacy tests and poll tax, Legislative Reference Service, LOC, all SJC-NARA. McCarthy to Loevy, Nov. 28, 1982; Freund to EMK, April 21, 1965; EMK to Parks, May 20, 1965, all AC-JFKL. For news coverage and praise: CR, April 13, May 7, 10, 1965. WP, May 16, 1965. NYHT, May 16, 1965. NYT, April 9, May 12, 1965. WS, May 12, 1965.

119 **revolt unveiled tactics:** William V. Shannon, "The Emergence of Senator Kennedy (D., Mass.)," NYT, Aug. 22, 1965. *Time* correspondent file, autumn 1965, NM-DC. Arduous study: "By the time you finish those many hours . . . with a briefing book *this* high . . . he has crammed and moot-courted himself so that he knows every nuance of the issue," said women's rights activist Judith Lichtman in her UVA oral history. "He gets it. He gets the law. He gets the strategy. The substance. Understands the weak points." Bipartisan: JAF interview with Kenneth Feinberg. Michael Enzi, Burt Wides OH, UVA. See also David Nexon, "Senator Edward M. Kennedy: The Master Legislative Craftsman," *Health Affairs*, Sept. 17, 2009.

120 **had profound effects:** "Statement by the President," First Anniversary of The Voting Rights Act of 1965, Aug. 6, 1965; "Memorandum for the President," Nov. 1, 1965; Marshall to LBJ, Jan. 14, 1966; report to Katzenbach, Feb. 2, 1966, LBJL. In Mississippi, the percentage of eligible Black voters registered jumped from 7 percent to 67 percent in five years. The number of Black elected officials

in southern states covered by the act leapt from seventy-two to nigh one thousand in a decade. See James Cobb, "The Voting Rights Act at 50: How It Changed the World," Time.com, Aug. 6, 2015.

120 **issue was immigration:** U.S. Census tables, racial and ethnic composition, 1960, 2010, U.S. Department of Commerce. Waters and Ueda, *New Americans*, introduction.

121 **a family legacy:** Goodwin tells the tale in *Fitzgeralds*, 101–3. She writes, "While Fitzgerald's influence was probably not as large as he liked to believe, history does record that on March 2, 1897 . . . Cleveland vetoed the literacy bill as a radical departure from U.S. national policy related to immigration, thereby keeping America's doors open for another twenty years." Her source, Fitzgerald biographer John Henry Cutler, cited Fitzgerald's "twilight days" recollections as the basis for the story of the Lodge-Fitzgerald clash. See Cutler, *"Honey Fitz,"* 64.

121 **revisions in immigration:** John F. Kennedy, "Letter to the President of the Senate and to the Speaker of the House on Revision of the Immigration Laws," July 23, 1963, UCSB. EMKOH-UVA. "A Conversation with Senator Edward Kennedy on Immigration," June 9, 2006, JFKL.

122 **"a civil rights issue":** "A Conversation with Senator Edward Kennedy on Immigration," June 9, 2006, JFKL. EMKOH-UVA. Sen. Paul Douglas testimony, March 1, 1965, hearing, Subcommittee on Immigration and Naturalization, SJC-NARA. Hart to Sorensen, Dec. 14, 1962; Hart to Mobley, Aug. 25, 1965, Hart-UM. Sen. Hiram Fong OH, former members of Congress, LOC. Michael Myers OH, UVA. Kennedy, *Nation of Immigrants.* Gjelten, *A Nation of Nations,* 86–88. Aristide Zolberg, "Immigration Control Policy: Law and Implementation," in Waters and Ueda, *New Americans.*

122 **America's southern border:** Albert M. Camarillo, "Mexico," in Waters and Ueda, *New Americans.* Importation of Foreign Agricultural Workers, Hearings before the Committee on Agriculture and Forestry, United States Senate, Jan. 15 and 16, 1965.

123 **the second tier:** EMK opening statement, Subcommittee on Immigration and Naturalization, Feb. 10, 1965, hearing; Address by Senator Edward M. Kennedy at the American Immigration and Citizenship Conference, March 4, 1965; Fact sheet, Some Highlights of Kennedy Involvement in Immigration and Refugee Issues, SJC-NARA. The legislation was a collection of amendments to the existing law, known variously as the Immigration Act, the Immigration and Naturalization Act of 1965, or the Hart-Celler bill, after sponsors Phil Hart and Emanuel Celler. Orchowski, *Law That Changed,* 39.

123 **Kennedy to manage:** Ervin comments, Subcommittee on Immigration and Naturalization, Feb.19, 1965 (Congo), and Feb. 24, 1965 (Ethiopia), and Feb. 25, 1965 (Anglo-Saxon), hearings, SJC-NARA.

The nativist witnesses were blunt. "Go into the stinking, steaming ghettoes in our large cities . . . and then let us ask ourselves sincerely, should we lower the immigration bars?" said Charles McCarthy of the

Council for Individual Freedom at the July 28, 1965, hearing.

"The average white citizen is losing his rights to your phony cause," said Mrs. Anni Wagenforh, representing the Baltimore Anti-Communist League, on July 22, 1965. "You are condoning the most inhumane practice by trying to destroy a nation's beautiful culture and personality, to replace it with ignorance, crime, disease and greed."

On Dirksen role see SJC, executive sessions, Aug. 31, 1965 ("Forget about the immigration bill today," the Illinois senators told his colleagues), and Sept. 8, 1965. On Eastland see Manatos to O'Brien, Aug. 16, 1965; Humphrey to EMK, April 30, 1965, LBJL. Daniel Tichenor, "Lyndon Johnson's Ambivalent Reform: The Immigration and Nationality Act of 1965," *Presidential Studies Quarterly*, Sept. 2016, and *Time* correspondent files NM-DC, July 5, 1957, Sept. 23, 1965. On Irish see David Burke OH, UVA.

125 **relationship with syntax:** Report of Proceedings, Subcommittee on Immigration and Naturalization, March 16, 1965, SJC-NARA. Kennedy to Kling, April 27, 1966, EMK-JFKL.

125 **just and capable:** Sen. Jacob Javits remarks, Subcommittee on Immigration and Naturalization, Feb. 24, 1965 hearing, SJC-NARA. WP, April 8, 1964. BH, Feb. 25, 1965. Meg Greenfield, "The Senior Senator Kennedy," *The Reporter*, Dec. 15, 1966.

125 **war of wills:** EMK and LBJ, White House tape recording, March 8, 1965; Celler and LBJ, White House tape recording, May 5, 1964; Carl Albert and LBJ, White House tape recording, May 18, 1965, LBJL. Feighan to RFK, Feb. 4, 1965, AW-JFKL. Feighan was chairman of a dormant joint committee on immigration, which he hoped to use the bill as an occasion to revive, and chairman as well of the House Judiciary subcommittee on immigration.

125 **closing the Mexican border:** EMK, "The Immigration Act of 1965," draft, SJC-NARA; the published version is in *The Annals of the American Academy*, American Academy of Political and Social Science, Sept. 1966. Celler, LBJ, and Katzenbach, White House tape recording, Aug. 26, 1965, LBJL. *Time* correspondent file, Sept. 23, 1965, NM-DC. Orchowski, *Law That Changed*, 72–73. NYT, Aug. 25, 26, 27, 28, 1965.

125 **should be family reunification:** Deane and Davie Heller, "Our New Immigration Law," *American Legion* magazine, Feb. 1966. David Reimers, "An Unintended Reform: the 1965 Immigration Act and Third World Immigration to the United States," *Journal of American Ethnic History*, Fall 1983. Gjelten, *A Nation of Nations*, 125–27. Gabriel Chin, "Was the 1965 Immigration Act Anti-Racist?," in Gabriel Chin and Rose Cuison Villazor, *The Immigration and Nationality Act of 1965: Legislating a New America* (New York: Cambridge University Press, 2015), 47.

126 **a bitter dose:** O'Brien to LBJ ("Concerning the news story that Senator Robert Kennedy would move to eliminate the western hemisphere quota, we have checked this out carefully and the Attorney General has talked to Bobby, as well as Teddy,

and we are assured this will not occur"), Sept. 20, 1965, LBJL.

Rainbow: Typed notes, attached to a copy of the Sept. 30, 1965, conference report, Emanuel Celler papers, LOC, cited in Philip E. Wolgin, "Beyond Natural Origins: The Development of Modern Immigration Policymaking 1948–1968," Spring 2011 PhD dissertation, University of California, Berkeley, 54. See also William Hartley, "United States Immigration Policy: The Case of the Western Hemisphere," *World Affairs*, Summer, 1972.

No White House tape has surfaced of Johnson informing Kennedy or Hart about the deals his administration cut with Feighan, Ervin, and Dirksen. But there is a recording of the president as he prepares to break the news to Manny Celler.

The president called the congressman to the Oval Office, to what Celler thought was a strategy meeting with Katzenbach on how to defeat the nativists. Johnson gave Celler the full treatment. He launched into a long soliloquy, larded with flattery, and described the historic bill-signing ceremony that lay on the horizon, in Celler's own glistening New York harbor.

"We'll take the pen that we sign the bill with," Johnson told Celler and Katzenbach, "and then we'll go up there to Ellis Island with old Manny, and get a picture in the paper with him, and salute him, and kick our heels." But when Celler, encouraged, tried to shift the conversation to the fight over the Western Hemisphere quotas, Johnson's voice turned cold.

"I'll talk to him . . . Nick," Johnson said, dismissing Katzenbach and turning off the tape machine. And Celler was told how things stood. See Celler, LBJ, and Katzenbach, White House tape recording, Aug. 26, 1965, LBJL. As LBJ's adviser, Lawrence O'Brien put it in his oral history for the LBJL, "We're not going to walk away from this because we didn't get a whole loaf. We'll take half a loaf."

126 **was seeing Congress:** EMK, "The Immigration Act of 1965."

128 **He was successful:** David Burke OH, UVA. *Time* correspondent files, Jan. 3–4, 1969, Sept. 23, 1965, NM-DC. BG, Sept. 23, 1965.

128 **far-reaching, unintentional results:** Kevin Johnson, "The Beginning of the End: The Immigration Act of 1965 and the Emergence of the Modern U.S.-Mexico Border State," in Chin and Villazor, *Legislating*; Chin and Villazor, introduction, and Zolberg, "Immigration Control Policy," in Waters and Ueda, *The New Americans*. Gjelten, *A Nation of Nations*, chapter 10. U.S. Census Bureau, "America's Foreign Born in the Last 50 Years," www.census.gov.

128 **labeled "chain migration":** Zolberg, "Immigration Control Policy," in Waters and Ueda, *The New Americans*. Orchowski, *Law That Changed*, 121. Gjelten, *A Nation of Nations*, 142.

129 **Crisscrossing the border:** "A Conversation with Senator Edward Kennedy on Immigration," June 9, 2006, JFKL. Johnson and James Farmer, White House tape recording, Feb. 24, 1964, LBJL. Douglas Massey and Karen Pren, "Unintended Consequences of US Immigration Policy: Explaining the

Post-1965 Surge from Latin America," *Population And Development Review*, March 21, 2012. Timothy Henderson, *Beyond Borders: A History of Mexican Migration to the United States* (Malden, MA: Wiley-Blackwell, 2011). Jeannette Money and Kristina Victor, "The 1965 Immigration Act: The Demographic and Political Transformation of Mexicans and Mexican Americans in U.S. Border Communities," in Chin and Villazor, *Legislating*. For results see NYT, May 26, 1966, and Walinsky to RFK, "Re: Irish immigration," undated, 1966–1968, AW-JFKL.

130 **been more wrong:** CQW, Oct. 8, 1965. Gjelten, *Nation of Nations*, 132, 137–42. Frank Bean and B. Lindsay Lowell, "Unauthorized Migration," and Camarillo, "Mexico," in Waters and Ueda, *The New Americans*. Orchowski, *Law That Changed*, 43. CFN to Bayh, "Summary of Main Points of New Immigration Act," Oct. 29, 1965, Bayh-IU. Valenti to O'Brien, Oct. 1, 1965, LBJL. As a political palliative, the 1965 fix lasted less than a decade. Immigration, most notably illegal immigration from Latin America, quickly returned to presidential agendas. See Cannon to Ford, June 16, 1975, with attached Domestic Council Committee on Illegal Aliens, Background and Proposed Organization Plan; Parsons to Cannon, Cavanaugh, and Lynn, Sept. 27, 1976, with attached Preliminary Report of the Domestic Council Committee on Illegal Aliens ("The law must be revised to incorporate current and future realities not envisaged in the 1965 deliberations"), GFL.

Seven: Loyalties

131 **family coat-holder:** JAF interviews with Charles Tretter, Robert Healy. EMKOH-UVA. Burt Wides OH, UVA. James King interview, AC-JFKL.

132 **old man's spy:** JAF interview with Gerard Doherty. JFK to Morrissey, Sept. 27, 1951, JFKL. "Nomination of Francis X. Morrissey," confirmation hearing transcripts, Oct. 13, 1965; Morrissey bar application, June 15, 1932; Remarks of Walter McLaughlin, Oct. 12, 1965, SJC-NARA. TCF-HI, June 30, 1961, Whelan papers. BG, Oct. 3, 1965. TCF-Harvard, Oct. 14, 1965. Blair and Blair, *Search*, 454–56, 553. Mary Frackleton OH, UVA.

132 **eyes and ears:** Morrissey to JPK, May 19, 26, June 17, 1954, JFKL. EMKOH-UVA. Anthony Galluccio interview, Clay Blair papers, University of Wyoming.

133 **cries of hackery:** JAF interviews with Gerard Doherty, Robert Healy, James Doyle. McCarthy to JFK, July 25, 1961; Griswold to Bundy, Nov. 21, 1963, JFKL. JPK to RFK, Aug. 15, 1961, KFP-JFKL. TCF-HI, June 30, 1961, Whelan papers. NYT, July 3, 1961. BG, July 12, 1961. NYHT, May 16, 1961.

The *Boston Globe* and *New York Times* columnist Anthony Lewis led the press coverage on the prospective nomination in 1961. Robert Healy, in his oral history at UVA, said that he told the Kennedys in 1963 that their hometown paper would continue to oppose them if they insisted on appointing the "dented fender judge" to the federal bench. See Healy OH, UVA.

On Morrissey and EMK see EMKOH–UVA: "Every lunchtime I was free, and every lunchtime Frank Morrissey would arrange that I would go to a different place in Boston and give a talk." See also BH, Sept. 27, 1965. *Boston Traveler*, Dec. 16, 1959. Milton Gwirtzman OH, UVA. Milton Gwirtzman OH, JFKL. See JPK to Morrissey, June 3, 1960, JFKL, cited in Nasaw, *Patriarch*, 768. See also Schlesinger, *Robert Kennedy*, 375–76: "Look: my father has come to me and said that he has never asked me for anything, that he wants to ask me only this one thing—to make Frank Morrissey a federal judge," JFK told his staff. "What can I do?"

134 **Morrissey's primary advocate:** "Conversation with Joseph Kennedy and Edward Kennedy," Sept. 24, 1965; "Conversation with Nicholas Katzenbach," Sept. 28, 1965, Johnson White House tapes, UVA. RFK to LBJ, Sept. 2, 1964; Dodd to LBJ, Sept. 22, 1964; EMK to LBJ, Sept. 29, 1965, LBJL. Griswold to Bundy, Nov. 21, 1963, JFKL. BG, March 8, 1965. News briefing transcripts, Sept. 26, 27, 1965, LBJL. *Time*, Oct. 8, 1965. Milton Gwirtzman, David Burke OH, JFKL. The LBJ-EMK conversation is from Kennedy's notes, cited by Gwirtzman in his UVA oral history, supported by EMKOH-UVA.

134 **most unqualified candidate:** JAF interviews with George Abrams, Robert Healy, James Doyle. Wyzanski to Eastland et al., Sept. 27, 1965, SJC-NARA. "Nomination of Francis X. Morrissey," confirmation hearing transcripts, Oct. 12, 13, 1965. See also Morison to LBJ, Oct. 23, 1965, LBJL. BG, Aug 27, 28, Sept. 27, 28, 29, 1965. WP, Aug. 31, Sept. 29, 1965. WS, Sept. 27, 1965.

135 **a good whacking:** JAF interviews with George Abrams, Charles Tretter. "Nomination of Francis X. Morrissey," confirmation hearing transcripts, Oct. 12, 13, 1965; minutes and transcript of the executive session Oct. 13, 1965; Kennedy to Eastland, Sept. 29, 1965; Jenner to Eastland, Oct. 1, 1965; committee records and tally of favorable and unfavorable letters, SJC-NARA. BG, Oct. 1, 15, 17, 18, 1965. EMK remarks, CR, Sept. 28, 1965. WP, Oct. 3, 15, 1965. NYT, Oct. 14, 1965, See also Charles Ferris OH, UVA: "I was afraid to ask him what a tort was."

On Dirksen see TCF-Harvard, Oct. 14, 1965; David Burke OH, JFKL, and Milton Gwirtzman OH, JFKL: "Frank felt that if he could show the senators that he was a nice, obliging fellow, that they would confirm him. He regarded it sort of like being interviewed for admission to a Boston club."

135 **an awkward witness:** Robert Healy recalled that President Kennedy and his staff used to needle Morrissey about his feeble 1934 campaign, and that Kenneth O'Donnell (a friend to John and Robert but no intimate of Ted) called Healy after the first Senate hearing to remind him that Morrissey had been a candidate in Massachusetts at the same time he was supposedly practicing law in Georgia. "I'm going to just tell you this once, and then I'm going to hang up," O'Donnell said. See Robert Healy OH, UVA. The *Globe* stories ran on Oct. 15 and 17, 1965.

136 **mobster Michael Spinella:** Library of Congress translation: "Edward Kennedy and Wife Photographed at Capodichino Airport," *Il Mattino*, May 28, 1961, and supporting documents regarding legal status of Michael Spinella, Francis X. Morrissey folder, Dirksen Senate files, ED-DC.

See EMKOH-UVA: "We had a night in Capri. Our group was eating at this restaurant, and a fellow came up to Morrissey. . . . He said, 'My son has just been killed in Vietnam, and I'd like to go back to the United States, but I'm having difficulty with a visa, getting back in. Will you be of some help?' And he said, 'Do you mind if I get a picture with you?' Fine. And so he got a picture with me.

"When I came back . . . I was going to dinner with [John Kennedy] because he was interested in my trip. There was a phone call from my brother Bobby. . . .

"And he said, 'Jack, I just want you to know that your brother Teddy just had his picture taken with the biggest Mafioso figure in all of Italy. . . .'

"Jack said: 'Can't we keep you out of trouble, Teddy?' "

See also Conversation with Everett Dirksen, Oct. 20, 1965, Johnson White House tapes, UVA. BG, May 18, 1961. TCF-Harvard, Oct. 14, 1965. WP, Oct. 21, 1965. WSJ, Oct. 21, 1965. NYT, Oct. 22, 1965. EMKOH-UVA. Milton Gwirtzman, David Burke OH, JFKL.

136 **pull the nomination:** JAF interviews with George Abrams, Charles Tretter. Katzenbach to LBJ, Sept 2, 24, 1965; Watson to LBJ, Sept. 13, 1965; EMK to colleagues, Oct. 19, 1965; Katzenbach to Eastland, Oct. 18, 1965, LBJL. Gwirtzman to EMK, Oct. 1965, SJC-NARA. EMK remarks, CR, Oct. 21, 1965. BG, Oct. 13, 21, 1965. WP, Oct. 1, 22, 1965. NYT, Oct. 21, 22, 1965. Adam Walinsky OH, JFKL. Howard Baker interview, AC-JFKL.

On EMK's efforts, see David Burke OH, JFKL: "The price we'd have to pay for those votes was very, very high. I used to say to Edward Kennedy that he'd be speaking in front of ladies' teas in Altoona and Peoria . . . for the rest of his life."

Said Gerard Doherty in his JFKL oral history, "We went from, 'We're in pretty good shape,' to 'Well, with a little bit of luck we can do it,' [to] 'Well, we're going to need a lot of luck.' And then I remember saying to him it was mathematically impossible." The EMK "Harvard" quote is from Gerard Doherty interview, LD-WYO.

On RFK's decisive action see Milton Gwirtzman OH, JFKL; Adam Walinsky interview, LT-CU; Charles Ferris OH, UVA: "Bobby just sort of stepped in, and that was the end of Frank Morrissey." Technically, EMK moved that the nomination be recommitted to the Judiciary Committee. All understood that this would kill the nomination. See Senate Judiciary Committee, minutes of executive session, Sept. 20, 1965, SJC-NARA. Two weeks later, Morrissey wrote the president, asking him to withdraw his name. Morrissey to LBJ, Nov. 3, 1965, and LBJ to Morrissey, Nov. 5, 1965; Clark to LBJ, Nov. 3, 1965, LBJL.

Morrissey remained on the municipal bench. In 1974 he was censured by the Supreme Judicial Court after the *Boston Globe* Spotlight team revealed that he had accepted $4,000 from a Massachusetts man under investigation for stock fraud. See BG, May 17, 1973.

137 **nomination was a snare:** The notion that Morrissey's nomination was a plot by LBJ was advanced by Kennedy sympathizers almost immediately and maintained through the years. Arthur Schlesinger Jr., in his 1978 biography of RFK, contended that LBJ made the nomination knowing (and relishing) that it would be a flytrap: "The Kennedys would suffer the obloquy for the nomination. . . . It would place them under obligation to him while at the same time exposing their own pious pretentions." See Schlesinger, *Robert Kennedy*, 684. See also Joseph Califano OH, Jan. 28, 1988, LBJL: "Johnson was willing to do it . . . and he was going to stick the Kennedys . . . all the way out front. And that was calculated at every stage." See also Califano, *Governing America*, 90. The president "was enjoying this tarnishing of the Kennedy glamour," said Mansfield's aide Charles Ferris in his oral history for the Kennedy library. "Johnson could have put Morrissey over the line. It would have been cake," Charles Tretter recalled. "Johnson spun the trap." See JAF interviews with Charles Tretter, Joseph Califano.

The White House tapes and archives, however, show that LBJ named Morrissey only after repeated requests (in writing and in person) by RFK and EMK. If they were only going through the motions, pro forma, for their father, they did not tell the president. EMK never claimed to have been played—the most he conceded was that once the avalanche of opprobrium began, there may have been satisfaction at the White House; see EMKOH-UVA.

Johnson was aware when he recorded conversations, and so the tapes should be listened to with care. But his Sept. 28, 1965, telephone conversation with Nicholas Katzenbach shows no sign of scheming. "I don't give a damn who's judge," LBJ told Katzenbach. "Bobby asked me." See "Conversation with Nicholas Katzenbach," Sept. 28, 1965, Johnson White House tapes, UVA.

Johnson's conversation with Ted and Joseph Kennedy, on Sept. 24, 1965, is similarly innocuous. Ted Kennedy sounds touched and grateful, and Johnson sincere. See "Conversation with Joseph and Edward Kennedy," Sept. 24, 1965, Johnson White House tapes, UVA.

137 **young Galahad's armor:** TCF-Harvard, Oct. 14, 1965.

138 **shoulder in the chest:** JAF interviews with Joseph Tydings, Mark Shields, Charles Tretter. EMKOH-UVA. David Burke, Milton Gwirtzman, Adam Walinsky, Joseph Tydings OH, JFKL. WSJ, Oct. 21, 1965. Shields was a young floor aide for Senator William Proxmire at the time and recalled RFK's remark. Tydings, in his memoirs, recounts an incident in which "Bobby gave me a pretty hard shoulder into the chest, knocked me back toward the wall, and just kept on walking. It could have been an accident, but I don't think so." See Tydings and Frece, *Against the Grain*, chapter 15.

139 **alluring Vietnamese courtesan:** JAF interview with Joseph Tydings. EMKOH-UVA. Vladimir Lehovich, diplomatic oral history, ADST, March 25,

1977. On EMK overseas see also Edward M. Kennedy, FBI file, Sullivan to Belmont, "Ted Kennedy," Dec. 28, 1961; Jones to DeLoach, Oct. 20, 1964. The unredacted FBI files were obtained in a Freedom of Information Act lawsuit by the group Judicial Watch.

140 **into the Parker House:** Dun Gifford OH, JFKL. Hersh, *Education*, 249. Tretter, a driver and advance man, hit dangerous speeds taking EMK to the airport for his flight to Vietnam. EMK thanked him at the curb, saying with a grin, "Charlie, all I could think about when withdrawing Morrissey is the day I will have to defend you for a judgeship on the floor of the Senate." JAF interview with Charles Tretter.

Eight: A Senator to Be Reckoned With

141 **righteousness of the cause:** JAF interviews with George Abrams, Donald Luce. See David Burke and John Tunney OH, UVA, for description of the "movable cocoon" in which the visitors traveled. On dutiful EMK, see Vladimir Lehovich, diplomatic oral history, ADST, March 25, 1977. For accounts of the trip see NYT, Oct. 25, 26, 28, 1965. BG, Oct. 25, 26, 1965. See also Paul Healy, "The Education of Ted Kennedy," *The Sign,* June 1966.

The number of U.S. troops in Vietnam rose to 180,000 in 1965, the first year of LBJ's massive escalation of the war. In what the *Boston Globe* described as his first public commentary on the conflict, EMK had sent a letter to a Boston University "teach-in" on the Vietnam War that spring. He told the war's critics that American credibility was at stake, and that nations "vital to our security," like Burma and the Philippines, could fall to Chinese communist dominance if the United States withdrew; see BG, May 6, 1965. Six weeks before leaving for Vietnam, EMK continued to define the war with Cold War terminology. The United States "must make it clear to the Communist world that they cannot win in Vietnam by guerilla warfare any more than they could win in Berlin by blockade," he told a huge crowd of Ohio Democrats; see BG, Sept. 13, 1965.

142 **hub of expertise:** JAF interviews with Dale de Haan, George Abrams, Donald Luce. "Refugee Fact Book: Vietnam," Oct. 1965, SJC-NARA. EMKOH-UVA. Cooper to Bundy, Oct. 9, 1965, FRUS, 1964–1968, Volume III, Vietnam, June–Dec. 1965. The refugee subcommittee gave Kennedy a valuable jurisdictional entry to the field of foreign affairs. But it could generously be described as a congressional backwater. When Kennedy took over the Subcommittee on Refugees and Escapees, as it was titled, it had six employees and a yearly budget of $87,500. The Subcommittee on Antitrust and Monopoly, by contrast, had a staff of forty and a budget of $512,000. See "Tentative Budget, Subcommittee on Refugees and Escapees, Feb. 1, 1964 through Jan. 31, 1965," and "Confidential, Budget, Antitrust," SJC-NARA.

142 **the "hearts and minds":** JAF interview with Charles Tretter. On RFK see Arthur Schlesinger to "the children," May 9, 1965, Schlesinger, *Letters,* 293. For JFK see "Transcript of CBS Broadcast with Walter Cronkite, 2 September 1963," JFKL, in which JFK told the newsman, "I don't think that unless a greater effort is made by the government to win popular support that the war can be won out there. In the final analysis it is their war. They are the ones who have to win it or lose it."

143 **terrorized the peasantry:** JAF interviews with George Abrams, Don Luce. "Refugee Problems in South Vietnam and Laos," Hearings before the Subcommittee on Refugees and Escapees, July 13–Sept. 30, 1965, SJC-NARA; see testimony of Stephen Cary, assistant executive director, American Friends Service Committee, 234, and Roger Hilsman, former assistant secretary of state, 318.

On Fulbright see de Haan to EMK, May 19, 1965, SJC-NARA. Kennedy's hearings were held several months before Fulbright had the Foreign Relations Committee stage the first, and famous, congressional investigation of the war. Schlesinger, *Robert Kennedy,* 730.

On Johnson administration reaction and subcommittee successes see TCF-Harvard, Sept. 1, 2, 1965. "In negotiating the treacherous path between advising the administration and offending it, Ted Kennedy's tiny committee operated cautiously, but not without speed. Kennedy's speech on the Senate floor on this topic was carefully couched so as not to appear to damn or blame the administration."

144 **a bullish essay:** JAF interview with George Abrams.

145 **The article, published:** Edward Kennedy, "A Fresh Look at Vietnam," *Look,* Feb. 8, 1966. Fredrik Logevall, "Bernard Fall: The Man Who Knew the War," NYT, Feb. 21, 2017.

145 **briefers had lied:** JAF interviews with George Abrams, Mrs. David Burke, Charles Tretter, William vanden Heuvel. EMKOH-UVA, as transcribed in Perry, *Oral History.* See also Churnick to EMK, Dec. 8, 1965, and Eccles to EMK, Dec. 27, 1965, EMK-JFKL. Fredrik Logevall, "Bernard Fall: The Man Who Knew the War," NYT, Feb. 21, 2017. Edward Kennedy, "A Fresh Look at Vietnam," *Look,* Feb. 8, 1966. Fall died on Feb. 21, 1967, when he stepped on a land mine while accompanying a patrol of U.S. Marines in South Vietnam. David Burke's wife, Trixie, recalled, "The Kennedys were famous for being cheap. Not frugal. Cheap." But when the check came from *Look,* Ted gave half—$1,000—to Burke, and the family bought one of the newfangled color televisions. JAF interview with Mrs. David Burke.

146 **haven for skeptics:** For the examples of EMK's wavering on the war see EMK to Acker and EMK to Commager, both March 17, 1966, both EMK-JFKL. See also JAF interviews with Don Luce, Daniel Ellsberg, George Abrams. John Sommer interview, AC-JFKL. Address by Senator Edward M. Kennedy, Harvard Medical School, Oct. 25, 1967; Address by Senator Edward M. Kennedy Before the International Rescue Committee, NY, Oct. 31, 1967; Minutes, Senate Judiciary Committee, March 2, 1966, SJC-NARA. BG, Oct. 26, 1967.

146 **inequities of the Selective Service System:** The study of students from South Boston High School and graduates of elite colleges was made by former secretary of the Navy and U.S. senator James

Webb. See Farrell, *Tip O'Neill*, 229. BG, Nov. 2, 1999. On EMK and the draft see NJ, Nov. 29, 1969; BG, June 13, 30, 1966, Jan. 13, 1967; NYT, June 30, 1966, March 5, 7, 21, 23, June 15, 1967, Dec. 1, 1969. *Time*, Dec. 1, 1967. Dun Gifford interview, AC-JFKL.

See also EMK op-ed, "Inequities in the Draft: The Case Against a Volunteer Army of the Disadvantaged," contending that an all-volunteer force would rely on economically disadvantaged young Americans, and so encourage U.S. militarism by muting the voices of middle-class and wealthy families, NYT, Feb. 24, 1971.

Kennedy's opposition failed to stop the Nixon administration from adopting an all-volunteer force in 1973. See EMK testimony, Senate Armed Services Committee, Feb. 4, 1971; BG, April 18, 1967; and Martin Anderson, "The Making of the All-Volunteer Armed Force," paper submitted to Hofstra University, 1987 conference on the Nixon presidency, included in Friedman and Levantrosser, *Cold War Patriot*, 171–77.

148 **Supreme Court had concluded:** "The yokels have ruled the Republic since its first days—often, it must be added, very wisely. But now they decay," H. L. Mencken wrote in 1928. "Old apportionments give them unfair advantage. The vote of a malarious peasant on the lower Eastern Shore counts as much as the votes of twelve Baltimoreans."

In 1960, a Vermont town with thirty-eight residents elected the same number of representatives as the state capital, Burlington, with its population of thirty-three thousand. In ten states, senators representing less than 20 percent of the population could make a majority in the state senate. For a perceptive account of the controversy, see Smith, *Doorstep*.

In a series of cases the Supreme Court decided to enter what Justice Felix Frankfurter had called "the political thicket" of apportionment and elections, and, once there, how to rule on the equal protection issue. *Baker v. Carr* (369 U.S. 186) was the landmark decision that brought the court into the arena. Two years later, *Reynolds v. Sims* (377 U.S. 533) concluded that "legislators represent people, not trees or acres. . . . A citizen, a qualified voter, is no more nor no less so because he lives in the city or on the farm. This is the clear and strong command of our Constitution's Equal Protection Clause."

Many states, of course, modeled their legislatures on Congress, where the composition of the Senate, with tiny states like Rhode Island having as many senators as Texas or California, flouts the one-person, one-vote principle. Senators representing less than 20 percent of the American population (those from the smallest twenty-six states) can form a majority in the U.S. Senate (see NYT, Nov. 20, 2016; *Atlantic*, Oct. 10, 2018). The distorted representation offered in the Senate is enshrined in the Constitution, however, and not affected by the redistricting cases. On Warren see Abraham, *Freedom*, 17.

148 **Dirksen made it:** Senate Judiciary Committee, Executive Session, minutes, Aug. 4, 1964, SJC-

NARA. "A Plan of Campaign for the Committee for Government of the People," Whitaker & Baxter Advertising Agency, Sept. 1965; Markley to Dirksen, Dec. 2, 1965; list of invitees, pledged donations, Whitaker to Flynn, Sept. 20, 1965; Report to the Advisory Committee, Committee for Government of the People, on the Campaign of Public Information in behalf of the Reapportionment Constitutional Amendment, May 6, 1966, ED-DC. Peter Irons, "The Race to Control the States," *The Progressive*, May 1965.

151 **"one man, one vote" argument:** Senate Judiciary Committee transcript, May 23, 1967, SJC-NARA. Smith, *Doorstep*, 277. MacNeil, *Dirksen*, 296. James Flug interview, LT-CU. James Flug, Howard Baker interviews, AC-JFKL. EMKOH-UVA. The Kennedy-Baker substitute capped deviations to 10 percent and included a provision limiting gerrymandering. See BG, June 9, 1967. NYT, June 7, 9, 12, 1967. WP, June 9, Nov. 9, 1967. CR, March 22, May 10, June 6, 8, 1967. WSJ, Dec. 2, 1965. *Time*, Aug. 13, 1965. See Smith, *Doorstep*, 99–100, 190. On JFK see John F. Kennedy, "The Shame of the States," NYT, May 18, 1958. On RFK argument before the Supreme Court see NYT, Jan. 18, 1963.

152 **"surely been underestimated":** David Broder column WP, Nov. 14, 1967. A *Washington Post* editorial on Nov. 10, 1967, called the work of Kennedy and Baker "a great achievement for two promising young men," particularly in overcoming the "legislative anarchy" of Dirksen and his allies. "Edward Kennedy Is Gaining Stature in the Senate" was the headline in a similar appraisal in NYT, June 12, 1967. See also *Time*, Dec. 1, 1967. James Flug interview, LT-CU.

Nine: Robert's Time

154 **few other superstars:** Smith, *Hostage*, introduction, xvii. JAF interview with Peter Hart. EMK address, ADA, Roosevelt Day Dinner, Boston, March 4, 1967, SJC-NARA. Adam Walinsky OH, JFKL. "Robert F. Kennedy, Chrono," TW-JFKL. Tom Brokaw interview, LT-CU. Evan Thomas letter to Seigenthaler and Guthman, quoted in John Corry, "The Manchester Papers," *Esquire*, June 1967. See also Halberstam, *Odyssey*: "They wanted to be able to complain about the lack of privacy given them by the press, and yet be able to summon photographers and reporters from important magazines to reveal all kinds of innermost thoughts at opportune moments."

154 **media was infiltrated:** For accounts of the changes in American political journalism see Downie, *Muckrakers*; Wolfe, *New Journalism*; and Halberstam, *Powers*.

154 **pretty young women:** see Clymer, *Edward M. Kennedy*, 92, citing May 1, 12, and 17, 1967, gossip items in *Women's Wear Daily*.

155 **he split the party:** JAF interview with Victoria Reggie Kennedy. Schlesinger diaries, Feb. 27, 1966, AS-NYPL. EMK address, ADA, Roosevelt Day Dinner, Boston, March 4, 1967, SJC-NARA. Watson to Johnson, Oct. 23, 1967, with attached EMK remarks, Jefferson-Jackson Day dinner, Des Moines, Iowa, Oct. 9, 1967, LBJL. Schlesinger to

Clymer, Feb. 10, 1996, AC-JFKL. Adam Walinsky OH, JFKL. "Robert F. Kennedy, Chrono," TW-JFKL.

155 **victory of arms was not possible:** Schlesinger, *Robert Kennedy*, chapter 32, "The Breach Widens: Vietnam." Said antiwar congressman Don Edwards, "Teddy was late in opposing the war. Bobby was late in opposing the war. Even [Eugene] McCarthy was late." McCarthy Historical Project, EM-MHS. JAF interview with Charles Tretter.

155 **his brother's lee:** Chronology of EMK and the refugee subcommittee's actions between 1965 and the fall of 1967, "Senator Edward M. Kennedy's Involvement in Civilian Casualties and General Health Problems," Sept. 19, 1967; "Refugee Problems in South Vietnam," Report of the Committee on the Judiciary, Subcommittee on Refugees and Escapees, March 4, 1966; Haugerud to EMK, Nov. 21, 1968; EMK to McNamara, Aug. 11, 1967, and McNamara to EMK, Aug. 17, 1967; Kennedy to Rusk, May 23, 1967, and Macomber to EMK, June 29, 1967; Dillon to Sanders, Oct. 12, 1967, all SJC-NARA. Acker to EMK, March 17, 1966, EMK-JFKL. NYT, March 5, 7, July 15, 1966, Aug. 18, 1967. Mankiewicz and Swerdlow, *As I Was Saying*. Kennedy was "the only political figure in Washington to take a consistent interest in the plight of the Vietnamese civilians," wrote Neil Sheehan in *A Bright Shining Lie*, 620. On civilian casualties see Ralph Nader Congress Project, Citizens Look at Congress, Edward M. Kennedy, 1972. Schaap, *R.F.K*, 33.

156 **ingenue to oracle:** JAF interview with George Abrams. Holbrooke to Komer and Leonhart, "Lunch with Senator Edward Kennedy," Jan. 20, 1967, LBJL. O'Neill to White, June 21, 1967; O'Brien to LBJ, Sept. 29, 1967, with Desautels to O'Brien, Sept. 27, 1967, TON-BC. Abrams to EMK, Aug. 16, 1967; Shannon to EMK, Aug. 18, 1967, with EMK notation, SJC-NARA. Neil Sheehan, "Edward Kennedy Finds Vietnam Toll of Civilians High," NYT, May 8, 1967. NYT, July 31, Sept. 22, Oct. 9, 28, Nov. 1, 1967.

157 **"the other war":** "Civilian Casualty, Social Welfare and Refugee Problems in South Vietnam," Hearings before the Subcommittee on Refugees and Escapees, May 10–Oct. 16, 1967; Enthoven to EMK, Oct. 17, 1967, SJC-NARA. Kennedy's opening remarks were on Oct. 9; Luce testified on Oct. 10; Hilsman on Oct. 13; and Bundy on Oct. 16. See also Abrams to EMK, Oct. 5 and 6, 1967, de Haan to EMK, Oct. 16, 1967. RFK, *Face the Nation*, Nov. 26, 1967, quoted in Newfield, *Robert Kennedy*, 51. EMKOH-UVA. NYT, Oct. 17, 1967. WP, Oct. 26, 1967.

159 **an independent itinerary:** EMK diary excerpts, transcripts of taped EMK conversations with Vietnamese hospital staff: Can Tho, Quang Nam, Da Nang, Vietnam, Jan. 1968; Briefing for IV Corps Dinner, SJC-NARA. David Burke OH, UVA. Rosenblatt to Leonhart, Dec. 5, 1967; Leonhart to Rostow, Gaud, Habib, and Steadman; Bunker and Komer to Katzenbach and Katzenbach to Komer, Dec. 29, 1967, all LBJL. BG, Dec. 30, 1967. NYT, Jan. 6, 1968.

It is difficult to consider a tactic more at odds with winning hearts and minds than the military's practice of blindly firing nighttime "harassment and interdiction" salvos into the countryside, without the guidance of forward observers, at places where suspected Viet Cong might gather. "Excessive unobserved firepower expenditures by allied forces during the Vietnam War defied the traditional counterinsurgency principle that population protection should be valued more than destruction of the enemy," yet the U.S. Army devoted the majority of its artillery missions, and fired nearly half of its ammunition, as "H&I" in 1966 and 1967. The practice was ultimately phased out not because of concern over civilian casualties but because it was viewed as wasteful and expensive. See "The Limits of Fire Support: American Finances and Firepower Restraint During the Vietnam War," John Michael Hawkins, PhD dissertation, Texas A&M University, Aug. 2013, and John Michael Hawkins, "The Costs of Artillery: Eliminating Harassment and Interdiction Fire During the Vietnam War," *Journal of Military History*, Jan. 2006.

Kennedy's advance team, organized by David Burke, was E. Barrett Prettyman, John Nolan, N. Thompson Powers, and Don Luce's friend John Sommer. Kennedy was joined in Vietnam by Burke and a physician, John Levinson. See Barrett Prettyman OH, JFKL. John Nolan and John Levinson interviews, AC-JFKL. EMK to Eastland, Nov. 22, 1967; Prettyman to EMK, "Trip to Vietnam," March 5, 1968; "Summary of History of Refugee Problem and Civilian Health and Casualty Programs fron 1965 to 1967," Dec. 6, 1967, SJC-NARA.

160 **A torrent of scenes:** "Address by Senator Edward M. Kennedy, before the World Affairs Council of Boston on his recent trip to South Vietnam," Jan. 25, 1968; "Address by Senator Edward M. Kennedy, before the American Advertising Foundation," Washington, DC, Feb. 5, 1968; "Summary of Particulars re Civilian War Casualties Said to Have Been Caused by American Action," Rehabilitation Center Admission Records, Nov.–Dec. 1967; Sommer to EMK, Dec. 25, 1967, SJC-NARA. EMKOH-UVA.

160 **aid worker David Gitelson:** Gitelson's death was officially attributed to the Viet Cong, but Luce and other friends wondered if he had not been murdered by corrupt South Vietnamese soldiers. JAF interview with Don Luce. John Sommer interview, AC-JFKL. Gitelson report on airstrike, Dec. 1967, SJC-NARA. Kennedy remarks, CR, Feb. 1, 1968. *Time*, Feb. 9, 1968. William Seraile, "Disillusionment in the Delta," *Peace Corps Worldwide*, July 13, 2017. John Balaban, *Remembering Heaven's Face*, chapter 6, "The Poor American." There are somewhat garbled versions of the Gitelson meeting in Clymer, *Edward M. Kennedy*, 97, and EMK-TC, 255–56.

161 **the phantasma, Vietnam:** EMK diary, and itinerary, Vietnam, SJC-NARA. Thomas Durant, John Levinson, John Nolan, John Sommer interviews, AC-JFKL. "Address by Senator Edward M. Kennedy, before the World Affairs Council of Boston

on his recent trip to South Vietnam," Jan. 25, 1968, SJC-NARA. There are several versions of Kennedy's confrontation with the army over free-fire zones—this one is from David Burke OH, UVA.

On Vann: "Edward Kennedy and John Vann had become friends because Edward Kennedy had shared Vann's concern for the anguish of the Vietnamese peasantry," wrote Vann's biographer, Neil Sheehan. "Kennedy had made it his special mission to alleviate the suffering of the civilian war wounded and the peasants who had been reduced to homeless refugees. He had traveled to Vietnam to see their plight, had held Senate hearings, and had brought political pressure to bear for more humane conditions in the refugee camps, for adequate hospitals and for an end to the indiscriminate bombing and shelling of the countryside." Sheehan, *A Bright Shining Lie*, 11–12.

162 **"What a clusterfuck":** JAF interview with John Hamill.

162 **"atrocity of a war":** EMK-TC, 257. John Levinson interview, AC-JFKL. "Address by Senator Edward M. Kennedy, before the World Affairs Council of Boston on his recent trip to South Vietnam," Jan. 25, 1968, SJC-NARA. Rostow to Johnson, Jan. 16, 1968, with attached report, Komer to Johnson, Jan. 13, 1968, LBJL.

162 **"the futility of the military":** E. Barrett Prettyman OH, JFKL.

163 **litany of dissent:** Burke let Johnson's dog sit on his lap and accepted a soft drink he didn't want ("Well, Dave, your president is going to have a Fresca and you mean you won't have one with me?"), acts of submission for which he was heckled that night at Hickory Hill. See David Burke OH, UVA.

163 **he urged Johnson:** William Leonhart, Memorandum of Conversation: LBJ, EMK, Burke, and Leonhart, Jan. 24, 1968; Leonhart; Memorandum for the President, Leonhart to LBJ, Jan. 25, 1968.

163 **Kennedy's public critique:** "Notes of the President's Tuesday National Security Lunch," Jan. 23, 1968; "Notes of Meeting of the National Security Council," Jan. 24, 1968; "Notes of Meeting" with the chiefs of staff, Jan. 29, 1968; "Notes of Meeting" from the Foreign Affairs Luncheon, FRUS, 1964–1968, Volume VI, Vietnam, Jan.–Aug. 1968. Leonhart to Bunker, Jan. 24, 1968; Read to Rostow, Jan. 27, 1968; Bunker to Rusk, Jan. 28, 1968; Rostow to LBJ, Jan. 30, 1968; Rostow to LBJ with attached Lodge to Rostow, Jan. 30, 1968; Lodge to LBJ, Jan. 30, 1968, LBJL. WP, Jan. 25, 1968. Humphrey to Rostow, Jan. 30, 1968, CS-MHS. Adam Walinsky OH, JFKL.

The Pentagon Papers would later demonstrate that at the very same time that Bunker was accusing EMK of reckless bias, U.S. pacification officials were writing their own bitter internal reports about South Vietnamese corruption: "The primary interest of GVN officials in Bien Hoa Province is money. . . . Unless major revisions are brought about . . . there is only to be a continuation of the same ordeal with the accompanying frustrations, inactions, corruption." See Gibbons, *U.S. Government*, Part V draft, quoting Pentagon Papers, Vol. II, 406–7.

164 **the Tet holidays:** JAF interview with Daniel Ellsberg. FRUS, 1964–1968, Volume VI, Vietnam, Jan.–Aug. 1968, Editorial Note 33. Adam Walinsky OH, JFKL. Daniel Ellsberg, Memorandum for the Record, "Impact of the VC Winter-Spring Offensive," Feb. 28, 1968, AW-JFKL. Theodore White, "The Tet Offensive, 1968"; Chrono Jan. 31, 1968; Chrono March 11, 1968, TW-JFKL. NYT, March 10, 1968.

The news that Westmoreland wanted another 206,000 troops was a contributing factor to the decline of support for the war after Tet. "That particular leak probably changed the policy. Because of it, you know, that just raised such a storm on the Hill that [LBJ] just couldn't do it," said Walinsky. Walinsky believed that RFK's office leaked the news of the Pentagon troop request to the *New York Times*, and that RFK got the information from Daniel Ellsberg. Ellsberg confirmed to the author that he gave the information to RFK—but said that the *Times* got the same data from another source, unconnected to the Kennedys.

Ellsberg was an early source for EMK's staff, which shared Ellsberg's written critiques of the war with RFK. "He and Dave Burke were playing real cloak and dagger, sneaking around street corners, meeting outside of hotel lobbies, that kind of stuff," said Walinsky. By 1968, Ellsberg was advising both RFK and EMK.

Ellsberg would become famous in 1971 after leaking the Pentagon Papers to the *Times* with the peripheral assistance of a former EMK aide, Dun Gifford. Then, when the *Times* was ordered by a federal judge to stop publishing the papers, Gifford was "absolutely critical," said Ellsberg, in persuading him to give a set of the secret documents to the *Washington Post*, which carried on for the muzzled *Times*. See Ellsberg, *Secrets*, 202; Schlesinger, *Robert Kennedy*, 843.

165 **the dark maze:** "Notes of the President's Meeting with General Earle Wheeler, JCS and General Creighton Abrams," March 26, 1968, FRUS, 1964–1968, Volume VI, Vietnam, Jan.–Aug. 1968, 156.

165 **unrelenting pressure to challenge:** JAF interviews with William vanden Heuvel, Peter Edelman. Ted joined in the meetings of Kennedy advisers, without his brother on Oct. 8 and Oct. 17 and with Robert on hand on Dec. 10. EMKOH-UVA. E. Barrett Prettyman OH, JFKL. Roche to LBJ, Dec. 18, 1967; Watson, "WMW Conversation with Larry O'Brien," Jan. 24, 1968, LBJL. For "music" see Sylvia Wright remembrance, undated, AS-NYPL, also in Stein and Plimpton, *American Journey*, 232. Schlesinger, *Robert Kennedy*, 846. O'Donnell, *Common Good*, Open Road Integrated Media Edition, 470, 536, and 546: "Teddy hated the 'you must run' crowd," who defined the choice as one of moral courage, said Kenneth O'Donnell. "They would go on and on, as if Bobby was the only one who could stop the madness. Teddy resented the pressure it put on Bobby, thought the times were dangerous. He felt that Bobby could still have an effect on the course of the war and wait and run in

1972." EMK had given RFK similarly practical advice in 1964, urging him to run for the Senate in New York rather than campaign for the vice presidential nomination. "Teddy was the strongest that he ought to run for Senate," O'Donnell said.

166 **Ted was intransigent:** Goodwin to RFK, "Conversation with EMK on Feb. 13," JFKL. Eugene McCarthy won twenty of the twenty-four delegates awarded in New Hampshire and finished within a few hundred votes of Johnson in the total votes cast.

167 **The final council:** "Conversation with Richard Goodwin, April 28, 1969," AS-NYPL. *Time,* Mar. 22, 1968. NYT, March 15, 1968. William vanden Heuvel OH, UVA. Boomhower, *Indiana Primary,* 25. Chafe, *Never Stop Running,* 287. EMKOH-UVA. Schlesinger, *Robert Kennedy,* 846, 850; see also Schlesinger diary, March 17, 1968, partially reprinted in Schlesinger, *Journals,* 282–84.

168 **"a terrible feeling":** The scenes at Hickory Hill are from Schlesinger's diary, and included in his biography of RFK. So is his conversation with JKO. See Schlesinger, *Robert Kennedy,* 855–57. David Burke OH, UVA: "Ted was opposed to Bobby's running for the presidency, because he had a feeling of dread. . . . He thought Bobby was volatile and hence vulnerable to some crazy human who was looking for a twofer or some historic moment." See also Dun Gifford OH, UVA, who listed EMK's concerns about RFK: "A, he might not win, and B, he might get killed." Edelson to Bayh, "The Man for All Reasons," March 18, 1968, Bayh-IU. O'Donnell, *Common Good,* Open Road Integrated Media Edition, 548.

169 **Robert now raged:** RFK address to students at Kansas State University, March 18, 1968. The audio and a transcript of the speech are available on the KSU website.

169 **to the "boiler room girls":** Esther Newberg, Rosemary Keough OH, JFKL. JAF interviews with Nance Lyons and Rosemary Keough Kerrebrock. See Dun Gifford OH, UVA: "They were very valuable people, smart and strong. It was a closed access, big room with no windows and a lot of phone lines . . . ultra top secret." The other term for the boiler room operation was "The Hen Party." See Dun to The Hen Party, April 8, 1968; also "Key Inside People," with list of boiler room assignments; memo to Stephen Smith; Memo from Dave Hackett to Boiler Room, Dun Gifford papers, JFKL.

169 **did not look promising:** JAF interview with Jerome Grossman. Roche to LBJ, "Massachusetts Primary," Dec. 6, 1967, LBJL. NYT, Dec. 1, 4, 1967. A robust peace movement in Massachusetts was backing McCarthy. Had EMK run as a favorite son, the McCarthy forces would have branded him as a stalking horse for the president. So EMK remained neutral, and when LBJ then declined to enter the primary, he ceded the state and its seventy-two delegates to McCarthy. See McCarthy, *Year of the People.*

169 **Ted Kennedy dispatched:** JAF interview with Michael Riley, Gerard Doherty. EMK memo, March 21, 1968, RFK 1968 Presidential Campaign Papers, JFKL, cited in Boomhower, *Indiana Primary.*

170 **its marching band:** JAF interviews with Gerard Doherty, Michael Riley, Louie Mahern. Gerard Doherty OH, UVA. See also Doherty, *They Were My Friends,* chapter 4. See also Boomhower, *Indiana Primary,* 2008, an insightful single-volume account of the primary. Riley, Mahern, and fellow young Democrat William Schreiber were the nucleus of early Kennedy supporters.

171 **backed his man:** JAF interviews with Michael Riley, Gerard Doherty. Notes of Morning Meeting at Hickory Hill, April 3, 1968: "RFK thinks Indiana is the *key* . . . thinks he will win in Oregon and California but they will fall apart if Indiana is lost. Analogy to West Virginia. McC kids will flood the place—must be countered," Dun Gifford papers, JFKL. Martin Plissner to CBS Special Events and Election Units, April 15, 1968, TW-JFKL. David Halberstam, "Travels with Bobby Kennedy," *Harper's,* July 1968. EMKOH-UVA. Gerard Doherty OH, JFKL. Halberstam, *Odyssey.*

171 **Robert campaigned furiously:** JAF interviews with Michael Riley, Gerard Doherty. EMKOH-UVA. Notes of Morning Meeting at Hickory Hill, April 3, 1968; see also Doherty to Smith, "Campaign Personnel in Indiana and Their Financial Support," April 13, 1968, both Dun Gifford papers, JFKL. Richard Goodwin OH, McCarthy Historical Project, EM-MHS. Gerard Doherty OH, JFKL. David Burke OH, UVA. Boomhower, *Indiana Primary,* 39–43, 75. Doherty memo, March 22, 1968, RFK 1968 Presidential Campaign Papers, JFKL, cited in Boomhower, *Indiana Primary,* 9. NYT, April 10, 1968. Edgar Berman diary, April 1, 11, 15, 1968, CS-MHS. WP, April 14, 1968. Paul Wieck, "The Indiana Trial Run," TNR, May 11, 1968. Hal Higdon, "Indiana: A Test for Bobby Kennedy," NYT, May 5, 1968. David Halberstam, "Travels with Bobby Kennedy," *Harper's,* July 1968. *Newsweek,* May 19, 1968. Halberstam, *Odyssey.*

172 **Johnson's national address:** JAF interviews with Michael Riley, Lou Mahern. David Burke OH, UVA. David Burke OH, JFKL. The limits of human memory are intriguing. Of those who were with EMK at the moment Johnson announced he was abdicating, one said EMK was eating a club sandwich, another said it was a chicken sandwich, and the third said just as certainly that it was an ice cream cone.

Roche to LBJ, "Conversations with Members," March 21, 1968. Notes of Meeting at Hickory Hill, Friday, April 19, 1968; Gifford "Fragments," 1968; Notes of Meeting, April 1, 1968; Notes of Morning Meeting at Hickory Hill, April 3, 1968; "Night Reading," Ty Fain, May 15, 1968, Dun Gifford papers, JFKL. With Johnson out of the race, Sorensen spelled out the Kennedy strategy at the April 1 strategy meeting. "RFK will be nominated and elected without a single vote from the South. Key is in Indiana. If we beat McCarthy in Nebraska, Indiana, Oregon, California, South Dakota; if we carry election for delegates in DC; win in West Virginia; district delegates in New York, we will have sizable jump," he said. "McCarthy voters will come with us. . . . We have reason to believe we will get Illinois."

173 **the grieving crowd:** Robert Kennedy, "Statement on Assassination of Martin Luther King, Jr., Indianapolis, Indiana, April 4, 1968," JFKL. "To tame the savageness of man, and to make gentle the life of this world" is a quotation that RFK borrowed from scholar Edith Hamilton's work on ancient Greece, which he took to reading after JFK died. RFK most memorably included it in his extemporaneous remarks on the evening that King was assassinated, and EMK adopted the sentiment. See Thomas Rollins OH, UVA, and JAF interview with Thomas Rollins. See also Boomhower, *Indiana Primary*, chapter 4, "The Speech." RFK's address is also available on YouTube.

174 **Robert Kennedy won:** JAF interview with Michael Riley. RFK's reception in the nonprimary states was "cold as hell," David Burke recalled. David Burke OH, JFKL. State-by-state analysis, with suggested EMK duties, March 25, 1968; Owens to EMK, May 7, 1968; Kirk to Gifford, May 8, 1968, Dun Gifford papers, JFKL. Newfield, *Robert Kennedy*, 299–300. Kennedy garnered 42 percent of the Indiana vote, Branigin 31 percent, and McCarthy 27 percent. The notes of Theodore White, who was in RFK's room as the returns were broadcast, read "Bobby growls: 'That's not the way I was brought up.'" White notes, Indiana primary, TW-JFKL.

174 **Charisma, and cash:** JAF interviews with Michael Riley, Lou Mahern. Michael Riley, Jerry Kretchmer interviews, LT-CU. Reese to O'Donnell, April 4, 1968; O'Brien to EMK, April 27, 1968; "Materials," April 27, 1968, Dun Gifford papers, JFKL. On Racine background see Kennedy, *The Fruitful Bough*, 49. Riley said he distributed $100,000 in Indianapolis alone. Mahern remembers getting $10,000, with the bills still in their Federal Reserve wrappers. See also Boomhower, *Indiana Primary*, 104.

Lawrence O'Brien told Humphrey that the RFK campaign spent a million dollars in Indiana "They bought the militants, the churches, the negroes, the community center leaders," Humphrey told an aide. "Larry says he disapproved of this, but Bobby overrode him." The Branigin campaign, said Humphrey, got its own $200,000 infusion from the Johnson-Humphrey team. See EMKOH-UVA and David Burke OH, JFKL. See also Edgar Berman Diary, EB-MHS and CS-MHS.

175 **"Bobby and California":** EMKOH-UVA. "Notes of Morning Meeting at Hickory Hill," April 3, 1968, Dun Gifford papers, JFKL. On Oregon see David Burke OH, JFKL.

Ten: To Sail Beyond . . . the Western Stars

176 **election night rally:** SFC, June 6, 1968. SFE, June 5, 1968. John Seigenthaler OH, UVA. Sixties: Hunter S. Thompson, *Fear and Loathing in Las Vegas*, New York: Popular Library, 1971, 66–68, 178–180.

177 **tide of killing:** "The grotesque horror of Senator Kennedy's killing convulses the body politic again in this astonishing, incredible and frightening year," *Time* magazine correspondent Neil MacNeil

would write his editors that week; MacNeil dispatch, June 6, 1968, NM-DC. "The greatest immediate danger arising out of the . . . assassination of Senator Kennedy is the rapidly developing sense of national guilt and the feeling there is a sickness in our society," wrote aide George Reedy to LBJ, June 5, 1968, LBJL.

177 **It was a smashmouth year:** David Burke OII, UVA. SFE, June 5, 1968. Emma Rothschild, "Notes from a Political Trial," *New York Review of Books*, July 10, 1969. The Kempton telegram is from Goodwin, *Remembering America*, and Jon Bradshaw, "Richard Goodwin: The Good, the Bad, and the Ugly," *New York* magazine, Aug. 18, 1975. For smashmouth and Black Panthers also see Didion, *White Album*. For portents see Schlesinger, *Robert Kennedy*, 908–9, 912. Chester, Hodgson, and Page, *Melodrama*, 352. There was a frightening "hysterical dimension" to the crowds that surged from the sidewalks to surround Robert Kennedy's car, said William vanden Heuvel in his UVA oral history: "There was nobody more intensely hated . . . and more intensely loved."

177 **dose of charisma:** John Seigenthaler, David Burke OH, UVA. John Seigenthaler interview, AC-JFKL. SFC, June 6, 1968.

178 **shot three times:** EMK-TC. John Seigenthaler OH, UVA. John Seigenthaler, taped interview, LD-WYO. John Seigenthaler interview, AC-JFKL. Moldea, *Killing*. SFE, June 5, 1968.

179 **controlling his emotions:** JAF interview with John Seigenthaler. David Burke OH, UVA. SFE, June 5, 1968. Jacobs, *Rage*. According to Jacobs, EMK liked to tell the story of how Burton had bullied an uncertain Air Force officer: "This is Congressman Phillip Burton. I am standing here with Senator Edward Kennedy, whose brother has just been shot and who may be the next president of the United States. You are at a point I call a career decision, Major. Either you get that plane now or your career is over."

On Humphrey see Edgar Berman diary, June 5, 1968, CS-MHS. Berman's diary lists two different times for the Humphrey-EMK call. The earlier time is more likely, as in both versions it includes the request for a government airplane to fly a neurosurgeon from Boston, which was made before EMK left San Francisco.

179 **Kennedy remained silent:** EMKOH-UVA. Robert Fitzgerald, John Seigenthaler, David Burke OH, UVA. John Seigenthaler interview, AC-JFKL. SFE, June 5, 1968.

179 **first saw his brother:** EMKOH-UVA. John Seigenthaler, Dun Gifford, Milton Gwirtzman OH, UVA. Gifford remembers him arriving in Los Angeles as "grim . . . like a frozen man he was so angry. . . . He had figured out by then that Bobby was really going to be sick, if he made it." Mankiewicz and Swerdlow, *As I Was Saying*, 159. Manatos to LBJ; Hill to LBJ, June 5, 1968, LBJL. Joseph Kraft OH, JFKL. Komisarow et al., "The Assassination of Robert F. Kennedy: An Analysis of the Senator's Injuries and Neurosurgical Care," *Journal of Neurosurgery*, June 2018. The Associated Press, after consulting experts, said Kennedy faced "an

indefinite life of limited usefulness" if he survived. David Hackett OH, JFKL. Stein, *American Journey*. On RFK death see also Goodwin, *Remembering America*.

180 **Lowenstein told Kennedy:** John Tunney OH, UVA. John Tunney, Milton Gwirtzman interview, AC-JFKL. Kennedy recalled Lowenstein's comment in his memoir: EMK-TC, 272.

180 **"the political whirlwind":** The pressure on EMK was immediate. As in *Hamlet*, the funeral meats furnished the marriage table. While RFK was dying, Humphrey and his staff were analyzing what EMK could add to the ticket. Humphrey and McCarthy discussed it at a meeting on the eve of RFK's funeral, where McCarthy told Humphrey that EMK was a "lightweight" and not fit to be a heartbeat away from the Oval Office. See Edgar Berman diary, June 5, 7, and 8, 1968. In the hours after RFK's death, the *Times* prepared an analysis of EMK's political prospects and reported "talk" of a Humphrey-Kennedy ticket. See NYT, June 7, 1968. Within a week after RFK's death, EMK was getting memos from his staff on the need to make a decision about the vice presidential nomination; see Gwirtzman, AC-JFKL. And also as RFK was dying, the *New York Times* had an advance obituary for EMK set in type. For that and more on the Lowenstein encounter, see Honan, *Survivor*, 129–30: "He had suddenly become a major figure in national politics—conceivably even his party's presidential nominee." See also WP, June 8, 1968.

180 **"we know death":** JAF interviews with Michael Schwartz, James Doyle. Fred Dutton OH, JS-JFKL. Frank Mankiewicz OH, JFKL. Regarding death, JKO, "As a matter of fact, if it weren't for the children, we'd overlook it." On Air Force One see Gaither to Johnson, June 6, 1968, LBJL. NYT, June 7, 1968. WP, June 3, 2018. *Newsweek*, June 16, 1968. Honan, *Survivor*, 128.

182 **the cool cathedral:** Milton Gwirtzman, John Culver OH, UVA. Ronnie Eldridge, Carter Burden, Art Buchwald, Dun Gifford OH, JS-JFKL. NYT, June 7, 8, 1968. TNY, June 15, 1968. "Ted had just lost his greatest friend, the closest brother he had ever had; he had no sleep," Gwirtzman said. "He was really in very difficult shape."

182 **his brother's funeral:** Milton Gwirtzman, John Culver, William vanden Heuvel, Paul Kirk OH, UVA. JAF interview with William vanden Heuvel. NYT, June 9, 1968. Speech notes, AW-JFKL; John Culver OH, JFKL. BG, Sept. 30, 1968.
"When Jack Kennedy was a senator . . . he had his eyes on the presidential prize," said Paul Kirk. "When Bobby was a senator, he had his eyes on the prize. When Senator Ted Kennedy came to the Senate, because of the normal actuarial tables, as a first matter I think he decided, *This is where I'm going to be*. . . . Now the actuarial tables are violently upset." See Paul Kirk OH, UVA.
For RFK text see Robert Kennedy, "Day of Affirmation Address," University of Cape Town, South Africa, June 6, 1966, JFKL: "Each time a man stands up for an ideal, or acts to improve the lot of others, or strikes out against injustice, he sends forth a tiny ripple of hope, and crossing each other from a million different centers of energy

and daring those ripples build a current which can sweep down the mightiest walls of oppression and resistance."

Eleven: Wildness

184 **Ted was weighted:** NYT, June 16, 1968. BG, June 16, 1968.

184 *Mira* **carried Ted:** Dun Gifford OH, UVA. Hadley Harbor: Joseph Gargan interview, LD-KS. *Life*, Nov. 1, 1968.

185 **its consort, despair:** EMKOH-UVA. JAF interviews with Patrick Kennedy, Victoria Reggie Kennedy. See also John Tunney, David Burke, Gerard Doherty, Milton Gwirtzman OH, UVA.

186 **"He had a hard time":** Dun Gifford OH, UVA. EMKOH-UVA. The press tracked EMK and his political future that summer. See BG, June 22, July 6, Sept. 30, 1968. NYT, July 10, 24, Aug. 14, 1968. WP, July 20, 1968. BH, July 22, 1968. *Newsweek*, Aug. 5, 1968. Burns, *Camelot Legacy*, 148. Hersh, *Education*, 334. Rogers, *Look*, March 4, 1969. See White, *Making, 1968*, 331: "Anguished and brooding, numbed by love, hurt and shock, grieving for his murdered brother, he had earlier given friends days of concern that he might abandon politics altogether and retreat into some inner silence."

186 **"thought of Bobby":** EMK-TC, 279. North Star: EMK-TC, 274–75. Kennedy was helped in the writing of his memoir by the accomplished journalist and biographer Ron Powers.

187 **"a fallen standard":** CR, Sept. 4, 1968. "Points Concerning Senator Edward Kennedy's Speech," Aug. 24, 1968, LBJL. NYT, Aug. 22, 1968. BG, Aug. 22, 1968.

187 **Humphrey-Kennedy ticket:** Edgar Berman Diary, Aug. 23, 30, 1968, CS-MHS. In their meeting, EMK deterred Humphrey from choosing Sargent Shriver as a running mate. Shriver had his own national ambitions, and had angered the clan when, during RFK's campaign, he accepted LBJ's offer to serve as ambassador to France. It was perceived as an act of disloyalty.
Humphrey dangled the nomination before EMK all summer. His willingness to have Kennedy as a running mate was reported in the *New York Times* within a week of RFK's death, on June 11, 1968. It was a steady theme in the press, and in Humphrey's meetings with his advisers. Humphrey told his aides that he "respected and loved John, and actually sort of liked Bobby," but "felt closer to Teddy than anyone else in the family." There were tangible moves in July, when Humphrey met with Stephen Smith and Theodore Sorensen and urged them to persuade EMK to join the ticket. They closed no doors, but cited Humphrey's support of the Vietnam War as a major obstacle. See Edgar Berman diary, July 13, 16, Aug. 18, 21, 22, 23, 1968, EB-MHS. See also BR, June 10, 1968; *National Observer*, June 17, 1968; BG, July 20, 23, 26, 27, 1968; WP, July 20, 1968; NYT, July 11, 24, 26, 27, 1968.

188 **zeniths of ambivalence:** There is much discussion about the effect of the Kennedy assassination on Eugene McCarthy in the McCarthy Historical Project oral histories at the University of Minne-

sota. "The same bullet that killed Bobby Kennedy may well have penetrated McCarthy because between that moment . . . and Chicago, Gene McCarthy didn't seem to be the same man," said campaign ad man Jack Canaan. "The lift, the light, the glee of the campaign disappeared," said Arleen Hynes. "He gave up," said Frances Julian. See John Shattuck, Erwin Kroll, Frances Julian, Jack Canaan, Thomas McCoy, Don Peterson, Arleen Hynes OH, EM-MHS.

Conversely, if the war was the overriding issue, why didn't the Kennedy forces unite behind McCarthy after the assassination? The clan was not temperamentally suited to play the role of supporting actors. "The Kennedys were quite willing to give up their lives," a McCarthy supporter marveled, "but not one ounce of political power." See Robert M. Smith OH, EM-MHS.

188 **Kennedy for President!:** The notion of drafting Kennedy as a presidential candidate was independently initiated by former Ohio governor Michael DiSalle on July 13, 1968. See DiSalle to Bayh, July 14, 1968, and Bayh to DiSalle, Aug. 6, 1968, Bayh-IU. It was embraced by various Democratic officials, most notably Jesse Unruh, Speaker of the California Assembly. See NYT, July 14, 15, 1968. On McGovern's role, see "Vietnam and the 1968 Election," Remarks by Senator George McGovern, Platform Hearing of Kennedy Volunteers, Los Angeles, CA, July 27, 1968; Announcement by Senator George McGovern, Aug. 10, 1968; Statement by William J. vanden Heuvel, Aug. 14, 1968, GM-Princeton.

188 **Daley wished to speak:** JAF interviews with William vanden Heuvel, Dan Rostenkowski. Stephen Smith was weighing his own political career in New York, and so allowed a *New York* magazine reporter, Peter Maas, to accompany him to Chicago for the convention. Maas's Oct. 7, 1968, article, "Ted Kennedy—What Might Have Been," gave a behind-the-scenes look into the Kennedy camp. See also Richard Goodwin, "The Night McCarthy Turned to Kennedy," *Look*, Oct. 15, 1968.

On Daley see John Criswell to Kim Jones, July 27, 1968; on Daley press conference and Fred Panzer, Memorandum to the President, June 22, 1968; on Harris poll, LBJL. See also *Newsweek*, Aug. 5, 1968. *New York Daily News*, July 26, 1968. BG, July 26 and 27, 1968. NYT, July 25, 27, 1968. EMK-TC, 272–73. Robert Shrum OH, UVA. Bradlee, *A Good Life*, 212–13.

The Stonington phone booth call was described by William vanden Heuvel in 1970, when it was a fresh memory, to Burton Hersh, and cited in *Education*, 338–39. It appeared as well in bits and pieces in the press in late July 1968. EMK spoke about the call in his oral history at UVA but—apparently mistakenly—said it took place during the Democratic convention.

On Kennedy's wariness, see Chalmers Roberts to Theodore White, Dec. 2, 1968, TW-JFKL. See also Al Lowenstein OH, McCarthy Historical Project, EM-MHS.

189 **promote a Kennedy candidacy:** JAF interviews with William vanden Heuvel, Barbara Souliotis. William vanden Heuvel OH, UVA. WP, Aug. 26, 1968.

190 **a mighty peak:** JAF interviews with William vanden Heuvel, Paul Kirk, James Doyle. David Burke, John Tunney, John Culver, Milton Gwirtzman, John Seigenthaler OH, UVA. William Daley interview, LT-CU. Richard Goodwin interview, AC-JFKL. Galbraith to EMK, Sept. 5, 1968, JKG-JFKL. Al Lowenstein, David Mixner, Richard Stout, Don Edwards OH, McCarthy Historical Project, FM-MHS. See also *New York* magazine, Oct. 7, 1968. Honan, *Survivor*, 38. Goodwin, *Look*, Oct. 15, 1968. Warren Rogers, "Ted Kennedy Talks About the Past, and His Future," *Look*, March 4, 1969. ("We had it. . . . All he had to do is say yes," Smith said.) BG, Aug. 27, 29, 1968. WS, Aug. 28, 1968. "Kennedy Wave Sweeps over the Convention" was the headline in the *New York Times* on Tuesday, Aug. 27, 1968.

McCarthy said later that Smith told him, "Teddy wouldn't go for it if he had to fight with me. I told him he wouldn't have to fight with me. I told him I was willing to give all the strength I had to Kennedy on the first ballot, or any ballot." See Edgar Berman Diary, Aug. 30, 1968, CS-MHS.

Lowenstein believed that, save for a few holdouts, the McCarthy delegates would have flocked to Kennedy whether McCarthy urged them to or not. "McCarthy could have stood like King Canute, and not kept votes from going to Ted Kennedy," he would say in his oral history.

There are several fine accounts in the 1968 campaign books of the events in Chicago. On the Kennedy boom see Witcover, *Dream*, 329–32; Chester, Hodgson, and Page, *Melodrama*, "The Ted Offensive," 564–76; and White, *Making, 1968*, 328–33.

191 **"Coos Bay, Oregon":** JAF interviews with Matt Storin, Trixie Burke. Clymer, *Edward M. Kennedy*, 122. Another version has Kennedy saying, "I want you guys to know that I expect you to be around in 1976 when I call from Coos Bay, Oregon, and tell you to get out there in a hurry because Jay Rockefeller is about to whip my ass in the Oregon primary." See WSJ, May 5, 1972. See also Rogers, *Look*, March 4, 1969, and Shrum, *No Excuses*, 78. You cannot choose your time, EMK told Shrum: When the door was open you had to go through it.

On *Julius Caesar* see Honan, *Survivor*, 165. In June 1969 Kennedy mused about the sentiment when talking to an Associated Press reporter, Joseph Mohbat. "The thing about being a Kennedy," he told Mohbat, "is that you come to know there's a time for Kennedys, and it's hard to know when that time is, or if it will ever come again."

191 **could-have-beens:** David Burke, Milton Gwirtzman, Neil MacNeil OH, UVA. Hersh, *Education*, 351. For "vulnerable" see *Look*, March 4, 1969. Kennedy was emotionally torn, and doubted his own abilities, said Burke. He usually worked through such feelings by intensive study and calculation. "When he prepares for something . . . he has books, he has endless documentation, papers. Because he's never, ever sure he has it all," Burke said. But now, "Mayor Daley said, 'If you want to have the nomination for President of the United States, you could have it tomorrow morning. . . . Come into town, and Chicago will be stood on its ear and you will, by acclamation. . . .'

"Ted said, 'I don't know what I stand for. I don't know where I am. I don't know what my preparation is. I haven't looked at it. I haven't thought about it. I haven't talked to enough people. . . .'
"There was not time to talk to people. This was underway. The momentum was there, and the madness was in the air," said Burke. "Suddenly the presidency . . . something that may have been in the back of his mind, was now staring him in the face."

192 **being ripped apart:** David Burke, Milton Gwirtzman OH, UVA. Al Lowenstein OH, McCarthy Historical Project, EM-MHS. Schlesinger to Harriman, *Letters*, Aug. 29, 1968, 375. Evans and Novak, "Why Ted Refused," BG, Aug. 29, 1968. NYT, Aug. 29, 1968. White, *Making, 1968*, 326–331. Chester, Hodgson, and Page, *Melodrama*, 576–78. On Joan's fears see Betty Hannah Hoffman, "Joan Kennedy's Story," LHJ, July 1970.
EMK was almost drafted anyway. He put out the word, late Tuesday night, that he would not be a candidate. Early on Wednesday, he called and spoke to Humphrey as the vice president was having breakfast with Daley. EMK said he was disavowing all efforts to make him the nominee, and Daley then swung the Illinois delegation to Humphrey.
Yet a rump group of Black delegates, Lowenstein, and other McCarthyites, still hoping to stop Humphrey, conspired to nominate EMK for president over his wishes. Their effort dissolved just as the civil rights figure Fannie Lou Hamer of Mississippi was preparing to put EMK's name in nomination. See Frank McDonald, Mark Siegal, Phil Moore OH, McCarthy Historical Project, EM-MHS. See also Edgar Berman diary, Aug. 28, 1968, CS-MHS, and Edgar Berman diary, Aug. 28, 1968, EB-MHS.

193 **"right to stop it":** White, *Making, 1968*, 331. Galbraith to EMK, Sept. 5, 1968, JKG-JFKL.

193 **now the flagbearer:** Dun Gifford OH, UVA. *Life*, July 17, 1970. Ted was now "a solitary figure," RK told the magazine. "There is no point denying that he is—and for the rest of his life will be—alone."

194 **assassination attempts:** JAF interview with William vanden Heuvel. Al Lowenstein OH, McCarthy Historical Project, EM-MHS. John Tunney, John Culver, William vanden Heuvel, Robert Shrum OH, UVA. When Edward Kennedy's FBI file was released in 2010 it was found to contain hundreds of pages on threats to his life. In addition to his brothers, the civil rights leaders Martin Luther King, Medgar Evers, and Malcolm X were gunned down in the 1960s. Lowenstein himself would be shot and killed in 1980; Kennedy would give the eulogy.

195 **a psychological wreck:** JAF interviews with Patrick Kennedy, Victoria Reggie Kennedy, Kandy Stroud. EMKOH-UVA. John Tunney, John Culver, David Burke, Gerard Doherty OH, UVA. Anne Taylor Fleming, "The Kennedy Mystique," NYT, June 17, 1979. "T.M.B.S.": See *Life*, Aug. 1, 1969.

196 **premier anodyne for Ted:** JAF interviews with Patrick Kennedy, Victoria Reggie Kennedy. David Burke, John Tunney OH, UVA. "right size": Caro, *Master*, 136. Helga Wagner: WP, May 16, 1978,

March 13, 1980; Helga Wagner interview, "Cover-Up," *People* magazine podcast, Elizabeth McNeil editor, Christina Everett producer, June 21, 2018; *Palm Beach Daily News*, Nov. 22, 2013; NYT, March 12, 1980; see also Hersh, *Intimate*, 508.

197 **flagbearer for a restoration:** Gwirtzman to Marshall, Dec. 4, 1968, with attached memo, BM-JFKL.

198 **so 1968 passed:** "Address of Senator Edward M. Kennedy on the Urgent Need for International Action to Meet Humanitarian Needs in the Nigerian Civil War," Jan. 22, 1969, SJC-NARA. Woozy: see *Look*, March 4, 1969. NYT, Sept. 20, 22, 1968. On House of Representatives, see Dun Gifford interview, AC-JFKL. On Humphrey, see Glenn Weaver interview, CS-MHS.

198 **challenging Russell Long:** Charles Ferris, David Burke OH, UVA. Charles Ferris OH, SHO. Charles Ferris, Dun Gifford interviews, AC-JFKL.

199 **erratic and unpredictable:** Peabody, *Leadership*, chapter 12. *Newsweek*, Jan. 13, 1969. NYT, May 25, 1977. WP, Dec. 31, 1968, Jan. 6, 1969. David Burke, Charles Ferris OH, UVA. Charles Ferris OH, SHO. Said Ferris about Mansfield, "He knew exactly what I was doing, and it was very convenient because there were never any Mansfield fingerprints."

200 **youth and vigor:** Paone to Clymer, June 6, 1997, with Muskie remarks from Democratic caucus, AC-JFKL. David Burke, Charles Ferris OH, UVA. Honan, *Survivor*, 135. *Time*, Jan. 10, 1969. *Newsweek*, Jan. 13, 1969. Peabody, *Leadership*, chapter 12.
Despite appeals from Kennedy and intermediaries like Galbraith, Eugene McCarthy stuck with Long, who had done him favors as Finance chairman. When asked why he would support Kennedy for president in Chicago, but not for the lowly job of whip, McCarthy replied, "I can think of a lot of people I would like to see as Pope but would not like to see as my pastor." See Galbraith to EMK, Jan. 2, 1969, JKG-JFKL. *Time*, Jan. 10, 1969. NYT, Dec. 31, 1968, Jan. 4, 1969. WP, Jan. 2, 5, 1969.
Peabody's 1976 study of leadership challenges in the House and Senate from 1955 to 1974 is a scholarly and colorful text. Hersh, who was following Kennedy around in 1968 and 1969, gives a similarly detailed and stylistic account of the contest in his 1972 biography, *Education*, 355–62.

201 **the ABM program:** FRUS, 1969–1976, Volume XXXIV, National Security Policy, 1969–1972, Note 25. EMK remarks, CR, Feb. 4, 1969. Address by Senator Edward M. Kennedy before The Economic Club of Detroit, April 8, 1969. WP, Feb. 2, 1969. NYT, Feb. 2, 9, 1969. "We had to have it to be able to agree to forgo it," Nixon wrote in his memoirs. See Nixon, *RN*, 415–17. CQW, July 11, 1969. *Science*, May 16, Aug. 8, 1969. Carey Parker, Dun Gifford OH, UVA. Ralph Nader Congress Project, Citizens Look at Congress, Edward M. Kennedy, 1972.

201 **Kennedy's high profile:** Owens to EMK, "Your Leadership on ABM," April 10, 1969, JFKL. Chayes and Wiesner, *ABM*. Carey Parker OH, UVA. David C. Phillips, "Ballistic Missile Defense: Evolution of the Decision-Making Process," System Development Corporation, Nov. 1969. WP,

April 10, 1969. *Science*, May 16, Aug. 8, 1969. NYT, April 2, 6, 8, 1969. Kennedy's inscription in the copy of the book he gave to Dun Gifford was to the effect: "All because they tried to put a couple of crummy missiles in North Andover."

202 **the Democratic front-runner:** Haldeman diary, April 8, 1969, Buchanan to Nixon, March 19, 1969, RNL. David Burke OH, UVA.

202 **a marquee name:** David Burke OH, UVA. NYT, April 5, 1969. "A Tribute to Martin Luther King, Jr. by Senator Edward M. Kennedy in Memphis, Tennessee," April 4, 1969. Diary of White House Leadership Meetings, Oct. 7, 1969, GFL.

203 **spare the killer's life:** JAF interview with Dolores Huerta. *Imperial Valley Press* (California), May 19, 1969. *El Malcriado*, United Farm Workers, May 1–31, 1969. Burke quoted in Hersh, *Education*, 366. On Sirhan: EMK to Younger, May 18, 1969, reprinted in WP, May 22, 1969. *Time*, May 30, 1969.

204 **the concerned neighbors:** Milliken to EMK, Sept. 26, Oct. 15, 1968; EMK to Milliken, Oct. 8, 1968, BM-JFKL. Years later, the boys would confirm their rowdy behavior. They called themselves the Hyannis Port Terrors: see Lawford, *Symptoms*, 97; Collier and Horowitz, *The Kennedys*, 373–75.

204 **call it Hamburger Hill:** JAF interview with Trixie Burke. David Burke, Dun Gifford OH, UVA. WP, May 21, 1969. *Time*, May 30, 1969. *Life*, June 27, 1969. NYT, May 21, 23, 30, June 3, 8, 1969. BG, May 28, 1969. Zaffiri, *Hamburger Hill*, 275–76. CQW, May 23, 1969. David Burke told a reporter that Kennedy had been fuming over the indifferent attitude about the costs of war displayed by Henry Kissinger in a forty-five-minute meeting at the White House in early May. See also John Lindsay memo to *Newsweek* editors, May 22, 1969, AC-JFKL.

205 **To carry on:** WP, June 9, 11, 1969. Associated Press, June 18, 1969. Guthman to Noyes, June 20, 1969; Flug to Marshall, undated, summer 1969; Marshall to EMK, July 3, 1969, BM-JFKL. Kennedy wrote the note about carrying on to Christie Coombs, whose husband was killed in the September 11, 2001, attacks. Barack Obama cited it in his eulogy for Kennedy. See "Eulogy at the Funeral Service for Senator Edward M. Kennedy in Boston, Massachusetts, August 29, 2009," UCSB.

206 **took him to Alaska:** *Time*, April 18, 1969. BR, April 11, 1969. BA, April 13, 1969. BH, April 12, 1969. NYT, April 8, 11, 1969.

206 **tasting the pressures:** EMK-TC, 281–82. BA, April 13, 1969. Hersh, *Education*, 379. Clymer, *Edward M. Kennedy*, 134. Wright quoted in Anne Taylor Fleming, "The Kennedy Mystique," NYT, June 17, 1979. John Lindsay memos to *Newsweek* editors, April and May 22, 1969, AC-JFKL. The hip flask was noted by Brock Brower in *Life*, Aug. 1, 1969. NYT, April 10, 1972. Lindsay was turned off by the "arrogance" Kennedy displayed on the way home from Alaska, the kind that "young men born to wealth and new to power exhibit." But his recklessness also hinted at a yearning for escape or self-destruction, said Lindsay, in the fact that Kennedy controlled his drinking on military aircraft in Alaska, "where the damage would have been

minimal," and then "just plain let himself go on the flight home where it would do the most damage."

207 **wildness in his brain:** Joseph E. Mohbat "For Ted, the Fun Has Gone Out of Politics," BG, June 8, 1969. John Tunney, Edmund Reggie, David Burke OH, UVA. See also William vanden Heuvel OH, UVA: "This is a person who's in trouble. . . . He didn't have any real help in handling those enormous burdens of grief and responsibility that were put upon him. . . . He didn't have a good marriage. He'd lost the two men in his life who meant the most to him. . . . All this had to greatly affect his subconscious behavior."

Twelve: Chappaquiddick

209 **boiler room girls arrived:** The activities of the Chappaquiddick partygoers, except where noted, are taken from the transcript of their testimony at the January 5–8, 1970, inquest (Inquest re Mary Jo Kopechne, Dukes County, Docket No. 15220) in Edgartown.

210 **Kopechne could be quiet:** JAF interviews with Clark Hoyt, Melody Miller, Michael Schwartz, Rosemary Keough Kerrebrock. Melody Miller OH, UVA. McKeown to Joseph and Gwen Kopechne, July 24, 1969; Kopechne family history from Potoski and Nelson, *Our Mary Jo*. *Time*, Aug. 1, 1969. *The Citizens' Voice* (Wilkes-Barre, PA), July 26, 2015.

211 **work with Robert Kennedy:** Melody Miller OH, UVA. Potoski and Nelson, *Our Mary Jo*. Keough's remarks are from the BBC documentary *Chappaquiddick*.

211 **"the whole world":** April Reese to Kopechnes, July 20, 1969, *Our Mary Jo*.

212 **"girls" were career women:** JAF interview with Nance Lyons. Nance Lyons OH, UVA. Marie Ritter OH, McCarthy Historical Project, Eugene McCarthy papers, University of Minnesota. Rosemary Keough Kerrebrock interview, LT-CU. Esther Newberg and Rosemary Keough OH, JFKL.

212 **Kennedy would attend:** JAF interviews with Nance Lyons, Melody Miller, Charles Tretter, Rosemary Keough Kerrebrock. EMK interview, Spotlight team, BG, 1974. Dun Gifford interview, AC-JFKL. Keough in *Philadelphia Bulletin*, Aug. 24, 1969, and BBC documentary *Chappaquiddick*. Joseph Gargan, James Smith, Paul Redmond interviews, LD-KS. Martin Nolan, Melody Miller, Dun Gifford OH, UVA.

213 **one-lane humpbacked bridge:** Inquest testimony. JAF interview with Timothy Leland. On JBK pregnancy, see JBK interview, LD-WYO.

214 **high-spirited event:** Inquest testimony, EMK and others. EMK testified that he was "absolutely sober" when he drove off the bridge. Stan Moore, who was a friend of Richards, told Leo Damore that Kennedy had three rum-and-Cokes in twenty minutes on the Richards boat; Gargan, who was not there for the entire interval, disputed that. See the Moore and Gargan interviews in LD-KS. The account of EMK's cookout drinking—three drinks—is from Arthur Schlesinger's diary, Aug. 27, 1969, AS-NYPL. The historian and Kennedy family friend spoke with EMK, Ethel Kennedy,

and Stephen and Jean Kennedy Smith in the days immediately after the accident and recorded their unvarnished comments in a revealing, unpublished Aug. 27 entry.

The Joe Jr. and JFK lockup tale is from Damore, *Cape Cod Years*. For regatta tales see also Benjamin Smith interview, Joan and Clay Blair, Clay Blair papers, University of Wyoming, excerpted in Blair and Blair, *Search*, 56.

214 **not a great party:** JAF interviews with Charles Tretter, Nance Lyons, and Rosemary Keough Kerrebrock. Charles Tretter, Nance Lyons OH, UVA. Schlesinger diary, Aug. 27, 1969, AS-NYPL. Because her mother was ill, Betty Gargan missed the party as well.

215 **decidedly unglamorous men:** Miller OH, UVA. JAF interviews with Charles Tretter, Nance Lyons, Rosemary Keough Kerrebrock. Inquest testimony. Newberg quoted in *Time*, Aug. 1, 1969. Schlesinger diary, Aug. 27, 1969, AS-NYPL.

215 **"I needed to get out":** This guarded account, from EMK's memoir *True Compass*, was the first to indicate that EMK and Kopechne shared an emotional moment at the party, and that it stirred a response in them "to get out, to get outside." His motivation to leave, therefore, was not entirely what he always said it was: to catch the late ferry and rest up for the next day's races. This raises the question whether he and Kopechne wanted to continue their talk elsewhere on the island, perhaps while walking on the beach, as some of the boiler room girls speculated. EMK would report a similar need to escape, prompted by another emotional discussion about RFK's death, when testifying in the rape trial of his nephew William Smith in Palm Beach in 1991. EMK set the events of that Palm Beach night in motion by waking his son and his nephew and taking them drinking. EMK-TC. In his oral history, Dun Gifford reasoned that EMK and Kopechne were going to the beach. "It's pretty clear where they were headed. They never got there," he said. "That could have been innocent or not." See Dun Gifford OH, UVA.

216 **car left the bridge:** EMK generally said that he could not remember how he got free, but the senator told his doctor on the afternoon of the accident that he had "grabbed the side of an open window and pulled himself out." See Michael Putzel and Richard Pyle, Associated Press Special Assignment Team report, Feb. 1976. EMK, John Farrar inquest testimony. EMK statement to police, July 19, 1969, and televised speech, July 25, 1969. EMK Spotlight interview, BG, 1974. EMK-TC. Schlesinger diary, July 25, Aug. 14, 27, 1969, AS-NYPL. Dun Gifford OH, UVA. Reckless driving was a family tradition: see Nancy Morse, Torbert Macdonald oral histories in Clay Blair papers, University of Wyoming; Harry Muheim, "Rich, Young and Happy," *Esquire*, Aug. 1966; Patsy Mulkern OH, JFKL.

216 **Kennedy's subsequent behavior:** Concussion: A doctor's statement (Affidavit of Doctor Robert D. Watt) was included in the record of the inquest as exhibit No. 27. EMK would label his behavior as "irrational and indefensible and inexplicable" (BG,

Spotlight interview, 1974). He wrote in his memoir, "I am not proud of these hours. . . . I was afraid. I was overwhelmed, I made terrible decisions" (EMK-TC, 291). In his televised address on the night of July 25, 1969, he said, "I regard as indefensible the fact that I did not report the accident to the police immediately. . . . I was overcome . . . by a jumble of emotions—grief, fear, doubt, exhaustion, panic, confusion, and shock." The Stephen and Jean Kennedy Smith remarks are from Schlesinger diary, Aug. 14, 27, 1969, AS-NYPL: "Jack and Bobby saved me," Kennedy told his sister Jean. "They got me out of that car."

217 **there was recklessness:** John Tunney OH, UVA. Lindsay *Newsweek* memo. Schlesinger diary re JFK health, July 19, 1959, AS-NYPL.

217 **proposing a rationale:** Gargan interviews, LD-KS. Markham, Gargan inquest testimony. Damore, *Senatorial Privilege*, 77–80. Stephen Smith account of the accident and rescue attempts, Schlesinger diary, Aug. 14, 1969, AS-NYPL. It is worth noting that in July 1974, rather than calling the Coast Guard, EMK and his crew rescued five amateur mariners whose boat had gotten swamped. See BG, July 24, 1974. *Boston Herald American*, July 25, 1974.

218 **a forgiving interpretation:** EMK inquest testimony. EMK interview, Spotlight team, BG, 1974. Schlesinger diary, Aug. 14, 1969, AS-NYPL. Damore, *Senatorial Privilege*, 80.

219 **less charitable explanation:** Jean Kennedy Smith told Schlesinger that her brother "panicked" and hoped "to find some way to cover it all up." After visiting the Kennedys at Hyannis Port, Schlesinger informed his diary, in an Aug. 27, 1969 entry, that EMK had told Gargan and Markham "not to alarm the girls at the cottage. They accepted this unquestioningly as an instruction and evidently supposed that Ted would report the affair to the police. . . . and he didn't know how he could cover up; there was no plan, but he told [Gargan and Markham] to say nothing and do nothing until they heard from him. Then, in some confused way, he made his appearance before the hotel clerk, perhaps to establish an alibi." Here is another instance where EMK used *True Compass* to disclose more information than he previously acknowledged. In *Senatorial Privilege*, in 1988, Damore wrote of how Kennedy proposed, then abandoned, a scenario in which Kopechne was alone in the car and drove off the bridge herself. The book was dismissed. It was not until *True Compass* was published that Kennedy admitted to "devising and rejecting scenarios . . . that flashed compulsively through my feverish thoughts." EMK-TC. See Gargan interviews, LD-KS, and Anderson columns, Aug. 1969.

In her oral history with the Miller Center at UVA, Nance Lyons said that the idea of blaming the crash on someone else was still alive on Saturday morning but that "the women . . . derailed that brilliant idea. We refused to go along." JAF interviews with Charles Tretter, Nance Lyons, Rosemary Keough Kerrebrock.

220 **plunged into the water:** EMK, Gargan inquest testimony. Charles Tretter OH, UVA. JAF interview,

Charles Tretter. Damore, *Senatorial Privilege*, 81–91. EMK called Wagner, he said later, to try to track down Smith, who was on vacation in Spain. See Helga Wagner interview, "Cover-Up," *People* magazine podcast, June 21, 2018. EMK tried unsuccessfully to get in touch with Burke Marshall as well.

221 **wants to establish an alibi:** Stephen and Jean Kennedy Smith accounts, Schlesinger diary, July 25, Aug. 14, 27, 1969, AS-NYPL. MacNeil to *Time* editors, July 25, 1969, NM-DC. Damore interviews, Joseph Gargan et al., LD-KS. On July 27, the *New York Times* reported that "the most damaging innuendo had to do with speculation that the Senator had delayed reporting the accident—and possibly even thereby sacrificed whatever slight chance there might have been of saving Mary Jo—in the hope of somehow keeping his name out of it." The suspicion that Kennedy was drunk surfaced immediately as well: see *Time*, Aug. 1, 1969.

221 **awed local authorities:** The *Boston Globe* Spotlight team, after studying the law and legal practices in similar cases, reached the conclusion that "inept" and "apprehensive" investigators showed "overwhelming deference to Kennedy's power and prestige." But they did so by their own volition, the reporters Stephen Kurkjian and Gerard O'Neill concluded, "not from a conspiracy among themselves or with Kennedy." Given their lack of evidence and the "archaic" laws, the Spotlight team concluded, the local prosecutors would be "highly unlikely" to have obtained a conviction for manslaughter or vehicular homicide. See BG, Oct. 31, 1974, April 4, 2018. JAF interviews with Stephen Kurkjian, Gerard O'Neill. As conservative publisher William F. Buckley Jr. wrote in Oct. 1969, "Nobody believes that Senator Kennedy committed a serious crime. . . . There are advantages to being a public figure. . . . But there are disadvantages, as anyone can see who asks himself how much call would there be for an inquest or a grand jury proceeding if it had been other than Senator Kennedy involved," *National Review*, Oct. 7, 1969.

Leo Damore's book *Senatorial Privilege*, and the transcripts of his interviews at Kent State University, give a thorough account of the state of the law, the challenges posed to the prosecutors by the statute, and how the prosecution and defense attorneys reached the deal in which Kennedy pleaded guilty. Damore did find instances where sympathetic Massachusetts authorities performed favors, cloaked evidence, and leaked information to the Kennedy camp, but he unearthed no orchestrated cover-up.

The overriding attitude may best have been captured by the local special prosecutor, Walter Steele, who later told the BBC, "I was not going to participate in any unjust assault on Kennedy, because I am a Democrat. . . . On the other hand, I was not going to suppress anything. I was going to do my job—but not happily." See BBC documentary *Chappaquiddick*.

See also *Newsweek*, July 28, Aug. 3, 1969; *Time*, Aug. 1, 1969; and NYT, July 21, 1969.

224 **compose a statement:** James Arena, John Farrar inquest and exhumation hearing testimony. Arena transcript and personal notes, LD-KS. Arena,

police report, July 19, 1969. Damore, *Senatorial Privilege*. For a full-length and immediate account of the behavior of the Massachusetts authorities, see Olsen, *Bridge*. Olsen conducted his interviews with Arena, Steele, Farrar, Dr. Donald Mills, and others in the days and weeks after the accident, when what they had witnessed was fresh in their minds, and before they were staggered by ill-founded allegations that they had orchestrated a cover-up.

On whether Kopechne could have been saved, see *Newsweek*, Aug. 3, 1969, in which diver Farrar is quoted saying that there was no way Kennedy could have rescued Kopechne from the inky waters, but that there was a "slim chance" she may have been saved if rescue workers had been called to the wreck immediately.

The Associated Press's eight-month investigation of the accident in 1975–76 cited experts in concluding that "breathable air drained quickly from the car" through the three broken windows and the floor drains, and that the car "would not retain an air pocket sufficient in size to enable an individual to remain in the vehicle, breathe the trapped air and survive."

225 **"Death by drowning":** Donald Mills inquest testimony. Mills exhumation hearing testimony. Dun Gifford OH, UVA. Olsen, *Bridge*. In his UVA oral history, Gifford describes his examination of Kopechne's body, and his finding that her hands and fingernails showed no marks of a frantic attempt to escape. On the lurid claims, see Schlesinger diary entries, July 25, Aug. 27, 1969, AS-NYPL.

226 **hold the statement:** Registry inspector George Kennedy inquest testimony. Damore, *Senatorial Privilege*.

Thirteen: Inquest

228 **"that he panicked":** Schlesinger diary, July 25, Aug. 14, Aug. 27, 1969, AS-NYPL. NYT, July 20, 23, 1969. Theodore Sorensen, Milton Gwirtzman OH, UVA. "He was wearing . . . quite ostentatiously, a huge bandage around his head, possibly because he needed it and his doctors insisted on it but possibly to gain some sympathy," said Sorensen.

228 **senator suffered a concussion:** The doctor's statement (Affidavit of Doctor Robert D. Watt) was included in the record of the inquest as exhibit No. 27. While in college, the author was awakened by a friend who, riding alone to see me one morning, had driven his car off a bridge. It flipped and landed upside down in a creek. Stunned, he had crawled from the wreck and hiked for more than a mile to my door, passing occupied homes on the way.

229 **"still-possible charge of manslaughter":** JAF interview with William vanden Heuvel. Milton Gwirtzman OH, UVA. Schlesinger diary, July 25, 1969, AS-NYPL. Hersh, *Education*, 413. "Had they been able to prove DUI [driving under the influence] the consequences would have been much more severe," William vanden Heuvel, an adviser, recalled in his UVA oral history. Theodore Sorensen OH, UVA.

230 **her own raw feelings:** Chellis, *Living*, 86. See also JBK interview, AC-JFKL.

230 **to Helga Wagner:** Helga Wagner interview, "Cover-Up," *People* magazine podcast, Elizabeth McNeil editor, Christina Everett producer, June 21, 2018. Chellis, *Living*, 86.

230 **was maddeningly inconsistent:** EMK, Markham inquest testimony. Schlesinger diary, Aug. 14 and 27, 1969, AS-NYPL. Milton Gwirtzman, Theodore Sorensen, John Tunney, Martin Nolan OH, UVA. *Life*, Oct. 3, 1969.

232 **the minimum sentence:** Damore, *Senatorial Privilege*. Walter Steele, Robert Clark interview transcripts, LD-KS. BG, NYT, July 26, 1969. Transcript of hearing, NYT, July 26, 1969.

233 **plea for forgiveness:** Sorensen, Gwirtzman OH, UVA. NYT, BG, July 26, 1969. Nixon compared the speech to his Checkers talk as well. Nixon recognized how the accident crippled Kennedy's presidential prospects in the era of the nuclear arms race. "God. That's a damn thing to have on his record. . . . Didn't he say in the speech: 'I panicked'?" See Nixon and Ehrlichman, April 18, 1972, RNL.

234 **more magical thinking:** Galbraith to EMK, July 26, 1969, JKG-JFKL. NYT, July 31, 1969. Look gave many interviews, and testified at the exhumation hearing, and again at the inquest. For examples of the impact of his testimony, see NYT, July 27, 1969; WP, Nov. 11, 12, 1979; *Los Angeles Times*, Dec. 24, 1979; and the Associated Press Special Assignment Team report, Feb. 1976.

235 **"with a blonde":** Olsen, *Bridge*, 272.

235 **moved to exhume:** Herbert Miller to Burke Marshall, Dec. 15, 1969, with attached ruling of Judge Bernard Brominski, Burke Marshall papers, JFKL. Exhumation hearing transcript, LD-KS. NYT, Oct. 21, 22, 1969. Schlesinger diary ("Steve . . . says, in addition, that Dinis does not think that Ted was in the car; he claims that it would have been impossible for anyone to have got out of the upturned car in several feet of water. The presumable implication is that the accident was staged and, I suppose, that Mary Jo was murdered.") Aug. 27, 1969, AS-NYPL. JBK interview, LD-WYO.

237 **legal team triumphed:** Damore, *Senatorial Privilege*, 310–13. BG, July 26, 1991.

239 **"the moral strength, to call":** Inquest transcript and Report: James A. Boyle, Justice, District Court, Dukes County, Inquest: re Mary Jo Kopechne, Docket No. 15220. The transcript of Kennedy's inquest testimony, Judge Boyle's report, and the findings of the exhumation hearing (In the Court of Common Pleas of Luzerne County, Pennsylvania, In Re: Kopechne, Criminal 1114 of 1969) can be found, as well, in the appendices of Lange and DeWitt, *Chappaquiddick*.

240 **finding of negligence:** JAF interview with Alan Simpson. John Tunney OH, UVA. New York mayor John Lindsay, after hearing about the accident, had tartly recited some rules of politics: Never travel alone, "never take girls out, and never drown them." See Schlesinger diary, July 29, 1969, AS-NYPL. The first part of that advice—don't go out alone with a woman—had been conveyed to his sons by Joseph Kennedy; Ted was "quite stupid" to ignore it, his mother concluded. See RK, Coughlan interview, Jan. 1972, RCP-NW. Golfer: Sherrill, *Last Kennedy*, 129.

241 **"very sad summer":** JBK to Schlesinger, Oct. 27, 1969, AS-NYPL. JAF interview with Patrick Kennedy. Kennedy and Fried, *Common Struggle*, 34.

241 **with customary stoicism:** "Personal Notes of Mrs. Joseph P. Kennedy Regarding Ted's Tragic Accident, July, 1969," Saturday, July 19, 1969, KFP-JFKL.

242 **the patriarch succumbed:** JAF interview with Burton Hersh. Dallas with Ratcliffe, *Kennedy Case*, 338–40, 349. RK diary, KFP-JFKL.

242 **"almost completely devoid":** EMK-TC, 294–95. Hurt anymore: NYT, Nov. 28, 1971. "There was a joy in the guy that came from deep within," EMK's Harvard classmate Richard Clasby told LHJ in January 1972. "Now he has to reach for the enjoyment. It's not spontaneous anymore. The fun he gets out of things never lasts very long."

Fourteen: Unlikely Savior

244 **weighed the repercussions:** H. R. Haldeman diary, RNL, July 19, 20, 21, 22, 26, 30, 1969. Safire, *Fall*. Farrell, *Nixon*.

245 **a dark side:** JAF interview with Thomas Korologos. Paul Kirk OH, UVA. See also Kissinger on Nixon's Kennedy obsession, Schlesinger diary, Jan. 27, 1975, AS-NYPL. Caulfield to Ehrlichman, July 31, 1969, RNL. Senate Watergate Report (The Final Report of the Senate Select Committee on Presidential Campaign Activities), June 1974. WP, Aug. 1, 1973. Ulasewicz and McKeever, *Private Eye*.

246 **pulled Kennedy aside:** Safire, *Fall*. EMK interview, June 2, 1997, AC-JFKL. O'Connor to Clymer, AC-JFKL. In his diary, Haldeman reports that Nixon passed on good advice to Kennedy: "Told him how he understood how tough it was, etc. Said he was surprised to see how hard the press had been on him. . . . Realize they are your enemy at heart even if they *do* like you, because their prime motivation is the story." Haldeman diary, RNL, Aug. 4, 1969.

246 **taste of defeat:** CQA, 1969, 271–73, 335–36. Gun Control Act: In a 65–19 vote, his colleagues freed vendors of rifle and shotgun ammunition from having to register their customers.

246 **was hemorrhaging clout:** JAF interview with Matthew Storin. Milton Gwirtzman, Mary Frackleton OH, UVA. EMK to O'Brien, Dec. 16, 1970, TS-UMASS. John William Honan, "Can Teddy Kennedy Survive His Reputation?," *New York Times Magazine*, May 24, 1970. Dun Gifford and Fred Dutton interviews, AC-JFKL. CQW, Dec. 12, 1969. Andrew Butrica and Steven Dick, "Electronics Research Center," National Aeronautics and Space Administration. On the draft, see White House News Summary, Sept. 30, 1969, quoted in Ambrose, *Triumph*. "As you indicate in your letter," Kennedy wrote to a constituent, "President Nixon has not looked upon Massachusetts with special kindness." Kennedy to Andreis, Jan. 1, 1971, EMK-JFKL. Peabody, *Leadership*, 395.

247 **Republican southern strategy:** Richard Nixon interview, Aug., 1968, Haldeman notes, White House Special Files, Nixon Presidential Returned Materials Collection, RNL. JAF interview with Lee Atwater.

247 **cloaked in euphemisms:** See Balzano to Nixon, "The Ethnic Vote in the 1972 Election," Dec. 31, 1971; Harry S. Dent, "Report on Meeting of Southerners and Other Conservatives with the President," Aug. 6, 1970, White House Special Files, Nixon Presidential Returned Materials Collection: Contested Materials, RNL. Dan T. Carter lecture series, "George Wallace, Richard Nixon and the Transformation of American Politics," Baylor University, April 15 and 16, 1991. John A. Farrell, "Divided We Stand," *National Journal*, Feb. 25, 2012. For background on Nixon's southern strategy see aide John Ehrlichman's memo, *Witness to Power*, 222. The Nixon record on racial justice was strong in some areas—like its opposition to de jure segregation of public schools—but "the subliminal appeal to the antiblack voter was always in Nixon's statements and speeches on schools and housing," Ehrlichman recalled. The key, he said, was to cloak the issues so that a voter could "avoid admitting to himself that he was attracted by a racist appeal." On southern transformation, air-conditioning, and migration see Polsby, *How Congress Evolves*.

248 **"a Supreme Court judge":** Lee Atwater was a Republican Party chairman and adviser to Republicans Strom Thurmond, Ronald Reagan, and George H. W. Bush. Political scientist Alexander Lamis published excerpts of this 1981 interview, without attributing it to Atwater, in 1984. After Atwater's death in 1991, Lamis revealed his source. See Rick Perlstein, "Lee Atwater's Infamous 1981 Interview on the Southern Strategy," *The Nation*, Nov. 13, 2012.

248 **court to starboard:** JAF interviews with Wallace Johnson, Thomas Korologos. SJC executive session transcript, July 24, 1968; Sept. 10, 13, 1968; Fortas nomination files, SJC-NARA. John H. to McGovern, July 17, 1968, GM-Princeton. U.S. Senate Historical Office: "The Senate Rejects a Supreme Court Nominee." CQA, 1969, 337–49. John A. Farrell, "The Inside Story of Richard Nixon's Ugly, 30-Year Feud with Earl Warren," *Smithsonian* magazine, March 21, 2017. See also Abraham, *Justices*; Woodward and Armstrong, *Brethren*.

249 **Old South sensibility:** JAF interview with Birch Bayh. Bayh speech, Boston, Nov. 21, 1969, and Bayh constituent form letter, 1969; Connaughton to Bayh, Oct. 15, 1969; "The Haynsworth Nomination in Perspective," issue paper, 1969, Bayh-IU. Charles "Mac" Mathias OH, UVA. EMKOH-UVA. NYT, Sept. 21, 1969. CQW, Sept. 12, 1969. The Fortas scrap: "The methodology they used in stopping [the Fortas] appointment . . . was really what taught the rest of the Senate what to do when the Carswell and Haynsworth nominations came up," EMK aide James Flug recalled in 1990. Eastland aide John Holloman, in the same forum, agreed. See *America & the Courts*, C-SPAN, June 9, 1990. For a book-length account of the Haynsworth nomination see Frank, *Haynsworth*.

249 **the Haynsworth nomination:** JAF interviews with Birch Bayh and Jason Berman. Connaughton to Bayh, Sept. 30, 1969; Jerry to Senator, Nov. 1969, "Recent Press Coverage," Bayh-IU. Reuther to Eastland, Oct 15, 1969; AFL chronology: "Con-

flict of Interest Charge Against Judge Haynsworth"; Biemiller to Eastland, with analyses of Haynsworth ethics and record, Sept. 12 and 16, 1969; Haynsworth to Marion, Oct. 15, 1963; Rehnquist to Hruska, Sept. 1969; Haynsworth Nomination Files; *Hearings*, Sept. 17, 1969, all SJC-NARA. Burt Wides interview ("Kennedy was ineligible because . . . of Chappaquiddick. So Bayh took up the cudgels"), AC-JFKL. EMKOH-UVA. Alexander to Harlow, undated, Jan. 1970, RNL. James Flug-John Holloman interview C-SPAN, June 9, 1990. William Eaton, "Why Haynsworth Lost," *Chicago Daily News*, Nov. 22–23, 1969. CQW, Sept. 26, 1969. See also Kalman, *Sixties*. EMK made the front page once in the hearings—when he and Sam Ervin "erupted in heated argument" over a 1964 letter written by RFK as attorney general, clearing Haynsworth of bribery in the vending case. The letter was not exculpatory, EMK argued, as it covered only the charge of bribery, not a conflict of interest. See WP, Sept. 18, Nov. 23, 1969.

250 **indefatigable James Flug:** JAF interviews with Wallace Johnson, James Flug, Thomas Susman. Thomas Susman, Charles "Mac" Mathias OH, UVA. David Burke interview, AC-JFKL. James Flug interview, AC-JFKL. See also Rehnquist to Eastland, Sept. 19, 1969, Haynsworth nomination files, SJC-NARA. Looking back decades later, EMK called it a "not insignificant, but not significant" conflict of interest and expressed his regard for Haynsworth. He had no such regrets about Carswell, who he thought was "a buffoon." See EMKOH-UVA. "The ethical questions . . . were nonsense," Holloman said. "It was a smokescreen to block a man who was considered a very conservative appointment." James Flug-John Holloman interview, C-SPAN, June 9, 1990. NYT, Dec. 13, 1970. On Flug and the nominations see Ralph Nader Congress Project, Citizens Look at Congress, Edward M. Kennedy, 1972.

250 **Haynsworth was defeated:** CQA, 1969. Diary of White House Leadership Meetings, Oct. 14, 1969, Hartmann papers, GFL. Goldwater to Harlow, April 8, 1970; Alexander to Harlow, undated, Jan. 1970, RNL. See also Bobelian, *Battle*; Abraham, *Justices*; Frank, *Haynsworth*. To retaliate, Nixon prodded House minority leader Gerald Ford to initiate the impeachment of liberal justice William O. Douglas, a crude tactic that further alienated Robert Griffin. See Ehrlichman, *Witness*, 122, and MacNeil file to *Time* editors, April 16, 1970, NM-DC. See also Dean Kotlowski, "Nixon, the Senate, and Haynsworth Nomination," *The Nixon Presidency, Presidential Studies Quarterly*, Winter 1996.

251 **Carswell was nominated:** JAF interview with Jason Berman. Carswell chronology, Bayh-IU. Burger to Mitchell, April 4, 1969, Ehrlichman papers, Hoover Institution. Ed Roeder interview, AC-JFKL. NYT, Jan. 23, 1970. Abraham, *Justices*. Frank, *Haynsworth*. CQA, 1970, 154–62. After Haynsworth was defeated, the president ordered aide Harry Dent to look "farther South and further right": see Bruce H. Kalk, "The Carswell Affair: The Politics of a Supreme Court Nomination in the Nixon Administration," *American Journal of*

Legal History 42, no. 3 (July 1998). If Carswell was defeated, Nixon told GOP congressional leaders, "I will send them someone from Mississippi": see Diary of White House leadership meetings, Oct. 14, 1969, and March 3, 1970, GFL. See also James Flug-John Holloman interview C-SPAN, June 9, 1990.

251 **"we call Flug off"**: David Burke, Senate Aide A (Carey Parker) interview, AC-JFKL. Carswell chronology; Wilkins to Bayh, Jan. 28, 1970, Bayh-IU. CQA, 1970, 154–62. JAF interviews with Jason Berman, Burt Wides.

252 **"segregationist and white-supremacist"**: Carswell chronology, and Seymour to Edelman, Jan. 24 and 26, 1970, Bayh-IU. Journalist Richard Harris used the Carswell nomination as a window on the Senate's ways in long articles published in *The New Yorker* on December 5 and 12, 1970, which were gathered and published as a book, *Decision*; see 18, 26–27, 101. The Flug memo to Kennedy, January 24, 1970, is cited on page 37. Ed Roeder interview, AC-JFKL. Burt Wides OH, UVA. NYT, April 12, 1970.

252 **the lovefest marred:** Hearings before the Committee on the Judiciary, United States Senate, Nomination of George Harrold Carswell, Jan. 27, 28, 29, and Feb. 2, 3, 1970. Charles Horsky and Norman Ramsey, "Memorandum to Senators Tydings and Kennedy," April 2, 1970; "Judge Carswell: The Candor Question," undated staff memorandum; Carswell chronology, Bayh-IU. Harris, *Decision.* NYT, Jan. 28, 1970.

253 **"I smell blood"**: Harris, *Decision.* Carswell hearing, SJC, Jan. 27, 1970. JAF interview with Ralph Neas. CQA, 1970, 154–62. Transcript of remarks by Senator Robert Griffin, March 17, 1970, Bayh-IU. BG, March 29, 1970.

253 **could they stall:** Carswell chronology, Bayh-IU. CQA, 1970. Harris, *Decision.* The press then detonated another bombshell that made Mansfield's decision seem prescient: Carswell had been an organizer of the "Seminole Boosters," a segregated club supporting the Florida State University athletic program. Senators began to worry: What else was in his background?

254 **nation's legal establishment:** Carswell chronology; petition of former Supreme Court clerks, undated, 1970; "Key Data" compiled by "Law Students Concerned for the Court," Bayh-IU. Harris, *Decision.* NJ, April 4, 1970. "Opposition Chronology," CQW, April 3, 1970. Charles "Mac" Mathias OH, UVA.

254 **"Carswell's a boob"**: Ehrlichman, *Witness*, 126.

255 **"a lot of mediocre judges"**: James Flug-John Holloman interview, C-SPAN, June 9, 1990. Bayh speech to Fordham University Law School, April 21, 1970; Carswell chronology, Bayh-IU. MacNeil file to *Time* editors, April 10, 1970, NF-DC. Harris, *Decision.* Hruska was not alone in his anti-intellectualism. Senator Russell Long argued that a "C student" was preferable to the "upside-down, corkscrew thinkers" of the Warren court. See Abraham *Justices*, 7.

255 **Nixon reacted badly:** Carswell chronology, Bayh-IU. Diary of White House leadership meetings, April 7, 1980, GFL. Ehrlichman papers,

March 6, 1970 notes, Hoover Institution. MacNeil file to *Time* editors, April 10, 1970, NM-DC. NYT, April 20, 1970. Harris, *Decision.* "Subtle and skillful in his approach to the Chinese, he was stubborn and spiteful in his approach to the Senate," wrote one Nixon biographer: see Ambrose, *Triumph.*

255 **Senate rejected Carswell:** CQA, 1970, 154–62. "Presidential Statement to Congress: Nixon's Statements on Carswell Nomination Rejection," UCSB. "It is difficult—it is, in fact, impossible—to recall any Presidential statement in this century as intemperate and as divisive as the one issued by Richard Nixon," wrote Richard Rovere in the *New Yorker*, April 18, 1970. "To succeed by appropriating the rhetoric of George Wallace is really to concede the failure of his Administration." In the course of the nomination, Senator Robert Dole brought up the Morrissey debacle, charging EMK with hypocrisy. EMK noted wryly how, once his colleagues had signaled their dissatisfaction with poor Morrissey, he at least had the courtesy to withdraw the nomination, and that Carswell's supporters should now do the same. Tydings also evoked Morrissey's name, telling a swing vote—Senator Margaret Chase Smith—how hard it had been for him to split from the Kennedys in the Morrissey saga, but how he'd felt compelled to do the right thing, and maybe she should too.

255 **Blackmun would write:** CQA, 1970, 163–64. The defeat of Haynsworth and Carswell, wrote legal scholar John P. Frank, were "political retaliation" for what Nixon did to Fortas, "a sort of legislative murder in response to an executive assassination," and so transformed the character of Supreme Court confirmations. See Frank, *Haynsworth.*

256 **of moral behavior:** NYT, July 13, 1970, July 1, 1976. JAF interviews with James Flug, Jason Berman. Flug said the Democrats had reports of Carswell's sexual preferences but declined to use them in the 1970 confirmation fight, in part because they feared it was disinformation. "Did you know the whole time that Carswell was a homo?" Eastland asked him after the battle was over. "Mr. Chairman, we heard that about all your nominees. We figure we were being set up," Flug replied. James Flug, Ed Roeder interviews, AC-JFKL.

256 **"Investigators on Kennedy"**: Haldeman diary, April 9, 1970, RNL.

256 **"great silent majority"**: Richard Nixon, "Address to the Nation on the War in Vietnam," Nov. 3, 1969, UCSB.

256 **Nixon dispatched Agnew:** NYT, Oct. 6, 1971. On polarization see also Buchanan to Nixon, May 21, 1970, "Media Memorandum for the President," RNL, in which the speechwriter argues, "We are in a contest for the soul of the country now. . . . It will be their kind of society or ours; we will prevail or they shall prevail."

257 **clandestine air campaign:** Nixon was withdrawing troops and needed to bloody the North Vietnamese to buy time for Vietnamization of the war. For background see Kimball, *Nixon's Vietnam War*; Kissinger, *White House Years.*

257 **would invade Cambodia:** Nixon to Kissinger, Jan. 8, 1969, White House Special Files, Nixon Presi-

dential Returned Materials Collection, RNL.
Nixon "Address to the Nation on the Situation in
Southeast Asia," April 30, 1970, UCSB.
257 **vanished in the storm:** NYT, April 30, May 1,
1970. BH, May 3, 1970. Word of the inquest transcript's release pulled EMK from a White House
briefing on the Cambodia invasion; see Ehrlichman notes, April 30, 1970, Hoover Institution.
258 **"dealing with deities":** BG Spotlight Series, Oct.
27–31, 1974. "Address by Senator Edward M. Kennedy to the Advertising Club of Greater Boston and
the Broadcasting Executives Club of Greater New
England," Boston, May 1, 1970, SJC-NARA. Buchanan to Nixon, "Media Memorandum for the
President," May 21, 1970, RNL. NYT, April 30, May
1, 1970. BSA, May 3, 1970. BH, May 2, 1970. *Time,*
May 11, 1970.

Fifteen: Bubble and Toil and Trouble

259 **"world of loneliness":** Robert Byrd OH, Byrd-SU.
Robert Byrd OH, UVA. WP, Oct. 4, 1967.
260 **so he maneuvered:** Robert Byrd OH, Byrd-SU.
Robert Byrd OH, UVA. WP, Oct. 4, 1967.
261 **The animosity between:** Corbin, *Last Great Senator.* O'Donnell and Powers, *Memories.*
262 **Then came a clash:** Fred Harris, Joseph Tydings
OH, JFKL. JAF interview with Joseph Tydings.
Harris, *Does People.*
263 **make the Social Security bill:** Fred Harris, Joseph
Tydings OH, JFKL. CR, Dec. 14, 1967. Harris, *Does
People.*
264 **"dealing with men":** CR, Dec. 14, 1967.
264 **Don't get mad:** The saying is variously attributed
to Joseph P. Kennedy or Robert Kennedy or to the
Boston Irish in general. In his 1975 memoir, *Conversations with Kennedy,* Benjamin Bradlee called it
"that wonderful law of the Boston Irish political
jungle."
264 **Kennedy "leapfrogged over me":** Robert Byrd
OH, UVA.
265 **"Bubble and toil":** Robert Byrd OH, UVA. David
Burke OH, UVA. Owens to EMK, March 4, 1970,
EMK-JFKL. Charles Ferris OH, SHO. Wayne
Owens, Charles Ferris, Dun Gifford interviews, AC-
JFKL. David Burke recalled that EMK's goal was to
"make policy and attempt to apply pressures on issues, rather than merely seeing that the senators
would be on the floor. We would spend less time
getting cabs for the airport after a roll call vote—
the kind of thing that was traditional with the office." Burke interview in Peabody, *Leadership.* NYT,
June 30, 1970. Burke's reference to "bubble and
toil" is from the witches' scene in Shakespeare's
play *Macbeth.*
266 **washed the sweatshirts:** Two excellent books—
Bibby, Mann, and Ornstein, *Vital Statistics,* and
Davidson and Oleszek, *Congress and Its Members,* capture the change on Capitol Hill. See also Mark J.
Oleszek and Walter J. Oleszek, "Legislating in the
Senate: From the 1950s into the 2000s," author's
collection, and John A. Farrell, "The O'Neill
Speakership," U.S. House of Representatives, The
Cannon Centenary Conference: The Changing
Nature of the Speakership, Nov. 12, 2003, U.S.
Government Printing Office, 15–17.

266 **Bobby Byrd would:** George McGovern OH, UVA.
Charles Ferris interview, AC-JFKL. BG, Nov. 7, 1970.
267 **avidity was cloaked:** Charles Ferris OH, UVA.
George Smathers OH, SHO. TNR, Dec. 12, 1970.
WP, Oct. 4, 1967. NYT, Feb. 28, 1971. Peabody,
Leadership. "Serviceable and soft-spoken, toiling
and moiling, he is the Uriah Heep of the Senate":
see NYT, Oct. 12, 1971. Heep is the obsequious
villain in Charles Dickens's *David Copperfield.*
269 **Americans the right to vote:** JAF interview with
Pat Keefer. EMK to Byrd, Sept. 9, 1986, SHO.
Charles Ferris, Carey Parker OH, UVA. Charles
Ferris OH, SHO. Wayne Owens interview, AC-
JFKL. Carey Parker interview, Pat Keefer files.
Time, May 11, 1970. NYT, Feb. 23, March 13, 29,
Sept. 11, 1970. CQW, Sept. 25, 1971.
Dublin: Kennedy was denounced as a capitalist "para-
site" by rowdy Maoist protesters in Ireland and
heckled to a point even Nixon found objection-
able. See Nixon handwritten notation, Buchanan
to Nixon, March 16, 1970, RNL: "I take no comfort in this regardless who is the target." *Irish
Times,* Nov. 4, 1997. BH, May 2, 1970. The text of
the speech can be found at CR, March 17, 1970,
7775.
270 **poised to forgive:** Martin Nolan OH, UVA. BG,
Dec. 3, 1969, March 17, 18, 1970, July 11, 1993. *Chicago Daily News,* March 17, 1970. Murray Kempton,
"The Last Senator Kennedy," *New York Post,* Aug.
1969. Peabody, *Leadership.*
271 **like a dervish:** Kennedy to Harrison, Dec. 18,
1969; minutes, campaign staff meeting, Dec. 22,
1969, AC-JFKL. Kirk to Keedy, Dec. 22, 1970, TS-
UMASS. Paul Kirk OH, UVA. Burke to RK, Sept.
16, 1970, KFP-JFKL. NYT, Aug. 27, 1970. BH, Oct.
30, 1970. WP, Sept. 20, 1970. CQA, 1970. Kennedy
got 62 percent of the vote. JBK interview, AC-
JFKL.
271 **requisite political cover:** JAF interview with Richard Arenberg. On Massachusetts voters, see David
Burke OH, UVA. Rejecting EMK "would have
been a heretical act. You don't do that to Jack's
brother, to Bobby's brother."
272 **"couldn't justify Chappaquiddick":** JAF interview
with Joseph Tydings. Walter Mondale, David
Burke, Charles Ferris OH, UVA. Joseph Tydings,
Wayne Owens interviews, AC-JFKL. Bayh Chappaquiddick letters, 1969, Bayh-IU. For a more critical view, see Dole to Bomar, Nov. 11, 1971,
Dole-KU. Hart to Goodwin, Jan. 14, 1970; Hart to
Mykamp, Jan. 22, 1970, Hart-UM. EMK to
Mankiewicz, Aug. 6, 1969; Mankiewicz to Kennedy, Dec. 3, 1969, Frank Mankiewicz papers-
JFKL. Galbraith to Kennedy, July 26, 1969, Dec.
18, 1969; EMK to Galbraith, Sept. 7, 1969, JKG-
JFKL. CQW, July 25, Aug 1, 1969. *Life,* Oct. 3, 1969.
272 **on the whip race:** Martin Nolan OH, UVA. Robert
Byrd OH, Byrd-SU. George Smathers OH, SHO.
McGrory column, BG, Dec. 30, 1970. NYT, Nov.
12, 1970. BG, Nov. 18, 1970.
273 **trouble out west:** Kirk to EMK, Jan. 19, 1971, TS-
UMASS. EMKOH-UVA. WP, Evans & Novak, Nov.
12, 1970. Peabody, *Leadership,* chapter 13.
275 **a proxy ballot:** JAF interviews with Thomas
Korologos, James Wyatt, Ray Smock. Fite, *Richard*

B. Russell. Russell Long interview and vote analysis in Peabody, *Leadership,* chapter 13. BG, Jan. 22, 1971. NYT, Jan. 22, 1971.
275 **"a huge humiliation":** "After Chappaquiddick he lost. . . . That's right and that's why," said Burke. Charles Ferris, however, disagreed: "Bob Byrd got it because he was made for the job and Ted was not." See David Burke, Charles Ferris OH, UVA. See also Walter Mondale, Thomas Oliphant, Melody Miller, Carey Parker OH, UVA. EMKOH-UVA. Galbraith to EMK, Jan. 21, 1971, JKG-JFKL. *Christian Science Monitor,* Jan. 23, 1971. BG, Jan. 22, 1971.
EMK invited a few reporters back to his home that night for a "very wet" Irish wake, steeped in dark humor, the *Boston Globe*'s Thomas Oliphant recalled. Representative Morris Udall of Arizona, who had lost his challenge of Democratic Speaker John McCormack that week, phoned Kennedy to say, "As soon as I finish picking this liberal buck shot out of my ass, I'll come over and help you extract those liberal knives from your back." See NM-DC.
At the Gridiron Club dinner that spring, Kennedy told the assembled press and guests, "I want to take this opportunity to thank the 28 Democratic senators who pledged to vote for me—and especially the 24 who actually did." See Peabody, *Leadership,* chapter 13.
Toward the end of his career, in his oral history, Kennedy spun it as best he could. "With the exception of the losing part, it was good to get out of the whip's job because you get absorbed in the knick-knacks of the Senate," he recalled. "With my position in history, I had more ability to have an impact and influence in the Senate than from the position as whip. And since I was a target at that time of the Republicans, they had an opportunity to make life more difficult for me. If they knew that I had to go someplace, make a speech, they would delay the recessing of the Senate, and all those games were being played."

Sixteen: A Fortuitous Preoccupation

278 **faith and death and duty:** James Wechsler to file, copy to Schiff, "Conversation with Ted Kennedy, April 13, 1971," AS-NYPL. JAF interviews with Paul Kirk, Melody Miller, Thomas Rollins. John Seigenthaler OH, UVA. Federal Bureau of Investigation, Edward M. Kennedy, Mary Jo Kopechne files. BG, Sept. 24, 1973, March 18, 1980.
278 **an open door:** Honan, *Survivor,* 20. The book is an outgrowth of a series of articles he wrote for the *New York Times Magazine.* JAF interviews with Paul Kirk, Victoria Reggie Kennedy. *Time,* Nov. 29, 1971. "Go along quietly" is from Wechsler to file, copy to Schiff, "Conversation with Ted Kennedy, April 13, 1971," AS-NYPL. The cuff links, said Kirk, were worn by EMK for years in reverent memory of JFK.
278 **a good father:** Betty Hannah Hoffman, LHJ, July 1970. Edward M. Kennedy Jr., Kara Kennedy, Patrick Kennedy OH, UVA. Honan, *Survivor,* 166.
279 **the senator's marriage:** JBK acknowledged her fragile mental state, and her alcoholism, in interviews

with magazine reporters beginning in the mid-1970s. For confirmation and commentary see John Tunney, Lester Hyman, Melody Miller, Milton Gwirtzman, Betty Taymor, Stuart Shapiro, Michael Dukakis, Mary Frackleton, Wyche Fowler, Ellis Mottur OH, UVA; EMKOH-UVA; EMK-TC; and Paul Kirk, Lester Hyman, Ed Martin, Dun Gifford, Lawrence Horowitz, John Seigenthaler, Tip O'Neill interviews, AC-JFKL. The "pretty face" quote is from *Newsweek,* July 28, 1969. For descriptions of Joan's outfits see Lester David, "Joan—The Tormented Kennedy," LHJ, March 1974. See also NYT, April 21, 1971.
280 **the family's image:** Galbraith to EMK, June 9, 1971, JKG-JFKL For more on the debunking of the Kennedy myth, see Nixon and Haldeman and Colson, Aug. 5, 1971, White House tape, RNL, and Buchanan to Nixon ("Socially, Kennedy is out of touch with the political mood. The Jet Set, Swinger, See-Through Blouse cum Hot Pants crowd, the Chappaquiddick Hoe-down and Paris highjinks—the more publicity they all get, the better"), June 9, 1971, RNL.
280 **"jet set types":** Nixon and Haldeman and Ziegler, April 9, 1971, White House tape, RNL. In a 1972 interview, Joan admitted that she was "a little ridiculous" and "naive" when wearing provocative clothing to the White House and other events. "I was probably trying to get some attention for myself," she said. "I had really lost my sense of self-confidence. . . . The only thing I knew, that I was sure of, was that I was a very attractive young woman. I had a pretty good figure." See JBK interview, LD-WYO.
282 **these dominoes toppled:** LeRoy Goldman, Max Fine OH, UVA. Because Ben Smith had resigned to let Kennedy claim the seat immediately after the 1962 election, Kennedy had a few months' seniority over another senator on the health panel—Gaylord Nelson of Wisconsin—who was also elected in 1962, but not sworn in until January 1963. See Lippman, *Senator Ted Kennedy,* 217.
282 **community health centers:** Briefing sheet, "Kennedy Early Involvement with Neighborhood Health Centers," undated, SLC-NARA. Clymer, *Edward M. Kennedy,* 83–84.
283 **expected "great ferment":** EMK to Galbraith, Feb. 12, 1968, with "Proposed Health Legislation" attachment, JKG-JFKL. "Insurance for High Quality Medical Care," by EMK, CR, Dec. 16, 1969. "National Health Insurance and Health Security," by EMK, CR, Aug. 27, 1970. NJ, Dec. 27, 1969. EMK interview, AC-JFKL. Stuart Altman, David Burke OH, UVA. Nexon to EMK, Feb. 22, 1995, SLC-NARA. Wechsler to file, copy to Schiff, "Conversation with Ted Kennedy, April 13, 1971," AS-NYPL.
285 **launching a war on cancer:** EMKOH-UVA. Stan Jones, LeRoy Goldman, Phil Caper OH, UVA. Benno Schmidt, James Cavanaugh interviews, AC-JFKL. Mary Lasker OH, CU. Mukherjee, *Emperor.* Nexon and O'Rourke to EMK, Jan. 18, 1996, SLC-NARA. Cavanaugh to Cole to Nixon, draft, April 30, 1971, RNL. Jonathan Rhoads, "Recollections of the First Chairman of the National Cancer Advisory Board at the National Institutes of Health,"

and Alan Davis, "The Legislative Process of the National Cancer Act, 1970–71," both in *Cancer*, Dec. 15, 1996. "Nixon Buys Plan for Attack on Cancer," *Nature*, Jan. 29, 1971. Elizabeth Brenner Drew, "The Health Syndicate," *Atlantic Monthly*, Dec. 1967. John Iglehart, "Proposals for Cancer Research: A New Agency, or an Expanded NIH Program?" NJ, March 27, 1971. Langley Grace Wallace, "Catalyst for the National Cancer Act: Mary Woodard Lasker," *Concord Review*, Winter 2016. For a comprehensive account of the birth of the war on cancer, see Rettig, *Cancer Crusade*.

285 **in Captain Hook:** Ehrlichman to Morgan, Nov. 25, 1970; Haldeman diary, Jan. 21, 1971, Nixon and Haldeman, May 28, 1971, and Nixon and Kissinger, May 18, 1971, White House tapes, RNL.

286 **launch a preemptive strike:** LeRoy Goldman OH, UVA. Cavanaugh files, "Revised Health Game Plan," early 1971; Ehrlichman to Nixon, Dec. 16, 1970; Cavanaugh and Cole to Nixon, draft, April 30, 1971, RNL. Richard Nixon, "Annual Message to the Congress on the State of the Union," Jan. 22, 1971, UCSB. U.S. Senate, March 9, 10, and June 10, 1971, Conquest of Cancer Act of 1971, Hearings before the Subcommittee on Health of the Committee on Labor and Public Welfare; see Schmidt to EMK, March 22, 1971, in "Additional Information."

287 **new cancer agency:** LeRoy Goodman OH, UVA. Schmidt to Nixon, Dec. 8, 1970, RNL. EMK, statement on introducing the Conquest of Cancer Act, Jan. 25, 1971, AC-JFKL. Richard Nixon, "Special Message to the Congress Proposing a National Health Strategy," Feb. 18, 1971, UCSB. EMK comments, witness testimony, and Shannon to Smith, Feb. 24, 1971, "Additional Information," Conquest hearings. Arturo Casadevall and Ferric C. Fang, "Moonshot Science—Risks and Benefits," *mBio*, July–Aug. 2016. NJ, March 27, 1971. Rettig, *Cancer Crusade*.

288 **the turning point:** Richardson to EMK, and attachments, April 2, 1971; American Medical Association to EMK, March 15, 1971; National Academy of Science to EMK, March 15, 1971; Robst to Adams, May 13, 1971, "Additional Information," Conquest hearings Woods to Chapin and Haldeman, April 23, 1971; Ehrlichman memo to files, May 5, 1971; Cole and Ehrlichman to Nixon, May 6, 1971; Parker to Cole, May 19, 1971; Nixon and Haldeman and Kissinger, White House tape, April 28, 1971, RNL. Haldeman diary, April 28, May 11, 1971. Nexon and O'Rourke to EMK, Jan. 18, 1996, SLC-NARA. John Iglehart, "House Subcommittee Questions Wisdom of Establishing Independent Cancer Agency," NJ, July 31, 1971. Davis, "Legislative Process." Rettig, *Cancer Crusade*.

289 **a disease to be survived:** EMK, Benno Schmidt interviews, AC-JFKL. EMKOH, UVA. LeRoy Goldman OH, UVA. Cole and Cavanaugh to Nixon, draft, April 30, 1971; Nixon and Colson, White House tape, Dec. 23, 1971, RNL. Mary Lasker OH, CU. Nexon and O'Rourke to EMK, Jan. 18, 1996, SLC-NARA. Cancer is still the second-highest cause of death, claiming more than six hundred thousand lives in the United States each year. But

there has been significant progress in childhood cancers, and notable long-term declines in death rates for the four leading maladies—lung, colorectal, breast, and prostate cancer. See Rebecca Siegel, Kimberly Miller, and Ahmedin Jemal, "Cancer Statistics, 2020," American Cancer Society.

290 **a "decent interval":** Kimball, *Vietnam War Files*. Kimball, *Nixon's Vietnam War*. Kissinger, *White House Years*. Kissinger remarks, U.S. Department of State, "The American Experience in Southeast Asia, 1946–1975," Sept. 29, 2010. Ferguson, *Kissinger*. The destructive power of the bombing in Southeast Asia exceeded that of the Allied campaigns in World War II, including the atomic bombing of Hiroshima and Nagasaki. For statistics see Edward Miguel and Gerard Roland, "The Long Run Impact of Bombing Vietnam," National Bureau of Economic Research, 2006, and Clodfelter, *Vietnam in Military Statistics*. For Nixon's views of the morality of war, see Farrell, *Nixon*, 367, and Nixon White House tape, June 2, 1971, RNL.

291 **a more open policy:** Memorandum, Kissinger to Nixon, Sept. 29, 1969, with notes, FRUS, 1969–1976, Volume XVII, China, 1969–1972. Vanden Heuvel to Wakaizumi, "Scheduled trip to Japan by Senator Edward M. Kennedy," Sept. 9, 1965; Hoffmann to EMK, May 27, 1966, and EMK to Hoffmann, June 13, 1966; Beer to EMK, May 28 and July 18, 1966, and EMK to Beer, June 20, 1966, all EMK-JFKL. For examples of Kennedy tapping academic expertise see Burke to Shriver, July 13, 1966, and 1966 correspondence between EMK and Benjamin Schwartz and Richard Neustadt at Harvard and Lucien Pye and Jerome Wiesner at MIT, all EMK-JFKL. See also EMK to Galbraith, July 1 and 25, 1966, and Galbraith to EMK, Aug. 1, 1966, JKG-JFKL. "Statement by Senator Edward M. Kennedy," Center for the Study for Democratic Institutions, Santa Barbara, CA, Jan. 24, 25, 1969, and "Address by Senator Edward M. Kennedy before the National Committee on United States–China Relations," New York City, March 20, 1969, SJC-NARA. Jerome A. Cohen, "Ted Kennedy's Role in Restoring Diplomatic Relations with China," *Legislation and Public Policy* 14, no. 2 (2011): 347, Richard Nixon, "Asia After Viet Nam," *Foreign Affairs*, Oct. 1967. NYT, July 21, 1966, Jan. 25, Feb. 2, March 21, 1969. BG, May 4 and July 24, 1966.

292 **the country was then:** Larry Niksch, "The India-Pakistan War of November–December 1971: Background, Causes and the Role of American Diplomacy," Congressional Research Service, April 20, 1972. Archer Blood OH, ADST.

292 **a cataclysmic typhoon:** Alfred Sommer and Wiley Mosley, "East Bengal Cyclone of November, 1970," *Lancet*, May 13, 1972. Heitzman and Worden, *Bangladesh*. GAO report, "US Disaster Relief to Pakistan Following the November 1970 Cyclone," Feb. 23, 1972. The 1970 storm was the deadliest tropical cyclone in history. As a means of comparison, the deadliest U.S. hurricane and tidal surge, which struck Galveston in 1900, killed some ten thousand people.

292 **fumbling the response:** CR, Nov. 20 and 24, 1970. EMK press release, Nov. 20, 1970, SJC-NARA.

292 **bordered on genocide:** Senator Edward Kennedy, "Tragedy in Bengal: The Role of American Foreign Policy," *Washington Monthly*, Nov. 1971. "Questions for Mr. Blood on Conditions in East Pakistan," Kennedy staff, undated; Dale to Senator, re Pakistan, April 13, 1971; Jerry/Dale to Senator, re Hearing on Pakistan, June 25, 1971, SJC-NARA. Christopher Van Hollen, Archer Blood OH, ADST. Retzlaff and Metcalf, The Berkeley South Asia Study Group, "US Policy in South Asia 1971: A Tragic Failure," Jan. 25, 1972, GM-Princeton. ("There can be no doubt that the Pakistani authorities had embarked on a carefully thought-out plan of exterminating the intellectual and professional elite . . . and of cowing the remainder of the population by terror and intimidation," this panel of contemporary scholars concluded.) "The Events in East Pakistan, 1971," The Secretariat of the International Commission of Jurists, Geneva, 1972. WS, July 26, 1971. Bass, *Blood Telegram*, is a most instructive and complete account.

293 **leading congressional critic:** CR, April 1, May 18, June 2, 1971. "Relief Problems in East Pakistan and India, Part 1," Hearing before the Subcommittee to Investigate Problems Connected with Refugees and Escapees, Committee on the Judiciary, U.S. Senate, June 28, 1971. "Crisis in East Pakistan," Hearings before the Subcommittee on Asian and Pacific Affairs, House Committee on Foreign Affairs, May 11, 1971. "EMK Statements on Bangladesh," EMK statements, June 25, 28, 1971, and EMK to Rogers, April 6, 1971, and May 27, 1971, SJC-NARA. Chronology of EMK actions and statements, Embassy of Pakistan, undated, RNL. WP, July 5, 23, 1971. Bass, *Blood Telegram*, 201–3.

293 **"Don't squeeze Yahya":** Kissinger to Nixon, April 28, 1971, FRUS. Kissinger and Nixon, White House tape recording, June 4, 1971, RNL. Christopher Van Hollen, Harold Saunders OH, ADST. Christopher Van Hollen, "The Tilt Policy Revisited: Nixon-Kissinger Geopolitics and South Asia," in *The Regional Imperative: The Administration of U.S. Foreign Policy Towards South Asian States Under Presidents Johnson and Nixon* (Atlantic Highlands, NJ: Humanities Press, 1980). FRUS, 1969–1976, Volume XI, South Asia Crisis, 1971, contains many of the relevant administration documents, and transcripts of White House tapes. The refugee subcommittee files in the Senate Judiciary Committee collection (SJC-NARA) tell the congressional side of the story. Harold Saunders, "What Really Happened in Bangladesh," *Foreign Affairs*, July/Aug. 2014. "The most sexless, nothing, these people," Nixon told aides Henry Kissinger and H. R. Haldeman. "What about the black Africans? Well, you can see something, the vitality there, I mean they have a little animal-like charm, but God, those Indians, ack, pathetic." See Gary Bass, "The Terrible Cost of Presidential Racism," NYT, Sept. 3, 2020.

294 **attention to Bangladesh:** NYT, Aug. 2, 1971. "India and Bangla Desh," John P. Lewis diary of Kennedy trip, Sept. 20, 1971, SJC-NARA.

294 **"suffering and the misery":** Kennedy diary, "Thoughts for Speech from Tape," undated; Hilaly

to Kennedy, Embassy of Pakistan, Aug. 2, 1971; "For Press Inquiries: EMK India/Pakistan Trip," internal staff memo, undated, SJC-NARA. Nevin Scrimshaw interview, courtesy of Gary J. Bass. Lewis, "India and Bangla Desh."

296 **"the number of tortured":** "Thoughts for Speech from Tape," "Tape 1 of EMK Trip to India," taped diary of meetings with Indian officials, "Tape 3 . . . Meetings with Mrs. Gandhi," "Some Talking Points for PM Meeting," SJC-NARA. Nevin Scrimshaw, "A Trip to India with Senator Ted Kennedy," Feb. 21, 2012, courtesy of Gary J. Bass. Lewis, "India and Bangla Desh." Christopher Van Hollen OH, ADST. "Relief Problems in East Pakistan and India," Part II (Sept. 30, 1971) and Part III (Oct. 4, 1971), Hearings before the Subcommittee to Investigate Problems Connected with Refugees and Escapees, Committee on the Judiciary, U.S. Senate. *Life*, Aug. 27, 1971. Summary of Kennedy trip, Embassy New Delhi to Secretary of State, Aug. 18, 1971, RNL.

297 **results back home:** Drafts and final copy, "Address by Senator Edward M. Kennedy to the National Press Club," Aug. 26, 1971; "Suggested Revisions to the Speech . . . by Dean Lewis"; "EMK Statements on Bangladesh," chronology; EMK to Fulbright, Sept. 28, 1971; Dale to EMK, Sept. 28, Oct. 1, 1971; "Key Questions to Clarify the Record on Military Shipments to Pakistan," SJC-NARA. The original version of EMK's speech was toned down after Lewis suggested it was "too vicious in its attack on the [Nixon] Administration." For speech, see also CR, Sept. 8, 1971. Kissinger and Nixon, White House tape recordings, Aug. 11 and 13, 1971, RNL. Galbraith to EMK, Aug. 23, 1971, JKG-FKL. Christopher Van Hollen OH, ADST. "Relief Problems in East Pakistan and India," Part II (Sept. 30, 1971) and Part III (Oct. 4, 1971), Hearings before the Subcommittee to Investigate Problems Connected with Refugees and Escapees, Committee on the Judiciary, U.S. Senate. WS, Oct. 18, 1971. Memorandum for the Record, The President, Henry Kissinger et al., Aug. 11, 1972; Kissinger, Memorandum for the President, "Implications of the Situation in South Asia," Aug. 18, 1971, both NSC files, NSA. In "Tilt Policy Revisited," Van Hollen credits Kennedy for the Nixon administration's generosity: "By expending large sums of money for the refugees in India, the White House hoped to reduce the barrage of criticism it was receiving from the media and the Congress, led by Senator Edward Kennedy as Chairman of the Judiciary Committee's Subcommittee on Refugees."

298 **"smear the hell":** Jerry to EMK, Oct. 7, 1971, with EMK notation and annotated pages of Dole remarks from CR, Oct. 6, 1971; Jerry to EMK, Dec. 8, 1971, with EMK notation, SJC-NARA. Nixon and Kissinger, White House tape recordings, July 30, Aug. 11, Oct. 20, 1971, RNL.

298 **Cold War showdown:** Kissinger and Nixon, White House tape recordings, Dec. 12, 1971, RNL. Luke Nichter and Richard Moss, in "Superpower Relations, Backchannels and the Subcontinent: Using the Nixon Tapes to Examine the 1971 India-Pakistan War," nixontapes.org; FRUS, 1969–1976,

Volume XI, South Asia Crisis, 1971. Retzlaff and Metcalf, "Tragic Failure." Bass, *Blood Telegram*, 289–309. Van Hollen, "Tilt Policy Revisited."

298 **Kennedy condemned Nixon:** Jerry to EMK, Dec. 8, 1971, with EMK notations; "Talking points" for Kennedy speech, undated; EMK to Sheikh Mujibur Rahman, Jan. 11, 1972, and Rahman to EMK, Jan. 16, 1971; Dale/Jerry to Dick, "Press Info on Senator's Trip to Bangladesh," Feb. 5, 1972; trip itinerary; EMK remarks, Dacca, Bangladesh, Feb. 14, 1972; "The Birth of Bangladesh": A Report by the Chairman, Senator Edward M. Kennedy of the Subcommittee to Investigate Problems Connected with Refugees and Escapees of the Committee on the Judiciary, U.S. Senate, April 4, 1972; Kennedy diary, "Meeting of EMK with President Bhutto," Sept. 18, 1973, all SJC-NARA. EMK testimony, Committee on Foreign Relations, U.S. Senate, March 6 and 7, 1972. EMK Senate speech, CR, Dec. 7, 1971. Background briefing with Henry Kissinger, Dec. 7, 1971, NSC files, NSA. An account of U.S. military aid, requested by Kennedy and confirming his charges, was released by the General Accounting Office in February 1972. WS, Dec. 7, 1971. NYT, Feb. 15, 1972. WP, Feb. 15, 1972.

299 **the continual preoccupation:** The record of the Nixon administration's preoccupation with EMK is extensive. See Rogers and Kissinger, telephone transcript, April 6, 1971; Haig to Nixon, memorandum, June 25, 1971, FRUS, Volume XI, South Asia Crisis. Background briefing with Henry Kissinger, Dec. 7, 1971, NSC files, NSA. Hoskinson to Kissinger, May 20, 1971; Saunders to Kissinger, Sept. 8, 1971; Saunders to Haig, Sept. 30, 1971; Saunders and Hoskinson to Kissinger, Oct. 29, 1971; Nixon and Kissinger, White House tape recording, May 18, 1971; Nixon and Rogers, White House tape recording, May 21, 1971; Nixon and Kissinger et al., White House tape recording, July 30, 1971; Nixon and Kissinger, White House tape recording, Aug. 11, 1971; Nixon and Kissinger, White House tape recording, Aug. 13, 1971; Nixon and Ehrlichman, White House tape recording, Sept. 8, 1971; Nixon and Colson, White House tape recording, Oct. 20, 1971; Nixon, Haldeman, and Kissinger, White House tape recording, Nov. 5, 1971; Nixon and Kissinger, White House tape recording, Nov. 10, 1971; Kissinger and Nixon, White House tape recording, Dec. 6, 1971; Nixon, Kissinger, and Mitchell, White House tape recording, Dec. 8, 1971; Nixon and Colson, White House tape recording, Jan. 18, 1972, all RNL. The Republican National Committee maintained an opposition research file on Kennedy throughout this period that tracked his movements and activities for top White House and Republican officials. See Robert J. Dole, RNC Chairman's Files, Dole-KU.

Seventeen: A Dramatic Public Proceeding of Historic Proportions

300 **murderous to civilians:** Jerry Tinker, Subcommittee on Refugees, Memorandum, July 8, 1970; "Refugee and Civilian War Casualty Problems in Indochina,"

staff report, Sept. 28, 1970; unsigned staff memo on My Lai massacre, circa 1970–71, "Suggested Theme"; EMK statements, May 25, June 28, Dec. 13, 1970, Feb. 21, 1971, Feb. 6, April 5, April 17, May 8, Aug. 3, Sept. 26, Oct. 9, Dec. 4, 1972, Feb. 27, June 4, 1973, SJC-NARA. JAF interviews with Dale de Haan, Daniel Ellsberg. Edward Miguel and Gerard Roland, "The Long Run Impact of Bombing Vietnam," Department of Economics, University of California, Berkeley. Daniel Ellsberg, "Laos: What Nixon Is Up To," *New York Review of Books*, March 11, 1971.

301 **"monumental and historic catastrophe":** EMK to Alsop, CR, May 25, 1970. EMK also said, publicly, that RFK's role in the bugging of Martin Luther King was a mistake "and wrong"; see transcript, EMK and Elizabeth Drew, "Thirty Minutes With . . . ," PBS, June 28, 1973.

301 **Kennedy was tenacious:** For the slop over comments see the White House tapes, May 4 and 8, 1972, RNL. For "morally bankrupt" see EMK, "The Forgotten Casualties," *Commonweal* magazine, Oct. 30, 1970. For other writings see EMK, "Indochina: A Slaughter of Innocents," *The Nation*, June 28, 1971; EMK, "The Tragedy of Indochina: Ten Million Civilian Victims," *Compton Yearbook*, 1972; EMK, "And This Should Outrage the Conscience of All Americans," NYT, Dec. 27, 1972, and EMK, "Editorial Submitted to the New England Journal of Medicine," SJC-NARA, published in the journal May 13, 1971. For a sampling of the many stories inspired by the Kennedy subcommittee reports see NYT, March 15, April 22, Nov. 21, 1971, May 25, Oct. 4, 15, 1972; WP, Dec. 2, 1972, and *New York Review of Books*, March 11, 1971.

301 **John Kerry, a Navy lieutenant:** JAF interview with John Kerry. John K. Galbraith to EMK, June 21, 1971, JFKL. Nixon and Haldeman, June 1, 1971; Nixon, Haldeman, and Kissinger and Nixon, Timmons, and Devine, June 11, 1971, White House tapes, RNL. WP, April 22, 1971. Kerry was a teenage volunteer on EMK's 1962 campaign. He would go on to serve as EMK's seatmate in the Senate, as secretary of state, and as the Democratic presidential nominee in 2004. He made his mark in the Vietnam Veterans Against the War protests by asking the Senate Foreign Relations Committee, "How do you ask a man to be the last man to die in Vietnam? How do you ask a man to be the last man to die for a mistake?" For Kerry see Kranish, Mooney, and Easton, *Kerry*, and Brinkley, *Tour of Duty*.

302 **segments in the Pentagon Papers:** JAF interviews with Daniel Ellsberg and Thomas Oliphant. Nixon and Haldeman ("entitled to know"), June 16, 1971; Nixon, Haldeman, and Colson ("writhing"), June 23, 1971; Nixon, Haldeman, and Colson, June 15, 1971; Nixon, Ehrlichman, and Mitchell, June 15, 1971; Nixon and Haldeman, June 17, 1971, White House tapes, RNL. For overview see Ellsberg, *Secrets*. Rudenstine, *Presses*.

302 **known as the Plumbers:** "The Final Report of the Select Committee on Presidential Campaign Activities" (hereafter Senate Watergate Report), U.S. Senate, June 1974. Dun Gifford interview, AC-JFKL.

303 **Secret Service detail:** Nixon, Haldeman, and Ehrlichman (Secret Service), and Nixon, Haldeman, and Butterfield (Secret Service and Burden), Sept. 7, 1972; Nixon, Haldeman, and Colson, Sept. 11, 1972 (Teddy story), White House tapes, RNL. For transcripts, see Kutler, *Abuse*. WP, Feb. 10, 1973. In the 1970s, while still married to Joan, EMK was linked by gossip in the press to Helga Wagner, Amanda Burden, Olympic skier Suzy Chaffee, and others. Only Wagner, many years later, confirmed a relationship.

303 **placed him under surveillance:** Nixon and Kissinger, Aug. 2, 1972; Nixon and Haldeman, July 6, 1971; Nixon and Ehrlichman, Sept. 8, 1971, White House tapes, RNL; Haldeman diary ("total animal"), June 23, 1971, RNL. According to Haldeman, Kissinger told Nixon that EMK groped Ford under a table, and snuck upstairs to pound on her door at a New York hotel. "He walked up to her floor, said he wanted to screw her, and she said that they couldn't because of the press, and he said that the press will never touch me. He pulled the same thing on Edgar Bergen's daughter." Nightclub: Aitken, *Charles W. Colson*. Haldeman diary, Dec. 5, 1970, RNL.

303 **advice from Rose:** Joan Kennedy interview, AC-JFKL.

303 **the Moscow summit:** The Nixon campaign's repeated attempts to break into the Democratic National Committee offices and McGovern campaign headquarters began in May, when Nixon was on his trip to Moscow, and continued for almost a month. The burglars were ultimately arrested on June 17. See Kutler, *Wars*; Emery, *Watergate*; and Lukas, *Nightmare*.

304 **not well in Nixonland:** The word "Nixonland" was coined by Democratic presidential candidate Adlai Stevenson in a speech in 1956: "a land of slander and scare; the land of sly innuendo, the poison pen, the anonymous phone call and hustling, pushing, shoving; the land of smash and grab and anything to win." See Farrell, *Nixon*, 243.

304 **restoration of Camelot:** See Nixon handwritten comment, "John F. Kennedy Center," White House news digest, May 28, 1971; Nixon handwritten comment, Woods to Nixon, Nov. 20, 1972; Butterfield to Nixon, "Sanitization of the EOB," Jan. 16, 1970, RNL. William Safire, Nixon diary, Feb. 27, 1969, Safire papers, LOC. For JKO, see Farrell, *Nixon*, 409–10.

304 **his slithery courtiers:** Magruder to Mitchell, April 12, 1972, with attached memo, Fore to Marik, April 4, 1972; for surveillance see Chotiner to Mitchell, Nov. 8, 1971, "Chapman's Friend Reports" (which captured Gene McCarthy calling EMK a "barefoot boy with balls of brass and an intellect of the same metal"); Nixon and Ehrlichman, March 16, 1973; Nixon and Kissinger, May 18, 1971, White House tapes, RNL. See also Dole to Panselow, April 17, 1972, and Dole to Steinmeyer, May 11, 1972, RNC Chairman's Files, Dole-KU. For samples of polling see Robert Teeter papers, Box 64, GFL. For Nixon and EMK, see Haldeman diary, June 9, 1971, and Nixon, Mitch-

ell, and others, Sept. 18, 1971, White House tapes, RNL.

304 **warning to Haldeman:** Safire to Haldeman, "Kennedy Victory Scenario," Nov. 16, 1971, RNL. For similar analysis see Buchanan to Nixon, "EMK-Political Memorandum," June 9, 1971, RNL.

305 **bugging and surveillance:** Nixon and Haldeman, May 28, 1971; see also Nixon and Haldeman discussing financing, July 2, 1971, White House tapes, RNL.

305 **the "IT&T affair":** JAF interview, Wallace Johnson. EMKOH-UVA. John Tunney OH, UVA. Nixon to Kleindienst, April 19, 1971, White House tape, RNL. "Hearings Before the Committee on the Judiciary, United States Senate, on Nomination of Richard G. Kleindienst, of Arizona, to be Attorney General," U.S. Senate. Beard to Merriam, June 25, 1971; "Kleindienst Briefing Paper," unsigned, EMK staff, March 1972; Flug to EMK, undated, "Judiciary Exec.—Kleindienst—ITT"; Flug, "Talking Notes," March 21, 1972, all SJC-NARA. Susman to EMK, Jan. 15, 1974; Susman to EMK, "Kleindienst's Testimony before Judiciary," June 14, 1974; ITT chronology, TS-UMASS. Brecher to Bayh, March 1, 1972; "Chronology of Events"; Brecher to Bayh, April 13, 1972, "Review of Basic Facts and Testimony Through April 12"; "Kleindienst—ITT Hearings, Beard Testimony and Present Status of Hearings," Bayh-IU. NYT, April 23, 1972. Senate Watergate Report.

306 **"collapse or die":** EMKOH-UVA. Goldman to EMK, March 24, 1972; "Interview with Dita Beard," SJC-NARA. Kennedy should not be thought cruel—a week later Beard felt well enough to appear on the CBS newsmagazine *60 Minutes*. NYT, March 27, 1972.

306 **wept in court:** NYT, May 17, June 8, 1974. CQW, Jan. 12, May 18, 1974. Haldeman diary, March 8, 14, 1972, RNL. In a White House tape recording, Nixon is quoted saying, "Oh God yes. . . . That's part of this ballgame," when asked if IT&T would be making donations after settling the case. "This is very, very hush-hush and it has to be engineered very delicately." Nixon to Haldeman and Ehrlichman, May 13, 1971, White House tapes, RNL.

307 **at the Watergate:** Nixon and Kissinger, April 15, 17, and May 5, 1972, Aug. 2, 1972, White House tapes, RNL. Senate Watergate Report.

307 **known as Ad Prac:** JAF interviews with James Flug, Thomas Susman. EMKOH-UVA. The formal title was the Subcommittee on Administrative Practice and Procedure. Flug to EMK, memos: "Why Ad Prac Should Stay Out of Watergate," by "X," and "Why Ad Prac should announce Watergate Hearings Now," by "Y," and "Watergate—The lawyerlike approach," by "Z," Sept. 28, 1972; unsigned, undated memo on "press source" contact with unnamed *Washington Post* reporter; Flug to EMK, undated, mid-August 1972; Flug to EMK, Aug. 25, 1972; Flug to EMK, undated, Sept. 1972, SJC-NARA.

308 **opportunity to be immunized:** George McGovern OH, UVA: "I always thought it would help clear the air on Chappaquiddick for him." Nixon and Agnew, White House tapes, June 22, 1971; Nixon

and Colson, Nixon, Burns, and Connolly, Nixon and Haldeman, White House tapes, Jan. 18, 1972; Colson to Haldeman, June 14, 1972, with transcript of Colson and Healy telephone conversation; Finkelstein to Magruder, March 7, 1972; Marik to Magruder, April 5, 1972; Fore to Marik, April 4, 1972, RNL. BG, July 9, 1972. NYT, June 16, 1972. WSJ, May 5, 1972. Thompson, *Campaign Trail*. White, *Making, 1972*. At one point, Theodore Sorensen sent EMK a memo outlining an arrangement in which EMK could serve as both vice president and a member of McGovern's cabinet. EMK was intrigued, but not persuaded. See EMKOH-UVA.

309 **a disastrous start:** JAF interview with Burt Solomon. EMKOH-UVA. George McGovern OH, UVA. Matty Troy, Kevin White interviews, AC-JFKL. White and EMK had a somewhat flinty relationship, going back to White's support for McCormack in 1962, and White's failure to help the Kennedys find a site for the John F. Kennedy Presidential Library. See Joe Klein and Burt Solomon, *The Real Paper*, June 12, 1974, and O'Neill, *Rogues*, 221, 237. *Life*, Dec. 29, 1972. BG, Jan. 12, 1973. Mark Shields, syndicated column, Feb. 4, 2012. NYT, July 13, 1972.

For background on Eagleton see James Giglio, "The Eagleton Affair: Thomas Eagleton, George McGovern and the 1972 Vice Presidential Nomination," *Presidential Studies Quarterly*, Dec. 2009, and Hart, *Right from the Start*, and White, *Making, 1972*.

On Shriver: Johnson had appointed Shriver as ambassador to France in the midst of the 1968 presidential campaign. Many in the Kennedy clan thought he should have spurned the offer and campaigned for RFK. See EMKOH-UVA: "There was a general sense among the Kennedy people that Sarge hadn't come back from France in 1968 to help Bobby. So there was a good deal of anxiety about that." EMK said he did not share that resentment, but the feeling was still alive in 1976, when Shriver ran for president.

Kenneth O'Donnell was not coy when explaining the clan's lukewarm support for Shriver. He attributed it to EMK: "Who is Shriver? Head of the Peace Corps? How'd he get that job? He was Eunice Kennedy's husband. Head of the Merchandise Mart? How'd he get the job? He was Eunice Kennedy's husband. Ambassador to France? How'd he get the job? And why didn't he help Bobby? Because of Johnson! Sure, Shriver has asked for our help, but I'll do what the senior senator of the state of Massachusetts tells me to." See Stroud, *How Jimmy Won*, 249.

See also McGovern OH, UVA, and Schlesinger diary, July 13, 1972 (White), Aug. 6, 1972, and March 6, 1976 (Shriver), and Oct. 4, 1972 (McGovern), AS-NYPL.

309 **McGovern's final hope:** JAF interviews with Thomas Susman, Wallace Johnson, Joseph Califano. EMKOH-UVA. James Flug, EMK interviews, AC-JFKL. McGovern-Shriver Political Research, "Memorandum on the Watergate Break-In and Bugging," with attached chronology, Sept. 22, 1972, Bayh-IU. The "fine hand" quote is from Nixon and Dean, Feb. 28, 1973, White House

tapes, RNL. The dilemma facing EMK, and the anger expressed by McGovern supporters ("with unprintable expletives"), was captured by columnist Stewart Alsop, BG, Oct. 6, 1972.

By law, a senator's office files are his to dispense, but a committee or subcommittee file belongs to the Senate and is supposed to be transferred to the National Archives at the end of a senator's service. Like many colleagues, EMK saw this rule as something more honored in the breach.

Researchers like Adam Clymer and Geoff Shepard, writing while EMK was alive, searched in vain for the subcommittee files on Watergate. (See McCulley to Gillette re "Adam Clymer request," March 18, 1993, AC-JFKL, and EMK to Jaworski, July 30, 1974, TS-UMASS, and Shepard, *Plot*.) As it turns out, the Watergate files—and others that cover a wide spectrum of EMK's work on the Judiciary Committee—had not been turned over to the National Archives as required. They were kept with the office collection, closed to researchers, and shipped to the John F. Kennedy Presidential Library. It was only because Kennedy, writing his memoir, sought to refresh his memory that Flug's Watergate files (including transcripts of his interview with Baldwin) were shipped to the senator, and only then, after his death, placed in the National Archives, where they should have been all along.

309 **a prize catch:** EMKOH-UVA. Ervin to EMK, Oct. 10, 1972, SJC-NARA.

310 **the family advisers:** EMKOH-UVA. Unsigned, undated memo on "press source" contact with unnamed *Washington Post* reporter; Flug to EMK, undated, mid-August 1972; Flug to EMK, Aug. 25, 1972; Flug to EMK, undated, Sept. 1972, SJC-NARA.

310 **"X," "Y," and "Z":** EMKOH-UVA. Transcript of Baldwin interview by Flug, undated, Sept. 1972; Flug to EMK, memos: "Why Ad Prac Should Stay Out of Watergate," by "X," and "Why Ad Prac should announce Watergate Hearings Now," by "Y," and "Watergate—The lawyerlike approach," by "Z," Sept. 28, 1972—for preliminary inquiry see EMK "Dear Colleague" to Ad Prac subcommittee members, Oct. 12, 1973, all SJC-NARA. For press reports on EMK dilemma see Alsop, BG, Oct. 6, 1972, and NJ, Nov. 11, 1972, and NYT, Oct. 13, 1972. Segretti stories, WP, Oct. 10, 15, 1972. Reporters from the *Los Angeles Times* eventually got to Baldwin and placed his story before the public; CBS News did two specials on Watergate, and *Time* magazine and the *New York Times* traded scoops with the *Post* that winter, before Judge John Sirica threatened the convicted burglars with heinous prison sentences, causing one of them, James McCord, to confess. Two fine accounts of the scandal unfolding in 1972 are Bernstein and Woodward, *President's Men*, and Sussman, *Coverup*.

312 **"no decision was made":** EMKOH-UVA: "We've missed an opportunity . . . but we clearly did not have enough at this time to do the kind of hearing that was called for. . . . Because I had such high visibility—it still seemed that the best we could do was to have someone else do it." JAF interview with

Bob Woodward. Ed Martin, James Flug, Thomas Susman interviews, AC-JFKL. EMK to subcommittee, Oct. 17, Nov. 15, 1972; Flug to EMK, "Espionage Sabotage Summary, Nov. 6, 1972; Fact Sheet, "How and Why Ad Prac Got In," undated, fall 1972; Memo, "Mike to EMK, Eddie, Paul, Dick, Jim and Tommy," Jan. 8, 1973, all SJC-NARA. Among the tricksters interviewed by the committee was a young Republican named Karl Rove. See "Memorandum re Carl Rove," TS-UMASS. For the Bernstein interview see Bernstein and Woodward, *President's Men*, 247. For Goldwater see BH, July 13, 1973; for Thurmond see Wayne Owens interview, AC-JFKL. Luce, NYT, Aug. 31, 1974.

312 **On Nixon's birthday:** Nixon and Haldeman, Sept. 26, 1972, White House tapes; "Collect Telegram," staff to Nixon, Jan. 9, 1973, RNL.

313 **"with the playboy":** Schlesinger diary, Nov. 26, 1972, AS-NYPL.

314 **known as the Senate Watergate Committee:** Mansfield to Ervin, Nov. 17, 1972, Mike Mansfield papers, University of Montana. EMK to Ervin, Feb. 7, 1973; Ervin to EMK, Feb. 8, 1973, SJC-NARA. Oberdorfer, *Senator Mansfield*, 432–33. CR, Feb. 6, 1973. Mansfield worried about the credibility of a Kennedy-led probe, but he told Oberdorfer that another consideration for giving the job to Ervin was the danger of assassination that EMK would face in such a high-profile role.

314 **Kennedy expressed relief:** EMKOH-UVA. EMK to Ervin, Feb. 7, 1973; EMK to Ervin, June 6, 1973; Flug to EMK, Oct. 9, 1972; Flug to EMK, undated, Nov. 1972; Flug to EMK, undated, January 1972, SJC-NARA. See Charles Ferris OH, SHO: "Ted Kennedy wanted to head the investigation" but Mansfield insisted that the investigation be bipartisan, with no presidential hopefuls on the panel. See Thompson, *At That Point*, 11.

314 **They trapped Gray:** Confidential Memo to Flug and other Judiciary Committee aides on Feb. 23, 1973, meeting, unsigned, SJC-NARA. NYT, March 7, 14, 1973. WP, March 1, 1973. WS, March 1, 1973. David Corbin, "Senator Robert C. Byrd, The 'Unsung Hero' of Watergate," *West Virginia Law Review*, Spring 2006. Sussman, *Coverup*, 152. Louis Patrick Gray III, hearings before the Committee on the Judiciary, United States Senate, Feb. 28–March 22, 1973. See also Gray and Gray, *Nixon's Web*.

315 **Dean told the prosecutors:** Senate Watergate Report, 53–55, for break-ins and bugging, 65–66 for Ellsberg psychiatrist.

315 **Richardson's confirmation hearings:** EMKOH-UVA: "I had talked to Richardson . . . and had been very clear that he wasn't going to get confirmed unless he appointed a special prosecutor. . . . This was a *quid pro quo* for his being able to get through." Burt Wides OH, UVA. Will Hastings, James Flug interviews, AC-JFKL. "Summary of Events Surrounding the Confirmation of Elliot Richardson and the Appointment of Archibald Cox," unsigned, Bayh-IU. Memoranda, "Judiciary Committee Executive Session," Oct. 24, 1973; "Statements of Cox at Richardson Confirmation Hearings," TS-UMASS. Richardson to EMK, May 17, 1973; EMK to Richardson, May 18, 1973; Char-

ter revisions, May 17, 1973; Clymer to Hastings, June 29, 1997. Nixon and Haig, May 20, 1973; Nixon and Haldeman and Ehrlichman, Oct. 14, 1972, White House tapes, RNL. "Nomination of Elliot L. Richardson to Be Attorney General," Hearings before the Committee on the Judiciary, United States Senate, May 9–22, 1973.

315 **as special prosecutor:** In the days after the Massacre, the Judiciary Committee, with EMK's enthusiastic support, considered legislation to establish a permanent special prosecutor. See EMK et al. to Sirica, Oct. 23, 1973; Eastland to Bork, Oct. 24, 1973; EMK statements, Oct. 23, 25, 1973; CR, Oct. 26, 1973; Susman to EMK, Oct. 30, 1973; memo and outline of legislation, Judiciary Committee Executive Session, Oct. 24, 1973; Susman to EMK, Jan. 14, 1974, TS-UMASS. Burt Wides OH, UVA. Nixon's agreement to have Leon Jaworski take over from Cox cooled that effort, but the idea lived on and the independent counsel provisions were included in the Ethics in Government Act of 1978.

315 **it is too facile:** JAF interview with Geoff Shepard. Shepard, *Plot*.

315 **at first dismissed Cox:** JAF interview with Geoff Shepard. Nixon and Haig, May 18, 1973, White House tape, RNL. NYT, June 12, 1973. William Spragens, "Kennedy Era Speechwriting, Public Relations and Public Opinion," *Presidential Studies Quarterly*, Winter 1984, 78–86. For a listing of the more prominent Kennedy affiliates hunting Nixon during Watergate see Farrell, *Nixon*, 679. EMK offered no apologies—at a college commencement speech in June 1974 he praised Cox, Ervin, and others "who ask and give no quarter when the integrity of government is at stake." See BH, June 2, 1974.

316 **outraged by the "Saturday Night Massacre":** JAF interviews with Neil MacNeil, Gerald Ford, James Doyle, Ron Liebman. EMK and MacNeil OH, UVA. EMK statement, Nov. 2, 1973; unsigned memo, "Impeachment—Questions and Answers," TS-UMASS. Carl Albert OH, Carl Albert Center, University of Oklahoma. O'Neill, Albert, Rodino statements, Oct. 23, 1973; O'Neill statement, Oct. 24, 1973; "The Saturday Night Massacre and the Impetus to Impeachment," n.d., TON-BC. "Chronology of Events Re Special Prosecutor," n.d., late 1973; Bill to Senator, "Summary of Events since Thursday," n.d.; Richardson, "Summary of Reasons Why I Must Resign," Oct. 19, 1973, Bayh-IU. Buchanan to Nixon, Nov. 5, 1973, RNL. Schlesinger diary, Oct. 21, 1973, AS-NYPL. WP, Oct. 24, 1973, Nov. 28, 1982.

Eighteen: Health Cares

318 **his son might die:** Philip Caper, Barbara Souliotis, Ellis Mottur OH, UVA. The Kennedys cooperated with Geraldo Rivera, who wrote a chapter on Ted Jr. in his book *A Special Kind of Courage*, 191–214.

319 **niece down the aisle:** JAF interview with Kathleen Kennedy Townsend. WP, Nov. 18, 1973. NYT, Nov. 18, 1973. "bittersweet chorus": *When Irish eyes are smiling / sure 'tis like a morn in spring / In the lilt of Irish laughter / you can hear the angels sing / When*

Irish hearts are happy / all the world seems bright and gay / And when Irish eyes are smiling / sure they steal your heart away. Lyrics by Chauncey Olcott and George Graff Jr., music by Ernest Ball.

319 **toxic anticancer drug:** Philip Caper, Melody Miller OH, UVA. Luella Hennessey Donovan interview, LD-WYO. WP, March 8, 1974. *People*, April 8, 1974. *Good Housekeeping*, Oct. 1974 and Dec. 1986.

320 **song was bleak:** *Good Housekeeping*, Dec. 1986. "It was a very dangerous type of cancer, and there was a real question about his survival," EMK recalled. See EMKOH-UVA. On "open marriage": The *Globe* carried the story that Joan was free to "pursue her own interests" after she was spotted in Venice. When asked where her husband was, she said that he was home, "babysitting." See BG, Sept. 9, 1973. Joan confirmed the arrangement in an interview with Adam Clymer, AC-JFKL. A book, *Open Marriage: A New Life Style for Couples*, spent forty weeks on the *New York Times* bestseller list and sold thirty-five million copies after being published in 1972. See NYT, March 26, 2006.

320 **stay in rehab:** NYT, Sept. 13, 24, Oct. 10, 1974. LHJ, Aug., Sept. 1974. *Time*, Oct. 7, 1974. BG, Sept. 9, 1973.

321 **the Kennedy marriage:** Kennedy and Fried, *Common Struggle*, 33–45, 254–55. Lesley Stahl, "Patrick Kennedy Breaks His Silence," *60 Minutes*, Oct. 4, 2015. John Tunney, Lester Hyman, Mary Frackleton, Wyche Fowler OH, UVA. Schlesinger diary, Dec. 16, 1973, AS-NYPL. Hersh, *Intimate*, 461–62. Richard Kaplan interview, LD-WYO. John Seigenthaler interview, AC-JFKL.

321 **reports of his infidelity:** Joan Braden, "Joan Kennedy Tells Her Own Story," *McCall's*, Aug. 1978.

322 **like an O'Neill tragedy:** Kennedy and Fried, *Common Struggle*, 33–45, 254–55. Patrick Kennedy, *60 Minutes*, Oct. 4, 2015. Schlesinger diary, Nov. 8, 1972, AS-NYPL. Edward M. Kennedy Jr., Kara Kennedy, Patrick Kennedy, David Burke, Ellis Mottur OH, UVA. Alcoholism has a genetic component, and there are numerous incidents of the disease reported in RK's line (see Goodwin, *Fitzgeralds*, 83, 127–28) as well as in JBK's family. Though JFK's and Eunice Kennedy's children evaded addiction, several of their cousins—most notably Pat Kennedy Lawford's son, Christopher, and RFK's sons Robert and David—abused drugs. On the genetic component see Howard Edenberg and Tatiana Foroud, "Genetics and Alcoholism," *Nature Reviews Gastroenterology & Hepatology*, Aug. 10, 2013.

322 **preparing for the 1976 election:** Milton Gwirtzman interview, AC-JFKL. Julie Baumgold, "Teddy at the Tiller," *New York* magazine, Oct. 9, 1972. BA, Nov. 19, 1972. NYT, Sept. 15, 1972. Carter: Witcover, *Marathon*, 111. Aide Hamilton Jordan advised Carter on Nov. 4, 1972, "I believe it would be very difficult for Senator Kennedy to win a national election, as the unanswered questions of Chappaquiddick run contrary to this national desire for trust and morality in government."

322 **by Theodore Sorensen:** Theodore Sorensen, "Private and Confidential to Senator Kennedy, Messrs. Burke, Kirk, Marshall, Martin, Seigenthaler & Smith," March 9, 1973, TS-JFKL.

324 **embraced George Wallace:** Martin to Casey, March 17, 1972, RNC chairman files, Dole-KU. On "trimming," see Milton Gwirtzman interview and diary notes, AC-JFKL. William Safire, ex–Nixon speechwriter turned columnist for the *New York Times*, wrote admiringly of Kennedy's trip to Alabama, "He played upon his audiences' resentment of Northern hypocrisy on racial matters . . . and reprised his theme of a Kennedy-Wallace kinship of tragic violence." See NYT, July 5, 1973.

325 **résumé on foreign policy:** "Refugee and Humanitarian Problems in Chile, Part II," Hearings of the Subcommittee on Refugees and Escapees, Senate Judiciary Committee, July 23, 1974. See also "Refugee and Humanitarian Problems in Chile," Hearings of the Subcommittee to Investigate Problems with Refugees and Escapees, Senate Judiciary Committee, Sept. 28, 1973. Re Chile: CR, Oct. 2, 1974. Re Portugal: BG, Dec. 2, 1974, and NYT, Dec. 14, 1974. In addition to Soviet leader Leonid Brezhnev and Portugal's president, Francisco da Costa Gomes, EMK had meetings in his credentialing tours with French president Valéry Giscard d'Estaing, Israeli prime minister Yitzhak Rabin, former Israeli prime minister Golda Meir, Jordan's King Hussein, Egyptian premier Anwar Sadat, and German chancellor Willy Brandt.

327 **dissidents to set free:** Robert Hunter, Mark Schneider OH, UVA. Joan Kennedy, Milton Gwirtzman, Christopher Ogden, Jim King interviews, AC-JFKL. Schlesinger diary, May 1, 1974, AS-NYPL. EMK met with dissidents in a September 1978 trip to Moscow, and again won exit visas for refuseniks. See WP, Sept. 12, 13, 1978; BG, Sept. 12, 1978. For 1974 trip see NYT, April 24, 1974. BG, May 14, 1974. *Christian Science Monitor*, April 26, 1974. *Boston Herald American*, April 25, 1974. *Good Housekeeping*, Oct. 1975. On his 1978 trip to China, on which he nudged the U.S.-Chinese relationship toward full diplomatic recognition, EMK won permission for Johnny Foo, a Chinese citizen, to visit his exiled parents in Massachusetts. Clymer's papers at the JFKL include an excerpt of Walter Stoessel's diary, and EMK's correspondence with Epelman and Portugal's new leaders, President Francisco da Costa Gomes and Foreign Minister Mario Soares.

327 **costs of medical care:** EMKOH-UVA. EMK to Nixon, undated, January 1974, RNL.

327 **moved by personal experience:** Nixon and Hoffman, Sept. 25, 1972, White House tapes, RNL. Fine descriptions of Nixon-era health care policy are given in Blumenthal and Morone, *Heart*, and Altman and Shactman, *Power*. See Charles Ferris OH, SHO: "Some of the most progressive legislation was passed during Nixon's term. If you blindfolded yourself you would think that Lyndon Johnson was still in office."

329 **top of the Senate Finance Committee:** JAF interviews with LeRoy Goldman, Lawrence O'Donnell. LeRoy Goldman, James Mongan OH, UVA. EMK interview, AC-JFKL. "Statement by Senator Edward M. Kennedy upon Introduction of the Comprehensive National Health Insurance Act," April 2, 1974, SLC-NARA. For Long opposition to

national health insurance see Nixon, Long, White House staff, and Senate leaders, White House tapes, April 26, 1971, RNL; for White House reaction to the EMK-Mills alliance, see Michel to Harper, "Kennedy and Mills on Health Insurance," with attached EMK-Mills testimony and fact sheet, June 19, 1972; for White House analysis of the troubled health care system, see the health care section ("An Alternative National Health Insurance Proposal: A Maximum Liability Health Insurance Plan") of the "Mega Proposal," a comprehensive plan for reorganizing social welfare policy, January 1973, RNL. See also Nexon to EMK, undated, Stan Jones notes on history of Kennedy-Mills and negotiations with Nixon, SLC-NARA. NYT, Aug. 28, 1970, March 9, April 3, 1974. *Time*, June 7, 1971.

329 **"something with nothing":** Nixon and cabinet, June 8, 1971; see also Nixon, Haldeman, Dole, and Mitchell, June 3, 1971, White House tapes, and "Proposed Health Game Plan," 1971, and "Regulation of the Health Insurance Industry," 1971, "Kennedy HMO Proposal," 1972, RNL. For "something with nothing," see Blumenthal, *Heart*, chapter 6. EMK condensed the testimony from a year of hearings he conducted and published them as a book; see Kennedy, *Critical Condition*. The states he visited included New York, California, Ohio, Iowa, Tennessee, Colorado, and West Virginia; the countries were Great Britain, Denmark, Sweden, and Israel. For White House fear of EMK and the health care issue, and account of EMK hearings, see LeRoy Goldman OH, UVA. See also Starr, *Remedy*, 53. Starr notes, "Nixon's effort to compete with Kennedy on liberal terrain was entirely in keeping with his general pattern as president. Politically, Nixon and liberal Democrats detested and distrusted each other, but substantively they were closer than their mutual hostility suggested. Throughout Nixon's presidency, liberal assumptions dominated national debate and the Democrats continued to control Congress, but Nixon often sought to defeat them by offering alternative policies in an effort to co-opt their supporters."

330 **an HMO experiment:** Richard Nixon, "Address on the State of the Union," Jan. 30, 1974, UCSB. "Kennedy HMO Proposal," 1972; Richardson to Nixon, memorandum on the "Mega Proposal," Jan. 29, 1973, RNL. Phil Caper, Paul Rogers, Caspar Weinberger interviews, AC-JFKL. NYT, Jan. 4, Feb. 19, 1971. CQW, Feb. 26, 1971, May 19, 1973. NJ, Sept. 2, 1972, March 16, 1974. Stuart Altman, in *Power, Politics, and Universal Health Care*, 40, notes that the HMO experiment became a lasting legacy of the Nixon-Kennedy collaboration. "The HMO concept gradually took hold and eventually changed the nature of health insurance in America." By 2009, some form of managed care covered three out of four insured Americans.

330 **made national health insurance:** Richard Nixon, "Address on the State of the Union," Jan. 30, 1974, UCSB; Richard Nixon, "Special Message to the Congress Proposing a Comprehensive Health Insurance Plan," Feb. 6, 1974, UCSB. McDonald to Price, "Health Insurance," June 19, 1972; Wein-

berger to Nixon, memoranda on national health insurance, Nov. 2, Dec. 7, 1973; Cavanaugh to Cole, "Game Plan on the Health Issue," March 2, 1974, RNL. Munnell to Bentsen and Altman, "The National Health Care Proposals of Presidents Truman and Nixon," Nov. 3, 1993, WCL. Democratic Policy Committee, Special Report—Health Care, "The Nixon Years," TD-SDS. Hearing Before the Committee on Finance, U.S. Senate, "Administration Health Proposal," Caspar Weinberger testimony, Jan. 31, 1974. White House Message to Congress and Fact Sheet, "The Comprehensive Health Insurance Plan," Feb. 6, 1974, Dole-KU. Blumenthal, *Heart*, chapter 6. NYT, Feb. 7, 1974. CQW, Feb. 9, 1974. Alice Rivlin, "Agreed: Here Comes National Health Insurance," *New York Times Magazine*, July 21, 1974. Nixon's proposal was historic, and an inspiration for reformers who followed. As Altman writes (p. 42), "It is striking to consider how much of its structure and provisions are similar to plans proposed thirty-five years later. Employer mandates, subsidized insurance for the poor, cost sharing, insurance pools and catastrophic insurance limits have been included in nearly all subsequent plans."

331 **The time was ripe:** JAF interviews with LeRoy Goldman and Paul Kirk. EMK OH-UVA. Stan Jones, Max Fine OH, UVA. Yarmolinsky to EMK, April 25, 1974; "Notes on Health Politics" newsletter, Health Professionals for Political Action, April 1974, Yarmolinsky papers, JFKL. Onek to Eizenstat and Butler, March 13, 1978, JCL. Rashi Fein, Max Fine interviews, AC-JFKL. Malcolm Gladwell, "The Risk Pool," TNY, Aug. 28, 2006. "Narrative Comparison of NHIPA, Kennedy Bill and Kennedy-Mills Proposal," July 1972, RNL. Nexon to EMK, undated, Stan Jones notes on history of Kennedy-Mills and negotiations with Nixon, SLC-NARA. NJ, March 16, 1974. CQW, May 25, July 20, 1974. NYT, July 21, 1974. BG, July 15, 1974.

332 **questioned Labor's sincerity:** EMKOH-UVA. Quadagno, *Uninsured.*

333 **He and Mills sat down:** JAF interview with Stuart Altman. Stuart Altman OH, UVA. Altman, Frank Samuel, and Theodore Cooper represented the administration, Stan Jones was there for Kennedy, and William Fullerton attended on behalf of Mills. See also Caspar Weinberger interview, AC-JFKL. NJ, July 27, 1974.

333 **worst tactical mistake:** JAF interview with EMK. Stuart Altman, James Mongan, Michael Dukakis OH, UVA. Weinberger statement on the Kennedy-Mills bill, April 2, 1974; Clawson to White House Staff, April 4, 1974; O'Neill to Nixon, via Ash, "Kennedy-Mills Health Insurance Proposal," April 10, 1974, RNL. Medical historian David Blumenthal and others believe the Nixon-Kennedy-Mills negotiations were the closest the United States would get to national health insurance in Kennedy's life, yet Kennedy chose to omit the episode from his memoirs.

333 **let it slide:** Timmons to Ford, Sept. 5, 1974, Friedersdorf to Cannon, Nov. 28, 1975, Lynn to Ford, Jan. 12, 1976, GFL. The Ford administration slipped from endorsing national health insur-

ance, to mandated catastrophic coverage, to no action at all. Rashi Fein interview, AC-JFKL.

333 **an inebriated Mills:** WP, Oct. 11, 1974. *Time*, Dec. 16, 1974. Stuart Altman OH, UVA: "If it wasn't for Fanne Foxe, we might have had national health insurance in 1974." Caspar Weinberger interview, AC-JFKL: "The reasons we didn't succeed grew out of the loss of authority of the chairman of the House Ways and Means Committee. If he had been able to maintain the immense authority that he had, I was quite confident that we would be able to get something. It was very close—it was a very close thing. That comparatively trivial issue upset the apple cart. Kennedy was receptive to Wilbur Mills, and he also wanted to accomplish something." James Mongan, who worked for Russell Long's Finance Committee, had a different perspective. He believed that Long was resolute—"It wasn't going to happen"—and the most that might have passed was a modest protection from catastrophic costs. See James Mongan OH, UVA. For EMK on insurance industry see Philip Caper OH, UVA.

334 **wake of Watergate:** Robert Sherrill, "Chappaquiddick + 5," NYT, July 14, 1974. The *Times* article "raised all the issues and questions again, and by the fall, I had really made up my mind that I wouldn't be running," Kennedy recalled. "There were numbers of factors: the well-being of the children—mine, and also the other children. If something happened to me, what was going to happen to the family? I had also the consideration of the impact on Joan, who was having a difficult, challenging time. If I was going to get into this in a serious way, what was going to happen to her? And in '76, I was supposed to run for the Senate, so I'd be giving up a Senate seat." EMKOH-UVA. Said Burton Hersh of Sherrill's piece, "A suppurating editorial corpse, oozing speculative gasses, worm-riddled with inaccuracies." See Hersh, "The Survival of Edward Kennedy," *Washingtonian*, Feb. 1979.

335 **gunman would fire:** EMKOH-UVA. Milton Gwirtzman interview and diary notes, AC-JFKL. *Newsweek*, Oct. 7, 1974. BG, Sept. 23, 24, 25, 1974. WP, Sept. 24, 1974. NYT, Sept. 9, 24, 1973, Aug. 18, 1974. The *Globe's* euphemism for Joan's treatment for alcoholism was "hospitalized . . . as a result of emotional stress."

Nineteen: ROAR

336 **outside City Hall:** JAF interviews with Barbara Souliotis, Mike Barnicle. Paul Kirk, Mary Frackleton, Alice McGoff, Lisa Collins OH, UVA. The quote is from William James, on the unveiling of the Robert Gould Shaw monument, May 31, 1897.

336 **a different cause:** JAF interview with Barbara Souliotis. Gerard Doherty, Mary Frackleton OH, UVA. For accounts of the busing crisis see Lupo, *Liberty's*, Formisano, *Boston*, and Lukas, *Common Ground*. See also Pete Hamill, "The Revolt of the White Lower Middle Class," *New York* magazine, April 14, 1969.

337 **and liberal dogma:** JAF interview with Dolores Huerta. "Awake," see RFK OH, JFKL. For liberal dogma see Statement of Clarence Mitchell,

Director, Washington Bureau of the NAACP, Senate Subcommittee on Education, Senate Labor and Public Welfare Committee, March 28, 1972, and Harvard Law School faculty petition, April 12, 1972, and Staff Study on Busing, 1972, TON-BC. Also Alexander to Bayh, Feb. 16, 1970, Bayh-IU. BG, June 21, 1965. Celler to Boggs, May 11, 1972, Hale Boggs papers, Tulane University.

338 **harried working class:** JAF interview with Mike Barnicle. Martin Nolan OH, UVA. Charles Ferris OH, SHO. For Coles interview see BG, Oct. 15, 1971. For O'Neill see BG, Feb. 25, 1975. On Garrity see Clark to Watson, May 17, 1966, LBJL.

For EMK support of busing, see text of EMK statement, U.S. Commission on Civil Rights, BH, Oct. 5, 1966. See also Griswold to EMK, Oct. 7, 1966, and EMK to Griswold, Oct. 21, 1966; "Anti-Civil Rights Provisions in H.R. 18037," summer 1968; for EMK on cross-jurisdictional busing see Logue to EMK, April 17, 1967, and EMK to Logue, May 1, 1967; "Racial Imbalance Briefing Note," undated; S. Francis Overlan, Sidney Aronson, and John Noble, "Urban-Suburban School Mixing: A Feasibility Study," West Hartford Public Schools, March 1967, all EMK-JFKL.

On Boston school committee history and segregation, see Kerrigan to Ford, Aug. 15, 1974; undated fact sheet, "Boston School Case," and DOJ memorandum, Oct. 10, 1974, K. William O'Connor, "Boston School Case"; Office of Civil Rights to Secretary, HEW, "Proposed Action Regarding Boston Public Schools," Nov. 19, 1971; Pottinger to Ohrenberger, Nov. 30, 1971, and Colburn and Pottinger, "Deployment of United States Marshals in Boston School Desegregation Process," Aug. 11, 1975, all GFL.

For federal, state, and local officials ducking responsibility, see Colburn and Pottinger, Aug. 11, 1975, Cole to Ford, Oct. 10, 1974, and Ford to Hicks, Dec. 16, 1974, Bulger to Ford, Jan. 2, 1975, and Ford to Bulger, Jan. 9, 1975, Parsons to Cannon, April 14, 1975, Parsons to Buchen and Cannon, Oct. 23, 1975, and Kennedy to Ford (requesting a presidential audience for Louise Day Hicks and other busing foes), all GFL.

339 **they would not listen:** JAF interview with Mike Barnicle. Anthony Lewis OH, UVA. BG, Sept. 8, 1974. Barnicle said his column was prompted by the *Globe's* editor, Thomas Winship, who suggested to the columnist that EMK had gone AWOL as the crisis unfolded. EMK did not indicate if he had been influenced by the column, or its reference to RFK—but Barnicle was personally invited by EMK's staff to accompany the senator to the rally the following day. On King and Cicero, see William vanden Heuvel OH, UVA.

340 **Things turned ugly:** EMKOH-UVA. Barbara Souliotis, Mark Schneider, Paul Kirk OH, UVA. BG, "The First Year," May 25, 1975; Sept. 10, 1974. Formisano, *Boston*, 76. Lupo, *Liberty's*, 204. Two years later, the plaza was the scene of a Pulitzer Prize–winning photograph of a white protester leveling an American flag, like a lance, at a Black attorney being beaten by a crowd.

340 **institutions failed Boston:** Robert Bates OH, UVA. BG, "The First Year," May 25, 1975. Formisano, *Boston*, 69–82.

342 **had no solutions:** EMKOH-UVA. BG, Sept. 10, 1974. Lupo, *Liberty's*, 5, 205, 210. See BG, "The First Year," May 25, 1975; Feb. 25, 1975. On Bulger see Cullen and Murphy, *Whitey Bulger*, 116–17. See also BG, April 22, 2001. JAF interviews with Mike Barnicle, Kenneth Feinberg, Kathleen Sullivan.

342 **employed issues like busing:** "Chronology of School Desegregation Decisions," GFL. The integration cases were *Green v. New Kent County School Board* in 1968 and *Alexander v. Holmes* in 1969. The busing decision came in *Swann v. Charlotte-Mecklenburg Board of Education* in 1971. Nixon pollster Robert Teeter found that while Americans "overwhelmingly support the principle of school desegregation," by a 75–20 margin, "there is no doubt that the American public is opposed to busing to achieve a racial balance," by an almost identical 76–20 margin. See Teeter to Mitchell, Feb. 27, 1972, GFL. By 1975, the opposition to busing remained the same, but support for desegregation had slipped, in a Harris poll, to 56 percent.

342 **extra federal funding:** CQW, Sept. 20, 27, Oct. 18, 1975. EMK to Morse, March 3, 1966; EMK to Campbell, Oct. 21, 1966; EMK to Logue, April 17, 1967, EMK-JFKL. Cole to Ford, "Busing in Boston," Oct. 10, 11, 1974; Silberman to Rumsfeld, Dec. 12, 1974; "Talking Points for Telephone Conversation with Governor Sargent," undated, GFL.

342 **He was heckled:** EMKOH-UVA. BG, Oct. 15, 1974; Feb. 16, March 8, 1975. BH, Feb. 15, 1975.

343 **bigger and nastier:** JAF interview with Barbara Souliotis. EMKOH-UVA. Barbara Souliotis OH, UVA. BG, April 7, 8, 1975. BH, April 7, 1975. NYT, April 7, 1975, March 8, 1976.

343 **white parents fled:** Formisano, *Boston*, 209–12.

344 **cause of disillusionment:** Teeter to Cheney, Nov. 12, 1975, GFL. For a properly kaleidoscopic tour of the era, see Perlstein, *Invisible Bridge*. See also Patterson, *Restless Giant*, the relevant volume of the Oxford History of the United States.

344 **costs of war:** De Haan to EMK, Nov. 1972, "Indochina visit," Summary of Chronology, SJC-NARA. NYT, Dec. 27, 1972.

345 **the Paris Accords:** Suggested Talking Points for Rogers Meeting, Sept. 21, 1972; Halberstam to de Haan, Sept. 26, 1972; Eastland to Rogers, Oct. 17, 1972; de Haan Memo for File on Indochina trip, Nov. 1972; Summary of Meeting with the North Vietnamese Deputy Prime Minister, Dr. Nguyen Duy Trinh, March 16, 1973; de Haan to EMK, Oct. 27, 1972, April 6, 1973; Michael Halberstam, report of study mission on trip to Hanoi, undated, 1973; Itinerary and Summary of Findings ("There is no peace . . . the cease fire has yet to work, and probably will not. It is called only half jokingly the 'ceaseless fire' and from our nights in the provinces the night-time artillery fire and day-time actions remain distressingly the same"), Tinker and de Haan to EMK, undated, 1973, SJC-NARA.

345 **"The Ceasefire War":** "The Ceasefire War," report on 1973 Study Mission to Southeast Asia, Refugee Subcommittee, Jan. 27, 1974; Kennedy statement, April 15, 1973, SJC-NARA. WP, April 15, 1973. CR, May 29, 1973.

"They'll be fighting again, and you know it . . . and I know it," Kissinger told former secretary of de-

fense Mel Laird on Jan. 17, 1973. "There's going to be fighting in Southeast Asia for many years to come," Laird confirmed. "We know the goddamned agreement will probably not work," Kissinger told Alexander Haig, his former deputy, on March 15, 1973. See also Stearman to Kissinger, May 9, 1973: "There is still no ceasefire." On South Vietnam initial cease-fire violations, see Nixon and Kissinger, transcript of telephone call, Jan. 31, 1973. All from FRUS, 1969–1976, Volume X, Vietnam, Jan. 1973–July 1973.

345 **attempting to cut off funding:** CQW, May 11, 1974. WS, May 7, 1974. NYT, March 20, 1974. WP, May 6, 1974.

345 **Graham Martin, advised Kissinger:** Martin had lost his foster son, a Marine, who died in the fighting in Vietnam. Confidential, Martin to Kissinger, March 21, 1974; Kennedy to Kissinger, March 13, 1974, and Kissinger to Kennedy, March 25, 1974; Martin to Kissinger, March 6, May 15, 1974, SJC-NARA. CR, April 1, 2, 1974.

345 **would blame Congress:** Kennedy statement, May 31, 1973; CR, June 29, 1973.

Nixon signed: The original measure was designed to end funding for U.S. bombing of Cambodia and Laos, but in return for an extension until Aug. 15, 1973, Nixon agreed to sign a bill that cut off U.S. military action in all of Southeast Asia, including South and North Vietnam. See John H. Sullivan, "The War Powers Resolution: A Special Study of the Committee on Foreign Affairs," U.S. House of Representatives, 1982, 109.

In January, Kennedy had successfully pushed to make the cutoff a matter of party policy in the Democratic caucus. See Saffold to EMK, Feb. 10, 1995, with excerpts from the Jan. 4, 1973, debate in the party conference, AC-JFKL.

"We can scratch South Vietnam," said Goldwater in late March. "It is imminent that South Vietnam is going to fall into the hands of North Vietnam." See NYT, March 20, 1975.

346 **flee as fight:** For EMK $100 million, see CR, March 26, 1975. For EMK opposition to Ford requests see CR, March 21, 1975. See also EMK to Ford, March 21, 1975; Kissinger to Ford, April 22, 29, 1975; Friedersdorf to Ford, April 21, 23, 24, 1975, GFL.

Congress did not "lose" the Vietnam War. For more than a decade the lawmakers gave three U.S. presidents carte blanche to prevail in Southeast Asia. The cutoff of funds for bombing and other military operations in Indochina, signed into law by Nixon in the summer of 1973, was the first legal halter on presidential warmaking in the region and, as EMK and others argued, long overdue. By then, "to most people the war was over and Vietnam was past," a House Foreign Affairs Committee study on presidential war powers concluded. The mood in Congress was captured by Republican senator Norris Cotton of New Hampshire, who said, "I want to get the hell out of there as quickly as possible, and I don't want to fool around to the point that they might take more prisoners." See Sullivan, "The War Powers Resolution," 109.

Congress never "cut off" aid to South Vietnam. The Nixon administration asked Congress for $1.6 billion for South Vietnam in FY 1974, and Congress authorized $1.1 billion. In FY 1975 the Nixon-Ford administrations requested $1.4 billion, and Congress authorized $700 million. In January 1975, Ford requested an emergency $300 million for the South—but it was not approved by the time Saigon fell. In those same years, Congress okayed some $250–$300 million in aid each year to Cambodia. See Kissinger, *Ending.*

346 **Saigon fell on April 30:** "Indochina Evacuation and Refugee Problems, Part I: Operation Babylift & Humanitarian Needs," Hearing before the Subcommittee to Investigate Problems Connected with Refugees and Escapees, April 8, 1975; "Indochina Evacuation and Refugee Problems," study mission report, June 9, 1975; EMK statement, April 30, 1975; "The Aftermath of War: Humanitarian Problems of Southeast Asia," staff report, Subcommittee to Investigate Problems Connected with Refugees and Escapees, May 17, 1976, SJC-NARA. Closing the book: See Nessen to Staff Secretary, April 28, 1975; Kissinger to Ford, May 14, 1975; Marrs to Buchen, June 12, 1975, GFL. See also de Haan to EMK, April 21, 28, 1975; EMK to Meany, May 8, 1975; Tinker to de Haan, undated, spring 1975; Fact Sheet—Report on Conditions in Camp Pendleton, CA, SJC-NARA. CQW, April 12, 1975. Edward M. Kennedy, "Refugee Act of 1980," *International Migration Review,* Spring–Summer 1981, 141–56.

346 **plotted to kill:** NYT, Dec. 22, 1974. "Alleged Assassination Plots Involving Foreign Leaders," November 1975 interim report of the Select Committee to Study Governmental Operations with Respect to Intelligence Activities, United States Senate (the Church Committee). Some of the revelations had made their way into the public record via scattered press reports. The FBI bugging of Martin Luther King, for example, was disclosed in 1968. In 1971, antiwar activists broke into an FBI field office outside Philadelphia and unearthed evidence of the COINTELPRO dissident surveillance and disruption project. Drew Pearson and Jack Anderson mentioned the assassination plots in columns in 1967 and 1971. On Ford and assassinations, see Olmsted, *Challenging,* 61.

347 **The raft of wrongdoing:** "Intelligence Activities and the Rights of Americans," Report of the Select Committee to Study Governmental Operations with Respect to Intelligence Activities, United States Senate. EMK was among those public figures whose mail was opened, along with Hubert Humphrey and the pre-presidential Richard Nixon. See WP, Sept. 25, 1975.

CIA-Mafia plot: According to the Church Committee, the plotting at CIA started in the final months of the Eisenhower administration, after Castro came to power and threatened the Mob's gambling interests in Havana. The CIA turned to Robert Maheu, a former FBI agent working as a private investigator, who in turn reached out to mobster John Rosselli. Rosselli put them in touch with Sam Giancana and Santos Trafficante, the Cosa Nostra chieftain in Cuba. Giancana was shot dead on the eve of his testimony to the Church Committee in

1975. Rosselli's body was found in an oil drum off the coast of Florida one year later.

Assassination: John Kennedy asked Senator George Smathers and newsman Tad Szulc about the advisability of assassinating Castro. See Church Committee, Interim Report, "Alleged Assassination Plots Involving Foreign Leaders," Nov. 20, 1975, 123, 138. On RFK briefing, see 104 and 133.

Exner affair: The committee report that led to exposure of the Exner affair elliptically noted, "Evidence before the Committee indicates that a close friend of President Kennedy had frequent contact with the president. . . . FBI reports and testimony indicate that the President's friend was also a close friend of John Rosselli and Sam Giancana and saw them often during this same period."

348 **relationship with Judith Campbell Exner:** JAF interview with Kitty Kelley. Judith Exner testimony, Sept. 20, 1975, and EMK testimony, Sept. 22, 1975, both to Select Committee to Study Governmental Operations with Respect to Intelligence Activities, United States Senate. In her Church Committee testimony, Exner denied that she had ever conveyed messages between John Kennedy and Sam Giancana. Later in life, battling cancer and needing money, she changed her story several times and claimed to have been a courier in the Kennedy-Mafia plot against Castro. See Hersh, *Dark Side,* chapter 18, "Judy"; Michael O'Brien, "The Exner File: Truth and Fantasy from a President's Mistress," *Washington Monthly,* Dec. 1999; and Kitty Kelley, "The Dark Side of Camelot," *People,* Feb. 29, 1988.

348 **Tintagel was tawdry:** Tom Wicker, "Kennedy Without End, Amen," *Esquire,* June 1977. For a history of the investigations see Olmsted, *Challenging.*

348 **the middle stage:** Lawrence, *Class of '74,* introduction. Lacking a compelling program: See Hart, *Right from the Start,* epilogue: "The fields of liberalism failed to provide a crop. . . . The soil is worn out."

349 **"the imperial presidency":** For a review of executive abuses and reform, see Kutler, *Wars,* chapter 22, "In the Shadow of Watergate," 574–611. See also the report of the Senate Select Committee to Study Governmental Operations with Respect to Intelligence Activities (the Church Committee hearings and report), 1975–76. NYT, June 13, 1982.

349 **left a vacuum:** Ervin to EMK, Jan. 16, 1973, TS-UMASS. The same spirit gripped the House: "The ingredients are present, and the timing right, for a somewhat historic confrontation with executive power and its gradual usurpation of congressional prerogatives," the new House whip, James Wright of Texas, wrote Majority Leader Tip O'Neill. It was time, Wright said, for coordinated resistance to "the dismemberment of legislative power." Wright to O'Neill, Jan. 19, 1973, and O'Neill to Wright, Jan. 24, 1973, TON-BC. See also Barriere to Albert, Jan. 15, Feb. 14, Aug. 3, 1973, Carl Albert Center, University of Oklahoma.

Kennedy agreed with Ervin on the question of congressional competency. The executive agencies were expanding in size and sophistication, and the issues facing Congress required growing technical expertise. Kennedy was a midwife to the 1973 establishment of the congressional Office of Technology Assessment, which survived for twenty years before succumbing to Republican attacks over its cost and effectiveness. See Ellis Mottur OH, UVA, and Colin Norman, "OTA Caught in Partisan Crossfire," *Technology Review*, Oct./Nov. 1977, and NYT, Sept. 24, 1995.

349 **"unique and spectacular":** Susman to EMK, Jan. 18, 1973, with EMK notation, and Susman memos, "Impoundment I," Jan. 31, 1973, and "Impoundment II," Feb. 2, 1973, TS-UMASS. Sundquist, *Decline*, 201–13.

350 **was the pocket veto:** Edward M. Kennedy, "Congress, the President, and the Pocket Veto," *Virginia Law Review* 63, no. 3 (April 1977): 355–82. EMK to Ford, Oct. 10, 1974, GFL. Louis Fisher, "The Pocket Veto: Its Current Status," Congressional Research Service, March 30, 2001. NYT, March 1, Aug. 16, 1973, June 1, 1974. WP, March 1, 1973, June 1, 1974. *Kennedy v. Sampson*, 511 F. 2d 430 (D.C. Cir. 1974).

350 **Foreign Intelligence Surveillance Act:** JAF interview with Kenneth Feinberg. Kenneth Feinberg OH, UVA. CR, May 18, 1977. NYT, March 17, 1976. See also Kennedy to Colby, April 24, 1975, and a May 2, 1975, internal memo from CIA general counsel John Warner to CIA director William Colby revealing the agency's displeasure at EMK's initial efforts to put curbs on electronic eavesdropping, both on CIA FOIA website. EMK statement, War Powers Resolution, Nov. 7, 1973, TS-UMASS.

350 **Freedom of Information Act:** JAF interview with Thomas Susman. CQW, June 8, Oct. 12, Nov. 23, 1974. Ford to EMK, Aug. 20, 1974; EMK and Moorhead to Ford, Sept. 23, 1974; Ash to Nixon, June 28, 1974; Timmons to Korologos, April 27, 1974; Scowcroft to Timmons, April 15, 1974; Timmons to Ford, Aug. 19, 1974; Cole to Ford, Oct. 8, 1974, Ash to Ford, Oct. 16, 1974, O'Donnell and Korologos to Timmons, Oct. 30, 1974, all GFL.

According to the National Security Archive, a nonpartisan watchdog group, the 1974 amendments represent a "milestone in the quest to secure the public's right to information." Since their passage, "the FOIA has allowed citizens to learn more about their family histories and personal files; it has brought to light government oversights, shortfalls and transgressions; it has forced improvement in government regulations and activities." See "Veto Battle 30 Years Ago Set Freedom of Information Norms," Nov. 23, 2004, NSA website.

351 **campaign finance reform:** R. Sam Garrett, "The State of Campaign Finance Policy: Recent Developments and Issues for Congress," Congressional Research Service, June 23, 2016.

351 **"first effective curbs":** NYT, July 27, 1973. CQA, 1971. Ford statement, Oct. 15, 1974, GFL. Lukas, *Nightmare*, chapter 5, "Dirty Money," 109–45. "Americans found it difficult to distinguish between campaign contributions and outright bribes," the *New York Times* reported in a Dec. 4, 1973, analysis by David Rosenbaum. "Moreover, from the Senate Watergate hearings, television

viewers from coast to coast saw what some of these vast sums were spent for: wiretapping, burglaries, political sabotage." And so the public demand for reform was overwhelming. "That hit, just at the time of . . . intensity in the Watergate thing . . . at the right time," Kennedy recalled. As Senator John Pastore, a Democrat from Rhode Island, remembered, the senators "were running like a bunch of scared rats." See Mutch to Clymer, May 10, 1995, with transcript of Senator Hugh Scott interview; EMK interview, AC-JFKL.

Once EMK had gone through his process of self-education, he tended to stay active on an issue for at least a few years. He traced his 1973 interest in campaign finance to his battles over voter suppression and the Voting Rights Act, the poll tax, and the "whole concept of expanding the franchise" in 1965. He was successful in defending the Supreme Court one-man, one-vote ruling in 1966, and in his 1970 battle to get eighteen-year-olds the vote. He failed, however, in his long campaign to bring voting rights to residents of the nation's capital. See EMK interview, AC-JFKL.

The law—a series of amendments to a 1971 act—required full disclosure and placed restraints on what individuals could donate to a candidate for federal office ($1,000 per contest), or to a political party or committee ($5,000), and set an aggregate limit for an individual donor of $25,000 a year. Presidential campaigns were capped at spending $10 million in the primaries, and $20 million in the general election. If the presidential candidates qualified, and chose to do so, they could obtain public funding for their campaigns. The independent FEC was empowered to punish violators.

351 **Scott and Kennedy:** EMK press releases, Nov. 13, Dec. 6, 1973; EMK testimony, Senate Finance Committee, Nov. 15, 1973, TS-UMASS. NYT, Dec. 4, 12, 1973. CQW, April 13, 1974. As always, the legislation had many important sponsors in the Senate, aside from Kennedy and Scott: Democratic senators Phil Hart of Michigan, Alan Cranston of California, Walter Mondale of Minnesota, and Adlai Stevenson of Illinois, and Republicans Charles Mathias of Maryland, Richard Schweiker of Pennsylvania, and Robert Stafford of Vermont. For an account of the post-Watergate debate about campaign financing, see Mutch, *Campaigns*.

351 **the Supreme Court declared:** *Buckley v. Valeo*, 424 U.S. 1 (1976). "The Supreme Court really mangled the concept of freedom of expression," Senator Hugh Scott said afterward, and he quoted Mr. Bumble from *Oliver Twist*: "If the law supposes that, the law is a ass—a idiot." It was a "ridiculous" decision, said Scott. "In effect, it says that if you're poor, the Court has no concern for you. If you're rich, go for it. Spend all you want." Archibald Cox filed a brief, on behalf of Scott and Kennedy, as amicus curiae in the case. See Hugh Scott and Carey Parker interviews, Mutch to Clymer, May 10, 1995, AC-JFKL.

352 **dollars of "dark money":** Liberal Democrats have helped undermine reform as well. In 1984, Ronald Reagan campaigned for reelection without holding a single general election fundraiser, as he

and his opponent, Walter Mondale, both accepted $40 million in federal funding. That provision of EMK's legislation seemed an accepted success. But in 2008, Barack Obama became the first major-party presidential candidate to reject public financing in a general election—and suffered no apparent penalty from the voters. The Nixon years were back. Jeffrey Toobin, "Money Unlimited," TNY, May 14, 2012. Lear Jiang, "Disclosure's Last Stand? The Need to Clarify the 'Informational Interest' Advanced by Campaign Finance Disclosure," *Columbia Law Review* 119, no. 2 (2019). WP, June 16, 2012, Feb. 9, 2016.

Twenty: Deacon

353 **Law Day address:** Susman to EMK, April 23, 1974, re Law Day Speech, TS-UMASS. Opposition research report on Edward "Ted" Kennedy, Carter 1976 campaign, JCL. Jimmy Carter, Hamilton Jordan OH, Jimmy Carter collection, UVA. Peter Bourne interview, AC-JFKL. Thompson, *Shark Hunt*, 452–95. Paul Kirk, James King OH, AC-JFKL. For Anderson analysis see Anderson, *Electing*, 72–73. The awkwardness was compounded by Carter's eleventh-hour recanting of an invitation to give Kennedy and his entourage a ride in the governor's airplane from Atlanta to the university in Athens. See WP, Aug. 10, 1980. The first staff memo to propose that Carter run for the presidency, by aide Peter Bourne in 1972, captured the Georgians' poor opinion of Kennedy: "Both he and his wife seem to be drifting from one emotional crisis to another, he has repeatedly handled stress poorly, and in fact has never been tested by a knock down drag out campaign." See Bourne to Carter, July 25, 1972, reprinted in Stroud, *How Jimmy Won*, 23–27.

354 **blinding self-regard:** JAF interview with Hamilton Jordan. Jimmy Carter, Hamilton Jordan OH, Jimmy Carter collection, UVA. WP, May 14, 1977. The "strengths are weaknesses" maxim was introduced to the author by then senator Gary Hart in a 1982 interview. Carter's "naivete was a strength and a weakness," Eizenstat said in an Oct. 9, 2018, speech to the Washington Book Club, attended by the author. In a letter to Ursula Niebuhr, Arthur Schlesinger Jr. called Carter "a humorless, ungenerous, cold-eyed, crafty, rigid, sanctimonious and possibly vindictive man." See Schlesinger to Niebuhr, May 24, 1976, *Letters*, 440. See also Alter, *His Very Best*, 196–97.

354 **themes, not issues:** EMKOH–UVA. Patrick Caddell interview, AC-JFKL. *Rolling Stone*, June 31, 1976. Witcover, *Marathon*, is the benchmark account of Carter's campaign and features the "kiss his ass" exchange, 341–42. See also Alter, *His Very Best*, and Stroud, *How Jimmy Won*. The transcript of a December 1976 post-election conference at the Institute of Politics of the John F. Kennedy School of Government at Harvard College, published in 1977, Moore and Fraser, eds., *Campaign for President*, is a valuable collection of remarks by campaign strategists. NYT, March 21, 1976. For EMK and 1976 convention see NYT, July 15, 1976; BG, July 12, 14, 1976.

Carter had another reason to be grateful to EMK, who had not used his power to actively promote his brother-in-law Sargent Shriver's 1976 presidential campaign. Shriver joined the race regardless. The Kennedy legacy, Shriver said, "awaits the leader who can claim it. I intend to claim that legacy." But EMK did not join Shriver when he declared his candidacy. See Witcover, *Marathon*, 151–52, 250.

355 **already taut relationship:** BG, Aug. 24, 1976.

355 **The debacle that followed:** EMKOH-UVA. Patrick Caddell, "Initial Working Paper on Political Strategy," Dec. 10, 1976, JCL.

356 **"clearly civil war":** Patrick Caddell interview, AC-JFKL. For Carter on EMK drinking see Carter, *Diary*, 457, and for woman-killer remark see Clymer, *Edward M. Kennedy*, 241. See Powell, *Story*, 185. Peter Bourne told Clymer that Carter deplored Kennedy's sybaritic lifestyle. See Bourne interview, AC-JFKL. As Walter Mondale put it, "Why, at this point in American history [did Kennedy] decide to act in a way that would elect Reagan? The answer is that he thought that Carter was unworthy of being president. That was just plain irresponsible." See Alter, *His Very Best*, 495. On assassination see EMKOH-UVA.

357 **dicker and deal:** EMK-TC, 359–60. Carter often cited philosopher Reinhold Niebuhr that "the sad duty of politics is to establish justice in a sinful world." See NYT, June 19, 1977. What Carter saw as a sad duty, the Kennedys embraced as an energizing challenge.

357 **put a barracuda:** Patrick Caddell interview, AC-JFKL. Carter, *Diary*, 378.

358 **saw things in black and white:** JAF interviews with Jimmy Carter, Hamilton Jordan, Anne Wexler. Jimmy Carter interview, undated early 1980s, "Channel 4," TON-BC. Alonzo McDonald, James Schlesinger OH, Jimmy Carter collection, UVA. Powell and Rafshoon to Carter, Feb. 9, 1979; Moore to Carter, Feb. 4, 1977, Feb. 27, 1978, April 3, 1978; Dye to Moore, July 12, 1977, April 6, 1978; Tate to Moore, Feb. 20, 1977, Sept. 12, 1978; Gonzalez to Carter, Oct. 20, 1978; Donilon to Moore, Aug. 16, 1977; Moore to Mondale, June 6, 1977, all JCL. Norman Ornstein, "The Open Congress Meets the President," in King, ed., *Both Ends*.

358 **thirst for oil:** Yergin, *Prize*, 567, 588–90, 608, 613, 791. "The embargo and its consequences sent shock radiating through the social fabric. . . . The age of shortage was at hand," Yergin wrote (pp. 615–17). "In the United States, the shortfall struck at fundamental beliefs in the endless abundance of resources . . . deeply rooted in the American character."

358 **phenomenon called "stagflation":** Weiss and Lew to Speaker O'Neill, Sept. 7, 1979; Weiss to Lew, May 6, 1980, TON-BC. Eizenstat, *President Carter*, 277–78. Michael Bordo and Athanasios Orphanides, eds., *The Great Inflation: The Rebirth of Modern Central Banking*, papers and transcripts from a 2008 conference of the National Bureau of Economic Research (Chicago: University of Chicago Press, 2013), Bordo and Orphanides introduction. For Nixon's browbeating of Arthur Burns, and stagflation, see Burns, *Secret Diary*.

359 **clashed with his party:** "He's a Republican," Schlesinger told a reporter. "He has the temperament of a small-businessman who happened to become President." *Newsweek*, Jan. 29, 1979. Caddell memo to Carter, JCL. Eizenstat, *President Carter*, 830. NJ, Nov. 25, 1978.

359 **foreign policy initiatives:** JAF interview with Jimmy Carter. Jan Kalicki interview, AC-JFKL. Oksenberg to Brzezinski, Nov. 18, 1977; Far East desk to Brzezinski, Jan. 5, 1978; Brzezinski to Carter, May 5, 1978, and Vance to Carter, Jan. 3, 1979 ("Ted will continue as a strong ally on China policy"), all Digital National Security Archive, NSA. Eizenstat, *President Carter*, 293, 572, 582, 610. The canal treaty began as a Nixon administration goodneighbor initiative, but Senators Jesse Helms and Strom Thurmond ("We own it. We bought it. It's ours."), Ronald Reagan, and an emerging New Right movement saw it as a symbol of American decline. Clymer, *Drawing the Line*, 8–9. Alter, *His Very Best*, 383–84.

359 **fixer Griffin Bell:** On cost containment see Eizenstat and Onek to Carter, Feb. 14, 1978; Califano to Carter, Feb. 14, 1978, JCL; and Carter to O'Neill, March 20, 1979, TON-BC. On Bell see Susman to EMK, Jan. 7, 24, 1977; EMK to (Aaron) Henry, Feb. 3, 1977: "You and Clarence [Mitchell] and Jesse [Jackson] cannot be lightly written off by any conscientious senator," Kennedy wrote, trying to ease their disappointment, TS-UMASS. But Bell had this going for him as well: he had been a Georgia coordinator for John F. Kennedy's campaign in 1960 and appointed to the federal bench by President Kennedy in 1961. See also Kaufman and Kaufman, *Presidency*, 27, 103. When Bell departed in 1979, Kennedy helped the White House get Benjamin Civiletti confirmed as attorney general as well.

360 **battled Long on tax reform:** Moe to Mondale, Aug. 1, 1979, Walter Mondale papers, Minnesota Historical Society. On tax reform, see Paul McDaniel OH, UVA. Stanley Surrey, "Reflections on the Tax Reform Act of 1976," *Cleveland State Law Review*, 1976. NYT, March 7; July 19, 20, 24, 1976. Kennedy aided Carter when the president launched his own tax reform bill in 1977, targeting deductions like three-martini lunches and country club dues, but the president fared no better than the Senate liberals in 1976. When genuflecting to wealthy donors with its *Buckley v. Valeo* decision in 1976, the Supreme Court struck a blow to the post-Watergate reform impulse. Carter's defeat on tax reform "spoke volumes about how American democracy was captured then—and still is now—by highly organized special interests that keep their benefits through large donations," said Eizenstat, *President Carter*, 116.

360 **Deregulation would transform:** Stephen Breyer OH, UVA. Susman to Kennedy, Oct. 9, 1973; Susman to Kennedy, Dec. 16, 1975; Martin to Kennedy, March 5, 1974, with March 1, 1974, attachment, TS-UMASS. OMB briefing paper, "Summary of Independent Regulatory Commissions," July 8, 1975, GFL. Breyer interview, *Commanding Heights*, PBS. Lippman, *Senator Ted*

Kennedy, 160. Hot pants: See Kathryn Harrigan and Daniel Kasper, "Senator Kennedy and the CAB," Harvard Business School, case study 4-378-055, 1978, 6. The authors cite then Federal Trade Commission chairman Lewis Engman: "The average airline commercial looks like an ad for a combination bawdy house and dinner theater." The Harrigan and Kasper paper was condensed from a Kennedy School of Government case study— "Senator Kennedy and the Civil Aeronautics Board: Parts I, II, and Sequel," C94-77-157, -158, -158S, written by Donald Simon. It includes Breyer's account, and early memos to EMK and staff outlining the task before them.

362 **another senator's turf:** Stephen Breyer OH, UVA. EMK interview, AC-JFKL. Magnuson and Cannon to Kennedy, Oct. 4, 1974; Kennedy to Magnuson and Cannon, Oct. 4, 1974, TS-UMASS. Stephen Breyer, "The Genesis of Airline Deregulation: The Role of the Kennedy Hearings and Report," manuscript draft, 1979, GFL. NYT, March 30, 1975.

On Cannon, see Derthick and Quirk, *Politics*, 109: "To protect the committee's prerogatives Cannon had to dispel suspicion (encouraged by Kennedy . . . and given general currency by the press) that Commerce would abjectly defer to the regulated interests and obstruct reform."

See also Simon case study, "Senator Kennedy and the Civil Aeronautics Board," II: A Department of Transportation official told Breyer he was "a lunatic college professor who would drive Pan Am into bankruptcy," and that Kennedy would be blamed. Breyer brought the threat to Kennedy. "Would we drive them into bankruptcy?" Kennedy asked. "No . . . but we'll get blamed for it," Breyer replied. "Hold the hearing," said Kennedy.

Breyer never ruled out the possibility that Cannon thought Kennedy was just padding the subcommittee budget, a common practice in the Senate, and was not really serious about the airlines and the CAB. It was not until the hearings were over that Cannon personally, and angrily, accused Kennedy of "trespassing" on his territory and threatened to cut his funding: "Your committee is getting into an area where it has no jurisdiction and I object to it," he told Kennedy.

363 **man of substance:** JAF interview with Thomas Susman. Susman to EMK, June 6, 1974; Breyer to Kennedy, Sept. 27, 1974; Parker to Kennedy, Oct. 30, 1974, TS-UMASS. Harrigan and Kasper, "Senator Kennedy and the CAB," 7–9. Carey Parker, anonymous interview, AC-JFKL. Otten quoted in Lippman, *Senator Ted Kennedy*, 159. Derthick and Quirk, *Politics*, 106: "Looking in 1974 for a project to undertake . . . Kennedy noticeably lacked a significant record of legislative achievement." Given his role in immigration, redistricting, draft reform, voting rights, the voting age, and the war on cancer, this is too harsh a judgment—but reflects the lack of a major statute bearing his name.

363 **An effective hearing:** Breyer to Kennedy, undated, early 1975, "CAB Hearings," TS-UMASS. Breyer, Susman, and others would school Kennedy for three to five hours the night before or arrive at

his home with thick briefing binders around dawn on the day of a hearing. See Simon case study, "Senator Kennedy and the Civil Aeronautics Board," II. On preparation see "Senator's Cushion," unsigned, undated staff memo, SJC-NARA.

364 **Kennedy zinged him:** Pacific Southwest Airlines had 158 seats on its California planes, vs. 121 on a comparable American Airlines jet flying the Boston–Washington route under CAB regulation. Both were usually around 55 to 60 percent full. "Thus, if American carried 95 passengers on average, as did PSA, instead of 66 it could have reduced its fares 30 percent," wrote Breyer, "Genesis," 27–28. For the "apples and oranges" exchange and analysis, see Harrigan and Kasper, "Senator Kennedy and the CAB," 13–14.

365 **Americans took advantage:** Alfred Kahn, David Rubenstein, Charles Schultze OH, Jimmy Carter collection, UVA. EMK remarks, American Enterprise Institute, May 21, 1979; "Summary of the Chronology" of CAB actions regarding Pan American, undated, fall 1974; Bakes to EMK, Jan. 31, 1978, TS-UMASS. Kennedy to Ford, June 26, 1975; Marsh to Cannon, re "Kennedy letter," July 7, 1975; "Senate Members Attending Regulatory Reform Meeting," WH briefing paper, June 25, 1975, GFL. NYT, Nov. 8, 1974, Feb. 19, June 30, 1975. NJ, July 28, 1979. WP, July 2, 1980. Breyer, "Genesis," preface. Eizenstat, *President Carter*, 361–72. Breyer interview, *Commanding Heights*, PBS. See also Derthick and Quirk, *Politics*, 43–44.

Eizenstat notes that reform has a half-life. With the dismantling of the CAB, regulation fell to the Federal Aviation Administration, which had its own "symbiotic" relationship with the airlines and okayed mergers that created an "oligopoly" of firms carrying 80 percent of all passengers.

366 **two men could cooperate:** For assessments of deregulation see Alter, *His Very Best*, 491–92.

366 **eat its peas:** EMKOH-UVA. EMK-TC, 358. Eizenstat Q&A, Washington Book Club, Oct. 9, 2018. Transition memo, unsigned, Peter Bourne papers, JCL. Blumenthal and Morone, *Heart*, 263–64, 276–78. Carter, *Diary*, 76, 102.

366 **A systemic solution:** EMKOH-UVA. Califano to Carter, May 22, 1978; Eizenstat to Carter, Feb. 22, 1979, JCL. Blumenthal and Morone, *Heart*, 264–74.

367 **did not mourn:** Carter, *Diary*, 210. Califano, *Governing*, 88–119. Eizenstat, *President Carter*, 815–33.

367 **The final dose:** EMKOH-UVA. Stuart Eizenstat OH, Jimmy Carter collection, UVA. Kennedy to Carter with attached summary, April 14, 1978; Onek to Eizenstat, May 19, 1978; Califano to Carter, May 30, 1978; Eizenstat to Carter, May 31, 1978; Eizenstat and Onek to Carter, "Meeting with Kennedy on NHI," July 27, 1978; Eizenstat and Onek to Carter, "National Health Plan," March 20, 1979; Summary Fact Sheet: President Carter's National Health Plan Legislation, June 12, 1979; Mongan to Eizenstat and Carp, Nov. 9, 1979, all JCL. Eizenstat to Carter, July 27, 1978; Eizenstat and Onek to Carter, "Meeting with Kennedy on NHI," July 27, 1978, AC-JFKL. Burke to Dole, May 12, 1979, with talking points and

May 14, 1979, press release, Dole-KU. BH, Nov. 19, 1978. NJ, July 29, Dec. 2, 1978. NYT, July 29, 30, 1978. Eizenstat, *President Carter*, 815–33. Califano, *Governing*, 88–119. On health care as a "right" see Burton Hersh, "The Survival of Edward Kennedy," *Washingtonian*, Feb. 1979.

In 1979, as he prepared to run for reelection, Carter offered his own health insurance plan that he proclaimed, many years later, would have passed Congress with EMK's support and obviated the need for President Barack Obama's Affordable Care Act ("Obamacare"). Despite Democratic control of both houses of Congress, however, Carter could not persuade either the House or the Senate to act on his legislation. See Bird, *Outlier*, 304–9. A bitter Carter ratcheted up the charge after Kennedy's death, when he told *60 Minutes* in 2010, "We would have had comprehensive health care now, had it not been for Ted Kennedy's deliberately blocking the legislation that I proposed. . . . It was his fault. Ted Kennedy killed the bill. . . . He did not want to see me have a major success in that realm of life." See Frank James, "Jimmy Carter Blames Ted Kennedy for Killing Earlier Health Overhaul," *It's All Politics*, NPR, Sept. 16, 2010.

368 **sidled to the right:** Califano to Carter, May 30, 1978; Schultze to Carter, May 2, 1978; Schultze and McIntyre to Carter, May 31, 1978; Moore to Carter, Dec. 7, 1978, JCL. Fein to Kennedy and Fein to Glasser, May 30, 1978, AC-JFKL: "We are engaged with an Administration that uses words loosely, makes conflicting commitments, attempts to negotiate beyond the point that is negotiable, and accuses others of backing out of the process or out of agreements or of being inflexible." Jimmy Carter OH, Jimmy Carter collection, UVA.

368 **gathered in Memphis:** NYT, Dec. 7, 11, 1978. WP, Dec. 9, 11, 1978. BG, June 10, 1979.

368 **"against the wind":** JAF interview with Joseph Califano. Remarks of Senator Edward M. Kennedy, Workshop on Health Care, Democratic National Committee, Mid-term Convention, Memphis, Tennessee, Dec. 9, 1978, EMKI. Telephone Interview of the President by *The New Yorker*, Feb. 14, 1997, WCL. Califano, *Inside*, 336–38. Moore, *1980 in Retrospect*, 17. EMK interview, AC-JFKL.

370 **declaration of war:** Jimmy Carter interview, AC-JFKL. WP, Dec. 11, 1978.

370 **Jody Powell had watched:** Powell, *Story*, 182.

370 **Jordan told Carter:** Eizenstat Q&A, Washington Book Club, Oct. 9, 2018. Gerald Rafshoon OH, Jimmy Carter collection, UVA. Pat Caddell interview; Jordan to Carter, undated, Sept. 1979, and undated, autumn 1979, AC-JFKL. Jordan to Carter, "Eyes Only," Jan. 17, 1979, memo excerpted in WP, June 8, 1980. BG, June 10, 1979. Bourne, *Carter*, 431.

370 **Carter looked petty:** Lipshutz to Carter, May 3, 1979, AC-JFKL. NYT, June 14, 1979. *Washington Monthly*, Sept. 1979. NJ, March 3, 1979. *Time*, June 25, 1979. When the news of the Kennedy snub reached the press, the White House reversed itself and Kennedy was invited. See Stahl, *Reporting*, 86–87.

371 **benefit Ronald Reagan:** JAF interviews with Jimmy Carter, Victoria Reggie Kennedy. EMKOH-UVA. Susman to EMK, undated, 1979, TS-UMASS. Moe to Mondale, Aug. 1, 1979, Walter Mondale papers, Minnesota Historical Society. NJ, Sept. 8, 1979. Carter pushed allies like O'Neill to tears (see Farrell, *Tip O'Neill*, 516) and Rosten-kowski to vengeance (see Eizenstat, *President Carter*, 819) over federal appointments. Years later, Carter confessed that he did not appreciate how angry the Cox episode left Kennedy or how it would fuel the senator's decision to challenge him. See Jimmy Carter interview, AC-JFKL. For Kennedy and Bell and Cox see also Powell, *Story*, 188. Nantucket Sound: EMKOH-UVA. Carter signed a measure creating the Chattahoochee River National Recreation Area in 1978.

372 **were not fantasists:** Germond and Witcover, *Blue Smoke*, 50–51. According to the authors, the family was represented in McLean by Jean and Stephen Smith and RFK's son Joseph, the New Frontier and RFK eras by Arthur Schlesinger, Theodore Sorensen, John Douglas, and John Seigenthaler, and the senator's contemporary staff and advisers by Paul Kirk, David Burke, Carey Parker, Dr. Larry Horowitz, Rick Burke, and others. For Wagner and itinerary see WP, Feb. 4, 1979.

372 **woes were spiking:** *Newsweek*, July 23, 1979. NYT, June 10, Aug. 26, 1979. Perlstein, *Reaganland*, 558, 561–68.

373 **a national malaise:** NJ, July 28, 1979. *Newsweek*, July 30, 1979. WP, July 9, 10, 16, 1979. BG, July 20, 1979. NYT, Aug. 1, 1979. Gillon, *Dilemma*, 265. For lively accounts of the Camp David saga, see Mattson, *"What the Heck"*; Eizenstat, *President Carter*, 671–707; and Perlstein, *Reaganland*, 558–94. Malaise: The word did not appear in the Camp David speech but was a Carter favorite going back to his 1974 Law Day address. It was picked up by the press from Carter's Camp David guests that summer, after being cited by Pat Caddell in his April memo to Carter (Patrick Caddell, "Of Crisis and Opportunity," April 23, 1979, JCL), which began, "America is a nation deep in crisis. Unlike civil war or depression this crisis, nearly invisible, is unique from those that previously have engaged Americans in their history. Psychological more than material, it is a crisis of confidence marked by a dwindling faith in the future. It cannot be 'seen' in ordinary ways—there are no armies of the night, no street demonstrations, no powerful lobbys [*sic*]. It can be read in the polls which monitor the vital signs of the body politic, it can be heard in the growing real despair of elites and ordinary citizens alike as they struggle to articulate in concepts the malaise which they themselves feel. The crisis is not your fault."

Twenty-One: The Cause of the Common Man

374 **the worst way:** EMK fared better than California governor Jerry Brown, who, in the second of three unsuccessful presidential campaigns (1976, 1980, 1992), won no primaries and made little dent. "My principles are simple," Brown declared. "Protect the earth. Serve the people. And explore the universe." Broder et al., *Pursuit*. In this compendium by the *Washington Post* campaign writers, see "Kennedy," by T. R. Reid, 68, 78–79, 81.

375 **"problem of character":** Tuchman quoted in Natalie Gittelson, "Chappaquiddick: The Verdict on Ted Kennedy," *McCall's*, Aug. 1979. In the Sept. 24, 1979, issue of *Newsweek*, columnist Meg Greenfield wrote of Chappaquiddick, "Kennedy's closer friends and staff and supporters who argue that this is a concern only to soreheads, cranks and a few right-wing bananas do him a terrible disservice. What happened that night and the senator's attitude toward it and conduct thereafter represent a legitimate subject of interest and anxiety and this casts a huge moral shadow over his candidacy. It emerges as a failure of personal and public responsibility so large and deep as to overwhelm much of the undeniable goodness and strength of the man."

375 **"going to be geniuses":** WP, June 8, 1980.

375 **an adoring audience:** EMK 1980 Democratic convention address, EMKI.

376 **newsman Roger Mudd:** EMK's answer: "Well, I'm—were I to—to make the—the announcement and—to run, the reasons that I would run is because I have a great belief in this country, that it is—has more natural resources than any nation in the world, has the greatest educated population in the world, the greatest technology of any country in the world, the greatest capacity of innovation in the world, and the greatest political system in the world. . . . And the energies and the resourcefulness of this nation, I think, should be focused on these problems in a way that brings a sense of restoration in this country by its people to—in dealing with the problems that we face—primarily the issues on the economy, the problems of inflation and the problems of energy. And I would basically feel that—that it's imperative for this country to either move forward, that it can't stand still, or otherwise it moves back."

376 **he winged it:** JAF interview with Roger Mudd. EMKOH-UVA. A tape of the broadcast, complete with the commercials that ran in 1979, is available on YouTube. Broder et al., *Pursuit*, 41. EMK's mind was churning, said aide Melody Miller. He did not want his son Patrick to hear an exchange with Mudd about the dangers of assassination, and he bridled at a hypothetical question Mudd asked about his daughter Kara. He knew immediately that the interview "was a disaster. I remember getting on the boat afterward with Patrick and telling him it was a disaster." See Melody Miller OH, UVA. EMKOH-UVA.

376 **The *Teddy* documentary:** JAF interview, Kandy Stroud. EMKOH-UVA. Melody Miller OH, UVA. Perlstein, *Reaganland*, 656. To the Carter team's distress, the motion picture *Jaws* made its television debut that night on ABC, commanding one of the largest television audiences ever. The country was watching the mechanical shark, Jordan recalled, while "I wanted everyone to see what I saw: the Kennedy legend reduced to a bumbling inarticulate man." Jordan, *Crisis*, 21.

377 **second abysmal performance:** JAF interviews with Roger Mudd, Victoria Reggie Kennedy.

EMKOH-UVA. Melody Miller OH, UVA. EMK-TC, 368–71. *Time*, Nov. 19, 1979.

377 **"something psychologically going on":** Warren Rudman OH, UVA.

377 **"sort of going through the motions":** Milton Gwirtzman, Edmund Reggie OH, UVA. Charles Ferris OH, SHO. Anthony Lewis, video interview, *Boston Globe* special series, "Ted Kennedy," video. Donald Ritchie, "Where Is Ted Kennedy When We Need Him? The Possibilities for Legislating in a Polarized Congress," speech given at U.S. Embassy, Dublin, Ireland, June 22, 2017. Lawrence Horowitz interview, AC-JFKL. "The guy doesn't want it," wrote *Globe* columnist Ellen Goodman, after following EMK through the purgatory that was winter in Iowa. "It's written in his body language. It's in his eyes, his speech patterns, his erratic behavior. . . . The man doesn't really want to be in Iowa, Maine, New Hampshire. He doesn't want to be asked again about Chappaquiddick, about his sex life, about the shah. . . . I see a man running for president dutifully, fatalistically, unhappily . . . a complicated man with a lot to win by losing: Privacy, peace, family, personal freedom. He exorcises the past. He's done it, he's run for President and doesn't have to do it again. . . . He exorcises the fear. He has survived. He is, in a very real sense, a free man." See Goodman, BG, Jan. 24, 1980. "He always gave the impression of a man who had lived his life for everybody but himself," wrote Lewis Lapham that fall. "I don't know how it is possible not to feel sympathy for the man, and I'm sure that he possesses all the virtues that his admirers ascribe to him—courage, fortitude, sentimental good nature, and a bewildered decency of intent." Lapham, "Edward Kennedy and the Romance of Death," *Harper's*, Dec. 1979. For more expressions of belief that Kennedy's "heart was not in it"—that he ran reflexively, or from a sense of obligation, or that losing in 1980 was an act of self-liberation—see UVA oral histories of Betty Taymor, Stu Shapiro, Melody Miller, Lester Hyman, Dan Fenn, Robert Bates, and Richard Clasby. Also JAF interviews with Peter Edelman, Janet Heffinger, Roger Mudd, William vanden Heuvel, and Peter Hart.

378 **as self-sabotage:** "Many apparently accidental injuries happening to such patients are really self-inflicted," wrote Sigmund Freud in 1901. "This is brought about by the fact that there is a constantly lurking tendency to self-punishment, usually expressing itself in self-reproach, or contributing to the formation of a symptom, which skillfully makes use of an external situation. The required external situation may accidentally present itself or the punishment tendency may assist it until the way is open for the desired injurious effect. Such occurrences are by no means rare even in cases of moderate severity, and they betray the portion of unconscious intention." See Sigmund Freud, *Psychopathology of Everyday Life*, 1901, chapter 8, cited in Clinch, *Kennedy Neurosis*. Assassination: see Melody Miller OH, UVA. NYT, Nov. 29, 1979. Letter: see Kennedy and Fried, *Common Struggle*, 61.

379 **onus of splitting:** Milton Gwirtzman OH, UVA. WP, Sept. 12, 1979. White, *America in Search*, 270, 291.

379 **Kennedy wanted it:** BG, Jan. 24, 1980.

379 **"don't underestimate commitment":** Healy comment from BG, June 10, 1979. JAF interview with Joseph Dolan. Edward Kennedy Jr., Kara Kennedy, Patrick Kennedy OH, UVA. Mudd. CBS, *Teddy*. EMK was "almost as much trapped by the legend as propelled by it," said Theodore White, *America in Search*, 272. Assessing the power of the Kennedy myth, White (who, with Jacqueline Kennedy, manufactured the Camelot parable) quoted Tennyson's *Idylls of the King*: "The city is built / To music, therefore never built at all / and therefore built forever."

379 **a Kennedy legacy:** JAF interview with Victoria Reggie Kennedy. EMKOH-UVA. Edward Kennedy Jr., Kara Kennedy, Patrick Kennedy, Paul Kirk OH, UVA. Germond and Witcover, *Blue Smoke*, 53–54. White, *America in Search*, 270, 274. BG, Nov. 11, 1980. Moore, *1980 in Retrospect*, 22–24. Drew, *Portrait*, 166, 171.

381 **"nothing but ragtime":** JAF interview with Peter Hart. EMKOH-UVA. Milton Gwirtzman, Paul Kirk OH, UVA. Lawrence Horowitz, Susan Estrich interviews, AC-JFKL. Ragtime: WP, Feb. 5, 1980. BG, Sept. 18, 1979. NYT, Sept. 7, Oct. 12, 19, 30, Nov. 2, 15, Dec. 3, 1979, Jan. 23, 1980. WP, Sept. 12, 1979. NJ, March 10, 1979. Drew, *Portrait*, 123. Schlesinger, *Robert Kennedy*. Moore, *1980 in Retrospect*, 18, 26–27. On polling, and Mackin and Wagner, see L. Patrick Devlin, "An Analysis of Kennedy's Communication in the 1980 Campaign," *Quarterly Journal of Speech*, Nov. 1982, 398. On Carter's early start see Drew, *Portrait*, 123. For Doherty see BM, Nov. 30, 2009.

381 **offering centrist bromides:** JAF interview with Robert Shrum. Shrum to Senator, Dec. 17, 1979, AC-JFKL. On same theme see also Mankiewicz to Shrum, circa Jan. 4, 1980, AC-JFKL. For discussion of conservative climate see Hart to Kennedy Campaign, Dec. 1979; Orren to Hart and Smith, undated, winter 1979–80, all AC-JFKL. EMK address to Investment Association of New York, Sept. 28, 1979, cited in Timothy Stanley, "'Sailing Against the Wind': A Reappraisal of Edward Kennedy's Campaign for the 1980 Democratic Party Presidential Nomination," *Journal of American Studies* 43, issue 2 (Aug. 2009). See also NYT, Sept. 16, 1979. *Village Voice*, Oct. 15, 1979. *Time*, Nov. 5, 1979. WP, June 4, 1980. Devlin, "An Analysis of Kennedy's Communication in the 1980 Campaign," 400.

382 **the dedication ceremonies:** EMKOH-UVA. Butler to Jordan, Sept. 10, 1979, JCL. Broder et al., *Pursuit*, 233–34. NYT, Oct. 21, Nov. 11, 1979.

382 **word came from Tehran:** NYT, Nov. 5, 8, 1979. Moore, *1980 in Retrospect*, 26. Paul Kirk interview, AC-JFKL.

383 **"every single evening":** EMK quoted in Germond and Witcover, *Blue Smoke*, 144. Jordan, *Crisis*, 19. One story, related in a memo by a *Washington Post* staffer, captures EMK's frustration. On January 20, the senator appeared on the ABC Sunday morning talk show *Issues and Answers*. Twice, the

show was interrupted by bulletins reporting the news that Carter made when talking about Iran that morning on NBC's *Meet the Press*. After noting "the utterly brazen arrogance of Carter in agreeing to go on that show one day before the Iowa caucuses after he had said in writing that he would have to forego personal appearances until the Tehran hostages were freed," the *Post* memo went on to describe how, as EMK was giving a "fairly thoughtful" reply to a question on domestic policy, the senator was interrupted by the host, who said, "People might think we were derelict if we don't get one Chappaquiddick question into this show." Kennedy then had forty seconds to respond. See Broder et al., *Pursuit*, 58.

384 **a political gaffe:** EMKOH-UVA. Shrum to EMK, undated, AC-JFKL. William Cohen interview, HJ-UW. NYT, Dec. 4, 1979. For representative critiques of Kennedy, see the editorials in the *Baltimore Sun*, Dec. 4, 1979, and *Washington Star*, Dec. 5, 1979. Mondale to Carter, Dec. 12, 1979, and Kraft to Carter, Dec. 13, 1979, JCL. Moore, *1980 in Retrospect*, 34–35, 48–49. Devlin, "An Analysis of Kennedy's Communication in the 1980 Campaign," 404–6. Essayist Michael Kinsley widely credited with coining this definition of a political gaffe. See Kinsley, "Jerseygate," TNR, June 18, 1984.

384 **his own flaws:** WP, June 9, 1980. Devlin, "An Analysis of Kennedy's Communication in the 1980 Campaign," 404–6. Kirk quoted in Moore, *1980 in Retrospect*, 48. For Kennedy, "each failure to live up to his prior billing"—his slips of the tongue and other mistakes—left him "faced with what was probably the most painful criticism of all: that he was not as good as his brothers," wrote Elizabeth Drew in *Portrait*, 40.

384 **rebel Muslims in Afghanistan:** Parker to EMK, Jan. 3, 1980; Kaliki to EMK, "Interviews with James Reston and Walter Cronkite," Jan. 3, 1980, AC-JFKL. Jody Powell leaked a memo he had ostensibly written to Carter, listing the urgent need to debate in Iowa, with the president's handwritten reply—the unctuous vow of self-sacrifice. See Powell to Carter, undated, JCL. Nixonian: Reporters chundered at the ploy. "Abbott had never served up a better straight line to . . . Costello," wrote Germond and Witcover. See *Blue Smoke*, 91. See also Zelizer, *Jimmy Carter*, Kindle edition, loc. 1780. Threat to peace: Jimmy Carter, State of the Union Address, Jan. 23, 1980, JCL.

385 **The flag, the flag:** Hilsman to EMK, Dec. 24, 1979, AC-JFKL. Stuart Eizenstat OH, UVA.

385 **"fat rich kid":** WP, June 9, 1980. The phenomenon was deeply frustrating for Kennedy, who was left exposed to the media's scrutiny and could only shadowbox as Carter hid in the White House. "The Kennedy campaign was premised on the idea that Carter was not a leader; then, of all things, just as the campaign began he was being hailed as one," Elizabeth Drew wrote. See *Portrait*, 40.

385 **shameless, and lucky:** For Carter ad see WP, Jan. 22, 1980. Jimmy Carter, "State of the Union Address," Jan. 23, 1980, UCSB. Vacillations: Alter,

His Very Best, 504–7, 510; Bird, *Outlier*, 487, 489. Afghan aid: David Gibbs, "Afghanistan: The Soviet Invasion in Retrospect," *International Politics*, June 2000. See also Editorial Note 56, and Item 59, "Report Prepared by the Central Intelligence Agency," Aug. 22, 1979, both from FRUS, 1977–1980, Volume XII, Afghanistan, U.S. Department of State, 2018, 162–68 and 172–74. The FRUS documents show that the prospect that the Soviet Union could be drawn into a quagmire in Afghanistan was widely discussed in the Carter administration throughout the summer and fall of 1979. See, for example, Brement to Brzezinski and Aaron, Sept. 8, 1979, Item 61, 176: "The more over-extended the Soviets feel, the better off we will be and the less likely that they will undertake reckless future action. Afghanistan has all the earmarks of a situation in which the Soviets could become embroiled endlessly." See also Bird, *Outlier*, 504–5; Gates, *Shadows*, 144–47. And see Glad, *Outsider*, 197–200.

386 **Character was the killer:** JAF interview with Peter Hart. Pat Caddell interview, AC-JFKL.

386 **as an immunization:** "Everybody underestimated it . . . it may already be fatal," an EMK adviser told Elizabeth Drew in early January. See Drew, *Portrait*, 50.

387 **the media joined in:** Powell was being cute. The Carter campaign's opposition research highlighted the charge "Panics in a crisis." See also "Kennedy" talking points, and Riegle to EMK, Jan. 25, 1980, AC-JFKL. For 1976, see opposition research report on Edward "Ted" Kennedy, Carter 1976 campaign, JCL. On Chappaquiddick and womanizing, see NYT, Sept. 22, 26, 27, 1979, Jan. 19, 1980. *Time*, Oct. 8, 1979, Feb. 4, 1980. WP, Nov. 13, 1979, June 9, Aug. 10, 1980. For Jordan memo see Jones, *Passages*, 31. For Mondale phone call, see Gillon, *Dilemma*.

Despite the press onslaught on Chappaquiddick, Powell still griped in his memoirs that Kennedy had "one of the most loyal and effective claques" of journalists in Washington, whose "responsibility was to avoid saying anything bad about Teddy personally—keeping rumors about women and drugs out of the press," while portraying Carter as "a vindictive little redneck." See Powell, *Story*, 186.

387 **Feminists added their concerns:** Associated Press, Sept. 20, 1979. Suzannah Lessard, "Kennedy's Woman Problem, Women's Kennedy Problem," *Washington Monthly*, Dec. 1979. The coverage of Kennedy's private life followed a pattern in the years after Chappaquiddick. The supermarket tabloids and gossip columns would report on his reputed dalliances; the mainstream press would then allude to them, and once a decade or so a reputable magazine would address them directly.

388 **withstand the pressures:** EMKOH-UVA. Kennedy and Fried, *Common Struggle*, 54–55. In the course of this exercise, Patrick added, Ted discovered that Joan's issues with drinking began in college, before their marriage.

389 **doing for herself:** EMKOH-UVA. Chellis, *Joan Kennedy*, 129, 146, 151, 173. Devlin, "An Analysis of

Kennedy's Communication in the 1980 Campaign." Years later, in an interview with the author, Walcott said of EMK, "Far better father than he was a husband." Edward Kennedy Jr., Kara Kennedy, Patrick Kennedy OH, UVA.

389 **prepared briefing sheets:** EMKOH-UVA. Clymer, *Edward M. Kennedy,* 276. Gwirtzman, "Personal Questions," Briefing paper for campaign announcement, Nov. 4, 1979, AC-JFKL. *Time,* Nov. 19, 1979. Chellis, *Joan Kennedy,* 80-81, 129, 146, 151.

390 **The kids learned early:** Edward Kennedy Jr., Kara Kennedy, Patrick Kennedy OH, UVA. Edward Kennedy Jr. interview, AC-JFKL. NYT, March 30, 1980.

391 **had confronted Joan:** WP, Jan. 19, 1980. Broder et al., *Pursuit,* 82.

392 **Carter's imperial trappings:** Hamilton Jordan, Patrick Caddell OH, UVA. At ABC, the network chieftains had opted to send a late-night news show on a suicide mission: battling Johnny Carson's *Tonight Show* in the ratings wars. On November 8, Frank Reynolds anchored the twenty-minute nightly update, which would run four days a week, called *The Iran Crisis—America Held Hostage.* Reynolds was replaced by mop-haired Ted Koppel, and the show rechristened as *Nightline.* It became a huge success, and Koppel would anchor it for twenty-five years. For the year and more that the hostages were held captive, *Nightline* would mark each passing day. So, at the completion of his evening news broadcast on CBS, would Walter Cronkite.

392 **gave thought to quitting:** On Warhol and Wyeth, see EMKOH-UVA. WP, July 21, 1980. Jetliner and budget see WP, June 9, 1980. From March to December, the veteran hands in the Carter campaign kept to their budget and spent $2.8 million. The Kennedy campaign spent $2.4 million in November and December alone, according to the *Post.* By the end of the contest in Iowa, Kennedy had raised and spent $4.4 million and had just $200,000 left. See *Time,* Feb. 4, 1980. For the rolling debate about withdrawal and Smith see EMKOH-UVA, EMK-TC, 377, and Germond and Witcover, *Blue Smoke,* 145-46. For Kirk see Moore, *1980 in Retrospect,* 64-66. Kennedy's organizers did their job well in Iowa but failed to predict that the Democratic caucuses would triple in size from 1976 to 1980, resulting in a contest that was more like a primary than a caucus.

394 **found his cause:** The text of the Georgetown University speech was printed in NYT, Jan. 29, 1980. After leaving office, Carter acknowledged that he had been warned about admitting the shah, and of Soviet interference in Afghanistan. See Jimmy Carter OH, UVA. See Jordan, *Crisis,* 32. On Afghanistan see Kaufman and Kaufman, *Presidency,* 162. See also transcript, "Jimmy Carter," *The American Experience,* PBS. For EMK and Iowa defeat and Georgetown speech see *Time,* Feb. 4, 1980, and *The Progressive,* Feb. 1980.

394 **coherence and motive:** Safire, NYT, Jan. 31, 1980. "Three months into his campaign, Ted Kennedy at last had answered the question Roger Mudd had asked," wrote Germond and Witcover, *Blue*

Smoke, 148. Devlin, "An Analysis of Kennedy's Communication in the 1980 Campaign," 412-13.

395 **candidate seemed happier:** WP, Feb. 13, 1980. *Time,* Feb. 11, 1980. NJ, Feb. 23, 1980. Moore, *1980 in Retrospect,* 64.

395 **Pietistic as ever:** WP, Feb. 14, 1980. BG, Feb. 15, 1980.

395 **winning for losing:** EMKOH-UVA. Moore, *1980 in Retrospect,* 73-74. WP, March 21, 1980. NYT, March 21, 1980.

396 **"a marvelous veneer":** Devlin, "An Analysis of Kennedy's Communication in the 1980 Campaign," 411-12. Cohen interview, HJ-UW.

396 **manipulative and unsporting:** Patrick Caddell OH, UVA. Jack Watson and Stuart Eizenstat also noted that, by declaring the crisis of paramount concern, Carter was playing into the ayatollah's hands. See Watson OH, UVA, and Eizenstat, Washington Book Club speech, Oct. 9, 2018: "Four hundred and forty-four humiliating days . . . he holes himself up in the White House. . . . All that did was make him a hostage . . . and give the press all the reason to focus on this issue. . . . It was just brutal." NJ, Feb. 16, 1980. WP, April 21, 1980. Moore, *1980 in Retrospect,* 52-54. Devlin, "An Analysis of Kennedy's Communication in the 1980 Campaign," 411-12.

397 **assembling a coalition:** EMKOH-UVA. Shrum New York texts, undated, AC-JFKL. Stanley, *Kennedy vs. Carter.* Carter, *Diary,* 412. Carter was wrong to malign New York: as Senator Daniel P. Moynihan annually noted, the federal taxes paid by the state's residents almost always outweighed the funds it got back from Washington. NYT, Aug. 8, 1985.

397 **signs of panic:** Jordan, *Crisis,* 245. WP, June 10, 1980.

398 **a fateful decision:** JAF interviews with Jimmy Carter, Hamilton Jordan. Hamilton Jordan OH, UVA. Patrick Caddell, Jack Watson interviews, AC-JFKL.

398 **"man in the street":** WP, April 21, 1980.

398 **political had become personal:** Jordan, *Crisis,* 315. When the primaries were over, Jordan wrote Carter, making the case that Ted Kennedy was to blame for the disaster to come—and the end of the liberal era. Kennedy's challenge left the Democratic president "damaged severely," Jordan told his boss. "Support for you based on your being a likable, well-intentioned, compassionate and at times atypical politician has eroded badly. The Kennedy attacks . . . have made you seem more like the manipulative politician bent on re-election at all costs." State and local Democratic organizations were divided, the electorate was tuning Carter out, and liberals were flirting with the independent candidacy of Republican representative John Anderson of Illinois. See Jordan to Carter, June 25, 1980, reprinted in Jordan, *Crisis,* 305-9. Jimmy Carter, Gerald Rafshoon OH, UVA. Carter diary entry, June 5, 1980, AC-JFKL.

399 **Senator Daniel Inouye:** JAF interview with Tad Devine. (Inouye was awarded the Medal of Honor for the courage he displayed, despite horrible wounds, leading his men against a Nazi

machine-gun nest in Italy, only days before Germany surrendered.) EMKOH-UVA. Moore to Carter, June 4, Aug. 25, 1980, JCL. Kennedy briefing notes, undated, spring/summer 1980; Shrum notes, Carter-Kennedy meeting; Moe to Jordan, May 29, June 5, 1980, AC-JFKL. Lew to O'Neill, July 17, 1980; Ross to Peterson, July 21, 1980; O'Donnell to O'Neill, July 23, 1980, TON-BC. *Newsweek*, May 12, Aug. 4, 1980. WP, Aug. 10, 1980. Moore, *1980 in Retrospect*, 87.

399 **odyssey had informed him:** Devlin, "An Analysis of Kennedy's Communication in the 1980 Campaign," 416.

401 **"the cause endures":** At a political event in Washington State in June 1959, JFK passed his wife, Jacqueline, a note with the scribbled plea, "Give me last lines from 'Ulysses,'" the ones that began, he noted, "Come my friends." From memory (for she had been taught the poem by her grandfather) she wrote out, "'Tis not too late to seek a newer world / Sitting well in order, let us smite the sounding furrow / For my purpose holds to sail beyond the sunset / And the baths of all the western stars until I die / It may be that the gulfs will wash us down / It may be we shall reach the Happy Isles / and see the great Achilles whom we knew / Though we are not now which we once were / That strength which in the old days moved earth and heaven / That which we are, we are / One equal temper of heroic hearts / Made weak by time and fate but strong in will / To strive, to seek, to find, and not to yield." JFK used the poem in his closing remarks that night after crossing out the words "made weak by time and fate" and replacing them with "dealt harshly perhaps by time and fate." After JFK's death, RFK continued the theme, naming his 1967 book of political essays and speeches *To Seek a Newer World*. For the text of EMK's speech see EMK, Address to the Democratic National Convention, Aug. 12, 1980, JFKL.

402 **shake his hand:** White, *America in Search*, 342. NYT, Aug. 12, 1980.

The story of the EMK "slight" would grow over the years. It began that night with the television newsmen, filling the airtime during the sluggish demonstration after Carter's speech, and the sharp-eyed Myra McPherson, who wrote in the next morning's *Washington Post* (Aug. 15, 1980) that EMK upstaged Carter and stopped "far short of the traditional upraised hand-holding." Bert Lance, watching the proceedings on television, "couldn't believe that Jimmy Carter was standing around, milling around on that platform at the convention waiting for Ted Kennedy" when, because of Iran and the economy, Carter was "being perceived as being weak." The episode, said Lance, "cost him dearly." The *New York Times* had its story about the encounter a day later, when it reported that EMK "withheld the final firm political embrace of his rival," and that the incident was "the talk among departing delegates." See NYT, Aug. 16, 1980.

In his 1980 diary entry, Carter noted the media's infatuation with the tale but said he personally did not notice anything untoward—except that EMK "seemed to have had a few drinks, which I probably would have done myself." EMK's performance was "fairly cool" but "adequate," the president wrote at the time. See Carter, *Diary*, 457–58.

By 1993, when he was interviewed by historian Douglas Brinkley, the incident had grown in Carter's mind. "He wouldn't shake my hand," Carter said. "It was obvious Kennedy was drinking heavily. . . . He was wandering around and I went up to him several times and stuck out my hand and he didn't shake it." In fact, the videotape shows them shaking hands five times. (See Brinkley to Clymer, with transcript of Oct. 29, 1993, interview, AC-JFKL.)

The evidence didn't stop Carter from perpetrating the myth. When he published his diary in 2010, he wrote that "ostentatiously, Kennedy refused to shake my extended hand." And at age ninety in 2015, Carter repeated the slur to author Jon Ward; see Ward, *Camelot's End*.

The story reflected the Carter clan's hard feelings. In 1984, a still-seething Rosalynn Carter slammed EMK in a televised interview. After failing to stop Carter in the primary process, EMK "should have quit," she said. "He was a poor loser. I thought that once he saw he could not win he would try to help the Democratic Party because I thought it was so important to keep Ronald Reagan out of the White House. . . . Instead, he tore the Democratic Party to pieces." See NYT, May 2, 1984.

For his part, EMK said that his actions were cool after Carter's speech because "it was the president's night" and he did not want to steal the limelight. His staff and liberal supporters were divided, he recalled. Some wanted him to embrace the victor, others said it would look phony. He added, a bit sharply, that the arms-aloft tableau must not have meant that much to Carter, since the campaign invited so many other Democratic politicos to mill about the platform before EMK arrived. (See EMKOH-UVA.)

The Carter camp bears part of the fault for that. EMK had proposed to watch the president's speech from the convention hall, but Carter's team did not want the network television cameras straying from the rostrum to catch the senator's reactions. Nor, for that reason, did they want EMK's motorcade to leave his rooms at the Waldorf-Astoria hotel until after Carter finished.

EMK's caravan to the hall was then delayed by traffic. Waiting for Kennedy, as the delegates became restless, Carter's chieftains filled the time by inviting the host of Democratic functionaries—"every freeholder from New Jersey," as EMK put it—to the rostrum. And, as EMK noted, there was no reason that Carter, in the course of shaking EMK's hand five times, could not have raised their arms in victory. "He made no point to elevate mine!" EMK remembered. "If he had raised both of our hands, I would not have resisted it, certainly." (See EMKOH-UVA.)

Shrum says that he and EMK practiced the gesture in the senator's hotel room. Shrum told him it wasn't that hard. "Maybe not for you," said EMK. At the convention hall, Shrum reminded EMK, "Don't

forget to raise his hand," and EMK replied, "I won't." When EMK came down from the platform, Shrum asked, "What happened?" and EMK said, "It just didn't work out." JAF interview with Robert Shrum; Shrum, *No Excuses*, 127–29.
In the end, Kennedy took satisfaction in how things turned out. "For a guy who said, 'I don't have to kiss his ass,'" Carter had certainly been solicitous, EMK would recall. (See Germond and Witcover, *Blue Smoke*, 195.)

Twenty-Two: Reagan

404 **John Hinckley Jr.:** Reagan was shot by Hinckley as the president approached his limousine after making a speech at a Washington, DC, hotel. The shooting took place at 2:25 p.m. on March 30. Kennedy watched the breaking news stories on a television in the Senate cloakroom with Senators Gary Hart, Russell Long, and others, and made brief remarks on the Senate floor. Just before 3 p.m. he phoned the hospital emergency room, but the call was not completed. See Reagan daily diary, March 30, 1981, RRL, and Associated Press and NYT, March 31, 1981. JAF interview with Greg Craig. Craig was Hinckley's attorney. He later served on Kennedy's staff as a foreign policy adviser, and then represented President Bill Clinton in the 1999 impeachment trial. See also Greg Craig OH, UVA.

404 **typically gracious performance:** Ronald Reagan, Remarks on Presenting the Robert F. Kennedy Medal to Mrs. Kennedy, June 5, 1981; Deaver to Ethel Kennedy, June 21, 1981; EMK to Reagan, Nov. 13, 1981; EMK to Reagan, March 7, 1985; JFK Jr. and Caroline Kennedy to Reagan, March 10, 1985; Deaver to Reagan, March 12, 1985; JFK Jr. to Reagan, March 12, 1985; Reagan to JFK Jr. and Caroline Kennedy, undated, April 1985; Timmons to Noonan, June 17, 1985; Noonan speechwriting file, June 24, 1985, dinner; EMK to Ronald and Nancy Reagan, June 25, 1985, RRL. Remarks of President Ronald Reagan, McLean, VA, June 24, 1985; EMK to Reagan, Oct. 24, 1985, JFKL. WP, June 6, 1981, June 25, 1985; BG, June 6, 1981, June 25, 1985. NYT, June 6, 1981. EMKOH-UVA. Carey Parker, John Seigenthaler OH, UVA.
At Kennedy's first meeting with the new president, he was struck by how Reagan stuck to staged remarks and old Hollywood stories, and Kennedy later told his staff that the visit removed any qualms he may have had about measuring up to the office. Yet Seigenthaler remembers that as Kennedy escorted Reagan through the Rose Garden crowd on the day of the medal presentation, they came across a Cape Cod yachtsman who invited the president to come up and race with him against Kennedy. "I'd love to," said Reagan, "but I don't believe I'd get my horse in the water." It taught them, said Seigenthaler, not to underestimate Reagan's wits. See Seigenthaler OH, UVA.

404 **fought like curs:** JAF interviews with James A. Baker III, Kenneth Duberstein, Michael Deaver, Thomas Korologos, Kirk O'Donnell. JFK quote on politics from Kennedy biographical dictation, JFK

tapes, undated, 1960, JFKL. EMK quote on Reagan and leadership, AC-JFKL. On Reagan vs. Carter see "Reagan Campaign Action Plan," Oct. 1983 (The 1980 victory was "first and foremost, a referendum on the failure of national leadership: the disarray, mismanagement and malaise of the Carter administration"), RRL. Thomas Oliphant, Max Friedersdorf OH, UVA. Kirk O'Donnell interview, Hedrick Smith papers, LOC. Lew to O'Neill, "Interest Rates, Inflation and Federal Reserve Policy," Feb. 28, 1980; Hoffman to O'Neill, Nov. 10, 1980, TON-BC. Mann and Ornstein, eds., *American Elections*, 136. NJ, Nov. 8, 1980.

406 **"government is the problem":** Ronald Reagan, "Inaugural Address," Jan. 20, 1981, UCSB. "The Combined Effects of Major Changes in Federal Taxes and Spending Programs Since 1981," Congressional Budget Office, April 1984. The long-term effects of the nation's turn to the Right, said political analysts Thomas and Mary Edsall at the end of the Reagan era, were extraordinary. "The collapse of the political left and the ascendance of a hybrid conservative populism dominated by the affluent have had enormous policy consequences," they wrote. "The holders of power under the new conservative regime encouraged and endorsed, through tax, debt and budgetary policy, a substantial redistribution of income from the bottom to the top . . . what may well have been the most accelerated upwards redistribution of income in the nation's history." See Edsall and Edsall, *Chain Reaction*, 4–6.

406 **appoint Stephen Breyer:** JAF interview with Stephen Breyer. Gershengorn to Perrilli, "Senate Confirmation Proceedings—Appointment to First Circuit," June 9, 1993, WCL. EMKOH-UVA. "Stephen Breyer Circuit Court Nomination," EMK briefing book, Blattner collection, Judicial Nominations II, Feb. 12, 2007. According to EMK's briefing book, Kennedy had elicited a promise from Carter to name Breyer when they met after the 1980 Democratic convention, as a condition of supporting the president that fall. See also Eizenstat, *President Carter*, 372–73. On Morgan, see NYT, Dec. 1, 1980. There was bad blood between Kennedy and Morgan because the Judiciary Committee, under Breyer's direction, had blocked the appointment of Morgan's former campaign manager as a federal judge over questions about his ethics and ability. See also Powell, *Story*, 188, and Carey Parker OH, UVA.

407 **landmark Voting Rights Act:** EMK interview, AC-JFKL. Burt Wides OH, UVA. JAF interview with Ralph Neas, Burt Wides. NYT, April 8, 19, May 3, July 2, 1981. Mounger to Reagan, July 27, 1981; Gressette to Reagan, Sept. 8, 1981; Meese and Uhlmann to Reagan, Nov. 3, 1981; Cooksey to Duberstein, Jan. 28, 1982; Smith to Reagan, Feb. 2, 1982; Thurmond to Reagan, Feb. 8, 1982; Harper to Reagan, March 5, 1982; Frey to Reagan, June 23, 1982; Ervin to Reagan, July 16, 1981, with Ervin essay, "The Truth Respecting the Highly Praised and Constitutionally Devious Voting Rights Act"; Statement by the President, Nov. 6, 1981, RRL. CQW, April 11, 1981. Thomas Boyd

and Stephen Markman, "The 1982 Amendments to the Voting Rights Act: A Legislative History," *Washington & Lee Law Review* 40 (1983): 1347. May, *Bending*, 214–31. See also Pertschuk, *Giant Killers*, chapter 6, "A Not So Splendid Misery."
Outside the South, there were nine Massachusetts towns covered under the Section Five preclearance requirement, three in Connecticut, and ten in New Hampshire, as well as two New York counties. See "Experience of the Department of Justice Under the Voting Rights Act," Attachment B, RRL. The reach of the preclearance requirement was later extended to include jurisdictions with heavy Native American or Latino populations.
The Supreme Court, in *Shelby County v. Holder*, the 2013 decision, struck down the preclearance requirement of the act as unnecessary. "Coverage today is based on decades-old data and eradicated practices," wrote Chief Justice John Roberts. But white southern Republicans, after arguing for decades that the South had atoned and matured, immediately revived their old tactics. Justice Ruth Bader Ginsburg, in dissent, chided Roberts and the majority when writing that "throwing out preclearance when it has worked and is continuing to work to stop discriminatory changes is like throwing away your umbrella in a rainstorm because you are not getting wet." See Vance Newkirk, "How *Shelby County v. Holder* Broke America," *Atlantic*, July 10, 2018.
409 **Dole's wit was:** JAF interview with Robert Dole. Dole, a fierce partisan, was elected to the House in 1960 and the Senate in 1968. He served as GOP leader in the Senate from 1985 to 1996. Dole also served as Republican Party chairman under Nixon and was the Republican vice presidential candidate on Gerald Ford's losing ticket in 1976. Dole ran for president but was beaten in the Republican primaries in 1980 by Ronald Reagan, and by George H. W. Bush in 1988. In 1996 he clinched the Republican nomination but lost to Democrat Bill Clinton.
There is a fine portrait of Dole in Cramer, *What It Takes*. See also Charles Ferris OH, SHO. EMK aide Jeff Blattner recalled the time in 1989 that Kennedy voted against the nomination of a former colleague, John Tower of Texas, to be Secretary of Defense. The headlines that day had also featured stories about poisoned grapes from Chile. Walking by Kennedy in the Senate, Dole said, solicitously: "Ted, did you get that basket of grapes John Tower sent you?"
"Dole is a very private person," said his Republican ally Senator John Chafee of Rhode Island. "He has a lot of charisma, but he's not a guy who . . . has many close friends here. That doesn't mean everybody doesn't respect him and like him, but I don't think he extends himself that way." See John Chafee interview, Sheila Burke interview, both HJ-UW. "He's intensely private," Burke said. "He survived extraordinarily difficult times by developing a very caustic sense of humor. . . . [But] he is someone who is personally far more caring than he's ever given credit for. . . . He feels some things very deeply."

Al Gore, who served in the Senate with Dole, told Bill Clinton that Dole was a mean person with a nice streak, as opposed to a warm person with a mean streak. See Clinton to Branch, Jan. 29, 1994, TB-UNC.
409 **endorsed a compromise:** JAF interviews with Ralph Neas, Burt Wides. EMK, Ralph Neas, William Taylor interviews, AC-JFKL. Ronald Weich OH, UVA. Thurmond to Reagan, Aug. 5, 1981; Lott to Baker, Sept. 18, 1981; Lott to Reagan, Oct. 13, 1981; Uhlmann to Meese, Oct. 16, 1981; Horowitz and McConnell to Harper, Nov. 13, 1981; Darman to Meese, Baker, and Deaver, Jan. 20, 1982; OMB to Reagan, "Dole Bill," April 13, 1982 ("There are . . . problems with the Dole version . . . but, as noted, we can clearly live with it—it is a genuine compromise between two dug-in Senate positions"); Fielding to staff, April 26, 1982; Frey to Reagan, June 23, 1982; Jackson to Reagan, June 27, 1982; Young to Reagan, June 30, 1982; Kennedy to Reagan, July 13, 1982, RRL. See also Clymer, *Edward M. Kennedy*, 322–26. NYT, May 1, 1982.
Reagan was of two minds on the Voting Rights Act. On one hand, he wanted to help Thurmond, Representative Trent Lott of Mississippi, and other Republicans make inroads in the South. Countering this interest was a fear of seeming racist, especially after his administration, in a widely condemned move, had reversed a Nixon-era practice that denied tax-exempt status to private schools that practiced racial discrimination. If it now opposed the Voting Rights Act, wrote deputy chief of staff Richard Darman to Reagan, it would "continue to raise the political wrath of the Black and civil rights community . . . [and] continue to create the impression that this President is insensitive." See Darman and Rollins to Reagan, Feb. 26, 1982, RRL. When pressuring White House aides to accept the legislation, EMK's staff threatened to use Reagan's waffling to drive up minority turnout in the 1982 congressional elections. See Louisell and Williams to Harper, Feb. 9, 1982, RRL.
410 **attributes: Orrin Hatch:** See Orrin Hatch, *Square Peg*. See also Roderick, *Leading the Charge*. The diary references on EMK are on pp. 66 and 78, the Electoral College debate is featured on pp. 136–40.
410 **victims of discriminatory *intent*:** The case was *Mobile v. Bolden* (446 U.S. 55, 1980), a class action suit in which Black Alabamans cited the race of local white officeholders as evidence of discrimination.
410 **to quota systems:** Boyd and Markman, "Amendments," 1392.
411 **tax and budget cuts:** Orrin Hatch interview, AC-JFKL. On O'Neill and Kennedy, see Peter D. Hart Research Associates, focus group report, Portland, OR, Oct. 1981, TON-BC. On tax vote see Shrum, *No Excuses*, 132.
The Labor Committee's liberals and conservatives scrapped for months over Reagan's efforts to move hundreds of categorical social programs into block grants, cutting costs by a billion

dollars. Some notably wasteful endeavors—like the CETA public jobs program—were eliminated, and nine block grants, subsuming more than fifty categorical programs and consolidating others, were created, giving Reagan his billion dollars in savings.

Yet when the dust settled, more than four hundred categorical social programs remained, and many of the programs that were packaged into block grants—like EMK's cherished community health centers—were protected by earmarks or restrictions that preserved their original intent and functions. (Briefing sheet, "Kennedy Early Involvement with Neighborhood Health Centers," undated, SLC-NARA.) For the seesaw battle in committee and the Senate see NYT, March 10, April 3, May 18, June 11, 14, 1981, and CQW, March 14, June 13, July 25, Aug. 1, 1981. See also Hatch to Kennedy, May 15, 1981, AC-JFKL, and Darman to Baker et al., "Meeting with the Legislative Strategy Group," June 17, 1981, RRL. On the block grant battle, see U.S. General Accounting Office, "Block Grants: Characteristics, Experience, and Lessons Learned," Feb. 1995. See also Richard Williamson, "Block Grants: One Year Later," *Journal of Legislation* 10, issue 2 (May 1983), and Timothy Conlan, "The Politics of Federal Block Grants: From Nixon to Reagan," *Political Science Quarterly* 99, no. 2 (Summer 1984), and David Nexon, "The Politics of Congressional Health Policy in the Second Half of the 1980s," *Medicare Care Review*, Spring 1987.

412 **revolution was attitudinal:** JAF interviews with James Baker, Kirk O'Donnell, Newt Gingrich. CQW, Dec. 19, 1981. Wirthlin to Richards, July 29, 31, 1981, RRL. O'Donnell to O'Neill, Aug. 4, 1981, TON-BC. For a discussion of Reagan's "revolution," see Farrell, *Tip O'Neill*, 602–6, and Stockman, *Triumph*. Stockman's analysis of the failed "revolution" is contained in the epilogue, 408–28. He described the block grants as "cosmetic reforms," 233.

For "fairness" see Patrick Caddell, "Memorandum to the Democratic Leadership," Feb. 20, 1982; Lynch to Manatt, Sept. 23, 1981, TON-BC, and White House Office of Policy Information, "Fairness Issues," June 1, 1982, RRL, and "The Combined Effects of Major Changes in Federal Taxes and Spending Programs Since 1981," Congressional Budget Office, April 1984. Jackson used the phrase "they catch the early bus" to describe low-income workers throughout the 1988 primary campaign, and in his address to the Democratic national convention that year. See NYT, July 20, 1988: "They catch the early bus. They work every day. They raise other people's children. They work every day. They clean the streets. They work every day."

412 **passage of the Sentencing Reform Act:** Michael Tonry, "Federal Sentencing 'Reform' Since 1984: The Awful as Enemy of the Good," *Crime and Justice* 44, no. 1 (Sept. 2015): 99–164, quote on 100.

412 **soaring crime rates:** See Susman to EMK, May 20, 1975, and Susman to Kirk and Parker, n.d., circa 1975, TS-UMASS. For the Baby Boom generation and crime see Goldwin to Cannon, Sept. 8, 1976,

GFL. For crime and the national political agenda see Connor to Buchen, April 4, 1975, GFL. The criminal code was widely seen as in need of reform. See Lazarus to Buchen, Nov. 26, 1974, GFL: "Our body of criminal law on the Federal level is a haphazard hodgepodge of conflicting, contradictory and imprecise law piled one upon the other. . . . It is possible to identify at least five different formulas for insanity . . . the word 'willful' has some 78 interpretations . . . never-used statutes also clutter up our law, e.g., operating a pirate ship on behalf of a 'foreign prince,' detaining a United States carrier pigeon; and seducing a female steamship passenger." JAF interview with Kenneth Feinberg. Burton Hersh, "The Survival of Edward Kennedy," *Washingtonian*, Feb. 1979.

413 **Kennedy stifled yawns:** EMK, "Punishing the Offenders," NYT, Dec. 6, 1975. See also EMK, "Symposium on Sentencing, Part I, Introduction," *Hofstra Law Review*, Fall 1978: "Sentencing in America today is a national scandal. Every day our system of sentencing breeds massive injustice. Judges are free to roam at will, dispensing ad hoc justice in ways that defy both reason and fairness." Hersh, *Washingtonian*, Feb. 1979, "Survival." Kenneth Feinberg OH, UVA: "Kennedy saw it as an important opportunity for him to be perceived as somebody who could not be labeled automatically liberal."

413 **led to unsurety:** On abuse of discretion see Goldwin to Cannon, Sept. 8, 1976, and Cannon to Ford, undated, 1976, GFL. "Decisions on similarly situated persons are widely inconsistent and the decision-making process is unregulated and invisible to the public," Cannon told the president. "There is substantial evidence which suggests that the uncertainty caused by this standardless and invisible sentencing process contributes heavily to unrest in prisons and to attitudes of contempt by inmates toward the law even after their release." See Kennedy remarks in Murakawa, *First Civil Right*, 110, and David Jaros, "Flawed Coalitions and the Politics of Crime," *Iowa Law Review* 99 (2014): 1473, 1491. Frankel dinner: NYT, June 16, 1977. Also present at the 1975 dinner were Norval Morris, dean of the University of Chicago Law School, and Harvard professors James Q. Wilson and James Vorenberg.

413 **became more punitive:** Lynn Adelman, "How Congress, the U.S. Sentencing Commission and Federal Judges Contribute to Mass Incarceration," *Litigation*, American Bar Association, Fall 2017, 8–11. Adelman notes that in a 2005 decision, *United States v. Booker*, the Supreme Court struck down the mandatory feature of the sentencing guidelines—but that federal judges, conditioned by the guidelines, "almost totally failed to . . . ameliorate the harshness of the federal sentencing regime." Murakawa, *First Civil Right*, 99–100. Evans, *Leadership in Committee*, 114–117.

414 **"the sentencing machine":** Tonry, "Federal Sentencing 'Reform' Since 1984," 144. JAF interview with Kenneth Feinberg. Adelman, "How Congress," 8–11. The Judiciary senators had input on Reagan's nominees, and at Kennedy's request Stephen Breyer was appointed to the sentencing

commission and played a role in what followed. Tonry, who worked as a consultant to the commission, attributes the blame for the sentencing catastrophe as follows: "Part of it was bad management. Part of it was the commissioners' lack of sentencing experience and knowledge of sentencing guidelines. Part was hubris. The largest part was that the crime control policies of the Reagan administration were oriented more towards toughness than fairness. The commissioners Reagan appointed sought to show that they too were tough on crime."

414 **mandatory sentences soared:** Tonry, "Federal Sentencing 'Reform' Since 1984." The crime bills were the Anti-Drug Abuse Acts of 1986 and 1988, the Violent Crime Control and Law Enforcement Act of 1994, the Federal Death Penalty Act of 1994, and the Antiterrorism and Effective Death Penalty Act of 1996. See Murakawa, *First Civil Right*, 113. On the politics of the crime bills see Reed to Reno, April 1, 1993; Reed and Cerda to Clinton, Oct. 25, 1993 ("As the crime issue takes on increasing urgency in Congress and the countryside, we face the prospect of a bidding war in both houses, in which Republicans and even liberal Democrats compete. . . . There is no way to stop this train in the Senate. . . . Biden strongly believes that the administration needs to seize control of the issue by upping the ante."); Reed and Cerda to Clinton, Oct. 27, 1993 ("You have a chance to seize one of the two most powerful realignment issues . . . that will come your way, at a time when public concern about crime is the highest it has been since Richard Nixon stole the issue from the Democrats in 1968."); and Reed to Clinton, Aug. 11, 1994, WCL.

414 **mass incarceration produced:** Adelman, "How Congress," 8–11. See also Murakawa, *First Civil Right*, 103–4.

On prisons see NYT, Aug. 18, 1981, April 12, 1992. "No country in the world imprisons as many people as America does, or for so long," *The Economist* reported in its June 20, 2015, issue. It placed the cost to American taxpayers at $80 billion a year.

On the sentencing reform bill in the Senate see NYT, Jan. 31, 1978, Feb. 3, 1984. The ACLU predicted at the time that EMK's proposals "by abolishing parole and good time . . . close the safety valves . . . and risk even longer periods of incarceration." See Levin and Repak, *Myth of Leadership*, 98.

415 **common rite of passage:** Ta-Nehisi Coates, "The Black Family in the Age of Mass Incarceration," *Atlantic*, Oct. 2015.

415 **"kingpins and the traffickers":** See EMK hearing testimony and Chairman Biden opening remarks, Subcommittee on Crime and Drugs, Committee on the Judiciary, "Federal Cocaine Sentencing Laws: Reforming the 100-to-1 Crack/Powder Disparity," Feb. 12, 2008.

On Clinton and incarceration see NYT, July 15, 2015: "I signed a bill that made the problem worse and I want to admit it." On Biden see WP, Jan. 11, 2021.

On crack cocaine see Reed and Kagan to Clinton, July 3, 1997, and "The Clinton Administration Crack-Powder Initiative," Oct. 1997, which outlines the EMK, Clinton, and Biden efforts to equalize cocaine penalties, and EMK's prodding of Clinton. ("Senator Edward Kennedy supports a move toward equalization of crack and powder sentencing. At the present time, he is not prepared to support the administration's position because he does not believe the proposal goes far enough toward equalization," Reed and Kagan told the president.) WCL.

415 **a national political hysteria:** On blame see National Research Council, *Incarceration*. See also JAF interviews with Kenneth Feinberg and Ronald Weich.

EMK soon had misgivings. By early 1985 he was issuing unheeded warnings about mandatory sentencing, incarceration, and the costs of new prisons. See EMK, "Prison Overcrowding: The Law's Dilemma," *Annals of the American Academy of Political and Social Science*, March 1985, 113–22, in which he urges judges to follow a policy of more "selective incapacitation." See also Ronald Weich, "The Battle Against Mandatory Minimums: A Report from the Front Lines," *Federal Sentencing Reporter*, Sept./Oct. 1996, and Ronald Weich, "Who Built Prison America? Not Ted Kennedy," *The Crime Report*, Center on Media, Crime and Justice, John Jay College, Aug. 20, 2015. "Kennedy and other liberals can be faulted for voting in favor of the 1986 crime bill and other bills which contained mandatory minimums, but they did not lead the charge," Weich wrote. "In fact, Sen. Kennedy was a leader in opposing mandatory minimums once their effect became clear."

On the other hand, Kennedy was still citing sentencing and bail reform among his crime-fighting accomplishments when he ran for reelection in 1994. See "Senator Kennedy on Crime," undated, circa 1994, NL-UMASS.

415 **critic and facilitator:** Joshua Muravchik, "Kennedy's Foreign Policy: What the Record Shows," *Commentary*, Dec. 1979. Kalicki to EMK, Nov. 1, 1979, "Foreign and Defense Policy Positions," AC-JFKL. WS, Oct. 11, 1979. Telegram from the Embassy in the Soviet Union to the Department of State, Aug. 10, 1974, FRUS, Volume XVI, Soviet Union, Aug. 1974–Dec. 1976. Clymer, in *Edward M. Kennedy*, offers the most detailed account of the senator's foreign travel and diplomacy.

416 **soldiered for "legacy":** EMK interview, AC-JFKL. EMK was drawn to the test ban idea because, he reasoned, if the nuclear powers could not be sure that their increasingly more complex weapons would work as expected, they would be more hesitant to use them, especially in a first strike upon an enemy.

416 **the nuclear freeze:** JAF interview with Richard Arenberg. Randall Forsberg interview, WGBH, *War and Peace in the Nuclear Age*, PBS, 1989. Nyhan, *The Duke*, 4–5. On EMK feelings about JFK and the "missile gap" see Dobrynin, *In Confidence*, 367.

EMK was alerted to the political potential of the freeze when voters in fifty-nine of sixty-two towns in western Massachusetts endorsed the concept via local referenda in 1980. Of the thirty-three of those towns carried by Reagan that night, thirty passed the freeze resolution. By June 1981, the

Massachusetts legislature had endorsed the freeze and friendly organizations like the Federation of American Scientists were urging Kennedy to sign on. See Robert Leavitt, "Freezing the Arms Race: The Genesis of a Mass Movement," Kennedy School of Government, Case Program C14-83-557, Harvard University, 1983, and "Freezing the Arms Race: The Campaign in Washington," C14-83-558.

417 **justify the arms race:** EMK interview, AC-JFKL. Forsberg interview, WGBH. Daryl G. Kimball, "In Memoriam: Randall Caroline Forsberg," *Arms Control Today*, Dec. 2007. NYT, June 13, 1982. Leavitt, "Freezing the Arms Race." The freeze sponsors in the House were Representatives Ed Markey and Silvio Conte of Massachusetts, and Jonathan Bingham of New York: soon they were joined by more than 180 colleagues. Schell's book was serialized in the *New Yorker* and then published in book form in early 1982. More than one hundred million people saw *The Day After* in 1983—one of the highest-rated dramas of its time.

419 **the Soviet Union's economy:** See also Ronald Reagan, "Address to Members of the British Parliament," June 8, 1982, RRL: "Overcentralized, with little or no incentives, year after year the Soviet system pours its best resources into the making of instruments of destruction. The constant shrinkage of economic growth combined with the growth of military production is putting a heavy strain on the Soviet people." See the chapters on Reagan in Gaddis, *Strategies*. See also Reagan, *An American Life*, 238.

419 **Strategic Defense Initiative (SDI):** "Reagan Campaign Action Plan," Oct. 1983, RRL. When asked to list their greatest fear of Reagan's reelection, 38 percent of the respondents said nuclear war, and only 6 percent listed the issue that had brought political ruin to Reagan's two predecessors—inflation. The "shovel" theory was advanced by Thomas K. Jones, a deputy undersecretary of defense for strategic nuclear forces. "If there are enough shovels to go around, everybody's going to make it," he told the *Los Angeles Times* in 1982. "Dig a hole, cover it with a couple of doors and then throw three feet of dirt on top. It's the dirt that does it." NYT, March 19, 1982.

420 **man of parts:** Cannon, *President Reagan*, 281. Forsberg interview, WGBH. EMK interview, AC-JFKL.

421 **as an envoy:** Larry Horowitz interview, AC-JFKL. Matlock, *Reagan and Gorbachev*, 92–94. On Gorbachev see Taubman, *Gorbachev*.

421 **the 1984 election:** Germond and Witcover, *Wake Us When It's Over*, 35–36.

422 **"eagerly dehumanize themselves":** Greenfield, *Washington* (New York: PublicAffairs, 2001), 7.

422 **not challenge Reagan:** Edward Kennedy Jr., Kara Kennedy, Patrick Kennedy OH, UVA. Edward Kennedy Jr. interview, AC-JFKL. For detailed accounts of the decision not to run in 1984 see Clymer, *Edward M. Kennedy*, 3–8, and Goldman and Fuller et al., *Quest*, 59–68. EMK's memory of the family parley, as recounted in his memoir, was slightly different—he said that his children were silent at the family gathering but conveyed their strong objections in private at his Squaw Island home later that weekend.

Kennedy's son Patrick, in his memoir, *A Common Struggle*, says that the children's objections served as a public excuse for EMK, who had made a private decision to forsake the presidency and focus on the Senate; see 68–69. Tunney agreed; see John Tunney OH, UVA. See EMKOH-UVA and EMK-TC, 400–404. JAF interviews with Adam Clymer, Robert Shrum, Thomas Rollins. Thomas Oliphant, Thomas "Tip" O'Neill, Larry Horowitz interview, AC-JFKL. Harrison to Leslie, Oct. 6, 1981, AC-JFKL. BG, Sept. 24, 1982. WSJ, Oct. 5, 1982. WP, Oct. 26, Nov. 8, 1982. *Newsweek*, Dec. 13, 1982. Transcript, EMK news conference, NYT, Dec. 2, 1982. NYT, June 27, 1984.

423 **his new status:** *The Times* (London), Feb. 2, 1992. The 1983 approach to Moscow has been the source of controversy. The opening was initiated by John Tunney, who lost his bid for reelection to the Senate in 1976, was practicing law and had clients whose international interests took him to the USSR. Tunney seems to have conveyed a request that EMK be received in Moscow to a Soviet intermediary who passed it to Victor Chebrikov, the head of the KGB, who in turn sent a May 14, 1983, memo to Andropov.

Chebrikov wrote in the toadying, flattering manner of an underling ("Kennedy is very impressed with the activities of Y. V. Andropov and other Soviet leaders, who expressed their commitment to heal international affairs, and improve mutual understanding between peoples"). Based on the memo, dippy propagandists from the American Right, like talk radio host Rush Limbaugh and Fox personality Greg Gutfeld, would charge in years to come that Kennedy was giving comfort to the enemy and undermining Reagan. If Kennedy had his way, Gutfeld blithered, "we would still have the USSR." For an analysis of these claims see PolitiFact, Poynter Institute, March 13, 2015 ("Limbaugh: Ted Kennedy Undercut Reagan with Back-Door Line to Soviets"), and July 18, 2017 ("Fox News Host Cites Kennedy-KGB Meeting That Never Happened").

The Chebrikov memo was, in fact, a distant relay of whatever Kennedy or an aide advised Tunney to convey, translated from English to Russian by the KGB—and then back again to English by *The Times*, which came upon the memo in the Russian archives. The *Times* translation contains such garbled phrasing as "In order to neutralize criticism that the talks between the USA and the USSR are non-constructive, Reagan will grandiose, but subjectively propagandistic."

Tunney told *The Times* that Chebrikov's memo was self-aggrandizing "bullshit." The supposed quid pro quo conveyed by the KGB chief—that, in return for a trip to Moscow, Kennedy would help Andropov get a prime-time appearance on U.S. television with a broadcaster like Walter Cronkite or Barbara Walters—was a cheap enough blandishment. Any American newsman would have leaped at the chance to interview the new Soviet leader and would not need Kennedy to persuade them.

The record of the times shows that, far from undercutting Reagan, Kennedy worked arm in arm with the administration on Soviet affairs. Reagan's arms negotiator, Max Kampelman, wrote in his memoirs, "The senator never acted or received information without informing the appropriate United States agency or official." See PolitiFact, Poynter Institute, March 13, 2015. Reagan White House aide Jack F. Matlock lauds Kennedy in *Reagan and Gorbachev*, 92–94. Secretary of State George Shultz said in his memoir that he trusted and appreciated Kennedy and urged Reagan to work with him. See George P. Shultz, *Turmoil and Triumph*, 703, 869, 884–85. For further assessment of the Kennedy back channel, see Memorandum from the President's Assistant for National Security Affairs (Carlucci) to Secretary of State Shultz, Jan. 10, 1987, and Note from Ambassador-at-Large Nitze and the Counselor of the Department of State (Kampelman) to Secretary of State Shultz, May 10, 1987, both FRUS, 1981–1988, Volume VI, Soviet Union, Oct. 1986–Jan. 1989.

423 **when Horowitz returned:** Larry Horowitz interview, AC-JFKL. Matlock, *Reagan and Gorbachev*, 92–94. *Time*, Jan. 2, 1984.

424 **Kennedy back channel:** EMK interview, AC-JFKL. EMK fact sheet, undated, 1994 campaign, NL-UMASS. For the Reagan administration's assessment of the Kennedy back channel, see Memorandum from the President's Assistant for National Security Affairs (Carlucci) to Secretary of State Shultz, Jan. 10, 1987, and Note from Ambassador-at-Large Nitze and the Counselor of the Department of State (Kampelman) to Secretary of State Shultz, May 10, 1987, both FRUS, 1981–1988, Volume VI, Soviet Union, Oct. 1986–Jan. 1989. The Kennedy channel survived the bureaucratic skirmishing between the NSC and Secretary of State George Shultz. By 1987, Gorbachev and Reagan had grown close enough to schedule summit meetings every six months, ending the need for middlemen. Kennedy was not the only discreet avenue employed by the Soviets to send their signals: they used Richard Nixon, businessman Duane Andreas, and others.

425 **clashing with Reagan:** JAF interview with Greg Craig. EMK op-ed, "Support the Peace Effort of Nicaragua's Indians," NYT, Nov. 27, 1984. EMK to Clark, May 26, 1982, and Fontaine to Clark, June 1, 1982; Bingaman and EMK, "Dear Colleague" letter on cutting U.S. support for Contras, June 6, 1984; North, Lehman, and Menges to McFarlane, June 11, 1984; Denton to Buchanan with Denton-Kennedy staff report on Nicaraguan Indians, April 12, 1985; talking points, "Boland Amendments," undated, RRL. CQW, April 9, 1983. NYT, March 30, April 11, 1984.

426 **the soccer stadium:** Associated Press, Jan. 15, 1986. EMK interview, AC-JFKL.

426 **involvement in South Africa:** JAF interview with Greg Craig. Desmond Tutu OH, UVA. Rostow to Johnson, Aug. 10, 1967, LBJL. MacArthur to Kennedy, March 31, 1967, EMK-JFKL. EMK to Reagan, Oct. 10, 1984; Ringdahl to Poindexter, "Terrorist Threat Against Senator Kennedy and Jesse Jackson," Dec. 21, 1984, RRL. "Senator Edward Kennedy—South Africa Legislation," EMK staff chronology, undated, AC-JFKL.

426 **the daunting expectations:** JAF interview with Greg Craig. Kennedy to Reagan, Oct. 10, 1984. The administration detailed an assistant secretary of state to reply. See Bennett to Kennedy, Nov. 7, 1984 ("US policy under this administration has sought—and continues to seek—to nurture evolutionary change . . . to help curb violence by seeking avenues for peaceful change, not to create further polarization by expressing confrontational, if well-intentioned, statements"), RRL.

427 **Ethiopia and Sudan:** JAF interview with Eileen McNamara. EMK, "Ethiopian Journal," *People*, Jan. 28, 1985.

428 **reviews were harsh:** JAF interviews with Greg Craig, Kathleen Kennedy Townsend, Robert Shrum. Desmond Tutu OH, UVA. EMK, Desmond Tutu interviews, AC-JFKL. EMKOH-UVA. Remarks of Sen. Edward M. Kennedy, Martin Luther King Jr. Memorial Breakfast, Boston, MA, Jan. 15, 1985; Craig to EMK, undated, 1985, AC-JFKL. NYT, Jan. 6, 10, 12, 14, 15, 1985. WP, Jan. 14, 1985. Cable traffic, Nickel U.S. Embassy Pretoria to Shultz, U.S. State Department, Jan. 8, 11, 14, 23, 1985; Botha to EMK, Jan. 11, 1985; Nickel, introductory remarks, Jan. 8, 1985, AC-JFKL.

428 **"not my life":** Clymer, *Edward M. Kennedy*, 374–75. Shrum, *No Excuses*, 151–52. JAF interview with Robert Shrum. Among those who believed that Kennedy made the correct choice when withdrawing from the 1988 race was Richard Nixon. "As far as Teddy Kennedy is concerned the train has left the station," he wrote to friends at the end of 1984. "Chappaquiddick may well be forgotten, but 20 years will have elapsed since the death of Bobby and a quarter of a century since the death of Jack. . . . Teddy, who in 1988 will be prematurely old, will have lost his major base of support." See Nixon to friends, Oct. 29, 1984, in "Appendix: The Campaign Papers," Goldman and Fuller et al., *Quest*.

429 **endorsed the sanctions:** JAF interview with Greg Craig. Richard Lugar OH, UVA. Chapman to McManus and Deaver, April 12, 1984; Blankley and Chapman to Jenkins and Meese, April 25, 1984; Shultz to Regan, "US Policy in Southern Africa After Four Years," undated; Lugar and Kassebaum to Reagan, Nov. 30, 1984; McFarlane to Reagan, Feb. 20, 1985; Reagan to Kassebaum, Feb. 22, 1985, RRL. For an overview see Love, *U.S. Anti-apartheid Movement*, and Anne Mariel Peters, "U.S. Sanctions on South Africa," UVA, April 3, 2006.

430 **veto was overridden:** JAF interview with Greg Craig: "He ended apartheid. There is no doubt in my mind that the United States of America would not have imposed sanctions without Ted Kennedy." EMKOH-UVA. Buchanan to McFarlane and Regan, Aug. 20, 1985; Charen to Buchanan, July 29, 1985, RRL. NYT, Oct. 3, 1986. CQA, 1986, 359–72. EMK interview, AC-JFKL.

430 **sanctions were effective:** Cohen to Powell, "South Africa Policy" ("Sanctions struck a serious symbolic and psychological blow"), National Security Council, Jan. 15, 1988, RRL. For Weicker see BM, Nov. 30, 2009.

430 **decide which gavel:** WP, Dec. 21, 1986.

431 **"A public law":** JAF interviews with EMK, Thomas

Rollins. EMK, Anthony Podesta interviews, AC-JFKL. Thomas Rollins OH, UVA.

Twenty-Three: Vehemence and Vitriol

432 **young gay men:** Centers for Disease Control, *MMWR Weekly*, June 5, 1981. Anthony Fauci OH, UVA. Shilts, *Band*, 62–76. The AIDS virus—HIV—was identified by French researchers in 1983. Pamela Smith, "AIDS: An Overview of Issues," Congressional Research Service, Dec. 24, 1987. "Review of the Public Health Service's Response to AIDS," Feb. 1985, Office of Technology Assessment, U.S. Congress.

433 **to scare off:** The Supreme Court case was *Bowers v. Hardwick*, 478 U.S. 186 (1986). The Constitution contains no "fundamental right to engage in homosexual sodomy," even in private by consenting adults, the court ruled. For a cinematic review of the rise of the New Right, see Perlstein, *Reaganland*. Buchanan's column from the *New York Post* is cited in Shilts, *Band*, 311. See also Nancy Lee Jones, "AIDS: A Brief Overview of the Major Legal Issues," Congressional Research Service, Feb. 10, 1987.

433 **virus was insidious:** Drake and Burke to Dole, "AIDS UPDATE," June 30, 1987, Dole-KU. On Reagan administration response see Donald Francis transcript and Francis to Dowdle, April 12, 1983, "The Age of AIDS," *Frontline*, PBS. "We want you to look pretty and do as little as you can," Francis and the other CDC scientists were told by their superiors in Washington. "We literally had nothing for the first two years, essentially nothing," Francis recalled. "We had to steal equipment from the other laboratories." By the time the first cases of AIDS were diagnosed, a CDC expert told *Frontline*, 250,000 Americans were already infected. Reagan did not address AIDS in his speeches until May 1987. See "Remarks by the President to the American Foundation for AIDS Research Awards Dinner," May 31, 1987, UCSB. Shilts, *Band*, 525–26. See also Cannon, *President Reagan*, 814–19.

434 **harbored baying bigots:** JAF interviews with Lynn Drake, Tim Westmoreland. Waxman was concerned about Reagan's shortchanging of disease prevention even before AIDS was identified as a threat. A member of his staff, visiting the CDC in Atlanta, was told in early 1981 that proposed budget cuts would leave the country vulnerable to epidemics. It was on that same trip that Waxman's staff was informed about the outbreak of *Pneumocystis* pneumonia among gay men in West Hollywood, within his congressional district. Waxman, *Waxman Report*, chapter 3, "HIV/AIDS and the Ryan White Act." Another early foe of the disease was Representative Ted Weiss, who represented the west side of Manhattan, including parts of Greenwich Village. Their efforts in the House are chronicled by Shilts and others, but the Senate's initial response to the epidemic is something of a scholarly black hole. See also Andriote, *Victory Deferred*, 220–23. For Buckley see NYT, March 18, 1986.

435 **gay community's support:** EMKOH-UVA. Anthony Fauci OH, UVA. Susan Estrich interview,

AC-JFKL. Susman to EMK, March 11, 1975, TS-UMASS. Clymer, *Edward M. Kennedy*, 301. Shilts, *Band*, 29–32. EMK's cluelessness was matched by members of his staff. "I could be a bit dull back then," Thomas Rollins confessed. "You just didn't know any gay people." See also Shrum, *No Excuses*, 112.

435 **His reputation gave:** JAF interview with Robert Shrum. Drake to Burke, April 27, 1987, Dole-KU. The gay community was itself divided on health measures that might curb the liberating sexual atmosphere, like closing bathhouses. Shilts, *Band*, covers the controversy at length, beginning on page 19: "Promiscuity . . . was central to the raucous gay movement of the 1970s." He and Andriote, *Victory Deferred*, 72–76, also note how gay sex was an influential commercial interest.

437 **Kennedy apologized for the tardy:** JAF interviews with Kitty Higgins, Thomas Rollins, Maureen Byrnes, Vic Basile, Tim Westmoreland. EMKOH-UVA. Thomas Rollins, Anthony Fauci, Mona Sarfaty OH, UVA. EMK remarks, National AIDS Network, Washington, DC, June 3, 1987; Dole to Koch, Nov. 14, 1985 ("I do not believe that a dramatic increase in Federal involvement is likely at a time when we are facing massive deficits which must be brought under control," Dole wrote New York mayor Ed Koch); Dole and EMK, "Face Off" script, April 30, 1986, Dole-KU. "Acquired Immune Deficiency Syndrome (AIDS)," April 16, 1986, hearing, Senate Committee on Labor and Human Resources. Rollins et al. to EMK, "Agenda for 1986," Jan. 24, 1986, Thomas Rollins papers. See also Mark Merlis, "AIDS: Health Care Financing and Services," Congressional Research Service, Feb. 29, 1988, who noted, almost seven years after the disease was discovered, "As it begins to focus on the AIDS epidemic, Congress is also confronting larger questions." Shilts, *Band*, 371.

437 **Weicker was chairman:** JAF interview with Vic Basile, Maureen Byrnes. Anthony Fauci, Lowell Weicker OH, UVA. NYT, Sept. 12, 1986. NIH news release, "NIH Dedicates Lowell P. Weicker Building," May 4, 2015. See Zimmerman to Chiles, with GAO briefing report B-228706, Aug. 12, 1987. On early funding, see "Review of the Public Health Service's Response to AIDS," Washington DC: U.S. Congress, Office of Technology Assessment, Feb. 1985, 7.

437 **He needed Hatch:** Sheila Burke, Nancy Soderberg OH, UVA.

439 **Hatch and Dole had national:** On EMK operating style, see JAF interviews with Jeff Blattner, Chris Dodd, Joseph Tydings, Donald Ritchie, Ranny Cooper, Robert Shrum, Chris Jennings, James Manley.

On AIDS see JAF interview with Tim Westmoreland. Anthony Fauci ("Hatch was terrific") OH, UVA. EMK, Orrin Hatch interviews, AC-JFKL. David Sundwall, Oct. 25, 2017, Sundwall Lecture on Public Health Policy, Salt Lake City, Utah. "Acquired Immune Deficiency Syndrome (AIDS)" hearing, Committee on Labor and Human Resources, U.S. Senate, April 16, 1986. "Dole Urges Caution on AIDS Testing," May 21, 1987; Dole to Hatch, June 12, 1987; Devine to Burke, with attached Schlafly memo, June 12, 1987, Dole-KU. Nexon to EMK, "Meeting with Waxman," Feb. 22, 1990, NL-UMASS. Shilts, *Band*, 296, 399.

The Mormon church has a code—the "Word of Wisdom"—for healthy behavior that makes for health-conscious congregations. Hatch's religious orientation may have played a role in his willingness to take more progressive stands on issues like child health care, AIDS, and the dangers of tobacco. Thomas Korologos, Republican lobbyist, believed that Hatch's faith played another key role in the relationship with EMK: "Hatch was a Mormon through and through. He is a Mormon missionary. He wanted to save Kennedy's soul. He believed he was straightening Kennedy out."

440 **was fully engaged:** JAF interview, Thomas Rollins. EMKOH-UVA. Anthony Fauci, Thomas Rollins OH, UVA. Michael Iskowitz interview, AC-JFKL. "AIDS Epidemic," hearing, Committee on Labor and Human Resources, U.S. Senate, Jan. 16, 1987. NYT, Jan. 16, 1987. On Dole and EMK, see CQW, June 20, 1987. "Kennedy is there when it does nothing for him, nothing for him except [political] heartache . . . [and] grief," women's rights activist Judith Lichtman said in her UVA oral history. "I never think that he's there for me because there's some political equation."

441 **his considerable relief:** EMKOH-UVA. Thomas Rollins OH, UVA.

441 **disease opened doors:** JAF interviews with Thomas Rollins, Kitty Higgins. Thomas Rollins, Mona Sarfaty, Anthony Fauci OH, UVA. EMKOH-UVA. Michael Iskowitz, Sandra Thurman interviews, AC-JFKL.

On Beirn and Iskowitz see Mathilde Krim, American Foundation for AIDS Research, "Remembering Terry: The Ryan White (CARE) Act," *The AmFAR Newsletter*, Summer 1996. See also Bob Gatty, "Ryan White: The Inside Story," *HIV Specialist*, Summer 2010.

EMK remarks, National AIDS Network, Washington, DC, June 3, 1987; EMK to Reagan, May 29, 1987; Taylor to Dole, March 27, 1990, Dole-KU.

Fauci was the director of the National Institute of Allergy and Infectious Diseases, and the coordinator of AIDS research at NIH. Krim's husband, Arthur, was a prominent Democratic Party fundraiser; John Kennedy's famous forty-fifth birthday party, with Marilyn Monroe attending, was held in the Krims' New York home.

442 **Dole murmured to:** JAF interview with Lynn Drake. Michnick and Burke to Dole, Oct. 24, 1986; Drake to Burke, April 7, 1987; Burke to Dole, May 22, June 4, 1987; "Dear Colleague" letter on members-only briefing, Kennedy, Byrd, Weicker, and Dole, June 30, 1987; Burke and Drake to Dole, June 16, July 29, 1987; Burke and Drake to Dole, "Meeting with Senator Kennedy—AIDS," July 29, 1987; Questionnaire on AIDS, *San Francisco Chronicle*, Senator Robert Dole, Aug. 14, 1987; Talking Points—AIDS, Nov. 4, 1987, Dole-KU. NYT, March 21, 1987. *Human Events*, June 6, 1987. Sheila Burke, Robert Dole OH, UVA.

442 **That left Helms:** CQA, 1987. EMK remarks, National AIDS Network, Washington, DC, June 3, 1987, Dole-KU. Helms supported mandatory

testing and quarantines and banning immigrants with AIDS, and opposed safe sex programs, which he said condoned immoral behavior. See also *Human Events*, June 6, 1987. CQW, June 29, 1987. The Democrats, after two Reagan landslides, feared being seen as "coddling homosexuals," said Randy Shilts, UPI, Nov. 19, 1987.

443 **and accused Helms:** CR, Oct. 18, 1983. EMKOH-UVA. If RFK was alive, "he would be the first person to say that it was wrong to wiretap Martin Luther King" and "the first person to say that J. Edgar Hoover's reckless campaign against Martin Luther King was a shame and a blot on American history," EMK said. As evidence of RFK's admiration for King, he quoted from his brother's remarkable speech in Indianapolis on the night the civil rights leader was killed.

The sparring between Helms and EMK continued. In 1993, in a loud debate over AIDS and immigrants, Helms ostentatiously played with his hearing aid and said, "Let me adjust my hearing aid. It could not accommodate the decibels of the senator from Massachusetts. I can't match him in decibels or Jezebels." See WP, Feb. 19, 1993. Ronald Weich OH, UVA.

444 **safe sex comic:** CR, Oct. 14, 1987. Associated Press, Oct. 14, 1987. New York mayor Ed Koch criticized EMK and the Senate for complicity in Helms's mischief, which "ignores the proven effectiveness of AIDS education efforts and severely impedes our ability to expand them." Koch charged that Kennedy and the other senators, "fearing an adverse reaction that a homophobic demagogue might inflame in their home state . . . gave in to homophobic hysteria." NYT, Nov. 7, 1987. Richard Kusserow, Inspector General, Department of Health and Human Services, "Report on Review of Centers for Disease Control Funds Awarded to the Gay Men's Health Crisis," Nov. 17, 1987. Senate Record Vote Analysis, Oct. 14, 1987, Republican Policy Committee, Dole-KU.

445 **gotten a whipping:** Sarfaty, Beirn and Iskowitz, two memos to EMK, Oct. 16, 1987, NL-UMASS.

445 **bill in hand:** Sarfaty et al. to EMK, Oct. 30, 1987, Nov. 19, 1987; Iskowitz to EMK, Dec. 18, 1987, NL-UMASS.

446 **Byrd and Kennedy:** EMKOH-UVA. Robert Byrd OH, UVA. Sarfaty et al. to EMK, Oct. 23, 1987, March 5, April 15, 1988; Keith to EMK, Feb. 5, 1988, NL-UMASS.

448 **Hatch at his best:** CR, April 28, 1988. JAF interview with Thomas Rollins. Thomas Rollins OH, UVA. Iskowitz to Littlefield, April 10, 1989, NL-UMASS. The AIDS Research and Information Act of 1988 expanded AIDS research and established the first national AIDS prevention campaign. CQW, June 20, 1987. EMK statement, May 15, 1987, Dole-KU. CR, May 15, 1987.

449 **Again, Hatch replied:** CR, May 14, 1990. The Ryan White Comprehensive AIDS Resources Emergency (CARE) Act was modeled on federal disaster relief programs. Among other things, it provided federal money for local hospitals, hospice and home care, and AIDS drugs.

The political decision to emphasize the impact of AIDS on White and other patients outside the gay community was not without controversy, even within EMK's office. "Goddamn it, this is a lie," Rollins told Beirn, as reports about heterosexual transmission scared the straight population. "Well, it's a pretty goddamn helpful lie, isn't it?" Beirn replied. "That is all we need to agree on, my brother." See Rollins OH, UVA.

450 **tide had turned:** JAF interview with David Sundwall. Orrin Hatch, Michael Iskowitz interviews, AC-JFKL. WP, May 5, 1990. Burke and Willis to Dole, April 19, 1990, Dole-KU. There were four major steps taken by the Senate in the first decade of the AIDS crisis. The first were the hikes in research funding for the NIH and CDC and other agencies, guided by Lowell Weicker. The Hatch-EMK team then pushed the Health Omnibus Programs Extension (HOPE) Act through the chamber in 1988. The two men then worked together on the Ryan White Comprehensive AIDS Resources Emergency (CARE) Act, which provided almost a billion dollars in targeted aid for impacted communities and other programs and became law in 1990. Finally, there was the American with Disabilities Act, which included AIDS victims, and protected them from discrimination, which was signed into law in July 1990. Congress also passed the Terry Beirn Community Based Clinical Trials Program Act in 1991, to establish local treatment trials for AIDS sufferers, and AIDS-related bills on housing and other issues.

450 **privacy and discrimination:** Iskowitz to Littlefield, April 10, 1989, NL-UMASS.

451 **his consistent enthusiasm:** There are several fine accounts of the political and legislative process that engendered the ADA. See Davis, *Enabling Acts*, and Jonathan Young, "Equality of Opportunity: The Making of the Americans with Disabilities Act," National Council on Disability, 1997.

452 **task for Harkin and Kennedy:** JAF interview with Maureen Byrnes. Tom Harkin, Carolyn Osolinik interviews, AC-JFKL. Carey Parker OH, UVA. Porter and Bates to Sununu, April 21, 1989, GHWBL. Kennedy's personal connection to the cause of the disabled was shared by many players in the ADA saga. Dole was disabled. Hatch had a brother-in-law stricken by polio. Weicker had a son with Down syndrome. Harkin had a deaf brother. The House sponsor, Representative Tony Coelho, suffered from epilepsy, as did the wife of the ADA's top advocate in the chamber, Representative Steny Hoyer. President George H. W. Bush had children with disabilities. Attorney General Richard Thornburgh had a disabled son, who suffered brain damage in a car accident. "I didn't get elected to get re-elected," Harkin told an aide who advised him to be cautious. "My brother is deaf. I understand discrimination. . . . We are doing this legislation." See Young, "Equality of Opportunity," and Davis, *Enabling Acts*, 3–5.

453 **pounded the table:** Paul Donovan OH, UVA. Tom Harkin, William Roper, Pat Wright, Carolyn Osolinik interviews, AC-JFKL. Young, "Equality of Opportunity." Anne Mariel Peters, "The Americans with Disabilities Act," UVA, 2006. Said Sununu, "We argued a lot, we got hot under the collar a lot, but to this day, I probably respect Ted

Kennedy more than most Republicans respect him. I think he did his homework; he was always prepared, he was smart and articulate for his side and really was willing to give and take to get results done. . . . When the going got tough on those two bills [the ADA and the Civil Rights Act of 1991] and they could have been killed . . . [EMK's skills] gave us enough confidence to cross the extra last fifty yards." William Barr, who negotiated on civil rights issues for the Department of Justice, had a similar impression: "I always enjoyed dealing with Kennedy because he was very direct and he knew how to make a deal. . . . He'd call up and say, 'Look, I know you don't want to go too far in this direction, but here's an issue we can isolate where I think you would agree with me. And if I guarantee you that this bill will stay at that dimension and we won't use it as a vehicle, can we work together on it? And in return, here's something I can do for you.' We'd just cut a deal, and it was done. . . . He would stand by his deals. It was the art of the possible." See John Sununu, William Barr, Richard Thornburgh OH, George H. W. Bush collection, UVA.

454 **a harsh choice:** Young, "Equality of Opportunity."

Twenty-Four: Robert Bork's America

457 **"Robert Bork's America":** The Simpson-EMK exchange is from the full transcript of Simpson's interview for the *Frontline* documentary "Supreme Revenge," broadcast on PBS in 2019. Not all of the interview is included in the film itself. Simpson told a similar story in his oral history at UVA.

JAF interview with Jeff Blattner (re Bork), EMK (re Cuomo). Statement of Senator Edward M. Kennedy on the Nomination of Robert Bork to the Supreme Court, CR, July 1, 1987. NJ, Sept. 12, 1987. EMK was presiding over a hearing on July 1 when Attorney General Meese called to give him the news of Bork's appointment, Blattner said. When he resumed the chair, Kennedy told the Reagan lieutenant who was testifying, "I think I will have something to say about that."

As Adam Clymer notes, EMK had made a similarly harsh attack on Rehnquist, which the chief justice managed to survive, and which has not entered the history books like the remarks on Bork. "The schools of America would . . . be segregated. Millions of citizens would be denied the right to vote under scandalous malapportionment laws. Women would be condemned to second-class status as second-class Americans. Courthouses would be closed to individual challenges against police brutality and executive abuse," Kennedy said, upbraiding Rehnquist in a Senate speech on Sept. 11, 1986. "Government would embrace religion and the wall of separation between church and state would be in ruins. State and local majorities would tell us what we can read, how to lead our private lives, whether to bear children, how to bring them up, what kinds of people we may become." Clymer, *Edward M. Kennedy*, 394. See also Jenkins, *Partisan*, 215–22.

"I never mind seeing people wade into the fray and fight the fight, but the hypocrisy . . . is just too much,"

Simpson told his diary, amid the fight over Rehn-quist. "Ted Kennedy, with his past capers—some of which match my own—can ill be seen making those kinds of judgments." See Hardy, *Shooting*, 116.

457 **the original intent:** JAF interviews with Peter Edelman, Antonin Scalia. EMKOH-UVA. Laurence Tribe OH, UVA. In its briefing books on Bork, the Reagan administration variously described his philosophy as "judicial restraint" and "interpretiv-ism," and labeled him an "intentionalist." The term "originalism" became more in vogue in later years. See "Robert Bork," White House counsel briefing paper, and "Robert H. Bork: Biographical Information," RRL. NYT, July 5, Sept. 13, 1987.

458 **a theoretical invention:** JAF interview with Ralph Neas. "Robert Bork," White House counsel brief-ing paper, RRL. The Ninth Amendment of the Bill of Rights states, "The enumeration, in the Constitution, of certain rights, shall not be con-strued to deny or disparage others retained by the people." Originalists like Bork, finding this amend-ment inconvenient, dismiss it as an extraneous, inoperable "ink blot" in the Constitution.

458 **been a swing vote:** Powell was the author of a fa-mous memo, from the first Nixon term, calling on conservatives to organize their resistance to liber-alism. See Powell to Sydnor, "Confidential Memo-randum," Aug. 23, 1971. The memo is in the justice's papers at Washington & Lee University. It is reprinted in Smith, *Who Stole*, 445.

458 **craft the creed:** EMKOH-UVA. JAF interview with Jeff Blattner. Laurence Tribe OH, UVA. Jeff Blatt-ner interview, "Supreme Revenge," *Frontline*, PBS, Jan. 11, 2019. Summary, briefing book on Bork for Senate colleagues, EMK briefing book, Blattner collection, Judicial Nominations II, Feb. 12, 2007, Robert Bork Nomination. "Hearings on Saxbe Nomination to be Attorney General," undated; "Confirmation of Judges," undated, Alan Simp-son papers, University of Wyoming. Cranston to Democratic colleagues, June 29, 1987; Biden to Daschle, July 23, 1987, TD-SDS. WP, July 2, 1987.

460 **pulling a fire alarm:** JAF interviews with Jeff Blattner, Ricki Seidman. EMK briefing book, Blatt-ner collection, Judicial Nominations II, Feb. 12, 2007, Robert Bork Nomination: "The timing of the statement is designed to make it clear the nom-ination will face major opposition in the Senate and discourage centrist Senators who might oth-erwise commit themselves prematurely." EMKOH-UVA. Anthony Lewis, Melody Barnes, Marcia Greenberger OH, UVA. NYT, July 3, 1987. Garry Wills, "The Decline and Fall of a Sure Thing," NYT, Sept. 10, 1989. *Philadelphia Inquirer*, Nov. 16, 1986. NJ, Sept 12, 1987. David Sutphen OH, UVA.

460 **"stark and direct":** BG, Oct. 11, 1987. EMKOH-UVA. In his UVA oral history EMK explained how the nomination process works to the advantage of a nominee, whose backers generally have a pre-planned strategy that can overwhelm resistance "before people who have reservations have a chance." EMK's attack bought time for the coali-tion of liberal interest groups who opposed the nomination, and they responded with a sophisti-cated public relations campaign.

Conservatives parried with a briefing paper mimick-ing Kennedy's speech on Bork—"The Liberal Spe-cial Interest Group's America" (RRL)—that cited the more extreme liberal pleadings on issues like homosexuality, crime, free speech, pornography, and abortion filed over the years by the American Civil Liberties Union and others. To keep the fo-cus on Bork, Biden and Kennedy asked the lib-eral groups to forfeit their opportunity to testify at the hearings, and they reluctantly agreed. See BG, Oct. 11, 1987.

461 **Biden and Kennedy:** Carolyn Osolinik, Marcia Greenberger OH, UVA. JAF interview with Jeff Blattner, James Doyle. Early whip count; EMK to Biden, Aug. 4, 1987; EMK to Cox, Aug. 7, 1987, and Cox reply, undated; Blattner to EMK, July 17, 1987; Osolinik to EMK, Aug. 6, 1987; EMK brief-ing book, Blattner collection, Judicial Nomina-tions II, Feb. 12, 2007, Robert Bork Nomination. Early White House whip count (which closely matched the Democratic count, with fifty-five sen-ators listed as pro-Bork), RRL. NYT, Sept. 19, 1986. For a critical view of Bork's role in the Saturday Night Massacre, see Anthony Lewis, "Bork and Wa-tergate," NYT, Aug. 23, 1987.

462 **a "confirmation conversion":** JAF interview with Thomas Korologos. EMKOH-UVA. White House "Materials on Judge Robert H. Bork," and Senate Judiciary Committee, "Response Prepared to White House Analysis of Judge Bork's Record"; Stephens to Culvahouse, July 31, 1987; Blackwell to Reagan, Sept. 30, 1987, and Reagan response, Oct. 21, 1987; Weyrich to Bork, Oct. 21, 1987; Rader to Ball, Korologos, Reynolds, and Bolton, Aug. 20, 1987; Culvahouse to Baker, Duberstein, Ball, and Griscom, Sept. 8, 1987, RRL. WSJ, Oct. 7, 1987. *Time*, Oct. 12, 1987. For excellent contem-porary accounts of the Bork nomination see Bron-ner, *Battle*, and Gitenstein, *Matters*. Bronner covered the battle for the *Boston Globe* and Giten-stein served as the chief Judiciary Committee counsel.

462 **to biracial coalitions:** EMK to "Dear Friend," Aug. 12, 1987; Osolinik, Blattner, and Podesta to EMK, July 31, 1987; EMK briefing book, Blattner collec-tion, Judicial Nominations II, Feb. 12, 2007, Rob-ert Bork Nomination. BG, Oct. 11, 1987. WSJ, Oct. 7, 1987. EMKOH-UVA. Carolyn Osolinik OH, UVA. JAF interview with Jeff Blattner. Five south-ern freshmen—John Breaux of Louisiana, Bob Graham of Florida, Richard Shelby of Alabama, Wyche Fowler of Georgia, and Terry Sanford of North Carolina—were special targets of the civil rights forces. On the Judiciary Committee, the swing votes were Republican Arlen Specter of Pennsylvania and Democrats Robert Byrd of West Virginia, Howell Heflin of Alabama, and Dennis DeConcini of Arizona.

On Republican diddling see "Bork Meeting," Aug. 18, 1987 ("The mobilization is not nearly at the level it ought to be. . . . We need more people and we need to get them soon or it will be too late"), and Weyrich to Bork, Oct. 21, 1987 ("I will never for-give myself and the rest of the conservative move-ment for not being ready"), and Rader to Ball,

Korologos, Reynolds, and Bolton, Aug. 20 1987 ("We need better answers"), all RRL.

462 **was in jeopardy:** Culvahouse to Baker, Duberstein, Ball, and Griscom, Sept. 8, 1987, RRL. Gitenstein, *Matters*, 180, 203.

463 **Senate Caucus Room:** John and Robert Kennedy had declared their presidential candidacies in the Caucus Room. In 2009 the Senate renamed it the Kennedy Caucus Room, to honor the three brothers.

463 **fidgety, bearded professor:** JAF interviews with Janet Heininger, Jeff Blattner. Laurence Tribe, Carolyn Osolinik, Alan Simpson OH, UVA. Jeff Blattner interview, AC-JFKL. Address of Senator Edward M. Kennedy, Nomination of Robert Bork to the Supreme Court, Georgetown University Law Center, Washington, DC, Sept. 11, 1987. EMK briefing book, Blattner collection, Judicial Nominations II, Feb. 12, 2007, Robert Bork Nomination. NYT, July 29, 1987. WP, Sept. 16, 1987.

464 **nominee was "borked":** Six Republicans voted to reject the nomination. JAF interviews with Thomas Korologos, Ralph Neas, Jeff Blattner. Carolyn Osolinik OH, UVA. Tom Shales, "The Bork Turnoff; On Camera, the Judge Failed to Save Himself," WP, Oct. 9, 1987. NYT, Feb. 9, 1988. WSJ, Oct. 7, 1987. EMK to Simpson, undated, quoted in Hardy, *Shooting*, 215. Five years later, Supreme Court nominee Ruth Bader Ginsburg was shown videotapes of the Bork showdown to help prepare her for her own Senate hearings. She concluded that Bork had been "unjustly crucified" for his "candid" scholarly responses and she deplored the demeaning process. See Klain to Gergen, "Judge Ginsburg: Performance Pitfalls," July 14, 1993, WCL.

Twenty-Five: Relapse

466 **Kennedy had shown he was:** The press was beginning to take notice. *U.S. News & World Report*, in its April 4, 1988, issue, dubbed him "The King of the Hill."

466 **scuttle for headlines:** JAF interview with Thomas Rollins. Thomas Rollins OH, UVA. Lawrence Horowitz interview, AC-JFKL. Rollins to EMK, "Weekly Book," Jan. 16, 1986, NL-UMASS.

467 **he was leading:** Galbraith to EMK, June 28, 1989, and April 23, 1990, JKG-JFKL.

467 **Grove City College:** The case was *Grove City College v. Bell*, 465 U.S. 555 (1984). For a case study, and discussion of the ruling and Title IX, see Hugh Davis Graham, "The Storm over Grove City College: Civil Rights Regulation, Higher Education, and the Reagan Administration," *History of Education Quarterly*, Winter 1998, 407–29. Cribb, "Grove City legislation briefing," March 9, 1988, RRL. Weinberger to Ford, Feb. 28, 1975, GFL. Burke to Dole, March 16, 1988, Dole-KU. NYT, Oct. 3, 1984; March 17, 23, 1988. EMKOH-UVA. Marcia Greenberger, Barbara Souliotis OH, UVA.

469 **substance abuse problems:** JAF interview with John Warner. Lawrence Horowitz interview, AC-JFKL. John Culver, Charles Tretter, Robert Hunter OH, UVA. Lawford, *Symptoms*, 108. NYT,

May 31, 1991. Sally Jacobs, "Prime Time with Joan Kennedy," *Boston Globe Magazine*, July 9, 2000. Michele McPhee and Dave Wedge, "The Fall of Joan," BM, Aug. 2005. Kennedy and Fried, *Common Struggle*, 66–67, 80, 82, 95. Several of EMK's nephews did not survive. In 1984, RFK's son David was found dead from a drug overdose in a Palm Beach hotel, while his brother Michael was killed in a skiing accident on New Year's Eve 1997 in Aspen. John F. Kennedy Jr. died when the plane he was piloting crashed in 1999, on his way to a family wedding.

469 **culture of silence:** Edward Kennedy Jr., Kara Kennedy, Patrick Kennedy OH, UVA. On the family culture, see this oral history interview and others by Maria and Robert Shriver, and the Patrick Kennedy and Christopher Lawford memoirs.

470 **great white shark:** Edward M. Kennedy Jr., Kara Kennedy, Patrick Kennedy OH, UVA. EMK to JAF, 1991, author collection.

470 **empty years emotionally:** Korman to EMK, undated 1982, March 15, 1982, Dec. 4, 1985, Oct. 28, 1991. ("It is never easy being vulnerable, but unless one decides to express real feelings, there is no hope for real relationships," Korman wrote. "You and I have been writing for over 15 years and only one of us has ever behaved in a vulnerable fashion.") Korman collection, JFKL. Elizabeth Shannon OH, UVA.

The portrait of EMK in the 1980s is drawn from JAF interviews over many years with those who knew him, including Terri Robinson, Patrick Kennedy, Alan Simpson, Orrin Hatch, Lawrence Horowitz, Richard Goodwin, John Warner, Thomas Rollins, Melody Miller, Robert Shrum, Christopher Dodd, and Victoria Reggie Kennedy; from Patrick Kennedy's memoir, *A Common Struggle*; and from the EMK oral history interviews with John Culver, Elizabeth Shannon, John Tunney, and the senator's children.

Shannon attributed Kennedy's problems with intimacy to the nigh-abusive treatment he received from a cold and negligent mother as a child. "I don't think she was ever cruel to her children . . . just indifference—that's hurtful to a child," Shannon said. It left Kennedy with "this odd inarticulateness when it comes to expressing something personal or maybe somewhat hurtful in himself." Before he died, her husband, the journalist and diplomat William Shannon, worked as a potential biographer with EMK and conducted hours of interviews with the senator about his childhood and family. She was deeply versed in the family background and the senator's psyche.

471 **"There were groupies":** JAF interview with Melody Miller. "Tabloid Noise and Judicial Silence: The Nadir of Ted Kennedy," Boston.com, 2009. Tom Harkin interview, AC-JFKL. Former aides Shrum and Rollins recall a day when the Rolling Stones were touring the United States, and EMK's staff was delighted to set up a meeting between frontman Mick Jagger and the senator. EMK asked Jagger how, in his advancing years, he trained to give such energetic performances. He worked out in the gym, said the singer, drank Gatorade, and

had lots of sex. "Hmmm. Gatorade, you say?" said Kennedy. JAF interview with Thomas Rollins, Robert Shrum.

471 **his antics might:** Michael Kelly, "Ted Kennedy on the Rocks," *GQ*, Feb. 1990. Speedboat: When the speedboat photograph was published, Howell Heflin was credited with joking that Kennedy "has changed his position on offshore drilling." See BG, Feb. 19, 2009. BH, July 15, 1991. American Trash: BH, Jan. 20, 1989. Convention: JAF interview with Walter Robinson. Aground: BH, Aug. 19, 1987. Bistro: Lawford, *Symptoms*, 272. See also John Tunney, John Seigenthaler OH, UVA; JAF interviews with Orrin Hatch, Christopher Dodd. Patrick Kennedy, *60 Minutes*, Oct. 4, 2015.

473 **terminate Murdoch's waiver:** JAF interview with Thomas Rollins. Remarks of Senator Edward M. Kennedy on Murdoch, Open Forum, Lexington, MA, Jan. 5, 1988, AC-JFKL. The *Herald* diligently kept track throughout the 1980s of the women who came and went in Kennedy's life. See BH, June 17, 1985, April 10, Aug. 9, 1986, Sept. 18, 1987, Aug. 6, 1992. See also *Washingtonian*, Aug. 1982. On the Murdoch-Kennedy "vendetta" see NYT, Jan. 7, 11, 1988, and *Time*, Jan. 18, 1988, and BG, Jan. 11, 1988, and Clymer, *Edward M. Kennedy*, 418–21. Kennedy's friend Senator Lowell Weicker called Murdoch "the No. 1 dirt bag owner of any publication or electronic media in this nation."

473 **Senator Bedfellow figure:** Michael Kelly assembled incidents like those at La Brasserie from interviews and the gossip columns of *Penthouse* magazine, the *Washington Times*, the *Boston Herald*, and other sources for an influential February 1990 article in *GQ* magazine: "Ted Kennedy on the Rocks." Kennedy's son Patrick called it "a devastating (although basically accurate) piece about his aggressively single lifestyle and its possible ramifications for his political authority." See Kennedy and Fried, *Common Struggle*, 95, 99. On La Brasserie see also NYT, Aug. 9, 2020.

474 **conduct in Palm Beach:** Anne Mercer deposition; Detective Hohnholz deposition; Edward Kennedy deposition; Patrick Kennedy deposition, author's collection. BG, April 3, 1991.

474 **"impulse of self-destruction":** Schlesinger diary, April 6, 9, 1991, AS-NYPL.

474 **more young women:** BG, July 24, 1991. WP, July 23, 1991. NYT, July 23, 24, 1991. Smith became "animal-like" and "violent" and acted like a "sicko" as he tried to force himself on them, the three women told the Florida authorities. In Matoesian, *Discourse*, 14–15, Smith's attorney, Roy Black, critiques the women's testimony, defends the judge's decision, and minimizes its impact. None of the women filed charges against Smith after they were allegedly assaulted, Black noted; the one who had sex with Smith stayed the night and raised no alarm as she lay beside him while he answered a phone call from his girlfriend.

475 **shirt or nightshirt:** Schlesinger diary, May 23, 1991, NYPL. Michelle Cassone, statement to police, May 5, 1991; statement by Senator Edward M. Kennedy, May 15, 1991, both in author's collection. The author covered the Palm Beach story

while working for the *Boston Globe* in 1991. BG, April 6, 7, 1991. NYT, April 6, 1991.

475 **polls showed him losing to:** BG, April 9, 1991.

475 **named Clarence Thomas:** Laurence Tribe, Jeff Blattner OH, UVA. Phyllis Berry Myers interview, Timothy Phelps collection. John Sununu OH, George H. W. Bush collection, UVA.

476 **his friend Souter:** JAF interview with Jeff Blattner. Rudman privately assured EMK that Souter was fair and objective "and will not try to push the Court in a conservative direction." But Kennedy objected to the "stealth" nominee. "The Senate is still in the dark about this nomination, and all of us are voting in the dark," he told the Senate. "David Souter Nomination," EMK briefing book, Blattner collection, Judicial Nominations II, Feb. 12, 2007.

476 **He met with Kennedy:** On EMK's initial dealings with Thomas see "Clarence Thomas Nomination," EMK briefing book, Blattner collection, Judicial Nominations II, Feb. 12, 2007. Butt: Floyd Brown, a right-wing striver who founded a group called Citizens United, used Republican Party funds to produce a cable television advertisement attacking Senate liberals on character issues that summer. It brought up Biden's blemish as a law school plagiarist and EMK on Chappaquiddick, and featured a screenshot of the tabloid *New York Post*'s coverage of the Palm Beach scandal, with the front-page headline "Teddy's Sexy Romp." Bush disavowed it, yet it caused a stir. See NYT, Sept. 4, 6, 1991. Floyd Brown, Gary Bauer interviews, Timothy Phelps collection. "We were framing the debate early on," said Brown. "Ted Kennedy was on trial . . . because how can this man who has acted like this . . . sit up there and judge Judge Thomas, this man of integrity?"

477 **pending Civil Rights Act of 1991:** Like the Civil Rights Restoration Act of 1988, the Civil Rights Act of 1991 was designed to correct and reinstate statutes ruled invalid by the Supreme Court, most notably concerning employment discrimination. EMK had come close to a deal in 1990, but Bush vetoed the legislation as "a quota bill." Throughout the summer of 1991, Danforth's simultaneous status as a proponent of both Thomas and the civil rights bill complicated matters for EMK and the civil rights community. "That stayed our hand," said Jeff Blattner. "We didn't want to get into a fractious situation with Danforth." By pledging to help get the civil rights bill passed, Danforth had elicited a deadline from the Democratic majority for a vote on the Thomas nomination, which limited the time that Hill's charges could be investigated, or further hearings held. The final negotiations that led to the bill's passage started as the White House held its victory party for Thomas, with Danforth operating as the intermediary between Bush and Kennedy. The White House remained steadfast in its opposition, but Dole and other Senate Republicans saw a need to repair the political damage done to the party among civil rights and women's groups by the Thomas-Hill hearings. Some of Danforth's colleagues were furious at the notion that the president would rebuff him after he

had gone to the mat for Bush and Thomas. "You're going to screw Jack Danforth after he just got your Supreme Court nominee confirmed?" Senator Ted Stevens of Alaska told Bush aides. "Well, not with my vote."

Kennedy, meanwhile, successfully kept the Democrats, especially southern Democrats, in line. "Kennedy was the one who cut the deal," White House counsel C. Boyden Gray remembered. The final version of the bill included a provision by which women plaintiffs could, for the first time, receive damages for sexual harassment and discrimination. Women's rights leaders noted caustically, however, that the amount of damages was capped in gender cases—unlike the uncapped damages for complaints based on race. It was the best he could get, Kennedy told them.

"How upset I was that night at him," Lichtman recalled. But "I think he was taking us all out of our misery. He was taking himself out of his misery—with Clarence Thomas and his palpable lack of leadership and the debacle that ensued." Judith Lichtman, Jeff Blattner OH, UVA. C. Boyden Gray interview, AC-JFKL. John Sununu OH, George H. W. Bush collection, UVA.

See EMK diary transcripts, June 8, 28, July 11, 12, and 16, Sept. 20, 1990; civil rights bill "Chronology"; EMK talking points, "Questions and Answers," re the Civil Rights Act of 1991; EMK to Sununu, June 29, 1990, and Sununu to EMK, July 10, 1990; Coleman to Sununu, Sept. 7, 1990; Coleman to Bush, Sept. 18, 1990, all Blattner collection. "Bill Summary," Jan. 12, 1990, NL-UMASS. NYT, Dec. 30, 1989, July 7, Oct. 25, 1991.

For fine accounts of the Thomas-Hill story, see Phelps and Winternitz, *Capitol Games*, and Mayer and Abramson, *Strange Justice*. NYT, July 7, 29, 1991.

477 **the Left temporized:** JAF interviews with Timothy Phelps, Jeff Blattner, Ricki Seidman. "Clarence Thomas Nomination," EMK briefing book, Blattner collection, Judicial Nominations II, Feb. 12, 2007. Laurence Tribe, William Taylor, Carolyn Osolinik, Jeff Blattner, Judith Lichtman OH, UVA. EMKOH-UVA. Redacted portions, Jeff Blattner OH-UVA, Blattner collection.

477 **felt sexually harassed:** "Nomination of Judge Clarence Thomas to be Associate Justice of the Supreme Court of the United States," hearings before the Committee on the Judiciary, United States Senate, Oct. 11, 12, and 13, 1991, Part 4 of 4. Report of Temporary Special Independent Counsel pursuant to Senate Resolution 202, May 13, 1992. "Revised Hill Statement," Alan Simpson papers, University of Wyoming.

477 **bosses to stand down:** JAF interviews with Ricki Seidman, Timothy Phelps, James Manley. Judith Lichtman, Laurence Tribe OH, UVA.

"Kennedy's already well-documented personal problems, exacerbated by the Palm Beach drinking and sex escapade on Easter weekend, had gotten in the way of his political responsibilities. The overindulgence in alcohol and lack of discipline in the senator's life showed in both his swollen facial features and his decrepit performance," wrote Timothy Phelps, the *Newsday* reporter who broke

Anita Hill's story (closely followed by NPR's Nina Totenberg) and went on to write a book about the hearings. "Kennedy had proved to be a tongue-tied embarrassment to himself rather than a moral beacon to others." Phelps and Winternitz, *Capitol Games*, 359–60.

477 **looking grimly uncomfortable:** Carolyn Osolinik OH, UVA. NYT, Oct. 8, 1991. Simpson to Frick, Nov. 20, 1991; FBI 302 report, Oct. 11, 1991; Statement of Sen. Joseph R. Biden Jr. on the Nomination of Judge Clarence Thomas, with chronology, Oct. 7, 1991, Alan Simpson papers, University of Wyoming. Seidman to EMK, June 1, 1992, Blattner collection. Phelps, Mayer, Abramson, and others who covered the Thomas-Hill hearings believe that EMK's early, spirited intervention might have transformed the political terrain and could well have changed the outcome. If not for the Palm Beach scandal, "Clarence Thomas would not be on the US Supreme Court," Phelps told the author. The *Boston Globe* reached a similar conclusion at the time of the hearings: "His silence was so notable. . . . It may have made a difference in the result." See BG editorial, "Sen. Kennedy's baggage," Oct. 20, 1991. Blattner, citing Danforth's effective work, disagreed. JAF interview with Jeff Blattner.

478 **"a high-tech lynching":** Hearings, Part 4, 157–58. Mayer and Abramson, *Strange Justice*, 300. NYT, Oct. 12, 1991. WP, Oct. 12, 1991.

478 **story rang true:** Jill Abramson, "Do You Believe Her Now?," *New York* magazine, Feb. 19, 2018. NYT, Oct. 10, 1991. WP, Oct. 12, 1991; Nov. 22, 2017. BG, Oct. 12, 13, 1991.

478 **the feminist complaint:** Simpson to Frick, Nov. 20, 1991; "Facts About Angela Wright," undated; Dick/Carl to Simpson, "Preparation for Thomas Hearing," Oct. 9, 1991, Alan Simpson papers, University of Wyoming. Alan Simpson OH, UVA. In his oral history, and elsewhere, Simpson recalled that Kennedy suspected that an unresolved personal and perhaps romantic tension between Thomas and Hill lay at the heart of their clash. See Hardy, *Shooting*, 384. See also Hearings, Part 4. Phelps and Winternitz, *Capitol Games*. David Brock, "The Real Anita Hill," *American Spectator*, March 1992.

478 **Kennedy's strategy of maintaining:** JAF interview with Ricki Seidman. Carolyn Osolinik, Ronald Weich OH, UVA. EMK handwritten notes, Judiciary Committee stationery, EMK briefing book, Blattner collection, Judicial Nominations II, Feb. 12, 2007. Carolyn Osolinik interview, AC-JFKL. BG, Oct. 12, 1991. Mayer and Abramson, *Strange Justice*, 303. The Gallup poll found that Kennedy had a 54 percent disapproval rating—the highest among the Judiciary Committee senators. BG, Oct. 16, 1991.

479 **"issue isn't discrimination":** EMK handwritten notes, Judiciary Committee stationery, EMK briefing book, Blattner collection, Judicial Nominations II, Feb. 12, 2007. Thomas hearings, Oct. 11–13, 1991, Part 4.

479 **Specter roasted Kennedy:** BG, Oct. 16, 1991. JAF, "Comeback Kid," *Boston Globe Magazine*, Nov. 21, 1993.

480 **"this disconnect between":** Anita Hill interview, "Tabloid Noise and Judicial Silence: The Nadir of Ted Kennedy," Boston.com, 2009.

480 **have a drinking problem:** JAF interview of EMK; a transcript is available in the Clymer papers, AC-JFKL, and the author's collection. JAF, "Kennedy Says Lifestyle Will Change," BG, June 9, 1991. JAF interview with Thomas Rollins. Tom Harkin interview, AC-JFKL. Ronald Weich OH, UVA. McNamara, *Eunice,* 272.

481 **"his moral authority":** Editorial, "Sen. Kennedy's Baggage," BG, Oct. 20, 1991. Littlefield to Buntain, Nov. 5, 1991, NL-UMASS.

482 **speak at Harvard:** NYT, Oct. 26, 1991. BG, Oct. 27, 1991. "He arrived with a speech written for him by someone else and promptly delivered it—head down, eyes on a stranger's text—with a passion you would use to recite a recipe," Mike Barnicle wrote. "The speech was . . . hyped . . . as some sort of apology, a public epiphany, a confession." Jimmy Breslin likened Kennedy to a drunk on a pay phone, promising his wife he would leave the bar soon: "A speech . . . drinkers make with a borrowed quarter," he wrote. See TNY, May 23, 1994.
Kennedy's son Patrick was as critical as the columnists: "Many people thought this was his great mea culpa," he wrote. "To me, the speech reinforced the denial I had lived with all my life." See Kennedy and Fried, *Common Struggle,* 98.

483 **Smith went free:** Paul Donovan, Melody Miller OH, UVA. BG, Dec. 1, 7, 12, 1991. NYT, Dec. 3, 1991. Charles Pierce, "Kennedy Unbound," *Boston Globe Sunday Magazine,* Jan. 5, 2003. Smith's attorney, Roy Black, said Ted Kennedy's testimony was a turning point in the trial. See Matoesian, *Discourse,* 17.

483 **"I am an enjoyer":** EMK-TC, 421–22.

483 **children confronted him:** JAF interview with Patrick Kennedy. Patrick Kennedy, *60 Minutes,* Oct. 4, 2015. Kennedy and Fried, *Common Struggle,* 102–5. EMK-TC, 422.

Twenty-Six: A Different Kind of Democrat

485 **an impending wedding:** It was a fine example of the capital's social grapevine at work. Caroline and her playground friends attended the Maret School, a private school in northwest Washington, DC, favored by *Washington Post* reporters for their children. Children told parents; parents called the newsroom. JAF interviews with Victoria Reggie Kennedy, Paul Donovan, and Lois Romano. Clymer interview with Victoria Reggie Kennedy AC-JFKL. WP, March 15, 1992.

487 **was Victoria Reggie:** JAF interviews with Victoria Reggie Kennedy, Doris Reggie. Victoria Reggie Kennedy, Edmund and Doris Reggie, Trina Vargo OH, UVA. JAF, "Comeback Kid," BG, Nov. 21, 1993. BG, March 16, July 5, Sept. 8, 1982. NYT, Aug. 28, 2009. At the Democratic convention in 1980, Doris was the lone Kennedy delegate to refuse the call to make Jimmy Carter the unanimous nominee of their party.

487 **though Kennedy's three children:** JAF interview with Victoria Reggie Kennedy. Trina Vargo,

Edward M. Kennedy Jr., Kara Kennedy, Patrick Kennedy OH, UVA.

488 **Vicki loved deeply:** JAF interview with Victoria Reggie Kennedy. Caroline Raclin, Gregory Craig OH, UVA. EMK-TC, 449.

488 **"uninhibited and confident":** Gregory Craig OH, UVA.

489 **a fine stepfather:** JAF interviews with Victoria Reggie Kennedy, John Kerry, Robert Caro. Caroline Raclin, Curran Raclin OH, UVA. Paul Donovan interview, AC-JFKL. Donald Ritchie, "Where Is Ted Kennedy When We Need Him? The Possibilities for Legislating in a Polarized Congress," speech given at U.S. Embassy, Dublin, Ireland, June 22, 2017. BG, Nov. 21, 1993. On one occasion, Vicki recalled, Curran had upset her by staying out late with a date. Vicki asked EMK to chasten her son, which, given Ted's own reputation as a ladies' man, the senator judged might not seem credible. He told Curran instead of a son's responsibility to not alarm his mother.

491 **woman like Vicki:** John Tunney, Victoria Reggie Kennedy OH, UVA.

491 **warmer, richer anodyne:** JAF interview with EMK, 1993, quoted in Farrell, "Comeback Kid," BG, Nov. 21, 1993. JAF interview with Victoria Reggie Kennedy. On weight see EMK interview, AC-JFKL; Victoria Reggie Kennedy OH, UVA. NYT, Feb. 1, 1985. BG, Sept. 8, 1992. TNY, March 31, 1997. On Reggie influence see Klein, *Ted Kennedy,* xv–xvi.

492 **Irish, stoics, fatalists:** JAF interview with Victoria Reggie Kennedy. "Kennedys don't talk about themselves," said the somewhat frustrated oral historian James Young, who led the EMK oral history project at UVA.

492 **stepchildren were impressed:** Curran and Caroline Raclin OH, UVA. EMK was no self-flagellating penitent, consciously atoning and striving for redemption, Curran said. "I think what drove him was he felt that . . . it was his duty to help other people. . . . If he hadn't made mistakes, these well-documented mistakes in the past, he would be exactly the same."

492 **repair his image:** Paul Donovan OH, UVA. EMK eulogy for Jacqueline Onassis, NYT, May 24, 1994. BG, Sept 8, 1992, Aug. 25, 1993. Telephone Interview of the President by *The New Yorker,* Feb. 14, 1997, WCL. TNY, May 23, 1994.

493 **the Clinton telenovela:** Nancy Soderberg, Elizabeth Shannon, Sean O'Huiginn, Niall O'Dowd OH, UVA. On Smith see BG, Dec. 3, 1992, March 18, 1993. In 1988, EMK backed Governor Michael Dukakis for president, and in 2000 Senator John Kerry.

494 **Clinton named Breyer:** JAF interview with Kenneth Feinberg. Stephen Breyer, Jeff Blattner OH, UVA. Klein to Nussbaum, "Judge Breyer's Opinions and Legal Scholarship," June 10, 1993; Klein to Nussbaum, "Judge Ginsburg's Opinions and Legal Scholarship," June 11, 1993; Klain to Nussbaum, "Areas of Discussion for the President," June 11, 1993; Verrilli to Klein, "Review of Judge Breyer's Opinions," June 8, 1993; Perrelli and Gershengorn to Klein, "Judge Breyer's Civil Rights, Privacy and National Security Opinions," June 7, 1993, WCL. Clinton to Branch, April 20, May 31,

1994, TB-UNC. Instead of keeping a diary, Clinton had his friend the author Taylor Branch drop by the White House to periodically debrief him, ask questions, and record his thoughts.

See also Klain to Paster and Nussbaum, "Hill Consultations Regarding Breyer & Social Security Problem," June 8, 1993, WCL. Clymer, *Edward M. Kennedy*, 525–26. EMKOH-UVA.

495 **missed their opportunity:** On Democrats and the Supreme Court see EMKOH-UVA.

495 **aligned for national health insurance:** "President Clinton Forms Health Care Taskforce," Jan. 25, 1993, and "Main Points for President Clinton to Stress at Monday's Meeting," Jan. 25, 1993, WCL. For the Clinton health care wars, see Johnson and Broder, *System*. The transcripts of the interviews that Broder and Johnson conducted, available in Johnson's papers at the University of Wisconsin, are invaluable in reconstructing the narrative of Kennedy in the early Clinton years, as were interviews JAF conducted with David Nexon, Lawrence O'Donnell, and Chris Jennings. The papers of Taylor Branch, at the University of North Carolina, contain transcripts of his extensive interviews with Bill Clinton.

496 **1993, a grand bipartisan bargain:** Sheila Burke OH, UVA. Burke to Dole, "Congressional Outlook," March 4, 1991; Diane Rowland, "Testimony Before Senate Finance Committee," Feb. 10, 1994, Dole-KU. Nexon to Werner, "Whip Meeting with Senator Biden," June 15, 1992, WCL. EMK diary notes, "White House Dinner—Feb. 22, 1993"; Nexon to EMK, "Overview of health care polling data," Feb. 9, 1992, both NL-UMASS. Marcia Angell, "How Much Will Health Care Reform Cost?," *New England Journal of Medicine*, June 17, 1993. Democratic Policy Committee, special report, "Believe It or Not: Incredible Facts About America's Health Care Crisis," May 20, 1993, TD-SDS.

496 **round or flat:** JAF interview with David Nexon. EMK interview tape, HJ-UW. Thomas Rollins OH, UVA. "Senators Mitchell, Kennedy, Riegle & Rockefeller, 'HealthAmerica: Affordable Health Care for All Americans Act (S. 1227),'" undated briefing paper; Nexon to Werner, "Whip Meeting with Senator Nunn," June 6, 1992, both from Health Care Task Force Records, WCL.

On health care, and other issues, Kennedy stole a fable from Russell Long about the advantages of political flexibility, in which three finalists for a teaching job in rural Louisiana go before a school board split down the middle by evolutionists and fundamentalists. When asked if he will teach that the world is round or flat, the first candidate promises to teach that it is round, and is blackballed by the fundamentalists. The next candidate promises to teach that the earth is flat, and is shot down by the progressives. The third candidate gets the job. "I told them," he explains, "that I can teach it round, or I can teach it flat." See Kennedy remarks, "Crisis in American Math, Science and Engineering Education," Hearing of the Committee on Labor and Human Resources, U.S. Senate, Nov. 14, 1989, 11. See also Statement of James Roosevelt, CEO of Tufts Health Plan, on the death of EMK, State House News Service, Aug. 26,

2009. Michael Dukakis OH, UVA. EMK interview, AC-JFKL.

Kennedy also liked to tell his aides, "There is more than one way to skin a cat." JAF interview with Thomas Rollins.

See also Nexon to EMK, Sept. 22, 1989, on play-or-pay plan, with EMK notation "This is urgent," and EMK to Mitchell and Daschle, Dec. 28, 1989, NL-UMASS.

496 **"the bottom line":** On pragmatist see Jennings and Edelstein to Hillary Clinton, Aug. 9, 1993, WCL, and Littlefield to Wofford, Nov. 12, 1991, NL-UMASS.

497 **urged the Clintons:** JAF interviews with David Nexon, Chris Jennings. John Dingell OH, UVA. Hillary Clinton, Nick Littlefield, David Abernathy, John Rother, Judith Feder interviews, HJ-UW. Talking points, "Meeting with President Clinton," n.d., 1992; Littlefield to EMK, "Talking points for telephone conversation with Warren Christopher," Nov. 20, 1992; Nexon to EMK, "Comprehensive Health Care Reform," Nov. 5, 1992; Littlefield to Hilley and Davis, Dec. 23, 1992, NL-UMASS.

The Labor Committee files are marked by missives to and from Kennedy, urging the White House to strike immediately. "The bill needs to get up here fast," aide Nexon urged Kennedy. "If we don't keep the pressure up, this bill will get bogged down. The special interest groups are on the run now—even the Chamber of Commerce has said they will accept an employer mandate—but if the bill slows down, the whole dynamic will change for the worse." Nexon to Kennedy, April 20, 1993, NL-UMASS.

Nor were some on the White House staff blind to the danger: "If we delay," a briefing paper sent to the president warned, "reform will be thwarted." Another memo alerted Hillary Clinton that the Democratic leaders in both houses of Congress saw the reconciliation process as the only path with a chance for success: "Without exception, these Members stated or implied that there is NO chance a comprehensive health reform initiative can pass the Congress on a separate legislative track." "Main Points for President Clinton to Stress at Monday's Meeting," Jan. 25, 1993, and Jennings to Hillary Rodham Clinton, Feb. 22, 1993, "Health Care," and Magaziner to Bill and Hillary Rodham Clinton, March 7 and March 8, 1993, WCL. See also Adam Clymer, Robert Pear, and Robin Toner, "What Went Wrong? How the Health Care Campaign Collapsed," NYT, Aug. 29, 1994.

497 **Hillary's task force:** JAF interview with Lawrence O'Donnell. John Hilley OH, UVA. EMK interview tape; Nick Littlefield ("We were the old Democrats. They were the New Democrats, so they had to come up with a different plan"), Pat Griffin ("Being hard-nosed and analytical . . . there was this sense that you were sinning"), HJ-UW. CQW, Feb. 26, 1994.

Burke to Dole, "Clinton Health Care," Dec. 7, 1992, Dole-KU. House Republicans captured the Clintons' ambition succinctly: "The Clinton health plan envisions a massive, experimental government-run system with a global budget that sets and enforces a limit on all health care expenditures at the national level. It empowers the federal government to control one-seventh of the nation's economy through an array of institutions and ill-defined mechanisms. All Americans would be required to enroll in the national program and change the manner in which they receive health care." House Republican Conference, "Health Care Update," Oct. 20, 1993.

For a detailed examination of the economic impact see William Dudley, "The Clinton Healthcare Plan: No Free Lunch," U.S. Economic Research, Goldman Sachs, Jan. 1994, Dole-KU. See also Beth Fuchs and Mark Merlis, "Health Care Reform: President Clinton's Health Security Act," Nov. 22, 1993, Congressional Research Service, LOC.

The Clintons were warned about the clout of the small business lobby, especially with the moderate Democrats on the Finance Committee, and likely opposition to an employer mandate: See Jennings to Clinton Campaign, "Transition from Campaigning to Legislating on Health Care—Focusing on the Small Business Issue and the Congress," Oct. 21, 1992, WCL; on the bill's complexity, and Clinton priorities, see Lux to Ickes and Lawler, Jan. 27, 1994, WCL. For an analysis of the emergence, and flaws, of the "managed competition" theory see Hacker, Road.

498 **mishmash of liberal:** JAF interviews with Lawrence O'Donnell, David Nexon, James Manley, Janet Heininger. EMK interview tape; Bill Clinton interview, July 17, 1995; Hillary Clinton, Nick Littlefield, George Mitchell interviews, HJ-UW. John Hilley OH, UVA. Telephone Interview of the President by *The New Yorker*, Feb. 14, 1997; Magaziner to WJC and HRC, "Health Care Reform and the Economic Package," March 7, 1993; Munnell and De Long to Altman, "Comments on the Health Care Reform Plan," Sept. 7, 1993, all WCL. Nexon to Kennedy ("Most of the economic advisers—CEA, OMB, Treasury—would essentially prefer that the administration never do a comprehensive health plan or postpone it to as distant a date as possible"), April 22, 1993, NL-UMASS. Simon to EMK, Dec. 30, 1993, NL-UMASS.

498 **Clinton was overwhelmed:** EMKOH-UVA, Sheila Burke OH, UVA. EMK interview tape; Bill Clinton interview, July 17, 1995; John Chafee interview; George Stephanopoulos interview, HJ-UW. "The people who didn't want anything to happen had time to get organized, raise money, mass their forces, develop their strategy, and they saw us getting weaker under the welter of this Whitewater thing," Clinton said. "It was maddening. . . . I was lost in the funhouse."

On Whitewater see "Investigation conducted by independent counsel Kenneth Starr," Feb. 9, 1999, TD-SDS. Moldea, *Washington Tragedy*. William Kristol to Republican Leaders, "Defeating President Clinton's Health Care Proposal," Project for a Republican Future, Dec. 2, 1993, author's collection. For Limbaugh see Johnson and Broder, *System*, 266–67. Alligators: See Clinton to Branch, Dec. 6, 1993, TB-UNC. Sean Wilentz, "Presumed Guilty," *New York Review of Books*, March 7, 2019.

The Republican resentment of the Clintons was deep, rooted in the Vietnam War era and the culture wars of the 1960s, and perhaps best captured by Vice President Dan Quayle's wife, Marilyn, when she told the Republican National Convention in 1992, "Not everyone joined the counterculture, not everyone demonstrated, dropped out, took drugs, joined in the sexual revolution, or dodged the draft. Not everyone concluded that American society was so bad that it had to be radically remade by social revolution. Not everyone believed that the family was so oppressive that women could only thrive apart from it.

"The majority of my generation lived by the credo our parents taught us. We believed in God, in hard work and personal discipline, in our nation's essential goodness, and in the opportunity it promised those willing to work for it. And so, most of us went to school, to church, and to work. We married and started families. We had a stake in the future, and though we knew some changes needed to be made, we did not believe in destroying America to save it.

"I sometimes think that the liberals are always so angry because they believed the grandiose promises of the liberation movements," she added. "They're disappointed because most women do not wish to be liberated from their essential natures."

499 **Kennedy soldiered on:** For examples of EMK cooperation see Nancy Kassebaum, George Mitchell OH, UVA. EMK to HRC, Aug. 13, Sept. 16, Oct. 19, 1993; Nexon to Magaziner, Sept. 16, 1993; Nexon to Jennings, Sept. 27, 1993; Griffin to William J. Clinton, March 9, 1994; "Summary of the Health Security Act, as Reported by the Senate Committee on Labor and Human Resources," June 9, 1994, WCL.

499 **the brilliant, erratic:** Though it was not dispositive, the relationship between the Clinton White House and the two committee chairmen—Kennedy and Moynihan—consumed a great deal of time and effort.

Kennedy was, from the start, the Senate good cop for the White House. "Senator Kennedy wants to continue to be a player in health care reform and has been seeking ways to embrace managed competition while maintaining his liberal consumerism views," White House aides reported. "As long as Bentsen chaired the Finance Committee, Kennedy was confined to a minor role in health care reform. Kennedy's desire to have a seat at the decision-making table keeps moving him toward the middle making him more pragmatic."

Kennedy pressed the White House to write the bill in such a way that the Labor Committee had primary jurisdiction, which was fine with the Clintons, except that it complicated their relationship with the Finance Committee and Moynihan.

Moynihan, meanwhile, played the Senate bad cop. Given a chance, on Capitol Hill or the Sunday talk shows, he took shots at health care reform.

"The Finance Committee is viewed by many insiders as in disarray," White House aide Chris Jennings explained in a memo to his bosses. "The transition, like most changes of the guard, from Chairman Bentsen to Chairman Moynihan has not been very smooth. The staff, with perhaps the exception of the staff director, Lawrence O'Donnell, does not appear to have much influence with, or much authority from the chairman. As a result, decisions and actions have been slow to occur."

Moynihan and O'Donnell "have been relatively pessimistic about the chances of passing health reform this year," Jennings wrote. "There are a number of reasons for this, but there is no doubt that one of them is that Moynihan and O'Donnell are not overly familiar with the issue. What they do know is that health care reform will be complex, controversial, and potentially expensive, and they are extremely nervous about taking on this issue as their first big initiative." Hillary Clinton came to call Moynihan "weak-spined and stupid . . . an idea person—but could never produce anything."

Moynihan and O'Donnell, however, gave as good as they got. The health care plan's underlying assumptions were "fantasy," Moynihan announced. There was no health care crisis. There was a welfare crisis, but Clinton's solution for that was just "boob bait for the bubbas."

"It was over at the outset," O'Donnell said of Clinton's health care plan. With no chance of earning moderate Democratic or Republican support, "it was the dream of the cultists" at the White House—"a doomed ship of disconnected fools."

Clinton "is a poor boy from Arkansas and can only think in terms of . . . people who are deprived, who don't have access," Moynihan said. In fact, the senator argued, the issue was not access but cost, in part from excess care: "Our problem is we are not deprived and we have too much access."

The jurisdictional gridlock between Moynihan and Kennedy was ultimately resolved by not being resolved: neither committee got exclusive jurisdiction, and both reported their own bills, leaving Majority Leader Mitchell to compose the final legislation.

JAF interviews with Lawrence O'Donnell, Chris Jennings, Jeff Blattner, David Nexon. See Clinton to Branch, July 21, 1994, TB-UNC. See also "Background Information," Health Care Task Force Records, undated; Griffin to William J. Clinton, Jan. 25, March 16, May 18, 1994; Jennings to HRC, April 19, May 3, 1993, and "Senate Committee Jurisdiction over President Clinton's Comprehensive Health Reform Legislation," June 19, 1993; Jennings and Edelstein to HRC with attached Nexon and Littlefield to EMK, Aug. 9, 1993, and "Health Care Legislative Strategy," Nov. 23, 1993, all WCL.

See also Nexon to EMK, "Update on Durenberger," Jan. 11, 1994; Nexon to EMK, "Follow-up conversation with Specter staff," Jan. 1994; Nexon to EMK, "Meeting with Senator Kassebaum," Jan. 26, 1994; Nexon to EMK, "Meeting with Stephanopoulos and Griffin," Jan. 21, 1994; Nexon to EMK, "Update on Senators," April 6, 1994, all SLC-NARA, and Littlefield to EMK, April 16, 1993; Nexon to EMK, May 7, 1993, and Nexon to EMK, Nov. 30, 1993, all NL-UMASS.

See also EMK interview tape and Daniel P. Moynihan, Sheila Burke, Lawrence O'Donnell, Chris Jennings, David Nexon, George Stephanopoulos, Nick Littlefield, Christy Ferguson interviews,

HJ-UW. Willis Gradison OH, UVA. The RFK quote about Moynihan is from Stein and Plimpton, *American Journey*, 185. The quote about consensus is from Moynihan to Sulzberger, Jan. 11, 2001, in Weisman, *A Portrait*, 648–49.

500 **good at muddying:** On dying reform see Munnell to Altman, Sept. 21, 1993; Magaziner to WJC and HRC, June 22, 1994; Jennings to HRC, Oct. 17, 1993; White House Senate vote count, July 14, 1994; Griffin, "Meeting with Senator Conrad," July 14, 1994; Griffin, "Meeting with Senator Mitchell," Aug. 1, 1994; Dingell to WJC, Sept. 20, 1994.

See also "Rostenkowski Analyzes Health Reform Failure," Dec. 5, 1994, address, Harvard School of Public Health, WCL. Rostenkowski was a skilled and veteran deal-maker from Chicago who was indicted in 1994 on corruption charges, pleaded guilty, and spent seventeen months in jail. His problems, the rise of Newt Gingrich in the House, and the lame-duck status of George Mitchell all affected events. The Packwood quote on fingerprints is from NYT, Sept. 18, 1994. See also Bill McInturff interview, HJ-UW.

500 **so politically toxic:** JAF interview with Lawrence O'Donnell, Jeff Blattner. Ronald Weich OH, UVA. Clymer, *Edward M. Kennedy*, 532. Johnson and Broder, *System*, 284–85, 490–91. The luckless CBO official was Robert Reischauer, see Nick Littlefield, Robert Reischauer interviews, HJ-UW, on Kennedy phone call: "He screamed at me for 35 minutes: 'You're going to bring the Clinton administration down. This is the one chance in American history to do something as important as this. And you, some minor staff official, is taking it upon yourself to thwart the will of the American people.'" See also CBO, "An Analysis of the Administration's Health Proposal," Feb. 8, 1994; "Statement of Senator Edward M. Kennedy on the CBO Analysis of the Health Security Act," Feb. 8, 1994, and Rima and Jeffrey to Daschle, "Finance Hearing: CBO Report," Feb. 8, 1994, TD-SDS.

For a chronicle of Kennedy floor statements, see Vachon to Paull, "Summaries of Democratic Health Care Reform Floor Debate," Sept. 1, 1994, Dole-KU. For vote counts see "Coverage Coalition," and whip count, Aug. 4, 1994, TD-SDS.

500 **Kennedy and Packwood:** JAF interview with Lawrence O'Donnell. Christy Ferguson interview, HJ-UW. NJ, Aug. 13, 1994. Clinton also believed that Dole was using the ethics case to neuter Packwood. "As long as Packwood has his ethics problem . . . Dole owns him," Clinton told Branch, Aug. 25, 1994, TB-UNC.

Packwood's maneuvering did not save him. He resigned his Senate seat in 1995 after the Ethics Committee issued a devastating report. "These were not merely stolen kisses, as Senator Packwood has claimed," Senator Mitch McConnell, chairman of the committee, announced. "There was a habitual pattern of aggressive, blatantly sexual advances, mostly directed at members of his own staff or others whose livelihoods were connected in some way to his power and authority as a Senator."

501 **"Kennedy believed longer":** Steve Richetti interview, HJ-WU.

Twenty-Seven: Sweet Jack Falstaff

502 **fretting about reelection:** The 1994 omnibus crime bill—the Violent Crime Control and Law Enforcement Act—followed passage of the Brady Handgun Violence Prevention Act of 1993. Both were endorsed and signed by Clinton and shepherded through the Senate by Biden. EMK voted for each on final passage.

The 1994 bill had many appealing elements for Democrats, including a ban on assault weapons, funds for one hundred thousand new local police officers, and measures to curtail violence against women. EMK was aghast, however, at its radical expansion of the federal death penalty. "I didn't come to the Senate to put thirteen-year-olds to death," he told his wife, Vicki. By the end of the debate, sixty offenses were made capital crimes, and prosecutors were allowed to charge even the youngest teenagers as adults. Meanwhile, the ban on assault weapons did not last—it had a sunset provision that allowed it to expire in 2004.

The more lasting—and controversial—elements of the 1994 bill were its billions of dollars for prison construction and its mandatory sentencing provisions, which, together with the sentencing laws passed with EMK's support a decade earlier, helped fuel a monstrous increase in the number of incarcerated Americans.

On EMK and sentencing reform see Kate Stith and Steve Yoh, "The Politics of Sentencing Reform: The Legislative History of the Federal Sentencing Guidelines," *Wake Forest Law Review* 28 (1993); Edward M. Kennedy, "Toward a New System of Criminal Sentencing: Law with Order," *American Criminal Law Review* 16 (1979); and Edward M. Kennedy, "Symposium on Sentencing, Part I, Introduction," *Hofstra Law Review*, Fall 1978.

502 **Kennedy neglected Massachusetts:** See Mimi to EMK, Dec. 13, 1993, NL-UMASS. At one point, Dole's aides urged him to "strongly" oppose yet "another foray by Kennedy into [the defense budget] to help pay for broader economic problems in his state." See Burke and Whittinghill to Dole, March 12, 1991, Dole-KU.

502 **cleanup of Boston's harbor:** Mary to EMK, Sept. 20, 1991, NL-UMASS; Jeka to Brody, English, Harrington, Sept. 27, 1996, with attachment, J. Joseph Moakley papers, Suffolk University. Andrew T. Savage, "Boston Harbor: The Anatomy of a Court-Run Cleanup," *Boston College Environmental Affairs Law Review*, Dec. 1, 1995.

502 **traffic-choked Fitzgerald Expressway:** Carey Parker OH, UVA. Associated Press, April 2, 1987. UPI, April 6, 1987. David Luberoff and Alan Altshuler, "Mega-Project: A Political History of Boston's Multibillion Dollar Artery/Tunnel Project," JFK School of Government, Harvard University. NJ, April 26, 2000. Farrell, *Tip O'Neill*, 666–70.

On Democratic identity see Senator Paul Simon to Senator Thomas Daschle, Dec. 2, 1995: *"Who are we and what do we stand for?* It is not as clear as it should be," and Shrum to Campaign Leadership, "Message/Media," May 21, 1993 ("Right now, there is no perceived national Democratic economic policy"), NL-UMASS.

503 **their kitchen table:** JAF interviews with representative J. Joseph Moakley, Tad Devine, Fred Salvucci, David Luberoff. George Miller, George Mitchell, John McCain OH, UVA. Kavanaugh to Littlefield, Sept. 15, 1993; Shrum to Campaign Leadership. "Message/Media," May 21, 1993, NL-UMASS.

504 **"a subtle destroyer":** Franklin D. Roosevelt, State of the Union Address, Jan. 4, 1935, Franklin D. Roosevelt Presidential Library.

505 **blue-collar America:** Farrell, *Tip O'Neill*, 590–93, 647–48. The classic account of the Democratic Party's efforts and success raising funds from corporate America is Jackson, *Honest Graft.* "rising tide": EMK, "The Rising Tide Must Lift More Boats," speech at the Center for National Policy, Washington, DC, Feb. 8, 1996, NL-UMASS.

On the postwar evolution of the Democratic Party see Edsall and Edsall, *Chain Reaction*, 4–10, 26, 267; William Schneider, "The New Shape of American Politics," *Atlantic*, Jan. 1987; Schneider, "An Insider's View of the Election," *Atlantic*, July 1988; Schneider, "The Suburban Century Begins," *Atlantic*, July 1992. Bill Keller, "The State of the Unions: Organized Labor's Vital Signs Show Waning Political Clout; But Numbers Don't Tell All," CQ, Aug. 28, 1982. "Joe O" to Burke and EMK, undated, circa May 1970, TS-UMASS. Teeter to Haldeman, Jan. 6, 1972; Teeter to Mitchell, Feb. 15, 1972; Teeter to Callaway, Dec. 8, 1975, GFL. See Balz and Brownstein, *Storming*, and Hacker and Pierson, *Let Them Eat Tweets.* The Moynihan letter to EMK was written on July 25, 1968, and included in Weisman, *A Portrait*, 150–53. It is not clear, said Weisman, whether EMK received it.

505 **protected from foreign imports:** Peterson, *Changing World*, 2–5, 49.

506 **trade adjustment assistance:** Peterson, *Changing World*, 39–41. Alden, *Failure.* Alden gives a comprehensive account of America's failures to address the downsides of free trade, and contrasts the stuttering U.S. effort with successful trade adjustment policies in western Europe. See chapter 5, "Helping the Losers: The Tragedy of Trade Adjustment Assistance." He writes, "The failure to help American workers adjust to the new scale and intensity of global competition is one of the bigger mistakes of U.S. government economic policy in the last half century, one that has resulted in an enormous waste of human capacity," 113.

507 **called themselves "New Democrats":** *Newsweek*, June 28, 1982; WP, March 13, 1984; Richard Cohen, "Democratic Leadership Council Sees Party Void and Is Ready to Fill It," NJ, Feb. 1, 1986. JAF, "The Troubled Presidency of Bill Clinton," *Boston Globe Magazine*, Jan. 22, 1995. Reich, *System*, 156, 162–63: "They . . . drank from the same campaign funding trough as the Republicans—big corporations, Wall Street, and the very wealthy."

507 **Economic inequality reached:** Reich, *System*, Kindle edition, 15–16: "Between 1980 and 2019, the share of the nation's total household income going to the richest 1 percent more than doubled, while the earnings of the bottom 90 percent barely rose," wrote Reich, a Berkeley economist and former secretary of labor. "CEO pay increased 940 percent but the typical worker's pay increased

12 percent. . . . The share of total wealth held by the richest 0.1 percent—about 160,000 American households—went from less than 10 percent to 20 percent over the last four decades. They now own almost as much wealth as the bottom 90 percent of households combined. . . . The only other country with similarly high levels of wealth concentration is Russia. . . . This power shift is related to a tsunami of big money into politics. In the election cycle of 2016 the richest one-hundredth of 1 percent of Americans—24,949 extraordinarily wealthy people—accounted for a record-breaking 40 percent of all campaign contributions." On inequality see also "The Economy We Need," NYT, July 5, 2020, and Gordon, *Rise and Fall*, 609–13. See also Sitaraman, *Crisis*, and Smith, *Who Stole*.

507 **offer was palliative care:** Clinton's 1992 platform, "Putting People First," promised to provide literacy classes, completion of high school, and occupational training to workers. After the president's GI Bill for America's Workers foundered in his first term, he and EMK joined others to enact the Workforce Investment Act of 1998, a palliative act to reform the job training system. See Reich through Rubin to Clinton, "The Reemployment Act of 1994," March 1, 1994; Waldman to Gore, June 14, 1994; REA Task Group Meeting Notes, June 14, 1994; Dimond to Rasco, Rivlin, and Tyson, "G.I. Bill for America's Workers," June 12, 1995; Rivlin, Tyson, Rasco, Riley, Reich to Clinton, Aug. 10, 1995; Clinton to EMK, May 20, 1996; Lew and Tyson to Clinton, June 25, 1996; White House release, "The Workforce Investment Act of 1998 Signing Ceremony," Aug. 7, 1998, WCL, and EMK remarks, CR, June 22, 1994. See also Lew to Weiss, "UAW Speech: Trade Issues," May 6, 1980, TON-BC. Reich, *System*, 130.

"A storm is coming": EMK, "The Rising Tide Must Lift More Boats," speech at the Center for National Policy, Washington, DC, Feb. 8, 1996, NL-UMASS.

508 **"helpful but frustratingly small":** Reich, *System*, 130.

508 **"kill every time":** Thomas Rollins to JAF, June 3, 2020, author's collection. NAFTA: Slavet and McGahey to EMK, April 22, 1993, NL-UMASS.

508 **change was wrenching:** Robert Reich, Speech before the Democratic Leadership Council, Nov. 22, 1994, C-SPAN. See also David Leonhardt and Stuart Thompson, "How Working-Class Life Is Killing Americans," NYT, March 6, 2020, and Kuttner, *Survive*, xvi–xx, 2–6. Mack Truck: BG, July 5, 1988. Moynihan to Wirtz, May 6, 1964, Weisman, *A Portrait*. "The greatest single danger facing the Negroes of America is that the whites are going to put them on welfare," Moynihan wrote. "It will be a good deal easier just to pension the Negroes off, as it were, than to accept the major and sometimes wrenching changes in our way of doing things that will be required if we are going to bring them in as full-fledged members of the larger community . . . we have already done as much to whole sections of Appalachia . . . as also to the Indian reservations."

509 **Kennedy was left with a handful:** Fox to EMK, July 11, 1991; for EMK view and his prescription, see "The Rising Tide Must Lift More Boats,"

speech at the Center for National Policy, Washington, DC, Feb. 8, 1996, both NL-UMASS. NYT, March 8, 1996.

509 **Jacqueline Onassis died:** NYT, May 24, 1994. Toxins: See Lewis to HRC, "Political Briefing—Boston, Massachusetts," Dec. 6, 1993, WCL.

510 **Sir John Falstaff:** Martin Nolan, "Ted Staying Power," BG, July 11, 1993. Jonathan Yardley, "Missing Bobby," WP, May 31, 1993. JAF interview with Joe McGinniss. The two more notable books, each of which spurred attendant publicity, were by Kennedy's former aide Richard E. Burke (*The Senator*), and by writer Joe McGinniss (*Last Brother*). Each book had its flaws, providing Kennedy's staff the opportunity to dismiss them.

McGinniss, in a portrait of Kennedy's life through Chappaquiddick, employed the public and written record to concoct Kennedy's thoughts and dialogue. With so reticent a subject, it was the only way, the author said, to convey the life more "richly and fully." He was slammed by critics for purporting to read the senator's mind.

Burke's credibility was suspect, as he wrote the book amid midlife mental and financial crises and admitted to creating fictional characters in his tales of sex and cocaine abuse.

In October 1994, the bipartisan Senate Ethics Committee, after interviewing Burke and investigating his charges, unanimously found "no basis" for the allegations that Kennedy harassed his female staff members or used illegal drugs. Senators tend to protect one another, but the committee was half Republican, and issued its ruling in the midst of a rough campaign season when the Senate majority was at stake. The harsh treatment afforded Senators Robert Packwood and John Tower in that era showed that there were limits to their colleagues' willingness to look the other way. Packwood resigned under threat of expulsion after being accused of sexual harassment in 1995, and Tower's nomination as defense secretary was defeated, amid charges of womanizing and drinking, in 1989.

510 **ne'er-do-wells:** "The political power of the health care issue does *not* come primarily from covering the poor—and the 37 million uninsured," Shrum told Kennedy and his advisers. "It comes from three *middle class* concerns: People want costs controlled; people don't want to lose health insurance if they lose their jobs; people don't want their insurance cancelled if they get sick." See Shrum to Campaign Leadership, "Message/Media," May 21, 1993, NL-UMASS.

And so the Clinton strategy stressed the notion that health care reform must be sold as a universal benefit—"We cannot just focus on the 'have-nots that will now have' but must address everyone"—but the message got muddied along the way. See Prunty to Boorstin, Feb. 2, 1993, WCL. By October 1993 almost half the country believed that Clinton's reform was for "the poor" as opposed to "everybody." See Bill McInturff, John Breaux interviews, HJ-UW. "We targeted the 15 percent of the people who didn't have health insurance and the Republicans targeted the 85 percent who do," said Breaux.

On Democratic woes, see Debra to Daschle, Oct. 14, 1994, "New Poll," TD-SDS: "One would think that the wrangling that took place in Washington made the public think 'a pox on both your houses.' Instead, the Republicans really do seem poised to 'inherit the rubble.'"
On voter surliness see Michael Kennedy, Tom Kiley interviews, AC-JFKL.
See also Nexon to Jennings, "Health Care and the 1994 Election: Evidence from the Polls and Implications for Democratic Strategy," Dec. 12, 1994, WCL: "The failure to pass health reform fed the voters' anger about the perceived failure of the Democrats to bring about change and the continuance of 'business as usual' in Washington."

510 **a formidable opponent:** Martin Nolan, Michael Dukakis, John Tunney, Robert Shrum OH, UVA. Romney was the one great reelection test. Kennedy beat Howard Whitmore in 1964, Josiah Spaulding in 1970, Michael Robertson in 1976, Ray Shamie in 1982, and Joseph Malone in 1988. After defeating Romney, he would breeze again in 2000 vs. Jack E. Robinson and in 2006 against Kenneth Chase. Only George Cabot Lodge, in 1962, and Romney kept Kennedy's winning percentage below 60 percent.

510 **Mitt Romney, at forty-seven:** JAF interviews with Robert Shrum, Jim Manley, Tad Devine, Jeff Blattner, Gerard Doherty. David Burke, Carey Parker, Paul Kirk, Gerard Doherty OH, UVA. Tom Kiley interview, AC-JFKL. Edelstein and Shea to HRC, "Briefing for Kennedy Fundraiser," Sept. 22, 1994, WCL. Donovan to EMK, "Planning for 1994," Dec. 14, 1993, NL-UMASS. BG, Sept. 25, Oct. 30, Nov. 10, 1994. WP, Sept. 25, 1994.

512 **arrived like minutemen:** JAF interviews with Robert Shrum, Ranny Cooper, Jack Corrigan, Paul Donovan. In addition to Burke and Cooper, the cadre included Paul Kirk, John Sasso, Charles Baker, Jim King, Jack Corrigan, and Shrum's partner Tad Devine—all skilled at running state and presidential races. See also NYT, Oct. 19, 1994. Ronald Weich, David Broder OH, UVA. Graham: JAF interview with Jeff Blattner.

512 **a certain ruthlessness:** JAF interviews with Robert Shrum and Tad Devine. Tom Kiley interview, AC-JFKL. BG, Nov. 10, 1994. NYT, Oct. 10, 1994.

513 **angry Ampad workers:** Memorandum for the President, Lewis to William J. Clinton, "Massachusetts Political Update," Nov. 1, 1994, WCL. Charles Manning interview, "The Choice 2012," *Frontline*, PBS. BG, Oct. 30, Nov. 10, 1994. Gerard Doherty OH, UVA. EMK was willing to do what had to be done. He and his nephew Joe committed what they had forsworn—given the family's own experience with religious discrimination—by questioning whether Romney's Mormon faith cloaked racist and sexist beliefs. Both Kennedys retracted their remarks, but not before seeding the notion in the electorate. See Charles Manning interview, "The Choice 2012"; BG, May 22, Sept. 28, 1994.

513 **cinched the outcome:** On expectations and podium, see Charles Manning interview, "The Choice 2012." JAF interview with Robert Shrum. Anthony Lewis, David Burke, Carey Parker, Paul Kirk OH, UVA. Burke threatened to quit the

campaign if Kennedy's other advisers would not let the senator debate. "If you know your staff . . . thinks you'd lose the debate, that's a lousy way to get up every morning and campaign. And that's what it was," he recalled. Once Kennedy agreed to debate Romney, "the campaign changes its complexion. . . . This barge now has a prow. . . . We're going to debate. We're going to beat his ass." See also Michael Kennedy interview, AC-JFKL. BG, Oct. 26, 28, 1994. Collection of national political commentary, 1994 Massachusetts Senate race, SHO, including Ronald Brownstein, *Los Angeles Times*, Oct. 7, 1994; George Will, WP, Sept. 25, 1994. See also R. W. Apple Jr., NYT, Oct. 26, 1994. Shrum, *No Excuses*, 249–50. For Healy see BG, Oct. 29, 1994. For debate verdict see Balz and Johnson, *Battle*, 238.

514 **on election day, Massachusetts:** JAF interviews with Mrs. David Burke, Victoria Reggie Kennedy. Tom Kiley interview, AC-JFKL.

Twenty-Eight: Catskinning

516 **the Republican takeover:** JAF interviews with Robert Shrum, James Manley. EMKOH-UVA.

516 **"revolution" was Gingrich:** EMKOH-UVA. JAF interview with Janet Heininger. Maraniss and Weisskopf, *"Tell Newt."* The bathtub quote is from Grover Norquist, a Gingrich adviser, from *Morning Edition*, NPR, May 25, 2001. Newt Gingrich, 1978 Atlanta speech to College Republicans, see "The Long March of Newt Gingrich," *Frontline*, PBS. *Time*, Dec. 25, 1995/Jan. 1, 1996. BG, Jan. 25, 1995. NJ, Feb. 23, 2012. Joe Klein, "The Town That Ate Itself," TNY, Nov. 23, 1998. Farrell, *Tip O'Neill*, 626–28. Ronald M. Peters Jr., "The Republican Speakership," paper delivered at the 1996 meeting of the American Political Science Association. Donald Ritchie, "Where Is Ted Kennedy When We Need Him?," speech delivered at the U.S. Embassy, Ireland, June 22, 2017. For the legacy of Gingrich's nastiness, see Mann and Ornstein, *Even Worse*.

518 **plot a counterrevolution:** Littlefield and Nexon, *Lion*, 49. JAF interview with Robert Shrum.

519 **Kennedy found unanimity:** JAF interview with Victoria Reggie Kennedy. EMK to Richard and Doris Kearns Goodwin, Nov. 29, 1994; EMK to Sasso, Nov. 29, 1994; EMK to Brinkley, Nov. 29, 1994, NL-UMASS. Littlefield and Nexon, *Lion*, chapter 5, "Preparing the Resistance."

519 **Kennedy and Clinton met:** JAF interviews with Chris Jennings, James Manley, David Nexon. Memo, "Meeting with President Clinton," Dec. 13, 1994; EMK office memo, "Overall Budget Strategy—Condensed Form," NL-UMASS. Nexon to Jennings, "Analysis of poll data on the role of health care in the 1994 elections/implications for Democratic strategy," Dec. 8, 1994; Jennings to Hillary Clinton, "Polling Data Analysis by Senator Kennedy's Office," Dec. 12, 1994; Telephone Interview of the President by *The New Yorker*, Feb. 14, 1997, WCL. Littlefield and Nexon, *Lion*, 114–17. George Tames OH, SHO. Elsa Walsh, "How Ted Kennedy Won the White House," TNY, March 31, 1977. NYT, Jan. 24, 30, 1995.

520 **"stand for something":** NYT, Jan. 12, 1995.
521 **wise was not their nature:** EMK statement, "Protection of Medicare," Jan. 31, 1995; Kennedy briefing book, "Budget Book," fall 1995, with backup material; Nexon to EMK, "Medicare Trust Fund Solvency," April 5, 1995; Nexon to EMK, "Medicare Update," April 18, 1995; Nexon to EMK, "DPC Talking Points on Republican Medicare/Medicaid Cuts," with attached memoranda, April 10, 1995; Danica to EMK, "Effects of a Year-Long 75% Continuing Resolution on the Departments of Education, Labor and HHS," Dec. 6, 1995; Lauren and David to EMK, "Preliminary Analysis of Discretionary Spending in the Budget Bills," Jan. 5, 1996, SLC-NARA. Rima and Ron to Daschle, "Medicare Post-Recess Strategy," Sept. 5, 1995; Rima and Cybele to Daschle, "Kennedy & Rockefeller Medicare Meeting," Sept. 7, 1995; "Daschle Unveils Democratic Plan to Preserve Medicare Without Increasing Costs to Seniors," Oct. 2, 1995, TD-SDS. Shalala to Bill and Hillary Clinton, "Public Portrayal of the Medicare Program," June 7, 1995; Telephone Interview of the President by *The New Yorker*, Feb. 14, 1997, WCL. Littlefield to EMK, June 1, 1995, NL-UMASS. Littlefield and Nexon, *Lion*, 239–40. Maraniss and Weisskopf, *"Tell Newt,"* 148. Walsh, TNY, March 31, 1997.
521 **and scooped soil:** BG, Nov. 7, 1995. Kennedy and Fried, *Common Struggle*, 127.
522 **to stop his surge:** EMK to Sasso, Nov. 29, 1994, NL-UMASS. "A History of the US Department of the Treasury During the Clinton Administration, 1993–2001," WCL.
523 **"his emotions raw":** JAF interview with Victoria Reggie Kennedy. Littlefield and Nexon, *Lion*, 145–47. NYT, Jan. 11, 2004. Telephone Interview of the President by *The New Yorker*, Feb. 14, 1997, WCL. EMK aide David Nexon had a slightly different take from his co-author, Littlefield, on the minimum age meeting. Kennedy's blowup "seemed to me to be calculated, rather than spontaneous," said Nexon. "He was trying to get the bipartisan group Kerry was working with off the dime." When EMK made his blistering phone call to CBO director Reischauer on the Clinton health care bill, said Nexon, there may have been a similar element of calculation. "Since the reasoned approach hadn't worked, Kennedy may have decided to try the emotional one," Nexon said. JAF interview with David Nexon.
524 **as Clinton's proxy:** EMK to Mellman, Oct. 23, 1995, NL-UMASS. EMK interview, AC-JFKL. Littlefield and Nexon, *Lion*, 313. For Kennedy's efforts and Dole's frustration see NYT, March 27, April 17, 18, May 4, 9, 10, 15, 16, July 10, 1996.
525 **raise the minimum wage:** One measure of Kennedy's importance in the politics of the minimum wage is the sorry fact that since his death, it has not been raised by Congress, leaving the issue to the states and municipalities. JAF interviews with James Manley, Thomas Korologos, Trent Lott. John Hilley OH, UVA. Rollins to EMK, 2008, Rollins papers. Littlefield and Nexon, *Lion*, 383, 401, 408. NYT, Aug. 4, 1996. Kennedy and Clinton returned to the issue in better political and economic times after Clinton's reelection, but the

next increase did not occur until 2007–09. See Caplan to Clinton, Jan. 26, 1998, and Sperling to Clinton, Jan. 26, 1998, and Herman to Kennedy, draft, April 20, 1999, WCL. EMK interview, AC-JFKL.
On Lott see Lott, *Herding Cats*, 130–34. In clandestine talks with a political consultant (Dick Morris) whom they shared, Clinton and Lott agreed that the passage of significant legislation would help the president and Senate Republicans in the 1996 elections and so worked quietly together at the expense of congressional Democrats and the Republican presidential candidate, Robert Dole. See also Hilley, *Challenge*, 24. After working in the Senate for George Mitchell, Hilley led the White House office of legislative liaison.
526 **for incremental help:** JAF interviews with Chris Jennings, David Nexon, Robert Shrum. Nexon to EMK, Nov. 23, 1994, NL-UMASS. Vachon to Paull, "Summaries of Democratic Health Care Reform Floor Debate," Sept. 1, 1994; Burke to Dole, May 1, 1992, Dole-KU. "A History of the White House Domestic Policy Council, 1993–2001," Clinton Administration History Project, 2001; Stern to Clinton, Aug. 17, 1996, WCL. "Health Insurance Portability: Reform Could Ensure Continued Coverage for up to 25 Million Americans," GAO, Sept. 1995. On strategy of incremental reform see Nexon to Magaziner, June 25, 1994; "Possible Fall-Back Option," undated, unsigned, WCL. See also Littlefield to committee staff, Jan. 8, 1996, NL-UMASS. NYT, Nov. 11, 1996. Kennedy went public with his plans for incremental reform while the body of the Clinton health care program was still warm; see EMK, "Why We're Still Trying," *Roll Call*, Sept. 26, 1994.
527 **liked Nancy Kassebaum:** EMKOH-UVA. EMK interview, AC-JFKL. Edward Kennedy Jr., Kara Kennedy, Patrick Kennedy, George Mitchell OH, UVA. Nexon to EMK, Nov. 23, 1994, NL-UMASS. Rasco to Clinton, July 28, 1995; Brophy, Hilley, and Jennings to Clinton, "Signing of the Health Insurance Portability and Accountability Act of 1996," Aug. 20, 1996; "Summary of Health Insurance Reform Act of 1995," WCL.
At passage, the bill's title was the Health Insurance Portability and Accountability Act. It also included tax breaks for health insurance for self-employed workers and an $8 billion tax break for Americans bearing the costs of long-term care.
HIPAA, as it is known, built on another reform introduced by Kennedy during the Reagan administration: a law requiring midsized and large firms to let employees who have lost their jobs keep group health insurance benefits for eighteen months at their own expense. It was part of the Consolidated Omnibus Budget Reconciliation Act in 1986, and so became known as COBRA. See Jane Hiebert-White, "Who Won What in the Kassebaum/Kennedy Struggle?," *Health Progress*, Sep.–Oct. 1996.
In that same year that COBRA became law, Kennedy was instrumental in passage of the Emergency Medical Treatment and Active Labor Act (EMTALA), which prohibits hospitals from turning away emergency room patients because they lack health insurance.

Kennedy did not live to see a grand national health insurance system—"the cause of his life"—enacted, but his record is stocked with these kinds of patches, which paved the way for passage of the Affordable Care Act in 2009. See David Nexon, "Senator Edward Kennedy: Architect of Reform, Builder of Compromise," *Health Affairs*, Aug. 27, 2009. With the above reforms, Nexon listed EMK initiatives on mental health parity, health personnel, child health care, tobacco, cancer, genetic testing, and FDA reform.

527 **Their alliance was tested:** David Nexon, "Senator Edward M. Kennedy: The Master Legislative Craftsman," *Health Affairs*, Sept. 17, 2009.

528 **deal was reached:** JAF interview with Chris Jennings. "Legislative History of Kennedy-Kassebaum Health Insurance Reform Act," SLC-NARA. See Brophy, Hilley, and Jennings to Clinton, "Signing of the Health Insurance Portability and Accountability Act of 1996," Aug. 20, 1996; Telephone Interview of the President by *The New Yorker*, Feb. 14, 1997, WCL. Clymer, *Edward M. Kennedy*, 566. WP, Jan. 25, 1996. NYT, March 9, Oct. 2, 1996. Nexon, "Architect," *Health Affairs*. A key to the breakthrough, Lott recalled, was Kennedy's ability to reach agreement with another of his Republican "unlikely allies"—Ways and Means chairman Bill Archer, a conservative from Texas. See Lott, *Herding Cats*, 134. See also Nexon, "Craftsman."

For 1996 reappraisals of Kennedy see David Shribman, "Kennedy's Week of Opportunities," BG, April 26, 1996; Lloyd Grove, "The Liberal Lion Roars Back," WP, July 9, 1996; Adam Clymer, "Big Man in Congress: Kennedy, of All People," NYT, Aug. 11, 1996.

Twenty-Nine: Ireland

530 **other favored reform:** In Massachusetts, John Kerry had concluded that his best bet for reelection in 1996, in a race against the popular governor William Weld, lay in reassembling the liberal coalition that had prevailed for EMK two years earlier. Kerry asked for help, and EMK responded by handing Kerry a role in the jousting with Dole on the minimum wage, and by agreeing to let Kerry be a figurehead for children's health that year. JAF interview, Mary Beth Cahill. BG, June 21, 2003. NYT, Jan. 11, 2004. Nexon to EMK, "Health Policy Objectives/Status Update," June 1995, NL-UMASS.

530 **thirty years of violence:** EMK interview, AC-JFKL. Sean O'Huiginn, Carey Parker OH, UVA. *Baltimore News American*, May 3–10, 1983. Clymer, *Edward M. Kennedy.* "The IRA and Sinn Fein," *Frontline*, PBS, Oct. 21, 1977.

531 **an emotional attachment:** Elizabeth Shannon, Garret Fitzgerald, Sean Donlon, Michael Lillis OH, UVA.

531 **ripped into British policy:** EMKOH-UVA. EMK interview, AC-JFKL. Carey Parker OH, UVA. O'Neill and Burton, "Dear Colleague," June 24, 1969, with attached letter to Nixon and press release, "Congressmen Protest Discrimination in Northern

Ireland"; "Report on the fact-finding mission to the United Kingdom, Belgium, Hungary and Ireland, April 11–23, 1979," with accounts of O'Neill meetings with Ambassador Shannon and Irish prime minister Lynch, British prime minister Thatcher and officials, Irish opposition parties, and Ulster political leaders, Kirk O'Donnell papers, TON-BC. Kennedy remarks, CR, Oct. 20, 1971. See also Hinckley to McDaniel, "Northern Ireland Visit and Anglo-American Information Talks," June 7, 1985. ("The underlying problems are political, relating to social justice and human rights," National Security Council aide Ron Hinckley reported. "The economic inequalities merely reflect the long history of social injustice and the subordination of human rights on sectarian bases. . . . The lack of social and human rights progress continues to breed political extremism. . . . The government maintains the order necessary to perpetuate Protestant advantages at the expense of Catholics. . . . Without IRA violence and Sinn Fein ballot success as a prod, Great Britain will opt for the status quo.") RRL.

531 **spite and fury:** Sean O'Huiginn OH, UVA. The Irish government was surprised and dismayed as well. Kennedy "doesn't know what he's talking about," said the prime minister, Jack Lynch. See Garret Fitzgerald, Sean Donlon, Michael Lillis OH, UVA.

531 **"is Britain's Vietnam":** Northern Ireland, Hearings before the Subcommittee on Europe, Committee on Foreign Affairs, U.S. House of Representatives, Feb. 28, 29, and March 1, 1972. For EMK testimony, see also CR, Feb. 28, 1972. The domestic press response was in line with the British newspapers: see Nofziger to Dole, Dec. 20, 1971, Dole-KU, and NYT, Feb. 3, 1972. Georgetown University professor Samuel Dash, who would earn fame as chief counsel of the Senate Watergate Committee, conducted an investigation for a United Nations affiliate and concluded that the British Army was guilty of reckless or deliberate homicidal behavior. See WP, June 8, 1972. Harlow to O'Neill, July 7, 1969, RNL. For accounts of the involvement of the American Irish and Kennedy's role in the "Troubles" of Northern Ireland see Garret Fitzgerald, Sean Donlon, Michael Lillis OH, UVA; Stacie L. Pettyjohn and Rob Martin, "Northern Ireland Timeline," UVA, June 19, 2007, and Wilson, *Irish America*. For the first stirrings of Kennedy's involvement in Ulster's affairs, see 58–65.

532 **Hume's Londonderry home:** JAF interview with John Hume. EMKOH-UVA. Carey Parker OH, UVA. EMK, "Ulster Is an International Issue," *Foreign Policy* 11 (Summer 1973): 57–71. EMK, "Northern Ireland—A View from America," Tip O'Neill Memorial Lecture, Derry, Jan. 9, 1998. John Hume OH, UVA. ("Force was seen as patriotism . . . particularly in Irish America," Hume recalled. "Our argument was to challenge that traditional approach because that had never succeeded and never would. That when you have a divided people, what does violence do? It only deepens the division and makes the problem more difficult to resolve.") Fitzpatrick, *John Hume*, 35–36.

532 **"a profound influence"**: EMKOH-UVA. It is important to recognize, in the Ulster story, the fortuitous nature of progress. In the 1970s and 1980s the Horsemen had a stable of smart and able aides who were interested in the Irish question. O'Neill relied on Kirk O'Donnell; Moynihan had Tim Russert; Carey had David Burke; Carter had Robert Hunter; and Kennedy had Parker, who was not of Irish ancestry, but fond of Irish poetry, and chose to educate himself on Irish affairs and so became the "intellectual coordinator" of their efforts. A decade later, the serendipitous assembly of parties at another moment—the debate over the Gerry Adams visa—spurred more than one participant to cite Shakespeare: "There is a tide in the affairs of men." See Trina Vargo, Niall O'Dowd, Garret Fitzgerald, Sean Donlon, Michael Lillis OH, UVA, and Nancy Soderberg, Bill Clinton OH Project, UVA.

532 **"a healing process"**: John Hume OH, UVA. While writing a biography of Tip O'Neill, and when covering the Clinton presidency for the *Boston Globe*, the author interviewed EMK and other important players in the Northern Ireland saga, including John Hume, Niall O'Dowd, Jimmy Carter, George Mitchell, William Clark, Gerry Adams, Michael Deaver, Trina Vargo, Garret Fitzgerald, Sean Donlon, Michael Lillis, Bill Clinton, Carey Parker, and Nancy Soderberg.

533 **"sending us death"**: Wilson, *Irish America*, 5, 42–44, 66, 125. An August 1994 cable to Nancy Soderberg from Val Martinez, the American consul in Belfast, reported on the status of Northern Ireland as it marked the first quarter century of the Troubles. "Twenty-five years is a long stretch indeed," Martinez wrote. When the IRA fired its first shot amid the rioting of 1969, young Americans were gathering at Woodstock. "In 1969, no one could know it could get so bad." The initial IRA arsenal was compiled of three submachine guns, one rifle, and nine pistols. Yet the first quarter century saw 3,167 deaths, 9,983 explosions, and 36,603 injuries. "The equivalent numbers for a country with the population of the United States would be: 500,000 dead; 5.5 million injured," Martinez wrote. "No one in Northern Ireland seems to believe that it will last another 25 years—but no one wants to predict a quick end to it all either." Martinez to Soderbergh, Aug. 12, 1994, WCL.

533 **where Caroline Kennedy**: NYT, Oct. 24, 1975.

534 **The Four Horsemen**: The nickname did not come from the Apocalypse, at least not directly. The reference, known to Irish Americans, came from Notre Dame football and a legendary paragraph in American journalism. In an October 1924 edition of the *New York Herald Tribune*, Grantland Rice began his story, "Outlined against a blue-gray October sky, the Four Horsemen rode again. In dramatic lore they are known as Famine, Pestilence, Destruction and Death. These are only aliases. Their real names are Stuhldreher, Miller, Crowley and Layden. They formed the crest of the South Bend cyclone before which another fighting Army football team was swept over the precipice at the Polo Grounds yesterday."

For the Four Horsemen and Carter statements see JAF interview with John Hume, Carey Parker. Parker to Farrell, Sept. 21, 1988, author's collection. Sean O'Huiginn, Charles Ferris OH, UVA. EMK, Moynihan, Carey, and O'Neill, "Joint St. Patrick's Day Appeal for Peace in Northern Ireland," March 17, 1977, and O'Neill to Vance, June 3, 1977, with attachment, "Basic Agenda," and Ferris to O'Neill, "Meeting with Secretary Vance on Northern Ireland," June 8, 1977, all TON-BC, and Brzezinski to Carter, "Proposed Statement on Northern Ireland," Aug. 23, 1977, JCL. For reaction of IRA sympathizers and the Horsemen's response, see Carroll to O'Neill, Oct. 27, 1977, and O'Neill to Carroll, Nov. 3, 1977, and Parker to Diehl, Dec. 1, 1977, TON-BC. NYT, Aug. 31, 1977. WP, Sept. 4, 1977.

For Hume and Irish diplomats see JAF interview with Michael Lillis, Sean Donlon. See also Lillis to O'Donnell, recounting Hume's search for Speaker O'Neill's ancestral home and a proposed itinerary for O'Neill's trip to Ireland, April 2, 1979, and Mairead Corrigan and Ciaran McKeown statements, April 20, 1979, on O'Neill's "strong identification" with Hume and the Irish government. See also BG, April 19, 20, 1979, and Holland, *American Connection*.

For Irish diplomatic initiative see Sharkey to O'Donnell, Nov. 30, 1982, on meeting between Irish embassy staff and House Democratic leadership staff, with attached memo, "Meeting to Review 'Friends of Ireland' Initiative," Nov. 23, 1982, TON-BC. See also State Department briefing paper for Reagan lunch with Irish ambassador Sean Donlon, March 17, 1981.

534 **They feted Reagan**: While coping with Thatcher's arrival at 10 Downing Street, the Horsemen also had to deal with Irish prime minister Charles Haughey, a republican who didn't think that Sean Donlon, the Irish ambassador to Washington, was sufficiently devoted to the cause. O'Neill, Kennedy, and Hume called Haughey and made it clear that their support for Irish interests was contingent on Hume's strategy of moderation and Donlon's continued employment. See Garret Fitzgerald, Sean Donlon, Michael Lillis OH, UVA. Fitzpatrick, *John Hume*, 77–81. WP, July 9, 1980. EMKOH-UVA.

On Horsemen lobbying Carter to intercede with Thatcher, see O'Neill to Vance, May 10, 1979; O'Neill to Carter, June 22, 1979; Carter to O'Neill, "personal and confidential," Aug. 4, 1979; and O'Donnell to O'Neill, "Mrs. Thatcher's Visit—Irish Update," Dec. 17, 1979, TON-BC.

On Irish diplomats wooing Reagan, see Allen to Reagan, "Irish Embassy Project," Feb. 3, 1981; Allen to Reagan on Irish embassy lunch, March 17, 1981; State Department briefing paper, March 17, 1981, all RRL.

On Kennedy and O'Neill lobbying Reagan to intercede with Thatcher, see JAF interview with Sean Donlon. See also EMK to Reagan, Feb. 13, 1981, with EMK handwritten notation "I'm still trying to find Ballyporeen on my map of Ireland. Why don't we visit there together?" and Blair to Allen, June 10,

1981, and Allen to Reagan, June 15, 1981, and O'Neill to Reagan, May 19, 1981, and Sept. 27, 1983. WP, May 14, 1981, Feb. 24, 1985. NYT, Aug. 4, 1981. *Financial Times*, Feb. 22, 1985. *Irish Press*, March 15, 1985. See also Wilson, *Irish America*, chapter 8. Bertie Ahern, Carey Parker OH, UVA.
For the evolving Reagan response to the Kennedy and O'Neill entreaties see JAF interviews with Garret Fitzgerald, Sean Donlon, Michael Lillis, John Hume. See also Allen to Friedersdorf, April 24, 1981, and Reagan to O'Neill, June 18, 1981; see also O'Neill to Reagan, Dec. 13, 1984; Kennedy, O'Neill, and congressional "Friends of Ireland" to Reagan, Dec. 20, 1984, McFarlane to Reagan, Jan. 8, 1985, with Reagan to O'Neill, January 9, and January 11, 1985, and cable from the U.S. embassy in Dublin to the State Department, Jan. 17, 1985, RRL. See also BG, June 30, 2000, and JAF interviews with Michael Deaver, William Clark, and Sean Donlon. See Sean O'Huiginn, Carey Parker OH, UVA.
For Irish government lobbying see July 28, 1981, and Oct. 19, 1982, cables from the U.S. embassy in Dublin to the State Department conveying the Irish government's desire that Reagan intercede with Thatcher and relaying Prime Minister Garret Fitzgerald's condemnation of her "obduracy and hypocrisy," RRL. NYT, Oct. 13, 1981. WP, Oct. 22, 1981. See also Garret Fitzgerald, Sean Donlon, Michael Lillis OH, UVA. "We have a small industry in Ireland to find relatives for American politicians," said Donlon. See also Holland, *American Connection*, 143.
On State Department position, and quid pro quos, see BG, June 30, 2000, and Kennedy to Reagan, Feb. 13, 1981, with attached "Defense-Related Initiative on Northern Ireland," and Friedersdorf and Turner to Reagan, Feb. 24, 1981, briefing on Feb. 26, 1981, phone call to EMK on Thatcher and Northern Ireland, RRL.
On Clark's views and influence see JAF interview with William Clark. See also Garret Fitzgerald, Sean Donlon, Michael Lillis OH, UVA. See also Blair and Rentschler to Clark, Jan. 15, 1982, and cable from the embassy in Dublin to the State Department, Jan. 24, 1985; for the "nudge" see U.S. embassy in London to the State Department, Dec. 7, 1984, all RRL. See EMKOH-UVA.
On the Anglo-Irish accord see Statement by the President, joint appearance with Speaker O'Neill, Nov. 15, 1985, and Platt to Poindexter, "State Department Position Regarding Aid to Northern Ireland," Feb. 7, 1986, and Shultz to Miller, undated, 1986, RRL. See also William Shannon, "The Anglo-Irish Agreement," *Foreign Affairs*, Spring 1986.
See also Thatcher, *Downing Street*, chapter 14, "Shadows of Gunmen."
535 **would need a visa:** JAF interview with Bill Clinton. Gerry Adams OH, UVA. Nancy Soderberg, Bill Clinton OH Project, UVA. Clinton to Dinkins, Oct. 30, 1993; Reno to Lake, Nov. 23, 1994 ("We oppose lifting the visa restrictions," Reno wrote. The DOJ and FBI "are very concerned that funds raised by Mr. Adams might be used to purchase weapons"); Unsigned, undated note, circa late

1993 or early 1994, from "Peter" re: State Department opposition ("Secretary Christopher strongly opposes issuing the visa. . . . Furthermore, Secretary Christopher objects to our appearing to be willing to enter into the negotiations over Northern Ireland—an issue that he considers has demonstrated it is hopelessly difficult to resolve"); Vargo to Soderberg, Nov. 11, 1993, all Soderberg papers, WCL. BG, Feb. 10, 1995. NYT, Nov. 4, 1993.
535 **Ambassador Jean Kennedy Smith:** JAF interview with Victoria Reggie Kennedy. EMKOH-UVA. John Hume, Gerry Adams, Sean O'Huiginn, Carey Parker OH, UVA. Smith interview, AC-JFKL. Holl to Lake, "Travel of Ambassador Jean Kennedy Smith to Northern Ireland," Dec. 14, 1993, WCL. O'Clery, *Daring*, 63, 80, 84. "There's no ambiguity about the Kennedys in Ireland, so doors opened for her," Irish parliamentarian Maurice Manning told the *Boston Globe*. "She was a very unorthodox ambassador. . . . She had her own agenda, which was essentially to bring Gerry Adams and company in from the cold. She was hugely successful and hugely influential for doing that." BG, Aug. 30, 2009. NYT, July 29, 1994.
537 **a covert chain:** JAF interviews with EMK, Nancy Soderberg, Niall O'Dowd. EMKOH-UVA. Niall O'Dowd, Trina Vargo OH, UVA. Nancy Soderberg, Bill Clinton OH Project, UVA. Gerry Adams statement, Jan. 28, 1994, Soderberg papers, WCL.
Kennedy personally interceded with U.S. labor leaders, Secretary of State Warren Christopher, National Security Adviser Anthony Lake, and Vice President Al Gore. Kennedy aides called their friends on the White House staff. On January 25, Kennedy and Christopher Dodd met with the president at the White House. By then, Kennedy was familiar with the arguments of the naysayers, which he dismantled. "I felt that at the end of the meeting with Clinton that we were going to get it," said Kennedy. "The substance of this thing was so powerful. The politics were so powerful. . . . He was going to take the chance."
Lake and his deputy Soderberg put their reputations on the line by advising Clinton to spurn the recommendations of his own Departments of Justice and State. The Irish came to respect Soderberg (they gave her the nickname "Fancy Sodabread") and her insistence that they toe the path to peace. Gore, another of Hume's confidants, also supported the visa decision.
But Kennedy made one last call to Lake, when word reached the senator that there were concerns that Adams had not sufficiently renounced violence. If the answer was no, then give it to us straight, Kennedy told Lake. "To . . . flyspeck it and sink it in that way was, I thought, devious . . . and unbecoming and unacceptable way of dealing with it."
Kennedy told Lake that the reaction to a negative decision would be loud and quick in Irish America, and that he was prepared to offer an amendment in the Senate and put Congress on record in favor of the visa.
Ultimately, with the help of Kennedy's staff, Adams issued a statement to give Clinton cover: "My sole purpose in coming to the United States is to

advance the cause of peace and move the process forward," he said. "I want to see an end to all violence and an end to this conflict. I don't advocate violence. It is my personal and political priority to see an end to the IRA and an end to all other organizations involved in armed actions. I am willing to seek to persuade the IRA to make definitive decisions on the conduct of its campaign." See EMKOH-UVA; O'Clery, *Daring*, 101–3.

The chain of communication worked both ways, Adams recalled. "There were all sorts of back channels going on. If somebody got a formalization from source A, then the Nancys of this world would go on to Teddy and Teddy could go on to John Hume, or Teddy could go on to Jean Kennedy Smith and Jean Kennedy Smith could go on to Father Reid." Gerry Adams OH, UVA.

537 **With Kennedy leading:** JAF interview with Niall O'Dowd. Bill Clinton interview with JAF, Conor O'Clery, Martin Fletcher, Susan Flavella-Geraghty, Feb. 1995, WCL. BG, Feb. 10, 1995. O'Clery, *Daring*, 109.

537 **typified Britain's outrage:** EMK et al. to Clinton, Jan. 15, 1994; Lake to Adams, Oct. 2, 1994, Bruce Morrison papers, University of Connecticut. *Financial Times*, Dec. 27, 2018. *Irish Times*, Dec. 31, 2018. *The News Letter* (Belfast), Dec. 27, 2018. Her majesty's government was not helped by the fact that it had assisted the Bush campaign in the 1992 election, something Clinton and his political advisers did not forget. The member of the royal family killed by the IRA was Lord Louis Mountbatten, whose boat was destroyed by a bomb off the coast of Sligo in 1979.

538 **Adams traveled to New York:** JAF interviews with EMK, Bill Clinton, John Hume, Niall O'Dowd, Nancy Soderberg, Peter Bean. O'Dowd was more than a publisher. He had helped assemble a group of Irish American advocates for the peace process that included Mayor Raymond Flynn of Boston, former congressman Bruce Morrison, and corporate executives like William Flynn and Charles Feeney. The Kennedy family friend Bill Barry served as a security consultant.

On Soderberg and the backdoor maneuvering, see Soderberg to Lake et al. ("My contact to Adams is Neill O'Dowd who can be reached most easily through Trina"), Aug. 8, 1994; see also Sinn Fein to O'Dowd to Trina to Nancy, Jan. 19, 1994, with proposed Adams remarks, Jan. 21, 1994, both in Soderberg papers, WCL. "She had to have her deniability," O'Dowd recalled, "so if anything went wrong, it was just Senator Kennedy's office she was dealing with." Soderberg also relied on Hume, the Irish government, and Smith for information and insight. See also Trina Vargo OH, UVA.

On the practice grenades see BG, Feb. 10, 1995, and unsigned, undated U.S. law enforcement "Update on San Diego Bombs" ("The FBI notes that Southern California is not a hot bed of IRA activity"), Soderberg papers, WCL.

On Adams trip see "USUN Readout of National Committee on Foreign Policy Conference on Northern Ireland," Feb. 1, 1994, WCL. O'Clery, *Daring*, 107–8, 111–12, 124. O'Dowd, *Irish Voice*, 248–53.

In 1998 when John Hume and unionist David Trimble were awarded the Nobel Peace Prize, Kennedy felt that Gerry Adams should have been included. Carey Parker OH, UVA.

538 **no easy road:** Trina Vargo OH, UVA.

539 **when Adams returned:** Transcript, Telcon Between President Clinton and Irish Prime Minister Reynolds, Aug. 31, 1994, Soderberg papers, WCL. Gerry Adams, Trina Vargo OH, UVA. "Teddy was pivotal again in terms of the Joe Cahill thing," said Adams. Kennedy and Smith realized that "if there were skeptics out there or if there were people who thought this was a surrender or they were being sold out, there was no better man to tell them what the story was than Joe Cahill, and no better example of proof that things had changed." In his oral history at UVA, the Irish diplomat Sean O'Huiginn agreed. "The campaign of violence was becoming a very murderous and unproductive cul-de-sac," he recalled. But Sinn Fein and the IRA "were obviously going to need something that they could represent, at a minimum, as an honorable outcome." The respect and support they got from the U.S. government represented that kind of outcome. O'Clery, *Daring*, 131–33. Wilson, *Irish America*, 296–97.

539 **the greatest journey:** EMK, O'Neill Lecture, Jan. 9, 1998. EMKOH-UVA. Bertie Ahern, Gerry Adams OH, UVA. "Our argument within Republicanism was that you can only use armed struggle if there's no alternative. But if there was an alternative, why on earth would you be involved in anything other than peaceful and democratic means?" Adams said. "This showed that we did have some clout." BG, Dec. 1, 1995. O'Clery, *Daring*, 249.

540 **On Good Friday that spring:** Soderberg notes, 1995; Adams to Lake, Jan. 31, 1995, with attachment, Gerry Adams, "Sinn Fein Perspective on the Current Situation," Jan. 25, 1995; Morrison, Feeney, Jamison, and O'Dowd, "We are at a crisis," June 23, 1997, Soderberg papers, WCL. Bertie Ahern, George Mitchell OH, UVA. Andrew Sanders, "Senator Edward Kennedy and the 'Ulster Troubles': Irish and Irish-American Politics, 1965–2009," *Historical Journal of Massachusetts* 39 (Summer 2011). Adams said he learned from Kennedy. "He might describe the [opposition] in colorful language if he's talking privately, but he also understands that [his foe] has his point of view, and part of the job is to try to see if there's any common ground, to get toward your objectives," said Adams. "He made—I asked him to—a lot of phone calls. . . . He went to senior British representatives numerous times. . . . This isn't just haggling and groveling stuff, this is the tedium of making progress." Gerry Adams OH, UVA. Said Kennedy's longtime aide Carey Parker, "Apart from national health insurance, I don't know of any other issue that he has spent so much time on." Carey Parker OH, UVA.

Thirty: Troubled Waters

541 **horror and grief:** National Transportation Safety Board Aviation Accident Final Report, Accident

Number NYC99MA178, July 16, 1999. WP, July 18, 1999. NYT, July 22, 1999. BG, July 18, 1999. English et al., *Last Lion*, 341–42.

542 **"just shut down":** JAF interview with Robert Shrum. The *Boston Globe* and *Washington Post* coverage of July 18 through 24 offers a thorough chronicle of that week's events, as did many other media outlets. National Transportation Safety Board Aviation Accident Final Report, Accident Number NYC99MA178, July 16, 1999. Kennedy and Fried, *Common Struggle*, 166–67. Alan Simpson, who served as the director of the Institute of Politics at the John F. Kennedy School of Government, remembered that John Jr. had once arrived at a board meeting there and told EMK he had flown his own plane, following the coastline on a beautiful night, from New York to Boston. "I've told you not to do that," EMK told his nephew. "You're not an instrument pilot and you know damn well that just irritates me. Dammit John, you can't do that. . . . Stop it." See Simpson OH, UVA.

542 **splendor and loss:** JAF interview with Patrick Kennedy. Maria and Robert Shriver, Ronald Weich OH, UVA. Kennedy and Fried, *Common Struggle*, 3, 34.

543 **Patrick was thrilled:** Bob Hohler, "The UnKennedy," *Boston Globe Magazine*, June 6, 1999. Kennedy and Fried, *Common Struggle*, 78. Edward M. Kennedy Jr. interview, AC-JFKL. Mark Leibovich, "Ted Kennedy, Jr. Is (Finally) Ready for the Family Business," *New York Times Magazine*, March 13, 2013. With Ted Jr. out of the way, RFK's son Joseph entered the campaign and captured O'Neill's seat. See Sullivan and Kenney, *Race*.

544 **they said goodbye:** BG, July 23, 24, 1999. WP, July 24, 1999. *Time*, Aug. 2, 1999. Christopher Lawford, *Symptoms*, 375. The line, "What made us dream that he could comb grey hair?," is from "In Memory of Major Robert Gregory," by William Butler Yeats, from the 1919 collection *The Wild Swans at Coole*.

544 **there was Ted Kennedy:** David Sutphen OH, UVA. For similar accounts see JAF interview with Stephanie Cutter, Jeff Blattner, and Trina Vargo, Melody Miller OH, UVA, and Charles Ferris OH, SHO.

545 **part of a complex relationship:** Thurgood Marshall Jr. OH, UVA. Reed and Kagan to Clinton, April 3, 1998; Jennings to Bowles, Nov. 27, 1996; EMK to Verveer, March 16, 1998; Reed, Sperling, Jennings, Johnson to Clinton, Jan. 12, 1999; Remarks by the President at Signing Ceremony, Work Incentives Improvment Act, Dec. 17, 1999; Remarks at a Dinner for Lt. Gov. Kathleen Kennedy Townsend of Maryland in Hyannis Port, Massachusetts, Aug. 5, 2000, WCL. Kennedy Statement, Patient's Bill of Rights, Feb. 25, 1997, SLC-NARA.

545 **differences came down:** JAF interview with Chris Jennings, David Nexon. Nexon to Magaziner, June 25, 1994, SLC-NARA. Nexon to Jennings, Dec. 8, 1994, "Possible Fall-Back Option," undated, unsigned; Jennings and Min to Clinton, Jan. 15, 1997; Reed and Sperling to Clinton, Feb. 21, 1997; Jennings to Clinton, Reed, Sperling, Hilley, March 13, 1997, WCL.

545 **Orrin Hatch agreed:** Littlefield to EMK, March 27, 1992 ("We need to rebuild the old Kennedy-Hatch axis, which is a bit rusty right now"), Dec. 29, 1994, NL-UMASS. Jennings to Clinton, Reed, Sperling, Hilley, March 13, 1997; Jennings to Bowles, March 31, 1997; Jennings to Clinton, Reed, Sperling, Hilley, Verveer, WCL. Littlefield and Nexon, *Lion*, 421. NYT, March 14, 1997.

546 **"off on his own":** John Hilley OH, UVA. NYT, May 22, 1997. Hatch, *Square Peg*, 111–20. Hilley, *Challenge*, 133–36.

546 **Kennedy was incensed:** EMKOH-UVA. John Hilley, John Tunney, Esther Olavaria OH, UVA. Edelman to Littlefield, July 31, 1997, NL-UMASS. NYT, Aug. 11, 1997. Hilley, *Challenge*, 155. Nexon and Littlefield, *Lion*, 441–42. Hatch, *Square Peg*, 111–20.

548 **White House intern:** On Foster, see Robert B. Fiske Jr., Report of the Independent Counsel In Re Vincent W. Foster Jr., June 30, 1994, Brett Kavanaugh papers, National Archives. *Newsweek*, Feb. 2, 1998. See also Moldea, *Washington Tragedy*. On Whitewater see "Investigation conducted by independent counsel Kenneth Starr," Feb. 9, 1999, TD-SDS.

548 **independent counsel statute that Starr:** There was nothing "independent" about Kenneth Starr. The original Whitewater counsel, Republican Robert Fiske, was on his way toward acquitting the Clintons of serious wrongdoing and had released his finding that Vincent Foster's death was a suicide, when right-wing outrage spurred two conniving judges to oust him and install Starr, who had no prosecutorial experience and had been working as an adviser for Clinton's accusers. For critiques of the office, in general, see Abraham Dash, "The Office of Independent Counsel and the Fatal Flaw: 'They Are Left to Twist in the Wind,'" *Maryland Law Review* 60, no. 1 (2001): 26–40; Justice Antonin Scalia dissent in *Morrison v. Olson*, 487 U.S. 654, 706 (1988); and Elaine W. Stone, "The Genesis of the Independent Counsel Statute," Brookings Institution, Washington, DC, 1999.

For Kennedy and independent counsel law see EMK et al. to Sirica, Oct. 23, 1973; Eastland to Bork, Oct. 24, 1973; EMK statements, Oct. 23, 25, 1973; CR, Oct. 26, 1973; Susman to EMK, Oct. 30, 1973; memo and outline of legislation, Judiciary Committee Executive Session, Oct. 24, 1973; Susman to EMK, Jan. 14, 1974, TS-UMASS.

548 **impeached the president:** The hypocrisy of Newt Gingrich, who led the persecution of the president while conducting his own adulterous affair with Callista Bisek, a House aide, reached the level of farce when Gingrich divorced his (second) wife, married Bisek, and engineered her appointment (by the sexually predatory Donald Trump) as the American ambassador to the Vatican. Representative Robert Livingston of Louisiana, next in the line of succession to Speaker Gingrich in 1998, stepped down as his own adulterous behavior was disclosed. Representative Henry Hyde, the chairman of the Judiciary Committee that impeached Clinton, confessed to marital infidelity. Supreme Court justice Brett

Kavanaugh, who made his mark as an apparatchik on Starr's team, was accused of sexual assault during his 2018 confirmation hearings. Starr was fired as Baylor University's president in 2016 for his role in a campus-wide cover-up of rape and other sexual assaults at the school. On Kavanaugh's role for Starr see Brett Kavanaugh papers, National Archives. "sordid": *Time*, Feb. 2, 1998. *Newsweek*, Feb. 2, 1998.

549 **a key role:** JAF interview with Trent Lott, James Manley, Norman Ornstein. Thomas Daschle, Melody Barnes OH, UVA. Gormley, *Virtue*, 620–21. Baker, *Breach*, 261. Lott and Daschle, *Crisis Point*, 129–36. Lott, *Herding Cats*, 178, 180.

549 **the senators assembled:** Gormley, *Virtue*, 620.

550 **"the Gramm-Kennedy Miracle":** JAF interview with Greg Craig. David Sutphen, Trent Lott, Melody Barnes, Carey Parker OH, UVA. Gormley, *Virtue*, 621. Baker, *Breach*, 289–95. BG, Jan. 9, 1999. The Gramm-Kennedy agreement "averted further confrontation over rival Republican and Democratic trial plans that had threatened to send the Senate into the same partisan spiral as the House," the *New York Times* reported, see NYT, Jan. 9, 1999. Lott and Daschle, *Crisis Point*, 131–35.

Thirty-One: Fortunate Sons

551 **fears and resentments:** JAF interviews with Chris Dodd, Lawrence O'Donnell, Trent Lott, Janet Heininger. EMK-TC, 487. Obama, *Promised*, 57.

551 **new, polarized era:** JAF interviews with Victoria Reggie Kennedy, Lawrence O'Donnell, Chris Jennings, Richard Arenberg, Donald Ritchie, Norman Ornstein. *Time*, July 2, 2001. NYT, Jan. 23, 2002. Thomas Daschle, James Sasser, Ronald Weich, David Sutphen, John Jennings OH, UVA. Kennedy campaigned for Gore in Iowa and New Hampshire and helped the vice president stave off a challenge from Senator Bill Bradley of New Jersey, who EMK viewed as something of a dilettante. Clymer, *Edward M. Kennedy*, 2009 ed., 590–92.

552 **CIA's distinct warnings:** *The 9/11 Commission Report* (New York: Norton, 2004), 115–19, 201–2, 212–13, 254–65. "The system was blinking red," CIA director George Tenet told the commission. The warnings could not have been clearer. In the months before 9/11, both Clinton and Bush were warned by the intelligence community that Al Qaeda hoped to attack the American homeland. See also Coll, *Ghost Wars*, 566–70.

552 **he asked Kennedy and other:** William Taylor, Terry Hartle, Ellen Guiney, Margaret Spellings, Danica Petroshius OH, UVA. The standards and accountability movement dated back to the growing realization, in the Reagan and Bush years, that public education in the United States was putting major portions of the population, and the health of the nation, "at risk." EMK-TC, 489–92. NYT, Jan. 14, 2002. *Time*, July 2, 2001. The "big four" lawmakers on the act were Kennedy, Senator Judd Gregg, a Republican from New Hampshire, Representative George Miller, a Democrat from California, and Representative John Boehner, a Republican from Ohio.

553 **followed the Reagan template:** Sandy Kress OH, UVA. Remarks by the President at Dedication of the Robert F. Kennedy Department of Justice Building, Washington, DC, Nov. 20, 2001, George W. Bush Presidential Library. EMK-TC, 487–88. NYT, Jan. 14, 2002. *Time*, July 2, 2001.

553 **"most unlikely partnership":** Bush, *Decision Points*, 275. NYT, July 4, 2007. Bush's education adviser, Margaret Spellings, remembered that EMK was not invited to a preinaugural meeting in Texas because Republicans had demonized him for years in party handouts and fund-raising appeals. But once in Washington, "in the first fifteen seconds you could tell that he's a guy with a heart and with a commitment," she said. Margaret Spellings OH, UVA. Her colleague Sandy Kress had a similar memory. "The president was extremely passionate, knowledgeable, caring, interested in Senator Kennedy and his reaction and views, which I think was surprising to Senator Kennedy," he said. "Senator Kennedy was respectful, interested, giving off the feeling of wanting to be a partner, very committed to the issue, and respectful of the president and the office, all of which I think was somewhat surprising to the president." Sandy Kress OH, UVA.

554 **Wellstone accused Kennedy:** JAF interviews with James Manley, Michael Myers, Lawrence O'Donnell. EMK-TC, 489. TNY, Oct. 18, 2004. See Bush, *Decision Points*, 276 ("I would not be the education president. I was a war president"). NYT, Feb. 13, 2002; April 7, 2004. Thomas Daschle, William Taylor, Danica Petroshius, George Miller, Sandy Kress, Michael Myers OH, UVA.

"No bill Kennedy got passed has ever been the subject of such sustained criticism over many years as the No Child Left Behind Act," wrote Kennedy biographer Adam Clymer. The lack of promised funding made the new law a target of liberals, who believed that it demanded too much from underfunded schools, while conservatives resisted what they saw as an unwanted federal incursion on the authority of local school boards.

The promises of new funding for schools, a balanced budget, and paying down the national debt evaporated once the Bush tax cuts of 2001 and the spending authorized by both parties after 9/11—and then for the war in Iraq—emptied the U.S. Treasury. "Obviously the war and other calamities, 9/11 etc., took over the budget," said Margaret Spellings. "There were other equities . . . and Kennedy and Bush parted ways." Margaret Spellings OH, UVA.

"He took a risk," said EMK aide David Sutphen. "If you put skin in the game, you're going to get burned sometimes."

See Clymer, *Edward M. Kennedy*, 2009 ed., 594–95, and Jean Edward Smith's account of the Bush presidency in his biography, *Bush*, and chapter 4, "Making Sure Kids Learn," in Graham, *Home Front*.

555 **September 11, 2001:** Laura Bush, *Spoken*, 198–200. Carey Parker OH, UVA.

556 **to destroy the Capitol:** The senator called the families of all the 9/11 victims from Massachusetts. "No one else" called—not John Kerry, not

the governor, not the airline—said Cindy Mc-
Ginty, one of the 9/11 widows from Massachusetts, and a Republican. "And he didn't do it for
political gain; you never heard about this." He
helped arrange therapists for her and her children and took them sailing and called the family
every year on September 11. See Cindy McGinty
OH, UVA. JAF interviews with James Manley, Paul
Donovan, Victoria Reggie Kennedy. EMK-TC,
492–93. Fourth hijacked airline: see Bill Stern-
berg, "What Was Flight 93's Target on 9/11?," WP,
Sept. 9, 2021, and *The 9/11 Commission Report*.

556 **a nobler man:** Rob Martin, Hilde Eliassen Restad,
and Randi Lewis, "Iraq Timeline," UVA, Nov. 21,
2007. Sharon Waxman OH, UVA.

556 **"the reality-based community":** Ron Suskind,
"Faith, Certainty and the Presidency of George W.
Bush," *New York Times Magazine*, Oct. 17, 2004. The
full quote, from an unnamed senior White House
official, is, "People like you are still living in what
we call the reality-based community. You believe
that solutions emerge from your judicious study of
discernible reality. That's not the way the world
really works anymore. We're an empire now, and
when we act, we create our own reality. And while
you are studying that reality—judiciously, as you
will—we'll act again, creating other new realities,
which you can study too, and that's how things will
sort out. We're history's actors, and you, all of you,
will be left to just study what we do."

557 **war with Iraq:** JAF interview with William vanden
Heuvel. Sharon Waxman OH, UVA. On the folly
and flawed assumptions of the Bush administration and the Iraq War see Robert Draper, *Start*;
Thomas E. Ricks, *Fiasco*; and Packer, *Assassins'
Gate*. The documentary record on the decision to
invade Iraq is available in the Report of the Iraq
Inquiry, by a Committee of Privy Counsellors
chaired by Sir John Chilcot, London, available at
www.iraqinquiry.org.uk, and in "The Iraq Project,"
National Security Archive, Washington, DC, available at www.nsarchive.gwu.edu.

557 **He railed at:** NYT, Dec. 17, 2005.

557 **"been down that road":** JAF interviews with
Stephanie Cutter, William vanden Heuvel. EMK,
Speech Against the Invasion of Iraq, Johns Hop-
kins School of Advanced International Studies,
Sept. 27, 2002, EMKI. William vanden Heuvel
OH, UVA. On Vietnam see Phil Johnston, BM,
Nov. 30, 2009.

558 **one of only twenty-three:** CR, Oct. 7, 10, 11, 2002.

558 **his daughter, Kara:** Edward M. Kennedy Jr., Kara
Kennedy, Patrick Kennedy, Melody Miller OH,
UVA. "He had so many powerful feelings," his son
Ted Jr. said of EMK, but "because everyone in our
family was relying on him to be the strong guy, I
think he really felt like he had to be stoic, even
though he was an emotional man. . . . But I do
agree with Kara. Perhaps it was his Irish Catholic
upbringing that made it difficult for him to easily
talk about intimate feelings." See Ted Kennedy Jr.
OH, UVA.

559 **a treatable cancer:** JAF interview with Victoria
Reggie Kennedy. On persevering see BG, May 25,
2008. Kara Kennedy died at the age of fifty-one in

September 2011, after suffering a heart attack at
her health club. NYT, Sept. 17, 2011.

559 **insurgency took root:** Rob Martin, Hilde Eliassen
Restad, and Randi Lewis, "Iraq Timeline," UVA,
Nov. 21, 2007. Brian and Alma Hart OH, UVA.
Mike Barnicle, "Of Memory and the Sea," *Time*,
Aug. 26, 2009. As a senior Democrat, Kennedy
had sought and been granted a seat on a third
major committee—Armed Services—during the
Reagan years.

560 **known for such gestures:** For Biden see CR, Feb.
26, 2002. For Kerry and for 9/11 see Kerry and
Stephen Kerrigan, BM, Nov. 30, 2009. For others
see Kandy Stroud, *Cosmopolitan*, Dec. 1979, and
Melody Miller, Burt Wides OH, UVA. If he could
not get there in person, Kennedy often phoned or
sent a note. At one point in the 2004 election,
Kennedy campaigned on an Indian reservation in
New Mexico with John Kerry's daughter Vanessa,
where they were blessed in a ceremony by a chanting tribal spiritual leader. "I think we just got married," he whispered to Vanessa. As the election
approached, Kennedy sent her a note, recalling the
Humphrey Bogart line from *Casablanca*: "No matter what happens, we will always have New Mexico."

560 **the jingoistic ruckus:** Sharon Waxman OH, UVA.
BG, Oct. 16, 2003.

561 **"George Bush's Vietnam":** JAF interview with
Stephanie Cutter. BG, Sept. 19, Oct. 16, 2003.
NYT, Sept. 25, 27, 2003, March 5, April 5, 2004.
EMK, Speech on Iraq Policy, Center for American
Progress, C-SPAN, Jan. 14, 2004. EMK, Speech to
the Council on Foreign Relations, March 5, 2004.
Bush, *Decision Points*, 304. Rob Martin, Hilde Eli-
assen Restad, and Randi Lewis, "Iraq Timeline,"
UVA, Nov. 21, 2007. John McCain, Ronald Weich,
Sharon Waxman, William vanden Heuvel OH,
UVA.

562 **"very lonely times":** JAF interviews with James
Manley, Paul Donovan. Sharon Waxman OH,
UVA. BG, Jan. 17, 2005. *Los Angeles Times*, Jan. 28,
2005. NYT, Jan. 28, 2005, Jan. 9, 2007. EMK, National Press Club, Newsmaker Luncheon, Jan. 9,
2007, Federal News Service.

562 **Democratic presidential nominee:** Kennedy was
an important player at key moments in the 2000
and 2004 presidential campaigns. He gave Al
Gore a needed endorsement, campaign time, and
staff help in New Hampshire in 2000, and did the
same for Kerry in Iowa in 2004. JAF interviews
with Robert Caro, Robert Shrum. Though the
2004 Democratic convention was held in Boston,
Kennedy's role was truncated by the Kerry campaign, which was stressing the nominee's military
background and centrist leanings that month.

562 **working with Bush:** JAF interviews with Chris Jennings, James Manley. Fred Barnes, "Teddy's Triumph," *Weekly Standard*, July 7, 2003. NYT, June
22, 2003, July 4, 2007. Paul Kirk, Michael Myers,
Antonia Hernandez, Melody Barnes OH, UVA.

563 **and Kennedy signed on:** JAF interviews with Chris
Jennings, David Nexon, James Manley. EMK to Po-
desta, May 14, 1998; Reed and Kagan to Clinton,
April 9, 1999; Jennings and Jeanne L. to Hillary
Clinton, March 30, 1999, WCL. David Nexon,

"Senator Edward M. Kennedy: The Master Legislative Craftsman," *Health Affairs*, Sept. 17, 2009. Thomas Oliver, Philip Lee, Helene Lipton, "A Political History of Medicare and Prescription Drug Coverage," *The Milbank Quarterly*, June 2004. Henry Aaron, "Prescription Drug Bill: The Good, the Bad, and the Ugly," www.brookings.edu, Jan. 15, 2004. NYT, June 22, Nov. 23, 2003. Rashi Fein, Michael Myers OH, UVA. Graham, *Home Front*, chapter 5, "Drug Coverage for Seniors." McDonough, *Inside*, 28–31. English et al., *Last Lion*, 381.

564 **collaborator on immigration:** EMKOH-UVA. Esther Olavarria OH, UVA. Salter, *Luckiest Man*, 322–23. For an evocative glimpse at the inner workings of Congress and the immigration issue, see "Twelve Stories—How Democracy Works Now," by Shari Robertson and Michael Camerini, a twelve-part documentary series, 2001–13.

565 **waves of illegal immigration:** A Conversation with Senator Edward Kennedy on Immigration, June 9, 2006, JFKL. EMKOH-UVA. Cannon to Ford, "Domestic Council Committee on Illegal Aliens," June 16, 1975; Parsons to Cannon, Cavanaugh, and Lynn, Sept. 27, 1976, "Preliminary Report of the Domestic Council Committee on Illegal Aliens," Sept. 27, 1976, GFL. Henderson, *Beyond Borders*. Douglas Massey and Karen Pren, "Unintended Consequences of US Immigration Policy: Explaining the Post-1965 Surge from Latin America," *Population and Development Review*, March 2012. "Illegal Immigration," *CQ Researcher*, April 24, 1992. NYT, Feb. 12, 1979. JAF interview with Tom Tancredo.

566 **but helped Simpson:** EMKOH-UVA. Carey Parker OH, UVA. Hardy, *Shooting*, 79–81, 86. After his own attempt at immigration reform failed, President Jimmy Carter appointed a commission to study immigration, led by Notre Dame president Theodore Hesburgh. Kennedy and Simpson were representatives from the Senate. It issued its findings in 1981; see NYT, Feb. 27, 1981.

567 **legal immigration policies:** NYT, Feb. 14, March 13, 16, April 10, 1988; Oct. 29, 1990.

567 **sealed the porous border:** Epstein to Emanuel, May 27, 1993; Rubin to Clinton with Clinton annotation and attached Reich to National Economic Council, July 16, 1993, WCL. Myers to EMK, "Immigration and Refugee Agenda," June 1, 1995, NL-UMASS. Kennedy and Simpson statements, Reform of Legal Immigration, Hearing before the Subcommittee on Immigration, SJC-NARA, Sept. 13, 1995. *Newsweek*, Aug. 9, 1993.

567 **to crack down:** EMK, A Conversation with Senator Edward Kennedy on Immigration, June 9, 2006, JFKL. EMKOH-UVA. Reich to Simpson, draft letter with attached White House analysis, March 1996, WCL. Ruth Ellen Wasem, "Immigration Reform: Brief Synthesis of Issue," CRS Report, May 10, 2007. David Grable, "Personhood Under the Due Process Clause: A Constitutional Analysis of the Illegal Immigration Reform and Immigrant Responsibility Act of 1996," *Cornell Law Review*, 1998. NYT, May 3, 1996.

568 **McCain and Kennedy went:** EMKOH-UVA. EMK, A Conversaton with Senator Edward Kennedy on

Immigration, June 9, 2006, JFKL. JAF interview with Dolores Huerta. James Sasser, Esther Olavarria, Carey Parker OH, UVA. Balz and Johnson, *Battle*, 40. Clymer, *Edward M. Kennedy*, 610–12. Salter, *Luckiest Man*, 322–23. "Twelve Stories," Robertson and Camerini. Kennedy was not a knee-jerk supporter of all immigration. He was sensitive to the needs of American workers. When U.S. businesses took advantage of the H1-B visa program to hire skilled foreign workers who could be paid less than their American counterparts, Kennedy was a critic and maintained that any increase in the program be temporary. See Sperling and Reed to Clinton, Feb. 24, 1998; Reed and Kagan to Clinton, March 13, 1998; Kagan and Katzen to DPC/NEC Principals, March 30, 1998, WCL. "Brief History of Comprehensive Immigration Reform Efforts in the 109th and 110th Congresses to Inform Policy Discussions in the 113th Congress," Congressional Research Service report, Feb. 27, 2013. Marc R. Rosenblum, "U.S. Immigration Policy Since 9/11: Understanding the Stalemate over Comprehensive Immigration Reform," Migration Policy Institute, Aug. 2011.

568 **clash like rams:** On McCain and Kennedy see Salter, *Luckiest Man*, 109–10, 236, 287, 341. Over time, Kennedy and McCain became good friends, and EMK was once chosen by Senate Democrats to approach the notoriously independent McCain and see if he might switch parties. McCain declined. The two also shared respect for national service, and McCain worked with EMK to try to boost the size of the Clinton-era program Ameri-Corps.

569 **After leaving office:** Bush, *Decision Points*, 304–6. EMKOH-UVA. President Bush Addresses the Nation on Immigration Reform, May 15, 2006, George W. Bush Presidential Library. *Time*, April 7, 2006. NYT, April 12, 2006. Salter, *Luckiest Man*, 322–23. "Twelve Stories," Robertson and Camerini. Rosenblum, "Stalemate."

571 **rank political cowardice:** JAF interview with Trent Lott, Victoria Reggie Kennedy. EMKOH-UVA. John McCain, Esther Olavarria OH, UVA. Bush, *Decision Points*, 304–6. Lott and Daschle, *Crisis Point*, 188–91. WP, June 29, 2007. NYT, May 19, June 9, June 26, 2007. Bush statement, President Bush Disappointed by Congress's Failure to Act on Comprehensive Immigration Reform, June 28, 2007, George W. Bush Presidential Library. Reid was "scared" to give a victory to the Republicans and contended that "We need the issue," said Kennedy; see EMK, A Conversation with Senator Edward Kennedy on Immigration, June 9, 2006, JFKL. "Twelve Stories," Robertson and Camerini. Rosenblum, "Stalemate." See also Graham, *Home Front*, chapter 9, "Illegal Immigration: Punishment or Amnesty?"

571 **immigrants in New Bedford:** William Cohen interview, HJ-UW. "Twelve Stories," Robertson and Camerini.

572 **Roberts and Alito were:** For accounts of the continued politicization of the Supreme Court, see Hulse, *Confirmation Bias*, and Marcus, *Supreme Ambition*.

572 **"has to be our continuum"**: EMK diary excerpt, July 21, 2005, Blattner collection, Judicial Nominations II, Feb. 12, 2007.

574 **were not "partisan hacks"**: EMK diary excerpt, Nov. 15, 2005; Remarks of Senator Edward M. Kennedy on Repairing the Supreme Court Nominations Process, made to the Alliance for Justice, Feb. 1, 2007, both Blattner collection, Judicial Nominations II, Feb. 12, 2007. WP, Sept. 13, 2021. Alito was the author of a majority opinion, overturning Roe *v. Wade*, which leaked from the Supreme Court in the spring of 2022.

574 **"the wonderful daffodils"**: EMK diary excerpt, May 18, 2005, Blattner collection, Judicial Nominations II, Feb. 12, 2007.

Thirty-Two: The Fires of Sunset

575 **his seventy-fifth birthday:** JAF interview with Victoria Reggie Kennedy. NYT, May 17, 2008.

576 **father was infuriated:** Kennedy and Fried, *Common Struggle*, 1–5, 200–202, 265. NYT, May 5, Sept. 19, 2006. Edward Kennedy Jr., Kara Kennedy, Patrick Kennedy, Victoria Reggie Kennedy OH, UVA.

576 **"all on his back":** Lawford, *Symptoms*, 379–81. Kennedy and Fried, *Common Struggle*, 77–78, 278. See also John Culver OH, UVA. The family motorboat on the Cape was christened the *Grande Fromage*. House Speaker Nancy Pelosi called him "Senator." Not "the senator" but as in, "Senator thinks the strategy is sound." Nancy Pelosi OH, UVA.

577 **Barack Obama, Joseph Biden:** JAF interviews with David Axelrod, Stephanie Cutter, Victoria Reggie Kennedy, Robert Shrum, Christopher Dodd. Axelrod, *Believer*. Ken Feinberg, Michael Dukakis OH, UVA.

578 **an unlikely partnership:** When Kennedy convened a "workhorse group" of legislative aides, activists, and lobbyists in the fall of 2008, they considered three avenues of reform: Constitution Avenue, a single-payer system; Independence Avenue, a minimal approach; and Massachusetts Avenue, a replica of Romneycare. See John E. McDonough, *Inside*, 36–43. Barry R. Furrow, "Health Reform and Ted Kennedy: The Art of Politics . . . and Persistence," *Journal of Legislation and Public Policy*, New York University, May 1, 2011.

578 **tackle the issue:** Thomas Stemberg, the founder of Staples Inc., and a longtime Romney business associate, suggested to Romney that the savings in emergency room care of the uninsured justified the effort on economic as well as political grounds: "Mitt, if you really want to do a service to the people . . . you should find a way of getting health care coverage to them." See Brian C. Mooney, "Romney and Health Care: In the Thick of History," BG, May 30, 2011, the lead story in a multipart series on Romney and Romneycare. See also Brill, *Bitter Pill*, 31–36.

579 **of personal responsibility:** Romney was supported, and influenced, by the work of the conservative and then-respected Heritage Foundation. Mooney, BG, May 30, 2011.

The individual mandate was not especially favored by liberals because they disliked the proposed enforcement measures and feared they might encourage businesses to drop health insurance from employee benefits. See "Hillary Rodham Clinton's Briefing Book for Congressional Testimony Relating to Health Care," 1993–94; Hart to Clinton, Oct. 27, 1993, WCL. John Holahan, Colin Winterbottom, Sheila Zedlewski, "The Distributional Effects of Employer and Individual Health Insurance Mandates: A Summary," The Urban Institute, July 1994, Dole-KU. McDonough to EMK, "Review of Health Reform Efforts in Massachusetts," Feb. 20, 1993, SLC-NARA.

579 **"perhaps for the rest":** JAF interview with David Nexon. Mooney, BG, May 30, 2011. Romneycare has been adjusted via court challenges, political tinkering, and the passage of the Affordable Care Act. Through all, it has been judged to be successful. Health care costs remained high, but six years after its passage, 97 percent of working-age adults, and virtually every child in the state, was covered by some form of health insurance. An artist included the law in Romney's official portrait, which hangs in the State House. Charles Pierce, "Life Under Romneycare," *Esquire*, Oct. 2012. Barbara Anthony, "Beyond Obamacare: Lessons from Massachusetts," Harvard Kennedy School working paper No. 82, Sept. 2017. BG, Jan. 28, 2020. Ryan Lizza, "Romney's Dilemma," TNY, May 30, 2011. *Time*, Feb. 26, 2009. NYT, May 13, 2003. McDonough, *Inside*, 24, 35. Michael Myers, James Mongan OH, UVA.

580 **turned to Obama:** JAF interview with Stephanie Cutter. EMK interview transcript, April 21, 2008, HJ-UW. Balz and Johnson, *Battle*, 170. EMK and Caroline Kennedy interviews, *Time*, Jan. 28, 2008.

581 **"time chooses you":** Obama, *Promised*, 69. EMK interview transcript, April 21, 2008, HJ-UW. Balz and Johnson, *Battle*, 171.

582 **Kennedy's great cause:** Balz et al., *Landmark*, 11–12. Obama, *Promised*, 86–88, 378–79. Brill, *Bitter Pill*, 45–47. Politico.com, Sept. 22, 2013. Jonathan Cohn, "How They Did It," TNR, May 21, 2010. "What's she not telling you about her health care plan?" an Obama television ad asked. "It forces everyone to buy insurance, even if you can't afford it, and you pay a penalty if you don't." See McDonough, *Inside*, 60.

582 **vow of intent:** JAF interviews with David Axelrod, Stephanie Cutter, Victoria Reggie Kennedy, Christopher Dodd, Chris Jennings, David Nexon. There was no explicit quid pro quo struck in the Kennedy-Obama phone call, said Axelrod and Victoria Reggie Kennedy, but there was an understanding. EMK interview transcript, April 21, 2008, HJ-UW. Balz and Johnson, *Battle*, 177. "Obama's Deal," *Frontline*, PBS, April 13, 2020.

583 **"I feel change":** NYT, Jan. 27, 28, 2008. *Time*, Jan. 28, 2008.

583 **series of taunts and jeers:** JAF interviews with David Axelrod, Robert Shrum, Stephanie Cutter, Chris Jennings. EMK interview transcript, April 21, 2008, HJ-UW. Balz to Johnson, "Kennedy-Obama" chronology, June 14, 2008, HJ-UW. Balz and Johnson, *Battle*, 173. Greg Craig, Thomas Daschle OH, UVA. For the Clinton camp's approach, see Heilemann and Halperin, *Game Change*, 161, 163, 185, 197–99, 207–11, 214, 218.

584 **belling the cat:** EMK interview transcript, April 21, 2008, HJ-UW.

584 **chair, and suffered a seizure:** JAF interviews with Victoria Reggie Kennedy, David Nasaw. Kennedy and Fried, *Common Struggle*, 283. NYT, Feb. 2, May 17, June 3, 2008. English et al., *Last Lion*. Phil Johnston, Lawrence Horowitz, BM, Nov. 30, 2009.

585 **"never felt sorry":** JAF interview with Victoria Reggie Kennedy.

585 **"Where's my bill?":** David Bowen OH in Abrams, *Obama*, 113.

585 **way of dying:** JAF interview with Victoria Reggie Kennedy, Christopher Dodd. Barbara Souliotis OH, UVA. NYT, July 9, 10, 2008, Feb. 21, Dec. 23, 2009. Barnicle, *Time*, Aug. 26, 2009. Lawrence Horowitz, BM, Nov. 30, 2009.

586 **travel to Denver:** JAF interviews with Robert Shrum, Victoria Reggie Kennedy. Edward M. Kennedy Jr., Kara Kennedy, Patrick Kennedy OH, UVA. Curran Raclin, Barbara Souliotis OH, UVA. NYT, Aug. 26, 2008. *Denver Post*, Aug. 25, 2008. Author's notes, 2008 Democratic National Convention. Kennedy and Fried, *Common Struggle*, 289–90.

587 **"Call the roll!":** JAF interview with Victoria Reggie Kennedy.

587 **lines of Romneycare:** JAF interview with Victoria Reggie Kennedy. Kennedy explored the idea of a bipartisan deal, like those he had reached with Hatch and other Republicans over the years, but with low expectations. Republicans would later blame his failing health for the partisan rancor that followed, but Kennedy had read his adversaries well. The GOP was determined to wreck the Democratic presidency, as Minority Leader Mitch McConnell admitted to *National Journal* correspondent Major Garrett in October 2010: "The single most important thing we want to achieve is for President Obama to be a one-term president." Another Republican senator, Jim DeMint of South Carolina, told conservative activists, "If we're able to stop Obama on this, it will be his Waterloo. It will break him."
Kennedy urged Baucus and the White House to prepare to use the budget reconciliation process, if necessary, to skirt a Republican filibuster. Obama and Baucus tried for months to get an influential Republican, like the Finance Committee's ranking Republican, Senator Charles Grassley of Iowa, to join them. In November 2008, Baucus called a bipartisan meeting in Kennedy's hideaway office, with Dodd and Kennedy and top Republicans, to open negotiations. The group grew to include Hatch and other GOP leaders. But the Tea Party rebellion of 2009 thoroughly intimidated the Republican senators, and ended any hope for a compromise. See McDonough, *Inside*, 66–69, 82, and Obama, *Promised*, 400–401.

588 **blueprint for the Affordable Care Act:** Obama would recall, "Fortunately we had a model to work with, one that, ironically, had grown out of a partnership between Ted Kennedy and . . . Mitt Romney." Kennedy "despite his reputation as a wide-eyed liberal was ever practical" and "understood that trying to dismantle the existing system and replace it with an entirely new one would be not only a po-

litical nonstarter but hugely disruptive economically." See Obama, *Promised*, 382–83. NYT, March 31, 2009. Cohn, "How They Did It," TNR, May 21, 2010.

588 **"I'm still fighting":** JAF interviews with David Axelrod, Joseph Califano, Peter Hart. Author's notes, Barack Obama inauguration ceremony. *Time*, Jan. 20, 2009. NYT, Feb. 21, 2009. Kennedy and Fried, *Common Struggle*, 298.

589 **"This is the time, Mr. President":** JAF interview with Victoria Reggie Kennedy. Obama, *Promised*, 374–75.

589 **"better not lose":** Obama, *Promised*, 378. See also Peter Baker, "The Limits of Rahmism," NYT, March 8, 2010, and Axelrod, *Believer*, 371–76. At one meeting, after Axelrod had presented Obama with some gloomy survey research, the president replied, "I'm sure you're right. But I just came back from Green Bay, Wisconsin. I met a woman there who was thirty-five years old, had a job, a husband and two children, and health insurance. But she also has stage three breast cancer, and now she's hit her lifetime caps, so her insurance company is refusing to pay her bills, and she's terrified that she's going to die and leave her family bankrupt. That's not the country we believe in. So let's just keep fighting."

589 **Even hardened politicians:** Carey Parker OH, UVA. Nicholas Lemann, "Kennedy Care," TNY, Sept. 7, 2009. "The passage of a substantive health-care bill would be immensely to Obama's credit, but he would not be its only begetter," Lemann wrote. "If he winds up being able to shift the trajectory of American politics, it will be because the country was ready. Ted Kennedy spent a career making sure it would be."

589 **something for Ted:** JAF interviews with David Axelrod, David Nexon. Nancy Pelosi OH, UVA. Furrow, "Health Reform and Ted Kennedy." "Obama's Deal," *Frontline*, PBS, April 13, 2020. Politico.com, Sept. 22, 2010. Axelrod, *Believer*. Cohn, "How They Did It," TNR, May 21, 2010.

590 **In May, he started:** JAF interviews with Christopher Dodd, Chris Jennings. Brill, *Bitter Pill*, 373. Kennedy and Fried, *Common Struggle*, 293–94. Lawrence Horowitz, BM, Nov. 30, 2009.

590 **one last card:** JAF interview with Victoria Reggie Kennedy. Caroline Raclin OH, UVA. Kennedy to Obama, May 12, 2009, obamawhitehouse.archives .gov.

591 **thrilled, and proud:** JAF interviews with Christopher Dodd, Victoria Reggie Kennedy, Robert Shrum. Caroline Raclin, Edward M. Kennedy Jr., Kara Kennedy, Patrick Kennedy, OH, UVA. Young quote from John Culver OH, UVA. NYT, July 16, 2009. Kennedy and Fried, *Common Struggle*, 299, 303. EMK to Patrick, Murray, and DeLeo, July 2, 2009, Boston.com. EMK to Pope Benedict XVI, BG, Aug. 30, 2009.

593 **"fell a burden":** JAF interviews with Ranny Cooper, Stephanie Cutter. Barbara Souliotis, John Culver, Melody Miller OH, UVA. "Eulogy at the Funeral Service for Senator Edward M. Kennedy in Boston, Massachusetts, August 29, 2009," UCSB. The name of the Wordsworth poem was "Character of the Happy Warrior."

Bibliography

Abraham, Henry J. *Freedom and the Court: Civil Rights and Liberties in the United States.* New York: Oxford University Press, 1972.
———. *Justices, Presidents, and Senators: A History of the U.S. Supreme Court Appointments from Washington to Bush II.* Lanham, MD: Rowman & Littlefield, 2007.
Abrams, Brian. *Obama: An Oral History 2009–2017.* New York: Little A, 2018.
Aitken, Jonathan. *Charles W. Colson: A Life Redeemed.* New York: Crown, 2010.
———. *Nixon: A Life.* Washington, DC: Regnery, 1993.
Alden, Edward. *Failure to Adjust: How Americans Got Left Behind in the Global Economy.* Lanham, MD: Rowman & Littlefield, 2017.
Alford, Mimi. *Once Upon a Secret: My Affair with President John F. Kennedy and Its Aftermath.* New York: Random House, 2012.
Allison, William T. *The Tet Offensive: A Brief History with Documents.* New York: Routledge, 2008.
Alter, Jonathan. *His Very Best: Jimmy Carter, a Life.* New York: Simon & Schuster, 2020.
Alterman, Eric. *The Cause: The Fight for American Liberalism from Franklin Roosevelt to Barack Obama.* New York: Penguin, 2013.
Altman, Stuart, and David Shactman. *Power, Politics, and Universal Health Care: The Inside Story of a Century-Long Battle.* Amherst, NY: Prometheus, 2011.
Ambrose, Stephen. *Nixon.* Vol. 2, *The Triumph of a Politician.* New York: Simon & Schuster, 1989.
———. *Nixon.* Vol. 3, *Ruin and Recovery.* New York: Simon & Schuster, 1991.
Amory, Cleveland. *The Proper Bostonians.* New York: E. P. Dutton, 1947.
Andelic, Patrick. *Donkey Work: Congressional Democrats in Conservative America, 1974–1994.* Lawrence: University Press of Kansas, 2019.
Anderson, Patrick. *Electing Jimmy Carter: The Campaign of 1976.* Baton Rouge: Louisiana State University Press, 1994.
Andriote, John-Manuel. *Victory Deferred: How AIDS Changed Gay Life in America.* Chicago: University of Chicago Press, 1999.
Annis, James Lee, Jr. *Big Jim Eastland: The Godfather of Mississippi.* Jackson: University Press of Mississippi, 2016.
———. *Howard Baker: Conciliator in an Age of Crisis.* Lanham, MD: Madison Books, 1995.
Arenberg, Richard A. *Congressional Procedure: A Practical Guide to the Legislative Process in the U.S. Congress; The House of Representatives and Senate Explained.* Alexandria, VA: TheCapitol.Net, 2018.
Arenberg, Richard A., and Robert B. Dove. *Defending the Filibuster: The Soul of the Senate.* Bloomington: Indiana University Press, 2012.
Ashby, LeRoy, and Rod Gramer. *Fighting the Odds: The Life of Senator Frank Church.* Pullman: Washington State University Press, 1994.
Axelrod, David. *Believer: My Forty Years in Politics.* New York: Penguin Press, 2015.
Bai, Matt. *All The Truth Is Out: The Week Politics Went Tabloid.* New York: Vintage, 2014.
Bailey, Stephen. *The New Congress.* New York: St. Martin's Press, 1966.
Baker, Bobby, with Larry L. King. *Wheeling and Dealing: Confessions of a Capitol Hill Operator.* New York: Norton, 1980.
Baker, Peter. *The Breach: Inside the Impeachment and Trial of William Jefferson Clinton.* New York: Scribner, 2000.
Baker, Richard A. *200 Notable Days: Senate Stories, 1787 to 2002.* Washington, DC: U.S. Government Printing Office, 2006.
Baker, Richard A., and Roger H. Davidson, eds. *First Among Equals: Outstanding Senate Leaders of the Twentieth Century.* Washington, DC: Congressional Quarterly, 1991.
Baker, Russell. *The Good Times.* New York: Penguin, 1989.
Balaban, John. *Remembering Heaven's Face: A Story of Rescue in Wartime Vietnam.* Athens: University of Georgia Press, 1991.
Ball, George. *The Past Has Another Pattern: Memoirs.* New York: Norton, 1982.

Balz, Dan, and Ronald Brownstein. *Storming the Gates: Protest Politics and the Republican Revival.* Boston: Little, Brown, 1996.

Balz, Dan, and Haynes Johnson. *The Battle for America 2008: The Story of an Extraordinary Election.* New York: Viking, 2009.

Balz, Dan, Ceci Connolly, and the staff of *The Washington Post. Landmark: The Inside Story of America's New Health-Care Law and What It Means for Us All.* New York: PublicAffairs, 2010.

Barlett, Donald L., and James B. Steele. *America: What Went Wrong?* Kansas City, MO: Andrews & McMeel, 1992.

———. *America: Who Stole the Dream?* Kansas City, MO: Andrews & McMeel, 1996.

Barone, Michael, and Grant Ujifusa. *The Almanac of American Politics.* Washington, DC: *National Journal,* various editions.

Barry, John M. *The Ambition and the Power: The Fall of Jim Wright; A True Story of Washington.* New York: Viking, 1989.

Bass, Gary. *The Blood Telegram: Nixon, Kissinger, and a Forgotten Genocide.* New York: Knopf, 2013.

Beatty, James. *The Rascal King: The Life and Times of James Michael Curley (1878–1958).* Reading, MA: Addison-Wesley, 1992.

Beauchamp, Cari. *Joseph P. Kennedy Presents: His Hollywood Years.* New York: Knopf, 2009.

Beran, Michael Knox. *The Last Patrician: Bobby Kennedy and the End of American Aristocracy.* New York: St. Martin's Press, 1998.

Bernstein, Carl, and Bob Woodward. *All the President's Men.* New York: Simon & Schuster, 1974.

Bernstein, Irving. *Guns or Butter: The Presidency of Lyndon Johnson.* New York: Oxford University Press, 1996.

———. *Promises Kept: John F. Kennedy's New Frontier.* New York: Oxford University Press, 1991.

Beschloss, Michael. *Kennedy and Roosevelt: The Uneasy Alliance.* New York: Norton, 1980.

———. *Reaching for Glory: Lyndon Johnson's Secret White House Tapes, 1964–1965.* New York: Simon & Schuster, 2001.

———. *Taking Charge: The Johnson White House Tapes, 1963–1964.* New York: Simon & Schuster, 1997.

Beschloss, Michael, ed. *Jacqueline Kennedy: Historic Conversations on Life with John F. Kennedy.* New York: Hyperion, 2011.

Bibby, John, and Roger H. Davidson. *On Capitol Hill: Studies in the Legislative Process.* Hinsdale, IL: Dryden Press, 1972.

Bibby, John, Thomas Mann, and Norman Ornstein. *Vital Statistics on Congress, 1980.* Washington, DC: American Enterprise Institute, 1981.

Biden, Joseph. *Promises to Keep.* New York: Random House, 2007.

Binder, Sarah A., and Steven S. Smith. *"Politics or Principle?": Filibustering in the United States Senate.* Washington, DC: Brookings Institution, 1997.

Bird, Kai. *The Outlier: The Unfinished Presidency of Jimmy Carter.* New York: Crown, 2021.

Blaemire, Robert. *Birch Bayh: Making a Difference.* Bloomington: Indiana University Press, 2019.

Blair, Joan, and Clay Blair. *The Search for J.F.K.* New York: Berkley, 1976.

Blakey, George Robert. *The Plot to Kill the President.* New York: Times Books, 1981.

Blumenthal, David, and James Morone. *The Heart of Power: Health and Politics in the Oval Office.* Berkeley: University of California Press, 2009.

Bobelian, Michael. *Battle for the Marble Palace: Abe Fortas, Lyndon Johnson, Earl Warren, Richard Nixon and the Forging of the Modern Supreme Court.* Tucson, AZ: Schaffner Press, 2019.

Bohrer, John. *The Revolution of Robert Kennedy: From Power to Protest After JFK.* New York: Bloomsbury, 2017.

Boomhower, Ray E. *Robert F. Kennedy and the 1968 Indiana Primary.* Bloomington: Indiana University Press, 2008.

Boot, Max. *The Road Not Taken: Edward Lansdale and the American Tragedy in Vietnam.* New York: Liveright, 2018.

Bourne, Peter. *Jimmy Carter: A Comprehensive Biography from Pains to Post-Presidency.* New York: Scribner, 1997.

Bowden, Mark. *Guests of the Ayatollah: The Iran Hostage Crisis; The First Battle in America's War with Militant Islam.* New York: Atlantic Monthly Press, 2006.

Bowen, Michael. *The Roots of Modern Conservatism: Dewey, Taft, and the Battle for the Soul of the Republican Party.* Chapel Hill: University of North Carolina Press, 2011.

Boyle, Kevin. *The Shattering: America in the 1960s.* New York: Norton, 2021.

———. *The UAW and the Heyday of American Liberalism, 1945–1968.* Ithaca, NY: Cornell University Press, 1995.

Bradlee, Benjamin. *Conversations with Kennedy.* New York: Norton, 1975.

———. *A Good Life.* New York: Simon & Schuster, 1995.

Branch, Taylor. *At Canaan's Edge: America in the King Years, 1965–68.* New York: Simon & Schuster, 2006.

———. *The Clinton Tapes: Wrestling History with the President.* New York: Simon & Schuster, 2009.

———. *Parting the Waters: America in the King Years, 1954–63.* New York: Simon & Schuster, 1988.

———. *Pillar of Fire: America in the King Years, 1963–65.* New York: Simon & Schuster, 1998.

Brands, H. W. *Reagan: The Life.* New York: Doubleday, 2015.

Brill, Steven. *America's Bitter Pill: Money, Politics, Background Deals, and the Fight to Fix Our Broken Healthcare System.* New York: Random House, 2015.

Brinkley, Douglas. *Tour of Duty: John Kerry and the Vietnam War.* New York: William Morrow, 2004.

———. *The Unfinished Presidency: Jimmy Carter's Journey Beyond the White House.* New York: Viking, 1998.

Brinkley, Douglas, and Luke Nichter. *The Nixon Tapes, 1971–1972.* New York: Houghton Mifflin Harcourt, 2014.

———. *The Nixon Tapes, 1973.* New York: Houghton Mifflin Harcourt, 2015.

Broder, David, et al., *The Pursuit of the Presidency 1980.* New York: Washington Post/Berkley Books, 1980.

Brogan, Hugh. *Kennedy.* New York: Longman, 1996.

Bronner, Ethan. *Battle for Justice: How the Bork Nomination Shook America.* New York: Norton, 1989.

Brzezinski, Zbigniew. *Power and Principle: Memoirs of the National Security Adviser, 1977–1981.* New York: Farrar, Straus & Giroux, 1983.

Bundy, William. *A Tangled Web: The Making of Foreign Policy in the Nixon Presidency.* New York: Hill & Wang, 1998.

Burke, Richard, with William and Marilyn Hoffer. *The Senator: My Ten Years with Ted Kennedy.* New York: St. Martin's Press, 1992.

Burleigh, Nina. *A Very Private Woman: The Life and Unsolved Murder of Presidential Mistress Mary Meyer.* New York: Bantam, 1999.

Burner, David, and Thomas R. West. *The Torch Is Passed: The Kennedy Brothers and American Liberalism.* New York: Atheneum, 1984.

Burns, Arthur. *Inside the Nixon Administration: The Secret Diary of Arthur Burns.* Edited by Robert Ferrell. Lawrence: University Press of Kansas, 2010.

Burns, James MacGregor. *Edward Kennedy and the Camelot Legacy.* New York: Norton, 1976.

———. *John Kennedy: A Political Profile.* New York: Harcourt Brace, 1960.

Bush, George H. W. *All the Best, George Bush: My Life in Letters and Other Writings.* New York: Scribner, 1999.

Bush, George W. *Decision Points.* New York: Crown, 2010.

Bush, Laura. *Spoken from the Heart.* New York: Scribner, 2010.

Byrd, Robert. *The Senate, 1789–1989.* 4 vols. Washington, DC: U.S. Government Printing Office, 1989–1994. Vols. 1 and 2, *Addresses on the History of the United States Senate*; Vol. 3, *Classic Speeches, 1830–1993*; Vol. 4, *Historical Statistics, 1789–1992.*

Califano, Joseph A., Jr. *Governing America: An Insider's Report from the White House and the Cabinet.* New York: Simon & Schuster, 1981.

———. *Inside: A Public and Private Life.* New York: PublicAffairs, 2005.

Campbell, Karl E. *Senator Sam Ervin, Last of the Founding Fathers.* Chapel Hill: University of North Carolina Press, 2007.

Cannon, James. *Time and Chance: Gerald Ford's Appointment with History.* New York: HarperCollins, 1994.

Cannon, Lou. *President Reagan: The Role of a Lifetime.* New York: Simon & Schuster, 1991.

Caro, Robert. *Master of the Senate: The Years of Lyndon Johnson.* New York: Knopf, 2002.

———. *Means of Ascent: The Years of Lyndon Johnson.* New York: Knopf, 1990.

———. *The Passage of Power: The Years of Lyndon Johnson.* New York: Knopf, 2012.

Carroll, James. *One of Ourselves: John Fitzgerald Kennedy in Ireland.* Bennington, VT: Images from the Past, 2003.

Carter, Dan. *From George Wallace to Newt Gingrich: Race in the Conservative Counterrevolution, 1963–1994.* Baton Rouge: Louisiana State University Press, 1996.

———. *The Politics of Rage: George Wallace, the Origins of the New Conservatism and the Transformation of American Politics.* Baton Rouge: Louisiana State University Press, 1995.

Carter, Jimmy. *White House Diary.* New York: Farrar, Straus & Giroux, 2010.

Casey, Shaun. *The Making of a Catholic President: Kennedy vs. Nixon 1960.* New York: Oxford University Press, 2009.

Chafe, William. *Never Stop Running: Allard Lowenstein and the Struggle to Save American Liberalism.* New York: Basic Books, 1993.

Chayes, Abram, and Jerome B. Wiesner, eds. *ABM: An Evaluation of the Decision to Deploy an Anti-Ballistic Missile System.* Introduction by Edward M. Kennedy. New York: Harper & Row, 1969.

Chellis, Marcia. *Living with the Kennedys: The Joan Kennedy Story.* New York: Simon & Schuster, 1985.

Chester, Lewis, Godfrey Hodgson, and Bruce Page. *An American Melodrama: The Presidential Campaign of 1968.* New York: Viking, 1969.

Chin, Gabriel, and Rose Cuison Villazor. *The Immigration and Nationality Act of 1965: Legislating a New America.* New York: Cambridge University Press, 2015.

Clapp, Charles. *The Congressman: His Work as He Sees It.* Washington, DC: Brookings Institution, 1963.

Clarke, Thurston. *JFK's Last Hundred Days: The Transformation of a Man and the Emergence of a Great President.* New York: Penguin, 2013.

———. *The Last Campaign: Robert F. Kennedy and 82 Days That Inspired America.* New York: Henry Holt, 2008.

Clendinen, Dudley, and Adam Nagourney. *Out for Good: The Struggle to Build a Gay Rights Movement in America.* New York: Simon & Schuster, 1999.

Clifford, Clark, with Richard Holbrooke. *Counsel to the President: A Memoir.* New York: Random House, 1991.

Clinch, Nancy Gager. *The Kennedy Neurosis: A Psychological Portrait of a Political Dynasty.* New York: Grosset & Dunlap, 1973.

Clinton, Bill. *My Life.* New York: Knopf, 2004.

Clodfelter, Micheal. *Vietnam in Military Statistics: A History of the Indochina Wars, 1772–1991.* Jefferson, NC: McFarland, 1995.

Clymer, Adam. *Drawing the Line at the Big Ditch: The Panama Canal Treaties and the Rise of the Right.* Lawrence: University Press of Kansas, 2008.

———. *Edward M. Kennedy: A Biography.* New York: Morrow, 1999.

Cohn, Jonathan. *The Ten Year War: Obamacare and the Unfinished Crusade for Universal Coverage.* New York: St. Martin's Press, 2021.

Coll, Stephen. *Ghost Wars: The Secret History of the CIA, Afghanistan, and Bin Laden, from the Soviet Invasion to September 10, 2001.* New York: Penguin Press, 2004.

Collier, Peter, and David Horowitz. *The Kennedys: An American Drama.* New York: Summit Books, 1984.

Coogan, Tim Pat. *The IRA.* London: HarperCollins, 1987.

———. *The Troubles: Ireland's Ordeal and the Search for Peace*. London: Hutchinson, 1995.

Corbin, David A. *The Last Great Senator: Robert C. Byrd's Encounters with Eleven U.S. Presidents*. Washington, DC: Potomac Books, 2012.

Cramer, Richard Ben. *What It Takes: The Way to the White House*. New York: Random House, 1992.

Cullen, Kevin, and Shelley Murphy. *Whitey Bulger: America's Most Wanted Gangster and the Manhunt That Brought Him to Justice*. New York: Norton, 2013.

Curley, James Michael. *I'd Do It All Again: A Record of All My Uproarious Years*. Englewood Cliffs, NJ: Prentice Hall, 1957.

Cutler, John Henry. *"Honey Fitz": Three Steps to the White House; The Life and Times of John F. (Honey Fitz) Fitzgerald*. Indianapolis: Bobbs-Merrill, 1962.

Dallas, Rita, with Jeanira Ratcliffe. *The Kennedy Case*. New York: G. P. Putnam's Sons, 1973.

Dallek, Robert. *Camelot's Court: Inside the Kennedy White House*. New York: HarperCollins, 2013.

———. *Flawed Giant: Lyndon Johnson and His Times, 1961–1973*. New York: Oxford University Press, 1998.

———. *An Unfinished Life: John F. Kennedy, 1917–1963*. New York: Little, Brown, 2003.

Damore, Leo. *The Cape Cod Years of John Fitzgerald Kennedy*. New York: Four Walls Eight Windows, 1993.

———. *Senatorial Privilege: The Chappaquiddick Cover-Up*. New York: Regnery Gateway, 1988.

David, Lester. *Good Ted, Bad Ted: The Two Faces of Edward M. Kennedy*. Secaucus, NJ: Carol Publishing, 1993.

———. *Joan—The Reluctant Kennedy: A Biographical Profile*. New York: Funk & Wagnalls, 1974.

———. *Ted Kennedy: Triumphs and Tragedies*. New York: Grosset & Dunlap, 1972.

Davidson, Roger, and Walter Oleszek. *Congress and Its Members*. Washington DC: CQ Press, 1990.

Davis, John. *The Kennedys: Dynasty and Disaster*. New York: McGraw-Hill, 1984.

Davis, Lennard. *Enabling Acts: The Hidden Story of How the Americans with Disabilities Act Gave the Largest US Minority Its Rights*. Boston: Beacon Press, 2015.

Derthick, Martha, and Paul Quirk. *The Politics of Deregulation*. Washington, DC: Brookings Institution, 2001.

Didion, Joan. *The White Album*. New York: Simon & Schuster, 1979.

Dinneen, Joseph. *The Kennedy Family*. Boston: Little, Brown, 1959.

Dobrynin, Anatoly. *In Confidence: Moscow's Ambassador to America's Six Cold War Presidents*. New York: Times Books, 1995.

Doherty, Gerard. *They Were My Friends—Jack, Bob and Ted, My Life in and out of Politics*. West Wareham, MA: Omni Publishing, 2017.

Donaldson, Gary. *The First Modern Campaign: Kennedy, Nixon and the Election of 1960*. Lanham, MD: Rowman & Littlefield, 2007.

Donovan, Robert. *PT-109: John F. Kennedy in World War II*. New York: McGraw-Hill, 1961.

Downie, Leonard, Jr. *The New Muckrakers*. New York: New American Library, 1976.

Doyle, James. *Not Above the Law: The Battles of Watergate Prosecutors Cox and Jaworski*. New York: William Morrow, 1977.

Draper, Robert. *To Start a War: How the Bush Administration Took America into Iraq*. New York: Penguin Press, 2020.

Drew, Elizabeth. *On the Edge: The Clinton Presidency*. New York: Simon & Schuster, 1994.

———. *Portrait of an Election: The 1980 Presidential Campaign*. New York: Simon & Schuster, 1981

———. *Showdown: The Struggle Between the Gingrich Congress and the Clinton White House*. New York: Simon & Schuster, 1997.

Duncliffe, William. *The Life and Times of Joseph P. Kennedy*. New York: Macfadden-Bartell, 1965.

Edsall, Thomas, and Mary Edsall. *Chain Reaction: The Impact of Race, Rights and Taxes on American Politics*. New York: Norton, 1991.

Ehrlichman, John. *Witness to Power: The Nixon Years*. New York: Simon & Schuster, 1982.

Eizenstat, Stuart E. *President Carter: The White House Years*. New York: Thomas Dunne, 2018.

Ellsberg, Daniel. *Secrets: A Memoir of Vietnam and the Pentagon Papers*. New York: Penguin, 2003.

Emery, Fred. *Watergate: The Corruption of American Politics and the Fall of Richard Nixon*. New York: Times Books, 1994.

English, Bella, et al. *Last Lion: The Fall and Rise of Ted Kennedy*. By the Team at *The Boston Globe*. Edited by Peter Canellos. New York: Simon & Schuster, 2009.

Erie, Steven. *Rainbow's End: Irish Americans and the Dilemmas of Urban Machine Politics, 1840–1985*. Berkeley: University of California Press, 1988.

Ervin, Sam. *The Whole Truth: The Watergate Conspiracy*. New York: Random House, 1980.

Evans, C. Lawrence. *Leadership in Committee: A Comparative Analysis of Leadership Behavior in the U.S. Senate*. Ann Arbor: University of Michigan Press, 1991.

Evans, Rowland, and Robert Novak. *Lyndon B. Johnson: The Exercise of Power*. New York: New American Library, 1966.

Exner, Judith, and Ovid Demaris. *My Story*. New York: Grove Press, 1977.

Farrell, John A. *Richard Nixon: The Life*. New York: Doubleday, 2017.

———. *Tip O'Neill and the Democratic Century*. New York: Little, Brown, 2001.

Fay, Paul. *The Pleasure of His Company*. New York: Harper & Row, 1966.

Feeney, Mark. *Nixon at the Movies: A Book About Belief*. Chicago: University of Chicago Press, 2004.

Fenno, Richard. *The Making of a Senator: Dan Quayle*. Washington, DC: Congressional Quarterly Press, 1989.

———. *Senators on the Campaign Trail: The Politics of Representation*. Norman: University of Oklahoma Press, 1996.

Ferguson, Niall. *Kissinger*. Vol. 1, *1923–1968: The Idealist*. New York: Penguin, 2015.

Fite, Gilbert C. *Richard B. Russell, Jr., Senator from Georgia*. Chapel Hill: University of North Carolina Press, 1991.

Fitzpatrick, Maurice. *John Hume in America: From Derry to DC*. Newbridge: Irish Academic Press, 2017.
Formisano, Ronald P. *Boston Against Busing: Race, Class and Ethnicity in the 1960s and 1970s*. Chapel Hill: University of North Carolina Press, 1991.
Foster, R. F. *Modern Ireland: 1600–1972*. London: Allen Lane, 1988.
France, David. *How to Survive a Plague: The Inside Story of How Citizens and Science Tamed AIDS*. New York: Knopf, 2016.
Frank, Barney. *Frank: A Life in Politics from the Great Society to Same-Sex Marriage*. New York: Farrar, Straus & Giroux, 2015.
———. *Speaking Frankly: What's Wrong with the Democrats and How to Fix It*. New York: Times Books, 1992.
Frank, John P. *Clement Haynsworth, the Senate, and the Supreme Court*. Charlottesville: University Press of Virginia, 1991.
Friedman, Leon, and William Levantrosser. *Cold War Patriot and Statesman: Richard Nixon*. Westport, CT: Greenwood Press, 1993.
Frum, David. *How We Got Here: The 70's; The Decade That Brought You Modern Life—For Better or Worse*. New York: Basic Books, 2000.
Gabler, Neal. *Catching the Wind: Edward Kennedy and the Liberal Hour*. New York: Crown, 2020.
Gaddis, John Lewis. *The Cold War: A New History*. New York: Penguin, 2005.
———. *George F. Kennan: An American Life*. New York: Penguin, 2011.
———. *Strategies of Containment: A Critical Appraisal of American National Security Policy During the Cold War*. New York: Oxford University Press, 2005 edition.
Galbraith, John Kenneth. *Name-Dropping: From FDR On*. Boston: Houghton Mifflin, 1999.
Gargan, Joseph. Unpublished memoirs.
Garment, Leonard. *Crazy Rhythm: From Brooklyn and Jazz to Nixon's White House, Watergate, and Beyond*. New York: Times Books, 1997.
Garrow, David. *Protest at Selma: Martin Luther King, Jr. and the Voting Rights Act of 1965*. New Haven, CT: Yale University Press, 1978.
Gates, Robert. *From the Shadows: The Ultimate Insider's Story of Five Presidents and How They Won the Cold War*. New York: Simon & Schuster, 1996.
Gellman, Irwin. *Campaign of the Century: Kennedy, Nixon and the Election of 1960*. New Haven, CT: Yale University Press, 2022.
Germond, Jack W., and Jules Witcover. *Blue Smoke and Mirrors: How Reagan Won and Why Carter Lost the Election of 1980*. New York: Viking, 1981.
———. *Wake Us When It's Over: Presidential Politics of 1984*. New York: Macmillan, 1985.
Gibbons, William Conrad. *The U.S. Government and the Vietnam War*. Vols. I–IV. Committee on Foreign Relations, U.S. Senate, 1984. Unpublished Vol. V, courtesy of the Gibbons estate.
Giglio, James. *The Presidency of John F. Kennedy*. Lawrence: University Press of Kansas, 1991.
Gillon, Steven M. *The Democrats' Dilemma: Walter F. Mondale and the Liberal Legacy*. New York: Columbia University Press, 1992.
———. *The Pact: Bill Clinton, Newt Gingrich, and the Rivalry That Defined a Generation*. New York: Oxford University Press, 2008.
Gitenstein, Mark. *Matters of Principle: An Insider's Account of America's Rejection of Robert Bork's Nomination to the Supreme Court*. New York: Simon & Schuster, 1992.
Gitlin, Todd. *The Sixties: Years of Hope, Days of Rage*. New York: Bantam, 1987.
Gjelten, Tom. *A Nation of Nations: A Great American Immigration Story*. New York: Simon & Schuster, 2015.
Glad, Betty. *An Outsider in the White House: Jimmy Carter, His Advisors, and the Making of American Foreign Policy*. Ithaca, NY: Cornell University Press, 2009.
Glazer, Nathan, and Daniel P. Moynihan. *Beyond the Melting Pot: The Negroes, Puerto Ricans, Jews, Italians and Irish of New York City*. Cambridge, MA: MIT Press, 1963.
Goldman, Peter, and Tony Fuller. *The Quest for the Presidency 1984*. New York: Bantam, 1985.
Goodwin, Doris Kearns. *The Fitzgeralds and the Kennedys: An American Saga*. New York: Simon & Schuster, 1987.
———. *Lyndon Johnson and the American Dream. 1976*. New York: St. Martin's Press, 1991.
Goodwin, Richard. *Remembering America: A Voice from the Sixties*. Boston: Little, Brown, 1988.
Gordon, Colin. *Dead on Arrival: The Politics of Health Care in Twentieth-Century America*. Princeton, NJ: Princeton University Press, 2003.
Gordon, Robert J. *The Rise and Fall of American Growth*. Princeton, NJ: Princeton University Press, 2016.
Gormley, Ken. *Archibald Cox: Conscience of a Nation*. Reading, MA: Addison-Wesley, 1997.
———. *The Death of American Virtue: Clinton vs. Starr*. New York: Crown, 2010.
Gould, Lewis. *The Most Exclusive Club: A History of the Modern United States Senate*. New York: Basic Books, 2009.
Graham, John. *Bush on the Home Front: Domestic Policy Triumphs and Setbacks*. Bloomington: Indiana University Press, 2010.
Gray, Ed, and L. Patrick Gray. *In Nixon's Web: A Year in the Crosshairs of Watergate*. New York: Times Books, 2008.
Greenberg, Stanley. *Middle Class Dreams: The Politics and Power of the New American Majority*. New York: Times Books, 1995.
Greenburg, Jan Crawford. *Supreme Conflict: The Inside Story of the Struggle for Control of the United States Supreme Court*. New York: Penguin, 2007.
Greenfield, Meg. *Washington*. New York: PublicAffairs, 2001.

Greider, William. *Secrets of the Temple: How the Federal Reserve Runs the Country.* New York: Simon & Schuster, 1987.
———. *Who Will Tell the People: The Betrayal of American Democracy.* New York: Simon & Schuster, 1992.
Guthman, Edwin O. *We Band of Brothers: A Memoir of Robert F. Kennedy.* New York: Harper & Row, 1971.
Guthman, Edwin O., and C. Richard Allen, eds. *RFK: Collected Speeches.* New York: Viking, 1993.
Guthman, Edwin O., and Jeffrey Shulman, eds. *Robert Kennedy, in His Own Words: The Unpublished Recollections of the Kennedy Years.* New York: Bantam, 1988.
Haas, Lawrence J. *The Kennedys in the World: How Jack, Bobby and Ted Remade America's Empire.* Lincoln, NE: Potomac Books, 2021.
Hacker, Jacob. *The Road to Nowhere: The Genesis of President Clinton's Plan for Health Security.* Princeton, NJ: Princeton University Press, 1997.
Hacker, Jacob, and Paul Pierson. *Let Them Eat Tweets: How the Right Rules in an Age of Extreme Inequality.* New York: Liveright, 2020.
Halberstam, David. *The Best and the Brightest.* New York: Random House, 1972.
———. *The Powers That Be.* New York: Knopf, 1979.
———. *The Unfinished Odyssey of Robert Kennedy.* New York: Random House, 1969.
Haldeman, H. R. *The Haldeman Diaries: Inside the Nixon White House.* New York: G. P. Putnam's Sons, 1994.
Hamill, Pete. *Irrational Ravings.* New York: G. P. Putnam's Sons, 1971.
Hamilton, Nigel. *Bill Clinton: Mastering the Presidency.* New York: PublicAffairs, 2007.
———. *JFK: Reckless Youth.* New York: Random House, 1992.
Handlin, Oscar. *Boston's Immigrants.* New York: Atheneum, 1975.
———. *The Uprooted.* New York: Grosset & Dunlap, 1951.
Hardeman, D. B., and Donald Bacon. *Rayburn: A Biography.* Lanham, MD: Madison, 1989.
Hardy, Donald Loren. *Shooting from the Lip: The Life of Senator Al Simpson.* Norman: University of Oklahoma Press, 2011.
Harris, Fred. *Does People Do It? A Memoir.* Norman: University of Oklahoma Press, 2008.
Harris, John F. *The Survivor: Bill Clinton in the White House.* New York: Random House, 2006.
Harris, Richard. *Decision.* New York: E. P. Dutton, 1971.
Hart, Gary. *Right from the Start: A Chronicle of the McGovern Campaign.* New York: Quadrangle, 1973.
Hastings, Max. *Vietnam: An Epic Tragedy, 1945–1975.* New York: HarperCollins, 2018.
Hatch, Orrin. *Square Peg: Confessions of a Citizen Senator.* New York: Basic Books, 2002.
Heileman, John, and Mark Halperin. *Game Change: Obama and the Clintons, McCain and Palin, and the Race of a Lifetime.* New York: Harper, 2010.
Heitzman, James, and Robert Worden, eds. *Bangladesh: A Country Study.* Washington, DC: U.S. Government Printing Office for the Library of Congress, 1989.
Henderson, Timothy. *Beyond Borders: A History of Mexican Migration to the United States.* Malden, MA: Wiley-Blackwell, 2011.
Hersh, Burton. *The Education of Edward Kennedy: A Family Biography.* New York: William Morrow, 1972.
———. *Edward Kennedy: An Intimate Biography.* Berkeley, CA: Counterpoint, 2010.
———. *The Shadow President: Ted Kennedy in Opposition.* South Royalton, VT: Steerforth Press, 1997.
Hersh, Seymour. *The Dark Side of Camelot.* Boston: Little, Brown, 1997.
Heymann, C. David. *RFK: A Candid Biography of Robert F. Kennedy.* New York: Dutton, 1998.
———. *A Woman Named Jackie.* Boston: G. K. Hall, 1990.
Hilley, John. *The Challenge of Legislation: Bipartisanship in a Partisan World.* Washington, DC: Brookings Institution, 2008.
Hodgson, Godfrey. *The Gentleman from New York: Daniel Patrick Moynihan: A Biography.* Boston: Houghton Mifflin, 2000.
Holland, Jack. *The American Connection: U.S. Guns, Money and Influence in Northern Ireland.* Niwot, CO: Roberts Rinehart Publishers, 1999.
Honan, William. *Ted Kennedy: Portrait of a Survivor.* New York: Quadrangle, 1972.
Horowitz, Craig. *The Legislative Legacy of Edward M. Kennedy: Eleven Milestones in Pursuit of Social Justice, 1965–2007.* Jefferson, NC: McFarland, 2014.
Hulse, Carl. *Confirmation Bias: Inside Washington's War Over the Supreme Court from Scalia's Death to Justice Kavanaugh.* New York: Harper, 2019.
Hutschnecker, Arnold. *The Drive for Power.* New York: Evans, 1974.
Hyman, Lester. Unpublished memoirs.
Jackson, Brooks. *Honest Graft: Big Money and the American Political Process.* Washington, DC: Farragut Publishing, 1990.
Jacobs, John. *A Rage for Justice: The Passion and Politics of Phillip Burton.* Berkeley: University of California Press, 1995.
Jenkins, John. *The Partisan: The Life of William Rehnquist.* New York: PublicAffairs, 2012.
Jentleson, Adam. *Kill Switch: The Rise of the Modern Senate and the Crippling of American Democracy.* New York: Liveright Publishing Corporation, 2021.
Johnson, Haynes, and David Broder. *The System: The American Way of Politics at the Breaking Point.* Boston: Little, Brown, 1996.
Johnson, Loch. *A Season of Inquiry: Congress and Intelligence.* Lexington: University Press of Kentucky, 1985.
Johnson, Paul. *Modern Times: The World from the Twenties to the Eighties.* New York: HarperCollins, 1983.

Jones, Charles O. *Passages to the Presidency: From Campaigning to Governing.* Washington, DC: Brookings Institution, 1998.

———. *The Trusteeship Presidency: Jimmy Carter and the United States Congress.* Baton Rouge: Louisiana State University Press, 1988.

Jordan, Hamilton. *Crisis: The Last Year of the Carter Presidency.* New York: Putnam, 1982.

Kaiser, Robert. *"R.F.K. Must Die!" A History of the Robert Kennedy Assassination and Its Aftermath.* New York: Dutton, 1970.

Kallina, Edmund, Jr. *Courthouse over White House; Chicago and the Presidential Election of 1960.* Orlando: University Press of Florida, 1988.

———. *Kennedy v. Nixon: The Presidential Election of 1960.* Gainesville: University Press of Florida, 2010.

Kalman, Laura. *The Long Reach of the Sixties: LBJ, Nixon and the Making of the Contemporary Supreme Court.* New York: Oxford University Press, 2017.

Kampelman, Max. *Entering New Worlds: The Memoirs of a Private Man in Public Life.* New York: HarperCollins, 1991.

Karabel, Jerome. *The Chosen: The Hidden History of Admission and Exclusion at Harvard, Yale and Princeton.* Boston: Houghton Mifflin, 2005.

Karnow, Stanley. *Vietnam: A History: The First Complete Account of Vietnam at War.* New York: Viking, 1983.

Katcher, Leo. *Earl Warren: A Political Biography.* New York: McGraw-Hill, 1967.

Katzenbach, Nicholas DeB. *Some of It Was Fun: Working with RFK and LBJ.* New York: Norton, 2008.

Kaufman, Burton Ira, and Scott Kaufman. *The Presidency of James Earl Carter, Jr.* 2nd ed. Lawrence: University Press of Kansas, 2006.

Kelley, Kitty. *Jackie Oh!* Secaucus, NJ: Lyle Stuart, 1978.

Kelly, Michael. *Things Worth Fighting For: Collected Writings.* New York: Penguin Press, 2004.

Kempton, Murray. *America Comes of Middle Age.* Boston: Little, Brown, 1963.

———. *Rebellions, Perversities and Main Events.* New York: Times Books, 1994.

Kennedy, David M. *Freedom From Fear: The American People in Depression and War, 1929–1945.* New York: Oxford University Press, 1999.

Kennedy, Edward M. *The Fruitful Bough: A Tribute to Joseph Kennedy,* a privately printed collection of reminiscences edited by Edward M. Kennedy. West Hanover, MA: Halliday Lithograph Corporation, 1965.

———. *In Critical Condition: The Crisis in America's Health Care.* New York: Simon & Schuster, 1972.

———. *True Compass: A Memoir.* New York: Twelve, 2009.

Kennedy, Edward M., and Mark O. Hatfield. *Freeze!: How You Can Help Prevent Nuclear War.* New York: Bantam, 1982.

Kennedy, John F. *A Nation of Immigrants.* Rev. ed. New York: Harper Perennial, 2008.

———. *Profiles in Courage.* 1956; reprint New York: HarperCollins, 2003.

Kennedy, John F., ed. *As We Remember Joe.* Cambridge, MA: University Press, 1945.

Kennedy, Patrick J., and Stephen Fried. *A Common Struggle.* New York: Blue Rider Press, 2015.

Kennedy, Robert. *Thirteen Days, A Memoir of the Cuban Missile Crisis.* New York: Norton, 1969.

Kennedy, Rose Fitzgerald. *Times to Remember.* New York: Doubleday, 1974.

Kenney, Charles, and Robert Turner. *Dukakis: An American Odyssey.* Boston: Houghton Mifflin, 1988.

Kerry, John. *Every Day Is Extra.* New York: Simon & Schuster, 2018.

Kimball, Jeffrey. *Nixon's Vietnam War.* Lawrence: University Press of Kansas, 1998.

———. *The Vietnam War Files: Uncovering the Secret History of Nixon-Era Strategy.* Lawrence: University Press of Kansas, 2004.

King, Anthony, ed. *Both Ends of the Avenue: The Presidency, the Executive Branch, and Congress in the 1980s.* Washington, DC: American Enterprise Institute for Public Policy Research, 1983.

King, Martin Luther, Jr. *The Papers of Martin Luther King Jr.* Berkeley: University of California Press, 2000.

Kissinger, Henry. *Ending the Vietnam War: A History of America's Involvement In and Extrication From the Vietnam War.* New York: Simon & Schuster, 2003.

———. *White House Years.* New York: Little, Brown, 1979.

———. *Years of Renewal.* New York: Simon & Schuster, 1999.

———. *Years of Upheaval.* New York: Little, Brown, 1982.

Klein, Edward. *Ted Kennedy: The Dream That Never Died.* New York: Crown, 2009.

Knock, Thomas J. *The Rise of a Prairie Statesman: The Life and Times of George McGovern.* Princeton, NJ: Princeton University Press, 2016.

Koskoff, David. *Joseph P. Kennedy: A Life and Times.* Englewood Cliffs, NJ: Prentice Hall, 1974.

Kranish, Michael, Brian C. Mooney, and Nina J. Easton. *John F. Kerry: The Complete Biography by the* Boston Globe *Reporters Who Know Him Best.* New York: PublicAffairs, 2004.

Kruse, Kevin, and Julian Zelizer. *Fault Lines: A History of the United States Since 1974.* New York: Norton, 2019.

Kutler, Stanley. *The Wars of Watergate: The Last Crisis of Richard Nixon.* New York: Norton, 1992.

Kutler, Stanley, ed. *Abuse of Power: The New Nixon Tapes.* New York: Free Press, 1997.

Kuttner, Robert. *Can Democracy Survive Global Capitalism?* New York: Norton, 2018.

Lange, James, and Katherine DeWitt. *Chappaquiddick: The Real Story.* New York: St. Martin's Press, 1993.

Larson, Kate Clifford. *Rosemary: The Hidden Kennedy Daughter.* Boston: Houghton Mifflin Harcourt, 2015.

Lawford, Christopher. *Symptoms of Withdrawal: A Memoir of Snapshots and Redemption.* New York: HarperCollins, 2005.

Lawford, Patricia Kennedy, ed. *That Shining Hour.* New York: Halliday Lithograph Corporation, 1969.

Lawrence, John A. *The Class of '74: Congress After Watergate and the Roots of Partisanship.* Baltimore: Johns Hopkins University Press, 2018.
Leamer, Laurence. *The Kennedy Men: 1901–1963.* New York: William Morrow, 2001.
———. *The Kennedy Women: The Saga of an American Family.* New York: Villard, 1994.
———. *The Sons of Camelot: The Fate of an American Dynasty.* New York, William Morrow, 2004.
Leaming, Barbara. *Kick Kennedy: The Charmed Life and Tragic Death of the Favorite Kennedy Daughter.* New York: Thomas Dunne, 2016.
Lehr, Dick, and Gerard O'Neill. *Black Mass: The Irish Mob, the FBI and a Devil's Deal.* New York: PublicAffairs, 2000.
Lepore, Jill. *These Truths: A History of the United States.* New York: Norton, 2018.
Lerner, Max. *Ted and the Kennedy Legend.* New York: St. Martin's Press, 1980.
Levin, Murray B., and T. A. Repak. *Edward Kennedy: The Myth of Leadership.* Boston: Houghton Mifflin, 1980.
———. *Kennedy Campaigning: The System and the Style as Practiced by Senator Edward Kennedy.* Boston: Beacon Press, 1966.
Lewis, Finlay. *Mondale: Portrait of an American Politician.* 1980. Rev. ed. New York: Perennial Library, 1984.
Link, William A. *Righteous Warrior: Jesse Helms and the Rise of Modern Conservatism.* New York: St. Martin's Press, 2008.
Lippman, Theo, Jr. *Senator Ted Kennedy: The Career Behind the Image.* New York: Norton, 1976.
Littlefield, Nick, and David Nexon. *Lion of the Senate: When Ted Kennedy Rallied the Democrats in a GOP Congress.* New York: Simon & Schuster, 2015.
Loevy, Robert D. *To End All Segregation: The Politics of the Passage of the Civil Rights Act of 1964.* Lanham, MD: University Press of America, 1990.
Logevall, Fredrik. *Embers of War: The Fall of an Empire and the Makings of America's Vietnam.* New York: Random House, 2012.
———. *JFK: Coming of Age in the American Century, 1917–1956.* New York: Random House, 2020.
Lott, Trent. *Herding Cats: A Life in Politics.* New York: Regan Books, 2005.
Lott, Trent, and Thomas Daschle. *Crisis Point: Why We Must—and How We Can—Overcome Our Broken Politics in Washington and Across America.* New York: Bloomsbury, 2016.
Love, Janice. *The U.S. Anti-apartheid Movement.* New York: Praeger, 1985.
Lukas, J. Anthony. *Common Ground: A Turbulent Decade in the Lives of Three American Families.* New York: Knopf, 1985.
———. *Nightmare: The Underside of the Nixon Years.* New York: Viking, 1976.
Lupo, Alan. *Liberty's Chosen Home: The Politics of Violence in Boston.* Boston: Beacon Press, 1988.
Lyons, Louis. *Newspaper Story: One Hundred Years of the Boston Globe.* Cambridge, MA: Belknap Press of Harvard University Press, 1971.
Mackaman, Frank H. *An Idea Whose Time Has Come: The Civil Rights Act of 1964.* Pekin, Illinois: The Dirksen Congressional Center, 2014.
———. *The Long Hard Furrow: Everett Dirksen's Part in the Civil Rights Act of 1964.* Pekin, Illinois: The Dirksen Congressional Center, 2014.
MacNeil, Neil. *Dirksen: Portrait of a Public Man.* New York: World Publishing Co., 1970.
MacNeil, Neil, and Richard A. Baker. *The American Senate: An Insider's History.* New York: Oxford University Press, 2013.
Mahoney, Richard D. *Sons & Brothers: The Days of Jack and Bobby Kennedy.* New York: Arcade, 1999.
Maier, Thomas. *The Kennedys: America's Emerald Kings.* New York: Basic Books, 2003.
Mailer, Norman. *Miami and the Siege of Chicago.* New York: New American Library, 1968.
———. *The Presidential Papers.* New York: Berkley, 1976.
———. *Some Honorable Men: Political Conventions, 1960–1972.* Boston: Little, Brown, 1976.
Manchester, William. *The Death of a President: November 23–November 25, 1963.* New York: Harper & Row, 1967.
———. *One Brief Shining Moment: Remembering Kennedy.* Thorndike, ME: Thorndike Press, 1984.
Mankiewicz, Frank, and Joel Swerdlow. *So As I Was Saying . . . My Somewhat Eventful Life.* New York: Thomas Dunne, 2016.
Mann, Robert. *The Walls of Jericho: Lyndon Johnson, Hubert Humphrey, Richard Russell and the Struggle for Civil Rights.* New York: Harcourt Brace, 1996.
Mann, Thomas, and Norman Ornstein. *The Broken Branch: How Congress Is Failing America and How to Get It Back on Track.* New York: Oxford University Press, 2006.
———. *It's Even Worse Than It Looks.* New York: Basic Books, 2012.
Mann, Thomas, and Norman Ornstein, eds. *The American Elections of 1982.* Washington, DC: American Enterprise Institute, 1983.
Maraniss, David. *First in His Class: The Biography of Bill Clinton.* New York: Simon & Schuster, 1995.
Maraniss, David, and Michael Weisskopf. *"Tell Newt to Shut Up!"* New York: Simon & Schuster, 1996.
Marcus, Ruth. *Supreme Ambition: Brett Kavanaugh and the Conservative Takeover.* New York: Simon & Schuster, 2019.
Martin, John Bartlow. *Adlai Stevenson of Illinois.* New York: Doubleday, 1976.
———. *A Hero for Our Time: An Intimate Story of the Kennedy Years.* New York: Macmillan, 1983.
Martin, Ralph G. *Seeds of Destruction: Joe Kennedy and His Sons.* New York: G. P. Putnam's Sons, 1995.
Matlock, Jack F., Jr. *Autopsy on an Empire: The American Ambassador's Account of the Collapse of the Soviet Union.* New York: Random House, 1995.
———. *Reagan and Gorbachev: How the Cold War Ended.* New York: Random House, 2004.

Matoesian, Gregory. *Law and the Language of Identity: Discourse in the William Kennedy Smith Rape Trial.* New York: Oxford University Press, 2001.

Matthews, Christopher. *Bobby Kennedy: A Raging Spirit.* New York: Simon & Schuster, 2017.

———. *Jack Kennedy: Elusive Hero.* New York: Simon & Schuster, 2011.

———. *Kennedy and Nixon: The Rivalry That Shaped Postwar America.* New York: Touchstone, 1996.

Matthews, Donald R. *U.S. Senators and Their World.* Chapel Hill: University of North Carolina Press, 1960.

Mattson, Kevin. *"What the Heck Are You Up To, Mr. President?": Jimmy Carter, America's "Malaise," and the Speech That Should Have Changed the Country.* New York: Bloomsbury, 2009.

May, Ernest R., and Philip D, Zelikow, eds. *The Kennedy Tapes: Inside the White House During the Cuban Missile Crisis.* Cambridge, MA: Belknap Press of Harvard University Press, 1997.

May, Ernest R., Timothy Naftali, and Philip D. Zelikow, eds. *The Presidential Recordings: John F. Kennedy; The Great Crises.* 3 vols. New York: Norton, 2001.

May, Gary. *Bending Toward Justice: The Voting Rights Act and the Transformation of American Democracy.* Durham, NC: Duke University Press, 2014.

Mayer, Jane. *Dark Money: The Hidden History of the Billionaires Behind the Rise of the American Right.* New York: Doubleday, 2016.

Mayer, Jane, and Jill Abramson. *Strange Justice: The Selling of Clarence Thomas.* Boston: Houghton Mifflin, 1994.

McCaffrey, Lawrence. *Textures of Irish America.* Syracuse, NY: Syracuse University Press, 1992.

McCain, John, with Mark Salter. *Faith of My Fathers: A Family Memoir.* New York: Random House, 1999.

———. *Worth the Fighting For: A Memoir.* New York: Random House, 2002.

McCarthy, Eugene. *The Year of the People.* Garden City, NY: Doubleday, 1969.

McCarthy, Joe. *The Remarkable Kennedys.* New York: Popular Library, 1960.

McDonough, John. *Inside National Health Reform.* Berkeley: University of California Press, 2011.

McGinniss, Joe. *The Last Brother: The Rise and Fall of Teddy Kennedy.* New York: Simon & Schuster, 1993.

———. *The Selling of the President 1968.* New York: Penguin, 1988.

McGrory, Mary. *The Best of Mary McGrory: A Half-Century of Washington Commentary.* Edited by Phil Gailey. Kansas City, MO: Andrews McMeel, 2006.

McLuhan, Marshall. *Understanding Media: The Extensions of Man.* New York: McGraw-Hill, 1966.

McNamara, Eileen. *Eunice: The Kennedy Who Changed the World.* New York: Simon & Schuster, 2018.

McNamara, Robert. *In Retrospect: The Tragedy and Lessons of Vietnam.* New York: Times Books, 1995.

McPherson, Harry. *A Political Education: A Journal of Life with Senators, Generals, Cabinet Members and Presidents.* Boston: Little, Brown, 1972.

Meacham, Ellen. *Delta Epiphany: Robert F. Kennedy in Mississippi.* Jackson: University Press of Mississippi, 2018.

Meacham, Jon. *Destiny and Power: The American Odyssey of George Herbert Walker Bush.* New York: Random House, 2015.

Moldea, Dan. *The Killing of Robert F. Kennedy: An Investigation of Motive, Means and Opportunity.* New York: Norton, 1995.

———. *A Washington Tragedy: How the Death of Vincent Foster Ignited a Political Firestorm.* Lanham, MD: Regnery, 1998.

Moore, Jonathan, ed. *The Campaign for President: 1980 in Retrospect.* Cambridge, MA: Ballinger, 1981.

———. *Campaign for President: The Managers Look at '84.* Dover, MA: Auburn House, 1986.

Moore, Jonathan, and Janet Fraser, eds. *Campaign for President: The Managers Look at '76.* Cambridge, MA: Ballinger, 1977.

Morris, Edmund. *Dutch: A Memoir of Ronald Reagan.* New York, Random House, 1999.

Moynihan, Daniel Patrick. *Came the Revolution: Argument in the Reagan Era.* New York: Harcourt Brace Jovanovich, 1988.

Mukherjee, Siddhartha. *The Emperor of All Maladies: A Biography of Cancer.* New York: Scribner, 2010.

Murakawa, Naomi. *The First Civil Right: How Liberals Built Prison America.* New York: Oxford University Press, 2014.

Mutch, Robert. *Campaigns, Congress and Courts: The Making of Federal Campaign Finance Law.* New York: Praeger, 1988.

Nasaw, David. *The Patriarch: The Remarkable Life and Turbulent Times of Joseph P. Kennedy.* New York: Penguin, 2012.

National Research Council. *The Growth of Incarceration in the United States: Exploring Causes and Consequences.* Washington, DC: National Academies Press, 2014.

Nelson, Garrison. *John William McCormack: A Political Biography.* New York: Bloomsbury, 2017.

Nelson, Michael, Barbara Perry, and Russell Riley. *42: Inside the Presidency of Bill Clinton.* Ithaca, NY: Cornell University Press, 2016.

Nesbitt, Francis. *Race for Sanctions: African Americans Against Apartheid, 1946–1994.* Bloomington: Indiana University Press, 2004.

Newfield, Jack. *Robert Kennedy: A Memoir.* New York: Dutton, 1969.

Newton, Jim. *Justice for All: Earl Warren and the Nation He Made.* New York: Riverhead, 2006.

Nixon, Richard. *RN: The Memoirs of Richard Nixon.* New York: Grosset & Dunlap, 1978.

Nyhan, David. *The Duke: The Inside Story of a Political Phenomenon.* New York: Warner Books, 1988.

Oates, Joyce Carol. *Black Water.* New York: Penguin, 1992.

Obama, Barack. *A Promised Land.* New York: Crown, 2020.

Oberdorfer, Don. *Senator Mansfield: The Extraordinary Life of a Great American Statesman and Diplomat.* Washington, DC: Smithsonian Books, 2003.

———. *Tet! The Story of a Battle and Its Historic Aftermath.* Garden City, NY: Doubleday, 1971.

O'Brien, Lawrence. *No Final Victories: A Life in Politics from John F. Kennedy to Watergate.* Garden City, NY: Doubleday, 1974.

O'Brien, Michael. *John F. Kennedy: A Biography.* New York: Thomas Dunne, 2005.

———. *Philip Hart: The Conscience of the Senate.* East Lansing: Michigan State University Press, 1995.

O'Clery, Conor. *Daring Diplomacy: Clinton's Secret Search for Peace in Ireland.* Boulder, CO: Roberts Rinehart Publishers, 1997.

O'Connor, Edwin. *The Last Hurrah.* Boston: Atlantic Monthly Press, 1956.

O'Connor, Thomas. *The Boston Irish: A Political History.* Boston: Northeastern University Press, 1995.

O'Donnell, Helen. *A Common Good: The Friendship of Robert F. Kennedy and Kenneth P. O'Donnell.* New York: William Morrow, 1998.

———. *The Irish Brotherhood: John F. Kennedy, His Inner Circle, and the Improbable Rise to the Presidency.* Berkeley, CA: Counterpoint, 2015.

O'Donnell, Kenneth, and David Powers, *"Johnny, We Hardly Knew Ye": Memories of John Fitzgerald Kennedy.* Boston: Little, Brown, 1972.

O'Dowd, Niall. *An Irish Voice.* Dublin: The O'Brien Press, 2010.

Offner, Arnold A. *Hubert Humphrey: The Conscience of the Country.* New Haven, CT: Yale University Press, 2018.

Okrent, Daniel. *Last Call: The Rise and Fall of Prohibition.* New York: Scribner, 2010.

Oleszek, Walter J., et al. *Congressional Procedures and the Policy Process.* Thousand Oaks, CA: CQ Press, 2020.

Oliphant, Thomas, and Curtis Wilkie. *The Road to Camelot: Inside JFK's Five-Year Campaign.* New York: Simon & Schuster, 2017.

Olmsted, Kathryn. *Challenging the Secret Government: The Post-Watergate Investigations of the CIA and FBI.* Chapel Hill: University of North Carolina Press, 1996.

Olsen, Jack. *The Bridge at Chappaquiddick.* Boston: Little, Brown, 1969.

O'Neill, Gerard. *Rogues and Redeemers: When Politics Was King in Irish Boston.* New York: Crown, 2012.

O'Neill, Tip, with William Novak. *Man of the House: The Life and Political Memoirs of Speaker Tip O'Neill.* New York: St. Martin's Press, 1987.

Orchowski, Margaret. *The Law That Changed the Face of America: The Immigration and Nationality Act of 1965.* Lanham, MD: Rowman & Littlefield, 2015.

Oudes, Bruce. *From: The President: Richard Nixon's Secret Files.* New York: Harper & Row, 1989.

Packer, George. *The Assassins' Gate, America in Iraq.* New York: Farrar, Straus & Giroux, 2005.

———. *Our Man: Richard Holbrooke and the End of the American Century.* New York: Knopf, 2019.

Palermo, Joseph. *In His Own Right: The Political Odyssey of Senator Robert F. Kennedy.* New York: Columbia University Press, 2001.

Parmet, Herbert S. *Jack: The Struggles of John F. Kennedy.* New York: Dial Press, 1980.

———. *JFK: The Presidency of John F. Kennedy.* New York: Dial Press, 1983.

Patterson, James T. *Grand Expectations: The United States, 1945–1974.* The Oxford History of the United States. New York: Oxford University Press, 1996.

———. *Mr. Republican: A Biography of Robert A. Taft.* Boston: Houghton Mifflin, 1972.

———. *Restless Giant: The United States from Watergate to Bush v. Gore.* The Oxford History of the United States. New York: Oxford University Press, 2005.

Peabody, Robert L. *Leadership in Congress: Stability, Succession, and Change.* Boston: Little, Brown, 1975.

Peck, Don. *Pinched: How the Great Recession Has Narrowed Our Futures and What We Can Do About It.* New York: Crown, 2011.

Perlstein, Rick. *Before the Storm: Barry Goldwater and the Unmaking of the American Consensus.* New York: Hill & Wang, 2001.

———. *The Invisible Bridge: The Fall of Nixon and the Rise of Reagan.* New York: Simon & Schuster, 2014.

———. *Nixonland: The Rise of a President and the Fracturing of America.* New York: Scribner, 2008.

———. *Reaganland: America's Right Turn, 1976–1980.* New York: Simon & Schuster, 2020.

Perry, Barbara. *Edward M. Kennedy: An Oral History.* New York: Oxford University Press, 2019.

———. *Rose Kennedy: The Life and Times of a Political Matriarch.* New York: Norton, 2013.

Pertschuk, Michael. *Giant Killers.* New York: Norton, 1986.

Peterson, Peter G. *The United States in the Changing World Economy.* Washington, DC: U.S. Government Printing Office, 1971.

Phelps, Timothy M., and Helen Winternitz. *Capitol Games: Clarence Thomas, Anita Hill, and the Story of a Supreme Court Nomination.* New York: Hyperion, 1992.

Phillips, Kevin. *The Emerging Republican Majority.* New Rochelle, NY: Arlington House, 1969.

———. *The Politics of Rich and Poor: Wealth and the American Electorate in the Reagan Aftermath.* New York: Random House, 1990.

Pietrusza, David. *1960: LBJ vs. JFK vs. Nixon.* New York: Sterling Publishing Co., 2008.

Pipes, Kasey. *Ike's Final Battle: The Road to Little Rock and the Challenge of Equality.* Los Angeles: World Ahead Media, 2007.

Polsby, Nelson. *Congress and the Presidency.* Englewood Cliffs, NJ: Prentice-Hall, 1976.

———. *How Congress Evolves: Social Bases of Institutional Change.* New York: Oxford University Press, 2003.

Posner, Gerald. *Case Closed: Lee Harvey Oswald and the Assassination of JFK.* New York: Random House, 1993.

Potoski, Georgetta, and William Nelson. *Our Mary Jo.* Amazon Kindle edition. 2017.

Powell, Jody. *The Other Side of the Story.* New York: William Morrow, 1984.

Purdum, Todd. *An Idea Whose Time Has Come: Two Presidents, Two Parties and the Battle for the Civil Rights Act of 1964.* New York: Henry Holt, 2014.

Quadagno, Jill. *One Nation Uninsured: Why the U.S. Has No National Health Insurance.* New York: Oxford University Press, 2005.

Rainie, Harrison, and John Quinn. *Growing Up Kennedy: The Third Wave Comes of Age.* New York: Putnam, 1983.

Reagan, Ronald. *An American Life.* New York: Simon & Schuster, 1990.

———. *The Reagan Diaries.* New York: HarperCollins, 2007.

Redman, Eric. *The Dance of Legislation: An Insider's Account of the Workings of the United States Senate.* New York: Simon & Schuster, 1973.

Reeves, Richard. *President Kennedy: Profile of Power.* New York: Simon & Schuster, 1993.

———. *President Nixon: Alone in the White House.* New York: Touchstone, 2001.

Reeves, Thomas. *A Question of Character: A Life of John F. Kennedy.* New York: Free Press, 1991.

Reich, Robert. *Locked in the Cabinet.* New York: Random House, 1997.

———. *The System: Who Rigged It, How We Fix It.* New York: Knopf, 2020.

Rettig, Richard. *Cancer Crusade: The Story of the National Cancer Act of 1971.* Princeton, NJ: Princeton University Press, 1971.

Ricks, Thomas E. *Fiasco: The American Military Adventure in Iraq.* New York: Penguin Press, 2006.

Risen, Clay. *The Bill of the Century: The Epic Battle for the Civil Rights Act.* New York: Bloomsbury Press, 2014.

Ritchie, Donald A. *Press Gallery: Congress and the Washington Correspondents.* Cambridge, MA: Harvard University Press, 1991.

Rivera, Geraldo. *A Special Kind of Courage: Profiles of Young Americans.* New York: Simon & Schuster, 1976.

Roderick, Lee. *Leading the Charge: Orrin Hatch and 20 Years of America.* Carson City, NV: Gold Leaf Press, 1994.

Rooks, Douglas. *Statesman: George Mitchell and the Art of the Possible.* Camden, ME: Down East Books, 2016.

Rorabaugh, W. J. *The Real Making of the President: Kennedy, Nixon and the 1960 Election.* Lawrence: University Press of Kansas, 2009.

Rothenberg, Randall. *The Neo-Liberals: Creating the New American Politics.* New York: Simon & Schuster, 1984.

Rudenstine, David. *The Day the Presses Stopped: A History of the Pentagon Papers Case.* Berkeley: University of California Press, 1996.

Rudman, Warren. *Combat: Twelve Years in the U.S. Senate.* New York: Random House, 1996.

Rudolph, Lloyd, and Susan Rudolph. *The Regional Imperative: U.S. Foreign Policy Towards South Asian States.* Atlantic Highlands, NJ: Humanities Press, 1980.

Ryan, Dennis. *Beyond the Ballot Box: A Social History of the Boston Irish, 1845–1917.* Amherst: University of Massachusetts Press, 1983.

Sabato, Larry. *The Kennedy Half Century: The Presidency, Assassination and Lasting Legacy of John F. Kennedy.* New York: Bloomsbury, 2013.

Safire, William. *Before the Fall: An Inside View of the Pre-Watergate White House.* New York, Doubleday, 1975.

Salinger, Pierre, ed. *"An Honorable Profession": A Tribute to Robert F. Kennedy.* Garden City, NY: Doubleday, 1968.

Salter, Mark. *The Luckiest Man: Life with John McCain.* New York: Simon & Schuster, 2020.

Samuelson, Robert J. *The Great Inflation and Its Aftermath: The Past and Future of American Affluence.* New York: Random House, 2008.

Sandbrook, Dominic. *Eugene McCarthy: The Rise and Fall of Postwar American Liberalism.* New York: Knopf, 2004.

Sandler, Martin, ed. *The Letters of John F. Kennedy.* New York: Bloomsbury, 2013.

Scammon, Richard, and Ben Wattenberg. *The Real Majority: An Extraordinary Examination of the American Electorate.* New York: Capricorn, 1971.

Schaap, Dick. *R.F.K.* New York: Signet, 1967.

Schlesinger, Arthur, Jr. *Journals, 1952–2000.* New York: Penguin, 2007.

———. *The Letters of Arthur Schlesinger.* New York: Random House, 2013.

———. *Robert Kennedy and His Times.* Boston: Houghton Mifflin, 1978.

———. *A Thousand Days: John F. Kennedy in the White House.* Boston: Houghton Mifflin, 1965.

Schlesinger, Marian Cannon. *I Remember: A Life of Politics, Painting and People.* Cambridge, MA: TidePool Press, 2012.

Schlight, John. *A War Too Long: The USAF in Southeast Asia.* Air Force History and Museums Program, 1996.

Selverstone, Marc, ed. *A Companion to John F. Kennedy.* West Sussex, UK: John Wiley & Sons, 2014.

Shannon, William V. *The American Irish.* New York: Macmillan, 1963.

———. *The Heir Apparent: Robert Kennedy and the Struggle for Power.* New York: Macmillan, 1967.

Shapiro, Ira. *The Last Great Senate: Courage and Statesmanship in Times of Crisis.* New York: PublicAffairs, 2012.

Shawcross, William. *Sideshow: Kissinger, Nixon and the Destruction of Cambodia.* New York: Simon & Schuster, 1979.

Sheehan, Neil. *A Bright Shining Lie: John Paul Vann and America in Vietnam.* New York: Random House, 1988.

Shenon, Philip. *A Cruel and Shocking Act: The Secret History of the Kennedy Assassination.* New York: Holt, 2013.

Shepard, Geoff. *The Secret Plot to Make Ted Kennedy President: Inside the Real Watergate Conspiracy.* New York: Sentinel, 2008.

Sherrill, Robert. *The Last Kennedy.* New York: Dial Press, 1976.

Shesol, Jeff. *Mutual Contempt: Lyndon Johnson, Robert Kennedy and the Feud That Defined a Decade.* New York: Norton, 1997.

Shilts, Randy. *And the Band Played On: Politics, People and the AIDS Epidemic.* New York: St. Martin's Press, 1987.

Shlaes, Amity. *The Forgotten Man: A New History of the Great Depression.* New York: HarperCollins, 2007.

————. *Great Society: A New History.* New York: HarperCollins, 2019.

Shrum, Robert. *No Excuses: Concessions of a Serial Campaigner.* New York: Simon & Schuster, 2007.

Shultz, George P. *Turmoil and Triumph: My Years as Secretary of State.* New York: Charles Scribner's Sons, 1993.

Simpson, Alan K. *Right in the Old Gazoo: A Lifetime of Scrapping with the Press.* New York: William Morrow, 1997.

Sinclair, Barbara. *The Transformation of the U.S. Senate.* Baltimore: Johns Hopkins University Press, 1989.

Sitaraman, Ganesh. *The Crisis of the Middle-Class Constitution: Why Economic Inequality Threatens Our Republic.* New York: Knopf, 2017.

Sloyan, Patrick. *The Politics of Deception: JFK's Secret Decisions on Vietnam, Civil Rights and Cuba.* New York: Thomas Dunne, 2015.

Small, Melvin, ed. *A Companion to Richard M. Nixon.* Malden, MA: Wiley-Blackwell, 2011.

Smith, Amanda, ed. *Hostage to Fortune: The Letters of Joseph P. Kennedy.* New York: Viking, 2001.

Smith, Hedrick. *The Power Game: How Washington Works.* New York: Random House, 1988.

————. *Who Stole the American Dream?* New York: Random House, 2012.

Smith, J. Douglas. *On Democracy's Doorstep: The Inside Story of How the Supreme Court Brought "One Person, One Vote" to the United States.* New York: Hill & Wang, 2014.

Smith, Jean Edward. *Bush.* New York: Simon & Schuster, 2016.

Smith, Jean Kennedy. *The Nine of Us: Growing Up Kennedy.* New York: Harper Collins, 2016.

Smith, Steven. *Call to Order: Floor Politics in the House and Senate.* Washington, DC: Brookings Institution, 1989.

————. *The Senate Syndrome: The Evolution of Procedural Warfare in the Modern U.S. Senate.* Norman: University of Oklahoma Press, 2014.

Smith, Steven, and Christopher J. Deering. *Committees in Congress.* Washington, DC: CQ Press, 1990.

Solberg, Carl. *Hubert Humphrey: A Biography.* New York: Norton, 1984.

Sorensen, Theodore. *Counselor: A Life at the Edge of History.* New York: Harper, 2008.

————. *Kennedy.* New York: Harper & Row, 1965.

————. *The Kennedy Legacy: A Peaceful Revolution for the Seventies.* 1969. Special ed. New York: Macmillan, 1993.

Stahl, Lesley. *Reporting Live.* New York: Touchstone, 1999.

Stanley, Timothy. *Kennedy vs. Carter: The 1980 Battle for the Democratic Party's Soul.* Lawrence: University Press of Kansas, 2010.

Starr, Paul. *Remedy and Reaction: The Peculiar American Struggle over Health Care Reform.* New Haven, CT: Yale University Press, 2011.

Stein, Jean. *American Journey: The Times of Robert Kennedy.* Edited by George Plimpton. New York: Harcourt Brace Jovanovich, 1970.

Stephanopoulos, George. *All Too Human: A Political Education.* New York: Little, Brown, 1999.

Stockman, David. *The Triumph of Politics: Why the Reagan Revolution Failed.* New York: Harper & Row, 1986.

Stossel, Scott. *Sarge: The Life and Times of Sargent Shriver.* Washington, DC: Smithsonian Books, 2004.

Strober, Gerald, and Deborah H. Strober. *Let Us Begin Anew: An Oral History of the Kennedy Presidency.* New York: HarperCollins, 1993.

————. *The Nixon Presidency: An Oral History of the Era.* New York: HarperCollins, 1994.

Stroud, Kandy. *How Jimmy Won: The Victory Campaign from Plains to the White House.* New York: William Morrow, 1977.

Sullivan, Gerald, and Michael Kenney. *The Race for the Eighth: The Making of a Congressional Campaign; Joe Kennedy's Successful Pursuit of a Political Legacy.* New York: Harper & Row, 1987.

Sundquist, James L. *The Decline and Resurgence of Congress.* Washington, DC. Brookings Institution, 1981.

Sussman, Barry. *The Great Coverup: Nixon and the Scandal of Watergate.* New York: New American Library, 1974.

Swanson, Gloria. *Swanson on Swanson.* New York: Random House, 1980.

Swift, Will. *The Kennedys Amidst the Gathering Storm: A Thousand Days in London, 1938–1940.* New York: HarperCollins, 2008.

Takiff, Michael. *A Complicated Man: The Life of Bill Clinton as Told by Those Who Know Him.* New Haven, CT: Yale University Press, 2010.

Talbot, David. *Brothers: The Hidden History of the Kennedy Years.* New York: Free Press, 2007.

Taraborrelli, J. Randy. *After Camelot: A Personal History of the Kennedy Family, 1968 to the Present.* New York: Grand Central Publishing, 2012.

————. *Jackie, Ethel, Joan: Women of Camelot.* New York: Warner Books, 2000.

Taubman, William. *Gorbachev: His Life and Times.* New York: Norton, 2017.

Thatcher, Margaret. *The Downing Street Years, 1979–1990.* New York: HarperCollins, 1993.

Thernstrom, Stephan. *The Other Bostonians: Poverty and Progress in the American Metropolis, 1880–1970.* Cambridge, MA: Harvard University Press, 1973.

Thomas, Evan. *Robert Kennedy: His Life.* New York: Simon & Schuster, 2000.

Thompson, Fred. *At That Point in Time: The Inside Story of the Senate Watergate Committee.* New York: Quadrangle, 1975.

Thompson, Hunter S. *Fear and Loathing in Las Vegas.* New York: Popular Library, 1971.

————. *Fear and Loathing on the Campaign Trail '72.* New York: Popular Library, 1973.

————. *The Great Shark Hunt.* New York: Summit Books, 1979.

Thompson, Kenneth W., ed. *The Carter Presidency.* Lanham, MD: University Press of America, 1990.

Trout, Charles H. *Boston, the Great Depression, and the New Deal.* New York: Oxford University Press, 1977.

Tydings, Joseph, and John W. Frece. *My Life in Progressive Politics: Against the Grain.* College Station: Texas A&M University Press, 2018.

Tye, Larry. *Bobby Kennedy: The Making of a Liberal Icon.* New York: Random House, 2016.

Ulasewicz, Tony, and Stuart McKeever. *The President's Private Eye.* Westport, CT: MACSAM Publishing Co., 1990.

U.S. Congress. *Memorial Addresses and Other Tributes.* 111th Cong., 1st sess., 2010. Washington, DC: U.S. Government Printing Office, 2010.

U.S. Department of Defense. *The Pentagon Papers.* Boston: Beacon Press, 1971.

Valeo, Francis R. *Mike Mansfield, Majority Leader: A Different Kind of Senate, 1961–1976.* Armonk, NY: Sharpe, 1999.

vanden Heuvel, William J., and Milton Gwirtzman. *On His Own: Robert F. Kennedy, 1964–1968.* Garden City, NY: Doubleday & Co., 1970.

Waldman, Michael. *The Fight to Vote.* New York: Simon & Schuster, 2016.

Waldman, Steven. *The Bill: How Legislation Really Becomes Law; A Case Study of the National Service Bill.* New York: Penguin Books, 1996.

Ward, Jon. *Camelot's End: Kennedy vs. Carter and the Fight That Broke the Democratic Party.* New York: Twelve, 2019.

Washington Post. *The Fall of a President.* New York: Delacorte Press, 1974.

———. *The Presidential Transcripts.* New York: Dell, 1974.

Waters, Mary, and Reed Ueda, eds. *The New Americans: A Guide to Immigration Since 1965.* Cambridge, MA: Harvard University Press, 2007.

Watson, Denton. *Lion in the Lobby: Clarence Mitchell Jr.'s Struggle for the Passage of Civil Rights Laws.* New York: William Morrow, 1990.

Waxman, Henry. *The Waxman Report: How Congress Really Works.* New York: Twelve, 2009

Weisman, Steven R., ed. *Daniel Patrick Moynihan: A Portrait in Letters of an American Visionary.* New York: PublicAffairs, 2010.

Wells, Tom. *The War Within: America's Battle over Vietnam.* Berkeley: University of California Press, 1994.

Whalen, Charles, and Barbara Whalen. *The Longest Debate: A Legislative History of the 1964 Civil Rights Act.* Washington, DC: Seven Locks Press, 1985.

Whalen, Richard. *Catch the Falling Flag: A Republican's Challenge to His Party.* Boston: Houghton Mifflin, 1972.

———. *The Founding Father: The Story of Joseph P. Kennedy.* Washington, DC: Regnery Gateway, 1993.

———. *Kennedy Versus Lodge: The 1952 Massachusetts Senate Race.* Boston: Northeastern University Press, 2000.

———. *Taking Sides: A Personal View of America from Kennedy to Nixon to Kennedy.* Boston: Houghton Mifflin, 1974.

White, Theodore. *America in Search of Itself: The Making of the President 1956–1980.* New York: Harper & Row, 1982.

———. *Breach of Faith: The Fall of Richard Nixon.* New York: Atheneum Publishers, 1975.

———. *The Making of the President 1960.* New York: Atheneum, 1961.

———. *The Making of the President 1964.* New York: Atheneum, 1965.

———. *The Making of the President 1968.* New York: Atheneum, 1969.

———. *The Making of the President 1972.* New York: Atheneum, 1973.

White, William S. *The Citadel: The Story of the U.S. Senate.* New York: Harper & Brothers, 1957.

Whitehill, Walter M. *Boston in the Age of John Fitzgerald Kennedy.* Norman: University of Oklahoma Press, 1966.

Widmer, Ted, ed. *Listening In: The Secret White House Recordings of John F. Kennedy.* New York: Hyperion, 2012.

Wilentz, Sean. *The Age of Reagan: A History, 1974–2008.* New York: HarperCollins, 2008.

Williams, Juan. *Eyes on the Prize: America's Civil Rights Years, 1954–1965.* New York: Penguin, 1987.

Wills, Garry. *The Kennedy Imprisonment: A Meditation on Power.* Boston: Little, Brown, 1982.

Wilson, Andrew J. *Irish America and the Ulster Conflict, 1968–1995.* Washington, DC: Catholic University of America Press, 1995.

Witcover, Jules. *85 Days: The Last Campaign of Robert Kennedy.* New York: Putnam, 1969.

———. *Joe Biden: A Life of Trial and Redemption.* New York: William Morrow, 2010.

———. *Marathon: The Pursuit of the Presidency, 1972–1976.* New York: Viking, 1977.

———. *The Year the Dream Died: Revisiting 1968 in America.* New York: Warner, 1997.

Wofford, Harris. *Of Kennedys and Kings.* Pittsburgh: University of Pittsburgh Press, 1980.

Wolfe, Tom. *The New Journalism.* New York: Harper & Row, 1973.

Woodham-Smith, Cecil. *The Great Hunger: Ireland, 1815–1849.* New York: Harper & Row, 1962.

Woods, Randall Bennett. *Fulbright: A Biography.* New York: Cambridge University Press, 1995.

Woodward, Bob. *The Agenda: Inside the Clinton White House.* New York: Simon & Schuster, 1994.

———. *The Choice: How Clinton Won.* New York: Simon & Schuster, 1996.

———. *The Last of the President's Men.* New York: Simon & Schuster, 2015.

Woodward, Bob, and Scott Armstrong. *The Brethren: Inside the Supreme Court.* New York: Simon & Schuster, 1979.

Woodward, Bob, and Carl Bernstein. *The Final Days.* New York: Simon & Schuster, 1976.

Yang, Jia Lynn. *One Mighty and Irresistible Tide: The Epic Struggle over American Immigration, 1924–1965.* New York: Norton, 2020.

Yergin, Daniel. *The Prize: The Epic Quest for Oil, Money and Power.* New York: Simon & Schuster, 1991.

Zaffiri, Samuel. *Hamburger Hill: The Brutal Battle for Dong Ap Bia, May 11–20, 1969.* New York: Ballantine, 1988.

Zelizer, Julian E. *Burning Down the House: Newt Gingrich and the Rise of the New Republican Party.* New York: Penguin Press, 2020.

———. *The Fierce Urgency of Now: Lyndon Johnson, Congress and the Battle for the Great Society.* New York: Penguin, 2015.

———. *Jimmy Carter.* New York: Times Books, 2010.

———. *On Capitol Hill: The Struggle to Reform Congress and Its Consequences, 1948–2000.* Cambridge: Cambridge University Press, 2004.

Illustration Credits

page 6, top   Joe Dennehy/*The Boston Globe*
page 6, middle   Boston Public Library
page 6, bottom   Boston Public Library
page 7, top   Courtesy: The Richard Nixon Presidential Library and Museum (National Archives and Records
                           Administration)
page 7, bottom   Library of Congress, Prints & Photographs Division, U.S. News & World Report Magazine
                           Collection, LC-DIG-ppmsca-50448
page 8, top   Joe Dennehy/*The Boston Globe*
page 8, middle   Everett/Shutterstock
page 8, bottom   Stan Grossfeld/*The Boston Globe*
page 9, top   Ronald Reagan Presidential Library
page 9, bottom   U.S. Senate Historical Office
page 10, top   Marcy Nightswander/AP/Shutterstock
page 10, bottom   John Tlumacki/*The Boston Globe*
page 11, top   John Tlumacki/*The Boston Globe*
page 11, bottom   David L. Ryan/*The Boston Globe*
page 12, top   Courtesy, William J. Clinton Presidential Library
page 12, bottom   Library of Congress, Prints & Photographs Division, CQ Roll Call Photograph Collection,
                           LC-DIG-ppmsca-38876 DLC
page 13, top   Courtesy of the George W. Bush Presidential Library and Museum
page 13, bottom   Shutterstock
page 14, top left, top right, and bottom left of series
                           Library of Congress, Prints & Photographs Division, CQ Roll Call Photograph Collection,
                           LC-CQ06-WR98092411
page 14, bottom right of series
                           Library of Congress, Prints & Photographs Division, CQ Roll Call Photograph Collection,
                           LC-CQ06-WR98092410
page 14, bottom   Mark Garfinkel
page 15, top   Bill Greene/*The Boston Globe*
page 15, middle   Matthew J. Lee/*The Boston Globe*
page 15, bottom   Matthew J. Lee/*The Boston Globe*
page 16, top   Courtesy Barack Obama Presidential Library
page 16, middle   Courtesy Barack Obama Presidential Library
page 16, bottom   Courtesy Barack Obama Presidential Library

Index